Roget's Thesaurus
of the Bible

Roget's Thesaurus of the Bible

by

A. Colin Day

Marshall Pickering
An Imprint of HarperCollins*Publishers*

Marshall Pickering is an imprint of
HarperCollins*Religious*
Part of HarperCollins*Publishers*
77–85 Fulham Palace Road, London W6 8JB

First Published in Great Britain
in 1992 by Marshall Pickering
This edition 1997

1 3 5 7 9 10 8 6 4 2

A catalogue record for this book is
available from the British Library

ISBN 0 551 03133 6

Printed and bound in the USA by
R R Donnelley & Sons Co

Contents

Preface

This is a reference book for people studying the Bible. It may be used to find the answer to the question, 'What does the Bible say about . . . ?' That is to say, it groups together verses and passages of the Bible which are about the same subject.

Traditionally a Bible concordance has been used to find sets of verses or passages on the same subject, so it is necessary to understand how a thesaurus differs from a concordance.

Bible concordances enable one to find verses containing the same *word*. This usually works only for a particular version (or translation) of the Bible in a particular language. For example, in English, passages on faith will be found by searching for such words as 'believe', 'faith', 'trust', 'rely on' etc. Where you find particular verses depends on which word has been used when translating them.

A Bible thesaurus links together passages with similar *meanings*. Those passages may then be linked together irrespective of the version or the language. So, for example, passages on faith may be found grouped together under category **485 Belief**.

I am very grateful to Susan M. Lloyd, editor of *Roget's Thesaurus of English Words and Phrases* (Longman, 1982 edition) for her encouragement to use the categories of that work as a basis for my thesaurus. This in general I have done, with certain adjustments mentioned below in the section entitled **About this book**.

I must record my indebtedness to my wife Jean, who has believed in the scheme even when few others did and when I nearly lost hope myself, and who by her quiet encouragement and understanding has been just the impetus I needed. I am also very grateful to Roger Forster for his encouragement and help in the later stages.

That this work is imperfect and incomplete no one knows better than I. However, from the reactions already received I have reason to believe that it will be of use, which is what I sincerely hope it will be.

How to use this book

● Exploring a topic

This book may be used to find Bible verses and passages referring to a certain topic. Let us suppose, for example, that you want to find passages about who Jesus is.

First it is necessary to think of a word which specifies the topic. You may think of the word 'identity' ('the identity of Jesus'), or simply the word 'is' ('who is this man?').

● Using the index

Look up this word in the index at the back of the book. If your word was 'is' you will see

is
  exist 1
  . . .
  Who is Jesus? 13c

This signifies that the word 'is' may be used in different ways. One can use it to indicate that something exists ('God is!'). This meaning is dealt with in category number **1**. The second way one can use the word 'is' is to talk about someone's identity ('Who is this man?') This meaning is dealt with under category **13**. In particular, the subject of who Jesus is will be found in paragraph *c* of category **13**. (The phrase *Who is Jesus?* appears in italics to show that this is a side-heading of category **13**, as described below.)

The sense in which you are interested is the second one. Turn to the categories (the major part of the book) and look up category **13**. Bible references on the theme of **Identity** are listed there. These references are grouped into paragraphs, many of which have side-headings (in the left margin). The side-headings may be considered as the rungs of a ladder, down which you can climb to the section of interest.

The first few paragraphs of category **13** are on the identity of God. Paragraph *c* has the side-heading *Who is Jesus?*, introducing several paragraphs on this subject. You may want to browse among these, and for contrast you may wish to look at the neighbouring paragraphs on the identity of other people (such as John the Baptist).

The word 'is' is not the only one you could have used. Looking in the index for any of the terms 'identity', 'am', 'be', 'are', 'who are', or 'who is' would also have led you to category **13**.

Paragraph indications (such as the *c* above) give you a hint as to the best place to begin searching.

● Bible references

The words accompanying each Bible reference should not be taken as a formal quotation. These are merely my informal paraphrase. Sometimes the content of several references needs to be summarised, and therefore an exact translation could not be given. The need to keep the book to a reasonable size means that the text should be as brief as possible, and an exact translation may be too long. The wording given should be enough to remind you of what the Bible says without quoting it exactly.

● Browsing

You may find it useful to browse not only in the category you have reached, but also in neighbouring ones. If, for instance, you are exploring category **485 Belief**, you might also find relevant material in the next category, **486 Unbelief**.

Sometimes cross-references to other related categories are given. For instance, at the end of category **125 Past time** there is a cross-reference to category **68 Beginning**.

When you have found Bible references which appear to be promising for your search, look them up and browse in the Bible itself to see the context in which those references appear.

● Using the Bible index

It may be that you have difficulty finding a single word or phrase which you can look up in the index. However, you may already know a verse which exemplifies the meaning you have in mind. In this case, you can use the Bible index to see which categories refer to that verse, and to discover which of those categories conveys the meaning in which you are interested.

As an example, you may want to find verses on the subject of the wicked being visited by their own wickedness, but perhaps you find it difficult to summarise this concept in one word. If you can find one verse which demonstrates this principle, such as Psalm 9:16, you can look it up in the Bible index. This will tell you that Psalm 9:16 is referred to in two places within the categories, category **280** paragraph *a* and category **913** paragraph *a*. Investigating these paragraphs will show you that **280***a* is the one which is on the subject required, as category 280 is entitled **Rebounding**, and paragraph *a* has a side-heading *Evil rebounds*.

About this book

This book grew out of a desire to have a file of Bible verses so arranged as to group together references to the same subject. Before embarking on such a project, the existing possibilities were of course examined.

● Concordances

One of the most widely-used Bible reference books is the concordance. This lists occurrences of each word, with some context to show how the word fits into the verse. Concordances are normally tied to a particular version of the Bible in a particular language. Trying to find a verse which you remember has the word 'believe' in it, when the concordance is based on a version which uses 'has faith' in its place can be frustrating. As mentioned in the preface, exploring one topic may require searching the concordance for a range of different words. On the other hand, if you need to find every occurrence of one word (especially if it is the name of a person or place) then the concordance is what you need.

● Bible topics

An alternative approach is a book which compiles a large number of Bible topics, with the references given for each. Perhaps the most exhaustive work of this kind is *Nave's Topical Bible* by Orville J. Nave (Baker Book House, reprinted 1979). This boasts over 20,000 topics and subtopics, which are listed in alphabetical order. The book is voluminous (1615 pages), including 151 pages of Bible index. Often whole verses (and sometimes lengthy passages) are rendered verbatim from the King James Version, but where convenient a summarising gloss is included with a list of references.

The difficulty with using English words as headings is that they may not be mutually exclusive. Nave, for example, has topics 'Evidence', 'Testimony', and 'Witness', which overlap in meaning. Such a system of headings may also fail to suggest to the compiler all that could be included. Nave has no section on the identity of Jesus, for example. In saying this my intention is not to be critical of Nave's work, which has proved valuable to countless people, but simply to point out that such an approach has its limitations.

● Roget's Thesaurus

The thesaurus which has descended from P. M. Roget was intended to categorise the whole field of meaning under 1000 heads (now reduced in Longman's edition to 990). When these heads are used as categories for Bible references, then the version or language used is immaterial providing that the meaning conveyed is the same. The heads cover all branches of meanings, and so should provide places for filing topics as diverse as one cares to list. Moreover, similar topics will often be listed near one another, to enhance browsing.

This, then, seemed to provide a suitable framework for a Bible reference book. As mentioned above, I have in general used the categories of the 1982 Longman's revision of Roget's Thesaurus. The names of some categories seemed to be somewhat unduly abstruse for my purposes, so I have in these cases chosen other names, and indicated my revision in the **List of categories** (pp. 7–22) by printing the name in italics. In some cases the distinctions in the Thesaurus of English words have proved too subtle for the task of distinguishing Bible references. For this reason, for instance, category **615 Good** has not been distinguished from **644 Goodness** (nor **616 Evil** from **645 Badness**). This is not to quarrel with the basic categories, but simply to exploit them more comfortably for this particular application.

- Empty categories

In some cases there are no Bible references to be found under certain categories. I have not been able to find any Bible verses which have a bearing on **276 Aircraft**, for instance (though some interpreters might claim to do so). In such cases it seemed best to leave the category in place, although empty, so that the structure of all the categories might remain intact. Wherever possible, I have include cross-references from these empty categories to categories containing Bible references. For instance, category **276 Aircraft**, though empty, has a cross reference to category **271 Aviation**, which includes references to some flying things.

The idea of producing a thesaurus of Bible references seemed a sound one; the problem lay in the implementation. It has taken over fifteen years of trying various schemes in order to arrive at a methodology with which I am reasonably satisfied.

- The ordering

I have attempted to group references so that similar verses are recorded together. This has been attempted both by grouping like references into paragraphs and also by arranging references within paragraphs so that like came near to like.

However, these references could have been grouped in completely different ways. If my arrangements do not suit your needs, treat the references as items laid out at a rummage sale. Though the material may lack complete order, yet there is value for those who will browse.

It is impossible to carry out such arranging without some interpretation of the references. This does not mean that there is any profit in wondering too deeply what my reasons were for arranging things as I did. You may feel that my arrangements run quite counter to your interpretations (and indeed they may). In this case I suggest that you consider the rummage sale to have been laid out quite poorly, but you may nevertheless find what you need.

● The method

The only feasible way to write this book has been by successive approximations.

The whole Bible was surveyed, extracting references which appeared to be obviously of interest to a Bible student. Next a pass was made through each of the 990 categories, putting in order and subdividing the references which had fallen into that category. An index was compiled at the same time, which often led to the discovery that similar references had been filed in more than one category, and so needed reorganising.

When this had been accomplished with a minimum of references, a computer program was written to generate a Bible index for these. This Bible index was used when surveying the whole Bible once again, as for each verse it showed what aspects had already been used to generate references. More references were now culled, and fitted into the existing framework of categories and subdivisions. This again led to reorganisation, an expanded index, revised subheadings, and so on.

In order to check the index, a computer program was written to produce a reverse index, with the index entries sorted according to category and paragraph. The Bible references were checked (to see that the chapter and verse numbers were correct) by using a copy of the Bible on computer disk, to which was fed the list of all the references used in the book. This way, from each reference, the verse could be displayed in full on the screen. After this had been checked, the next reference could be used to display its verse on the screen with a delay of only half a second.

● Reference books

Various books have been used in the compilation of this Thesaurus. Although the renderings used are merely loose paraphrases of the text, I have found it useful to work with the Revised Standard, the New International and the New American Standard versions. No attempt has been made to distinguish variations in the original manuscripts; if these versions included a textual variant, I considered it for inclusion. There have been many occasions when the King James version and Young's *Analytical*

Concordance to the Holy Bible have proved very useful. When it seemed necessary, I have used the original Hebrew and Greek, aided by:

A Concordance to the Greek Testament, Moulton and Geden, Edinburgh (1957).

The Englishman's Hebrew and Chaldee Concordance of the Old Testament, George V. Wigram, Zondervan (1970).

A Greek-English Lexicon of the New Testament, Arndt and Gingrich, University of Chicago Press (1979).

A Hebrew and English Lexicon of the Old Testament, Brown, Driver and Briggs, Oxford (1951).

I have often found help from consulting the *Tyndale Commentaries* (IVP), and the *New Bible Dictionary* (IVP).

● Is it complete?

No such work as this can ever hope to be complete. The semantics of the Bible is inexhaustible, so how can it be categorised with anything like finality?

Those who want to find every occurrence of a particular word (especially proper names) are recommended to use a concordance as their tool rather than this thesaurus.

Even allowing for the fact that a thesaurus could never be complete, I am very conscious that this thesaurus is nowhere near as comprehensive as I would like it to be. Limitations have had to be imposed due to time, effort, and cost of publication. It is also true that one reason for the limitation of this work is identical to that given by Dr Johnson for mistakes in his dictionary: 'Ignorance, ma'am, sheer ignorance!' I tender my apologies along with my hope that this work will nevertheless be found useful by those who have a love for the Bible and who want to explore more of its riches.

List of categories

Class one: Abstract relations

1 Existence

Abstract:	1 Existence	2 Nonexistence
Concrete:	3 Substantiality	4 Insubstantiality
Formal: (internal/external)	5 *Nature*	6 Extrinsicality
Modal: (absolute/relative)	7 State	8 Circumstance

2 Relation

Absolute:	9 *Fellowship*	10 Unrelatedness
	11 *Relations of kindred*	
	12 Correlation	
	13 Identity	14 Contrariety
	15 Difference	
Continuous:	16 Uniformity	17 Non-uniformity
Partial:	18 Similarity	19 Dissimilarity
	20 Imitation	21 *Uniqueness*
	22 Copy	23 *Model*
General:	24 Agreement	25 Disagreement

3 Quantity

Simple: (absolute/relative)	26 Quantity	27 Degree
	28 Equality	29 Inequality
Comparative:	30 Mean	
	31 Compensation	
(by comparison with a standard)	32 *Much*	33 *Not much*
(by comparison with an object)	34 Superiority	35 Inferiority
(changes in quantity)	36 Increase	37 Decrease
Conjunctive:	38 Addition	39 Subtraction
	40 Adjunct	41 Remainder
		42 Decrement
	43 Mixture	44 *Unmixed*
	45 *Joining*	46 *Separating*
	47 Bond	
	48 *Cohesion*	49 *Non-cohesion*
	50 Combination	51 Decomposition
Concrete:	52 Whole	53 Part
	54 Completeness	55 Incompleteness
	56 Composition	57 Exclusion

> **Note**
> Category names in italics are not identical to those in *Roget's Thesaurus of English words and Phrases* (Longman, 1982).

58	Component	59	*Foreigner*

4 Order

General:

60	Order	61	Disorder
62	Arrangement	63	Derangement

Consecutive:

64	Precedence	65	Sequence
66	*Forerunner*	67	Sequel
68	Beginning	69	End

70 Middle

71	Continuity	72	Discontinuity
73	*Ranking*		

Collective:

74	*Gathering*	75	*Scattering*
76	*Meeting place*		

Distributive:

77	Class		
78	Inclusion		
79	Generality	80	*Self*

Categorical:

81	*Principle*	82	*Multiple*
83	Conformity	84	Nonconformity

5 Number

Abstract:

85	Number		
86	*Counting*		
87	List		

Determinate:

88	*One*	89	Accompaniment
90	*Two*		
91	*Doubling*	92	*Half*
93	*Three*		
94	*Three times*	95	*Third*
96	*Four*		
97	*Four times*	98	*Quarter*
99	Five and over	100	Multisection

Indeterminate:

101	Plurality	102	Fraction
		103	Zero
104	*Numerous*	105	*Few*
106	Repetition		
107	Infinity		

6 Time

Absolute:
(definite/indefinite)

108	Time	109	Neverness
110	Period	111	Course
112	Contingent duration		
113	Long duration	114	*Brief*
115	*For ever*	116	*Instantly*
117	Chronometry	118	Anachronism

Relative: (to succession)

119	*First*	120	Posteriority
121	Present time	122	Different time
123	Synchronism		

(to a period)

124 *Future time*	125 Past time
126 Newness	127 Oldness
128 Morning	129 Evening
130 *Youthfulness*	131 Age
132 Young person	133 Old person

134 Adultness

(to an effect or purpose)

135 Earliness	136 Lateness
137 *Opportunity*	138 Untimeliness

Recurrent:

139 Frequency	140 Infrequency
141 *Regularity*	142 *Irregularity*

7 Change

Simple:

143 Change	144 Permanence
145 Cessation	146 *Unceasing*
147 Conversion	148 *Returning*
149 Revolution	
150 Substitution	151 Interchange

Complex: 152 Changeableness 153 Stability

(present/future) 154 Present events 155 Destiny

8 Causation

Constancy of sequence:

156 Cause	157 Effect
158 Attribution	159 Chance

Connection between cause and effect:

160 Power 161 Impotence

Power in operation:

162 Strength	163 Weakness
164 *Making*	165 Destruction
166 *Reproducing*	
167 *Reproduction*	168 Destroyer
169 Parentage	170 *Descendant*
171 Productiveness	172 Unproductiveness
173 Agency	
174 Vigour	175 Inertness
176 Violence	177 Gentleness

Indirect power:

178 Influence
179 Tendency
180 Liability

Combination of causes: 181 Concurrence 182 Counteraction

Class two: Space

1 Space in general

Abstract space: (indefinite) 183 Space

(definite) 184 Region

(limited) 185 Place

Relative space: 186 Situation

Existence in space:	187 Location	188 Displacement
	189 Presence	190 Absence
	191 Inhabitant	192 Abode
	193 Contents	194 Receptacle

2 Dimensions

General:	195 Size	196 Littleness
	197 Expansion	198 Contraction
	199 Distance	200 Nearness
	201 *Gap*	202 Contiguity
Linear:	203 Length	204 Shortness
	205 Breadth	206 Narrowness
	207 Layer	208 Filament
	209 Height	210 Lowness
	211 Depth	212 Shallowness
	213 Summit	214 Base
	215 *Vertical*	216 *Horizontal*
	217 *Hanging*	218 Support
	219 Parallelism	220 *Tilting*
	221 *Turning upside down*	
	222 Crossing	
Centrical: (general)	223 *Outside*	224 *Inside*
		225 Centrality
	226 Covering	227 Lining
	228 Dressing	229 *Uncovering*
	230 Surroundings	231 *Interposing*
	232 Circumscription	
	233 Outline	
	234 Edge	
	235 Enclosure	
	236 Limit	
(special)	237 Front	238 Rear
	239 Side	240 *Opposite side*
	241 *Right side*	242 *Left side*

3 Form

General:	243 Form	244 *Formlessness*
	245 Symmetry	246 Distortion
Special:	247 Angularity	
	248 Curvature	249 Straightness
	250 Circularity	251 Convolution
	252 *Roundness*	
Superficial:	253 Convexity	
	254 Prominence	255 Concavity
	256 Sharpness	257 Bluntness
	258 Smoothness	259 Roughness
	260 Notch	261 Fold

262 Furrow	
263 Opening	264 Closure

4 Motion
General:

265 Motion	266 *Stillness*
267 Land travel	268 Traveller
269 Water travel	270 Mariner
271 *Aviation*	
272 Transference	273 Carrier
274 Vehicle	275 Ship
	276 Aircraft

Degrees of motion:
Conjoined with force:
With reference to direction:

277 *Swiftness*	278 Slowness
279 *Impact*	280 *Rebounding*
281 Direction	282 Deviation
283 Preceding	284 Following
285 *Advance*	286 Regression
287 Propulsion	288 *Pulling*
289 Approach	290 Recession
291 Attraction	292 Repulsion
293 Convergence	294 Divergence
295 Arrival	296 Departure
297 *Entrance*	298 *Emergence*
299 Reception	300 Ejection
301 Food	302 Excretion
303 Insertion	304 Extraction
305 Passage	
306 Overstepping	307 Shortfall
308 Ascent	309 Descent
310 *Lifting up*	311 Lowering
312 Leap	313 Plunge
314 *Circling*	315 *Rotation*
316 Evolution	
317 Oscillation	
318 Agitation	

Class three: Matter

1 Matter in general

319 Materiality	320 *Spirituality*
321 Universe	
322 *Weight*	323 Lightness

2 Inorganic matter
Solids:

324 Density	325 Rarity
326 Hardness	327 Softness
328 Elasticity	
329 Toughness	330 Brittleness

	331 Structure	332 Powderiness
	333 Friction	334 Lubrication
Fluids: (in general)	335 *Liquids*	336 Gaseousness
	337 Liquefaction	338 Vaporization
(specific)	339 Water	340 Air
	341 Moisture	342 Dryness
	343 Ocean	344 Land
	345 Gulf	
	346 Lake	347 Marsh
		348 Plain
		349 Island
(in motion)	350 Stream	
	351 *Channel*	352 Wind
		353 Air-pipe
	354 Semiliquidity	355 *Cloud*
	356 Pulpiness	357 *Oiliness*

3 Organic matter

Vitality: (general)	358 Organisms	359 Mineral
	360 Life	361 Death
		362 Killing
		363 Corpse
		364 Interment
(special)	365 *Animals*	366 *Plants*
	367 Zoology	368 Botany
	369 Animal husbandry	370 Agriculture
	371 *Mankind*	
	372 Male	373 Female
Sensation: (general)	374 Physical sensibility	375 Physical insensibility
	376 Physical pleasure	377 Physical pain
(touch)	378 Touch	
(heat)	379 Heat	380 Cold
	381 Heating	382 Refrigeration
	383 Furnace	384 Refrigerator
	385 Fuel	
(taste)	386 Taste	387 *Insipidness*
	388 Pungency	
	389 Condiment	
	390 Savouriness	391 Unsavouriness
	392 Sweetness	393 Sourness
(odour)	394 Odour	395 *Odourlessness*
	396 Fragrance	397 Stench
(sound: general)	398 Sound	399 Silence
	400 Loudness	401 Faintness
(specific sounds)	402 Bang	403 *Roar*
	404 Resonance	405 Nonresonance
	406 Sibilation	407 Stridor

	408 Human cry	409 *Animal sounds*
(musical sounds)	410 Melody	411 Discord
	412 Music	
	413 Musician	414 Musical instrument
(perception of sound)	415 Hearing	416 Deafness
(light: general)	417 Light	418 Darkness

419 Dimness

	420 *Light source*	421 Screen
	422 Transparency	423 Opacity

424 Semitransparency

(specific light)	425 Colour	426 *Colourlessness*
	427 Whiteness	428 Blackness
	429 Greyness	430 Brownness
	431 Redness	432 Orange
	433 Yellowness	434 Greenness
	435 Blueness	436 Purpleness
	437 Variegation	
(perception of light)	438 Vision	439 Blindness

440 *Defective vision*

	441 Spectator	442 Optical instrument
	443 Visibility	444 Invisibility
	445 Appearance	446 Disappearance

Class four: Intellect: the exercise of the mind

Division one: Formation of ideas

1 Intellectual operations in general

447 Intellect	448 Absence of intellect
449 Thought	450 Absence of thought
451 Idea	
452 Topic	

2 Precursory conditions and operations

453 Curiosity	454 Incuriosity
455 Attention	456 Inattention
457 Carefulness	458 Negligence
459 Enquiry	460 Answer
461 Experiment	
462 Comparison	
463 Discrimination	464 Indiscrimination
465 Measurement	

3 Materials for reasoning

466 Evidence	467 Counterevidence

468 Qualification

(degrees of evidence)	469 Possibility	470 Impossibility

592 Compendium
593 Poetry. Prose
594 Drama

Class five: Volition: the exercise of the will

Division one: Individual volition

1 Volition in general

Acts:

595 Will	596 Necessity
597 Willingness	598 Unwillingness
599 Resolution	
600 Perseverance	601 Irresolution
602 Obstinacy	603 *Change of mind*
	604 Caprice
605 Choice	606 Absence of choice
	607 Rejection
608 Predetermination	609 Spontaneity
610 Habit	611 *Weaning*

Causes:

612 Motive	613 Dissuasion
614 Pretext	

Objects:

615 Good	616 Evil

2 Prospective volition

Conceptional:

617 Intention	618 Nondesign
619 Pursuit	620 Avoidance
	621 Relinquishment
622 Business	
623 Plan	
624 Way	
625 Middle way	626 Circuit
627 Requirement	

Subservience to ends:

628 Instrumentality
629 Means
630 Tool
631 Materials
632 Store

633 Provision	634 Waste

635 Sufficiency

636 Insufficiency	637 *Excess*

(degrees of subservience)

638 Importance	639 Unimportance
640 *Usefulnes*	641 *Uselessness*
642 Good policy	643 Inexpedience
644 Goodness	645 Badness
646 Perfection	647 Imperfection
648 Cleanness	649 Uncleanness
650 Health	651 Ill health

	652 Salubrity	653 Insalubrity
	654 Improvement	655 Deterioration
	656 Restoration	657 Relapse
	658 Remedy	659 Bane
(contingent subservience)	660 Safety	661 Danger
	662 Refuge	663 Pitfall
	664 Warning	665 Danger signal
	666 Preservation	
	667 Escape	
	668 Deliverance	
Precursory measures:	669 Preparation	670 *Unpreparedness*
	671 Attempt	
	672 Undertaking	
	673 Use	674 Nonuse
		675 Misuse

3 Voluntary action

Simple:	676 Action	677 Inaction
	678 Activity	679 Inactivity
	680 Haste	681 Leisure
	682 Exertion	683 Repose
	684 Fatigue	685 Refreshment
	686 *Worker*	
	687 Workshop	
Complex:	688 Conduct	
	689 Management	
	690 Director	
	691 Advice	
	692 Council	
	693 Precept	
	694 Skill	695 Unskilfulness
	696 Proficient person	697 Bungler
	698 Cunning	699 Artlessness

4 Antagonism

Conditional:	700 Difficulty	701 Facility
Active:	702 Hindrance	703 Aid
	704 Opposition	705 Opponent
	706 Cooperation	707 *Co-worker*
	708 Party	
	709 Dissension	710 Concord
	711 Defiance	
	712 Attack	713 Defence
	714 Retaliation	715 Resistance
	716 Contention	717 Peace
	718 War	719 Pacification
	720 Mediation	

721 Submission
722 Combatant
723 *Weapons*
724 Arena

5 Results of action

725 Completion	726 Noncompletion
727 Success	728 Failure
729 Trophy	
730 Prosperity	731 Adversity

732 Averageness

Division two: Social volition

1 General social volition

733 Authority	734 *Anarchy*
735 Severity	736 Leniency
737 Command	
738 Disobedience	739 Obedience
740 Compulsion	
741 Master	742 Servant
743 Badge of rule	
744 Freedom	745 Subjection
746 Liberation	747 Restraint
	748 Prison
749 Keeper	750 Prisoner
751 Commission	752 Abrogation
	753 Resignation
754 *Nominee*	
755 Deputy	

2 Special social volition

756 Permission	757 Prohibition
758 Consent	
759 Offer	760 Refusal
761 Request	762 Deprecation
763 Petitioner	

3 Condition social volition

764 Promise	
765 *Covenant*	
766 Conditions	
767 Security	
768 Observance	769 Nonobservance

770 Compromise

4 Possessive relations

Property in general:	771 Acquisition	772 Loss
	773 Possession	774 Nonownership
	775 Joint possession	
	776 Possessor	
	777 Property	
	778 Retention	779 Nonretention
Transfer of property:	780 Transfer	
	781 Giving	782 Receiving
	783 Apportionment	
	784 Lending	785 Borrowing
	786 Taking	787 Restitution
	788 Stealing	
	789 Thief	
	790 Booty	
Interchange of property:	791 *Trade*	
	792 Purchase	793 Sale
	794 Merchant	
	795 Merchandise	
	796 Market	
Monetary relations:	797 Money	
	798 Treasurer	
	799 Treasury	
	800 Wealth	801 Poverty
	802 Credit	803 Debt
	804 Payment	805 Nonpayment
	806 Expenditure	807 Receipt
	808 Accounts	
	809 Price	810 Discount
	811 Dearness	812 Cheapness
	813 Liberality	814 Economy
	815 Prodigality	816 Parsimony

Class six: Emotion, religion and morality

1 General

817 Affections	
818 Feeling	
819 Sensibility	820 Insensibility
821 *Excitement*	
822 Excitability	823 Inexcitability

2 Personal emotion

Passive:	824 Joy	825 Suffering
	826 Pleasurableness	827 Painfulness
	828 Content	829 Discontent

		830 Regret
	831 *Comfort*	832 Aggravation
	833 Cheerfulness	834 *Sadness*
	835 *Signs of joy*	836 Lamentation
	837 Amusement	838 Tedium
	839 Wit	840 Dullness
Discriminative:	841 Beauty	842 Ugliness
	843 Beautification	
	844 Ornamentation	845 Blemish
	846 Good taste	847 Bad taste
	848 Fashion	849 Ridiculousness
		850 Affectation
		851 Ridicule
Prospective:	852 Hope	853 Hopelessness
		854 Fear
	855 Courage	856 Cowardice
	857 Rashness	858 Caution
	859 Desire	860 Indifference
		861 Dislike
		862 Fastidiousness
		863 Satiety
Contemplative:	864 Wonder	865 Lack of wonder
Extrinsic:	866 Repute	867 Disrepute
	868 Nobility	869 Commonalty
	870 Title	
	871 Pride	872 Humility
	873 Vanity	874 Modesty
	875 Ostentation	
	876 Celebration	
	877 Boasting	
	878 Insolence	879 Servility

3 Interpersonal emotion

Social:	880 Friendship	881 Enmity
	882 Sociality	883 Unsociability
	884 Courtesy	885 Discourtesy
	886 Congratulation	
	887 Love	888 Hatred
	889 Endearment	
	890 Darling	891 *Anger*
		892 *Quick temper*
		893 Sullenness
	894 Marriage	895 Celibacy
		896 Divorce. Widowhood
Diffusive:	897 Benevolence	898 Malevolence
		899 *Curse*
		900 Threat

	901 Philanthropy
	903 Benefactor
Special	905 Pity
Retrospective:	907 Gratitude
	909 Forgiveness

901 Philanthropy	902 Misanthropy
903 Benefactor	904 Evildoer
905 Pity	906 Pitilessness
907 Gratitude	908 Ingratitude
909 Forgiveness	910 Revenge
	911 Jealousy
	912 Envy

4 Morality

Obligation:	913 *Righteousness*	914 Wrong
	915 Dueness	916 Undueness
	917 Duty	918 Undutifulness
		919 *Exemption*
Sentiments:	920 Respect	921 Disrespect
		922 Contempt
	923 *Approval*	924 *Disapproval*
	925 Flattery	926 *Calumny*
	927 Vindication	928 Accusation
Conditions:	929 *Faithfulness*	930 *Unfaithfulness*
	931 *Unselfishness*	932 Selfishness
	933 Virtue	934 Wickedness
	935 Innocence	936 Guilt
	937 Good person	938 Bad person
	939 Penitence	940 Impenitence
	941 Atonement	
Practice:	942 Temperance	943 Intemperance
		944 Sensualism
	945 Asceticism	
	946 Fasting	947 Gluttony
	948 Sobriety	949 Drunkenness
	950 Purity	951 Impurity
		952 Libertine
Institutions:	953 Legality	954 Illegality
	955 Jurisdiction	
	956 Tribunal	
	957 *Magistrate*	
	958 Lawyer	
	959 Litigation	
	960 Acquittal	961 Condemnation
	962 Reward	963 Punishment
		964 Means of punishment

5 Religion

Superhuman beings and	965 *Deity*	
regions	966 Deities in general	
	967 *Pagan gods*	
	968 Angel	969 Devil

	970 *Ghost*	
	971 Heaven	972 Hell
Doctrines:	973 Religion	974 Irreligion
	975 *Scriptures*	
	976 Orthodoxy	977 Heterodoxy
		978 Sectarianism
Sentiments:	979 *Holiness*	980 Impiety
Acts:	981 Worship	982 Idolatry
		983 Sorcery
		984 Occultism
Institutions:	985 The church	
	986 *Priests and elders* 987 Laity	
	988 Ritual	
	989 *Priests' garments*	
	990 Temple	

Abbreviations

Old testament

Gen.	Genesis
Exod.	Exodus
Lev.	Leviticus
Num.	Numbers
Deut.	Deuteronomy
Josh.	Joshua
Judg.	Judges
Ruth	Ruth
1 Sam.	1 Samuel
2 Sam.	2 Samuel
1 Kgs.	1 Kings
2 Kgs.	2 Kings
1 Chr.	1 Chronicles
2 Chr.	2 Chronicles
Ezra	Ezra
Neh.	Nehemiah
Esther	Esther
Job	Job
Ps.	Psalms
Prov.	Proverbs
Eccles.	Ecclesiastes
S. of S.	Song of Solomon
Isa.	Isaiah
Jer.	Jeremiah
Lam.	Lamentations
Ezek.	Ezekiel
Dan.	Daniel
Hos.	Hosea
Joel	Joel
Amos	Amos
Obad.	Obadiah
Jonah	Jonah
Mic.	Micah
Nahum	Nahum
Hab.	Habakkuk
Zeph.	Zephaniah
Hag.	Haggai
Zech.	Zechariah
Mal.	Malachi

New testament

Matt.	Matthew
Mark	Mark
Luke	Luke
John	John
Acts	Acts
Rom.	Romans
1 Cor.	1 Corinthians
2 Cor.	2 Corinthians
Gal.	Galatians
Eph.	Ephesians
Phil.	Philippians
Col.	Colossians
1 Thess.	1 Thessalonians
2 Thess.	2 Thessalonians
1 Tim.	1 Timothy
2 Tim.	2 Timothy
Titus	Titus
Philem.	Philemon
Heb.	Hebrews
Jas.	James
1 Pet.	1 Peter
2 Pet.	2 Peter
1 John	1 John
2 John	2 John
3 John	3 John
Jude	Jude
Rev.	Revelation

Class one: Abstract relations

Section one: Existence

1 Existence

● Existence of God

a God is the I AM (Exod. 3:14); God is and was (Rev. 1:4, 8; 4:8; 11:17; 16:5); he who comes to God must believe that he exists (Heb. 11:6).

● Existence of Christ

b The Word existed at the beginning (John 1:1); before Abraham, I AM (John 8:58); when you lift up the Son of man you will know that I AM (John 8:28); you will believe that I AM (John 13:19); unless you believe that I AM, you will die in your sins (John 8:24).

● It is I

c Do not be afraid, I AM [it is I] (Matt. 14:27; Mark 6:50; Luke 24:39; John 6:20); Jesus said 'I AM' and they fell to the ground (John 18:5–8).
I am the . . . see **13*h***.

● Existence through God

d God calls into existence what does not exist (Rom. 4:17); by your will they existed (Rev. 4:11); in God we live and move and have our being (Acts 17:28); in the Son all things hold together (Col. 1:17).

● Boastful existence

e Nineveh says, 'I am, with no one beside me' (Zeph. 2:15).

2 Nonexistence

● No God

a The fool says there is no God (Ps. 10:4; 14:1; 53:1).
Where is God?, see **190*a***.

● Never born

b One who has never been is better off than the living or the dead (Eccles. 4:2–3); Job wished he had never been born (Job 3:1–19); better for the betrayer if he had never been born (Matt. 26:24; Mark 14:21); like a miscarriage I would not have been (Job 3:16; 10:19); woe to me, my mother, that you bore me (Jer. 15:10).

● Ceasing to exist

c Heaven and earth will pass away (Matt. 5:18; 24:35; Mark 13:31; Luke 16:17; 21:33); the heavens will pass away (2 Pet. 3:10); changed like a garment (Heb. 1:11–12); shaken and removed (Heb. 12:26–7); the heavens and earth will grow old and be changed (Heb. 1:10–12).

d There shall no longer be sea (Rev. 21:1); death (Rev. 21:4); night (Rev. 22:5).

e The world and its lusts are passing away (1 John 2:17); the form of this present world is passing away (1 Cor. 7:31); the beast was and is not (Rev. 17:8, 11); the rulers of this age are passing away (1 Cor. 2:6); those who attack you will be non-existent (Isa. 41:11–12); nations will be as if they had never been (Obad. 16); Tyre will be no more (Ezek. 26:21; 27:36).

f Rachel's children are no more (Jer. 31:15; Matt. 2:18).

● Nonentities   *g* God has chosen things that are not (1 Cor. 1:28).

3 Substantiality
See **319**.

4 Insubstantiality
See **320**.

5 Nature

● Nature
of people

a What will this child turn out to be? (Luke 1:66); what is Apollos, what is Paul? (1 Cor. 3:5).
Nature of man, see **371a; nature of fools**, see **501c**.

● Nature
of Christ

b What sort of man is this? (Matt. 8:27).
Who is Jesus?, see **13c**.

6 Extrinsicality
See **59**.

7 State: absolute condition

● State

a Let each lead the life God has assigned (1 Cor. 7:17); let every one remain in the station in which he was called (1 Cor. 7:20–4); it is good for a man to remain as he is (1 Cor. 7:26); the widow is happier if she remains as she is (1 Cor. 7:40).

8 Circumstance: relative condition

● Welfare

a Is it well with Laban? (Gen. 29:6); is it well with Absalom? (2 Sam. 18:29, 32); see if it is well with your brothers (Gen. 37:14); they asked the Levite of his welfare (Judg. 18:15); David asked about the welfare of the army (2 Sam. 11:7); every day Mordecai asked how Esther was (Esther 2:11).

b Is it well with you? (2 Sam. 20:9; 2 Kgs. 4:26); is all well? (2 Kgs. 5:21; 9:11, 17, 18, 19, 22, 31).

c Seek the welfare of the city to which you are exiled (Jer. 29:7).

● Circumstances

d Content in all things (Phil. 4:11–12); give thanks in everything (1 Thess. 5:18).

Section two: Relation

9 Fellowship

● Fellowship
with God

a Fellowship with God (1 John 1:6); with the Father and his Son (1 John 1:3); fellowship with his Son (1 Cor. 1:9); the fellowship of the Spirit (2 Cor. 13:14; Phil. 2:1).

● Fellowship
with others

b The apostles' fellowship (Acts 2:42); fellowship with one another (1 John 1:7); fellowship with us (1 John 1:3); the right hand of fellowship (Gal. 2:9).

c Throw in your lot with us (Prov. 1:14).

Kindred, see **11**.

10 Unrelatedness: absence of relation

● What in
common?

a What have we in common?: Jephthah and the king of the Ammonites (Judg. 11:12); God and the Gileadites (Josh. 22:24);
David and the sons of Zeruiah (2 Sam. 16:10; 19:22); Elijah and
the widow (1 Kgs. 17:18); Elisha and the king of Israel (2 Kgs.
3:13); Neco and Josiah (2 Chr. 35:21); Israel and their enemies
(Ezra 4:3); demons and Jesus (Matt. 8:29; Mark 1:24; 5:7; Luke
4:34; 8:28); Jesus and his mother (John 2:4).

● Good and bad
separated

b What relation can exist between: righteousness and lawlessness
(2 Cor. 6:14); light and darkness (2 Cor. 6:14); a believer and an
unbeliever (2 Cor. 6:15).

c The ruler of this world has nothing in me (John 14:30); they are
not of the world just as I am not (John 17:14, 16).

d If we say we have fellowship with God and walk in darkness, we
lie (1 John 1:6).

● Have no
dealings

e Do not share with them (Eph. 5:7); take no share in the unfruitful
works of darkness (Eph. 5:11).

f Have nothing to do with that righteous man (Matt. 27:19).
Leaving others alone, see **620s**; **no dealings**, see **833a**.

11 Relations of kindred

● Related
people

a You are my bone and my flesh (Gen. 29:14); I am your bone and
your flesh (Judg. 9:2–3); Amasa is my bone and my flesh (2 Sam.
19:13); we are your bone and flesh (2 Sam. 5:1; 1 Chr. 11:1);
you elders of Judah are my brothers, my bone and my flesh
(2 Sam. 19:12).

b Jacob told Rachel he was a relative (Gen. 29:12); the king is our
close relative (2 Sam. 19:42); those killed were Gideon's brothers (Judg. 8:19); Ben-hadad is my brother (1 Kgs. 20:32);
Joseph was of the house of David (Luke 2:4).

c Two brothers, Simon and Andrew (Matt. 4:18; 10:2; Mark 1:16;
Luke 6:14; John 1:40); two other brothers, James and John (Matt.
4:21; 10:2; Mark 1:19; 3:17).
Father and mother, see **169**; **children**, see **170**.

● Marrying
relatives

d Abraham told Sarah to say she was his sister (Gen. 12:13, 19;
20:2, 5, 12); as Isaac told Rebekah (Gen. 26:7, 9).

e A wife for Isaac from his relatives (Gen. 24:4, 38); take a wife
from your cousins (Gen. 28:2).

f Sex forbidden between close relatives (Lev. 18:6–18).

● Related
nations

g Your older sister is Samaria and your younger sister Sodom
(Ezek. 16:46–56).

● Attitudes
between kin

h Relatives should not quarrel (Gen. 13:8); you must not fight
against your relatives (1 Kgs. 12:24); it is good for brothers to
live in unity (Ps. 133:1); a believer should take care of relatives

(1 Tim. 5:4, 8, 16); a priest was not to defile himself except for near kin (Lev. 21:1–4).

Kinsman-redeemer, see **792*m***; **Levirate marriage**, see **894*l***.

i Brother will deliver up brother to death (Matt. 10:21; Mark 13:12); a man's enemies will be his own family (Mic. 7:6; Matt. 10:36); betrayed by kinsmen (Luke 21:16).

Killing brothers, see **362*ac***.

j Go from your family (Gen. 12:1; Acts 7:3).

● Christ's
earthly family

k Christ's mother and brothers came to speak with him (Matt. 12:46; Mark 3:31–2; Luke 8:19); his brothers are named (Matt. 13:55; Mark 6:3); are not his sisters with us? (Matt. 13:56; Mark 6:3); his brothers did not believe (John 7:3–5); his brothers married (1 Cor. 9:5); James the Lord's brother (Gal. 1:19); his mother and brothers in the upper room (Acts 1:14).

● Christ's
true family

l Christ's true relatives are those who obey God (Matt. 12:48–50; Mark 3:33–5; Luke 8:21); he calls them brothers (Heb. 2:11–12); he is the firstborn among many brothers (Rom. 8:29); made like his brothers (Heb. 2:17); what is done to his brothers is done to him (Matt. 25:40); tell my brothers to go to Galilee (Matt. 28:10).

● God's
family

m The Father, from whom every family is named (Eph. 3:15).

n Members of God's household (Eph. 2:19); the household of faith (Gal. 6:10).

o You are all brothers (Matt. 23:8–9); treat younger people as brothers and sisters (1 Tim. 5:1–2); Onesimus is no longer a slave but a beloved brother (Philem. 16).

12 Correlation: double or reciprocal relation

● In proportion

a According to the number of people: take a lamb (Exod. 12:4); gather manna (Exod. 16:16); take an inheritance (Num. 26:53–4; 33:54); give the Levites cities (Num. 35:8); God set boundaries according to the number of the sons of Israel (Deut. 32:8).

According to the number, see **85**.

● Interdependent

b Man and woman are interdependent (1 Cor. 11:11–12).

13 Identity

● I am God

a I am Yahweh (Gen. 15:7; Exod. 6:2, 6, 29; 12:12; 20:2; 29:46); I am God Almighty [El Shaddai] (Gen. 17:1; 35:11); I am the God of Abraham (Gen. 26:24); of Abraham and Isaac (Gen. 28:13); of Abraham, Isaac and Jacob (Exod. 3:6; Acts 7:32).

I am, see **1*a***.

● Who is
God?

b Who is the Lord? (Exod. 5:2); lest I say, 'Who is the Lord?' (Prov. 30:9); who is the Almighty? (Job 21:15); who is the King of glory? (Ps. 24:8, 10).

● Who is
Jesus?

c Who are you? (John 8:25, 53; Acts 9:5; 22:8; 26:15); who is this? (Matt. 21:10; Mark 4:41; Luke 8:25; 9:9); who is the Son of Man? (John 9:36); who is this Son of man? (John 12:34); who is this who forgives sins? (Luke 7:49); Zacchaeus wanted to see who Jesus was (Luke 19:3); who do people say I am? (Matt. 16:13; Mark 8:27; Luke 9:18); are you he who is to come? (Matt. 11:3; Luke 7:19); this can't be the son of David, can it? (Matt. 12:23); are you the Christ? (Matt. 26:63; Mark 14:61; Luke 22:67; John 10:24); are you the Son of God? (Matt. 26:63; Luke 22:70); if you are the Son of God . . . (Matt. 4:3, 6; 27:40; Luke 4:3, 9).

Nature of Christ, see **5b**.

d They said he was John the Baptist, Elijah or one of the prophets (Matt. 16:14; Mark 6:14–16; 8:28; Luke 9:7–8, 19); this is John the Baptist raised from the dead (Matt. 14:2); this is the prophet Jesus from Nazareth (Matt. 21:11); just the carpenter (Mark 6:3); the carpenter's son (Matt. 13:55); Joseph's son (Luke 4:22; John 6:42); behold, the man! (John 19:5).

- Jesus is the Christ

e Some said he was the Christ (John 7:41); can this be the Christ? (John 4:29); the demons knew he was the Christ (Luke 4:41); Peter confessed him to be the Christ (Matt. 16:16; Mark 8:29; Luke 9:20); Paul proclaimed him as the Christ (Acts 9:22; 17:3; 18:5); demonstrating from the Scriptures that Jesus was the Christ (Acts 18:28); the Son of God (Matt. 27:54; Mark 3:11; Luke 4:41; Acts 9:20); the Holy One of God (Mark 1:24; Luke 4:34; John 6:69).

f He admitted he was the Christ, the Son of God (Matt. 26:63–4; Mark 14:61–2; Luke 22:67–70; John 4:26); he called himself the Son of God (John 19:7); who is the liar but he who denies that Jesus is the Christ? (1 John 2:22); it is the Lord (John 21:7).

g Many will come saying 'I am the Christ' (Matt. 24:5; Mark 13:6; Luke 21:8).

- I am the . . .

h I am: the bread of life (John 6:35, 41, 48, 51); the light of the world (John 8:12); the door (John 10:7, 9); the good shepherd (John 10:11, 14); the resurrection and the life (John 11:25); the way, the truth and the life (John 14:6); the vine (John 15:1, 5).

I AM (without an object), see **1a**.

- Who is John the Baptist?

i Who are you? (John 1:19, 22); they wondered whether John was the Christ (Luke 3:15); he was not the Christ (John 1:20; 3:28; Acts 13:25); nor the prophet (John 1:21); nor Elijah (John 1:21); except figuratively (Matt. 11:14; 17:12–13; Mark 9:13); he was not the light (John 1:8).

- Who is?

j Whose daughter are you? (Gen. 24:23, 47); whose son is this? (1 Sam. 17:55–8); whose maid is this? (Ruth 2:5); who is that man? (Gen. 24:65); who are you? (Gen. 27:18, 32; Ruth 3:9; 1 Sam. 26:14; 2 Sam. 1:8; Acts 19:15); no one dared ask, 'Who are you?' (John 21:12); the chiliarch asked who Paul was (Acts 21:33); who are these? (Gen. 48:8; Num. 22:9); who are these in white robes? (Rev. 7:13); argument over the identity of the harlots' children (1 Kgs. 3:21–7).

      k Who is he who would do this? (Esther 7:5); who is it you are speaking about? (John 13:24, 25).

● What is?   *l* Manna—what is it? (Exod. 16:15).
             Unimportant, see **639**.

● Is it really?   *m* Are you the man who spoke to her? (Judg. 13:11); is this Naomi? (Ruth 1:19); is that you, Asahel? (2 Sam. 2:20); are you Ziba? (2 Sam. 9:2); are you Joab? (2 Sam. 20:17); are you the man of God? (1 Kgs. 13:14); is it you, Elijah? (1 Kgs. 18:7); is it you, you troubler of Israel? (1 Kgs. 18:7); is this the man who made the earth tremble? (Isa. 14:16); are you the one of whom I spoke? (Ezek. 38:17); is this the one who used to sit and beg? (John 9:8–9); is this your son? (John 9:19); Lord, if it is you (Matt. 14:28).

● Is it me?   *n* It is not me, is it? (Matt. 26:22, 25; Mark 14:19).

● True identity   *o* I am Esau (Gen. 27:19, 32); it was Leah (Gen. 29:25); I am Joseph (Gen. 45:3, 4); is this not Bathsheba? (2 Sam. 11:3); it is Elijah (2 Kgs. 1:8).

      p I am the woman who prayed (1 Sam. 1:26); this is the man (1 Sam. 9:17); this is he (1 Sam. 16:12).

      q You are the man! (2 Sam. 12:7).
             Nature of people, see **5a**.

14 Contrariety

See **84**.

15 Difference

● Differentiating *a* Differentiating between clean and unclean animals (Lev. 11:47; 20:25); between holy and profane (Lev. 10:10); which Israel failed to do (Ezek. 22:26); you will distinguish betwen the righteous and the wicked (Mal. 3:18).
             Unequal, see **29**.

      b God made a distinction between Egypt and Israel (Exod. 8:22; 9:4; 11:7); God's presence made Israel distinct from other nations (Exod. 33:16).

● Different   *c* A different gospel (2 Cor. 11:4; Gal. 1:6–9); a different Jesus or
  doctrines ·   spirit (2 Cor. 11:4); different doctrine (1 Tim. 6:3); no one can lay another foundation from what has been laid (1 Cor. 3:11).

16 Uniformity

● All treated   *a* One fate comes to the righteous and the wicked (Eccles. 9:2–3);
  alike   God destroys the righteous and the wicked (Job 9:22); what befalls the fool will also befall me (Eccles. 2:15); there is no difference, for all have sinned and are justified by grace (Rom. 3:22–4); while the heir is a child he is no different from a slave (Gal. 4:1).
             Equal treatment, see **28o**.

● Uniform grace	*b* In Christ there are no distinctions between: Jew, Greek (Rom. 10:12; Gal. 3:28; Col. 3:11); slave, free, male, female (Gal. 3:28).
	c God justifies both Jew and Gentile by faith (Rom. 3:29–30); God made no distinction between Jews and Gentiles (Acts 15:9). **Jew and Gentile**, see **371ai**.
● Is God the same?	*d* Speaking of God as if he were just the same as the gods of the nations (2 Chr. 32:19); you thought that I was just like you (Ps. 50:21). **Equality with God**, see **28a**.

17 Non-uniformity

● Variety of function

● Variety of form

a Limbs do not have the same function (Rom. 12:4); believers are given diverse gifts (Rom. 12:6; 1 Cor. 12:4–31).

b Gathering fish of every kind (Matt. 13:47); flesh of different creatures differs (1 Cor. 15:39); heavenly bodies differ in splendour (1 Cor. 15:40–1).
Different, see **15**.

18 Similarity

● Made like God

a Mankind—male and female—was created in the image of God (Gen. 1:26–7; 9:6); people are made in the likeness of God (Gen. 5:1; Jas. 3:9); a man—male—is the image and glory of God (1 Cor. 11:7).
Who is like God?, see **21a**.

● Christ like God

● Becoming like God

b Christ is the image of God (2 Cor. 4:4; Col. 1:15); an exact representation of God's nature (Heb. 1:3).

c When you eat of the tree you will be like God (Gen. 3:5); the man has become like one of us (Gen. 3:22); I will make myself like the Most High (Isa. 14:14).

d The house of David will be like God (Zech. 12:8); God is renewing us according to his own image (Col. 3:10); we are being changed into the image of God (Rom. 8:29; 2 Cor. 3:18); we shall bear the image of the man of heaven (1 Cor. 15:49); when he appears we shall be like him (1 John 3:2).

● Like people

e Seth was born in the image of Adam (Gen. 5:3); like Adam they have broken the covenant (Hos. 6:7); we have borne the image of the man of earth (1 Cor. 15:49); like people, like priest (Isa. 24:2; Hos. 4:9).

f Our flesh is like our brethren's flesh (Neh. 5:5); Barnabas and Paul had the same nature as other men (Acts 14:15); as did Elijah (Jas. 5:17); Gideon's brothers were like him (Judg. 8:18); I would that all people were like me (1 Cor. 7:7).

g Mountain shadows like men (Judg. 9:36); men like trees, walking (Mark 8:24).

h May all your enemies be like Absalom! (2 Sam. 18:32).

● Christ like people

i Christ came in the likeness of sinful flesh (Rom. 8:3); born in the likeness of men (Phil. 2:7); made like his brothers (Heb. 2:17).

● Like
creatures

j Do not make a likeness of anything (Exod. 20:4; Deut. 4:16–18; 5:8); the Philistines made images of tumours and mice (1 Sam. 6:5).

Like lions, see **365ae**.

● Like the
nations

k They wanted a king, to be like all the nations (Deut. 17:14; 1 Sam. 8:5, 20); we will be like the nations, serving wood and stone (Ezek. 20:32); Moab and Seir said Judah was like all the nations (Ezek. 25:8).

l We would have been like Sodom and Gomorrah (Isa. 1:9; Rom. 9:29).

● Like other
things

m Those who make idols will be like them (Ps. 115:8; 135:18); they became detestable like the thing they loved (Hos. 9:10).

● Likening

n To what shall I liken this generation? (Matt. 11:16; Luke 7:31).

o The kingdom of heaven may be likened to: a king settling accounts (Matt. 18:23); a man sowing seed (Matt. 13:24); a mustard seed (Matt. 13:31; Luke 13:18–19); a landowner hiring men (Matt. 20:1); a king giving a wedding feast (Matt. 22:2); ten virgins (Matt. 25:1); yeast (Luke 13:20–1).

Compare, see **462**.

19 Dissimilarity

● Not like
other people

a We are not to be like the Gentiles: praying repetitiously (Matt. 6:8); lording it over others (Matt. 20:26; Mark 10:43; Luke 22:26).

b The Pharisee thanked God he was not like others (Luke 18:11).

● Not matching

c The new patch will not match the old (Luke 5:36).

20 Imitation

● Imitating
God

a Imitate God, as beloved children (Eph. 5:1); imitators of the Lord (1 Thess. 1:6); be imitators of me as I am of Christ (1 Cor. 11:1); whatever the Son sees the Father doing he also does (John 5:19); Christ suffered leaving us an example to imitate (1 Pet. 2:21); foot-washing is an example for us to imitate (John 13:15).

Conforming, see **83**.

● Imitating
believers

b Imitate the faith of your leaders (Heb. 13:7); you should imitate us (2 Thess. 3:7); follow our example (2 Thess. 3:9).

c Be imitators of me (1 Cor. 4:16; 11:1); the things you have seen in me, do (Phil. 4:9); you followed my teaching, conduct etc. (2 Tim. 3:10).

d You imitated the churches of God (1 Thess. 2:14); imitators of those who inherit the promises (Heb. 6:12); go and do the same as the good Samaritan (Luke 10:37).

● Imitating others

e Do what I do (Judg. 7:17).

● Imitating good

f Imitate good, not evil (3 John 11).

● Imitating evil

g Israel must not imitate the nations (Exod. 23:24; Lev. 18:3; Deut. 12:30; 18:9); but that is what they did (2 Kgs. 17:15); do not imitate the scribes and Pharisees (Matt. 23:3); do not be like the Gentiles (Matt. 6:8).

21 Uniqueness

● God is unique

a Who is like me? (Isa. 44:7; Jer. 49:19; 50:44); who is like you, O Lord? (Exod. 15:11); who is like the Lord? (Ps. 89:6; 113:5); is there any God besides me? (Isa. 44:8); who is a God like you? (Mic. 7:18); who is God besides the Lord? (2 Sam. 22:32; Ps. 18:31); what god is great like our God? (Ps. 77:13).

b No one is like the God of Israel (Deut. 33:26); there is no one else like him (Exod. 8:10; 9:14; 15:11; Deut. 3:24; 2 Sam. 7:22; 1 Kgs. 8:23; Ps. 35:10; 71:19; 86:8; 89:6, 8); there is no one like you (1 Chr. 17:20; 2 Chr. 6:14; 14:11; Jer. 10:6, 7).
Made like God, see **18***a*.

c You alone are God (2 Kgs. 19:15; Ps. 86:10; Isa. 37:16, 20); you alone are the Most High (Ps. 83:18); you alone are the Lord (Neh. 9:6); besides him there is no God (Isa. 45:5, 14, 18, 21); there is no god beside me (Deut. 32:39; Isa. 44:6); there is no other (Deut. 4:35, 39; 1 Kgs. 8:60; Isa. 45:6, 22; 46:9); there is no God but one (1 Cor. 8:4); the only God (1 Tim. 1:17); God is one and there is no other but him (Mark 12:32); there was no God before me or after me (Isa. 43:10); no one has heard or seen a god besides you (Isa. 64:4).

d There is no saviour but me (Hos. 13:4).

● Unique nations

e No other nation is like Israel (Deut. 4:7; 33:29; 2 Sam. 7:23; 1 Chr. 17:21; Ps. 147:20).

f Pharaoh, whom are you like in your greatness? (Ezek. 31:2); who is like Tyre? (Ezek. 27:32); there is no one besides Nineveh (Zeph. 2:15).

● Unique people

g My perfect one is unique (S. of S. 6:9); nothing can compare with wisdom (Prov. 8:11).

h There was no one like: Saul (1 Sam. 10:24); Solomon (1 Kgs. 3:12–13; 2 Chr. 1:12; Neh. 13:26); Hezekiah (2 Kgs. 18:5); Josiah (2 Kgs. 23:25); Job (Job 1:8; 2:3).

● Unique creatures

i Nothing on earth is like the crocodile (Job 41:33); who is like the beast? (Rev. 13:4).

● Unique events

j Has there been anything like this? (Deut. 4:32–4); whoever heard anything like this? (Jer. 18:13); nothing like this was ever seen in Israel (Matt. 9:33); we never saw anything like this (Mark 2:12).

● Unique trouble

k Nothing like what was done to Jerusalem (Dan. 9:12); see if there is any pain like my pain (Lam. 1:12); to what can I liken you? (Lam. 2:13); great tribulation such as has never been before (Matt. 24:21; Mark 13:19).

● Unique feasts

l No Passover like it since the days of Solomon (2 Chr. 30:26); since the days of Samuel (2 Chr. 35:18); no Feast of Booths like that since the time of Joshua (Neh. 8:17).

● Unique things

m There is no sword like Goliath's (1 Sam. 21:9); nothing like Solomon's throne (1 Kgs. 10:20; 2 Chr. 9:19); what is like the great city? (Rev. 18:18); a weight of glory beyond comparison (2 Cor. 4:17).

22 Copy

● Copying

a The king had to write out a copy of the law (Deut. 17:18).

b Artaxerxes gave Ezra a copy of the decree (Ezra 7:11).

● Shadows of the true

c The earthly sanctuary was a shadow of the true (Heb. 8:5; 9:23–4); the festivals and sabbath are a shadow of things to come (Col. 2:17); the law has only a shadow of good things to come (Heb. 10:1).
Type, see **23***b*.

● Portrait

d Whose likeness and inscription is this? (Matt. 22:20; Mark 12:16; Luke 20:24).

23 Model

● Pattern

a The tabernacle was made according to the pattern shown to Moses (Exod. 25:9, 40; 26:30; 27:8; Num. 8:4; Acts 7:44; Heb. 8:5).

● Type

b Adam was a type foreshadowing the Adam to come (Rom. 5:14); these things happened as types for us (1 Cor. 10:6, 11).
Shadows of the true, see **22***c*.

24 Agreement

See **710**.

25 Disagreement

See **709**.

Section three: Quantity

26 Quantity

● Amounts of food

a An omer of manna per head (Exod. 16:16); two omers per head on the sixth day (Exod. 16:22); a seah of flour and two of barley for a shekel (2 Kgs. 7:1, 16, 18); a quarter of a kab of dove's dung (2 Kgs. 6:25).

● Amounts of spices

b Amounts of spices: in the anointing oil (Exod. 30:23–4); in the incense (Exod. 30:34).

● Amounts of resources

c Amounts of materials for the tabernacle (Exod. 38:24–9).

d God gave Solomon wisdom like the sand of the seashore (1 Kgs. 4:29).
Dimensions, see **195**; **measurement**, see **465**.

27 Degree: relative quantity
Rank, see **73**.

28 Equality: sameness of quantity or degree

● Equality
with God

a Jesus made himself out to be equal to God (John 5:18); he who believes in me believes in him who sent me (John 12:44); he who sees me sees him who sent me (John 12:45).

b Am I in place of God? (Gen. 50:19); he did not grasp at equality with God (Phil. 2:6).

● Equality
with Christ

c As he is, so are we (1 John 4:17); receiving a believer is receiving Christ and the one who sent him (Matt. 10:40; 18:5; Mark 9:37; Luke 9:48; John 13:20); you received me as Christ himself (Gal. 4:14); listening to a disciple is listening to Christ (Luke 10:16); whatever is done for his brothers is done for Christ himself (Matt. 25:40).

d Be obedient to masters as to Christ (Eph. 6:6); as to the Lord, not to men (Eph. 6:6); work heartily, as to the Lord (Col. 3:23).

e Rejecting a disciple is rejecting Christ and the one who sent him (Luke 10:16); whatever is not done for his brothers not done for him (Matt. 25:45); sinning against the brothers, you sin against Christ (1 Cor. 8:12).

● Equality
between people

f Before God, as you are, so is the alien (Num. 15:15); one law for both you and the alien (Exod. 12:49; Lev. 24:22; Num. 9:14; 15:14–16, 29); the alien shall be as the native (Lev. 19:34).
All treated alike, see **16a**.

g You are as Pharaoh (Gen. 44:18); accept him as you would me (Philem. 17).

● Financial
equality

h The labourers were given equal wages, irrespective of hours worked (Matt. 20:12, 14); the aim is financial equality among believers (2 Cor. 8:13–14); Levites to receive equal portions (Deut. 18:8).

i The rich shall not pay more nor the poor less (Exod. 30:15).

● Equal measure

j They all had one omer per person (Exod. 16:18).

k All the stands were identical (1 Kgs. 7:37).

● Squares
and cubes

l The length, breadth and height of the city are equal (Rev. 21:16); the holy of holies was 20 cubits in length, breadth and height (1 Kgs. 6:20); 20 cubits in length and breadth (2 Chr. 3:8; Ezek. 41:4).

m The temple area was 500 cubits each side (Ezek. 42:16–20; 45:2); the central area of the land was 25 000 cubits square (Ezek. 48:20).

n Square items: the bronze altar (Exod. 27:1; 2 Chr. 4:1); the incense altar (Exod. 30:2; 37:25); the breastpiece (Exod. 28:16; 39:9); the openings of the stands (1 Kgs. 7:31); the doorposts (Ezek. 41:21).

● Equal
treatment

   o Equality in injuries caused and exacted (Exod. 21:23–5; Lev. 24:17–22); an eye for an eye and a tooth for a tooth (Matt. 5:38); your life for his life (1 Kgs. 20:39, 42; 2 Kgs. 10:24).

   p I will do to you as I plan to do to them (Num. 33:56).
All treated alike, see **16a**.

29 Inequality: difference of quantity or degree

● Unequal
mates

   a Do not plough with an ox and donkey together (Deut. 22:10); do not be misyoked with unbelievers (2 Cor. 6:14).
Difference, see **15**; **mixture**, see **43**.

● Unequal
weights

   b Do not have large and small weights (Deut. 25:13).

30 Mean

● Average

   a You are lukewarm, neither cold nor hot (Rev. 3:15–16).

31 Compensation

See **787**.

32 Much

● Gathering
much

   a Some gathered much (Exod. 16:17); he who gathered much had nothing over (Exod. 16:18; 2 Cor. 8:15).

● Faithful
in much

   b He who is faithful in little is faithful also in much (Luke 16:10).

33 Not much

● Not much
food

   a Some gathered little (Exod. 16:17); he who gathered little had no lack (Exod. 16:18; 2 Cor. 8:15); you looked for much but it came to little (Hag. 1:9); better a little with the fear of the Lord (Prov. 15:16); better a little with righteousness (Prov. 16:8); better a dry morsel with quiet (Prov. 17:1).

● Faithful
in little

   b He who is faithful in little is faithful also in much (Luke 16:10); you have been faithful in a very little (Luke 19:17).
Small, see **196**.

34 Superiority

● Greatness
of God

   a Ascribe greatness to our God (Deut. 32:3); the Father is greater than I (John 14:28); my Father is greater than all (John 10:29).

● Greatness
of Jesus

   b Jesus would be great (Luke 1:32); are you greater than our father Jacob? (John 4:12); than our father Abraham? (John 8:53); something greater than the temple is here (Matt. 12:6); greater than Solomon (Matt. 12:42; Luke 11:31); greater than Jonah (Matt. 12:41; Luke 11:32); he who comes after me is greater than me (John 1:15, 30).

● Greatness
of John

   c John would be great before the Lord (Luke 1:15); among those born of women none was greater than John (Matt. 11:11; Luke 7:28).

● Greatness in the kingdom	*d* Who is greatest in the kingdom? (Matt. 18:1); they had discussed who was the greatest (Mark 9:34; Luke 9:46; 22:24). *e* The least among you in the one who is great (Luke 9:48); he who humbles himself is the greatest (Matt. 18:4); whoever wants to be great must be the servant (Matt. 20:26–7; 23:11; Mark 9:35; 10:43–4; Luke 22:26); whoever keeps the least commandment will be greatest in the kingdom of heaven (Matt. 5:19). *f* He who is least in the kingdom is greater than John (Matt. 11:11; Luke 7:28); the believer will do greater works than these (John 14:12). *g* I am not inferior to these superlative apostles (2 Cor. 11:5; 12:11). **Importance**, see **638**.
● Advantages	*h* What advantage has a wise man over a fool? (Eccles. 6:8); what advantage has the Jew? (Rom. 3:1).

35 Inferiority

● Lowliness in the kingdom	*a* A disciple is not above his teacher (Luke 6:40); nor a slave above his master (Matt. 10:24; John 13:16; 15:20). *b* The least among you is the one who is great (Luke 9:48); he who is least in the kingdom is greater than John (Matt. 11:11; Luke 7:28); whoever annuls the least commandment will be least in the kingdom of heaven (Matt. 5:19).
● Least of all	*c* Paul counted himself the least of the apostles (1 Cor. 15:9); the least of all the saints (Eph. 3:8); the foremost of sinners (1 Tim. 1:15–16). **Unimportance**, see **639**.

36 Increase

● Growth in body	*a* Those who grew and became strong: Samuel (1 Sam. 2:21, 26; 3:19); John the Baptist (Luke 1:80); Jesus (Luke 2:40, 52). *b* You grew up in maidenhood (Ezek. 16:7). *c* Samson's hair grew again (Judg. 16:22); stay in Jericho until your beards grow (2·Sam. 10:5; 1 Chr. 19:5). *d* Her abdomen will swell up (Num. 5:21, 22, 27); they expected him to swell up and fall down dead (Acts 28:6).
● Growth in wealth	*e* You had little and it has increased greatly (Gen. 30:30).
● Kingdom growth	*f* The seed on good soil grew up (Mark 4:8; Luke 8:8); the seed sprouts and grows (Mark 4:27); mustard seed grows into a tree (Matt. 13:32; Mark 4:32; Luke 13:19). *g* Increase our faith! (Luke 17:5); desire the pure milk of the word that you may grow (1 Pet. 2:2); grow in grace and the knowledge of our Lord (2 Pet. 3:18).
● Growth of the word	*h* The word of God grew and multiplied (Acts 12:24); the word of the Lord was growing (Acts 19:20).

● Growth of the church	*i* The body of Christ grows and builds itself up (Eph. 4:16); grows with a growth from God (Col. 2:19); God gives the growth (1 Cor. 3:6–7); the structure grows into a holy temple (Eph. 2:21).

37 Decrease: no increase

● Reducing	*a* He must not reduce food, clothing or marriage rights (Exod. 21:10).
	b No reduction in the quota of bricks (Exod. 5:8–19).
	c The flood receded (Gen. 8:1–13).

38 Addition

● Adding to God	*a* God spoke these words and added no more (Deut. 5:22); do not add to God's words (Deut. 4:2; 12:32; Prov. 30:6); if anyone adds to the words, God will add to him the plagues (Rev. 22:18).
	b Nothing can be added to God's work (Eccles. 3:14).
● Adding blessing	*c* To him who has will more be given (Matt. 13:12; 25:29; Mark 4:25; Luke 8:18; 19:26); all these things will be added to you (Matt. 6:33; Luke 12:31); add to your faith virtue etc. (2 Pet. 1:5–7).
	d Hezekiah had fifteen years added to his life (2 Kgs. 20:6; Isa. 38:5).
● Adding people	*e* Joseph, may the Lord add another son (Gen. 30:24); may the Lord add a hundred times as many people (2 Sam. 24:3; 1 Chr. 21:3); the Lord added to them those who were being saved (Acts 2:47).

39 Subtraction

● Subtracting from God	*a* Do not take away from God's commands (Deut. 4:2; 12:32); if anyone subtracts from the words, God will subtract his share in the tree of life (Rev. 22:19); nothing can be taken away from God's works (Eccles. 3:14).
● Subtracting blessing	*b* From him who has not, what he has will be taken away (Matt. 13:12; 25:29; Mark 4:25; Luke 8:18; 19:26).

40 Adjunct: thing added

See **38**.

41 Remainder: thing remaining

● Offerings left over	*a* Any left from the Passover must be burned (Exod. 12:10); nothing to be left till morning (Exod. 34:25; Lev. 22:30; Num. 9:12); anything remaining from the ram of ordination must be burned (Exod. 29:34; Lev. 8:32); remainders from the peace offering to be burned (Lev. 7:15–18; 19:6–7).
● Food left over	*b* Leftovers of manna went bad (Exod. 16:19–20); except on the sabbath (Exod. 16:23–4).
	c The priests had much food left over (2 Chr. 31:10); twelve

baskets left over from feeding the five thousand (Matt. 14:20; Mark 6:43; 8:19; Luke 9:17; John 6:13); seven baskets from the four thousand (Matt. 15:37; Mark 8:8, 20); do you not remember how many baskets you gathered? (Matt. 16:9–10); they ate and had some left over (2 Kgs. 4:43–4).

d Dogs eat the crumbs that fall from the table (Matt. 15:27; Mark 7:28); the poor man wanted to eat what fell from the rich man's table (Luke 16:21).

e Moab has settled on his lees (Jer. 48:11).

● Gleaning

f Do not harvest all your field, go back for a sheaf, beat olive boughs again, or gather grapes a second time (Lev. 19:9, 10; 23:22; Deut. 24:19–21); like the gleanings of olives and grapes (Isa. 24:13); would not grape gatherers leave gleanings? (Jer. 49:9; Obad. 5).

g Ruth gleaning (Ruth 2:2–23); the gleaning of Ephraim exceeds the vintage of Abiezer (Judg. 8:2–3).

● Survivors

h Noah and his family (Gen. 7:23); Benjamin of Rachel's children (Gen. 44:20); Caleb and Joshua out of their generation (Num. 26:65); Jotham of Gideon's sons (Judg. 9:5); Mephibosheth of Saul's family (2 Sam. 9:1–4); Elijah of the prophets (1 Kgs. 18:22; 19:10, 14; Rom. 11:3).

i A few of the Anakim were left (Josh. 11:22); 600 Benjaminites were left (Judg. 20:47); of 1000 only 100 left and of 100 only 10 left (Amos 5:3); a few hairs bound in the hem and a few of those burned (Ezek. 5:3–4).

j Survivors will be terrified (Lev. 26:36).

● Stump of a tree

k Like a tree whose stump remains (Isa. 6:13); a branch from the stump of Jesse (Isa. 11:1); leave the stump with a band round it (Dan. 4:15, 23, 26).

● Remnant

l God sent me to preserve a remnant (Gen. 45:7); they will leave my husband neither name nor remnant (2 Sam. 14:7).

m Seven thousand followers of the Lord were left (1 Kgs. 19:18; Rom. 11:4).

● Remnant in the land

n None was left except Judah (2 Kgs. 17:18); the poorest people were left in the land (2 Kgs. 24:14; 25:12; Jer. 39:10; 40:7; 52:16); I will make the lame the remnant (Mic. 4:7); the king of Babylon left a remnant (Jer. 40:11); a leader was appointed for those left in the land (2 Kgs. 25:22); the remnant were taken into Egypt (Jer. 43:5–7).

● Remnant by grace

o A remnant will escape (Ezek. 6:8; 12:16); an escaped remnant (Ezra 9:13, 15); out of Zion a remnant (2 Kgs. 19:31; Isa. 37:32); survivors will be left from Jerusalem (Ezek. 14:22); the remnant who survived (Neh. 1:3); pray for the remnant (2 Kgs. 19:4; Isa. 37:4); save your people, the remnant of Israel (Jer. 31:7); the Lord left a few survivors (Isa. 1:9; Rom. 9:29); the Lord will recover the remnant (Isa. 11:11); gleanings would be left (Isa. 17:6); only a remnant (Isa. 10:21–2; Rom. 9:27).

p The remnant will lean on the Lord (Isa. 10:20); he who is left in Zion will be called holy (Isa. 4:3); the remnant will be like dew from the Lord (Mic. 5:7); a highway for the remnant (Isa. 11:16).

q By God's favour a remnant is left (Ezra 9:8); a remnant chosen by grace (Rom. 11:5).

● Remnant abandoned

r I will abandon the remnant (2 Kgs. 21:14); a remnant will not be left of the men of Anathoth (Jer. 11:23); I will take away the remnant who entered Egypt (Jer. 44:12–14); like a vine they will glean the remnant of Israel (Jer. 6:9); a lion for the remnant of Moab (Isa. 15:9).

● Land left

s Much land remains to be possessed (Josh. 13:1).

42 Decrement: thing deducted
See **39**.

43 Mixture

● Mixing unlike things

a Do not mix: seeds planted (Lev. 19:19; Deut. 22:9); animals for ploughing (Deut. 22:10; cf. 2 Cor. 6:14); animals for breeding (Lev. 19:19); materials for clothes (Lev. 19:19; Deut. 22:11).

b The image had feet of iron mixed with clay (Dan. 2:33, 41–3).

● Mixing people

c Israel mixed with the nations (Ezra 9:2; Ps. 106:35; Hos. 7:8); a mixed multitude went up with them from Egypt (Exod. 12:38); they separated themselves from the mixed multitude (Neh. 13:3); do not be unequally yoked together with unbelievers (2 Cor. 6:14).

44 Unmixed

● Singleness

a Singleness of eye (Matt. 6:22; Luke 11:34); singleness of heart (Eph. 6:5; Col. 3:22).

b Led astray from singleness and purity towards Christ (2 Cor. 11:3).

Pure in heart, see **950*b***.

45 Joining

● Physical union

a In marriage the two will become one flesh (Gen. 2:24; Matt. 19:5; Mark 10:8; Eph. 5:31); as also with a prostitute (1 Cor. 6:16); man should not separate what God has joined (Matt. 19:6; Mark 10:9).

b The bones came together (Ezek. 37:7).

● Sexual union

c If a man goes in to his wife and finds her not a virgin (Deut. 22:13–21); kill every woman who has known a man (Num. 31:17).

d Going in to the brother's widow (Deut. 25:5).

e Intercourse between: Adam and Eve (Gen. 4:1, 25); Cain and his wife (Gen. 4:17); the sons of God and the daughters of men (Gen. 6:4); Jacob and Leah (Gen. 29:23; 30:16); Jacob and Rachel (Gen. 29:30); Jacob and Bilhah (Gen. 30:3–4); Judah and Shua

(Gen. 38:2); Onan and Tamar, spilling the semen (Gen. 38:8–9); Boaz and Ruth (Ruth 4:13); Elkanah and Hannah (1 Sam. 1:19); Ithra and Abigail (2 Sam. 17:25); Ephraim and his wife (1 Chr. 7:23).

f Intercourse between: Lot's daughters and their father (Gen. 19:32–5); Reuben and Bilhah (Gen. 35:22); Judah and Tamar (Gen. 38:16–18); Eli's sons and the serving women (1 Sam. 2:22); Abner and Rizpah (2 Sam. 3:7); David and Bathsheba (2 Sam. 11:4; 12:24; Ps. 51:t); Amnon and Tamar (2 Sam. 13:14); Absalom and his father's concubines (2 Sam. 16:21–2). **Rape**, see **981***z*.

g Animals mating (Gen. 30:39, 41; 31:10).

● Sex limited

h David did not go in to the concubines again (2 Sam. 20:3); David did not know Abishag (1 Kgs. 1:4); Joseph did not know Mary until Jesus was born (Matt. 1:25).

● Prospect of sex

i There is no man to come in to us (Gen. 19:31); give me my wife that I may go in to her (Gen. 29:21); Samson wanted to go in to his wife (Judg. 15:1); lie with me (Gen. 39:7, 10, 12; 2 Sam. 13:11); he came in to lie with me (Gen. 39:14); you may go in to the captive woman (Deut. 21:13); shall I go home to lie with my wife? (2 Sam. 11:11); another will lie with your wives (2 Sam. 12:11). **Sexual desire**, see **859***n*.

● Unclean through sex

j A pair having intercourse are unclean (Lev. 15:18); sex with a menstruating woman forbidden (Lev. 15:24; 18:19; 20:18; Ezek. 18:6; 22:10); a man lying with a menstruating woman is unclean seven days (Lev. 15:24); a man lying with an unclean woman (Lev. 15:33). **Immorality**, see **951**.

● Spiritual union

k United with him in death and resurrection (Rom. 6:5); whoever is united to the Lord becomes one spirit with him (1 Cor. 6:17).

l In him the whole building is joined together (Eph. 2:21); the body is knit together (Eph. 4:16; Col. 2:19); knit together in love (Col. 2:2).

m The Israelites were united as one man (Judg. 20:11); the people of Judah were of one heart (2 Chr. 30:12); two sticks joined to represent the union of Judah and Israel (Ezek. 37:16–22); a staff called Union (Zech. 11:7, 14); Jerusalem is a city bound firmly together (Ps. 122:3).

n Gentiles were grafted in (Rom. 11:17–19, 24); God can graft Jews back in (Rom. 11:23, 24).

46 Separating

● Dividing up a body

a The Levite cut up his concubine's body (Judg. 19:29; 20:6); his master will cut him in pieces (Matt. 24:51; Luke 12:46); Samson tore the lion (Judg. 14:6); Saul cut up the yoke of oxen (1 Sam.

11:7); the chiliarch was afraid Paul would be torn in pieces (Acts 23:10).

- Severing parts of the body

b Cut off the woman's hand (Deut. 25:12); if your hand or foot causes you to sin, cut it off (Matt. 5:30; 18:8; Mark 9:43–5); they cut off their hands and feet (2 Sam. 4:12); the head and hands of Dagon were cut off (1 Sam. 5:4); they cut off Adoni-bezek's thumbs and big toes (Judg. 1:6, 7); Peter cut off the ear of the high priest's slave (Matt. 26:51; Mark 14:47; Luke 22:50; John 18:10, 26).

c Zipporah cut off her son's foreskin (Exod. 4:25); beware of the mutilators (Phil. 3:2).

d The large horn was broken (Dan. 8:8); Judas burst open (Acts 1:18).

e That what is lame may not be dislocated (Heb. 12:13).
Castration, see **172i**; **pluck out**, see **304f**; **parts of corpses**, see **363j**; **circumcision**, see **988m**.

- Beheading

f David promised to take off Goliath's head (1 Sam. 17:46); which he did (1 Sam. 17:51); they cut off Saul's head (1 Sam. 31:9); they beheaded Ishbosheth (2 Sam. 4:7); they cut off Sheba's head (2 Sam. 20:22); 70 sons of Ahab beheaded (2 Kgs. 10:6–8); let me go cut off his head (2 Sam. 16:9); those beheaded for their witness to Jesus (Rev. 20:4).

- Gashing bodies

g Do not cut your bodies mourning for the dead (Lev. 19:28; 21:5; Deut. 14:1; Jer. 16:6); the priests of Baal cut themselves with swords (1 Kgs. 18:28); how long will you gash yourselves? (Jer. 47:5); 80 men with their bodies gashed (Jer. 41:5); every hand is gashed (Jer. 48:37); gashing himself with stones (Mark 5:5).

- Breaking bones

h Like a lion he breaks all my bones (Isa. 38:13); he has broken my bones (Lam. 3:4).

i No bone of the Passover was to be broken (Exod. 12:46; Num. 9:12); none of his bones shall be broken (Ps. 34:20; John 19:36); their legs were broken (John 19:32).

- Divided things

j I will put you in the cleft of a rock (Exod. 33:22); Samson lived in the cleft of the rock at Etam (Judg. 15:8, 11); not an altar of cut stones (Exod. 20:25).

k Animals with divided hoofs (Lev. 11:3; Deut. 14:6–8).

- Dividing waters

l He separated waters from waters (Gen. 1:6–7); the waters of the Red Sea were divided (Exod. 14:16, 21); God divided the sea (Neh. 9:11; Ps. 74:13; 78:13; 136:13); he who divided the waters before them (Isa. 63:12); the waters of the Jordan were divided for Elijah (2 Kgs. 2:8); for Elisha (2 Kgs. 2:14).

- Breaking rocky things

m God split rocks in the wilderness (Ps. 78:15); is not my word like hammer which shatters the rocks? (Jer. 23:29); rocks were split when Jesus died (Matt. 27:51); God split the hollow place in Lehi (Judg. 15:19); the altar was split apart (1 Kgs. 13:3, 5); the tablets were broken (Exod. 32:19; Deut. 9:17).

n The mount of Olives will be split in two (Zech. 14:4).

- Breaking earthenware

 o They broke the pitchers (Judg. 7:19–20); breaking contaminated earthenware (Lev. 11:33, 35; 15:12); you will shatter them like earthenware with a rod of iron (Ps. 2:9); break the jar (Jer. 19:10); they will break Moab's jars (Jer. 48:12).

- Breaking bread

 p Jesus broke the loaves (Matt. 14:19; 15:36; 26:26; Mark 6:41; Luke 22:19; 24:30; 1 Cor. 11:24); he was recognised by the breaking of bread (Luke 24:35).

 q On the first day of the week they gathered to break bread (Acts 20:7, 11); Paul gave thanks and broke bread (Acts 27:35); the bread which we break is a sharing in the body of Christ (1 Cor. 10:16).

- Breaking sticks

 r I broke the staff called Favour (Zech. 11:10); I broke the staff called Union (Zech. 11:14); a bruised reed he will not break (Isa. 42:3; Matt. 12:20).

- Tearing

 s There is a time to rend (Eccles. 3:7).

 t Saul tore the edge of Samuel's robe (1 Sam. 15:27); the Lord has torn the kingdom from you (1 Sam. 15:28; 28:17); Ahijah tore his cloak in 12 pieces (1 Kgs. 11:30); David cut off the edge of Saul's robe (1 Sam. 24:4–5, 11); Elisha tore his garments in two (2 Kgs. 2:12); the high priest tore his clothes (Matt. 26:65; Mark 14:63); the new patch is torn (Luke 5:36); their nets began to break (Luke 5:6).

 Tearing clothes in grief, see **836g**.

 u The veil of the temple was torn in two (Luke 23:45) from top to bottom (Matt. 27:51; Mark 15:38).

- Dividing things

 v God separated light from darkness (Gen. 1:4); by means of sun, moon and stars (Gen. 1:14, 18).

 w New wine bursts old wineskins (Matt. 9:17; Mark 2:22; Luke 5:37); the ropes melted from Samson's arms (Judg. 15:14); Samson snapped the new ropes (Judg. 16:12); the bowstrings (Judg. 16:9); Hananiah broke Jeremiah's yoke (Jer. 28:10–12); he broke the chains and fetters (Mark 5:4).

 x The king cut pieces off the scroll and burnt them (Jer. 36:23).

 y The stern of the ship was broken up by the waves (Acts 27:41).

- Cutting trees

 z Sidonians cutting cedar (1 Kgs. 5:6); felling good trees (2 Kgs. 3:19, 25); sons of the prophets cutting trees (2 Kgs. 6:4).

 aa I cut down cedars and cypresses of Lebanon (Isa. 37:24); they will cut down your choicest cedars (Jer. 22:7); they have cut down the forest of Egypt (Jer. 46:23).

 ab The voice of the Lord breaks cedars of Lebanon (Ps. 29:5); the Lord will lop the boughs and cut down Lebanon (Isa. 10:33–4); cut down the trees and cast up a siege (Jer. 6:6); the tree of Assyria cut down (Ezek. 31:12).

 ac Every fruitless tree is felled and burned (Matt. 3:10; 7:19; Luke 3:9); chop down the tree and cut off the branches (Dan. 4:14, 23); cut it down (Luke 13:7, 9).

- Separation from God

ad Your iniquities have separated you from God (Isa. 59:2); Uzziah was cut off from the house of the Lord (2 Chr. 26:21); separated from Christ (Eph. 2:12); eternal destruction away from the face of the Lord (2 Thess. 1:9); branches were broken off the olive tree (Rom. 11:17–24); continue in his kindness or you too will be cut off (Rom. 11:22); you who would be justified by the law are estranged from Christ (Gal. 5:4).

ae Paul could wish himself accursed from Christ for the sake of his kinsmen (Rom. 9:3).

af Nothing can separate us from the love of Christ (Rom. 8:35, 38–9).

- Nazirites

ag The Nazirite took a vow of separation (Num. 6:1–21); Samson would be a Nazirite from the womb (Judg. 13:5; 16:17); a razor would never come on Samson's head (1 Sam. 1:11).

ah I raised up some of your young men to be Nazirites (Amos 2:11); you made the Nazirites drink wine (Amos 2:12).

- Separation of kingdoms

ai The nations were separated (Gen. 10:5, 32); in Peleg's time the earth was divided (Gen. 10:25; 1 Chr. 1:19); God had made a breach in Israel (Judg. 21:15).

aj Division into the two kingdoms of Israel and Judah (1 Kgs. 12:16–20); Israel divided into two parts (1 Kgs. 16:21); I tore the kingdom from the house of David (1 Kgs. 14:8); Israel torn from the house of David (2 Kgs. 17:21).

ak A divided kingdom or family must fall, so how can Satan's kingdom be divided? (Matt. 12:25–6; Mark 3:24–6; Luke 11:17–18); PERES—your kingdom is divided (Dan. 5:28).

al Abraham divided his forces against the kings (Gen. 14:15).

- People separating

am Abraham and Lot separated (Gen. 13:9); Paul separated from Barnabas (Acts 15:39); a wife must not separate from her husband (1 Cor. 7:10); what God has joined together, let not man separate (Matt. 19:6; Mark 10:9).
Mourning parting, see **836ad**.

an He parted from them (Luke 24:51).

- People divided

ao The people were divided about Jesus (John 7:43; 9:16; 10:19); the city was divided about the gospel (Acts 14:4); households will be divided (Luke 12:52–3); I came to bring division (Luke 12:51).

ap Let there be no divisions (1 Cor. 1:10; 12:25); warn a man who is factious (Titus 3:10); divisions among the Corinthians (1 Cor. 11:18); these are the ones who cause divisions (Jude 19); is Christ divided? (1 Cor. 1:13).

- Separate from evil

aq Be separate, says the Lord (2 Cor. 6:17); the Israelites had to separate themselves from the people of the land (Ezra 6:21; 9:1–2; 10:11; Neh. 9:2; 13:3, 30); God separated them from other people (Lev. 20:24, 26; 1 Kgs. 8:53); I will separate my people and your people (Exod. 8:23); a people dwelling by itself (Num. 23:9); those who had separated from the people of the land (Neh.

10:28); the world has been crucified to me and I to the world (Gal. 6:14); the Levites were separated from the other Israelites (Num. 8:14; 16:9; Deut. 10:8).

ar Keep back from the tents of Korah's men (Num. 16:24, 26); get away from this congregation (Num. 16:45); Kenites, get out from Amalek (1 Sam. 15:6).

as He will separate them as sheep from goats (Matt. 25:32).

47 Bond: connecting medium

● Clasps

a Clasps for: the veil (Exod. 26:33); the linen curtains (Exod. 26:6; 36:13); goats' hair curtains (Exod. 26:11; 36:18).

● Tent pegs

b Pegs for the court (Exod. 27:19; 38:20; 38:31; 39:40); Merari looked after the pegs (Num. 3:37); Jael killed Sisera with a tent peg (Judg. 4:21; 5:26).

● Tenons and bars

c Tenons for the boards (Exod. 26:19; 36:22–4); bars to connect the boards (Exod. 26:26–8; 36:31–4; 39:33).

● Binding clothing

d Binding so that the robe of the ephod not be torn (Exod. 28:32; 39:23); there is a time to sew together (Eccles. 3:7).

e Patching clothing with unshrunk cloth (Matt. 9:16; Mark 2:21).

● Chains

f Peter was bound with two chains (Acts 12:6); Paul was bound with two chains (Acts 21:33); like me, except for these chains (Acts 26:29); this chain is due to the hope of Israel (Acts 28:20); Onesiphorus was not ashamed of my chains (2 Tim. 1:16); an angel with a great chain in his hand (Rev. 20:1).

g His chains fell off his hands (Acts 12:7); everyone's chains were unfastened (Acts 16:26).

h Chains to connect the breastpiece and ephod (Exod. 28:22–8).

● Anchors

i They cast four anchors from the stern (Acts 27:29); pretending to lay out anchors from the bow (Acts 27:30); they cast off the anchors (Acts 27:40).

j This hope we have as an anchor of the soul (Heb. 6:19).

● Spiritual bonds

k Preserve the unity of the Spirit in the bond of peace (Eph. 4:3); love is the bond of unity (Col. 3:14); the body of Christ is held together with sinews (Col. 2:19).

48 Cohesion

● Clinging to God

a Cling to the Lord (Josh. 23:8); Hezekiah clung to the Lord (2 Kgs. 18:6); my soul clings to you (Ps. 63:8).

● Clinging to people

b Ruth clung to Naomi (Ruth 1:14); the lame man clung to Peter and John (Acts 3:11).

● Clinging to things

c In the Son all things hold together (Col. 1:17).

d Eleazar's hand stuck to the sword (2 Sam. 23:10).

49 Non-cohesion

Slippery, see **258*b***.

50 Combination

Mixture, see **43**; **joining**, see **45**.

51 Decomposition

● Things
decaying

a Leftovers of manna bred worms (Exod. 16:20); except on the sabbath (Exod. 16:24).

b Your riches have rotted and your garments are moth-eaten (Jas. 5:2); treasures on earth, where moth and rust devour (Matt. 6:19–20); he who sows to the flesh will reap corruption (Gal. 6:8); woe to the city, the pot with the rust in it (Ezek. 24:6); let its rust be consumed (Ezek. 24:11–12).
Wear out, see **655c**.

c The mountain crumbles away (Job 14:18).

● People
decaying

d Putrefaction instead of perfume (Isa. 3:24); I am like a moth and rot to Israel and Judah (Hos. 5:12); the moth will eat them like a garment (Isa. 51:8); our outward man is decaying (2 Cor. 4:16); David saw corruption (Acts 13:36).

e Maggots are your bed and worms your covering (Isa. 14:11); their worm will not die (Isa. 66:24); where their worm does not die (Mark 9:48); Herod was eaten by worms (Acts 12:23).

● No decay

f Treasure in heaven, where no moth destroys (Luke 12:33); you will not allow your holy one to see decay (Acts 2:27; 13:35); he whom God raised saw no corruption (Acts 13:37).

52 Whole. Principal part

See **54**.

53 Part

● Discipline
of limbs

a Do not yield your limbs to sin (Rom. 6:13); yield your limbs as slaves to righteousness (Rom. 6:19); put to death your earthly limbs (Col. 3:5).

● Christ's
limbs

b Believers are members in Christ's body (Rom. 12:4–5; 1 Cor. 6:15–16; 12:12–27; Eph. 5:30); we are members of one another (Eph. 4:25).

● Hands and
fingers

c Hand for hand, foot for foot (Exod. 21:24; Deut. 19:21); cut off the woman's hand (Deut. 25:12); if your right hand makes you stumble, cut it off (Matt. 5:30; 18:8); better that one limb perish rather than the whole body perish (Matt. 5:29–30; 18:8–9; Mark 9:43–8).

d Bind these words on your hand (Deut. 6:8; 11:18); a sign on your hand (Exod. 13:9, 16).

e Solomon prayed with hands raised to heaven (1 Kgs. 8:54; 2 Chr. 6:12–13).
Lifting hands, see **310i**.

f Moses' hand became leprous (Exod. 4:6–7); a man with a withered hand (Matt. 12:10; Mark 3:1; Luke 6:6); stretch out your hand (Matt. 12:13; Mark 3:5; Luke 6:10); strengthen the weak hands (Heb. 12:12).

g Nebuchadnezzar's nails were like bird's claws (Dan. 4:33); the fingers of a man's hand wrote on the wall (Dan. 5:5).

h The cherubim had human hands under their wings (Ezek. 1:8; 10:8, 21); his hands are gold (S. of S. 5:14).
Wave hands, see **317d**; **laying on of hands**, see **378t**.

● Christ's hands

i See my hands and feet (Luke 24:39–40); he showed them his hands and his side (John 20:20); put out your finger and see my hands (John 20:27).

● Feet and legs

j Mephibosheth had not seen to his feet (2 Sam. 19:24); she caught hold of Elisha's feet (2 Kgs. 4:27); Asa had diseased feet (2 Chr. 16:12); as a shepherd snatches away two legs or part of an ear (Amos 3:12); strengthen the weak knees (Heb. 12:12).

k Washing the disciples' feet (John 13:5–14); not my feet only, but also my hands and my head (John 13:9); if she has washed the saints' feet (1 Tim. 5:10).

l Their feet were like calves' feet (Ezek. 1:7); his legs are alabaster pillars (S. of S. 5:15); his feet like burnished bronze (Rev. 1:15; 2:18); how lovely are your feet (S. of S. 7:1); the feet of him who brings good news (Isa. 52:7; Nahum 1:15; Rom. 10:15); feet shod with the preparation of the gospel (Eph. 6:15).

m Creatures with many feet are detestable (Lev. 11:42).

n If the foot should say, 'I am not a hand' (1 Cor. 12:15).

● Digits

o On right thumb and right big toe: blood (Exod. 29:20; Lev. 8:23–4; 14:14); oil (Lev. 14:17, 28).

p Tables written with the finger of God (Exod. 31:18; Deut. 9:10); this is the finger of God (Exod. 8:19); if I cast out demons by the finger of God (Luke 11:20); Jesus wrote on the ground with his finger (John 8:6).

q Cutting off thumbs and big toes (Judg. 1:6, 7).

r Six fingers and six toes (2 Sam. 21:20).

● Fins

s Sea creatures with fins and scales are clean (Lev. 11:9–12; Deut. 14:9–10).

● Organs

t Offering kidneys, liver, fat tail etc. (Lev. 3:4, 10, 15; 4:9; 7:4; 8:16, 25; 9:10, 19).

● Branches

u Branches spread on the road (Matt. 21:8; Mark 11:8); they took palm branches to meet him (John 12:13); palm branches in their hands (Rev. 7:9).

v The branch of the Lord will be glorious (Isa. 4:2); a righteous branch will reign (Jer. 23:5; 33:15); my servant the Branch (Zech. 3:8); a man whose name is the Branch will build the temple (Zech. 6:12); a branch from the roots of Jesse (Isa. 11:1); he shall be called a Nazarene [Heb. *nezer* 'branch'] (Matt. 2:23).

w I am the vine, you are the branches (John 15:5); unfruitful branches are severed (John 15:2, 6); branches of the olive tree are broken off and Gentiles grafted in (Rom. 11:16–24).

- Subdivisions   *x* 24 divisions of priests (1 Chr. 24:3–31); divisions of priests and Levites (1 Chr. 28:13, 21; 2 Chr. 8:14); Hezekiah appointed the divisions of priests and Levites (2 Chr. 31:2); priests and Levites appointed according to their divisions (Ezra 6:18); stand in the holy place according to your divisions (2 Chr. 35:4–5, 10).

    y Divisions of the gatekeepers (1 Chr. 26:1; 2 Chr. 8:14); 12 divisions of the army (1 Chr. 27:1–15).

54 Completeness

- Filling things   *a* The boat was filling with water (Mark 4:37; Luke 8:23); they filled both the boats with fish (Luke 5:7); they filled the jars to the brim (John 2:7).

    b The house was full of people (Judg. 16:27).

- Filling the earth   *c* Mankind was to fill the earth (Gen. 1:28).

    d All the earth will be filled with the glory of God (Num. 14:21); the earth will be filled with the knowledge of the Lord (Isa. 11:9); all the earth will be filled with the knowledge of the glory of the Lord (Hab. 2:14).

- Filling people   *e* I went out full, but returned empty (Ruth 1:21); I am filled (Phil. 4:18).

- Fullness of God   *f* In Christ all fullness dwells (Col. 1:19); in him all the fullness of God dwells in a body (Col. 2:9); the measure of the stature of the fullness of Christ (Eph. 4:13); he ascended so that he might fill all things (Eph. 4:10); the church is the fullness of him who fills all in all (Eph. 1:23).

- Filled with God   *g* May the whole earth be filled with his glory (Ps. 72:19).

    h Be filled with the Spirit (Eph. 5:18); the seven men should be full of the Spirit (Acts 6:3).

    i People filled with the Holy Spirit: Bezalel (Exod. 31:3; 35:31); John the Baptist—from his mother's womb (Luke 1:15); Elizabeth (Luke 1:41); Zacharias (Luke 1:67); Jesus (Luke 4:1); the disciples in Jerusalem (Acts 2:4; 4:31); Peter (Acts 4:8); Stephen (Acts 6:5; 7:55); Paul (Acts 9:17; 13:9); Barnabas (Acts 11:24); the disciples in Antioch of Pisidia (Acts 13:52).

    Filled with the Spirit, see **965*q***.

    j You have been filled in him (Col. 2:10); already you are filled! (1 Cor. 4:8); filled with all the fullness of God (Eph. 3:19); from his fullness we have all received (John 1:16).

- Fullness of God's kingdom   *k* The wedding hall was filled with guests (Matt. 22:10); that my house may be filled (Luke 14:23); when the net was full they drew it ashore (Matt. 13:48).

    l Israel is hardened until the full number of the Gentiles come in (Rom. 11:25); they rest until the full number of their martyred brothers should be complete (Rev. 6:11); what will the fullness of Israel be! (Rom. 11:12); all Israel will be saved (Rom. 11:26).

55 Incompleteness
See **726**.

56 Composition
Arrangement, see **65**.

57 Exclusion
See **300**.

58 Component
See **53**.

59 Foreigner

● Gentiles'
nature

a Gentiles: greet their brothers (Matt. 5:47); pray repetitiously (Matt. 6:7); are concerned about food and clothing (Matt. 6:32; Luke 12:30); are liars and deceitful (Ps. 144:7–8, 11); are darkened in their minds (Eph. 4:17–18); strangers to the covenants of promise (Eph. 2:12); do not know God (1 Thess. 4:5).

b Kings collect tax from strangers (Matt. 17:25–6); the rulers of the Gentiles lord it over them (Matt. 20:25).

● Suffering from
foreigners

c I will give you into the hands of aliens (Ezek. 11:9); they will deliver him to the Gentiles (Matt. 20:19; Mark 10:33; Luke 18:32); I will bring strangers upon Tyre (Ezek. 28:7).

d How can we sing the Lord's song on foreign soil? (Ps. 137:4).

e He came as an alien and is acting the judge (Gen. 19:9).

● Foreigners in
the holy places

f Our inheritance has been turned over to foreigners (Lam. 5:2); Jerusalem will be trampled by the Gentiles (Luke 21:24); the Gentiles will trample on the holy city for 42 months (Rev. 11:2); aliens have entered the holy places of the temple (Jer. 51:51); nations you forbade have entered her sanctuary (Lam. 1:10).

g You brought foreigners into God's sanctuary (Ezek. 44:7, 9); they thought Paul had brought Greeks into the temple (Acts 21:28–9).

h Strangers will no more pass through Jerusalem (Joel 3:17).

● Foreigners
restricted

i No foreigner may eat of the Passover (Exod. 12:43); no Ammonite or Moabite should ever enter God's assembly (Deut. 23:3–4; Neh. 13:1–3); foreigners excluded from Israel (Neh. 13:3).

Nations, see **371**.

j David set foreigners to quarry stones (1 Chr. 22:2); Solomon set foreigners to labour (2 Chr. 2:17–18).

k The king may not be a foreigner (Deut. 17:15).

● Foreigners'
hope

l Regulations for a sojourner who wants to keep the Passover (Exod. 12:48; Num. 9:14); or who wants to make a sacrifice (Num. 15:14).

m May the foreigner's prayer be heard (1 Kgs. 8:41–3; 2 Chr. 6:32–3); the foreigner should not think that God will exclude him

(Isa. 56:3); God will make the foreigners joyful in his house of prayer (Isa. 56:6).

n Rejoice, Gentiles, with his people (Deut. 32:43; Rom. 15:10); praise the Lord, all you Gentiles (Ps. 117:1; Rom. 15:11); I will give praise to you among the Gentiles (2 Sam. 22:50; Ps. 18:49; Rom. 15:9).

o Sojourners will join the house of Jacob (Isa. 14:1); foreigners will rebuild your walls (Isa. 60:10); foreigners will be your shepherds and farmers (Isa. 61:5); foreigners come cringing (2 Sam. 22:44–5; Ps. 18:45); aliens will be as native-born (Ezek. 47:22); we are no longer foreigners but fellow-citizens (Eph. 2:19).

p The foreigner will rise higher and higher (Deut. 28:43); he will proclaim justice to the Gentiles (Isa. 42:1; Matt. 12:18); in his name will the Gentiles hope (Matt. 12:21; Rom. 15:12); the Gentiles who are called by my name (Acts 15:17); Galilee of the Gentiles (Isa. 9:1; Matt. 4:15).

● Salvation for Gentiles

q The Lord's servant will be a light for the Gentiles (Isa. 42:6; 49:6; Acts 13:47); a light to lighten the Gentiles (Luke 2:32); Greeks wanted to see Jesus (John 12:20–1); the Gentiles had received the word of God (Acts 11:1); God has granted repentance to the Gentiles (Acts 11:18); God had opened a door of faith to the Gentiles (Acts 14:27); in Antioch the gospel was first preached to Greeks (Acts 11:20); Gentiles can hear the word of the gospel and believe (Acts 15:7); the salvation of God is sent to the Gentiles (Acts 28:28); taking from the Gentiles a people for his name (Acts 15:14); for the obedience of faith among all the Gentiles (Rom. 1:5).

r We turn to the Gentiles (Acts 13:46); from now on I go to the Gentiles (Acts 18:6); I am an apostle to the Gentiles (Rom. 11:13); God sent Paul to the Gentiles (Acts 26:17; Gal. 2:7); I will send you to the Gentiles (Acts 22:21); I am a debtor both to Greeks and barbarians (Rom. 1:14); God chose that by my mouth the Gentiles should hear (Acts 15:7); what God had done among the Gentiles through him (Acts 21:19).

● Specific foreigners

s David left his parents with the king of Moab (1 Sam. 22:3–4); David lived with the king of Gath (1 Sam. 27:2–3); I am the son of an alien (2 Sam. 1:13).

t David told Ittai the Gittite to go back (2 Sam. 15:19–22); Elijah was only sent to a widow of Sidon (Luke 4:26); Elisha only cleansed Naaman the Syrian of leprosy (Luke 4:27); the Samaritan was the only one to give thanks (Luke 17:16–18); the Samaritan was the only one to take pity (Luke 10:33); the Canaanite woman's daughter was healed (Matt. 15:22–8; Mark 7:26); Philip preached to the Samaritans (Acts 8:5–8).

● Reckoned as foreigners

u Abraham was a sojourner (Gen. 23:4); Abraham lived as an alien in the land (Heb. 11:9); Abraham's descendants would be sojourners in another land (Gen. 15:13; Acts 7:6); Gershom—a sojourner (Exod. 2:22; 18:3).

v Laban treated his daughters as foreigners (Gen. 31:15); I have become a stranger to my brothers (Ps. 69:8); if I do not know the meaning of the language I will be a foreigner (1 Cor. 14:11).

w You are just strangers and sojourners (Lev. 25:23); all God's people are sojourners on earth (1 Chr. 29:15); foreigners and exiles in this world (Heb. 11:13; 1 Pet. 2:11); sojourners scattered abroad (1 Pet. 1:1); I am a stranger in the earth (Ps. 119:19).

x I am like a stranger to God (Ps. 39:12); God has become like a sojourner in the land (Jer. 14:8).

- Foreigners avoided

y The Levite would not spend the night with foreigners (Judg. 19:12); a Jew may not associate with a foreigner (Acts 10:28); Ephraim mixes with the nations and foreigners sap his strength (Hos. 7:8–9); do not go to the Gentiles or Samaritans (Matt. 10:5); a stranger they will not follow (John 10:5).

z Treat an obdurate brother as you would a Gentile or tax collector (Matt. 18:17); Christian workers went out, accepting nothing from Gentiles (3 John 7).

- Kindness to strangers

aa God loves aliens and gives them food and clothing (Deut. 10:18); the Lord protects strangers (Ps. 146:9).

ab Support foreigners as you do the poor (Lev. 25:35); invite the alien to the Feast of Booths (Deut. 16:14); do not overlook hospitality to foreigners, for some have entertained angels (Heb. 13:2).

ac Give the alien: food (Deut. 14:29); firstfruits (Deut. 26:11); gleanings (Lev. 19:10; 23:22; Deut. 24:19–21); the tithe (Deut. 26:12–13).

ad I was a stranger and you welcomed me (Matt. 25:35); when did we see you a stranger? (Matt. 25:38, 44).

- Unkindness to strangers

ae Do not ill-treat foreigners because you were sojourners yourselves in Egypt (Exod. 22:21; 23:9; Lev. 19:33–4; Deut. 10:19; 23:7); do not pervert justice due to an alien (Deut. 24:17; 27:19).

af Evildoers murder strangers (Ps. 94:6); they have oppressed the alien (Ezek. 22:7, 29); I was a stranger and you did not welcome me (Matt. 25:43).

- Wisdom towards foreigners

ag An elder must have a good reputation with those outside (1 Tim. 3:7); behave rightly towards outsiders (1 Thess. 4:12); act wisely towards outsiders (Col. 4:5).

ah Solomon loved many foreign women (1 Kgs. 11:1).

Section four: Order

60 Order

- Orderliness

a Let all things be done in an orderly manner (1 Cor. 14:40); I rejoice to see your orderliness (Col. 2:5).

● Orderly
things

   b The fixed order of the universe (Jer. 31:35, 36); to write an orderly account (Luke 1:3).

   c Ahithophel put his house in order (2 Sam. 17:23); the unclean spirit found the house swept and put in order (Matt. 12:44; Luke 11:25).

   d They trimmed their lamps (Matt. 25:7).

● Orderly
army

   e Belts are not undone nor sandal thongs broken (Isa. 5:27); there is no straggler in the ranks (Isa. 14:31); the locusts march in order (Joel 2:7–8).

61 Disorder

● Disorder
at large

   a The people were running loose (Exod. 32:25); I saw a great tumult (2 Sam. 18:29); there was uproar over Paul (Acts 17:5; 19:29, 32, 40; 20:1); uproar at a funeral (Matt. 9:23); possible uproar over Christ's arrest and death (Matt. 26:5; 27:24; Mark 14:2).

● Enemies
disordered

   b God will throw your enemies into confusion (Deut. 7:23); there was a commotion among the Philistines (1 Sam. 14:19, 20).

● Disorder in
the church

   c God is not a God of disorder (1 Cor. 14:33); Paul feared there may be disorder in the church (2 Cor. 12:20); where jealousy exists there will be disorder (Jas. 3:16).

62 Arrangement: reduction to order
See **65**.

63 Derangement
See **61**.

64 Precedence
See **283**.

65 Sequence

● In turn

   a All are raised in their own order (1 Cor. 15:23); the natural is first, then the spiritual (1 Cor. 15:46).

   b Those speaking in tongues should speak in turn (1 Cor. 14:27); prophesying should be done one at a time (1 Cor. 14:31).

● Order of
march

   c The order of march from the camp of Israel (Num. 2:1–34; 10:13–28).

   Ordered according to seniority, see **73**.

66 Forerunner

● Forerunner

   a Jesus has entered the shrine as a forerunner (Heb. 6:20).

   b John was a forerunner for Jesus (Matt. 3:3–12; Mark 1:2–8; Luke 3:3–17; John 1:23).

67 Sequel
See **284**.

68 Beginning

● God the
beginning

a Christ the beginning of God's creation (Rev. 3:14); Jesus the Alpha and the Omega (Rev. 22:13); also said of God (Rev. 21:6); of the Lord God (Rev. 1:8); Jesus the Beginning and the End (Rev. 22:13); also said of God (Rev. 21:6); Jesus the First and the Last (Rev. 1:17; 2:8; 22:13); also said of God (Isa. 44:6; 48:12); I am the first and with the last (Isa. 41:4).
Creation, see **164**.

● Start of
all things

b In the beginning God created heavens and earth (Gen. 1:1; Heb. 1:10); in the beginning was the Word (John 1:1); him who has been from the beginning (1 John 2:13–14); God set up wisdom at the beginning of his way (Prov. 8:22–3); the Word was in the beginning with God (John 1:2); what was from the beginning (1 John 1:1).

c Before the foundation of the world: the Father loved the Son (John 17:24); the kingdom prepared for the elect (Matt. 25:34); their names written in the book of life (Rev. 13:8; 17:8); God chose them (Eph. 1:4); Christ the Lamb of God was foreknown (1 Pet. 1:20); the Son had glory together with the Father (John 17:5).

d God chose you from the beginning to be saved (2 Thess. 2:13).

e The first month of the year, the beginning of months (Exod. 12:2).

f Were you the first man? (Job 15:7); it was not like this from the beginning (Matt. 19:8).

g The devil sinned from the beginning (1 John 3:8).

● First to act

h Who should be the first to fight? (Judg. 1:1; 10:18; 20:18; 1 Kgs. 20:14); Abijah began the battle (2 Chr. 13:3).

i The first of the house of Joseph to greet the king (2 Sam. 19:20).

● First one

j The first will be last and the last first (Matt. 19:30; Mark 10:31); the last will be first and the first last (Matt. 20:16; Luke 13:30); whoever wants to be first must be your slave (Matt. 20:27); if anyone wants to be first he must be last of all and servant of all (Mark 9:35).

● Beginning of
the gospel

k Christ is the originator of our salvation (Heb. 2:10); the originator of our faith (Heb. 12:2); the beginning, the firstborn from the dead (Col. 1:18); Christ would be the first to rise from the dead (Acts 26:23); the firstfruits of those who slept (1 Cor. 15:20, 23).

l The beginning of the gospel of Jesus Christ (Mark 1:1); from that time Jesus began to preach (Matt. 4:17); the first of his signs (John 2:11); he began to speak to them in parables (Mark 12:1); from that time he began to teach them about his sufferings (Matt. 16:21; Mark 8:31).

m He who began a good work in you will complete it (Phil. 1:6); let what you heard from the beginning remain in you (1 John 2:24).

- **To the Jew first**

  n The word preached thoughout Judea, beginning from Galilee (Acts 10:37); the gospel to be preached beginning from Jerusalem (Luke 24:47; Acts 1:8); God sent Christ to the Jews first (Acts 3:26); the word of God to be spoken first to the Jews (Acts 13:46); the gospel is to the Jew first (Rom. 1:16; cf. 2:9, 10).

- **First among the Gentiles**

  o In Antioch the disciples were first called Christians (Acts 11:26); how God first visited the Gentiles (Acts 15:14); the first day Paul set foot in Asia (Acts 20:18); Epaenetus was the first convert in Asia (Rom. 16:5); Paul was the first to bring the gospel to Corinth (2 Cor. 10:14).

  Firstborn, see **119**; **firstfruits**, see **171***l*.

69 End

- **End of things**

  a The end of a thing is better than its beginning (Eccles. 7:8); on the last day of the feast Jesus stood (John 7:37).

  b The end of all flesh (Gen. 6:13); Christ is the end of the law (Rom. 10:4).

- **Last one**

  c The first will be last and the last first (Matt. 19:30; Mark 10:31); the last will be first and the first last (Matt. 20:16; Luke 13:30).

- **End of the ages**

  d Christ has appeared at the end of the ages (Heb. 9:26); manifested in the last time (1 Pet. 1:20); the Holy Spirit would be poured out in the last days (Acts 2:17); children, it is the last hour (1 John 2:18); the end of the ages has come upon us (1 Cor. 10:11); the end of all things is at hand (1 Pet. 4:7); the end is not yet (Luke 21:9); you have stored up treasure in the last days (Jas. 5:3).

  e The vision is for the time of the end (Dan. 8:17, 19); the end of the age (Matt. 13:39, 49; 24:3); I am with you to the end of the age (Matt. 28:20); the gospel will be preached in all the world and then the end will come (Matt. 24:14); then comes the end (1 Cor. 15:24); salvation to be revealed in the last time (1 Pet. 1:5); afterwards you will receive me to glory (Ps. 73:24).

  f He who endures to the end will be saved (Matt. 10:22; 24:13; Mark 13:13).

  g The seven last plagues (Rev. 15:1).

  The Beginning and the End, see **68***a*.

- **End of the ungodly**

  h Your end has come (Jer. 51:13); the end has come (Ezek. 7:6); the end is coming to the land (Ezek. 7:2–3); the end has come for Israel (Amos 8:2); he will make a full end of the inhabitants of the earth (Zeph. 1:18).

  i What will be the end of those who do not obey the gospel? (1 Pet. 4:17); I perceived their end (Ps. 73:17); their end will be according to their deeds (2 Cor. 11:15); their end is destruction (Phil. 3:19); if it bears thorns and thistles, its end is to be burned (Heb. 6:8).

  The end of liars, see **545***d*.

- **Final words**

  j The last words of David (2 Sam. 23:1); the prayers of David are ended (Ps. 72:20); the words of Job are ended (Job 31:40); thus

far are the words of Jeremiah (Jer. 51:64); when Jesus had
finished these parables (Matt. 13:53); when Jesus had finished
these sayings (Matt. 26:1; Luke 7:1).

70 Middle
Average, see **30**.

71 Continuity: uninterrupted sequence
See **65**.

72 Discontinuity: interrupted sequence
Separating, see **46**.

73 Ranking

● Rank

a The brothers were positioned according to age (Gen. 43:33);
beginning with the oldest and ending with the youngest (Gen.
44:12); according to their birth (Exod. 28:10).

74 Gathering

● Gathering
waters

a Gathering the waters into seas (Gen. 1:9–10).

● God
gathering

b God will gather his people from the nations where they have been
scattered (Deut. 30:4; Neh. 1:9; Ps. 106:47; Isa. 11:11–12; Jer.
29:14; 32:37; Ezek. 11:17; 20:34, 41; 28:25; 34:13; 36:24;
37:21); from Egypt and Assyria (Zech. 10:10); from east and
west (Isa. 43:5); when I gather them from the lands (Ezek.
39:27); he gathered in the redeemed from all the lands (Ps.
107:2–3); from the ends of the earth (Jer. 31:8); from the four
winds (Matt. 24:31; Mark 13:27).

c Gather us from the nations (1 Chr. 16:35); he who scattered
Israel will gather them (Jer. 31:10); I will gather you (Mic. 2:12;
Zeph. 3:20); after 40 years I will gather Israel (Ezek. 29:13); you
will be gathered one by one (Isa. 27:12); God gathers the dispersed of Israel (Isa. 56:8); I will gather my sheep (Jer. 23:3); I
longed to gather your children as a hen gathers her chicks (Matt.
23:37; Luke 13:34); he will gather the wheat into his barn (Matt.
3:12; 13:30; Luke 3:17); Jesus died to gather into one the
children of God scattered abroad (John 11:52); bringing everything together in Christ (Eph. 1:10); our gathering together to
meet him (2 Thess. 2:1); all nations will be gathered before him
(Matt. 25:32).

● Gathering
with God

d He who does not gather with me scatters (Matt. 12:30; Luke
11:23); he who reaps gets wages and gathers fruit for eternal life
(John 4:36).

● Mustering
the people

e Trumpets to signal an assembly (Num. 10:3); they assembled
them at the place called Armageddon (Rev. 16:16).

f The Levites gathered to Moses (Exod. 32:26); Joshua mustered the people (Josh. 8:10); Joshua gathered the tribes (Josh. 24:1); all Israel assembled as one man (Judg. 20:1); Samuel called the people together (1 Sam. 7:5–6; 10:17).

g   Let all Israel be gathered (2 Sam. 17:11; 1 Kgs. 18:19); muster Judah within three days (2 Sam. 20:4); David assembled all Israel (1 Chr. 13:5; 15:3; 19:17); Rehoboam mustered Judah and Benjamin (1 Kgs. 12:21); the leaders were assembled to bring up the ark (1 Kgs. 8:1); all the people came to the king (2 Sam. 19:8).

● Gathering together

h   The church gathered together at Pentecost (Acts 2:1); for prayer (Acts 4:31; 12:12); in Solomon's portico (Acts 5:12); on the first day of the week to break bread (Acts 20:7, 8); to hear a letter (Acts 15:30); for a missionary report (Acts 14:27); in council (Acts 15:6).

i   Instructions concerning meeting for discipline (1 Cor. 5:4); for the Lord's supper (1 Cor. 11:17–34); for worship and teaching (1 Cor. 14:23, 26).

j   Where two or three are gathered together in Christ's name (Matt. 18:20); do not neglect to meet together (Heb. 10:25).

k   Holy convocations on days one and seven (Exod. 12:16).

● Groups

l   The angels, God's company (Gen. 32:2).

m   Esau coming with 400 men (Gen. 32:6; 33:1).

● Crowds doing evil

n   Do not follow a crowd to do evil (Exod. 23:2); a great crowd with swords and clubs (Matt. 26:47; Mark 14:43); the high priests and elders persuaded the crowds (Matt. 27:20; Mark 15:11).

o   The crowd returned beating their breasts (Luke 23:48).

● Crowds pressing round

p   Great crowds followed Jesus (Matt. 4:25; 8:1; 14:13; 19:2; 20:29; Mark 3:7–8; 5:24; Luke 9:11; 14:25; 23:27; John 6:2); a great crowd gathered round him (Mark 5:21; Luke 8:4); the crowds pressed round him (Luke 5:1; 8:42, 45); a crowd was sitting round him (Mark 3:32); a large crowd went with him (Luke 7:11); a large crowd around the disciples (Mark 9:14).

q   So many gathered they trod on one another (Luke 12:1); so many were gathered together there was no room (Mark 2:2); they could not get near him because of the crowds (Luke 5:19; 8:19); Zaccheus could not see for the crowd (Luke 19:3); crowds gathered so he could not eat (Mark 3:20; 6:31); crowds before and behind were shouting out (Matt. 21:9); when Jesus saw a crowd was gathering (Mark 9:25).

r   The crowds were seeking him (Luke 4:42); the crowd was waiting for him (Luke 8:40; 9:37); the crowd went out to meet him (John 12:18); the crowd ran up to him (Mark 9:15); great crowds brought sick people to him (Matt. 15:30).

● Crowds amazed

s   The crowds were amazed at his teaching (Matt. 7:28; 22:33; Mark 11:18); the crowds were awestruck at his authority (Matt.

9:8); the crowds were amazed at his healing (Matt. 12:23; 15:31; Mark 2:12).

● Crowds
helped

t Seeing the crowds he had compassion on them (Matt. 9:36; 14:14; 15:32; Mark 6:34; 8:1–2); Jesus called the crowd to him (Matt. 15:10; Mark 7:14); they came to the crowd (Matt. 17:14); Jesus spoke to the crowds (Matt. 23:1; 26:55); Jesus talked to the crowds about John (Matt. 11:7); Jesus taught the crowds (Mark 2:13; 10:1); great crowds gathered so he taught them from a boat (Matt. 13:2; Mark 4:1; Luke 5:3); Jesus spoke to the crowds in parables (Matt. 13:34); crowds gathered to hear him and be healed (Luke 5:15; 6:17–18); the crowd heard him gladly (Mark 12:37).

● Avoiding
crowds

u When he saw the crowds he went up into a mountain (Matt. 5:1); when Jesus saw crowds around him he gave orders to depart (Matt. 8:18); he sent the crowds away (Matt. 14:22; 15:39; Mark 6:45; 8:9); leaving the crowd, they crossed over (Mark 4:36).

v Herod feared the crowd (Matt. 14:5).

75 Scattering

● Scattering
the peoples

a God scattered the people of Babel all over the earth (Gen. 11:8); scatter them by your power (Ps. 59:11); God has scattered the proud (Luke 1:51); may God's enemies be scattered (Ps. 68:1); God promised to scatter the Egyptians among the nations (Ezek. 29:12; 30:23, 26); Elam would be scattered (Jer. 49:36).

b Followers of Theudas were scattered (Acts 5:36); followers of Judas of Galilee were scattered (Acts 5:37).

● Scattering
Israel

c God would scatter disobedient Israel among the nations (Lev. 26:33; Deut. 4:27; 28:64; Ps. 106:27; Jer. 9:16; Ezek. 12:15; 20:23; 22:15; Zech. 10:9); if you are unfaithful I will scatter you (Neh. 1:8); he will scatter them beyond the River (1 Kgs. 14:15); a people scattered and dispersed (Esther 3:8); you have scattered us among the nations (Ps. 44:11); I scattered them among the nations (Ezek. 36:19; Zech. 7:14); I will scatter your remnant to the winds (Ezek. 5:10); these are the horns which scattered them (Zech. 1:19); one third scattered (Ezek. 5:2, 12); though I scattered them I was a sanctuary to them (Ezek. 11:16); the Dispersion of the Jews (John 7:35).

d They have scattered my people among the nations (Joel 3:2).

e The people were scattering from Saul (1 Sam. 13:11); no one will be with you by tonight (2 Sam. 19:7).

f Simeon and Levi would be scattered in Israel (Gen. 49:7).

● Scattered
like sheep

g Israel scattered like sheep without a shepherd (1 Kgs. 22:17; 2 Chr. 18:16); scattered because there was no shepherd (Ezek. 34:5); woe to the shepherds who are scattering my sheep (Jer. 23:1–2); strike the shepherd and the sheep will be scattered (Zech. 13:7; Matt. 26:31; Mark 14:27); you will be scattered (John 16:32).

● Church
scattered

    h The church was scattered after the death of Stephen (Acts 8:1, 4; 11:19); the church referred to as the Dispersion (Jas. 1:1; 1 Pet. 1:1); the word of the Lord spread (Acts 13:49).

    i He who does not gather with me scatters (Matt. 12:30; Luke 11:23).

● Sowing

    j Those who sow in tears will reap with joy (Ps. 126:5–6); whatever a man sows, that he will reap (Gal. 6:7–8); sow righteousness (Hos. 10:12); he who sows righteousness gets a sure reward (Prov. 11:18); the fruit of righteousness is sown in peace (Jas. 3:18); sowing spiritual good (1 Cor. 9:11); one sows and another reaps (John 4:37); he who sows and he who reaps will rejoice together (John 4:36).

    k Sow your seed morning and evening (Eccles. 11:6); happy you who sow beside all waters (Isa. 32:20); do not sow among thorns (Jer. 4:3); he who watches the wind will not sow (Eccles. 11:4); does he not sow dill and cummin? (Isa. 28:25).

    l One scatters yet increases (Prov. 11:24); sowing as a picture of generous giving (2 Cor. 9:6, 10).

    m The parable of the sower (Matt. 13:3–8; Mark 4:3–9; Luke 8:5–8); with interpretation (Matt. 13:18–23; Mark 4:14–20; Luke 8:11–15).

    n The parable of the tares (Matt. 13:24–30); interpreted (Matt. 13:37–43); the parable of the mustard seed (Matt. 13:31–2; Mark 4:31–2; Luke 13:18–19); the parable of the sprouting seed (Mark 4:26–9).

    o The Rechabites were not to sow seed (Jer. 35:7).

    p The body sown in death (1 Cor. 15:36–7, 42–4).

76 Meeting place
See **192**.

77 Class

● Species

    a Creatures according to their kind: plants with their seed (Gen. 1:11–12); sea creatures (Gen. 1:21); land creatures (Gen. 1:24–5); birds (Gen. 1:21; 6:20); animals (Gen. 6:20); creeping things (Gen. 6:20); all creatures (Gen. 7:14).

78 Inclusion
In one another, see **224*d***.

79 Generality
All, see **54**.

80 Self

● Yourself

    a If you are wise, you are wise for yourself (Prov. 9:12).
Not acting alone, see **88*r*; selfish**, see **932**.

81 Principle

● Principles

   a The principle of sin and death (Rom. 7:21–5; 8:2).

   b The principle of faith (Rom. 3:27); the principle of the Spirit of life (Rom. 8:2).

82 Multiple

See **104**.

83 Conformity

● Conforming

   a Conformed to the image of his Son (Rom. 8:29); conformed to his death (Phil. 3:10); conformity with the body of his glory (Phil. 3:21).

   b A disciple must be like his teacher, a slave like his master (Matt. 10:25); a fully-trained pupil will be like his teacher (Luke 6:40).

   c All things to all men (1 Cor. 9:19–22).

   d Do not be conformed to this age (Rom. 12:2); do not be conformed to your former ignorant passions (1 Pet. 1:14).

   Imitating, see **20**.

● Example

   e Christ washed their feet as an example (John 13:15); Christ suffered, leaving you an example (1 Pet. 2:21); in me Christ demonstrated his patience as an example (1 Tim. 1:16).

   f Observe those who live according to Paul's example (Phil. 3:17); we offer ourselves as a model for you (2 Thess. 3:9); the Thessalonians were an example to all the believers (1 Thess. 1:7); the prophets were an example of suffering and patience (Jas. 5:10).

   g Be an example to believers (1 Tim. 4:12); show yourself to be an example of good deeds (Titus 2:7); elders should be examples to the flock (1 Pet. 5:3).

84 Nonconformity

● Awkward

   a A wild donkey of a man, against everyone (Gen. 16:12).

Section five: Number

---

85 Number

● Total

   a According to the number of people: take a lamb (Exod. 12:4); gather manna (Exod. 16:16); take an inheritance (Num. 26:53–4; 33:54); give the Levites cities (Num. 35:8); God set boundaries according to the number of the sons of Israel (Deut. 32:8).

   In proportion, see **12a**.

86 Counting

● Counting
people

   a Soldiers being numbered off (Num. 31:49; 1 Sam. 14:17; 2 Sam. 18:1); the numbers of those equipped for war (1 Chr. 12:23–37).

   b Censuses taken by: Moses (Exod. 38:25–6; Num. 1:2–46; 3:40–3; 26:2–4, 63); Saul (1 Sam. 15:4); David (2 Sam. 24:1–2;

1 Chr. 21:1–2; 27:1–24); Solomon (2 Chr. 2:17); Amaziah (2 Chr. 25:5); Caesar Augustus (Luke 2:1–5); in the days of the census (Acts 5:37).

c The people were numbered (Judg. 21:9); Saul numbered the men (1 Sam. 11:8; 13:15); Joab began the count but did not finish (1 Chr. 27:24); the numbers of people returning from exile in Babylon (Ezra 2:2–67).

d When a census is taken, each must pay a ransom (Exod. 30:12).

● Counting Levites

e The Levites were not counted with the others (Num. 1:47–9); the Levites were counted (Num. 3:15–16, 22, 28, 34, 39; 4:46–9; 26:57–62; 1 Chr. 23:3); the Kohathites (Num. 4:2–3, 34–7); the Gershonites (Num. 4:22–3, 38–41); and the Merarites (Num. 4:29–30, 42–5).

● Counting things

f Count the towers of Zion (Ps. 48:12); where is he who counted the towers? (Isa. 33:18); you counted the houses of Jerusalem (Isa. 22:10).

g God counts my steps (Job 14:16; 31:4); God counts the stars (Ps. 147:4); the hairs of your head are all numbered (Matt. 10:30; Luke 12:7).

h They counted the money in the chest (2 Kgs. 12:10); they counted out the articles from the temple (Ezra 1:8–11).

i Flocks passing under the hand of one who counts them (Jer. 33:13).

Measurement, see **465**.

87 List

See **586**.

88 One

● One God

a The Lord our God is one Lord (Deut. 6:4; Mark 12:29); God is one (Job 23:13; Mark 12:32; Rom. 3:30; Gal. 3:20); the Lord will be one and his name one (Zech. 14:9); there is no God but one (1 Cor. 8:4); there is one God (1 Tim. 2:5); even the demons believe there is one God (Jas. 2:19); one God the Father and one Lord Jesus Christ (1 Cor. 8:6); the only God (John 5:44; 1 Tim. 1:17; Jude 25).

b The only true God (John 17:3); the only wise God (Rom. 16:27); the only ruler (1 Tim. 6:15).

No other God, see **21a**.

c I and the Father are one (John 10:30).

● One church

d One body (Rom. 12:5; 1 Cor. 10:17; 12:12–13, 20; Eph. 2:16; 4:4; Col. 3:15); all one in Christ Jesus (Gal. 3:28).

e Jesus dies to gather into one the children of God (John 11:52); Jew and Gentile made one (Eph. 2:14–15); one flock, one shepherd (John 10:16); Jesus prays that believers may be one (John 17:11, 21–3).

f Keep the unity of the Spirit (Eph. 4:3); the unity of the faith (Eph.

4:13); when brothers live together in unity (Ps. 133:1); the believers were of one heart and mind (Acts 4:32).

One flesh, see **45a**.

● Redemption once for all

g Once for all Christ appeared to put away sins (Heb. 9:26); once for all Christ offered himself as a sacrifice (Heb. 7:27; 9:28); once for all Christ entered the holy place (Heb. 9:12); one offering (Heb. 10:12, 14); an offering once for all (Heb. 10:10).

● Only child

h Your only son (Gen. 22:2, 12, 16); Jephthah's only child (Judg. 11:34); the only son of a widow (Luke 7:12); Jairus had an only daughter (Luke 8:42); the man's only son (Luke 9:38).

● Only begotten Son

i Glory as of the only begotten of the Father (John 1:14); the only begotten God (John 1:18); God gave his only begotten Son (John 3:16); he has not believed in the name of the only begotten Son of God (John 3:18).

● Only one

j When Abraham was one I called him (Isa. 51:2); Elijah said he was the only one left (1 Kgs. 18:22; 19:10, 14; Rom. 11:3).

k I have trodden the wine press alone (Isa. 63:3); there was no one to help (Isa. 63:5).

● Living alone

l It is not good for the man to be alone (Gen. 2:18); the leper had to live alone (Lev. 13:46); how lonely the city that was full of people (Lam. 1:1).

m Unless a grain of wheat falls into the ground and dies it remains alone (John 12:24).

● On one's own

n Jacob was left alone (Gen. 32:24); why are you alone? (1 Sam. 21:1); a messenger running alone brings good news (2 Sam. 18:25, 26); I alone have escaped to tell you (Job 1:15, 16, 17, 19); Paul was left behind in Athens alone (1 Thess. 3:1).

o Jesus went to pray alone (Matt. 14:23); they saw no one but Jesus alone (Matt. 17:8; Mark 9:8; Luke 9:36).

p Rebuke your brother on his own (Matt. 18:15).

q In Sheol a man mourns only for himself (Job 14:22); I sat alone because of your hand on me (Jer. 15:17).

Isolation, see **883d**.

● Not acting alone

r I do nothing on my own (John 8:28); I did not come of my own accord (John 8:42); I did not speak of my own accord (John 12:49).

89 Accompaniment

● God with his people

a God in the midst of his people (Exod. 33:14; 34:9; Num. 14:14; 35:34; Deut. 7:21; 23:14; Josh. 3:10; 22:31); God is in the midst of her (Ps. 46:5); the Lord goes with you (Deut. 31:6, 8); the Lord is with Israel (Num. 23:21; Deut. 20:1, 4); I am in the midst of Israel (Joel 2:27); is not the Lord is our midst? (Mic. 3:11); my Spirit is among you (Hag. 2:5); God will dwell among them (Rev. 21:3); the Lord your God is in your midst (Zeph. 3:15, 17); men will hear that God is with a Jew (Zech. 8:23); the Lord is with them (Zech. 10:5); he will declare that God is among you (1 Cor. 14:25).

b The Lord be with you all (2 Thess. 3:16); the Lord be with your spirit (2 Tim. 4:22); the God of love and peace will be with you (2 Cor. 13:11).

c God will bring with him those who have fallen asleep (1 Thess. 4:14).

● God with us

d Immanuel, God with us (Isa. 7:14; 8:10; Matt. 1:23); God is with us (2 Chr. 13:12); God is with you (Isa. 45:14); the Lord is with us (Num. 14:9; 2 Chr. 32:8; Ps. 46:7, 11); God will be with you (Gen. 48:21); the Lord is with you (2 Chr. 20:17); I will be with you (Exod. 3:12); I am with you (Hag. 1:13; 2:4); they will know that I am with them (Ezek. 34:30); when we pass through the waters he will be with us (Isa. 43:2); do not be afraid, for I am with you (Isa. 41:10; 43:5; Jer. 42:11; 46:28); may the Lord be with you (Ruth 2:4; 2 Sam. 14:17; 1 Chr. 22:11, 16; Amos 5:14); may the Lord be with us (1 Kgs. 8:57); perhaps the Lord will be with me (Josh. 14:12); I am always with God (Ps. 73:23); you are with me (Ps. 23:4); son, you are always with me (Luke 15:31); is not the Lord with you? (1 Chr. 22:18); is the Lord in our midst or not? (Exod. 17:7); the Lord is with you when you are with him (2 Chr. 15:2).

e Those with us are more than those with them (2 Kgs. 6:16).

f God stands at the right hand of the needy (Ps. 109:31); the Lord stood with me (2 Tim. 4:17); you set me in your presence for ever (Ps. 41:12); when I awake I am still with you (Ps. 139:18).

● Walking
with God

g Enoch walked with God (Gen. 5:22, 24) as did Noah (Gen. 6:9); walk before me and be blameless (Gen. 17:1); walk humbly with your God (Mic. 6:8); I will walk among them (Lev. 26:12; 2 Cor. 6:16).

● God with
specific people

h God with: Abraham (Gen. 21:22); Asa (2 Chr. 15:9); David (1 Sam. 16:18; 18:12, 14, 28; 20:13; 2 Sam. 5:10; 7:3, 9; 1 Chr. 11:9; 17:2); Gideon (Judg. 6:12–13, 16); Hezekiah (2 Kgs. 18:7); Isaac (Gen. 26:28); Ishmael (Gen. 21:20); Israel (Jer. 30:11); Jacob (Gen. 28:15, 20; 31:5; 35:3); Jehoshaphat (2 Chr. 17:3); Jeremiah (Jer. 1:8, 19; 15:20; 20:11); Job (Job 29:5); Joseph (Gen. 39:2, 3, 21, 23; Acts 7:9); the house of Joseph (Judg. 1:22); Joshua (Deut. 31:23; Josh. 1:9; 6:27); Joshua as with Moses (Josh. 1:5; 3:7); each judge (Judg. 2:18; 2 Chr. 19:6); Mary (Luke 1:28); Paul (Acts 18:10); Samuel (1 Sam. 3:19); Saul (1 Sam. 10:7; 20:13); Solomon (1 Chr. 28:20; 2 Chr. 1:1); Solomon as with David (1 Kgs. 1:37).

● God with
Jesus

i The Word was with God (John 1:1); he was in the beginning with God (John 1:2); God was with Jesus (Acts 10:38); the Father was with him (John 16:32); no one could do these signs if God were not with him (John 3:2); he who sent me is with me (John 8:29); God is at my right hand (Acts 2:25).

● Jesus with
his people

j Jesus chose apostles that they might be with him (Mark 3:14); you have been with me in my trials (Luke 22:28); you have been with me from the beginning (John 15:27); Jesus prayed for his own people to be with him (John 17:24); Peter was accused of being with Jesus (Matt. 26:69, 71; Mark 14:67; Luke 22:56; John 18:26); these men had been with Jesus (Acts 4:13); I am with you always (Matt. 28:20); where I am, there will my servant be (John 12:26); that where I am you may be also (John 14:3); where two or three are gathered together, there am I (Matt. 18:20).

k The dying thief would be with Jesus in paradise (Luke 23:43); better to depart and be with Christ (Phil. 1:23); preferring to be absent from the body and at home with the Lord (2 Cor. 5:8); for ever with the Lord (1 Thess. 4:17).

l Jesus took Peter, James and John with him (Matt. 17:1; 26:37; Mark 5:37, 40; 9:2; Mark 14:33; Luke 8:51; 9:28); the former demoniac wanted to be with him (Mark 5:18; Luke 8:38); Jesus drew near and walked with them (Luke 24:15).

m You will not always have me with you (Matt. 26:11; Mark 14:7; John 12:8); for a little longer I am with you (John 7:33; 13:33); do wedding guests mourn when the bridegroom is with them? (Matt. 9:15; Mark 2:19; Luke 5:34).

● People with
people

n He who walks with wise men will be wise (Prov. 13:20); bad company ruins good morals (1 Cor. 15:33); do two walk together without an appointment? (Amos 3:3).

o Lot went with Abraham (Gen. 12:4; 13:1); come with us (Num. 10:29–32); come with me from Lebanon (S. of S. 4:8); go with the men (Num. 22:20, 35); Saul wanted Samuel to return with him (1 Sam. 15:25–31); I would go with the throng to the house of God (Ps. 42:4); go with them without hesitation (Acts 10:20; 11:12); Peter went with them (Acts 10:23).

p David told Abiathar to stay with him (1 Sam. 22:23); Ruth kept with Boaz' maids (Ruth 2:8, 23).

q Joshua was to accompany the people into the land (Deut. 31:7); Judah and Simeon went to war together (Judg. 1:3, 17); Deborah went with Barak (Judg. 4:8–9); Jonathan's armour bearer was with him (1 Sam. 14:7); Abishai went down into the camp with David (1 Sam. 26:6–7); David was to go with Achish into battle (1 Sam. 28:1; 29:2).

r Where you go I will go (Ruth 1:16–18); I will not leave you (2 Kgs. 2:2, 4, 6; 4:30); please go with us (2 Kgs. 6:3); where the king goes, there I will be (2 Sam. 15:21); only Luke is with me (2 Tim. 4:11); Saul and Jonathan were not parted in death (2 Sam. 1:23); tomorrow you will be with me (1 Sam. 28:19).

s I will remain with the one this people have chosen (2 Sam. 16:18); the people accompanied the king (2 Sam. 19:40); David was going to go into battle with the people (2 Sam. 18:2); will you go with me to battle? (1 Kgs. 22:4; 2 Kgs. 3:7); let my servants go with your servants (1 Kgs. 22:49); Ahaziah went with Joram to fight Hazael (2 Kgs. 8:28).

t Why did you not go with me, Mephibosheth? (2 Sam. 19:25); we forbade him because he does not follow with us (Luke 9:49). **Not with**, see **190**.

90 Two

- Two are better   *a* Two are better than one (Eccles. 4:9).
- Twins   *b* Rebekah gave birth to twins (Gen. 25:24); Tamar bore twins to Judah (Gen. 38:27); the twin boys as figurehead (Acts 28:11).

    c All of them bear twins (S. of S. 4:2; 6:6); twins of a gazelle (S. of S. 4:5; 7:3).

- Two witnesses   *d* The evidence of two or three witnesses needed for confirmation (Deut. 17:6; 19:15; cf. Num. 35:30; Matt. 18:16; 2 Cor. 13:1; Heb. 10:28); an accusation against an elder requires two or three witnesses (1 Tim. 5:19); the testimony of two men is true (John 8:17).

    e Two false witnesses accused Jesus (Matt. 26:60).

- Two olive trees   *f* Two olive trees (Zech. 4:3); the two olive trees are two anointed ones (Zech. 4:11–14); the two witnesses are two olive trees and two lampstands (Rev. 11:3–4).

- Two disciples   *g* Take one or two along with you to the sinning brother (Matt. 18:16); if two of you agree on earth, it shall be done (Matt. 18:19); where two or three are gathered in my name (Matt. 18:20).

    h Jesus sent out the apostles two by two (Mark 6:7); the seventy were sent out two by two (Luke 10:1); Jesus sent two disciples (Matt. 21:1; Mark 11:1; 14:13; Luke 19:29); John sent two disciples (Luke 7:19).

    i Two going to Emmaus (Luke 24:13); two walking in the country (Mark 16:12).

- Two people   *j* No one can serve two masters (Matt. 6:24; Luke 16:13).

    k Two demonised men (Matt. 8:28); two blind men (Matt. 20:30); a man had two sons (Matt. 21:28; Luke 15:11); two debtors (Luke 7:41); two men went up to the temple to pray (Luke 18:10); two men in the field, one taken and one left (Matt. 24:40; Luke 17:36); two women grinding at the mill, one taken and one left (Matt. 24:41; Luke 17:35); two men in one bed, one taken and one left (Luke 17:34).

    l Two criminals were led out with him (Luke 23:32); two thieves were crucified with him (Matt. 27:38; Mark 15:27; John 19:18).

- Two angels   *m* Two men in white clothing (Acts 1:10); two angels in white (John 20:12).

- Two nations   *n* Two nations are in your womb (Gen. 25:23).

- Two animals   *o* Two of all animals in the ark (Gen. 6:19; 7:8, 9, 15); two of unclean animals (Gen. 7:2).

    p Two lambs were sacrificed every day (Exod. 29:38–42).

● Two things	*q* Two tablets of the testimony (Exod. 31:18; 32:15; Deut. 4:13; 5:22; 9:10–11, 15, 17); two other tablets (Exod. 34:1, 4; 34:29; Deut. 10:1).
	r Two silver trumpets (Num. 10:2).
	s A two-edged sword (Judg. 3:16; Ps. 149:6; Prov. 5:4; Heb. 4:12; Rev. 1:16; 2:12).
	t I have become two companies (Gen. 32:10).

91 Doubling

● Double portion	*a* The firstborn had a double portion (Deut. 21:17); Hannah was given a double portion (1 Sam. 1:5); Elishah wanted a double portion of Elijah's spirit (2 Kgs. 2:9); instead of shame you will have a double portion (Isa. 61:7).
	b A double portion of manna (Exod. 16:5, 22).
	c Take double money (Gen. 43:12, 15); elders who rule well should be given double honour (1 Tim. 5:17).
	d She has received double for all her sins (Isa. 40:2).
	Double-minded, see **601*a***.
● Twice over	*e* The doubling of Pharaoh's dream (Gen. 41:32); the Lord had appeared to Solomon twice (1 Kgs. 11:9); you make him twice as much a son of hell (Matt. 23:15).

92 Half

● Halving bodies	*a* Abraham cut the animals in two (Gen. 15:10); they cut the calf in two and passed between the parts (Jer. 34:18–19); dividing the dead ox (Exod. 21:35); divide the child in two (1 Kgs. 3:25–6); some were sawn in two (Heb. 11:37).
● Halving things	*b* Hanun cut the men's beards and garments in half (2 Sam. 10:4; 1 Chr. 19:4).
● Half of groups	*c* If half of us die, they will not care about us (2 Sam. 18:3).
	d Jacob divided people and animals into two companies (Gen. 32:7); half the people worked while half carried arms (Neh. 4:16, 21).
● Halving possessions	*e* Manasseh inherited by two halves (Josh. 22:7); Mephibosheth and Ziba would divide the land (2 Sam. 19:29); even to half my kingdom (Esther 5:3, 6; 7:2; Mark 6:23).
	f Half of my possessions I give to the poor (Luke 19:8).
	Half-hearted, see **518**.

93 Three

● Trinity	*a* Baptized in the name of the Father, Son and Holy Spirit (Matt. 28:19); the grace of the Lord Jesus, the love of God, the fellowship of the Spirit (2 Cor. 13:14); same Spirit ... same Lord ... same God (1 Cor. 12:4–6); one Spirit ... one Lord ... one God and Father (Eph. 4:4–6); foreknowledge of the Father, sanctification of the Spirit, to obey Jesus Christ (1 Pet. 1:2).
● Three men	*b* Three men came to Abraham (Gen. 18:2); three men from each

tribe to survey the land (Josh. 18:4); David's three mighty men (2 Sam. 23:9, 13–17, 19, 22–3; 1 Chr. 11:12, 15–19, 21, 24–5); three sons of Anak (Judg. 1:20).

● Three things   *c* Three branches—three days (Gen. 40:10, 12–13); three baskets—three days (Gen. 40:16, 18–19); Joab pierced Absalom with three spears (2 Sam. 18:14); yeast in three measures of meal (Matt. 13:33; Luke 13:21); let us make three booths (Matt. 17:4; Mark 9:5; Luke 9:33); I offer you three things (2 Sam. 24:12; 1 Chr. 21:10).

      d Three cities of refuge (Num. 35:14; Deut. 4:41; 19:2, 7, 9). **The three woes**, see **830h**.

● Three   *e* Three witnesses, the Spirit, the water and the blood (1 John 5:8). witnesses   **Two or three witnesses**, see **90d**.

94 Three times

● Three times   *a* Three times a year all the men must attend the feasts (Exod. a year   23:14, 17; 34:23; Deut. 16:16); three times a year Solomon made offerings (1 Kgs. 9:25; 2 Chr. 8:13). **Thrice daily**, see **139a**.

● Thrice   *b* Peter would deny Christ three times (Matt. 26:34, 75; Mark 14:30, 72; Luke 22:34, 61; John 13:38); Peter three times asked whether he loved Christ (John 21:17); Paul three times begged the Lord to remove his thorn in the flesh (2 Cor. 12:8); Peter was three times urged to eat (Acts 10:16; 11:10); this is the third time I am coming to you (2 Cor. 12:14; 13:1).

      c The king only struck the arrows three times on the ground (2 Kgs. 13:18); three times Joash defeated Aram (2 Kgs. 13:19, 25); three times beaten with rods (2 Cor. 11:25).

● Threefold   *d* A threefold cord is not easily broken (Eccles. 4:12).

95 Third

● Destruction   *a* The destruction of a third of: the earth and trees (Rev. 8:7); sea, of a third   sea creatures and ships (Rev. 8:8–9); rivers and waters (Rev. 8:10–11); stars (Rev. 12:4); and sun and moon (Rev. 8:12); mankind (Rev. 9:15, 18).

      b One third will be brought through fire (Zech. 13:9).

● Dividing   *c* Divide the land into three (Deut. 19:3); divide your hair into three into three   parts (Ezek. 5:1–2).

      d The great city split into three parts (Rev. 16:19).

      e Gideon divided the men into three companies (Judg. 7:16); David divided his army into three parts (2 Sam. 18:2); the temple guard divided into thirds (2 Kgs. 11:5–6; 2 Chr. 23:4–5); David spared one third of the Moabites (2 Sam. 8:2).

96 Four

● Four angels   *a* Four angels holding the four winds (Rev. 7:1); four angels bound at the Euphrates (Rev. 9:14, 15).

● Four creatures   *b*   The four living creatures of Ezekiel (Ezek. 1:5–18); of Revelation (Rev. 4:6–8); four great beasts (Dan. 7:3).

● Four people   *c*   The four great beasts are four kings (Dan. 7:17); four smiths to cast down the horns (Zech. 1:20–1); four men carrying a paralytic (Mark 2:3); four daughters of Philip (Acts 21:9).

● Four things   *d*   Each creature had four faces and four wings (Ezek. 1:6; 10:14, 21); a leopard with four wings and four heads (Dan. 7:6); four horns in place of the one broken (Dan. 8:8); four horns which scattered Israel and Judah (Zech. 1:18–19).

   e   Four chariots (Zech. 6:1).

97 Four times

● Fourfold   *a*   Fourfold restitution (2 Sam. 12:6; Luke 19:8); the enemies sent to me four times (Neh. 6:4).

98 Quarter

● A fourth part   *a*   Power over a quarter of the earth (Rev. 6:8); Herod the tetrarch (Matt. 14:1).

   b   They read from the law for a quarter of the day and confessed and worshipped for a quarter of the day (Neh. 9:3).

● Quartering   *c*   Dividing Jesus' garments into four lots (John 19:23).

99 Five and over

● Five   *a*   Five: times more for Benjamin (Gen. 43:34); sets of garments for Benjamin (Gen. 45:22); brothers presented to Pharaoh (Gen. 47:2); tumours and mice (1 Sam. 6:4, 17–18); lords of the Philistines (Josh. 13:3); smooth stones (1 Sam. 17:40); will chase 100 (Lev. 26:8); talents (Matt. 25:15); foolish virgins and wise virgins (Matt. 25:2); loaves and two fish (Matt. 14:17; 16:9; Mark 6:38, 41; 8:19; Luke 9:13; John 6:9); brothers (Luke 16:28); husbands (John 4:18); times the 39 lashes (2 Cor. 11:24).

● Six   *b*   Six: cities of refuge (Num. 35:6, 13–15); fingers per hand and toes per foot (2 Sam. 21:20; 1 Chr. 20:6); wings for the seraphim (Isa. 6:2); stone jars (John 2:6).

● Seven animals   *c*   Seven: pairs of clean animals (Gen. 7:2); lambs at Beersheba (Gen. 21:28–31); ears of corn and cows for years of plenty and famine (Gen. 41:1–36); altars, bulls and rams (Num. 23:1, 4, 14, 29); bulls, rams, lambs and goats for a sin offering (2 Chr. 29:21); bulls and rams for a burnt offering (Job 42:8).

● Seven people and groups   *d*   Seven: nations in the land (Deut. 7:1; Acts 13:19); sons of Saul to be hung (2 Sam. 21:6); brothers (Matt. 22:25; Mark 12:20); sons of Sceva (Acts 19:14); churches of Asia (Rev. 1:4, 11, 20).

● Seven spirits   *e*   Seven: spirits of God (Rev. 1:4; 3:1; 4:5; 5:6); angels (Rev. 1:20; 8:2, 6; 15:1, 6, 7, 8; 16:1; 17:1; 21:9); demons from Mary (Mark 16:9; Luke 8:2); spirits more evil than the first (Matt. 12:45; Luke 11:26).

● Seven things   *f*   Seven: lamps on lampstand (Exod. 25:32–7; 37:18–23; Num.

8:2; Zech. 4:2); lampstands (Rev. 1:12, 20); torches of fire (Rev. 4:5); trumpets (Josh. 6:4, 6, 13; Rev. 8:2, 6); fresh bowstrings (Judg. 16:7–9); locks of Samson's hair (Judg. 16:13–14, 19); pillars for wisdom's house (Prov. 9:1); loaves and a few fish (Matt. 15:34; 16:10; Mark 8:5–6, 20); baskets left over (Matt. 15:37; Mark 8:8, 20); horns and eyes (Rev. 5:6); thunders (Rev. 10:3, 4); stars (Rev. 1:16, 20; 2:1; 3:1); seals (Rev. 5:1, 5; 6:1); heads (Rev. 12:3; 13:1; 17:3, 7); diadems (Rev. 12:3); plagues (Rev. 15:1, 6, 8; 21:9); golden bowls (Rev. 15:7; 16:1; 17:1; 21:9); hills (Rev. 17:9); kings (Rev. 17:10).

● Seven times   g   Seven times: march round Jericho (Josh. 6:4, 15); sprinkling of blood (Lev. 4:6, 17; 16:14, 19; Num. 19:4); sprinkling of oil (Lev. 8:11; 14:16, 27); washing in Jordan (2 Kgs. 5:10, 14); Elijah sending his servant to see (1 Kgs. 18:43); the boy sneezing (2 Kgs. 4:35); shall I forgive? (Matt. 18:21).

       h   Seven times a day I praise you (Ps. 119:164); if he sins seven times a day, forgive him (Matt. 18:21–2; Luke 17:4).

● Sevenfold   i   Sevenfold: vengeance on Cain's killer (Gen. 4:15; Gen. 4:24); punishment (Lev. 26:18, 21, 28); a thief must repay (Prov. 6:31); brightness of the sun (Isa. 30:26); furnace heated (Dan. 3:19).

● Eight   j   Jesse had eight sons (1 Sam. 16:10–11; 17:12); eight people saved in Noah's ark (1 Pet. 3:20).

● Ten   k   Ten: righteous? (Gen. 18:32); brothers (Gen. 42:3); linen curtains (Exod. 26:1); stands and lavers (1 Kgs. 7:27, 38, 43; 2 Chr. 4:6); commandments (Deut. 10:4); elders (Ruth 4:2); concubines (2 Sam. 15:16; 20:3); shares in the king (2 Sam. 19:43); golden lampstands (1 Kgs. 7:49; 2 Chr. 4:7); tables (2 Chr. 4:8); pieces given to Jeroboam (1 Kgs. 11:31); tribes (1 Kgs. 11:35); horns (Dan. 7:7, 20, 24; Rev. 12:3; 13:1; 17:3, 7, 12, 16); diadems (Rev. 13:1); kings (Dan. 7:24; Rev. 17:12); virgins (Matt. 25:1); lepers (Luke 17:12); slaves each given one mina (Luke 19:13).

● Eleven   l   Eleven: goat's hair curtains (Exod. 26:7); disciples (Matt. 28:16; Mark 16:14; Luke 24:9, 33; Acts 1:26; 2:14).

● Twelve people and groups   m   Twelve: princes of Ishmael (Gen. 25:16); patriarchs (Gen. 35:22–6; Acts 7:8); tribes of Israel (Matt. 19:28; Luke 22:30; Acts 26:7; Jas. 1:1; Rev. 7:4–8; 21:12); men from the tribes (Num. 13:2–16; 34:18–28; Deut. 1:23; Josh. 3:12; 4:2); pillars for the tribes (Exod. 24:4); male goats for the number of the tribes of Israel (Ezra 6:17); divisions of the army (1 Chr. 27:1–15); men for Ishbosheth and David (2 Sam. 2:15); prefects (1 Kgs. 4:7); apostles (Matt. 10:1–2; 11:1; Mark 3:14, 16; Luke 6:13); disciples of John in Ephesus (Acts 19:7); angels (Rev. 21:12); legions of angels (Matt. 26:53).
The twelve, see **538a**.

● Twelve things   n   Twelve: pieces of Ahijah's cloak (1 Kgs. 11:30); oxen under the 'sea' (1 Kgs. 7:25, 44; 2 Chr. 4:4, 15; Jer. 52:20); jewels (Exod. 28:10, 21; 39:14); rods (Num. 17:2); pieces of the concubine

(Judg. 19:29); loaves (Lev. 24:5); baskets of broken pieces (Matt. 14:20; Mark 6:43; 8:19; Luke 9:17; John 6:13); stones (Josh. 4:2–7; 1 Kgs. 18:31); stars (Rev. 12:1); foundations with names (Rev. 21:14); gates of the city (Ezek. 48:30–4; Rev. 21:12); gates and pearls (Rev. 21:21); kinds of fruit (Rev. 22:2).

- Fourteen   *o* 14 generations three times over (Matt. 1:17).

- 20s   *p* 20 righteous? (Gen. 18:31); 24 divisions of priests (1 Chr. 24:4–18); 24 divisions of musicians (1 Chr. 25:9–31); 24 elders seated on 24 thrones (Rev. 4:4, 10; 5:8; 11:16; 19:4).

- 30s   *q* 30 righteous? (Gen. 18:30); 30 sons on 30 donkeys with 30 cities (Judg. 10:4); 30 sons and 30 daughters (Judg. 12:9); 30 mighty men (2 Sam. 23:13–39; 1 Chr. 11:11, 15, 20, 25; 27:6); 37 in all (2 Sam. 23:39).

- 40s and 50s   *r* 40 righteous? (Gen. 18:29); 40 stripes (Deut. 25:3) less one (2 Cor. 11:24); 40 sons and 30 grandsons on 70 donkeys (Judg. 12:14); 40 men plotted to kill Paul (Acts 23:13); 45 righteous? (Gen. 18:28); 48 cities for the Levites (Num. 35:6–7); 50 righteous? (Gen. 18:24, 26); 50 men to run before Absalom (2 Sam. 15:1); recline in groups of 50 (Luke 9:14).

- 60s and 70s   *s* 70 people came into Egypt (Gen. 46:27; Exod. 1:5; Deut. 10:22); 70 elders (Exod. 24:1, 9; Num. 11:16, 24; Ezek. 8:11); Gideon had 70 sons (Judg. 8:30; 9:2, 5, 18, 24, 56); Ahab had 70 sons (2 Kgs. 10:1, 6); the 70 appointed to preach (Luke 10:1, 17); 75 people in Egypt (Acts 7:14); 77 leaders of Succoth (Judg. 8:14).

- 100s   *t* 99 out of 100 sheep (Matt. 18:12; Luke 15:4); 100 men fed (2 Kgs. 4:42–4); Isaac reaped 100-fold (Gen. 26:12); he will receive 100 times as much (Mark 10:30); 100-fold, 60-fold, 30-fold (Matt. 13:8, 23); 30-fold, 60-fold, 100-fold (Mark 4:8, 20); 100-fold (Luke 8:8); 100 Philistine foreskins (1 Sam. 18:25); he had them recline by 100s and 50s (Mark 6:40); 120 brethren in the upper room (Acts 1:15); the wall was 144 cubits high (Rev. 21:17); 153 fish (John 21:11); 200 Philistine foreskins (1 Sam. 18:27); 276 people on board ship (Acts 27:37); 300 men lapped the water (Judg. 7:6–8); 70 times seven times [490] (Matt. 18:22); 600 men with Saul (1 Sam. 13:15; 14:2); 600 foreign troops with David (2 Sam. 15:18); the number of the beast is 666 (Rev. 13:18).

- 1000s   *u* 3000 baptised (Acts 2:41); 4000 fed (Matt. 15:38; 16:10; Mark 8:9, 20); 5000 fed (Matt. 14:21; 16:9; Mark 6:44; 8:19; Luke 9:14; John 6:10); 5000 men believing (Acts 4:4); 7000 left as a remnant (1 Kgs. 19:18; Rom. 11:4).

- 10 000 and above   *v* 12 000, 1000 from each tribe (Num. 31:4–5); 12 000 from each tribe (Rev. 7:5–8); 12 000 men of Ai killed (Josh. 8:25); 12 000 stadia (Rev. 21:16); 40 000 men Reuben, Gad and half Manasseh (Josh. 4:13); 70 000 died (2 Sam. 24:15; 1 Chr. 21:14); 144 000 redeemed (Rev. 7:4; 14:1, 3); 600 000 men went up out of Egypt (Exod. 12:37; Num. 11:21); 601 730 (Num. 26:51); numbered at

603 550 (Exod. 38:26; Num. 1:46; 2:32); 800 000 of Israel and 500 000 of Judah (2 Sam. 24:9); 1 100 000 of Israel and 470 000 of Judah (1 Chr. 21:5); 200 million horsemen (Rev. 9:16).

100 Multisection
See **102**.

101 Plurality
See **104**.

102 Fraction: less than one

● Tithing for God

a Bring the whole tithe into the storehouse (Mal. 3:8–10); bring your tithes every three days (Amos 4:4); priests collect the tithe (Heb. 7:5).

b Jacob promised to give God a tenth of all he received (Gen. 28:22); a tenth of all produce of the land and of all animals is the Lord's (Lev. 27:30–2); a tenth of all flocks is holy to the Lord (Lev. 27:32).

c A tenth of all produce is to be eaten before the Lord with rejoicing (Deut. 12:17–18; 14:22–7); bring your tithe there (Deut. 12:6, 11).

d The third year the tithe is for the Levite and the deprived (Deut. 14:28–9; 26:12–13); the tithe is for the Levites (Num. 18:21); and from it they must present a tenth of the tithe (Num. 18:26–8); Hezekiah commanded the people to resume the tithe for the Levites (2 Chr. 31:4–10); the tithe was stored in rooms in the temple (2 Chr. 31:11–12; Neh. 12:44); Nehemiah had the tithes for the Levites restored (Neh. 10:37–9; 13:10–13).

e Pharisees tithed garden herbs (Matt. 23:23; Luke 11:42); the Pharisee tithed all his income (Luke 18:12).

● Tithing for people

f Abraham gave a tenth of everything to Melchizedek (Gen. 14:20; Heb. 7:2, 4–9); a king would take a tenth of their produce and flocks (1 Sam. 8:15, 17).

● A tenth of people

g A tenth of the people would supply the food (Judg. 20:10); one in ten of the people would live in Jerusalem (Neh. 11:1); a tenth will remain in it (Isa. 6:13).

h A tenth of the city fell (Rev. 11:13).

● A fifth

i Restitution to be made, paying a fifth more than the value (Lev. 5:16; 6:5; 22:14; Num. 5:7); redemption paying a fifth more than the value (Lev. 27:13, 15, 19, 27, 31).

j A fifth of the produce of Egypt was taken for Pharaoh (Gen. 41:34; 47:24, 26).

● Small fractions

k One fiftieth of the booty was to be given to the Levites (Num. 31:30); give them back one hundredth of what you are exacting (Neh. 5:11); one in five hundred of the people and livestock as an offering to the Lord (Num. 31:28–9).

103 Zero

Nothing, see **639**.

104 Numerous

● God make
you numerous

a May you become thousands (Gen. 24:60); may God make you a
company of peoples (Gen. 28:3); may they become many (Gen.
48:16); may God increase you a thousandfold (Deut. 1:11); may
Reuben's men not be few (Deut. 33:6).

● God will multiply
his people

b Abraham was to become a great nation (Gen. 12:2); the father
of many nations (Gen. 17:5; Rom. 4:16–17); I will multiply you
very much (Gen. 17:2; Heb. 6:14); I will make you very fruitful
(Gen. 17:6); I blessed him and multiplied him (Isa. 51:2); Sarah
would become many nations (Gen. 17:6); I will multiply your
offspring (Gen. 26:24); I will make you a great nation (Gen.
46:3); I will make you a company of peoples (Gen. 48:4); I will
make you fruitful and many (Gen. 48:4).

c God had said he would multiply Israel (Deut. 7:13): like the stars
(Gen. 15:5; 22:17; 26:4; Exod. 32:13; 1 Chr. 27:23); like the dust
(Gen. 13:16; 28:14; 2 Chr. 1:9); like the sand (Gen. 22:17; 32:12;
Hos. 1:10); too many to count (Gen. 16:10); as numerous as
sheep (Ezek. 36:37); they will be fruitful and multiply (Jer. 23:3);
I will multiply them (Jer. 30:19); the ten thousand thousands of
Israel (Num. 10:36); may God add 100 times as many people
(2 Sam. 24:3; 1 Chr. 21:3).

d Nations will come from you (Gen. 35:11); they will become a
multitude of peoples (Gen. 48:19).

● God multiplied
his people

e I multiplied Abraham's offspring (Josh. 24:3); the Israelites
increased in numbers (Gen. 47:27; Exod. 1:7, 12, 20; Deut. 26:5;
Acts 7:17); God multiplied them (Lev. 26:9); you have multiplied the nation (Isa. 9:3; 26:15); God made his people very
fruitful (Ps. 105:24); God made them as numerous as the stars
(Deut. 1:10; 10:22; 28:62; Neh. 9:23); as the sand (2 Sam. 17:11;
1 Kgs. 4:20; Rom. 9:27); too many to count (1 Kgs. 3:8); offspring as numerous as the stars and the sand (Heb. 11:12); who
can count the dust of Jacob? (Num. 23:10); he blesses them and
they multiply (Ps. 107:38).

f The sons of Joseph were a numerous people (Josh. 17:14–15);
David's offspring would be numerous as the stars and the sand
(Jer. 33:22–3).

g Moab feared the Israelites because they were numerous (Num.
22:3); it was not because you were numerous that God loved you
(Deut. 7:7).

● Multiplied
conditionally

h Multiplication was conditional on obedience (Deut. 6:3; 8:1;
13:17); your offspring would have been like the sand (Isa.
48:19).

● Numerous
after exile

i After exile, God would multiply them more than their fathers
(Deut. 30:5); I will multiply on you man and beast (Ezek.

36:10–11); they will be as many as of old (Zech. 10:8); Jerusalem will be inhabited without walls because of the multitudes within (Zech. 2:4).

● Multiplying people

j I will multiply Ishmael very much (Gen. 17:20); I will make Ishmael a nation (Gen. 21:13, 18); Nineveh, multiply yourselves like the locust (Nahum 3:15); I will make Moses a great nation instead (Exod. 32:10; Num. 14:12; Deut. 9:14); your descendants will be many (Job 5:25).

k The sons of the desolate will be more than those of the married (Isa. 54:1); widows more numerous than the sand (Jer. 15:8).

● Multitudes saved

l Multitudes added to the church (Acts 2:41, 47; 4:4; 5:14; 6:1, 7; 9:42; 11:24; 14:1; 16:5; 17:12); they made many disciples (Acts 14:21); many believed (Acts 11:21); thousands of Jews believed (Acts 21:20); many priests obedient to the faith (Acts 6:7); the church was built up and multiplied (Acts 9:31); the word of God grew and multiplied (Acts 12:24); I have many people in this city (Acts 18:10).

m 144 000 were sealed from all the tribes of Israel (Rev. 7:4); a great multitude which no one could count (Rev. 7:9); myriads of myriads and thousands of thousands (Rev. 5:11).

● Multitudes of the ungodly

n Many enter the gate leading to destruction (Matt. 7:13); many seek in vain to enter the narrow door (Luke 13:24); many called but few chosen (Matt. 22:14).

● Many enemies

o Those who hate me without a cause are more than the hairs on my head (Ps. 69:4).

p Saul has slain his thousands and David his ten thousands (1 Sam. 18:7–8; 21:11; 29:5).

● Numerous armies

q In the multitude of people is the glory of a king (Prov. 14:28).

r Opposing armies like the sand (Josh. 11:4; Judg. 7:12; 1 Sam. 13:5); like locusts (Judg. 6:5; Jer. 46:23); without number (2 Chr. 12:3); a great multitude (1 Kgs. 20:13; 2 Chr. 20:2); the Arameans filled the country (1 Kgs. 20:27).

s The number of Satan's army is like the sand (Rev. 20:8); the name was legion because the evil spirits were many (Mark 5:9; Luke 8:30).

t There were too many soldiers with Gideon (Judg. 7:2, 4).

● Many ruling

u When a land transgresses it has many rulers (Prov. 28:2); you have as many gods as cities (Jer. 2:28; 11:13).

● Many ministering

v Myriads attended him (Dan. 7:10); the priests were many in number (Heb. 7:23).

● Multitudes of creatures

w Numerous locusts (Exod. 10:14); camels as numerous as the sand (Judg. 7:12); so many sacrifices they could not be counted (1 Kgs. 8:5; 2 Chr. 5:6).

● Many thoughts

x Your thoughts to us are too numerous to count (Ps. 40:5); more numerous than the sand (Ps. 139:18).

God's thoughts, see **449a**.

● Many sins   *y* My iniquities are more than the hairs on my head (Ps. 40:12).

105 Few

● Few in Israel
a Jacob's men were few (Gen. 34:30); the men of Israel were like two little flocks of goats (1 Kgs. 20:27); you were the least numerous of people (Deut. 7:7); he went down to Egypt few in number (Deut. 26:5); when they were few in number (1 Chr. 16:19; Ps. 105:12).

b If the household is too small for a lamb (Exod. 12:4).

c You will be left few in number (Deut. 4:27; 28:62); the people in Jerusalem were few (Neh. 7:4); few men are left (Isa. 24:6); we are left but a few of many (Jer. 42:2).

d The priests were too few, so the Levites helped them (2 Chr. 29:34); not enough priests had consecrated themselves (2 Chr. 30:3).

● Few in the kingdom
e Will only a few be saved? (Luke 13:23); few find the narrow gate leading to life (Matt. 7:14; Luke 13:24); many are called but few are chosen (Matt. 22:14); not many wise, powerful or noble are saved (1 Cor. 1:26); God can save by many or by few (1 Sam. 14:6); the harvest is plentiful but the labourers are few (Matt. 9:37; Luke 10:2).

● Few enemies
f The men of Ai are few (Josh. 7:3); a few Arameans beat many of Judah (2 Chr. 24:24); the rest of his trees will be so few a child could count them (Isa. 10:19).

Few chasing many, see **619c**.

106 Repetition

● Saying repeatedly
a Jesus prayed again, saying the same words (Matt. 26:44; Mark 14:39); Paul wrote the same things again (Phil. 3:1).

b If your brother sins and repents repeatedly, forgive repeatedly (Matt. 18:21–2; Luke 17:4).

● Doing repeatedly
c Priests offer the same sacrifices repeatedly (Heb. 9:25–6; 10:11); daily (Heb. 7:27; 10:11); yearly (Heb. 9:25; 10:1, 3).

107 Infinity

Eternity, see **115**.

Section six: Time

108 Time

● Time in general
a Redeem the time, because the days are evil (Eph. 5:16); are there not 12 hours in the day? (John 11:9); my times are in your hands (Ps. 31:15).

Wasting time, see **634b**.

● Extremity of periods
b The first day of the week: they came to the tomb (Matt. 28:1; Mark 16:2); Christ rose from the dead (Mark 16:9; Luke 24:1;

John 20:1, 19); breaking bread (Acts 20:7); making a contribution (1 Cor. 16:2); the Lord's day (Rev. 1:10).

c New moon (1 Sam. 20:5, 18, 24); blow the silver trumpets on the
first of each month (Num. 10:10); blow the trumpet at new moon
(Ps. 81:3); it is not new moon (2 Kgs. 4:23); at full moon he will
come home (Prov. 7:20).

d At the turn of the year the Arameans attacked (1 Kgs. 20:22, 26);
at the end of the third year give the tithe away (Deut. 14:28;
26:12); at the end of seven years, a remission (Deut. 15:1; 31:10);
start of the year of Jubilee (Lev. 25:9).

● Month 1

e **Month 1**, Abib / Nisan: (Exod. 12:2; 13:4; 23:15; 34:18; Deut.
16:1): **1st day** of 2nd year the tabernacle set up (Exod. 40:2, 17);
starting to cleanse the temple (2 Chr. 29:17); Ezra set out from
Babylon (Ezra 7:9); Nehemiah served wine to the king (Neh.
2:1); the lot was cast before Haman (Esther 3:7); Ezekiel had a
word (Ezek. 29:17); the sanctuary cleansed (Ezek. 45:18); **7th
day** the word of the Lord came to Ezekiel (Ezek. 30:20); a
sacrifice for those who sin ignorantly (Ezek. 45:20); **10th day** a
lamb taken (Exod. 12:3); from Jordan to Gilgal (Josh. 4:19); **13th
day** the scribes were summoned (Esther 3:12); **14th day** Passover (Exod. 12:6, 18; Lev. 23:5; Num. 9:1–5; 28:16; Josh. 5:10;
2 Chr. 35:1; Ezra 6:19; Ezek. 45:21); **15th day** they set out from
Egypt (Num. 33:3); the Feast of Unleavened Bread (Lev. 23:6;
Num. 28:17; Ezek. 45:25); until **21st day** (Exod. 12:18); **24th
day** Daniel saw a vision (Dan. 10:4).

● Month 2

f **Month 2**, Ziv: in the 480th year after coming out of Egypt, the
temple was begun (1 Kgs. 6:1); 4th year, foundation of the
temple laid (1 Kgs. 6:37; 2 Chr. 3:2); **1st day** 2nd year a census
taken (Num. 1:1, 18); **14th day** alternative Passover (Num. 9:11;
2 Chr. 30:15); Hezekiah held the Passover (2 Chr. 30:2, 13);
15th day to the wilderness of Sin (Exod. 16:1); **20th day** cloud
lifted (Num. 10:11).

● Month 3

g **Month 3**, Sivan: arrival at Sinai (Exod. 19:1); Asa assembled
the people (2 Chr. 15:10); **1st day** the word of the Lord to Ezekiel
(Ezek. 31:1); **23rd day** the scribes summoned (Esther 8:9).

● Month 4

h **Month 4**: fast of the fourth month (Zech. 8:19); **5th day** Ezekiel
saw visions (Ezek. 1:1); **9th day** wall of Jerusalem breached (Jer.
39:2; 52:6–7).

● Month 5

i **Month 5**: fast of the fifth month (Zech. 7:3, 5; 8:19); **1st day**
40th year from Egypt Aaron died (Num. 33:38); Ezra arrived in
Jerusalem (Ezra 7:9); **10th day** Jerusalem burned (Jer.
52:12–13); elders came to enquire of the Lord (Ezek. 20:1).

● Month 6

j **Month 6**, Elul: **1st day** word of the Lord by Haggai (Hag. 1:1);
5th day Ezekiel saw a vision (Ezek. 8:1); **24th day** work resumed on the temple (Hag. 1:15); **25th day** the wall finished (Neh.
6:15).

● Month 7

k **Month 7**, Tishri / Ethanim: at the feast (1 Kgs. 8:2; 2 Chr. 5:3);

Gedaliah killed (2 Kgs. 25:25); fast of the seventh month (Zech. 7:5; 8:19); **1st day** the Feast of Trumpets (Lev. 23:24; Num. 29:1); sacrifices restarted (Ezra 3:6); **10th day** Day of Atonement (Lev. 16:29; 23:27; Num. 29:7); **15th day** Feast of Booths (Lev. 23:34, 39; Num. 29:12; Neh. 8:14); **21st day** word of the Lord by Haggai (Hag. 2:1); **23rd day** returning home after dedicating the temple (2 Chr. 7:10).

● Month 8

l **Month 8**, Bul: 11th year, temple was finished (1 Kgs. 6:38); word of the Lord to Zechariah (Zech. 1:1); **15th day** Jeroboam made a feast like that in Judah (1 Kgs. 12:32, 33); **24th day** word of the Lord to Haggai (Hag. 2:10, 20); foundation of temple laid (Hag. 2:18).

● Month 9

m **Month 9**, Chislev: Nehemiah received visitors from Judah (Neh. 1:1); **4th day** word of the Lord to Zechariah (Zech. 7:1); **20th day** returned exiles assembled (Ezra 10:9).

● Month 10

n **Month 10**, Tebeth: the fast of the tenth month (Zech. 8:19); Esther went in to the king (Esther 2:16); **5th day** Ezekiel heard of the fall of Jerusalem (Ezek. 33:21); **10th day** Nebuchadnezzar besieged Jerusalem (2 Kgs. 25:1; Jer. 52:4); **12th day** Ezekiel's word against Egypt (Ezek. 29:1).

● Month 11

o **Month 11**, Shebat: **1st day** 40th year Moses addressed the people (Deut. 1:3); **24th day** word of the Lord to Zechariah (Zech. 1:7).

● Month 12

p **Month 12**, Adar: temple was rebuilt (Ezra 6:15); the lot was satisfactory for Haman (Esther 3:7); **1st day** word of the Lord to Ezekiel (Ezek. 32:1); **13th day** the Jews were to be annihilated (Esther 3:13; 9:1); the Jews were to kill and plunder (Esther 8:12; 9:17); **14th day** Jews in Susa killed their enemies (Esther 9:15, 18); country Jews feasted (Esther 9:17, 19, 21); **15th day** Jews in Susa feasted (Esther 9:18, 21); **25th day** Jehoiachin released (Jer. 52:31); **27th day** Jehoiachin was released (2 Kgs. 25:27).

● Time of day

q Beginning of the middle watch (Judg. 7:19); in the fourth watch of the night [3–6 am] (Matt. 14:25; Mark 6:48); at the time of the evening offering (Dan. 9:21).

r **[6 am]** Sixth hour [Roman time] (John 19:14).

s **[9 am]** Third hour (Matt. 20:3; Mark 15:25; Acts 2:15).

t **[10 am]** Tenth hour [Roman time] (John 1:39).

u **[Noon]** Sixth hour (Matt. 20:5; Acts 10:9); Elijah mocked them (1 Kgs. 18:27); darkness until the ninth hour (Matt. 27:45; Mark 15:33; Luke 23:44).

v **[3 pm]** Ninth hour (Matt. 20:5; 27:45; Mark 15:33–4; Luke 23:44; Acts 3:1; 10:3, 30); Jesus cried out (Matt. 27:46).

w **[5 pm]** Eleventh hour (Matt. 20:6, 9).

x **[6 pm]** Sixth hour [Roman time] (John 4:6).

y **[7 pm]** Seventh hour [Roman time] (John 4:52).

Midnight, see **129*k***; **tomorrow**, see **124*a***.

- Timing of redemption

z A plan for the fullness of time (Eph. 1:10); the time of the promise was approaching (Acts 7:17); the prophets enquired what time was indicated (1 Pet. 1:11); when the time had fully come, God sent his Son (Gal. 4:4); from that time Jesus began to preach (Matt. 4:17); the time is fulfilled (Mark 1:15); times which the Father has fixed (Acts 1:7); as to times, you do not need me to write (1 Thess. 5:1).

aa Herod found out what time the star appeared (Matt. 2:7); according to the time he had ascertained (Matt. 2:16); in the sixth month Gabriel was sent to Nazareth (Luke 1:26).

ab My time has not yet come (John 2:4; 7:6, 8, 30; 8:20); the time is at hand (Matt. 26:18, 45); the time has come (Mark 14:41; John 17:1); the time has come for the Son of Man to be glorified (John 12:23); for him to leave the world (John 13:1); at the right time Christ died (Rom. 5:6); the Pharisees asked when the kingdom of God was coming (Luke 17:20).

ac In a day of salvation I have helped you (Isa. 49:8); now is the acceptable time (2 Cor. 6:2); to proclaim the year of the Lord's favour (Isa. 61:2); the acceptable year of the Lord (Luke 4:19); it is time for you to awaken from sleep (Rom. 13:11).

ad This is your hour and the power of darkness (Luke 22:53).
Right time, see **137**.

- Day of the Lord

ae The day of the Lord is near (Ezek. 30:3; Joel 1:15; 3:14; Obad. 15; Zeph. 1:7, 14); the day of the Lord is coming (Joel 2:1); the great and terrible day of the Lord (Joel 2:31; Mal. 4:5); the day of the Lord is darkness, not light (Amos 5:18, 20); a day of darkness and gloom (Zeph. 1:15); wail, for the day of the Lord is near (Isa. 13:6); the day of the Lord will be cruel (Isa. 13:9).

af The day of the Lord Jesus Christ (1 Cor. 1:8; 5:5; 2 Cor. 1:14; Phil. 1:6, 10; 2:16); the day of God (2 Pet. 3:12; Rev. 16:14); the great day of the Lord (Acts 2:20).

- Timing of the day of the Lord

ag When will this be? (Matt. 24:3; Mark 13:4; Luke 21:7); no one knows but the Father (Matt. 24:36; Mark 13:32); you do not know the time (Matt. 24:42; 25:13; Mark 13:33); whether the second watch or the third (Luke 12:38); when you do not expect (Matt. 24:44; Luke 12:40); as when the master of the house returns unexpectedly (Matt. 24:50; Mark 13:35; Luke 12:46).

ah The day of the Lord will come like a thief (Luke 12:39; 1 Thess. 5:2, 4; 2 Pet. 3:10); if the householder had known when the thief was coming (Matt. 24:43); do not think the day of the Lord has already come (2 Thess. 2:2).

- Day of judgement

ai The day of judgement (Matt. 10:15; 11:22, 24; 12:36; 2 Pet. 2:9; 3:7; 1 John 4:17); the time for the dead to be judged (Rev. 14:7); a day on which he will judge (Acts 17:31; Rom. 2:16); the judgement of the great day (Jude 6); the day of wrath (Rom. 2:5; Rev. 6:17); the hour to reap (Rev. 14:15).

● Time of restoration	*aj*	The day of redemption (Eph. 4:30); the time for restoring everything (Acts 3:21).

109 Neverness

Never been, see *2b*.

110 Period

● Periods in general	*a*	The day of creation (Gen. 2:4); the days of creation (Gen. 1:5, 8, 13, 19, 23, 31; 2:2); this is the day which the Lord has made (Ps. 118:24); let the day I was born perish (Job 3:3).
	b	For every day a year (Num. 14:34; Ezek. 4:5, 6); I will pay you back for the years the locust has eaten (Joel 2:25).
● Seasons	*c*	God made sun and moon to mark seasons, days and years (Gen. 1:14); he made the moon for the seasons (Ps. 104:19).
	d	God determined the times of all the nations (Acts 17:26).
	e	Some regard one day as better than another (Rom. 14:5); concern that they observed special days, months, seasons and years (Gal. 4:10).
	f	There is a time and a procedure for everything (Eccles. 3:6); even the stork in the sky knows her seasons (Jer. 8:7); man does not know his time (Eccles. 9:12); it is an evil time (Amos 5:13).
● Periods of hours	*g*	**Half an hour**: there was silence in heaven (Rev. 8:1).
	h	**One hour**: these have worked only one hour (Matt. 20:12); could you not keep watch for one hour? (Matt. 26:40).
	i	**Two hours**: the Ephesians shouted (Acts 19:34).
● Periods of days	*j*	**A day and a night**: adrift at sea (2 Cor. 11:25).
	k	**Two days**: until passover (Matt. 26:2).
	l	**Three days**: until fulfilment (Gen. 40:12–13, 18–19); Joseph's brothers in prison (Gen. 42:17); darkness over Egypt (Exod. 10:22); the spies hid (Josh. 2:16, 22); mustering Judah (2 Sam. 20:4); pestilence (2 Sam. 24:13; 1 Chr. 21:12); Rehoboam considered (1 Kgs. 12:5; 2 Chr. 10:5); taking the spoil (2 Chr. 20:25); fasting for Esther (Esther 4:16); Jonah in the fish (Jonah 1:17; Matt. 12:40); Christ in the heart of the earth (Matt. 12:40); rebuilding the temple (Matt. 26:61; 27:40; Mark 14:58; 15:29; John 2:19–20); until Christ rose (Matt. 16:21; 17:23; 20:19; 27:63; Mark 8:31; 9:31; 10:34; Luke 9:22; 18:33; 24:7; Acts 10:40); the third day I complete my course (Luke 13:32); raised on the third day (1 Cor. 15:4); Mary and Joseph searching for Jesus (Luke 2:46); the crowd had been with Jesus (Matt. 15:32; Mark 8:2); Paul was blind (Acts 9:9); **three and a half days** the witnesses' bodies will lie unburied (Rev. 11:9–11).
	m	**Four days** Lazarus was in the tomb (John 11:17, 39).
	n	**Six days** for God to make heaven and earth (Gen. 1:1–31; Exod. 20:11; 31:17); until the transfiguration (Matt. 17:1; Mark 9:2).

o **Seven days**: between dove flights (Gen. 8:10, 12); between marriages (Gen. 29:27–8); eating unleavened bread (Exod. 12:15; 13:6–7; 34:18; Lev. 23:8; Num. 28:17; Deut. 16:4; 2 Chr. 30:21, 22; 35:17; Ezra 6:22); Feast of Booths (Lev. 23:36, 39–42; Deut. 16:15; Neh. 8:18); firstborn animal to remain with its mother (Exod. 22:30; Lev. 22:27); mother of male child unclean (Lev. 12:2); suspected leper in quarantine (Lev. 13:4, 5, 21, 26, 31, 33); leprous garment shut up (Lev. 13:50, 54); cleansed leper outside his tent (Lev. 14:8); house in quarantine (Lev. 14:38); man remains unclean (Lev. 15:24; Num. 19:11, 14, 16; 31:19); for cleansing (Lev. 15:13); Miriam outside camp (Num. 12:14–15); Saul had to wait for Samuel (1 Sam. 10:8; 13:8); high priest being ordained (Exod. 29:30, 35; Lev. 8:33–5); seven days and seven days for the feast (1 Kgs. 8:65; 2 Chr. 7:8–9); unleavened bread for another seven days (2 Chr. 30:23); Zimri ruled (1 Kgs. 16:15); seven days and seven nights Job's friends sat with him (Job 2:13); Ezekiel sat among the exiles (Ezek. 3:15–16); Paul at Troas (Acts 20:6); Paul at Tyre (Acts 21:4).

p **Eight days**: until the transfiguration (Luke 9:28).

q **10 days** tribulation (Rev. 2:10); **14 days** adrift at sea (Acts 27:27, 33); **15 days** Paul stayed with Peter (Gal. 1:18); **21 days** Gabriel was hindered (Dan. 10:13).

● A month and more

r **40 days**: there was rain (Gen. 7:4, 17); before Noah sent the raven (Gen. 8:6); for embalming (Gen. 50:3); Moses was on the mountain (Exod. 24:18; 34:28; Deut. 9:9, 11, 18, 25; 10:10); the twelve men spied out Canaan (Num. 13:25; 14:34); Goliath challenged Israel (1 Sam. 17:16); Elijah fasted in Horeb (1 Kgs. 19:8); Ezekiel lay on his right side (Ezek. 4:6); until Nineveh's overthrow (Jonah 3:4); Jesus fasted in the wilderness (Matt. 4:2; Mark 1:13; Luke 4:2); the risen Jesus appeared to them (Acts 1:3).

s **One month**: captive woman mourning parents (Deut. 21:13); Shallum ruled (2 Kgs. 15:13); **50 days** from Firstfruits to the feast of weeks (Lev. 23:15–16); seven weeks (Deut. 16:9); **two months** Jephthah's daughter bewailed her virginity (Judg. 11:37–9); **three months** Moses was hidden (Heb. 11:23); the ark in the house of Obed-edom (2 Sam. 6:11); fleeing? (2 Sam. 24:13; 1 Chr. 21:12); Jehoahaz ruled (2 Kgs. 23:31; 2 Chr. 36:2); Jehoiachin ruled (2 Kgs. 24:8; 2 Chr. 36:9); Mary stayed with Elizabeth (Luke 1:56); Paul in the synagogue at Ephesus (Acts 19:8); Paul in Greece (Acts 20:3); **four month** to harvest (John 4:35); **150 days** the flood was on the earth (Gen. 7:24); **five months** Elizabeth hid herself (Luke 1:24); locusts tormented (Rev. 9:5, 10); **180 days** Ahasuerus displayed his wealth (Esther 1:4); **six months** Zechariah ruled (2 Kgs. 15:8); **seven months** the ark with the Philistines (1 Sam. 6:1); burying the slain (Ezek.

39:12, 14); **nine months 20 days** registering the people (2 Sam. 24:8); **390 days** Ezekiel lay on his left side (Ezek. 4:5, 9).

● Periods
of years

t **One year**: redemption rights in a town (Lev. 25:29–30); a newly-wed at home (Deut. 24:5); Ahaziah ruled (2 Kgs. 8:26; 2 Chr. 22:2); Barnabas and Paul taught in Antioch (Acts 11:26); **12 months** beautification (Esther 2:12); **one year and four months** David lived with the Philistines (1 Sam. 27:7); **one year and six months** Paul taught in Corinth (Acts 18:11).

u **Two years** Ishbosheth ruled (2 Sam. 2:10); Absalom lived in Jerusalem without seeing the king (2 Sam. 14:28); Nadab ruled (1 Kgs. 15:25); Elah ruled (1 Kgs. 16:8); Ahaziah ruled (1 Kgs. 22:51); Pekahiah ruled (2 Kgs. 15:23); Amon ruled (2 Kgs. 21:19; 2 Chr. 33:21); Paul taught daily in the school of Tyrannus (Acts 19:10); Paul lived in Rome (Acts 28:30).

v **Three years** Abimelech ruled (Judg. 9:22); famine (2 Sam. 21:1; 24:13; 1 Chr. 21:12); Abijam [Abijah] ruled (1 Kgs. 15:2; 2 Chr. 13:2); until the ships returned (1 Kgs. 10:22); Samaria besieged (2 Kgs. 17:5; 18:10); until Moab is brought low (Isa. 16:14); Isaiah went naked and barefoot (Isa. 20:3); being educated (Dan. 1:5); Paul admonished them (Acts 20:31); Paul was in isolation (Gal. 1:18).

w **Three and a half years** of drought (Luke 4:25; Jas. 5:17); a period variously described as: **1260 days** (Rev. 11:3; 12:6); **42 months** (Rev. 11:2; 13:5); a time, times and half a time (Dan. 7:25; 12:7; Rev. 12:14).

x **1290 days** after the regular sacrifice stops (Dan. 12:11); **1335 days** to wait (Dan. 12:12); **2300 evenings and mornings** (Dan. 8:14).

y **Six years**: a Hebrew slave to serve (Exod. 21:2; Deut. 15:12); Jephthah judged (Judg. 12:7); Joash was hidden (2 Kgs. 11:3; 2 Chr. 22:12); **seven years**: Jacob served for Rachel (Gen. 29:18, 20); twice over (Gen. 29:27, 30; 31:41); of plenty and of famine (Gen. 41:26–36); a sabbath (Lev. 25:2–4); serving Midian (Judg. 6:1); Ibzan judged (Judg. 12:9); famine (2 Kgs. 8:1, 2); building Solomon's temple (1 Kgs. 6:38); weapons will be used for fuel (Ezek. 39:9); let seven times pass over him (Dan. 4:16, 23, 32); Anna lived with her husband (Luke 2:36); **seven years six months** David in Hebron (2 Sam. 2:11; 5:5; 1 Chr. 3:4; 29:27); **eight years**: serving Cushan-rishathaim (Judg. 3:8); Abdon judged (Judg. 12:14); Jehoram ruled (2 Kgs. 8:17; 2 Chr. 21:5, 20); Aeneas had been bedriden (Acts 9:33); **nine years** Hoshea ruled (2 Kgs. 17:1).

● Ten years
and more

z **Ten years** Elon judged (Judg. 12:11); Menahem ruled (2 Kgs. 15:17); **11 years** Jehoiakim ruled (2 Kgs. 23:36; 2 Chr. 36:5); Zedekiah ruled (2 Kgs. 24:18; 2 Chr. 36:11; Jer. 52:1); **12 years** serving Chedorlaomer (Gen. 14:4); Omri ruled (1 Kgs. 16:23); Jehoram ruled (2 Kgs. 3:1); a woman had bled (Matt. 9:20; Mark

5:25; Luke 8:43); **13 years** Solomon building his own house (1 Kgs. 7:1); **14 years** until Paul returned to Jerusalem (Gal. 2:1); **16 years** Jehoash ruled (2 Kgs. 13:10); Jotham ruled (2 Kgs. 15:33; 2 Chr. 27:1, 8); Ahaz ruled (2 Kgs. 16:2; 2 Chr. 28:1); **17 years** Rehoboam ruled (1 Kgs. 14:21; 2 Chr. 12:13); Jehoahaz ruled (2 Kgs. 13:1); **18 years** serving Eglon (Judg. 3:14); serving the Ammonites (Judg. 10:8); a woman had a spirit of infirmity (Luke 13:11, 16).

- 20 years and more

aa **20 years** Jacob had served (Gen. 31:38, 41); serving Sisera (Judg. 4:3); Samson judged (Judg. 15:20; 16:31); the ark at Kiriath-jearim (1 Sam. 7:2); Pekah ruled (2 Kgs. 15:27); **22 years** Jair judged (Judg. 10:3); Jeroboam ruled (1 Kgs. 14:20); Ahab ruled (1 Kgs. 16:29); **23 years** Tola judged (Judg. 10:2); Jeremiah had spoken the word of the Lord (Jer. 25:3); **24 years** Baasha ruled (1 Kgs. 15:33); **25 years** Jehoshaphat ruled (1 Kgs. 22:42; 2 Chr. 20:31); **28 years** Jehu ruled (2 Kgs. 10:36); **29 years** Amaziah ruled (2 Kgs. 14:2; 2 Chr. 25:1); Hezekiah ruled (2 Kgs. 18:2; 2 Chr. 29:1).

- 30 years and more

ab **31 years** Josiah ruled (2 Kgs. 22:1; 2 Chr. 34:1); **33 years** David ruled Israel and Judah (2 Sam. 5:5; 1 Chr. 3:4; 29:27); **38 years** to the brook Zered (Deut. 2:14); a man had been ill (John 5:5).

- 40 years and more

ac **40 years**: Moses was in Midian (Acts 7:30); Israel in the wilderness (Num. 14:33–4; 32:13; Deut. 2:7; 8:2, 4; 29:5; Josh. 5:6; Neh. 9:21; Amos 2:10; 5:25; Acts 7:36, 42; 13:18; Heb. 3:9); for every day a year (Num. 14:34); Israel ate manna (Exod. 16:35); God was grieved with them (Ps. 95:10; Heb. 3:17); serving the Philistines (Judg. 13:1); the land had rest (Judg. 3:11; 5:31; 8:28); Eli judged (1 Sam. 4:18); Saul ruled (Acts 13:21); David ruled (2 Sam. 5:4; 1 Kgs. 2:11; 1 Chr. 29:27); Solomon ruled (1 Kgs. 11:42; 2 Chr. 9:30); Joash ruled (2 Kgs. 12:1; 2 Chr. 24:1); for the iniquity of Judah (Ezek. 4:6); Egypt will be uninhabited (Ezek. 29:11–12); **41 years** Asa ruled (1 Kgs. 15:10; 2 Chr. 16:13); Jeroboam ruled (2 Kgs. 14:23); **46 years** to build the temple (John 2:20); **seven weeks** [of years] until Messiah (Dan. 9:25).

- 50 years and more

ad **50 years** a year of jubilee (Lev. 25:8–12); **52 years** Uzziah ruled (2 Kgs. 15:2; 2 Chr. 26:3); **55 years** Manasseh ruled (2 Kgs. 21:1; 2 Chr. 33:1).

- 70 years and more

ae **70 years**: of exile in Babylon (2 Chr. 36:21; Jer. 25:11, 12; 29:10; Dan. 9:2; Zech. 1:12; 7:5); a typical lifetime (Ps. 90:10); Tyre will be forgotten (Isa. 23:15, 17).

- 80 years and more

af **80 years** the land had rest (Judg. 3:30); lifetime, due to strength (Ps. 90:10).

- Hundreds of years

ag **300 years** Israel had lived in Gilead (Judg. 11:26); **390 years** for the iniquity of Israel (Ezek. 4:5); **400 years** enslaved and oppressed (Gen. 15:13); **430 years** in Egypt (Exod. 12:40–1); **430 years** till the law came (Gal. 3:17); **62 weeks** [of years] (Dan.

9:25–6); **450 years** to gain the inheritance of the land (Acts 13:19); **70 weeks** [of years] to make an end of sin (Dan. 9:24).

- 1000 years
ah **1000 years**: as one day (Ps. 90:4; 2 Pet. 3:8); Satan bound (Rev. 20:2–3, 7); martyrs reigning (Rev. 20:4–6).

111 Course: indefinite duration
Period, see **110**.

112 Contingent duration
See **112c**.

113 Long duration

- Long life
a I will fill up the number of your days (Exod. 23:26); the Lord will give you many years in the land (Deut. 30:20); with long life I will satisfy him (Ps. 91:16); prolong the king's life! (Ps. 61:6).

b I will multiply my days like the sand (Job 29:18); though a sinner prolongs his life (Eccles. 8:12); if a man lives many days, the days of darkness will be many (Eccles. 11:8).

- How to
live long
c Length of life as a result of obedience (Exod. 20:12; Deut. 4:40; 25:15; 1 Kgs. 3:14; 1 Pet. 3:10); keep God's commands, that you may live long in the land (Deut. 4:40; 5:33; 6:2; 11:9, 21; 32:47); the fear of the Lord prolongs life (Prov. 10:27).

d Honour your father and mother so that you may live long (Exod. 20:12; Deut. 5:16; Eph. 6:2–3); do not take a mother bird with her young, that you may live long (Deut. 22:7).

e Keeping wisdom's commands will prolong your life (Prov. 3:2); wisdom gives length of days (Prov. 3:16); accept my words and your years will be many (Prov. 4:10); by me your days will be multiplied (Prov. 9:11).

- Long life not
achieved
f If you turn to other gods you will not live long in the land (Deut. 30:18); who by worrying can add a cubit to his life span? (Matt. 6:27; Luke 12:25).

g Solomon did not ask for long life (1 Kgs. 3:11; 2 Chr. 1:11).

- Long time
h Place the title deeds in an earthenware jar so they may last a long time (Jer. 32:14); after a long time the master returned (Matt. 25:19).

i They spent a long time with the disciples (Acts 14:28); Paul spoke for a long time (Acts 20:7, 11).
Eternal, see **115**; **since youth**, see **130**.

114 Brief

- Shortness
of life
a Let me know how brief my life is (Ps. 39:4; 89:47); a hundred and twenty years (Gen. 6:3); seventy years, or at most eighty (Ps. 90:10).

b There will no more be anyone who dies prematurely (Isa. 65:20).

- Life is short
c Our days on earth are like a shadow (1 Chr. 29:15; Job 8:9); man

is like a breath, his days a passing shadow (Ps. 144:4); between morning and evening they are broken in pieces (Job 4:20); man's days are like grass (Ps. 103:15; 1 Pet. 1:24); like grass sprouting in the morning and withering by evening (Ps. 90:5–6); all flesh is grass, soon withering (Isa. 40:6–8); man who is made like grass (Isa. 51:12); man withers like a flower and flees like a shadow (Job 14:2); my days are like a lengthened shadow and I wither like grass (Ps. 102:11); a mist that appears briefly (Jas. 4:14); a breath (Job 7:7, 16); short-lived (Job 14:1).

Man a mere breath, see **352d**.

- Life is swiftly gone

d My life has been shorter than my ancestors (Gen. 47:9); he cut short my life (Ps. 102:23–4); he cuts me off from the loom (Isa. 38:12); my days are swifter than a weaver's shuttle (Job 7:6); swifter than a runner (Job 9:25); my days are extinguished (Job 17:1, 11); you will seek me and I will not exist (Job 7:21); in the middle of my days I must enter Sheol (Isa. 38:10).

- Evildoers soon die

e Evildoers will wither like grass (Ps. 37:2); like grass on the housetops (Ps. 129:6); the rich man will wither like grass (Jas. 1:10–11); like flowers of the pasture they will vanish (Ps. 37:20); a lying tongue is only for a moment (Prov. 12:19); a little while and the wicked will be no more (Ps. 37:10); he was no more (Ps. 37:36).

f The godless die in youth (Job 36:14); such men will not live out half their days (Ps. 55:23); you have shortened the days of his youth (Ps. 89:45); the years of the wicked will be short (Prov. 10:27); the wicked will not lengthen his days like a shadow (Eccles. 8:13).

g Your descendants will die in the prime of life (1 Sam. 2:33); God has numbered your reign and ended it (Dan. 5:26); let his days be few (Ps. 109:8).

- Christ's life was short

h Made for a little while lower than the angels (Heb. 2:7, 9); with them for a little while (John 13:33; 14:19; 16:16–19); a little longer (John 7:33; 12:35).

- Short time till the end

i God has shortened the days (Matt. 24:22; Mark 13:20); the time has grown short (1 Cor. 7:29); as the devil knows (Rev. 12:12); a little while and the coming one shall come (Heb. 10:37).

j Suffer for a little while (1 Pet. 1:6; 5:10); light affliction for a moment (2 Cor. 4:17).

k The devil must be loosed for a little while (Rev. 20:3).

- Transient world

l The things that are seen are transient (2 Cor. 4:18); grass alive today and burned tomorrow (Matt. 6:30; Luke 12:28).

m Wealth sprouts wings and flies off (Prov. 23:5); riches are not for ever (Prov. 27:24); woe to him who heaps up what is not his—for how long? (Hab. 2:6); perishable things like silver and gold (1 Pet. 1:18); the joy of the wicked is short (Job 20:5).

n The body is sown as a perishable thing (1 Cor. 15:42); the perishable does not inherit the imperishable (1 Cor. 15:50); this perishable must put on the imperishable (1 Cor. 15:53).

● Transient devotion

o Your love is like the dew (Hos. 6:4); they will be like the dew (Hos. 13:3); some have no root and endure only for a while (Matt. 13:21; Mark 4:17; Luke 8:13); your people possessed your sanctuary for a little while (Isa. 63:18).

● Transient hardship

p His anger is but for a moment (Ps. 30:5); for a brief moment I forsook you (Isa. 54:7).

q The seven years seemed like a few days (Gen. 29:20).

● Hireling time

r The days of a hireling (Job 7:1); according to the years of a hireling (Isa. 16:14; 21:16).

115 For ever

● Eternity

a What is not seen is eternal (2 Cor. 4:18); he has set eternity in man's heart (Eccles. 3:11).

● Eternal God

b The eternal God (Gen. 21:33; Isa. 40:28; Rom. 16:26); the immortal God (Rom. 1:23); from everlasting to everlasting you are God (Ps. 90:2); you are from everlasting (Ps. 93:2; Hab. 1:12); from eternity I am he (Isa. 43:13); he who lives for ever (Rev. 4:9, 10; 10:6; 15:7); the Lord who abides for ever (Ps. 9:7; 102:12); the living God who endures for ever (Dan. 6:26); the number of God's years is unsearchable (Job 36:26); King of the ages (Rev. 15:3); the Lord will be your everlasting light (Isa. 60:20).

● Eternal attributes

c His eternal attributes: power and deity (Rom. 1:20); righteousness (2 Cor. 9:9); purpose (Eph. 3:11); reign (Rev. 11:15); dominion (1 Tim. 6:16); kingdom (Ps. 145:13; Dan. 4:3; 7:27); love (Jer. 33:11); name (Ps. 135:13).

Everlasting rule, see **733*b***.

● Eternal praise

d The Creator, blessed for ever (Rom. 1:25); praised from everlasting to everlasting (Neh. 9:5); eternal glory to God (Rom. 11:36; 16:27; Gal. 1:5; Eph. 3:21; Phil. 4:20; 1 Tim. 1:17; 2 Tim. 4:18; Heb. 13:21; 1 Pet. 4:11; 2 Pet. 3:18; Jude 25; Rev. 1:6; 5:13; 7:12).

● Eternal Christ

e Jesus Christ the same yesterday, today and for ever (Heb. 13:8); without beginning or end (Heb. 7:3); he lives for ever (Heb. 7:24–5); his years will never end (Ps. 102:27; Heb. 1:12); you gave him length of days for ever (Ps. 21:4); alive for evermore (Rev. 1:18); the power of an indestructible life (Heb. 7:16); a perfect high priest for ever (Heb. 5:6; 6:20; 7:3, 17, 21, 24, 28); the Christ remains for ever (John 12:34); the Son remains for ever (John 8:35); with us always (Matt. 28:20); Christ is God over all, blessed for ever (Rom. 9:5).

● Eternal Spirit

f The eternal Spirit (Heb. 9:14); another Counsellor, to be with you for ever (John 14:16).

- Eternal reign

   g His throne is for ever and ever (Ps. 45:6; Heb. 1:8); the Lord will reign for ever (Exod. 15:18); he will reign for ever and his kingdom will not end (Luke 1:33).

- Eternal dealings

   h What God does is done for ever (Eccles. 3:14); as long as the earth remains, the seasons will not cease (Gen. 8:22).

   i The land given as an everlasting possession (Gen. 17:8; 48:4); the passover, a feast for ever (Exod. 12:14, 24); a perpetual priesthood (Exod. 40:15; Num. 25:13); Israel are God's people for ever (2 Sam. 7:24).

   j I will establish his kingdom for ever (2 Sam. 7:13, 16); I said your house would walk before me for ever (1 Sam. 2:30).

   k Eternal: comfort (2 Thess. 2:16); covenant (Gen. 17:7, 19; Num. 18:19; Ps. 105:10; Isa. 55:3; Jer. 32:40; 50:5; Ezek. 16:60; 37:26; Heb. 13:20); destruction (2 Thess. 1:9); dominion (Dan. 7:14); glory (2 Tim. 2:10; 1 Pet. 5:10); fire (Jude 7); weight of glory (2 Cor. 4:17); inheritance (Heb. 9:15); joy (Isa. 35:10; 51:11; 61:7); lovingkindness (Ps. 103:17); redemption (Heb. 9:12); reproach (Jer. 23:40); righteousness (Dan. 9:24); salvation (Isa. 45:17; Heb. 5:9).

   l God's salvation is for ever (Isa. 51:6); we receive an imperishable wreath (1 Cor. 9:25); a building for us, eternal in heaven (2 Cor. 5:1); eternal habitations (Luke 16:9); the body is raised imperishable (1 Cor. 15:42); the dead will be raised imperishable (1 Cor. 15:52); an inheritance imperishable and undefiled (1 Pet. 1:4); born again of imperishable seed (1 Pet. 1:23); with the Lord for ever (1 Thess. 4:17); he who does the will of God remains for ever (1 John 2:17).

- Eternal truth

   m God's word abides for ever (1 Pet. 1:25); the truth with us for ever (2 John 2); the Lord's word is eternal (Ps. 119:89); his testimonies founded for ever (Ps. 119:152); the word of our God stands for ever (Isa. 40:8); the fear of the Lord endures for ever (Ps. 19:9); Christ's words will never pass away (Matt. 24:35; Mark 13:31; Luke 21:33).

- Eternal sin

   n Blaspheming against the Holy Spirit is an eternal sin (Mark 3:29).

   Eternal life, see **360**. **Eternal punishment**, see **963**.

116 Instantly

- Suddenly

   a Joshua came on them suddenly (Josh. 10:9; 11:7); the thing happened suddenly (2 Chr. 29:36); his calamity will come suddenly (Prov. 6:15).

   b Lest he come suddenly (Mark 13:36); lest that day come upon you suddenly (Luke 21:34); they thought the kingdom of God would appear at once (Luke 19:11).

- In a short time

   c In a short time you would have me a Christian (Acts 26:28); we shall be changed in a moment, in a wink (1 Cor. 15:52).

117 Chronometry

See **108***a*.

118 Anachronism

Premature birth, see **138***b*.

119 First

- **Firstborn**

a Abel offered the firstlings of his flock (Gen. 4:4); every firstborn male, man or animal, belongs to God (Exod. 13:2, 12; 22:29–30; 34:19; Num. 3:13; 8:16–17; Luke 2:23); the firstborn belongs to the priests (Num. 18:15); give me your firstborn sons (Exod. 22:29); set apart every firstborn male of your animals (Lev. 27:26; Deut. 12:6; 15:19); to bring the firstborn to the temple (Neh. 10:36); census of firstborn males (Num. 3:40–51); the Levites are God's in place of the firstborn males (Num. 3:12; 8:16); Israel is God's firstborn son (Exod. 4:22).

b Jether was Gideon's firstborn (Judg. 8:20).

- **Rights of the firstborn**

c If the firstborn is the son of an unloved wife, his rights should not be lost (Deut. 21:15–17); it is not the custom to marry the younger before the firstborn (Gen. 29:26); the firstborn was seated according to his birthright (Gen. 43:33); Jehoram was given the kingdom because he was the firstborn (2 Chr. 21:3).

- **Birthrights transferred**

d Esau sold his birthright (Gen. 25:31, 34; Heb. 12:16); Jacob stole the blessing of the firstborn (Gen. 27:19, 32); Jacob blessed Ephraim, though Manasseh was the firstborn (Gen. 48:14–19); Reuben was Jacob's firstborn (Gen. 49:3; 1 Chr. 5:1); but the rights of the firstborn were Joseph's (1 Chr. 5:2); having one portion more than his brothers (Gen. 48:22); Hosah made his son Shimri the first though he was not the firstborn (1 Chr. 26:10).

- **Death of the firstborn**

e The firstborn of the Egyptians killed (Exod. 4:23; 11:5; 12:12, 29; 13:15; Num. 8:17; 33:4; Ps. 78:51; 105:36; 135:8; 136:10).

f The builder of Jericho will lose his firstborn (Josh. 6:26); as Hiel did (1 Kgs. 16:34).

- **Sacrificing the firstborn**

g The king of Moab sacrificed his firstborn son (2 Kgs. 3:27); they made their firstborn pass through the fire (Ezek. 20:26); shall I give my firstborn for my transgression? (Mic. 6:7).

- **Christ the firstborn**

h I will make him the firstborn (Ps. 89:27); Christ is the firstborn of all creation (Col. 1:15); he is before all things (Col. 1:17); the firstborn from the dead (Col. 1:18; Rev. 1:5); the first among many brothers (Rom. 8:29); the assembly of the firstborn (Heb. 12:23).

120 Posteriority

Days to come, see **124**.

121 Present time

• Present
age

a Do you not know how to interpret the present time? (Luke 12:56); Christ saves us from the present evil age (Gal. 1:4); the sufferings of the present time (Rom. 8:18); Demas, in love with this present world (2 Tim. 4:10); the tabernacle symbolizes the present time (Heb. 9:9).

b Things present cannot separate us from the love of God (Rom. 8:38); the present and the future are yours (1 Cor. 3:22).

• Now

c Now is the day of salvation (2 Cor. 6:2); today you will be with me in Paradise (Luke 23:43).

122 Different time

123 Synchronism

124 Future time

• Tomorrow

a When? tomorrow (Exod. 8:9–10; 9:5); tomorrow we will go to such a place and make a profit (Jas. 4:14).

b Do not boast about tomorrow (Prov. 27:1; Jas. 4:13–16); you do not know about tomorrow (Jas. 4:14); do not be anxious about tomorrow (Matt. 6:34).

c Let us eat and drink, for tomorrow we die (1 Cor. 15:32).

• Future
generations

d They will tell his righteousness to a people yet unborn (Ps. 22:30–1); a people yet unborn will praise the Lord (Ps. 102:18).

• Things
to come

e The wrath to come (Matt. 3:7; Luke 3:7; 1 Thess. 1:10); future judgement (Acts 24:25).

f Things to come: the age (Matt. 12:32; Mark 10:30; Luke 18:30; Eph. 1:21; Heb. 6:5); life (1 Tim. 4:8); world (Heb. 2:5); city (Heb. 13:14); blessings (Heb. 11:20).

g High priest of the good things to come (Heb. 9:11).

h In the last days the mountain of the house of the Lord will be established (Isa. 2:2; Mic. 4:1); the vision he sees is for many years hence (Ezek. 12:27); in the latter years God will attack Israel (Ezek. 38:8).

• Future hope

i Plans to give you a future and a hope (Jer. 29:11); surely there is a future (Prov. 23:18).

j Things to come cannot separate us from the love of God (Rom. 8:38); the present and the future are yours (1 Cor. 3:22).

• Knowing
the future

k Tell us what is going to happen in the future (Isa. 41:23; 44:7); God has made known what will happen in the future (Dan. 2:45).

l The Holy Spirit will declare things to come (John 16:13); Jacob told his sons things to come (Gen. 49:1).
Predicting the future, see **511***b*.

125 Past time: retrospective time

• Ages ago

a Before the world was formed, you are God (Ps. 90:2); his goings forth are from eternity (Mic. 5:2).

b Grace given in Christ ages ago (2 Tim. 1:9); wisdom God decreed before the ages (1 Cor. 2:7); from ancient times God planned it (2 Kgs. 19:25; Isa. 37:26); eternal life which God promised ages ago (Titus 1:2); God announced it long ago (Isa. 45:21; 48:5); I will utter things hidden from the foundation of the world (Matt. 13:35).

c From of old their condemnation has not been idle (2 Pet. 2:3); long ago they were marked out for condemnation (Jude 4).

● Bygone days
d Ask about former days (Deut. 4:32; 32:7); ask of past generations (Job 8:8); I have considered the days of old (Ps. 77:5).

e In ancient times your fathers lived beyond the River (Josh. 24:2); our fathers have told us what you did in days of old (Ps. 44:1).

f God spoke of old by the prophets (Heb. 1:1; Luke 1:70; Acts 3:21; 15:18); I declared the former things (Isa. 48:3); things written in former times (Rom. 15:4); it was said to men of old (Matt. 5:21, 33); the mystery was not made known to previous generations (Eph. 3:5).

g Job longs for the days gone by (Job 29:2); I remember the days of old (Ps. 143:5); do not ask why former days were better (Eccles. 7:10); Jerusalem remembers the precious things from days gone by (Lam. 1:7).

h Let the time past suffice for bad conduct (1 Pet. 4:3).
Beginning, see **68**.

126 Newness

● Unused
a A red heifer which has never been yoked (Num. 19:2; Deut. 21:3); two milch cows, never yoked (1 Sam. 6:7); a colt on which no one had ever sat (Mark 11:2; Luke 19:30); a tomb where no one had even been laid (Luke 23:53; John 19:41).

b The ark on a new cart (1 Sam. 6:7; 2 Sam. 6:3; 1 Chr. 13:7); Samson was bound with ropes never before used (Judg. 15:13; 16:11); Ahijah wore a new cloak (1 Kgs. 11:29); bring me a new jar with salt in it (2 Kgs. 2:20).

c You have not been this way before (Josh. 3:4).

● New creation
d I make all things new (Rev. 21:5); I am doing a new thing (Isa. 43:19); I declare new things (Isa. 42:9; 48:6); the Lord's mercies are new every morning (Lam. 3:23).

e New: commandment (John 13:34; 1 John 2:7–8; 2 John 5); covenant (Jer. 31:31; 1 Cor. 11:25; 2 Cor. 3:6; Heb. 8:8, 13; 9:15; 12:24); heaven and earth (Isa. 65:17; 66:22; 2 Pet. 3:13; Rev. 21:1); Jerusalem (Rev. 3:12; 21:2); song (Ps. 33:3; 40:3; 96:1; 98:1; 144:9; 149:1; Isa. 42:10; Rev. 5:9; 14:3); teaching (Mark 1:27; Acts 17:19, 21); tomb (Matt. 27:60); way into the sanctuary (Heb. 10:20).
New covenant, see **764l**.

f A new creation (2 Cor. 5:17; Gal. 6:15); the new man (Eph. 4:24; Col. 3:10); one new man in place of the two (Eph. 2:15); walk in newness of life (Rom. 6:4); serve in the new life of the Spirit (Rom. 7:6); the renewing of the Holy Spirit (Titus 3:5); the renewal of your mind (Rom. 12:2); renewed in the spirit of your minds (Eph. 4:23); renewed daily (2 Cor. 4:16); a householder with old and new in his treasure (Matt. 13:52).

g I will put a new spirit within them (Ezek. 11:19); I will give you a new heart and a new spirit (Ezek. 36:26); make yourselves a new heart and a new spirit (Ezek. 18:31).

h A new patch is no good for an old garment (Matt. 9:16; Mark 2:21; Luke 5:36); new wine is for unused wineskins (Matt. 9:17; Mark 2:22; Luke 5:37–9); till I drink new wine with you (Matt. 26:29; Mark 14:25); fresh dough with no leaven (1 Cor. 5:7).

● Nothing new

i There is nothing new under the sun (Eccles. 1:9); everything has already been (Eccles. 1:9; 3:15).

127 Oldness

● Old is good

a The old is good (Luke 5:39); ask for the ancient paths (Jer. 6:16).

b Whatever is obsolete and growing old is ready to vanish (Heb. 8:13).

● Traditions of men

c It is not our custom to marry the younger first (Gen. 29:26); commemorating Jephthah's daughter became a tradition (Judg. 11:39–40); custom for the young men to give a marriage feast (Judg. 14:10); the sharing of booty became a lasting statute (1 Sam. 30:25); the governor was accustomed to release one prisoner at the feast (Matt. 27:15; Mark 15:6).

d The Israelites do not eat the sinew of the hip (Gen. 32:32); the priests of Dagon do not tread on the threshold (1 Sam. 5:5).

e Zealous for the traditions of my fathers (Gal. 1:14); I had done nothing against the customs of our fathers (Acts 28:17); the Pharisees observed the traditions of the elders by washing before eating (Mark 7:3–4); you break God's command for the sake of your tradition (Matt. 15:3, 6; Mark 7:8–9, 13); see no one deludes you by human tradition (Col. 2:8).

Old sayings, see **496c**.

● Customs changed

f Disciples transgress the tradition of the elders (Matt. 15:2; Mark 7:5); Jesus would alter the traditions (Acts 6:14); new wine is not put into old wineskins (Matt. 9:17; Mark 2:22); a new patch is not put on an old garment (Matt. 9:16; Mark 2:21); Paul was said to be against Jewish customs (Acts 21:21).

g Such a thing is not done in Israel (2 Sam. 13:12); it is not the custom of the Romans to give up a man untried (Acts 25:16).

● Customs of Jesus

h As his custom was: he taught them (Mark 10:1); he went to the synagogue on the sabbath (Luke 4:16); he went to the Mount of Olives (Luke 22:39).

● Customs of Paul

i As his custom was, Paul went to the synagogue on the sabbath (Acts 17:2).

● Christian
traditions

j Holding to the traditions as Paul delivered them (1 Cor. 11:2); hold to the traditions (2 Thess. 2:15); those who live not according to the tradition (2 Thess. 3:6); he brings out of his treasure things new and old (Matt. 13:52).

● Old nature

k Our old man was crucified (Rom. 6:6); put off the old man (Eph. 4:22; Col. 3:9); old things have gone (2 Cor. 5:17); cleanse out the old leaven (1 Cor. 5:7–8).

128 Morning. Spring. Summer

● Provision
of day

a God called the light 'day' (Gen. 1:5); day and night will not cease (Gen. 8:22); if you can break my covenant with day and night (Jer. 33:20, 25); yours is the day, yours the night (Ps. 74:16); have you commanded the dawn to take place? (Job 38:12).

● Rising early

b Rising early: God (Jer. 7:13, 25; 11:7; 25:3, 4; 26:5; 29:19; 32:33; 35:14, 15; 44:4); the angels (Gen. 19:2); Abraham (Gen. 19:27; 21:14; 22:3); Abimelech (Gen. 20:8); Isaac and Abimelech (Gen. 26:31); Jacob (Gen. 28:18); Laban (Gen. 31:55); Moses (Exod. 8:20; 9:13; 24:4); the Israelites (Exod. 32:6; Num. 14:40; Josh. 6:15); Joshua (Josh. 7:16; 8:10); the men of Ai (Josh. 8:14); Abimelech (Judg. 9:33); Elkanah's family (1 Sam. 1:19); Philistines (1 Sam. 5:3); Samuel (1 Sam. 15:12); David (1 Sam. 17:20; 29:10); Absalom (2 Sam. 15:2); the Moabites (2 Kgs. 3:22); Judah (2 Chr. 20:20); Hezekiah (2 Chr. 29:20); Job (Job 1:5); Jesus (Mark 1:35); people wanting to hear Jesus (Luke 21:38).

c The good wife rises while it is still light (Prov. 31:15); early on the first day of the week (Mark 16:2).

d It is in vain that you rise early (Ps. 127:2); woe to those who rise early to pursue strong wine (Isa. 5:11).

● In the
morning

e Manna in the morning (Exod. 16:13–15); bread in the morning (Exod. 16:8, 12); in the morning you will see (Exod. 16:7); in the morning they took counsel how to kill Jesus (Matt. 27:1; Mark 15:1).

f The sun had risen when Lot reached Zoar (Gen. 19:23); at break of day the king went to the lions' den (Dan. 6:19); in the morning Jesus returned to Jerusalem (Matt. 21:18); they came to the tomb at dawn (Luke 24:1).

g In the morning watch the Lord looked (Exod. 14:24).

● Joy in the
morning

h Joy comes in the morning (Ps. 30:5); the Lord's mercies are new every morning (Lam. 3:23); you make the dawn and sunset shout for joy (Ps. 65:8); he who blesses with a loud voice early in the morning is like one who curses (Prov. 27:14).

● Worship in
the morning

i One lamb sacrificed each morning (Exod. 29:39; Num. 28:4); in the morning I will pray to you (Ps. 5:3); I will awake the dawn (Ps. 57:8); I rise before dawn and cry for help (Ps. 119:147); I wait for the Lord more than watchmen for the morning (Ps. 130:6).

● Hopeless morning

j In the morning you will long for evening, and at evening for morning (Deut. 28:67); through the night Job longed for morning (Job 7:4).

● Dawn from heaven

k Dawn from heaven (Luke 1:78); Christ the morning star (Rev. 2:28; 22:16); till day dawns and the morning star rises in your hearts (2 Pet. 1:19); the day is at hand (Rom. 13:12).

● Using the day

l We are sons of the day (1 Thess. 5:5, 8); conduct yourselves as in the day (Rom. 13:13); I must work while it is day (John 9:4); if any one walks in the day (John 11:9).

● Spring of the year

m In the spring, when kings go to war (2 Sam. 11:1; 1 Chr. 20:1); winter is past and plants are growing (S. of S. 2:11–13).

● Summer

n Summer and winter will not cease (Gen. 8:22); you have made summer and winter (Ps. 74:17); when the fig tree sprouts, summer is near (Matt. 24:32; Mark 13:28; Luke 21:30); harvest is past, summer is ended (Jer. 8:20).

129 Evening. Autumn. Winter

● Provision of night

a God called the darkness 'night' (Gen. 1:5); while the earth remains, day and night will not cease (Gen. 8:22); in the evening you will long for morning (Deut. 28:67); through the night Job longed for morning (Job 7:4); there shall be no night (Rev. 21:25; 22:5).

● In the evening

b The angels came to Sodom in the evening (Gen. 19:1); the servant came at evening (Gen. 24:11); Isaac meditated at evening (Gen. 24:63); David rose from his bed at evening (2 Sam. 11:2); the sun had set when Jacob came to Bethel (Gen. 28:11); at evening the disciples wanted to dismiss the crowds (Matt. 14:15); at evening the wages were paid (Matt. 20:8); at evening you say it will be fair weather (Matt. 16:2).

c Quails in the evening (Exod. 16:13); meat in the evening (Exod. 16:8, 12); in the evening you will know (Exod. 16:6).

d Kill the lamb at twilight (Exod. 12:6); one lamb sacrificed at twilight (Exod. 29:41; Num. 28:8); at evening he was reclining at table (Matt. 26:20).

e In the evening they brought the sick to Jesus (Matt. 8:16; Mark 1:32; Luke 4:40); when evening came they went out of the city (Mark 11:19); when it was evening he came with the twelve (Mark 14:17); at sunset, hanged bodies were taken down (Josh. 8:29; 10:27); when evening came Nicodemus asked for Jesus' body (Matt. 27:57); when evening came Joseph asked for the body (Mark 15:42–3); stay with us, for evening is near (Luke 24:29); when it was evening on the first day of the week (John 20:19).

● Using the night

f By night: Gideon cut down the Asherah (Judg. 6:27); Saul came to the witch (1 Sam. 28:8); Nehemiah examined the walls (Neh. 2:12, 13, 15); Joseph fled to Egypt with Mary and the child (Matt. 2:14); Nicodemus came to Jesus (John 3:2; 19:39); Judas went out (John 13:30); his disciples were supposed to have stolen him away (Matt. 28:13).

● Danger at night

g Do not spend the night at the fords (2 Sam. 17:16); they are coming at night to kill you (Neh. 6:10); Paul was lowered down the walls in a basket (Acts 9:25); the brethren sent Paul and Silas away (Acts 17:10); Paul was brought to Antipatris (Acts 23:31).

● Attacking by night

h Abraham attacked the kings by night (Gen. 14:15); Jehoram attacked the Edomites by night (2 Kgs. 8:20); let us take spoil by night (1 Sam. 14:36); lie in wait by night (Judg. 9:32, 34).

i Those who marched all night: Joshua (Josh. 10:9); Abner and his men (2 Sam. 2:29); Joab and his men (2 Sam. 2:32).

● Prayer at night

j I meditate on you in the night watches (Ps. 63:6); I meditate on your word in the night watches (Ps. 119:148); I remember your name in the night (Ps. 119:55); at midnight I rise to praise you (Ps. 119:62); those who serve by night in the house of the Lord (Ps. 134:1); Jesus spent all night in prayer (Luke 6:12).

● Midnight

k Who would ask a friend for food at midnight? (Luke 11:5).

l God acted at midnight (Exod. 11:4; 12:29); at midnight Samson arose (Judg. 16:3); at midnight Paul and Silas were praying and singing hymns (Acts 16:25); Paul spoke until midnight (Acts 20:7); at midnight the sailors thought they were nearing land (Acts 27:27).

● Spiritual night

m You are not sons of night (1 Thess. 5:5); at night people sleep and get drunk (1 Thess. 5:7).

n No one can work in the night (John 9:4); if any one walks at night he stumbles (John 11:10).

o The day of the Lord like a thief in the night (1 Thess. 5:2); at midnight the bridegroom came (Matt. 25:6); the night is far gone (Rom. 13:12).

● Autumn

p As in my autumn days (Job 29:4); trees in autumn without fruit (Jude 12).

● Winter

q It was winter (John 10:23); come before winter (2 Tim. 4:21); pray that your flight will not be in winter (Matt. 24:20; Mark 13:18); the winter is past (S. of S. 2:11).

r Wintering (Acts 27:12; 1 Cor. 16:6; Titus 3:12).

130 Youthfulness

● From the womb

a You have been my God from my mother's womb (Ps. 22:10); the name given by the angel before he was conceived in the womb (Luke 2:21).

b From the womb: a Nazirite (Judg. 13:5, 7); set apart (Gal. 1:15); called (Isa. 49:1, 5); known and consecrated (Jer. 1:5); filled with the Holy Spirit (Luke 1:15); a man lame (Acts 3:2; 14:8).

● From birth

c The wicked go astray from birth (Ps. 58:3); on you I have leaned from birth (Ps. 71:6).

d A man blind from birth (John 9:1); our son, born blind (John 9:19, 20); a person born blind (John 9:32).

● From youth

    e He had been demonised since childhood (Mark 9:21).

    f All these I have observed from my youth (Mark 10:20; Luke 18:21); my manner of life from my youth (Acts 26:4); from childhood you have known the Scriptures (2 Tim. 3:15); you have taught me from my youth (Ps. 71:17).

    g A warrior from his youth (1 Sam. 17:33); Moab has been at ease from his youth (Jer. 48:11); afflicted and close to death from my youth (Ps. 88:15); we have sinned from our youth (Jer. 3:25).

● Benefits
of youth

    h Remember your Creator in the days of your youth (Eccles. 12:1); I remember the devotion of your youth (Jer. 2:2); while Josiah was still a youth he sought the Lord (2 Chr. 34:3).

    i Let no one despise your youth (1 Tim. 4:12); rejoice during your childhood (Eccles. 11:9); the older will serve the younger (Gen. 25:23; Rom. 9:12).

    j Your youth is renewed like the eagle's (Ps. 103:5).

● Limitations
of youth

    k Jether was afraid because he was only a youth (Judg. 8:20); you are only a youth (1 Sam. 17:33); Solomon is young and inexperienced (1 Chr. 22:5; 29:1); when Rehoboam was young (2 Chr. 13:7); Elihu waited to speak because others were older (Job 32:4, 6); even youths grow weary (Isa. 40:30); while the heir is a child he is no different from a slave (Gal. 4:1).

    l An elder should not be a recent convert (1 Tim. 3:6); shun youthful passions (2 Tim. 2:22); it is good for a man that he bear the yoke in his youth (Lam. 3:27).

131 Age

● Lifespan

    a Man's lifespan shall be 120 years (Gen. 6:3); the length of our life is 70 years, or 80 (Ps. 90:10); the youth will die at 100 (Isa. 65:20).

    b A man's lifespan is predetermined (Job 14:5); who can add a cubit to his span of life ? (Matt. 6:27).

● Age ranges

    c Census of Levites males one month up (Num. 3:15, 22, 28, 34, 39; 26:62); census of firstborn males a month up (Num. 3:40); valuation of people from 5 to 20 (Lev. 27:5); valuation of people from 20 to 60 (Lev. 27:3–4); census of males 20 and up (Num. 1:3, 18, 20–45; 26:2, 4; 2 Chr. 25:5); David did not count those under 20 (1 Chr. 27:23); men aged 20 and over could go to war (Num. 1:3, 18); 20 and up shall pay the tax (Exod. 30:14; 38:26); Levites numbered from 20 up (1 Chr. 23:24, 27); Levites 20 and up to oversee the work (Ezra 3:8); Levites start work at 25 and retire at 50 (Num. 8:24–5); widows not enrolled under 60 (1 Tim. 5:9).

    d Census of those between 30 and 50 of: Gershonites (Num. 4:22–3, 38–9); Merarites (Num. 4:29–30, 42–3); Kohathites (Num. 4:2–3, 34–5); Levites (Num. 4:3, 23, 30; 1 Chr. 23:3).

    e Herod killed the boys two and under (Matt. 2:16); none of the people 20 and upward would see the land (Num. 32:11); from 20 and upward they would die in the wilderness (Num. 14:29).

- **Specific ages** *f* Eight days old when circumcised (Gen. 17:12; 21:4; Lev. 12:3; Luke 1:59; 2:21; Acts 7:8; Phil. 3:5); a firstborn animal sacrificed at eight days old (Exod. 22:30).

g People at specific ages: Mephibosheth 5 (2 Sam. 4:4); Joash 7 (2 Kgs. 11:21; 2 Chr. 24:1); Josiah 8 (2 Chr. 34:1); Jehoiachin 8 [18?] (2 Chr. 36:9); Jesus 12 (Luke 2:42); Jairus' daughter 12 (Mark 5:42; Luke 8:42); Ishmael 13 (Gen. 17:25); Joseph 17 (Gen. 37:2); Zedekiah 21 (2 Chr. 36:11); Ahaziah 22 (2 Chr. 22:2); Amon 22 (2 Chr. 33:21); Hezekiah 25 (2 Chr. 29:1); Joseph 30 (Gen. 41:46); David 30 (2 Sam. 5:4); Jesus 30 (Luke 3:23); Jehoram 32 [sic] (2 Chr. 21:5, 20); Isaac 40 (Gen. 25:20); Esau 40 (Gen. 26:34); Moses 40 (Acts 7:23); Caleb 40 (Josh. 14:7); Ishbosheth 40 (2 Sam. 2:10); the lame man over 40 (Acts 4:22); Rehoboam 41 (2 Chr. 12:13); Jesus not yet 50 (John 8:57); Isaac 60 (Gen. 25:26); Hezron 60 on marrying (1 Chr. 2:21); Darius about 62 (Dan. 5:31); Enoch 65 (Gen. 5:21); Abraham 75 (Gen. 12:4); Moses 80 (Exod. 7:7); Barzillai 80 (2 Sam. 19:32, 35); Aaron 83 (Exod. 7:7); Anna 84 (Luke 2:37); Caleb 85 (Josh. 14:10); Sarah 90 (Gen. 17:17); Abraham 99 (Gen. 17:1, 24); Abraham 100 (Gen. 17:17; 21:5); Moses 120 (Deut. 31:2); Jacob 130 (Gen. 47:9); Noah 600 (Gen. 7:6, 11).

- **Age at fatherhood** *h* Nahor 29 (Gen. 11:24); Peleg 30 (Gen. 11:18); Serug 30 (Gen. 11:22); Shelah 30 (Gen. 11:14); Reu 32 (Gen. 11:20); Eber 34 (Gen. 11:16); Arpachsad 35 (Gen. 11:12); Malalel 65 (Gen. 5:15); Enoch 65 (Gen. 5:21); Kenan 70 (Gen. 5:12); Terah 70 (Gen. 11:26); Abraham 86 (Gen. 16:16); Enosh 90 (Gen. 5:9); Shem 100 (Gen. 11:10); Abraham 100 (Gen. 17:17; 21:5; Rom. 4:19); Seth 105 (Gen. 5:6); Adam 130 (Gen. 5:3); Jared 162 (Gen. 5:18); Lamech 182 (Gen. 5:28); Methusaleh 187 (Gen. 5:25); Noah 500 (Gen. 5:32).

- **Age when crowned** *i* Joash 7 (2 Kgs. 11:21); Josiah 8 (2 Kgs. 22:1); Manasseh 12 (2 Kgs. 21:1; 2 Chr. 33:1); Azariah [Uzziah] 16 (2 Kgs. 14:21; 15:2; 2 Chr. 26:1, 3); Jehoiachin 18 (2 Kgs. 24:8); Ahaz 20 (2 Kgs. 16:2; 2 Chr. 28:1); Zedekiah 21 (2 Kgs. 24:18; Jer. 52:1); Ahaziah 22 (2 Kgs. 8:26); Amon 22 (2 Kgs. 21:19); Jehoahaz 23 (2 Kgs. 23:31; 2 Chr. 36:2); Amaziah 25 (2 Kgs. 14:2; 2 Chr. 25:1); Hezekiah 25 (2 Kgs. 18:2); Jehoiakim 25 (2 Kgs. 23:36; 2 Chr. 36:5); Jotham 25 (2 Kgs. 15:33; 2 Chr. 27:1, 8); Jehoram 32 (2 Kgs. 8:17); Jehoshaphat 35 (1 Kgs. 22:42; 2 Chr. 20:31); Rehoboam 41 (1 Kgs. 14:21).

- **Age at death** *j* Eli 98 (1 Sam. 4:15); Joseph 110 (Gen. 50:22, 26); Joshua 110 (Josh. 24:29; Judg. 2:8); Moses 120 (Deut. 34:7); Aaron 123 (Num. 33:39); Sarah 127 (Gen. 23:1); Jehoiada 130 (2 Chr. 24:15); Kohath 133 (Exod. 6:18); Ishmael 137 (Gen. 25:17); Amram 137 (Exod. 6:20); Levi 137 (Exod. 6:16); Job 140 (Job

42:16); Jacob 147 (Gen. 47:28); Abraham 175 (Gen. 25:7); Isaac 180 (Gen. 35:28); Terah 205 (Gen. 11:32); Lamech 777 (Gen. 5:31); Mahalalel 895 (Gen. 5:17); Enosh 905 (Gen. 5:11); Kenan 910 (Gen. 5:14); Seth 912 (Gen. 5:8); Adam 930 (Gen. 5:5); Noah 950 (Gen. 9:29); Jared 962 (Gen. 5:20); Methusaleh 969 (Gen. 5:27).

k Enoch 365 when he was not (Gen. 5:23–4).

132 Young person. Young animal. Young plant

● Younger greater *a* The younger shall be greater (Gen. 48:19).

● Youngest child *b* Gideon was the youngest (Judg. 6:15); Jotham the youngest son of Gideon (Judg. 9:5); David was the youngest (1 Sam. 16:11; 17:14).

c The rebuilder of Jericho will lose his youngest son (Josh. 6:26); as Hiel did (1 Kgs. 16:34).

● Young people *d* Jonathan had a little lad with him (1 Sam. 20:35); the Arameans captured a little Israelite girl (2 Kgs. 5:2); a young man called Eutychus (Acts 20:9); the streets of Jerusalem will be filled with boys and girls (Zech. 8:5).

e When Israel was a youth I loved him (Hos. 11:1).
Youthfulness, see **130**.

● Mocked *f* Youths mocked Elishah (2 Kgs. 2:23); even children despise me
by youths (Job 19:18); those younger than I mock me (Job 30:1).

● Childlikeness *g* You must receive the kingdom of God like a child (Matt. 18:2–4; Mark 10:15; Luke 18:17); receive the word like newborn babies (1 Pet. 2:2); let the greatest become as the youngest (Luke 22:26); in evil be babies (1 Cor. 14:20); Solomon considered himself a little child (1 Kgs. 3:7); as did Jeremiah (Jer. 1:6).

● Children and *h* From the mouth of infants God established strength (Ps. 8:2);
the kingdom God revealed these things to babies (Matt. 11:25; Luke 10:21); children crying Hosanna in the temple (Matt. 21:15); praise from the mouths of children (Matt. 21:16); they brought children to him (Matt. 19:13; Mark 10:13; Luke 18:15); the kingdom of heaven belongs to such as these (Matt. 19:14; Mark 10:14; Luke 18:16).

i Receiving a child in Christ's name (Matt. 18:5; Mark 9:36–7; Luke 9:47–8); the seriousness of harming a little one (Matt. 18:6, 10, 14; Mark 9:42; Luke 17:2).

j I am writing to you little children (1 John 2:12, 13).

● Childishness *k* This generation is like children sitting in the marketplace (Matt. 11:16; Luke 7:32); do not be children in your thinking (1 Cor. 14:20); you were not mature, but as babes in Christ (1 Cor. 3:1); those who need milk are babies (Heb. 5:13); that we may no longer be children (Eph. 4:14); when I was a child, I acted as a child (1 Cor. 13:11).

● Young animal *l* A newborn animal is to be left with its mother for seven days (Exod. 22:30; Lev. 22:27); you shall not kill a mother animal and its young on the same day (Lev. 22:28); do not take a mother bird with its young (Deut. 22:6–7); do not boil a kid in its mother's milk (Exod. 23:19; 34:26; Deut. 14:21); take their calves home (1 Sam. 6:7, 10); Samuel offered a suckling lamb (1 Sam. 7:9).

133 Old person

- Character of old people

a Older men are to be temperate (Titus 2:2); older women are to be reverent (Titus 2:3).

b Wisdom is with the aged (Job 12:12); many years should teach wisdom (Job 32:7); old people may not be wise (Job 32:9); I understand more than the aged (Ps. 119:100).

- Hope in old age

c They will bring forth fruit in old age (Ps. 92:14); do not cast me off in old age (Ps. 71:9, 18); even to old age I will carry you (Isa. 46:4); old men and women will again sit in the streets of Jerusalem (Zech. 8:4).

d Respect old people (Lev. 19:32); do not rebuke an old man (1 Tim. 5:1).

e There will not be an old man in your house (1 Sam. 2:31–2).

- Regarding old age

f I was young and now I am old (Ps. 37:25); when you are old (John 21:18); may he be a sustainer of your old age (Ruth 4:15).

- Those who were old

g People who were old: Lot (Gen. 19:31); Abraham and Sarah (Gen. 18:11–12); Sarah bore a son in old age (Gen. 24:36); Abraham (Gen. 21:2, 5, 7; 24:1; 25:8); Abraham would be buried at a good old age (Gen. 15:15); Isaac (Gen. 27:1–2; 35:29); Joshua (Josh. 13:1; 23:1–2); Gideon (Judg. 8:32); Eli (1 Sam. 2:22; 4:18); Samuel (1 Sam. 8:1, 5; 12:2); Jesse (1 Sam. 17:12); Barzillai (2 Sam. 19:32, 35); David (1 Kgs. 1:1, 15; 1 Chr. 23:1); Ahijah's eyes were dim with age (1 Kgs. 14:4); the Shunamite's husband (2 Kgs. 4:14); Jehoiada (2 Chr. 24:15); Job (Job 42:17); Zachariah and Elizabeth (Luke 1:7, 18).

h An old man is coming up (1 Sam. 28:14); people older than your father are with us (Job 15:10).

i The Ancient of Days (Dan. 7:9, 13, 22).
Elders, see **986*ae*.**

134 Adultness

- Maturity

a Go on to maturity (Heb. 6:1); in thinking be mature (1 Cor. 14:20); until we reach mature manhood (Eph. 4:13); that you may stand mature (Col. 4:12); to present every man mature in Christ (Col. 1:28); solid food is for the mature (Heb. 5:14); we do speak wisdom among those who are mature (1 Cor. 2:6); when I became a man I gave up childish things (1 Cor. 13:11).

b Ask him, he is of age (John 9:21, 23).

135 Earliness

- Work soon done

a Why are you back so soon? (Gen. 27:20; Exod. 2:18).

b What you do, do quickly (John 13:27).

- God will not delay

c The Lord is not slow concerning his promise (2 Pet. 3:9); he who is coming will not delay (Hab. 2:3; Heb. 10:37); none of my words will be delayed any longer (Ezek. 12:25, 28); will God delay over his elect? (Luke 18:7).

d My salvation will not delay (Isa. 46:13); God will soon crush Satan under your feet (Rom. 16:20); he will vindicate them speedily (Luke 18:8); salvation is nearer than when we first believed (Rom. 13:11–12); there would be no more delay (Rev. 10:6); to show his servants what must soon happen (Rev. 1:1; 22:6); I will come soon (Rev. 2:16; 3:11; 22:7, 12, 20); this generation will not pass away till all this takes place (Mark 13:30; Luke 21:32).

Haste, see **680**; **rising early**, see **128***b*.

136 Lateness

- God's delay

a Lord, how long? (Ps. 6:3; 13:1; 35:17; 74:10; 79:5; 89:46; 90:13; Isa. 6:11; Rev. 6:10); do not delay (Ps. 40:17); when will you comfort me? (Ps. 119:82); how long must I call for help? (Hab. 1:2); how long will you have no mercy on Jerusalem? (Zech. 1:12); how long will the wicked exult? (Ps. 94:3); how long will you leave us in doubt? (John 10:24); when will you judge my persecutors? (Ps. 119:84); because sentence against evil is not executed promptly (Eccles. 8:11).

b For the sake of my name I delay my anger (Isa. 48:9); days lengthen, visions fail (Ezek. 12:22); my master is delayed (Matt. 24:48; Luke 12:45); the bridegroom was delayed (Matt. 25:5).

c I will not do it in your days but in your son's (1 Kgs. 11:12; 21:29).

d How long must I endure you? (Matt. 17:17; Mark 9:19; Luke 9:41).

- People who delayed

e Those who delayed: Lot (Gen. 19:16); Moses (Exod. 32:1); Sisera (Judg. 5:28); Amasa (2 Sam. 20:5); the Levites (2 Chr. 24:5); Zacharias (Luke 1:21).

f They wanted to delay Rebekah's going (Gen. 24:55); why are you last to bring the king back? (2 Sam. 19:11–12).

g How long will you love being simple? (Prov. 1:22); how long will they prophesy lies? (Jer. 23:26).

- Delay

h Do not delay giving (Prov. 3:28); if the serpent bites before being charmed (Eccles. 10:11).

- Late

i It is in vain that you go to bed late (Ps. 127:2); woe to those who stay up late drinking wine (Isa. 5:11); the hour is late (Mark 6:35); it was already late (Mark 11:11).

137 Opportunity

- Right time for God

a The time has come to be gracious to Zion (Ps. 102:13); it is time for the Lord to act (Ps. 119:126).

b At the right time Christ died for the ungodly (Rom. 5:6).

● Right time
for people

   c Be ready in season and out of season (2 Tim. 4:2); making the most of the opportunity (Col. 4:5); you were concerned for me but you had no opportunity (Phil. 4:10).

   d Perhaps you have come to kingship for such a time as this (Esther 4:14); when I have an opportunity I will summon you (Acts 24:25).

   e He looked for an opportunity to betray him (Matt. 26:16; Mark 14:11; Luke 22:6); an opportunity came on Herod's birthday (Mark 6:21).

   Door of opportunity, see **263h**.

● Opportunity
for the devil

   f The devil departed from him until an opportune time (Luke 4:13); do not give the devil an opportunity (Eph. 4:27).

   Time, see **108**.

138 Untimeliness

● Not the time

   a Is it a time to receive presents? (2 Kgs. 5:26); is it time for you to live in panelled houses? (Hag. 1:4); the time has not come to build the temple (Hag. 1:2).

● Premature birth

   b As to one untimely born (1 Cor. 15:8).

   Occasion, see **137**.

139 Frequency

● Thrice daily

   a Daniel prayed three times a day (Dan. 6:10, 13).

   In turn, see **65a**; **Unceasing**, see **146**.

140 Infrequency

● Rare

   a The word of the Lord and visions were rare (1 Sam. 3:1).

141 Regularity

● Regular
periods

   a While the earth remains the seasons will not cease (Gen. 8:22); give us this day our daily bread (Matt. 6:11; Luke 11:3).

   b Forced labourers in relays, one month in Lebanon and two at home (1 Kgs. 5:14).

● Regular feasts
and fasts

   c Men must attend the feasts three times a year (Exod. 23:14, 17; 34:23; Deut. 16:16); every year his parents went up to the passover (Luke 2:41).

   d I fast twice a week (Luke 18:12).

● Regular burnt
offerings

   e Two male lambs as a daily offering (Exod. 29:38; Num. 28:3–8); every sabbath, two extra (Num. 28:9–10); at the start of every month (Num. 28:11–15).

● Birthdays

   f Birthdays: Pharaoh (Gen. 40:20); Herod (Matt. 14:6; Mark 6:21).

142 Irregularity

Fickleness, see **152**.

Section seven: Change

143 Change: difference at different time

See **152**.

144 Permanence: absence of change

● God is
the same

   a God is always the same (Ps. 102:27); I the Lord do not change (Mal. 3:6); Jesus is the same yesterday, today and for ever (Heb. 13:8); the Father shows no variableness (Jas. 1:17).

● The world is
the same

   b The universe is unchanging (Eccles. 1:4–7). **Stable**, see **153**.

145 Cessation: change from action to rest

● Stopping
building

   a They stopped building Babel (Gen. 11:8); Baasha stopped fortifying Ramah (1 Kgs. 15:21; 2 Chr. 16:5); the Jews were forced to stop building Jerusalem (Ezra 4:21–4); we will stop them working (Neh. 4:11); why should the work stop? (Neh. 6:3).

● Stopping
activity

   b No more treading out wine (Isa. 16:10); I have made the wine cease (Jer. 48:33).

   c Voices of joy, of bride and bridegroom will cease (Jer. 7:34; 16:9; 25:10; Rev. 18:23); sounds of songs and harps heard no more in Tyre (Ezek. 26:13); I will put an end to her gaiety (Hos. 2:11); the voice of your messengers will be heard no more (Nahum 2:13); the oppressor has ceased (Isa. 14:4).

   d The bearers halted (Luke 7:14).

● Things
stopping

   e The manna ceased (Josh. 5:12); the wind stopped (Matt. 14:32; Mark 6:51); prophecy, tongues and knowledge will cease (1 Cor. 13:8).

146 Unceasing

● Continuing
to pray

   a They ought to pray at all times (Luke 18:1); pray without ceasing (1 Thess. 5:17); pray at all times in the Spirit (Eph. 6:18).

   b Night and day we pray that we may see you (1 Thess. 3:10); I remember you constantly in my prayers (2 Tim. 1:3).

● Always
rejoicing

   c Rejoice always (1 Thess. 5:16); rejoice in the Lord always (Phil. 4:4); sorrowful yet always rejoicing (2 Cor. 6:10).

● God always
works

   d The Lord's mercies are unceasing (Lam. 3:22); Jesus Christ will sustain you to the end (1 Cor. 1:8); he who began a good work will perform it (Phil. 1:6); my Father is working still (John 5:17).

● People
continuing

   e Tell them to go forward (Exod. 14:15); always abounding in the work of the Lord (1 Cor. 15:58).

147 Conversion: change to something different

● People
transformed

   a You will be changed into another man (1 Sam. 10:6); Jesus was transfigured (Matt. 17:2; Mark 9:2–3; Luke 9:29).

● Being
changed

   b We are being changed into his likeness (2 Cor. 3:18); be transformed by the renewing of your mind (Rom. 12:2); he will change our bodies to be like his glorious body (Phil. 3:21); we will all be changed (1 Cor. 15:51–2).

c Can the Ethiopian change his skin or the leopard his spots? (Jer. 13:23).

Turned to blood, see **335*k*.**

● Converts

d Unless you are converted and become like children you shall not enter (Matt. 18:3); lest they be converted (John 12:40).

e They described the conversion of the Gentiles (Acts 15:3); Epaenetus, the first convert to Christ from Asia (Rom. 16:5); an overseer should not be a new convert (1 Tim. 3:6).

f You cross sea and land to make one proselyte (Matt. 23:15); Nicolas, a proselyte from Antioch (Acts 6:5).

148 Returning

● Returning to God

a Return to me, says the Lord (Jer. 4:1; Joel 2:12–13); return to the Lord (Hos. 12:6; 14:1); return, faithless Israel (Jer. 3:12); return, faithless sons (Jer. 3:14, 22); return to him from who you have revolted (Isa. 31:6); let him return to the Lord (Isa. 55:7).

b You will return to the Lord (Deut. 4:30); when you return to the Lord (Deut. 30:2); let us return to the Lord (Lam. 3:40; Hos. 6:1); if you return to the Almighty (Job 22:23); if you return to the Lord with all your heart (1 Sam. 7:3); if you return to the Lord, your brothers will return from captivity (2 Chr. 30:9).

c Return to me and I will return to you (Zech. 1:3; Mal. 3:7); return to the Lord that he may return to you (2 Chr. 30:6); return, O Lord (Num. 10:36).

d Yet you have not returned to me (Amos 4:6, 8, 9, 10, 11); they have not returned to the Lord (Hos. 7:10).

● Returning to people

● Let them go home

e The dove returned to Noah (Gen. 8:9); return to your mistress (Gen. 16:9); let us return and visit the brethren (Acts 15:36).

f Soldiers given a chance of returning home (Deut. 20:5–8); in the year of Jubilee property reverts (Lev. 25:10, 13, 28, 31, 33); returning home after the death of the high priest (Num. 35:28; Josh. 20:6).

g Let them return home in peace (1 Kgs. 22:17; 2 Chr. 18:16); let me return to my own country (1 Kgs. 11:21–2); they all wanted David to come back (2 Sam. 19:14).

● Go home!

h Go home! (2 Sam. 3:16; 14:8; 1 Kgs. 14:12); go to your homes (Ruth 1:8, 11–12, 15; 1 Sam. 8:22; 10:25; 13:2; 1 Kgs. 12:24); send David back home (1 Sam. 29:4); please return (1 Sam. 29:7, 10–11); let us go back home (1 Sam. 9:5); he was commanded not to return the way he came (1 Kgs. 13:9–10).

i David told Uriah to go home (2 Sam. 11:8–10); David told Ittai the Gittite to return (2 Sam. 15:19–20).

j Everyone to your tents, Israel! (2 Sam. 20:1; 1 Kgs. 12:16; 2 Chr. 10:16); every one to his city and country! (1 Kgs. 22:36).

● Going home

k When Abimelech died they all returned home (Judg. 9:55); every one went home (Judg. 21:23–4; 1 Chr. 16:43); the people were dispersed, each to his tent (2 Sam. 20:22); the Philistines went home (1 Sam. 14:46); Absalom's servants returned to Jerusalem (2 Sam. 17:20).

l Naomi returned home (Ruth 1:6–7, 22); Elkanah and family returned home (1 Sam. 1:19; 2:11, 20); Ahithophel went home and strangled himself (2 Sam. 17:23); David came to his house (2 Sam. 20:3); the Queen of Sheba returned to her own land (1 Kgs. 10:13; 2 Chr. 9:12); the Shunammite returned home (2 Kgs. 8:3); the magi returned home another way (Matt. 2:12); they returned to Jerusalem that very hour (Luke 24:33).

● Returning to the old

m Shall I take your son back to the land you came from? (Gen. 24:5–8); they wanted to return to Egypt (Num. 14:3–4); he shall not cause the people to return to Egypt (Deut. 17:16); the Lord will bring you back to Egypt (Deut. 28:68); they will return to Egypt (Hos. 9:3; 11:5); in their hearts they turned back to Egypt (Acts 7:39).

● Returning to their land

n Abraham returned to where his tent and altar had been (Gen. 13:3–4); in the fourth generation they shall return here (Gen. 15:16); Jacob wanted to go back to his land (Gen. 30:25); return to the land of your fathers (Gen. 31:3).

● Returning after exile

o The redeemed of the Lord will return to Zion (Isa. 35:10; 51:11); I will bring you back to the land (Ezek. 37:12); I will bring Israel back (Jer. 50:19); your children will return to their land (Jer. 31:17); I will bring you back to this place (Jer. 29:10); they will return from the land of the enemy (Jer. 31:16).

p Manasseh was brought back to Jerusalem from Babylon (2 Chr. 33:13); the exiles returned from captivity (Ezra 1:11; 2:1); those who returned from exile (Ezra 6:21); Ezra and others returned from Babylon (Ezra 7:1–9); the book of the genealogy of those who returned (Neh. 7:5–60).

● Jesus returning to God

q I am going back to the Father (John 16:28; 20:17).

● Jesus coming again

r I will come back and receive you to myself (John 14:3); I am going away and I am coming back (John 14:28); this Jesus will come back in the same way (Acts 1:11); like those waiting for their Lord to return (Luke 12:36).

149 Revolution: sudden or violent change
Conversion, see **147**.

150 Substitution: change of one thing for another

● Vicarious substitution

a Abraham offered the ram instead of his son (Gen. 22:13); Judah asked to be a slave instead of Benjamin (Gen. 44:33); Levites were taken instead of the firstborn (Num. 3:40–5; 8:16–18).

● Exchange

b Leah instead of Rachel (Gen. 29:23); please send someone else

(Exod. 4:13); the harlot exchanged the children (1 Kgs. 3:20); you have reigned in place of Saul (2 Sam. 16:8).

c A votive animal must not be exchanged (Lev. 27:10); the tithe animals cannot be exchanged (Lev. 27:33); exchange the tithe for money (Deut. 14:25).

d I gave Ethiopia and Seba in exchange for you (Isa. 43:3); I give peoples in exchange for you (Isa. 43:4).

● Exchanging good for bad

e They exchanged the truth about God for a lie (Rom. 1:25); they exchanged the glory of God for idols (Ps. 106:20; Rom. 1:23); has a nation changed gods? (Jer. 2:11); women exchanged natural sexual relations for unnatural (Rom. 1:26).

151 Interchange: double or mutual change
See **150**.

152 Changeableness

● Staggering

a The drunken man is like one who lies down in the sea (Prov. 23:34); as a drunken man staggers in his vomit (Isa. 19:14); priest and prophet reel from strong drink (Isa. 28:7); they reeled and staggered like drunken men (Ps. 107:27); the nations will drink and stagger (Jer. 25:16); the earth reels like a drunkard (Isa. 24:20); if anyone walks in the night he stumbles (John 11:10).

● Fickleness

b A reed swayed by the wind (Matt. 11:7; Luke 7:24); tossed about by every wind of doctrine (Eph. 4:14); a double-minded man, unstable in all his ways (Jas. 1:8).

c Reuben, unstable as water (Gen. 49:4); her ways are unstable (Prov. 5:6); Paul was not fickle, saying yes and no (2 Cor. 1:17).

● Without root

d Plants on the rocky ground had no root (Matt. 13:6; Mark 4:6); he has no root in himself (Matt. 13:21; Mark 4:17).

153 Stability

● Unchanging things

a The law of the Medes and Persians cannot be changed (Dan. 6:8, 12, 15).

b Love never fails (1 Cor. 13:8).

● Stability of the world

c The world is firmly established (1 Chr. 16:30; Ps. 93:1; 96:10); you established the earth (Ps. 119:90); since the fathers fell asleep everything remains the same (2 Pet. 3:4).

d The new heavens and the new earth will endure (Isa. 66:22).

● God's things established

e Heaven and earth will pass away, but: not the law (Matt. 5:18; Luke 16:17); not Christ's words (Matt. 24:35; Mark 13:31; Luke 21:33); God will endure (Ps. 102:26–7; Heb. 1:11–12).

f For ever your word is established in the heavens (Ps. 119:89); may the Lord establish his word (1 Sam. 1:23); you have founded your testimonies for ever (Ps. 119:152).

● Stable foundation

g The Lord will be the stability of your times (Isa. 33:6); the righteous has an everlasting foundation (Prov. 10:25); the Lord has founded Zion (Isa. 14:32); God showed the unchangeableness of his purpose by an oath (Heb. 6:17).

h The house did not fall because its foundation was on a rock (Matt. 7:24–5; Luke 6:48); the house of the righteous will stand (Prov. 12:7).

● Firm footing

i He makes my feet like hinds' feet (2 Sam. 22:34; Ps. 18:33); my feet have not slipped (2 Sam. 22:37; Ps. 18:36); your foot will not stumble (Prov. 3:23); if you run you will not stumble (Prov. 4:12); he set my feet on a rock (Ps. 40:2); he will not allow your foot to be moved (Ps. 121:3).

j Establish my steps in your work (Ps. 119:133); his steps do not slip (Ps. 37:31).

k Eliakim will be like a peg in a firm place (Isa. 22:23).

● God establishes us

l God establishes us in Christ (2 Cor. 1:21); Christ will establish you to the end (1 Cor. 1:8); may he establish your hearts (1 Thess. 3:13); God will establish you (1 Pet. 5:10); he is able to establish you (Rom. 16:25); his master is able to make him stand (Rom. 14:4).

m Your offspring and your name will endure (Isa. 66:22).

● Standing firm in God

n Rooted and established in the faith (Col. 2:7); established in the truth (2 Pet. 1:12); we sent Timothy to establish your faith (1 Thess. 3:2); the gospel in which you stand (1 Cor. 15:1); the stability of your faith (Col. 2:5); you stand fast only through faith (Rom. 11:20); we have a secure anchor of the soul (Heb. 6:19); you stand firm in the Lord (1 Thess. 3:8).

● God's people planted

o I will plant my people Israel (2 Sam. 7:10; 1 Chr. 17:9); Judah will again take root (2 Kgs. 19:30; Isa. 27:6; 37:31); the righteous will be planted in the house of the Lord (Ps. 92:12–13).

● Secure kingship

p If a king judges justly his throne will be established for ever (Prov. 29:14); by justice a king gives stability to the land (Prov. 29:4).

q I will establish your throne (1 Kgs. 9:5); I will establish his throne (1 Chr. 17:11–14; 22:10; 28:7); the house of David is established before you (1 Chr. 17:24); Solomon established his kingdom (2 Chr. 1:1); the Lord established Jehoshaphat's kingdom (2 Chr. 17:5).

● Not moved

r The king trusts in the Lord and will not be moved (Ps. 21:7); believers are like Mount Zion, which cannot be moved (Ps. 125:1); the city of God will not be moved (Ps. 46:5); he who does these things will never be moved (Ps. 15:5).

s He will never allow the righteous to be moved (Ps. 55:22); the righteous will never be moved (Ps. 112:6; Prov. 10:30); the root of the righteous will not be moved (Prov. 12:3); we receive a kingdom which cannot be shaken (Heb. 12:28).

t I will not be moved (Ps. 62:2, 6); because he is at my right hand I will not be shaken (Ps. 16:8; Acts 2:25); I said in my prosperity I would not be moved (Ps. 30:6).

u The wicked says 'I shall not be moved' (Ps. 10:6); a man is not established by wickedness (Prov. 12:3).

● Stability of
people

v The Kenites' dwelling-place was enduring (Num. 24:21); you felt secure in your wickedness (Isa. 47:10).
Permanence, see **144**.

154 Present events

See **121**.

155 Destiny: future events

See **124**.

Section eight: Causation

156 Cause: constant antecedent

● Elements

a We were in bondage under the elements of the universe (Gal. 4:3); you turn back to the weak and worthless elements (Gal. 4:9); according to the elements of the world rather than Christ (Col. 2:8); you have died with Christ to the elements of the world (Col. 2:20).

157 Effect: constant sequel

Growth, see **36**.

158 Attribution: assignment of cause

Explanation, see **520***d*.

159 Chance: no assignable cause

● At random

a Time and chance happen to everyone (Eccles. 9:11); we will know whether it happened by chance (1 Sam. 6:9); a man drew his bow at random (1 Kgs. 22:34; 2 Chr. 18:33).

160 Power

● Power
of God

a God Almighty (Gen. 17:1; 35:11; 48:3); the Almighty (2 Cor. 6:18; Rev. 1:8; 4:8; 11:17; 15:3; 16:7, 14; 19:6, 15; 21:22); the great, mighty and awesome God (Neh. 9:32); the Lord on high is mightier than the waters (Ps. 93:4); God is mighty (Job 36:5); mighty in deed (Jer. 32:19); the Lord comes with power (Isa. 40:10).

b God brought them out of Egypt by his mighty hand (Exod. 6:1; 13:3, 9, 14, 16; 32:11; Deut. 7:19); with an outstretched arm (Exod. 6:6; Deut. 7:19); your right hand was majestic in power (Exod. 15:6); the hand of the Lord is powerful (Josh. 4:24); your right hand and your arm brought them victory (Ps. 44:3); do you have an arm like God? (Job 40:9–14).

c Yours is the greatness and the power (1 Chr. 29:11); in your hands are strength and power (1 Chr. 29:12); he who is with us is greater than he who is with him (2 Chr. 32:7); God raised up Pharaoh to show his power (Exod. 9:16); the Israelites saw the power of the Lord (Exod. 14:31); exalted in his power (Job 36:22; 37:23); no one can withstand God (2 Chr. 20:6); who can resist his will? (Rom. 9:19).

d You do not perceive the Scriptures nor the power of God (Matt. 22:29; Mark 12:24).

● Power of Christ

e Christ is the power of God (1 Cor. 1:24); power to the Lamb (Rev. 5:12); by what power have you done this? (Acts 4:7); God anointed Jesus with the Spirit and with power (Acts 10:38); a prophet mighty in deed and word (Luke 24:19); the power of our Lord Jesus (1 Cor. 5:4; 2 Pet. 1:16); more powerful than John (Mark 1:7); he who comes after me is mightier than I (Matt. 3:11; Luke 3:16).

f Power to subject all things to himself (Phil. 3:21); power to heal (Luke 5:17); power went out from him (Mark 5:30; Luke 6:19; 8:46); with power and authority he commands evil spirits (Mark 1:27; Luke 4:36); he lives by the power of God (2 Cor. 13:4); coming with great power and glory (Matt. 24:30; Mark 13:26; Luke 21:27).

g If you can do anything... (Mark 9:22).

● Power of God's people

h Joseph has the horns of the wild ox (Deut. 33:17); I will make a horn sprout for David (Ps. 132:17); I will make a horn sprout for Israel (Ezek. 29:21); Zedekiah made horns of iron (1 Kgs. 22:11; 2 Chr. 18:10).

Horn, see **254**.

i No one would be able to stand before Joshua (Josh. 1:5); David became more and more powerful (2 Sam. 5:10; 1 Chr. 11:9); David's mighty men (2 Sam. 23:8–39; 1 Chr. 11:10–47); John the Baptist would have the power of Elijah (Luke 1:17).

j Let not the mighty man boast in his might (Jer. 9:23); to each according to his ability (Matt. 25:15).

● Power through God

k Why stare at us as if by our power we made this man walk? (Acts 3:12); the surpassing power is from God, not from us (2 Cor. 4:7); his power is made perfect in weakness (2 Cor. 12:9); the power at work in us is the power which raised Christ from the dead (Eph. 1:19–20); the power at work within us (Eph. 3:20); striving according to his working which works in me in power (Col. 1:29); we commend ourselves in the power of God (2 Cor. 6:7).

l Greater is he who is in you than he who is in the world (1 John 4:4); he is powerful among you (2 Cor. 13:3); all things are possible to him who believes (Mark 9:23).

● Power through the Spirit

m Not by might nor by power but by my Spirit (Zech. 4:6); Jesus was anointed with the Spirit and with power (Acts 10:38); you will receive power when the Holy Spirit comes upon you (Acts

1:8); clothed with power from on high (Luke 24:49); God has given us a spirit of power (2 Tim. 1:7); the power of the Spirit (Luke 4:14; Rom. 15:13, 19); filled with power with the Spirit of the Lord (Mic. 3:8).

● Power of
the gospel

n The gospel is the power of God (Rom. 1:16); the message of the cross is the power of God (1 Cor. 1:18); a horn of salvation (Luke 1:69).

o The kingdom of God is not talk but power (1 Cor. 4:20); not persuasive words but the demonstration of the Spirit and power (1 Cor. 2:4); our Gospel came not in word only but in power in the Holy Spirit (1 Thess. 1:5).

Strength, see **162**; **nothing impossible**, see **469**.

161 Impotence

● God's
limitations

a I cannot do anything until you come there (Gen. 19:22).

b Is the Lord's arm shortened? (Num. 11:23; Isa. 50:2); the Lord's hand is not shortened (Isa. 59:1); lest people say the Lord was not able to bring them into the land (Num. 14:16; Deut. 9:28).

c Christ could do no mighty work there (Mark 6:5); I can do nothing on my own authority (John 5:30).

d Some people have the form of godliness but deny its power (2 Tim. 3:5).

Impossible, see **470**.

● Unable
to expel

e Judah could not drive out the Jebusites (Josh. 15:63); the Manassites were not able to drive out the Canaanites (Josh. 17:12); the men of Judah could not drive out the inhabitants of the plain (Judg. 1:19); the Benjaminites could not dislodge the Jebusites (Judg. 1:21).

f The disciples were not able to cast out the evil spirit (Matt. 17:16; Mark 9:18; Luke 9:40); why could we not drive it out? (Matt. 17:19; Mark 9:28).

● Unable to
serve God

g You cannot serve the Lord (Josh. 24:19); the carnal mind cannot submit to God's law (Rom. 8:7); the law, weakened by the flesh, could not save (Rom. 8:3); many will seek to enter and will not be able (Luke 13:24); while we were helpless Christ died (Rom. 5:6).

● Unable
to harm

h No one could withstand the Israelites (Josh. 23:9); Jesus' enemies could not catch him (Luke 20:26).

● Impotence
of Satan

i He disarmed principalities and powers (Col. 2:15); I will dash your weapons from your hands (Ezek. 39:3); the ruler of this world has no power over me (John 14:30); some can kill the body but can do no more (Matt. 10:28; Luke 12:4).

● Impotence
of idols

j Idols can neither do harm nor good (Jer. 10:5); have other gods been able to deliver their lands? (2 Kgs. 18:34–5).

Weakness, see **163**.

162 Strength

● Strength
of God

a Ascribe to the Lord glory and strength (Ps. 29:1); ascribe strength to God (Ps. 68:34); God is mighty in strength (Job 9:4); show yourself strong, O God (Ps. 68:28); you are strong, O God (Ps. 62:11); their Redeemer is strong (Jer. 50:34); he has shown strength with his arm (Luke 1:51); the strength of his might (Eph. 6:10); the weakness of God is stronger than men (1 Cor. 1:25); worthy is the Lamb to receive might (Rev. 5:12).

● Strong
through
God

b The Lord is my strength (Exod. 15:2; Ps. 28:7; Hab. 3:19); God is our refuge and strength (Ps. 46:1); you are my strength (Ps. 31:4); God is the strength of my heart (Ps. 73:26); the horn of my salvation (2 Sam. 22:3); by your favour our horn is exalted (Ps. 89:17); you have exalted my horn like that of the wild ox (Ps. 92:10); the horns of the righteous will be lifted up (Ps. 75:10); in my name his horn shall be exalted (Ps. 89:24); he has raised up a horn for his people (Ps. 148:14).

c The Lord is the strength of his people (Ps. 28:8); the Lord is their strength (Ps. 37:39); the Lord will give strength to his people (Ps. 29:11); God is the horns of a wild ox for Israel (Num. 23:22; 24:8); he gives strength to the weary, to those who wait for him (Isa. 40:29–31); he will give strength to his king (1 Sam. 2:10); strengthen me according to your word (Ps. 119:28); Samson prayed for strength just once more (Judg. 16:28); Jonathan strengthened David in God (1 Sam. 23:16); David found strength in God (1 Sam. 30:6).

d May you be strengthened through his Spirit in the inner man (Eph. 3:16); may you be strengthened with all power (Col. 1:11); may he strengthen your hearts in every good deed and word (2 Thess. 2:17); I can do everything through him who strengthens me (Phil. 4:13); the Lord strengthened me (2 Tim. 4:17).

● Strength
of people

e The glory of young men is their strength (Prov. 20:29); a wise man is strong (Prov. 24:5); overpower the strong man and you can plunder his goods (Matt. 12:29; Mark 3:27; Luke 11:22).

f Moses was still strong when he died aged 120 (Deut. 34:7); you will come to your grave in full vigour (Job 5:26); Joshua was still strong at 85 (Josh. 14:11); Saul and Jonathan, stronger than lions (2 Sam. 1:23); Amnon was stronger than Tamar (2 Sam. 13:14).

g Where does Samson get his strength? (Judg. 16:5–6); keep the commandments that you may be strong (Deut. 11:8); John the Baptist grew strong in spirit (Luke 1:80); Jesus grew and became strong (Luke 2:40); an angel strengthened him (Luke 22:43).

h One people will be stronger than the other (Gen. 25:23); David's house grew stronger (2 Sam. 3:1); the feeble gird on strength (1 Sam. 2:4).

i The people of the land are strong (Num. 13:28, 31).

- Strengthening others

j The hands of those with you will be strengthened (2 Sam. 16:21); you have strengthened weak hands and feeble knees (Job 4:3–4); strengthen the feeble arms and the weak knees (Heb. 12:12).

k Paul and Silas strengthened the churches (Acts 15:41); the churches were being strengthened in the faith (Acts 16:5); strengthening all the disciples (Acts 14:22; 18:23); they strengthened the brethren (Acts 15:32); when you have turned, strengthen your brethren (Luke 22:32); we sent Timothy to strengthen you (1 Thess. 3:2); the one like a man touched Daniel and strengthened him (Dan. 10:18); we who are strong ought to bear the failings of the weak (Rom. 15:1).

- Be strong!

l Be strong! (Deut. 31:6, 7, 23; Josh. 1:6, 7, 9, 18; 10:25; 1 Sam. 4:9; 2 Sam. 10:12; 1 Kgs. 2:2; 1 Chr. 19:13; 22:13; 28:10, 20; 2 Chr. 15:7; 25:8; 32:7; Isa. 35:4; Dan. 10:19; Hag. 2:4; Zech. 8:9, 13; 1 Cor. 16:13); strengthen yourself! (1 Kgs. 20:22); be strong in the Lord (Eph. 6:10); be strong in grace (2 Tim. 2:1).

- Strength of animals

m Out of the strong came something sweet (Judg. 14:14); what is stronger than a lion? (Judg. 14:18); the strength of a hippopotamus (Job 40:16).

- Limitations of strength

n A man does not prevail by strength (1 Sam. 2:9); God's delight is not in the horse's strength, nor in a man's legs (Ps. 147:10); a warrior is not saved by great strength (Ps. 33:16); those whose strength is their god (Hab. 1:11); when he became strong he was proud (2 Chr. 26:16).

- Angels' strength

o Angels, mighty in strength (Ps. 103:20).

Power, see **160**.

163 Weakness

- God's weakness

a The weakness of God is stronger than men (1 Cor. 1:25); Christ was crucified in weakness (2 Cor. 13:4); he took our weaknesses and carried our diseases (Matt. 8:17).

- Human weakness

b The weakness of the children and animals (Gen. 33:13); man's frailty (Job 4:19); the wife as the weaker vessel (1 Pet. 3:7); is my strength the strength of stones? (Job 6:12); all hands are limp, all knees like water (Ezek. 7:17).

c If I am shaved I will become weak (Judg. 16:17); Samson's strength left him (Judg. 16:19); Saul had no strength in him (1 Sam. 28:20); though king, I am weak (2 Sam. 3:39); the house of Saul grew weaker (2 Sam. 3:1); therefore their inhabitants were short of strength (2 Kgs. 19:26); I am not strong enough to dig (Luke 16:3).

d Every high priest is beset with weakness (Heb. 5:2); the law appoints men in their weakness as high priests (Heb. 7:28).

e I was with you in much weakness (1 Cor. 2:3); his bodily presence is weak (2 Cor. 10:10); the spirit is willing but the flesh is weak (Matt. 26:41; Mark 14:38); we are weak in him (2 Cor. 13:4); to the weak I became weak that I might win the weak

(1 Cor. 9:22); we are weak but you are strong (1 Cor. 4:10; 2 Cor. 13:9); who is weak and I am not weak? (2 Cor. 11:29).

f The body is sown in weakness and raised in power (1 Cor. 15:43).

Women in weakness, see **373k**.

● Weak people

g Gideon's clan was the weakest in Manasseh (Judg. 6:15); we have no power against this great army (2 Chr. 20:12); we are unable to build the wall (Neh. 4:10); no one was able to bind him (Mark 5:3–4); when the foundations are destroyed, what can the righteous do? (Ps. 11:3); without me you can do nothing (John 15:5); I know you have only a little power (Rev. 3:8).

● Using weakness

h I will boast of my weakness (2 Cor. 11:30; 12:5, 9); I am content with weakness, for when I am weak, then I am strong (2 Cor. 12:10); they won strength out of weakness (Heb. 11:34); Christ's power is made perfect in weakness (2 Cor. 12:9).

● Help the weak

i Help the weak (1 Thess. 5:14); strengthen the weak knees (Heb. 12:12); blessed is he who considers the weak (Ps. 41:1); bear with the failings of the weak (Rom. 15:1); the weak man eats only vegetables (Rom. 14:1–2); the man with a weak conscience (1 Cor. 8:7–12).

● God helps the weak

j God chose what is weak (1 Cor. 1:27); the Spirit helps us in our weakness (Rom. 8:26); a high priest able to sympathise with our weaknesses (Heb. 4:15).

● Weak things

k A fox would break their wall down (Neh. 4:3).

164 Making

● Creation of the world

a God created the heavens and the earth (Gen. 1:1; 14:19, 22; 2 Kgs. 19:15; 1 Chr. 16:26; 2 Chr. 2:12; Neh. 9:6; Ps. 121:2; 124:8; 134:3; 146:6; Isa. 42:5; 44:24; 45:18; 51:13; Jer. 32:17; Jonah 1:9; Acts 4:24; 14:15; 17:24; Rev. 10:6; 14:7); in six days (Exod. 20:11; 31:17); you made heaven and earth (Isa. 37:16; Jer. 32:17); the Lord who made heaven and earth (Ps. 115:15).

b God hangs the earth on nothing (Job 26:7); he has founded the earth upon the seas (Ps. 24:2); God laid the earth's foundation (1 Sam. 2:8; Job 38:4; Ps. 102:25; 104:5; Isa. 48:13; 51:16; Zech. 12:1; Heb. 1:10); he made the earth by his power (Jer. 51:15).

c God is the maker of all things (Eccles. 11:5; Jer. 10:16; 51:19; Eph. 3:9); the builder of all things (Heb. 3:4); my hand made all these things (Acts 7:50); God's eternal power and deity are seen by what has been made (Rom. 1:20).

d The heavens are the work of his hands (Ps. 8:3); God made the mountains (Ps. 65:6); mountains and wind (Amos 4:13); sea and land (Ps. 95:5); the earth, mankind and animals (Jer. 27:5); light and darkness (Isa. 45:7); sun, moon and stars (Gen. 1:14–16); the Pleiades and Orion (Amos 5:8); God made the moon for seasons (Ps. 104:19).

Creation of the seas, see **343a**.

- **How God created**

  e Creation by wisdom (Ps. 136:5; Prov. 3:19; 8:27; Jer. 10:12); by God's word (Ps. 33:6; Heb. 11:3); by God's will (Rev. 4:11); he commanded and they were created (Ps. 148:5).

  f Through the Word all things were made (John 1:3); the world was made through him (John 1:10); all things are by Jesus Christ (1 Cor. 8:6); all things were created by him (Col. 1:16); through him God made the universe (Heb. 1:2); he is the beginning of God's creation (Rev. 3:14).

- **Creation of life**

  g Creation of: vegetation (Gen. 1:11–12); sea creatures and birds (Gen. 1:20–1); land creatures (Gen. 1:24–5); beasts and birds from the ground (Gen. 2:19); I made behemoth along with you (Job 40:15).

  Creatures from dust, see **332c**.

- **Creation of man**

  h God created mankind (Gen. 1:26–27; 5:1–2; Deut. 4:32; Matt. 19:4; Mark 10:6); man formed from dust (Gen. 2:7); I created mankind (Isa. 45:12).

  i Woman made from man's rib (Gen. 2:22); Adam was created first, then Eve (1 Tim. 2:13); man was not from woman but woman from man (1 Cor. 11:9).

  j Your hands made me (Job 10:8; Ps. 119:73); you curdled me like cheese (Job 10:10); the Spirit of God has made me (Job 33:4); you wove me in my mother's womb (Ps. 139:13); God made us (Ps. 100:3); remember your Creator (Eccles. 12:1); men will look to their Maker (Isa. 17:7); the Creator of Israel (Isa. 43:15).

  k Who gave man his mouth? (Exod. 4:11); God has made both ears and eyes (Prov. 20:12); does he who made ear and eye not hear and see? (Ps. 94:9).

  l We are the clay, you are the potter (Isa. 64:8); you are like clay in the hand of the potter (Jer. 18:6); can the pot criticise the potter? (Isa. 29:16; 45:9; Rom. 9:20–1); God was sorry he had made man (Gen. 6:6, 7).

- **Creator of all**

  m He is the maker of rich and poor (Prov. 22:2); he who made me in the womb made my slave also (Job 31:15); God made every nation of men (Acts 17:26); has not one God created us all? (Mal. 2:10); they served the creature rather than the Creator (Rom. 1:25).

  New creation, see **126d**..

- **Building**

  n I will watch over them to build and to plant (Jer. 31:28).

  o The one who has built a new house should return to it (Deut. 20:5); unless the Lord builds the house the builders work in vain (Ps. 127:1); by wisdom a house is built (Prov. 24:3); the wise man built his house on rock (Matt. 7:24; Luke 6:48); the foolish man on sand (Matt. 7:26; Luke 6:49); woe to him who builds his house with unrighteousness (Jer. 22:13–14); woe to him who builds a city with bloodshed (Hab. 2:12).

  Stones for building, see **344r**.

● Building
cities

p Cain was building the city called Enoch (Gen. 4:17); let us build a city and a tower (Gen. 11:4); the Israelites built Egyptian store cities (Exod. 1:11); let a faithless city never be rebuilt (Deut. 13:16); cursed be the man who rebuilds Jericho (Josh. 6:26); Hiel rebuilt Jericho (1 Kgs. 16:34); he built a city and called it Luz (Judg. 1:26); the Danites rebuilt Laish [Dan] (Judg. 18:28); they rebuilt their cities (Judg. 21:23); David built up Jerusalem (2 Sam. 5:9; 1 Chr. 11:8).

q Solomon rebuilt Gezer and other cities (1 Kgs. 9:17–19; 2 Chr. 8:2–6); Rehoboam built cities for defence (2 Chr. 11:5–10); Jeroboam built Shechem (1 Kgs. 12:25); Asa built Geba and Mizpah (1 Kgs. 15:22); Asa built fortified cities (2 Chr. 14:6–7); Omri built Samaria (1 Kgs. 16:24); Ahab built cities (1 Kgs. 22:39); Jehoshaphat built store cities (2 Chr. 17:12); Uzziah built Elath (2 Kgs. 14:22; 2 Chr. 26:2); Uzziah built cities among the Philistines (2 Chr. 26:6); Jotham built cities (2 Chr. 27:4); Hezekiah built cities (2 Chr. 32:29); Sheerah built upper and lower Beth-horon (1 Chr. 7:24).

r God will build the cities of Judah (Ps. 69:35); I will rebuild the fallen booth of David (Amos 9:11); they will rebuild the ruined cities (Amos 9:14).

● Rebuilding
Jerusalem

s Solomon built the Millo (1 Kgs. 9:24; 11:27); they are rebuilding that rebellious city, Jerusalem (Ezra 4:12); let us rebuild the wall of Jerusalem (Neh. 2:17, 18); rebuilding the wall (Neh. 3:1–32); build up the walls of Jerusalem (Ps. 51:18); the Lord builds up Jerusalem (Ps. 147:2); the Lord will rebuild Zion (Ps. 102:16); Cyrus will say of Jerusalem, Let it be rebuilt (Isa. 44:28); they will rebuild the ancient ruins (Isa. 61:4); the city will be rebuilt on her ruins (Jer. 30:18); I will build you up again (Jer. 31:4); this city will be rebuilt (Jer. 31:38); the ruins will be rebuilt (Isa. 44:26, 28; Ezek. 36:10); Nehemiah wanted to rebuild Jerusalem (Neh. 2:5); the decree to rebuild Jerusalem (Dan. 9:25); the day for building your walls (Mic. 7:11).

● Building
houses

t I built houses (Eccles. 2:4); build houses in exile and live in them (Jer. 29:5); the bricks and sycamores have fallen but we will rebuild with stones and cedar (Isa. 9:10).

u A palace built for David (2 Sam. 5:11; 1 Chr. 14:1; 15:1); for Solomon (1 Kgs. 3:1; 7:1; 9:10; 2 Chr. 8:1); Solomon built a house for Pharaoh's daughter (1 Kgs. 9:24).

v Wisdom has built her house (Prov. 9:1); the wise woman builds her house (Prov. 14:1).

w It is not time to build houses (Ezek. 11:3); the Rechabites were not to build houses (Jer. 35:9).

x You will build a house but not live in it (Deut. 28:30); they will build houses but not live in them (Zeph. 1:13).

● Building
  the temple

    y David wanted to build the temple (1 Kgs. 8:17–18; 1 Chr. 28:2–3; 2 Chr. 6:7); David could not build it (1 Kgs. 5:3; 1 Chr. 22:8; 28:3); I will rebuild the tabernacle of David (Acts 15:16).

    z David's son would build it (1 Kgs. 5:5; 8:19; 1 Chr. 22:9–10; 2 Chr. 6:9); Solomon will build it (1 Chr. 28:6, 10); David charged Solomon to build it (1 Chr. 22:6); build the Lord's sanctuary (1 Chr. 22:19); Solomon gave orders to build the temple (2 Chr. 2:1); Solomon built the temple (1 Kgs. 6:1–38; 2 Chr. 3:1); Jotham rebuilt the Upper Gate of the temple (2 Kgs. 15:35).

    aa God appointed Cyrus to build a temple in Jerusalem (2 Chr. 36:23; Ezra 1:2); Cyrus issued a decree to rebuild the temple (Ezra 5:13); Zerubbabel and Jeshua started to rebuild the temple (Ezra 5:2); we are rebuilding the temple (Ezra 5:11); let the temple be rebuilt (Ezra 5:15; 6:3); build the house (Hag. 1:8); my house will be rebuilt (Zech. 1:16); enemies wanted to build with them (Ezra 4:2–3).

    ab Jesus promised to rebuild the temple (Matt. 26:61; 27:40; Mark 14:58; John 2:19–21); the man called the Branch will build the temple (Zech. 6:12–13).

● Building
  the church

    ac On this rock I will build my church (Matt. 16:18); built upon the foundation of the apostles and prophets (Eph. 2:20); you are God's building (1 Cor. 3:9); living stones built into a spiritual house (1 Pet. 2:5); I laid a foundation as a master-builder (1 Cor. 3:10).

    ad Building up the body of Christ (Eph. 4:12); it upbuilds itself in love (Eph. 4:16); authority given by the Lord for building you up (2 Cor. 10:8; 13:10); pursue the building up of one another (Rom. 14:19); build yourselves up (Jude 20).

    ae Love edifies (1 Cor. 8:1); a tongue edifies the speaker but prophecy edifies the church (1 Cor. 14:4); the other man is not edified (1 Cor. 14:17).

    af Seek the edification of the church (1 Cor. 14:12); let all things be done to edify (1 Cor. 14:26); build one another up (1 Thess. 5:11).

165 Destruction

● God
  destroying

    a God tears down and it cannot be rebuilt (Job 12:14); what I have built I am tearing down (Jer. 45:4); he destroys nations (Job 12:23); with you I shatter nations (Jer. 51:20–3); utterly destroy Babylon (Jer. 50:26); I was at ease and he shattered me (Job 16:12–14).

    b The Lord brings disaster on Jerusalem and Judah (2 Kgs. 21:12; 2 Chr. 34:24; Jer. 44:11); the angel was about to destroy Jerusalem (2 Sam. 24:16; 1 Chr. 21:15); the Lord sent bands against Judah to destroy it (2 Kgs. 24:2); I will make Jerusalem a heap of ruins (Jer. 9:11); I will ruin the pride of Judah and Jerusalem

(Jer. 13:9); I will lay waste your cities (Lev. 26:31); I will devastate this city (Jer. 19:8, 11); you saw the disaster I brought on Jerusalem (Jer. 44:2); you have made the city into a heap (Isa. 25:2); a ruin, ruin, ruin I will make it (Ezek. 21:27); I will make Samaria a heap of ruins (Mic. 1:6).

c God will destroy: the high places and idolatrous altars of Israel (Lev. 26:30; Ezek. 6:3–4); the idols of Egypt (Ezek. 30:13); their altars and pillars (Hos. 10:2); Samariah's idols (Mic. 1:7); the idols of Nineveh (Nahum 1:14).

● Destruction in Israel

d The city has fallen (Ezek. 33:21); the wall of Jerusalem was breached (Jer. 39:2); Jerusalem in ruins (Neh. 2:3, 17; Ps. 79:1); you have broken through his walls and ruined his strongholds (Ps. 89:40); for seventy years (Dan. 9:2); Edom wanted Jerusalem razed to its foundations (Ps. 137:7); Zion will be ploughed like a field (Jer. 26:18; Mic. 3:12).

e Your land is desolate (Isa. 1:7); the whole land will be a desolation (Jer. 4:27); his cities have been destroyed (Jer. 2:15).

f Tearing down the tower of Penuel (Judg. 8:9, 17); Abimelech destroyed Shechem (Judg. 9:45); why destroy the inheritance of the Lord? (2 Sam. 20:19–20); the Lord commanded me to destroy this place (2 Kgs. 18:25); let us wipe out Israel (Ps. 83:4). **Destruction of walls, see 235*k*.**

● Destruction of the temple

g This house will become a heap of ruins (1 Kgs. 9:8); the temple was burnt (2 Kgs. 25:9; 2 Chr. 36:19); there will not be one stone left upon another (Matt. 24:2; Mark 13:2; Luke 19:44; 21:6).

h Jesus would rebuild the temple after it had been destroyed (Matt. 26:61; Mark 14:58; John 2:19–21); you who would destroy the temple! (Matt. 27:40; Mark 15:29); Jesus of Nazareth will destroy this place (Acts 6:14).

● Destruction of the church

i Saul began to destroy the church (Acts 8:3); if any one destroys God's temple, God will destroy him (1 Cor. 3:17); the weak brother is destroyed by your knowledge (1 Cor. 8:11).

● Destruction of Satan's works

j Destroy all the idols and high places (Num. 33:52); destroy the places where they worshipped their gods (Deut. 12:2); destroy their altars and their sacred pillars (Exod. 34:13; Deut. 7:5; 12:3); smash their sacred pillars (Exod. 23:24); tear down their altars (Judg. 2:2); demolish the altar of Baal and the Asherah (Judg. 6:25).

k Moses ground up the golden calf (Deut. 9:21); they destroyed the pillar of Baal (2 Kgs. 10:26–7); they demolished the temple of Baal (2 Kgs. 11:18; 2 Chr. 23:17); destroying the high places and idols (2 Kgs. 18:4; 23:6–20; 2 Chr. 14:3; 15:8; 31:1; 33:15; 34:3–7); Asa destroyed the Asherah (1 Kgs. 15:13; 2 Chr. 15:16); they removed the altars and incense altars (2 Chr. 30:14). **Destroying high places, see 209*ag*.**

l He drove out the enemy and said, 'Destroy!' (Deut. 33:27); our weapons are mighty through God for the destruction of strong-holds (2 Cor. 10:4–5).

m Have you come to destroy us evil spirits? (Mark 1:24; Luke 4:34); the Son of God came to destroy all the works of the devil (1 John 3:8); to destroy him who had the power of death (Heb. 2:14); the time for destroying those who destroy the earth (Rev. 11:18); the Lord Jesus will destroy the lawless one (2 Thess. 2:8).

n The Lord will swallow up death for ever (Isa. 25:8).

● Destruction of the wicked

o God was going to destroy all people (Gen. 6:13); all flesh (Gen. 6:17); I will sweep away everything (Zeph. 1:2); God sent angels to destroy Sodom (Gen. 19:13–14); God ruined Egypt (Exod. 8:24; 9:25, 31; 10:7); I will destroy the people of the land (Exod. 23:23); God will ruin: Moab (Num. 21:29; 24:17; Isa. 15:1–9; Jer. 48:1); Edom (Num. 24:19; Jer. 49:13); Amalek (Exod. 17:14; Num. 24:20); Damascus (Isa. 17:1); Tyre (Ezek. 26:17); Babylon (Jer. 51:2); Egypt (Ezek. 30:12); Ammon (Ezek. 25:7).

p Fallen, fallen is Babylon (Isa. 21:9); they will destroy the walls of Tyre (Ezek. 26:4).

Disaster for ships, see **275*h***.

q Hormah—destruction (Num. 21:2–3; Judg. 1:17); they broke down the wall of Gath, Jabneh and Ashdod (2 Chr. 26:6).

r I will destroy the Israelites (Exod. 32:10); the Lord your God is a consuming fire (Deut. 9:3); this disaster is from the Lord (2 Kgs. 6:33); the Lord is laying waste the earth (Isa. 24:1); God will break you down for ever (Ps. 52:5); God destroys the wicked in a moment (Ps. 73:19); evildoers will be destroyed (Ps. 92:7); destruction of the ungodly (2 Pet. 3:6); sin destroyed the house of Jeroboam (1 Kgs. 13:34); I will consume the house of Baasha (1 Kgs. 16:3).

s The wide gate and the broad road that leads to destruction (Matt. 7:13); the house on sand fell with a great fall (Matt. 7:27); they distort the Scriptures to their own destruction (2 Pet. 3:16); destruction will come upon them suddenly (1 Thess. 5:3).

t One tenth of the city was destroyed (Rev. 11:13); Babylon was destroyed (Rev. 14:8; 16:19; 18:2, 17, 21); the heavens will be destroyed by fire (2 Pet. 3:10, 12); as the world was formerly destroyed by water (2 Pet. 3:6); created things will be removed (Heb. 12:27).

Killing, see **362**; **burning**, see **381**.

● Swallowing up

u Aaron's rod swallowed the others (Exod. 7:12); the earth swallowed the Egyptians (Exod. 15:12); the earth swallowed Korah's company (Num. 16:31–3; 26:10; Deut. 11:6).

● Blotted out

v Blot me out of your book (Exod. 32:32); whoever has sinned I will blot out of my book (Exod. 32:33).

● Abominations

w Anything under a ban is most holy (Lev. 27:28); and may not be redeemed (Lev. 27:29); Jericho was under a ban of destruction (Josh. 6:17–19; 7:1; 1 Chr. 2:7); the Israelites became a thing devoted to destruction (Josh. 7:12); no one is lost except the one doomed to destruction (John 17:12).

x The abomination of desolation (Dan. 9:27; 11:31; 12:11; Matt. 24:15; Mark 13:14); the man of sin, the son of destruction (2 Thess. 2:3).

● Shipwreck

y Jehoshaphat's ships were wrecked (1 Kgs. 22:48; 2 Chr. 20:37); shipwrecked three times (2 Cor. 11:25); the shipwreck of Tyre (Ezek. 27:26–7); description of one shipwreck (Acts 27:14–44).

z Some have made shipwreck of their faith (1 Tim. 1:19).

● Destruction of crops

aa The little foxes ruin the vineyards (S. of S. 2:15); the people of the east ruined the crops like swarms of locusts (Judg. 6:4–5); swarms of locusts (Joel 1:4; Amos 7:1).

Destroying trees, see **366p.**

● Destruction of people

ab The demon tried to destroy him (Mark 9:22); Tamar was a devastated woman (2 Sam. 13:20).

166 Reproducing
See **167**.

167 Reproduction

● Genitals

a A man with his male member cut off (Deut. 23:1); a woman seizing an opponent's genitals (Deut. 25:11); 100 Philistine foreskins (1 Sam. 18:25); 200 Philistine foreskins (1 Sam. 18:27).

b Eating her own afterbirth (Deut. 28:57); blessed is the womb that bore you (Luke 11:27).

● Physical birth

c There is a time to give birth (Eccles. 3:2); how can a man be born when he is old? (John 3:4); when a woman gives birth she forgets the anguish (John 16:21); can a man give birth? (Jer. 30:6); woe to him who says, 'What are you begetting?' (Isa. 45:10).

d A woman who gives birth becomes unclean (Lev. 12:2); I was conceived and born in sin (Ps. 51:5).

e When Hebrew women are giving birth (Exod. 1:16, 19).

● Pregnancies

f Lot's daughters were pregnant by their father (Gen. 19:36–8); Judah's wife Shua bore three sons (Gen. 38:3–5); Tamar was pregnant by Judah (Gen. 38:18, 24); Hannah conceived and bore Samuel (1 Sam. 1:20); and three sons and two daughters (1 Sam. 2:21); if I had a husband tonight and gave birth (Ruth 1:12); the two harlots gave birth (1 Kgs. 3:17–18).

g Pregnancy of: Hagar (Gen. 16:4); Bathsheba (2 Sam. 11:5); the Shunamite woman (2 Kgs. 4:17); the prophetess (Isa. 8:3); Elizabeth (Luke 1:13–14, 24, 36); Mary (Matt. 1:18; Luke 1:31; 2:5).

h You will rip up pregnant women (2 Kgs. 8:12); Menahem ripped up all the pregnant women (2 Kgs. 15:16); woe to those with child in those days (Matt. 24:19; Mark 13:17; Luke 21:23).

Pregnant by the Spirit, see **965af.**

- **Conceptions and births**

  i Conception and birth of: Cain (Gen. 4:1); Abel (Gen. 4:2); Seth (Gen. 4:25); Enoch by Cain's wife (Gen. 4:17); Isaac by Sarah (Gen. 17:17; 18:10; 21:2; Heb. 11:11); Isaac and Esau by Rebekah (Gen. 25:21–6; Rom. 9:10); Reuben, Simeon, Levi and Judah by Leah (Gen. 29:31–5); Dan and Naphtali by Bilhah (Gen. 30:4–8); Gad and Asher by Zilpah (Gen. 30:10–13); Issachar, Zebulun and Dinah by Leah (Gen. 30:17–21); Joseph by Rachel (Gen. 30:23); Benjamin by Rachel (Gen. 35:16–18); Beriah by Ephraim's wife (1 Chr. 7:23); Moses (Exod. 2:2; Acts 7:20); Obed by Ruth (Ruth 4:13); Samson (Judg. 13:3–5, 7, 24); Solomon by Bathsheba (2 Sam. 12:24); Jezreel by Gomer (Hos. 1:3–4); Lo-ruhamah by Gomer (Hos. 1:6); Lo-ammi by Gomer (Hos. 1:8–9).

- **Births**

  j Birth of: Ichabod (1 Sam. 4:19–21); John (Luke 1:57); a son to David by Bathsheba (2 Sam. 11:27).

  k Birth of Jesus (Matt. 1:18; 2:1, 4; Luke 2:6–7); the virgin will bear a son (Isa. 7:14; Matt. 1:23); God sent his Son, born of a woman (Gal. 4:4); the woman gave birth to a male child (Rev. 12:4–5).

  l Do you know when mountain goats and deer give birth? (Job 39:1–3); like a partridge hatching eggs she did not lay (Jer. 17:11).

  m Why did I not die at birth? (Job 3:11); you were born in sin (John 9:34).

- **Labour pains**

  n Pain in childbearing would be increased (Gen. 3:16); a woman in travail has sorrow (John 16:21).

  o They will be in anguish like a woman in labour (Isa. 13:8); pangs like a woman in childbirth (Jer. 13:21; 22:23; 30:6; 49:24; 50:43); I am in anguish like a woman in labour (Isa. 21:3; Jer. 6:24); I groan like a woman in labour (Isa. 42:14); we were like a pregnant woman crying out in her pangs (Isa. 26:17–18); I heard a cry as of a woman in travail (Jer. 4:31); writhe like a woman in childbirth, daughter of Zion (Mic. 4:10); I am in travail again until Christ be formed in your (Gal. 4:19).

  p This is but the beginning of the birth pangs (Matt. 24:8; Mark 13:8); sudden destruction like birth pangs (1 Thess. 5:3); the woman cried out in labour pains (Rev. 12:2); the whole creation groans and travails (Rom. 8:22).

  q The pains of childbirth come on the child (Hos. 13:13).

- **Born of God**

  r God who gave you birth (Deut. 32:18); this one and that one were born in Zion (Ps. 87:4–6); before she travailed she brought forth (Isa. 66:7–9).

  s You must be born again (John 3:3, 7); he has given us new birth to a living hope (1 Pet. 1:3); he who believes Jesus is the Christ is born of God (1 John 5:1); born again through the word of God (1 Pet. 1:23); he brought us forth by the word of truth (Jas. 1:18); born not of blood but of God (John 1:13); born of water and the

Spirit (John 3:5); what is born of the Spirit is Spirit (John 3:6); so is everyone who is born of the Spirit (John 3:8).

t No one born of God goes on sinning (1 John 3:9; 5:18); whatever is born of God overcomes the world (1 John 5:4).

u This day I have begotten you (Ps. 2:7); they will be saved through the birth of the Child (1 Tim. 2:15).

● Spiritual birth

v Children have come to the birth and there is no strength to deliver them (2 Kgs. 19:3; Isa. 37:3); we brought forth as it were wind (Isa. 26:18).

w You conceive chaff and bring forth stubble (Isa. 33:11); they conceive mischief and bring forth iniquity (Isa. 59:4); he conceives mischief and gives birth to falsehood (Ps. 7:14); they hatch adders' eggs (Isa. 59:5); when desire has conceived it gives birth to sin (Jas. 1:15); sin gives birth to death (Jas. 1:15).

x Your origin and birth and from the Canaanites (Ezek. 16:3–4).

168 Destroyer

● Destroyer

a A destroyer of nations has set out (Jer. 4:7).

b The destroying angel (Exod. 12:23); woe to you, destroyer who have not been destroyed! (Isa. 33:1); the time has come to destroy the destroyer (Rev. 11:18); the angel of the Abyss, called Abaddon and Apollyon [Destroyer] (Rev. 9:11).

169 Parentage

● Genealogies

a Genealogy of: Cain (Gen. 4:17–22); Adam to Noah's sons (Gen. 5:3–32; 1 Chr. 1:1–4); Noah's sons (Gen. 10:1–32; 1 Chr. 1:5–23); Shem to Abraham (Gen. 11:10–26; 1 Chr. 1:24–7); Abraham (1 Chr. 1:28–42); Nahor (Gen. 22:20–4); Abraham's wife Keturah (Gen. 25:1–4); Ishmael (Gen. 25:12–16; 1 Chr. 1:29–33); Isaac (1 Chr. 1:34); Jacob (Gen. 35:22–6); Esau (Gen. 36:1–19; 1 Chr. 1:35–42); Horites (Gen. 36:20–30); Ezra (Ezra 7:1–5).

b All Israel was enrolled by genealogies (1 Chr. 9:1); the sons of Israel (Gen. 46:8–27; Num. 26:4–60; 1 Chr. 2:1–2); Asher (1 Chr. 7:30–40); Benjamin (1 Chr. 7:6–12; 8:1–40; 9:7–9); Jeiel and Saul (1 Chr. 9:35–44); Ephraim (1 Chr. 7:20–7); Gad (1 Chr. 5:11–17); Issachar (1 Chr. 7:1–5); Levi (Exod. 6:16–25; Num. 3:17–21, 27, 33; 1 Chr. 6:1–30; 9:14–21; 23:7–23; 24:20–30); Moses and Aaron (Exod. 6:20–5); Aaron (Num. 3:2; 1 Chr. 6:50–3; 24:1–2); Manasseh (1 Chr. 7:14–19); Naphtali (1 Chr. 7:13); Reuben (Exod. 6:14; 1 Chr. 5:1–10); Simeon (Exod. 6:15; 1 Chr. 4:24–43); Judah (1 Chr. 2:3–55; 4:1–23; 9:4–6); Perez (Ruth 4:18–22); David's sons (2 Sam. 3:2; 5:13–16; 1 Chr. 3:1–24); Korahites (1 Chr. 26:1–11); Jehielites (1 Chr. 26:21–5); Jeshua (Neh. 12:10); Christ (Matt. 1:1–17; Luke 3:23–38).

c The Levites were enrolled in genealogical records (2 Chr.

31:15–19); some returned exiles did not have proof of descent from Israel (Ezra 2:59–62; Neh. 7:61–4); genealogical enrolment of the returned exiles (Ezra 8:1–14; Neh. 7:5); the book of genealogy of those who returned (Neh. 7:5–60); lists of the chiefs who lived in Jerusalem (Neh. 11:3–19, 22).

d Joseph belonged to the house and family of David (Luke 2:4); Christ's human ancestry is from Israel (Rom. 9:5); our Lord was descended from Judah (Heb. 7:14).

e Melchizedek was without genealogy (Heb. 7:3).

f Avoid controversies and genealogies (Titus 3:9); myths and endless genealogies (1 Tim. 1:4).

● Generations

g The generations of: heaven and earth (Gen. 2:4); Adam (Gen. 5:1); Noah (Gen. 6:9); Shem, Ham, Japheth (Gen. 10:1); Shem (Gen. 11:10); Terah (Gen. 11:27); Ishmael (Gen. 25:12); Isaac (Gen. 25:19); Esau (Gen. 36:1, 9); Jacob (Gen. 37:2); Aaron and Moses (Num. 3:1).

h The whole earth was populated from Noah's sons (Gen. 9:18–19).

● Parenthood

i Honour your father and mother (Exod. 20:12; Lev. 19:3; Deut. 5:16; Matt. 15:4; 19:19; Mark 7:10; 10:19; Luke 18:20; Eph. 6:2); obey your parents (Eph. 6:1; Col. 3:20); David left his parents with the king of Moab (1 Sam. 22:3–4); let me kiss my father and mother (1 Kgs. 19:20); let me first bury my father (Matt. 8:21; Luke 9:59).

j I will turn the hearts of fathers to their children and children to their fathers (Mal. 4:6); parents should save for their children (2 Cor. 12:14).

k A man will leave his parents (Gen. 2:24; Matt. 19:5; Eph. 5:31); my parents forsake me but the Lord takes me up (Ps. 27:10).

l I came to set people against their parents (Matt. 10:35; Luke 12:53); if anyone does not hate father and mother he cannot be my disciple (Luke 14:26).

m Children will rise against parents (Matt. 10:21; Mark 13:12); they are disobedient to parents (Rom. 1:30); men will be disobedient to parents (2 Tim. 3:2).

n Put to death a son disobedient to his parents (Deut. 21:18–21); or who curses his parents (Exod. 21:17; Lev. 20:9; Prov. 20:20; Matt. 15:4; Mark 7:10); or who strikes his parents (Exod. 21:15); he who harms his parents is a shameful son (Prov. 19:26); cursed be he who despises his parents (Deut. 27:16; Prov. 30:17); father and mother have been despised in Jerusalem (Ezek. 22:7).

o They called the parents of the man born blind (John 9:18).

● Father
Abraham

p Abraham became the father of many nations (Gen. 17:4–5; Rom. 4:17); the father of circumcised and uncircumcised who believe (Rom. 4:11–12); look to Abraham, your father (Isa. 51:2); Abraham is our father (John 8:39); do not say Abraham is your father (Matt. 3:9; Luke 3:8); eating with Abraham, Isaac and

Jacob in the kingdom of heaven (Matt. 8:11); Abraham our fore-father (Rom. 4:1); our father Abraham (Rom. 4:12); Abraham is the father of us all (Rom. 4:16).

● God our
   Father

q Our Father in heaven (Matt. 6:9; Luke 11:2); you have one Father, in heaven (Matt. 23:9); your Father in heaven (Matt. 5:48; 6:1); he spoke to them of the Father (John 8:27); our father is God (John 8:41–2); I will be a Father to you (2 Cor. 6:18); the Father from whom every family derives its name (Eph. 3:14–15); his name will be called Everlasting Father (Isa. 9:6); you have known the Father (1 John 2:13); is the Lord who made you not your Father? (Deut. 32:6); do we not all have one Father? has not one God created us? (Mal. 2:10); God is a father to the fatherless (Ps. 68:5); the Father of spirits (Heb. 12:9); the Father of lights (Jas. 1:17).

r As a father pities his children (Ps. 103:13); he reproves as a father his children (Prov. 3:12; Heb. 12:5–9); if I am a father, where is my honour? (Mal. 1:6).

s David will call out, 'You are my Father, my God' (Ps. 89:26); God will be Father to David's offspring (2 Sam. 7:14; 1 Chr. 17:13); to Solomon (1 Chr. 22:10; 28:6); I am Israel's Father (Jer. 31:9); you will call me, 'My Father' (Jer. 3:19); you are our Father (Isa. 64:8); you are our Father though Abraham does not know us (Isa. 63:16); my Father, the friend of my youth (Jer. 3:4).

● Father of
   the Christ

t You are my Son, today I have become your Father (Ps. 2:7; Heb. 1:5); I must be in my Father's house (Luke 2:49); he was calling God his Father (John 5:18); the God and Father of our Lord Jesus Christ (Eph. 1:3; Col. 1:3; 1 Pet. 1:3); his God and Father (Rev. 1:6); as I received from my Father (Rev. 2:27).

● Abba!
   Father!

u Abba! Father! (Mark 14:36); a spirit of adoption, crying, Abba! Father! (Rom. 8:15); the Spirit of his Son in our hearts, crying, Abba! Father! (Gal. 4:6).

God the Father, see **965g**.

● Spiritual
   fathers

v Be a father and a priest to me (Judg. 17:10); to us (Judg. 18:19); calling a tree or stone their father (Jer. 2:27); your father was an Amorite (Ezek. 16:3, 45).

w I became your father through the gospel (1 Cor. 4:15); we dealt with you as a father (1 Thess. 2:11); I am writing to you, fathers (1 John 2:13, 14).

● Sins of the
   fathers

x Iniquities of the fathers visited on the children (Exod. 20:5; 34:7; Num. 14:18; Deut. 5:9); God stores a man's sins for his sons (Job 21:19); slaughter for the children because of the iniquity of the fathers (Isa. 14:21); I will repay both their iniquities and their fathers' (Isa. 65:7); the fathers have eaten sour grapes and the children's teeth are set on edge (Jer. 31:29; Ezek. 18:2); you repay the guilt of fathers to their children (Jer. 32:18); our fathers have sinned and we have borne their iniquities (Lam. 5:7).

y Fathers shall not be put to death for the children nor vice versa (Deut. 24:16; 2 Kgs. 14:6; 2 Chr. 25:4); sons shall not bear the iniquity of their fathers nor vice versa (Ezek. 18:19, 20).

z Israel are beloved for the sake of their fathers (Rom. 11:28).

● Satan your father

aa If God were your Father you would love me (John 8:42); you are of your father the devil (John 8:44).

Children of evil, see **170y**.

● Motherhood

ab Though a woman forget her sucking child, God will not forget you (Isa. 49:15).

ac Eve—the mother of all living (Gen. 3:20); you are children of Sarah (1 Pet. 3:6); Deborah was a mother in Israel (Judg. 5:7); your grandmother Lois and mother Eunice shared your faith (2 Tim. 1:5).

ad The mother of Zebedee's sons came (Matt. 20:20); the mother of the sons of Zebedee watched the crucifixion (Matt. 27:56).

ae Peter's mother-in-law was sick (Matt. 8:14; Mark 1:30; Luke 4:38).

● Jesus' mother

af The mother of Jesus was there (John 2:1); Jesus' mother and brothers came seeking him (Matt. 12:46–50; Mark 3:31–5; Luke 8:19–21); the mother of my Lord (Luke 1:43); behold, your mother! (John 19:27); Mary, the mother of Jesus (Acts 1:14); blessed is the womb that bore you (Luke 11:27).

ag My mother and brothers are those who obey God's word (Matt. 12:50; Mark 3:35; Luke 8:21).

● Spiritual mothers

ah Jerusalem above is the mother of us all (Gal. 4:26); Babylon, mother of harlots (Rev. 17:5).

ai A city which is a mother in Israel (2 Sam. 20:19); your mother was a Hittite (Ezek. 16:3, 45).

● Animal mothers

aj A newborn animal is to be left with its mother for seven days (Exod. 22:30; Lev. 22:27); you shall not kill a mother animal and its young on the same day (Lev. 22:28); do not take a mother bird with its young (Deut. 22:6–7); do not boil a kid in its mother's milk (Exod. 23:19; 34:26; Deut. 14:21); take their calves home (1 Sam. 6:7, 10).

170 Descendant

● Concerning children

a Children are a gift from the Lord (Ps. 127:3); like a warrior's arrows (Ps. 127:4); like olive shoots around your table (Ps. 128:3); let our sons be like plants and our daughters pillars (Ps. 144:12); children of believers are holy (1 Cor. 7:14); grandchildren are the crown of the old (Prov. 17:6); his descendants will be mighty (Ps. 112:2); Jonadab shall not lack a man to stand before me (Jer. 35:19).

Youngest child, see **132b**.

b Tell your son and grandson what I did (Exod. 10:2); tell your children (Exod. 12:26–7; 13:8); that the generation yet unborn should tell it to their children (Ps. 78:5–6).

c If a slave is given a wife, the wife and children belong to the master (Exod. 21:4).

d Korah's sons did not die (Num. 26:11); the tenth generation of the illegitimate may not enter the assembly (Deut. 23:2); nor that of Ammonites or Moabites (Deut. 23:3); the third generation of an Edomite or Egyptian may enter the assembly (Deut. 23:8).

e Children will have parents put to death (Matt. 10:21).

Children rising against parents, see **169m**; **disobedient children**, see **738a**.

f The seed of the woman will bruise the serpent's head (Gen. 3:15).

● Particular children

g God gave the midwives families (Exod. 1:21); Hannah prayed that God would give her a son (1 Sam. 1:11); Elijah promised that the Shunamite woman would have a son (2 Kgs. 4:16); the angel promised that Zechariah and Elizabeth would have a son (Luke 1:13).

h Through Isaac your descendants will be reckoned (Gen. 21:12; Rom. 9:7–8; Heb. 11:18); take your only son Isaac whom you love (Gen. 22:2); names of the sons of Israel (Exod. 1:1–4); Ephraim and Manasseh are mine as Reuben and Simeon are (Gen. 48:5); a son shall be born to David's house, Josiah (1 Kgs. 13:2).

i The daughters of Zelophehad were to inherit (Num. 27:1–7; 36:2; Josh. 17:3–4); Jephthah's daughter came out to meet him (Judg. 11:34); my daughter has just died (Matt. 9:18).

j Your daughter-in-law is better than seven sons (Ruth 4:15); am I not better than ten sons? (1 Sam. 1:8); woman, behold your son! (John 19:26).

● Adoption

k Moses was adopted by Pharaoh's daughter (Exod. 2:10; Acts 7:21); Moses refused to be called the son of Pharaoh's daughter (Heb. 11:24).

l He predestined us to be adopted as sons (Eph. 1:5); you have received the Spirit of adoption as sons (Rom. 8:15); we receive adoption as sons (Gal. 4:5); we wait for adoption as sons (Rom. 8:23); the adoption of sons belongs to Israel (Rom. 9:4).

● Son of God

m You are my Son, today I have begotten you (Ps. 2:7; Acts 13:33; Heb. 1:5; 5:5); this is my Son, my beloved (Matt. 3:17; 17:5; Mark 1:11; 9:7; Luke 3:22; 2 Pet. 1:17); my Son, whom I have chosen (Luke 9:35); out of Egypt have I called my Son (Matt. 2:15).

n Son of God (Matt. 14:33; Mark 1:1; Luke 1:35; John 1:34, 49); declared Son of God with power (Rom. 1:4); this was the Son of God! (Matt. 27:54; Mark 15:39); Son of the Most High (Luke 1:32); Son of the Most High God (Mark 5:7; Luke 8:28); to us a child is born, a son is given (Isa. 9:6); I believe you are the Christ, the Son of God (John 11:27); these are written that you may believe that he is the Christ, the Son of God (John 20:31).

o Are you the Son of God?—I am (Luke 22:70); I am the Son of God (John 10:36); he said 'I am the Son of God' (Matt. 27:43); he made himself out to be the Son of God (John 19:7); if you are the Son of God (Matt. 4:3, 6; 27:40; Luke 4:3, 9).

p How can they say Christ is the son of David? (Matt. 22:42–5; Mark 12:35–7; Luke 20:41–4); God's Son, by the flesh descended from David (Rom. 1:3); Jesus Christ, descended from David (2 Tim. 2:8); the root and the offspring of David (Rev. 22:16).

q God has spoken to us by his Son (Heb. 1:2); Christ is faithful as a Son over God's house (Heb. 3:6); the owner of the house sent his son (Matt. 21:37; Mark 12:6; Luke 20:13); whoever confesses that Jesus is the Son of God (1 John 4:15); no one knows the Son except the Father (Matt. 11:27).

Chosen son, see **605d**.

● Children of God

r We are God's offspring (Acts 17:28–9); you are sons of the Lord (Deut. 14:1); the sons of God saw the daughters of men (Gen. 6:2); the sons of the resurrection are sons of God (Luke 20:36).

s Israel is God's firstborn son (Exod. 4:22–3); is Ephraim my dear son? (Jer. 31:20); they have acted corruptly and are not his children (Deut. 32:5).

t The Spirit testifies with our spirit that we are sons of God (Rom. 8:16); because you are sons, God sent the Spirit of his son (Gal. 4:6); all who are led by the Spirit of God are sons of God (Rom. 8:14); sons of God through faith in Christ Jesus (Gal. 3:26); he gave the right to become children of God (John 1:12–13); you shall be my sons and daughters (2 Cor. 6:18); sons of the living God (Hos. 1:10; Rom. 9:26); you will be sons of the Most High (Luke 6:35); now we are children of God (1 John 3:2); what love, that we should be called children of God (1 John 3:1); I will be his God and he will be my son (Rev. 21:7); he will see his offspring (Isa. 53:10); bringing many sons to glory (Heb. 2:10).

● Living as God's children

u The peacemakers will be called sons of God (Matt. 5:9); be sons of your Father in heaven (Matt. 5:45); be imitators of God as beloved children (Eph. 5:1); children of God in a crooked generation (Phil. 2:15); when God disciplines you he treats you as sons (Heb. 12:7).

● Children of Abraham

v The promise was to Abraham's seed (Gal. 3:16); you are Abraham's seed (Gal. 3:29); those who are of faith are sons of Abraham (Gal. 3:7); a daughter of Abraham (Luke 13:16); he also is a son of Abraham (Luke 19:9); the promise is to all the descendants, not just those of the law (Rom. 4:16).

● Spiritual descendants

w Paul's sons in the faith, Timothy (1 Tim. 1:2), Titus (Titus 1:4) and Onesimus (Philem. 10); Timothy served Paul like a child serving his father (Phil. 2:22); Timothy, my beloved child in the Lord (1 Cor. 4:17).

x Here am I and the children God has given me (Isa. 8:18; Heb.

2:13); the children of your elect sister (2 John 13); your sons and daughters come from afar (Isa. 60:4).

● Children
of evil

y You son of the devil! (Acts 13:10); sons of the evil one (Matt. 13:38); you are sons of those who murdered the prophets (Matt. 23:31).

Satan your father, see **169***aa*; **children of the devil**, see **969***n*.

171 Productiveness

● Procreation

a God commanded all creatures to multiply (Gen. 1:22); let the waters teem with creatures (Gen. 1:20); God commanded mankind to multiply (Gen. 1:28; 9:1, 7); all creatures from the ark were to multiply (Gen. 8:17); be fruitful and multiply (Gen. 35:11); may the Lord increase you and your children (Ps. 115:14).

b Let our flocks produce thousands (Ps. 144:13–14).

Multiplying, see 104*a*.

● Barren
producing

c The barren woman has more children than she who has a husband (Isa. 54:1; Gal. 4:27); God makes the barren woman a mother (Ps. 113:9); the barren woman has borne seven children (1 Sam. 2:5); Abimelech's household bore children again (Gen. 20:17); who would have said that Sarah would nurse children? (Gen. 21:7); none shall be barren among you (Exod. 23:26; Deut. 7:14).

d Your wife will be like a fruitful vine (Ps. 128:3).

● Blossoming

e The vines are in blossom (S. of S. 2:13, 15); I went down to see the blossoms (S. of S. 6:11); let us see whether the vine has blossomed (S. of S. 7:12).

● Fertility

f The spies were to see whether the soil was fertile or poor (Num. 13:20); I brought you into a fruitful land (Jer. 2:7); I will dig around and apply fertilizer (Luke 13:8); rain and snow make the earth bring forth and sprout (Isa. 55:10); land which bears useful vegetation is blessed by God (Heb. 6:7).

● Land
producing
fruit

g The land will yield its produce (Lev. 26:4–5; Ps. 67:6; 85:12); the trees and the land will yield fruit (Ezek. 34:27; Zech. 8:12); the produce of the ground will be rich and plentiful (Isa. 30:23); we shall be fruitful in the land (Gen. 26:22).

h God will bless the fruit of your ground (Deut. 7:13); blessed will be your offspring and produce (Deut. 28:4, 11; 30:9); before the sabbath year the land will give fruit for three years (Lev. 25:21); trees whose fruit is offered will yield more (Lev. 19:25).

i The ploughman will overtake the reaper (Amos 9:13); the wilderness will blossom (Isa. 35:1); the desert becomes a fertile field (Isa. 32:15); Lebanon will become a fruitful field (Isa. 29:17); may there be abundance of grain on top of the mountains (Ps. 72:16); trees bearing fruit every month (Ezek. 47:12; Rev. 22:2).

j The land brought forth abundantly (Gen. 41:47); the land of a rich man bore abundantly (Luke 12:16); some fell on good soil and produced grain (Matt. 13:8; Mark 4:8; Luke 8:8).

Wilderness blooming, see **172*aa***.

● Fruit

k Aaron's rod sprouted and bore almonds (Num. 17:8); they took a bunch of grapes from Eshcol (Num. 13:23; Deut. 1:25); two baskets of figs (Jer. 24:1–5); a basket of summer fruit (Amos 8:1–2).

● Firstfruits

l Bring the firstfruits (Exod. 23:16, 19; 34:22, 26; Lev. 23:10–14; Deut. 26:2, 10; Neh. 10:35; 12:44); honour the Lord with the firstfruits (Prov. 3:9); firstfruits belong to the priests (Num. 18:13; Ezek. 44:30); honey and leaven acceptable as firstfuits (Lev. 2:12).

m Israel was the firstfuits of his harvest (Jer. 2:3); Christ is risen, the firstfruits of those who slept (1 Cor. 15:20, 23); the redeemed are firstfruits (Jas. 1:18; Rev. 14:4); the household of Stephanas were the firstfruits of Achaia (1 Cor. 16:15); we have the first-fruits of the Spirit (Rom. 8:23).

● Spiritual
fruit

n I found Israel like grapes in the wilderness (Hos. 9:10); Israel will fill the whole earth with fruit (Isa. 27:6); Judah will again take root downward and bear fruit upward (2 Kgs. 19:30; Isa. 37:31).

o He sent his servants to collect the fruit (Matt. 21:34); he will give the vineyard to those who will hand over the fruit (Matt. 21:41, 43); the seed on good soil brings forth a crop (Matt. 13:23; Mark 4:20; Luke 8:15); every branch that bears fruit he prunes that it may produce more fruit (John 15:2); he who abides in Christ bears much fruit (John 15:4–5); by bearing much fruit you prove to be Christ's disciples (John 15:8); I appointed you to go and bring forth fruit (John 15:16); bearing fruit in every good work (Col. 1:10); that we might bear fruit for God (Rom. 7:4); bring forth fruit worthy of repentance (Matt. 3:8; Luke 3:8); God has made me fruitful (Gen. 41:52).

p These things will keep you from being unfruitful (2 Pet. 1:8); that they may not be unfruitful (Titus 3:14); filled with the fruit of righteousness (Phil. 1:11); discipline yields the peaceful fruit of righteousness (Heb. 12:11); the fruit of righteousness is sown in peace (Jas. 3:18); the fruit of light is all goodness (Eph. 5:9); the fruit of the Spirit (Gal. 5:22–3).

q He will be like a tree bearing fruit in season (Ps. 1:3); he will not cease to yield fruit (Jer. 17:8); I am like a cypress, from me comes your fruit (Hos. 14:8); if a grain of wheat dies it bears much fruit (John 12:24).

Good fruit, see **644*f***.

r They will eat the fruit of their own way (Prov. 1:31).

● Fruitful
labour

s The harvest is plentiful (Matt. 9:37); that I might have a harvest among you, as among the other Gentiles (Rom. 1:13); to continue in the flesh means fruitful labour for me (Phil. 1:22); all over the world the gospel is bearing fruit (Col. 1:6).

● Known by
their fruit

t You will know them by their fruit (Matt. 7:16–20); bearing fruit for death (Rom. 7:5); every tree is known by its fruit (Matt. 12:33; Luke 6:44); can a fig tree bear olives or a vine figs? (Jas. 3:12); can thorns bear grapes or thistles figs? (Matt. 7:16; Luke 6:44).

Distinguishing people, see **463b**.

● Catch
of fish

u They could not haul in the net because of the multitude of fish (John 21:6); so many fish the nets were breaking and the boats sinking (Luke 5:6–7).

172 Unproductiveness

● Childless

a Those who were barren: Abraham and Sarah (Gen. 11:30; 15:2–3; 16:1–2; Rom. 4:19); the women of Abimelech's household (Gen. 20:18); Rebekah (Gen. 25:21); Rachel (Gen. 29:31; 30:1–2); Manoah's wife (Judg. 13:2); Hannah (1 Sam. 1:2); Michal (2 Sam. 6:23); Elizabeth (Luke 1:7, 36); Sarah was past childbearing (Gen. 18:11).

b Those who had no sons: Zelophehad (Num. 26:33; 27:3–4; 1 Chr. 7:15); the Shunamite woman (2 Kgs. 4:14); Eleazar (1 Chr. 23:22; 24:28); Jether (1 Chr. 2:32); Sheshan (1 Chr. 2:34); Seled (1 Chr. 2:30); Nadab and Abihu (Num. 3:4; 1 Chr. 24:2).

c Levirate marriage if someone dies leaving no son (Deut. 25:5; Matt. 22:24; Mark 12:19; Luke 20:28); seven brothers died childless (Matt. 22:25–6; Mark 12:20–2; Luke 20:29–31).

d Shimei's brothers did not have many sons (1 Chr. 4:27); Jeush and Beriah did not have many sons (1 Chr. 23:11); Eliezer had no other sons (1 Chr. 23:17).

e Barrenness as the act of God (Gen. 16:2; 30:2; 1 Sam. 1:5); those who marry near relatives will be childless (Lev. 20:20–1); as will the adulterous woman (Num. 5:27–8); the wicked has no offspring (Job 18:19).

f As your sword made women childless, your mother shall be childless (1 Sam. 15:33); write this man down as childless (Jer. 22:30).

g The barren will one day be considered happy (Luke 23:29).

● Eunuchs

h The eunuch should not consider himself worthless (Isa. 56:3); eunuchs who are born so, made so by men or choose to be so for the kingdom (Matt. 19:12).

i No one who has been castrated may enter the assembly (Deut. 23:1); would that they might castrate themselves! (Gal. 5:12).

j Seven eunuchs who served King Ahasuerus (Esther 1:10); Hegai the king's eunuch (Esther 2:3); the eunuch in charge of the king's concubines (Esther 2:14); one of the king's eunuchs (Esther 4:5; 7:9); king's eunuchs who were doorkeepers (Esther 6:2); Ebed-melech, an Ethiopian eunuch (Jer. 38:7); the Ethiopian eunuch (Acts 8:27).

Barren producing, see **171c**.

- Miscarriage
  - *k* If a woman is struck and has a miscarriage (Exod. 21:22); give them a miscarrying womb and dry breasts (Hos. 9:14).
  - *l* Like a miscarriage I would not have been (Job 3:16); the miscarriages which never see the sun (Ps. 58:8).
  - *m* Your animals have not miscarried (Gen. 31:38); none shall miscarry (Exod. 23:26).

- Fruitless land
  - *n* The ground would not be fruitful: for Cain (Gen. 4:12); for the disobedient Israelites (Lev. 26:20; Deut. 11:17; 28:38–40; 29:23).
  - *o* Esau would dwell away from fertile ground (Gen. 27:39); the land is unfruitful (2 Kgs. 2:19); he will live in parched places of the wilderness (Jer. 17:6).
  - *p* The ground will no longer yield its strength (Gen. 4:12); I will make the sky like iron and the earth bronze (Lev. 26:19); you will plant seed in vain (Lev. 26:16); ten acres will yield but a bath and a homer of seed an ephah of grain (Isa. 5:10); the vintage will fail and the fruit harvest will not come (Isa. 32:10); harvest destroyed by locusts (Joel 1:11–12); the harvest will be taken away (Jer. 8:13); because of you the earth has withheld its produce (Hag. 1:10); you will plant a vineyard but not eat its fruit (Deut. 28:30); you will sow much but harvest little (Deut. 28:38); you planted much but harvest little (Hag. 1:6); cursed will be your offspring and produce (Deut. 28:18).
  - *q* He changes a fruitful land into a salt waste (Ps. 107:34); fruitful land will become worthless (Isa. 7:23).
  - *r* The word is choked and is unfruitful (Matt. 13:22; Mark 4:19); the seed among thorns gave no fruit (Mark 4:7); they bring no fruit to maturity (Luke 8:14); it produced only wild grapes (Isa. 5:2, 4); trees in autumn without fruit (Jude 12).
  - *s* Though there be no fruit, yet I will rejoice in the Lord (Hab. 3:17–18).

- Fruitless things destroyed
  - *t* Land yielding thorns and thistles is near to being cursed (Heb. 6:8); every unproductive tree will be cut down and burnt (Matt. 3:10; 7:19; Luke 3:9); if it does not bear fruit next year, cut it down (Luke 13:6–9); every branch which bears no fruit is cut off (John 15:2); the fig tree without fruit was cursed (Matt. 21:19; Mark 11:13–14, 20).

- Wilderness
  - *u* Ishmael lived in the wilderness (Gen. 21:21); the west side of the wilderness (Exod. 3:1); God led them by way of the wilderness (Exod. 13:17); set out for the wilderness (Num. 14:25); your corpses will fall in the wilderness (Num. 14:29, 32–3); you lived in the wilderness a long time (Josh. 24:7); 40 years in the wilderness (Deut. 8:2); he led his people through the wilderness (Ps. 136:16); God found his people in the wilderness (Deut. 32:10); Elijah went a day's journey into the wilderness (1 Kgs. 19:4); some wandered in the wilderness (Ps. 107:4).

v The goat of removal was sent into the wilderness (Lev. 16:10, 21–2).

w Wilderness of: Beersheba (Gen. 21:14); Edom (2 Kgs. 3:8); Gibeon (2 Sam. 2:24); Jeruel (2 Chr. 20:16); Kedemoth (Deut. 2:26); Moab (Deut. 2:8); Shur (Exod. 15:22); Sin (Exod. 16:1; Num. 33:11–12); Sinai (Exod. 19:1–2; Num. 33:15–16); Zin (Num. 20:1; 27:14; 33:36; 34:3; Deut. 32:51; Josh. 15:1).

x David stayed in the wilderness of: Engedi (1 Sam. 24:1); Maon (1 Sam. 23:24–5); Paran (1 Sam. 25:1); Ziph (1 Sam. 23:14, 15; 26:2); Judea (Matt. 3:1).

● John in the wilderness

y John in the wilderness (Matt. 3:1; Luke 3:2); John lived in the wilderness before his public appearance (Luke 1:80); John the Baptist appeared in the wilderness (Mark 1:4); one shouting in the wilderness (Isa. 40:3; Matt. 3:3; Mark 1:3); what did you go into the wilderness to see? (Matt. 11:7; Luke 7:24).

● Jesus in the wilderness

z Jesus was led by the Spirit into the wilderness (Matt. 4:1; Luke 4:1); the Spirit drove him into the wilderness (Mark 1:12); Jesus had to stay out in the wilderness (Mark 1:45).

● Wilderness blooming

aa The wilderness will rejoice and blossom (Isa. 35:1); the Lord will make Zion's wilderness like Eden (Isa. 51:3).

● Lack of fish

ab They caught nothing all night (Luke 5:5; John 21:3); have you caught nothing? (John 21:5).

173 Agency
Power, see **160**.

174 Vigour: physical energy
See **571**.

175 Inertness
Sluggishness, see **679***h*.

176 Violence

● Force

a The earth was full of violence (Gen. 6:11, 13); Simeon and Levi have weapons of violence (Gen. 49:5); Edom's violence against Jacob (Obad. 10); the priests threatened to take meat by force (1 Sam. 2:16); two men so violent no one could pass (Matt. 8:28); do not rob anyone by force (Luke 3:14).
Fierce men, see **892***b*.

b The kingdom of heaven comes with violence (Matt. 11:12; Luke 16:16).

c The Lord will strike Israel like a reed shaken in water (1 Kgs. 14:15); I will shake Jacob as in a sieve (Amos 9:9).

d God has broken out against my enemies (2 Sam. 5:20; 1 Chr. 14:11); God broke out against Uzzah (2 Sam. 6:7–8; 1 Chr. 13:11; 15:13); the three mighty men broke through at Bethlehem (2 Sam. 23:16).

e You will not be afraid of violence (Job 5:21); you rescue me from violent men (2 Sam. 22:49; Ps. 18:48); violence will not be heard again in the land (Isa. 60:18).

Death penalty for violence, see **963***m*.

● Earthquakes

f The mountain quaked (Exod. 19:18); an earthquake in the Philistine garrison (1 Sam. 14:15); the earth quaked (2 Sam. 22:8; Ps. 18:7); there was a great earthquake (Matt. 28:2; Acts 16:26; Rev. 16:18); the earth shook at the noise of rejoicing (1 Kgs. 1:40); the place where they gathered was shaken (Acts 4:31); there was an earthquake (Rev. 6:12; 8:5; 11:13, 19).

g When God went forth, the earth quaked (Judg. 5:4, 5; Ps. 68:8); he looks at the earth and it trembles (Ps. 104:32); God shakes the earth (Job 9:6); you made the land quake (Ps. 60:2); mountains quake before him (Nahum 1:5); the mountains saw you and quaked (Hab. 3:10).

h The earthquake in the days of Uzziah (Zech. 14:5); two years before the earthquake (Amos 1:1).

i There will be earthquakes (Matt. 24:7; Mark 13:8; Luke 21:11); the earth is shaken violently (Isa. 24:19); there will be an earthquake in the land of Israel (Ezek. 38:19); when Jesus died the earth shook (Matt. 27:51); the Lord was not in the earthquake (1 Kgs. 19:11).

● Storms

j A fierce squall came on the lake (Matt. 8:24; Mark 4:37; Luke 8:23); out of the south comes the storm (Job 37:9); the violent Northeaster wind (Acts 27:14); Jonah in the wind and storm (Jonah 1:4).

● Thunder and lightning

k Thunder and lightning (Exod. 19:16; 20:18); God answered Moses with thunder (Exod. 19:19); the Lord thundered against the Philistines (1 Sam. 7:10); thunder and rain during wheat harvest (1 Sam. 12:17–18); God thundered from heaven (2 Sam. 22:14; Ps. 18:13); thunder as God's voice accompanied by lightning (Job 37:2–5; Ps. 29:3–9); lightning was his arrows (2 Sam. 22:15; Ps. 18:14; 77:17–18); flash forth lightning and scatter them (Ps. 144:6); can you send out lightnings? (Job 38:35); his lightnings light up the world (Ps. 97:4); lightning flashed from the fire (Ezek. 1:13–14); he makes lightnings for the rain (Ps. 135:7; Jer. 10:13; 51:16).

l Thunder and lightning from: the throne (Rev. 4:5); the censer (Rev. 8:5); the temple (Rev. 11:19); there was thunder and lightning (Rev. 16:18).

m Some said it thundered (John 12:29); the seven thunders sounded (Rev. 10:3–4); a voice like loud thunder (Rev. 14:2); the sound of many thunders (Rev. 19:6).

n Sons of thunder (Mark 3:17).

177 Gentleness

● Gentleness
of God

   a The wisdom from above is gentle (Jas. 3:17); your gentleness has made me great (2 Sam. 22:36; Ps. 18:35).

● Gentleness
of Christ

   b I am gentle and lowly in heart (Matt. 11:29); your king comes, gentle and on a donkey (Matt. 21:5); a bruised reed he will not break and a smouldering wick he will not quench (Isa. 42:3; Matt. 12:20); I exhort you by the meekness and gentleness of Christ (2 Cor. 10:1).

● Gentleness of
God's people

   c The fruit of the Spirit is gentleness (Gal. 5:23); God has given us a spirit of moderation (2 Tim. 1:7).

   d Put on gentleness (Col. 3:12); pursue gentleness (1 Tim. 6:11); an elder must be gentle (1 Tim. 3:3); remind them to be gentle (Titus 3:2); a gentle and quiet spirit (1 Pet. 3:4); let your gentleness be known to all (Phil. 4:5).

   e The Lord's servant must in gentleness instruct those who oppose him (2 Tim. 2:25); restore the sinner in a spirit of gentleness (Gal. 6:1); give a reply with gentleness (1 Pet. 3:15).

   f We were gentle as a nursing mother among you (1 Thess. 2:7); a high priest can deal gently with the ignorant (Heb. 5:2).

● Gentle
words

   g A soft answer turns away wrath (Prov. 15:1); will Leviathan speak soft words? (Job 41:3); a soft tongue may break bones (Prov. 25:15).

178 Influence
See **612**.

179 Tendency

180 Liability

● Responsible
to warn

   a The responsibility of the watchman to give warning (Ezek. 3:17–21; 33:2–9); if anyone does not heed the warning, his blood will be upon his own head (Ezek. 33:4–5); if the watchman gives no warning, he will be held accountable for the man's blood (Ezek. 3:18, 20; 33:6, 8).

● Responsible
for own death

   b If anyone goes out, his blood shall be on his own head (Josh. 2:19); your blood will be on your own head (2 Sam. 1:16; Acts 18:6).

● Responsible
for others'
death

   c We must give an accounting for his blood (Gen. 42:22); if anyone is harmed inside, his blood be on our heads (Josh. 2:19); his blood be on us and on our children (Matt. 27:25).

   d May Abner's blood be on Joab (2 Sam. 3:28–9); I will require Ishbosheth's blood at your hand (2 Sam. 4:11); this generation will be held responsible for the blood of all the prophets (Matt. 23:35; Luke 11:50).

   e You intend to bring this man's blood on us (Acts 5:28).

   f Do not put innocent blood on us (Jonah 1:14).

● Accountable   *g* That the whole world may be accountable to God (Rom. 3:19); every one will give account of himself to God (Rom. 14:12).

                  h They are without excuse (Rom. 1:20); you are without excuse (Rom. 2:1).

181 Concurrence: combination of causes
Cooperation, see **706**.

182 Counteraction
Opposition, see **704**.

Class two: Space

Section two: Space in general

---

183 Space: indefinite space

● Roomy

a Rehoboth, the Lord has made room for us (Gen. 26:22); God brought me into a broad place (2 Sam. 22:20; Ps. 18:19; 31:8); oh, that you would bless me and enlarge my border! (1 Chr. 4:10); I will enlarge your borders (Exod. 34:24); still there is room (Luke 14:22).

b The city was roomy (Neh. 7:4); the work was spread wide (Neh. 4:19).

c God's limits are high, deep, long and broad (Job 11:7–9).

● No room

d There was no room in the inn (Luke 2:7); you will be too cramped for all your children (Isa. 49:19–20).

● Territory

e Their area would extend north, south, east and west (Gen. 13:14; 28:14); from the river of Egypt to the Euphrates (Gen. 15:18); from the desert to the river (Exod. 23:31); from the desert to Lebanon (Josh. 1:4); every place you tread on (Deut. 11:24; Josh. 1:3).

● Worldwide

f His dominion will be from sea to sea, from the river to the ends of the earth (Ps. 72:8; Zech. 9:10).

g Wherever I go, you are there (Ps. 139:8–10); from the rising of the sun to its setting my name will be great (Mal. 1:11); their voice has gone out into all the world (Ps. 19:4; Rom. 10:18).

h Wherever they go I will search them out (Amos 9:2–4).

i Go into all the world (Mark 16:15); witnesses to the uttermost parts of the earth (Acts 1:8); many will come from east and west in the kingdom of heaven (Matt. 8:11; Luke 13:29); wherever the gospel is preached, she will be remembered (Matt. 26:13); the gospel preached to every creature under heaven (Col. 1:23).

j The coming of the Son of Man will be like lightning, visible from east to west (Matt. 24:27; Luke 17:24); he will gather his elect from the four winds (Mark 13:27).

● Firmament

k Expanse of the firmament (Gen. 1:6–8); lights in the expanse (Gen. 1:14).

184 Region: definite space

● The land given

a To your offspring I will give this land (Gen. 12:7; 13:15; 15:18; 17:8; 24:7; 26:3; 28:13; 35:12; 48:4; Exod. 32:13); I have given you this land (Gen. 15:7); the land God gives you (Exod. 20:12; Num. 15:2; Deut. 4:1); the land God is giving us (Deut. 2:29; 11:31; 27:2–3); to give you the land (Lev. 25:38); the Lord has given the land (Deut. 1:21; 3:18; Josh. 2:9, 24); to you I will give the land of Canaan (1 Chr. 16:18; Ps. 105:11); the land you gave to their fathers (1 Kgs. 8:48); the Lord gave the land to Israel

(Josh. 21:43; Ps. 135:12; 136:21–2); to Abraham's offspring (2 Chr. 20:7); Joshua will give them the land (Deut. 3:28; 31:7, 23); he gave them the lands of the nations (Ps. 105:44); then I will let you dwell in the land I gave your fathers for ever (Jer. 7:7).

b The land he swore to give (Gen. 50:24; Deut. 1:8; 6:23; 10:11; 11:9, 21; Jer. 32:22); covenant to give them the land (Exod. 6:4); a covenant to give Abraham the land (Neh. 9:8).

● What kind of land

c See what the land is like (Num. 13:18); Moses was to see the land (Num. 27:12; Deut. 34:1); it is a good land (Num. 14:7; Deut. 1:25; 8:7); the land is very good (Judg. 18:9); a broad and rich land (Neh. 9:35); a land with cities you did not build (Deut. 6:10; Josh. 24:13); the beautiful land (Dan. 11:16, 41); the borders of the land (Num. 34:1–12).

Flowing with milk and honey, see **635**.

● Going to the land

d Go to the land I will show you (Gen. 12:1; Acts 7:3); go up to the land (Exod. 33:1); go back to the land (Gen. 31:3, 13); I will take you back to the land (Gen. 48:21); God will bring them into the land (Exod. 3:8; 6:8; 13:11; 23:23); I will bring Caleb into the land (Num. 14:24); and Joshua (Num. 14:30); I led you into the land (Judg. 2:1); stay in the land (Gen. 26:2–3; Jer. 42:10); Jacob lived in the land (Gen. 37:1); I have come to the land the Lord swore to give us (Deut. 26:3); he brought them to his holy land (Ps. 78:54); Joseph brought Jesus and his mother to the land of Israel (Matt. 2:20–1).

● The land inherited

e You told them to enter and possess the land (Neh. 9:15); dwell in the land (Ps. 37:3; Jer. 25:5).

f The land inherited by: those blessed by the Lord (Ps. 37:22); those God exalts (Ps. 37:34); those with the blessing of Abraham (Gen. 28:4); the righteous (Ps. 37:29); he who makes God his refuge (Isa. 57:13); those who hope in the Lord (Ps. 37:9); the meek (Ps. 37:11; Matt. 5:5); your children (Deut. 1:39).

g Follow the commands so that you may possess the land (Deut. 4:1; 8:1; 11:8; 1 Chr. 28:8); pursue justice, that you may possess the land (Deut. 16:20); the land is ours because we have sought the Lord (2 Chr. 14:7); the upright will inhabit the land (Prov. 2:21); to us this land is given (Ezek. 11:15).

The land an inheritance, see **777***h*.

● Not entering the land

h Those who did not enter the land: Aaron (Num. 20:12, 24); Moses (Num. 20:12; Deut. 3:25–6; 32:52); all that generation (Num. 14:23; Deut. 1:35).

i Moses viewed the land (Deut. 32:49, 52); the wicked will not dwell in the land (Prov. 10:30); you commit abominations and should you possess the land? (Ezek. 33:25–6).

● Judgement on the land

j I will desolate the land (Lev. 26:32–3); land, land, land, hear the word of the Lord (Jer. 22:29); the end is coming on the land (Ezek. 7:2–3).

- Returning
  to the land

  k The Lord will bring you back to the land after exile (Deut. 30:5); bring them back to the land (1 Kgs. 8:34; 2 Chr. 6:25); they will come from the land of the north to the land I gave your fathers for an inheritance (Jer. 3:18); you will live in the land I gave to your fathers (Ezek. 36:28); they will live in the land I gave to Jacob (Ezek. 37:25); I will bring them to the land of Israel (Ezek. 37:12, 14); I will gather you and give you the land of Israel (Ezek. 11:17; 20:42); when I gather them they will live in the land (Ezek. 28:25).

- A better
  land

  l They desired a better land, a heavenly one (Heb. 11:16); they are seeking a homeland (Heb. 11:14).

- Other
  lands

  m Those who went down to Egypt: Abraham (Gen. 12:10); Joseph (Gen. 39:1); Israel (Gen. 46:3–7; Ps. 105:23); the remnant (Jer. 43:7).

  n Joseph bought all the land for Pharaoh (Gen. 47:20).

  o Till I take you away to a land like your own (2 Kgs. 18:32).

- Regions

  p Gilead given to Reuben, Gad and half of Manasseh (Num. 32:5, 29–42; 34:14–15; Deut. 3:12, 15–17; 29:8; Josh. 1:13, 15); Israel took Gilead and Bashan, the land of the Amorites (Num. 21:24; Deut. 3:12–17; 4:47–9; 29:8; 31:4; Josh. 12:2–6; 13:8–33; 14:3; 17:1–6; 18:7; 24:8; Judg. 11:21–2); Gilead, land of Sihon and Og (1 Kgs. 4:19; Neh. 9:22); the Amorites had taken the land from Moab (Num. 21:26–30); Gilead disputed by the Ammonites (Judg. 11:13–27); the land of Gilead was cut off from Israel (2 Kgs. 10:33).

  q Territory of: Reuben (Josh. 13:15–23; Ezek. 48:6); Gad (Josh. 13:24–8; Ezek. 48:27); half Manasseh (Josh. 13:29–31); Judah (Josh. 15:1–12; Ezek. 48:7); Joseph (Josh. 16:1–4); Ephraim (Josh. 16:5–8; Ezek. 48:5); Manasseh (Josh. 17:7–10; Ezek. 48:4); Benjamin (Josh. 18:11–20; Ezek. 48:23); Simeon (Josh. 19:1–9; Ezek. 48:24); Zebulun (Josh. 19:10–16; Ezek. 48:26); Issachar (Josh. 19:17–23; Ezek. 48:25); Asher (Josh. 19:25–31; Ezek. 48:2); Naphtali (Josh. 19:32–9; Ezek. 48:3); Dan (Josh. 19:40–8; Ezek. 48:1).

  r I have given Mount Seir to Esau (Deut. 2:5); I have given Ar to the sons of Lot (Deut. 2:9, 19).

- Samaria

  s Purchase of the hill of Samaria (1 Kgs. 16:24); aliens resettled in Samaria (2 Kgs. 17:24; Ezra 4:10); Jesus had to pass through Samaria (John 4:4); he came to Sychar and Samaria (John 4:5); you will be witnesses to me in Samaria (Acts 1:8); the church was scattered throughout Samaria (Acts 8:1); Philip preached Christ in Samaria (Acts 8:5).

  Samaritans, see **371ab**.

- Galilee

  t Galilee of the Gentiles (Isa. 9:1; Matt. 4:15); the region of Zebulun and Naphtali (Matt. 4:13–15); surely Christ does not come from Galilee? (John 7:41); no prophet is to arise from Galilee (John 7:52).

u Joseph went up from Galilee (Luke 2:4); Joseph headed for Galilee (Matt. 2:22–3); Jesus returned to Galilee (Luke 4:14); he went into Galilee (John 4:3, 43); he stayed in Galilee (John 7:9).

v Jesus came into Galilee preaching (Mark 1:14); teaching from Galilee as far as here (Luke 23:5); Jesus withdrew into Galilee (Matt. 4:12); news of him spread through all Galilee (Mark 1:28); Jesus went about all Galilee (Matt. 4:23; Mark 1:39; John 7:1); they were going through Galilee (Mark 9:30); they were gathering in Galilee (Matt. 17:22); Jesus left Galilee (Matt. 19:1); a great crowd from Galilee followed (Mark 3:7).

w After I am raised I will go before you to Galilee (Matt. 26:32; Mark 14:28); he is going before you to Galilee (Matt. 28:7; Mark 16:7); tell my brethren to go to Galilee (Matt. 28:10); the eleven disciples went to Galilee (Matt. 28:16); remember what he said in Galilee (Luke 24:6).

● Jesus in various regions

x Jesus in: the country of the Gadarenes (Matt. 8:28); the country of the Gerasenes (Mark 5:1; Luke 8:26); the region of Tyre (Mark 7:24); the district of Tyre and Sidon (Matt. 15:21; Mark 7:31); Gennesaret (Matt. 14:34; Mark 6:53); the region of Magadan (Matt. 15:39); the district of Dalmanutha (Mark 8:10); the region of Caesarea Philippi (Matt. 16:13; Mark 8:27); trans-Jordan (Matt. 19:1; Mark 10:1).

● Cities in general

y A city set on a hill cannot be hid (Matt. 5:14); I have made you a fortified city (Jer. 1:18).

Walled towns, see **235*g***; **fortified cities**, see **713*c***; **capturing cities**, see **786*j***.

● Looking for a city

z Some found no way to a city to settle in (Ps. 107:4); the Lord led them to a city to settle in (Ps. 107:7); there they establish a city (Ps. 107:36); we have a strong city with salvation as walls (Isa. 26:1); Abraham was looking for the city God built (Heb. 11:10); we are looking for a city to come (Heb. 13:14); God has prepared a city for them (Heb. 11:16).

● Cities in Israel

aa Israel took the cities of Sihon (Num. 21:25–7); and the cities of Og (Deut. 3:4–6); cities you did not build (Deut. 6:10); building cities (Num. 32:16–17, 24, 34–8); cities of the Gibeonites (Josh. 9:17); 30 cities, Havvoth-jair (Judg. 10:4); Jair had 23 cities in Gilead (1 Chr. 2:22); 60 cities in Bashan (1 Kgs. 4:13); Hebron, formerly called Kiriath-arba (Josh. 14:13–15; 15:13; Judg. 1:10; 2 Sam. 2:1, 3); Timnath-serah was given to Joshua (Josh. 19:50); Jericho, city of palm trees (Judg. 3:13); Achish gave David Ziklag (1 Sam. 27:5–6); Philistines came to live in Israelite cities (1 Sam. 31:7); cities restored to Israel (1 Sam. 7:14; 1 Kgs. 20:34); Joash and David took Rabbah (2 Sam. 12:26–9); Hiram did not like the cities Solomon gave him (1 Kgs. 9:11–13); Ahab built cities (1 Kgs. 22:39); the cities of Aroer will be a place for flocks (Isa. 17:2–3).

ab If he retreats into a city we will drag it into the valley (2 Sam. 17:13).

ac They will resettle the desolate cities (Isa. 54:3); he reproached the cities where his miracles were done (Matt. 11:20); you will not have gone through all the cities of Israel before the Son of man comes (Matt. 10:23).

● Cities for the tribes

ad Cities for: Judah (Josh. 15:21–62; Neh. 11:25–30); Ephraim (Josh. 16:9; 1 Chr. 7:28–9); Manasseh (Josh. 17:11–12); Benjamin (Josh. 18:21–8; Neh. 11:31–5); Simeon (Josh. 19:2–8); Zebulun (Josh. 19:15); Issachar (Josh. 19:22); Asher (Josh. 19:30); Naphtali (Josh. 19:35–8); Dan (Josh. 19:41–6); Aaron (Josh. 21:4, 13–19); the Levites (1 Chr. 6:54–81); the Kohathites (Josh. 21:5, 20–6); the Gershonites (Josh. 21:6, 27–33); the Merarites (Josh. 21:7, 34–40).

● Cities of refuge

ae Cities for the Levites, cities of refuge (Num. 35:1–15; Deut. 4:41–3; 19:1–13; Josh. 14:4; 20:2, 7–9; 21:2–42; 1 Chr. 6:57–60, 67–70).

● Jerusalem's history

af Melchizedek king of Salem (Gen. 14:18); Adonizedek king of Jerusalem (Josh. 10:1–5; 12:10); the border of Judah was at Jerusalem (Josh. 15:8); as also the border of Benjamin (Josh. 18:16); Jebusites in Jerusalem (Josh. 15:63); Jerusalem belonged to Benjamin (Josh. 18:28; 1 Chr. 8:32); Benjamin did not drive the Jebusites out of Jerusalem (Judg. 1:21); some of Judah, Benjamin, Ephraim and Manasseh lived in Jerusalem (1 Chr. 9:3); Judah captured Jerusalem (Judg. 1:8); they came near Jebus, Jerusalem (Judg. 19:10–11); David took the fortress and called it the city of David (2 Sam. 5:6–9; 1 Chr. 11:4–8); the angel was about to destroy Jerusalem (2 Sam. 24:16; 1 Chr. 21:15); Jerusalem beseiged (Isa. 29:3); Zion has become a wilderness (Isa. 64:10); when you see Jerusalem surrounded by armies (Luke 21:20).

Burning Jerusalem, see **381f.**

ag Jerusalem, killing the prophets (Matt. 23:37; Luke 13:34); it cannot be that a prophet perishes away from Jerusalem (Luke 13:33); the present Jerusalem is in slavery with her children (Gal. 4:25).

ah Jesus went up to Jerusalem for passover (John 2:13, 23); Jesus went up to Jerusalem for the feast (John 5:1); Jesus going up to Jerusalem (Matt. 20:17–18; 21:1; Mark 10:32–3; Luke 9:51, 53; 13:22; 17:11; 18:31; 19:28); he was drawing near Jerusalem (Luke 19:11); they came to Jerusalem (Mark 11:15, 27); his departure, to be accomplished at Jerusalem (Luke 9:31).

ai Repentance is to be preached, beginning at Jerusalem (Luke 24:47); you will be witnesses in Jerusalem (Acts 1:8); Paul going up to Jerusalem (Acts 21:4, 12, 13, 17; Rom. 15:25).

● Jerusalem's value

aj Glorious things are spoken of you, city of God (Ps. 87:3); Mount Zion, the city of our God (Ps. 48:1–3); the city of God (Ps. 46:4);

the city you have chosen (1 Kgs. 8:48); Jerusalem, your holy mountain (Dan. 9:16); Zion, the city of our appointed feasts (Isa. 33:20); Jerusalem is built as a compact city (Ps. 122:3); the city of the great King (Ps. 48:2; Matt. 5:35).

ak You say Jerusalem is where one should worship (John 4:20–1).

● Concern for   *al* Pray for the peace of Jerusalem (Ps. 122:6); do good to Zion (Ps.
Jerusalem   51:18); walk about Zion, count her towers, ramparts and palaces (Ps. 48:12–13); take no rest till he makes Jerusalem a praise in the earth (Isa. 62:7); if I forget Jerusalem, may my right hand forget her skill (Ps. 137:5).

● New   *am* The redeemed of the Lord will return with singing to Zion (Isa.
Jerusalem   35:10); I create Jerusalem a rejoicing (Isa. 65:18); Jerusalem will be called the city of Truth (Zech. 8:3); they will call you the city of the Lord, Zion of the Holy One of Israel (Isa. 60:14); Jerusalem will be called the throne of the Lord (Jer. 3:17); the Lord will reign in Jerusalem (Isa. 24:23).

an Heavenly Jerusalem (Heb. 12:22); the Jerusalem above is free (Gal. 4:26); the city of my God, new Jerusalem, coming down out of heaven from God (Rev. 3:12; 21:2, 10).

Mount Zion, see **209***l*.

● Bethlehem   *ao* Rachel buried near Bethlehem (Gen. 35:19; 48:7); a Levite from Bethlehem (Judg. 17:7, 9); a Levite took a concubine from Bethlehem (Judg. 19:1, 2, 18); Ephrathites from Benjamin sojourning in Moab (Ruth 1:1–2); Naomi and Ruth returning to Bethlehem (Ruth 1:19, 22); Samuel came to Bethlehem (1 Sam. 16:4); David of Bethlehem (1 Sam. 17:12); water from the well at Bethlehem (2 Sam. 23:14–16; 1 Chr. 11:16–18); Bethelehem, the city of David (Luke 2:4); Bethlehem as the birthplace of the Christ (Mic. 5:2; Matt. 2:1, 5–6; John 7:42); let us go to Bethlehem (Luke 2:15).

● Nazareth   *ap* Can any good thing come out of Nazareth? (John 1:46); the sect of the Nazarenes (Acts 24:5).

aq Gabriel was sent to Nazareth (Luke 1:26); Joseph settled in Nazareth (Matt. 2:23); they returned to Nazareth (Luke 2:39, 51); Jesus came from Nazareth in Galilee (Mark 1:9); this is the prophet Jesus, from Nazareth (Matt. 21:11); he came to Nazareth where he had been brought up (Luke 4:16); Jesus of Nazareth (Matt. 26:71; Luke 18:37; John 1:45; Acts 10:38; 26:9); Jesus the Nazarene (Mark 1:24; Luke 24:19; John 18:5, 7; 19:19; Acts 2:22; 4:10; 6:14; 22:8); what you did in Capernaum, do in your home town too (Luke 4:23).

● Capernaum   *ar* Jesus left Nazareth and settled in Capernaum (Matt. 4:13); he came to Capernaum, a city of Galilee (Luke 4:31); he came to his own city (Matt. 9:1; 13:54; Mark 6:1); he went down to Capernaum (John 2:12); he came back to Capernaum (Mark 2:1); they came to Capernaum (Matt. 17:24); they came to Capernaum seeking Jesus (John 6:24).

as Jesus taught in the synagogue at Capernaum (Mark 1:21; John 6:59); a sick son in Capernaum (John 4:46); Capernaum, will you be exalted? (Matt. 11:23; Luke 10:15).

● Bethany near
Jerusalem

at Bethany is about two miles from Jerusalem (John 11:18); when Jesus was at Bethany (Matt. 26:6; Mark 14:3); Jesus came to Bethany (John 12:1); as he approached Bethphage and Bethany (Luke 19:29); Lazarus of Bethany, the village of Mary and Martha (John 11:1); he led them out as far as Bethany (Luke 24:50).

● Jericho

au Marching round Jericho (Josh. 6:1–15); the walls of Jericho fell down (Josh. 6:20; Heb. 11:30); cursed be he who builds Jericho (Josh. 6:26); Hiel rebuilt Jericho (1 Kgs. 16:34); they came to Jericho (Mark 10:46; Luke 18:35); he was passing through Jericho (Luke 19:1); as they went out of Jericho (Matt. 20:29); a man was going down to Jericho when he fell among thieves (Luke 10:30).

● Cities of
the plain

av Sodom and Gomorrah and the cities round them committed immorality (Jude 7); Lot settled in the cities of the valley, near Sodom (Gen. 13:12); when Lot went out of Sodom (Luke 17:29); Zoar, a little town (Gen. 19:20, 22); God overthrew the cities of the plain (Gen. 19:24–5).

aw We would have been like Sodom and Gomorrah (Isa. 1:9–10; Rom. 9:29); they have become like Sodom and Gomorrah to me (Jer. 23:14); your younger sister was Sodom (Ezek. 16:46–56); as when God overthrew Sodom and Gomorrah (Jer. 50:40); my people's sin is greater than that of Sodom (Lam. 4:6); how can I make you like Admah and Zeboiim? (Hos. 11:8); I overthrew you like Sodom and Gomorrah (Amos 4:11).

ax Babylon will be like the overthrow of Sodom and Gomorrah (Isa. 13:19); as will Edom (Jer. 49:18); Moab will be like Sodom and the Ammonites like Gomorrah (Zeph. 2:9); the great city called Sodom and Egypt (Rev. 11:8).

ay It will be more tolerable for Sodom and Gomorrah than for them (Matt. 10:15; 11:23–4; Luke 10:12); if God condemned Sodom and Gomorrah (2 Pet. 2:6).

● Babylon

az The city was called Babel (Gen. 11:9); oracle concerning Babylon (Isa. 13:1–14:23); after 70 years I will punish the king of Babylon (Jer. 25:12); Babylon will be destroyed (Isa. 14:22–3); Babylon will be like the overthrow of Sodom and Gomorrah (Isa. 13:19); God remembered Babylon the great (Rev. 16:19); fallen is Babylon the great (Rev. 14:8; 18:2); so will Babylon be thrown down (Rev. 18:21).

ba Babylon the great, mother of harlots (Rev. 17:5); lamenting over Babylon (Rev. 18:9–19); the great city called Sodom and Egypt (Rev. 11:8); the harlot is the great city that rules over the kings of the earth (Rev. 17:18).

● Nineveh

bb Go to Nineveh, that great city (Jonah 1:2; 3:2); Nineveh was a very great city (Jonah 3:3); the oracle of Nineveh (Nahum 1:1); Nineveh was like a pool of water (Nahum 2:8); Nineveh is devastated (Nahum 3:7); Jonah was a sign to Nineveh (Luke 11:30); the men of Nineveh will condemn this generation (Matt. 12:41; Luke 11:32).

● Tyre and Sidon

bc Oracles concerning Tyre (Isa. 23:1–18; Ezek. 26:2–28:19); oracle concerning Sidon (Ezek. 28:21–4); for three transgressions of Tyre (Amos 1:9–10); it will be more tolerable for Tyre and Sidon (Matt. 11:21–2; Luke 10:13–14).

● Other cities

bd Cain built a city called Enoch (Gen. 4:17); Susa the capital (Esther 1:5; 3:15; 8:14); Susa (Dan. 8:2); judgement on all the cities of Moab (Jer. 48:21–4; Ezek. 25:9); oracle about Damascus (Isa. 17:1–3).

be John baptised in Bethany beyond Jordan (John 1:28); John baptised in Aenon near Salim (John 3:23).

bf He went to a city called Nain (Luke 7:11); a city called Ephraim (John 11:54); he went to Cana in Galilee (John 2:1, 11; 4:46); he withdrew to Bethsaida (Luke 9:10); Philip was from Bethsaida (John 1:44); woe to you, Chorazin and Bethsaida! (Matt. 11:21; Luke 10:13).

185 Place: limited space

See **184**.

186 Situation

State, see **7**.

187 Location

● Where?

a Where are you? (Gen. 3:9); where is your brother Abel? (Gen. 4:9); where is Sarah? (Gen. 18:9); where is the prostitute? (Gen. 38:21); where are Samuel and David? (1 Sam. 19:22); where is Jonathan's son? (2 Sam. 9:4); where are Ahimaaz and Jonathan? (2 Sam. 17:20).

b Where have you come from and where are you going? (Gen. 16:8); where are you from? (Gen. 29:4; John 19:9); where are you going? (John 13:36); no one asks me, 'Where are you going?' (John 16:5); where are they feeding the flock? (Gen. 37:16); I did not ask where he came from (Judg. 13:6); where did you glean today? (Ruth 2:19); where is the seer's house? (1 Sam. 9:18); where has your beloved gone? (S. of S. 6:1).

c Where is the Lord? (Jer. 2:6, 8).

d Where Christ was to be born (Matt. 2:4–6); no one knows where Christ comes from (John 7:27); we do not know where this man is from (John 9:29–30).

● Depositing

e Lay sins on the head of the goat (Lev. 16:21).

Lay hands on, see **378***t*.

188 Displacement

• Exile possible

a You and your king will come to a nation they have not known (Deut. 28:36); the Lord will uproot Israel and scatter them beyond the Euphrates (1 Kgs. 14:15); I will cut off Israel from the land (1 Kgs. 9:7); the Lord cast them into another land (Deut. 29:28); the land to which God has banished you (Deut. 30:1); if they are taken away to another land (1 Kgs. 8:46; 2 Chr. 6:36); if they pray in exile (1 Kgs. 8:48; 2 Chr. 6:37–8); till I take you away to a land like your own (2 Kgs. 18:32; Isa. 36:17); I will not remove Israel from the land if they obey (2 Chr. 33:8).

• Exile in prospect

b Prepare baggage for exile (Ezek. 12:3–7); they will go into exile (Ezek. 12:11); Gilgal will go into exile (Amos 5:5); you will go into exile beyond Damascus (Amos 5:27); they will be the first to go into exile (Amos 6:7); Israel will go into exile (Amos 7:11, 17); Judah will go into exile (Mic. 1:16); Judah will be carried into exile in Babylon (Jer. 20:4–6); I will remove you beyond Babylon (Acts 7:43); half of Jerusalem will be exiled (Zech. 14:2).

• Deportation

c Tiglath-pileser [Tilgath-pilneser] took captive to Assyria: part of Israel (2 Kgs. 15:29); Beerah (1 Chr. 5:6); the two and a half tribes (1 Chr. 5:26).

d Israel carried into exile to Assyria (2 Kgs. 17:6, 23; 18:11); the king of Aram took captives to Damascus (2 Chr. 28:5); Benjaminites going into exile (1 Chr. 8:6, 7); Judah carried into exile (2 Kgs. 24:14; 25:11, 21; 1 Chr. 9:1; 2 Chr. 36:20; Ezra 2:1; Jer. 13:19; 39:9; 40:1; 52:15; Lam. 1:3); the exile of Jerusalem (Jer. 1:3); the deportation to Babylon (Matt. 1:11, 12, 17); because you were delighted when Judah was sent into exile (Ezek. 25:3).

e My people go into exile for lack of knowledge (Isa. 5:13); you contended with them by exiling them (Isa. 27:8); I sent them into exile (Ezek. 39:28).

• Exiled people

f Manasseh was taken to Babylon (2 Chr. 33:11); Jehoiachin / Jeconiah was taken to Babylon (2 Chr. 36:10; Jer. 24:1; 27:20); Zedekiah taken to Babylon (Jer. 32:5; 52:11); Jehozadak the priest carried into exile (1 Chr. 6:15); chief people taken to Babylon (2 Kgs. 25:18–21); Jehoahaz was removed to Egypt (2 Kgs. 23:34; 2 Chr. 36:4); Mordecai was exiled from Jerusalem with Jeconiah (Esther 2:6); the number of those carried into exile (Jer. 52:28–30); I came to the exiles (Ezek. 3:15).

• Exiled foreigners

g Egypt to prepare for exile (Jer. 46:19); Milcom will go into exile (Jer. 49:3); the people of Aram will be exiled to Kir (Amos 1:5); the king of Ammon will go into exile (Amos 1:15).

h Damascus carried into exile into Assyria (2 Kgs. 16:9); aliens resettled in Samaria (2 Kgs. 17:24; Ezra 4:10); Thebes went into exile (Nahum 3:10).

• Sojourn

i Elimelech went to sojourn in Moab (Ruth 1:1).

189 Presence

God's presence

a God is here (Gen. 28:16); God is in her palaces (Ps. 48:3); the name of the city will be, The Lord Is There (Ezek. 48:35); the Lord was there (Ezek. 35:10); I am Gabriel who stand in the presence of God (Luke 1:19).

b You make him joyful with your presence (Ps. 21:6; Acts 2:28); in your presence is fulness of joy (Ps. 16:11); he stood in their midst (Luke 24:36).

c God is present everywhere (Ps. 139:7–9).
God with us, see **89***d*; **death due to God's prsence**, see **361***aa*.

Bread of the Presence

d The bread of the Presence [showbread] (Exod. 25:30; 35:13; 39:36; Num. 4:7; 1 Kgs. 7:48; 1 Chr. 23:29; 2 Chr. 2:4; 4:19; 13:11; Neh. 10:33); prepared by the Kohathites (1 Chr. 9:32); eaten by David (1 Sam. 21:6; Matt. 12:4; Mark 2:26; Luke 6:4).
Table of showbread, see **218***ae*.

190 Absence

God absent

a Where is your God? (Ps. 42:3, 10); where is their God? (Ps. 79:10; 115:2; Joel 2:17); where is the Lord your God? (Mic. 7:10); where is the Lord, God of Elijah? (2 Kgs. 2:14); where is God my Maker? (Job 35:10); is there no God in Israel? (2 Kgs. 1:3, 6, 16); is the Lord not in Zion? (Jer. 8:19); where are your gods? (Jer. 2:28).
No God, see **2***a*.

b God would not be in their midst (Exod. 33:3); the Lord is not with you (Num. 14:42–3; Deut. 1:42); the Lord is not with Israel (2 Chr. 25:7); is it not because God is not among us? (Deut. 31:17); you do not go out with our armies (Ps. 44:9; 60:10; 108:11); I go forward and backward but he is not there (Job 23:8).

c The Lord had departed from Saul (1 Sam. 16:14; 18:12; 28:15, 16).

People removed

d Cain went out from God's presence (Gen. 4:16); while we are at home in the body we are absent from the Lord (2 Cor. 5:6).

e Enoch was not, for God took him (Gen. 5:24); he is not here, but risen (Matt. 28:6).

People missing

f Saul could not be found (1 Sam. 10:21); Jonathan and his armour bearer were not there (1 Sam. 14:17); Thomas was not with them (John 20:24); if your father misses me (1 Sam. 20:6); you will be missed (1 Sam. 20:18); the prisoner was gone (1 Kgs. 20:40); why did you go to war without us? (Judg. 12:1); I am absent in body but with you in spirit (Col. 2:5).

g One tribe was cut off from Israel (Judg. 21:3, 6); no combatant was missing (Num. 31:49).

h My husband is not at home (Prov. 7:19); my beloved had gone (S. of S. 5:6).

i What is lacking cannot be counted (Eccles. 1:15).

- None to
  plead

j God saw that there was no one to intercede (Isa. 59:16); there is no one who calls on your name (Isa. 64:7).

- Uninhabited

k Your cities will be without inhabitant (Jer. 4:7; 9:11; 34:22); Jerusalem will be without inhabitant (Jer. 26:9; 33:10); no one will live in Edom (Jer. 49:18; Ezek. 35:9); no one will live in Hazor (Jer. 49:33); Babylon will not be inhabited (Isa. 13:20; Jer. 50:13, 40; 51:29).

l There was no man (Jer. 4:25); every city is forsaken (Jer. 4:29); the fortified city is empty (Isa. 27:10); the populous city is empty (Isa. 32:14).

- Empty

m The earth was formless and empty (Gen. 1:2); the city once full of people is deserted (Lam. 1:1); the highways were deserted (Judg. 5:6).

n Sisera wanted Jael to say no one was there (Judg. 4:20); there was no one in the Aramean camp (2 Kgs. 7:5, 10).

o The unclean spirit finds his house empty (Matt. 12:44); let his habitation be desolate and empty (Acts 1:20); the prison was empty (Acts 5:23); your seat will be empty (1 Sam. 20:18); David's place was empty (1 Sam. 20:25, 27); the ark was empty apart from the stone tablets (1 Kgs. 8:9; 2 Chr. 5:10).

191 Inhabitant

- Roman
  citizens

a Men who are Roman citizens (Acts 16:37–8); Paul was a Roman citizen (Acts 22:25–9; 23:27); a citizen of no mean city (Acts 21:39).

- Citizens
  of heaven

b Fellow-citizens with the saints (Eph. 2:19); our citizenship is in heaven (Phil. 3:20).

192 Abode: place of habitation or resort

- God's
  dwelling

a Your dwelling (Exod. 15:13, 17; 1 Kgs. 8:13); I love the place where your glory dwells (Ps. 26:8); how dear are your dwelling-places! (Ps. 84:1).

b Will God really dwell on earth? (1 Kgs. 8:27; 2 Chr. 6:18); who can build a house for him? (2 Chr. 2:6); God does not live in houses made by men (Acts 7:48; 17:24); God said he would dwell in thick cloud (1 Kgs. 8:12).

c You are being built into a dwelling of God by his Spirit (Eph. 2:22); that Christ may dwell in your hearts by faith (Eph. 3:17); Christ in you, the hope of glory (Col. 1:27); we are his house (Heb. 3:6); my Father and I will make our abode with him (John 14:23); the Spirit of God lives in you (1 Cor. 3:16).

d David sought a dwelling for God (Ps. 132:5; 2 Sam. 7:2; 1 Chr. 17:1; Acts 7:46); but he was not the one to build (2 Sam. 7:5; 1 Chr. 17:4); the site (1 Chr. 22:1); Solomon built (2 Sam. 7:13; 1 Chr. 22:10; 2 Chr. 6:2; Acts 7:47); come to your resting place (2 Chr. 6:41; Ps. 132:8); the house I built for your name (1 Kgs. 8:48).

- God lives
  with men

e I will dwell among the children of Israel (Exod. 29:45–6; Lev. 26:11; Num. 35:34; 1 Kgs. 6:13; Ezek. 37:27; 43:7, 9); I will live among you (Zech. 2:10); the camp where I live in their midst (Num. 5:3); I live in a high and holy place, also with him who is contrite (Isa. 57:15); the upright will dwell in your presence (Ps. 140:13); the dwelling-place of God is with men and he will live among them (Rev. 21:3); God gives the lonely a home (Ps. 68:6).

f The Word became flesh and dwelt among us (John 1:14); the Holy Spirit who lives within us (2 Tim. 1:14).

- Bethel

g Bethel, the house of God (Gen. 28:17–19, 22; 35:1, 15).

- God living in
  the tabernacle

h A sanctuary that I may live among them (Exod. 25:8); the Lord's tabernacle (Josh. 22:19).

Doorway of the tent of meeting, see **263d**.

- Shiloh

i The tent of meeting set up at Shiloh (Josh. 18:1); the house of God was at Shiloh (Judg. 18:31); the house of the Lord in Shiloh (1 Sam. 1:24); he forsook the tabernacle at Shiloh (Ps. 78:60); I will make this house like Shiloh (Jer. 26:6, 9).

- God lives in
  Jerusalem

j The Lord dwells in Jerusalem for ever (1 Chr. 23:25); the Lord dwells in Zion (Ps. 9:11; 76:2; Joel 3:17, 21; Zech. 8:3); the Lord wanted Zion for his habitation (Ps. 132:13–14).

Temple, see **990n**.

- Living
  with God

k I will dwell in the house of the Lord for ever (Ps. 23:6); all the days of my life (Ps. 27:4); let me live in your tent for ever (Ps. 61:4); you have been our dwelling-place throughout all generations (Ps. 90:1); the eternal God a dwelling-place (Deut. 33:27); better one day in your courts than a thousand elsewhere (Ps. 84:10); planted in the house of the Lord (Ps. 92:13); he who dwells in the shelter of the Most High (Ps. 91:1); if you make the Most High your dwelling (Ps. 91:9); Lord, who may dwell in your tent? (Ps. 15:1).

l In my Father's house are many dwelling-places (John 14:2); longing to be clothed with our heavenly dwelling, built by God (2 Cor. 5:1–4).

Abiding in Christ, see **224d**.

- Synagogue

m Jesus taught in synagogues (Matt. 9:35; 13:54; Mark 1:39; 6:2; Luke 4:15; 6:6; 13:10); Jesus preached in the synagogues of Judea (Luke 4:44); Jesus went into the synagogue (Matt. 12:9; Mark 1:21; 3:1; Luke 4:16); this he said in the synagogue at Capernaum (John 6:59); I always taught in synagogues (John 18:20).

n Barnabas and Paul preached in the synagogues in Salamis (Acts 13:5); on the sabbath they went to the synagogue in Pisidian Antioch (Acts 13:14); they entered the synagogue in Iconium (Acts 14:1); there was a synagogue in Thessalonica (Acts 17:1); they entered the synagogue at Berea (Acts 17:10); Paul reasoned in the synagogue at Athens (Acts 17:17); at Corinth (Acts 18:4);

at Ephesus (Acts 18:19; 19:8); Apollos spoke out boldly in the synagogue at Ephesus (Acts 18:26).

o Moses is read in the synagogues every sabbath (Acts 15:21); the centurion built our synagogue (Luke 7:5); Jairus, a ruler of the synagogue (Luke 8:41); the synagogue of the Freedmen (Acts 6:9); Paul asked for letters to the synagogues in Damascus (Acts 9:2).

p Hypocrites love to stand and pray in synagogues (Matt. 6:5); they love the chief seats in the synagogues (Matt. 23:6; Mark 12:39; Luke 11:43; 20:46).

q A synagogue of Satan (Rev. 2:9; 3:9); they burned all the meeting places of God in the land (Ps. 74:8).

- Persecution from synagogues

r They will flog you in their synagogues (Matt. 10:17; Mark 13:9); some you will scourge in your synagogues (Matt. 23:34); when they bring you before the synagogues (Luke 12:11; 21:12); in every synagogue I beat believers (Acts 22:19); in every synagogue I punished them (Acts 26:11).

s They will put you out of the synagogues (John 16:2); if any should confess Christ he would be put out of the synagogue (John 9:22); they did not confess him lest they be put out of the synagogue (John 12:42).

- Tents

t Those who lived in tents: Jabal (Gen. 4:20); Jacob (Gen. 25:27); Israel and Judah (2 Sam. 11:11); the Rechabites (Jer. 35:7); Abraham, Isaac and Jacob (Heb. 11:9); the ark (2 Sam. 6:17; 7:2, 6; 1 Chr. 15:1; 16:1; 17:1).

u Absalom had a tent pitched on the roof (2 Sam. 16:22); he will pitch his tents between the sea and the holy mountain (Dan. 11:45); I will make you live in tents again (Hos. 12:9).

v How lovely are your tents, Israel! (Num. 24:5); your tent will be secure (Job 5:24).

- Camping

w Locations of the tribes in the camp (Num. 2:2–34); camping tribe by tribe (Num. 24:2); where the cloud settled they would camp (Num. 9:17); God seeks out a place for you to camp (Deut. 1:33).

x David came to where Saul was camped (1 Sam. 26:5); Israel and Absalom camped in Gilead (2 Sam. 17:26).

- Booths

y Jacob made booths for his animals (Gen. 33:17); the Israelites lived in booths when they came out of Egypt (Lev. 23:43); the feast of booths (Lev. 23:34, 39–43; Neh. 8:14–17); three booths for Jesus, Moses and Elijah (Matt. 17:4; Mark 9:5; Luke 9:33).

z Like a hut in the field (Isa. 1:8).

- Houses

aa David lived in his house (2 Sam. 7:1); a house of cedar (2 Sam. 7:2; 1 Chr. 17:1); the House of the Forest of Lebanon (1 Kgs. 7:2; 10:17; 2 Chr. 9:16); when the Queen of Sheba saw the house he had built (1 Kgs. 10:4; 2 Chr. 9:3); those who wear soft clothes are in kings' houses (Matt. 11:8; Luke 7:25).

ab Consecrating your house to the Lord (Lev. 27:14).

ac Samuel's house was in Ramah (1 Sam. 7:17); Shimei was told to build a house in Jerusalem (1 Kgs. 2:36).

ad Houses which you did not fill (Deut. 6:11); is it time for you to live in your panelled houses? (Hag. 1:4); each of you is busy with his own house (Hag. 1:9); woe to him who builds a big house without righteousness (Jer. 22:13–14); summer houses, winter houses, houses of ivory will all be destroyed (Amos 3:15).

ae Leprosy in a house (Lev. 14:33–57).

af They led Jesus to the praetorium (John 18:28); Pilate entered the praetorium (John 18:33).

Building houses, see **164*t***; **caves**, see **255*f*.**

- **A place to live**

ag Is there place for us to stay? (Gen. 24:23–5).

ah Teacher, where do you live? (John 1:38–9); they stayed with him that day (John 1:39); Jesus lodged in Bethany (Matt. 21:17); today I must stay at your house (Luke 19:5); the Samaritans asked him to stay with them (John 4:40); stay with us for it is nearly evening (Luke 24:29); Lydia urged them to stay with her (Acts 16:15); prepare a guest room for me (Philem. 22).

ai Birds build nests in the trees (Ps. 104:17); birds nest in the branches (Ezek. 17:23; Matt. 13:32; Mark 4:32; Luke 13:19); sparrow and swallow find a place to nest in your temple (Ps. 84:3).

aj Badgers make homes in the rock (Prov. 30:26); wild animals living in places once inhabited (Isa. 13:21–2; 32:14; 34:11, 13–17).

ak Living in the tombs (Mark 5:3; Luke 8:27).

- **Homeless**

al Foxes have holes and birds nests, but Jesus had nowhere (Matt. 8:20; Luke 9:58); we apostles are homeless (1 Cor. 4:11).

193 Contents: things contained

194 Receptacle

- **The ark of the covenant**

a The ark made (Exod. 25:10–16; 31:7; 35:12; 37:1–5; 39:35; Deut. 10:1, 3); placed in the tent (Exod. 40:3, 21); anointed (Exod. 30:26); screened by the veil (Exod. 40:3, 21); covered with the veil (Num. 4:5); looked after by the Kohathites (Num. 3:31); containing manna (Exod. 16:32–4; Heb. 9:4); and Aaron's rod (Num. 17:10; Heb. 9:4); and the tablets (Deut. 10:5; Heb. 9:4).

Cover of the ark, see **226*l***; **ark of the Testimony**, see **466*i*.**

- **The ark moved around**

b The ark going before the Israelites (Num. 10:33, 35; Josh. 3:3, 6, 11); carried round Jericho (Josh. 6:4, 6, 8, 12–13); at Bethel (Judg. 20:27); brought into the camp (1 Sam. 4:3–6); captured (1 Sam. 4:11, 17, 21–2); causing havoc among the Philistines (1 Sam. 5:1–12); restored to Israel (1 Sam. 6:1–21); bringing death to the men who look inside (1 Sam. 6:19); brought to the house of Abinadab (1 Sam. 7:1); brought to enquire of God

(1 Sam. 14:18); in the house of Obed-edom (2 Sam. 6:10–11; 1 Chr. 13:13–14); with the army under shelter (2 Sam. 11:11); the ark in a tent (2 Sam. 7:2; 1 Chr. 15:1; 16:1; 17:1).

● The ark in Jerusalem

c David brought the ark up (2 Sam. 6:2–10, 12–17; 1 Chr. 13:3; 1 Chr. 15:3, 12, 25; 2 Chr. 1:4); despite unwillingness (2 Sam. 6:10); Abiathar had carried the ark before David (1 Kgs. 2:26); Asaph ministering before the ark (1 Chr. 16:37); the ark taken back when David fled (2 Sam. 15:24, 29).

● The ark in the temple

d David wanted to build a house for the ark (1 Chr. 28:2); the ark placed in the temple (1 Kgs. 6:19; 8:1–9; 1 Chr. 22:19; 2 Chr. 5:2–10; 6:11); to be left in the temple (2 Chr. 35:3); the priests took up the ark (1 Kgs. 8:3); Solomon stood before the ark (1 Kgs. 3:15); I have set a place for the ark (1 Kgs. 8:21).

e The ark of the covenant in the temple in heaven (Rev. 11:19).

● State of the ark

f Nothing in the ark except the stone tablets (1 Kgs. 8:9; 2 Chr. 5:10); men will no longer think of the ark of the covenant (Jer. 3:16).

● Temple utensils

g The utensils made for the table (Exod. 25:29; 37:16); for the altar of burnt offering (Exod. 27:3; 38:3); the utensils made for the temple (2 Chr. 4:8, 11); the plan for the utensils of the temple (1 Chr. 28:13–18); Hiram made the basins, shovels and bowls (1 Kgs. 7:40, 45); cups, snuffers, bowls and spoons (1 Kgs. 7:50); pails, shovels and forks (2 Chr. 4:16); the rest of the money was made into utensils (2 Chr. 24:14); the money was not used for making utensils (2 Kgs. 12:13).

h Each tribal leader offered a silver dish, a silver bowl, one gold pan (Num. 7:13–14, 19–20, 25–6, 31–2, 37–8, 43–4, 49–50, 55–6, 61–2, 67–8, 73–4, 79–80); twelve plates, bowls and ladles for the dedication of the altar (Num. 7:84–6).

i A jar with an omer of manna (Exod. 16:33); the gold objects put in a box beside the ark (1 Sam. 6:8, 11, 15).

j Levites looked after the utensils (1 Chr. 9:28–9); utensils carried on the table (Num. 4:7); you who bear the vessels of the Lord (Isa. 52:11).

k Ahaz cut them in pieces (2 Chr. 28:24); Nebuchadnezzar cut in pieces the gold vessels (2 Kgs. 24:13); taken away to Babylon (2 Kgs. 25:14–15; Jer. 52:18–19; Dan. 1:2); Belshazzar's guests drank from the vessels of the temple (Dan. 5:2–3, 23); the vessels of the Lord's house will not soon be brought back (Jer. 27:16–22); will the vessels be brought back within two years? (Jer. 28:3); the utensils restored (Ezra 1:9–10; 5:14; 6:5; 7:19); Ezra weighed out the utensils (Ezra 8:25–30).

● Various vessels

l Joseph's silver cup (Gen. 44:2–17); basins and vessels were brought for David (2 Sam. 17:28); all Solomon's drinking vessels were gold (1 Kgs. 10:21; 2 Chr. 9:20); drinks were served in golden vessels (Esther 1:7); borrow as many empty vessels as you can (2 Kgs. 4:3).

m Open vessels unclean due to a corpse (Num. 19:15); Gideon's men had empty pitchers (Judg. 7:16, 19–20); Jeremiah and the earthenware jar (Jer. 19:1–13); the deed placed in an earthenware jar (Jer. 32:14); John the Baptist's head on a platter (Matt. 14:8, 11; Mark 6:25, 28).

n On boiling the sin offering, an earthenware vessel must be broken, a bronze vessel scoured (Lev. 6:28).

o Parable of the boiling pot (Ezek. 24:3–14); I see a boiling pot (Jer. 1:13); this is the pot and we are the meat (Ezek. 11:3); this is the pot and the slain are the meat (Ezek. 24:3–14).

p Many types of vessels, to honour and dishonour (2 Tim. 2:20).

q Who can tip the water jars of heaven? (Job 38:37); seven golden bowls full of the wrath of God (Rev. 15:7).

r They took worn-out wineskins (Josh. 9:4); I am like a wineskin in the smoke (Ps. 119:83); new wine into old wineskins (Matt. 9:17; Mark 2:22; Luke 5:37–8).

● Containers   *s* Moses in a reed basket (Exod. 2:3); Paul was lowered in a basket (Acts 9:25; 2 Cor. 11:33); sacks for grain (Gen. 42:25, 27–8, 35; 43:12, 18, 21–3; 44:1–2, 8, 11–12); David put the stones in his bag (1 Sam. 17:40); they broaden their phylacteries (Matt. 23:5).

● Rooms   *t* An inner chamber of the tower of Shechem (Judg. 9:46, 49); side chambers round the temple (1 Kgs. 6:5; 1 Chr. 28:11–12); rooms in the temple were used to store the tithe (2 Chr. 31:11–12); a room in the temple for Tobiah (Neh. 13:5, 7); side chambers in the house of the forest of Lebanon (1 Kgs. 7:3); the hall of pillars (1 Kgs. 7:6); the hall of the throne (1 Kgs. 7:7); where is my guest room? (Mark 14:14; Luke 22:11); a large upper room (Mark 14:15; Luke 22:12; Acts 1:13); the Shunammite woman made an upper room for Elisha (2 Kgs. 4:10); prepare a guest room for me (Philem. 22); go to your room and pray in secret (Matt. 6:6).

● Decks   *u* Noah's ark had three decks (Gen. 6:16).

Section three: Dimensions

---

195 Size

● Dimensions   *a* Dimensions of: Noah's ark (Gen. 6:15); ark of the covenant (Exod. 25:10; 37:1); mercy seat (Exod. 25:17; 37:6); table (Exod. 25:23; 37:10); linen curtains (Exod. 26:2; 36:9); goats' hair curtains (Exod. 26:8; 36:15); boards (Exod. 26:16; 36:21); bronze altar (Exod. 27:1; 2 Chr. 4:1; Ezek. 43:13–17); court (Exod. 27:9–18; 38:9–18); breastpiece (Exod. 28:16); altar of incense (Exod. 30:2; 37:25); the temple (1 Kgs. 6:2–3, 17; 2 Chr. 3:3–4); the rebuilt temple (Ezra 6:3); Ezekiel's temple (Ezek. 40:5–42:20); the holy of holies (2 Chr. 3:8); the cherubim (1 Kgs. 6:23–6; 2 Chr. 3:11–13); pillars of the temple (1 Kgs. 7:15; 2 Kgs. 25:17; Jer. 52:21); capitals of the pillars (1 Kgs.

7:16; Jer. 52:22); the 'sea' (1 Kgs. 7:23; 2 Chr. 4:2); each stand (1 Kgs. 7:27); openings at the top of each stand (1 Kgs. 7:31); wheels of the stands (1 Kgs. 7:32); the lavers (1 Kgs. 7:38); the house of the forest of Lebanon (1 Kgs. 7:2); the hall of pillars (1 Kgs. 7:6); the flying scroll (Zech. 5:2).

b Each storey was five cubits high (1 Kgs. 6:10); stones eight and ten cubits long (1 Kgs. 7:10); a gallows 50 cubits high (Esther 5:14; 7:9).

- Capacity

c The 'sea' held 2000 baths (1 Kgs. 7:26); 3000 baths (2 Chr. 4:5); each basin held 40 baths (1 Kgs. 7:38).
Volume measures, see **465c.**

- Fat things

d Seven fat cows (Gen. 41:2, 4, 18, 20); seven plump ears (Gen. 41:5–6, 22, 24).

e Israel grew fat and kicked (Deut. 32:15); Eglon was very fat (Judg. 3:17); they were fatter than the other youths (Dan. 1:15); you have fattened yourselves in a day of slaughter (Jas. 5:5).

- Tall people

f Saul was a head taller than anyone else (1 Sam. 9:2; 10:23); do not look at his height (1 Sam. 16:7); a nation tall and smooth (Isa. 18:2, 7).

- Giants

g There were giants in those days (Gen. 6:4); the giants, the sons of Anak, before whom we were like grasshoppers (Num. 13:22, 28, 32–3); the people, sons of the Anakim, are bigger and taller than we (Deut. 1:28); tall sons of the Anakim (Deut. 9:2); Joshua destroyed the Anakim (Josh. 11:21–2); the Anakim were there (Josh. 14:12, 15); Caleb drove out the three sons of Anak (Josh. 15:13–14; Judg. 1:20); I destroyed before them the Amorites, tall as cedars (Amos 2:9).

h Those tall as the Anakim: Emim (Deut. 2:10–11); Zamzummim (Deut. 2:20–1).

i Goliath's height was six cubits and a span (1 Sam. 17:4); Lahmi, brother of Goliath (1 Chr. 20:5); Ishi-benob, a descendant of the giants (2 Sam. 21:16); as was Saph (2 Sam. 21:18); and others (1 Chr. 20:4–8); at Gath was a very tall man (2 Sam. 21:20; 1 Chr. 20:6); an Egyptian five cubits tall (1 Chr. 11:23).
Killing giants, see **362y.**

196 Littleness

- Short

a A dwarf could not serve as priest (Lev. 21:20); Zacchaeus was short in stature (Luke 19:3); the Lord's hand is not too short to save (Isa. 59:1).

b Four things small but wise, ants, badgers, locusts, lizards (Prov. 30:24–8); we were like grasshoppers (Num. 13:33); the inhabitants of the earth are like grasshoppers (Isa. 40:22).

- Thin

c I have become thin (Ps. 109:24); the fatness of Jacob will become lean (Isa. 17:4).

d Seven thin cows (Gen. 41:3–4, 19–20, 27); seven thin ears (Gen. 41:6, 23–4, 27).

- Small

e The bronze altar was too small for all the offerings (1 Kgs. 8:64; 2 Chr. 7:7); where we live is too small for us (2 Kgs. 6:1); Zoar, a little town (Gen. 19:20, 22); Benjamin, the smallest tribe (1 Sam. 9:21); I have made you small among the nations (Jer. 49:15); a cloud as small as a man's hand (1 Kgs. 18:44).

f Mustard seed is the smallest seed (Matt. 13:31; Mark 4:31); if you have faith as a grain of mustard seed (Matt. 17:20; Luke 17:6); the kingdom of God is like a grain of mustard seed (Luke 13:19).

g Why notice the speck in your brother's eye? (Matt. 7:3–5; Luke 6:41–2); not a jot or tittle shall pass from the law (Matt. 5:18; Luke 16:17).

h The bed is too short and the blanket too narrow (Isa. 28:20).

197 Expansion

- Enlarge

a May God enlarge Japheth (Gen. 9:27); enlarge my border (1 Chr. 4:10); enlarge the place of your tent (Isa. 54:2–3); if God enlarges your territory (Deut. 19:8); you have extended the borders of the land (Isa. 26:15).

- Spread

b Leprosy spreads in the skin (Lev. 13:7–8, 22, 27, 35); or in a garment (Lev. 13:51).

198 Contraction

- Reduce

a The Lord began to reduce Israel (2 Kgs. 10:32); God has shrivelled me up (Job 16:8).

199 Distance

- From far away

a The Gibeonites said they had come from a far country (Josh. 9:6, 9, 22); the queen of Sheba came from the ends of the earth to hear the wisdom of Solomon (Matt. 12:42; Luke 11:31); from a far country, from Babylon (2 Kgs. 20:14; Isa. 39:3); the Lord's army is coming from a far country (Isa. 13:5).

- Going far away

b I will send you far away to the Gentiles (Acts 22:21); the prodigal son went into a far country (Luke 15:13); a man went into a far country to receive a kingdom (Luke 19:12); however far away I go, your hand leads me (Ps. 139:9–10).

c Do not go very far (Exod. 8:28).

- At a distance

d Laban put a three-days journey between the flocks (Gen. 30:36); the people stood at a distance (Exod. 20:18, 21); they were afraid to come near Moses (Exod. 34:30); he withdrew from them about a stone's throw (Luke 22:41).

e You will see the land at a distance (Deut. 32:52); they saw Joseph from a distance (Gen. 37:18); seen the promises from a distance (Heb. 11:13).

f Peter followed at a distance (Matt. 26:58; Mark 14:54); women looking on from a distance (Matt. 27:55; Mark 15:40; Luke

23:49); seeing Jesus from a distance (Mark 5:6); 10 lepers stood at a distance (Luke 17:12).

g If the arrows are beyond you, go (1 Sam. 20:22); the arrow is beyond you (1 Sam. 20:37).

h Keep far away from the adulteress (Prov. 5:8).

i As far as the east is from the west, so far has he removed our transgressions (Ps. 103:12); this far the Lord has helped us (1 Sam. 7:12).

● Particular distances

j About 200 cubits from land (John 21:8); pasture lands 1000 cubits from the city wall (Num. 35:4–5); 2000 cubits between you and the ark (Josh. 3:4).

k The Mount of Olives was a sabbath day's journey from Jerusalem (Acts 1:12); Emmaus was 60 stadia from Jerusalem (Luke 24:13); Bethany is about two miles from Jerusalem (John 11:18); blood for a distance of 1600 stadia (Rev. 14:20); if someone forces you to go one mile, go two (Matt. 5:41).

● God far away

l Why do you stand far off? (Ps. 10:1); the Lord is far from the wicked (Prov. 15:29); the rich man in Hades saw Abraham far away (Luke 16:23).

● Far from God

m The exiles had gone far from God (Ezek. 11:15); their heart is far from God (Matt. 15:8; Mark 7:6); you are near to their lips but far from their heart (Jer. 12:2); they are far from your law (Ps. 119:150); they went far from me (Jer. 2:5); the promise is to those far off (Acts 2:39); you who are far off, hear what I have done (Isa. 33:13); you who were far off (Eph. 2:13, 17); while he was far off his father ran to him (Luke 15:20); peace to the far and near (Isa. 57:19).

200 Nearness

● God near

a God brought the Levites near himself (Num. 16:9–10); no plague when they come near the sanctuary (Num. 8:19); only Moses was to approach God (Exod. 24:2); the Lord spoke with Moses face to face (Exod. 33:11; Num. 12:8; Deut. 34:10); the Lord spoke to Israel face to face (Deut. 5:4); I have seen God face to face (Gen. 32:30); what nation has a god so near as the Lord is to us? (Deut. 4:7); the children of Israel, a people near to him (Ps. 148:14); you are near, Lord (Ps. 119:151); the Lord is near to all who call on him (Ps. 145:18); he is not far from each of us (Acts 17:27); the Lord is at hand (Phil. 4:5); do not be far from me (Ps. 22:11, 19); am I a God near at hand and not far off? (Jer. 23:23); then we will see face to face (1 Cor. 13:12).

b It is good for me to be near God (Ps. 73:28); the Lord will bring near those whom he chooses (Num. 16:5); blessed is the one you choose and bring near (Ps. 65:4).

c You who are near, acknowledge my might (Isa. 33:13); call on him while he is near (Isa. 55:6).

d The kingdom is near (Matt. 3:2; 4:17; 10:7; Mark 1:15; Luke

10:9, 11; 21:31); the word is near you (Deut. 30:11–14; Rom. 10:8); the Lord is at hand (Phil. 4:5).

- Drawing
  near to God

e You are not far from the kingdom (Mark 12:34); peace to those who were near (Isa. 57:19; Eph. 2:17); those far off have been brought near through the blood of Christ (Eph. 2:13); a better hope by which we draw near to God (Heb. 7:19); those who draw near to God through him (Heb. 7:25); come near to God (Heb. 10:22; Jas. 4:8); let us draw near with confidence to the throne of grace (Heb. 4:16); draw near, nations (Isa. 34:1).

f They delight in drawing near to God! (Isa. 58:2); Jerusalem did not draw near to God (Zeph. 3:2).

- Drawing near
  to Jesus

g Bring them to me (Matt. 14:18); bring him here to me (Matt. 17:17; Mark 9:19); they brought children to Jesus (Matt. 19:13).

- Close to
  people

h Joseph told his brothers to come closer (Gen. 45:4); let us look one another in the face (2 Kgs. 14:8); better a neighbour who is near than a friend far away (Prov. 27:10); Zedekiah will speak to the king of Babylon face to face (Jer. 32:4; 34:3).

i The Gibeonites were near neighbours (Josh. 9:16, 22).

j If the arrows are on this side, come (1 Sam. 20:21); why go so near the city wall? (2 Sam. 11:20–1).

k Do not come near me for I am holier than you (Isa. 65:5).

- Neighbours

l Love your neighbour as yourself (Lev. 19:18; Matt. 22:39; Mark 12:31; Luke 10:27); love your neighbour and hate your enemy (Matt. 5:43); who is my neighbour? (Luke 10:29); which one proved to be neighbour? (Luke 10:36).
Love your neighbour, see **887t**.

- The end
  is near

m The day of their calamity is near (Deut. 32:35); the end of all things is at hand (1 Pet. 4:7); the coming of the Lord is near (Jas. 5:8); he is near, at the very gates (Matt. 24:33; Mark 13:29); your redemption is drawing near (Luke 21:28).

201 Gap

- Chasm

a Between us and you a great chasm is fixed (Luke 16:26).

202 Contiguity

Neighbours, see **200l**.

203 Length

See **195**.

204 Shortness

Short, see **204a**.

205 Breadth. Thickness

- Handbreadth
- Broad

a The 'sea' was a handbreadth thick (1 Kgs. 7:26; 2 Chr. 4:5).

b The broad way leads to destruction (Matt. 7:13).

206 Narrowness. Thinness

● Narrow   *a* Balaam's donkey on narrow paths (Num. 22:24, 26); enter by the narrow gate that leads to life (Matt. 7:13–14); strive to enter by the narrow door (Luke 13:24).

● Neck   *b* Your neck is like the tower of David (S. of S. 4:4); your neck is like a tower of ivory (S. of S. 7:4).

207 Layer

● Boards   *a* Boards for the tabernacle (Exod. 26:15–25; 36:20–30; 39:33); the altar made of boards (Exod. 27:8); carried by the Merarites (Num. 4:31); some got to shore on planks (Acts 27:44).

● Plates   *b* Censers beaten into plates for the altar (Num. 16:38–9).

208 Filament

● Cord / thread   *a* The plate fastened to the turban with a blue cord (Exod. 28:37; 39:31); before the silver cord is broken (Eccles. 12:6).

   b Gold sheets cut into thread (Exod. 39:3).

● Rope   *c* Rahab let the spies down by a rope (Josh. 2:15); scarlet cord tied to the window (Josh. 2:18, 21); seven fresh bowstrings (Judg. 16:7–9); Samson bound with new ropes (Judg. 15:13; 16:11); we will bring ropes to that city (2 Sam. 17:13); let us put ropes on our heads (1 Kgs. 20:31–2).

209 Height

● Highness   *a* God is higher than the heavens (Job 22:12); as high as the heavens his lovingkindness is great (Ps. 103:11); as the heavens are higher than the earth, so are God's ways higher than man's (Isa. 55:9); your righteousness is like great mountains (Ps. 36:6).

   b I am from above (John 8:23).

   God is exalted, see **866g**.

● Heights   *c* The eagle nests high on the cliff (Job 39:27–8); though you make your nest as high as the eagle's (Jer. 49:16; Obad. 4).

   d Get up on a high mountain, bearer of good news (Isa. 40:9); a city set on a hill cannot be hid (Matt. 5:14).

   e Neither height nor depth can separate us from the love of God (Rom. 8:39).

● Mountains in general   *f* The mountains rose and the valleys sank (Ps. 104:8); the mountains were covered by the flood (Gen. 7:20).

   g Their gods are gods of the mountains (1 Kgs. 20:23, 28); I lift up my eyes to the hills (Ps. 121:1); the high mountains are for the wild goats (Ps. 104:18).

   h I am against you, destroying mountain (Jer. 51:25); prophesy to the mountains of Israel (Ezek. 36:1–8); the mountains and hills will sing for joy (Isa. 55:12).

● Removing mountains   *i* Before Zerubbabel the mountain will become a plain (Zech. 4:7); God removes mountains (Job 9:5); every mountain will be made low (Isa. 40:4; Luke 3:5); the mountain will move when commanded (Matt. 17:20; 21:21; Mark 11:23); if I have faith to remove mountains (1 Cor. 13:2); every mountain was removed (Rev. 6:14; 16:20); mountains melt before the Lord (Ps. 97:5; Mic. 1:4); though the mountains slip into the sea (Ps. 46:2–3); touch the mountains so that they smoke (Ps. 144:5); the mountains skipped like rams (Ps. 114:4, 6); that the mountains might quake at your presence! (Isa. 64:1); the mountains may shift but my love will not (Isa. 54:10).

- Escape to the mountains

j They will call on mountains and hills to cover them (Hos. 10:8; Luke 23:30; Rev. 6:15–16); escape to the mountains! (Gen. 19:17, 19); Lot lived in the mountains (Gen. 19:30).

- Mount Sinai

k Mount Sinai (Exod. 19:2–23; 34:2–4; Neh. 9:13) also called Mount Horeb (Deut. 1:6, 19; 4:10); the burning bush on Mount Sinai (Exod. 3:1–2; Acts 7:30); the angel spoke to Moses on Mount Sinai (Acts 7:38); the Lord came from Sinai (Deut. 33:2); the mountain of God (Exod. 4:27; 18:5); you will worship at this mountain (Exod. 3:12); the Lord made a covenant with us at Horeb (Deut. 5:2); Sinai quaked (Judg. 5:5); you have been long enough at this mountain (Deut. 1:6); you have circled this mountain long enough (Deut. 2:3); Elijah came to Horeb, the mountain of God (1 Kgs. 19:8); Mount Sinai corresponds to the present Jerusalem (Gal. 4:24–5); you have not come to a mountain burning with fire (Heb. 12:18–21).

- Mount Zion

l The mountain of the house of the Lord (Isa. 2:2–3; Mic. 4:1); Mount Zion where you dwell (Ps. 74:2); the mountain where God chooses to live (Ps. 68:16); the mountain of the Lord of hosts will be called the holy mountain (Zech. 8:3); his holy mountain (Ps. 3:4); the city of our God, his holy mountain (Ps. 48:1–2); the holy mountain at Jerusalem (Isa. 27:13); Jerusalem, your holy mountain (Dan. 9:16); you have come to Mount Zion, the heavenly Jerusalem (Heb. 12:22); the Lamb stood on Mount Zion (Rev. 14:1).

m Mount Zion which he loves (Ps. 78:68); the Lord loves the gates of Zion (Ps. 87:2); Mount Zion, the place of the name of the Lord (Isa. 18:7); dwelling in Zion, my holy mountain (Joel 3:17); the Lord will reign on Mount Zion and in Jerusalem (Isa. 24:23).

n Let them bring me to your holy hill (Ps. 43:3); who may live on your holy hill? (Ps. 15:1); I have set my king on Zion, my holy mountain (Ps. 2:6); the house of Israel will serve me on my holy mountain (Ezek. 20:40).

o Its foundations is in the holy mountains (Ps. 87:1); those who trust in the Lord are like Mount Zion (Ps. 125:1); like mountains round Jerusalem so the Lord surrounds his people (Ps. 125:2).
Jerusalem, see **184***af*.

- Mountain of God

p Tyre, you were on the holy mountain of God (Ezek. 28:14); I cast you from the mountain of God (Ezek. 28:16).

- **The mount of Olives**

  q David went up the Mount of Olives (2 Sam. 15:30); the mount of Olives (Matt. 21:1; 24:3; 26:30; Mark 11:1; 13:3; 14:26; Luke 19:29; 19:37; 21:37; 22:39; John 8:1; Acts 1:12); the mountain east of the city (Ezek. 11:23); the mount of Olives will be split (Zech. 14:4).

- **Mount Moriah**

  r Isaac offered on Mount Moriah (Gen. 22:2); the temple built on Mount Moriah (2 Chr. 3:1).

- **Jesus' mountains**

  s The devil took Jesus to a high mountain (Matt. 4:8); the sermon on the mount (Matt. 5:1–7:27); the mount of transfiguration (Matt. 17:1; Mark 9:2; Luke 9:28); the holy mountain (2 Pet. 1:18); Jesus went up a mountain (Matt. 15:29; John 6:3); Jesus went into the mountains (Mark 3:13); Jesus went into a mountain to pray (Mark 6:46; Luke 6:12; 9:28); he withdrew to the mountain (John 6:15); a mountain in Galilee (Matt. 28:16).

- **Various named mountains**

  t The ark rested on Mount Ararat (Gen. 8:4); Aaron died on Mount Hor (Num. 20:22–8; 33:37–41); Moses viewed the land from Mount Nebo/Abarim (Num. 27:12; Deut. 32:49–50); Jotham shouted from Mount Gerizim (Judg. 9:7); Abijah shouted from Mount Zemaraim (2 Chr. 13:4).

  u Mount: Baalah (Josh. 15:11); Carmel (1 Kgs. 18:20; 2 Kgs. 4:25); Ebal (Deut. 11:29; 27:4, 13; Josh. 8:30, 33); Ephron (Josh. 15:9); Gaash (Josh. 24:30); Gerizim (Deut. 11:29; 27:12; Josh. 8:33; Judg. 9:7); Gilboa (2 Sam. 1:6, 21); Gilead (Judg. 7:3); Halak (Josh. 11:17); Hermon [Sion] (Deut. 4:48; Josh. 11:17; 12:1, 5; 13:5, 11; Ps. 42:6; Ps. 89:12); Hor (Num. 34:7–8); Jearim (Josh. 15:10); Mizar (Ps. 42:6); Nebo (Deut. 34:1); Paran (Hab. 3:3); Perazim (Isa. 28:21); Pisgah (Deut. 3:17, 27; 4:49; Josh. 12:3); Seir (Deut. 1:2; 2:1–5; Josh. 15:10; 24:4; Ezek. 35:2–15); Tabor (Judg. 4:6, 12, 14; Ps. 89:12); Zalmon (Judg. 9:48).

  v The mountains of Abarim (Num. 33:48); the mountains of Bashan (Ps. 68:15); the hill of Ammah (2 Sam. 2:24); the hill of Hachilah (1 Sam. 26:3); the hill of Moreh (Judg. 7:1); the hill of Samaria (1 Kgs. 16:24); our fathers worshipped in this mountain (John 4:20); Areopagus—Mars' hill (Acts 17:19, 22).

- **Unnamed mountains**

  w A crag on each side of the pass (1 Sam. 14:4); the forces were on opposing mountains (1 Sam. 17:3); David was on one side of the mountain and Saul on the other (1 Sam. 23:26); David shouted from a distant mountain (1 Sam. 26:13).

  x The mountain of your inheritance (Exod. 15:17); in visions the Lord set me on a very high mountain (Ezek. 40:2); he carried me away in the Spirit to a high mountain (Rev. 21:10); a burning mountain was thrown into the sea (Rev. 8:8).

  y The seven heads are seven hills (Rev. 17:9).

- **Mounds**

  z A heap of stones: at Galeed (Gen. 31:46–52); over Achan (Josh. 7:26); over the king of Ai (Josh. 8:29); over Absalom (2 Sam. 18:17).

  aa Heaps of the tithe (2 Chr. 31:6–9); two heaps of heads (2 Kgs.

10:8); the waters stood in a heap (Exod. 15:8; Josh. 3:13, 16; Ps. 33:7; 78:13).

ab Cities on mounds (Josh. 11:13); they cast up a mound against the city (2 Sam. 20:15).

● Sacrificing on high places

ac Balak brought Balaam to the high places of Baal (Num. 22:41); a sacrifice on the high place (1 Sam. 9:12–14); the high place at Gibeath-elohim (1 Sam. 10:5); Gibeon was the great high place (1 Kgs. 3:4); the tabernacle was at the high place at Gibeon (1 Chr. 21:29); Solomon went to the high place at Gibeon (2 Chr. 1:3); the people sacrificed at the high places (1 Kgs. 3:2; 22:43; 2 Chr. 33:17); as did Solomon (1 Kgs. 3:3); and Ahaz (2 Kgs. 16:4; 2 Chr. 28:4); the high places were not removed (1 Kgs. 15:14; 2 Kgs. 12:3; 14:4; 15:4, 35; 2 Chr. 15:17; 20:33).

ad Sacrificing on every high hill (Ezek. 20:28); they sacrifice on the tops of mountains (Hos. 4:13); why the high place Bamah? (Ezek. 20:29); if he eats on the mountains (Ezek. 18:11); if he does not eat on the mountains (Ezek. 18:6, 15); Moab has gone to the high places to weep (Isa. 15:2).

● Building high places

ae They built high places (1 Kgs. 14:23; 2 Kgs. 17:9); Solomon built a high place for Chemosh and Molech (1 Kgs. 11:7); Jeroboam built houses on the high places (1 Kgs. 12:31; 13:32); Jehoram made high places (2 Chr. 21:11); Ahaz built high places (2 Chr. 28:25); Manasseh rebuilt the high places (2 Kgs. 21:3; 2 Chr. 33:3, 19); they have built the high places of Topheth (Jer. 7:31); they built the high places of Baal (Jer. 19:5; 32:35).

● Worship on high places

af Priests of the high places (1 Kgs. 12:32; 13:33; 2 Kgs. 17:32; 23:9); they put their own gods in the houses of the high places (2 Kgs. 17:29).

● Destroying high places

ag The hills are a deception (Jer. 3:23); I will destroy your high places (Lev. 26:30; Ezek. 6:3); demolish their high places (Num. 33:52); destroy worship places on mountains and hills (Deut. 12:2).

ah Those who removed the high places: Asa (2 Chr. 14:3, 5); Jehoshaphat (2 Chr. 17:6); Hezekiah (2 Kgs. 18:4, 22; 2 Chr. 31:1; 32:12); Josiah (2 Chr. 34:3).

ai Josiah defiled the high places (2 Kgs. 23:8, 13); Josiah removed the houses of the high places (2 Kgs. 23:19).

● Towers

aj Count her towers (Ps. 48:12); anyone who wants to build a tower must count the cost (Luke 14:28).

ak Uzziah built towers in Jerusalem (2 Chr. 26:9); Uzziah built towers in the wilderness (2 Chr. 26:10); Jotham built towers (2 Chr. 27:4); they will break down Tyre's towers (Ezek. 26:4, 9).

al The tower of: Babel (Gen. 11:4–5); David (S. of S. 4:4); the Furnaces (Neh. 3:11; 12:38); Hananel (Neh. 3:1; 12:39; Jer. 31:38; Zech. 14:10); the Hundred (Neh. 3:1; 12:39); Penuel

(Judg. 8:9, 17); Shechem (Judg. 9:46–9); Siloam (Luke 13:4); Thebez (Judg. 9:51–2).

am The devil set him on the pinnacle of the temple (Matt. 4:5; Luke 4:9).

an The Lord is a tower of salvation (2 Sam. 22:51); you have been a strong tower (Ps. 61:3); the name of the Lord is a strong tower (Prov. 18:10).

210 Lowness

● Underneath

a Underneath are the everlasting arms (Deut. 33:27).
Under God's wings, see **271***d*.

● Under
the sun

b Nothing new under the sun (Eccles. 1:9); no profit under the sun (Eccles. 1:3; 2:11); under the sun (Eccles. 2:17; 4:1, 7, 15; 6:1, 12; 9:6, 9, 13; 10:5).

c Under heaven (Eccles. 1:13; 2:3; 3:1).

211 Depth

● Deep
places

a Can you search the depths of God? (Job 11:7); the inward mind and heart of a man are deep (Ps. 64:6); have you explored the subterranean regions? (Job 38:16–17); put out into deep water (Luke 5:4); the well is deep (John 4:11).

b Neither height nor depth can separate us from the love of God (Rom. 8:39); the Spirit searches the depths of God (1 Cor. 2:10); the deep things of Satan (Rev. 2:24).

● Sounding
depths

c The sailors took soundings (Acts 27:28); 20 fathoms, then 15 fathoms (Acts 27:28); water ankle-deep (Ezek. 47:3); knee-deep (Ezek. 47:4); deep enough to swim in (Ezek. 47:5).

212 Shallowness

● No depth

a On rocky ground there was no depth of soil (Matt. 13:5; Mark 4:5).

213 Summit

● Top

a David approached the summit (2 Sam. 15:32; 16:1).

b The capitals of the pillars (1 Kgs. 7:16–20, 41; 2 Chr. 4:12–13).

● Heads

c The head cannot say it does not need the feet (1 Cor. 12:21).

d Do not swear by your head (Matt. 5:36); his head is like gold (S. of S. 5:11); your head crowns you like Carmel (S. of S. 7:5).

e Oil on the head of the cleansed leper (Lev. 14:18, 29); she poured the perfume on Jesus' head (Matt. 26:7; Mark 14:3).
Lifting heads, see **310***j*.

f My head, my head! (2 Kgs. 4:19).

g A donkey's head cost 80 shekels (2 Kgs. 6:25); a leopard with four heads (Dan. 7:6).

h You will be the head and not the tail (Deut. 28:13); the alien will be the head and you the tail (Deut. 28:44).

i The husband is the head of the wife (Eph. 5:23); Christ is the

head of every man, the husband is the head of the wife, God is the head of Christ (1 Cor. 11:3); Christ is the head of all rule and authority (Col. 2:10); Christ is the head of the church (Eph. 1:22; 5:23; Col. 1:18); the whole body is fitted to the head (Eph. 4:16; Col. 2:19); grow up into Christ, the head (Eph. 4:15).
Severed heads, see **363*j*.**

- Roof
j Make a parapet for your roof (Deut. 22:8); they made an opening in the roof (Mark 2:4; Luke 5:19).

k The spies were hidden on the roof (Josh. 2:6, 8); they fled to the roof of the tower (Judg. 9:51); 3000 people were on the roof (Judg. 16:27); Samuel spoke to Saul on the roof (1 Sam. 9:26); a tent pitched on the roof (2 Sam. 16:22); why have you all gone up to the housetops? (Isa. 22:1); let him on the housetop not go down (Matt. 24:17; Mark 13:15; Luke 17:31).

214 Base

- Earth's foundation
a God marked out the foundations of the earth (Prov. 8:29); God laid the foundation of the earth (Job 38:4, 6); the earth's foundations were laid bare (2 Sam. 22:16; Ps. 18:15); earth's foundations shake (Isa. 24:18).

b If the foundations are destroyed, what can the righteous do? (Ps. 11:3).

- City foundation
c Laying Jericho's foundation cost the firstborn (Josh. 6:26; 1 Kgs. 16:34); on the foundations were the names of the twelve apostles (Rev. 21:14); the foundation stones were adorned with precious stones (Rev. 21:19–20).

- Temple foundation
d Large stones for the foundation of the temple (1 Kgs. 5:17); laying the foundation of the temple in the time of: Solomon (1 Kgs. 6:37; 2 Chr. 3:3); Ezra (Ezra 3:10–12; 5:16).

- Church foundation
e God's foundation stands (2 Tim. 2:19); no other foundation but Christ (1 Cor. 3:11); Christ as the cornerstone (Eph. 2:20); the stone rejected by the builders has become the head of the corner (Ps. 118:22; Matt. 21:42; Mark 12:10; Luke 20:17; Acts 4:11; 1 Pet. 2:7); I am laying in Zion a precious cornerstone for the foundation (Isa. 28:16; 1 Pet. 2:6).

f On the foundation of the apostles and prophets (Eph. 2:20); on this rock I will build my church (Matt. 16:18); I laid a foundation (1 Cor. 3:10).

215 Vertical

- Plumb line
a I will stretch over Jerusalem the plumb line of Samaria and Ahab (2 Kgs. 21:13); a plumb line amongst Israel (Amos 7:7–8); the plumb line in the hand of Zerubbabel (Zech. 4:10); I will make righteousness the plumb line (Isa. 28:17).

- Standing up
b When Ezra opened the book the people stood up (Neh. 8:5); they stood on their feet, a great army (Ezek. 37:10); stand on your feet

and I will speak to you (Ezek. 2:1); he made me stand upright (Dan. 8:18); the Spirit set me on my feet (Ezek. 2:2).
Standing in the gateway, see **263o**.

c The lion was made to stand on two legs (Dan. 7:4).

216 Horizontal
See **348**.

217 Hanging

● People hanging

a Cursed be every one who hangs on a tree (Deut. 21:22–3; Gal. 3:13).

b Pharaoh hanged the chief baker (Gen. 40:19, 22; 41:13); Joshua hanged the king of Ai on a tree (Josh. 8:29); Joshua hung the kings on five trees (Josh. 10:26); David had the men hanged (2 Sam. 4:12); the Gibeonites hanged Saul's sons (2 Sam. 21:6, 9); the Philistines hanged Saul and Jonathan's bodies (2 Sam. 21:12); the two officials were hanged (Esther 2:23); Haman wanted to hang Mordecai (Esther 5:14; 6:4); Haman was hanged (Esther 7:9–10; 8:7); and his sons (Esther 9:13–14, 25).

c Jesus was killed by hanging him on a tree (Acts 5:30; 10:39).

d Ahithophel hanged himself (2 Sam. 17:23); Judas hanged himself (Matt. 27:5).

e Absalom hung by his hair in a tree (2 Sam. 18:9–10); princes are hung up by their hands (Lam. 5:12).

● Things hanging

f The veil was hung from pillars (Exod. 26:32–33); better a millstone hung round his neck (Matt. 18:6).

g They will hang on him all the weight of his father's house (Isa. 22:24).

218 Support

● Moses' staff

a With his staff Moses was to perform miracles (Exod. 4:17); Moses' staff became a snake (Exod. 4:2; 7:9–10); he took the staff of God with him (Exod. 4:20); with it he struck the Nile (Exod. 7:15–20); he stretched out his staff over the rivers (Exod. 8:5); over the dust (Exod. 8:16–17); to the sky (Exod. 9:23; 10:21–2); over the land of Egypt (Exod. 10:13); over the Red Sea (Exod. 14:16, 26–7); he struck the rock (Exod. 17:5–6; Num. 20:8–11); while he held up the staff, Israel beat Amalek (Exod. 17:9–12).

● Various staffs

b A rod from each of the tribal leaders (Num. 17:2–10); Aaron's rod that budded (Heb. 9:4); Judah's staff as security (Gen. 38:18, 25); Jonathan dipped his staff in the honey (1 Sam. 14:27, 43); David took his stick (1 Sam. 17:40, 43); Elisha's staff was laid on the dead boy (2 Kgs. 4:29, 31); a stick made the iron float (2 Kgs. 6:6); the angel touched the food with his staff (Judg. 6:21).

c Do not take a staff (Matt. 10:10; Luke 9:3); they put a reed in his hand (Matt. 27:29); they beat him on the head with a reed (Mark 15:19); a sponge put on a reed (Matt. 27:48; Mark 15:36; John 19:29).

d Two staffs, Favour and Union (Zech. 11:7, 10, 14); two sticks joined into one (Ezek. 37:16–20).

e Egypt is a stick of crushed reed (2 Kgs. 18:21; Isa. 36:6); Israel has been a staff of reed to Israel (Ezek. 29:6–7); a bruised reed he will not break (Isa. 42:3; Matt. 12:20).

f You will break them with a rod of iron (Ps. 2:9); your rod and your staff comfort me (Ps. 23:4).

Staff of bread, see **636d.**.

- **Supports**

g Ten stands for the lavers (1 Kgs. 7:27–39, 43; 2 Chr. 4:14; Jer. 27:19); supports at the corners of the stands (1 Kgs. 7:30, 34); the stands were broken up (Jer. 52:17, 20).

h Solomon made a bronze platform (2 Chr. 6:13); Ezra stood on a wooden podium (Neh. 8:4).

- **Poles**

i Poles for: the ark (Exod. 25:13–15; 37:4–5; 39:35; Num. 4:6; 1 Kgs. 8:7–8; 1 Chr. 15:15; 2 Chr. 5:9); the table (Exod. 25:27–8; 37:14–15; Num. 4:8); the bronze altar (Exod. 27:6–7; 38:6–7; Num. 4:14); the altar of incense (Exod. 30:4–5; Num. 4:11).

j The lampstand was carried on bars (Num. 4:10, 12).

- **Beams**

k The shaft of his spear was like a weaver's beam (1 Sam. 17:7; 2 Sam. 21:19; 1 Chr. 11:23; 20:5).

l Every one get a beam (2 Kgs. 6:2); beams are laid in the walls (Ezra 5:8); a beam from the house used in punishment (Ezra 6:11); the beams of our houses are cedar (S. of S. 1:17).

m You do not notice the beam in your own eye (Matt. 7:3–5; Luke 6:41–2).

- **Pillars**

n Pillars for: the tent (Exod. 39:33); the veil (Exod. 26:32; 36:36); the screen (Exod. 26:37; 36:38); the court (Exod. 27:10–17; 38:10–19; 39:40). The Merarites looked after the frames, bars and pillars (Num. 3:36–7; 4:31–2).

o Samson pulled the pillars of the temple (Judg. 16:26, 29); 45 pillars for the house of the forest of Lebanon (1 Kgs. 7:3); the hall of pillars (1 Kgs. 7:6).

p Two bronze pillars were made for Solomon's temple (1 Kgs. 7:15–22, 41; 1 Chr. 18:8; 2 Chr. 3:15–17; 4:12; 2 Kgs. 25:16–17; Jer. 27:19; 52:20–3); later broken up (2 Kgs. 25:13; Jer. 52:17); Joash was made king, standing by the pillar (2 Kgs. 11:14; 2 Chr. 23:13); Josiah renewed the covenant near the pillar (2 Kgs. 23:3).

q Marble pillars (Esther 1:6).

r The pillars of heaven tremble (Job 26:11); God keeps the pillars of the earth steady (Ps. 75:3); wisdom has set up her seven pillars (Prov. 9:1).

s The church is the pillar and foundation of the truth (1 Tim. 3:15);

the overcomer will be made a pillar in the temple (Rev. 3:12); let our daughters be as corner pillars (Ps. 144:12); I have made you an iron pillar (Jer. 1:18).

● Sacred pillars

t Do not set up a pillar (Deut. 16:22); the oak of the pillar in Shechem (Judg. 9:6).

u They built pillars on every high hill (1 Kgs. 14:23; 2 Kgs. 17:10); Jehoram put away the pillar of Baal (2 Kgs. 3:2); the pillars of the house of Baal were destroyed (2 Kgs. 10:26); Hezekiah broke down the pillars (2 Kgs. 18:4; 2 Chr. 31:1); Josiah cut the pillars in pieces (2 Kgs. 23:14); Asa tore down the pillars (2 Chr. 14:3). **Stone as pillar**, see **344f**; **pillar of cloud**, see **355c**; **pillar of fire**, see **381q**.

● Seats and beds

v An unlean person's seat and bed become unclean (Lev. 15:4, 6, 9–10, 20–4, 26–7).

w Beds were brought for David (2 Sam. 17:28); a bed for Elishah (2 Kgs. 4:10); the bed of Solomon (S. of S. 3:7); King Solomon made himself a palanquin (S. of S. 3:9).

x Israel bowed at the head of the bed (Gen. 47:31); sat up in bed (Gen. 48:2); gathered his feet up into the bed (Gen. 49:33); Saul sat on the bed (1 Sam. 28:23); Ishbosheth was lying in bed (2 Sam. 4:7, 11); at evening David got out of bed (2 Sam. 11:2); those who recline on beds of ivory (Amos 6:4).

y Frogs on your bed (Exod. 8:3); teraphim in the bed (1 Sam. 19:13–16).

z A paralytic lying on a bed (Matt. 9:2); they let down the paralytic's bed (Mark 2:4); take up your bed (Matt. 9:6; Mark 2:9, 11–12).

aa My bed will comfort me (Job 7:13); he plans wickedness on his bed (Ps. 36:4); woe to those who devise wickedness on their beds (Mic. 2:1).

ab Couches of gold and silver (Esther 1:6); he was asleep on the cushion (Mark 4:38).

● Footstool

ac David wanted to build a house for God's footstool (1 Chr. 28:2); let us worship at his footstool (Ps. 99:5; 132:7); the Lord has not remembered his footstool (Lam. 2:1); the earth is God's footstool (Isa. 66:1; Matt. 5:35; Acts 7:49).

ad Till I make your enemies your footstool (Ps. 110:1; Mark 12:36; Luke 20:43; Acts 2:35; Heb. 1:13; 10:13); sit here by my footstool (Jas. 2:3).

● Table

ae The table of showbread (Exod. 25:23–30; 31:8; 37:10–16; 39:36; 40:4, 22–3; Lev. 24:6; Num. 4:7; 1 Kgs. 7:48; 1 Chr. 28:16; 2 Chr. 4:19; 13:11; 29:18; Ezek. 41:22; Heb. 9:2); looked after by the Kohathites (Num. 3:31); ten tables (2 Chr. 4:8); tables on which to slaughter the offerings (Ezek. 40:39–43).

af A table and chair for Elisha (2 Kgs. 4:10).

ag He overturned the tables of the money-changers (Matt. 21:12; Mark 11:15).

<table>
<tr><td>● Giving
support</td><td>ah They supported Moses' hands (Exod. 17:12); they used supports to undergird the ship (Acts 27:17).

ai The Lord was my support (2 Sam. 22:19; Ps. 18:18).</td></tr>
</table>

219 Parallelism

220 Tilting

● Tipping   *a* I will send those to tip Moab over (Jer. 48:12).

221 Turning upside down

● Overturn   *a* He overturned the tables of the money-changers (Matt. 21:12; Mark 11:15; John 2:15).

              b These men who have turned the world upside down have come here (Acts 17:6).

222 Crossing: intertexture

● Crossing
rivers

a Jacob crossed the ford (Gen. 32:22–3); cross the brook Zered (Deut. 2:13–14); cross Ar, the border of Moab (Deut. 2:18).

b Crossing the Jordan (Deut. 11:31; 12:10; 27:2, 4; 31:2–3; 32:47; Josh. 1:2, 11; 3:1, 6, 11–17; 4:1, 10–13, 22–3; 7:7; 24:11); until I cross over Jordan (Deut. 2:29).

c Moses wanted to cross over (Deut. 3:25); God swore that Moses would not cross (Deut. 4:21–2; 31:2).

d Reuben and Gad would cross over to battle (Num. 32:21, 27, 29, 32; Josh. 1:14); they did not allow anyone to cross the fords (Judg. 3:28); without the password (Judg. 12:5–6); Israelites crossed the Jordan to escape (1 Sam. 13:7); Gadites crossed Jordan in flood (1 Chr. 12:15); David crossed the Jordan to battle (1 Chr. 19:17).

e Those who crossed the Jordan: Ammonites (Judg. 10:9); David (2 Sam. 10:17); David and all the people (2 Sam. 17:22; 19:18, 39, 41); Absalom (2 Sam. 17:24); Barzillai escorting David (2 Sam. 19:31, 36); Joab and the commanders (2 Sam. 24:5).

f They pursued them as far as the fords of Jordan (Josh. 2:7); David would wait at the fords (2 Sam. 15:28); do not spend the night at the fords but cross over (2 Sam. 17:16, 21); they have crossed the brook of water (2 Sam. 17:20); cross over with me (2 Sam. 19:33); Moab at the fords of the Arnon (Isa. 16:2).

g The province beyond the River (Ezra 4:10, 11, 16, 17, 20; 5:3, 6; Neh. 2:7, 9; 3:7).

● Crossing
over

h Your messengers crossed the sea (Isa. 23:2); Jesus crossed over (Matt. 8:18; 9:1; Mark 5:21; 8:13); the disciples crossed ahead of him (Matt. 14:22; Mark 6:45; John 6:17); they crossed over (Matt. 14:34); they crossed to the other side (Mark 4:35; Luke 8:22); Jesus went to the other side of the sea of Galilee (John 6:1).

i No one may cross between us and you (Luke 16:26)

- Crossing hands
- Spinning and weaving

j Jacob crossed his hands (Gen. 48:14).

k Spinning thread (Exod. 35:25–6); weaving Samson's hair (Judg. 16:13–14); weaving hangings for the Asherah (2 Kgs. 23:7); the workers in combed flax and the weavers of white cotton will despair (Isa. 19:9).

l The lilies of the field do not toil or spin (Matt. 6:28; Luke 12:27); they plaited a crown of thorns (Mark 15:17).

m They weave spiders' webs (Isa. 59:5); he cuts me off from the loom (Isa. 38:12).

- Networks

n Networks on the capitals of the pillars (1 Kgs. 7:17–18, 41; 2 Chr. 4:12–13).

223 Outside

- Outward appearance

a Outwardly you appear righteous (Matt. 23:27–8); man looks on the outward appearance (1 Sam. 16:7); you are looking at externals (2 Cor. 10:7).
Appearance, see **445**.

- Outside a person

b Nothing outside a man can defile him (Mark 7:15, 18); you clean the outside of cup and dish (Matt. 23:25).

c Being a Jew and circumcised are not external matters (Rom. 2:28).

- Outside the house

d Do not go outside your house (Exod. 12:22; Josh. 2:19); duties outside the sanctuary (1 Chr. 26:29).
Going outside, see **298c**.

- Outside the camp

e Outside the camp: the sin offering was burnt (Exod. 29:14; Lev. 4:12, 21; 8:17; 9:11; 16:27; Heb. 13:11); site of the tent of meeting (Exod. 33:7); where lepers must live (Lev. 13:46).

f Miriam outside the camp seven days (Num. 12:14–15); Nadab and Abihu carried outside the camp (Lev. 10:4–5); Jesus suffered outside the camp (Heb. 13:12–13).

g Outside are the dogs and the sorcerers and the immoral (Rev. 22:15).

- Outside the kingdom

h The sons of the kingdom will be cast into outer darkness (Matt. 8:12); cast him into outer darkness (Matt. 22:13); cast the worthless servant into outer darkness (Matt. 25:30).

i For those outside everything is in parables (Mark 4:11); conduct yourself wisely with regard to those outside (Col. 4:5).
Outsiders, see **59ag**.

- On the outside

j A book written inside and on the back (Rev. 5:1).

224 Inside

- In the heart

a From within come evil things (Mark 7:21–3); inwardly they are ravenous wolves (Matt. 7:15); inside there is robbery (Matt. 23:25; Luke 11:39); hypocrisy (Matt. 23:28); dead men's bones (Matt. 23:27); first clean the inside (Matt. 23:26).

b The Lord looks on the heart (1 Sam. 16:7); he who made the outside also made the inside (Luke 11:40); true Jewhood and circumcision are inward matters (Rom. 2:29); give what is within for alms and all is clean (Luke 11:41).

c His Spirit in the inner man (Eph. 3:16); the Spirit of truth will be in you (John 14:17).

● In one another

d The Father is in me and I in the Father (John 10:38; 14:10, 11); I in my Father and you in me and I in you (John 14:20); as you are in me and I in you, that they may be in us (John 17:21); I in them and you in me (John 17:23); that your love may be in them and I in them (John 17:26); remain in me and I in you (John 15:4–7).

● Stomach

e The curse will make her belly swell (Num. 5:21–2, 27); your belly is a heap of wheat (S. of S. 7:2); food is for the stomach and the stomach for food (1 Cor. 6:13).

f Striking in the belly: Ehud to Eglon (Judg. 3:21–2); Abner to Asahel (2 Sam. 2:23); Joab to Abner (2 Sam. 3:27); Rechab and Baanah to Ishbosheth (2 Sam. 4:6–7); Joab to Amasa (2 Sam. 20:10).

g Judas' bowels gushed out (Acts 1:18); Levi was still in the loins of his father (Heb. 7:10).

● Contained within

h Simeon's portion was within Judah (Josh. 19:1, 9).

225 Centrality

● Navel

a Your navel is a rounded bowl (S. of S. 7:2).

226 Covering

● Covering the body

a Adam and Eve sewed fig leaves to cover themselves (Gen. 3:7); Noah's sons covered him with a garment (Gen. 9:23); God covered Moses with his hand (Exod. 33:22); Rahab covered the spies with flax (Josh. 2:6); Jael covered Sisera with a rug (Judg. 4:18–19); Ruth asked Boaz to cover her with his garment (Ruth 3:9); God spread his garment over Israel (Ezek. 16:8); Elijah threw his cloak over Elisha (1 Kgs. 19:19); an old man wrapped in a robe (1 Sam. 28:14); two wings covering the seraph's body (Ezek. 1:11, 23).

b Mary wrapped Jesus in cloths (Luke 2:7); you will find a baby wrapped in cloths (Luke 2:12).

c They will call on the mountains and hills to cover them (Hos. 10:8; Luke 23:30).

d They covered Amasa's body (2 Sam. 20:12); Joseph wrapped Jesus' body in a linen cloth (Matt. 27:59; Mark 15:46; Luke 23:53; John 19:40); they saw the linen wrappings (Luke 24:12; John 20:6–7); Lazarus was bound hand and foot with wrappings (John 11:44).

● Covering the face

e The leper must cover his lip (Lev. 13:45); Rebekah veiled herself before Isaac (Gen. 24:65); a woman must cover her head whilst praying or prophesying (1 Cor. 11:4–15); Moses veiled his face after speaking with God (Exod. 34:33–5; 2 Cor. 3:13–16); woe to the women who make veils for people of every height (Ezek. 13:18, 21); Elijah covered his face with his mantle (1 Kgs. 19:13); David and the people covered their heads (2 Sam. 15:30); David covered his face in mourning (2 Sam. 19:4); Haman covered his head and mourned (Esther 6:12); they covered Haman's face (Esther 7:8); a bandage over his eyes (1 Kgs. 20:38).

f He will cover his face so he cannot see the land (Ezek. 12:6, 12); two wings to cover the face and two to cover the feet (Isa. 6:2).

g A woman's hair is given to her as a covering (1 Cor. 11:15).

- **Covering things**

h The woman covered the well with the messengers in it (2 Sam. 17:19); spreading sackcloth on the rock (2 Sam. 21:10).

i They put their clothes under Jehu on the steps (2 Kgs. 9:13); I have spread my couch with coverings (Prov. 7:16); the crowd used their cloaks and branches to cover the donkey and the road (Matt. 21:7–8; Mark 11:7–8; Luke 19:35–6).

j The angel sheathed his sword (1 Chr. 21:27); go into your scabbard, sword of the Lord (Jer. 47:6); put your sword in its sheath (John 18:11).

k The Lord will destroy the covering which is over all peoples (Isa. 25:7).

- **Cover of the ark**

l The cover of the ark [mercy seat]: made (Exod. 25:17; 31:7; 37:6; 39:35); put on the ark (Exod. 40:20); sprinkled with blood (Lev. 16:14, 15).

m Cherubim's wings covered the mercy seat (Exod. 37:9; Heb. 9:5); the cherubim's wings covered the ark (1 Kgs. 8:6–7); I will appear in the cloud over the mercy seat (Lev. 16:2); Moses heard a voice from above the mercy seat (Num. 7:89).

- **Covering holy things**

n A covering of skins for the tabernacle (Exod. 26:14; 39:34; 40:19); the tabernacle and its furniture was to be covered before being moved (Num. 4:5–15); the ark to be covered with the veil and skins (Num. 4:5–6).

o The Gershonites looked after the coverings (Num. 3:25).

- **Overlaying**

p Covered with pitch: the ark (Gen. 6:14); the basket of reeds (Exod. 2:3).

q Overlaid with gold: the ark (Exod. 25:11; 37:2); its poles (Exod. 25:13; 37:4); the table (Exod. 25:24; 37:11); its poles (Exod. 25:28; 37:15); the boards and bars of the tabernacle (Exod. 26:29; 36:34); pillars (Exod. 26:32, 37; 36:34, 36, 38); the altar of incense (Exod. 30:3; 37:26; 1 Kgs. 6:22); its poles (Exod. 30:5; 37:28); the inside of the temple and the holy place (1 Kgs. 6:20–2; 2 Chr. 3:4–9); the walls of the temple (1 Chr. 29:4); the doors and doorposts (2 Kgs. 18:16); the cherubim (1 Kgs. 6:28; 2 Chr. 3:10); the cherubim on the doors (1 Kgs. 6:32); the floor of the temple (1 Kgs. 6:30); Solomon's throne (1 Kgs. 10:18; 2 Chr. 9:17).

r Overlaid with bronze: the altar (Exod. 27:2; 38:2); its poles (Exod. 27:6; 38:6); the doors for the court (2 Chr. 4:9).

s The house was covered with cedar planks (1 Kgs. 6:9); the walls and floor were overlaid with wood (1 Kgs. 6:15–16); the altar was overlaid with cedar (1 Kgs. 6:20); the hall of the throne was panelled with cedar (1 Kgs. 7:7).

Roof, see **213***j*.

● Skins

t God made garments of skin for Adam and Eve (Gen. 3:21); kids' skins on Jacob's hands and neck (Gen. 27:16).

u The skin of the burnt offering was the priest's (Lev. 7:8); Gideon's fleece (Judg. 6:36–40).

v Rams' skins and porpoise skins for the tabernacle (Exod. 25:5; 26:14; 35:7, 23; 39:34; Num. 4:25); covering of porpoise skins (Num. 4:6, 8, 10, 11, 12, 14).

w Sea creatures with fins and scales are clean (Lev. 11:9–12; Deut. 14:9–10); something like scales fell from his eyes (Acts 9:18); the crocodile's skin is like a double coat of mail (Job 41:13).

x Skin for skin! (Job 2:4).

227 Lining

228 Dressing

● Clothed

a Having food and clothing we will be content (1 Tim. 6:8); the former demoniac was clothed and in his right mind (Mark 5:15; Luke 8:35); put your clothes on (Acts 12:8); when you were young you girded yourself (John 21:18).

● Clothes

b Paul looked after the clothes of those stoning Stephen (Acts 7:58; 22:20).

c Bring the cloak I left at Troas (2 Tim. 4:13); let him in the field not return for his cloak (Matt. 24:18; Mark 13:16); throwing off his cloak he sprang up (Mark 10:50).

● Using clothes

d They used worn-out clothes and rags to lift Jeremiah (Jer. 38:11–12).

e Elijah struck the water with his mantle (2 Kgs. 2:8); Elisha struck the water with Elijah's mantle (2 Kgs. 2:13–14); prophets will not put on a hairy mantle to deceive (Zech. 13:4); buy and wear a linen waistcloth (Jer. 13:1).

Tearing clothes in grief, see **836***g*; **tearing clothes in anger**, see **891***t*.

● Touching garments

f If I only touch his garment (Matt. 9:21; Mark 5:28); she touched his cloak (Mark 5:27); who touched my garments? (Mark 5:30–1).

g Handkerchiefs and aprons were carried from Paul to the sick (Acts 19:12).

● Modest
clothes

h Women should dress modestly (1 Tim. 2:9); a woman must not wear men's clothing, nor a man women's (Deut. 22:5).

i Remove her captive's clothes (Deut. 21:13); Jehoiachin changed his prison clothes (2 Kgs. 25:29; Jer. 52:33); put on mourning garments (2 Sam. 14:2); Joshua in filthy garments (Zech. 3:3–4).

j Jesus had a towel round his waist (John 13:4); some went about in sheepskins and goatskins (Heb. 11:37); Elijah wore a leather belt (2 Kgs. 1:8); as did John the Baptist (Matt. 3:4; Mark 1:6); we are poorly clothed (1 Cor. 4:11); do not take two tunics (Matt. 10:10; Mark 6:9; Luke 9:3).

k Garments with 'leprosy' (Lev. 13:47–59).

● Sackcloth

l Instead of fine robes, sackcloth (Isa. 3:24); let us wear sackcloth (1 Kgs. 20:31–2); the king wore sackcloth underneath (2 Kgs. 6:30); they have put on sackcloth (Isa. 15:3); they all put on sackcloth (Jonah 3:5–8); Isaiah had worn sackcloth (Isa. 20:2); repenting in sackcloth and ashes (Matt. 11:21).

● Fine
clothes

m Esau's best clothes for Jacob (Gen. 27:15); a special coat for Joseph (Gen. 37:3, 31–2); Joseph dressed in fine linen (Gen. 41:42); Daniel clothed in purple (Dan. 5:29); Saul clothed you in scarlet (2 Sam. 1:24); the princess's clothing is interwoven with gold (Ps. 45:13); Jesus arrayed in a scarlet robe (Matt. 27:28); in purple (Mark 15:17; John 19:2); in a gorgeous robe (Luke 23:11); bring the best robe and put it on him (Luke 15:22); festal garments (Isa. 3:22); Zion, put on your beatiful garments (Isa. 52:1); a golden girdle around his breasts (Rev. 1:13); golden girdles around their chests (Rev. 15:6).

n Achan coveted a beautiful robe (Josh. 7:21); purple robes captured from Midian (Judg. 8:26); Ahijah wore a new cloak (1 Kgs. 11:29); the scribes like long robes (Mark 12:38; Luke 20:46); the rich man dressed in purple and fine linen (Luke 16:19); a rich man in fine clothes (Jas. 2:2); the woman was dressed in purple and scarlet (Rev. 17:4); did you go out to see a man wearing soft clothes? (Matt. 11:8; Luke 7:25); even Solomon was not clothed like them (Matt. 6:29; Luke 12:27).

Red clothes, see **431***d*; **purple clothes**, see **436***c*; **clean clothes**, see **648***l*.

● Special
clothes

o Royal robes worn by: the kings of Israel and Judah (1 Kgs. 22:10; 2 Chr. 18:9); the king of Judah into battle (1 Kgs. 22:30; 2 Chr. 18:29); Esther (Esther 5:1); Mordecai (Esther 6:8, 11; 8:15); Herod (Acts 12:21).

p Virgin daughters of the king wore a special robe (2 Sam. 13:18); a man dressed in linen with a gold belt (Dan. 10:5); Christ wore a long robe with a gold sash (Rev. 1:13); a man without a wedding garment (Matt. 22:11, 12).

q Samuel wore a linen ephod (1 Sam. 2:18); as did David (1 Chr. 15:27); praising God in holy attire (2 Chr. 20:21).

r Tassels on the corners of your garments (Num. 15:38–9; Deut. 22:12).

Fringe of clothes, see **234a**.

s A woman dressed as a harlot (Prov. 7:10).

Priests' clothes, see **989**.

● Bright clothes

t White clothes for the Ancient of Days (Dan. 7:9); for the angel at the tomb (Matt. 28:3; Mark 16:5); those in Sardis who have not soiled their clothes will be dressed in white (Rev. 3:4–5); white clothes to cover your nakedness (Rev. 3:18); the twenty-four elders were dressed in white (Rev. 4:4); each martyr was given a white robe (Rev. 6:11); the great multitude before the Lamb wore white robes (Rev. 7:9, 13); the armies of heaven clothed in clean white linen (Rev. 19:14).

u At the transfiguration Jesus' clothes became bright and gleaming (Mark 9:3; Luke 9:29); white as light (Matt. 17:2); the angels at the tomb had dazzling clothes (Luke 24:4); a man in shining garments (Acts 10:30); the seven angels in clean, bright linen (Rev. 15:6).

White clothes, see **427a**.

● God clothing people

v Garments of skin for Adam and Eve (Gen. 3:21); if God will give me clothes to wear (Gen. 28:20–1); do not worry about what you will wear (Matt. 6:25, 28; Luke 12:22); if God clothes weeds he will clothe you (Matt. 6:30; Luke 12:28); God gives aliens food and clothing (Deut. 10:18); I gird you though you have not known me (Isa. 45:5); I clothed you with embroidered cloth (Ezek. 16:10).

● Clothing the needy

w Clothe the naked (Isa. 58:7); if he clothes the naked (Ezek. 18:7, 16); from the plunder they clothed the naked prisoners (2 Chr. 28:15); he must not reduce her clothing (Exod. 21:10); if I have seen anyone perish for lack of clothing (Job 31:19–20); Dorcas made garments (Acts 9:39); I was naked and you clothed me (Matt. 25:36); I was naked and you did not clothe me (Matt. 25:43).

● Giving clothes

x Abraham's servant gave garments to Rebekah (Gen. 24:53); Joseph gave garments to his brothers (Gen. 45:22); Jonathan gave his own robe to David (1 Sam. 18:4); robes brought out for the priests of Baal (2 Kgs. 10:22); Samson promised clothes to those who solved his riddle (Judg. 14:12, 19); Micah offered a suit of clothes per year (Judg. 17:10); Hannah made Samuel a new garment each year (1 Sam. 2:19); the Israelites asked the Egyptians for clothes (Exod. 3:22; 12:35); I would have given you a belt (2 Sam. 18:11); Esther sent garments to clothe Mordecai (Esther 4:4).

y If anyone wants your tunic, give him your cloak also (Matt. 5:40); if he wants your cloak, give him your tunic as well (Luke 6:29).

● Transferred
clothes

z The wicked multiplies garments but the just will wear them (Job 27:16–17); I will clothe him with your robe and sash (Isa. 22:21); false prophets come in sheeps' clothing (Matt. 7:15); Saul wore other robes to disguise himself (1 Sam. 28:8).
Disguise, see **527a**.

aa They divided Jesus' clothing (Matt. 27:35; Mark 15:24; Luke 23:34; John 19:23).

● Figurative
clothes

ab The Lord is clothed with majesty (Ps. 93:1; 104:1); covering yourself with light as a cloak (Ps. 104:2); with the remainder of wrath you gird yourself (Ps. 76:10); he put on righteousness as a breastplate (Isa. 59:17); righteousness and faithfulness will be his belt (Isa. 11:5); garments of vengeance for clothing (Isa. 59:17).

ac Meadows clothed with flocks and grain (Ps. 65:13); the earth is covered with the deep as with a garment (Ps. 104:6); the heavens and the earth will be changed like a garment (Ps. 102:26; Heb. 1:11–12).

ad I clothed myself with righteousness (Job 29:14); our righteous deeds are like filthy clothes (Isa. 64:6); rich robes in place of the filthy clothes of sin (Zech. 3:3–5); fine clean linen, which is the righteous deeds of the saints (Rev. 19:8); let your priests be clothed with righteousness (Ps. 132:9); I will clothe her priests with salvation (Ps. 132:16); he has clothed me with garments of salvation (Isa. 61:10).

ae Clothed with a garment dipped in blood (Rev. 19:13); robes washed in the blood of the Lamb (Rev. 7:14).

af Clothed with: strength and dignity (Prov. 31:25); Christ (Rom. 13:14; Gal. 3:27); power from on high (Luke 24:49); strength for battle (2 Sam. 22:40; Ps. 18:39); the imperishable (1 Cor. 15:53–4); our dwelling from heaven (2 Cor. 5:2–3); the new self (Eph. 4:24; Col. 3:10); a heart of compassion etc. (Col. 3:12); humility tied around you (1 Pet. 5:5).

ag He clothed himself with cursing (Ps. 109:18–19); clothed with shame (Ps. 109:29; 132:18).

229 Uncovering

● Nakedness
and shame

a Adam and Eve were naked and were not ashamed (Gen. 2:25); realised they were naked (Gen. 3:7); afraid because they were naked (Gen. 3:10–11).

b Lest I strip her naked (Hos. 2:3); I will expose your nakedness before them (Ezek. 16:37); I will uncover her lewdness (Hos. 2:10); I will show the nations your nakedness (Nahum 3:5); I will lift your skirts up over your face and your shame will be seen (Jer. 13:26); your nakedness will be uncovered and your shame seen (Isa. 47:3); they have seen her nakedness (Lam. 1:8); you will serve your enemies in nakedness (Deut. 28:48); your lovers will leave you naked (Ezek. 16:39); they will leave you naked

(Ezek. 23:29); the Assyrians uncovered Oholah's nakedness (Ezek. 23:10).

c Captives from Egypt and Assyria will be led away naked and barefoot (Isa. 20:4); strip yourselves and wear sackcloth (Isa. 32:11).

d Hanun cut off the men's clothes at the waist (2 Sam. 10:4; 1 Chr. 19:4); a young man ran away naked (Mark 14:51–2); the bravest will flee naked (Amos 2:16); the exorcists fled naked and wounded (Acts 19:16).

e Do not go up on to the altar, lest your nakedness be exposed (Exod. 20:26); blessed is he who keeps his garments that he may not go naked (Rev. 16:15).

● Nakedness and poverty

f Naked from his mother's womb and naked to return (Job 1:21; Eccles. 5:15); nakedness will not separate us from the love of Christ (Rom. 8:35); the poor are left naked (Job 24:7, 10).

g I was naked and you clothed me (Matt. 25:36); I was naked and you did not clothe me (Matt. 25:43); when did we see you naked? (Matt. 25:38, 44); if a brother or sister is without clothing (Jas. 2:15).

h We long to be clothed with our new house and not be naked (2 Cor. 5:3).

i Tyre will be a bare rock (Ezek. 26:4, 14).

● Unaware of nakedness

j Noah became drunk and lay naked (Gen. 9:21–3); woe to him who makes his neighbours drunk so that he can gaze on their nakedness (Hab. 2:15); the demon-possessed man did not wear clothes (Luke 8:27); you do not know that you are naked (Rev. 3:17); you were naked and I covered you (Ezek. 16:7–8); keep your feet from going unshod (Jer. 2:25).

● Naked prophets

k Saul prophesied naked before Samuel (1 Sam. 19:24); Isaiah went naked and barefoot as a sign (Isa. 20:2–4).

● Stripping people

l They stripped Joseph of his robe (Gen. 37:23); they stripped Aaron of his garments and put them on his son (Num. 20:26, 28); the Philistines stripped Saul's dead body (1 Sam. 31:8–9; 1 Chr. 10:8–9); stripping the slain (2 Sam. 23:10); the robbers stripped him (Luke 10:30); they stripped Jesus (Matt. 27:28); they took the robe off Jesus (Matt. 27:31; Mark 15:20); the magistrates tore the clothes off them (Acts 16:22); the ten horns will strip the harlot naked (Rev. 17:16).

m You have taken pledges and stripped people naked (Job 22:6).

n Ruth uncovered Boaz' feet (Ruth 3:4, 7); I am not fit to remove his sandals (Matt. 3:11).

● People stripping

o The high priest taking off his garments (Lev. 16:23); Jonathan stripped off his clothes and gave them to David (1 Sam. 18:4).

p Take off your sandals for you are standing on holy ground (Exod. 3:5; Josh. 5:15; Acts 7:33); my lord uncovered himself shamelessly (2 Sam. 6:20); a sandal removed from the man who would not marry his brother's widow (Deut. 25:8–10; Ruth 4:7–8); I had taken off my garments (S. of S. 5:3).

q Joseph left his garment and fled (Gen. 39:12–13, 15–16).

r Jesus laid aside his clothes (John 13:4); Peter was stripped for work (John 21:7); whilst building the wall of Jerusalem, no one took off his clothes (Neh. 4:23).

s A woman who prays or prophesies with her head uncovered dishonours her head (1 Cor. 11:5); is it proper for a woman to pray with head uncovered? (1 Cor. 11:13).

t The Lord has bared his holy arm (Isa. 52:10).

● Baldness

u Go up, you baldhead! (2 Kgs. 2:23); if a man becomes bald (Lev. 13:40–2); they shall not make their heads bald (Lev. 21:5); make yourselves bald because your children are exiled (Mic. 1:16); every head is bald and every beard cut off (Isa. 15:2; Jer. 48:37); every head was made bald, every shoulder rubbed bare (Ezek. 29:18); shame on all faces and baldness on all heads (Ezek. 7:18); baldness has come upon Gaza (Jer. 47:5).

● Skinning

v Skinning sacrifices (Lev. 1:6; 2 Chr. 29:34; 35:11); they strip the skin from my people (Mic. 3:3).

230 Surroundings

● Surround

a All nations surrounded me like bees (Ps. 118:10–12); as the mountains surround Jerusalem, so the Lord surrounds his people (Ps. 125:2); I will be a wall of fire around Jerusalem (Zech. 2:5).

231 Interposing

● Interfering

a Meddling in a quarrel is like taking a passing dog by the ears (Prov. 26:17).

232 Circumscription

Enclosure, see **235**.

233 Outline

See **234**.

234 Edge

● Fringe of clothes

a Tassels on clothes (Num. 15:38; Deut. 22:12); they lengthen their tassels (Matt. 23:5); the woman touched the fringe of his garment (Matt. 9:20; Luke 8:44); as many as touched the fringe of his garment were healed (Matt. 14:36; Mark 6:56).

● Edge of things

b The brim of the 'sea' was like a cup (1 Kgs. 7:26; 2 Chr. 4:5).

c Solomon went to the seashore in Edom (2 Chr. 8:17); Jesus went by the seashore (Mark 2:13).

235 Enclosure

- Courtyards

a The courtyard of the tabernacle: made (Exod. 27:9; 38:9; 40:8); set up (Exod. 40:33).

b The Gershonites looked after the hangings for the courtyard (Num. 3:26).

c Solomon made the courtyard of the priests (2 Chr. 4:9); Solomon consecrated the courtyard for making offerings (1 Kgs. 8:64; 2 Chr. 7:7); do not measure the courtyard outside the temple (Rev. 11:2).

d Peter in the high priest's courtyard (Matt. 26:58, 69; Mark 14:54, 66).

- Walls

e Rahab's house was in the wall (Josh. 2:15); why go so near the wall? (2 Sam. 11:20–1); archers shot from the wall (2 Sam. 11:24); the Broad Wall (Neh. 12:38); the wall around the temple (Ezek. 40:5); like a bulge in a high wall (Isa. 30:13).

f The men were a wall to us (1 Sam. 25:16); I have made you walls of bronze (Jer. 1:18); I will make you a fortified wall of Bronze (Jer. 15:20); I will be a wall of fire around Jerusalem (Zech. 2:5); if she is a wall (S. of S. 8:9); I was a wall (S. of S. 8:10).

- Walled towns

g Property can be transferred in walled towns (Lev. 25:29–30); 60 cities with walls and bars (1 Kgs. 4:13).

h The new Jerusalem had a high wall (Rev. 21:12); measuring 144 cubits (Rev. 21:17); the wall had 12 foundation stones (Rev. 21:14).

- Building walls

i Solomon building the wall round Jerusalem (1 Kgs. 3:1); building the walls of the temple (1 Kgs. 6:15); Jotham built the wall of Ophel (2 Chr. 27:3); Manasseh made it higher (2 Chr. 33:14); Hezekiah rebuilt the walls (2 Chr. 32:5); Manasseh built the outer wall of the city of David (2 Chr. 33:14); build the walls of Jerusalem (Ps. 51:18).

j They are finishing the walls (Ezra 4:12); repairing the wall of Jerusalem (Neh. 3:1–32); the wall was built to half height (Neh. 4:6); the wall was completed (Neh. 6:15; 7:1); dedication of the wall (Neh. 12:27).

- Destruction of walls

k The wall of Jericho fell flat (Josh. 6:20); by faith the wall of Jericho fell down (Heb. 11:30).

l They were trying to break down the wall of Beth-maacah (2 Sam. 20:15); the wall of Aphek fell on 27 000 Arameans (1 Kgs. 20:30).

m The walls of Jerusalem broken down (2 Kgs. 14:13; 2 Chr. 25:23); the Chaldeans broke down the wall of Jerusalem (2 Kgs. 25:10; 2 Chr. 36:19; Jer. 39:8; 52:14); the wall of Jerusalem is broken down (Neh. 1:3); the wall of Jerusalem was breached (Jer. 39:2); you have broken down its walls (Ps. 80:12; 89:40).

n The sluggard's wall was broken down (Prov. 24:31); a whitewashed wall will be broken down (Ezek. 13:11–15); a man like a leaning wall, a tottering fence (Ps. 62:3).

o Christ has broken down the dividing wall between Jew and Gentile (Eph. 2:14).

● Fields

p Dedicating a field to the Lord (Lev. 27:16–24).

q The field of Ephron purchased (Gen. 23:8–20); Achsah asked Caleb for a field (Josh. 15:18; Judg. 1:14); redeeming Naomi's piece of land (Ruth 4:3–5); the king will take the best of your fields (1 Sam. 8:14); Jonathan and David went into the field (1 Sam. 20:11, 35); throw him into the field of Naboth (2 Kgs. 9:25–6); Judas obtained a field with the reward of wickedness (Acts 1:18); buying the potter's field (Matt. 27:7, 10); field of blood (Matt. 27:8).

r You are God's field (1 Cor. 3:9); I will remove its hedge and break down its wall (Isa. 5:5).

● Various enclosures

s Seal off the mountain (Exod. 19:12, 23); have you not made a hedge about Job? (Job 1:10).

t Make a parapet for your roof (Deut. 22:8).

236 Limit

● Borders of land

a I will set your boundary (Exod. 23:31); God determined the boundaries of man's habitations (Acts 17:26); he set the boundaries of the peoples (Deut. 32:8); you fixed the boundaries of the earth (Ps. 74:17).

b God has made Jordan the border between us (Josh. 22:25); the Arnon is the border between Moab and the Amorites (Num. 21:13–15; Judg. 11:18); Ar, the border of Moab (Deut. 2:18); the Jabbok, the border of Ammon (Josh. 12:2); the boundary of the land (Ezek. 47:13, 15–20).

c The border of: the land of Canaan (Num. 34:2–12); Gilead (Deut. 3:16–17); the Amorites (Judg. 1:36); Edom (Josh. 15:1).

d The border of: Judah (Josh. 15:1–12); Ephraim (Josh. 16:5–8); Manasseh (Josh. 17:7–10); Benjamin (Josh. 18:11–20); Zebulun (Josh. 19:10–14); Asher (Josh. 19:24–9); Naphtali (Josh. 19:32–4).

e Jeroboam restored the border of Israel (2 Kgs. 14:25).
Boundary mark, see **547*t*.**

● Limits for the sea

f God set limits for the sea (Job 38:10–11; Prov. 8:29); you set a boundary which the waters may not cross (Ps. 104:9); I placed the sand as the boundary of the sea (Jer. 5:22).

237 Front

● Face

a Each cherub had four faces (Ezek. 1:6; 10:14, 21); each cherub had two faces (Ezek. 41:18); the form of their faces (Ezek. 1:10; 10:22); his face was like the sun (Rev. 1:16).
Face to face, see **200*a*.**

● Foreheads

b Memorial bands between your eyes (Exod. 13:9, 16); these words shall be on your forehead (Deut. 6:8; 11:18); the plate on Aaron's forehead (Exod. 28:38); a mark on the foreheads of those who mourn the abominations (Ezek. 9:4); the name of the Lamb and his Father on their foreheads (Rev. 14:1); his name will be on their foreheads (Rev. 22:4).

c A mark on their right hand or forehead (Rev. 13:16; 14:9); a name on her forehead, Babylon the great (Rev. 17:5).

d Do not shave your forehead (Deut. 14:1); leprosy on Uzziah's forehead (2 Chr. 26:19, 20).

e Your nose is like a tower of Lebanon (S. of S. 7:4).

● Facing

f The cherubim faced the mercy seat (Exod. 37:9).

238 Rear

● Back

a You will see my back (Exod. 33:23); I will show them my back and not my face (Jer. 18:17); they have turned their back to me and not their face (Jer. 32:33).

b He was in the stern of the boat (Mark 4:38); the scroll was written on the front and the back (Ezek. 2:10).

● Tails

c The locusts have tails like scorpions (Rev. 9:10); his tail swept down a third of the stars (Rev. 12:4).

● Behind

d The angel and pillar went behind them (Exod. 14:19); get behind me, Satan (Mark 8:33).

e Attack them in the rear (Josh. 10:19).

● Looking
back

f Do not look back (Gen. 19:17); Lot's wife looked back (Gen. 19:26).

239 Side

● Cheeks

a Your cheeks are like pomegranates (S. of S. 4:3; 6:7); his cheeks are like beds of spices (S. of S. 5:13); turn the other cheek (Matt. 5:39; Luke 6:29).

● Side of
body

b A soldier pierced his side (John 19:34); he showed them his hands and his side (John 20:20); put your hand in my side (John 20:27); unless I put my hand in his side (John 20:25).

c God made the woman from one of the man's ribs (Gen. 2:21–2).

240 Opposite side

● Opposite

a The two Marys sat opposite the grave (Matt. 27:61).

241 Right side

● Right hand

a Your right hand is powerful (Exod. 15:6); the right hand of the Lord does valiantly (Ps. 118:15, 16); God stands at the right hand of the needy (Ps. 109:31); the Lord is at my right hand (Acts 2:25); the Lord is at your right hand (Ps. 110:5).

b Christ is seated at the right hand of God (Matt. 26:64; Mark 14:62; 16:19; Luke 22:69; Eph. 1:20; Col. 3:1; Heb. 1:3; 8:1; 10:12; 12:2); sit at my right hand (Ps. 110:1; Matt. 22:44; Mark 12:36; Luke 20:42; Acts 2:34; Heb. 1:13); God exalted Jesus at his right hand (Acts 2:33; 5:31); Stephen saw Jesus standing at the right hand of God (Acts 7:55–6); Jesus who is at God's right hand (Rom. 8:34; 1 Pet. 3:22).

c Joseph brought Manasseh towards his father's right hand (Gen. 48:13); Bathsheba sat on Solomon's right (1 Kgs. 2:19); he will set the sheep at his right hand (Matt. 25:33–4); they put a reed in his right hand (Matt. 27:29); lie down on your right side for 40 days (Ezek. 4:6); cast your net on the right side of the boat (John 21:6); a mark on their right hand or forehead (Rev. 13:16).

d Benjamin—son of the right hand (Gen. 35:18); the right hand of fellowship (Gal. 2:9).

● Right parts of body

e Anointing the right ears, right thumbs and right big toes with blood (Exod. 29:20; Lev. 8:23–4; 14:14, 25); with oil (Lev. 14:17, 28).

● Right and left

f The waters like a wall to right and left (Exod. 14:22, 29); not room to turn right or left (Num. 22:26); weapons of righteousness for the right hand and the left (2 Cor. 6:7).

Ambidextrous, see **242a**; **not turn to right or left**, see **249c**; **turn to right or left**, see **282h**.

g Request for Zebedee's sons to sit on Christ's right and left (Matt. 20:21, 23; Mark 10:37, 40); two robbers crucified on his right and left (Matt. 27:38; Mark 15:27; Luke 23:33).

242 Left side

● Left handed

a Ehud was left–handed (Judg. 3:15); seven hundred soldiers who were left–handed (Judg. 20:16); ambidextrous with sling and bow (1 Chr. 12:2).

● On left side

b Lie down on your left side for 390 days (Ezek. 4:4–5).

Section three: Form

243 Form

Create, see **164**.

244 Formlessness

● Formless

a The earth was formless and void (Gen. 1:2; Jer. 4:23).

245 Symmetry: regularity of form

Equal measure, see **28j**.

246 Distortion: irregularity of form

● Twisted

a A twisted and crooked generation (Deut. 32:5); they twisted like a deceitful bow (Ps. 78:57); what is crooked cannot be straightened (Eccles. 1:15); with the twisted you deal tortuously (2 Sam. 22:27; Ps. 18:26).

b She could not straighten (Luke 13:11).

c There is nothing crooked or perverted in my words (Prov. 8:8).

● Twisting

d Who can straighten what God has bent? (Eccles. 7:13); he has made my paths crooked (Lam. 3:9); you are making crooked the straight paths of the Lord (Acts 13:10); you twist everything that is straight (Mic. 3:9).

247 Angularity

Horns, see **254**.

248 Curvature

Circular, see **250**.

249 Straightness

● Straight paths

a Make his paths straight (Matt. 3:3; Mark 1:3; Luke 3:4); make straight the way of the Lord (John 1:23); make straight paths for your feet (Heb. 12:13); he will make your paths straight (Prov. 3:6); I will lead them on a straight path (Jer. 31:9); he led them by a straight way (Ps. 107:7); the crooked will become straight (Luke 3:5).

b You are making crooked the straight paths of the Lord (Acts 13:10); make your way straight before me (Ps. 5:8); my words are straight for him who understands (Prov. 8:9).

● Not turning aside

c We will not turn to right or left (Num. 20:17; Deut. 2:27); do not turn aside to right or left (Deut. 5:32; 17:11, 20; 28:14; Josh. 1:7; 23:6; Prov. 4:27); the milch cows did not turn to right or left (1 Sam. 6:12); Asahel did not turn to right or left (2 Sam. 2:19, 21); let your eyes look straight ahead (Prov. 4:25).

d The cherubim went straight ahead (Ezek. 1:9, 12, 17; 10:11, 22); people will go straight out of the temple (Ezek. 46:9).

Turn to right or left, see **282*h***.

250 Circularity: simple circularity

● Rings

a Rings on: the feet of the ark (Exod. 25:12; 37:3); the corners of the table (Exod. 25:26; 37:13–14); the corners of the bronze altar (Exod. 27:4, 7; 38:5, 7); the breastpiece and the ephod (Exod. 28:23–8; 39:16, 19–21).

Signet rings, see **743*k***.

● Loops

b Loops for: linen curtains (Exod. 26:4–5; 36:11–12); goats' hair curtains (Exod. 26:10–11; 36:17).

● Rainbow

c The rainbow as a sign of the covenant (Gen. 9:12–17); brightness round him like a rainbow (Ezek. 1:28); the rainbow on the angel's head (Rev. 10:1); a rainbow like an emerald round the throne (Rev. 4:3).

● Circular

d The 'sea' was circular (1 Kgs. 7:23).

e God inscribes a circle on the face of the waters (Job 26:10); when God drew a circle on the face of the deep (Prov. 8:29); God sits above the circle of the earth (Isa. 40:22).

251 Convolution: complex circularity

252 Roundness
See **250**.

253 Convexity

● Breasts

a Let her breasts satisfy you (Prov. 5:19); their breasts were pressed (Ezek. 23:3, 8, 21).

b Your two breasts are like two fawns (S. of S. 4:5; 7:3); your breasts are like clusters of the palm tree (S. of S. 7:7); may your breasts be like clusters of the vine (S. of S. 7:8); my breasts were like towers (S. of S. 8:10); a golden girdle round his breasts (Rev. 1:13).

c Our little sister has no breasts (S. of S. 8:8).
   Breast-feeding, see **301***o*.

254 Prominence

● Animal horns

a A ram caught by its horns (Gen. 22:13).

b A little horn came up and uprooted three horns (Dan. 7:8); a small horn which grew large (Dan. 8:9); a he-goat with a horn between its eyes (Dan. 8:5); the horn is the first king (Dan. 8:21).

c A ram with two horns (Dan. 8:3); the beast had two horns like a lamb (Rev. 13:11).

d Four horns in place of the one broken (Dan. 8:8, 22); four horns which scattered Israel and Judah (Zech. 1:18–19).

e A Lamb with seven horns and seven eyes (Rev. 5:6).

f A beast with ten horns (Dan. 7:7, 20); a beast with seven heads and ten horns (Rev. 12:3; 13:1; 17:3, 7); the ten horns you saw (Rev. 17:12, 16).

● Horns on altars

g The altar of burnt offering with four horns (Exod. 27:2; 38:2); blood on the horns (Exod. 29:12; Lev. 4:25, 30, 34; 8:15; 9:9).

h The altar of incense with horns (Exod. 30:2; 37:26); blood to be put on the horns (Exod. 30:10; Lev. 4:7, 18; 16:18); the four horns of the golden altar (Rev. 9:13).

i The horns of the altar of Bethel will be cut off (Amos 3:14).

255 Concavity

● Pit

a Penalty for a dangerous pit (Exod. 21:33–4); the arrogant have dug pits for me (Ps. 119:85); he has dug a pit and fallen in it (Ps. 7:15; 57:6); the nations have sunk in the pit they made (Ps. 9:15); may they be cast into pits (Ps. 140:10).

b Tar pits in the Valley of Siddim (Gen. 14:10); Joseph thrown into a pit (Gen. 37:20–9); they threw Absalom's body into a deep pit (2 Sam. 18:17); killing a lion in a pit on a snowy day (2 Sam. 23:20; 1 Chr. 11:22).
   Trench, see **262**.

c A harlot is a deep pit (Prov. 23:27); the mouth of an adulteress is a deep pit (Prov. 22:14); I called on your name from the depths of the pit (Lam. 3:55).

The pit, see **361*i*.**

1 Caves for burying

d The cave of Machpelah for burying (Gen. 23:9); burial place of: Abraham (Gen. 25:9); Jacob (Gen. 49:29–32; 50:13); Abraham, Sarah, Isaac, Rebekah, Leah (Gen. 49:31).

e Bodies put in the cave (Josh. 10:27).

1 People in caves

f Lot and his daughters lived in a cave (Gen. 19:30); you have made the temple a robbers' cave (Matt. 21:13; Mark 11:17; Luke 19:46).

g The cave of Adullam (1 Sam. 22:1; 2 Sam. 23:13; 1 Chr. 11:15); five kings hid in the cave at Makkedah (Josh. 10:16); Saul relieved himself in the cave (1 Sam. 24:3); David fled from Saul in the cave (Ps. 57:t); when David was in the cave (Ps. 142:t); the Israelites made dens and caves (Judg. 6:2); Israel hid in caves etc. (1 Sam. 13:6); he will have hidden himself in some cave (2 Sam. 17:9); Obadiah hid prophets in a cave (1 Kgs. 18:4, 13); Elijah came to a cave (1 Kgs. 19:9).

h People will go into caves and holes from before the terror of the Lord (Isa. 2:19, 21); everyone hid in caves from the Lord (Rev. 6:15); living in holes (Job 30:6).

Hiding holes, see **662*l*.**

1 Mine for ore

i There is a mine for silver (Job 28:1); mining ore in a dark mine shaft (Job 28:3–11).

1 Valley

j The valley of: Ben-hinnom (2 Chr. 28:3; 33:6; Jer. 19:2; 32:35); Beracah (2 Chr. 20:26); Elah (1 Sam. 17:19); Gibeon (Isa. 28:21); Kidron (2 Chr. 29:16; John 18:1); Rephaim (2 Sam. 23:13; 1 Chr. 11:15; 14:9); Salt (2 Sam. 8:13; 2 Chr. 25:11; Ps. 60:t); a valley near Ai (Josh. 8:11, 13).

k The valley of Ben-hinnom will be called the valley of Slaughter (Jer. 7:32; 19:6); the valley of dead bodies and ashes (Jer. 31:40); the valley of dry bones (Ezek. 37:1); the vally of Achor will be a door of hope (Hos. 2:15).

l Though I walk through the valley dark as death (Ps. 23:4); the valleys will be split under the Lord (Mic. 1:4); every valley will be filled in (Isa. 40:4; Luke 3:5).

1 Sockets

m Sockets for: the tent (Exod. 39:33); the boards (Exod. 26:19–25; 36:24–30); the pillars (Exod. 26:32, 37; 36:36, 38; 38:27); the court (Exod. 27:10–18; 38:10–19, 30–1; 39:40).

n The Merarites looked after the sockets (Num. 3:36–7; 4:31–2).

1 Hollow

o The altar was hollow (Exod. 27:8; 38:7).

256 Sharpness

1 Sharpening

a If he does not sharpen the axe, he must exert more strength (Eccles. 10:10); the Israelites went to the Philistines to sharpen tools (1 Sam. 13:20).

b As iron sharpens iron, so one man sharpens another (Prov. 27:17).

c God will sharpen his sword (Deut. 32:41; Ps. 7:12); a sword is sharpened (Ezek. 21:9–10).

d They have sharpened their tongue like a sword (Ps. 64:3); they sharpen their tongues like a serpent (Ps. 140:3).

1 **Sharp things**

e Flint knives for circumcision (Exod. 4:25; Josh. 5:2–3); use a sharp sword as a barber's razor (Ezek. 5:1); a three-pronged fork (1 Sam. 2:13).

f Jael pierced Sisera's temple with a tent-peg (Judg. 4:21; 5:26); Shamgar killed Philistines with an ox-goad (Judg. 3:31); it is hard for you to kick against the goads (Acts 26:14).

g A camel going through the eye of a needle (Matt. 19:24; Mark 10:25; Luke 18:25).

h The words of the wise are like goads (Eccles. 12:11).

i Their tongue is a sharp sword (Ps. 57:4); swords are in their lips (Ps. 59:7); your tongue is like a sharp razor (Ps. 52:2); he made my mouth like a sharp sword (Isa. 49:2); the word of God is sharper than a two-edged sword (Heb. 4:12).

j The adulteress is sharp as a two-edged sword (Prov. 5:4); death, where is your sting? (Hos. 13:14; 1 Cor. 15:55–6).

1 **Thorns and thistles**

k The ground will produce thorns and thistles (Gen. 3:18); if the ground produces thorns and thistles (Heb. 6:8); some seed fell among thorns (Matt. 13:7, 22; Mark 4:7, 18; Luke 8:7, 14); threshing the men of Succoth with thorns (Judg. 8:7, 16); they asked the bramble to reign (Judg. 9:15); the worthless will be burned like thorns (2 Sam. 23:6–7); the laughter of fools is like the crackling of thorns (Eccles. 7:6).

l Thorns and snares are in the way of the perverse (Prov. 22:5); briars and thorns will grow up (Isa. 5:6; 7:23–5); though thorns and thistles are with you (Ezek. 2:6).

m A crown of thorns (Matt. 27:29; Mark 15:17; John 19:2); Paul's thorn in the flesh (2 Cor. 12:7).

1 **Teeth**

n Tooth for tooth (Exod. 21:24; Lev. 24:20; Matt. 5:38); knocking out a slave's tooth (Exod. 21:27); shatter their teeth (Ps. 58:6); a beast with iron teeth (Dan. 7:7, 19).

o Your teeth are like ewes (S. of S. 4:2; 6:6); their teeth are spears and arrows (Ps. 57:4); the locusts had lions' teeth (Rev. 9:8).

p I have escaped by the skin of my teeth (Job 19:20).

Arrows, see **287*e***.

257 Bluntness

1 **Blunt**

a If the iron is blunt (Eccles. 10:10).

258 Smoothness

1 **Smooth**

a I am a smooth man (Gen. 27:11); the rough ways will become smooth (Luke 3:5).

ₗ Slippery

    b Let their way be dark and slippery (Ps. 35:6); you set them in slippery places (Ps. 73:18); their way will be like slippery paths (Jer. 23:12).

259 Roughness

ₗ Hairy

    a Esau was a hairy man (Gen. 27:11); as was Elijah (2 Kgs. 1:8); Esau's body was like a hairy garment (Gen. 25:25).

    b Elijah wore a garment of hair and a leather belt (2 Kgs. 1:8); as did John the Baptist (Matt. 3:4; Mark 1:6).

ₗ Hair of
the head

    c Your hair is like a flock of goats (S. of S. 4:1; 6:5); his hair is black as a raven (S. of S. 5:11); your flowing locks are like purple (S. of S. 7:5); his hair was like pure wool (Dan. 7:9); hair white as wool (Rev. 1:14); you cannot make one hair white or black (Matt. 5:36).

    White hair, see **427*i***; **grey hair**, see **429*a***.

    d The leper must let his hair hang loose (Lev. 13:45); as must an accused woman (Num. 5:18); Ezra plucked out some of his hair and beard (Ezra 9:3); Ezekiel was lifted by a lock of hair (Ezek. 8:3).

    e Mary wiped his feet with her hair (John 11:2; 12:3).

    f More than the hairs of my head: my iniquities (Ps. 40:12); those who hate me without cause (Ps. 69:4).

ₗ Long hair

    g Samson's strength lay in his hair (Judg. 16:17, 19); weaving Samson's hair (Judg. 16:13–14); his hair began to grow again (Judg. 16:22); Nebuchadnezar's hair grew like eagles' feathers (Dan. 4:33); if a woman has long hair it is her glory (1 Cor. 11:15); the locusts had women's hair (Rev. 9:8).

    h The priests are not to grow their hair long (Lev. 10:6; 21:10; Ezek. 44:20); if a man has long hair it is a dishonour (1 Cor. 11:14).

ₗ Hair cut

    i Absalom's hair weighed two hundred shekels when it was cut (2 Sam. 14:26); Paul cut his hair, for he had a vow (Acts 18:18); the Nazirite must burn his hair (Num. 6:18); cut off your hair and throw it away (Jer. 7:29).

    j Do not cut your hair at the sides of your head (Lev. 19:27); all who cut the corners of their hair (Jer. 9:26; 25:23); the Nazirite must not cut his hair while he is under the vow (Num. 6:5).

ₗ Hairs
protected

    k The hairs of your head are all counted (Matt. 10:30; Luke 12:7); not one of Jonathan's hairs shall fall to the ground (1 Sam. 14:45); no hair of your head shall fall to the ground (2 Sam. 14:11); not one of Adonijah's hairs would fall to the ground (1 Kgs. 1:52); not a hair of your head will perish (Luke 21:18; Acts 27:34).

ₗ Beards

    l Joab took Amasa by the beard (2 Sam. 20:9); Hanun cut off half their beards (2 Sam. 10:4, 5; 1 Chr. 19:4, 5); Mephibosheth had not seen to his moustache (2 Sam. 19:24); the oil running down Aaron's beard (Ps. 133:2).

m Ezra plucked out some of his hair and beard (Ezra 9:3); I gave my cheeks to those who pluck out the beard (Isa. 50:6).
Shave, see **648*i***.

1 Wool

n The king of Moab paid wool as tribute (2 Kgs. 3:4); the priests were not to wear wool (Ezek. 44:17); hair white as wool (Dan. 7:9; Rev. 1:14).
Sheep-shearing, see **369*e***.

260 Notch

261 Fold
See **262**.

262 Furrow

1 Trench

a Elijah made a trench around the altar (1 Kgs. 18:32); make this valley full of trenches (2 Kgs. 3:16).
Pit, see **255*a***.

263 Opening

1 Windows

a A window for the ark (Gen. 6:16); windows for the temple (1 Kgs. 6:4); window opposite window in three ranks (1 Kgs. 7:4, 5).

b Noah opened the window (Gen. 8:6); Sisera's mother looks out of the window (Judg. 5:28); Jezebel looked out of the window (2 Kgs. 9:30).

c Rahab lowered the spies from a window (Josh. 2:15); Michal lowered David from a window (1 Sam. 19:12); Michal saw David from the window (1 Chr. 15:29).

1 Doorways

d At the doorway of the tent of meeting: priests eating (Exod. 29:32); sacrifice offered (Lev. 1:3); pillar of cloud (Deut. 31:15); the Lord stood (Num. 12:5); people to assemble (Num. 10:3); Korah assembled the congregation (Num. 16:19); Zelophehad's daughters came before Moses (Num. 27:2); inheritances distributed (Josh. 19:51); Eli's sons lay with the serving women (1 Sam. 2:22).

e Guarding the doorway of the king's house (1 Kgs. 14:27); the Shunammite standing at the doorway (2 Kgs. 4:15); Naaman standing at the doorway (2 Kgs. 5:9); Abraham sitting at the doorway (Gen. 18:1); the wanton woman sits at the doorway of her house (Prov. 9:14).

f Blood on the doorposts and lintel (Exod. 12:7, 22); write these words on your doorposts (Deut. 6:9; 11:20); bring the slave to the doorpost (Exod. 21:6); doorposts for the temple (1 Kgs. 6:33); all the doors and doorposts were squared (1 Kgs. 7:5).

g The prison doors were opened (Acts 16:26).

1 Door of opportunity

h I have placed before you an open door (Rev. 3:8); a wide door was opened for me (1 Cor. 16:9); a door was opened for me in the Lord (2 Cor. 2:12); God opened a door of faith for the Gentiles (Acts 14:27); pray that God will open a door for the word (Col. 4:3).

1 **Gateways**

i The well by the gate of Bethlehem (2 Sam. 23:15, 16); show us the entrance to the city (Judg. 1:24–5); no one in sackcloth could enter the king's gate (Esther 4:2); Solomon's portico (John 10:23; Acts 3:11; 5:12); sitting by the Beautiful Gate (Acts 3:2, 10); the Jews watched the gates of Damascus day and night (Acts 9:24); the gate opened by itself (Acts 12:10); because of her joy, Rhoda did not open the gate (Acts 12:14).

j Open to me the gates of righteousness (Ps. 118:19–20); lift up your heads, you gates (Ps. 24:7, 9); open the gates that the righteous may enter (Isa. 26:2); your gates will be open day and night (Isa. 60:11); measuring the gateway of the temple (Ezek. 40:11).

k The river gates are opened (Nahum 2:6); your gates are opened wide to your enemies (Nahum 3:13).

1 **Sitting in the gateway**

l Those who sat in the gate: Lot (Gen. 19:1); Boaz (Ruth 4:1); David (2 Sam. 19:8); Mordecai (Esther 2:19, 21; 3:2; 5:9, 13; 6:10, 12); Job (Job 29:7).

m The princes sat in the entrance of the New Gate (Jer. 26:10); the king sat in the Benjamin Gate (Jer. 38:7); the officials of Babylon sat in the Middle Gate (Jer. 39:3).

n David sat between the two gates (2 Sam. 18:24); her husband sits in the gate among the elders (Prov. 31:23).

1 **Standing in the gateway**

o Moses stood in the gate of the camp (Exod. 32:26); the people assembled at the gates (Judg. 5:11); Absalom stood by the road to the gate (2 Sam. 15:2); David stood by the gate (2 Sam. 18:4); Jeremiah had to stand in the gate (Jer. 17:19–20); stand in the gate of the Lord's house (Jer. 7:2).

p At the gates of the city wisdom cries (Prov. 8:3); wisdom watching at her gates (Prov. 8:34).

1 **Mouth**

q Open your mouth and I will fill it (Ps. 81:10); I open my mouth, longing for your commandments (Ps. 119:131).

r Who can open the doors of his face? (Job 41:14); by faith they shut the mouths of lions (Heb. 11:33).

s The earth opened its mouth to receive Abel's blood (Gen. 4:11); the earth opened its mouth and swallowed Korah's company (Num. 16:30–4; 26:10; Ps. 106:17).

t Your lips drip honey (S. of S. 4:11); his lips are lilies (S. of S. 5:13).

u This people honours me with their lips (Matt. 15:8).

1 **Keys**

v Eliakim will be given the key to the house of David (Isa. 22:22); Christ holds the key of David (Rev. 3:7); Christ has the keys of death and Hades (Rev. 1:18); what he opens no one shuts (Isa. 22:22; Rev. 3:7); Peter was given the keys of the kingdom of heaven, to bind and loose (Matt. 16:19); you have taken away the key of knowledge (Luke 11:52).

w A star was given the key to the abyss (Rev. 9:1); he opened the abyss (Rev. 9:2); an angel had the key of the abyss (Rev. 20:1).

1 Openings

x Perez, what a breach you have made! (Gen. 38:29); their pregnant women will be ripped open (Hos. 13:16); they ripped open pregnant women in Gilead (Amos 1:13).

y An opening in the top of the robe of the ephod (Exod. 28:32).

z I arose to open to my beloved (S. of S. 5:5–6).

aa Ephphatha – be opened (Mark 7:34).

ab The stone had been removed from the tomb (John 20:1); remove the stone (John 11:39–41); open the mouth of the cave (Josh. 10:22).

ac A hole in the wall (Ezek. 8:7); dig through the wall (Ezek. 8:8); dig a hole through the wall (Ezek. 12:5); many breaches in the wall of the city of David (Isa. 22:9); they made an opening in the roof (Mark 2:4).

ad Easier for a camel to go through the eye of a needle (Matt. 19:24; Mark 10:25; Luke 18:25).

1 The Lord opening

ae Knock and it will be opened to you (Matt. 7:7–8; Luke 11:9–10); Lord, open to us! (Matt. 25:11; Luke 13:25).

1 Opening to the Lord

af If any one hears my voice and opens the door (Rev. 3:20); that they may open to him when he knocks (Luke 12:36); to him the gatekeeper opens (John 10:3); open to me, my sister (S. of S. 5:2); the Lord opened Lydia's heart to respond (Acts 16:14).

1 Heaven opened

ag The heavens were opened and I saw visions of God (Ezek. 1:1); in heaven an open door (Rev. 4:1); heaven opened at Christ's baptism (Matt. 3:16; Mark 1:10; Luke 3:21; John 1:51); to Stephen (Acts 7:56); before Peter (Acts 10:11); I saw heaven opened (Rev. 19:11).

1 Opening the temple

ah Samuel opened the doors of the house of the Lord (1 Sam. 3:15); Hezekiah opened the doors of the temple (2 Chr. 29:3); the temple in heaven was opened (Rev. 11:19; 15:5); the east gate of the inner court is to be opened on the Sabbath (Ezek. 46:1); do not open the gates of Jerusalem until the sun is hot (Neh. 7:3); the gates of the new Jerusalem shall never be shut (Rev. 21:25).

1 Opening the scroll

ai Who is worthy to open the scroll? (Rev. 5:2); the lion of the tribe of Judah can open the scroll (Rev. 5:5).

aj Opening of the: first seal (Rev. 6:1); second seal (Rev. 6:3); third seal (Rev. 6:5); fourth seal (Rev. 6:7); fifth seal (Rev. 6:9); sixth seal (Rev. 6:12); seventh seal (Rev. 8:1).

264 Closure

1 Doors

a A door for the ark (Gen. 6:16); doors for the temple (1 Kgs. 6:31–2, 34–5; 2 Chr. 4:22); doors for the court (2 Chr. 4:9); I will shatter the doors of bronze (Isa. 45:2).

| | *b* | If she is a door (S. of S. 8:9); I am the door of the sheep (John 10:7); I am the door (John 10:9). |

₁ Gates

c Setting up Jericho's gates cost the youngest son (Josh. 6:26; 1 Kgs. 16:34); Jotham built the upper gate of the temple (2 Chr. 27:3); the gates of Jerusalem have been burned (Neh. 1:3; 2:17); the gate is battered to ruins (Isa. 24:12); doors were not yet set up in the gateways (Neh. 6:1); measuring the gate of the temple (Ezek. 40:6–9); 12 gates of the city (Ezek. 48:30–4); the 12 gates of the city were 12 pearls (Rev. 21:12, 21).

d Beautiful Gate (Acts 3:2, 10); Benjamin Gate (Jer. 37:13; 38:7; Zech. 14:10); Corner Gate (Jer. 31:38; Zech. 14:10); East Gate (Neh. 3:29); Ephraim Gate (Neh. 8:16; 12:39); Fish Gate (2 Chr. 33:14; Neh. 3:3; 12:39); Fountain Gate (Neh. 2:14; 3:15; 12:37); Gate of the Guard (Neh. 12:39); Horse Gate (Neh. 3:28); Inspection Gate (Neh. 3:31); Middle Gate (Jer. 39:3); Old Gate (Neh. 3:6; 12:39); Refuse Gate (Neh. 2:13; 3:13, 14); Sheep Gate (Neh. 3:1, 32; 12:39; John 5:2); Valley Gate (Neh. 2:13, 15; 3:13); Water Gate (Neh. 3:26; 8:1, 3, 16; 12:37).

₁ Shutting
doors

e God closed up the ark (Gen. 7:16); the angels shut the door (Gen. 19:10); Ehud shut the doors behind him (Judg. 3:23); lock the door behind her (2 Sam. 13:17, 18); shut the door behind you (2 Kgs. 4:4); Elishah shut the door and prayed (2 Kgs. 4:33); the doors were shut for fear of the Jews (John 20:19); the prison was locked but empty (Acts 5:23); when the householder shuts the door you will knock (Luke 13:25); every house is closed up (Isa. 24:10).

₁ Shutting
temple
doors

f Ahaz shut the doors of the temple (2 Chr. 28:24); they have shut the doors of the porch (2 Chr. 29:7); the east gate of the sanctuary is to remain shut (Ezek. 44:1–2); oh, that one of you would shut the doors! (Mal. 1:10).

₁ Shutting
gates

g Shutting the gate at evening (Josh. 2:5, 7); Jericho was shut up (Josh. 6:1); David has shut himself into a city with gates and bars (1 Sam. 23:7); Nehemiah ordered the gates of Jerusalem to be shut (Neh. 13:19); the temple gates were shut (Acts 21:30).

h A nation without gates or bars (Jer. 49:31); Samson uprooted the gate and its posts (Judg. 16:3).

₁ Gatekeepers

i Gatekeepers for the house of the Lord (1 Chr. 9:17–27; 23:5); gatekeepers for the ark (1 Chr. 15:23, 24; 16:38); some of the Levites were gatekeepers (2 Chr. 34:13; Neh. 13:22); divisions of the gatekeepers (1 Chr. 26:1–19); Jehoiada stationed the gatekeepers (2 Chr. 23:19); the gatekeepers at each gate (2 Chr. 35:15; Neh. 11:19; 12:25).

j King's eunuchs who were doorkeepers (Esther 6:2).

₁ Stopping
wells

k The Philistines stopped up the wells (Gen. 26:15).

₁ Shutting the
kingdom

l You shut the kingdom of heaven against men (Matt. 23:13); the door of the marriage feast was shut (Matt. 25:10); what he shuts

181

no one will open (Isa. 22:22); he shuts and no one opens (Rev. 3:7).

1 Sealing   *m* They sealed the tomb (Matt. 27:66); they shut the abyss and sealed it over him (Rev. 20:3).

Stones as stoppers, see **344*i***.

n Solomon closed the breach in the city (1 Kgs. 11:27); Baasha blocked all entrance and exit for Judah (1 Kgs. 15:17; 2 Chr. 16:1).

o God shut the lions' mouths (Dan. 6:22).

1 Sealing the   *p* Like the words of a sealed book (Isa. 29:11); seal up the words
message   of the scroll (Dan. 12:4); the words are sealed up until the end time (Dan. 12:9); the scroll was sealed with seven seals (Rev. 5:1).

q Do not seal up the words of this book (Rev. 22:10).

Section four: Motion

265 Motion: successive change of plan
Changeableness, see **152**.

266 Stillness

1 Stilling   *a* Be still and know that I am God (Ps. 46:10); sun and moon, stand still (Josh. 10:12–13).

b He stills the roaring of the seas (Ps. 65:7); he stilled the storm (Ps. 107:29); when they threw Jonah overboard the sea grew calm (Jonah 1:12, 15); Jesus rebuked the wind and sea and there was calm (Matt. 8:26; Mark 4:39; Luke 8:24).

1 Motionless   *c* Enemies are motionless till your people pass over (Exod. 15:16); everyone stood still when they saw Asahel was dead (2 Sam. 2:23); Ahimaaz turned aside and stood still (2 Sam. 18:30); they stood still, looking sad (Luke 24:17).

1 Staying put   *d* Some tribes stayed away from the war (Judg. 5:16–17).

e Do not switch houses (Matt. 10:11; Mark 6:10; Luke 9:4; 10:7); Jesus stayed where he was two days longer (John 11:6).

267 Land travel

1 Journeying   *a* Abraham journeyed on south (Gen. 12:9); Israel travelled day and night (Exod. 13:21); they journeyed by stages (Exod. 17:1); the stages in the Israelites' journey from Egypt (Num. 21:10–20; 33:1–49).

b Jesus was setting out on a journey (Mark 10:17); like a man going on a journey (Matt. 25:14; Mark 13:34); Paul was on frequent journeys (2 Cor. 11:26); two disciples walking to Emmaus (Luke 24:13); my husband has gone on a journey (Prov. 7:19); you cross sea and land to make one proselyte (Matt. 23:15).

c The highways are empty, travellers gone (Isa. 33:8).

1 Marching	*d* The Israelites had to march around Jericho (Josh. 6:3–4); they have seen your procession (Ps. 68:24).
1 Walking	*e* Walk through the length and breadth of the land (Gen. 13:17); every place on which the sole of your foot treads is yours (Deut. 11:24; Josh. 1:3); the land on which your foot trod shall be your inheritance (Josh. 14:9).

f Four things are stately in walk, lions, cocks, goats and kings (Prov. 30:29–31); I taught Ephraim to walk (Hos. 11:3).

g The lame walk (Matt. 11:5; 15:31; Luke 7:22); take up your pallet and walk (Mark 2:9; John 5:8, 9, 11–12); in the name of Jesus Christ, walk (Acts 3:6); leaping up, he stood and walked (Acts 3:8–9, 12); the girl got up and walked (Mark 5:42); he sprang up and walked (Acts 14:8, 10).

h The priests of Dagon do not tread on the threshold (1 Sam. 5:5); idols have feet but cannot walk (Ps. 115:7).

Walking on water, see **269*e***.

1 Fast travel

i Jehu drove furiously (2 Kgs. 9:20); do not slow down for me (2 Kgs. 4:24).

1 Riding

j Abigail rode on a donkey (1 Sam. 25:20, 42); donkeys for the king's household to ride (2 Sam. 16:2); Absalom was riding on his mule (2 Sam. 18:9); Solomon was to ride on David's mule (1 Kgs. 1:33, 38, 44); the king's sons fled on mules (2 Sam. 13:29); your king comes riding on a donkey (Zech. 9:9; Matt. 21:5; John 12:15); Jesus rode on the donkey (Matt. 21:7; Mark 11:7; Luke 19:35; John 12:14).

k Horsemen were sent to meet Jehu (2 Kgs. 9:17–20); couriers riding on horses (Esther 8:10).

l I will give you 2000 horses if you can put riders on them (2 Kgs. 18:23; Isa. 36:8); mounts were provided for Paul (Acts 23:24); no animal except for Nehemiah's mount (Neh. 2:12).

m Ahithophel saddled his donkey (2 Sam. 17:23); I will saddle my donkey (2 Sam. 19:26); Shimei saddled his donkey (1 Kgs. 2:40); they saddled the donkey for the old prophet (1 Kgs. 13:13); the old prophet saddled the man of God's donkey (1 Kgs. 13:23); the Sunammite woman saddled a donkey (2 Kgs. 4:24).

n At God's rebuke rider and horse lay stunned (Ps. 76:6).

o God rode on a cherub (2 Sam. 22:11; Ps. 18:10); the Lord is riding on a swift cloud (Isa. 19:1).

Chariots and horsemen, see **274*a***.

268 Traveller

1 Wanderer

a Cain would be a wanderer on the earth (Gen. 4:12, 14); a wandering Aramean was my father (Deut. 26:5); they will be wanderers among the nations (Hos. 9:17); Israel wandered from nation to nation (1 Chr. 16:20; Ps. 105:13); wandering over deserts and mountains (Heb. 11:38).

b Shall I make you wander with us? (2 Sam. 15:20); God makes chiefs wander in a pathless waste (Job 12:24); you have taken account of my wanderings (Ps. 56:8).

c Satan came from roaming about on the earth (Job 1:7; 2:2).

ı Caravans

d A caravan of Ishmaelites (Gen. 37:25); they thought he was among the caravan (Luke 2:44).

269 Water travel

ı Rowing

a They rowed hard without avail (Jonah 1:13); they were distressed in rowing (Mark 6:48); when they had rowed about thirty stadia (John 6:19).

b Men of Sidon and Arvad were your rowers (Ezek. 27:8).

ı Sea travel

c They sailed from Attalia to Antioch (Acts 14:26); sea journey from Troas to Philippi (Acts 16:11–12); from Corinth bound for Syria (Acts 18:18); from Ephesus (Acts 18:21); Philippi to Troas (Acts 20:6); Troas to Assos (Acts 20:13); to Miletus (Acts 20:15); from Miletus to Tyre (Acts 21:1–3); to Ptolemais (Acts 21:7); the voyage and shipwreck to Malta (Acts 27:2–44); to Puteoli (Acts 28:11–13).

Sailors, see **270**; **ship travel**, see **275*c***; **sea transport**, see **343*o***.

ı Swimming

d They swam to shore (Acts 27:42–3); he will spread out his hands like a swimmer (Isa. 25:11).

ı Walking
on water

e Jesus came to them walking on the sea (Matt. 14:25–6; Mark 6:48–9; John 6:19); Peter walked on the water (Matt. 14:29).

ı Walking
in water

f The priests had to stand in the Jordan (Josh. 3:8, 15).

270 Mariner

ı Sailors

a Hiram sent sailors with Solomon's fleet (1 Kgs. 9:27; 2 Chr. 8:18); some went down to the sea in ships (Ps. 107:23); the sailors on the ship to Tarshish (Jonah 1:5–16); ships guided by the pilot (Jas. 3:4).

271 Aviation

ı Wings

a Oh, for wings like a dove! (Ps. 55:6); give wings to Moab so she can fly away (Jer. 48:9); two women with wings like a stork (Zech. 5:9); the woman was given the wings of the great eagle (Rev. 12:14); a leopard with four wings and four heads (Dan. 7:6); the lion's wings were plucked off (Dan. 7:4).

b The sun of righteousness with healing in its wings (Mal. 4:2).

ı Cherubim's
wings

c The wings of the cherubim (Exod. 25:20; 37:9; 1 Kgs. 6:27; 2 Chr. 3:11–13); the ark under the wings of the cherubim (1 Kgs. 8:6–7; 2 Chr. 5:7–8); cherubim with six wings (Isa. 6:2); each had four wings (Ezek. 1:6; 10:21); their wings touched one another (Ezek. 1:9); two wings covering their bodies (Ezek. 1:23); and two wings touching the wings of others (Ezek. 1:11); I heard the sound of their wings (Ezek. 1:24; 3:13); the sound of the cherubim's wings was heard (Ezek. 10:5).

<table>
<tr><td>1</td><td>Under God's
wings</td><td>*d*</td><td>Under the Lord's wings (Ruth 2:12); under his wings you will find refuge (Ps. 91:4); in the shadow of your wings men find refuge (Ps. 36:7; 57:1; 61:4); in the shadow of your wings I sing for joy (Ps. 63:7).</td></tr>
<tr><td>1</td><td>Flying things</td><td>*e*</td><td>A flying scroll (Zech. 5:1–2); their glory will fly away like a bird (Hos. 9:11).</td></tr>
</table>

272 Transference

1 Handing over

a Do not hand over an escaped slave to his master (Deut. 23:15); hand over the sons of Belial (Judg. 20:13); hand over the guilty son (2 Sam. 14:7); hand over Sheba (2 Sam. 20:21); they handed him over to Pilate (Matt. 27:2).

b Abner would transfer the kingdom to David (2 Sam. 3:10); let the king give her position to another (Esther 1:19); let another take his office (Ps. 109:8).

Birthrights transferred, see **119*d***.

c Binding Samson to hand him over to the Philistines (Judg. 15:12); will the men of Keilah hand me over to Saul? (1 Sam. 23:11–12) the Ziphites offered to surrender David (1 Sam. 23:20).

d God hands me over to the unjust (Job 16:11); God gave them up to impurity (Rom. 1:24); God gave them up to dishonourable passions (Rom. 1:26); God gave them up to a depraved mind (Rom. 1:28).

Transferring wives, see **894*v***; **handing over to the devil**, see **969*ab***.

1 Betraying

e Judas Iscariot who betrayed him (Matt. 10:4; 27:3; Mark 3:19); Judas became a traitor (Luke 6:16); he was to betray Jesus (John 6:71; 12:4); he sought an opportunity to betray him (Matt. 26:16; Mark 14:11; Luke 22:6); he discussed how to betray Jesus (Luke 22:4); Judas went to the chief priests to betray him (Mark 14:10); the devil put it into his heart to betray him (John 13:2).

f Jesus knew who would betray him (John 6:64; 13:11); one of you will betray me (Matt. 26:21; Mark 14:18; John 13:21); woe to the man who betrays him (Luke 22:22); he who dips his hand in the dish with me will betray me (Matt. 26:23); the betrayer's hand is with me on the table (Luke 22:21); do you betray the Son of man with a kiss? (Luke 22:48); the night he was betrayed, the Lord Jesus took bread (1 Cor. 11:23).

g The Son of man is to be betrayed into the hands of men (Mark 9:31; Luke 9:44); to be betrayed to the chief priests and scribes (Mark 10:33); my betrayer is at hand (Matt. 26:46; Mark 14:42); the Son of man is betrayed into the hands of sinners (Matt. 26:45; Mark 14:41).

h Brother will betray brother to death (Matt. 10:21; Mark 13:12); you will be betrayed by parents, brothers and friends (Luke 21:16); men will be traitors (2 Tim. 3:4).

<table>
<tr><td>1 Moving
house</td><td>*i* Esau moved to another land (Gen. 36:6).</td></tr>
</table>

273 Carrier

<table>
<tr><td>1 Carrying
holy things</td><td>*a* The Kohathites were to carry the holy articles (Num. 4:15) on their shoulders (Num. 7:9); the Gershonites were to carry the curtains and coverings (Num. 4:24–5); the Merarites were to carry the frames and posts (Num. 4:31–2); no one was to carry the ark but the Levites (1 Chr. 15:2); they carried the ark on their shoulders with poles (1 Chr. 15:15); the Levites took up the ark (2 Chr. 5:4); the ark would not be carried any more (2 Chr. 35:3); the Levites will no longer need to carry the tabernacle (1 Chr. 23:26).</td></tr>
<tr><td>1 Carrying
loads</td><td>*b* Do not carry a load on the Sabbath (Jer. 17:21, 24, 27); take up your mat and go home (Mark 2:11–12; Luke 5:24–5); on the Sabbath, carrying a pallet was not permitted (John 5:8–12); he would not allow anyone to carry anything through the temple (Mark 11:16).</td></tr>
<tr><td></td><td>*c* Samson carried the gate and posts on his shoulders (Judg. 16:3); they carried away the stones and timber of Ramah (1 Kgs. 15:22; 2 Chr. 16:6).</td></tr>
<tr><td></td><td>*d* Idols are loads carried by animals (Isa. 46:1); idols have to be carried (Jer. 10:5).</td></tr>
<tr><td></td><td>*e* A man carrying a pitcher of water (Mark 14:13; Luke 22:10).
Armour bearers, see **723***q*.</td></tr>
<tr><td>1 Carrying
the cross</td><td>*f* Jesus went out carrying his cross (John 19:17); they forced Simon of Cyrene to carry the cross (Matt. 27:32; Mark 15:21; Luke 23:26).
Crucifixion, see **964***d*.</td></tr>
<tr><td>1 Carrying
people</td><td>*g* Nadab and Abihu were carried outside the camp (Lev. 10:5); Elijah carried the boy to his own room (1 Kgs. 17:19); four people carried a paralytic to Jesus (Mark 2:3); the soldiers had to carry Paul (Acts 21:35).</td></tr>
<tr><td></td><td>*h* Aaron carried the names on his shoulders (Exod. 28:12); he will carry the lambs in his bosom (Isa. 40:11).</td></tr>
<tr><td>1 Bearing
sin</td><td>*i* The goat will bear their iniquities (Lev. 16:22); he bore our griefs and carried our sorrows (Isa. 53:4; Matt. 8:17); he will bear their iniquities (Isa. 53:11); he bore the sin of many (Isa. 53:12); he bore our sins in his body on the tree (1 Pet. 2:24); Ezekiel bore the iniquity of Judah (Ezek. 4:6); Ezekiel bore the iniquity of Israel (Ezek. 4:4–5).
Atonement, see **941**.</td></tr>
<tr><td>1 Bearing
people's
burdens</td><td>*j* Why should I carry the burden of all these people? (Num. 11:11–14); the seventy were to help Moses carry the burden of the people (Num. 11:16–17); bear one another's burdens (Gal. 6:2); every one will carry his own burden (Gal. 6:5).</td></tr>
<tr><td></td><td>*k* The Lord daily bears our burden (Ps. 68:19).</td></tr>
</table>

<table>
<tr><td>1 Metaphorical carrying</td><td>l God carried the Israelites on eagles' wings (Exod. 19:4; Deut. 32:11); God carried you as a father carries his son (Deut. 1:31); I have carried you from birth and to old age will carry you (Isa. 46:3–4); his angels will bear you up so that you will not hit your foot against a stone (Ps. 91:11–12; Matt. 4:6; Luke 4:10–11).</td></tr>
</table>

274 Vehicle

1 Chariots

a Pharaoh's chariots (Exod. 14:6–7, 9, 23–6); cast into the sea (Exod. 14:28; 15:4, 19).

b The kings had many horses and chariots (Josh. 11:4); the people of the plain had iron chariots (Josh. 17:16, 18; Judg. 1:19); Naaman came with horses and chariots (2 Kgs. 5:9); an army with horses and chariots (2 Kgs. 6:14, 15); Sisera had nine hundred iron chariots (Judg. 4:3, 13); Ahab struck the Arameans' horses and chariots (1 Kgs. 20:21); the Ammonites hired 32 000 chariots (1 Chr. 19:7); Shishak came with 1200 chariots and 60 000 horsemen (2 Chr. 12:3).

c David took horses and chariots from Hadadezer and kept horses for 100 chariots (2 Sam. 8:4; 1 Chr. 18:4); Absalom got a chariot and horses (2 Sam. 15:1); Adonijah got himself chariots and horsemen (1 Kgs. 1:5); Solomon had 4000 horses for his chariots and 12 000 horsemen (1 Kgs. 4:26; 2 Chr. 9:25); 1400 chariots and 12 000 horsemen (1 Kgs. 10:26; 2 Chr. 1:14); an imported chariot cost 600 shekels (1 Kgs. 10:29; 2 Chr. 1:17); Jehoahaz had no more than 50 horsemen and 10 chariots (2 Kgs. 13:7); no end to their horses and chariots (Isa. 2:7).

d Pharaoh had Joseph ride in a chariot (Gen. 41:43; 46:29); Rehoboam mounted his chariot hastily (1 Kgs. 12:18; 2 Chr. 10:18); prepare your chariot (1 Kgs. 18:44); Ahab brought Benhadad into the chariot (1 Kgs. 20:33); Jehu took Jonadab into his chariot (2 Kgs. 10:16); the Ethiopian eunuch had Philip sit in his chariot (Acts 8:31); Ahab was propped up in his chariot (1 Kgs. 22:35; 2 Chr. 18:34); two chariots sent out to find the Arameans (2 Kgs. 7:14); Jehu rode in a chariot (2 Kgs. 9:16); Joram and Ahaziah went out in their chariots (2 Kgs. 9:21); they took Josiah out of the chariot (2 Chr. 35:24); the Ethiopian eunuch sat in his chariot (Acts 8:28).

e The king will take your sons as charioteers (1 Sam. 8:11); cities for his chariots and horsemen (1 Kgs. 9:19; 2 Chr. 8:6); chariot cities (1 Kgs. 10:26).

f A chariot and horses of fire took Elijah (2 Kgs. 2:11); horses and chariots of fire round Elisha (2 Kgs. 6:17); my father! the chariots and horsemen of Israel! (2 Kgs. 2:12; 13:14); with myriads of chariots the Lord came to Sinai (Ps. 68:17); the chariot of the cherubim (1 Chr. 28:18); the Lord's chariots will be like the whirlwind (Isa. 66:15); the sound of their wings was like chariots and horses (Rev. 9:9).

ı Carts

g Horses and chariots for the sun at the gate of the temple (2 Kgs. 23:11).

h Some boast in horses and chariots (Ps. 20:7)

i Joseph sent carts for the children of Israel (Gen. 45:19, 21, 27; 46:5); six carts were used for carrying the tabernacle (Num. 7:3–7); the Philistines sent the ark away on a new cart (1 Sam. 6:7–8); David had the ark set on a new cart (2 Sam. 6:3–4; 1 Chr. 13:7).

275 Ship

ı Ships

a Solomon built ships at Ezion Geber (1 Kgs. 9:26); Huram sent Solomon ships (2 Chr. 8:18); Zebulun will be a haven for ships (Gen. 49:13); there go the ships (Ps. 104:26); a third of the ships were destroyed (Rev. 8:9).

ı Ships' tackle

b They threw the ship's tackle overboard (Acts 27:19); they slackened the ropes on the rudder and hoisted the foresail (Acts 27:40); ships guided by a small rudder (Jas. 3:4).

ı Ship travel

c The Lord will bring you back to Egypt in ships (Deut. 28:68); ships of Tarshish bring your sons from afar (Isa. 60:9); Jonah boarded a ship for Tarshish (Jonah 1:3).

Sea travel, see **269c**.

ı Noah's ark

d Noah was commanded to build an ark (Gen. 6:14–16); Noah constructed an ark (Heb. 11:7); during the building of the ark (1 Pet. 3:20); until Noah entered the ark (Matt. 24:38; Luke 17:27).

ı Ships for trading

e All who had ships at sea grew rich (Rev. 18:19); ships returned from sea every three years (1 Kgs. 10:22); Jehoshaphat built ships to go to Ophir for gold (1 Kgs. 22:48; 2 Chr. 20:36); the ships of Tarshish carried Tyre's merchandise (Ezek. 27:25).

f Tyre described as a sailing ship (Ezek. 27:4–9); your rigging lies slack (Isa. 33:23).

ı Ships for attacking

g Ships from Kittim will attack Assyria (Num. 24:24); ships of Kittim will come against him (Dan. 11:30).

ı Disaster for ships

h You break the ships of Tarshish (Ps. 48:7); a day against all the ships of Tarshish (Isa. 2:16); wail, ships of Tarshish (Isa. 23:1, 14).

i Rivers and wide canals where no ship shall pass (Isa. 33:21).

ı Boats

j Vessels of papyrus (Isa. 18:2); James and John in the boat mending their nets (Matt. 4:21; Mark 1:19); a boat was made ready for Jesus because of the crowd (Mark 3:9); he taught from a boat (Matt. 13:2; Mark 4:1; Luke 5:2–3); Jesus got into the boat with his disciples (Matt. 8:23; Mark 8:10; Luke 8:22); Jesus got into a boat and crossed over (Matt. 9:1; 15:39; Mark 4:36; 5:18; Luke 8:37); Jesus got into the boat and the wind stopped (Mark 6:51); he made the disciples get into the boat (Matt. 14:22; Mark 6:45); his disciples got into a boat (John 6:17); they went in a boat to a lonely place (Mark 6:32); the crowd saw there was no other boat there (John 6:22); they let down the ship's boat (Acts 27:30, 32).

276 Aircraft

Flying things, see **271***e*.

277 Swiftness

1 Fast runners

a Saul and Jonathan were swifter than eagles (2 Sam. 1:23); Asahel was as swift as a gazelle (2 Sam. 2:18).

b The ostrich laughs at horse and rider (Job 39:18).

1 People running

c A man ran from the battle to give news (1 Sam. 4:12); David ran to the battle line (1 Sam. 17:22, 48); the Cushite ran to give David news (2 Sam. 18:21); Ahimaaz wanted to run after (2 Sam. 18:22–3); the watchman saw one man running (2 Sam. 18:24, 26); his running is like that of Ahimaaz (2 Sam. 18:27); Peter ran to the tomb (Luke 24:12).

d Ahimaaz outran the Cushite (2 Sam. 18:23); Elijah outran Ahab (1 Kgs. 18:46); the other disciple outran Peter (John 20:4).

e If you have run with men on foot and they wearied you (Jer. 12:5); that he may run who reads it (Hab. 2:2).

1 Running after good

f I will run in the way of your commandments (Ps. 119:32); God's word runs swiftly (Ps. 147:15); be quick to hear, slow to speak (Jas. 1:19).

1 Running after evil

g Their feet run to evil and they hasten to shed blood (Prov. 1:16; Rom. 3:15); the Lord hates feet that hast to evil (Prov. 6:18).

1 Speed

h Do not slow down for me (2 Kgs. 4:24); go quickly and tell his disciples (Matt. 28:7–8).

i The race is not to the swift (Eccles. 9:11); the spoil speeds, the prey hastes (Isa. 8:1, 3); those who pursue you will be swift (Isa. 30:16).

Fast travel, see **276***i*; **haste**, see **680**.

278 Slowness

1 Gradual

a I will drive them out little by little (Exod. 23:30; Deut. 7:22); line upon line, here a little, there a little (Isa. 28:10, 13).

1 Slow

b We sailed along slowly and with difficulty (Acts 27:7); be slow to speak, slow to anger (Jas. 1:19).

279 Impact

1 Regulations on striking people

a Regulations for whoever strikes a man and kills him (Exod. 21:12); strikes his own slave and kills him (Exod. 21:20); strikes a man but does not kill him (Exod. 21:18); strikes his father or his mother (Exod. 21:15); strikes a pregnant woman (Exod. 21:22–5); if someone strikes you, turn the other cheek (Matt. 5:39; Luke 6:29).

b Judicial beating should not exceed forty lashes (Deut. 25:2–3); the forty stripes minus one (2 Cor. 11:24).

₁ Beating	*c* My father chastised you with whips, but I will use scorpions (1 Kgs. 12:11, 14; 2 Chr. 10:11, 14).
	d Moses saw an Egyptian beating a Hebrew (Exod. 2:11); the Israelite foremen were beaten (Exod. 5:14); Zedekiah slapped Micaiah in the face (1 Kgs. 22:24; 2 Chr. 18:23); Passhur had Jeremiah beaten (Jer. 20:2); they beat Jeremiah (Jer. 37:15); a prophet ordered someone to strike him (1 Kgs. 20:35, 37); Nehemiah beat some of the men (Neh. 13:25); the watchmen beat me (S. of S. 5:7); if he beats his fellow-servants (Matt. 24:49; Luke 12:45); they beat one of his servants (Matt. 21:35; Mark 12:3).
	e Balaam struck his donkey (Num. 22:23, 25, 27–8, 32).
	f I beat my body and make it my slave (1 Cor. 9:27); let the righteous strike me and rebuke me (Ps. 141:5); let him give his cheek to the smiter (Lam. 3:30); I gave my back to those who beat me (Isa. 50:6).
	g Crush a fool with a mortar and pestle and his folly will not leave him (Prov. 27:22); pressing milk produces butter and pressing the nose brings blood (Prov. 30:33).
	h The Lord will strike Israel (1 Kgs. 14:15); the Lord will strike Egypt (Isa. 19:22).
₁ Beating Jesus	*i* They will scourge and crucify him (Matt. 20:19; Mark 10:34; Luke 18:32); Pilate had Jesus flogged (Matt. 27:26; Mark 15:15; John 19:1); one of the officers struck Jesus (John 18:22–3); the guards received him with blows (Mark 14:65; John 19:3); they were mocking him and beating him (Luke 22:63); they beat him on the head (Matt. 27:30; Mark 15:19); they punched him and slapped him (Matt. 26:67); prophesy, who hit you? (Luke 22:64).
₁ Beating believers	*j* Men will beat you in their synagogues (Matt. 10:17; Mark 13:9); some you will scourge in your synagogues (Matt. 23:34); we commend ourselves in beatings (2 Cor. 6:5); some suffered scourging (Heb. 11:36).
	k Paul beat believers (Acts 22:19); Paul and Silas were flogged (Acts 16:22–23); the high priest ordered Paul to be struck on the mouth (Acts 23:2–3); they flogged the apostles (Acts 5:40); they have beaten us publicly (Acts 16:37); they beat Sosthenes in front of the judgement seat (Acts 18:17); they stopped beating Paul (Acts 21:32); Paul was to be examined by scourging (Acts 22:24–5); beaten numberless times (2 Cor. 11:23); three times beaten with rods (2 Cor. 11:25).
₁ Striking to death	*l* Abner struck Asahel in the belly (2 Sam. 2:23); Joab struck Abner in the belly (2 Sam. 3:27).
₁ Striking objects	*m* Moses was commanded to strike the rock (Exod. 17:6); he struck the rock when commanded to speak to it (Num. 20:11); Elisha commanded Joash to strike the ground with the arrows (2 Kgs. 13:18–19); battering rams against Tyre (Ezek. 26:9).
	n Lest you strike your foot against a rock (Ps. 91:12; Matt. 4:6;

Luke 4:11); happy he who dashes your little ones against a rock (Ps. 137:9).

o Elijah struck the water with his mantle (2 Kgs. 2:8); Elisha struck the water with Elijah's mantle (2 Kgs. 2:14).

1 **Knocking**

p The men of Gibeah pounded the door (Judg. 19:22); knock and it will be opened (Matt. 7:7; Luke 11:9–10); to open the door when he knocks (Luke 12:36); when the householder shuts the door, you will knock (Luke 13:25); Peter knocked on the door (Acts 12:13, 16); I stand at the door and knock (Rev. 3:20).

1 **Trampling**

q The official was trampled to death (2 Kgs. 7:17, 20); Jerusalem will be trampled by the Gentiles (Luke 21:24); the foot tramples the lofty city, brought low (Isa. 26:6); Moab will be trodden down like straw (Isa. 25:10); the crown of Ephraim's drunkards is trodden under foot (Isa. 28:3); it is hard for you to kick against the pricks (Acts 26:14).

r You will tread on the lion and the snake (Ps. 91:13); you will tread down the wicked (Mal. 4:3).

s Who requires of you this trampling of my courts? (Isa. 1:12); the Gentiles will trample the holy city for 42 months (Rev. 11:2).

t Why tread down the pasture? (Ezek. 34:18); seed on the road was trampled under foot (Luke 8:5); tasteless salt is fit only to be trampled under foot (Matt. 5:13); lest the swine trample the pearls under foot (Matt. 7:6).

Crushing, see **332f**.

1 **Clapping**

u Clap your hands (Ezek. 21:14); I will clap my hands (Ezek. 21:17).

280 Rebounding

1 **Evil rebounds**

a The wicked is ensnared in the work of his own hands (Ps. 9:16); his mischief will return on his own head (Ps. 7:16); a cruel man brings himself harm (Prov. 11:17); the wicked will fall by his own wickedness (Prov. 11:3, 5); they ambush themselves (Prov. 1:18); as you have done, it will be done to you (Obad. 15); their foot has been caught in the net they hid (Ps. 9:15–16); their sword will pierce their own heart (Ps. 37:15); because you have plundered, people will plunder you (Hab. 2:8).

b Those who dig a pit will themselves fall into it (Ps. 7:15–16; Prov. 26:27; Eccles. 10:8); they dug a pit, but they fell into it themselves (Ps. 9:15; 57:6); he who leads the upright astray will fall into his own pit (Prov. 28:10); suffering wrong for doing wrong (2 Pet. 2:13); do not judge lest you be judged (Matt. 7:1–2).

1 **Let evil rebound**

c Let the wicked fall into their own nets (Ps. 35:8; 141:10); bring the way of the wicked on his own head (1 Kgs. 8:32; 2 Chr. 6:23); return their reproach on their own heads (Neh. 4:4); do to her as she has done (Jer. 50:15, 29); may they be covered with the trouble their own lips have caused (Ps. 140:9); return sevenfold the reproach of our neighbours (Ps. 79:12); happy the one who repays Babylon with what they paid us (Ps. 137:8).

1 Evil
rebounding

d The Lord returned Nabal's evil on his own head (1 Sam. 25:39); he has brought their wickedness back on them (Ps. 94:23).

e Haman's scheme returned on his own head (Esther 9:25); the Lord has returned your bloodshed on you (2 Sam. 16:8); they shed the blood of your people and you gave them blood to drink (Rev. 16:6).

f Their own tongue is against them (Ps. 64:8); the talk of the foolish is a rod for his back (Prov. 14:3); he loved to curse and curses came (Ps. 109:17–18).

1 Good
rebounding

g Do to others as you would have them do to you (Matt. 7:12; Luke 6:31); forgive and you will be forgiven (Luke 6:37); the measure you give will be the measure you get (Matt. 7:2; Mark 4:24; Luke 6:38); a man's deeds return to him (Prov. 12:14).

h The kind man does himself good (Prov. 11:17); he who waters will himself be watered (Prov. 11:25).

281 Direction

1 North

a Proclaim these words to the north (Jer. 3:12); black horses patrol the north country (Zech. 6:6, 8); the king of the north (Dan. 11:6–45).

1 On the
north side

b Camping on the north side of the tabernacle: Dan (Num. 2:25); the Merarites (Num. 3:35).

c At the north of the altar gate was the image (Ezek. 8:5).

d The northern border (Num. 34:7–9); camped on the north side of Ai (Josh. 8:11).

1 Out of
the north

e Out of the north comes cold (Job 37:9); a stormy wind from the north (Ezek. 1:4); a violent wind called the Northeaster (Acts 27:14).

f Out of the north evil will break forth (Jer. 1:13–15); evil looms from the north (Jer. 6:1); I am bringing evil from the north (Jer. 6:1); a horsefly is coming from the north (Jer. 46:20); waters will rise from the north (Jer. 47:2).

g A people is coming from the north (Jer. 6:22); a commotion from the north (Jer. 10:22); see those coming from the north (Jer. 13:20); I will send for the tribes of the north (Jer. 25:9); I stirred up one from the north (Isa. 41:25); Nebuchadnezzar comes upon Tyre from the north (Ezek. 26:7); given into the hand of the people of the north (Jer. 46:24); God will come against Israel from the north (Ezek. 38:15; 39:2).

h A nation has come against Babylon out of the north (Jer. 50:3, 41); a horde of nations against Babylon out of the north (Jer. 50:9); slaughter in the land of the north by the river Euphrates (Jer. 46:10).

₁ Return from the north	*i* They will return from the land of the north (Jer. 3:18); the Lord will bring back Israel from the north land (Jer. 16:15; 23:8; 31:8); I will drive the northerner far from you (Joel 2:20).
₁ South	*j* Out of the south comes the storm (Job 37:9); the south wind brings heat (Job 37:17); a south wind sprang up (Acts 27:13; 28:13); the king of the south (Dan. 11:5–45); dappled horses patrol the south (Zech. 6:6).

k Abraham travelled on toward the south (Gen. 12:9; 20:1); the southern border (Num. 34:3–5).

l Camping on the south side of the tabernacle: Reuben (Num. 2:10); the Kohathites (Num. 3:29); those camped on the south set out (Num. 10:6).

₁ East   *m* The land of the sons of the east (Gen. 29:1); the sons of the east (1 Kgs. 4:30); I will give them to the sons of the east (Ezek. 25:4, 10); magi from the east (Matt. 2:1).

n Eden was to the east (Gen. 2:8); the Tigris flows east of Assyria (Gen. 2:14); cherubim east of the garden (Gen. 3:24); Cain settled east of Eden (Gen. 4:16); the sons of Shem settled in the hill country of the east (Gen. 10:30); men journeyed east (Gen. 11:2); as did Lot (Gen. 13:11); Ishmael would live east of his brethren (Gen. 16:12); Abraham sent his other sons eastward from Isaac (Gen. 25:6).

o The eastern border (Num. 34:10–12); Reuben and Gad inherited east of Jordan (Num. 32:19).

p Camping on the east side of the tabernacle: Judah (Num. 2:3); Moses and Aaron (Num. 3:38).

q Those camped on the east set out (Num. 10:5).

East wind, see **352k**.

₁ West   *r* The west side of the wilderness (Exod. 3:1); the western border (Num. 34:6); ambush to the west of Ai (Josh. 8:9, 12); a he-goat from the west (Dan. 8:5).

s Camping on the west side of the tabernacle: Ephraim (Num. 2:18); the Gershonites (Num. 3:23).

West wind, see **352k**.

₁ Combined directions   *t* You have created north and south (Ps. 89:12); Bethel on the west and Ai to the east (Gen. 12:8); the ram butting eastward, north-ward and southward (Dan. 8:4).

u Look north, south, east and west (Gen. 13:14; Deut. 3:27); you will spread out to west, east, north and south (Gen. 28:14).

v The tribes were to camp north, south, east and west of the tabernacle (Num. 2:3–25; 3:21–38); three oxen each facing north, west, south and east (1 Kgs. 7:25; 2 Chr. 4:4); the Lord gathered them from east, west, north and south (Ps. 107:3).

w A flaming sword turned in every direction (Gen. 3:24).

282 Deviation

1 Going astray

a If a neighbour's animal strays, bring it back (Deut. 22:1–3); like a bird wandering from its nest is a man who wanders from home (Prov. 27:8).

1 Turning from the Lord

b Are you turning away from the Lord? (Josh. 22:16, 18); if we are turning away (Josh. 22:23); if one of 100 sheep goes astray (Matt. 18:12–13); why do you make us stray from your ways? (Isa. 63:17); turn aside from the path (Isa. 30:11).

c Do not turn away from following the Lord (1 Sam. 12:20–1); I have told you this lest you go astray (John 16:1); lest any turn away from the Lord (Deut. 29:18); you will turn from the way (Deut. 31:29).

d Lot's wife looked back (Gen. 19:26); the people soon turned away (Deut. 9:12, 16); Saul has turned back from following me (1 Sam. 15:11); many of his disciples turned back from following him (John 6:66); some have turned aside to follow Satan (1 Tim. 5:15); they turn away from the holy commandment (2 Pet. 2:21).

e We were like sheep going astray (Ps. 119:176; Isa. 53:6; 1 Pet. 2:25); before I was afflicted I went astray (Ps. 119:67); they have strayed from me (Hos. 7:13); they always go astray (Heb. 3:10); forsaking the right way they have gone astray (2 Pet. 2:15); some have strayed from the faith (1 Tim. 6:21); some have strayed from the truth (2 Tim. 2:18); through love of money some have wandered from the faith (1 Tim. 6:10).

1 Turning from God's word

f Do not let me wander from your commandments (Ps. 119:10); I do not turn away from your law (Ps. 119:51); I do not turn aside from your testimonies (Ps. 119:157); I do not turn aside from your ordinances (Ps. 119:102); the arrogant wander from your commandments (Ps. 119:21); you reject those who go away from your statutes (Ps. 119:118).

1 Turning people away

g Solomon's wives turned away his heart after other gods (1 Kgs. 11:4); Elymas tried to turn the proconsul away from the faith (Acts 13:8); I am afraid you may be led astray (2 Cor. 11:3).

1 Change direction

h Turn aside to right or left! (2 Sam. 2:21); whenever you turn to right or left you will hear a word (Isa. 30:21); they will turn to you but you will not turn to them (Jer. 15:19).
Not turn to right or left, see **249c**.

1 Turning from evil

i Turn from your evil way (Jer. 25:5); perhaps they will turn from their evil way (Jer. 26:3).

283 Preceding: going before

1 God leading the way

a God led them in a pillar of cloud and fire (Exod. 13:21); God goes before you to show you the way you should go (Deut. 1:33); I will go before you (Isa. 45:2); the Lord will go before you (Isa. 52:12); you led your people like a flock (Ps. 77:20); he led his people through the wilderness (Ps. 136:16).

God guiding, see **689***d*.

b The ark went ahead of the people (Josh. 3:6, 11, 14); the star went on before them (Matt. 2:9).

1 Jesus going before

c I will go before you to Galilee (Matt. 26:32); he is going before you into Galilee (Matt. 28:7; Mark 16:7).

1 People leading the way

d Let the Lord appoint a man to go out and come in before the congregation (Num. 27:17); Joshua shall go across before this people (Deut. 3:28); the leaders led in Israel (Judg. 5:2).

e The shepherd goes before the sheep (John 10:4).

1 Coming before

f Why do the scribes say Elijah must come first? (Matt. 17:10; Mark 9:11); John would go before the Lord (Luke 1:17); to prepare the way (Luke 1:76; 7:27).

g Tax-collectors and harlots go into the kingdom of God before you (Matt. 21:31); another steps down before me (John 5:7).

h We who are alive will not precede those who have fallen asleep (1 Thess. 4:15).

284 Following: going after

1 Following Jesus

a The sheep follow the shepherd (John 10:4); my sheep follow me (John 10:27); if anyone serves me, let him follow me (John 12:26).

b Follow me (Matt. 4:19; 8:22; 9:9; 19:21; Mark 1:17; 2:14; 10:21; Luke 5:27; 9:59; 18:22; John 1:43; 21:19, 22); they followed Jesus (John 1:37); they left the boat and their father and followed him (Matt. 4:22); they left everything and followed him (Mark 1:18, 20; Luke 5:11).

c Great crowds followed him (Matt. 4:25; 14:13); many followed him (Matt. 12:15; Mark 2:15); the blind men followed him (Matt. 20:34; Mark 10:52; Luke 18:43).

d I will follow you wherever you go (Matt. 8:19; Luke 9:57); I will follow you, but first let me say goodbye (Luke 9:61); we left everything and followed you (Matt. 19:27; Mark 10:28; Luke 18:28).

e Whoever would come after me must take up his cross (Matt. 16:24; Mark 8:34; Luke 9:23; 14:27); whoever does not take up his cross and follow me is not worthy (Matt. 10:38).

f Peter followed him at a distance (Matt. 26:58; Mark 14:54; Luke 22:54; John 18:15).

g You cannot follow now, but you will follow later (John 13:36).

1 Following others

h They followed Sheba, not David (2 Sam. 20:2); whoever is for David, follow Joab (2 Sam. 20:11); Gehazi chased after Naaman (2 Kgs. 5:21); we forbade him because he was not following us (Mark 9:38); Jesus and his disciples followed the ruler (Matt. 9:19).

1 Coming after

i He who comes after me is mightier than I (Matt. 3:11; Mark 1:7).

285 Advance

₁ Promotion
    a Ahasuerus promoted Haman (Esther 3:1); Haman told how the king had promoted him (Esther 5:11); Nebuchadnezzar promoted Shadrach, Meshach and Abednego (Dan. 3:30); the king planned to promote Daniel (Dan. 6:3).
    God promoting, see **310e**.
    b He has exalted the humble (Luke 1:52).

₁ Going
 forward
    c They went straight forward (Ezek. 1:9, 12).

286 Regression: motion backwards

₁ Go
 backwards
    a You keep going backwards (Jer. 15:6).

287 Propulsion

₁ Throwing
 stones
    a Seven hundred Benjaminites could sling a stone at a hair and not miss (Judg. 20:16); David's men slung stones and shot arrows right- and left-handed (1 Chr. 12:2); David took his sling (1 Sam. 17:40); David slung a stone at Goliath (1 Sam. 17:49); Shimei threw stones at David (2 Sam. 16:6, 13); the slingers struck Kir-hareseth (2 Kgs. 3:25); engines for shooting arrows and stones (2 Chr. 26:15); Uzziah prepared bows and sling stones (2 Chr. 26:14).
    b He will be stoned or shot (Exod. 19:13).
    Stoning, see **344n**.
    c God will sling out the lives of your enemies as from a sling (1 Sam. 25:29).

₁ Throwing
 spears
    d Saul hurled a spear at David (1 Sam. 18:11); Saul hurled his spear at Jonathan (1 Sam. 20:33).

₁ Bows and
 arrows
    e Ishmael became an archer (Gen. 21:20); the sons of Ulam were archers (1 Chr. 8:40); I can bend a bow of bronze (2 Sam. 22:35; Ps. 18:34); take your quiver and bow (Gen. 27:3); Jonathan signalled by shooting arrows (1 Sam. 20:20, 36–8); taking a bow and arrows and shooting out of the window (2 Kgs. 13:15–17).
    f Saul was wounded by the archers (1 Sam. 31:3; 1 Chr. 10:3); a man drew his bow at random (1 Kgs. 22:34; 2 Chr. 18:33); Jehu drew his bow and shot Joram (2 Kgs. 9:24).
    g They would be shot from the wall (2 Sam. 11:20); archers shot from the wall (2 Sam. 11:24).
    h The fiery darts of the evil one (Eph. 6:16); lament called 'The Bow' (2 Sam. 1:18); they twisted like a deceitful bow (Ps. 78:57); children are like a warrior's arrows (Ps. 127:4–5); they bend their tongue like a bow (Jer. 9:3).

₁ God's bow
 and arrows
    i The Lord's arrow of victory over Aram (2 Kgs. 13:17); lightning is God's arrows (2 Sam. 22:15; Ps. 18:14); God has bent his bow (Ps. 7:12–13).
    j Your arrows are sharp in the heart of the king's enemies (Ps.

45:5); God will shoot his arrow at them (Ps. 64:7); send out your arrows and rout them (Ps. 144:6); arrows against the deceitful tongue (Ps. 120:4).

k He made me a polished arrow (Isa. 49:2); I will bend Judah as my bow (Zech. 9:13–14).

l He has bent his bow like an enemy (Lam. 2:4); he bent his bow and made me a target for his arrows (Lam. 3:12); God's arrows are within me (Job 6:4); your arrows have sunk deep into me (Ps. 38:2).

1 Throwing people

m Daniel was thrown into the lions' den (Dan. 6:16); Daniel's accusers were thrown into the lions' den (Dan. 6:24); they were thrown into the fiery furnace (Dan. 3:21); throwing Jonah into the sea (Jonah 1:12, 15); they wanted to throw Jesus over the cliff (Luke 4:29); the spirit dashes him to the ground (Mark 9:18); cast the worthless servant into outer darkness (Matt. 25:30).

n God is about to hurl you away (Isa. 22:17–18); I will hurl you out of this land (Jer. 16:13; 22:26); why has Coniah been hurled into an unknown land? (Jer. 22:28).

1 Throwing things

o Cast your bread on the waters (Eccles. 11:1); he threw the money into the temple (Matt. 27:5); whoever tells this mountain to be cast into the sea (Mark 11:23).

288 Pulling

1 Pulling people

a They pulled Lot back into the house (Gen. 19:10); they pulled them out of the city (Gen. 19:16); they dragged Paul out of the city (Acts 14:19); they dragged Paul and Silas into the market-place (Acts 16:19); the Jews dragged Jason before the authorities (Acts 17:6); they dragged Paul out of the temple (Acts 21:30).

1 Pulling things

b We will drag the city into the valley (2 Sam. 17:13); they dragged the net full of fish (John 21:8).

c Woe to those who drag iniquity with cords of falsehood (Isa. 5:18).

289 Approach: motion towards

1 Coming to people

a If they say, 'Come!', that will be the sign (1 Sam. 14:10); come up to us (1 Sam. 14:12).

b They came from all peoples to hear Solomon's wisdom (1 Kgs. 4:34); I hope to be coming shortly (Phil. 2:24; 1 Tim. 3:14).

1 Coming to Jesus

c No one can come to me unless the Father draws him (John 6:44, 65); come to me! (Matt. 11:28); no one comes to the Father but by me (John 14:6).

290 Recession: motion from

Departure, see **296**.

291 Attraction

Desire, see **859**.

292 Repulsion

Ejection, see **300**.

293 Convergence

Approach, see **289**.

294 Divergence

Deviation, see **282**.

295 Arrival

1 Meeting

a I will meet with you: at the ark (Exod. 25:22); at the doorway of the tent of meeting (Exod. 29:42–3).

b Prepare to meet your God (Amos 4:12); do two walk together without an appointment? (Amos 3:3); come out to meet the bridegroom (Matt. 25:6); Jesus met them and greeted them (Matt. 28:9).

c Whatever comes out to meet me I will sacrifice (Judg. 11:31); his daughter came out to meet him (Judg. 11:34).

d Let us meet in the plain of Ono (Neh. 6:2); let us meet in the temple (Neh. 6:10).

Visiting, see **882g**.

1 The Lord's coming

e The Lord comes to judge the earth (Ps. 96:13; 98:9); the Lord will come and all his holy ones (Zech. 14:5); blessed is he who comes in the name of the Lord (Ps. 118:26; Matt. 21:9; 23:39; Mark 11:9; Luke 13:35; 19:38; John 12:13); until he comes whose right it is (Ezek. 21:27).

f The coming of the Lord (1 Thess. 5:23; 2 Thess. 2:1); when our Lord Jesus comes (1 Thess. 3:13); when he comes to be glorified in his saints (2 Thess. 1:10); we who remain alive until the coming of the Lord (1 Thess. 4:15); be patient until the coming of the Lord (Jas. 5:7).

g Jesus is coming soon (Rev. 3:11; 22:7, 20); the coming of the Lord is at hand (Jas. 5:8); you will not have finished the towns of Israel before the Son of man comes (Matt. 10:23); the Son of man will come in the glory of his Father (Matt. 16:27; Mark 8:38; Luke 9:26); when the Son of man comes in his glory (Matt. 25:31); the Son of man coming on the clouds (Matt. 24:30; Mark 13:26; Luke 21:27); what will be the sign of your coming? (Matt. 24:3); the Lord will destroy the lawless one by his coming (2 Thess. 2:8).

h The coming of the Son of man will be like lightning (Matt. 24:27); like the days of Noah (Matt. 24:37); you do not know when your Lord is coming (Matt. 24:42); the Son of man comes when you do not expect (Matt. 24:44); where is the promise of his coming? (2 Pet. 3:4); I am coming like a thief (Rev. 16:15).

i Maranatha – our Lord, come! (1 Cor. 16:22); you proclaim the Lord's death until he comes (1 Cor. 11:26).

Waiting for the second coming, see **507***d*; **signs of Christ's return**, see **547***j*.

1 Destination   *j*   Immediately the boat was at their destination (John 6:21).

296 Departure

1 Setting out   *a*   When the cloud lifted the Israelites set out (Exod. 40:36–7; Num. 9:17); they set out at the Lord's command (Num. 9:18).

    b   Depart! go out from there! (Isa. 52:11).

1 Leaving   *c*   The Gadarenes asked Jesus to leave their country (Matt. 8:34); depart from me, for I am a sinful man (Luke 5:8); the Philippians begged Paul and Silas to depart (Acts 16:39).

Abandoning, see **621**.

    d   Please do not go away (Judg. 6:18).

1 Exodus   *e*   Joseph spoke of the exodus of Israel (Heb. 11:22); Moses and Elijah spoke with Jesus about his departure to be accomplished at Jerusalem (Luke 9:31).

297 Entrance

1 Entering places   *a*   Noah entered the ark (Gen. 7:1, 7, 13); how Aaron should enter the holy place (Lev. 16:3).

    b   Do not enter a house to take a pledge (Deut. 24:10); when you enter the house, greet it (Matt. 10:12); do not go into the house to retrieve anything (Mark 13:15).

    c   The Jebusites thought David could not get in (2 Sam. 5:6; 1 Chr. 11:5); Absalom entered Jerusalem (2 Sam. 15:37); they dared not be seen entering the city (2 Sam. 17:17); who will bring us into the fortified city? (Ps. 60:9); do not even enter the village (Mark 8:26).

    d   What enters the mouth does not defile a man (Matt. 15:11, 17; Mark 7:15, 18).

1 Entering the temple   *e*   The priests could not enter the temple for the cloud (2 Chr. 7:2); Uzziah entered the temple to burn incense (2 Chr. 26:16); Jotham did not enter the temple (2 Chr. 27:2).

The temple entered, see **990***q*.

1 Entering life   *f*   Strive to enter by the narrow door (Luke 13:24); the narrow gate that leads to life (Matt. 7:13–14); I am the gate; whoever enters through me will be saved (John 10:9); that they may enter the city by the gates (Rev. 22:14).

1 Access to God   *g*   We enter the holy of holies through the blood of Jesus (Heb. 10:19); we have access to the Father (Eph. 2:18); access in confidence through faith (Eph. 3:12).

1 Entering the gate   *h*   I shall enter through the gates of righteousness (Ps. 118:19–20); enter his gates with thanksgiving (Ps. 100:4); he who enters by the gate is the shepherd (John 10:2); that the king of glory may come in (Ps. 24:7, 9).

1 Entering the kingdom   *i*   How hard it is to enter the kingdom! (Mark 10:24); it is hard for the wealthy to enter (Matt. 19:23; Mark 10:23; Luke 18:24); not

everyone who says Lord! will enter (Matt. 7:21); it is better to enter maimed than not to enter (Matt. 18:8–9; Mark 9:43–7); abundant entrance into the kingdom (2 Pet. 1:11).

The kingdom entered, see **733*p*.**

j You will not enter the kingdom: unless your righteousness surpasses (Matt. 5:20); unless you become like children (Matt. 18:3; Mark 10:15; Luke 18:17); unless you are born again (John 3:5).

k You did not enter and you hindered those that did (Luke 11:52).

Entering
heaven

l Jesus has entered within the veil (Heb. 6:19–20); Christ entered heaven itself (Heb. 9:24).

m The twelve gates of the city were twelve pearls (Rev. 21:12, 21).

Demons
entering

n Satan entered Judas (Luke 22:3; John 13:27); many demons had entered the man (Luke 8:30); come out and do not enter him again (Mark 9:25); the demons entered the pigs (Matt. 8:32; Mark 5:12–13; Luke 8:32–3).

Demonised, see **969*u*.**

298 Emergence

Emerging

a Coming out of the ark (Gen. 8:16–19); Hebrews are coming out of their holes (1 Sam. 14:11).

Leaving
places

b They went out from Ur (Gen. 11:31); go from your country and family (Gen. 12:1); when Israel went forth from Egypt (Ps. 114:1).

Going
outside

c Do not go outside until morning (Exod. 12:22); the high priest must not go out of the sanctuary (Lev. 21:12); Joab would not come out of the tabernacle (1 Kgs. 2:30).

d Shimei was not to leave Jerusalem (1 Kgs. 2:36–7).

Coming out
of people

e What comes out of the mouth defiles a man (Matt. 15:11, 18; Mark 7:15, 20); out of the heart come evil things (Matt. 15:19; Mark 7:21)

Leaving evil

f Come out of her, my people (Jer. 51:45; Rev. 18:4); go forth from Babylon (Isa. 48:20; Jer. 50:8); come out from them and be separate (2 Cor. 6:17).

Leaving
the church

g They went out from us to demonstrate that they are not of us (1 John 2:19).

299 Reception

Welcoming
people

a That the Israelites may be accepted (Exod. 28:38); I know what to do so they will receive me into their homes (Luke 16:4).

b This man receives sinners and eats with them (Luke 15:2); he has gone to be the guest of a sinner (Luke 19:7); Zaccheus received Jesus gladly (Luke 19:6).

c He who receives you receives me (Matt. 10:40; John 13:20); he who receives such a child receives me (Matt. 18:5; Mark 9:37; Luke 9:48); accept one another as Christ accepted us (Rom.

15:7); accept him as you would me (Philem. 17); I was a stranger and you welcomed me (Matt. 25:35); you received me as an angel of God, as Christ (Gal. 4:14).

d Receive him who is weak in the faith (Rom. 14:1); receive Phoebe in the Lord (Rom. 16:2); receive Epaphroditus with all joy (Phil. 2:29); if Mark comes, welcome him (Col. 4:10).

e Those who receive him have the right to become children of God (John 1:12).

Greeting, see **884**.

f His own did not receive him (John 1:11); I come in my Father's name and you do not receive me (John 5:43); the Samaritan village would not receive him (Luke 9:53).

g If anyone does not bring this doctrine, do not receive him into the house (2 John 10).

h If anyone will not receive you, shake the dust off your feet (Matt. 10:14; Luke 9:5; 10:10–11); Diotrephes would not receive the brethren (3 John 10).

1 Not welcoming people

300 Ejection

1 Jesus casting out demons

a Begone, Satan! (Matt. 4:10); be quiet and come out of him (Mark 1:25–6); he was casting out a dumb demon (Luke 11:14).

b Jesus drove out many evil spirits (Matt. 8:16; Mark 1:34; Luke 4:41); Jesus was preaching and casting out evil spirits (Mark 1:39); I cast out demons today and tomorrow (Luke 13:32); he commanded the evil spirit to come out of the man in the synagogue (Luke 4:35); out of the Gadarene demoniac (Matt. 8:32; Mark 5:8; Luke 8:29); out of the man's son (Mark 9:25); the Syro-Phoenician woman begged Jesus to cast the demon out (Mark 7:26).

c He casts out demons by the ruler of demons (Matt. 9:34; 12:24, 27; Mark 3:22; Luke 11:15, 18–19); how can Satan cast out Satan? (Matt. 12:26); if I cast out demons by the Spirit of God (Matt. 12:28).

1 People casting out demons

d Cast out demons (Matt. 10:8); he gave them authority to cast out unclean spirits (Matt. 10:1); the twelve were to have authority to cast out demons (Mark 3:15); in my name they will cast out demons (Mark 16:17).

e The disciples cast out many demons (Mark 6:13); unclean spirits came out of many (Acts 8:7); in the name of Jesus Paul commanded the spirit to come out (Acts 16:18); evil spirits went out when garments from Paul were brought (Acts 19:12).

f The disciples could not cast out the evil spirit (Mark 9:18; Luke 9:40); why could we not cast it out? (Matt. 17:19; Mark 9:28).

g Did we not cast out demons in your name? (Matt. 7:22); someone was casting out evil spirits who did not follow them (Mark 9:38; Luke 9:49); itinerant Jewish exorcists tried to use the name of

Jesus (Acts 19:13); by whom do your sons cast out demons? (Matt. 12:27; Luke 11:19).

1 **Driving out the people of the land**

h The Lord will drive out these nations (Exod. 34:11; Deut. 6:19; 9:3–5; 11:23); I will drive them out (Exod. 33:2; 34:24; Josh. 13:6; 23:5); he drove out the enemy (Deut. 33:27); he drove out the nations before them (Ps. 78:55); I sent the hornet which drove them out (Josh. 24:12); you drove out the nations (Ps. 44:2; 80:8); the Lord has driven the Amorites out (Exod. 23:28; Josh. 24:18; Judg. 11:23); because of their wickedness the Lord is driving them out (Deut. 9:5; 18:12); driving out nations greater than you (Deut. 4:38; Josh. 23:9); did you not drive them out? (2 Chr. 20:7).

i Drive them out! (Exod. 23:31; Num. 33:52; Josh. 23:5); though they are strong, you can drive them out (Josh. 17:18); the Lord will be with me and I shall drive them out (Josh. 14:12); Caleb drove out the three sons of Anak (Josh. 15:14; Judg. 1:20).

j If you do not drive them out they shall vex you (Num. 33:55); the Israelites did not drive some of them out (Josh. 13:13; 15:63; 16:10; 17:13; Judg. 1:19, 21, 27–33).

k The Lord will not drive out these nations (Josh. 23:13; Judg. 2:3, 21, 23).

1 **Driving Israel out**

l Perhaps I can drive Israel out of the land (Num. 22:6, 11); they are coming to drive us out (2 Chr. 20:11); I am slinging out the inhabitants of the land (Jer. 10:18).

1 **Driven from God's presence**

m Adam was driven out of the garden (Gen. 3:23); Cain was driven from the ground and from the Lord's presence (Gen. 4:14, 16); men have driven me out from the Lord's inheritance (1 Sam. 26:19).

n Israel would be uprooted from the land (2 Chr. 7:20); I will cut off Israel from the land (1 Kgs. 9:7); the Lord removed Israel from his sight (2 Kgs. 17:18, 20, 23); removing Judah also from his sight (2 Kgs. 23:27; 24:3, 20; Jer. 52:3); I will cast you out of my sight (Jer. 7:15); the Lord would not cast them from his presence until now (2 Kgs. 13:23); I will cast you away from my presence (Jer. 23:39); I am cast out from your presence (Jonah 2:4).

o Uzziah was driven from the sanctuary (2 Chr. 26:18, 20); Tobiah's things were thrown out of the room in the temple (Neh. 13:8).

p I have cast you out from God's mountain, O cherub (Ezek. 28:16); the ruler of this world will be cast out (John 12:31); the great dragon was thrown down from heaven (Rev. 12:9).

1 **Jesus casting out people**

q Depart from me, you evildoers (Ps. 6:8; 119:115; Matt. 7:23; Luke 13:27); you cursed (Matt. 25:41); depart from me, men of blood (Ps. 139:19); the sons of the kingdom will be cast out (Matt. 8:12); all the prophets in the kingdom and you thrown out (Luke 13:28).

r Jesus drove the traders out of the temple (Matt. 21:12; Mark 11:15; Luke 19:45; John 2:15); Jesus sent the mourners away (Matt. 9:24; Mark 5:40); he sent the crowds away (Matt. 14:22).

s He who comes to me I will not cast out (John 6:37).

t The disciples wanted him to send the woman away (Matt. 15:23); send the crowds away (Matt. 14:15; 15:39; Mark 6:36).

1 Driven from God's people

u The diseased were to be sent out of the camp (Num. 5:2–4); anyone who did not come would be expelled from the assembly (Ezra 10:8); your brothers cast you out (Isa. 66:5).

v Drive out the slave woman (Gen. 21:10; Gal. 4:30); Abraham sent her off (Gen. 21:14); Abraham sent the sons of his concubines away (Gen. 25:6); Zebul drove out Gaal (Judg. 9:41); Gilead's sons drove out Jephthah (Judg. 11:2, 7).

1 Excommunicating

w They will expel you from the synagogue (John 16:2); whoever acknowledged that Jesus was the Christ would be put out of the synagogue (John 9:22); they did not confess him lest they be put out of the synagogue (John 12:42); they threw him out (John 9:34); blessed are you when men excommunicate you (Luke 6:22); the Jews drove us out (1 Thess. 2:15); do not let the wicked drive me away (Ps. 36:11).

x The one who did this should be removed from among you (1 Cor. 5:2); expel the wicked man (1 Cor. 5:13); Diotrephes puts brothers out of the church (3 John 10).

1 Jesus driven out

y The Spirit drove Jesus out into the wilderness (Mark 1:12); they cast Jesus out of Nazareth (Luke 4:29); they threw the heir out of the vineyard and killed him (Matt. 21:39; Luke 20:15).

1 Other driving out

z Abimelech sent Isaac away (Gen. 26:16, 27); the shepherds drove away Reuel's daughters (Exod. 2:17); Pharaoh drove out Moses and Aaron (Exod. 10:11, 28); and all Israel (Exod. 11:1; 12:31); the lords of the Philistines sent David away (1 Chr. 12:19); Abimelech drove David away (Ps. 34:t); Amaziah dismissed the soldiers from Ephraim (2 Chr. 25:10); Nehemiah drove away the son-in-law of Sanballat (Neh. 13:28); Amaziah told Amos to go away (Amos 7:12); Gallio drove them away from the judgement seat (Acts 18:16); Claudius had expelled all the Jews from Rome (Acts 18:2).

aa Joseph sent everyone else out when he made himself known to his brethren (Gen. 45:1); Amnon sent everyone out (2 Sam. 13:9); Amnon drove out Tamar (2 Sam. 13:15, 17); Gehazi tried to push her away (2 Kgs. 4:27); Peter sent the mourners out (Acts 9:40).

ab Abraham drove away the birds of prey (Gen. 15:11).

ac Send the ark away! (1 Sam. 5:11); they tell God to depart from them (Job 22:17).

1 Supplanting

ad Jacob—supplanter (Gen. 25:26); he has supplanted me twice (Gen. 27:36); in the womb he took his brother by the heel (Hos. 12:3).

ı Disqualified   *ae* Lest after preaching to others I should be disqualified (1 Cor. 9:27).

301 Food: eating and drinking

ı Food
defined

a God gave mankind plants and fruit for food (Gen. 1:29; 3:18); the garden of Eden contained trees good for food (Gen. 2:9); from which they could eat (Gen. 2:16; 3:2); God gives animals to man as food (Gen. 9:3); slaughtering and eating meat (Deut. 12:15–16, 20–5).

Clean animals, see **648z**.

b God gave plants to all creatures for food (Gen. 1:30).

ı The need
for food

c Food is for the stomach and the stomach for food (1 Cor. 6:13); do we not have a right to eat and drink? (1 Cor. 9:4); having food and clothing we will be content (1 Tim. 6:8); give us food! (Gen. 47:15); what shall we drink? (Exod. 15:24); he must not reduce her food (Exod. 21:10); command these stones to become bread (Matt. 4:3; Luke 4:3); a workman deserves his food (Matt. 10:10); if a son asks for a loaf, who will give him a stone? (Matt. 7:9); if he asks for a fish, who will give him a snake? (Luke 11:11–12).

ı Eating

d The disciples urged Jesus to eat (John 4:31); eat what is before you (Luke 10:7, 8; 1 Cor. 10:27); Paul encouraged them to eat (Acts 27:33–4).

e David ate (2 Sam. 12:20); when the child died, he ate (2 Sam. 12:21).

ı Drinking

f Those who lapped were chosen, but those who kneeled to drink were not (Judg. 7:5–7); he will drink from the brook (Ps. 110:7).

g They drink from your river of delights (Ps. 36:8).

h He took the cup and gave thanks (Matt. 26:27; Mark 14:23); one gave Jesus a drink of vinegar (Matt. 27:48; Mark 15:36); they gave me vinegar to drink (Ps. 69:21).

ı Eat, drink
and be merry

i Eating and drinking is God's gift to man (Eccles. 3:13); nothing better than to eat, drink and enjoy yourself (Eccles. 2:24; 5:18; 8:15); eat and drink, O lovers! (S. of S. 5:1); let us eat and drink for tomorrow we die (Isa. 22:13; 1 Cor. 15:32); eat, drink and be merry (Luke 12:19); in the days of Noah they were eating and drinking (Matt. 24:38; Luke 17:27); as they were in the days of Lot (Luke 17:28).

j God will visit his anger on him whilst he is eating (Job 20:23).

Eating, drinking and rejoicing, see **824z**; **savoury food**, see **390a**.

ı Limitations
of food

k The kingdom of God is not eating and drinking (Rom. 14:17); man does not live by bread alone (Deut. 8:3; Matt. 4:4; Luke 4:4); shall I go home to eat and drink? (2 Sam. 11:11); food will not commend us to God (1 Cor. 8:8); they serve their own stomach (Rom. 16:18); offerings under the law were only a matter of food and drink etc. (Heb. 9:10); the heart needs strengthening by grace, not food (Heb. 13:9).

1 **Providing food**

l Food provided: by Noah for the inhabitants of the ark (Gen. 6:21); by Abraham for Hagar (Gen. 21:14); by Joseph for his family (Gen. 47:12); for Ruth (Ruth 2:14; 3:15–17); for Saul by Jesse (1 Sam. 16:20); for Jesse's sons and the army commander (1 Sam. 17:17–18); by Ahimelech to David (1 Sam. 21:3–6; 22:10, 13); by Abigail for David (1 Sam. 25:18); for Israel making David king (1 Chr. 12:39–40); for all the Israelites by David (2 Sam. 6:19; 1 Chr. 16:3); for Mephibosheth at the king's table (2 Sam. 9:7, 10–13); for David and his men by Ziba (2 Sam. 16:1–2); by Barzillai and others (2 Sam. 17:27–9); by Solomon daily for his household (1 Kgs. 4:22); for Hiram's men by Solomon (1 Kgs. 5:9–11; 2 Chr. 2:10, 15); by Obadiah for the prophets (1 Kgs. 18:4, 13); for Elishah (2 Kgs. 4:42); for Esther (Esther 2:9); for Jeremiah during the siege of Jerusalem (Jer. 37:21); for Jehoiachin in Babylon (2 Kgs. 25:29; Jer. 52:33–4); by Nehemiah daily (Neh. 5:18); by the good wife for her husband (Prov. 31:15); for widows in the church (Acts 6:1–3).

m You will be given two loaves of bread (1 Sam. 10:4); a tenth of the people supplying food for the army (Judg. 20:10); when the Queen of Sheba saw the food of his table (1 Kgs. 10:5).

n I was hungry and you gave me food (Matt. 25:35); share your bread with the hungry (Isa. 58:7); if he gives his bread to the hungry (Ezek. 18:7, 16); you give them food (Matt. 14:16; Mark 6:37); if your enemy is hungry, give him food (Prov. 25:21; Rom. 12:20).

Stores of food, see **632a**.

1 **Breast-feeding**

o Sarah would nurse children (Gen. 21:7); Rebekah's nurse (Gen. 35:8); shall I get a nurse? (Exod. 2:7); nurse him for me (Exod. 2:9); Naomi became Obed's nurse (Ruth 4:16).

p Woe to those nursing babies in those days (Matt. 24:19; Luke 21:23); blessed are the breasts which never nursed (Luke 23:29); blessed are the breasts at which you nursed (Luke 11:27).

q Queens will be your nursing mothers (Isa. 49:23); you will suck the milk of nations and suck the breast of kings (Isa. 60:16); suck at Jerusalem's consoling breasts (Isa. 66:11).

1 **Man providing a meal**

r A meal provided: by Abraham for his visitors (Gen. 18:5–8); by Lot for his visitors (Gen. 19:3); for Abraham's servant (Gen. 24:33); by Jacob for Esau (Gen. 25:34); by Gideon for the angel (Judg. 6:19); by Manoah for the angel (Judg. 13:15–16); by Samuel for Saul (1 Sam. 9:23–4); by the medium for Saul (1 Sam. 28:20–5); for the Egyptian slave by David's men (1 Sam. 30:11); the rich man for the traveller (2 Sam. 12:4); for Amnon by Tamar (2 Sam. 13:5–10); for Elijah by the widow (1 Kgs. 17:13–16); for the Arameans in Samaria (2 Kgs.

6:22–3); for the risen Jesus (Luke 24:41–3); by the jailer for Paul and Silas (Acts 16:34).

s Boil stew for the sons of the prophets (2 Kgs. 4:38); they gave the captives food and drink (2 Chr. 28:15); bring bread and water for the fugitives (Isa. 21:14); Jesus told them to give Jairus's daughter something to eat (Mark 5:43; Luke 8:55); give my troops food (Judg. 8:5).

Preparing food, see **669j**; **feasting**, see **876a**; **social eating**, see **882a**.

Feeding crowds

t How can one feed people in the wilderness? (Mark 8:4); Elijah fed a hundred men with twenty loaves (2 Kgs. 4:42–4); the feeding of the five thousand (Matt. 14:15–21; Mark 6:35–44; Luke 9:12–17; John 6:5–13); the feeding of the four thousand (Matt. 15:32–8; Mark 8:1–9).

God gives food

u He supplies seed for sowing and bread for food (Isa. 55:10; 2 Cor. 9:10); God gives aliens food and clothing (Deut. 10:18); God gives food to the hungry (Ps. 146:7); bread to sustain man's heart (Ps. 104:15); he fills you with the finest wheat (Ps. 147:14).

v All creatures look to God for food (Ps. 104:27; 145:15–16); he gives food to every creature (Ps. 136:25); for cattle and ravens (Ps. 147:9); God feeds birds such as ravens (Matt. 6:26; Luke 12:24); who gives the raven food? (Job 38:41); God causes grass to grow for cattle and plants for man (Ps. 104:14); young lions seek their food from God (Ps. 104:21); can you hunt prey for the lion? (Job 38:39).

w Feed me with food sufficient for me (Prov. 30:8); can God prepare a table in the wilderness? (Ps. 78:19–20).

God feeds his people

x God gives food to those who fear him (Ps. 111:5); those who fear him will be fed with the finest of wheat and honey (Ps. 81:16); you prepare a table (Ps. 23:5); give us our daily bread (Matt. 6:11; Luke 11:3); do not be anxious about your food, but instead seek God's kingdom and it will be provided (Matt. 6:25–33; Luke 12:22–31); he fills the hungry with good things (Luke 1:53); my soul will be satisfied as with fat (Ps. 63:5); God gave Israel meat (Num. 11:18–22, 31–3; Ps. 78:27; 105:40); the Lord provided food for his people (Ruth 1:6); if God will give me food to eat he will be my God (Gen. 28:20); God nourished Israel with honey from the rock (Deut. 32:13); God appointed ravens to feed Elijah (1 Kgs. 17:4–6); God commanded a widow to feed Elijah (1 Kgs. 17:9); an angel provided a cake twice over for Elijah (1 Kgs. 19:5–8).

Plenty of food, see **635a**.

Feeding the flock

y Should not shepherds feed the flock (Ezek. 34:2); the shepherds fed themselves, not the flock (Ezek. 34:8); I will feed my sheep (Ezek. 34:13–16); my servant David will feed them (Ezek. 34:23); shepherds who will feed you with knowledge (Jer. 3:15); feed my lambs (John 21:15); feed my sheep (John 21:17); as a nurse cares for her children (1 Thess. 2:7); who will give the servants food at the proper time? (Matt. 24:45; Luke 12:42).

1 **Eating before God**

z Everyone in the household is to eat the Passover lamb (Exod. 12:4, 8); you shall eat before God (Deut. 12:7; 15:20); a tithe of produce eaten before the Lord (Deut. 12:18; 14:23–6); Jacob sacrificed and ate a meal with his kin (Gen. 31:54); the elders ate bread with Jethro before God (Exod. 18:12); the elders saw God and ate and drank (Exod. 24:11); they ate and drank before the Lord with joy (1 Chr. 29:22); eat and drink for this day is holy to the Lord (Neh. 8:10); the prince will eat bread before God (Ezek. 44:3).

1 **Eating offerings**

aa Sacrifices as God's food (Lev. 3:11; 21:6, 8; Num. 28:2; Mal. 1:7, 12); the bread of the presence set on the table (Exod. 25:30; 35:13; 39:36; 40:23; Lev. 24:5–8; Num. 4:7; 1 Kgs. 7:48; Heb. 9:2).

ab The priest to have some offerings as his food (Lev. 2:3, 10; 5:13; 6:16–18, 26; 7:6–10, 14, 32–6; Lev. 14:13; Num. 5:9–10; 18:19, 24, 30–2; 1 Sam. 2:28; Ezek. 42:13; 44:29); except for the sin-offering (Lev. 6:30); or the priests' grain offering (Lev. 6:23); the priests' portion specified (Deut. 18:3–4); the priests were to eat the ram of ordination (Exod. 29:31–3; Lev. 8:31); it must be eaten the same day (Lev. 22:30); Hezekiah commanded that the priests be given their portion (2 Chr. 31:4–5); temple workers eat food of the temple (1 Cor. 9:13); the priests were to eat the bread of the presence (Lev. 24:9).

ac Every male priest may eat the sacrifices (Lev. 6:18, 29; 7:6; 10:12–15; Num. 18:10); the priest's household could eat sacrifices (Lev. 10:14; Num. 18:11); even if deformed (Lev. 21:22); but no one outside (Lev. 22:10–13); restitution to be made if anyone eats an offering by mistake (Lev. 22:14–16); no one unclean may eat of it (Lev. 22:4–7); only the priests could eat holy bread (Mark 2:26; Luke 6:4); yet David ate it (1 Sam. 21:4–6; Matt. 12:4).

ad The Levites are to eat the sacrifices (Deut. 18:1, 8); Levites given the tithe to eat (Num. 18:30–2); the portions set apart for the Levites and priests (Neh. 12:47).

1 **Manna**

ae God gave the Israelites bread from heaven (Exod. 16:4, 15; Neh. 9:15; Ps. 78:24–5; 105:40; John 6:31); the manna (Exod. 16:31–5; Num. 11:6–9; Deut. 8:3, 16; Neh. 9:20); which stopped when they entered Canaan (Josh. 5:11–12); all ate the same spiritual food (1 Cor. 10:3–4); you have not eaten bread or drunk wine (Deut. 29:6); we hate this worthless food (Num. 21:5).

1 **Jesus our food**

af Jesus the bread of God (John 6:33); the bread of life (John 6:35, 48, 51); the bread which came down from heaven (John 6:33, 41, 50–1, 58); my Father gives the true bread from heaven (John 6:32); he who eats my flesh and drinks my blood has eternal life (John 6:53–7); the overcomer may eat from the tree of life (Rev.

2:7); the overcomer promised hidden manna (Rev. 2:17); Wisdom's invitation to eat and drink (Prov. 9:5).

Eating Christ's body, see **319e**.

1 The Lord's
supper

ag Instructions concerning the Lord's supper (1 Cor. 11:17–34); they devoted themselves to the breaking of bread (Acts 2:42); on the first day of the week they broke bread (Acts 20:7).

1 Particular
food

ah Prepare a savoury dish (Gen. 27:4, 7, 9, 14); who will give us meat? (Num. 11:4, 13, 18); we remember the fish, cucumbers, melons, leeks, onions, garlic (Num. 11:5); he will eat curds and honey (Isa. 7:15); everyone will eat curds and honey (Isa. 7:22); bread made from various grains (Ezek. 4:9).

ai Three baskets of bread (Gen. 40:16–17); pistachio nuts and almonds (Gen. 43:11); grain scattered on the well (2 Sam. 17:19); take ten loaves, cakes and a jar of honey (1 Kgs. 14:3); flour thrown into the pot (2 Kgs. 4:41); John ate locusts and wild honey (Matt. 3:4; Mark 1:6); the disciples plucked grain and ate it (Matt. 12:1; Mark 2:23; Luke 6:1); as sanctioned (Deut. 23:24–5); five loaves and two fish (Matt. 14:17; Mark 6:38; Luke 9:13; John 6:9); seven loaves and a few fish (Matt. 15:34; Mark 8:5–7).

1 Animals
eating

aj Animals chewing the cud are clean (Lev. 11:3; Deut. 14:6–8); barley and straw provided for the horses (1 Kgs. 4:28); searching for grass for the animals (1 Kgs. 18:5; 1 Chr. 4:39–40); the prodigal son feeding the pigs (Luke 15:15); the oxen and donkeys will eat salted fodder (Isa. 30:24); dogs eat the crumbs that fall from the table (Matt. 15:27; Mark 7:28).

ak Dogs will eat those who die in the city and birds those who die in the field (1 Kgs. 14:11; 16:4; 21:24); where dogs licked up Naboth's blood, dogs will lick up yours (1 Kgs. 21:19; 22:38); dogs will eat Jezebel (1 Kgs. 21:23–4; 2 Kgs. 9:10, 36); birds to eat the flesh of men (Ezek. 39:17–20; Rev. 19:17–18, 21); beasts of the field, come and eat! (Isa. 56:9); the birds and beasts will eat the corpses of this people (Jer. 7:33; 16:4; 19:7; 34:20); I give you as food to the beasts and birds (Ezek. 29:5; 39:4); out of the eater came something to eat (Judg. 14:14); the bear was told to eat much meat (Dan. 7:5).

Eating corpses, see **363m**.

al The hippopotamus eats grass (Job 40:15); the lion will eat straw like the ox (Isa. 11:7).

am The serpent would eat dust (Gen. 3:14); they will lick the dust like a serpent (Mic. 7:17).

an She laid him in a manger (Luke 2:7); you will find a baby lying in a manger (Luke 2:12, 16).

1 Food to be
avoided

ao Fruit from one tree forbidden (Gen. 2:17) but they ate from it (Gen. 3:6); fruit not to be eaten in the first four years (Lev. 19:23–4).

ap Do not eat the meat of an animal torn to pieces (Exod. 22:31); or which has died (Lev. 17:15; 22:8; Deut. 14:21; Ezek. 4:14; 44:31); people who eat pork (Isa. 65:4); those who eat pork and mice (Isa. 66:17); Peter had never eaten unclean food (Acts 10:14; 11:8); quadrupeds, reptiles and wild animals in a sheet (Acts 10:12; 11:6); Daniel and his friends would not defile themselves with the king's food (Dan. 1:5, 8, 12–16); let me not eat the delicacies of the wicked (Ps. 141:4); the Israelites do not eat the sinew of the hip (Gen. 32:32).

aq What a man eats does not make him unclean (Matt. 15:11; Mark 7:15); Jesus thus declared all foods clean (Mark 7:19); eat anything sold in the market (1 Cor. 10:25); no one should judge you by what you eat or drink (Col. 2:16); some forbid foods which God intended for us (1 Tim. 4:3); all food is clean, but do not eat anything which makes a brother stumble (Rom. 14:20–1); do not destroy your brother by your food (Rom. 14:15); receive the weak brother who eats only vegetables (Rom. 14:1–3).
Yeast, see **323*f***; **eating blood**, see **335*g***; **fat**, see **357*ag***; **honey**, see **392*a***; **unclean animals**, see **649*m***; **food offered to idols**, see **982*h***.

1 **Repulsive food**

ar The Israelites were made to eat the calf powdered (Exod. 32:20); I eat ashes like bread (Ps. 102:9); I will feed them with wormwood and poisoned water (Jer. 9:15); the woman accused of adultery had to drink the water of bitterness (Num. 5:23–8); men doomed to eat their own dung and drink their own urine (2 Kgs. 18:27; Isa. 36:12); Micaiah sentenced to eat only bread and water (1 Kgs. 22:27; 2 Chr. 18:26); they must eat what you tread down and drink what you foul (Ezek. 34:19); Nebuchadnezzar eating grass (Dan. 4:32, 33; 5:21); he would have filled his belly with the pods the pigs ate (Luke 15:16).

as Who will give a stone instead of bread? (Matt. 7:9–10); who will give a snake instead of a fish? (Luke 11:11–12).
Bitter food, see **391*a***.

1 **Cannibalism**

at You will eat your sons and your daughters (Lev. 26:29; Deut. 28:53–7; Jer. 19:9); fulfilled in the siege of Samaria (2 Kgs. 6:28–9); and in the sack of Jerusalem (Lam. 4:10); fathers will eat their sons and sons their fathers (Ezek. 5:10); should women eat their offspring? (Lam. 2:20); you who eat the flesh of my people (Mic. 3:3).

au I will make them eat their own flesh (Isa. 49:26).

1 **Not eating**

av Nehemiah did not eat the food allowance (Neh. 5:14–15, 18); I forget to eat my bread (Ps. 102:4); he loathes food (Job 33:20); they hated all kinds of food (Ps. 107:18); idols do not eat (Deut. 4:28).

aw Those whose ancestry could not be proved should not eat the offerings (Ezra 2:63; Neh. 7:65); they did not have time to eat (Mark 3:20; 6:31).

ax If food makes my brother stumble I will never eat meat again (1 Cor. 8:13).

Fasting, see **946**.

1 No food

ay Ammon and Moab did not provide food and water (Deut. 23:4); you have not given bread and water to the needy (Job 22:7).

az The disciples forgot to take bread (Matt. 16:5, 7; Mark 8:14, 16–17); a crowd with nothing to eat (Mark 8:1).

1 Allegorical food and drink

ba I have treasured his words more than my necessary food (Job 23:12); eating the scroll of God's words (Ezek. 2:8–10; 3:1–3; Rev. 10:9–10); your words were found and I ate them (Jer. 15:16); you need milk, not tough meat (1 Cor. 3:2; Heb. 5:12); long for the pure spiritual milk (1 Pet. 2:2); my food is to do the will of him who sent me (John 4:34); labour for the food which endures (John 6:27).

bb A loaf of barley bread—Gideon (Judg. 7:13–14).

bc You have given them tears to drink (Ps. 80:5); bread of adversity and water of affliction (Isa. 30:20); I will give her cup into your hand (Ezek. 23:31–4); I will lift up the cup of salvation (Ps. 116:13); drink water from your own cistern (Prov. 5:15).

302 Excretion

1 Discharges in general

a A man with a discharge is unclean (Lev. 15:2); and must be sent away from the camp (Num. 5:2); if he spits on a clean man, he makes him unclean (Lev. 15:8).

b May Joab's house always have someone with a discharge (2 Sam. 3:29).

1 Semen

c A man with an emission of semen is unclean (Lev. 15:16; 22:4; Deut. 23:10); Onan spilled his semen on the ground (Gen. 38:9); their semen is the semen of horses (Ezek. 23:20).

1 Menstruation

d A menstruating woman is unclean for seven days (Lev. 15:19); sexual intercourse with a menstruating woman forbidden (Lev. 18:19); Rachel said she was menstruating (Gen. 31:35).

1 Flow of blood

e A longer discharge of blood makes her unclean longer (Lev. 15:25); cleansed from her flow of blood (Lev. 12:7); a woman had a haemorrhage for twelve years (Matt. 9:20; Mark 5:25; Luke 8:43).

1 Defecation and dung

f Israelites to relieve themselves outside the camp and cover their excrement (Deut. 23:12–13); they thought Eglon was relieving himself (Judg. 3:24); Saul went into the cave to relieve himself (1 Sam. 24:3); the temple of Baal was used as a latrine (2 Kgs. 10:27).

g The dirt came out (Judg. 3:22); what enters the mouth goes into the stomach and is evacuated (Matt. 15:17).

h A fourth of a kab of dove's dung (2 Kgs. 6:25); doomed to eat their own dung (2 Kgs. 18:27; Isa. 36:12); the loaf to be cooked on human dung (Ezek. 4:12); or cow's dung (Ezek. 4:15).

i The wicked perishes like his dung (Job 20:7); they became as dung for the ground (Ps. 83:10); the bones will be like dung on the ground (Jer. 8:2); corpses will be like dung in the field (Jer. 9:22; 16:4; 25:33); I will spread the dung of your offerings on your faces (Mal. 2:3); as straw is trodden down in a dung heap (Isa. 25:10); I count all things as dung (Phil. 3:8).

1 Urinating

j Every male who urinates against a wall (1 Sam. 25:22, 34).

k Doomed to drink their own urine (2 Kgs. 18:27; Isa. 36:12).

1 Saliva and spitting

l If her father spat in her face she would be ashamed for seven days (Num. 12:14); his brother's wife shall spit in his face (Deut. 25:9); they spit in my face (Job 30:10).

m They spat on Jesus (Matt. 26:67; 27:30; Mark 14:65; 15:19); they will spit on him (Mark 10:34; Luke 18:32); I did not hide my face from shame and spitting (Isa. 50:6).

n Jesus spat and touched the man's tongue (Mark 7:33); Jesus spat on the man's eyes (Mark 8:23); spat and made clay (John 9:6).

o David let saliva run down his beard (1 Sam. 21:13); leave me alone while I swallow my saliva (Job 7:19).

1 Sweat

p By the sweat of your brow you will eat bread (Gen. 3:19); Jesus' sweat like drops of blood falling on the ground (Luke 22:44); the priests should not wear anything which causes sweat (Ezek. 44:18).

1 Vomit

q You will vomit the king's morsel (Prov. 23:8); lest you be filled with honey and vomit (Prov. 25:16); the fish vomited Jonah (Jonah 2:10); like a dog which returns to its vomit (Prov. 26:11; 2 Pet. 2:22); as a drunken man staggers in his vomit (Isa. 19:14); all tables are full of vomit (Isa. 28:8); be drunk and vomit (Jer. 25:27); make Moab drunk so he wallows in his vomit (Jer. 48:26); he swallows riches but will vomit them up (Job 20:15).

r The land vomited its inhabitants (Lev. 18:25, 28; 20:22); I will spew you out of my mouth (Rev. 3:16).

1 Sneezing

s The boy sneezed seven times (2 Kgs. 4:35); the crocodile's sneezes flash light (Job 41:18).

303 Insertion: forcible ingress

1 Impaling

a Ehud stabbed Eglon (Judg. 3:21); Jael impaled Sisera (Judg. 4:21; 5:26).

Striking to death, see **279*l*.**

b Beams were not inserted in the walls (1 Kgs. 6:6).

1 Dipping

c Jesus dipped a morsel and gave it to Judas (John 13:26).

Baptism, see **988*r*.**

304 Extraction: forcible egress

1 Bringing people out

a God brought: Abraham out of Ur (Gen. 15:7; 24:7; Neh. 9:7); Lot out of Sodom (Gen. 19:12, 16, 29); Israel out of Egypt (Exod. 3:10; 7:4; 12:17, 51; 13:9, 14, 16; 18:1; 20:2; 29:46; 32:7, 11; Lev. 19:36; 22:33; 25:38; 26:13; 25:42, 55; Num. 14:13; 15:41; 20:16; 23:22; 24:8; Deut. 4:20, 37; 5:6; 6:12, 21; 7:19; 8:14;

9:26; 13:5, 10; 16:1; 20:1; 26:8; 29:25; Josh. 24:5, 17; Judg. 2:1, 12; 6:8; 1 Sam. 8:8; 12:6, 8; 1 Kgs. 8:16, 21, 51, 53; 9:9; 2 Kgs. 17:36; 2 Chr. 6:5; 7:22; Ps. 81:10; 105:37; 136:11; Jer. 2:6; 7:22; 11:4, 7; 32:21; 34:13; Dan. 9:15; Amos 2:10; 3:1; 9:7; Mic. 6:4); out of Egypt I called my son (Hos. 11:1; 2:15); no longer talk of God bringing Israel up out of Egypt, but out of the north land (Jer. 16:14, 15; 23:7–8).

b These are your gods who brought you up out of Egypt (Exod. 32:4; 1 Kgs. 12:28; Neh. 9:18); because God hates us he brought us out of Egypt (Deut. 1:27).

c Rahab's family brought out of the house (Josh. 6:22–3); bringing the kings out of the cave (Josh. 10:22–3); I will bring you out of the city (Ezek. 11:7).

1 Drawing water

d Women drawing water (Gen. 24:11, 13, 43, 45; 1 Sam. 9:11); the three might men drew water at Bethlehem (2 Sam. 23:16; 1 Chr. 11:18).

e Moses, drawn out of the water (Exod. 2:10); he drew me out of the waters (2 Sam. 22:17; Ps. 18:16).

1 Plucking out

f Pulling up the weeds you may root out the wheat (Matt. 13:29); angels will pull the weeds out of the kingdom (Matt. 13:40–1); every plant not planted by my Father will be uprooted (Matt. 15:13); angels will extract the wicked from the righteous (Matt. 13:49).

g If your eye causes you to sin, pluck it out (Matt. 5:29; 18:9; Mark 9:47); you would have plucked out your eyes and given them to me (Gal. 4:15).

305 Passage: motion through

1 Passing by

a Do not pass me by (Gen. 18:3); do not pass this heap and pillar (Gen. 31:52); all David's men passed on before him (2 Sam. 15:18); he intended to pass them by (Mark 6:48).

1 Passing through

b A firepot and torch passed through the pieces (Gen. 15:17); the Lord will pass through (Exod. 12:23); Jesus passed through them (Luke 4:30).

c Israel passed through the Red Sea (Ps. 136:14); let us pass through your land (Num. 20:17; 21:22; Deut. 2:27; Judg. 11:17, 19); Edom refused to let them pass through (Num. 20:18–21).

1 Passing over

d The Lord will pass over the door (Exod. 12:23).
Passover, see **988c**.

306 Overstepping: motion beyond

1 Exceeding

a Solomon's wisdom surpassed that of the orientals and Egyptians (1 Kgs. 4:30); unless your righteousness exceeds that of the scribes and Pharisees (Matt. 5:20); what do you do more than others? (Matt. 5:47).

1 Giving more

b This widow put in more than all the rest (Mark 12:43; Luke 21:3).

307 Shortfall

1 Fall short   *a* All fall short of the glory of God (Rom. 3:23).

308 Ascent: motion upwards

1 God going
up

a Arise, O Lord! (Num. 10:35; Ps. 7:6; 9:19; 10:12; 17:13; 74:22; 82:8); let God arise! (Ps. 68:1); rise up, Judge of the earth! (Ps. 94:2); I will arise (Ps. 12:5; Isa. 33:10).

1 The
ascension

b I have not yet ascended (John 20:17); I am ascending to my Father and your Father (John 20:17); God has ascended with a shout (Ps. 47:5); when he ascended on high he led captives in his train (Ps. 68:18; Eph. 4:8); he ascended far above the heavens (Eph. 4:10); Jesus was taken up into heaven (Mark 16:19; Acts 1:2); he was lifted up and a cloud received him (Acts 1:9–11); he was taken up in glory (1 Tim. 3:16).

1 Going up
to God

c Moses went up the mountain to God (Exod. 19:3, 20; 34:2–4); come up to the Lord (Exod. 24:1); who may ascend the hill of the Lord? (Ps. 24:3); let us go up to Zion to the Lord (Jer. 31:6); let us go up to the mountain of the Lord (Isa. 2:3; Mic. 4:2).

d Do not go up steps on to my altar (Exod. 20:26).

1 Going up
to heaven

e The two witnesses went up to heaven in a cloud (Rev. 11:12); God raised us up with Christ and seated us with him in heaven (Eph. 2:6).

f A stairway to heaven with angels ascending and descending (Gen. 28:12); angels ascending and descending on the Son of Man (John 1:51); what if you saw the Son of man ascending? (John 6:62); the angel ascended in the flame (Judg. 13:20).

g Who has ascended into heaven and descended? (Prov. 30:4); do not say, Who will ascend into heaven? (Rom. 10:6); you said in your heart, I will ascend to heaven (Isa. 14:13).

h The path of life leads upward for the wise (Prov. 15:24).

1 Getting
up

i Get up! (Josh. 7:10); arise and stand on your feet (Acts 26:16); arise and talk to your people (2 Sam. 19:7); arise, my darling! (S. of S. 2:10, 13); little girl, arise! (Mark 5:41; Luke 8:54); Tabitha, arise! (Acts 9:40); young man, arise! (Luke 7:14); rise and do not be afraid (Matt. 17:7); rise, take up your bed (John 5:8); rise and make your bed (Acts 9:34); arise, let us go (John 14:31); arise, Peter (Acts 10:13; 11:7); get up quickly! (Acts 12:7).

j Jonathan climbed up on all fours (1 Sam. 14:13); Zaccheus climbed into a sycamore tree (Luke 19:4); the old men stood up before Job (Job 29:8).

k Friend, move up higher (Luke 14:10).

l Let every valley be lifted up (Isa. 40:4).

1 Steps

m Six steps to the throne (1 Kgs. 10:19; 2 Chr. 9:18); Solomon's staircase to the temple (1 Kgs. 10:5; 2 Chr. 9:4); staircase to the side chambers of the temple (1 Kgs. 6:8); algum wood for steps for the temple (2 Chr. 9:11); the steps of the city of David (Neh. 12:37); a stairway to heaven (Gen. 28:12).

309 Descent

1 People
falling

a The righteous man falls seven times and rises again (Prov. 24:16); he is set for the fall and rising of many in Israel (Luke 2:34); when he falls he will not go headlong (Ps. 37:24); my feet had nearly slipped (Ps. 73:2); if the blind leads the blind they will both fall into a pit (Matt. 15:14; Luke 6:39); let him who thinks he stands take heed lest he fall (1 Cor. 10:12).

b Virgin Israel has fallen (Amos 5:2); did they stumble so as to fall? (Rom. 11:11); how have the mighty fallen! (2 Sam. 1:19, 25, 27); everyone who falls on that stone will be broken to pieces (Luke 20:18).

c The kings fell into the tar pits (Gen. 14:10); the concubine fell at the doorway (Judg. 19:26); Eli fell backward off his seat (1 Sam. 4:18); Dagon fell before the ark (1 Sam. 5:3, 4); Saul fell full length (1 Sam. 28:20); Mephibosheth fell (2 Sam. 4:4); Ahaziah fell through the lattice (2 Kgs. 1:2); Haman was falling on the couch (Esther 7:8); my son falls into the fire or the water (Matt. 17:15); Judas fell headlong (Acts 1:18); Eutychus fell from the third floor (Acts 20:9); I fell at his feet like one dead (Rev. 1:17).

1 Things
falling

d The wall of Jericho fell down (Josh. 6:5, 20); by faith (Heb. 11:30); the house on sand fell down (Matt. 7:27; Luke 6:49); not a sparrow falls to the ground apart from your Father (Matt. 10:29).

1 Coming
down from
heaven

e The Lord came down on Mt Sinai (Exod. 19:11, 20; 34:5); God bowed the heavens and came down (2 Sam. 22:10; Ps. 18:9); bow your heavens and come down! (Ps. 144:5); oh, that you would rend the heavens and come down! (Isa. 64:1); how can he say, 'I came down from heaven'? (John 6:42); the Lord himself will descend from heaven (1 Thess. 4:16).

1 Falling from
heaven

f How you have fallen from heaven (Isa. 14:12); I saw Satan fall from heaven (Luke 10:18); the stars will fall from the sky (Matt. 24:29; Mark 13:25); a star fell from heaven (Rev. 8:10; 9:1); the stars fell to earth like figs (Rev. 6:13).

1 Come down!

g Man of God, come down! (2 Kgs. 1:9, 11); if you are the Son of God, come down from the cross (Matt. 27:40); let him come down from the cross (Matt. 27:42); come down from the cross (Mark 15:30, 32).

1 Going down

h The herd of swine rushed down into the sea (Matt. 8:32; Mark 5:13; Luke 8:33).

i Give place to this man (Luke 14:9).

j Do not say, Who will descend into the abyss? (Rom. 10:7); he descended into the lower parts of the earth (Eph. 4:9).

310 Lifting up

1 Lifting people up

a Better to be told to come up higher than to be put lower (Prov. 25:7); if one falls the other will lift him up (Eccles. 4:10).

b They tried to raise David up from the ground (2 Sam. 12:17); they lifted Jeremiah out of the cistern (Jer. 38:13); they took Daniel up out of the lions' den (Dan. 6:23).

c Jesus took him by the hand and raised him up (Mark 9:27); Jesus took her by the hand and raised her up (Luke 8:54); Peter took the lame man by the hand and raised him (Acts 3:7); he gave her his hand and raised her up (Acts 9:41).

1 God lifting up

d God taking Elijah to heaven (2 Kgs. 2:1); the Spirit lifted me up (Ezek. 3:12, 14; 8:3; 11:1, 24; 43:5).

e Lifting up does not come from east or west (Ps. 75:6); God puts one down and lifts up another (Ps. 75:7).

f You brought me up from Sheol (Ps. 30:3; Jonah 2:6); you lifted me up (Ps. 30:1); the Lord will set you high above the nations (Deut. 28:1); the Lord lifts me above my enemies (2 Sam. 22:49; Ps. 18:48); my head will be liften up above my enemies (Ps. 27:6); God lifts up my head (Ps. 3:3); he raises the poor from the dust (Ps. 113:7); God sets on high those that are low (Job 5:11); he brought me up out of the miry pit (Ps. 40:2).

1 Lifting up Jesus

g When you lift up the Son of man you will know (John 8:28); if I be lifted up I will draw all to me (John 12:32, 34); so must the Son of man be lifted up (John 3:14).

h The days drew near for him to be received up (Luke 9:51); who will descend to bring Christ up from the dead? (Rom. 10:7).
Going up, see **308**.

1 Lifting hands

i I lift up my hand to heaven (Deut. 32:40); I lift up my hands (Ps. 28:2; 63:4; 119:48); lift up your hands (Ps. 134:2; Lam. 2:19); we lift up heart and hands (Lam. 3:41); lifting up holy hands (1 Tim. 2:8).

1 Lifting heads

j Lift up your heads, O gates (Ps. 24:7, 9); lift up your heads for your redemption is near (Luke 21:28); the king of Babylon lifted up the head of Jehoiachin (2 Kgs. 25:27; Jer. 52:31); God lifts up my head (Ps. 3:3); Midian did not lift up their heads any more (Judg. 8:28); Pharaoh will lift up your head (Gen. 40:13, 19, 20).

1 Lifting animals

k Lift up a neighbour's animal which has fallen (Deut. 22:4); who will not lift a sheep out of a pit on the sabbath? (Matt. 12:11); who will not pull a donkey or an ox out of a well on the sabbath? (Luke 14:5).

311 Lowering

1 Bowing before men

a Bowing down: Abraham before his visitors (Gen. 18:2); Moses before Jethro (Exod. 18:7); Jacob before Esau (Gen. 33:3); Joseph's parents and brothers (Gen. 37:7, 9, 10); Joseph's brothers (Gen. 42:6; 43:26, 28; 44:14); Joseph before Israel (Gen. 48:12); Judah's brothers (Gen. 49:8); Ruth before Boaz (Ruth

2:10); David before Jonathan (1 Sam. 20:41); David before Saul (1 Sam. 24:8); Saul before the spirit of Samuel (1 Sam. 28:14); anyone before Absalom (2 Sam. 15:5); Adonijah before Solomon (1 Kgs. 1:53); Solomon before Bathsheba (1 Kgs. 2:19); Obadiah before Elijah (1 Kgs. 18:7); the captain before Elijah (2 Kgs. 1:13); the sons of the prophets before Elisha (2 Kgs. 2:15); the Shunammite woman before Elisha (2 Kgs. 4:37); everyone before Haman (Esther 3:2); Nebuchadnezzar before Daniel (Dan. 2:46); the slave before his master (Matt. 18:26); Cornelius fell at Peter's feet (Acts 10:25); the Philippian jailer fell down before Paul and Silas (Acts 16:29).

b May nations and your brothers bow down (Gen. 27:29); they will bow down at your feet (Rev. 3:9); the evil bow down before the good (Prov. 14:19); all your descendants will bow down to the faithful priest (1 Sam. 2:36); they will bow down to you (Isa. 49:23); those who despised you will bow down to you (Isa. 60:14).

c Mordecai would not bow down before Haman (Esther 3:2, 5).

1 Bowing before David

d Bowing down before David: Abigail (1 Sam. 25:23); a man (2 Sam. 1:2); Mephibosheth (2 Sam. 9:6); the wise woman (2 Sam. 14:4); Joab (2 Sam. 14:22); Absalom (2 Sam. 14:33); Ziba (2 Sam. 16:4); Ahimaaz (2 Sam. 18:28); Shimei (2 Sam. 19:18); Araunah [Ornan] (2 Sam. 24:20; 1 Chr. 21:21); Bathsheba (1 Kgs. 1:16, 31); Nathan (1 Kgs. 1:23).

1 Bowing before God

e Let us kneel before the Lord our Maker (Ps. 95:6); before me every knee will bow (Isa. 45:23; Rom. 14:11); all mankind will bow down before me (Isa. 66:23); I bow my knees before the Father (Eph. 3:14); Solomon prayed kneeling (1 Kgs. 8:54); Peter knelt and prayed (Acts 9:40); Paul knelt and prayed (Acts 20:36); the brethren knelt and prayed (Acts 21:5).

f Bowing down before God: Abraham (Gen. 17:3, 17); Abraham's servant (Gen. 24:26, 48, 52); Moses (Exod. 34:8; Deut. 9:18, 25); Balaam (Num. 22:31); Manoah and his wife (Judg. 13:20); Elijah (1 Kgs. 18:42); the Israelites (Exod. 4:31; 12:27; 1 Chr. 29:20; 2 Chr. 7:3; Neh. 8:6); Jehoshaphat (2 Chr. 20:18); Hezekiah (2 Chr. 29:29).

g Falling on their faces: Moses (Num. 16:4); Moses and Aaron (Num. 14:5; 16:22, 45; 20:6); Joshua (Josh. 5:14; 7:6); the people (1 Kgs. 18:39); David and the elders (1 Chr. 21:16); Ezekiel (Ezek. 3:23; 43:3; 44:4); Daniel (Dan. 8:17); Peter, James and John (Matt. 17:6); Jesus (Matt. 26:39); the angels, elders and living creatures (Rev. 7:11); the 24 elders (Rev. 11:16); the 24 elders and the four living creatures (Rev. 19:4).

h David lay on the ground all night (2 Sam. 12:16; 13:31).

1 Bowing before Jesus

i Kneeling before Jesus: a leper (Matt. 8:2; Mark 1:40); a rich man (Mark 10:17); soldiers (Matt. 27:29; Mark 15:19).

j Falling down before Jesus: Peter (Luke 5:8); Jairus (Mark 5:22;

Luke 8:41); a woman (Mark 5:33; Luke 8:47); the Syrophoeni-cian woman (Mark 7:25); a man (Matt. 17:14); unclean spirits (Mark 3:11); a demoniac (Luke 8:28); one of the ten lepers (Luke 17:16); Mary (John 11:32); the mob (John 18:6); Paul (Acts 9:4); the four living creatures and 24 elders (Rev. 5:8).

k The magi fell down and worshipped the child (Matt. 2:11); the demoniac bowed down before Jesus (Mark 5:6); the mother of Zebedee's sons bowed before Jesus (Matt. 20:20); at the name of Jesus every knee will bow (Phil. 2:10).

Bowing to false gods

l Seven thousand whose knees have not bowed to Baal (1 Kgs. 19:18); men bowing down to the sun (Ezek. 8:16); fall down and worship the golden image (Dan. 3:5–7, 10–11); those who bow down to the host of heaven (Zeph. 1:5).

m Bel bows down, Nebo stoops (Isa. 46:1).

Lowering people

n Rahab let the spies down the wall by a rope through the window (Josh. 2:15); Michal lowered David through a window (1 Sam. 19:12); Paul was let down the wall from the window in a basket (Acts 9:25; 2 Cor. 11:33); Jeremiah was lowered by ropes into the cistern (Jer. 38:6); the paralytic was let down through the roof (Mark 2:4; Luke 5:19); a sheet let down from the sky (Acts 10:11; 11:5).

o She laid the boy's body on the bed (2 Kgs. 4:21); he makes me lie down in green pastures (Ps. 23:2).

p Throwing Edomites from a cliff (2 Chr. 25:12); throwing Jezebel down (2 Kgs. 9:33).

Bringing down

q You bring down the haughty (2 Sam. 22:28; Ps. 18:27); God will bring the wicked down into the pit of destruction (Ps. 55:23); God puts one down and lifts up another (Ps. 75:7); the tall trees will be felled (Isa. 10:33); let every mountain and hill be made low (Isa. 40:4); who will bring me down? (Obad. 3); I will bring you down (Jer. 49:16); Capernaum will be brought down to Hades (Luke 10:15); you will be thrust down to Sheol (Isa. 14:15).

Stars thrown down, see **321*p***.

r There is no need to bring Christ down from heaven (Rom. 10:6).

s Making camels kneel (Gen. 24:11).

Crawling

t Sin lies down at the door (Gen. 4:7).

u On your belly you shall go (Gen. 3:14); insects which crawl are unlean (Lev. 11:20–3, 42).

Sitting down

v Boaz and the elders sat down (Ruth 4:1–2); David sat between the two gates (2 Sam. 18:24); David sat in the gate (2 Sam. 19:8); Job's friends sat down with him for seven days (Job 2:13).

Sitting in the gateway, see **263*l***.

w The boy sat on his mother's lap (2 Kgs. 4:20).

x Blessed is he who does not sit with scoffers (Ps. 1:1); I will not sit with the wicked (Ps. 26:4–5).

y Sit in the dust, daughter of Babylon! (Isa. 47:1); the elders of Zion sit on the ground (Lam. 2:10).

z Christ seated at God's right hand (Eph. 1:20; Col. 3:1; Heb. 1:3; 8:1; 10:12; 12:2); sit at my right hand (Ps. 110:1; Acts 2:34; Heb. 1:13); the Son of man will sit at the right hand of the power of God (Luke 22:69).

₁ Lying
down

aa Balaam's donkey lay down (Num. 22:27); when Boaz lay down (Ruth 3:4, 7).

ab Lie down on your left side for 390 days (Ezek. 4:4–5); lie down on your right side for 40 days (Ezek. 4:6).

₁ Sitting
to eat

ac He told the crowd to sit down (Mark 8:6); Jesus had them all recline on the ground (Matt. 14:19; 15:35; Mark 6:40–1; Luke 9:14–15; John 6:10).

ad Jesus reclined at table (Matt. 26:7); with his disciples (Matt. 26:20; Mark 14:18); with taxmen and sinners (Mark 2:15); a disciple reclining by Jesus' breast (John 13:23).

₁ Sitting
to teach

ae When Jesus sat down his disciples came and he taught them (Matt. 5:1); Jesus went up a mountain and sat down (Matt. 15:29); Jesus was sitting by the sea (Matt. 13:1); Jesus sat down in a boat and taught (Matt. 13:2; Mark 4:1); Jesus sat down to preach (Luke 4:20).

₁ Sitting at
the feet

af The demoniac at the feet of Jesus (Luke 8:35); Mary at the feet of Jesus (Luke 10:39); Paul at the feet of Gamaliel (Acts 22:3).

₁ Sitting
in glory

ag The Lord who sits above the cherubim (1 Sam. 4:4).

ah The Son of man sitting at the right hand of God (Matt. 26:64; Mark 14:62).

312 Leap

₁ People
jumping

a Through God I can jump over a wall (2 Sam. 22:30; Ps. 18:29); Michal saw David leaping (1 Chr. 15:29); they leaped about the altar of Baal (1 Kgs. 18:26).

b The baby jumped in her womb (Luke 1:41, 44); the lame man walked and leaped (Acts 3:8); the lame will leap like a deer (Isa. 35:6).

₁ Insects
jumping

c Insects which jump are clean (Lev. 11:21–2).

313 Plunge

₁ Throw
oneself
down

a Throw yourself down (Matt. 4:6; Luke 4:9).
Falling, see **309a**.

314 Circling

₁ Go
around

a March around the city (Josh. 6:3–4); circling around behind the enemy (2 Sam. 5:23; 1 Chr. 14:14).

b Samuel went round a circuit, judging (1 Sam. 7:16–17).

315 Rotation: motion in a continued circle

ı Wheels

a Problems with the chariot wheels (Exod. 14:25).

b Each stand had four bronze wheels (1 Kgs. 7:30, 32–3); a wheel for each of the four creatures (Ezek. 1:15–21; 10:9); I heard the sound of the wheels (Ezek. 3:13); called 'whirling wheels' (Ezek. 10:13); go in among the whirling wheels (Ezek. 10:2); wheels within wheels (Ezek. 1:16; 10:10).

ı Rolling

c Roll large stones over the cave mouth (Josh. 10:18); Joseph rolled a large stone over the mouth of the tomb (Matt. 27:60; Mark 15:46).

d Who will roll away the stone? (Mark 16:3); the stone had been rolled away (Mark 16:4; Luke 24:2); the angel of the Lord rolled away the stone (Matt. 28:2).

e Gilgal—rolling away reproach (Josh. 5:9).

ı Hinges

f Hinges for the doors (1 Kgs. 7:50); as a door turns on its hinges, so a sluggard on his bed (Prov. 26:14).

316 Evolution: motion in a reverse circle

317 Oscillation: reciprocating motion

ı Wave offering

a The wave offering (Exod. 29:24, 26; Lev. 7:30; 8:27, 29; 9:21; 14:12, 21, 24; Num. 6:19–20); the Levites were presented as a wave offering (Num. 8:13).

b Wave the sheaf of firstfruits (Lev. 23:11); loaves for a wave offering (Lev. 23:17, 20).

c Wave offering to be eaten by the priests (Lev. 10:15).

ı Wave hand

d I thought he would wave his hand over the place (2 Kgs. 5:11).

318 Agitation: irregular motion

ı Convulsions

a The demon threw him into convulsions (Mark 1:26; 9:18, 20, 26; Luke 9:39, 42).

ı Shaking

b I will shake the heavens and the earth (Hag. 2:6, 21); I will shake all nations (Hag. 2:7).

Sea stirred up, see **343***d*.

c Paul shook the viper off (Acts 28:5).

ı Trembling

d There was a great trembling in the camp (1 Sam. 14:15).

Class three: Matter

Section one: Matter in general

319 Materiality

1 Material bodies	*a* God remembered they were but flesh (Ps. 78:39); he knows we are dust (Ps. 103:14); Egyptian horses are flesh, not spirit (Isa. 31:3); the spirit is willing but the flesh is weak (Matt. 26:41; Mark 14:38).
	b Bone of my bones and flesh of my flesh (Gen. 2:23); people love their own flesh (Eph. 5:28–9).
	c With what kind of a body are the dead raised? (1 Cor. 15:35–44); sown as a natural body and raised as a spiritual body (1 Cor. 15:44); the flesh of men, animals, birds and fish is different (1 Cor. 15:39).
1 Jesus' body	*d* The Word became flesh (John 1:14); Jesus Christ has come in the flesh (1 John 4:2); since the children have flesh and blood, he also shared in the same (Heb. 2:14); a ghost does not have flesh and bones as I have (Luke 24:39); we have known Christ according to the flesh (2 Cor. 5:16); deceivers do not acknowledge that Jesus Christ has come in the flesh (2 John 7); the fulness of God dwells in him in a body (Col. 2:9); the veil is his flesh (Heb. 10:20); the temple of his body (John 2:21); a body you have prepared for me (Heb. 10:5).
1 Eating Christ's body	*e* This is my body (Matt. 26:26–8; Mark 14:22–4; Luke 22:19; 1 Cor. 11:24); sharing in the body and blood of Christ (1 Cor. 10:16); whoever eats my flesh has eternal life (John 6:54, 56); the bread I give for the life of the world is my flesh (John 6:51); how can he give us his flesh to eat? (John 6:52).
1 The church as Christ's body	*f* The church is Christ's body (Eph. 1:23); we are the body of Christ (Rom. 12:5); you are Christ's body (1 Cor. 12:27); we are members of his body (1 Cor. 12:12–27; Eph. 5:30); we who are many are one body (1 Cor. 10:17); preserve the unity of the one body (Eph. 4:3–4); the whole body is fitted together by every joint (Eph. 4:16); building up the body of Christ (Eph. 4:12).
1 Our bodies	*g* You clothed me with skin and flesh (Job 10:11); we have many limbs in one body (Rom. 12:4); his trunk is ivory work (S. of S. 5:14).
	h Husband and wife do not have authority over their own bodies, but that of the spouse (1 Cor. 7:4); he considered his own body as good as dead (Rom. 4:19).
	i The body is more than clothing (Matt. 6:25; Luke 12:23); your body is a temple of the Holy Spirit (1 Cor. 6:19); present your bodies a living sacrifice (Rom. 12:1); the body is not for immorality but for the Lord (1 Cor. 6:13).
	j Do not be afraid of those who kill the body (Luke 12:4); I beat

my body and make it my slave (1 Cor. 9:27); deliver him to Satan for the destruction of the flesh (1 Cor. 5:5); God gave them up to impurity, that their bodies be dishonoured (Rom. 1:24).

k Offerings under the law were only regulations for the body (Heb. 9:10); for the cleansing of the flesh (Heb. 9:13).

l I am carnal (Rom. 7:14); nothing good dwells in my flesh (Rom. 7:18); those who walk according to the flesh set their minds on things of the flesh (Rom. 8:5); the mind set on the flesh is hostile to God (Rom. 8:7); to set the mind on the flesh is death (Rom. 8:6); the flesh lusts against the Spirit (Gal. 5:17); the deeds of the flesh (Gal. 5:19–21); with my flesh I serve the law of sin (Rom. 7:25); they set their minds on earthly things (Phil. 3:19); sowing to the flesh (Gal. 6:8); the immoral man sins against his own body (1 Cor. 6:18); you were fleshly, babes in Christ (1 Cor. 3:1); while there is jealousy, are you not fleshly? (1 Cor. 3:3); the flesh profits nothing (John 6:63); having begun with the Spirit are you made perfect with the flesh? (Gal. 3:3); if you live according to the flesh you will die (Rom. 8:13).

m Flesh and blood cannot inherit the kingdom of God (1 Cor. 15:50).

n From now on we know no one according to the flesh (2 Cor. 5:16); make no provision for the flesh (Rom. 13:14); we do not live according to the flesh (Rom. 8:4–7); you are not in the flesh but in the Spirit (Rom. 8:9); it is not the children of the flesh but the children of the promise (Rom. 9:8); I do not put confidence in the flesh (Phil. 3:3–4).

o We do not wage war according to the flesh (2 Cor. 10:3); our struggle is not against flesh and blood (Eph. 6:12).

320 Spirituality

a The soul is more than food (Matt. 6:25); they kill the body but cannot kill the soul (Matt. 10:28); the spirit is willing but the flesh is weak (Matt. 26:41; Mark 14:38); worship in spirit and in truth (John 4:23, 24).

b No one knows the things of a man but the spirit of the man (1 Cor. 2:11); no one has power to imprison the spirit (Eccles. 8:8); the God of the spirits of all flesh (Num. 16:22; 27:16); give me a double portion of your spirit (2 Kgs. 2:9); the spirit of Elijah rests on Elisha (2 Kgs. 2:15).

c God is spirit (John 4:24); the spirit of the creatures was in the wheels (Ezek. 1:21; 10:17).
The Holy Spirit, see **965k**.

d The law is spiritual (Rom. 7:14); the words I have spoken are spirit and life (John 6:63); the Spirit gives life (John 6:63; 2 Cor. 3:6); it is raised as a spiritual body (1 Cor. 15:44).

e Test the spirits (1 John 4:1).

321 Universe

1 Creation of
the universe

a The creation of: the heavens and the earth (Gen. 1:1); the heavens (Ps. 96:5); the sky (Gen. 1:8); sun, moon and stars (Gen. 1:14–16; Ps. 136:7–9).

b God gave sun, moon and stars for light (Jer. 31:35); he made the Pleiades and Orion (Amos 5:8); sun, moon and stars differ in splendour (1 Cor. 15:41).

c Dry land called 'earth' (Gen. 1:9–10); the sun rises, sets and rises again (Eccles. 1:5); the sun like a bridegroom (Ps. 19:4–6).

d The stars fought against Sisera (Judg. 5:20); let those who love God be like the rising sun (Judg. 5:31).

1 God and
the universe

e God stretches out the heavens (Job 9:8); can you spread out the skies like a molten mirror? (Job 37:18); God makes the Bear, Orion and the Pleiades (Job 9:9); can you bind the Pleiades, loose Orion or guide the Bear? (Job 38:31–2); when I consider the heavens, the moon and stars which you have made (Ps. 8:3).

f The sky declares the glory of God (Ps. 19:1); praise him, sun, moon and stars (Ps. 148:3); the heavens declare his righteousness (Ps. 97:6).

g The heavens and earth belong to God (Deut. 10:14; Ps. 89:11); the world is mine and all it contains (Ps. 50:12); God fills the heaven and earth (Jer. 23:24); the earth is the Lord's (Exod. 9:29; Ps. 24:1; 1 Cor. 10:26); God counts the stars and names them (Ps. 147:4; Isa. 40:26); the earth is God's footstool (Matt. 5:35); the earth he has given to mankind (Ps. 115:16).

h The creation was subjected to futility (Rom. 8:20); the creation will be set free from its slavery to decay (Rom. 8:21); the creation groans and travails at present (Rom. 8:22).

i The Lord God is a sun and shield (Ps. 84:11); the city has no need of sun or moon, for God's glory shines on it (Rev. 21:23).

1 Worshipping
the universe

j Do not worship sun, moon and stars (Deut. 4:19; 17:3); burning incense to sun, moon and stars (2 Kgs. 23:5); 25 men worshipping the sun (Ezek. 8:16); the sun, moon and stars which they have served (Jer. 8:2); horses and chariots for the sun (2 Kgs. 23:11); Manasseh worshipped all the host of heaven (2 Chr. 33:3); and made altars for them (2 Kgs. 21:5; 2 Chr. 33:5); God gave them up to serve the host of heaven (Acts 7:42); if I have looked at the sun or moon (Job 31:26).

1 Stars as
signs

k A star will come from Jacob (Num. 24:17); we saw the star at its rising (Matt. 2:2); Herod found what time the star appeared (Matt. 2:7); the star stood over where the child lay (Matt. 2:9).

l Signs in sun, moon and stars (Luke 21:25); the sun, moon and eleven stars bowed down to Joseph (Gen. 37:9); a woman clothed with the sun, moon and stars (Rev. 12:1); the stars fell to earth (Rev. 6:13).

m Seven stars in his hand (Rev. 1:16; 2:1; 3:1); the seven stars are the angels of the seven churches (Rev. 1:20); I will give him the morning star (Rev. 2:28).

1 **The sky darkened**

n The stars, sun and moon will not give their light (Isa. 13:10); before sun, moon and stars are darkened (Eccles. 12:2); the stars, sun and moon will be darkened (Ezek. 32:7–8); the sun and moon grow dark and the stars are dimmed (Joel 3:15); the sun and moon will be darkened and the stars will fall (Matt. 24:29; Mark 13:24–5); the sun will be turned to darkness and the moon to blood (Joel 2:31); the sun turned black, the moon red and the stars fell (Rev. 6:12–13); a third of sun, moon and stars was struck (Rev. 8:12); the sun failed (Luke 23:45); the fourth bowl was poured on the sun (Rev. 16:8).

o The sky grew black with clouds and wind (1 Kgs. 18:45).

1 **Stars thrown down**

p The horn threw stars down (Dan. 8:10); a star called Wormwood (Rev. 8:10–11); a star from heaven fell to earth (Rev. 9:1); the dragon's tail swept stars from the sky (Rev. 12:4).

1 **Curbing the universe**

q God tells the sun not to shine (Job 9:7); the sun and moon stood still (Josh. 10:12–13); sun and moon stood in their places (Hab. 3:11); the moon and sun will be ashamed (Isa. 24:23).

r The sun shall not smite you by day nor the moon by night (Ps. 121:6); heat or sun will not smite them (Isa. 49:10).

1 **Universe passing away**

s Heaven and earth will pass away (Matt. 24:35; Mark 13:31; Luke 21:33; Rev. 21:1); I will shake heaven and earth (Hag. 2:6; Heb. 12:26); the earth will be shaken from its place (Isa. 13:13); the sky will be rolled up like a scroll (Isa. 34:4).

1 **New universe**

t I create new heavens and a new earth (Isa. 65:17); that will endure (Isa. 66:22); we look for new heavens and a new earth (2 Pet. 3:13); I saw a new heaven and a new earth (Rev. 21:1).

322 Weight

1 **Weights of things**

a David planned the weight for the gold vessels of the temple (1 Chr. 28:14–18); the weight of the gold earrings was 1700 shekels (Judg. 8:26); the crown weighed a talent of gold (2 Sam. 12:30; 1 Chr. 20:2); 50 shekels of gold in the nails (2 Chr. 3:9); 600 shekels of gold in each large shield (1 Kgs. 10:16; 2 Chr. 9:15); three minas of gold in each shield (1 Kgs. 10:17); 300 shekels in each shield (2 Chr. 9:16).

b Hiram sent Solomon 120 talents of gold (1 Kgs. 9:14); 420 talents of gold were brought from Ophir (1 Kgs. 9:28); 666 talents of gold in one year (1 Kgs. 10:14).

c Goliath's scale armour weighed 5000 shekels (1 Sam. 17:5); an iron spear weighing 600 shekels (1 Sam. 17:7); a bronze spear weighing 300 shekels (2 Sam. 21:16); Absalom's hair weighed 200 shekels (2 Sam. 14:26).

d 20 shekels weight of food per day (Ezek. 4:10); 100 pounds weight of myrrh and aloes (John 19:39); hailstones about a talent in weight (Rev. 16:21).

1 Weighing

e Ezra weighed out the silver, gold and utensils (Ezra 8:25–30); the silver, gold and utensils weighed out in Jerusalem (Ezra 8:33–4); I weighed out the silver (Jer. 32:9, 10).

f Weigh your hair into three parts (Ezek. 5:1–2); who has weighed the hills in a balance? (Isa. 40:12).

g Oh, that my vexation were weighed! (Job 6:2–3); let God weigh me in a true balance (Job 31:6); weighed in the balances and found wanting (Dan. 5:27).

Weighing scales, see **465***a*.

1 Beyond weighing

h The weight of the bronze was not determined (1 Kgs. 7:47; 2 Kgs. 25:16; 2 Chr. 4:18); more bronze than could be weighed (1 Chr. 22:3; Jer. 52:20); bronze and iron beyond weighing (1 Chr. 22:14); gold, silver, bronze and iron without reckoning (1 Chr. 22:16).

1 Heavy

i Eli was old and heavy (1 Sam. 4:18); a lead cover on the ephah (Zech. 5:7–8).

1 Sinking

j They sank like lead (Exod. 15:10); so will Babylon sink (Jer. 51:64); better a millstone hung round his neck (Matt. 18:6; Mark 9:42; Luke 17:2); Peter beginning to sink (Matt. 14:30); the boats began to sink (Luke 5:7).

1 Burdens

k I will add to your yoke (1 Kgs. 12:11, 14; 2 Chr. 10:11, 14); my iniquities are a heavy burden (Ps. 38:4); they put heavy loads on men's shoulders (Matt. 23:4; Luke 11:46).

l Why have you put the burden of all these people on me? (Num. 11:11); you are too heavy a burden for me (Deut. 1:9, 12); stone and sand are heavy but a fool's provocation is heavier (Prov. 27:3); lest we be burdensome to you (2 Sam. 13:25); why should I be a burden to the king? (2 Sam. 19:35); you will be a burden to me (2 Sam. 15:33); I was never a burden to you (2 Cor. 11:9; 12:13); working night and day so as not to burden you (2 Thess. 3:8); bear one another's burdens (Gal. 6:2).

Bearing people's burdens, see **273***j*.

m I will bring you out from under the burdens of the Egyptians (Exod. 6:6, 7); I removed the burden from his shoulder (Ps. 81:6); you will break the yoke of their burden (Isa. 9:4); the yoke and burden will be removed from your shoulders (Isa. 10:27); the burden of Assyria will be removed from their shoulders (Isa. 14:25); cast your burden on the Lord (Ps. 55:22).

Light yoke, see **323***c*.

n It seemed good to lay on you no other burden (Acts 15:28); I put no other burden on you (Rev. 2:24); his commands are not burdensome (1 John 5:3); come to me, all who are heavy-laden (Matt. 11:28).

o What is the burden of the Lord? (Jer. 23:33–8).

323 Lightness

<table>
<tr>
<td>₁ Buoyancy</td>
<td>a</td>
<td>The ark floated (Gen. 7:18); Elisha made the iron float (2 Kgs. 6:6).</td>
</tr>
</table>

₁ Buoyancy
   a The ark floated (Gen. 7:18); Elisha made the iron float (2 Kgs. 6:6).

   b Lightening a boat by thowing out: the cargo (Jonah 1:5); cargo and tackle (Acts 27:18–19); the wheat (Acts 27:38).

₁ Light yoke
   c Make our yoke lighter (1 Kgs. 12:4, 9, 10; 2 Chr. 10:4, 9, 10); my yoke is easy and my burden light (Matt. 11:30).
   Easy burdens, see **701***d*.

₁ Light as chaff
   d The wicked are like chaff driven away by the wind (Ps. 1:4); are the wicked like straw and chaff before the wind? (Job 21:18); evildoers will be like chaff (Mal. 4:1); your enemies will be like chaff (Isa. 29:5); let them be like chaff before the wind (Ps. 35:5; 83:13); he makes them like dust and chaff (Isa. 41:2); the nations will be like chaff before the wind (Isa. 17:13); they will be like chaff from the threshing floor (Hos. 13:3); in the balances they are lighter than breath (Ps. 62:9); he will burn up the chaff (Matt. 3:12).

   e The statue became like chaff (Dan. 2:35); a breath will carry the idols away (Isa. 57:13).

₁ Yeast
   f Peace offering with leavened bread (Lev. 7:13); loaves made with leaven as firstfruits (Lev. 23:17); bring a thankoffering from what is leavened (Amos 4:5).

   g Yeast which a woman hid in three measures of meal (Matt. 13:33; Luke 13:21).

   h Beware of the leaven of the Pharisees and Sadducees (Matt. 16:6); beware of the leaven of the Pharisees (Luke 12:1); beware of the leaven of the Pharisees and of Herod (Mark 8:15); clean out the leaven of malice (1 Cor. 5:8); a little leaven leavens the whole lump (Gal. 5:9).

₁ Unleavened
   i The Passover had to be eaten without yeast (Exod. 12:8, 15, 18–20; 13:3, 6–7; Num. 9:11; 28:17; Deut. 16:3–4; 1 Cor. 5:7–8); because the Israelites had no time to add yeast to the dough (Exod. 12:34, 39); the feast of Unleavened Bread (Lev. 23:6); they ate unleavened cakes (Josh. 5:11).

   j Sacrifices should not contain yeast (Exod. 23:18; 34:25; Lev. 2:4, 11; 6:17); unleavened bread for ordination (Exod. 29:2; Lev. 8:2, 26); grain offering eaten unleavened (Lev. 6:16–17); peace offering with unleavened bread (Lev. 7:12).

Section two: Inorganic matter

324 Density

Heaviness, see **322**.

325 Rarity

Infrequent, see **140**.

326 Hardness

Inflexible, see **602**.

327 Softness

Compliant, see **739**.

328 Elasticity

Rebounding, see **280**.

329 Toughness

Strength, see **162**.

330 Brittleness

ₗ Brittle   *a* Like clay, part of the kingdom will be brittle (Dan. 2:42).

331 Structure. Texture

332 Powderiness

ₗ Dust

a The serpent would eat dust (Gen. 3:14); dust from the tabernacle for the water of bitterness (Num. 5:17); the dust became gnats (Exod. 8:16–17); the dust of Samaria will not suffice for my people (1 Kgs. 20:10); the nations are like dust on the scales (Isa. 40:15).

b Shake the dust off your feet (Matt. 10:14; Luke 9:5; 10:11); they shook the dust off their feet (Acts 13:51); Shimei threw dust (2 Sam. 16:13); they were tossing dust in the air (Acts 22:23). **Dust on head**, see **836***l*.

ₗ Creatures from dust

c Man was made of the dust (Gen. 2:7; 3:19); he remembers that we are dust (Ps. 103:14).

d All come from dust and return to dust (Eccles. 3:20); all creatures die and return to their dust (Ps. 104:29); you turn man back to the dust (Ps. 90:3); if God withdrew his breath man would return to the dust (Job 34:14–15); would you turn me into dust again? (Job 10:9); the dust will return to the earth (Eccles. 12:7).

ₗ Soot   *e* Soot from the kiln (Exod. 9:8, 10).

ₗ Crushing

f Moses ground the golden calf to powder (Exod. 32:20; Deut. 9:21); Josiah ground the Asherah and idols to dust (2 Kgs. 23:6; 2 Chr. 34:4); Josiah ground the high place to dust (2 Kgs. 23:15); when they crush altar stones to powder (Isa. 27:9); the statue was crushed to pieces (Dan. 2:34–5, 44–5).

g Samson ground grain in the prison (Judg. 16:21); take the millstones and grind meal (Isa. 47:2); the grinders stand idle (Eccles. 12:3); the sound of the grinding is low (Eccles. 12:4).

h I crushed them like dust (2 Sam. 22:43; Ps. 18:42); you will thresh the mountains and pulverise them (Isa. 41:15); if this stone falls on anyone it will crush him (Matt. 21:44; Luke 20:18); the king of Aram had made Israel like the dust at threshing (2 Kgs.

13:7); the ostrich forgets that her eggs might be crushed (Job 39:15).

333 Friction

Scraping   *a* Job took a potsherd to scrape himself (Job 2:8); they will scrape off Tyre's soil (Ezek. 26:4).

334 Lubrication

Oiling the shield, see **357n**.

335 Liquids

Milk   *a* Jael gave Sisera milk (Judg. 4:19; 5:25); do not boil a kid in its mother's milk (Exod. 23:19; 34:26; Deut. 14:21).
Flowing with milk and honey, see **635d**.

Lifeblood   *b* I will require your lifeblood (Gen. 9:5–6); regulations concerning blood (Lev. 17:3–16); the life of the flesh is in the blood (Gen. 9:4; Lev. 17:11); blood to be poured out and covered (Lev. 17:13); blood pollutes the land (Num. 35:33); a man burdened with another's blood will be a fugitive until death (Prov. 28:17).

c Your brother's blood is crying to me (Gen. 4:10); earth, do not cover my blood (Job 16:18); the blood of all the prophets will be on this generation (Luke 11:50–1); in her was found the blood of prophets and saints (Rev. 18:24).

d They dipped Joseph's coat in goat blood (Gen. 37:31); clothed in a robe dipped in blood (Rev. 19:13); a bridegroom of blood (Exod. 4:26); Amasa wallowing in his blood (2 Sam. 20:12); dogs will lick up Ahab's blood (1 Kgs. 21:19); and they did (1 Kgs. 22:35, 38); he will wash his feet in the blood of the wicked (Ps. 58:10).

e I have betrayed innocent blood (Matt. 27:4); it is blood money (Matt. 27:6); Field of Blood (Matt. 27:8; Acts 1:19); blood, fire and smoke (Acts 2:19).

f They cut themselves till the blood gushed out (1 Kgs. 18:28); Jezebel's blood splashed on the wall (2 Kgs. 9:33); blood came out of the wine press of the wrath of God (Rev. 14:20).
Flow of blood, see **302e**; **bloodshed**, see **362**.

Eating blood   *g* You must not eat blood (Gen. 9:4; Lev. 3:17; 7:26–7; 17:10–12, 14; 19:26; Deut. 12:16, 23; 15:23); abstain from blood (Acts 15:20, 29; 21:25); the people ate the animals with the blood (1 Sam. 14:32–4); you eat meat with the blood still in it (Ezek. 33:25); shall I drink the blood of these men? (2 Sam. 23:17; 1 Chr. 11:19).

h Eat my flesh and drink my blood (John 6:53–5).

i They have shed blood and you gave them blood to drink (Rev. 16:6); drunk with the blood of the saints (Rev. 17:6).

j A lion drinks the blood of its prey (Num. 23:24); young eagles suck up blood (Job 39:30).

1 Turned to blood	*k*	Nile water turned to blood (Exod. 4:9; 7:17–20; Ps. 105:29); he turned their rivers to blood (Ps. 78:44); the sea turned into blood (Rev. 8:8; 16:3); rivers and springs became blood (Rev. 16:4); the witnesses have power to turn the waters into blood (Rev. 11:6); water as red as blood (2 Kgs. 3:22); the moon became like blood (Rev. 6:12).
1 Blood on the door	*l*	Blood was put on the door frame (Exod. 12:7, 22); when I see the blood I will pass over you (Exod. 12:13, 23).
1 Blood of sacrifices	*m*	The blood makes atonement (Lev. 17:11); without the shedding of blood there is no forgiveness (Heb. 9:22); blood poured on the altar (Deut. 12:27); blood was put on the horns of the altar and poured round its base (Exod. 29:12; Lev. 1:15; 8:15; 9:9); blood was sprinkled on the altar (Exod. 24:6; 29:16, 20; Lev. 1:5, 11, 15; 3:2, 8, 13; 7:2; 9:9, 12, 18; Num. 18:17; 2 Chr. 29:22); on the altar of incense (Exod. 30:10); on the people (Exod. 24:8); on priests (Lev. 8:30); blood on the ears, thumbs and toes for ordination (Exod. 29:20; Lev. 8:23); and on a cleansed leper (Lev. 14:14, 25); sprinkled seven times (Lev. 4:6, 17; 14:7; 16:14; Num. 19:4); the priests sprinkled the blood (2 Chr. 30:16; 35:11); Moses sprinkled the people with blood (Heb. 9:19–21); the live bird dipped in blood (Lev. 14:6, 51).
	n	Wash clothes splashed with blood from the offering (Lev. 6:27); Pilate mixed their blood with their sacrifices (Luke 13:1).
1 Blood of the covenant	*o*	A covenant is ratified by blood (Heb. 9:16–21); the blood of my covenant (Zech. 9:11); my blood of the covenant (Matt. 26:28; Mark 14:24); the new covenant in my blood (Luke 22:20; 1 Cor. 11:25); the blood of the covenant (Heb. 10:29; 13:20).
1 Blood of Christ	*p*	Redeemed by the precious blood of Christ (1 Pet. 1:19); redemption through his blood (Eph. 1:7); justified by his blood (Rom. 5:9); having made peace by the blood of his cross (Col. 1:20); taking not the blood of goats and calves but his own blood (Heb. 9:12–14); the blood of Christ cleanses the conscience (Heb. 9:14); the blood of Jesus cleanses us from all sin (1 John 1:7); the sprinkling of the blood of Jesus (1 Pet. 1:2); the sprinkled blood (Heb. 12:24); blood and water came out (John 19:34); he who came by water and blood (1 John 5:6); the water and blood bear witness (1 John 5:8).
	q	Brought near by the blood of Christ (Eph. 2:13); is not the cup a sharing in the blood of Christ? (1 Cor. 10:16); he freed us from our sins by his blood (Rev. 1:5); robes washed in the blood of the Lamb (Rev. 7:14); they overcame him by the blood of the Lamb (Rev. 12:11).

336 Gaseousness

Air, see **340**.

337 Liquefaction

1 Melting

a The manna melted away (Exod. 16:21); he sends his word and melts the ice (Ps. 147:18).

b Mountains melt like wax before the Lord (Ps. 97:5); the wicked perish as wax melts before the fire (Ps. 68:2).

c As metals are melted in the furnace, so I will melt you (Ezek. 22:20–2).

338 Vaporization

Cloud, see **355**.

339 Water

1 Water of the earth

a The Spirit of God hovered over the waters (Gen. 1:2); the earth was made out of water and by water (2 Pet. 3:5); God separated the waters (Gen. 1:6–7).

b God measured out the waters (Job 28:25); the Lord is over many waters (Ps. 29:3); the waters stood above the mountains (Ps. 104:6); at your rebuke they fled (Ps. 104:7); the waters saw you and were afraid (Ps. 77:16).

c Wings like the sound of many waters (Ezek. 1:24); a voice like the sound of many waters (Rev. 1:15; 14:2; 19:6).

1 Wells and springs

d The angel found Hagar by a spring (Gen. 16:7, 14); God showed Hagar a well of water (Gen. 21:19); Abraham complained to Abimelech about a well (Gen. 21:25); Isaac reopened his father's wells (Gen. 26:15, 18); disputes over wells (Gen. 26:19–22); Isaac's servants dug a well (Gen. 26:25); Jacob drew well water for Rachel (Gen. 29:2–10); Moses sat by the well in Midian (Exod. 2:15); at Elim there were 12 springs of water (Exod. 15:27; Num. 33:9); spring up, O well! (Num. 21:17); the spring of Harod (Judg. 7:1); David longed for water from the well of Bethlehem (2 Sam. 23:15; 1 Chr. 11:17); David's messengers were hidden in the well (2 Sam. 17:18); Jesus sat by the well in Samaria (John 4:6); I dug wells and drank foreign waters (2 Kgs. 19:24).

e The well of: Beer-lahai-roi (Gen. 16:14); Beersheba (Gen. 26:32–3); Nahor (Gen. 24:11–20); Sirah (2 Sam. 3:26); Dragon Well (Neh. 2:13).

1 Cisterns

f Drink the water from your own cistern (2 Kgs. 18:31); Uzziah hewed many cisterns (2 Chr. 26:10); hewn cisterns (Neh. 9:25); they have hewn for themselves broken cisterns (Jer. 2:13); they let Jeremiah down into a cistern (Jer. 38:6–9); Ishmael filled the cistern with corpses (Jer. 41:7, 9).

Pool, see **346**.

1 Drinking water

g To give drink to my chosen people (Isa. 43:20); David took Saul's jug of water (1 Sam. 26:11–12, 16); we have to pay for our own drinking water (Lam. 5:4).

Drawing water, see **304***d*.

1 Bad water	*h* Water turned into blood (Exod. 4:9; 7:17–24; Rev. 8:8; 16:3; 16:4, 6); the waters of Marah were bitter (Exod. 15:23–5); Wormwood made the waters bitter (Rev. 8:11); Elisha healed the bad waters with salt (2 Kgs. 2:19–22). **Turned to blood**, see **335*k*.** *i* The water of Bitterness that brings a curse (Num. 5:18). *j* Does a fountain put forth both fresh and bitter water? (Jas. 3:11).
1 God providing water	*k* Water from the rock (Exod. 17:6; Num. 20:8–11; Deut. 8:15; Neh. 9:15; Ps. 78:15–16, 20; Isa. 48:21); he opened the rock and water gushed out (Ps. 105:41); he turned the rock into a fountain (Ps. 114:8); you gave them water for their thirst (Neh. 9:20); God gave the people water from a well at Beer (Num. 21:16); Israel will have abundant water (Num. 24:7); God split the hollow at Lehi and water came out (Judg. 15:19); the valley was filled with water (2 Kgs. 3:17, 20). *l* God opened springs and streams (Ps. 74:15); he sends springs in the valleys (Ps. 104:10); he changes the desert into a pool of water (Ps. 107:35). **Lack of water**, see **342*e*.**
1 Water of life	*m* Waters will gush in the wilderness (Isa. 35:6); he will open rivers on bare heights (Isa. 41:18); I will pour water on the thirsty land (Isa. 44:3). *n* Water flowed from under the threshold of the temple (Ezek. 47:1–12); a spring will flow from the house of the Lord (Joel 3:18); living water will flow from Jerusalem (Zech. 14:8); there is a river whose streams make glad the city of God (Ps. 46:4); with you is the fountain of life (Ps. 36:9); all my springs are in you (Ps. 87:7); the river of the water of life flowing from the throne of God (Rev. 22:1); he will guide them to springs of water (Isa. 49:10; Rev. 7:17); everyone who thirsts, come to the water (Isa. 55:1). *o* God, the fountain of living waters (Jer. 2:13); they have forsaken the Lord, the fountain of living water (Jer. 17:13); he would have given you living water (John 4:10); from the spring of the water of life (Rev. 21:6); from the believer rivers of living water will flow (John 7:38); the water will be in him a well of water (John 4:14); they make the Valley of Baca a place of springs (Ps. 84:6). *p* Understanding is a fountain of life (Prov. 16:22); the fountain of wisdom is a flowing stream (Prov. 18:4); a well of living water (S. of S. 4:15); with joy you will draw water from the wells of salvation (Isa. 12:3).
1 Man providing water	*q* Give me a drink (Gen. 24:14, 17, 43, 45; John 4:7, 10); giving a cup of water to a disciple (Matt. 10:42; Mark 9:41); a man carrying a jug of water (Mark 14:13; Luke 22:10); give me springs of water (Josh. 15:19; Judg. 1:15); the Gibeonites became drawers of water (Josh. 9:21, 23, 27).

r I will water your camels (Gen. 24:14, 19, 44, 46); watering the flocks (Gen. 29:2–10; Exod. 2:16–19).

s We will not drink your water (Num. 20:17; 21:22); if we drink water we will pay for it (Num. 20:19).

1 Baptism
with water

t I baptise you with water (Matt. 3:11; Mark 1:8; Luke 3:16; John 1:26, 31, 33); John baptised with water (Acts 1:5); there was much water where John baptised (John 3:23); water for baptism (Acts 8:36).

Baptism, see **988r**.

1 Ceremonial
water

u The water of cleansing (Num. 8:7; 19:9, 13, 17); holy water (Num. 5:17); sprinkle water over the Levites (Num. 8:7); pass through the water what cannot stand the fire (Num. 31:23).

1 Other water

v Moses—drawn out of the water (Exod. 2:10); he drew me out of the waters (2 Sam. 22:17; Ps. 18:16); he who came by water and blood (1 John 5:6, 8).

w The waters were piled up in a heap (Exod. 15:8).

x The water was made wine (John 2:6–10).

y Joab captured the city of waters (2 Sam. 12:27).

z Cast your bread on the waters (Eccles. 11:1).

Walking on water, see **269e**; **flowing water**, see **350**.

340 Air

1 Air

a The seventh angel poured his bowl into the air (Rev. 16:17); we will meet the Lord in the air (1 Thess. 4:17).

1 Weather

b Predicting the weather (Matt. 16:2–3; Luke 12:54–6).

Hot weather, see **379a**; **cold weather**, see **380a**.

341 Moisture

1 Irrigation

a A mist watered the ground (Gen. 2:6); a river watered the garden of Eden (Gen. 2:10); the Jordan valley was well-watered (Gen. 13:10); Egypt was watered by the foot but the land of Israel drinks rain from heaven (Deut. 11:10–11); rain and snow water the earth (Isa. 55:10).

b God waters its furrows (Ps. 65:10); God waters the mountains from his high places (Ps. 104:13); I water the vineyard every moment (Isa. 27:3); God sends rain on land which is unpeopled (Job 38:26); he causes mists to ascend (Ps. 135:7).

c I made pools to water the trees (Eccles. 2:6).

d You will be like a watered garden (Isa. 58:11); I planted and Apollos watered (1 Cor. 3:6–8).

1 Dew

e God give you the dew of heaven (Gen. 27:28); who has begotten the dew? (Job 38:28); dew in the morning (Exod. 16:13–14); the manna fell with the dew (Num. 11:9).

f Gideon found dew on the fleece (Judg. 6:37–8); and on the ground (Judg. 6:39–40); my head is wet with dew (S. of S. 5:2); let him be wet with the dew of heaven (Dan. 4:15, 23, 25, 33; 5:21).

g Unity is like the dew of Hermon (Ps. 133:3); I will be like the
dew to Israel (Hos. 14:5); the remnant will be like dew from the
Lord (Mic. 5:7).

h Your love is like the dew than vanishes (Hos. 6:4); they will be
like the dew that vanishes (Hos. 13:3); we will fall on David like
dew on the ground (2 Sam. 17:12).

1 Moist   i The moist destroyed with the dry (Deut. 29:19); seven fresh
things   bowstrings, not dried (Judg. 16:7–8).

342 Dryness

1 Dry land   a God turned the sea into dry land (Exod. 14:16, 21–2, 29; 15:19;
Josh. 2:10; 4:23; Ps. 66:6); he rebuked the Dead Sea and it dried
up (Ps. 106:9); I dry up the sea with my rebuke (Isa. 50:2); God
dried up the sea (Isa. 51:10); God dries up sea and rivers (Nahum
1:4); passing the Red Sea as on dry land (Heb. 11:29; Neh. 9:11);
dry ground in the middle of the Jordan (Josh. 3:13, 17; 4:22–3;
5:1); Elisha and Elijah crossed the river on dry ground (2 Kgs.
2:8); the water of the Euphrates dried up (Rev. 16:12).

b The water was dried up from the earth (Gen. 8:13–14); like a root
out of dry ground (Isa. 53:2).

1 Drought   c If they do not obey, the Lord will send drought (Deut. 11:17;
28:23–4); God restrains the waters and they dry up (Job 12:15);
I will command the clouds not to rain on it (Isa. 5:6); I called for
a drought (Hag. 1:11); let no dew or rain be on you (2 Sam. 1:21);
no rain because the people have sinned (1 Kgs. 8:35; 2 Chr. 6:26;
7:13); the rebellious live in a parched land (Ps. 68:6); God sent
drought on some towns (Amos 4:7–8); Elijah announced the
drought (1 Kgs. 17:1, 7); Elijah prayed that it would not rain (Jas.
5:17); the two witnesses have power to stop the rain (Rev. 11:6);
the showers and spring rain have been withheld (Jer. 3:3);
Jeremiah on the drought (Jer. 14:1–6).

d The Nile will dry up (Isa. 19:5–7); the water brooks are dried up
(Joel 1:20); a drought on her waters that they may be dried up
(Jer. 50:38).

1 Lack of   e The skin of water was used up (Gen. 21:15); a wilderness with
water   no water (Deut. 8:15); no water for the Israelites (Exod. 15:22;
17:1; Num. 20:2, 5; 21:5; 33:14); the brook Cherith dried up
(1 Kgs. 17:7); the army had no water (2 Kgs. 3:9).

f You will be like a garden without water (Isa. 1:30); springs
without water (2 Pet. 2:17); clouds without water (Jude 12);
away from the dew of heaven (Gen. 27:39); in a dry and weary
land with no water (Ps. 63:1); the unclean spirit passes through
waterless places (Matt. 12:43).

g When the poor and needy seek water and there is none (Isa.
41:17).

1 Cutting   h God tells the rivers to dry up (Isa. 44:27); God turns rivers into
off water   a desert (Ps. 107:33); you dried up every-flowing streams (Ps.

74:15); I will dry up the Nile (Ezek. 30:12); I will dry up the pools (Isa. 42:15); God will dry up the river (Isa. 11:15).

i Stopping all springs of water (2 Kgs. 3:19, 25); Hezekiah stopped the springs outside Jerusalem (2 Chr. 32:3–4); with my foot I dried up the rivers of Egypt (2 Kgs. 19:24; Isa. 37:25).

₁ Dry things
j The dead bones were very dry (Ezek. 37:2); what will happen when the wood is dry? (Luke 23:31).

₁ Withering
k The king's hand withered (1 Kgs. 13:4); a man with a withered hand (Matt. 12:10; Mark 3:1; Luke 6:6); the fig tree withered (Matt. 21:19–20; Mark 11:20–1); will he not pull up the vine so that it withers? (Ezek. 17:9–10); the vine was plucked up and withered (Ezek. 19:12).

l His leaf will not wither (Ps. 1:3).

343 Ocean

₁ Creation of the seas
a Darkness over the surface of the deep (Gen. 1:2); the expanse separated waters below from waters above (Gen. 1:6–7); the gathering of the waters he called seas (Gen. 1:10); the channels of the sea appeared (2 Sam. 22:16; Ps. 18:15); God brought the sea to birth (Job 38:8–9); God pours the water of the sea on the earth (Amos 5:8; 9:6); the sea is his for he made it (Ps. 95:5).
Limits of the sea, see **236***f*.

₁ The seas
b Have you entered the springs of the sea? (Job 38:16); there is the sea, great and wide (Ps. 104:25); let the sea roar (1 Chr. 16:32); though the mountain slip into the sea (Ps. 46:2–3).

c Zebulun to have the abundance of the seas (Deut. 33:19); the Lord will cast Tyre's wealth into the sea (Zech. 9:4); the angel threw the stone into the sea (Rev. 18:21); better to be cast into the sea (Matt. 18:6; Mark 9:42); four beasts came out of the sea (Dan. 7:3).

₁ Sea stirred up
d The wind lifted up the waves of the sea (Ps. 107:25); the four winds of heaven stirred up the sea (Dan. 7:2); I am the Lord who stirs up the sea (Isa. 51:15); God stirs up the sea so that its waves roar (Jer. 31:35); the nations will be perplexed by the roaring of the sea (Luke 21:25); the boat was beaten by the waves (Matt. 14:24).

e The wicked are like the tossing sea (Isa. 57:20); they are wild waves of the sea (Jude 13); he who doubts is like a wave of the sea tossed by the wind (Jas. 1:6).

₁ Sea quelled
f The Lord has stretched out his hand over the sea (Isa. 23:11); God treads the waves of the sea (Job 9:8); you trampled the sea with your horses (Hab. 3:15); the Lord makes a way through the sea (Isa. 43:16); God shattered Rahab the sea monster (Job 26:12; Ps. 89:10); am I the sea or the sea monster that you muzzle me? (Job 7:12).

g You still the roaring of the sea (Ps. 65:7; 89:9); he rebuked the winds and the sea (Matt. 8:26; Mark 4:39; Luke 8:24); even winds and sea obey him (Matt. 8:27; Mark 4:41; Luke 8:25); the sea gave up the dead in it (Rev. 20:13); there was no more sea (Rev. 21:1).

ı Sea turned to blood

h A burning mountain thrown into the sea and a third of the sea became blood (Rev. 8:8); the bowl was poured into the sea and it became blood (Rev. 16:3).

ı Red Sea

i To the Red Sea (Exod. 13:18; Josh. 24:6–7); encamping by the sea (Exod. 14:2, 9; Num. 33:10–11); stretch out your staff over the sea (Exod. 14:16, 26–7); Moses performed wonders and signs at the Red Sea (Acts 7:36); they passed through the middle of the sea (Num. 33:8); all our fathers passed through the sea (1 Cor. 10:1).

j He gathered the waters of the sea as a heap (Ps. 33:7); the sea looked and fled (Ps. 114:3, 5); the sea engulfed their enemies (Ps. 78:53).

ı Sea of Galilee

k Boundary at the Sea of Chinnereth [Galilee / Gennesaret / Tiberias] (Num. 34:11; Deut. 3:17; Josh. 12:3; 13:27).

l Jesus settled in Capernaum by the sea (Matt. 4:13, 15); walking by the sea of Galilee (Matt. 4:18; 15:29; Mark 1:16); Jesus sat by the sea (Matt. 13:1); he was standing by the lake of Gennesaret (Luke 5:1); Jesus withdrew with his disciples to the sea (Mark 3:7); Jesus went to the other side of the sea of Galilee, of Tiberias (John 6:1); Jesus appeared at the sea of Tiberias (John 21:1).

ı Mediterranean

m The Great Sea [Mediterranean] (Josh. 15:12, 47); boundary at the Great Sea (Num. 34:5–7; Josh. 1:4; 23:4; Ezek. 47:20); the western sea (Deut. 11:24; 34:2).

ı Dead Sea

n The sea of the Arabah, the Salt Sea [Dead Sea] (Josh. 12:3); boundary at the Salt Sea (Num. 34:3, 12; Deut. 3:17; Josh. 15:2, 5; 18:19).

ı Sea transport

o Timber brought from the Lebanon by sea (1 Kgs. 5:9; 2 Chr. 2:16; Ezra 3:7).

Sea travel, see **269c**.

ı The 'sea'

p The 'sea' made (1 Kgs. 7:23–6, 39, 44; 1 Chr. 18:8; 2 Chr. 4:2, 15; Jer. 27:19); for the priests to wash in (2 Chr. 4:6); placed on the right of the house (2 Chr. 4:10); Ahaz removed the sea from the oxen under it (2 Kgs. 16:17); the sea broken up and taken away (2 Kgs. 25:13, 16; Jer. 52:17, 20).

ı Sea of glass

q A sea of glass (Rev. 4:6); mixed with fire (Rev. 15:2).

344 Land

ı Earth

a The ground cursed through Adam (Gen. 3:17); toil because of the ground the Lord has cursed (Gen. 5:29); Cain was cursed from the ground (Gen. 4:10–11).

Dry land, see **342a**.

b Naaman asked for two mules' burden of earth (2 Kgs. 5:17); the foolish man built his house on sand (Matt. 7:26); on the ground with no foundation (Luke 6:49).

1 Clay	*c* Cast in the clay ground (1 Kgs. 7:46; 2 Chr. 4:17); Jesus spat on the ground and made clay (John 9:6, 11, 15).
	d You made me like clay (Job 10:9); I too have been made out of clay (Job 33:6); you are like clay in the potter's hand (Jer. 18:6); we have this treasure in earthenware vessels (2 Cor. 4:7).
1 Stones	*e* You will be in league with the stones of the field (Job 5:23); the stones would cry out (Luke 19:40); a time to throw stones and a time to gether stones (Eccles. 3:5); God is able to raise up children to Abraham from these stones (Matt. 3:9; Luke 3:8).
1 Stones as monuments	*f* Jacob used a stone as a pillow (Gen. 28:11); and set it up at Bethel (Gen. 28:18); twelve stones taken from the Jordan (Josh. 4:3); and set up at Gilgal (Josh. 4:20); Joshua set up a stone as witness (Josh. 24:26–7).
	g Write the law on large stones (Deut. 27:2–3).

Heap of stones, see **209z**; **pillar**, see **218n**; **monuments**, see **548a**.

1 Named rocks	*h* Jacob set up a stone called Witness (Gen. 31:45–7); the Rock of Oreb (Judg. 7:25); the Rock of Rimmon (Judg. 20:47; 21:13); Ebenezer—stone of help (1 Sam. 7:12); hide by the stone Ezel (1 Sam. 20:19); the Rock of Escape (1 Sam. 23:28); Rocks of the Wild Goats (1 Sam. 24:2); stones at Gilgal (Judg. 3:19, 26); the stone of Zoheleth (1 Kgs. 1:9).
1 Stones as stoppers	*i* A large stone over the well (Gen. 29:2); stones rolled over the mouth of the cave (Josh. 10:18, 27); a stone over the mouth of the lions' den (Dan. 6:17); a stone rolled over the tomb (Matt. 27:60; Mark 15:46; John 11:38).
	j Who will roll away the stone? (Mark 16:3); the stone was rolled away from the tomb (Matt. 28:2; Mark 16:4; Luke 24:2; John 20:1).
1 Stones for harming	*k* Abimelech killed 70 men on one stone (Judg. 9:5); a millstone was thrown down on Abimelech (Judg. 9:53; 2 Sam. 11:21); animals slaughtered on a big rock (1 Sam. 14:33–4).
	l David chose five smooth stones (1 Sam. 17:40); David slung a stone (1 Sam. 17:49, 50); Shimei threw stones (2 Sam. 16:6, 13); lest you strike your foot against a stone (Ps. 91:12; Matt. 4:6; Luke 4:11); I will make Jerusalem a heavy stone for all the peoples (Zech. 12:3).

Throwing stones, see **287a**.

	m Spoil every good piece of land with stones (2 Kgs. 3:19, 25); some seeds fell on stony ground (Matt. 13:5, 20; Mark 4:5, 16; Luke 8:6, 13).
1 Stoning	*n* Achan's family were burned and stoned (Josh. 7:25); they stoned Stephen (Acts 7:59); they picked up stones to throw at Jesus (John 8:59; 10:31); the Gentiles and Jews tried to stone the apostles (Acts 14:5); they stoned Paul (Acts 14:19); once I was stoned (2 Cor. 11:25); some were stoned (Heb. 11:37).

o If even a beast touches the mountain, it will be stoned (Heb. 12:20).

Stones for protection

p He set my feet on a rock (Ps. 40:2); he will lift me up on a rock (Ps. 27:5); the wise man built his house on a rock (Matt. 7:24; Luke 6:48); they climb among the rocks [to hide] (Jer. 4:29); they called to the rocks to fall on them and hide them (Rev. 6:16).

Provision from rock

q Water out of the rock (Deut. 8:15; Isa. 48:21); he turned the rock into a pool of water (Ps. 114:8); strike the rock (Exod. 17:6); speak to the rock (Num. 20:8); but he struck it twice (Num. 20:11); they all drank from the spiritual rock (1 Cor. 10:4); honey and oil from the rock (Deut. 32:13); command these stones to become bread (Matt. 4:3; Luke 4:3); if a son asks for a loaf, who will give him a stone? (Matt. 7:9).

Stones for building

r Preparing stones for the temple (1 Chr. 22:2); they quarried large stones (1 Kgs. 5:17); the stones were prepared at the quarry (1 Kgs. 6:7); building the temple with huge stones (Ezra 5:8); three rows of cut stone (1 Kgs. 6:36); three courses of huge stones (Ezra 6:4); costly stones, cut to measure (1 Kgs. 7:9–11); the foundation of large stones (1 Kgs. 7:10); they will not leave one stone on another (Luke 19:44).

s Your servants hold dear the stones of Zion (Ps. 102:14).

Various literal stones

t They set Moses on a stone (Exod. 17:12); Samson lived in the cleft of the rock at Etam (Judg. 15:8, 11); the ark came to rest by a large stone (1 Sam. 6:14, 15, 18); the large stone in Gibeon (2 Sam. 20:8); Jeremiah hid stones in the mortar in Egypt (Jer. 43:9–10); tie a stone to the scroll and throw it in the Euphrates (Jer. 51:63); an angel took up a stone like a millstone (Rev. 18:21).

u A millstone is not to be taken in pledge (Deut. 24:6).

v A land whose stones are iron (Deut. 8:9); Tyre will be a bare rock (Ezek. 26:4, 14).

God the rock

w God the rock (Deut. 32:4, 30; 1 Sam. 2:2); you O rock (Hab. 1:12); the Lord God is an everlasting rock (Isa. 26:4); their rock is not like our rock (Deut. 32:31); there is no other rock (Isa. 44:8); the rock of Israel (Gen. 49:24; 2 Sam. 23:3; Isa. 30:29); the rock of his salvation (Deut. 32:15); the rock of my salvation (Ps. 89:26); the rock of our salvation (Ps. 95:1); the rock that begot you (Deut. 32:18); they remembered that God was their rock (Ps. 78:35); the rock that is higher than I (Ps. 61:2); who is a rock besides our God? (2 Sam. 22:32; Ps. 18:31); God my rock (Ps. 42:9; 144:1); my rock (2 Sam. 22:3; Ps. 18:2; 28:1; 31:3; 71:3; 92:15); my rock and my salvation (2 Sam. 22:2, 47; Ps. 18:46; 62:2, 6); my strong rock (Ps. 62:7); be a rock of strength to me (Ps. 31:2); be a rock of habitation to me (Ps. 71:3).

Christ the rock

x The stone the builders rejected has become the head stone (Ps. 118:22; Matt. 21:42; Mark 12:10; Luke 20:17; Acts 4:11; 1 Pet. 2:7); a stone of stumbling (Isa. 8:14; Rom. 9:33; 1 Pet. 2:8);

whoever falls on this stone will be broken to pieces (Matt. 21:44); a precious and trustworthy cornerstone (Isa. 28:16; 1 Pet. 2:6); a stone was cut out without hands (Dan. 2:34, 45); the stone became a mountain (Dan. 2:35); the rock which followed them was Christ (1 Cor. 10:4); a living stone (1 Pet. 2:4); to the overcomer I will give a white stone (Rev. 2:17).

ı People as rocks

y Simon was named Peter, the stone (John 1:42); on this rock I will build my church (Matt. 16:18); living stones built into a spiritual house (1 Pet. 2:5); look to Abraham, the rock from which you were hewn (Isa. 51:1–2).

345 Gulf: inlet

346 Lake

ı Named pools

a The pool of: Bethesda (John 5:2); Gibeon (2 Sam. 2:13); Hebron (2 Sam. 4:12); Shelah (Neh. 3:15); Siloam (John 9:7); the King's Pool (Neh. 2:14); the artificial pool (Neh. 3:16).

ı Reservoirs

b The conduit of the upper pool (2 Kgs. 18:17); Hezekiah made the pool and the conduit (2 Kgs. 20:20); you collected the waters of the lower pool (Isa. 22:9); you made a reservoir between the walls (Isa. 22:11); I will make the wilderness a pool of water (Isa. 41:18).

Lake of Galilee, see **343k**.

347 Marsh

ı Mire

a The hippopotamus lies down in the marsh (Job 40:21).

b He has thrown me into the mire (Job 30:19); I sink in deep mire (Ps. 69:2).

c Deliver me from the mire (Ps. 69:14); he brought me up out of the miry bog (Ps. 40:2).

348 Plain

ı Plains

a The plain of Dura (Dan. 3:1); the plain of the Jordan (1 Kgs. 7:46); the plain of Ono (Neh. 6:2); let us fight them in the plain (1 Kgs. 20:23, 25).

ı Level ground

b My foot stands on a level place (Ps. 26:12); lead me in a level path (Ps. 27:11); the way of the righteous is level (Isa. 26:7); let the rough ground become level (Isa. 40:4).

349 Island

ı Islands in general

a God takes up the islands like dust (Isa. 40:15); every island was moved from its place (Rev. 6:14); every island fled away (Rev. 16:20).

ı Islands specified

b A small island called Clauda (Acts 27:16); we must run aground on a certain island (Acts 27:26); called Malta (Acts 28:1); the island called Patmos (Rev. 1:9).

350 Stream: water in motion

<table>
<tr><td>1 Flood</td><td>

a The flood (Gen. 6:17; 7:6–24; 2 Pet. 2:5); until the flood came and destroyed them all (Luke 17:27); the world destroyed by flood (2 Pet. 3:6); never again shall a flood destroy the earth (Gen. 9:11); I swore that the waters of Noah should no more flood the earth (Isa. 54:9).

b God sends out waters and they flood the earth (Job 12:15); the floods lift up their pounding (Ps. 93:3); the floods burst on that house (Matt. 7:25, 27; Luke 6:48, 49).

c The King of Assyria will come like a flood on Judah (Isa. 8:7); Egypt rises to cover the earth (Jer. 46:8); waters from the north will overflow the land (Jer. 47:2).
</td></tr>
<tr><td>1 Swamped</td><td>

d I have come into deep waters and the flood flows over me (Ps. 69:1–2); all your waves have gone over me (Ps. 42:7; Jonah 2:3); waves were breaking over the boat (Matt. 8:24; Mark 4:37); may the flood not overflow me (Ps. 69:15); deliver me from the waters (Ps. 144:7); when you pass through the rivers they will not overflow you (Isa. 43:2).
</td></tr>
<tr><td>1 Rivers</td><td>

e Rivers flow into the sea, then return (Eccles. 1:7); you cleaved the earth with rivers (Hab. 3:9); were you angry with the rivers? (Hab. 3:8); man dams the streams (Job 28:11).

f The bird was killed over running water (Lev. 14:5–6, 50–1); bring the heifer to a valley with running water (Deut. 21:4).
</td></tr>
<tr><td>1 God provides rivers</td><td>

g I am making rivers in the desert (Isa. 43:19–20); running streams on every hill (Isa. 30:25); I will open rivers on the bare heights (Isa. 41:18); I will lead them by streams of water (Jer. 31:9).

h The Lord will be for us a place of rivers and wide canals (Isa. 33:21); the river of God is full of water (Ps. 65:9); the river of the water of life (Rev. 22:1); he will come like a rushing stream which the wind of the Lord drives (Isa. 59:19).
</td></tr>
<tr><td>1 Provision of rivers</td><td>

i Like cedars by the waters (Num. 24:6); his seed by many waters (Num. 24:7); like a tree planted by streams of water (Ps. 1:3); the king and princes will be like streams in a dry land (Isa. 32:2); rivers of living water flow from the believer (John 7:38); let justice flow like rivers (Amos 5:24).
</td></tr>
<tr><td>1 Failing rivers</td><td>

j My friends have been like the vanishing waters of a wadi (Job 6:15–18); will you be to me like a stream which fails? (Jer. 15:18).
</td></tr>
<tr><td>1 Rivers of people</td><td>

k The roaring of nations is like the roaring of many waters (Isa. 17:12–13); the great harlot sits on many waters (Rev. 17:1); the waters are peoples (Rev. 17:15).
</td></tr>
<tr><td>1 Jordan</td><td>

l Jordan overflows in harvest time (Josh. 3:15; 4:18); priests to stand in the Jordan (Josh. 3:8, 13); Jordan turned back (Ps. 114:3, 5); the raging of Jordan does not upset the hippopotamus (Job 40:23).

m The Jordan was the border of: Reuben (Josh. 13:23); Gad (Josh. 13:27); Judah (Josh. 15:5); Ephraim (Josh. 16:1, 7); Benjamin
</td></tr>
</table>

(Josh. 18:19–20); Issachar (Josh. 19:22); Naphtali (Josh. 19:34); the land (Ezek. 47:18).

n God has made Jordan the border between us (Josh. 22:25); from Jordan to the Great Sea (Josh. 23:4); they seized the fords of the Jordan (Judg. 3:28; 7:24; 12:5); they came as far as the Jordan (2 Sam. 19:15).

o Baptised in the river Jordan (Matt. 3:6; Mark 1:5; Luke 3:3); Jesus came to the Jordan to be baptised (Matt. 3:13).

1 Euphrates

p The great river, the Euphrates (Deut. 1:7; 11:24; Josh. 24:2–3; 2 Kgs. 23:29; 1 Chr. 5:9; 18:3; Rev. 16:12); the river Euphrates (Jer. 46:6, 10); the Euphrates (Jer. 51:63); the River (2 Sam. 8:3; 10:16; 1 Kgs. 4:21; 14:15; 1 Chr. 19:16; Ezra 4:10, 11, 16, 17, 20; Ps. 72:8; 80:11); from the river of Egypt to the Euphrates (Gen. 15:18; 2 Kgs. 24:7; Isa. 27:12); from the Euphrates (2 Chr. 9:26); from the River to the ends of the earth (Zech. 9:10); four angels bound at the river Euphrates (Rev. 9:14).

1 Nile

q Pharaoh by the Nile (Gen. 41:1); as Pharaoh comes to the water (Exod. 7:15; 8:20); Thebes [No Amon] by the Nile (Nahum 3:8).

r The land will rise like the Nile (Amos 8:8; 9:5); Egypt rises like the Nile (Jer. 46:7–8); the Nile is mine, I made it (Ezek. 29:3, 9); the depths of the Nile will dry up (Zech. 10:11).

1 Various rivers

s A river flowing from Eden with four tributaries (Gen. 2:10–14); Abanah and Pharpar, rivers of Damascus (2 Kgs. 5:12); Kishon swept them away (Judg. 5:21); the river of Ahava (Ezra 8:15, 21, 31).

t The brook: Besor (1 Sam. 30:10, 21); Cherith (1 Kgs. 17:3, 5); of Egypt (Josh. 15:4, 47); Jabbok (Josh. 12:2); of Kanah (Josh. 16:8); Kidron (2 Sam. 15:23; 1 Kgs. 15:13; 2 Kgs. 23:6, 12; 2 Chr. 30:14); Zered (Deut. 2:13).

u The waters of Merom (Josh. 11:7); Jotbatha, a land of streams (Deut. 10:7); a land of streams, fountains and springs (Deut. 8:7).

v By the streams of Babylon we sat down and wept (Ps. 137:1); by the Tigris (Dan. 10:4); by the river Chebar (Ezek. 1:1, 3; 3:15, 23; 10:15, 20, 22; 43:3).

Crossing rivers, see **222a**.

1 Pouring

w David poured out the water before the Lord (2 Sam. 23:16; 1 Chr. 11:18); they poured out water (1 Sam. 7:6); Elijah had water poured over the sacrifice (1 Kgs. 18:33–5); we are like water spilled on the ground (2 Sam. 14:14); the serpent poured out a river (Rev. 12:15).

x Pouring oil into the vessels (2 Kgs. 4:4–6); she poured the perfume on Jesus' head (Matt. 26:7).

y The love of God is poured into our hearts (Rom. 5:5).

The Spirit poured out, see **965s**.

1 Rain

z The Lord had not yet sent rain (Gen. 2:5); rain for forty days and nights (Gen. 7:4, 12); God provides rain (Ps. 147:8); the Lord gives the rain in its season (Jer. 5:24); when God went forth, the heavens dripped water (Judg. 5:4); God gives rain on the earth (Job 5:10); God distills water into rain (Job 36:27–8); God sent rain in abundance (Ps. 68:9); the Lord has poured down the early and the latter rain (Joel 2:23); God wraps up the water in his clouds (Job 26:8); God sends rain on good and bad (Matt. 5:45); he gave you rain from heaven (Acts 14:17).

aa Has the rain a father? (Job 38:28); who can tip the water-jars of heaven? (Job 38:37); can idols give rain or the heavens showers? (Jer. 14:22); if the clouds are full they pour rain on the earth (Eccles. 11:3); the farmer waits for the early and late rains (Jas. 5:7).

ab If you obey I will send rain (Lev. 26:4; Deut. 11:14; 28:12); send rain! (1 Kgs. 8:36; 2 Chr. 6:27); I will send rain (1 Kgs. 18:1); sound of much rain (1 Kgs. 18:41); after Elijah's prayer heavy rain came (1 Kgs. 18:45; Jas. 5:18); God will give you rain (Isa. 30:23); ask the Lord for rain (Zech. 10:1); I will give showers of blessing (Ezek. 34:26).

ac Thunder and rain during wheat harvest (1 Sam. 12:17); it had started to rain (Acts 28:2); trembling with the heavy rain (Ezra 10:9); it is the rainy season (Ezra 10:13).

ad Neither dew nor rain except by Elijah's word (1 Kgs. 17:1); you will not see wind and rain (2 Kgs. 3:17); rain on one city and none on another (Amos 4:7–8).

ae The just ruler is like sunshine after rain (2 Sam. 23:4); may he be like rain on the mown grass (Ps. 72:6); they waited for me as for the rain (Job 29:23); as the rain and snow come down from heaven (Isa. 55:10); God will come like the spring rain (Hos. 6:3).

Irrigate, see **341a**; **dew**, see **341e**.

1 Hailstones

af Heavy hail (Exod. 9:18, 23–4; Rev. 11:19); large hailstones (Josh. 10:11); hailstones a talent in weight (Rev. 16:21); hail and fire mixed with blood (Rev. 8:7); have you seen the storehouses of hail? (Job 38:22).

ag He gave them hail for rain (Ps. 105:32); he destroyed their vines with hail (Ps. 78:47); he gave over their cattle to hail (Ps. 78:48); I will rain hailstones, fire and brimstone on him (Ezek. 38:22); hail will sweep away the refuge of lies (Isa. 28:17).

ah God has one like a storm of hail (Isa. 28:2).

1 Snow

ai Killing a lion on a snowy day (2 Sam. 23:20; 1 Chr. 11:22); snow fell on Zalmon (Ps. 68:14).

aj God commands snow to fall on the earth (Job 37:6); God gives snow like wool (Ps. 147:16); have you entered the storehouses of the snow? (Job 38:22).

White as snow, see **427**.

1 Fountain

ak A fountain opened for sin and uncleanness (Zech. 13:1).

351 Channel

1 Water
channel

a Jerusalem was entered by way of the water tunnel (2 Sam. 5:8); Hezekiah made the pool and the conduit (2 Kgs. 20:20); Hezekiah directed water to the city of David (2 Chr. 32:30); the conduit of the upper pool (2 Kgs. 18:17; Isa. 7:3; 36:2).

1 Canal

b By the Ulai Canal (Dan. 8:2).

352 Wind: air in motion

1 Breath

a God breathed into man's nostrils the breath of life (Gen. 2:7); you send forth your breath and they are created (Ps. 104:30); God gives breath to the people on earth (Isa. 42:5); breathe on these slain, that they may live (Ezek. 37:9); I will cause breath to enter you that you may live (Ezek. 37:5–6); the breath came into them (Ezek. 37:10); Jesus breathed on his disciples (John 20:22).

b If God were to withdraw his breath all flesh would perish (Job 34:14–15); when you take away your breath, they die (Ps. 104:29); God in whose hand is your breath (Dan. 5:23); he gives to all men life and breath (Acts 17:25).

c There is no breath in the mouth of idols (Ps. 135:17); all scripture is God-breathed (2 Tim. 3:16).

1 Man a mere
breath

d Every man is a mere breath (Ps. 39:5, 11); man is like a breath (Ps. 144:4); a wind that does not return (Ps. 78:39); a man's thoughts are but a breath (Ps. 94:11).

1 Sighing

e Jesus looked up to heaven and sighed (Mark 7:34); Jesus sighed in his spirit (Mark 8:12); our years end like a sigh (Ps. 90:9).

1 Winds

f When God gave weight to the wind (Job 28:25); he brings the wind from his storehouses (Ps. 135:7; Jer. 51:16); stormy wind fulfilling his word (Ps. 148:8); his way is in whirlwind and storm (Nahum 1:3).

g God sent a wind and the flood receded (Gen. 8:1); the Lord drove the sea back with a strong east wind (Exod. 14:21); you blew with your wind (Exod. 15:10); God raised a stormy wind (Ps. 107:25); the Lord sent wind and storm on Jonah (Jonah 1:4); a great wind blew down the house (Job 1:19).

h The Lord was not in the wind (1 Kgs. 19:11); angels held back the four winds (Rev. 7:1).

i They sow the wind and reap the whirlwind (Hos. 8:7); Ephraim herds the wind (Hos. 12:1); striving after wind (Eccles. 1:14, 17; 2:11, 17, 26; 4:4, 6, 16; 6:9); toiling for the wind (Eccles. 5:16); we brought forth as it were wind (Isa. 26:18).

j You will not see wind and rain (2 Kgs. 3:17).

1 Wind from
various
directions

k Scorched by the east wind (Gen. 41:6, 23, 27); a hot wind from the desert (Jer. 4:11–12); an east wind which brought the locusts (Exod. 10:13); and a west wind to carry them away (Exod. 10:19); north and south winds, blow on my garden! (S. of S. 4:16); a stormy wind from the north (Ezek. 1:4); a fierce wind called the Northeaster (Acts 27:14); a south wind (Acts 28:13); as whirlwinds in the Negeb sweep on (Isa. 21:1).

l The wind blows from different directions, then returns (Eccles. 1:6); I will bring on Elam the four winds of heaven (Jer. 49:36); the four winds of heaven stirred up the great sea (Dan. 7:2).

₁ Wind of God

m God rode on the wind (2 Sam. 22:11; Ps. 18:10); God rides on the wings of the wind (Ps. 104:3); God makes winds his messengers (Ps. 104:4); he makes his angels winds (Heb. 1:7); God taking up Elijah in a whirlwind (2 Kgs. 2:1, 11); God answered Job from the whirlwind (Job 38:1).

n The wind blows where it will; so is everyone who is born of the Spirit [Wind] (John 3:8); at Pentecost a sound like a mighty wind (Acts 2:2).

₁ Wind in
opposition

o A storm of wind arose (Mark 4:37); the wind was against them (Matt. 14:24; Mark 6:48); when Peter saw the wind he was afraid (Matt. 14:30); Jesus rebuked the wind and the sea (Matt. 8:26; Mark 4:39; Luke 8:24); the wind stopped (Matt. 8:26; 14:32; Mark 6:51); even winds and sea obey him (Matt. 8:27; Mark 4:41; Luke 8:25).

353 Air-pipe

354 Semiliquidity
Marsh, see **347**.

355 Cloud

₁ Clouds

a I set my rainbow in the cloud (Gen. 9:13–14, 16); can you command the clouds? (Job 38:34); a cloud as small as a man's hand (1 Kgs. 18:44); the sky black with clouds (1 Kgs. 18:45); the clouds return after rain (Eccles. 12:2).

b So great a cloud of witnesses (Heb. 12:1); they are clouds without water (Jude 12); an angel clothed in a cloud (Rev. 10:1).

₁ God in
a cloud

c The Lord went ahead in a pillar of cloud (Exod. 13:21); with a pillar of cloud you led them (Neh. 9:12, 19); he led them with the cloud by day (Ps. 78:14); the pillar of cloud stood behind them (Exod. 14:19); the pillar of cloud came to the entrance of the tent (Exod. 33:9–10; Num. 12:5; Deut. 31:15); he spoke in the pillar of cloud (Ps. 99:7).

d The cloud covered the mountain (Exod. 19:16; 20:21; 24:15–16, 18); the cloud covered the tent (Exod. 40:34, 38; Num. 9:15; 16:42); the cloud filled the temple (1 Kgs. 8:10; 2 Chr. 5:13; Ezek. 10:3, 4).

e The glory of the Lord appeared in the cloud (Exod. 16:10); I will appear in the cloud (Lev. 16:2); thick clouds were God's cover (2 Sam. 22:12; Ps. 18:11); he spread a cloud for a covering (Ps. 105:39); God came to Moses in a cloud (Exod. 19:9; Num. 11:25); the Lord came down in the cloud (Exod. 34:5); the Lord said he would dwell in a thick cloud (1 Kgs. 8:12; 2 Chr. 6:1); clouds and darkness are round him (Ps. 97:2); you wrapped yourself in a cloud so no prayer could pass through (Lam. 3:44); God makes the clouds his chariot (Ps. 104:3); a cloud by day and fire by night (Num. 14:14; Deut. 1:33; Isa. 4:5).

f The cloud of the Lord over them when they set out (Num. 10:34); when the cloud was taken up they set out (Exod. 40:36; Num. 9:17–22); the cloud was lifted (Num. 10:11); when the cloud stayed, they stayed (Exod. 40:37; Num. 9:17–22); God does not see through the clouds (Job 22:14).

g The cloud of incense to cover the mercy seat (Lev. 16:13).

h Our fathers were all under the cloud (1 Cor. 10:1).

1 Jesus in a cloud

i A cloud on the mount of transfiguration (Matt. 17:5; Mark 9:7; Luke 9:34); a cloud took him out of their sight (Acts 1:9); one like a son of man, coming with the clouds of heaven (Dan. 7:13); the Son of Man will come in the clouds of heaven (Matt. 24:30; 26:64; Mark 13:26; 14:62; Luke 21:27); he is coming with the clouds (Rev. 1:7); one like a son of man seated on a cloud (Rev. 14:14); caught up to meet them in the clouds (1 Thess. 4:17).

1 Mist

j A mist watered the ground (Gen. 2:6); you are like a temporary mist (Jas. 4:14); they are mists driven by a storm (2 Pet. 2:17).

1 Foam

k He foams at the mouth (Mark 9:18); he foamed at the mouth (Mark 9:20).

356 Pulpiness

Marsh, see **347**.

357 Oiliness

1 Oil

a Oil for the lamps (Exod. 25:6; 27:20; 35:8, 14, 28; 39:37; Lev. 24:2); Eleazar has responsibility for the oil for the lamps (Num. 4:16); overseeing the stores of oil (1 Chr. 27:28); the olive tree answered, Should I give up my oil? (Judg. 9:9); pour oil into the jars (2 Kgs. 4:2–7); the wise maidens took oil for their lamps (Matt. 25:3–13); a good name is better than good oil (Eccles. 7:1).

b Asher will dip his foot in oil (Deut. 33:24); the rock gave streams of oil (Job 29:6).

1 Anointing oil

c The holy anointing oil (Exod. 25:6; 30:22–33; 31:11; 35:8, 28; 37:29; 39:38); looked after by Eleazar (Num. 4:16).

1 Anointing priests

d Aaron and his sons were anointed (Exod. 28:41; 29:7, 21, 29; 30:30; 40:13–15; Lev. 6:20; 8:12, 30); the high priest anointed with the holy oil (Num. 35:25); the anointing oil is on them (Lev. 10:7; 21:12); they anointed Zadok as priest (1 Chr. 29:22); unity is like the precious oil on Aaron's head (Ps. 133:2).

1 Anointing kings

e The trees went to anoint a king (Judg. 9:8); fill your horn with oil and go (1 Sam. 16:1).

f The anointing as king of: Saul (1 Sam. 9:16; 10:1; 15:1, 17);

David (1 Sam. 16:3, 12–13; 2 Sam. 2:4, 7; 3:39; 5:3, 17; 12:7; 1 Chr. 11:3; 14:8); Absalom (2 Sam. 19:10); Solomon (1 Kgs. 1:34, 39, 45; 1 Chr. 29:22); Hazael king of Syria (1 Kgs. 19:15); Jehu (1 Kgs. 19:16; 2 Kgs. 9:3, 6, 12); Joash (2 Kgs. 11:12; 2 Chr. 23:11); Jehoahaz (2 Kgs. 23:30).

g Saul was the Lord's anointed (1 Sam. 24:6, 10; 26:9, 11; 2 Sam. 1:14, 16); David was anointed by God (2 Sam. 23:1; Ps. 89:20); the Lord had anointed Hazael to cut off the house of Ahab (2 Chr. 22:7); Cyrus his anointed (Isa. 45:1).

h He cursed the Lord's anointed (2 Sam. 19:21); his anointed (2 Sam. 22:51; Ps. 18:50); the peoples plot against the Lord's anointed (Ps. 2:2).

1 **Anointing prophets**

i Anoint Elisha as prophet in your place (1 Kgs. 19:16).

1 **Anointed people**

j Oil on the right ears, thumbs and toes of the cleansed leper (Lev. 14:17, 28).

k You anoint my head with oil (Ps. 23:5); you have anointed me with fresh oil (Ps. 92:10); it is God who anointed us (2 Cor. 1:21); you have an anointing from the Holy One (1 John 2:20); the anointing remains in you (1 John 2:27); these are the two anointed ones (Zech. 4:14); do not touch my anointed ones (1 Chr. 16:22; Ps. 105:15).

1 **Anointing things**

l Anointing: the tabernacle (Exod. 30:26–9; 40:9–11; Lev. 8:10–11; Num. 7:1); the altar (Exod. 29:36); sprinkled seven times (Lev. 8:11).

m Jacob anointed the pillar (Gen. 28:18; 31:13; 35:14).

n Oil the shield (Isa. 21:5); Saul's shield, not anointed (2 Sam. 1:21).

1 **Oil on sacrifices**

o Oil on the cereal offering (Lev. 2:1, 4–7, 15–16; 6:15, 21; 7:12; 9:4; Num. 6:15; 7:13, 19, 25, 31, 37, 43, 49, 55, 61, 67, 73, 79; 8:8; 28:5).

p No oil on a sin offering (Lev. 5:11); nor on a grain offering of jealousy (Num. 5:15).

q Sprinkling oil seven times before the Lord (Lev. 14:16, 27).

1 **Cosmetic anointing**

r Oil to make man's face shine (Ps. 104:15); Ruth anointed herself (Ruth 3:3); David washed and anointed himself (2 Sam. 12:20); let oil not be lacking on your head (Eccles. 9:8); when you fast, anoint your head (Matt. 6:17); I anointed you with oil (Ezek. 16:9); the men of Judah anointed the men of Samaria with oil (2 Chr. 28:15).

s Do not anoint yourself (2 Sam. 14:2); I did not anoint myself (Dan. 10:3); you did not anoint my head with oil (Luke 7:46).

1 **Medicinal anointing**

t The good Samaritan poured on oil and wine (Luke 10:34); they anointed many who were sick (Mark 6:13); elders should anoint the sick with oil (Jas. 5:14).

1 **Anointed Christ**

u The Lord has anointed me to preach good news (Isa. 61:1; Luke 4:18); until the Anointed One [Messiah], the Prince (Dan. 9:25);

Jesus whom you anointed (Acts 4:27); God anointed you with the oil of gladness (Ps. 45:7; Heb. 1:9); she anointed his feet with perfume (Luke 7:38); she has anointed my body for burial (Mark 14:8); the women came to anoint Jesus' body (Mark 16:1).

1 **Jesus called Christ**

v Jesus called Christ (Matt. 1:16); the gospel of Jesus Christ, the Son of God (Mark 1:1); the genealogy of Jesus Christ (Matt. 1:1); a Saviour who is Christ the Lord (Luke 2:11); Simeon would not die before seeing the Christ (Luke 2:26); some said, 'This is the Christ' (John 7:41); will the Christ perform more signs than this man? (John 7:31); demons knew him to be the Christ (Luke 4:41); you are the Christ of God (Luke 9:20); you are the Christ, the Son of God (Matt. 16:16; Mark 8:29; John 11:27); Messiah, Christ, is coming (John 4:25); we have found the Messiah, Christ (John 1:41); that he may send you Jesus, the Christ appointed for you (Acts 3:20); who is the liar but he who denies that Jesus is the Christ? (1 John 2:22).

w Are you the Christ? (Mark 14:61); are you not the Christ (Luke 23:39); if you are the Christ, tell us (Luke 22:67; John 10:24); do the authorities know this is the Christ? (John 7:26); I adjure you to tell us if you are the Christ (Matt. 26:63); saying he is Christ, a king (Luke 23:2); what shall I do with Jesus called Christ? (Matt. 27:22).

1 **Christ's origin**

x Where Christ should be born (Matt. 2:4); no one knows where the Christ comes from (John 7:27); surely the Christ does not come from Galilee? (John 7:41); whose son is the Christ? (Matt. 22:42; Luke 20:41); why do scribes say Christ is the son of David? (Mark 12:35); the Christ comes from David and from Bethlehem (John 7:42); from Israel is the Christ according to the flesh (Rom. 9:5); son of David according to the flesh (Rom. 1:3).

1 **Christ's nature**

y You have one teacher, Christ (Matt. 23:10); John heard of the works of the Christ (Matt. 11:2); we have heard that the Christ remains for ever (John 12:34); Christ the power of God and the wisdom of God (1 Cor. 1:24).

Christ the Servant, see **742*k***.

1 **Christ suffering**

z God foretold that Christ would suffer (Acts 3:18); it was necessary for the Christ to suffer (Luke 24:26, 46); Christ had to suffer and rise again (Acts 17:3; 26:23); the prophets enquired about Christ and his suffering (1 Pet. 1:11); Christ our passover has been sacrificed (1 Cor. 5:7).

Suffering of Christ, see **825*j***.

aa If he is the Christ, let him save himself (Luke 23:35); let the Christ, the King of Israel, come down from the cross (Mark 15:32); rulers gathered against the Lord and his Christ (Acts 4:26).

Death of Christ, see **361*ai***.

1 Believing in Christ	*ab* If anyone confessed him to be the Christ, he would be expelled (John 9:22); these are written that you might believe that Jesus is the Christ, the Son of God (John 20:31).
1 Christ preached	*ac* They did not stop preaching Jesus as the Christ (Acts 5:42); God has made this Jesus both Lord and Christ (Acts 2:36); Philip preached Christ in Samaria (Acts 8:5); Paul testified that Jesus was the Christ (Acts 9:22; 18:5); Apollos demonstrated that Jesus was the Christ (Acts 18:28); this Jesus is the Christ (Acts 17:3). **Preaching Christ**, see **528***l*.
1 False Christs	*ad* False Christs will arise (Matt. 24:24; Mark 13:22); many will say, 'I am the Christ' (Matt. 24:5); do not believe one who says, 'Here is the Christ' (Matt. 24:23).
	ae Whether John might be the Christ (Luke 3:15); I am not the Christ (John 1:20; 3:28).
1 Fat	*af* All fat is the Lord's (Lev. 3:16); no fat was to be eaten (Lev. 3:17; 7:23–5); though it could be used (Lev. 7:24); Eli's sons wanted the meat with the fat (1 Sam. 2:15–16); the Lord's sword is gorged with fat (Isa. 34:6).
	ag Fat is not to be kept overnight (Exod. 23:18).
	ah The wicked man is covered with fat (Job 15:27). **Fat people**, see **195***e*.
1 Fat of the sacrifices	*ai* Abel brought fat portions as an offering (Gen. 4:4); fat of the sacrifices (Exod. 29:13, 22; Lev. 3:3–4, 9–10, 14–17; 4:8–10, 19, 26, 31, 35; 6:12; 7:3–4, 30–1, 33; 8:16, 25; 9:10, 19; 17:6; Num. 18:17).

Section three: Organic matter

---

358 Organisms: living matter

Life, see **360**.

359 Mineral: inorganic matter

1 Minerals	*a* Bdellium and onyx stone are found in Havilah (Gen. 2:12); the gold of Havilah is good (Gen. 2:11–12); there is a place for mining and refining metals (Job 28:1–11); a land where iron and copper can be dug (Deut. 8:9); silver, gold, bronze and iron are for the Lord's treasury (Josh. 6:19, 24). **Metals**, see **797***g*.

360 Life

1 Life of creatures	*a* The life of every creature is its blood (Gen. 9:4; Lev. 17:11, 14; Deut. 12:23); life is more than food (Matt. 6:25; Luke 12:23).
	b Eve, the mother of all living (Gen. 3:20); two of every creature to preserve life (Gen. 6:19); Joseph is still alive (Gen. 45:26, 28; 46:30); is Benhadad still alive? (1 Kgs. 20:32).

c [Long] live the king! (1 Sam. 10:24; 2 Sam. 16:16; 1 Kgs. 1:25, 31, 34, 39; 2 Kgs. 11:12; 2 Chr. 23:11); live for ever! (Dan. 6:6, 21); your life will be bound in the bundle of the living (1 Sam. 25:29).

d I have set before you life and death (Deut. 30:15); so choose life (Deut. 30:19); a live dog is better than a dead lion (Eccles. 9:4); why is life given to those who long for death? (Job 3:20–2).

e Let my life be given as my petition (Esther 7:3); all that a man has he will give for his life [soul] (Job 2:4); Haman begged for his life (Esther 7:7).

f They went down alive to Sheol (Num. 16:33); take them alive (1 Kgs. 20:18).

1 **God's life**

g The living God (1 Sam. 17:26, 36; Dan. 6:26); the Lord lives (2 Sam. 22:47; Ps. 18:46); this is the true God and eternal life (1 John 5:20); he is not God of the dead but of the living, for all live to him (Luke 20:38).

1 **Christ's life**

h I live because of the Father (John 6:57); he asked for life and you gave him length of days for ever (Ps. 21:4); the Father has granted the Son to have life in himself (John 5:26); the Prince of life (Acts 3:15); the life he lives, he lives to God (Rom. 6:10); the power of an indestructible life (Heb. 7:16); why seek the living among the dead? (Luke 24:5); angels said he was alive (Luke 24:23); the eternal life which was with the Father (1 John 1:2); we are saved through his life (Rom. 5:10).

1 **God giving life**

i God breathed the breath of life and man became a living being (Gen. 2:7); he gives to all men life and breath (Acts 17:25); you gave me life (Job 10:12); am I God to kill and make alive? (2 Kgs. 5:7); in him we live and move and have our being (Acts 17:28); you give life to all things (Neh. 9:6); the Lord kills and brings to life (1 Sam. 2:6); in his hand is the life of every living thing (Job 12:10); with you is the fountain of life (Ps. 36:9); whoever finds me finds life (Prov. 8:35); obeying the Lord is your life (Deut. 30:20); the breath of life from God entered them (Rev. 11:11); the last man became a life-giving spirit (1 Cor. 15:45).

1 **Eternal life promised**

j The tree of life (Gen. 2:9; 3:22, 24; Rev. 22:2); I have come that they might have life (John 10:10); I have set before you life and death (Deut. 30:19; Jer. 21:8); the Lord commanded the blessing, life for ever (Ps. 133:3); this is what he has promised us, eternal life (1 John 2:25); God promised eternal life (Titus 1:2; 1 John 2:25).

Promise of eternal life, see **764e**.

1 **Obtaining eternal life**

k Lest man eat of the tree of life and live for ever (Gen. 3:22, 24); what must I do to get eternal life? (Matt. 19:16; Mark 10:17; Luke 10:25; 18:18); the gate leading to life is narrow (Matt. 7:14).

l Lay hold of eternal life (1 Tim. 6:12); lay hold of that which is life indeed (1 Tim. 6:19).

m He was dead and is alive again (Luke 15:24, 32).

Eternal life by doing right

n Keep the statutes that you may live (Deut. 4:1, 40; 8:1); if a man observes God's ordinances he will live (Neh. 9:29; Ezek. 20:11, 13, 21); do good and you will abide for ever (Ps. 37:27); whoever loves life, keep your tongue from evil (Ps. 34:12–13); in the way of righteousness there is life (Prov. 12:28); the righteous man will surely live (Ezek. 18:9, 17); to those who do good and seek immortality he will give eternal life (Rom. 2:7); if the wicked man turns from sin, he will live (Ezek. 18:21–2, 28).

o I gave them bad statutes by which they could not live (Ezek. 20:25); if a law could give life, righteousness would be by law (Gal. 3:21).

p To inherit eternal life, love God (Luke 10:25–8); he who hates his life will keep it for eternal life (John 12:25); he who forsakes possessions and friends for Christ's sake will inherit eternal life (Matt. 19:29; Mark 10:30; Luke 18:30); he who sows to the Spirit will reap eternal life (Gal. 6:8); the righteous go into eternal life (Matt. 25:46); sanctification and its end, eternal life (Rom. 6:22).

Eternal life by God's word

q My words are life to those who find them (Prov. 4:22); you have the words of eternal life (John 6:68); if anyone keeps my word he will never die (John 8:51–2); the Father's commandment given to the Son is eternal life (John 12:50); you think that in the scriptures you have eternal life (John 5:39).

Eternal life through Christ

r In the Word was life (John 1:4); I am the way, the truth and the life (John 14:6); eternal life is Jesus Christ (1 John 1:2; 5:20); this life is in God's Son (1 John 5:11); if Christ is in you your spirit is alive (Rom. 8:10); eternal life is knowing God and Jesus Christ (John 17:3); we reign in life through Jesus Christ (Rom. 5:17).

s Christ gives eternal life (John 5:39–40; 17:2); I give my sheep eternal life (John 10:28); the Son gives life to whom he pleases (John 5:21); the gift of God is eternal life in Jesus Christ (Rom. 6:23); he gives a spring of water welling up to eternal life (John 4:14); he gives the food which endures to eternal life (John 6:27); the mercy of our Lord Jesus to eternal life (Jude 21); grace reigns to eternal life through Jesus Christ (Rom. 5:21); Jesus brought life and immortality to light (2 Tim. 1:10).

t When dead in sin, God brought us to life with Christ (Eph. 2:5; Col. 2:13); because I live, you will live also (John 14:19).

u Those who believe in Christ have eternal life (John 3:15, 16, 36; 6:40, 47; 1 Tim. 1:16); he who believes in him who sent Christ has eternal life (John 5:24); those who believe may know that they have eternal life (1 John 5:13); believing, you have life in his name (John 20:31); he who believes in me will never die (John 11:26).

    v He who eats Christ's flesh and drinks his blood has eternal life (John 6:27, 51, 54, 58).

    w The dead will hear the voice of the Son of God, and those who hear will live (John 5:25); in Christ will all be made alive (1 Cor. 15:22).

1 Recipients of eternal life

    x Heirs in hope of eternal life (Titus 3:7); ordained to eternal life (Acts 13:48); called to eternal life (1 Tim. 6:12).

1 Missing eternal life

    y You judge yourselves unworthy of eternal life (Acts 13:46); no murderer has eternal life (1 John 3:15).

1 Living the spiritual life

    z For me to live is Christ (Phil. 1:21); Christ lives in me and the life I now live is by faith in the Son of God (Gal. 2:20); whether awake or asleep, we live together with him (1 Thess. 5:10); that the life of Jesus may be manifested in our bodies (2 Cor. 4:10–11).

    aa Consider yourselves alive to God (Rom. 6:11); present yourselves to God as those alive from the dead (Rom. 6:13); if we live, we live to the Lord, not to ourselves (Rom. 14:7–8); we know we have passed from death to life because we love the brothers (1 John 3:14).

361 Death

1 Nature of death

    a The rider's name was Death (Rev. 6:8); have the gates of death been revealed to you? (Job 38:17); Sheol is open before God (Job 26:6); if I make my bed in Sheol, you are there (Ps. 139:8).

    b The meeting house for all mankind (Job 30:23); man dies and where is he? (Job 14:10); like sheep appointed for Sheol with death their shepherd (Ps. 49:14); Sheol has enlarged its throat (Isa. 5:14); greedy as Sheol, like death, never satisfied (Hab. 2:5). **Sleep of death**, see **679e.**

1 Effect of death

    c The dust returns to the earth and the spirit to God (Eccles. 12:7); to dust you will return (Gen. 3:19–20); like an animal from dust and to dust (Eccles. 3:19); his breath departs and he returns to the earth (Ps. 146:4).

    d You turn man back to the dust (Ps. 90:3); you overpower him and he departs (Job 14:20).

    e If her husband dies she is free to be married (Rom. 7:2; 1 Cor. 7:39). **Rest in death**, see **683q**; **mourning after a death**, see **836o.**

1 Inevitability of death

    f Man appointed to die (Heb. 9:27); in Adam all die (1 Cor. 15:22); death the end of every man (Eccles. 7:2); naked from the womb, and so departs (Eccles. 5:15); even rulers die like men (Ps. 82:7); even wise men die (Eccles. 2:16); we must surely die (2 Sam. 14:14); what man can live and not see death? (Ps. 89:48); do not all go to the one place? (Eccles. 6:6); death comes both to those who are satisfied and to those who are bitter (Job 21:23–26); there is a time to die (Eccles. 3:2); you will bring me to death (Job 30:23); worldly sorrow produces death (2 Cor. 7:10).

g We will not all sleep (1 Cor. 15:51).

1 Finality of death

h He who goes down to Sheol does not come up again (Job 7:9); man lies down and cannot be awakened (Job 14:12); the way of no return (Job 16:22); no one has authority over the day of death (Eccles. 8:8); they said the boy was dead (Mark 9:26).

1 Condition of the dead

i The dead tremble (Job 26:5); when the wicked dies his hope perishes (Prov. 11:7); a fire burns to the lowest Sheol (Deut. 32:22); there is no work nor thought nor wisdom in Sheol (Eccles. 9:10); the dead do not know anything (Eccles. 9:5); the stillborn does not know anything (Eccles. 6:3–5); the land of darkness and death-shadow (Job 10:21–2); there is no remembrance of God in Sheol (Ps. 6:5); the dead do not praise the Lord (Ps. 115:17); death cannot praise you (Isa. 38:18); God will profit nothing if I go down to the pit (Ps. 30:9); do I have pleasure in the death of the wicked? (Ezek. 18:23); lest I be like those who go down to the pit (Ps. 143:7); he made me dwell in darkness like those long dead (Lam. 3:6).

j Sheol rouses dead leaders to greet the king of Babylon (Isa. 14:9–11); the nations lying in Sheol (Ezek. 32:22–32).

k Christ is Lord of the dead and the living (Rom. 14:9); he is not God of the dead but of the living (Matt. 22:32; Mark 12:27); for all live to him (Luke 20:38).

1 Fear of death

l Through fear of death subject to bondage (Heb. 2:15); the cords of death surrounded me (2 Sam. 22:5–6; Ps. 18:4); the terrors of death are on me (Ps. 55:4); the valley of the shadow of death (Ps. 23:4); those sitting in the land of the shadow of death (Matt. 4:16).

1 Death is near

m My life draws near to Sheol (Ps. 88:3); I do not know the day of my death (Gen. 27:2); you bring me to Sheol in sorrow (Gen. 42:38; 44:29, 31); I am going the way of all the earth (Josh. 23:14; 1 Kgs. 2:2); I am about to die (Gen. 48:21; 49:29; 50:5, 24); I will go down to Sheol mourning for my son (Gen. 37:35); the cords of Sheol surrounded me (2 Sam. 22:6; Ps. 18:4); death gripped me (Ps. 116:3).

n You will be gathered to your people (Num. 31:2); you will die (2 Kgs. 1:4, 6, 16; 20:1; Isa. 38:1); the time is near for you to die (Deut. 31:14); about to lie down with your fathers (Deut. 31:16); when you lie down with your fathers (2 Sam. 7:12; 1 Kgs. 1:21); you will go to your fathers in peace (Gen. 15:15); you will be gathered to your people in peace (2 Chr. 34:28); you will die in peace (2 Kgs. 22:20; Jer. 34:4–5).

o Bathsheba's child will die (2 Sam. 12:14); I will go to him, not he return to me (2 Sam. 12:23); when your feet enter the city the child will die (1 Kgs. 14:12); Benhadad will certainly die (2 Kgs. 8:10); let them go down alive to Sheol (Ps. 55:15); those who are for death, let them go to death (Jer. 15:2; 43:11); apostles exhibited as men condemned to death (1 Cor. 4:9).

1 **Death may happen**	*p* Why bring us into the desert to die? (Exod. 14:11; Num. 16:13; 20:4; 21:5); give me children or I die! (Gen. 30:1); let them return from war lest they die (Deut. 20:5, 6, 7); we were like dead men before the king (2 Sam. 19:28); come down before my child dies (John 4:49).
1 **Resigned to death**	*q* Now let me die, since I see you are alive (Gen. 46:30); let me depart in peace, for I see your salvation (Luke 2:29–30); let me die with the Philistines (Judg. 16:30); let me die in my own city (2 Sam. 19:37); if they kill us, we will but die (2 Kgs. 7:4); if I welcome Sheol as my home (Job 17:13–14); the day of death is better than the day of birth (Eccles. 7:1); that we may eat it and die (1 Kgs. 17:12); the sword devours this one and that one (2 Sam. 11:25).
	r Where you die I will die (Ruth 1:17); if I must die with you I will not deny you (Matt. 26:35; Mark 14:31); I will lay down my life for you (John 13:37); let us go that we may die with him (John 11:16).
1 **Desire for death**	*s* Job wished he had died at birth (Job 3:11; 10:18); as did Jeremiah (Jer. 20:14–18); why is light given to those who long for death? (Job 3:20–2); Oh that God would crush me! (Job 6:8–9); hide me in Sheol! (Job 14:13); Elijah asked that he might die (1 Kgs. 19:4); better for me to die than to live (Jonah 4:3, 8); men call on hills to fall on them (Luke 23:30); men will seek death but not find it (Rev. 9:6); they will choose death rather than life (Jer. 8:3); better to have died in Egypt! (Exod. 16:3; Num. 14:2); would that we had died when our fathers did! (Num. 20:3); would that I had died instead of you! (2 Sam. 18:33).
1 **Death due to sin**	*t* When you eat of the tree you will surely die (Gen. 2:17; 3:3); by a man came death (1 Cor. 15:21); death reigned (Rom. 5:14, 17); a way which seems right to man but it ends in death (Prov. 16:25).
	u The soul who sins will die (Ezek. 18:4, 13, 18, 20, 24, 26); he who pursues evil will die (Prov. 11:19); death came on all men, for all sinned (Rom. 5:12); the wages of sin is death (Rom. 6:23); the end of those things is death (Rom. 6:21); when sin is completed it brings forth death (Jas. 1:15); you will die in your sins (John 8:21, 24); if you live according to the flesh you will die (Rom. 8:13); there is a sin which leads to death (1 John 5:16–17); everyone is to die for his own sin (Deut. 24:16; Jer. 31:30; Ezek. 3:18, 20); you deserve to die (1 Kgs. 2:26); wicked man, you will surely die (Ezek. 33:8); Saul died for his trespass (1 Chr. 10:13); this is why many are ill and some have fallen asleep (1 Cor. 11:30).
	v The wicked return to Sheol (Ps. 9:17); let the wicked be silent in Sheol (Ps. 31:17); the loose woman's house is the way to Sheol (Prov. 2:18; 7:27); her guests are in the depths of Sheol (Prov. 9:18); her feet go down to Sheol (Prov. 5:5); the pleasure seeker is dead while she lives (1 Tim. 5:6); they perish because they did

not love the truth (2 Thess. 2:10); all who hate wisdom love death (Prov. 8:36); why will you die? (Ezek. 18:31); what profit is it to gain the world and forfeit your life? (Matt. 16:26).

w   You will not die [for this sin] (2 Sam. 12:13).

1 Spiritually
dead

x   You have a name that you live but you are dead (Rev. 3:1); dead in sins (Eph. 2:1, 5; Col. 2:13); the mind set on the flesh is death (Rom. 8:6); the body is dead because of sin (Rom. 8:10); let the dead bury their dead (Matt. 8:22); the dead will hear the voice of the Son of God and will live (John 5:25); my son was dead and is alive again (Luke 15:24); your brother was dead and is alive again (Luke 15:32).

y   The commandment which should have brought life brought death instead (Rom. 7:10); when the law came, sin revived and I died (Rom. 7:9); sin deceived me and killed me (Rom. 7:11); the ministry of death (2 Cor. 3:7).

1 Death as
punishment

z   The man who did this deserves to die (2 Sam. 12:5); for breaking the oath Jonathan must die (1 Sam. 14:44); because Abimelech took Sarah he would die (Gen. 20:3, 7); the ten spies died of a plague (Num. 14:37); Nadab and Abihu died when they offered strange fire (Lev. 10:2; 16:1; Num. 3:4; 26:61; 1 Chr. 24:2); Dathan and Abiram died an unnatural death, the earth swallowing them (Num. 16:28–33); dying of snake bite (Num. 21:6); the whole congregation would die in the desert (Num. 14:35; 26:65); your corpses will fall in the wilderness (Num. 14:29, 32–3); all that generation of fighting men died (Deut. 2:15–16; Josh. 5:4, 6); if you are corrupt you will soon perish from the land (Deut. 4:26); all Eli's descendants would die in the prime of life (1 Sam. 2:33).

Death penalty, see **963k**.

1 Death due
to God's
presence

aa   Lest they die: the Egyptians urged them to leave (Exod. 12:33); let not God speak to us (Exod. 20:19; Deut. 5:25); Aaron to wear bells when entering the holy place (Exod. 28:35); priests must wear linen underclothing (Exod. 28:43); priests must wash (Exod. 30:21); Aaron must not enter the holy place any time (Lev. 16:2); incense must cover the mercy seat (Lev. 16:13); they must not touch the holy things (Num. 4:15); they must not see the holy things (Num. 4:18–20); the Levites must not come near (Num. 18:3).

ab   If we hear God more, we will die (Deut. 5:24–6; 18:16); he who comes near the tabernacle will die (Num. 17:12–13; 18:22); the stranger who comes near will be killed (Num. 1:51; 3:10, 38); lest there be a plague when they come near (Num. 8:19); Gideon feared he would die after he saw the angel (Judg. 6:22–3); we will die for we have seen God (Judg. 13:22); they have brought the ark here to kill us! (1 Sam. 5:10).

1 Death of
office holders

ac   Until the death of the high priest (Num. 35:25, 28, 32); when the judge died, they turned back (Judg. 2:19).

1 **Death of individuals**	*ad*	Death of: Aaron (Num. 20:24–8; 33:38; Deut. 10:6); Abdon (Judg. 12:15); Abijah (1 Kgs. 14:12, 17); Abraham (Gen. 25:8); Ananias (Acts 5:5); Dorcas (Acts 9:37); Eleazar (Josh. 24:33); Eli (1 Sam. 4:18); Elisha (2 Kgs. 13:20); Elon (Judg. 12:12); Eutychus (Acts 20:9); Gideon (Judg. 8:32); Hananiah the prophet (Jer. 28:17); Ibzan (Judg. 12:10); Isaac (Gen. 35:29); Ishmael (Gen. 25:17); Jacob (Gen. 49:33; Acts 7:15); Jair (Judg. 10:5); Jephthah (Judg. 12:7); Job (Job 42:17); Joseph (Gen. 50:26); Joshua (Josh. 24:29; Judg. 1:1; 2:8); Judas (Acts 1:18); Lazarus (John 11:11–14); Miriam (Num. 20:1); Moses (Num. 27:13; Deut. 32:50; 34:5; Josh. 1:1–2); Pelatiah the leader (Ezek. 11:13); Rachel (Gen. 35:18–19); Samuel (1 Sam. 25:1; 28:3); Sapphira (Acts 5:10); Sarah (Gen. 23:2); Saul and his sons (1 Sam. 31:6); Saul and Jonathan (2 Sam. 1:4–5); Terah (Gen. 11:32; Acts 7:4); Tola (Judg. 10:2).

	ae	Death of: David's child (2 Sam. 12:18, 19); Eli's sons (1 Sam. 2:34; 4:11, 17); Ezekiel's wife (Ezek. 24:18); the harlot's child (1 Kgs. 3:19); Jairus' daughter (Matt. 9:18; Mark 5:35; Luke 8:49); Judah's wife (Gen. 38:12); the poor man and the rich man (Luke 16:22); Rebekah's nurse (Gen. 35:8); the Shunammite's boy (2 Kgs. 4:20); Job's children (Job 1:19).

1 **Death of kings**	*af*	Death of: Abijam [Abijah] (1 Kgs. 15:8; 2 Chr. 14:1); Ahab (1 Kgs. 22:35, 37, 40; 2 Chr. 18:34); Ahaz (2 Kgs. 16:20; 2 Chr. 28:27; Isa. 14:28); Ahaziah (2 Kgs. 1:17); Asa (1 Kgs. 15:24; 2 Chr. 16:13); Baasha (1 Kgs. 16:6); David (1 Kgs. 2:1, 10; 11:21; 1 Chr. 29:28; Acts 2:29; 13:36); Hazael (2 Kgs. 13:24); Herod (Matt. 2:15, 19); [another] Herod (Acts 12:23); Hezekiah (2 Kgs. 20:21; 2 Chr. 32:33); Jehoahaz of Israel (2 Kgs. 13:9); Jehoahaz of Judah (2 Kgs. 23:34); Jehoiakim (2 Kgs. 24:6); Jehoram (2 Kgs. 8:24); Jehoshaphat (1 Kgs. 22:50; 2 Chr. 21:1); Jeroboam I (1 Kgs. 14:20); Jeroboam II (2 Kgs. 14:29); Jehu (2 Kgs. 10:35); Joash [Jehoash] of Israel (2 Kgs. 13:13; 14:16); Josiah (2 Chr. 35:24); Jotham (2 Kgs. 15:38; 2 Chr. 27:9); Menahem (2 Kgs. 15:22); Manasseh (2 Kgs. 21:18; 2 Chr. 33:20); Nahash (2 Sam. 10:1; 1 Chr. 19:1); Omri (1 Kgs. 16:28); Rehoboam (1 Kgs. 14:31; 2 Chr. 12:16); Saul (1 Sam. 31:6; 2 Sam. 1:4–5); Solomon (1 Kgs. 11:43; 2 Chr. 9:31); Tibni (1 Kgs. 16:22); Uzziah [Azariah] (2 Kgs. 15:7; 2 Chr. 26:23; Isa. 6:1).

1 **Death of groups**	*ag*	Every living creature died (Gen. 7:21–2); all the Egyptian army drowned (Exod. 14:28; 15:4–5).
1 **Death of animals**	*ah*	The pigs were drowned (Matt. 8:32; Mark 5:13; Luke 8:33).
1 **Death of Christ**	*ai*	The Anointed One [Messiah] will be cut off (Dan. 9:26); Jesus breathed his last (Matt. 27:50; Mark 15:37; Luke 23:46; John 19:30); Pilate was surprised he was already dead (Mark 15:44); a dead man named Jesus (Acts 25:19); Jesus indicated in what

way he would die (John 12:33; 18:32); I lay down my life (John 10:17–18); he poured himself out to death (Isa. 53:12); Christ Jesus died and was raised (Rom. 8:34).

aj Christ died for our sins (1 Cor. 15:3); he died for us (1 Thess. 5:10); he was delivered up for our transgressions (Rom. 4:25); a death for the redemption of transgressions (Heb. 9:15); Christ died for sins (1 Pet. 3:18); the death that he died, he died to sin (Rom. 6:10); while we were yet sinners, Christ died for us (Rom. 5:8); the good shepherd lays down his life for the sheep (John 10:11); redeemed with the precious blood of Christ (1 Pet. 1:18–19); giving his life as a ransom for many (Matt. 20:28); better that one man die for the people (John 11:50; 18:14); Jesus would die for the Jews and all the children of God (John 11:51–2); he laid down his life for his friends (John 15:13); Christ died for the ungodly (Rom. 5:6); he died for all (2 Cor. 5:14–15); unless a grain of wheat dies it remains alone (John 12:24); when I am lifted up I will draw all men to me (John 12:32); do not destroy him for whom Christ died (Rom. 14:15; 1 Cor. 8:11).

ak By death he would destroy him who had the power of death (Heb. 2:14); he might taste death for everyone (Heb. 2:9); he became obedient to death, even death on a cross (Phil. 2:8).

1 **Death of believers**

al Jesus indicated by what death Peter would glorify God (John 21:19); he would soon lay aside his earthly dwelling, as the Lord Jesus made clear to him (2 Pet. 1:14); the time of my departure has come (2 Tim. 4:6).

am We do not want you to be ignorant about those who have fallen asleep (1 Thess. 4:13); if there is no resurrection, those who have fallen asleeep in Christ have perished (1 Cor. 15:18); let me die the death of the righteous (Num. 23:10); precious in the Lord's sight is the death of his saints (Ps. 116:15); blessed are the dead who die in the Lord (Rev. 14:13); to die is gain (Phil. 1:21); far better (Phil. 1:23); death cannot separate us from the love of God (Rom. 8:38–9); what you sow does not come to life unless it dies (1 Cor. 15:36).

an I am ready to die for the name of the Lord Jesus (Acts 21:13); we ought to lay down our lives for the brothers (1 John 3:16); perhaps for a good man one would dare to die (Rom. 5:7); if we die, we die for the Lord, not for ourselves (Rom. 14:7–8).

1 **Dying to sin**

ao We died to sin (Rom. 6:2); those who are Christ's have crucified the flesh (Gal. 5:24); you died to the law (Rom. 7:4–6); I died to the law (Gal. 2:19); crucified with Christ (Gal. 2:20); our old self was crucified with him (Rom. 6:6); united with Christ in a death like his (Rom. 6:5); you have died with Christ to the elementary principles of the world (Col. 2:20); you have died and your life is hid with Christ (Col. 3:3); if we died with him we will live with him (Rom. 6:8; 2 Tim. 2:11); he who has died is freed from sin (Rom. 6:7).

ap Put to death the deeds of the body (Rom. 8:13); that we might die to sins and live to righteousness (1 Pet. 2:24); count yourselves dead to sin (Rom. 6:11); reckon your bodies as dead to immorality etc. (Col. 3:5).

1 Dying daily

aq I die daily (1 Cor. 15:31); as dying, and behold, we live (2 Cor. 6:9); the sentence of death was on us (2 Cor. 1:9); carrying about in our body the death of Jesus (2 Cor. 4:10).

ar He who finds his life will lose it and he who loses his life for my sake will find it (Matt. 10:39; 16:25; Mark 8:35; Luke 17:33); he who wants to save his life will lose it (Luke 9:24); he who loves his life will lose it (John 12:25); take up your cross (Matt. 10:38; 16:24; Mark 8:34; Luke 9:23; 14:27); I do not consider my life as of any account (Acts 20:24).

1 Death postponed

as He would not see death before he saw the Christ (Luke 2:26); some will not taste death until they see the Son of man in his glory (Matt. 16:28; Mark 9:1); what if he remains until I come? (John 21:22–3).

1 Second death

at The lake of fire is the second death (Rev. 20:14); he who overcomes will not be hurt by the second death (Rev. 2:11); the second death has no power over those in the first resurrection (Rev. 20:6).

1 Death avoided

au You will not die (Gen. 3:4); I will not die but live (Ps. 118:17–18); Enoch did not see death (Gen. 5:24; Heb. 11:5); Elijah was taken up into heaven (2 Kgs. 2:11); sons of the resurrection, like angels, do not die (Luke 20:36); the rumour spread that John would not die (John 21:23); you have delivered my soul from death (Ps. 56:13; 116:8).

av If you had been here my brother would not have died (John 11:21, 32); could he not have kept this man from dying? (John 11:37).

1 Death overcome

aw Christ destroyed death (2 Tim. 1:10); death has no more dominion over him (Rom. 6:9); the gates of Hades will not prevail against the church (Matt. 16:18); the last enemy to be destroyed is death (1 Cor. 15:26); death will be swallowed up (Isa. 25:8; 1 Cor. 15:54); where is your sting, O death? (Hos. 13:14; 1 Cor. 15:55); there will be no more death (Rev. 21:4); death and Hades gave up the dead in them (Rev. 20:13); death and Hades were thrown into the lake of fire (Rev. 20:14).

God delivers from death, see **668*j***.

362 Killing: destruction of life

1 Killing others

a Do not murder (Exod. 20:13; Deut. 5:17; Matt. 5:21; 19:18; Mark 10:19; Luke 18:20; Rom. 13:9; Jas. 2:11); the Lord hates hands that shed innocent blood (Prov. 6:17); cursed is he who kills in secret (Deut. 27:24–5); he who kills a thief after sunrise is guilty of bloodshed (Exod. 22:2–3).

b Murderers go to the lake of fire (Rev. 21:8); outside the city (Rev. 22:15); no murderer has eternal life (1 John 3:15); let none of you suffer as a murderer (1 Pet. 4:15); the law is for patricides, matricides, murderers (1 Tim. 1:9); from the heart come murders (Matt. 15:19; Mark 7:21); filled with murder (Rom. 1:29); their feet swift to shed blood (Isa. 59:7; Rom. 3:15); the murderer arises at dawn (Job 24:14); you lust and do not have, so you murder (Jas. 4:2); evildoers murder widows, strangers and orphans (Ps. 94:6); will you steal, murder and commit adultery? (Jer. 7:9); the thief comes only to steal, kill and destroy (John 10:10); this man is a murderer (Acts 28:4); Barabbas had murdered in the insurrection (Mark 15:7; Luke 23:19, 25); the devil was a murderer from the beginning (John 8:44); they did not repent of their murders (Rev. 9:21).

c There is a time to kill (Eccles. 3:3).
Death penalty, see **963*k***.

1 Manslaughter   *d* Killing another unintentionally (Exod. 21:13; Num. 35:11, 15, 22–3; Deut. 19:4); distinguishing murder from manslaughter (Exod. 21:12–13; Num. 35:16–24).
Manslayers fleeing, see **620*m***.

1 Bloodthirsty   *e* Saul and Jonathan did not hold back from killing (2 Sam. 1:22); Saul has slain his thousands and David his ten thousands (1 Sam. 18:7–8; 21:11; 29:5); David was a man who shed much blood (1 Chr. 22:8); Josheb-basshebeth killed 300 at one time (1 Chr. 11:11); 800 at one time (2 Sam. 23:8); Abishai killed 300 (2 Sam. 23:18; 1 Chr. 11:20).

f Joab killed in time of peace (1 Kgs. 2:5); get out, you man of blood! (2 Sam. 16:7–8); Manasseh shed much innocent blood (2 Kgs. 21:16; 24:3–4); you have filled the streets with the slain (Ezek. 11:6).

g Do not be afraid of those who kill the body (Luke 12:4).

1 Prospect of bloodshed   *h* Whoever finds me will kill me (Gen. 4:14); Abraham feared being killed because of Sarah (Gen. 12:12; 20:11); Isaac feared being killed because of Rebekah (Gen. 26:7); they will kill me (1 Kgs. 12:27); Ahab will kill me (1 Kgs. 18:9, 12, 14).

i Saul will kill me (1 Sam. 16:2); why does he seek my life? (1 Sam. 20:1); one of these days Saul will kill me (1 Sam. 27:1).

j Lest Absalom smite the city with the sword (2 Sam. 15:14); lest the king and all with him be destroyed (2 Sam. 17:16); not one of those with David will be left (2 Sam. 17:12); there will be a slaughter on Absalom's people (2 Sam. 17:9); you will kill men, children and pregnant women (2 Kgs. 8:12); the sword will never depart from your house (2 Sam. 12:10); the king of Assyria will fall by the sword in his own land (2 Kgs. 19:7); whoever escapes

Hazael, Jehu will kill and whoever escapes Jehu, Elisha will kill (1 Kgs. 19:17); bloodshed will pursue Edom (Ezek. 35:6).

Attempting to kill

k The wicked seeks to kill the righteous (Ps. 37:32); those who seek my life (Ps. 63:9; 70:2); they planned to kill me (Ps. 31:13); violent men sought my life (Ps. 54:3); those who seek my life lay snares (Ps. 38:12); do you mean to kill me as you killed the Egyptian? (Acts 7:28); the soldiers planned to kill the prisoners (Acts 27:42).

l Pharaoh tried to kill Moses (Exod. 2:15); those who sought to kill you are dead (Exod. 4:19); they wanted to stone Joshua and Caleb (Num. 14:10); Jonathan was to die (1 Sam. 14:39, 43–5); Jeremiah, you must die! (Jer. 26:8); they were trying to kill Paul (Acts 21:31).

m Saul tried to kill David with a spear (1 Sam. 18:11; 19:10); Saul wanted the Philistines to kill David (1 Sam. 18:17, 21, 25); Saul told Jonathan and his servants to kill David (1 Sam. 19:1–2); he sent messengers to kill him in the morning (1 Sam. 19:11, 15; Ps. 59:t); David must die! (1 Sam. 20:31–3); he who seeks my life seeks your life (1 Sam. 22:23); Saul was seeking his life (1 Sam. 23:15; 24:11); the people spoke of stoning him (1 Sam. 30:6); my son seeks my life (2 Sam. 16:11); I will strike down only the king (2 Sam. 17:2); Ishbi-benob tried to kill David (2 Sam. 21:16); they plotted to kill Jeremiah (Jer. 11:19); the men of Anathoth who seek your life (Jer. 11:21).

n Do not let Joab's grey hair go down to Sheol in peace (1 Kgs. 2:6); bring Shimei's grey hair down to Sheol in blood (1 Kgs. 2:9); Solomon sought Jeroboam's death (1 Kgs. 11:40); you have come to kill my son (1 Kgs. 17:18); shall I kill them? (2 Kgs. 6:21); let me go and kill Ishmael secretly (Jer. 40:15); the king gave orders to kill all the wise men (Dan. 2:12–13).

o They are coming to kill you (Neh. 6:10); Ishmael is coming to take your life (Jer. 40:14); they will not know or see until we kill them (Neh. 4:11); Bigthan and Teresh tried to kill the king (Esther 2:21; 6:2).

p Herod seeking to destroy Jesus (Matt. 2:13); those who sought the child's life are dead (Matt. 2:20); let us kill the heir (Matt. 21:38).

Restraint from killing

q Why kill David without a cause? (1 Sam. 19:5; 20:32); let me go! why should I kill you? (1 Sam. 19:17); the Lord has restrained you from killing (1 Sam. 25:26, 31, 33); you shall not die (2 Sam. 19:22–3); it is not for us to kill (2 Sam. 21:4); would you kill captives? (2 Kgs. 6:22); the sons were not put to death (2 Kgs. 14:6; 2 Chr. 25:4); Satan was not allowed to kill Job (Job 2:6).

r Let her not be killed in the temple (2 Kgs. 11:15; 2 Chr. 23:14).

Approval to kill

s You may kill my two sons (Gen. 42:37); whoever has it, let him die (Gen. 31:32; 44:9); why did you not kill Absalom? (2 Sam.

18:11); let Uriah be killed (2 Sam. 11:15); seven sons of Saul were handed over to be killed (2 Sam. 21:6–9).

t If there is sin in me, kill me yourself (1 Sam. 20:8); if there is iniquity in me, let him kill me (2 Sam. 14:32); Saul asked his armour bearer to kill him (1 Sam. 31:4; 1 Chr. 10:4); please kill me (2 Sam. 1:9).

1 **Smothering**   *u* The harlot lay on her child (1 Kgs. 3:19); Hazael smothered Ben-hadad (2 Kgs. 8:15); that they should abstain from what is strangled (Acts 15:20, 29; 21:25).

v The thorns choked the plants (Matt. 13:7; Mark 4:7; Luke 8:7); these things choke the word (Matt. 13:22; Mark 4:19; Luke 8:14).

Beheading, see **46f**.

1 **Killing rulers**   *w* Rechab and Baanah killed Ishbosheth (2 Sam. 4:6–7); Joab impaled Absalom (2 Sam. 18:14); Zimri killed Elah (1 Kgs. 16:10); Athaliah was put to death (2 Kgs. 11:16, 20; 2 Chr. 23:15, 21); Baasha killed Nadab (1 Kgs. 15:27, 28); Jehu killed Joram (2 Kgs. 9:24, 31); Jehu killed Ahaziah (2 Kgs. 9:27–8; 2 Chr. 22:9); Joash of Judah killed by his servants (2 Kgs. 12:20–1; 2 Chr. 24:25); they sent to Lachish and killed Amaziah (2 Kgs. 14:19; 2 Chr. 25:27); Shallum killed Zechariah (2 Kgs. 15:10); Menahem killed Shallum (2 Kgs. 15:14); Pekah killed Pekahiah (2 Kgs. 15:25); Hoshea killed Pekah (2 Kgs. 15:30); Amon killed by his servants (2 Kgs. 21:23; 2 Chr. 33:24); Pharaoh Neco killed Josiah (2 Kgs. 23:29); Ishmael killed Gedaliah (Jer. 41:2); Jeroboam will die by the sword (Amos 7:11).

x Joshua killed the five kings (Josh. 10:26); Ehud stabbed Eglon (Judg. 3:21–2); Gideon killed Zebah and Zalmunna (Judg. 8:20–1); Samuel hewed Agag in pieces (1 Sam. 15:33); I killed Saul (2 Sam. 1:10); Hazael smothered Benhadad (2 Kgs. 8:15); Sennacherib, king of Assyria, killed by the sword (2 Kgs. 19:37; 2 Chr. 32:21; Isa. 37:38); Belshazzar was killed (Dan. 5:30).

1 **Killing giants**   *y* David killed Goliath (1 Sam. 17:49–51); Abishai killed Ishbi-benob (2 Sam. 21:16); Sibbecai killed Saph [Sippai] (2 Sam. 21:18; 1 Chr. 20:4); Elhanan killed Goliath (2 Sam. 21:19); Elhanan killed Lahmi (1 Chr. 20:5); Jonathan killed a giant (2 Sam. 21:21; 1 Chr. 20:7); Benaiah killed the Egyptian with his own spear (1 Chr. 11:23).

1 **Killing families**   *z* Killing all the house of: Jeroboam by Baasha (1 Kgs. 15:29); Baasha by Zimri (1 Kgs. 16:11); Ahab by Jehu (2 Kgs. 10:11, 17); Ahaziah by Jehu (2 Kgs. 10:14).

aa The Philistines killed the sons of Saul (1 Chr. 10:2); they killed the 70 sons of Ahab (2 Kgs. 10:7); Athaliah killed all the royal children (2 Kgs. 11:1; 2 Chr. 22:10); Zedekiah's sons were killed before him (2 Kgs. 25:7; Jer. 39:6; 52:10).

ab Their little ones will be dashed in pieces (Isa. 13:16); happy the one who dashes your little ones against a rock (Ps. 137:9).

1 Killing
brothers

ac Cain killed his brother Abel (Gen. 4:8, 25; Matt. 23:35; 1 John 3:12); Esau planned to kill Jacob (Gen. 27:41); Joseph's brothers planned to kill him (Gen. 37:18); Abimelech killed his seventy brothers (Judg. 9:5, 18, 24, 56); Absalom had Amnon killed (2 Sam. 13:28–9); brother killed brother in the wise woman's story (2 Sam. 14:6); Jehoram killed all his brothers (2 Chr. 21:4, 13).

ad Everyone kill brothers, friends and neighbours (Exod. 32:27).

1 Suicide

ae Samson pulled the building down on himself (Judg. 16:30); Saul fell on his sword (1 Sam. 31:4; 1 Chr. 10:4); as did his armour-bearer (1 Sam. 31:5; 1 Chr. 10:5); Ahithophel hanged himself (2 Sam. 17:23); Zimri burnt the palace over himself (1 Kgs. 16:18); Judas hanged himself (Matt. 27:5); the Philippian jailer was about to kill himself (Acts 16:27); they thought Jesus contemplated suicide (John 8:22).

1 Killing
individuals

af I killed a man for wounding me (Gen. 4:23); Abraham took the knife to kill his son (Gen. 22:10); Moses killed the Egyptian (Exod. 2:12, 14); Balaam was killed by Israel (Josh. 13:22); Jael transfixed Sisera (Judg. 4:21; 5:26); Abimelech was killed by his armour bearer (Judg. 9:54); Saul's sons were killed (1 Sam. 31:2); Abner killed Asahel (2 Sam. 2:22; 3:30); Joab killed Abner (2 Sam. 3:27, 30); Rechab and Baanah were killed (2 Sam. 4:12); Uriah was killed (2 Sam. 11:17, 21, 24); you killed Uriah with the sword of Amon (2 Sam. 12:9); Joab stabbed Amasa (2 Sam. 20:10); Israel stoned Adoram [Hadoram] (1 Kgs. 12:18; 2 Chr. 10:18); Naboth was stoned (1 Kgs. 21:10, 13, 14); have you killed and taken possession? (1 Kgs. 21:19); Gedaliah was killed (2 Kgs. 25:25); the two officials were hanged (Esther 2:23).

ag Solomon had killed: Adonijah (1 Kgs. 2:24–5); Joab (1 Kgs. 2:30–4); Shimei (1 Kgs. 2:46).

ah The Amalekite who killed Saul was struck down (2 Sam. 1:15; 4:10); Amaziah killed those who had killed his father (2 Kgs. 14:5; 2 Chr. 25:3); they killed those who killed Amon (2 Kgs. 21:24; 2 Chr. 33:25).

Striking to death, see **279*l***; **stoning**, see **344*n***.

1 Killing one
another

ai The Midianites killed each other (Judg. 7:22); the Philistines killed one another (1 Sam. 14:20); the kings must have killed one another (2 Kgs. 3:23); every man's sword will be against his brother (Ezek. 38:21).

aj Gideon killed the men of Penuel (Judg. 8:17); Abimelech killed the people of Shechem (Judg. 9:43–5, 49); Gilead killed 42 000 of Ephraim (Judg. 12:6); killing the Benjaminites (Judg. 20:42–8); kill the inhabitants of Jabesh-gilead (Judg. 21:10–11); Judah killed 360 of Benjamin (2 Sam. 2:31); Judah killed 500 000 of Israel (2 Chr. 13:17); Jehu killed the princes of Judah (2 Chr. 22:8); Israel killed 3000 of Judah (2 Chr. 25:13); Zichri of Ephraim killed Maaseiah the king's son (2 Chr. 28:7); Pekah slew 120 000 of Judah in one day (2 Chr. 28:6); Ishmael slaughtered 80 men (Jer. 41:7).

1 Killing   *ak*   Israel was slaughtered (1 Sam. 4:2, 10); men of Ephraim killed
Israelites   by men of Gath (1 Chr. 7:21); 20 000 [of Israel] were slaughtered (2 Sam. 18:7); the chief people of Israel killed in Hamath (2 Kgs. 25:21); our fathers have been killed by the sword (2 Chr. 29:9); the Chaldeans slew the people of Judah (2 Chr. 36:17).

al   Haman planned to annihilate the Jews (Esther 3:6, 9, 13; 8:5; 9:24); we have been sold to be slaughtered (Esther 7:4); every Hebrew boy to be killed (Exod. 1:16) being thrown into the Nile (Exod. 1:22); Herod killed all the boys (Matt. 2:16).

1 Killing   *am*   Saul told his guards to kill the priests (1 Sam. 22:17); Doeg killed
priests   the priests and all their city (1 Sam. 22:16–19, 21); his priests fell by the sword (Ps. 78:64); Seraiah *et al.* killed (Jer. 52:27); should priest and prophet be slain in the temple? (Lam. 2:20).

an   They killed Mattan priest of Baal (2 Kgs. 11:18); Jehu killed the priests and prophets of Baal (2 Kgs. 10:19–25); Josiah killed the priests of the high places (2 Kgs. 23:20).

1 Killing   *ao*   Jezebel killed the prophets of the Lord (1 Kgs. 18:4, 13); they
prophets   killed your prophets (1 Kgs. 19:10, 14; Neh. 9:26; Rom. 11:3); Jezebel threatened to kill Elijah (1 Kgs. 19:2); they seek my life (1 Kgs. 19:10, 14); the king seeking to kill Elisha (2 Kgs. 6:31, 32); Jehoiakim killed Uriah (Jer. 26:21–3); let Jeremiah be put to death (Jer. 38:4); men seeking Jeremiah's life (Jer. 38:16); they stoned Zechariah in the court of the temple (2 Chr. 24:21; Matt. 23:35); Jerusalem, killing the prophets (Matt. 23:37; Luke 13:33–4); they beat and killed those sent to them (Matt. 21:35; 22:6; Mark 12:3–8; Luke 20:10–15); we would not have killed the prophets (Matt. 23:30); you are sons of those who killed the prophets (Matt. 23:31; Luke 11:47–8); they killed the Lord Jesus and the prophets (1 Thess. 2:15); the blood of all the prophets charged against this generation (Matt. 23:35; Luke 11:50–1).

ap   Elijah killed the prophets of Baal (1 Kgs. 18:40; 19:1); Nebuchadnezzar will kill Ahab and Zedekiah, the false prophets (Jer. 29:21).

1 Killing   *aq*   They will kill you (Matt. 24:9); some they will kill and some they
disciples   will persecute (Luke 11:49); some of you will be put to death (Luke 21:16); some you will kill and crucify (Matt. 23:34); those who kill you will think they are serving God (John 16:2); for your sake we are killed all day long (Ps. 44:22; Rom. 8:36); those killed because of the word of God (Rev. 6:9).

ar   Herod wanted to kill John (Matt. 14:5; Mark 6:19); they beheaded John (Matt. 14:10; Mark 6:27; Luke 9:9); they wanted to kill the apostles (Acts 5:33); they stoned Stephen (Acts 7:58–60); Paul persecuted the Way to death (Acts 22:4); James was killed with the sword (Acts 12:2); the kind of death by which Peter would glorify God (John 21:19); they tried to kill Paul (Acts 9:23–4, 29); they stoned Paul and thought he was dead (Acts 14:19); vowed not to eat or drink until they had killed Paul (Acts 23:12); the Jews tried to put Paul to death (Acts 26:21).

as The sword will not separate us from the love of Christ (Rom. 8:35).

1 **Killing peoples**

at David killed: Amalekites (1 Sam. 30:17); Philistines (1 Sam. 18:27; 19:8; 23:5; 2 Sam. 5:25); Arameans (2 Sam. 10:18; 1 Chr. 18:5; 19:18).

au They killed 10 000 Moabites (Judg. 3:29); Shamgar killed 600 Philistines (Judg. 3:31); Samson killed 30 Philistines (Judg. 14:19); 1000 Philistines with a donkey's jawbone (Judg. 15:16); David killed 22 000 Arameans (2 Sam. 8:5); 18 000 Arameans (2 Sam. 8:13); the Arameans were slaughtered (1 Kgs. 20:21); 100 000 Arameans killed (1 Kgs. 20:29); the Moabites were slaughtered (2 Kgs. 3:24); 10 000 Edomites (2 Kgs. 14:7); 12 000 Edomites (Ps. 60:t); Jehoram struck down the Edomites (2 Chr. 21:9).

av Samson killed more at his death than during his life (Judg. 16:30); Saul slaughtered the Ammonites (1 Sam. 11:11); Saul had killed Gibeonites (2 Sam. 21:1–2); ten thousand men of Seir were thrown from a cliff (2 Chr. 25:11–12); David slaughtered two thirds of the Moabites (2 Sam. 8:2); Pharaoh killed the Canaanites in Gezer (1 Kgs. 9:16).

1 **Annihilating**

aw Destroy the nations of the land (Deut. 7:2, 16, 24; 20:16); destroy the Amalekites (Deut. 25:19; 1 Sam. 15:3, 8, 18); on taking a city, destroy all the men (Deut. 20:13).

ax Simeon and Levi killed every male in Shechem (Gen. 34:25); Joab killed every male in Edom (1 Kgs. 11:15–16); Sihon and his people were wiped out (Deut. 2:34); as were Og and his people (Num. 21:35; Deut. 3:3–6); they destroyed every person (Josh. 10:40; 11:12, 14); all the Amorites (Josh. 10:20); all the Anakim (Josh. 11:21–2); no survivors were left (Josh. 11:8, 12); David left no survivors (1 Sam. 27:9, 11); the Hamites and Meunites were destroyed (1 Chr. 4:41).

ay Killing everyone in: Jericho (Josh. 6:21); Ai (Josh. 8:22, 24–6); Makkedah (Josh. 10:28); Libnah (Josh. 10:30); Lachish (Josh. 10:32); Gezer (Josh. 10:33); Eglon (Josh. 10:35); Hebron (Josh. 10:37); Debir (Josh. 10:39); Hazor (Josh. 11:11).

az Killing: Midianites (Num. 31:7–8, 17; Josh. 13:21); inhabitants of the land (Josh. 9:24); Ammonites (Judg. 11:33); people of Laish (Judg. 18:27); Philistines (Judg. 15:8; 1 Sam. 14:13–14, 31; 17:52).

Killing all males, see **372f**.

ba The Jews were given the right to exterminate their enemies (Esther 8:11); which they did (Esther 9:5–10, 12–15, 16).

bb They did not destroy the peoples (Ps. 106:34).

1 God killing

bc The Lord kills and brings to life (Deut. 32:39; 1 Sam. 2:6); those slain by the Lord will be many (Isa. 66:16); I will kill you with the sword (Exod. 22:24); can I kill and bring to life like God? (2 Kgs. 5:7); you sweep men away, they fall asleep (Ps. 90:5); he can destroy and cast into hell (Matt. 10:28; Luke 12:5); I am going to cut off the righteous and the wicked (Ezek. 21:4); he destroys the blameless and the wicked (Job 9:22); surely you will not sweep away the righteous with the wicked (Gen. 18:23–5); God will crush the head of his enemies (Ps. 68:21); kill my enemies before me (Luke 19:27); slay the wicked, O God (Ps. 139:19); with the breath of his mouth he will slay the wicked (Isa. 11:4); the king destroyed those murderers (Matt. 22:7); though he slay me, I will trust in him (Job 13:15).

bd God cuts off the nations (Deut. 19:1); the Lord will shatter kings (Ps. 110:5–6); God wanted the people of the land destroyed (Josh. 11:20).

1 God killing individuals

be The Lord put Er and Onan to death (Gen. 38:7, 10; Num. 26:19; 1 Chr. 2:3); the Lord was about to kill Moses (Exod. 4:24); the angel would have killed Balaam (Num. 22:33); God slew Sihon and Og (Ps. 135:10–11; 136:17–20); it was the Lord's will to put to death Eli's sons (1 Sam. 2:25); the Lord struck Nabal and he died (1 Sam. 25:38); the Lord will strike Saul (1 Sam. 26:10); the Lord put Saul to death (1 Chr. 10:14); the Lord struck down Uzzah (2 Sam. 6:7; 1 Chr. 13:10); the Lord struck down Jeroboam (2 Chr. 13:20); an angel of the Lord struck down Herod (Acts 12:23); are you causing the widow's son to die? (1 Kgs. 17:20).

1 God killing his people

bf Fire from the Lord consumed the 250 men (Num. 16:35); the Lord destroyed the followers of Baal-Peor (Deut. 4:3); the Lord struck Benjamin before Israel (Judg. 20:35); God struck down men of Beth Shemesh (1 Sam. 6:19); God killed the strongest of them (Ps. 78:31); when he killed them, they sought him (Ps. 78:34); he destroyed those who did not believe (Jude 5).

bg God was about to slay all the assembly (Num. 14:12–16; 16:21, 45; Deut. 9:14, 25); God would have destroyed you (Deut. 9:8, 19; Ps. 106:23); God would have destroyed Aaron (Deut. 9:20); the Lord will destroy you from the land (Deut. 6:15; Josh. 23:15, 16); I will send sword, famine and plague until they are destroyed from the land (Jer. 24:10); lest God bring pestilence or sword (Exod. 5:3); I will destroy them (Jer. 25:9); slaughter all who do not have the mark (Ezek. 9:6); I will destroy my people (Jer. 15:7); you have slain them in your anger (Lam. 2:21).

bh The Egyptians will say you brought them out to kill them (Exod. 32:12); please kill me (Num. 11:15).

1 God killing others

bi Will you kill an innocent nation? (Gen. 20:4); I could have wiped you off the earth with a plague (Exod. 9:15); I will strike down the firstborn (Exod. 12:12); the Lord killed the firstborn of Egypt

(Exod. 4:23; 12:29; 13:15); God smote the Egyptians (Exod. 12:27); God hurled the Egyptians into the waters (Neh. 9:11); the Lord slew the Amorites (Josh. 10:10–11); the angel of the Lord killed 185,000 Assyrians (2 Kgs. 19:35; Isa. 37:36); he killed all the Assyrian fighting men (2 Chr. 32:21); Assyria will fall by a sword not of man (Isa. 31:8); the Lord will destroy the Philistines (Jer. 47:4); I will kill her children with pestilence (Rev. 2:23).

bj I will wipe mankind off the face of the earth (Gen. 6:7); I will destroy every living creature (Gen. 7:4); God blotted out every creature (Gen. 7:23); I will never again destroy every living creature (Gen. 8:21).

1 **Killing Christ**

bk His killing foretold (Matt. 16:21; 17:23; 20:18–19; 26:2; Mark 8:31; 9:31; 10:34; Luke 9:22; 18:33; 24:7); they plotted to kill him (Matt. 26:4); crucify him! (Matt. 27:22–3; Mark 15:13–14; Luke 23:21; John 19:6, 15); they tried to kill him (Mark 11:18; Luke 19:47; John 8:40); they sought to kill him (Matt. 12:14; 26:3–4; 27:1; Mark 3:6; 14:1; Luke 22:2; John 5:18; 7:1, 19, 25; 8:37; 11:8, 53); and Lazarus also (John 12:10); Herod wanted to kill Jesus (Luke 13:31); they picked up stones to stone him (John 8:59; 10:31).

bl They killed him (Matt. 27:35; Mark 15:24; Luke 23:33; 24:20; John 19:18; Acts 2:23; 3:15; 7:52; 10:39; 13:28–9; 1 Thess. 2:15); they threw him out of the vineyard and killed him (Matt. 21:39; Mark 12:8); they crucified him and two others (Matt. 27:38; Mark 15:27; Luke 23:33; John 19:18); the rulers crucified the Lord of glory (1 Cor. 2:8); as a sheep to the slaughter (Isa. 53:7; Acts 8:32); he was crucified in weakness (2 Cor. 13:4); we preach Christ crucified (1 Cor. 1:23; 2:2); placarded as crucified (Gal. 3:1); was Paul crucified for you? (1 Cor. 1:13); a Lamb as if it had been slain (Rev. 5:6); the Lamb who was slain (Rev. 13:8).

bm You crucified him (Acts 2:36; 4:10; 5:30); they are crucifying the Son of God over again (Heb. 6:6).

1 **Killing animals**

bn Kill the lamb at twilight (Exod. 12:6); regulations for killing an animal (Lev. 17:3–4); killing animals on a large rock (1 Sam. 14:33–4); rise, Peter, kill and eat (Acts 10:13; 11:7); he who kills an animal must replace it (Lev. 24:18, 21); he goes like an ox to the slaughter (Prov. 7:22).

bo David had killed lions and bears (1 Sam. 17:35–6); Benaiah killed a lion in a pit on a snowy day (2 Sam. 23:20; 1 Chr. 11:22); the beast was slain (Dan. 7:11).

Sacrifices, see **981***h*.

1 **Animals killing**

bp Kill an ox which gores a person to death (Exod. 21:28–9); if one ox kills another (Exod. 21:35–6).

bq A lion killed a man of God (1 Kgs. 13:24; 20:36); lions killed the settlers in Samaria (2 Kgs. 17:25–6); two bears killed 42 youths (2 Kgs. 2:24).

363 Corpse

1 **Rules about corpses**

a What to do if a corpse is found in the country (Deut. 21:1–9); what to do if a man dies in a tent (Num. 19:14–15).

b Touching a dead body makes one unclean (Lev. 22:4; Num. 19:11, 16); priests must not defile themselves except for a near relative (Lev. 21:1–3; Ezek. 44:25); the high priest must not go near any dead body (Lev. 21:11); a Nazirite must not touch a dead body (Num. 6:6).

c A body must not be left hanging on a tree overnight (Deut. 21:22–3); they did not want the bodies to stay on the cross on the Sabbath (John 19:31).

1 **Corpses**

d Amasa's corpse was removed from the highway (2 Sam. 20:12); Jezebel's corpse will be like dung (2 Kgs. 9:37); they only found Jezebel's skull, feet and palms (2 Kgs. 9:35); the man of God's body was thrown on the road (1 Kgs. 13:24–5, 28); the prophet took up the man of God's body (1 Kgs. 13:29); Josiah's body was brought in a chariot to Jerusalem (2 Kgs. 23:30); they washed Dorcas' body (Acts 9:37).

e Corpses on the ground (2 Chr. 20:24); corpses lay like refuse in the streets (Isa. 5:25); corpses will fall like dung on the field (Jer. 9:22); Ishmael threw their bodies into the cistern (Jer. 41:7, 9); I will lay their dead bodies before their idols (Ezek. 6:5); there will be many corpses (Amos 8:3); countless corpses (Nahum 3:3); the valley of the dead bodies (Jer. 31:40).

1 **Bones**

f Joseph's bones were taken from Egypt (Gen. 50:25; Exod. 13:19; Josh. 24:32; Heb. 11:22); David took the bones of Saul and Jonathan (2 Sam. 21:12–13); touching Elisha's bones brought a dead man to life (2 Kgs. 13:21); our bones are scattered at the mouth of Sheol (Ps. 141:7).

g The millstone crushed his skull (Judg. 9:53); Golgotha—the place of the skull (Matt. 27:33; Mark 15:22; Luke 23:33; John 19:17); the jawbone of a donkey (Judg. 15:15–17).

h Bones were burned on altars to defile them (1 Kgs. 13:2; 2 Kgs. 23:16; 2 Chr. 34:5); he burned to lime the bones of the king of Edom (Amos 2:1); Josiah defiled idolatrous places with human bones (2 Kgs. 23:14, 20); bones will be left lying on the ground (Jer. 8:1–2); your bones will be scattered around your altars (Ezek. 6:5).

i The valley of dry bones (Ezek. 37:1–14).

1 **Parts of corpses**

j The heads of Oreb and Zeeb were brought to Gideon (Judg. 7:25); David took Goliath's head (1 Sam. 17:46, 51, 54, 57); the Philistines cut off Saul's head (1 Sam. 31:9; 1 Chr. 10:9–10); his head was put in the house of Dagon (1 Chr. 10:10); they took Ishbosheth's head to David (2 Sam. 4:7–8); they buried his head

(2 Sam. 4:12); Sheba's head will be thrown to you (2 Sam. 20:21–2); seventy heads were sent to Jehu (2 Kgs. 10:6–8); the girl was given the head of John the Baptist (Matt. 14:8–11; Mark 6:24–8).

k The concubine was cut into 12 pieces (Judg. 19:29; 20:6); Saul's body was fixed to the wall (1 Sam. 31:10–12); they cut off their hands and feet (2 Sam. 4:12).

ı Jesus' corpse

l Joseph of Arimathea asked for Jesus' body (Matt. 27:58; Mark 15:43; Luke 23:52; John 19:38); they did not break Jesus' legs (John 19:33); they did not find Jesus' body (Luke 24:3).
Stealing the body, see **788*l***.

ı Eating corpses

m Your bodies will be food for birds and beasts (Deut. 28:26); those who die in the city will be eaten by dogs and those who die in the field will be eaten by birds (1 Kgs. 14:11; 16:4; 21:24); dogs will eat Jezebel (1 Kgs. 21:23; 2 Kgs. 9:10, 36); their corpses will be food for birds and animals (Jer. 7:33; 16:4; 19:7; 34:20; Ezek. 39:17; Rev. 19:17–18); where the body is, there the eagles gather (Job 39:30; Matt. 24:28; Luke 17:37).

n I will give your flesh to the birds and beasts (1 Sam. 17:44); I will give the corpses of the Philistines to the birds and beasts (1 Sam. 17:46); they have given the bodies of your servants to birds and beasts for food (Ps. 79:2).
Burying corpses, see **364**.

ı Dead animals

o The carcasses of unclean animals must not be touched (Lev. 11:8, 11, 24–8, 31, 36–8); bees had nested in the lion's carcass (Judg. 14:8); do not eat what has died (Lev. 17:15; 22:8; Deut. 14:21; Ezek. 4:14).

364 Interment

ı Preparation for burial

a Where you die I will die and there be buried (Ruth 1:17).

b Joseph will close your eyes (Gen. 46:4); embalming of Jacob (Gen. 50:2); embalming of Joseph (Gen. 50:26); bringing out a man's bones from a house (Amos 6:10); she prepared my body for burial (Matt. 26:12; Mark 14:8; John 12:7); Jesus touched the bier (Luke 7:14).

c A pyre with fire and wood (Isa. 30:33); I have seen the wicked buried (Eccles. 8:10).
Funeral fires, see **381*l***.

d Jesus' body was wrapped in linen (John 19:40); they saw the wrappings (John 20:5–7).
Preparing for burial, see **669*l***.

ı Burial places

e The cave of Mamre purchased by Abraham as a burial site (Gen. 23:4–20); used for the burial of Abraham (Gen. 25:9–10); of Jacob (Gen. 47:30; 49:29–32; 50:5, 13); of the patriarchs (Acts 7:16).
Caves for burying, see **255*d***.

f Do not bury me in Egypt (Gen. 47:29); were there no graves in Egypt? (Exod. 14:11); Kibroth-Hattaavah—graves of greed (Num. 11:34; 33:16–17); the prophet buried the man of God in his own grave (1 Kgs. 13:30); bury me in the same grave (1 Kgs. 13:31); they threw a man in Elisha's grave (2 Kgs. 13:21); let me die near my parent's grave (2 Sam. 19:37).

g They bought the potter's field as a burial ground for foreigners (Matt. 27:7).

h Jerusalem, the city of my fathers' tombs (Neh. 2:3, 5); the tombs of David (Neh. 3:16); all the kings lie in glory in their own tombs (Isa. 14:18); what right do you have to hew a tomb for yourself here? (Isa. 22:16); I will give Gog a burial ground in Israel (Ezek. 39:11); you build the tombs of the prophets (Matt. 23:29; Luke 11:47–8).

i Josiah threw the dust of the Asherah on graves (2 Kgs. 23:6; 2 Chr. 34:4); demoniacs coming out of the tombs (Matt. 8:28); living in the tombs (Mark 5:2–3; Luke 8:27); people who sit in tombs (Isa. 65:4).

j I will open your graves and bring you out (Ezek. 37:12–13); the tombs were opened when Jesus died (Matt. 27:52).

1 Jesus' tomb

k Joseph of Arimathea had Jesus placed in his own new tomb (Matt. 27:59–60; Mark 15:46; Luke 23:53; John 19:40–2); they made his grave with the wicked man (Isa. 53:9); they made the tomb as secure as they could (Matt. 27:64–6); Mary Magdalene came to the tomb (Matt. 28:1); women went to the tomb (Luke 24:1, 22); Peter ran to the tomb (Luke 24:12); some of us went to the tomb (Luke 24:24).

1 Burying people

l The burial of: Aaron (Deut. 10:6); Abdon (Judg. 12:15); Abijah son of Jeroboam (1 Kgs. 14:13, 18); Abijam [Abijah] (1 Kgs. 15:8; 2 Chr. 14:1); Abner (2 Sam. 3:32); Abraham (Gen. 25:9); Absalom (2 Sam. 18:17); Ahab (1 Kgs. 22:37); Ahaz (2 Kgs. 16:20; 2 Chr. 28:27); Ahaziah (2 Kgs. 9:28; 2 Chr. 22:9); Ahithophel (2 Sam. 17:23); Amaziah (2 Kgs. 14:20; 2 Chr. 25:28); Amon (2 Kgs. 21:26); Ananias (Acts 5:6); Asa (1 Kgs. 15:24; 2 Chr. 16:14); Baasha (1 Kgs. 16:6); David (1 Kgs. 2:10; Acts 2:29); Deborah (Gen. 35:8); Eleazar (Josh. 24:33); Elisha (2 Kgs. 13:20); Elon (Judg. 12:12); Gideon (Judg. 8:32); Hezekiah (2 Chr. 32:33); Ibzan (Judg. 12:10); Ishbosheth's head (2 Sam. 4:12); Isaac (Gen. 35:29); Jacob (Gen. 50:13); Jair (Judg. 10:5); Jehoiada (2 Chr. 24:16); Jehoram (2 Chr. 21:20); Jehoshaphat (1 Kgs. 22:50; 2 Chr. 21:1); Jephthah (Judg. 12:7); Jesus (Matt. 27:60; Mark 15:46; Luke 23:53; John 19:42; 1 Cor. 15:4); Jezebel (2 Kgs. 9:34); Joab (1 Kgs. 2:34); Joash [Jehoash] of Israel (2 Kgs. 13:13; 14:16); Joash [Jehoash] of Judah (2 Kgs. 12:21; 2 Chr. 24:25); John the Baptist (Matt. 14:12; Mark 6:29); Joseph (Josh. 24:32); Joshua (Josh. 24:30; Judg. 2:9); Josiah (2 Kgs. 23:30; 2 Chr. 35:24); Jotham (2 Kgs. 15:38; 2 Chr.

27:9); Manasseh (2 Kgs. 21:18; 2 Chr. 33:20); Moses (Deut. 34:6); Omri (1 Kgs. 16:28); Rachel (Gen. 35:19; 48:7); Rehoboam (1 Kgs. 14:31; 2 Chr. 12:16); Samson (Judg. 16:31); Samuel (1 Sam. 25:1; 28:3); Sapphira (Acts 5:10); Saul and his sons (1 Sam. 31:11–13; 2 Sam. 2:4; 21:14; 1 Chr. 10:12); Solomon (1 Kgs. 11:43); Stephen (Acts 8:2); Tola (Judg. 10:2); Uzziah [Azariah] (2 Kgs. 15:7; 2 Chr. 26:23); the man of God from Judah (1 Kgs. 13:22, 29–31; 2 Kgs. 23:17).

m Joab burying the slain (1 Kgs. 11:15).

n Permit me first to buy my father (Matt. 8:21; Luke 9:59); let the dead bury their dead (Matt. 8:22; Luke 9:60).

1 Inadequate burial

o Better the stillborn than a man without a burial (Eccles. 6:3); my mother would have been my grave (Jer. 20:17); there was no one to bury them (Ps. 79:3); they will lie unburied (Jer. 25:33); their bones will not be buried (Jer. 8:2); there will be no one to bury them (Jer. 14:16); they will not be lamented or buried (Jer. 16:4, 6); their dead bodies will lie in the street of the city unburied (Rev. 11:8–9).

p Jehoiakim's body would not be buried (Jer. 36:30); you have been thrown out of your tomb (Isa. 14:19–20).

q I will put your corpses on the corpses of your idols (Lev. 26:30); he will have a donkey's burial (Jer. 22:19); they threw Uriah's body into the burial place of the common people (Jer. 26:23); it will take seven months to bury them all (Ezek. 39:11–16); they will bury in Topheth for lack of room elsewhere (Jer. 7:32; 19:11).

1 Figurative burial

r You are like unmarked tombs over which men walk (Luke 11:44); like whitewashed tombs (Matt. 23:27); their throat is an open grave (Ps. 5:9).

s We were buried with Christ in baptism (Rom. 6:4; Col. 2:12).

365 Animals

1 Animals in general

a God created all animals (Gen. 1:20–5; 2:19); sea creatures created (Gen. 1:20–2); land creatures created (Gen. 1:24–5); Solomon spoke of animals, birds, reptiles and fish (1 Kgs. 4:33); ask the beasts, birds and fish and let them teach you (Job 12:7–8); every animal of the forest and the cattle on a thousand hills are mine (Ps. 50:10).

b Man is like the beasts that perish (Ps. 49:12, 20); men are like beasts, for one fate comes to all (Eccles. 3:18–19, 21); like irrational animals (2 Pet. 2:12; Jude 10).

c No living creature was a helper suitable for man (Gen. 2:20); all creatures given into man's hand (Gen. 9:2); man is to rule all creatures (Ps. 8:6–8); beasts and birds are to fear man (Gen. 9:2); animals given to man for food (Gen. 9:3); all kinds of animals in the sheet (Acts 10:12; 11:6); images in the form of all kinds of creatures (Rom. 1:23).

d Two of every living creature was to be taken into the ark (Gen. 6:19–20); every living creature perished (Gen. 6:7; 7:21–3); Noah's covenant included every living creature (Gen. 9:10); you save man and beast (Ps. 36:6).

Lifting animals, see **310***k*; **killing animals**, see **362***bn*; **animals killing**, see **362***bp*; **clean and unclean animals**, see **649***z*; **animals released**, see **746***q*; **sex with animals**, see **951***n*.

1 Wild animals

e A wild beast has devoured him (Gen. 37:33); wild animals sent as a plague in judgement (Lev. 26:22; Deut. 32:24); wild beasts will eat your corpses (Deut. 28:26; Jer. 16:4); I will send wild beasts against you (Ezek. 5:17); beasts of the sky and the earth to devour and destroy (Jer. 15:3); to kill with wild beasts (Rev. 6:8); night when the beasts of the forest prowl (Ps. 104:20); wild animals will live in places once inhabited (Isa. 13:21–2; 32:14; 34:11, 13–17); if I cause wild beasts to pass through the land (Ezek. 14:15); I fought with wild beasts at Ephesus (1 Cor. 15:32).

f Wild animals will live with domesticated animals (Isa. 11:6–9; 65:25); you will not be afraid of wild beasts (Job 5:22); every kind of animal can be tamed (Jas. 3:7); the beasts of the field will be at peace with you (Job 5:23); I will make a covenant with the beasts and the birds (Hos. 2:18); Jesus was with the wild animals (Mark 1:13).

g I will destroy wild beasts from the land (Lev. 26:6; Ezek. 34:25); lest the wild beasts become too many for you (Deut. 7:22).

1 Insects etc.

h I am a flea (1 Sam. 24:14; 26:20).

i The plague of gnats (Exod. 8:16–19; Ps. 105:31); you strain out a gnat and swallow a camel (Matt. 23:24); swarms of flies (Ps. 78:45); a horsefly is coming from the north (Jer. 46:20); the plague of insects (Exod. 8:20–32); ants are not strong, but provide their food (Prov. 30:25); go to the ant, you sluggard (Prov. 6:6–8).

j Plagues of locusts (Exod. 10:4–20; Deut. 28:42; Ps. 78:46; 105:34; Joel 1:4–7; 2:25; Rev. 9:3); if there are locusts or grasshoppers (1 Kgs. 8:37; 2 Chr. 6:28; 7:13); Nineveh like locusts (Nahum 3:15–17); John the baptist ate locusts (Matt. 3:4; Mark 1:6).

Insects jumping, see **312***c*.

k God will send hornets (Exod. 23:28; Deut. 7:20; Josh. 24:12); the Amorites chased you like bees (Deut. 1:44).

l The leech has two daughters (Prov. 30:15); I am a worm (Ps. 22:6); man is a maggot and a worm (Job 25:6); God appointed a worm to eat the plant (Jonah 4:7); Herod was eaten by worms (Acts 12:23).

1 Frogs

m The plague of frogs (Exod. 8:1–15; Ps. 78:45; 105:30); three unclean spirits like frogs (Rev. 16:13).

1 Mice	*n*	The mouse is unclean (Lev. 11:29); five golden mice (1 Sam. 6:4–5, 11, 18); they eat mice (Isa. 66:17).
1 Snakes	*o*	The Lord sent fiery snakes (Num. 21:6); they were destroyed by serpents (1 Cor. 10:9); I am sending against you adders which cannot be charmed (Jer. 8:17); a man leans against a wall and a snake bites him (Amos 5:19); Moses' staff became a snake (Exod. 4:3; 7:9–10).
	p	They will pick up snakes and if they drink poison it will not harm them (Mark 16:18); authority to tread on snakes and scorpions (Luke 10:19); Moses put a snake on a pole (Num. 21:8–9; John 3:14); a viper came out of the sticks (Acts 28:3); if he asks for a fish, who will give him a snake? (Matt. 7:10).
	q	Dan is a snake (Gen. 49:17); men venomous and deaf as snakes (Ps. 58:4); you brood of vipers (Matt. 3:7; 12:34; 23:33; Luke 3:7); the horses' tails are like serpents (Rev. 9:19); wise as serpents and harmless as doves (Matt. 10:16).
	r	The snake deceived Eve (Gen. 3:1–5; 2 Cor. 11:3); the great dragon, the serpent, Satan (Gen. 3:1; Rev. 12:9; 20:2).
1 Scorpions	*s*	I will chastise you with scorpions (1 Kgs. 12:11, 14; 2 Chr. 10:11, 14); he led you through the wilderness with serpents and scorpions (Deut. 8:15); though you sit on scorpions (Ezek. 2:6); locusts given power like scorpions (Rev. 9:3); they have tails like scorpions (Rev. 9:10); like the sting of a scorpion (Rev. 9:5).
1 Foxes and jackals	*t*	Samson caught three hundred foxes (Judg. 15:4); a fox would break their wall down (Neh. 4:3); the little foxes ruin the vineyards (S. of S. 2:15); foxes prowl in Jerusalem (Lam. 5:18); even jackals suckle their young (Lam. 4:3); foxes have holes (Matt. 8:20).
	u	Your prophets have been like foxes among the ruins (Ezek. 13:4); that fox Herod (Luke 13:32).
1 Wolves	*v*	A wolf from the desert will destroy them (Jer. 5:6); the hireling sees the wolf coming and flees (John 10:12).
	w	Benjamin is a wolf (Gen. 49:27); her judges are wolves at evening (Zeph. 3:3); sheep among wolves (Matt. 10:16; Luke 10:3); ravenous wolves, not sparing the flock (Acts 20:29); her princes are like wolves tearing the prey (Ezek. 22:27); false prophets as wolves (Matt. 7:15).
1 Deer	*x*	Do you know when mountain goats or deer give birth? (Job 39:1); Naphtali is a doe (Gen. 49:21); they were swift as gazelles (1 Chr. 12:8); one's wife as a graceful deer (Prov. 5:19); my beloved is like a gazelle (S. of S. 2:9); be like a gazelle (S. of S. 2:17; 8:14); as the deer longs for the water (Ps. 42:1).
1 Bears	*y*	David had killed bears (1 Sam. 17:34–6); two bears killed 42 youths (2 Kgs. 2:24); as if a man flees from a lion and a bear meets him (Amos 5:19); a beast like a bear (Dan. 7:5); the beast's feet were like a bear's (Rev. 13:2).
	z	David is like a bear robbed of her cubs (2 Sam. 17:8); I will be

like a bear robbed of her cubs (Hos. 13:8); he is like a bear lying in wait (Lam. 3:10); a wicked ruler is like a charging bear (Prov. 28:15).

1 **Wild cattle**

aa Who set the wild donkey free? (Job 39:5–8); will the wild ox serve you? (Job 39:9–12); save me from the horns of the wild oxen (Ps. 22:21); many bulls have surrounded me (Ps. 22:12).

1 **Lions**

ab What is stronger than a lion? (Judg. 14:18); lions suffer hunger (Ps. 34:10); can you hunt prey for the lion? (Job 38:39); lions growling over their prey will not be frightened by shepherds (Isa. 31:4); like a lion, eager to tear (Ps. 17:12; 22:13); a lion has gone up from his thicket (Jer. 4:7); a lion from the forest will kill them (Jer. 5:6); the dens of lions (S. of S. 4:8); save me from the lion's mouth (Ps. 22:21); lions or ravenous beasts will not be found there (Isa. 35:9).

ac A young lion came roaring at Samson (Judg. 14:5); Daniel was thrown into the lions' den (Dan. 6:7, 16); a lion killed the man of God (1 Kgs. 13:24–8; 1 Kgs. 20:36); the Lord sent lions among them (2 Kgs. 17:25–6).

1 **Power over lions**

ad Samson tore the lion like a kid (Judg. 14:6); David had killed lions (1 Sam. 17:34–6); Benaiah killed a lion in a pit on a snowy day (2 Sam. 23:20; 1 Chr. 11:22); you will tread on lions and snakes (Ps. 91:13); by faith they shut the mouths of lions (Heb. 11:33); lions are quelled by God's anger (Job 4:10–11); I was delivered from the lion's mouth (2 Tim. 4:17).

1 **Like lions**

ae Each cherub had a lion's face (Ezek. 1:10; 10:14; 41:19); the first living creature was like a lion (Rev. 4:7); a beast like a lion with the wings of an eagle (Dan. 7:4); the locusts had lions' teeth (Rev. 9:8); horses with heads like lions (Rev. 9:17); the beast's head was like a lion (Rev. 13:2).

af Men like lions: Israel (Num. 23:24; 24:9; Ezek. 19:2–9); Gad (Deut. 33:20); Dan (Deut. 33:22); Judah (Gen. 49:9); Pharaoh (Ezek. 32:2).

ag They were stronger than lions (2 Sam. 1:23); their faces were like lions (1 Chr. 12:8); the remnant will be like a lion (Mic. 5:8); where is the den of lions? [Nineveh] (Nahum 2:11).

ah The Lord has left his hiding-place like a lion (Jer. 25:38); the Lord will roar like a lion (Hos. 11:10); I will be like a lion to Israel (Hos. 5:14); I will be like a lion or leopard to them (Hos. 13:7); he is like a lion in hiding (Lam. 3:10); the lion of Judah (Rev. 5:5).

ai A wicked ruler is like a roaring lion (Prov. 28:15); Jerusalem's princes are roaring lions (Zeph. 3:3); Israel is as sheep hunted by lions (Jer. 50:18); I am among lions (Ps. 57:4); my inheritance has become like a lion roaring against me (Jer. 12:8); the devil is like a roaring lion (1 Pet. 5:8).

1 **Leopards**

aj A leopard is watching them (Jer. 5:6); can the leopard change its spots? (Jer. 13:23); the mountains of leopards (S. of S. 4:8); a leopard with four wings and four heads (Dan. 7:6); the beast was like a leopard (Rev. 13:2); I will be like a lion or leopard to them (Hos. 13:7).

● Birds

ak Birds created (Gen. 1:20–2); birds will eat your corpses (Deut. 28:26); birds of the air do not sow or reap (Matt. 6:26; Luke 12:24); birds of the air nest in its branches (Ezek. 17:23; 31:6; Dan. 4:12, 21; Matt. 13:32; Mark 4:32; Luke 13:19); birds of the air have nests (Matt. 8:20); birds ate up the seed (Matt. 13:4; Mark 4:4; Luke 8:5); birds eating from the top basket (Gen. 40:17); birds of prey came to the carcasses (Gen. 15:11); to the corpses (2 Sam. 21:10); calling a bird of prey from the east (Isa. 46:11); like hovering birds the Lord will protect Jerusalem (Isa. 31:5); the fugitives of Moab are like fluttering birds (Isa. 16:2); they will come like birds (Hos. 11:11).

al Noah sent out a raven and a dove (Gen. 8:7–12); who gives food to the ravens? (Job 38:41); ravens fed Elijah (1 Kgs. 17:4, 6); does the hawk soar by your discernment? (Job 39:26); as a hen gathers her chicks (Matt. 23:37; Luke 13:34).

am Quail came over the camp (Exod. 16:13; Num. 11:31–2); I am like an owl in the wilderness (Ps. 102:6); a partridge on the mountains (1 Sam. 26:20); are not two sparrows sold for an assarion? (Matt. 10:29); five sparrows for two assaria (Luke 12:6).

an The ships brought apes and peacocks (1 Kgs. 10:22; 2 Chr. 9:21); the ostrich (Job 39:13–18); ostriches will live in Babylon (Jer. 50:39); cruel like ostriches (Lam. 4:3).

● Doves and pigeons

ao He overturned the seats of those selling doves (Matt. 21:12; Mark 11:15; John 2:14, 16).

ap Ephraim is like a silly dove (Hos. 7:11); be wise as serpents and harmless as doves (Matt. 10:16); the Holy Spirit descended like a dove (Matt. 3:16; Mark 1:10; Luke 3:22; John 1:32).

● Eagles

aq Does the eagle mount up by your command? (Job 39:27); an eagle flying in mid-heaven (Rev. 8:13); where the corpse is, the eagles will gather (Matt. 24:28; Luke 17:37).

ar Each creature had the face of an eagle (Ezek. 1:10; 10:14); the fourth creature was like a flying eagle (Rev. 4:7); the woman was given the wings of the great eagle (Rev. 12:14).

as They will mount up with wings like eagles (Isa. 40:31); they were swifter than eagles (2 Sam. 1:23); their horsemen fly like an eagle (Hab. 1:8).

at God stirs up the nest like an eagle (Deut. 32:11); God will swoop like an eagle (Jer. 49:22); an eagle is over the Lord's house (Hos. 8:1); two great eagles and a vine (Ezek. 17:3–10).

● Water creatures

au The hippopotamus [Behemoth] (Job 40:15–24); can you catch a crocodile [Leviathan] with a hook? (Job 41:1–3); Leviathan sports in the sea (Ps. 104:26); the Lord will punish Leviathan the twisting serpent (Isa. 27:1).

● Fish

av There will be many fish (Ezek. 47:9–10); the fish in the Nile died (Exod. 7:18, 21; Ps. 105:29); I will make fish stick to your scales (Ezek. 29:4); the Lord appointed a fish to swallow Jonah (Jonah 1:17); Jonah was three days and nights in the belly of the sea monster (Matt. 12:40); if he asks for a fish, who will give him a snake? (Matt. 7:10); you make men like fish without a ruler (Hab. 1:14).

● Domesticated animals

aw The law on animals which gore people or are killed (Exod. 21:28–36); if your neighbour's animal strays, bring it back (Deut. 22:1–4).

ax Saul spared the animals (1 Sam. 15:9); the horses, mules, camels and donkeys of those returning from exile (Ezra 2:66–7; Neh. 7:68–9).

● Cattle

ay If an ox gores someone to death (Exod. 21:28–36); do not muzzle an ox which is threshing (Deut. 25:4; 1 Cor. 9:9; 1 Tim. 5:18).

az Joseph bartered food for the Egyptians' livestock (Gen. 47:16); Pharaoh dreamed of seven cows (Gen. 41:2); the Egyptians' livestock died (Exod. 9:6); our livestock must go too (Exod. 10:24–6); the Philistines used two cows to draw the ark (1 Sam. 6:7); the second creature was like a calf (Rev. 4:7); each creature had the face of a bull (Ezek. 1:10).

ba Nebuchadnezzar would be like cattle (Dan. 4:15, 23, 25, 32, 33; 5:21); you cows of Bashan (Amos 4:1); Israel is like a stubborn heifer (Hos. 4:16); Ephraim is a heifer that loves to thresh (Hos. 10:11); Egypt is a pretty heifer (Jer. 46:20); if you had not ploughed with my heifer (Judg. 14:18); God's concern is not for oxen, is it? (1 Cor. 9:9).

● Camels

bb The servant took ten camels (Gen. 24:10); mounting camels (Gen. 31:17); a caravan of camels (Gen. 37:25); camels used in warfare (Judg. 6:5); camels without number (Judg. 7:12); 400 men escaped on camels (1 Sam. 30:17).

bc It is easier for a camel to go through the eye of a needle (Matt. 19:24; Mark 10:25; Luke 18:25); you strain out a gnat and swallow a camel (Matt. 23:24).

● Donkeys

bd Abraham saddled his donkey (Gen. 22:3, 5); ten loaded donkeys (Gen. 45:23); Moses put his family on a donkey (Exod. 4:20); Balaam's donkey (Num. 22:22–33); a donkey spoke with a man's voice (2 Pet. 2:16); 30 sons on 30 donkeys (Judg. 10:4); 40 sons and 30 grandsons on 70 donkeys (Judg. 12:14); the Levite took two donkeys (Judg. 19:3, 10); Abigail rode on a donkey (1 Sam. 25:20, 42); Ziba brought David provisions and donkeys (2 Sam. 16:1–2); Jesus rode on a donkey (Matt. 21:2–7; Mark 11:2–7; Luke 19:30–5; John 12:14–15).

be Issachar is a donkey (Gen. 49:14); Ishmael a wild donkey (Gen. 16:12).

Riding on animals, see **267***j*.

● Horses

bf The king must not multiply horses (Deut. 17:16); a horse is a vain hope for victory (Ps. 33:17); we put bits in horses' mouths (Jas. 3:3).

bg The Canaanites fled on horses (Judg. 5:22); Solomon had thousands of horses (1 Kgs. 4:26); Solomon imported horses from Egypt and Kue (1 Kgs. 10:28–9; 2 Chr. 1:16–17; 9:28); horses, war horses and mules were traded (Ezek. 27:14); Mordecai was paraded on the king's horse (Esther 6:8, 10–11); the war horse (Job 39:19–25); a man on a red horse (Zech. 1:8); a red horse (Rev. 6:4); a white horse (Rev. 6:2; 19:11); white horses (Rev. 19:14); a black horse (Rev. 6:5); a greenish horse (Rev. 6:8).

bh Horses with heads like lions (Rev. 9:17); the locusts were like war horses (Joel 2:4; Rev. 9:7)

bi Do not be like the horse or mule (Ps. 32:9); you are like my mare (S. of S. 1:9).

- **Pigs**

bj The boar from the forest ravages it (Ps. 80:13); the evil spirits entered the pigs (Matt. 8:30–2; Mark 5:11–13; Luke 8:32–3); do not throw pearls before swine (Matt. 7:6).

- **Dogs**

bk Against Israel not even a dog shall bark (Exod. 11:7); throw torn flesh to the dogs (Exod. 22:31); do not give what is holy to dogs (Matt. 7:6); it is not good to throw the children's bread to the dogs (Matt. 15:26; Mark 7:27); dogs eat the crumbs (Matt. 15:27; Mark 7:28); dogs licked his sores (Luke 16:21); the dog returns to his vomit (2 Pet. 2:22).

bl Am I a dog? (1 Sam. 17:43); I am a dead dog (1 Sam. 24:14); this dead dog (2 Sam. 16:9); I am only a dog (2 Kgs. 8:13).

bm Many dogs have surrounded me (Ps. 22:16); save me from the power of the dog (Ps. 22:20); they prowl around the city like dogs (Ps. 59:6, 14); outside are the dogs (Rev. 22:15); beware of the dogs (Phil. 3:2).

- **Sheep and goats**

bn The poor man had only little ewe lamb (2 Sam. 12:3).

bo We are the sheep of his hand (Ps. 95:7); the sheep of his pasture (Ps. 100:3).

bp The lost sheep of the house of Israel (Matt. 10:6; 15:24); all we like sheep have gone astray (Isa. 53:6); you were straying like sheep (1 Pet. 2:25); parable of the lost sheep (Matt. 18:12–14; Luke 15:4–7); the sheep and the goats (Matt. 25:32); little flock (Luke 12:32).

bq I am sending you as sheep among wolves (Matt. 10:16; Luke 10:3); you make us like sheep to be eaten (Ps. 44:11); like sheep for the slaughter (Ps. 44:22; Rom. 8:36); let them be like sheep for slaughter (Jer. 12:3); I was like a lamb led to the slaughter (Jer. 11:19); like sheep without a shepherd (Matt. 9:36); I will strike the shepherd and the sheep will be scattered (Zech. 13:7; Matt. 26:31).

br The Lamb of God (John 1:29, 36); the Lamb (Rev. 5:6–13; 14:1;

17:14); like a lamb to slaughter or a sheep to shearing (Isa. 53:7; Acts 8:32); as of a lamb without blemish (1 Pet. 1:19).

bs A ram with two horns (Dan. 8:3, 20); a he-goat from the west (Dan. 8:5, 21); a beast with two horns like a lamb (Rev. 13:11). **Sheep without a shepherd**, see **369**, **sacrificing animals**, see **981**.

● Cosmic creatures

bt Four living creatures (Ezek. 1:5–14; Rev. 4:6–8); living creatures identified as cherubim (Ezek. 10:6–22).

bu Four great beasts (Dan. 7:3–8); the great dragon, the serpent, Satan (Gen. 3:1; Rev. 12:9; 20:2); the Lord will kill the dragon who is in the sea (Isa. 27:1); did you not cut Rahab the dragon in pieces? (Isa. 51:9); the red dragon (Rev. 12:3); the beast from the abyss (Rev. 11:7); a beast out of the sea (Rev. 13:1–4); a beast out of the earth (Rev. 13:11–18); three unclean spirits like frogs (Rev. 16:13).

366 Plants

● Plants in general

a No plant had yet sprouted (Gen. 2:5); God created vegetation (Gen. 1:11); for food (Gen. 1:29–30; 3:18); the Lord made all kinds of trees in Eden (Gen. 2:9); Solomon spoke of plants (1 Kgs. 4:33).

b Every plant not planted by my Father will be uprooted (Matt. 15:13); Judah shall take root downward and bear fruit upward (2 Kgs. 19:30).

● Foliage

c Fig leaves for clothing (Gen. 3:7); the dove brought an olive leaf (Gen. 8:11); foliage for the Feast of Booths (Lev. 23:40; Neh. 8:15); branches cut from trees (Judg. 9:48–9; Matt. 21:8; Mark 11:8); they took branches of palm trees (John 12:13); the righteous will flourish like a green leaf (Prov. 11:28).

● Grass etc.

d God makes grass grow (Ps. 147:8); searching for grass for the animals (1 Kgs. 18:5); can papyrus grow without marsh? (Job 8:11).

e I am the rose of Sharon (S. of S. 2:1); the lilies of the field do not toil or spin (Matt. 6:28).

f All flesh is grass, soon withering (Isa. 40:6–8); all flesh is like grass (1 Pet. 1:24); they will wither like grass and herbs (Ps. 37:2); like grass sprouting in the morning and withering by evening (Ps. 90:5–6); like grass on the housetops, scorched (2 Kgs. 19:26; Isa. 37:27); let them be like grass on the housetops (Ps. 129:6); the rich man will pass away like grass (Jas. 1:10–11).

● Herbs

g Hyssop (Exod. 12:22; Lev. 14:4, 6, 49, 51–2; Num. 19:6, 18); gourds among the herbs (2 Kgs. 4:39); God appointed a plant to shade Jonah (Jonah 4:6); you tithe mint and dill and cummin (Matt. 23:23).

● Cereals and pulses

h Wheat and spelt are later than flax and barley (Exod. 9:31–2); a plot of ground full of barley (1 Chr. 11:13); a field of lentils (2 Sam. 23:11).

● Mandrakes	*i* Reuben found mandrakes (Gen. 30:14–16); the mandrakes are fragrant (S. of S. 7:13).
● Vines and olives	*j* Vineyards and olive trees (Neh. 9:25); every man under his vine and under his fig tree (1 Kgs. 4:25; 2 Kgs. 18:31; Mic. 4:4); the trees wanted the vine to reign over them (Judg. 9:12–13); can you use wood of the vine? (Ezek. 15:2–6).

k Dream of a vine (Gen. 40:9); Joseph is a fruitful vine (Gen. 49:22); Israel as a vine (Isa. 5:1–6; Hos. 10:1); I planted you as a choice vine (Jer. 2:21); a vine from Egypt (Ps. 80:8); parable of the two eagles and a vine (Ezek. 17:3–10); a vine in your vineyard (Ezek. 19:10); Israel like grapes (Hos. 9:10); your wife will be like a vine, your children like olive shoots (Ps. 128:3); I am the vine (John 15:5); I am the true vine (John 15:1); Jerusalem is like a useless vine (Ezek. 15:2–8); their vine is of Sodom (Deut. 32:32); the vine of Sibmah has withered (Isa. 16:8–9); I weep for you, vine of Sibmah (Jer. 48:32).

Growing vines, see **370k**.

l The trees wanted the olive tree to reign over them (Judg. 9:8–9); I am like an olive tree in the house of God (Ps. 52:8); two olive trees and two lampstands (Rev. 11:4).

● Trees — *m* God waters the trees he planted (Ps. 104:16); I will make many kinds of tree spring up in the desert (Isa. 41:19); the cypress and the myrtle instead of thorns (Isa. 55:13); the trees of the fields will clap their hands (Isa. 55:12); Ahaz sacrificed under every green tree (2 Chr. 28:4); I see men like trees, walking (Mark 8:24).

n 70 date palms at Elim (Exod. 15:27; Num. 33:9); your stature is like a palm tree (S. of S. 7:7–8); Saul was under the pomegranate tree (1 Sam. 14:2); the tamarisk tree at Gibeah (1 Sam. 22:6); I see a rod of almond (Jer. 1:11); balsam trees (2 Sam. 5:23–4; 1 Chr. 14:14–15); Elijah sat under a juniper tree (1 Kgs. 19:4–5); we hung our harps on the willows (Ps. 137:2).

o The burning bush (Exod. 3:2–4; Acts 7:30); he who dwelt in the bush (Deut. 33:16).

● Destroying trees — *p* Do not destroy the trees when besieging a town (Deut. 20:19–20); fell every good tree (2 Kgs. 3:19, 25); destroy worship places under every green tree (Deut. 12:2); God shattered the trees of the Egyptians (Ps. 105:33); you could tell this tree to be uprooted (Luke 17:6).

● Forests — *q* They entered the forest (1 Sam. 14:25–6); the forest of Hereth (1 Sam. 22:5); battle in the forest of Ephraim (2 Sam. 18:6); the forest devoured more than the sword (2 Sam. 18:8); the keeper of the king's forest (Neh. 2:8); the trees of the forest will sing for joy (1 Chr. 16:33; Ps. 96:12); the forest of cedars, cypresses and oaks is destroyed (Zech. 11:1–2).

● Fig trees — *r* Every man under his vine and under his fig tree (1 Kgs. 4:25; 2 Kgs. 18:31; Mic. 4:4); when you were under the fig tree I saw you (John 1:48, 50); the trees wanted the fig tree to reign over them (Judg. 9:10–11); the parable of the fig tree (Matt. 24:32; Mark 13:28; Luke 13:6; 21:29); Jesus cursed the fig tree (Matt. 21:19; Mark 11:13–14).

Trees bearing fruit, see **171**.

● Oaks   *s* The oaks of Moreh (Gen. 12:6; Deut. 11:30); oaks of Mamre (Gen. 13:18; 14:13; 18:1); the oak near Shechem (Gen. 35:4); Allon-Bacuth—oak of weeping (Gen. 35:8); the oak in Zaanannim (Josh. 19:33; Judg. 4:11); the oak in Ophrah (Judg. 6:11); the oak of the pillar in Shechem (Judg. 9:6); the oak of Tabor (1 Sam. 10:3); Absalom's head stuck in a great oak (2 Sam. 18:9–10); the man of God sitting under an oak (1 Kgs. 13:14); you will be ashamed of the oaks (Isa. 1:29); against the cedars of Lebanon and the oaks of Bashan (Isa. 2:13); they will be called oaks of righteousness (Isa. 61:3).

● Cedars   *t* The top of a cedar of Lebanon plucked off (Ezek. 17:3–4, 22); it will become a cedar (Ezek. 17:23); like a cedar they bring forth fruit in old age (Ps. 92:12–14).

● Metaphorical trees   *u* The trees went to anoint a king (Judg. 9:8); the thorn bush said to the cedar (2 Kgs. 14:9; 2 Chr. 25:18).

     v The tree of life (Gen. 2:9; 3:22, 24; Rev. 2:7; 22:2, 14, 19); wisdom is a tree of life (Prov. 3:18); the fruit of the righteous is a tree of life (Prov. 11:30); desire fulfilled is a tree of life (Prov. 13:12); a soothing tongue is a tree of life (Prov. 15:4); trees on both banks of the river (Ezek. 47:7, 12); a tree made the waters sweet (Exod. 15:25).

     w The tree of the knowledge of good and evil (Gen. 2:9; 3:2–7).

     x He will be like a tree planted by water (Ps. 1:3; Jer. 17:8); the righteous will flourish like the palm tree and like a cedar of Lebanon (Ps. 92:12); Assyria as a huge cedar (Ezek. 31:3–9); Israel will send down roots like Lebanon (Hos. 14:5); the Lord called you a green olive tree (Jer. 11:16); the two olive trees (Zech. 4:3); my beloved is like an apple tree (S. of S. 2:3).

     y Nebuchadnezzar pictured as a huge tree cut down (Dan. 4:10–15, 20–3); a violent man like a luxuriant tree (Ps. 37:35); the Lord will lop the boughs and cut down Lebanon (Isa. 10:33–4); I cut down the cedars of Lebanon (2 Kgs. 19:23); you will be like an oak whose leaf withers (Isa. 1:30); a shoot from the stump of Jesse (Isa. 11:1).

Thorns and thistles, see **256k**.

367 Zoology: the science of animals

Animals, see **365**.

368 Botany: the science of plants

Plants, see **366**.

369 Animal husbandry

● Tending animals

a Those who kept herds and flocks: Abel (Gen. 4:2); Jabal (Gen. 4:20); Rachel (Gen. 29:1–10); Jacob (Gen. 30:31); Joseph (Gen. 37:2); the sons of Israel (Gen. 37:12; 46:32–4; 47:3); Moses (Exod. 3:1); David (1 Sam. 16:11, 19; 17:15, 34); Amos (Amos 1:1; 7:14); shepherds near Bethlehem (Luke 2:8); Mesha king of Moab was a sheep-breeder (2 Kgs. 3:4); Uzziah had much livestock (2 Chr. 26:10); Job had thousands of sheep, camels, oxen and donkeys (Job 42:12).

b Strife between Abraham's and Lot's herdsmen (Gen. 13:7); shepherds for 40 years in the wilderness (Num. 14:33); the sons of Reuben and Gad had many livestock (Num. 32:1–4).

c Overseeing the animals (1 Chr. 27:29–31); a righteous man has regard for the life of his beasts (Prov. 12:10).

d Building sheepfolds (Num. 32:16, 24); Doeg was Saul's chief shepherd (1 Sam. 21:7); David left the flock with a keeper (1 Sam. 17:20); with whom have you left the sheep? (1 Sam. 17:28); I took you from following the sheep (2 Sam. 7:8; 1 Chr. 17:7).

e Sheep-shearing time: for Laban (Gen. 31:19); for Judah (Gen. 38:12); for Nabal (1 Sam. 25:2, 4, 7); for Absalom (2 Sam. 13:23).

● Shepherding God's people

f David will shepherd Israel (2 Sam. 5:2; 1 Chr. 11:2; Ps. 78:70–1); they will have one shepherd, David (Ezek. 34:23; 37:24); Cyrus is God's shepherd (Isa. 44:28).

g I will give you shepherds after my own heart (Jer. 3:15); I will raise up shepherds to tend them (Jer. 23:4); tend my sheep (John 21:16); he gave some to be shepherds and teachers (Eph. 4:11); shepherd the church of God (Acts 20:28); shepherd the flock of God (1 Pet. 5:2).

h Who tends a flock without using the milk? (1 Cor. 9:7).

i Woe to the shepherds who scatter the sheep (Jer. 23:1); the shepherds led them astray (Jer. 50:6); I will raise up a shepherd who will not care for the flock (Zech. 11:16–17); woe to the shepherds who only take care of themselves (Ezek. 34:2–10); many shepherds have ruined my vineyard (Jer. 12:10); shepherding only themselves (Jude 12); wail, you shepherds (Jer. 25:34–6).

j Strike the shepherd and the sheep will be scattered (Zech. 13:7; Matt. 26:31; Mark 14:27); they were scattered without a shepherd (Ezek. 34:5); the people wander and are afflicted for want of a shepherd (Zech. 10:2–3); sheep without a shepherd (Num. 27:17; 1 Kgs. 22:17; 2 Chr. 18:16; Matt. 9:36; Mark 6:34); shepherd the flock doomed to slaughter (Zech. 11:4, 7).

● God as shepherd

k God who has been my shepherd (Gen. 48:15); the Lord is my shepherd (Ps. 23:1); Shepherd of Israel (Gen. 49:24; Ps. 80:1); he will keep Israel as a shepherd keeps his flock (Jer. 31:10); he will tend his flock like a shepherd (Isa. 40:11); he leads his people like a flock of sheep (Ps. 78:52); he is their God and they are his flock (Ps. 95:7; Ezek. 34:31); they are the flock of his people (Zech. 9:16); I will shepherd my sheep (Ezek. 34:12); I will be their shepherd (Ps. 28:9); shepherd your people (Mic. 7:14).

l Out of Bethlehem will come a shepherd for Israel (Mic. 5:2–4; Matt. 2:6); parable of the good shepherd (John 10:1–5); I am the good shepherd (John 10:11, 14); one flock, one shepherd (John 10:16); the great Shepherd of the sheep (Heb. 13:20); the shepherd and guardian of your souls (1 Pet. 2:25); when the chief Shepherd appears (1 Pet. 5:4); the Lamb will be their shepherd (Rev. 7:17).

m Collected sayings given by one shepherd (Eccles. 12:11).

370 Agriculture

● Laws about agriculture

a When you reap, leave gleanings (Lev. 19:9, 10; 23:22); laws on planting fruit trees (Lev. 19:23–5); do not sow or reap in the seventh year (Lev. 25:4–5); or in the year of Jubilee (Lev. 25:12).

● Gardens

b The Lord planted a garden in Eden (Gen. 2:8); you were in Eden, the garden of God (Ezek. 28:13); the desolate land in exile has become like the garden of Eden (Ezek. 36:35).

c Plant gardens and eat their produce (Jer. 29:5); I made gardens and parks (Eccles. 2:5); like gardens beside the river (Num. 24:6); the king's garden (Neh. 3:15); the palace garden (Esther 7:7); the garden of Gethsemane (John 18:1); the garden of the tomb (John 19:41).

d My lover has gone down to his garden (S. of S. 6:2); my beloved is a locked garden (S. of S. 4:12); let my beloved come into his garden (S. of S. 4:16); I have come into my garden (S. of S. 5:1); you will be like a watered garden (Isa. 58:11); their life will be like a watered garden (Jer. 31:12).

● Tilling

e Not yet a man to till the ground (Gen. 2:5); agriculture would be through toil (Gen. 3:17–19); he who tills his land will have plenty of bread (Prov. 12:11; 28:19); he who puts his hand to the plough and looks back (Luke 9:62); the ploughman will overtake the reaper (Amos 9:13).

f Adam had to till the garden (Gen. 2:15); to till the ground from which he was taken (Gen. 3:23); Cain tilled the soil (Gen. 4:2); overseeing those who tilled the soil (1 Chr. 27:26); in the third year, sow, reap, plant vineyards (2 Kgs. 19:29; Isa. 37:30); Uzziah loved the soil (2 Chr. 26:10).

g Do not plough with an ox and a donkey (Deut. 22:10); does the farmer plough continually? (Isa. 28:24); Judah will plough, Jacob will harrow (Hos. 10:11); if you had not ploughed with my heifer (Judg. 14:18); cultivate Mephibosheth's land (2 Sam. 9:10); the king will appoint men to plough and harvest for him

(1 Sam. 8:12); Elisha was ploughing (1 Kgs. 19:19); Uzziah had ploughmen and vinedressers (2 Chr. 26:10); the poorest people were left to be vinedressers and ploughmen (2 Kgs. 25:12).

h Those who plough iniquity and trouble harvest it (Job 4:8); the ploughers ploughed on my back (Ps. 129:3); Zion will be ploughed as a field (Mic. 3:12).

● Planting

i Abraham planted a tamarisk tree (Gen. 21:33); Isaac planted crops and reaped a hundredfold (Gen. 26:12); here is seed for planting (Gen. 47:23); I planted and Apollos watered (1 Cor. 3:6–8).

● Fallow land

j This year and next year eat what grows of itself (2 Kgs. 19:29; Isa. 37:30); break up your fallow ground (Hos. 10:12).

● Vineyards

k Noah planted a vineyard (Gen. 9:20); again you will plant vineyards (Jer. 31:5); the Rechabites were not to plant a vineyard (Jer. 35:7); they will plant vineyards but not drink the wine (Zeph. 1:13).

l Harvesting and treading grapes (Judg. 9:27); treading the wine press on the sabbath (Neh. 13:15); the grapes of the earth are ripe for harvesting and treading (Joel 3:13; Rev. 14:17–20); the winepress of Zeeb (Judg. 7:25); why are your garments like one who treads in the wine press? (Isa. 63:2–3); the Lord has trodden Judah as in a wine press (Lam. 1:15); the wine press of the wrath of God (Rev. 14:19–20).

m He who has planted a vineyard and not yet tasted the fruit (Deut. 20:6); you will plant a vineyard and not have the fruit (Deut. 28:30, 39); who plants a vineyard without eating the fruit? (1 Cor. 9:7); vineyards you did not plant (Deut. 6:11; Josh. 24:13); they sow fields, plant vineyards and harvest (Ps. 107:37); will David give you fields and vineyards? (1 Sam. 22:7).

n I planted vineyards (Eccles. 2:4); Solomon had a vineyard (S. of S. 8:11); Ahab wanted Naboth's vineyard (1 Kgs. 21:1–18); overseeing the vineyards (1 Chr. 27:27).

o Everyone will eat of his own vine and fig tree (1 Kgs. 4:25; 2 Kgs. 18:31; Isa. 36:16).

p A song about a vineyard (Isa. 5:1–7; 27:2); you planted the vine (Ps. 80:8).

● Orchards

q You will plant olive trees and have no oil (Deut. 28:40); olive orchards you did not plant (Deut. 6:11; Josh. 24:13); overseeing the olive and sycamore trees (1 Chr. 27:28); he who tends a fig tree will eat its fruit (Prov. 27:18).

r An orchard of pomegranates (S. of S. 4:13); I went down to the nut orchard (S. of S. 6:11).

● Harvesting

s Seedtime and harvest will not cease (Gen. 8:22); harvest time (2 Sam. 23:13); he who watches the clouds will not reap (Eccles. 11:4); the ant gathers food at harvest (Prov. 6:8).

t Wheat harvest (Gen. 30:14; 1 Sam. 6:13; 12:17); barley harvest (Ruth 1:22; 2 Sam. 21:9); binding sheaves (Gen. 37:7); the boy went out to the reapers (2 Kgs. 4:18); when harvest time came he sent his servants (Matt. 21:34); the disciples plucked ears of grain (Matt. 12:1; Mark 2:23; Luke 6:1).

u The ploughman should plough in hope (1 Cor. 9:10); those who sow in tears will reap in joy (Ps. 126:5–6); he who sows and he who reaps will rejoice together (John 4:36); the ploughman will overtake the reaper (Amos 9:13); the farmer is the first to have a share of the crops (2 Tim. 2:6); if we sowed to the spirit, should we not reap material things? (1 Cor. 9:11).

v What a man sows, that will he reap (Gal. 6:7–9); he who sows sparingly will reap sparingly (2 Cor. 9:6); he who sows iniquity will reap vanity (Prov. 22:8); in due season we shall reap (Gal. 6:9); he will increase the harvest of your righteousness (2 Cor. 9:10); unless a grain of wheat falls into the ground (John 12:24).

w The fields are ripe for harvest (John 4:35); the harvest is plentiful (Matt. 9:37; Luke 10:2); pray the Lord of the harvest to send workers (Matt. 9:38; Luke 10:2); you reap that for which you have not worked (John 4:37–8); the harvest has come (Mark 4:29); the harvest of the earth was ripe (Rev. 14:15); he will gather the wheat into the barn (Matt. 3:12; Luke 3:17); at the time of harvest the wheat will be separated from the tares (Matt. 13:30); the harvest is the end of the age (Matt. 13:39).

x You will sow but not reap (Mic. 6:15); they have sown wheat and reaped thorns (Jer. 12:13).

y You reap what you do not sow (Luke 19:21–2); I knew you to reap where you did not sow (Matt. 25:24, 26); I sent you to reap where you have not laboured (John 4:38); the birds do not sow, reap or gather into barns (Matt. 6:26; Luke 12:24).

Gleaning, see **41f**.

● Threshing

z The threshing floor of Atad (Gen. 50:10–11); the threshing floor of Nacon (2 Sam. 6:6); the threshing floor of Chidon (1 Chr. 13:9); the threshing floor of Araunah [Ornan] (2 Sam. 24:16; 1 Chr. 21:15); Ornan was threshing wheat (1 Chr. 21:20); the threshing floor bought and an altar erected there (2 Sam. 24:18–25; 1 Chr. 21:18–28); the temple was built there (2 Chr. 3:1); Boaz at the threshing floor (Ruth 3:2–14); the threshing floor at the gate of Samaria (1 Kgs. 22:10; 2 Chr. 18:9); Gideon was threshing wheat in the winepress (Judg. 6:11); do not muzzle an ox when threshing (Deut. 25:4); dill and cummin are not threshed with a sledge (Isa. 28:27); bread grain is threshed but not crushed (Isa. 28:28); salted feed winnowed with shovel and fork (Isa. 30:24).

aa Threshing the men of Succoth with thorns (Judg. 8:7, 16); the Lord will thresh in that day (Isa. 27:12); I have made you into a threshing sledge (Isa. 41:15); arise and thresh, daughter of Zion! (Mic. 4:13); he has gathered them like sheaves to the threshing floor (Mic. 4:12); O my threshed and winnowed one! (Isa. 21:10); I will winnow them with a winnowing fork (Jer. 15:7).

● Parables of agriculture

ab Parables of: the sower (Matt. 13:3–9, 18–23; Mark 4:3–9, 14–20; Luke 8:4–8, 11–15); the growing seed (Mark 4:26–9); of the tares (Matt. 13:24–30); the mustard seed (Matt. 13:31–2; Mark 4:31–2; Luke 13:18–19); the vineyard and tenants (Matt. 21:33–41; Mark 12:1–11; Luke 20:9–18).

371 Mankind

● Nature of man

a Man created in the likeness of God (Gen. 1:26–7; 5:1–2; 9:6); a little lower than God, crowned with glory (Ps. 8:5); from dust (Gen. 2:7); named Man (Gen. 5:2); man's function to rule all creatures (Gen. 1:26); to subdue the earth (Gen. 1:28); to till the ground (Gen. 2:5); beasts and birds are to fear man (Gen. 9:2); all creatures given into man's hand (Gen. 9:2).

b Man [unlike God] lies and changes his mind (Num. 23:19; 1 Sam. 15:29); God is true though every man a liar (Rom. 3:4); things possible for God are impossible for man (Matt. 19:26; Mark 10:27; Luke 18:27).

Men are liars, see **545*a***.

c The first man is from the earth, the second from heaven (1 Cor. 15:47); the first man Adam and the last Adam (1 Cor. 15:45); Adam was a type of the one to come (Rom. 5:14).

Nature of people, see **5*a***; **man's knowledge**, see **490*v***.

d Each cherub had a man's face (Ezek. 1:10; 10:14; 41:19); the third creature was like a man (Rev. 4:7); the locusts had men's faces (Rev. 9:7).

● Man's value

e Of what account is man? (Isa. 2:22); a man is worth much more than a sheep (Matt. 12:12); what is man that you care about him? (Job 7:17; Ps. 8:4; 144:3–4; Heb. 2:6); who are you, O man, to answer back to God? (Rom. 9:20); what is man that he should be pure? (Job 15:14); men do not warrant worship (Acts 10:26; 14:15); as the heavens are higher than the earth, so are God's thoughts and ways compared with man's (Isa. 55:8–9); man is a maggot and a worm (Job 25:6).

Man a mere breath, see **352*d***; **greatness of man**, see **638*c***.

f The sabbath was made for man, not man for the sabbath (Mark 2:27); I will sweep away mankind from the earth (Zeph. 1:3).

● Human nature of Christ

g He emptied himself, taking human form (Phil. 2:7–8); the Word became flesh (John 1:14); Jesus the last Adam [man] (1 Cor. 15:45); one mediator between God and man, the man Christ Jesus (1 Tim. 2:5); behold, the man! (John 19:5); accused of blasphemy because he, a man, claimed to be God (John 10:33).

● 'Son of man'

h Who do men say the Son of man is? (Matt. 16:13); who is this Son of man? (John 12:34); do you believe in the Son of man? (John 9:35).

i God has set his seal on the Son of man (John 6:27); God gave him authority to judge because he is the Son of man (John 5:27).

j 'Son of man' used of Christ, with regard to: Lord of the Sabbath (Matt. 12:8; Mark 2:28; Luke 6:5); authority to forgive sins (Matt. 9:6; Mark 2:10; Luke 5:24); suffering (Matt. 17:12; Mark 9:12); being betrayed and killed (Matt. 17:22; 20:18; 26:2, 24, 45; Mark 8:31; 9:31; 10:33; 14:21, 41; Luke 9:22, 44; 22:22; 24:7); being lifted up (John 3:14; 8:28; 12:34); rising from the dead (Matt. 17:9; Mark 9:9); being given a kingdom (Dan. 7:13–14); being seated in heaven (Matt. 19:28; 25:31–2; 26:64; Mark 14:62; Luke 22:69); standing in heaven (Acts 7:56); returning (Matt. 10:23; Luke 12:40; 17:30; 18:8); coming in glory (Matt. 16:27; 24:30; 26:64; Mark 8:38; 13:26; Luke 9:26; 21:27); confessing his own before the Father (Luke 12:8).

k The Son of man: has nowhere to lay his head (Matt. 8:20); came eating and drinking (Matt. 11:19); did not come to be served but to serve (Matt. 20:28; Mark 10:45); has come to seek and save (Luke 19:10); will send forth his angels (Matt. 13:41); comes when you least expect (Matt. 24:44); will come like lightning (Luke 17:24).

l Everything written about the Son of man will be fulfilled (Luke 18:31); as in the days of Noah, so in the days of the Son of man (Luke 17:26); you will long to see one of the days of the Son of man (Luke 17:22); the hour has come for the Son of man to be glorified (John 12:23); now is the Son of man glorified (John 13:31); if you were to see the Son of man ascending (John 6:62); no one has ascended to heaven but he who descended, the Son of man (John 3:13).

m Pray for strength to stand before the Son of man (Luke 21:36); blessed are you when you are hated for the sake of the Son of man (Luke 6:22); do you betray the Son of man with a kiss? (Luke 22:48); speaking against the Son of man will be forgiven (Matt. 12:32); eat the flesh of the Son of man (John 6:53).

● Seen by man

n Do not practise your religious acts before men to be seen by them (Matt. 6:1, 18); they do all their works to be seen by men (Matt. 23:5); man looks at the outside but the Lord looks at the heart (1 Sam. 16:7).

● Man's teaching

o Peter with his mind on man's things, not on God's (Matt. 16:23; Mark 8:33); according to the teaching of men (Col. 2:22); teaching the traditions of men, not the commands of God (Mark 7:8); mere rules taught by men (Matt. 15:9; Mark 7:7).

p Was the baptism of John from men? (Matt. 21:25–6; Mark 11:30; Luke 20:4); the gospel I prached was not man's (Gal. 1:11–12); I did not consult with flesh and blood (Gal. 1:16); we must obey God rather than men (Acts 5:29); flesh and blood did not reveal this to you (Matt. 16:17); the message is not the word of men, but of God (1 Thess. 2:13); if this movement is of men it will fail

(Acts 5:38); he who rejects is not rejecting man but God (1 Thess. 4:8).

● Beware
of men

q He who relies on mankind, and not on God, is cursed (Jer. 17:5); trust in the Lord, not in man (Ps. 118:8; 146:3); man's deliverance is vain (Ps. 60:11; 108:12); the Egyptians are men, not God (Isa. 31:3); with him is an arm of flesh (2 Chr. 32:8); with God helping me, what can man do? (Ps. 56:4, 11; 118:6; Heb. 13:6); beware of men (Matt. 10:17); fear of men is a snare (Prov. 29:25); let me not fall into the hand of men (2 Sam. 24:14; 1 Chr. 21:13). **Trusting in men**, see **485***ag*; **fear of men**, see **854***ac*.

● Pleasing
men

r I do not receive glory from men (John 5:41); if I pleased men I would not be a slave of Christ (Gal. 1:10); not trying to please men but God (1 Thess. 2:4); not as men-pleasers (Eph. 6:6); some loved the praise of men more than praise from God (John 12:43); I did not look for praise from men (1 Thess. 2:6); what is highly valued among men is detestable before God (Luke 16:15).

s We seek what is honourable not only before God but also before men (2 Cor. 8:21).

● Witness
before men

t Acknowledgement of Christ before men brings acknowledgement before God (Matt. 10:32; Luke 12:8); denial of Christ before men brings denial before God (Matt. 10:33; Luke 12:9); Jesus increased in favour with God and man (Luke 2:52).

● The nations

u God made all nations from one man (Acts 17:26); and allotted their territories (Deut. 32:8; Acts 17:26); the nations are a drop from the bucket (Isa. 40:15); let the nations know they are but men (Ps. 9:20); why do the nations rage against the Lord? (Ps. 2:1–2).

v Kenite, Kennizite, Kadmonite, Hittite, Perrizzite, Rephaim, Amorite, Canaanite, Girgashite, Jebusite, Hivite (Gen. 15:19–21; Exod. 3:8, 17; 13:5; 23:23, 28; 33:2; 34:11; Deut. 7:1; 20:17; Josh. 3:10; 11:3; 24:11; Judg. 3:3–5; 1 Kgs. 9:20; 2 Chr. 8:7; Ezra 9:1; Neh. 9:8); the kingdoms of the earth listed (Jer. 25:19–26); the Jebusites in Jerusalem (Josh. 15:63); the kings of the Amorites and Canaanites afraid (Josh. 5:1); five kings of the Amorites fought Gibeon (Josh. 10:5); five lords of the Philistines (Josh. 13:3).

w The beast given authority over every tribe, people, tongue and nation (Rev. 13:7).

x **Nations from individuals**, see **104***b*; **restoring nations**, see **656***ag*; **nations as prostitutes**, see **951***y*.

● Oracles about
the nations

y Oracles concerning: Amalek (Num. 24:20); Ammon (Jer. 49:1–6; Ezek. 21:28–32; 25:2–7); Assyria (Isa. 14:24–7); Babylon (Isa. 13:1–14:23; Jer. 25:12–14; 50:1–51:64); Damascus (Isa. 17:1–3; Jer. 49:23–7); Edom (Isa. 21:11–17; Jer. 49:7–22; Ezek. 35:2–15; Obad. 1–21); Egypt (Isa. 19:1–25; Jer. 46:2–26; Ezek. 29:2–30:26); Elam (Jer. 49:34–9); Ethiopia (Isa. 18:1–7);

Kedar and Hazor (Jer. 49:28–33); Meshech and Tubal (Ezek. 38:2–39:16); Moab (Isa. 15:1–16:14; Jer. 48:1–47; Ezek. 25:8–11); Nineveh (Nahum 1:1–3:18); Philistia (Isa. 14:29–32; Jer. 47:1–7; Ezek. 25:15–17); Sidon (Ezek. 28:21–4); Tyre (Isa. 23:1–18; Ezek. 26:2–28:19).

Oracles, see **438ad**.

● Dealing with   z Vengeance on the Midianites (Num. 31:2–18); remember what
the nations   Amalek did (Deut. 25:17); blot out the memory of Amalek (Deut. 25:19); I will punish Amalek (1 Sam. 15:2–3); the remnant of Amalek destroyed (1 Chr. 4:43); Ammonites and Moabites not to enter the assembly (Deut. 23:3–6; Neh. 13:1–2); do not hate an Edomite or an Egyptian (Deut. 23:7).

● The nations   aa All nations would be blessed in Abraham (Gal. 3:8); you ran-
and God   somed them from every tribe, tongue, people and nation (Rev. 5:9); many nations will come seeking God (Jer. 16:19; Mic. 4:2; Zech. 8:22); all the nations called by my name (Amos 9:12; Acts 15:16); I will give you the nations as your inheritance (Ps. 2:8); the ends of the earth will turn to the Lord (Ps. 22:27); Ethiopia will stretch out her hands to God (Ps. 68:31); all flesh will see God's salvation (Luke 3:6); all the ends of the earth will see the salvation of God (Isa. 52:10); the field is the world (Matt. 13:38).

        ab God will call for a foreign nation (Isa. 5:26–30); the king of Assyria as God's razor (Isa. 7:20); Assyria the rod of my anger (Isa. 10:5).

● Samaritans   ac The mixed practices of the Samaritans (2 Kgs. 17:28–41); Jews have no dealings with the Samaritans (John 4:9); the Samaritans would not receive him (Luke 9:52–3); the good Samaritan (Luke 10:33); the leper who gave thanks was a Samaritan (Luke 17:16); they said Jesus was a Samaritan (John 8:48).

Samaria, see **184s**.

● God's people   ad They will be God's people and he their God (Exod. 6:7; Lev. 26:12; Deut. 29:13; Jer. 7:23; 24:7; 30:22; 31:1, 33; 32:38; Ezek. 11:20; 14:11; 37:23, 27; Zech. 8:8; 13:9; 2 Cor. 6:16; Heb. 8:10; Rev. 21:3); a covenant that they should be the Lord's people (2 Kgs. 11:17); God's own people (Exod. 33:13; Deut. 27:9; 2 Sam. 7:24; 1 Chr. 17:22; Isa. 51:16; Titus 2:14); they are my people (Isa. 63:8; Ezek. 34:30); Ammi—my people (Hos. 2:1); we are your people (Isa. 64:9); we are his people (Ps. 100:3); the people of his pasture (Ps. 95:7); blessed are the people whose God is the Lord (Ps. 144:15).

Chosen people, see **605h**; **holy people**, see **979f**.

● Israel and   ae Who is like God's people Israel? (2 Sam. 7:23); the Lord's
the Jews   vineyard is the house of Israel (Isa. 5:7); no other God has taken one nation for himself (Deut. 4:34); of all families on earth God chose Israel (Amos 3:2); Israel will not cease from being a nation before me (Jer. 31:36–7); blessed more than all peoples (Deut. 7:14); your people shall be my people (Ruth 1:16).

af I am a Hebrew (Jonah 1:9); Esther did not make her people known (Esther 2:10, 20); Mordecai had told them he was a Jew (Esther 3:4); if Mordecai is a Jew (Esther 6:13); Haman sought to destroy all Jews (Esther 3:6); evildoers crush your people (Ps. 94:5); let my people be my request (Esther 7:3); many became Jews for fear of the Jews (Esther 8:17).

ag What advantage has the Jew? (Rom. 3:1); salvation is from the Jews (John 4:22); the Jew is also a sinner (Rom. 2:17–29).

ah Nathanael was a true Israelite (John 1:47); Zacchaeus was a son of Abraham (Luke 19:9); Paul was an Israelite (Rom. 11:1; 2 Cor. 11:22); of the nation of Israel, of the tribe of Benjamin, a Hebrew of Hebrews (Phil. 3:5); Paul became like a Jew to win Jews (1 Cor. 9:20); we are Jews, not Gentile sinners (Gal. 2:15).

● Tribes of Israel

ai Reuben, Gad and half Manasseh (Num. 32:1–42; 34:14; Deut. 3:12–17; 4:43; 29:8; Josh. 1:12–18; 4:12–13; 22:1–34; 1 Chr. 26:32); officers of the tribes of Israel (1 Chr. 27:16–22); I will give one tribe to your son (1 Kgs. 11:13); Rehoboam reigned over Judah (1 Kgs. 12:17, 20; 2 Chr. 10:17); the brotherhood broken between Israel and Judah (Zech. 11:14); Judah and Israel will be reunited (Ezek. 37:16–20, 22).

● Jew and Gentile

aj All people on earth will be blessed through Abraham (Gen. 12:3; 22:18; 28:14; Acts 3:25); those physically descended from Abraham and Israel are not all children of Abraham, the true Israel (Rom. 9:6–8); true descendants of Abraham follow Abraham's example (John 8:33–9); Abraham is the father of those who copy his faith (Rom. 4:12); God can raise up children for Abraham even from stones (Matt. 3:9; Luke 3:8); a true Jew is one inwardly (Rom. 2:28–9); the Israel of God is based on a new creation (Gal. 6:15–16); some claim to be Jews and are not (Rev. 2:9; 3:9).

ak The gospel is first for the Jew, then the Gentile (Rom. 1:16); as is recompense for deeds done (Rom. 2:9–10); Jews and Greeks are all under sin (Rom. 3:9); some preached only to Jews (Acts 11:19); Gentiles rejoice with God's people (Rom. 15:8–12).

al Gentiles are now members of the same body with the Jews (Eph. 3:6); fellow-citizens (Eph. 2:19); Christ has made Jew and Gentile one (Eph. 2:14); Gentiles have been brought near through the blood of Christ (Eph. 2:11–13); there is no difference between Jew and Gentile (Rom. 10:12; Col. 3:11); there is neither Jew nor Greek (Gal. 3:28); those who were not God's people have become his people (Hos. 1:10; 2:23; Rom. 9:24–6; 1 Pet. 2:10); I will make them jealous with those who are not a people (Deut. 32:21).

Salvation for Gentiles, see 59*q*.

● Israel hardened

am Israel is hardened until the full complement of the Gentiles comes in (Rom. 11:25); the kingdom of God would be taken away from the Jews (Matt. 21:43); the sons of the kingdom will be cast out (Matt. 8:12); they are not his people and God is not their God (Hos. 1:9); Paul was in anguish about his kinsmen, the people of Israel (Rom. 9:3); reaching the lost sheep of Israel (Matt. 10:6; 15:24); the children should first be fed (Matt. 15:26; Mark 7:27); the full inclusion of the Jews will bring great richness (Rom. 11:12); God has not rejected his people whom he foreknew (Rom. 11:2).

372 Male

● Male and female

a God made them male and female (Gen. 1:27; 5:2; Matt. 19:4; Mark 10:6); male and female of every living creature was to be brought into the ark (Gen. 6:19; 7:2–3, 9, 16); unclean people, male or female, sent out (Num. 5:3).

b In Christ it is not a case of male and female (Gal. 3:28).

● Males

c Every male must be circumcised (Gen. 17:10–14, 23; 34:15, 22, 24; Exod. 12:48); a woman bearing a male child is unlean seven days (Lev. 12:2); firstborn males belong to the Lord (Exod. 13:12, 15); valuation of males (Lev. 27:3–7).

d Census of males: from 20 up (Num. 1:2); Levites, a month up (Num. 3:15); firstborn, a month up (Num. 3:40–3).

e Pharaoh was prepared to let the men go to worship (Exod. 10:11); three times a year your males shall come before God (Exod. 23:17; Deut. 16:16); I want the men to pray (1 Tim. 2:8); male priests may eat the sacrifices (Lev. 6:18, 29; 7:6; Num. 18:10). **Handsome men**, see **841***k*.

● Killing all males

f Kill all the males (Deut. 20:13); they killed every male (Gen. 34:25; Num. 31:7, 17); David intended to kill everyone who urinated against a wall (1 Sam. 25:22, 34); if the baby is a boy, kill him (Exod. 1:16, 22); Joab killed every male in Edom (1 Kgs. 11:15–16); I will cut off every male from Jeroboam (1 Kgs. 14:10); not a male left of the house of Baasha (1 Kgs. 16:11); I will cut off every male from Ahab (1 Kgs. 21:21; 2 Kgs. 9:8); Herod killed all boys up to two years old (Matt. 2:16).

● Male animals

g Male lambs (Exod. 12:5; Num. 28:3, 9, 19, 27); male goats (Lev. 4:23; 16:5; 22:19; Num. 15:24; 28:15, 22, 30); male animals (Lev. 1:3, 10).

h Male or female animals (Lev. 3:1, 6).

373 Female

● Women

a God made woman as man's helper (Gen. 2:21–3); called 'woman' because she came from man (Gen. 2:23); woman was created for man (1 Cor. 11:9).

b The woman gave me the fruit of the tree (Gen. 3:6, 12); consequences of the fall for the woman (Gen. 3:16).

c The women of Midian: captured (Num. 31:9); spared (Num. 31:15, 18); killed (Num. 31:17).

d A wench or two for every warrior (Judg. 5:30).

e Women who had followed Jesus from Galilee (Matt. 27:55–6; Mark 15:40–1; Luke 23:55); women who had been healed and who ministered to them (Luke 8:2–3); the women told the apostles (Luke 24:10); a woman of Samaria came to draw water (John 4:7).

f A woman clothed with the sun (Rev. 12:1); the locusts had women's hair (Rev. 9:8).

Lovely women, see **841g**.

- Instructions regarding women

g A woman bearing a female child is unclean two weeks (Lev. 12:5); valuation of females (Lev. 27:4–7); female slaves shall not go free like males (Exod. 21:7).

h A woman's vows may be annulled by her father (Num. 30:3–5); or her husband (Num. 30:6–15).

i A woman should have her head covered (1 Cor. 11:3–16); women should adorn themselves modestly (1 Tim. 2:9; 1 Pet. 3:3–5); let the women keep silent (1 Cor. 14:34–6); women are to learn in silence (1 Tim. 2:11); women are not to teach but to be quiet (1 Tim. 2:12); requirements for a woman involved in the activities of a deacon (1 Tim. 3:11).

j Rise up, you women who are at ease (Isa. 32:9).

- Women in weakness

k Give honour to the woman as the weaker vessel (1 Pet. 3:7); the Lord will sell Sisera into the hands of a woman (Judg. 4:9); lest they say a woman killed me (Judg. 9:53–4); the Egyptians will be like women (Isa. 19:16); your troops will be like women (Nahum 3:13); a woman protects a man! (Jer. 31:22); these people capture weak women (2 Tim. 3:6).

- Female animals

l Female goat (Num. 15:27); female animals (Lev. 4:28, 32; 5:6; 14:10; Num. 6:14).

Male and female, see **372a**.

374 Physical sensibility

Feeling, see **818**.

375 Physical insensibility

- Anaesthetic

a Jesus refused wine and gall (Matt. 27:34); wine and myrrh (Mark 15:23).

b God gave them a spirit of stupefaction (Rom. 11:8).

- No feeling

c Idols have hands but cannot feel (Ps. 115:7).

376 Physical pleasure

Pleasurableness, see **826**.

377 Physical pain

- Pain

a Man is chastened with pain (Job 33:19); Jehoram died in great pain (2 Chr. 21:19).

Suffering, see **825**.

378 Touch: sensation of touch

● Touching
people

a Isaac felt Jacob to see who he was (Gen. 27:22).

b The servant put his hand under Abraham's thigh (Gen. 24:9); put your hand under my thigh (Gen. 47:29); the man touched Jacob's thigh (Gen. 32:25, 32).

c Our hands have handled the word of life (1 John 1:1); Simeon took Jesus in his arms (Luke 2:28); who touched me? (Luke 8:45); touch me and see (Luke 24:39); they took hold of Jesus' feet (Matt. 28:9); unless I put my finger in the mark of the nails (John 20:25); put your finger in my hands (John 20:27); do not cling to me (John 20:17).

● Touching
things

d The Kohathites must not touch the holy things (Num. 4:15); whatever touches them shall be holy (Exod. 30:29); Uzzah took hold of the ark and was struck down (2 Sam. 6:6; 1 Chr. 13:9–10); whoever touches the mountain will be killed (Exod. 19:12–13; Heb. 12:20).

e Touching unclean things (Lev. 5:2–3); touching an unclean person makes one unclean (Lev. 15:7, 11); Jesus touched the bier (Luke 7:14).

Touching the unclean, see **649e**.

f Whoever touches thorns must be protected (2 Sam. 23:7).

g Let me feel the pillars (Judg. 16:26).

● Touching to
restore

h He touched me and made me stand (Dan. 8:18); a hand touched me and set me on my hands and knees (Dan. 10:10); he laid his right hand on me (Rev. 1:17); he touched me and strengthened me (Dan. 10:18); he touched my lips (Dan. 10:16); the Lord stretched out his hand and touched my mouth (Jer. 1:9); you hold my right hand (Ps. 73:23); you have laid your hand on me (Ps. 139:5).

i Elijah stretched himself on the child three times (1 Kgs. 17:21); Elisha stretched himself on the child (2 Kgs. 4:34–5).

j Jesus touched: the leper (Matt. 8:3; Mark 1:41; Luke 5:13); the blind men's eyes (Matt. 9:29; 20:34); the slave's ear (Luke 22:51).

k Jesus took by the hand: Peter's mother-in-law (Matt. 8:15; Mark 1:31); Jairus' daughter (Matt. 9:25; Mark 5:41; Luke 8:54); the man with dropsy (Luke 14:4); the boy (Mark 9:27).

l He put his fingers in the deaf man's ears (Mark 7:33).

m Jesus reached out and caught Peter (Matt. 14:31).

n Peter seized him by the hand and raised him up (Acts 3:7); he gave her his hand and raised her (Acts 9:41); Paul threw his arms around him (Acts 20:10).

o They begged him to touch the blind man (Mark 8:22); they brought babies for him to touch them (Luke 18:15); he laid his hands on children and blessed them (Matt. 19:13, 15; Mark 10:13, 16).

p The woman touched the edge of Jesus' garment (Matt. 9:20–1; Mark 5:27–8, 30–1; Luke 8:44–6); everyone tried to touch him (Mark 3:10; Luke 6:19); they begged to touch the edge of his garment (Matt. 14:36; Mark 6:56).

Touching garments, see **228***f*.

● Not touching
q The woman said God had told them not to touch the tree (Gen. 3:3); handle not, taste not, touch not (Col. 2:21).

r I did not let you touch her (Gen. 20:6); it is good for a man not to touch a woman (1 Cor. 7:1).

● The finger of God
s Tablets written by the finger of God (Exod. 31:18); this is the finger of God (Exod. 8:19); if I cast out demons by the finger of God (Luke 11:20).

● Laying on of hands
t Laying hands on the head of the sacrificial animal (Exod. 29:10, 15, 19; Lev. 1:4; 3:2, 8, 13; 4:4, 15, 24, 29, 33; 8:14, 18, 22; 16:21; Num. 8:12; 2 Chr. 29:23).

u Instructions about the laying on of hands (Heb. 6:2).

● Hands laid on to commission
v The Israelites laid hands on the Levites (Num. 8:10); Moses laid hands on Joshua (Num. 27:18, 23); the apostles laid hands on the seven (Acts 6:6); the leaders of the church in Antioch laid hands on Barnabas and Paul (Acts 13:3); a gift given to Timothy through the laying on of hands (1 Tim. 4:14; 2 Tim. 1:6); do not lay hands on anyone hastily (1 Tim. 5:22).

● Hands laid on for the Holy Spirit
w Joshua was filled with the spirit of wisdom because Moses laid his hands on him (Deut. 34:9); Peter and John laid hands on the Samaritans and they received the Holy Spirit (Acts 8:17–19); Ananias laid hands on Saul (Acts 9:12, 17); Paul laid hands on the Ephesians and they received the Holy Spirit (Acts 19:6).

● Hands laid on to heal
x Jesus laid hands on: a blind man (Mark 8:23); his eyes (Mark 8:25); the woman bent double (Luke 13:13); a few sick people (Mark 6:5); every one of the sick (Luke 4:40).

y They begged him to lay his hands on him (Mark 7:32); lay your hands on her (Matt. 9:18; Mark 5:23).

z They will lay hands on the sick and they will recover (Mark 16:18); Paul prayed and laid hands on Publius' father (Acts 28:8).

● Hands laid on to condemn
aa Witnesses laid hands on the head of the blasphemer (Lev. 24:14).

379 Heat

● Hot weather
a The south wind brings heat (Job 37:17); cold and heat will not cease (Gen. 8:22); sitting at the tent door in the heat of the day (Gen. 18:1); in the heat of the day Ishbosheth rested (2 Sam. 4:5); by day the heat consumed me (Gen. 31:40); we have borne the scorching heat (Matt. 20:12); God appointed a scorching east wind (Jonah 4:8); by the time the sun is hot you will be saved (1 Sam. 11:9).

b The sun will not beat on them (Rev. 7:16).

● Hot things

c The furnace was made seven times hotter (Dan. 3:19); a smouldering wick he will not extinguish (Isa. 42:3; Matt. 12:20).

380 Cold

● Cold weather

a Cold and heat will not cease (Gen. 8:22); out of the north comes cold (Job 37:9).

b Who has given birth to ice and frost? (Job 38:29–30); God's breath makes ice (Job 37:10); who can stand before his cold? (Ps. 147:17); God scatters frost like ashes (Ps. 147:16); he destroyed their trees with frost (Ps. 78:47).

c Frost by night (Gen. 31:40); it was cold (John 18:18; Acts 28:2); killing a lion on a snowy day (2 Sam. 23:20; 1 Chr. 11:22); in cold and exposure (2 Cor. 11:27); David could not keep warm (1 Kgs. 1:1).

Cold of snow, see **382***a*.

● Cool of the day

d God walked in the garden in the cool of the day (Gen. 3:8); a cool roof chamber (Judg. 3:20); until the cool of the day (S. of S. 2:17; 4:6).

● Cold things

e You are lukewarm, neither cold nor hot (Rev. 3:15–16).

381 Heating

● Fire in general

a As the sparks fly upward (Job 5:7); you who kindle a fire, walk by the light of your fire (Isa. 50:11).

b The tongue is a fire, set on fire by hell (Jas. 3:5–6); the beast made fire come down from heaven (Rev. 13:13); can a man take fire in his bosom and his clothes not be burned? (Prov. 6:27–8); wickedness burns like a fire (Isa. 9:18).

c By faith they quenched the power of fire (Heb. 11:34); when you walk through the fire you will not be burned (Isa. 43:2).

d Fire and smoke come from the crocodile's mouth (Job 41:19–21).

● Burning cities

e Cities being burned (Num. 31:10; Deut. 13:16; Josh. 6:24; 8:8, 19, 28; 11:11; Judg. 20:38, 48); your cities are burned (Isa. 1:7); the city of Laish was burnt (Judg. 18:27); the Amalekites had burnt Ziklag (1 Sam. 30:1, 3, 14); Pharaoh burned Gezer (1 Kgs. 9:16); the towns of the Ammonites will be set on fire (Jer. 49:2); I will set fire to the wall of Damascus (Jer. 49:27); they did not burn cities on their mounds (Josh. 11:13); they set on fire the tower of Shechem (Judg. 9:49); Abimelech tried to burn the door of the tower (Judg. 9:52); they burned their chariots (Josh. 11:6, 9).

● Burning Jerusalem

f Jerusalem was burnt (Judg. 1:8); the Chaldeans will set this city on fire (Jer. 32:29; 34:2, 22; 37:8, 10; 38:18, 23); burn a third of the hair at the centre of the city (Ezek. 5:1–2); the gates of Jerusalem have been burned (Neh. 2:17); he set fire to the royal palace (Jer. 39:8).

g He set fire to the temple of the Lord (2 Kgs. 25:9; 2 Chr. 36:19;

Jer. 52:13); our holy and beautiful house has been burned (Isa. 64:11); they burned your sanctuary (Ps. 74:7); they burned all the meeting places (Ps. 74:8).

● Burning idols

h Moses burned the calf (Exod. 32:20); burn their graven images (Deut. 7:5, 25); burn their Asherim (Deut. 12:3); David burned the Philistines' gods (1 Chr. 14:12); Asa burned the Asherah (1 Kgs. 15:13; 2 Chr. 15:16); Josiah burned the Asherah (2 Kgs. 23:6); they have cast their gods into the fire (2 Kgs. 19:18); burning the pillar of the house of Baal (2 Kgs. 10:26); they burnt the vessels made for Baal (2 Kgs. 23:4); the chariots of the sun burned (2 Kgs. 23:11); human bones would be burned on the altar (1 Kgs. 13:2; 2 Kgs. 23:16); the ashes were poured out (1 Kgs. 13:3, 5); the temples of the gods of Egypt will be burned (Jer. 43:12).

● Burning people

i If a priest's daughter becomes a prostitute she must be burned (Lev. 21:9); let fire consume Abimelech and his followers (Judg. 9:15, 20); we will burn your house down on you (Judg. 12:1); we will burn you and your house (Judg. 14:15); Zimri burned the king's house over himself (1 Kgs. 16:18); they burned her and her father (Judg. 15:6); they burned the bodies of Saul and his sons (1 Sam. 31:12); they burned Achan's family (Josh. 7:15, 25); Zedekiah and Ahab whom the king of Babylon roasted in the fire (Jer. 29:22).

● Burning things

j Fire burning grain or field (Exod. 22:6); Samson used foxes to set fire to the grain (Judg. 15:4–5); Joab's field was set on fire (2 Sam. 14:30); the plants on rocky ground were scorched (Matt. 13:6; Mark 4:6); how great a forest is kindled by a small fire! (Jas. 3:5); Jehoiakim burned Jeremiah's scroll (Jer. 36:22–3).

● Purifying by fire

k Metal objects should be purified by fire (Num. 31:22–3); gold is tested by fire (1 Pet. 1:7); a seraph flew with a burning coal and touched my mouth (Isa. 6:6–7).

● Funeral fires

l A large fire was made for Asa's funeral (2 Chr. 16:14); they did not make a fire for Jehoram (2 Chr. 21:19).

● Baking and cooking

m Baking unleavened bread (Exod. 12:39); Tamar baked cakes for Amnon (2 Sam. 13:8); the cake to be baked on dung (Ezek. 4:12); a charcoal fire with fish and bread on it (John 21:9); roasted ears of grain (Lev. 2:14); eat the lamb roasted (Exod. 12:8–9); bake or boil the manna (Exod. 16:23); boiling manna (Num. 11:8); places for baking and boiling the offerings (Ezek. 46:20–4); do not boil a kid in its mother's milk (Exod. 23:19; 34:26; Deut. 14:21); compassionate women boil their own children (Lam. 4:10).

n Baking bricks (Gen. 11:3).

● God as fire

o Our God is a consuming fire (Deut. 4:24; 9:3; Heb. 12:29); the light of Israel will become a fire (Isa. 10:17); I will be a wall of fire around Jerusalem (Zech. 2:5); his appearance was like fire (Ezek. 1:27; 8:2); smoke from his nostrils and fire from his mouth (2 Sam. 22:9; Ps. 18:8); a river of fire streamed from him (Dan. 7:10); the Lord has burned in Jacob like a flaming fire (Lam. 2:3); lest the Lord break out like a fire (Amos 5:6).

● Fire depicting
God

p   A firepot and a flaming torch (Gen. 15:17); God appeared in a burning bush (Exod. 3:2–3; Acts 7:30); the Lord descended on Mount Sinai in fire (Exod. 19:18; 24:17); the mountain burned with fire (Deut. 4:11; 9:15); fire ran down to the earth (Exod. 9:23, 24); the Lord will come in fire (Isa. 66:15); the Holy Spirit came with tongues of fire (Acts 2:3).

q   A pillar of fire by night (Exod. 13:21; Neh. 9:12, 19); cloud by day and fire by night (Num. 14:14; Deut. 1:33; Ps. 78:14; 105:39; Isa. 4:5); fire in the cloud at night (Exod. 40:38; Num. 9:15–16); as fire causes water to boil (Isa. 64:2); his throne blazed with fire (Dan. 7:9); in the midst of the creatures were coals of fire (Ezek. 1:13); the Lord spoke from the fire (Deut. 4:12; 5:4, 22, 24; 9:10; 10:4); you heard his words from the fire (Deut. 4:36); who can live with the consuming fire? (Isa. 33:14); you [Tyre] walked in the midst of the stones of fire (Ezek. 28:14); removed from the stones of fire (Ezek. 28:16).

r   The Lord was not in the fire (1 Kgs. 19:12).

● Fire from
God

s   A sea of glass mixed with fire (Rev. 15:2); God makes flame and fire his servants (Ps. 104:4); he makes his ministers a flame of fire (Heb. 1:7); cherubim with a flaming sword (Gen. 3:24).

t   Fire from the Lord burned up the offering (Lev. 9:24; Judg. 6:21; 1 Kgs. 18:38; 1 Chr. 21:26; 2 Chr. 7:1); the fire of God burned up Job's sheep and servants (Job 1:16); I will send fire upon Magog (Ezek. 39:6); fire devours before God (Ps. 50:3); from God's brightness coals were kindled (2 Sam. 22:13; Ps. 18:12); fire from heaven consumed them (2 Kgs. 1:10, 12, 14; Rev. 20:9); do you want us to call down fire from heaven? (Luke 9:54); fire from the Lord burned among them (Lev. 10:2; Num. 11:1–3); a fire is kindled in my anger (Deut. 32:22); the God who answers by fire (1 Kgs. 18:24); a chariot of fire and horses of fire (2 Kgs. 2:11); Israel will be a flame and Edom stubble (Obad. 18).

● Fire of
judgement

u   The worthless will be burned like thorns (2 Sam. 23:7); fire consumes the wicked (Ps. 106:18); the Lord will send judgement by fire (Amos 1:4, 7, 10, 12, 14; 2:2, 5; 7:4); God will rain fire and brimstone on the wicked (Ps. 11:6); God's anger will be seen in devouring fire (Isa. 30:30); in flaming fire taking vengeance (2 Thess. 1:7–8); everyone will be salted with fire (Mark 9:49); he will swallow up your enemies with fire (Ps. 21:9); fire goes before him and burns up his enemies (Ps. 97:3).

v   The Lord rained fire and sulphur on Sodom and Gomorrah (Gen. 19:24); the king set their city on fire (Matt. 22:7); I am about to kindle a fire in you (Ezek. 20:47–8); fire consumed 250 men

(Num. 16:35); Edom's land will become burning pitch and sulphur (Isa. 34:9).

w I have come to cast fire on the earth (Luke 12:49); when the Lord Jesus is revealed in flaming fire (2 Thess. 1:7); a fearful expectation of judgement and fire (Heb. 10:27).

x The heavens and earth are reserved for fire (2 Pet. 3:7); the heavens will be burned up and the elements melt (2 Pet. 3:12); the sun scorched people with fire (Rev. 16:8); a third of the earth, trees and grass were burned up (Rev. 8:7).

y Scattering coals from among the cherubim (Ezek. 10:2–7); coals of broom for the deceitful tongue (Ps. 120:4); may burning coals fall on them (Ps. 140:10); fire from the altar was cast on the earth (Rev. 8:5); the temple was filled with smoke (Rev. 15:8).

z God's word is a fire (Jer. 5:14; 20:9; 23:29); fire comes from the mouth of the witnesses (Rev. 11:5); each man's work will be revealed with fire (1 Cor. 3:13–15); baptism with the Holy Spirit and with fire (Matt. 3:11).

● Burning the unfruitful

aa He will burn the chaff with unquenchable fire (Matt. 3:12; Luke 3:17); evildoers will be set on fire like stubble (Mal. 4:1); tie the weeds in bundles to be burned (Matt. 13:30); as the tares are burned so it will be at the end of the age (Matt. 13:40); every unfruitful tree is thrown into the fire (Matt. 3:10); unfruitful branches are burned up (John 15:6); land bearing thorns and thistles will be burned (Heb. 6:8).

● Fire of hell

ab The angels will throw the wicked into the furnace (Matt. 13:50); to be thrown into the eternal fire of hell (Matt. 18:8–9).

ac The beast and false prophet were thrown into the lake of fire (Rev. 19:20); with the devil (Rev. 20:10); those whose names were not in the book of life were thrown into the lake of fire (Rev. 20:15); the lake of fire is the second death (Rev. 20:14; 21:8); worshippers of the beast will be tormented with fire and brimstone (Rev. 14:10).

ad The hell of fire (Matt. 5:22); hell, the unquenchable fire (Mark 9:43); their fire will not be quenched (Isa. 66:24); where their fire is not quenched (Mark 9:48).

Hell of fire, see **972a**.

● Saved from fire

ae Snatch some out of the fire (Jude 23); you were like a brand plucked from the burning (Amos 4:11); is this not a brand plucked from the fire? (Zech. 3:2); we went through fire and water (Ps. 66:12).

● Burning sacrifices

af Abraham took fire for the sacrifice (Gen. 22:6–7); burn the sin offering outside the camp (Exod. 29:14); fire for burning the sacrifice (Lev. 1:7); the fire must burn continuously on the altar (Lev. 6:13); a pan of coals for the incense (Lev. 16:12); Nadab and Abihu offered unauthorised fire (Lev. 10:1; Num. 3:4; 26:61).

ag The angel ascended in the flame from the altar (Judg. 13:20).

ah The ashes are to be taken to a clean place (Lev. 6:11); the ashes of a red heifer (Num. 19:9–10, 17).

ai Burn remainder of: the passover lamb (Exod. 12:10); the ram of ordination (Exod. 29:34; Lev. 8:32); the peace offering (Lev. 7:17; 19:6–7).

aj The priests' portion had been burned (Lev. 10:16).

ak Burning children as sacrifices (Deut. 12:31; 18:10; 2 Kgs. 21:6; 2 Chr. 28:3; 33:6; Jer. 7:31; 19:5).

al Ahaz made his son pass through the fire (2 Kgs. 16:3); they made their children pass through the fire (2 Kgs. 17:17, 31); Josiah defiled Topheth so it could not be used for making children pass through the fire (2 Kgs. 23:10).
Sacrifices, see **981***h*.

- Warming

am Do not light your fire on the sabbath (Exod. 35:3); they lit a fire (Luke 22:55; Acts 28:2); Peter warmed himself at the fire (Mark 14:54, 67; John 18:18, 25); I am warm, I have seen the fire (Isa. 44:15–16); be warmed and filled! (Jas. 2:16).

an A virgin to keep David warm (1 Kgs. 1:2); if two lie together they keep warm (Eccles. 4:11).

382 Refrigeration

- Cold of snow

a Like the cold of snow at harvest time is a faithful messenger (Prov. 25:13); she is not afraid of snow for her household is clothed in scarlet (Prov. 31:21).

- Cooling

b The rich man wanted Lazarus to cool his tongue (Luke 16:24).

383 Furnace

- Furnaces

a A furnace is for gold (Prov. 17:3; 27:21); as they melt metals in the furnace (Ezek. 22:20, 22)

b Whoever does not worship will be cast into a fiery furnace (Dan. 3:6, 11, 15); cast into the fiery furnace (Dan. 3:19–23); evildoers will be cast into the fiery furnace (Matt. 13:42); the day comes, burning like a furnace (Mal. 4:1); the smoke went up as from a furnace (Gen. 19:28).

c Out of the iron furnace of Egypt (Deut. 4:20; 1 Kgs. 8:51; Jer. 11:4); the Lord's furnace is in Jerusalem (Isa. 31:9).

- Oven

d Like an oven neglected by the baker (Hos. 7:4); they are hot as an oven (Hos. 7:6–7); our skin is hot as an oven from the heat of famine (Lam. 5:10).

384 Refrigerator

Cooling, see **382***b*.

385 Fuel

- Firewood

a Abraham took wood for the sacrifice (Gen. 22:3, 6–7); wood on the fire (Lev. 1:7); pile wood under the pot (Ezek. 24:5); a widow gathering sticks (1 Kgs. 17:10, 12); Paul gathered a bundle of sticks and put them on the fire (Acts 28:3).

b The Asherah was used as fuel for the altar (Judg. 6:26); the cart was used as fuel for the altar (1 Sam. 6:14); threshing sledges and yokes used for fuel (2 Sam. 24:22; 1 Chr. 21:23); Elijah boiled the oxen with the implements (1 Kgs. 19:21); using the wood of the vine for fuel (Ezek. 15:4–6).

c The Gibeonites became hewers of wood (Josh. 9:21, 23, 27); casting lots for the people to bring firewood (Neh. 10:34); Nehemiah provided for the supply of wood (Neh. 13:31); the wood we get must be paid for (Lam. 5:4).

d Lebanon would not suffice for fuel (Isa. 40:16).

e For lack of wood the fire goes out (Prov. 26:20); a contentious man is like fuel to a fire (Prov. 26:21); the strong man will become tinder (Isa. 1:31); I will make this people the wood (Jer. 5:14); you will be fuel for the fire (Ezek. 21:32).

- Dung for fuel

f The cake to be baked on human dung (Ezek. 4:12); or cow's dung (Ezek. 4:15).

- Weapons for fuel

g Weapons will be used for fuel (Ezek. 39:9–10); every warrior's boot and bloody cloak will be fuel (Isa. 9:5).

- Sulphur

h It rained fire and brimstone on Sodom and Gomorrah (Gen. 19:24; Luke 17:29); the land will be brimstone and salt (Deut. 29:23); its streams will be turned into pitch and its soil brimstone (Isa. 34:9); the breath of the Lord is like a stream of brimstone (Isa. 30:33); I will rain hailstones, fire and brimstone on him (Ezek. 38:22).

386 Taste

- Flavour

a The manna tasted like wafers made with honey (Exod. 16:31); like cakes baked with oil (Num. 11:8); Moab's taste remains in him (Jer. 48:11).

- Tasting

b The steward tasted the water become wine (John 2:9); the ear tastes words as the palate tastes food (Job 12:11; 34:3).

c Those who have tasted the heavenly gift (Heb. 6:4); those who have tasted the good word of God (Heb. 6:5); taste and see that the Lord is good (Ps. 34:8); tasting the kindness of the Lord (1 Pet. 2:3).

d 'Do not taste' (Col. 2:21).

387 Insipidness

- Tasteless

a If salt has become tasteless (Matt. 5:13; Mark 9:50; Luke 14:34–5); can something tasteless be eaten without salt? (Job 6:6).

- Unable to taste

b Barzillai could no longer taste his food (2 Sam. 19:35).

388 Pungency

● Salt

   a Lot's wife became a pillar of salt (Gen. 19:26); the land brimstone and salt (Deut. 29:23); Abimelech sowed Shechem with salt (Judg. 9:45); Elisha threw salt into the spring (2 Kgs. 2:20–2); salt water cannot yield fresh (Jas. 3:12).

   b The salt of the covenant on cereal offerings (Lev. 2:13); an everlasting covenant of salt (Num. 18:19; 2 Chr. 13:5).

   c The oxen and donkeys will eat salted fodder (Isa. 30:24); can something tasteless be eaten without salt? (Job 6:6).

   d You are the salt of the earth (Matt. 5:13); have salt in yourselves (Mark 9:50); let your speech be seasoned with salt (Col. 4:6).

● Smoke

   e The smoke went up as from a furnace (Gen. 19:28); the smoke of Ai went up (Josh. 8:20–1); a column of smoke from Gibeah was the signal (Judg. 20:38–40); the mountain smoking (Exod. 20:18); smoke went up from the abyss (Rev. 9:2); its smoke will go up for ever (Isa. 34:10); the smoke from her goes up for ever (Rev. 19:3); the smoke of their torment goes up for ever (Rev. 14:11).

   f I am like a wineskin in the smoke (Ps. 119:83).

   g The temple was filled with smoke (Isa. 6:4).

389 Condiment

Salt, see **388a**.

390 Savouriness

● Savoury food

   a Savoury food such as I love (Gen. 27:4, 7, 9, 14, 17, 31); the words of a whisperer are like tasty morsels (Prov. 18:8). **Sweetness**, see **392**.

391 Unsavouriness

● Bitter food

   a Eat the lamb with bitter herbs (Exod. 12:8; Num. 9:11); they gave me gall for my food (Ps. 69:21); the scroll will make your stomach bitter (Rev. 10:9–10); to a hungry man the bitter is sweet (Prov. 27:7).

   b I will feed them with wormwood (Jer. 9:15; 23:15); he has filled me with bitterness and wormwood (Lam. 3:19).

● Bitter water

   c Marah, bitter water (Exod. 15:23); wormwood made the waters bitter (Rev. 8:11); the water of bitterness (Num. 5:18, 23–4, 27); does a fountain give both sweet water and bitter? (Jas. 3:11).

● Bitterness of heart

   d Call me Mara for the Lord has dealt bitterly (Ruth 1:20); their soul was bitter (1 Sam. 30:6); God has made my soul bitter (Job 27:2); when my heart was bitter (Ps. 73:21); remember the wormwood and bitterness (Lam. 3:19).

   e A root bearing poison and wormwood (Deut. 29:18); their grapes are bitter (Deut. 32:32); the gall of bitterness (Acts 8:23); that no root of bitterness spring up (Heb. 12:15); it is evil and bitter for you to forsake the Lord (Jer. 2:19); those who turn justice into wormwood (Amos 5:7; 6:12); their mouth is full of cursing and bitterness (Rom. 3:14); more bitter than death is a woman who ensnares (Eccles. 7:26); the adulteress in the end is bitter as wormwood (Prov. 5:4).

f The bitterness of death is past (1 Sam. 15:32); put away all bitterness (Eph. 4:31).

392 Sweetness

● Honey

a Take some honey (Gen. 43:11); take a jar of honey (1 Kgs. 14:3); bees and honey in the carcase of the lion (Judg. 14:8); Samson and his parents ate the honey (Judg. 14:9); honey on the floor of the forest (1 Sam. 14:25–9); Jonathan tasted the honey (1 Sam. 14:27, 29, 43); the manna was like wafers with honey (Exod. 16:31); John the baptist ate locusts and wild honey (Matt. 3:4; Mark 1:6).

b He fed them honey from the rock (Deut. 32:13); with honey from the rock I would satisfy you (Ps. 81:16).

c Your lips drip honey (S. of S. 4:11); the lips of an adulteress drip honey (Prov. 5:3).

d Honey was not to be used in a burnt offering (Lev. 2:11).

e It is not good to eat too much honey (Prov. 25:27); do not eat too much honey lest you vomit it (Prov. 25:16); a sated man loathes honey (Prov. 27:7).

Flowing with milk and honey, see **635d.**

● Sweet

f Out of the strong came something sweet (Judg. 14:14); the fig tree would not leave its sweetness to reign (Judg. 9:11).

g What is sweeter than honey? (Judg. 14:18); honey is sweet, like wisdom (Prov. 24:13–14); pleasant words are a honeycomb (Prov. 16:24); your words are sweeter than honey (Ps. 19:10; 119:103); the scroll was sweet as honey (Ezek. 3:3; Rev. 10:9–10).

h The waters became sweet (Exod. 15:25); the waters of the sea became fresh (Ezek. 47:8); does a fountain give both sweet and bitter water? (Jas. 3:11).

i Evil is sweet in his mouth (Job 20:12).

393 Sourness

● Vinegar

a They offered Christ vinegar to drink (Matt. 27:48; Mark 15:36; Luke 23:36; John 19:29–30); they gave me vinegar to drink (Ps. 69:21).

b Undue cheerfulness is like vinegar on soda (Prov. 25:20).

● Sour grapes

c The fathers have eaten sour grapes (Ezek. 18:2).

394 Odour

● Smelling
● Sense of smell

a Isaac smelled his son's garments (Gen. 27:27).

b If all were hearing, where would be the sense of smell? (1 Cor. 12:17).

395 Odourlessness

● Unable   *a* Idols cannot smell (Deut. 4:28); idols have noses but cannot
to smell   smell (Ps. 115:6).

396 Fragrance

● Perfumed   *a* The perfumed anointing oil (Exod. 30:22–33); spices for the
anointing oil   anointing oil (Exod. 25:6; 35:8); your oils are fragrant (S. of S.
                1:3).

● Incense   *b* The holy incense (Exod. 25:6; 30:34–8; 31:11; 35:8, 15, 28;
37:29; 39:38); Eleazar looked after the incense (Num. 4:16);
incense burnt on the gold altar (Exod. 40:27); morning and
evening (Exod. 30:7–9); and when making atonement (Lev.
16:12–13; Num. 16:46); incense on the grain offering (Lev. 2:1,
15–16; 6:15); frankincense on the 12 loaves (Lev. 24:7); no
incense on a sin offering (Lev. 5:11); nor on grain offering of
jealousy (Num. 5:15); gold pans full of incense (Num. 7:14, 20,
26, 32, 38, 44, 50, 56, 62, 68, 74, 80, 86).

            c Only priests could burn incense (Num. 16:40; 1 Sam. 2:28;
1 Chr. 23:13); some Levites looked after it (1 Chr. 9:29–30);
Zacharias was chosen by lot to burn incense (Luke 1:9); a temple
in which to burn incense (2 Chr. 2:4).

● Incense   *d* Golden bowls of incense which are the prayers of the saints (Rev.
and prayer   5:8); incense was mixed with the prayers of the saints (Rev.
8:3–4); may my prayer be as incense (Ps. 141:2); people praying
at the hour of incense (Luke 1:10).

● Incense   *e* Korah and his men were to present incense to test whom God
offered amiss   had chosen (Num. 16:6–7, 17–18); their censers made into plates
for the altar (Num. 16:37–9); Uzziah entered the temple to burn
incense (2 Chr. 26:16).

            f Solomon burned incense at the high places (1 Kgs. 3:3); Jero-
boam burned incense on the altar (1 Kgs. 12:33; 13:1); Solomon's wives burned incense to their gods (1 Kgs. 11:8); Ahaz
burned incense in the valley of Ben-hinnom (2 Chr. 28:3); offering incense to idols (Ezek. 8:11).

            g I will cut down your incense altars (Lev. 26:30); Asa removed
the incense altars (2 Chr. 14:5).

● Aroma of   *h* Sacrifices are a pleasant aroma to God (Gen. 8:21; Exod. 29:18,
sacrifices   25, 41; Lev. 1:9; 6:21; 8:21, 28; 17:6; 23:13; Num. 15:3, 13, 14,
24; 18:17; 28:2, 8, 13, 24; 29:2, 6, 8, 13, 36); the sacrifice of
Christ is a fragrant aroma (Eph. 5:2); the gifts you sent are a
fragrant aroma, an acceptable sacrifice (Phil. 4:18); he spreads
the aroma of the knowledge of Christ (2 Cor. 2:14).

            i I will not smell your pleasant aromas (Lev. 26:31).

● Perfume   *j* An alabaster jar of expensive perfume (Matt. 26:7; Mark 14:3;
and spices   Luke 7:37–8; John 11:2; 12:3); while the king was at his table
my perfume gave out its fragrance (S. of S. 1:12); let its fragrance be wafted abroad (S. of S. 4:16).

k The smell of Esau's garments was like a field blessed by the Lord (Gen. 27:27); your garments are fragrant as myrrh, aloes and cassia (Ps. 45:8); the fragrance of your garments is like Lebanon (S. of S. 4:11).

l My beloved is a bag of myrrh (S. of S. 1:13); my beloved is a cluster of henna blossoms (S. of S. 1:14); perfumed with myrrh and frankincense (S. of S. 3:6); to the mountains of myrrh and incense (S. of S. 4:6); the finest spices (S. of S. 4:13–14); my hands dripped with myrrh (S. of S. 5:5); I have sprinkled my bed with myrrh, aloes and cinnamon (Prov. 7:17); six months of myrrh and six months spices (Esther 2:12).

m Gum, balm and myrrh (Gen. 37:25; 43:11); the Queen of Sheba brought a large quantity of spices (1 Kgs. 10:2, 10; 2 Chr. 9:1, 9).

n They will bring gold and frankincense (Isa. 60:6); gold, frankincense and myrrh were given to Jesus (Matt. 2:11); they offered him wine mixed with myrrh (Mark 15:23); they brought the spices (Luke 24:1); spices were prepared to anoint Jesus' body (Mark 16:1; Luke 23:56); Nicodemus and Joseph wrapped his body with the spices (John 19:39–40); Asa was buried with spices (2 Chr. 16:14).

397 Stench

● Stink

a Dead flies make the perfumer's oil stink (Eccles. 10:1); Egypt's canals will stink (Isa. 19:6); their fish stink for lack of water (Isa. 50:2); the piles of dead frogs stank (Exod. 8:14); I made the stench of your camp rise in your nostrils (Amos 4:10); Lazarus, dead for four days, would stink (John 11:39); the stench of their corpses will rise (Isa. 34:3).

398 Sound

● Noise

a The sound of the cherubim's wings (Ezek. 1:24; 3:13; 10:5).

399 Silence

● Quiet

a Silence in heaven for about half an hour (Rev. 8:1).
Silenced, see **578d**.

400 Loudness

● Noisy

a The laughter of fools is like the crackling of thorns (Eccles. 7:6); a noisy gong or clanging cymbal (1 Cor. 13:1).

401 Faintness

Whisper, see **578i**.

402 Bang: sudden and violent noise

See **400**.

403 Roar

● Lion's roar

a The lion has roared (Amos 3:8); does a lion roar without prey? (Amos 3:4); the Lord will roar like a lion (Hos. 11:10); the Lord roars from Zion (Joel 3:16; Amos 1:2); a loud voice like a lion roaring (Rev. 10:3).

b The devil is like a roaring lion (1 Pet. 5:8).

● Roar of nations

c The roar of nations is like the roar of many waters (Isa. 17:12–13).

404 Resonance
Roar, see **403**.

405 Nonresonance

406 Sibilation: hissing sound

407 Stridor: harsh sound
See **400**.

408 Human cry
Voice, see **577**.

409 Animal sounds

● Barking and howling

a Not even a dog will bark against Israel (Exod. 11:7); they howl like a dog (Ps. 59:6, 14).

● Lowing and bleating

b The cows lowed as they went (1 Sam. 6:12); what is this bleating and lowing? (1 Sam. 15:14).

● Crowing

c Before the cock crows you will deny me (Matt. 26:34; 26:75; Mark 14:30, 72; Luke 22:34, 61; John 13:38); the cock crowed (Matt. 26:74; Mark 14:72; Luke 22:60; John 18:27).

410 Melody: concord
Music, see **412**; **concord**, see **710**.

411 Discord
Dissension, see **709**.

412 Music

● Music to celebrate

a The sound of singing in the camp (Exod. 32:18); rejoicing with singing and instrumental music (1 Sam. 18:6; 1 Chr. 13:8); the elder brother heard music and dancing (Luke 15:25); Joab heard the trumpet (1 Kgs. 1:41); tambourines and dancing (Judg. 11:34); playing flutes (1 Kgs. 1:40); I would have sent you away with joy and with songs (Gen. 31:27); we played for you and you did not dance (Luke 7:32).

b The music of musicians will never be heard again in Babylon (Rev. 18:22).

● Singing
praise

c Singing praise to the Lord (Judg. 5:1–3; 1 Chr. 16:23; Ezra 3:11; Ps. 13:6; 68:4, 32); I will sing praise (2 Sam. 22:50; Ps. 18:49); let the mountains sing before the Lord (Ps. 98:8–9); singing to the Lord (Exod. 15:1, 21; 2 Sam. 22:1; Ps. 18:t); let my tongue sing of your word (Ps. 119:172); my tongue will sing of your righteousness (Ps. 51:14).

d Sing with psalms, hymns and spiritual songs (Eph. 5:19; Col. 3:16); come before him with singing (Ps. 100:2); let each one have a psalm (1 Cor. 14:26); when they had sung a hymn they went out to the Mount of Olives (Matt. 26:30; Mark 14:26); Paul and Silas were singing hymns of praise in prison (Acts 16:25); the priest and Levites praised the Lord with loud music (2 Chr. 30:21).

e If anyone is cheerful he should sing praises (Jas. 5:13); sing praise to him! (1 Chr. 16:9).

● Songs

f They sang the song of Moses (Deut. 32:1–44; Rev. 15:3); write this song (Deut. 31:19–22); this song will be sung in Judah (Isa. 26:1); the song of the vineyard (Isa. 5:1–6); the song of the harlot (Isa. 23:15–16); the song of songs, which is Solomon's (S. of S. 1:1); you will have a song as in the night (Isa. 30:29).

g Sing to him a new song (Ps. 33:1–3; 96:1; 40:3; 98:1; 144:9; 149:1; Isa. 42:10); they sang a new song (Rev. 5:9; 14:3); shout joyfully with psalms (Ps. 95:2); your statutes are my songs (Ps. 119:54); I will sing with the spirit and sing with the mind (1 Cor. 14:15).

h Our captors demanded songs (Ps. 137:3); those who sing idle songs to the harp (Amos 6:5); they listen to you as to a love song (Ezek. 33:32).

i I will not listen to your songs (Amos 5:23).

● Psalm titles

j A psalm (Ps. 66:t; 67:t; 92:t; 98:t); a psalm for thanksgiving (Ps. 100:t).

k A psalm of David (Ps. 3:t; 4:t; 5:t; 6:t; 8:t; 9:t; 12:t; 13:t; 15:t; 19:t; 20:t; 21:t; 22:t; 23:t; 24:t; 29:t; 31:t; 38:t; 39:t; 40:t; 41:t; 51:t; 62:t; 63:t; 64:t; 65:t; 68:t; 101:t; 108:t; 109:t; 110:t; 139:t; 140:t; 141:t; 143:t); of David (Ps. 11:t; 14:t; 18:t; 25:t; 26:t; 27:t; 28:t; 30:t; 32:t; 34:t; 35:t; 36:t; 37:t; 61:t; 69:t; 70:t; 103:t; 122:t; 124:t; 131:t; 133:t; 138:t; 144:t; 145:t); a maskil of David (Ps. 52:t; 53:t; 54:t; 55:t; 142:t); a mikhtam of David (Ps. 16:t; 56:t; 57:t; 58:t; 59:t; 60:t); a shiggaion of David (Ps. 7:t).

l A psalm of the sons of Korah (Ps. 47:t; 48:t; 49:t; 84:t; 85:t; 87:t; 88:t); a maskil of the sons of Korah (Ps. 42:t; 44:t; 45:t); of the sons of Korah (Ps. 46:t).

m A psalm of Asaph (Ps. 50:t; 73:t; 75:t; 76:t; 77:t; 79:t; 80:t; 82:t; 83:t); a maskil of Asaph (Ps. 74:t; 78:t); of Asaph (Ps. 81:t).

n Of Solomon (Ps. 72:t; 127:t); a maskil of Ethan (Ps. 89:t); a maskil of Heman (Ps. 88:t).

o A song of ascents (Ps. 120:t; 121:t; 122:t; 123:t; 124:t; 125:t; 126:t; 127:t; 128:t; 129:t; 130:t; 131:t; 132:t; 133:t; 134:t). **Musician**, see **413**; **Musical Instruments**, see **414**.

413 Musician

● Singers

a Singers were appointed by David (1 Chr. 15:16); by Jehoshaphat (2 Chr. 20:21); by Nehemiah (Neh. 12:31); the singers (1 Chr. 9:33–4; 2 Chr. 35:15); leaders of the singers (Neh. 12:46); 200 singing men and women (Ezra 2:65); the children of Asaph were the temple singers (Neh. 11:22); the singers were assembled (Neh. 12:28–9); singers and musicians in procession (Ps. 68:25).

● Instrument-alists

b Jubal was the father of all who play the lyre and flute (Gen. 4:21).

c Let a skilful harp-player be found (1 Sam. 16:16–17); David, a skilful musician (1 Sam. 16:18); David played his harp before Saul (1 Sam. 16:23; 18:10; 19:9); Elisha called for someone to play the harp (2 Kgs. 3:15); the sound was like harpists playing on their harps (Rev. 14:2).

d Temple musicians were appointed (1 Chr. 6:31–48; 15:16, 19–20; 16:5–6, 42; 23:5; 25:1, 6–8; 2 Chr. 5:12–13; 29:25–6); the foremen were skilful musicians (2 Chr. 34:12).

e Flute-players at a funeral (Matt. 9:23).

● Composers

f David was the sweet psalmist of Israel (2 Sam. 23:1); Solomon made 1005 songs (1 Kgs. 4:32).

414 Musical instruments

● Making musical instruments

a Gold bells were made for the high priest's robe (Exod. 28:33; 39:25); two trumpets to be made of silver (Num. 10:2); seven trumpets of ram's horns (Josh. 6:4, 6, 8, 13); lyres and harps were made of algum wood (1 Kgs. 10:12; 2 Chr. 9:11); David made musical instruments for praising the Lord (2 Chr. 7:6).

● Musical instruments in worship

b Singing to God with tambourines (Exod. 15:20); with the harp (Ps. 98:5); with the ten-stringed harp (Ps. 33:2; 92:3; 144:9); with lyres, harps, tambourines, cymbals etc. (2 Sam. 6:5; 2 Chr. 20:28; Ps. 150:3–5); prophets with harp, tambourine, flute and lyre (1 Sam. 10:5); praising the Lord with trumpets and cymbals (Ezra 3:10); thanksgiving with cymbals, harps and lyres (Neh. 12:27); the 24 elders had harps (Rev. 5:8); harps of God in their hands (Rev. 15:2); we hung our harps on the willows (Ps. 137:2).

c Bringing up the ark with trumpet sound (2 Sam. 6:15); the Lord has ascended with the sound of a trumpet (Ps. 47:5); they made an oath to the Lord with trumpets and horns (2 Chr. 15:14).

d When you hear the musical instruments you must fall down and worship (Dan. 3:5, 7, 10, 15).

● Trumpets for signalling

e Musical instruments need to make distinct sounds (1 Cor. 14:7–8); if the trumpet gives an uncertain sound, who will prepare for battle? (1 Cor. 14:8); the war horse responds to the trumpet (Job 39:24–5); a voice like a trumpet (Rev. 1:10; 4:1); when you give alms, do not sound a trumpet (Matt. 6:2).

● Trumpets to summon

f The trumpet blown to summon the people by Ehud (Judg. 3:27); by Gideon (Judg. 6:34); by Saul (1 Sam. 13:3); by Sheba (2 Sam. 20:1); wherever you hear the sound of the trumpet, rally there (Neh. 4:18–20).

g The ram's horn sounded for them to go up the mountain (Exod. 19:13, 16, 19); the blast of a trumpet (Exod. 20:18; Heb. 12:19).

● Trumpets for warning

h The trumpet sounded as a warning of invasion (Hos. 5:8; Jer. 4:5); priests with trumpets to sound the alarm (2 Chr. 13:12, 14); trumpets for the alarm (Num. 31:6); the watchman sounds the trumpet (Ezek. 33:3, 6); put the trumpet to your lips (Hos. 8:1); if a trumpet is blown in a city will the people not tremble? (Amos 3:6); listen to the sound of the trumpet (Jer. 6:17).

● Trumpets for battle

i When you go into battle the priests should sound the trumpets (Num. 10:9); a day of trumpet blast and battle cry (Zeph. 1:16); the sound of the trumpet, the alarm of war (Jer. 4:19); blow the trumpet in Tekoa (Jer. 6:1); how long must I hear the sound of the trumpet? (Jer. 4:21); they have blown the trumpet but no one goes to battle (Ezek. 7:14).

j Circle Jericho with the priests blowing trumpets (Josh. 6:4, 8–9, 13, 16, 20); Gideon's men blew their trumpets (Judg. 7:18, 19–20, 22); the 300 men had trumpets (Judg. 7:8, 16).

k Joab sounded the trumpet for the troops to stop fighting (2 Sam. 2:28; 18:16; 20:22).

● Trumpets for celebration

l The trumpet to sound the year of Jubilee (Lev. 25:9); a day for blowing the trumpets (Num. 29:1); blow the trumpet to proclaim a solemn assembly (Joel 2:15); blow the trumpet at the new moon (Ps. 81:3).

m The trumpet was sounded for the coronation of: Absalom (2 Sam. 15:10); Solomon (1 Kgs. 1:34, 39); Jehu (2 Kgs. 9:13); Joash (2 Kgs. 11:14; 2 Chr. 23:13).

● Trumpets at the end

n A great trumpet will sound to gather the exiles (Isa. 27:13); with a loud trumpet call the angels will gather the elect (Matt. 24:31); as the alarm for the day of the Lord (Joel 2:1); at the last trumpet (1 Cor. 15:52); the Lord will descend with the trumpet of God (1 Thess. 4:16).

● Seven trumpets

o Seven angels with seven trumpets (Rev. 8:2); seven trumpets of ram's horns (Josh. 6:4, 6, 8, 13).

p Sounding: the first trumpet (Rev. 8:7); the second trumpet (Rev. 8:8); the third trumpet (Rev. 8:10); the fourth trumpet (Rev. 8:12); the fifth trumpet (Rev. 9:1); the sixth trumpet (Rev. 9:13); the seventh trumpet (Rev. 11:15).

415 Hearing

● Listening

a Sarah was listening at the tent door (Gen. 18:10); Rebekah was listening (Gen. 27:5); go down to the camp and hear what they say (Judg. 7:10–11).

Listen!, see **455*p***.

● Hearing

b He who planted the ear, does he not hear? (Ps. 94:9); God made hearing ears (Prov. 20:12); no one has heard or seen a God besides you (Isa. 64:4).

c Do not speak in the hearing of a fool (Prov. 23:9); when one hears but does not understand (Matt. 13:19).

d Bells so that Aaron might be heard (Exod. 28:35); when you hear the sound of marching (2 Sam. 5:24); the people heard David charge the commanders (2 Sam. 18:5, 12); Adonijah and his guests heard the rejoicing (1 Kgs. 1:41); Ahijah heard the sound of her feet (1 Kgs. 14:6); the Lord made the Arameans hear the sound of an army (2 Kgs. 7:6); Athaliah heard the sound of the coronation (2 Chr. 23:12); Herod the tetrarch heard about Jesus (Matt. 14:1); if the governor hears about this (Matt. 28:14).

e My ears you have dug (Ps. 40:6); your ears will hear a word behind you (Isa. 30:21); to listen is better than the sacrifice of fools (Eccles. 5:1); blessed are your ears, for they hear (Matt. 13:16); many desired to hear what you hear (Matt. 13:17).

f He who hears my words and does them (Matt. 7:24); he who hears my words and does not do them (Matt. 7:26); be doers of the word and not merely hearers (Jas. 1:22).

Pay attention, see **455**.

● Ears

g Blood on right ear (Exod. 29:20; Lev. 8:23–4; 14:14, 25); oil on right ear (Lev. 14:17, 28); the slave's ear is pierced at the doorpost (Exod. 21:6; Deut. 15:17); my ear you have pierced (Ps. 40:6); if the ear should say, 'I am not an eye' (1 Cor. 12:16).

h Jesus put his fingers in the man's ears (Mark 7:33); Peter cut off the ear of the high priest's slave (Matt. 26:51; Mark 14:47; Luke 22:50).

i The ears of all who hear it will tingle (1 Sam. 3:11; 2 Kgs. 21:12; Jer. 19:3).

Deaf ears, see **416*b***.

416 Deafness

● Deaf

a It is God who makes man deaf (Exod. 4:11); do not curse the deaf (Lev. 19:14); Barzillai was deaf (2 Sam. 19:35); who is deaf as my messenger? (Isa. 42:19).

● Unhearing

b Idols have ears but cannot hear (Ps. 115:6; 135:17); idols do not hear (Deut. 4:28); people who are deaf yet have ears (Isa. 43:8); he has shut their ears so that they cannot hear (Isa. 44:18); the deaf cobra which stops up its ears (Ps. 58:4–5); this people have ears but hear not (Jer. 5:21; Ezek. 12:2); hearing they do not hear (Matt. 13:13–14, 15; Mark 4:12); having ears, do you not hear? (Mark 8:18).

● Deaf hearing

c Hear, you deaf! (Isa. 42:18); the ears of the deaf will be unstopped (Isa. 35:5); the deaf shall hear the words of a book (Isa. 29:18); Jesus healed a deaf man (Mark 7:32–7); he makes the deaf hear (Mark 7:37); the deaf hear (Matt. 11:5; Luke 7:22).

417 Light

- About light

a Light is pleasant (Eccles. 11:7); where is the way to where light dwells? (Job 38:19); what fellowship has light with darkness? (2 Cor. 6:14).

- God is light

b God is light (1 John 1:5); the Lord is my light (Ps. 27:1); the Lord will be your everlasting light (Isa. 60:19–20); the Lord will be my light (Mic. 7:8).

c A flaming torch passed between the pieces (Gen. 15:17); from God's brightness fire was kindled (2 Sam. 22:13; Ps. 18:12); the light dwells with him (Dan. 2:22).

d I am the light of the world (John 8:12; 9:5); I have come as light into the world (John 12:46); light has come into the world (John 3:19); the light that lightens every man (John 1:9); the light of men (John 1:4); the true light is already shining (1 John 2:8); the light is with you for a little longer (John 12:35); his face shone like the sun (Matt. 17:2); the Lord make his face shine upon you (Num. 6:25).

e God dwells in unapproachable light (1 Tim. 6:16); covering yourself with light as with a cloak (Ps. 104:2).

f There was a light from heaven (Acts 9:3; 22:6; 26:13); light shone in the prison (Acts 12:7).

g The angel of the Lord was like lightning (Matt. 28:3).

h Evildoers hate the light (John 3:20).

- God gives light

i Let there be light (Gen. 1:3); God makes light and darkness (Isa. 45:7); the heavenly lights were to give light on the earth (Gen. 1:15); the Israelites had light (Exod. 10:23); the pillar of cloud brought light to Israel (Exod. 13:21; 14:20); a pillar of fire to light their way (Neh. 9:12); God has shone from Zion (Ps. 50:2); God gives light to both the poor and the oppressor (Prov. 29:13); in your light we see light (Ps. 36:9).

- Personal light

j God lights my darkness (2 Sam. 22:29; Ps. 18:28); lift up the light of your face upon us (Ps. 4:6); the Lord has given us light (Ps. 118:27); God will be their light (Rev. 22:5); continual day with light at evening (Zech. 14:7); by his light I walked (Job 29:3); let us walk in the light of the Lord (Isa. 2:5); those who walk in the light of your countenance (Ps. 89:15); our secret sins in the light of your countenance (Ps. 90:8).

k The commandment of the Lord enlightens the eyes (Ps. 19:8); let your light and truth lead me (Ps. 43:3); your word is a light to my path (Ps. 119:105); the entrance of your words gives light (Ps. 119:130).

l The Lord make his face to shine upon you (Num. 6:25); let your face shine on me (Ps. 31:16; 80:3, 7, 19; 119:135); may God make his face shine upon us (Ps. 67:1).

● From darkness to light

m The people who walked in darkness have seen a great light (Isa. 9:2; Matt. 4:16; Luke 1:79); the light shines in darkness (John 1:5); believe in the light to become sons of light (John 12:36); God who commanded light to shine out of darkness has shone in our hearts the light of the knowledge of God (2 Cor. 4:6); daylight from on high dawns on us (Luke 1:78); he called you out of darkness into his marvellous light (1 Pet. 2:9).

n A light to illuminate the Gentiles (Isa. 42:6; Luke 2:32; Acts 13:47); walk while you have light (John 12:35); he who follows me shall not walk in darkness (John 8:12); Christ would be the first to announce light (Acts 26:23); Paul was sent to turn them from darkness to light (Acts 26:18).

o He who does the truth comes to the light (John 3:21); he who walks in the day does not stumble because he sees this world's light (John 11:9); if we walk in the light as he is in the light we have fellowship (1 John 1:7); if the eye is good the whole body is full of light (Matt. 6:22; Luke 11:34–6).

● Light of God's people

p You are the light of the world (Matt. 5:14); nations will come to your light (Isa. 60:3); the just ruler is like the sunrise (2 Sam. 23:4); once you were darkness but now you are light in the Lord (Eph. 5:8); you are children of the light (1 Thess. 5:5); live as children of light, exhibiting the fruit of the light (Eph. 5:8–9); let your light shine before men (Matt. 5:16); shine, for your light has come (Isa. 60:1).

q Moses' face shone (Exod. 34:29, 35); a man's wisdom makes his face shine (Eccles. 8:1); those who are wise will shine like the sky (Dan. 12:3); the light of the righteous shines brightly (Prov. 13:9); the path of the righteous is like dawn, increasing in brightness (Prov. 4:18); the righteous will shine like the sun (Matt. 13:43); the earth was made bright with the angel's splendour (Rev. 18:1).

r Light dawns for the righteous (Ps. 97:11); then your light will break out like dawn (Isa. 58:8); your light will rise in darkness (Isa. 58:10); light rises in the darkness for the upright (Ps. 112:4); I will make darkness into light before them (Isa. 42:16); darkness would become brighter than noon (Job 11:17).

s You are sure you are a light to those in darkness (Rom. 2:19); take care that the light in you may not be darkness (Luke 11:35); the sons of this generation are wiser than the sons of light (Luke 16:8).

Lightning, see **176k**.

418 Darkness

● Darkness over the earth

a Darkness was upon the face of the deep (Gen. 1:2); God separated the light from the darkness (Gen. 1:4); you appoint darkness and it becomes night (Ps. 104:20).

b When the sun had set it was dark (Gen. 15:17); as it grew dark before the sabbath (Neh. 13:19); the land darkened with the locusts (Exod. 10:15); darkness over the land at the crucifixion (Matt. 27:45; Mark 15:33; Luke 23:44).

c The sun will be darkened and the moon not give light (Matt. 24:29; Mark 13:24; Acts 2:20); I will darken the earth at noon (Amos 8:9).

The sky darkened, see **321n**.

● Shadow

d The shadow of the mountains looks like men (Judg. 9:36); the shadow went back ten steps (2 Kgs. 20:8–11; Isa. 38:8); Jonah sat in the shade of the plant (Jonah 4:5–6); the mountains were covered with the vine's shadow (Ps. 80:10).

e My days are like a lengthened shadow (Ps. 102:11); I am gone like a lengthening shadow (Ps. 109:23).

Valley of the shadow of death, see **255l**.

f Abiding in the shadow of the Almighty (Ps. 91:1); he hid me in the shadow of his hand (Isa. 49:2); I have hidden you in the shadow of my hand (Isa. 51:16); the Lord is your shade (Ps. 121:5); you have been a shade from the heat (Isa. 25:4); the king and princes will be like the shade of a great rock (Isa. 32:2); they wanted Peter's shadow to fall on the sick (Acts 5:15).

g The Father of lights with whom is no shifting shadow (Jas. 1:17).

● God and darkness

h God makes light and darkness (Isa. 45:7); God made darkness his canopy (2 Sam. 22:12; Ps. 18:11); darkness under his feet (2 Sam. 22:10; Ps. 18:9); clouds and darkness are round him (Ps. 97:2); the day of the Lord is a day of darkness (Joel 2:2; Amos 5:18, 20); even the darkness is not dark to you (Ps. 139:12); God knows what is in darkness (Dan. 2:22); in God there is no darkness (1 John 1:5).

i He put darkness between you and the Egyptians (Josh. 24:7); the plague of darkness over Egypt (Exod. 10:21–3); God sent darkness (Ps. 105:28); God spoke from the darkness (Deut. 5:23); I will give you the treasures of darkness (Isa. 45:3).

● People in darkness

j Terror and darkness fell on Abraham (Gen. 15:12); he has brought me into darkness and not light (Lam. 3:2); he has made me dwell in darkness like those long dead (Lam. 3:6); we look for light, and behold, darkness (Isa. 59:9); while you look for light he makes it darkness (Jer. 13:16).

k Some dwelt in darkness and the shadow of death (Ps. 107:10); the land of darkness and death-shadow (Job 10:21–2); darkness and distress in the land (Isa. 5:30); darkness will cover the earth and the peoples (Isa. 60:2); night will fall on the prophets (Mic. 3:6); who among you walks in darkness and has no light? (Isa.

50:10); formerly you were in darkness (Eph. 5:8); the enemy has made me dwell in darkness like those long dead (Ps. 143:3).

● Darkness of evil

l The power of darkness (Luke 22:53); men loved darkness rather than light (John 3:19); when your eye is bad your whole body is full of darkness (Matt. 6:23; Luke 11:34); if the light in you is darkness, how great is the darkness! (Matt. 6:23); have nothing to do with the unfruitful deeds of darkness (Eph. 5:11); lay aside the deeds of darkness (Rom. 13:12); if we say we have fellowship with him and walk in darkness, we lie (1 John 1:6); he who hates his brother is in darkness (1 John 2:9, 11).

m Evildoers work in the dark (Job 24:13–17); the way of the wicked is like darkness (Prov. 4:19); they meet darkness in daytime (Job 5:14); the fool walks in darkness (Eccles. 2:14).

● Out of darkness

n Those who sat in darkness saw a great light (Isa. 9:2; Matt. 4:16); the light shines in the darkness (John 1:5); he has delivered us from the domain of darkness (Col. 1:13); God called you out of darkness (1 Pet. 2:9); he brought them out of darkness (Ps. 107:14); you are not in darkness (1 Thess. 5:4, 5).
From darkness to light, see **417*m***.

● Outer darkness

o They will be driven away into darkness (Isa. 8:22); thrown into outer darkness (Matt. 8:12; 22:13; 25:30); black darkness has been reserved for them (2 Pet. 2:17); those for whom darkness has been reserved for ever (Jude 13); angels in everlasting bonds in darkness (Jude 6); the kingdom of the beast was thrust into darkness (Rev. 16:10).

● Extinguishing

p They have put out the lamps (2 Chr. 29:7); a dimly burning wick he will not extinguish (Isa. 42:3; Matt. 12:20); horse and army are extinguished like a wick (Isa. 43:17); by faith they quenched fire (Heb. 11:34); do not quench the Spirit (1 Thess. 5:19).

q For lack of wood the fire goes out (Prov. 26:20); our lamps are going out (Matt. 25:8).

419 Dimness
Shadow, see **418*d***.

420 Light source

● Sun and moon

a God created lights in the sky (Gen. 1:14); God gave sun, moon and stars for light (Jer. 31:35); you established light and sun (Ps. 74:16); God makes his sun rise on good and bad (Matt. 5:45).

b The light of the moon will be as the sun and the sun seven times brighter (Isa. 30:26).

c No more sun and moon for light (Isa. 60:19–20; Rev. 21:23).

● Lamps

d A firepot and a flaming torch (Gen. 15:17); Gideon's men had torches in the pitchers (Judg. 7:16, 20); a woman lights a lamp and sweeps the house (Luke 15:8); Judas came with lanterns, torches and weapons (John 18:3); the jailer called for lights (Acts

16:29); there were many lamps where we were gathered (Acts 20:8).

e The lamp of the body is the eye (Matt. 6:22).

● The lampstand   *f* The gold lampstand: made (Exod. 25:31–40; 31:8; 35:14; 37:17–24; 39:37; Lev. 24:1–4; Heb. 9:2); set up (Exod. 40:4, 24–5; Num. 8:2–4); anointed (Exod. 30:29); looked after by the Kohathites (Num. 3:31).

g The lamp of God had not yet gone out (1 Sam. 3:3); the golden lampstand is lit every evening (2 Chr. 13:11).

● Various   *h* Ten gold lampstands for the temple (1 Kgs. 7:49; 2 Chr. 4:7,
  lampstands   20–1); Zechariah saw a gold lampstand (Zech. 4:2); the seven lampstands are the seven churches (Rev. 1:12–13, 20; 2:1, 5); these are the two olive trees and the two lampstands (Rev. 11:4); a lampstand for Elisha (2 Kgs. 4:10).

● God is   *i* You are my lamp, O Lord (2 Sam. 22:29); seven lamps which
  a light   are the seven spirits of God (Rev. 4:5); the Father of lights (Jas. 1:17); no need of sun or moon in the city, for the Lamb is its lamp (Rev. 21:23); no need of lamp or sun, for God will give them light (Rev. 22:5); his face was like the sun shining in its strength (Rev. 1:16); the sun of righteousness will rise (Mal. 4:2); I have prepared a lamp for my anointed (Ps. 132:17).

● The word   *j* Your word is a lamp to my feet (Ps. 119:105); the commandment
  is a light   is a lamp (Prov. 6:23); a lamp shining in a dark place (2 Pet. 1:19).

● The light   *k* You light my lamp (Ps. 18:28); you appear as lights in the world
  of people   (Phil. 2:15); a lamp should not be put into a measure (Matt. 5:15; Mark 4:21; Luke 8:16; 11:33); John was a shining lamp (John 5:35); do not put out the lamp of God's people (2 Sam. 21:17); David will always have a lamp in Jerusalem (1 Kgs. 11:36; 15:4; 2 Kgs. 8:19; 2 Chr. 21:7).

l The virgins took their lamps to meet the bridegroom (Matt. 25:1); let your lamps be burning (Luke 12:35); her lamp does not go out at night (Prov. 31:18).

m How often is the light of the wicked put out? (Job 21:17); the lamp of the wicked will be put out (Prov. 24:20).

421 Screen

● Curtains   *a* Hangings of the tabernacle: of linen (Exod. 26:1–6; 36:8–13); of goat's hair (Exod. 26:7–13; 36:14–18); the screen for the door-way (Exod. 26:36–7; 36:37–8; 39:38; 40:28); Gershonites responsible for (Num. 3:25; 4:25).

b Hangings of the court: (Exod. 27:9–15; 38:9–16; 39:40; 40:33); the screen for the gateway (Exod. 27:16; 38:18; 39:40; 40:33); Gershonites responsible for (Num. 3:26; 4:26).

c He spreads out the heavens like a curtain (Isa. 40:22).

● The veil   *d* The veil of the tabernacle: (Exod. 26:31–5; 35:12; 36:35–6;

39:34; 40:3, 5; Heb. 9:3); Kohathites looked after (Num. 3:31); the ark was screened with the veil (Exod. 40:3, 21; Num. 4:5).

e The veil of the temple (2 Chr. 3:14); Jesus entered within the veil (Heb. 6:19); we enter the holy of holies through the veil, his body (Heb. 10:20); the veil of the temple was torn in two (Matt. 27:51; Mark 15:38; Luke 23:45).

● Various
veils

f Moses put a veil over his face (Exod. 34:33, 35; 2 Cor. 3:13); the Lord will destroy the veil over all nations (Isa. 25:7).

422 Transparency

● Transparent

a A platform gleaming like crystal (Ezek. 1:22); a sea of glass like crystal (Rev. 4:6); a sea of glass (Rev. 15:2); the street was pure gold, like transparent glass (Rev. 21:21); the river of the water of life, clear as crystal (Rev. 22:1).

423 Opacity

Cloud, see **355**.

424 Semitransparency

Cloud, see **355**; **transparent**, see **422**.

425 Colour

● Dying

a Dyed embroidered material (Judg. 5:30).
Multi-coloured, see **437**.

426 Colourlessness

427 Whiteness

● White
clothes

a The garment of the Ancient of Days was white as snow (Dan. 7:9); at the transfiguration Jesus' garments were shining white (Matt. 17:2; Mark 9:3; Luke 9:29); the angels' clothing was white (Matt. 28:3; Mark 16:5; John 20:12; Acts 1:10).

b Let your clothes be always white (Eccles. 9:8); they will walk with me in white (Rev. 3:4); he who overcomes will be clothed in white (Rev. 3:5); buy from me white garments (Rev. 3:18); 24 elders clothed in white (Rev. 4:4); white robes given to the martyrs (Rev. 6:11); a multitude clothed in white robes (Rev. 7:9); who are these in white robes? (Rev. 7:13); armies clothed in fine linen, white and clean (Rev. 19:14).

● White hair

c Christ's head and hair were white like wool, like snow (Rev. 1:14); the almond tree blossoms (Eccles. 12:5); you cannot make one hair white or black (Matt. 5:36).
Grey hair, see **429**.

d Leprosy turns hairs white (Lev. 13:3, 4, 10, 20, 21, 25, 26); leprous, like snow (Num. 12:10; 2 Kgs. 5:27).

● White things

e White horses (Zech. 1:8; 6:3, 6; Rev. 6:2; 19:11, 14); her princes were whiter than milk (Lam. 4:7); the fields are white for harvest (John 4:35); I saw a great white throne (Rev. 20:11).

● Made white

f Wash me and I shall be whiter than snow (Ps. 51:7); your sins will be white as snow (Isa. 1:18); robes washed and made white in the blood of the Lamb (Rev. 7:14).

g The false prophets whitewash any wall (Ezek. 13:10–15); her prophets have daubed whitewash (Ezek. 22:28); you white-washed wall! (Acts 23:3); whitewashed tombs (Matt. 23:27).

428 Blackness

● Black people

a My skin turned black (Job 30:30); I am black but comely (S. of S. 1:5); do not stare at me because I am swarthy (S. of S. 1:6); they are blacker than soot (Lam. 4:8).

● Black things

b His hair is black as a raven (S. of S. 5:11); you cannot make one hair white or black (Matt. 5:36).

c Black horses (Zech. 6:2, 6; Rev. 6:5); the sun became black as sackcloth (Rev. 6:12).

429 Greyness

● Grey hair

a A grey head is a crown of glory (Prov. 16:31); the glory of old people is their grey hair (Prov. 20:29); even to grey hairs I will carry you (Isa. 46:4); grey hairs come and he does not know it (Hos. 7:9).

White hair, see **427c.**

430 Brownness

● Brown

a Sorrel horses (Zech. 1:8).

431 Redness

● Red people

a Esau was red at birth (Gen. 25:25); called Edom [red] through his desire for red stew (Gen. 25:30); David was ruddy (1 Sam. 16:12; 17:42); my beloved is ruddy (S. of S. 5:10).

● Red cord

b Scarlet thread tied to one twin (Gen. 38:28, 30); scarlet cord dipped in blood (Lev. 14:4, 6, 49, 51–2); scarlet cord tied in the window (Josh. 2:18, 21); your lips are like a scarlet thread (S. of S. 4:3).

● Red material

c Rams' skins dyed red (Exod. 25:5; 26:14; 35:7, 23; 39:34); a cover of scarlet cloth (Num. 4:8); scarlet stuff (Num. 19:6).

● Red clothes

d Saul clothed you in scarlet (2 Sam. 1:24); her household are clothed in scarlet (Prov. 31:21); though you dress in scarlet (Jer. 4:30); why are your garments red? (Isa. 63:2); they put a scarlet robe on Jesus (Matt. 27:28); the woman was clothed in purple and scarlet (Rev. 17:4; 18:16).

● Red animals

e A red heifer (Num. 19:2); red horses (Zech. 1:8; 6:2; Rev. 6:4); a great red dragon (Rev. 12:3); a woman sitting on a scarlet beast (Rev. 17:3).

● Red things

f The water looked red like blood (2 Kgs. 3:22); the sky is red (Matt. 16:2–3); breastplates the colour of fire (Rev. 9:17).

g Though your sins be as scarlet, as red as crimson (Isa. 1:18). **Blue and purple**, see **435e**.

432 Orange
Red, see **431**; **yellow**, see **433**.

433 Yellowness
● Yellow

a Breastplates the colour of brimstone (Rev. 9:17).

434 Greenness
● Green

a A greenish horse (Rev. 6:8).

435 Blueness
● Blue cloth

a The robe of the ephod was blue (Exod. 28:31; 39:22).

b Blue cloths covering: the ark (Num. 4:6); the table (Num. 4:7); the lampstand (Num. 4:9); the golden altar (Num. 4:11); and its utensils (Num. 4:12).

c Royal robes of blue and white (Esther 8:15).

● Blue cords

d Loops of blue joining the curtains (Exod. 36:11); the holy crown fastened with a blue cord (Exod. 28:37; 39:31); cords of blue on tassels of garments (Num. 15:38).

● Blue and purple

e An awning of blue and purple (Ezek. 27:7).

f Blue, purple and scarlet material (Exod. 25:4; 26:1, 31, 36; 27:16; 28:5, 6, 8, 15, 33; 35:6, 23, 25, 35; 36:8, 35, 37; 38:18, 23; 39:1, 2, 3, 5, 8, 24, 29; 2 Chr. 3:14).

● Blue things

g Breastplates the colour of jacinth (Rev. 9:17).

436 Purpleness
● Purple cloth

a Purple cloth over the altar (Num. 4:13); the seat made of purple cloth (S. of S. 3:10); cords of purple linen (Esther 1:6); purple was traded (Ezek. 27:16); Lydia was a dealer in purple cloth (Acts 16:14); your flowing locks are like purple (S. of S. 7:5).

b Violet hangings (Esther 1:6).

● Purple clothes

c Purple robes (Judg. 8:26); a garment of fine linen and purple (Esther 8:15); her clothing is fine linen and purple (Prov. 31:22); those reared in purple lie on ash heaps (Lam. 4:5); the Assyrians were clothed in purple (Ezek. 23:6); whoever reads this writing will be clothed in purple (Dan. 5:7, 16); they clothed Daniel in purple (Dan. 5:29); a rich man dressed in purple (Luke 16:19); they dressed Jesus with purple (Mark 15:17; John 19:5); the woman was clothed in purple and scarlet (Rev. 17:4; 18:16); idols clothed in violet and purple (Jer. 10:9).
Blue and purple, see **435e**.

437 Variegation

- Black and
  white
- Multi-
  coloured

a Jacob exposed white stripes in the rods (Gen. 30:37–8); dappled horses (Zech. 6:3, 6).

b An eagle with plumage of many colours (Ezek. 17:3).
Speckled and spotted, see **647a**.

438 Vision

- Sight

a It is God who gives man sight (Exod. 4:11); God made seeing eyes (Prov. 20:12); God opened Hagar's eyes (Gen. 21:19); the Lord opened Balaam's eyes (Num. 22:31); Lord, open his eyes (2 Kgs. 6:17); open their eyes (2 Kgs. 6:20); Paul was sent to open their eyes (Acts 26:18); we want our eyes to be opened (Matt. 20:33); I want to receive my sight (Mark 10:51; Luke 18:41); the boy opened his eyes (2 Kgs. 4:35).

b We walk by faith, not by sight (2 Cor. 5:7).

- God seeing

c God who sees me (Gen. 16:13); Reuben—the Lord has seen my affliction (Gen. 29:32); he who formed the eye, does he not see? (Ps. 94:9); your eyes have seen my unformed substance (Ps. 139:16).
God watching, see **441f**.

- Seeing God

d Jacob saw God at Peniel (Gen. 32:30); seeing Esau was like seeing the face of God (Gen. 33:10); the people must not force their way through to see the Lord (Exod. 19:21); the seventy elders saw God (Exod. 24:9–11); Moses sees God's form (Num. 12:8); seeing a vision of the Almighty (Num. 24:4); I saw the Lord standing by the altar (Amos 9:1); I saw the Lord in the temple (Isa. 6:1); Gideon saw the angel of the Lord face to face (Judg. 6:22); David saw the angel (2 Sam. 24:17); we will die for we have seen God (Judg. 13:22); my eyes have seen the Lord (Isa. 6:5); now my eye sees you (Job 42:5).

e You saw no form when the Lord spoke to you (Deut. 4:12, 15); Moses saw God's back, for no one could see God and live (Exod. 33:20–3); no one has ever seen God (John 1:18; 1 John 4:12); you have never heard his voice or seen his form (John 5:37); no man has ever seen God or can see him (1 Tim. 6:16); no one has seen the Father except the one who came from God (John 6:46); the one who does evil has not seen God (3 John 11); no one who sins has seen him (1 John 3:6).

f In my flesh I will see God (Job 19:26); I will see your face in righteousness (Ps. 17:15); we will see him as he is (1 John 3:2); the pure in heart will see God (Matt. 5:8); they will see his face (Rev. 22:4); holiness, without which no one will see the Lord (Heb. 12:14); the upright will behold his face (Ps. 11:7).

- Seeing Christ

g Simeon would not die before seeing the Lord's Christ (Luke 2:26); we would see Jesus (John 12:21); he who has seen me has seen the Father (John 14:9); in a little while you will see me no more and then a little while and you will see me (John 16:16);

you will behold me (John 14:19); that which we have seen we proclaim (1 John 1:1, 3); he who sees me sees the one who sent me (John 12:45); he has appointed you to see the righteous one (Acts 22:14); have I not seen Jesus our Lord? (1 Cor. 9:1); beholding as in a mirror the glory of the Lord (2 Cor. 3:18); every eye will see him (Rev. 1:7).

● Eyes

h If the whole body were an eye, where would be the hearing? (1 Cor. 12:17); the eye cannot say it does not need the hand (1 Cor. 12:21).

i Leah had weak eyes (Gen. 29:17); David had beautiful eyes (1 Sam. 16:12); your eyes are like doves (S. of S. 4:1); his eyes are like doves (S. of S. 5:12); your eyes are like pools in Heshbon (S. of S. 7:4); Jonathan's eyes brightened after the honey (1 Sam. 14:27, 29); the eye is the lamp of the body (Matt. 6:22; Luke 11:34); the Son of God had eyes like fire (Rev. 1:14; 2:18; 19:12).

j The cherubim and the wheels were full of eyes (Ezek. 10:12); the rims of the wheels were covered with eyes (Ezek. 1:18); the horn had eyes (Dan. 7:8, 20); the four creatures were covered with eyes (Rev. 4:8).

k You will be as eyes for us (Num. 10:31); you would have plucked out your eyes and given them to me (Gal. 4:15); keep me as the apple of your eye (Ps. 17:8); he kept him as the apple of his eye (Deut. 32:10); he who touches you touches the apple of his eye (Zech. 2:8).

l If your right eye makes you stumble (Matt. 5:29; 18:9; Mark 9:47); I made a covenant with my eyes (Job 31:1); why notice the speck in your brother's eye and not the beam in your own? (Matt. 7:3–5; Luke 6:41–2).

Eyes enlightened, see **516h**.

● Eyes
destroyed

m Destroying a slave's eye (Exod. 21:26); they gouged out Samson's eyes (Judg. 16:21); Nahash wanted to gouge out their right eyes (1 Sam. 11:2); an eye for an eye (Exod. 21:24; Lev. 24:20; Deut. 19:21; Matt. 5:38); avenged for my two eyes (Judg. 16:28).

● Viewing

n Abraham looked down the valley (Gen. 19:28); Moses viewed the land (Deut. 32:49; 34:1–4); your eyes have seen all God did (Deut. 11:7); David rejoiced that his saw his successor reigning (1 Kgs. 1:48); turn my eyes away from vanity (Ps. 119:37).

o Everyone who looked at the bronze snake lived (Num. 21:9); if you see me when I am taken from you (2 Kgs. 2:10); gaze on king Solomon (S. of S. 3:11); why should you gaze at the Shulammite? (S. of S. 6:13).

p Blessed are your eyes, for they see (Matt. 13:16); many desired to see what you see (Matt. 13:17).

● Inspecting

q The priest examines: the leper (Lev. 13:3–44; 14:3); a leprous garment (Lev. 13:50–7); a leprous house (Lev. 14:36–7, 39, 44, 48).

r Nehemiah inspected the city walls (Neh. 2:13).

● Dreams

s God speaks in a dream (Job 33:15); I speak to prophets in dreams (Num. 12:6); your old men will dream dreams (Joel 2:28; Acts 2:17); God spoke to Israel in visions of the night (Gen. 46:2); Solomon's vision was a dream (1 Kgs. 3:15); Eliphaz received a message in a dream (Job 4:12–21); God did not answer Saul by dreams (1 Sam. 28:6, 15).

t Those to whom God spoke in a dream: Solomon (1 Kgs. 3:5); the wise men (Matt. 2:12); Joseph (Matt. 1:20; 2:13, 19, 22).

u Jacob had a dream at Bethel (Gen. 28:12); and in the house of Laban (Gen. 31:10); God came to Abimelech in a dream (Gen. 20:3); and to Laban (Gen. 31:24); Joseph's dreams (Gen. 37:5–11); this dreamer! (Gen. 37:19); the dreams of the butler and baker (Gen. 40:5–19); Pharaoh's dream (Gen. 41:1–32); the Amalekite's dream of Gideon (Judg. 7:13–14); Nebuchadnezzar's dream of the statue (Dan. 2:31–5); Nebuchadnezzar's dream of the tree (Dan. 4:10–18); Daniel's dream of the four beasts (Dan. 7:1–8).

v Nebuchadnezzar had dreams (Dan. 2:1, 3; 4:5); Pilate's wife suffered much in a dream (Matt. 27:19); you terrify me with dreams (Job 7:14).

● Dreams interpreted

w Joseph interpreted dreams (Gen. 40:12–13, 18–19; 41:12–13, 15, 25–32); Daniel understood visions and dreams (Dan. 1:17); the mystery was revealed to Daniel in a vision of the night (Dan. 2:19); do not interpretations of dreams belong to God? (Gen. 40:8; 41:16).

Interpreting dreams, see 520a.

● Misleading dreams

x If a dreamer of dreams arises to mislead you (Deut. 13:1); I had a dream, I had a dream (Jer. 23:25); let the prophet who had a dream tell the dream (Jer. 23:28); I am against those who prophesy false dreams (Jer. 23:32).

● Like a dream

y The wicked vanishes like a dream (Job 20:8); those who attack Jerusalem will be like a dream (Isa. 29:8); like the hungry dreaming of food (Isa. 29:8); like a dream when one awakes they are dismissed (Ps. 73:20); it was like a dream! (Ps. 126:1).

● Visions

z I reveal myself to prophets in visions (Num. 12:6); your young men will see visions (Joel 2:28; Acts 2:17); I will go on to visions and revelations of the Lord (2 Cor. 12:1); I was not disobedient to the heavenly vision (Acts 26:19).

aa Those who saw visions: Abraham (Gen. 15:1); Zechariah (2 Chr. 26:5); Isaiah (2 Chr. 32:32; Isa. 1:1); Ezekiel (Ezek. 1:1); Daniel (Dan. 8:1–8); Zacharias (Luke 1:22); Ananias (Acts 9:10); Paul, of Ananias (Acts 9:12); Peter (Acts 10:10–13; 11:5); Cornelius (Acts 10:3); Paul, of a man of Macedonia (Acts 16:9); Paul, in a trance (Acts 22:17–18).

ab What do you see? (Jer. 1:11, 13); Peter thought he was seeing a vision (Acts 12:9).

● No visions

ac Visions were infrequent (1 Sam. 3:1); they will seek a vision from the prophet (Ezek. 7:26); her prophets find no vision from the Lord (Lam. 2:9); where there is no vision the people run wild (Prov. 29:18); they say to the seers, You must not see visions (Isa. 30:10).

● Oracles   *ad* The oracle concerning: Amalek (Num. 24:20); Ammon (Jer. 49:1–6; Ezek. 21:28–32; 25:2–7); Damascus (Isa. 17:1); Egypt (Isa. 19:1); the wilderness of the sea (Isa. 21:1); Dumah [Edom] (Isa. 21:1); Arabia (Isa. 21:13); Moab (Isa. 15:1); the valley of vision (Isa. 22:1); Tyre (Isa. 23:1); beasts of the Negev (Isa. 30:6).

Oracles about the nations, see **371x**.

● Seers   *ae* The prophet used to be called a seer (1 Sam. 9:9); are you not a seer? (2 Sam. 15:27); the words of the seers (2 Chr. 33:18).

af Gad, David's seer (2 Sam. 24:11; 1 Chr. 21:9; 2 Chr. 29:25); Iddo the seer (2 Chr. 9:29; 12:15); Hanani the seer (2 Chr. 16:7); O seer (Amos 7:12).

439 Blindness

● Blind ones   *a* People who were blind through old age: Isaac (Gen. 27:1); Israel (Gen. 48:10); Ahijah (1 Kgs. 14:4); Eli (1 Sam. 3:2; 4:15).

b You offer blind animals as sacrifice (Mal. 1:8).

c Blind guides (Matt. 15:14; 23:16, 24); if a blind man leads a blind man they will both fall into a pit (Matt. 15:14; Luke 6:39); you are a guide to the blind (Rom. 2:19); you do not know that you are blind (Rev. 3:17); he who lacks these things is blind or short-sighted (2 Pet. 1:9).

d People who are blind yet have eyes (Isa. 43:8); this people have eyes but see not (Jer. 5:21; Ezek. 12:2); seeing they do not see (Matt. 13:13; Mark 4:12); having eyes, do you not see? (Mark 8:18); they have closed their eyes lest they should see (Matt. 13:15; Acts 28:27); you blind! (Matt. 23:19); you blind Pharisee! (Matt. 23:26); the blindness of the Pharisees (John 9:40–41); we grope for the wall like the blind (Isa. 59:10).

e Idols have eyes but cannot see (Ps. 115:5; 135:16); idols do not see (Deut. 4:28).

● Not seeing   *f* The Lord does not see (Ps. 94:7; Ezek. 9:9); the Lord does not see us (Ezek. 8:12); who is blind like the servant of the Lord? (Isa. 42:19–20).

g Shem and Japheth went backward so as not to see (Gen. 9:23); do not let me see the boy die (Gen. 21:16); do not look behind you (Gen. 19:17); we hope for what we do not see (Rom. 8:25).

h You will not see my face again (Exod. 10:28–9; Acts 20:25, 38); you will not see me again (Matt. 23:39); you will never see the Egyptians again (Exod. 14:13); they will not see the land (Num. 14:23; Josh. 5:6).

Insensible, see **375**.

● Blinded   *i* It is God who makes man blind (Exod. 4:11); God will strike you with blindness (Deut. 28:28); the angels struck the men with blindness (Gen. 19:11); Elisha asked the Lord to strike the soldiers with blindness (2 Kgs. 6:18); let their eyes be darkened so that they cannot see (Ps. 69:23); on the Damascus road Saul was blinded (Acts 9:8–9; 22:11); Elymas was struck blind (Acts 13:11).

j I have come that those who see may become blind (John 9:39); he has shut their eyes so that they cannot see (Isa. 44:18); he has blinded their eyes and hardened their heart (John 12:40); God gave them eyes that do not see (Rom. 11:8, 10); God has not given you eyes to see (Deut. 29:4); their eyes were prevented from recognising him (Luke 24:16).

k The Philistines gouged out Samson's eyes (Judg. 16:21); the king of Babylon put out Zedekiah's eyes (2 Kgs. 25:7; Jer. 39:7; 52:11); I will bring him to Babylon but he will not see it (Ezek. 12:13).

l The god of this world has blinded their minds (2 Cor. 4:4); the darkness has blinded his eyes (1 John 2:11).

m They blindfolded Jesus (Mark 14:65; Luke 22:64).

● Dealings with the blind

n Do not place a stumbling-block before the blind (Lev. 19:14); cursed is he who misleads the blind (Deut. 27:18); I was eyes to the blind (Job 29:15); I will lead the blind in a way they do not know (Isa. 42:16); invite the blind (Luke 14:13, 21).

o Blind men could not serve as priests (Lev. 21:18); the blind and the lame will keep you out (2 Sam. 5:6, 8).

● Blind healed

p God opens the eyes of the blind (Ps. 146:8); they eyes of the blind will be opened (Isa. 35:5); look, you blind, that you may see (Isa. 42:18); I appoint you to open the eyes of the blind (Isa. 42:7); the blind receive their sight (Luke 7:22); he has sent me to preach recovery of sight to the blind (Luke 4:18); Paul was sent to open their eyes (Acts 26:18).

q Two blind men called out to Jesus (Matt. 9:27–31; 20:30); blind Bartimaeus (Mark 10:46–52; Luke 18:35–43); the man born blind (John 9:1–7); the blind received sight (Matt. 11:5; 15:31; 21:14; Luke 7:21–2); he healed a blind and dumb demoniac (Matt. 12:22); they brought a blind man to Jesus to be healed (Mark 8:22–6).

440 Defective vision

● Seeing dimly

a Do not look at the speck in your brother's eye when you have a log in your own (Matt. 7:3–5; Luke 6:41–2).

b He saw men like trees, walking (Mark 8:24).

c We see dimly, as in a mirror (1 Cor. 13:12).

d He who lacks these things is blind or short-sighted (2 Pet. 1:9).

441 Spectator

- Looking at holy things

a The Kohathites must not go in to look at the holy things (Num. 4:20); they died because they had looked into the ark of the Lord (1 Sam. 6:19).

- Looking at people

b Moses' sister watched (Exod. 2:4); they watched Moses go into the tent (Exod. 33:10); Absalom went in to the concubines in the sight of all Israel (2 Sam. 16:22).

c They shall look on the one they pierced (Zech. 12:10; John 19:37).

d Shine so that they may see your good works (Matt. 5:16).

e Looking at a woman in lust (Matt. 5:28).

- God watching

f The eyes of the Lord range through the earth (2 Chr. 16:9; Zech. 4:10); the eyes of the Lord are everywhere, watching the evil and the good (Prov. 15:3).

g The Lord looks down on heaven and earth (Ps. 113:6); the Lord looks down from heaven to see if any one seeks him (Ps. 14:2; 53:2); the Lord looks down from heaven (Ps. 33:13; 102:19); I will quietly look from my dwelling (Isa. 18:4); his eyes keep watch on the nations (Ps. 66:7); the Lord looked down on the Egyptians (Exod. 14:24).

h God sees all a man's steps (Job 34:21); a man's ways are before the Lord's eyes (Prov. 5:21); your eyes are open to all the ways of men (Jer. 32:19); my eyes are on all their ways (Jer. 16:17); the eyes of the Lord are on those who fear him (Ps. 33:18); on the righteous (Ps. 34:15; 1 Pet. 3:12); God keeps his eyes on the righteous (Job 36:7); you have seen it (Ps. 35:22); you watcher of men (Job 7:20).

i Look down from heaven and see! (Isa. 63:15); open your eyes and see! (Dan. 9:18); until the Lord looks down from heaven and sees (Lam. 3:50); your Father sees in secret (Matt. 6:4); the Lord turned and looked at Peter (Luke 22:61).

- Seeing God's works

j You saw with your own eyes what God did in Egypt (Deut. 29:2; Josh. 24:7); what great things the Lord has done (Deut. 11:7); my eyes have seen your salvation (Luke 2:30–1); you will see it with your own eyes but you will not eat of it (2 Kgs. 7:2, 19).

- Watching Jesus

k Those who from the beginning were eyewitnesses (Luke 1:2); eyewitnesses of his majesty (2 Pet. 1:16); they watched him to see whether he would heal on the sabbath (Mark 3:2); the eyes of all in the synagogue were on him (Luke 4:20); the women were looking on (Mark 15:47; Luke 23:49, 55).

- Looking to God

l God, our eyes are on you (2 Chr. 20:12); my eyes are toward you (Ps. 141:8); the eyes of all look to you (Ps. 145:15).

442 Optical instrument

- Mirrors

a The mirrors of the serving women (Exod. 38:8).

b We behold the glory of the Lord as in a mirror (2 Cor. 3:18); now we see dimly as in a mirror (1 Cor. 13:12).

c A man who looks at his face in a mirror (Jas. 1:23).

443 Visibility

● Visible   a Light makes things become visible (Eph. 5:13).

444 Invisibility

● Invisible things   a By faith we understand that the visible things were made out of invisible (Heb. 11:3); we look at what is unseen and eternal (2 Cor. 4:18).

● Invisible God   b Moses endured, seeing him who is invisible (Heb. 11:27); though you do not see him, you believe in him (1 Pet. 1:8); Christ is the image of the invisible God (Col. 1:15); God's invisible attributes are clearly seen (Rom. 1:20); were God to pass by, I would not see him (Job 9:11).

● Unseen   c No one sees me (Isa. 47:10).

445 Appearance

● Apparition   a The Lord appeared to: Abraham (Gen. 18:1); Isaac (Gen. 26:24); Jacob (Gen. 35:1, 7, 9; 48:3); Solomon (1 Kgs. 9:2; 2 Chr. 1:7; 7:12); Joseph (Matt. 1:20; 2:13, 19); I appear in the cloud over the mercy seat (Lev. 16:2).

b The appearing of our Saviour (2 Tim. 1:10); he appeared once for all to put away sin (Heb. 9:26).

c After his resurrection he appeared to Mary Magdalene (Mark 16:9); to two walking in the country (Mark 16:12); to the apostles (Mark 16:14; 1 Cor. 15:5, 7); to Simon Peter (Luke 24:34; 1 Cor. 15:5); to his disciples (John 21:1, 14); to more than five hundred brethren (1 Cor. 15:6); to James (1 Cor. 15:7); to Paul (1 Cor. 15:8).

d When Christ, your life, appears, you also will appear with him (Col. 3:4); when he appears we will be like him (1 John 3:2); waiting for the appearing of our great God and Saviour Jesus Christ (Titus 2:13); keep the commandment until the appearing of our Lord Jesus Christ (1 Tim. 6:14); that when he appears we may have confidence (1 John 2:28).

e Elijah and Moses appeared to them (Matt. 17:3; Mark 9:4; Luke 9:30–1); resurrected saints appeared to many (Matt. 27:53).

● Appearances   f Do not look at his appearance or his height (1 Sam. 16:7); do not judge by the appearance (John 7:24); those who take pride in appearance (2 Cor. 5:12).

Outward appearance, see **223a**.

g The appearance of the likeness of the glory of the Lord (Ezek. 1:28).

● Spectacle   h Apostles have become a spectacle to the world (1 Cor. 4:9); you were made a spectacle (Heb. 10:33).

446 Disappearance

● Vanishing

a Christ vanished from their sight (Luke 24:31); the angel of the Lord vanished (Judg. 6:21); the sky will vanish like smoke (Isa. 51:6).

b Friendship vanishes like the waters of a wadi (Job 6:15–18).

Class four: Intellect: the exercise of the mind

4.1: Formation of ideas

Section one: Intellectual operations in general

447 Intellect

- Searching the heart

a The Lord searches all hearts (1 Chr. 28:9); you test the heart (1 Chr. 29:17); the hearts of men lie open before the Lord (Prov. 15:11).

- Evil hearts

b What goes out of the mouth comes from the heart (Matt. 15:18); the mouth speaks from that which fills the heart (Matt. 12:34; Luke 6:45).

c The depraved mind is filled with all wickedness (Rom. 1:28–9); the heart is deceitful (Jer. 17:9); puffed up by his fleshly mind (Col. 2:18); their mind and conscience are defiled (Titus 1:15).

d Nebuchadnezzar was given the mind of an animal (Dan. 4:16).

- Receptive hearts

e These words which I command you shall be on your heart (Deut. 6:6); I will write my law on their heart (Jer. 31:33; Heb. 8:10; 10:16); I will take from them their heart of stone and give them a heart of flesh (Ezek. 11:19; 36:26); oh, that they always had such a heart (Deut. 5:29); make yourselves a new heart and a new spirit (Ezek. 18:31).

f With the heart man believes (Rom. 10:10).

g We have the mind of Christ (1 Cor. 2:16); have this mind in Christ (Phil. 2:5).

448 Absence of intellect

- Irrational

a Like unreasoning animals (2 Pet. 2:12; Jude 10).

449 Thought

- God's thoughts

a My thoughts are not your thoughts, says the Lord (Isa. 55:8); God declares his thoughts to men (Amos 4:13).

b Many are your thoughts toward us (Ps. 40:5); how precious are your thoughts to me, O God (Ps. 139:17); what is man that you think of him? (Ps. 144:3).

c , see **104x**.

- Man's thoughts

d The Lord knows that the thoughts of a man are a mere breath (Ps. 94:11); I know their thoughts (Isa. 66:18); I know your thoughts (Ezek. 11:5); you know my thoughts from afar (Ps. 139:2).

e The thoughts of the righteous are just (Prov. 12:5); the righteous ponders how to answer (Prov. 15:28).

f Every thought was evil (Gen. 6:5); from the heart come evil thoughts (Matt. 15:19; Mark 7:21); let the unrighteous forsake his thoughts (Isa. 55:7); they became futile in their reasoning (Rom. 1:21); God gave them over to a depraved mind (Rom. 1:28); their thoughts accusing or defending them (Rom. 2:15); you do not think God's things but man's (Matt. 16:23).

● Right thoughts

g Think of what is true, honourable, right etc. (Phil. 4:8); set your mind on things above (Col. 3:2).

● Philosophy

h Epicurean and Stoic philosophers (Acts 17:18); see that you are not carried off through philosophy (Col. 2:8).

● Meditating

i Meditate on the law day and night (Josh. 1:8); in his law he meditates day and night (Ps. 1:2); your law is my meditation all the day (Ps. 119:97); I meditate on your word through the night watches (Ps. 119:148); I meditate on your precepts (Ps. 119:15, 78); on your statutes (Ps. 119:23, 48); on your wonders (Ps. 119:27; 145:5); your testimonies are my meditation (Ps. 119:99).

j Isaac went out to meditate in the field (Gen. 24:63); let my meditation be acceptable (Ps. 19:14); let my meditation be pleasing to him (Ps. 104:34).

● Mary pondering

k She pondered what kind of greeting this was (Luke 1:29); Mary pondered these things in her heart (Luke 2:19); his mother kept these things in her heart (Luke 2:51).

450 Absence of thought

● Thoughtless

a Swearing thoughtlessly (Lev. 5:4).

451 Idea

● Opinion

a I give my opinion (1 Cor. 7:25; 2 Cor. 8:10).
Thought, see **449**.

452 Topic

● Sound doctrine

a Pay attention to your teaching (1 Tim. 4:16); keep the form of sound words (2 Tim. 1:13); an elder must continue in sound doctrine (Titus 1:9); speak what befits sound doctrine (Titus 2:1); nourished on sound doctrine (1 Tim. 4:6); do not be carried away by strange teachings (Heb. 13:9).

b My teaching is not mine but his who sent me (John 7:16); he will know whether the teaching is of God (John 7:17); they were astonished at his teaching (Matt. 7:28; 22:33).
Amazed by teaching, see **864***w*.

● Unsound doctrine

c Teaching as doctrines the traditions of men (Matt. 15:9); doctrines of demons (1 Tim. 4:1).

d **Man's teaching**, see **371***o*.

e If anyone does not bring this teaching, do not receive him (2 John 10); he who does not abide in the teaching of Christ does not have God (2 John 9).

453 Curiosity: desire for knowledge
Enquiry, see **459**.

Section two: Precursory conditions and operations

---

454 Incuriosity
Inattention, see **456**.

455 Attention

● Hear our prayer!

a Let your eyes be open and your ears attentive to prayer here (1 Kgs. 8:29–30; 2 Chr. 6:20, 40); hear your people's prayer (1 Kgs. 8:33–4, 35–6, 38–9, 44–5, 47–9, 52; 2 Chr. 6:21, 23, 25, 27, 30, 35, 39; 20:9); hear the foreigner's prayer (1 Kgs. 8:42–3; 2 Chr. 6:33); incline your ear, Lord, and hear (2 Kgs. 19:16; Isa. 37:17); hear, O Lord (Ps. 27:7).

b Hear my prayer (1 Kgs. 8:28; Neh. 1:6, 11; Ps. 28:2; 54:2; 55:1; 61:1; 84:8; 86:6; 88:2; 102:1; 143:1); give ear to my words (Ps. 5:1; 17:6); Lord, hear my voice (Ps. 130:2; 141:1); hear my supplications (Ps. 140:6); give heed to me (Jer. 18:19); give heed to my cry (Ps. 142:6).
Hear prayer!, see **761y**.

● God hears prayer

c You who hear prayer (Ps. 65:2); the Lord hears the needy (Ps. 69:33); my eyes will be open and my ears attentive (2 Chr. 7:15); my eyes and heart will always be there (1 Kgs. 9:3; 2 Chr. 7:16); he will hear their cry (Ps. 145:19); the Lord hears the prayer of the righteous (Prov. 15:29); the Lord hears when I call (Ps. 4:3).

d Ishmael—'God hears' (Gen. 16:11); listen to me that God may listen to you (Judg. 9:7).
God answers prayer, see **721z**.

● God heard

e I love the Lord for he hears my voice (Ps. 116:1); he heard my voice (2 Sam. 22:7; Ps. 18:6); he has heard my supplication (Ps. 28:6); you heard my supplication (Ps. 31:22); the Lord has heard my prayer (Ps. 6:8–9); this poor man cried and the Lord heard him (Ps. 34:6); Father, thank you that you heard me (John 11:41–2).

f Because you prayed I have heard you (2 Kgs. 19:20); I have heard your prayer (2 Kgs. 20:5; 2 Chr. 34:27).

g God heard Ishmael (Gen. 21:17); God had regard for Abel and his offering (Gen. 4:4); the Lord listened to a man's voice (Josh. 10:14); God listened to Noah (Judg. 13:9); the Lord listened to Jehoahaz (2 Kgs. 13:4); the Lord heard Elijah's voice (1 Kgs. 17:22); the Lord heard Hezekiah (2 Chr. 30:20); the Lord regarded the prayer of the destitute (Ps. 102:17); when they cried to you, you heard them (Neh. 9:27, 28).

● God heeding

h God hears the cry of the orphan and widow (Exod. 22:22–3); of the poor (Exod. 22:27); God heard the groaning of the Israelites (Exod. 2:24); God heeded their cry (Exod. 3:7); you have heard my vows (Ps. 61:5).

i He who made ears and eyes hears and sees (Ps. 94:9); the Lord saw (Isa. 59:15); perhaps the Lord will hear the words of the Rabshakeh (2 Kgs. 19:4; Isa. 37:4); if I sin you take note of me (Job 10:14).

j I am watching over my word to do it (Jer. 1:12).

God answering, see **460***a*.

- Attentive to God

k Has any other people heard the voice of God? (Deut. 4:33); who has stood in the council of the Lord to hear his word? (Jer. 23:18); Mary was listening to the Lord's word (Luke 10:39); he wakens my ear to listen (Isa. 50:4); speak, Lord, for your servant is listening (1 Sam. 3:9); give me a hearing heart (1 Kgs. 3:9); this is my Son; hear him (Matt. 17:5); if any one hears my voice and opens the door (Rev. 3:20); to him you should give heed (Acts 3:22); he who is of God hears the words of God (John 8:47); if they hear him they will have prosperity (Job 36:11).

l Heed the Lord and you will escape the Egyptians' diseases (Exod. 15:26); to hearken is better than the fat of rams (1 Sam. 15:22); our eyes look to the Lord as servants to their masters (Ps. 123:2).

- Hearing the word

m Faith comes from hearing (Rom. 10:17); the hearing of faith (Gal. 3:2, 5); how shall they believe in the one they have not heard? (Rom. 10:14); have they not all heard? (Rom. 10:18); he has appointed you to hear a word from his mouth (Acts 22:14); come and hear what he has done for me (Ps. 66:16).

n The people were attentive to the book of the Law (Neh. 8:3); be doers of the word, not just hearers (Jas. 1:22).

o Make your ear attentive to wisdom (Prov. 2:2); be attentive to my words (Prov. 4:20; 5:7; 7:24); be attentive to wisdom (Prov. 5:1); blessed is he who listens to me (Prov. 8:34); everyone who is of the truth hears my voice (John 18:37); hear the words of the wise (Prov. 22:17).

- Listen!

p Let every one be quick to hear (Jas. 1:19); it is folly to give an answer before hearing (Prov. 18:13); does our law judge a man without first hearing him? (John 7:51).

q Hear, O Israel! (Deut. 6:4; 9:1); hear, O my people! (Ps. 81:8); pay heed! (Ps. 94:8); he who has ears, let him hear (Matt. 11:15; 13:9, 43; Mark 4:9, 23; Luke 8:8; 14:35; Rev. 13:9); let him hear what the Spirit says to the churches (Rev. 2:7, 11, 17, 29; 3:6, 13, 22); hear and understand! (Matt. 15:10); oh, that my people would listen to me! (Ps. 81:13); listen, that you may live (Isa. 55:3); whoever is wise should heed these things (Ps. 107:43); we must pay closer attention to what we have heard (Heb. 2:1); listen to the prophet who is like Moses (Deut. 18:15); looking to Jesus (Heb. 12:2).

r Listen to me that God may listen to you (Judg. 9:7); David listened to Abigail (1 Sam. 25:35); look at us! (Acts 3:4–5); hear your parents (Prov. 1:8; 4:1; 6:20; 23:22).
Listening, see **415***a*.

s Pay attention to the state of your herds (Prov. 27:23–7).

- Listening to people

t The eyes of all Israel are on you (1 Kgs. 1:20); Benhadad listened to Asa (1 Kgs. 15:20; 2 Chr. 16:4); the king of Assyria listened to Ahaz (2 Kgs. 16:9); Joash listened to the officials to do evil (2 Chr. 24:17); an evildoer listens to wicked lips (Prov. 17:4); the Samaritans gave heed to Simon Magnus (Acts 8:10).

u All the people hung on his words (Luke 19:48); the Lord opened Lydia's heart to respond (Acts 16:14).

v He who listens to you listens to me (Luke 10:16); he who knows God listens to us (1 John 4:6); blessed are your eyes and ears, for they see and hear (Matt. 13:16); the world listens to them (1 John 4:5).

456 Inattention

- God not heeding

a God does not pay heed (Ps. 94:7); how long shall I call and God will not hear? (Hab. 1:2); God disregards the justice due to me (Isa. 40:27); God's ear is not too dull to hear (Isa. 59:1).

b If I regard sin, the Lord will not hear (Ps. 66:18); God does not listen to sinners (John 9:31); for Cain and his offering God had no regard (Gen. 4:5); the Lord did not listen to you (Deut. 1:45))

c God overlooked the times of ignorance (Acts 17:30).
God not answering, see **460***j*.

- Refusing to hear the word

d Their ears are closed (Jer. 6:10); they stopped up their ears (Acts 7:57); you have become hard of hearing (Heb. 5:11); they have closed their eyes and ears (Matt. 13:15; Acts 28:27); eyes to see not and ears to hear not (Rom. 11:8); God has not given you ears to hear (Deut. 29:4); they will turn away their ears from the truth (2 Tim. 4:4); the time will come when they will not endure sound doctrine (2 Tim. 4:3).

- Refusing to heed the word

e How will Pharaoh listen? (Exod. 6:12); Pharaoh did not listen (Exod. 7:4, 13, 22; 8:15, 19; 9:12; 11:9); those who disregarded the word left people and animals outside (Exod. 9:21); they did not listen (2 Kgs. 17:14, 40; 21:9; Jer. 44:5); the Lord spoke, but they paid no attention (2 Chr. 33:10); they did not listen to the voice of the Lord (Ps. 106:25); they did not listen to me (Jer. 7:26; Zech. 1:4); I spoke but they did not listen (Jer. 35:17); I told you and you did not listen (John 9:27); you said, 'I will not listen' (Jer. 22:21); the Israelites will be unwilling to listen (Ezek. 3:7); they do not regard the deeds of the Lord (Isa. 5:12); you have not listened (Jer. 25:3; 35:15); they did not listen to the words the Lord had spoken (Jer. 37:2); we will not listen (Jer. 44:16); they paid no attention (Matt. 22:5).

f The Israelites would not listen (Exod. 6:9, 12); they would not listen (Isa. 28:12); Jehu was heedless of the law of the Lord (2 Kgs. 10:31); he who does not listen to him will be cut off from his people (Acts 3:23); if they will not hear, shake the dust off your feet (Matt. 10:14; Mark 6:11); if a sinning brother refuses to listen, treat him like a Gentile (Matt. 18:16–17); though prophets testified, they would not listen (2 Chr. 24:19; Neh. 9:30).

g Wisdom called and you did not pay attention (Prov. 1:24).

● Not heeding people

h We would not listen when we saw his distress (Gen. 42:21); Amnon would not listen to Tamar (2 Sam. 13:14, 16); Rehoboam did not listen to the people (1 Kgs. 12:15, 16; 2 Chr. 10:15, 16); he who stops his ears from hearing about bloodshed and shuts his eyes from looking at evil (Isa. 33:15).

i The king of Ammon disregarded Jephthah's message (Judg. 11:28); Amaziah would not listen to Joash (2 Kgs. 14:11; 2 Chr. 25:20); a prudent man ignores an insult (Prov. 12:16).

j They did not listen to the judges (Judg. 2:17); the Benjaminites would not listen (Judg. 20:13); Eli's sons would not listen to him (1 Sam. 2:25); the people would not listen to Samuel (1 Sam. 8:19); do not listen to Hezekiah (2 Kgs. 18:31, 32); let us not give heed to anything Jeremiah says (Jer. 18:18).

k Do not listen to the false prophets (Jer. 23:16); do not listen to your prophets and diviners (Jer. 27:9).

l Ichabod's mother took no notice (1 Sam. 4:20); they called to Baal but no one paid attention (1 Kgs. 18:29).

457 Carefulness

● Beware

a Beware the leaven of the Pharisees and Sadducees (Matt. 16:6–12; Mark 8:15); beware of the leaven of the Pharisees, hypocrisy (Luke 12:1); beware of the scribes (Mark 12:38; Luke 20:46); beware of dogs, evil workers, mutilators (Phil. 3:2); beware of covetousness (Luke 12:15).

Beware of men, see **371a**; **beware of your speech**, see **579d**; **beware of hundrances**, see **702a**.

● Keep watch

b May the Lord watch between us (Gen. 31:49); God guarded Israel as the apple of his eye (Deut. 32:10); the Lord's eyes are always on the land to care for it (Deut. 11:12); I am watching over my word (Jer. 1:12).

c Keep watch, for you do not know when your Lord is coming (Matt. 24:42–3); keep watch, for you do not know the time (Matt. 25:13; Mark 13:33–7); keep watch at all times (Luke 21:36); be on guard lest the day come suddenly (Luke 21:34); he commanded the gatekeeper to keep watch (Mark 13:34).

d Watch and pray that you may not enter into temptation (Matt. 26:41; Mark 14:38); keep watch with me (Matt. 26:38); could you not keep watch for one hour? (Matt. 26:40; Mark 14:37).

e Keep watch (Mark 13:37; 14:34); keep watch, stand firm in the faith (1 Cor. 16:13); watch yourself and your teaching (1 Tim. 4:16); guard your heart diligently (Prov. 4:23); be careful how you live (Eph. 5:15); let him who thinks he stands take heed lest he fall (1 Cor. 10:12).

f Be on guard for yourselves and the flock (Acts 20:28); we prayed to God and set a guard (Neh. 4:9); they sat down and kept watch over him (Matt. 27:36).

● Watchmen

g On your walls I have appointed watchmen (Isa. 62:6); I set watchmen over you (Jer. 6:17); when I choose someone and make him a watchman (Ezek. 33:2–6); I have made you a watchman (Ezek. 3:17; 33:7); set a watchman (Isa. 21:6); the prophet is the watchman of Ephraim (Hos. 9:8); watchmen on the hills of Ephraim (Jer. 31:6).

h The watchman stands continually on the watchtower (Isa. 21:8); the watchman saw people coming (2 Sam. 13:34; 18:24–7; 2 Kgs. 9:17); watchman, what of the night? (Isa. 21:11); your watchmen shout joyfully together (Isa. 52:8).

i When the watchmen of the house tremble (Eccles. 12:3); the watchmen found me (S. of S. 3:3; 5:7).

j Those sent to patrol the earth (Zech. 1:10–11; 6:7).

● Taking care

k Taking care of his victim (Exod. 21:19); take care of him (Luke 10:35); he who takes care of his master will be honoured (Prov. 27:18).

l They consecrated Eleazar to keep the ark (1 Sam. 7:1); ten concubines to look after the house (2 Sam. 15:16).

458 Negligence

● Neglecting the needy

a You must not neglect the Levite (Deut. 14:27); we will not neglect the house of our God (Neh. 10:39); he who shuts his ear to the cry of the poor will cry and not be answered (Prov. 21:13). **Not helping the poor**, see **801***k*.

b My own vineyard I have neglected (S. of S. 1:6).

● Neglecting God's things

c The Pharisees tithed herbs but neglected more important matters (Matt. 23:23; Luke 11:42); how shall we escape if we neglect such a great salvation? (Heb. 2:3); cursed be he who does the Lord's work with slackness (Jer. 48:10). **Inattention**, see **456**; **not seeking God**, see **459***ab*.

459 Enquiry

● Enquiring of God

a Those who enquired of God: Rebekah (Gen. 25:22); Balaam (Num. 22:8, 19); the Israelites (Judg. 1:1; 20:23, 27); Saul (1 Sam. 14:36–7; 28:6); David (1 Sam. 23:2, 4, 10–12; 2 Sam. 5:19, 23; 12:16; 21:1; 1 Chr. 14:10, 14; 21:30).

b They came to Moses to enquire of God (Exod. 18:15); enquire of God for us (Judg. 18:5; 2 Kgs. 22:13; Jer. 21:2); elders came to enquire of the Lord (Ezek. 20:1); they enquired of the Lord where Saul was (1 Sam. 10:22); Ahimelech enquired of the Lord for David (1 Sam. 22:10, 13, 15); enquire of the Lord through Elisha (2 Kgs. 8:8); enquire first for the word of God (1 Kgs. 22:5; 2 Kgs. 3:11; 2 Chr. 18:4); enquire of the Lord for me (2 Chr. 34:21); the advice of Ahithophel was like enquiring from God (2 Sam. 16:23); should I be consulted by such people (Ezek. 14:3).

c Enquiring by Urim (Num. 27:21); using an ephod to enquire (1 Sam. 23:9–12; 30:7–8); to enquire in his temple (Ps. 27:4); Saul called for the ark (1 Sam. 14:18–19); the bronze altar is for me to enquire by (2 Kgs. 16:15).

d The prophets enquired about the Christ (1 Pet. 1:10–11).

• Not enquiring of God

e They did not enquire of God about the Gibeonites (Josh. 9:14); we did not enquire of God about the ark (1 Chr. 15:13); I will not have you enquire of me (Ezek. 20:3, 31).

f Enquiring of Baal-zebub instead of God (2 Kgs. 1:2–3, 6, 16); Saul enquired of a medium, not of the Lord (1 Chr. 10:13–14); when they say consult mediums, should not a people consult their God? (Isa. 8:19); they enquire of a thing of wood (Hos. 4:12).

• Querying
• Asking questions

g No one can question what God does (Job 9:12).

h I was only asking (1 Sam. 17:29); Esther sent to enquire why Mordecai was mourning (Esther 4:5); Pilate asked whether he were already dead (Mark 15:44).

i When your children ask you about these things (Exod. 12:26; 13:14; Deut. 6:20; Josh. 4:6, 21); do not be ensnared by enquiring about their gods (Deut. 12:30); Herod enquired where Christ was to be born (Matt. 2:4).

j Let women ask their husbands at home (1 Cor. 14:35); the Queen of Sheba came with difficult questions (1 Kgs. 10:1; 2 Chr. 9:1).

• Jesus questioning

k Jesus was asking the teachers questions (Luke 2:46); who do men say I am? (Matt. 16:13; Mark 8:27; Luke 9:18); who do you say I am? (Matt. 16:15; Mark 8:29; Luke 9:20); Jesus asked the Pharisees a question (Matt. 22:41); if I ask you a question you will not answer (Luke 22:68); if you answer my question I will answer yours (Matt. 21:24; Mark 11:29; Luke 20:3).

• Questioning Jesus

l They asked him about the parables (Mark 4:10; 7:17); the disciples asked him why they could not cast it out (Matt. 17:19; Mark 9:28); in the house the disciples questioned him about divorce (Mark 10:10); Peter, John and James questioned him (Mark 13:3).

m The scribes and Pharisees assailed him with questions (Luke 11:53); the Pharisees asked Jesus when the kingdom of God was coming (Luke 17:20); a Pharisee asked him a question to test him (Matt. 22:35).

n They were afraid to ask him (Mark 9:32; Luke 9:45); no one dared ask him any more questions (Matt. 22:46; Mark 12:34; Luke 20:40); in that day you will ask me no questions (John 16:23).

● Interrogating   *o*   When Esau asks you (Gen. 32:17); the man questioned us about our family (Gen. 43:7); Gideon interrogated a youth from Succoth (Judg. 8:14); the governor interrogated Jesus (Matt. 27:11; Mark 15:2); Herod questioned Jesus at some length (Luke 23:9); the high priest questioned Jesus about his disciples and teaching (John 18:19); why question me? (John 18:21); the high priest questioned them (Acts 5:27); Paul was to be examined by scourging (Acts 22:24).

● Investigating   *p*   Investigate reports that some are following other gods (Deut. 13:14); investigate how this sin happened (1 Sam. 14:38); his father never pained him by asking what he did (1 Kgs. 1:6).

● Spying   *q*   The wicked spies on the righteous (Ps. 37:32); Joseph accused his brothers of being spies (Gen. 42:9–14, 30–1, 34); Moses sent men to spy out the land (Num. 13:2; 32:8; Deut. 1:22–5; Josh. 14:7); Moses sent men to spy out Jazer (Num. 21:32); Joshua sent out two spies (Josh. 2:1–3); Joshua sent men to spy out Ai (Josh. 7:2); men were sent to spy our Bethel (Judg. 1:23–4); the Danites sent five men to spy out the land (Judg. 18:2); David set out spies (1 Sam. 26:4); Abner came to find out all you are doing (2 Sam. 3:25); the Ammonites suspected David of sending spies (2 Sam. 10:3; 1 Chr. 19:3); Absalom sent spies throughout the land (2 Sam. 15:10); the priests sent spies to watch Jesus (Luke 20:20).

● Seeking   *r*   There is a time to seek (Eccles. 3:6); the preacher was seeking out everything done under heaven (Eccles. 1:13); seek and you will find (Matt. 7:7; Luke 11:9); he who seeks good seeks favour (Prov. 11:27); seek wisdom like silver (Prov. 2:4); they will seek wisdom but not find her (Prov. 1:28).
Aim at love, see **887b**.

● Seek God!   *s*   Seek God! (Job 8:5); seek the Lord while he may be found (Isa. 55:6); it is time to seek the Lord (Hos. 10:12); seek the Lord and live (Amos 5:4, 6); seek the Lord, all you humble of the earth (Zeph. 2:3); seek the Lord and his strength (1 Chr. 16:11; Ps. 105:4); set your heart to seek the Lord (1 Chr. 22:19); Asa commanded them to seek the Lord (2 Chr. 14:4); let us go to seek the Lord (Zech. 8:21–2).

   t   Seek first God's kingdom (Matt. 6:33; Luke 12:31); seek the things above, where Christ is (Col. 3:1).

   u   If my people humble themselves and seek my face (2 Chr. 7:14).

● Seeking God   *v*   I seek you (Ps. 63:1); I seek your precepts (Ps. 119:45); your face I will seek (Ps. 27:8); with my whole heart I have sought you (Ps. 119:10); I would seek God (Job 5:8); like you, we seek your God (Ezra 4:2); when he killed them they sought him (Ps. 78:34); yet they seek me day by day (Isa. 58:2); they will seek the Lord but not find him (Hos. 5:6); they will seek the word of the Lord but not find it (Amos 8:12).

   w   Those who sought God went to the tent of meeting (Exod. 33:7);

a covenant to seek the Lord (2 Chr. 15:12–13); in distress they sought you (Isa. 26:16); Jehoshaphat sought the Lord (2 Chr. 17:4; 19:3; 20:3; 22:9); Hezekiah sought the Lord (2 Chr. 31:21); Josiah began to seek God (2 Chr. 34:3).

x The Lord looks to see if any seek after God (Ps. 14:2; 53:2); for my people who seek me (Isa. 65:10); those who set their heart on seeking the Lord (2 Chr. 11:16); this is the generation of those who seek him (Ps. 24:6); afterwards Israel will seek the Lord (Hos. 3:5); Israel and Judah will come weeping, seeking the Lord (Jer. 50:4).

- Seeking and finding God

y If you seek him, he will be found by you (1 Chr. 28:9; 2 Chr. 15:2); you will seek him and find him when you seek with all your heart (Deut. 4:29; Jer. 29:13); that men would seek him and perhaps find him (Acts 17:27); they sought God and he was found by them (2 Chr. 15:4, 15).

z If I only knew where to find him! (Job 23:3).

- Good to seek God

aa The Lord is good to those who seek him (Lam. 3:25); those who seek the Lord shall not lack (Ps. 34:10); as long as Uzziah sought the Lord, he prospered (2 Chr. 26:5); I sought the Lord and he answered he (Ps. 34:4); let those who seek the Lord rejoice (1 Chr. 16:10; Ps. 105:3); happy are those who seek him (Ps. 119:2); those who seek him will praise him (Ps. 22:26).

- Not seeking God

ab No one seeks for God (Rom. 3:11); the wicked does not seek God (Ps. 10:4); they do not seek the Lord (Isa. 9:13); the shepherds do not seek the Lord (Jer. 10:21); they have not sought him (Hos. 7:10); they do not seek your statutes (Ps. 119:155); I was found by those who did not seek me (Isa. 65:1; Rom. 10:20); I will sweep away those who do not seek the Lord (Zeph. 1:6); I will go to my place until they seek me (Hos. 5:15).

- God searching

ac God searches minds and hearts (1 Chr. 28:9; Rom. 8:27; Rev. 2:23); Lord, you have searched me and known me (Ps. 139:1); search me and know my heart (Ps. 139:23); I the Lord search the heart (Jer. 17:10).

Trying hearts, see **461a**.

- God seeking

ad I myself will search for my sheep (Ezek. 34:11); seek me like a lost sheep! (Ps. 119:176); I will seek the lost (Ezek. 34:16); the Son of man has come to seek and to save what was lost (Luke 19:10); searching for the straying sheep (Matt. 18:12; Luke 15:4); the Father seeks such to worship him (John 4:23).

- Searching for things

ae Laban searched the tent (Gen. 31:34); Saul looked for the donkeys (1 Sam. 9:3; 10:14); a search was made in the royal archives (Ezra 5:17; 6:1); search in the books (Ezra 4:15); a search has been made (Ezra 4:19).

- Searching for people

af Joseph seeking his brothers (Gen. 37:15–16); they sought the spies but did not find them (Josh. 2:22); they searched but could not find the messengers (2 Sam. 17:20); Saul searched daily for David (1 Sam. 23:14); investigate and make sure where he is

(1 Sam. 23:22); Shimei went to look for his servants (1 Kgs. 2:40); everyone sought the wisdom of Solomon (1 Kgs. 10:24; 2 Chr. 9:23); Ahab searched for Elijah (1 Kgs. 18:10); the prophets searched for Elijah (2 Kgs. 2:16–17); I looked for my beloved but did not find him (S. of S. 3:1; 5:6); three men were looking for Peter (Acts 10:19); Herod searched for Peter and did not find him (Acts 12:19); Onesiphorus searched for Paul (2 Tim. 1:17).

● Searching for Jesus

ag Herod searched for the child Jesus (Matt. 2:8, 13); Mary and Joseph searched for Jesus (Luke 2:44–5, 48–9); the disciples searched for Jesus (Mark 1:36); they were seeking Jesus (John 11:56); the crowds were searching for him (Luke 4:42; John 6:24); everyone is seeking you (Mark 1:37); you seek me because you ate bread (John 6:26); whom do you seek? (John 18:4, 7; 20:15); you are looking for Jesus who was crucified (Matt. 28:5); you will seek me but not find me (John 7:34, 36; 8:21); you will seek me and not be able to come (John 13:33).

460 Answer

● God answering

a Answer me when I call! (Ps. 4:1); answer me, O Lord! (Ps. 69:16; 86:1; 119:145); I cry but you do not answer (Ps. 22:2); is there anyone who will answer? (Job 5:1).

b May the Lord answer you in the day of trouble (Ps. 20:1); you will answer (Ps. 38:15; 86:7); on the day I called you answered me (Ps. 138:3).

c God will give Pharaoh an answer (Gen. 41:16); the God who answers by fire is God (1 Kgs. 18:24); I cry to the Lord and he answers me (Ps. 3:4); I sought the Lord and he answered me (Ps. 34:4); you will call and the Lord will answer (Isa. 58:9); I called to the Lord and he answered me (Ps. 118:5; 120:1; Jonah 2:2); you have answered me (Ps. 118:21); they called to the Lord and he answered them (Ps. 99:6); Lord, you answered them (Ps. 99:8); before they call I will answer (Isa. 65:24); I will answer them (Zech. 10:6; 13:9).

God answers prayer, see **761z**.

● Answering God

d I called but no one answered (Isa. 65:12; 66:4); when I called, why was there no one to answer? (Isa. 50:2).

e He will call and I will answer him (Ps. 91:15).

f Who are you to answer back to God? (Rom. 9:20).

● Answering men

g An apt answer is a joy (Prov. 15:23); a right answer is a kiss on the lips (Prov. 24:26); the answer of the tongue is from the Lord (Prov. 16:1); it is folly to give an answer before hearing (Prov. 18:13); that you may give a true answer to him who sent you (Prov. 22:21); do not answer a fool according to his folly (Prov. 26:4–5); if you answer my question I will answer yours (Matt. 21:24; Mark 11:29; Luke 20:3).

h Be prepared to give an answer to everyone who asks for a reason

(1 Pet. 3:15); to know how to reply to each one (Col. 4:6); I will have an answer for him who reproaches me (Ps. 119:42).

i How will one answer the messengers of the nations? (Isa. 14:32); Solomon answered all the Queen of Sheba's questions (1 Kgs. 10:3; 2 Chr. 9:2); Artaxerxes sent an answer (Ezra 4:17); is that how you answer the high priest? (John 18:22).

● No answer

j God did not answer Saul that day (1 Sam. 14:37); the Lord did not answer him by dreams or Urim or prophets (1 Sam. 28:6, 15); the seers are ashamed because there is no answer from God (Mic. 3:7); God did not answer them (2 Sam. 22:42; Ps. 18:41); I cry out to you but you do not answer me (Job 30:20); he who neglects the poor will cry and not be answered (Prov. 21:13); they will cry to the Lord but he will not answer them (Mic. 3:4).
Prayer not answered, see **761***ae*.

k They will call, but wisdom will not answer (Prov. 1:28); we do not need to answer you (Dan. 3:16).

l Do you make no answer? (Matt. 26:62; Mark 14:60; 15:4); Jesus did not answer Herod (Luke 23:9).
Keep silent, see **582**.

m When they called on Baal no one answered (1 Kgs, 18:26, 29); though you cry to an idol it cannot answer (Isa. 46:7).

461 Experiment

● God testing men

a Test me, O Lord (Ps. 26:2); try me and know my thoughts (Ps. 139:23); I test the mind (Jer. 17:10); God tries the heart (1 Chr. 29:17; Ps. 7:9); God who tests our hearts (1 Thess. 2:4); his eyes test the sons of men (Ps. 11:4); God tests like one refining silver (Ps. 66:10; Prov. 17:3; Zech. 13:9); what is man that you examine him continually? (Job 7:17–18); I have tested you in the furnace of affliction, not like silver (Isa. 48:10); I will refine and assay them (Jer. 9:7); when he has tested me, I shall come forth like gold (Job 23:10); you have tested me and found nothing (Ps. 17:3).

b God tested Abraham (Gen. 22:1; Heb. 11:17); God tested Gideon's soldiers (Judg. 7:4); the word of the Lord tested Joseph (Ps. 105:19); you test the righteous (Jer. 20:12).

c God tested the Israelites to see whether: they would follow his commands (Exod. 16:4; Deut. 8:2; Judg. 3:1, 4); they would keep the way of the Lord (Judg. 2:22); they loved the Lord (Deut. 13:3).

d There the Lord tested them (Exod. 15:25); I tested you at the waters of Meribah (Ps. 81:7); God has come to test you (Exod. 20:20); God fed them manna to test them (Deut. 8:16); God left Hezekiah alone to test him (2 Chr. 32:31); he said this to test Philip (John 6:6).

● Man tested

e Count it all joy when you fall into testings (Jas. 1:2); that the proving of your faith may result in glory (1 Pet. 1:7); the fiery ordeal comes on you to test you (1 Pet. 4:12); a man is tested by his praise (Prov. 27:21).

● Men testing
God

f Do not put the Lord to the test (Deut. 6:16; Matt. 4:7; Luke 4:12); your fathers tested me (Ps. 95:9; Heb. 3:9); why put God to the test? (Exod. 17:2, 7; Acts 15:10); they put God to the test (Num. 14:22; Ps. 78:18, 41, 56; 106:14); you agreed to test the Spirit of the Lord (Acts 5:9); we should not test the Lord as they did (1 Cor. 10:9); I will not test the Lord (Isa. 7:12).

g Test me now (Mal. 3:10); evildoers put God to the test and escape (Mal. 3:15).

● Men testing
men etc.

h Joseph's brothers were to be tested (Gen. 42:15–16); test us for ten days (Dan. 1:12, 14); the Queen of Sheba came to test Solomon with hard questions (1 Kgs. 10:1; 2 Chr. 9:1); a man is tested by the praise given him (Prov. 27:21).

i I have made you an assayer and tester among my people (Jer. 6:27); deacons must first be tested (1 Tim. 3:10); you have put to the test those who claim to be apostles (Rev. 2:2); I wrote to test you (2 Cor. 2:9).

j Test everything (1 Thess. 5:21); test the spirits (1 John 4:1); the ear tests words as the palate tastes food (Job 12:11; 34:3); I tested all this with wisdom (Eccles. 7:23).

● Testing
Jesus

k The Pharisees and Sadducees asked for a sign to test Jesus (Matt. 16:1; Mark 8:11; Luke 11:16); a Pharisee asked Jesus a question to test him (Matt. 22:35); Pharisees tested him about divorce (Matt. 19:3; Mark 10:2); a lawyer put Jesus to the test (Luke 10:25); they said this to test him (John 8:6); why put me to the test? (Matt. 22:18; Mark 12:15).

Temptation, see **612*l*.**

● Testing
oneself

l Let us test and examine our ways (Lam. 3:40); test yourselves to see whether you are in the faith (2 Cor. 13:5); let a man examine himself before eating and drinking (1 Cor. 11:28).

Taste, see **386.**

462 Comparison

● Beyond
compare

a To whom will you compare God? (Isa. 40:18); to whom will you compare me? (Isa. 40:25; 46:5); the present sufferings are not worth comparing with the glory to come (Rom. 8:18).

● Comparing

b Some compare themselves with themselves (2 Cor. 10:12).

Liken, see **18*n*; who is like?** see **21*a*.**

463 Discrimination

● Discerning
God's word

a How shall we know a message which the Lord has not spoken? (Deut. 18:21); help me discern between good and evil (1 Kgs. 3:9); if the cart goes straight to Beth-shemesh we shall know it was the Lord (1 Sam. 6:9); the gift of distinguishing spirits (1 Cor. 12:10); that your love may abound in knowledge and discernment (Phil. 1:9).

- Distinguishing people

b The word 'Shibboleth' used to discriminate (Judg. 12:5–6); you will know them by their fruits (Matt. 7:16, 20); a tree is known by its fruit (Matt. 12:33); by this we know the children of God and the children of the devil (1 John 3:10).
Known by their fruit, see **171***t*.

464 Indiscrimination

- Confounding opposites

a Woe to those who confound good and evil, light and darkness, bitter and sweet (Isa. 5:20).

b You strain out a gnat and swallow a camel (Matt. 23:24).

465 Measurement

- Weights and measures

a Use honest weights and measures (Lev. 19:35–6; Ezek. 45:10); a just balance and scales are the Lord's (Prov. 16:11); the Levites are to assist the priest over measures of volume and size (1 Chr. 23:29); by the measure you measure it will be measured to you (Matt. 7:2; Mark 4:24; Luke 6:38); the rider had a pair of scales (Rev. 6:5).

b A shekel is 20 gerahs (Exod. 30:13; Ezek. 45:12); the maneh will be 60 shekels (Ezek. 45:12).
Weighing, see **322***e*.

c An omer is a tenth of an ephah (Exod. 16:36); an ephah is equal to a bath, a tenth of a homer (Ezek. 45:11, 14); the ephah measure with Wickedness inside (Zech. 5:6–8).

d The grain was beyond measuring (Gen. 41:49); each gathered at least ten homers (Num. 11:32); Ruth gleaned an ephah of barley (Ruth 2:17); given six measures of barley (Ruth 3:15, 17); three measures of meal (Matt. 13:33); a hundred measures of oil (Luke 16:6); a hundred measures of wheat (Luke 16:7); one sixth of a hin of water per day (Ezek. 4:11); each jar contained 20 or 30 gallons (John 2:6).
Capacity, see **195***c*.

- Dishonest measures

e Do not have different sets of weights and measures (Deut. 25:13–15); the Lord detests this (Prov. 20:10, 23); a trader with false balances (Hos. 12:7); cheating with dishonest scales (Amos 8:5; Mic. 6:11); the Lord hates dishonest scales (Prov. 11:1).

- Line measurement

f Measuring the temple with a measuring rod (Ezek. 40:3–42:20; Rev. 11:1); measuring Jerusalem with a measuring line (Zech. 1:16; 2:1–2); measuring new Jerusalem with a measuring rod (Rev. 21:15–17); I will make justice the measuring line (Isa. 28:17); the measuring line will go out further (Jer. 31:39).

g Measuring to the nearest city from a corpse (Deut. 21:2–3).

h David measured Moab with a line (2 Sam. 8:2).
Particular distances, see **199***j*.

- Measuring out the universe

i God measured out the waters (Job 28:25); who has measured the waters in his palm? (Isa. 40:12); who has put the dust of the earth in a measure? (Isa. 40:12); who stretched the measuring line over the earth? (Job 38:5); who has measured out the heavens with a span? (Isa. 40:12); if the heavens above can be measured (Jer. 31:37).

Counting, see **86**; **dimensions**, see **195**.

Section three: Materials for reasoning

466 Evidence

● Principles
of witness

    a Two or three witnesses are needed for a conviction, not just one (Num. 35:30; Deut. 17:6; 19:15; Matt. 18:16; John 8:17; 2 Cor. 13:1; 1 Tim. 5:19; Heb. 10:28); a witness must testify (Lev. 5:1); a truthful witness saves lives (Prov. 14:25).

● Bearing
witness

    b Seven lambs as a witness (Gen. 21:30); the stone heap was a witness (Gen. 31:44, 48, 50); the two and a half tribes built an altar as a witness (Josh. 22:27–8, 34); Joshua took a stone as a witness (Josh. 24:27); I have made David a witness to the peoples (Isa. 55:4); you are my witnesses (Isa. 43:10, 12; 44:8).

    c Witnesses against people: heaven and earth (Deut. 30:19; 31:28); this song (Deut. 31:19, 21); the book of the law (Deut. 31:26).

    d I got faithful witnesses (Isa. 8:2); I got witnesses [to the sale] (Jer. 32:10); you are witnesses (Ruth 4:9, 11); bear witness against me if I have defrauded you (1 Sam. 12:3).

    e While you are speaking, I will confirm your words (1 Kgs. 1:14).

    f They sought testimony against Jesus (Mark 14:55); how many things they testify against you! (Matt. 27:13).

● Witness to
oneself

    g You are witnesses against yourselves (Josh. 24:22); your own mouth is witness against you (2 Sam. 1:16); you testify against yourselves (Matt. 23:31); the rust of your gold and silver will be witness against you (Jas. 5:3).

    h Demetrius has received a good testimony (3 John 12).

● The
'testimony'

    i Two tablets of the testimony (Exod. 31:18; 32:15; 34:29); 'the testimony' (Num. 17:4, 7, 8, 10); the testimony put into the ark (Exod. 25:16, 21; 40:20); the ark of the testimony (Exod. 25:16, 22; 26:33, 34; 30:6, 26; 31:7; 39:35; 40:3, 5, 21; Num. 4:5; 7:89).

    j They gave Joash the testimony (2 Chr. 23:11).

● God is
witness

    k The Lord is witness (1 Sam. 12:5); God is my witness (Rom. 1:9; Phil. 1:8; 1 Thess. 2:5); you are witnesses and so is God (1 Thess. 2:10); God established a testimony in Jacob (Ps. 78:5); the Lord is witness between us (1 Sam. 20:23, 42); the Lord will witness against you (Mic. 1:2); God testifies against his people (Ps. 50:7); my witness is in heaven (Job 16:19); God has not left himself without witness (Acts 14:17); God bore witness to the Gentiles by giving them the Spirit (Acts 15:8); God bore witness to Abel's sacrifice (Heb. 11:4).

    l God bore witness to his word with signs and wonders (Acts 14:3;

Heb. 2:4); God confirmed the word by the signs which followed (Mark 16:20).

● Bearing
witness
to Jesus

m Bearing witness to Jesus: John (John 1:7, 32; 3:26; 5:33–4); works (John 5:36; 10:25); the Father (John 5:37; 8:18; 1 John 5:9–11); the Scriptures (John 5:39); the Spirit (John 15:26; Acts 5:32; 1 John 5:7–8); Jesus himself (John 5:31; 8:13–14, 18).

n A witness of the sufferings of Christ (1 Pet. 5:1); he who has seen has borne witness (John 19:35); you will be a witness of what you have seen and heard (Acts 22:15); we bear witness (John 3:11; 1 John 1:2); you will be witnesses to me to the ends of the earth (Acts 1:8); witnesses to the resurrection (Acts 1:22; 2:32; 3:15; 4:33; 5:32; 10:39–42; 13:31).

o God bore witness to Jesus (John 5:32; Acts 17:31); this is John's testimony (John 1:19); I have borne witness that this is the Son of God (John 1:34); many Samaritans believed because of the woman's testimony (John 4:39); on Patmos because of the testimony of Jesus (Rev. 1:9); Antipas, my witness (Rev. 2:13); they overcame him by the blood of the Lamb and the word of their testimony (Rev. 12:11); those slain for their testimony (Rev. 6:9); those who bear testimony to Jesus (Rev. 12:17); the testimony of Jesus is the spirit of prophecy (Rev. 19:10). **Proving,** see **478**.

● Jesus
bearing
witness

p Jesus bore witness against the world (John 7:7); Jesus testified the good confession before Pilate (1 Tim. 6:13); he came to bear witness to the truth (John 18:37); he gave many proofs that he was alive (Acts 1:3); he is the faithful witness (Rev. 1:5; 3:14); he bears witness of what he has seen and heard (John 3:32).

q I will confess his name before my Father (Rev. 3:5).

● Witness
with the
Spirit

r We are witnesses and so is the Holy Spirit (Acts 5:32); the Spirit bears witness with our spirit (Rom. 8:16); my conscience bears me witness in the Holy Spirit (Rom. 9:1); three witnesses, the Spirit, the water and the blood (1 John 5:7–8).

● Witness
to the
gospel

s You will be witnesses before kings and governors (Matt. 10:18; Mark 13:9; Luke 21:12–13); the gospel will be preached as a witness to all the world (Matt. 24:14); offer what Moses commanded, as a testimony (Matt. 8:4; Mark 1:44; Luke 5:14); you are witnesses of these things (Luke 24:48); you must bear witness for you have been with me from the beginning (John 15:27); we know this disciple's testimony is true (John 21:24); John bore testimony to the word of God (Rev. 1:2); Paul was appointed a witness (Acts 26:16); in Jerusalem and in Rome (Acts 23:11); you testified before many witnesses (1 Tim. 6:12); two witnesses clothed in sackcloth (Rev. 11:3); since we are surrounded by so great a cloud of witnesses (Heb. 12:1). **Witness before men**, see **371t**.

● False
witnesses

t You shall not bear false witness (Exod. 20:16; 23:1–3; Deut. 5:20; Matt. 19:18; Mark 10:19; Luke 18:20); do not witness against your neighbour without cause (Prov. 24:28); the Lord hates false witness (Prov. 6:19); a false witness will not go unpunished (Prov. 19:5, 9); a false witness will perish (Prov. 21:28); a worthless witness makes a mockery of justice (Prov. 19:28); a man who bears false witness is like a club, a sword, an arrow (Prov. 25:18).

u The investigation of a false witness (Deut. 19:16–21); from the heart comes false witness (Matt. 15:19); false witnesses have risen against me (Ps. 27:12; 35:11); will you commit false witness? (Jer. 7:9).

v Many false witnesses came forward against Jesus (Matt. 26:59–60; Mark 14:56–7); against Stephen (Acts 6:13); two worthless men to testify against Naboth (1 Kgs. 21:10, 13).

w If Christ did not rise, we are false witnesses against God (1 Cor. 15:15).

Inconsistent testimony, see **709*m***.

467 Counterevidence

Witness against, see **466*c***.

468 Qualification

Excuses, see **614**.

469 Possibility

● Possible for God

a With man this is impossible, but with God all things are possible (Matt. 19:26; Mark 10:27); what is impossible for men is possible for God (Luke 18:27); with God nothing is impossible (Luke 1:37); all things are possible for you (Mark 14:36); I know you can do all things (Job 42:2).

Power of God, see **160*a***; **nothing too difficult**, see **701*a***.

b If it be possible, let this cup pass (Matt. 26:39); if it were possible, the hour might pass from him (Mark 14:35).

● Possible for God's people

c Nothing will be impossible for them (Gen. 11:6); nothing will be impossible for you (Matt. 17:20); I can do all things through him who strengthens me (Phil. 4:13).

470 Impossibility

● Impossible for men

a With men it is impossible (Matt. 19:26; Mark 10:27); what is impossible for men is possible with God (Luke 18:27).

● Impossible for God

b It is impossible for God to lie (Heb. 6:18); God cannot lie (Titus 1:2); he cannot deny himself (2 Tim. 2:13).

c If God made windows in heaven, could this happen? (2 Kgs. 7:2, 19).

God's limitations, see **161*a***.

471 Probability

Certain, see **473**.

472 Improbability

Uncertain, see **474**.

473 Certainty

● Sure
knowledge

a How can I know I will possess the land? (Gen. 15:8); how can I be sure of this? (Luke 1:18); let every one be fully convinced in his own mind (Rom. 14:5).
Signs to convince, see **547***d*.

● Certain
beyond
doubt

b Every word of God is proved (Prov. 30:5); the gifts and calling of God are irrevocable (Rom. 11:29); it is inevitable that stumbling blocks come (Matt. 18:7).

● Faithful
sayings

c It is a faithful saying that Christ came to save sinners (1 Tim. 1:15); the saying is sure, deserving full acceptance (1 Tim. 4:9); the saying is sure (2 Tim. 2:11; Titus 3:8).

474 Uncertainty

● Puzzlement

a Susa was in confusion (Esther 3:15); when Herod heard John he was perplexed (Mark 6:20); Herod was perplexed about Jesus (Luke 9:7).

● Uncertain
things

b Refuse foolish controversies (2 Tim. 2:23).

c Not to trust in uncertain riches (1 Tim. 6:17).

Section four: Reasoning processes

---

475 Reasoning

● Reasoned
argument

a I would present my case before him (Job 23:4); scribes reasoning in their hearts about who could forgive sins (Mark 2:6, 8); they became futile in their reasoning (Rom. 1:21).

● Discussions

b What were you discussing on the way? (Mark 9:33); they discussed among themselves (Matt. 21:25; Mark 11:31; Luke 20:5); Paul conducted discussions (Acts 17:2, 17; 18:4, 19; 19:8, 9).
Argue, see **709**.

476 Intuition: absence of reason

● Instinct

a Creatures of instinct (2 Pet. 2:12); the things they know by instinct (Jude 10).

477 Sophistry: false reasoning

● False
reasoning

a We destroy sophistries (2 Cor. 10:5).

478 Demonstration

● Proving

a Proving that this Jesus is the Christ (Acts 9:22).
Bearing witness to Jesus, see **466***m*.

479 Confutation

● Refuting   *a* Apollos completely refuted the Jews (Acts 18:28).

Section five: Results of reasoning

480 Judgement: conclusion

● How you judge

a By the judgement you judge you will be judged (Matt. 7:2); do not judge according to appearance (John 7:24); you judge according to the flesh (John 8:15); why do you not judge what is right? (Luke 12:57); does our law judge a man without first hearing him? (John 7:51).

b Do not judge and you will not be judged (Matt. 7:1; Luke 6:37); let us not judge one another (Rom. 14:13); do not judge before the time (1 Cor. 4:5); mercy triumphs over judgement (Jas. 2:13).

● God, judge!

c Judge the earth, O God (Ps. 82:8); let the nations be judged (Ps. 9:19); may God judge between us (Gen. 16:5; 31:53; 1 Sam. 24:12, 15); judge me (Ps. 35:24); may the Lord judge you (Exod. 5:21); will you not judge them? (2 Chr. 20:12).

● God judges

d It is God who judges (Ps. 75:7); judgement belongs to God (Deut. 1:17); with him deeds are weighed (1 Sam. 2:3); God will bring every act to judgement (Eccles. 12:14); the Lord weighs the heart (Prov. 21:2); you bring men to judgement (Job 14:3); the Father judges each man's work (1 Pet. 1:17); the dead were judged according to what they had done (Rev. 20:11–13); man dies once, and after that comes judgement (Heb. 9:27); Paul spoke on the judgement to come (Acts 24:25); he will convict the world regarding judgement (John 16:8).

e The Lord will judge the earth (1 Sam. 2:10; 1 Chr. 16:33); the Lord judges the peoples (Ps. 7:8); there is a God who judges the earth (Ps. 58:11); I will judge that nation (Gen. 15:14); he will judge the living and the dead (1 Pet. 4:5); he will judge the nations (Ps. 96:10; Isa. 2:4; Joel 3:2, 12; Mic. 4:3); the Lord comes to judge everyone (Jude 15); God will judge those outside (1 Cor. 5:13); the hour of his judgement has come (Rev. 14:7); God has judged her (Rev. 18:20); the ruler of this world has been judged (John 16:11).

● God judges his people

f The Lord will judge his people (Heb. 10:30); the Lord stands to judge his people (Isa. 3:13); it is time for judgement to begin with the household of God (1 Pet. 4:17); I will judge between my sheep (Ezek. 34:17, 20, 22); he judges among the great ones (Ps. 82:1); we must all stand before the judgement seat of God (Rom. 14:10–11); we must all stand before the judgement seat of Christ (2 Cor. 5:10); Jesus Christ will judge the living and the dead (2 Tim. 4:1); if we sin wilfully there is a fearful expectation of judgement (Heb. 10:27).

g Act like those who will be judged by the law of liberty (Jas. 2:12); the Lord is the one to judge me (1 Cor. 4:4).

● God judges
righteously

h You will judge the peoples with righteousness (Ps. 67:4); you judge righteously (Jer. 11:20); you sit on your throne judging righteously (Ps. 9:4); he will judge the world in righteousness (Ps. 9:8; 96:13; 98:9); if God be unjust, how will he judge the world? (Rom. 3:6); will not the judge of all the earth do right? (Gen. 18:25).

● The Son
judging

i The king's son will judge the people in righteousness (Ps. 72:2); with righteousness he will judge (Isa. 11:3–4); the Father has committed all judgement to the Son (John 5:22); my judgement is true (John 8:16); for judgement I have come into the world (John 9:39); God will judge the world by the man he has appointed (Acts 17:31); God will judge men through Jesus Christ (Rom. 2:16); he gave him authority to execute judgement (John 5:27); Jesus Christ will judge the living and the dead (2 Tim. 4:1); my judgement is just (John 5:30).

j Who made me a judge? (Luke 12:14); I did not come to judge but to save (John 12:47); God did not send the Son to judge the world (John 3:17); I judge no one (John 8:15).

k This is the judgement, that light has come into the world (John 3:19); the word that I have spoken will judge him (John 12:48); now is the judgement of this world (John 12:31); he who believes in him is not judged (John 3:18); he who does not believe is judged already (John 3:18); whoever believes does not come into judgement (John 5:24).

● God's people
judging

l The breastpiece of judgement (Exod. 28:15, 29, 30); Aaron shall carry the judgement of Israel (Exod. 28:30); priests are to judge (Ezek. 44:24).

m Moses judged disputes (Exod. 18:13, 16); let them judge the people (Exod. 18:22); they judged the people (Exod. 18:26); the priests and the judge will decide (Deut. 17:9); thrones for judgement stand in Jerusalem (Ps. 122:5); you have appointed them to judge (Hab. 1:12).

n Samuel judging on circuit (1 Sam. 7:15–17); give me a hearing heart to judge your people (1 Kgs. 3:9); the hall of the throne where he was to judge (1 Kgs. 7:7); may the king judge your people with justice (Ps. 72:1–2); the king's mouth must not err in judgement (Prov. 16:10); the Lord is with you in giving judgement (2 Chr. 19:6); do you judge uprightly, you rulers? (Ps. 58:1).

o Lot wants to be the judge! (Gen. 19:9); Dan shall judge (Gen. 49:16).

● Judging
one another

p You will sit on thrones judging the twelve tribes of Israel (Matt. 19:28; Luke 22:30); thrones on which those given authority to judge were seated (Rev. 20:4); the spiritual man judges all things (1 Cor. 2:15); should you not judge those inside the church?

(1 Cor. 5:12); the saints will judge the world and angels (1 Cor. 6:2–3); I have already judged him as though present (1 Cor. 5:3).

q Let prophets speak and the others judge (1 Cor. 14:29).

r It is a small thing to be judged by you (1 Cor. 4:3); who are you to judge another man's servant? (Rom. 14:4); who are you to judge your neighbour? (Jas. 4:12); he who speaks against his brother judges the law (Jas. 4:11); let no one judge you regarding food and drink (Col. 2:16).

s If we judged ourselves we would not be judged (1 Cor. 11:31).

● Reckoning

t God reckoned his faith as righteousness (Gen. 15:6; Rom. 4:3–6, 9–11, 22; Gal. 3:6; Jas. 2:23); reckoned righteous by faith (Rom. 3:28; 4:24); Phinehas' intervention was reckoned to him for righteousness (Ps. 106:31); will not his uncircumcision be reckoned as circumcision? (Rom. 2:26).

u He was reckoned with the transgressors (Mark 15:28; Luke 11:50); reckon yourselves dead to sin (Rom. 6:11).

481 Misjudgement. Prejudice

● Partiality

a God shows no partiality (Deut. 10:17; Job 34:19; Acts 10:34; Rom. 2:11; Gal. 2:6; Eph. 6:9; Col. 3:25); will you plead God's case with partiality? (Job 13:8, 10).

b Do not show partiality (Deut. 16:19); either to small or great (Deut. 1:17); do not show partiality to a poor man (Exod. 23:3; Lev. 19:15); do not kill the innocent (Exod. 23:7).

c Follow these instructions without partiality (1 Tim. 5:21); do not show partiality as believers (Jas. 2:1–4, 9).

d You are not partial to any one (Matt. 22:16; Mark 12:14; Luke 20:21).

e How long will you show partiality to the wicked? (Ps. 82:2); showing partiality is not good (Prov. 18:5; 28:21); partiality in judging is not good (Prov. 24:23).

482 Overestimation

● Overestimating oneself

a Let no one think more highly of himself than he ought (Rom. 12:3); if anyone thinks he is something when he is nothing (Gal. 6:3).

483 Underestimation

● Underestimating

a You thought it an easy thing to go up and fight (Deut. 1:41); the people understimated Ai (Josh. 7:3); the complacency of fools destroys them (Prov. 1:32).

484 Discovery

● Finding

a The donkeys which were lost are found (1 Sam. 9:20; 10:2, 16).

b You will find God if you seek with all your heart (Deut. 4:29); seek and you will find (Matt. 7:7–8; Luke 11:9–10); I was found by those who did not seek me (Rom. 10:20).

Seeking and finding God, see **459y**.

● Not finding   *c* They searched but could not find the messengers (2 Sam. 17:20); men cannot find out all of God's work (Eccles. 3:11; 8:17); they will seek the Lord but not find him (Hos. 5:6).

485 Belief

● Faith in general   *a* Faith is the assurance of things hoped for, the certainty of things not see (Heb. 11:1); faith comes by hearing (Rom. 10:17); Jesus is the author and finisher of faith (Heb. 12:2); the spiritual gift of faith (1 Cor. 12:9); the heroes of faith (Heb. 11:4–40); faith, hope and love remain (1 Cor. 13:13); love believes all things (1 Cor. 13:7); what is this confidence of yours? (2 Kgs. 18:19); on whom do you rely? (2 Kgs. 18:20; 2 Chr. 32:10; Isa. 36:4–5); you would trust because there is hope (Job 11:18).

    b The shield of faith can extinguish flaming darts (Eph. 6:16); faith and love as a breastplate (1 Thess. 5:8); faith works through love (Gal. 5:6); we walk by faith, not by sight (2 Cor. 5:7); our aim is sincere faith (1 Tim. 1:5); pursue faith (1 Tim. 6:11–12; 2 Tim. 2:22); fight the good fight of faith (1 Tim. 6:12); I have kept the faith (2 Tim. 4:7); one Lord, one faith, one baptism (Eph. 4:5); the faith you have, have it between yourself and God (Rom. 14:22).

    c The simple man believes everything (Prov. 14:15).

● Trust in God   *d* Faith toward God (Heb. 6:1); your faith and hope are in God (1 Pet. 1:21); trust in the Lord (Ps. 4:5; 37:3, 5; 115:9; Prov. 3:5); have faith in God (Mark 11:22); hope in God (Ps. 42:5, 11; 43:5); trust in him at all times (Ps. 62:8); trust in the Lord for ever (Isa. 26:4); let him trust in the name of the Lord (Isa. 50:10); trust in the Lord and you will be established (2 Chr. 20:20); they should put their confidence in God (Ps. 78:7); that your faith not be in the wisdom of men but the power of God (1 Cor. 2:5); I have taught you so that your trust may be in the Lord (Prov. 22:19).

● I trust in God   *e* I trust in God (Ps. 25:2; 31:6, 14; 55:23; Acts 27:25); in God I put my trust (Ps. 56:4, 11); my God, in whom I trust (Ps. 91:2); I have trusted in the Lord (Ps. 26:1); I trust in you (Ps. 143:8); I trust in your lovingkindness (Ps. 13:5); my heart trusts in him (Ps. 28:7); we trust in the Lord (2 Kgs. 18:22); we trust in his holy name (Ps. 33:21); those who know your name will trust you (Ps. 9:10); we are relying on the Lord (Isa. 36:7); we rely on you (2 Chr. 14:11); so that we might trust in God (2 Cor. 1:9).

    f I will trust and not be afraid (Isa. 12:2); he will not fear for he trusts in the Lord (Ps. 112:7); when I am afraid I will put my trust in you (Ps. 56:3); in quietness and trust will be your strength (Isa. 30:15).

● Believers in God   *g* Those who believed God: Abraham (Rom. 4:20); Daniel (Dan. 6:23); the devils (Jas. 2:19); Hezekiah (2 Kgs. 18:5, 30); the people of Israel (Exod. 4:5, 31; 14:31); the house of Israel (Isa.

10:20); Jesus (Matt. 27:43); the king (Ps. 21:7); Mary (Luke 1:45); the people of Nineveh (Jonah 3:5); Shadrach, Meshach and Abednego (Dan. 3:28).

h People full of faith and of the Holy Spirit: Stephen (Acts 6:5); Barnabas (Acts 11:24).

i Do not let your God in whom you trust deceive you (2 Kgs. 19:10); do not let Hezekiah make you trust in the Lord (Isa. 36:15).

- Results of faith

j The one who believes: is blessed (Ps. 40:4; 84:12; Prov. 16:20; Jer. 17:7); will never thirst (John 6:35); is radiant (Ps. 34:5); is delivered (Ps. 22:4); is like Mount Zion (Ps. 125:1); will not be moved (Isa. 28:16; 1 Pet. 2:6); will not be disappointed (Rom. 9:33; 10:11); has prayers heard (1 Chr. 5:20); will prosper (Prov. 28:25); will be exalted (Prov. 29:25); is surrounded by loving-kindness (Ps. 32:10); is kept in perfect peace (Isa. 26:3); has rivers of living water flowing from him (John 7:38); does not remain in darkness (John 12:46).

k Judah conquered because they trusted the Lord (2 Chr. 13:18; 16:8); you will be delivered because you trusted in me (Jer. 39:18).

l We believe, therefore we speak (2 Cor. 4:13).

- Believe in Jesus

m The work of God is to believe in the one he sent (John 6:29); this is his commandment, that we believe on Jesus Christ (1 John 3:23); that the world may believe (John 17:21); that all might believe (John 1:7); blessed are those who have not seen yet have believed (John 20:29).

n Believe in God, believe also in me (John 14:1); believe in the light that you may become sons of light (John 12:36); whoever believes in me believes in him who sent me (John 12:44); repent and believe the gospel (Mark 1:15); repentance toward God and faith in Christ (Acts 20:21); Paul spoke of faith in Christ (Acts 24:24).

- Believers in Jesus

o I believe that Jesus Christ is the Son of God (Acts 8:37); I know whom I have believed (2 Tim. 1:12); Lord, I believe! (Mark 9:24; John 9:38); he saw and believed (John 20:8).

p Those who believed: his disciples (John 2:11); many people (John 2:23; 7:31; 8:30; Acts 4:4); many Samaritans (John 4:39, 41); an official (John 4:50); and his household (John 4:53); the man born blind (John 9:35–8); many across Jordan (John 10:42); many Jews (John 11:45; 12:11); many rulers (John 12:42); many men and women (Acts 5:14); Gentiles appointed for eternal life (Acts 13:48); the jailer and all his house (Acts 16:34); some Athenians (Acts 17:34); many Corinthians (Acts 18:8).

q Your faith is spoken of all over the world (Rom. 1:8); he was believed on in the world (1 Tim. 3:16); I have heard of your faith (Eph. 1:15); we heard of your faith in Christ (Col. 1:4); I hear of your faith in the Lord Jesus (Philem. 5); you have received a faith like ours (2 Pet. 1:1); your faith is more precious than gold (1 Pet. 1:7); sincere faith which your grandmother and mother also had (2 Tim. 1:5); one of these little ones who believe in me (Matt. 18:6); I pray for all who will believe through their word (John 17:20); I have prayed for you that your faith fail not (Luke 22:32).

r Let him come down from the cross and we will believe in him (Matt. 27:42; Mark 15:32).

● Righteous by faith

s Abraham believed God and it was reckoned to him as righteousness (Gen. 15:6; Rom. 4:3, 9; Gal. 3:6; Jas. 2:23); the father of all who believe unto righteousness (Rom. 4:11); those who believe are children of Abraham (Gal. 3:7–9); the promise comes by faith to all Abraham's offspring (Rom. 4:16); the righteous by faith shall live (Hab. 2:4; Rom. 1:17; Gal. 3:11; Heb. 10:38); faith is reckoned as righteousness (Rom. 4:5); the righteousness which is by faith (Rom. 3:22; 9:30; 10:4, 6–9; Phil. 3:9); a man is justified by faith (Rom. 3:28; 5:1; Gal. 2:16); God will justify both circumcised and uncircumcised by faith (Rom. 3:30); with the heart man believes to righteousness (Rom. 10:10); God justifies him who believes in Jesus (Rom. 3:26).

● Saved by faith

t Believe in the Lord Jesus and you will be saved (Acts 16:31); God saves those who believe (1 Cor. 1:21); we are of those who believe and are saved (Heb. 10:39); saved by grace through faith (Eph. 2:8); he who believes and is baptised will be saved (Mark 16:16); your faith has saved you (Luke 7:50); if you believe God raised him you will be saved (Rom. 10:9); our faith in Christ overcomes the world (1 John 5:4–5); lest they believe and are saved (Luke 8:12).

u Those who believe: have eternal life (John 3:15, 16, 36; 5:24; 6:40); become children of God (John 1:12); have life in his name (John 20:31); receive forgiveness (Acts 10:43); enter God's rest (Heb. 4:3).

v When Jesus saw their faith, he told the paralytic his sins were forgiven (Matt. 9:2; Mark 2:5; Luke 5:20).

w He who believes in him is not condemned (John 3:18); unless you believe that I am, you will die in your sins (John 8:24); now faith has come we are no longer under the law (Gal. 3:23–5).

x The devil takes away the word that they may not believe and be saved (Luke 8:12); they did not pursue it by faith but as if it were based on works (Rom. 9:32); if those of the law are heirs, faith is void (Rom. 4:14).

● Faith that works

y Faith without works is dead (Jas. 2:17, 20, 26); can faith without works save anyone? (Jas. 2:14); show me faith without works and I will show you my faith by my works (Jas. 2:18); faith is made complete by works (Jas. 2:22); a man is justified by works and not by faith alone (Jas. 2:24).

● Believing for miracles	*z*	Your faith has healed you (Matt. 9:22; Mark 5:34; 10:52; Luke 8:48; 17:19; 18:42); according to your faith be it done to you (Matt. 8:13; 9:29); do you believe I can do this? (Matt. 9:28); do not be afraid, just believe (Mark 5:36; Luke 8:50); faith in Jesus has healed this man (Acts 3:16); he had faith to be healed (Acts 14:9).
	aa	Faith to move mountains (Mark 11:23; Matt. 21:21; 1 Cor. 13:2); to uproot a tree (Luke 17:6); everything is possible to him who believes (Mark 9:23); he who believes in me shall do the works I do (John 14:12).
	ab	I have not found such faith even in Israel (Matt. 8:10; Luke 7:9); great is your faith! (Matt. 15:28); increase our faith (Luke 17:5); your faith is growing (2 Thess. 1:3); you excel in faith (2 Cor. 8:7).
	ac	Prayer is effective if you believe (Matt. 21:22; Mark 11:24); he must ask in faith, not doubting (Jas. 1:6); I believe; help my unbelief! (Mark 9:24); if you do not believe me, believe the works (John 10:38; 14:11).
● Believing the prophets	*ad*	The people trusted the Lord and Moses (Exod. 14:31); that they may believe in Moses for ever (Exod. 19:9); if you believed Moses you would believe me (John 5:46–7); believe in the Lord and in his prophets (2 Chr. 20:20); then they believed his words (Ps. 106:12); I trust in your word (Ps. 119:42); I believe in your commandments (Ps. 119:66); believing everything in the law and the prophets (Acts 24:14); they believed the scripture and Jesus' word (John 2:22); how slow you are to believe all the prophets have spoken! (Luke 24:25); who has believed what we have heard? (Isa. 53:1; John 12:38); do you believe the prophets, King Agrippa? (Acts 26:27); the tax-collectors and harlots believed John (Matt. 21:32).
● Trusting in riches	*ae*	If I have trusted in gold (Job 31:24); you trust in your own achievements and riches (Jer. 48:7); he who trusts in his riches will fall (Prov. 11:28); the man who trusted in his wealth (Ps. 52:7); those who trust in their wealth (Ps. 49:6); the Ammonites trusted in their treasures (Jer. 49:4); do not trust in extortion, robbery or riches (Ps. 62:10); not to trust in uncertain riches (1 Tim. 6:17).
● Trusting in ourselves	*af*	So that we might not trust in ourselves but in God (2 Cor. 1:9); they trusted in themselves that they were righteous (Luke 18:9); if a man trusts in his own righteousness (Ezek. 33:13); he who trusts in his own heart is a fool (Prov. 28:26); you trusted in your beauty (Ezek. 16:15).
● Trusting in men	*ag*	Cursed is he who trusts in man (Jer. 17:5); we put no confidence in the flesh (Phil. 3:3); I will not trust in bow or sword (Ps. 44:6); woe to those who rely on Egyptian horses and chariots (Isa. 31:1); do not trust in princes or men (Ps. 146:3); you have trusted in your army (Hos. 10:13); better to take refuge in the Lord than

trust in men or princes (Ps. 118:8–9); do not trust in neighbour or friend (Mic. 7:5); trust in a faithless man is like a bad tooth (Prov. 25:19).

ah Her husband's heart trusts in the good wife (Prov. 31:11).

ai The men of Shechem trusted Gaal (Judg. 9:26); you are relying on Egypt (2 Kgs. 18:21, 24); you relied on the king of Aram (2 Chr. 16:7); Achish trusted David (1 Sam. 27:12).

● Trusting
lies

aj His trust is fragile as a spider's web (Job 8:14); let him not trust in emptiness (Job 15:31); do not trust in deceptive words (Jer. 7:4); you are trusting in deceptive words (Jer. 7:8); you trusted in lies (Jer. 13:25); you made this people trust in a lie (Jer. 28:15); he made you trust in a lie (Jer. 29:31); they believe what is false (2 Thess. 2:11).

● Trusting
in idols

ak Everyone who trusts in idols will become like them (Ps. 115:8; 135:18); those who trust in idols will be put to shame (Isa. 42:17); the idolater trusts in his own creation (Hab. 2:18).

486 Unbelief. Doubt

● Unbelief in
general

a Whatever is not of faith is sin (Rom. 14:23); he who doubts is like a wave driven by the sea (Jas. 1:6).

b They were unable to enter because of unbelief (Heb. 3:19); the message was not combined with faith (Heb. 4:2); not all men have faith (2 Thess. 3:2); take care lest there be an unbelieving heart in any of you (Heb. 3:12).

● God doubting

c God puts no trust in his servants (Job 4:18; 15:15).

● Doubting God

d You did not trust the Lord (Deut. 1:32; 9:23); how long will they not believe in me? (Num. 14:11); they did not believe in God (Ps. 78:22); like their fathers, they did not believe in the Lord (2 Kgs. 17:14); Jerusalem did not trust in the Lord (Zeph. 3:2); they did not believe his word (Ps. 106:24); they did not believe in his wonders (Ps. 78:32); you did not rely on the one who made it (Isa. 22:11); I am doing something which you will never believe (Hab. 1:5; Acts 13:41); who has believed our report? (Isa. 53:1; Rom. 10:16).

e No strong trust, no trusty stronghold (Isa. 7:9); the branches were broken off through unbelief (Rom. 11:20); does their unbelief nullify God's faithfulness? (Rom. 3:3).

f Moses did not trust the Lord enough (Num. 20:12).

● Not believing
in Jesus

g O unbelieving generation! (Matt. 17:17; Mark 9:19; Luke 9:41); O you of little faith! (Matt. 6:30; 8:26; 14:31; 16:8; Luke 12:28); because of your little faith (Matt. 17:20); why have you no faith? (Mark 4:40); where is your faith? (Luke 8:25); he could not work many miracles because of their lack of faith (Matt. 13:58); he marvelled at their unbelief (Mark 6:6); after so many signs they did not believe in him (John 12:37); even his brothers did not believe in him (John 7:5); none of the rulers or Pharisees have believed, have they? (John 7:48); he will convict of sin because they do not believe in me (John 16:9).

h Unless you see signs and wonders you will not believe (John 4:48); you have seen me yet do not believe (John 6:36); some of you do not believe (John 6:64); you do not believe the one he has sent (John 5:38); because I speak the truth you do not believe me (John 8:45–6); how shall they call on him in whom they have not believed? (Rom. 10:14).

i When the Son of man comes, will he find faith on the earth? (Luke 18:8); how will you believe if I tell you heavenly things? (John 3:12); if I tell you, you will not believe (Luke 22:67); how can you believe when you seek glory from each other? (John 5:44).

● Not believing the gospel

j Whoever does not believe will be condemned (Mark 16:16); he who does not believe is condemned already (John 3:18); you do not believe because you are not of my sheep (John 10:26); the unbelieving will end up in the lake of fire (Rev. 21:8); he will put him with the unbelievers (Luke 12:46); tongues are a sign for unbelievers (1 Cor. 14:22); some would not believe (Acts 28:24); I told you and you do not believe (John 10:25).

k I received mercy because I acted ignorantly in unbelief (1 Tim. 1:13).

● Doubting the resurrection

l At the resurrection, some doubted (Matt. 28:17); they did not believe it (Mark 16:11, 13); they did not believe the women (Luke 24:11); they did not believe it through joy (Luke 24:41); Thomas refused to believe (John 20:25, 27); he reproached them for their unbelief (Mark 16:14); why do doubts arise in your hearts? (Luke 24:38).

m Why is it thought incredible that God raises the dead? (Acts 26:8).

● Not believing people

n The people might not believe Moses (Exod. 4:1); the Queen of Sheba did not believe until she came and saw it (1 Kgs. 10:7); you did not believe John (Matt. 21:32); he will say, 'Why did you not believe him?' (Matt. 21:25; Mark 11:31; Luke 20:5); Zacharias did not believe Gabriel (Luke 1:20).

o Sihon did not trust Israel (Judg. 11:20); do not trust neighbour or brother (Jer. 9:4); Gedaliah did not believe Johanan (Jer. 40:14).

p If they say the Christ is here, do not believe (Matt. 24:23, 26; Mark 13:21).

487 Credulity

● Gullible

a The simple man believes everything (Prov. 14:15).

488 Assent

● Assenting

a Let your word be 'Yes, yes' or 'No, no' (Matt. 5:37); you have said it (Matt. 26:25, 64; 27:11; Mark 15:2; Luke 22:70; 23:3; John 18:37).

b Paul was assenting to Stephen's death (Acts 8:1; 22:20).

● Amen!

c The woman shall say, 'Amen, amen!' (Num. 5:22); all the people said 'Amen' (1 Chr. 16:36; Neh. 5:13; 8:6); let all the people say 'Amen' (Ps. 106:48); amen! (1 Kgs. 1:36; Jer. 28:6); amen, Lord! (Jer. 11:5); amen and amen! (Ps. 41:13; 89:52); how will the other person say 'Amen' if he does not understand? (1 Cor. 14:16).

● Yes in Christ

d All the promises of God are Yes in Christ (2 Cor. 1:20); our amen is through him (2 Cor. 1:20); the Amen, the faithful and true witness (Rev. 3:14).

489 Dissent

● Dissenting

a Let your word be 'Yes, yes' or 'No, no' (Matt. 5:37).

490 Knowledge

● Knowledge in general

a Knowledge puffs up but love builds up (1 Cor. 8:1); the tree of the knowledge of good and evil (Gen. 2:9, 17); shepherds who will feed you with knowledge and understanding (Jer. 3:15); you have taken away the key of knowledge (Luke 11:52); in Christ are hid all the treasures of knowledge (Col. 2:3).

Knowing right and wrong, see **917g**.

b No one has yet known as he should (1 Cor. 8:2); knowledge will cease (1 Cor. 13:8); through your knowledge a weak brother is destroyed (1 Cor. 8:11).

c Then I shall know fully as I am fully known (1 Cor. 13:12); add to your virtue knowledge (2 Pet. 1:5); if I have all knowledge (1 Cor. 13:2).

d We know in part (1 Cor. 13:9, 12); knowledge falsely so-called (1 Tim. 6:20); do not rely on your own insight (Prov. 3:5).

● God knows all things

e God knows all things (1 John 3:20); a God of knowledge (1 Sam. 2:3); the riches of the knowledge of God! (Rom. 11:33); like God, knowing good and evil (Gen. 3:5, 22).

f No one knows of that day except the Father (Matt. 24:36; Mark 13:32).

g Your heavenly Father knows what you need (Matt. 6:8, 32; Luke 12:30).

h How does God know? (Ps. 73:11); you say, 'What does God know?' (Job 22:13).

● God knows the heart

i God knows the hearts of all men (1 Kgs. 8:39; Acts 1:24); God who knows the heart (Acts 15:8); God knows your hearts (Luke 16:15); God knows the secrets of the heart (Ps. 44:21); the Lord knows the thoughts of man (Ps. 94:11); I know your thoughts (Ezek. 11:5); I know their thoughts (Isa. 66:18); God, the Lord, he knows! (Josh. 22:22); you know me (1 Chr. 17:18; Jer. 12:3); Lord, you know my folly and my sins (Ps. 69:5); I know your sitting down and going out and coming in (2 Kgs. 19:27); you know my thoughts from afar (Ps. 139:2); you know all about me (Ps. 139:1–6).

● Jesus' knowledge

j Jesus, knowing all that was going to befall him (John 18:4); Jesus knew the Pharisees plotted against him (Matt. 12:14–15); he perceived their cunning (Luke 20:23); we know that you know all things (John 16:30); you know all things, you know I love you (John 21:17).

k I know where I came from and where I am going (John 8:14); knowing that he had come from God and went to God (John 13:3); knowing that the Father had given all things into his hands (John 13:3); knowing that his hour had come (John 13:1); knowing that all was accomplished (John 19:28).

l Jesus knew their thoughts (Matt. 9:4; 12:25; Luke 5:22; 6:8; 9:47); Jesus, knowing this (Matt. 16:8; 26:10; Mark 2:8); Jesus knew who did not believe (John 6:64); he knew who was going to betray him (John 13:11); Jesus knew all men and what was in man (John 2:24–5); if he were a prophet he would know what kind of woman she is (Luke 7:39).

● God knowing his people

m If anyone loves God he is known by him (1 Cor. 8:3); the Lord knows those who are his (2 Tim. 2:19); you have come to be known by him (Gal. 4:9); before I formed you in the womb I knew you (Jer. 1:5); I know Israel (Hos. 5:3); I know my own and my own know me (John 10:14); I know my sheep (John 10:27); I know whom I have chosen (John 13:18).

● Knowing about God

n They will know that I am the Lord (Exod. 7:5; 14:4, 18; 29:46; Jer. 16:21; Ezek. 6:10, 14; 7:27; 12:15, 16; 20:26; 24:27; 25:11, 17; 26:6; 28:22, 23, 24, 26; 29:6, 9, 16, 21; 30:8, 19, 25, 26; 33:29; 34:27; 35:15; 36:38; 38:23; 39:6, 28); you will know that I am the Lord (Exod. 6:7; 7:17; 10:2; 16:12; 1 Kgs. 20:13, 28; Ezek. 11:10, 12; 12:20; 13:9, 14; 13:21, 23; 14:8; 15:7; 16:62; 20:20, 38, 42, 44; 22:16; 23:49; 24:24; 25:7; 35:4; 36:11; 37:6, 13; Hos. 2:20; Joel 3:17); the nations will know (Ezek. 36:23; 39:7); the house of Israel will know (Ezek. 39:22); that everyone may know that you are God (2 Kgs. 19:19); then Manasseh knew that the Lord was God (2 Chr. 33:13); that they may know that you alone are the Most High (Ps. 83:18); may all peoples know that the Lord is God (1 Kgs. 8:60); that all peoples may know your name (1 Kgs. 8:43; 2 Chr. 6:33); he has known my name (Ps. 91:14).

o That your way may be known on earth (Ps. 67:2); make known his deeds among the nations (Isa. 12:4, 5); you will know it was the Lord who brought you out of Egypt (Exod. 16:6); that we might know the things given to us by God (1 Cor. 2:12); the elders who had known God's deeds (Josh. 24:31); when I make myself known to them (Ezek. 20:5).

● Knowing God

p The earth will be full of the knowledge of the Lord (Isa. 11:9);

the earth will be filled with the knowledge of the glory of the Lord (Hab. 2:14); the light of the knowledge of the glory of God (2 Cor. 4:6); the Egyptians will know the Lord (Isa. 19:21); Rahab and Babylon are among those who know me (Ps. 87:4); we Israel know you (Hos. 8:2); the people who know God will stand firm and take action (Dan. 11:32).

q God is known in Judah (Ps. 76:1); let him who boasts boast that he knows me (Jer. 9:24); is not that what it means to know me? (Jer. 22:16); I desire the knowledge of God and not sacrifice (Hos. 6:6); we demolish everything against the knowledge of God (2 Cor. 10:5); growing in the knowledge of God (Col. 1:10); you have come to know God, or rather be known by him (Gal. 4:9); they will all know me (Jer. 31:34; Heb. 8:11); you all know (1 John 2:20, 21).

r Let me know your ways (Exod. 33:13); know the God of your father (1 Chr. 28:9); let us press on to know the Lord (Hos. 6:3); I will give them a heart to know me (Jer. 24:7); then you will find the knowledge of God (Prov. 2:5).

s Though they knew God, they did not glorify him (Rom. 1:21); they profess to know God but deny him by their deeds (Titus 1:16); no one who sins has seen him or known him (1 John 3:6); always learning but never coming to a knowledge of the truth (2 Tim. 3:7).

● Christ knowing God

t The Father knows me and I know the Father (John 10:15); I know him (John 7:29; 8:55); no one knows the Father except the Son and those to whom the Son reveals him (Matt. 11:27; Luke 10:22); I know you and they know you have sent me (John 17:25).

● Knowing Christ

u That I may know Christ (Phil. 3:10); eternal life is knowing God and Jesus Christ (John 17:3); knowing the love of Christ (Eph. 3:18–19); the excellence of knowing Christ (Phil. 3:8); knowledge of God's mystery, that is, Christ (Col. 2:2); that we may know him who is true (1 John 5:20); grow in knowledge of our Lord Jesus Christ (2 Pet. 3:18); if you had known me, you would have known my Father (John 14:7); by this we know that we know him, if we keep his commands (1 John 2:3); many longed to see and hear what you see and hear (Luke 10:23–4).

● Man's knowledge

v Man became like God, knowing good and evil (Gen. 3:22); men know the command of God (Rom. 1:32); the one who knew his master's will but did not obey will be punished severely (Luke 12:47); through the law comes knowledge of sin (Rom. 3:20); he has appointed you to know his will (Acts 22:14); that you may know that you have eternal life (1 John 5:13); one thing I know, that I was blind and now I see (John 9:25).

w We speak of what we know (John 3:11); you are filled with all knowledge (Rom. 15:14); God gave the youths knowledge (Dan. 1:17); the word of knowledge (1 Cor. 12:8); I am not unskilled in knowledge (2 Cor. 11:6); we are not ignorant of Satan's devices (2 Cor. 2:11); we commend ourselves in knowledge (2 Cor. 6:6).

● Knowing
people

x Do you know Laban? (Gen. 29:5); the ox knows its master (Isa. 1:3).

y Obadiah recognised Elijah (1 Kgs. 18:7); Ahab recognised the prophet (1 Kgs. 20:41).

z The demons knew who Jesus was (Mark 1:34); Jesus I know and Paul I know, but who are you? (Acts 19:15); by this all men will know that you are my disciples (John 13:35).

aa They recognized Jesus (Matt. 14:35; Mark 6:54; Luke 24:31); by the breaking of bread (Luke 24:35).

491 Ignorance

● Ignorance
in general

a They hated knowledge (Prov. 1:29); have you not known? (Isa. 40:21, 28); idolaters have no knowledge (Isa. 45:20); if you plead ignorance, does not God know it? (Prov. 24:12); God overlooked the time of ignorance (Acts 17:30).

b The dead do not know anything (Eccles. 9:5); his sons are honoured and he does not know it (Job 14:21).

c My people are destroyed for lack of knowledge (Hos. 4:6); my people go into exile for lack of knowledge (Isa. 5:13); they are a nation lacking understanding (Deut. 32:28); God has not given you a heart to know (Deut. 29:4); Israel does not know (Isa. 1:3); I was stupid and ignorant (Ps. 73:22); who is this who is in the dark without counsel or knowledge? (Job 38:2; 42:3).

d I decided to know nothing except Christ and him crucified (1 Cor. 2:2).

● Not knowing
God

e I do not know the Lord (Exod. 5:2); the Gentiles who do not know God (1 Thess. 4:5); they do not know me (Jer. 9:3); another generation who did not know the Lord (Judg. 2:10); the sons of Eli did not know the Lord (1 Sam. 2:12); Samuel did not yet know the Lord (1 Sam. 3:7); an altar to an unknown god (Acts 17:23); there are those who have no knowledge of God (1 Cor. 15:34); you worship what you do not know (John 4:22); you do not know God (John 8:55); there is no knowledge of God in the land (Hos. 4:1); I gird you though you have not known me (Isa. 45:5); the world through wisdom did not know God (1 Cor. 1:21).

f Punishment for those who do not know God (2 Thess. 1:8); separated from the life of God because of ignorance (Eph. 4:18).

g They have known neither my Father nor me (John 8:19; 16:3); the world did not know him (John 1:10; 1 John 3:1); they did not recognise either him or the words of the prophets (Acts 13:27); among you stands one you do not know (John 1:26); the one who sent me you did not know (John 7:28); they do not know the one who sent me (John 15:21).

- Not knowing
God's ways

h They are only the poor who do not know the way of the Lord (Jer. 5:4); they have not known my ways (Ps. 95:10); my people do not know the ordinance of the Lord (Jer. 8:7); you know neither the sciptures nor the power of God (Matt. 22:29); zealous for God, but not according to knowledge (Rom. 10:2); they do not know how to do what is right (Amos 3:10).

i God is here and I did not know it (Gen. 28:16); they did not know that I healed them (Hos. 11:3).

j They do not know the way of peace (Isa. 59:8).

k You do not know what you are asking (Matt. 20:22; Mark 10:38); they said they did not know about John's authority (Matt. 21:27; Mark 11:33); not all have this knowledge (1 Cor. 8:7); I do not want you to be ignorant about spiritual gifts (1 Cor. 12:1).

- Ignorant
of Christ

l No one knows where the Christ comes from (John 7:27); you do not know where I come from (John 8:14); we do not know where he is from (John 9:29); they did not know that Jesus had stayed behind (Luke 2:43).

m John did not recognise Jesus (John 1:31, 33); they did not recognise Jesus (Luke 24:16); Mary did not (John 20:14); the disciples did not (John 21:4).

n The man did not know who had healed him (John 5:13); I do not know the man (Matt. 26:72, 74; Mark 14:71; Luke 22:57); I do not know what you are talking about (Matt. 26:70; Mark 14:68; Luke 22:60); Paul went to those who had never heard of Christ (Rom. 15:20–1).

o No one knew why Jesus said this to Judas (John 13:28); whether he is a sinner or not I do not know (John 9:25).

p Many desired to see and hear what you do, but they did not (Matt. 13:17); are you the only visitor to Jerusalem not to know of these things? (Luke 24:18); what eye has not seen nor ear heard, God has prepared (1 Cor. 2:9).

- Ignorant
of Christ's
return

q You do not know when the master of the house will return (Mark 13:35); you do not know when your Lord is coming (Matt. 24:42); I will come like a thief and you will not know at what hour (Rev. 3:3); be alert, for you do not know when he is coming (Matt. 24:42; Mark 13:33); neither people, angels nor the Son of man know the time (Matt. 24:36; Mark 13:32); the master does not know when the thief will come (Luke 12:39); it is not for you to know times and seasons (Acts 1:7).

- Not knowing
people

r A king who did not know of Joseph (Exod. 1:8; Acts 7:18); shall I give food to people I do not know? (1 Sam. 25:11); you will call a nation you do not know (Isa. 55:5).

s Isaac did not recognise Jacob (Gen. 27:23); Joseph's brothers did not recognise him (Gen. 42:8); Job's friends did not recognise him (Job 2:12); Elijah came but they did not recognise him (Matt. 17:12).

t As unknown and yet well-known (2 Cor. 6:9); Paul was unknown by sight to the Judean churches (Gal. 1:22).

u I do not know you (Matt. 7:23; 25:12); I do not know where you come from (Luke 13:25, 27).

● Not knowing where people are

v Cain said he did not know where Abel was (Gen. 4:9); we do not know what has become of Moses (Exod. 32:1, 23; Acts 7:40); no one knows where Moses is buried (Deut. 34:6).

● Sinning through ignorance

w Instructions concerning one who sins through ignorance (Lev. 5:17; Ezek. 45:20); I know that you acted in ignorance (Acts 3:17); I received mercy because I acted ignorantly in unbelief (1 Tim. 1:13); forgive them for they do not know what they are doing (Luke 23:34).

x The one who did not know his master's will will receive a lighter punishment (Luke 12:48); slaves do not know what their master is doing (John 15:15).

● Not knowing facts

y I will lead the blind in a way they do not know (Isa. 42:16); Abraham went out not knowing where he was going (Heb. 11:8); you do not know what a day may bring forth (Prov. 27:1); you do not know how bones grow in the womb nor the work of God (Eccles. 11:5).

z I do not know the day of my death (Gen. 27:2); grey hairs come and he does not know it (Hos. 7:9); we do not know what to do (2 Chr. 20:12); Jacob did not know Rachel had stolen the gods (Gen. 31:32).

aa They did not know what the manna was (Exod. 16:15); he does not know how the seed sprouts (Mark 4:27).

ab He did not know of the ambush (Josh. 8:14); they will not know or see till we come on them (Neh. 4:11); not knowing what will happen to me in Jerusalem (Acts 20:22); most in the theatre did not know why they had come together (Acts 19:32).

ac The people did not know that Jonathan had gone (1 Sam. 14:3); the officials did not know what Nehemiah had done (Neh. 2:16); the lad did not know anything of it (1 Sam. 20:39); Abimelech did not know anything of the matter (1 Sam. 22:15); David did not know that Abner was recalled (2 Sam. 3:26); the 200 men did not know anything (2 Sam. 15:11); not a thing was known about the messengers (2 Sam. 17:19); I did not know what the tumult was (2 Sam. 18:29); David does not know that Adonijah is king (1 Kgs. 1:11, 18); David did not know that Abner and Amasa were being killed (1 Kgs. 2:32).

492 Scholar

● Expert

a Agrippa was an expert in Jewish customs (Acts 26:3).

493 Ignoramus

● Uneducated

a How has this man learning since he never studied? (John 7:15); they saw that Peter and John were uneducated men (Acts 4:13).

b Those who do not know the law are accursed (John 7:49).

494 Truth

● Truth in
general

a What is truth? (John 18:38); buy truth and do not sell it (Prov. 23:23); whatever is true, think about it (Phil. 4:8); you will know the truth and the truth will set you free (John 8:32).

b Truth is lacking (Isa. 59:15).

● God is true

c God is true (John 3:33); let God be true though every man a liar (Rom. 3:4); he who sent me is true (John 8:26); I am the truth (John 14:6); he who is true (Rev. 3:7); truth is in Jesus (Eph. 4:21); the Word, full of grace and truth (John 1:14); grace and truth came through Jesus Christ (John 1:17).

● God's word
is true

d All your word is truth (Ps. 119:160); your word is truth (John 17:17); the word of the Lord in your mouth is truth (1 Kgs. 17:24); we commend ourselves in the word of truth (2 Cor. 6:7); your law is truth (Ps. 119:142); you teach the way of God in truth (Matt. 22:16; Mark 12:14; Luke 20:21); I came to bear witness to the truth (John 18:37).

e Speak nothing but truth in the name of the Lord (1 Kgs. 22:16; 2 Chr. 18:15).

● God's truth

f The Lord, abounding in truth (Exod. 34:6); send out your light and your truth (Ps. 43:3); the works of his hands are truth and justice (Ps. 111:7).

g The Spirit of truth (John 14:17; 15:26); he will guide you into all truth (John 16:13); by this we know the spirit of truth and the spirit of error (1 John 4:6); that you might know the truth (Luke 1:4); the truth which lives in us (2 John 2); my children walk in the truth (3 John 4); gird your waist with truth (Eph. 6:14); the truth which accords with godliness (Titus 1:1); the unleavened bread of sincerity and truth (1 Cor. 5:8); he is telling the truth that you may believe (John 19:35).

● Performing
the truth

h You desire inward truth (Ps. 51:6); worship in spirit and in truth (John 4:23, 24); men of truth as leaders (Exod. 18:21); if you made Abimelech king in truth and integrity (Judg. 9:16, 19). **Truthfulness**, see **540**.

● Against the
truth

i Men suppress the truth (Rom. 1:18); we can do nothing against the truth, only for it (2 Cor. 13:8); there is no truth in the devil (John 8:44).
Hiding the truth, see **525n**.

495 Error

● Do not
mislead

a Cursed is the one who leads a blind person astray (Deut. 27:18); if anyone does not make a mistake in what he says he is perfect (Jas. 3:2).
Lying, see **541**; **deception**, see **542**.

● Do not be
misled

b See that no one misleads you (Matt. 24:4; Luke 21:8); have nothing to do with worldly old wives' tales (1 Tim. 4:7); do not pay attention to Jewish myths (Titus 1:14); do not be carried away by the error of lawless men (2 Pet. 3:17).

● People
misled

c Hezekiah is misleading you (2 Kgs. 18:32; 2 Chr. 32:11; Isa. 36:14); have you also been led astray? (John 7:47); Manasseh misled Judah (2 Chr. 33:9); Jezebel misleads my servants into immorality (Rev. 2:20); your leaders mislead you (Isa. 3:12; 9:16); false prophets led Israel astray (Jer. 23:13); prophets who lead my people astray (Mic. 3:5); their shepherds have led them astray (Jer. 50:6); the princes have led Egypt astray (Isa. 19:13–14).

d You err greatly (Mark 12:27); you err, not knowing the scriptures or God's power (Matt. 22:29; Mark 12:24).

e Men speaking perverse things will seek to draw away the disciples (Acts 20:30); false prophets will mislead many (Matt. 24:11, 24); they will turn aside to myths (2 Tim. 4:4).

● No misleading

f Our exhortation is not from error (1 Thess. 2:3); we did not follow clever myths (2 Pet. 1:16).

496 Maxim

● Wise proverbs

a A proverb in the mouth of fools is like lame legs (Prov. 26:7); is like a thorn in a drunkard's hand (Prov. 26:9).

b Solomon spoke three thousand proverbs (1 Kgs. 4:32); I will listen to a proverb (Ps. 49:4); the proverbs of Solomon (Prov. 1:1; 10:1; 25:1); the Preacher arranged many proverbs (Eccles. 12:9).

● Old sayings

c 'Saul among the prophets' became a proverb (1 Sam. 10:12); 'from the wicked comes wickedness'—a proverb (1 Sam. 24:13); a saying, 'the blind or lame shall not enter the house' (2 Sam. 5:8); 'ask advice at Abel' (2 Sam. 20:18); 'the days grow long and every vision fails' (Ezek. 12:22); 'like mother, like daughter' (Ezek. 16:44); 'fathers eat sour grapes and the children's teeth are set on edge' (Ezek. 18:2); 'physician, heal yourself' (Luke 4:23); ' a dog returns to its vomit' (2 Pet. 2:22).

● Bywords
of horror

d You will be a byword of horror (Deut. 28:37); you will become a proverb and a byword among all peoples (1 Kgs. 9:7); this house will be a proverb and a byword (2 Chr. 7:20); I will make them a reproach and a proverb (Jer. 24:9); I will make the idolater a sign and a proverb (Ezek. 14:8); you make us a byword (Ps. 44:14).

e I have become a byword (Job 30:9); he has made me a byword (Job 17:6); I became a byword to them (Ps. 69:11).

497 Absurdity
Folly, see **499**.

498 Intelligence. Wisdom

● Wisdom
in general

a I considered wisdom, madness and folly (Eccles. 1:17; 2:12); wisdom exceeds folly as light exceeds darkness (Eccles. 2:13); in much wisdom there is much grief (Eccles. 1:18).

b Wisdom is with the aged (Job 12:12); many years should teach wisdom (Job 32:7); teach us to number our days that we may get a heart of wisdom (Ps. 90:12); wisdom will die with you! (Job 12:2).

c Wisdom is better than strength (Eccles. 9:16); wisdom strengthens a wise man (Eccles. 7:19); wisdom is better than weapons of war (Eccles. 9:18); a poor wise lad is better than an old foolish king (Eccles. 4:13); better to get wisdom than gold (Prov. 16:16); wisdom is sweet to the soul (Prov. 24:14); the wisdom from above is pure, peaceable etc. (Jas. 3:17); would that they were wise! (Deut. 32:29); wisdom is justified by her deeds (Matt. 11:19; Luke 7:35).

d Get wisdom! (Prov. 4:5); the beginning of wisdom is, get wisdom! (Prov. 4:7); to know wisdom and instruction (Prov. 1:2); who is wise and understanding? (Jas. 3:13); who has put wisdom in the mind? (Job 38:36); where can wisdom be found? (Job 28:12); God knows where wisdom is to be found (Job 28:23).

e Wisdom personified cries out (Prov. 1:20–33; 8:1–36; 9:1–6).

● Wisdom
of God

f God is wise in heart (Job 9:4); with God are wisdom and power (Job 12:13, 16); wisdom and power belong to God (Dan. 2:20); the Lord is great in wisdom (Isa. 28:29); God's wisdom and insight (Eph. 1:8); the riches of the wisdom and knowledge of God! (Rom. 11:33); the only wise God (Rom. 16:27).

g By wisdom the Lord founded the earth (Prov. 3:19); in wisdom you made them all (Ps. 104:24).

h The Spirit of wisdom and understanding (Isa. 11:2); the Spirit of wisdom and revelation (Eph. 1:17); the Wisdom of God sent prophets and apostles (Luke 11:49).

i Christ the wisdom of God (1 Cor. 1:24, 30); God's hidden wisdom (1 Cor. 2:7); all the treasures of wisdom and knowledge are hidden in Christ (Col. 2:3); that the manifold wisdom of God might be made known (Eph. 3:10).

j In the wisdom of God the world could not know God by wisdom (1 Cor. 1:21); no wisdom can avail against the Lord (Prov. 21:30).

● God gives
wisdom

k The fear of the Lord is wisdom (Job 28:28); the fear of the Lord is the beginning of wisdom (Ps. 111:10; Prov. 1:7; 9:10); the Lord gives wisdom (Prov. 2:6); may the Lord give you prudence (1 Chr. 22:12); you will make me know wisdom (Ps. 51:6); would that God would show you the secrets of wisdom! (Job 11:6); God gives wisdom to the wise (Dan. 2:21); Bezalel filled with the Spirit in wisdom (Exod. 35:31); if any one lacks wisdom, let him ask God (Jas. 1:5); the word of wisdom (1 Cor. 12:8); a wisdom not of this age nor its rulers (1 Cor. 2:6).

● **God's word gives wisdom**

l Keeping the statutes is your wisdom (Deut. 4:6); your commandments make me wiser than my enemies (Ps. 119:98); the law of the Lord makes the simple wise (Ps. 19:7); proverbs giving prudence to the simple (Prov. 1:4); pay attention and gain understanding (Prov. 4:1); the scriptures make one wise to salvation (2 Tim. 3:15); rejecting the Lord's word, what wisdom is theirs? (Jer. 8:9).

● **Being wise**

m The mouth of the righteous utters wisdom (Ps. 37:30); those who are wise will give understanding to many (Dan. 11:33); those who are wise will shine (Dan. 12:3); the Queen of the South came to hear the wisdom of Solomon (Luke 11:31); Rehoboam acted wisely (2 Chr. 11:23); the prince of Tyre is wiser than Daniel (Ezek. 28:3); is there no wisdom remaining in Edom? (Jer. 49:7).

n Be wise as serpents (Matt. 10:16); be wise as to good, innocent as to evil (Rom. 16:19); act according to your wisdom (1 Kgs. 2:6); the sons of this generation are wiser than the sons of light (Luke 16:8).

Wisdom of Solomon, see **500***d*.

● **Jesus' wisdom**

o Jesus was filled with wisdom (Luke 2:40); increased in wisdom (Luke 2:52); where did this man get this wisdom? (Matt. 13:54).

● **False wisdom**

p The tree was desirable to make one wise (Gen. 3:6).

q The wisdom of this world is folly with God (1 Cor. 3:19); the Greeks seek wisdom (1 Cor. 1:22); to preach not in wise words (1 Cor. 1:17); the wisdom of the wise will perish (Isa. 29:14; 1 Cor. 1:19); the wise are put to shame (Jer. 8:8–9); God captures the wise in their cunning (Job 5:13); God turns the knowledge of the wise to foolishness (Isa. 44:25).

r Let us deal wisely with them (Exod. 1:10); this wisdom is not from above, but is earthly (Jas. 3:15).

s Do not be wise in your own eyes (Prov. 3:7; Rom. 12:16); woe to those who are wise in their own eyes (Isa. 5:21); the rich man is wise in his own eyes (Prov. 28:11); there is more hope for a fool than for a man who is wise in his own eyes (Prov. 26:12); by my own wisdom I did this (Isa. 10:13); let not the wise man boast in his wisdom (Jer. 9:23).

499 Unintelligence. Folly

● **Folly in general**

a A little foolishness outweighs wisdom (Eccles. 10:1); folly is joy to one without sense (Prov. 15:21); folly is bound up in the heart of a child (Prov. 22:15); God has made the ostrich forget wisdom (Job 39:17).

b Whoever is foolish, turn in here! (Prov. 9:4, 16).

● **Foolishness of God**

c The foolishness of God is wiser than the wisdom of man (1 Cor. 1:25); Christ crucified is foolishness to the Gentiles (1 Cor. 1:23); the message of the cross is foolishness for those who are perishing (1 Cor. 1:18); the foolishness of what is preached (1 Cor. 1:21); I did not come preaching with wisdom (1 Cor. 2:1); God has chosen the foolish things (1 Cor. 1:26–7); to the natural man the things of the Spirit are foolishness (1 Cor. 2:14).

● Foolishness of men

d Claiming to be wise, they became fools (Rom. 1:22); senseless (Rom. 1:31); every man is stupid (Jer. 10:14); from the heart comes foolishness (Mark 7:22); God has made foolish the wisdom of the world (1 Cor. 1:20); their folly will become apparent to all (2 Tim. 3:9); idolaters are foolish (Jer. 10:8; 51:17); my people are foolish (Jer. 4:22); Ephraim is like a silly dove (Hos. 7:11); you foolish Galatians! (Gal. 3:1).

e I do not know how to come in or go out (1 Kgs. 3:7).

f You have acted foolishly (1 Sam. 13:13); Job speaks without wisdom (Job 34:35); I have acted foolishly (2 Sam. 24:10; 1 Chr. 21:8); I have played the fool (1 Sam. 26:21); Lord, you know my folly (Ps. 69:5); do not do this folly (2 Sam. 13:12).

g Once we were foolish (Titus 3:3); let him become foolish that he may become wise (1 Cor. 3:18); the Lord knows that the reasonings of the wise are useless (1 Cor. 3:20); God has chosen foolish things to shame the wise (1 Cor. 1:27).

h Bear with me in a little foolishness (2 Cor. 11:1, 16–19).

i Turn Ahithophel's advice to foolishness (2 Sam. 15:31).
Fools, see **501**; **wordy folly,** see **581***b*.

500 Wise man

● Wise people

a A wise man is strong (Prov. 24:5); the wise man will hear and increase in learning (Prov. 1:5); the wise man built his house on the rock (Matt. 7:24); the excellent woman speaks wisdom (Prov. 31:26); a wise son makes a glad father (Prov. 10:1; 15:20; 23:24–5; 29:3); five of the virgins were wise (Matt. 25:2); live as wise men (Eph. 5:15); whoever is wise, let him understand these things (Hos. 14:9); who is the man wise enough to understand this? (Jer. 9:12).

b You hid these things from the wise and prudent (Matt. 11:25; Luke 10:21); the wise men are put to shame (Jer. 8:9); wise men will be destroyed from Edom (Obad. 8); I am a debtor to both wise and foolish (Rom. 1:14).

● People who were wise

c Let Pharaoh look for a discerning and wise man (Gen. 41:33); no one was so wise as Joseph (Gen. 41:39); choose wise men as leaders of the tribes (Deut. 1:13, 15); Joshua was filled with the spirit of wisdom (Deut. 34:9); Abigail was intelligent (1 Sam. 25:3); the wise woman from Tekoa (2 Sam. 14:2); a wise woman of Abel Beth-Maacah (2 Sam. 20:16); Jonadab was very wise (2 Sam. 13:3); David had wisdom like an angel of God (2 Sam. 14:20); God gave the four youths wisdom (Dan. 1:17, 20); Sergius Paulus was an intelligent man (Acts 13:7).

● Solomon

d Solomon prayed for wisdom (1 Kgs. 3:9; 2 Chr. 1:10); wisdom would be given him (1 Kgs. 3:12; 2 Chr. 1:12); God gave Solomon surpassing wisdom (1 Kgs. 4:29–31; 5:12); Israel saw he had wisdom from God (1 Kgs. 3:28); he was greater in wisdom than all other kings (1 Kgs. 10:23; 2 Chr. 9:22); exceeding what the Queen of Sheba had heard (1 Kgs. 10:7; 2 Chr. 9:6); she came to hear the wisdom of Solomon (1 Kgs. 10:4; 2 Chr. 9:3; Matt. 12:42); they came to hear Solomon's wisdom (1 Kgs. 4:34; 10:24); God has given David a wise son (1 Kgs. 5:7).

● Magicians

e Pharaoh sent for his wise men (Gen. 41:8); the wise men, sorcerors and magicians of Egypt (Exod. 7:11, 22; 8:7, 18; 9:11); seven wise men of Ahasuerus (Esther 1:13–14); where are your wise men? (Isa. 19:12); the magicians, conjurers, sorcerers and Chaldeans (Dan. 2:2; 5:7); Daniel was appointed chief of the magicians, sorcerers, Chaldeans and diviners (Dan. 5:11); the visit of the magi (Matt. 2:1–12); Elymas the magos (Acts 13:6, 8).

Sorcery, see **983**.

● Wise men in
the church

f I send you prophets, wise men and scribes (Matt. 23:34); choose men full of the Spirit and wisdom (Acts 6:3); they could not withstand Stephen's wisdom (Acts 6:10).

501 Fool

● Fools against
God

a The fool says in his heart, There is no God (Ps. 14:1; 53:1); a foolish people reviles your name (Ps. 74:18); the foolish man reviles you all the day (Ps. 74:22).

● God against
fools

b God said, 'You fool!' (Luke 12:20); you fools and blind! (Matt. 23:17); a sword against the diviners that they may become fools (Jer. 50:36).

● Nature of fools

c The characteristics of a fool (Prov. 26:1–12); the fool walks in darkness (Eccles. 2:14); fools through their sinful ways (Ps. 107:17); fools despise wisdom (Prov. 1:7); the fool encounters problems (Job 5:3–5); an idiot will be wise when a donkey is born a man (Job 11:12).

● Work of fools

d The foolish man built his house on the sand (Matt. 7:26); foolish and slow of heart to believe! (Luke 24:25).

e A foolish woman is noisy (Prov. 9:13); you speak like a foolish woman (Job 2:10); a foolish son makes a sad mother (Prov. 10:1); a foolish son despises his mother (Prov. 15:20); a foolish son is a grief to his parents (Prov. 17:25); a foolish son is destruction to his father (Prov. 19:13); the father of a fool has no joy (Prov. 17:21).

● Those who
were fools

f Nabal's name meant Fool (1 Sam. 25:25); five of the virgins were foolish (Matt. 25:2); the princes of Zoan are fools (Isa. 19:11).

g Leave fools and live! (Prov. 9:6).

● Counted
as fools

h Should Abner die like a fool? (2 Sam. 3:33); you will be like a fool (2 Sam. 13:13); whoever says to his brother, 'You fool' (Matt. 5:22).

i The prophet is a fool (Hos. 9:7); we are fools for Christ's sake (1 Cor. 4:10).

502 Sanity

● Regaining
sanity

a Nebuchadnezzar's sanity returned (Dan. 4:34, 36); the man possessed by legion was clothed and in his right mind (Mark 5:15; Luke 8:35); the prodigal came to himself (Luke 15:17).

● Sane

b If we are sane, it is for you (2 Cor. 5:13).

503 Insanity

● Studying
insanity

a I set myself to know madness and folly (Eccles. 1:17; 2:12).

● Striking
insane

b The Lord will strike you with madness (Deut. 28:28); you will be driven mad by what you see (Deut. 28:34); I will strike every rider with madness (Zech. 12:4); the nations will drink and stagger and go mad (Jer. 25:16); the nations drink Babylon's wine and go mad (Jer. 51:7).

● Reckoned
insane

c David pretended to be insane (1 Sam. 21:13–15; Ps. 34:t); why did this madman come to you? (2 Kgs. 9:11).

d They said Jesus was out of his mind (Mark 3:21; John 10:20); Festus said Paul was out of his mind (Acts 26:24–5); they said Rhoda was out of her mind (Acts 12:15).

e Every madman who prophesies (Jer. 29:26); the man of the Spirit is mad (Hos. 9:7); if all speak in tongues, outsiders will say you are mad (1 Cor. 14:23); if we are beside ourselves, it is for God (2 Cor. 5:13); I am speaking like a madman (2 Cor. 11:23).

504 Madman
See **503**.

Section six: Extension of thought

505 Memory

● Remember,
O God!

a Remember me, O God (Neh. 5:19; 13:14, 29, 31; Ps. 106:4); remember your word to me (Ps. 119:49); remember me when you come into your kingdom (Luke 23:42); remember your congregation and Mount Zion (Ps. 74:2); remember David's affliction (Ps. 132:1); remember the day of Jerusalem (Ps. 137:7); remember what has befallen us (Lam. 5:1); God, remember Abraham! (Exod. 32:13); remember Tobiah and Sanballat (Neh. 6:14).

b You who remind the Lord, take no rest (Isa. 62:6).

● God remem-
bering

c God remembers: Noah (Gen. 8:1); Abraham (Gen. 19:29); Ra-chel (Gen. 30:22); his covenant (Gen. 9:15–16; Exod. 2:24; Lev. 26:42, 45; Deut. 4:31; Ps. 106:45; Ezek. 16:60); the days of old (Isa. 63:11).

d You will be remembered by the Lord (Num. 10:9); though a mother may forget, I will not forget you (Isa. 49:15); you will not be forgotten by me (Isa. 44:21); the needy will not always be forgotten (Ps. 9:18); sparrows are not forgotten by God (Luke 12:6); God will not forget your work and love (Heb. 6:10).

e I remember their wickedness (Hos. 7:2); he will remember their iniquity (Hos. 8:13; 9:9).

● Remembering
God

f Remember the Lord (Neh. 4:14); remember the Lord from afar (Jer. 51:50); they will remember me in far countries (Zech. 10:9); remember your Creator (Eccles. 12:1); remember Jesus Christ (2 Tim. 2:8); do this in remembrance of me (Luke 22:19; 1 Cor. 11:24, 25).

g Remember his wonderful deeds (1 Chr. 16:12); I will remember the deeds of the Lord (Ps. 77:11); remember his covenant (1 Chr. 16:15–17); I will remind you of these things so you will be able to remember them (2 Pet. 1:12–15); the Holy Spirit will bring to your remembrance all I said (John 14:26); after he was raised they remembered his word (John 2:22); do not forget my teach-ing (Prov. 3:1).

h I will not forget your word (Ps. 119:16); I do not forget your law (Ps. 119:61, 109, 153); I do not forget your statutes (Ps. 119:83); I will never forget your precepts (Ps. 119:93, 141); I do not forget your commandments (Ps. 119:176).

i We have not forgotten you (Ps. 44:17); when I remember you on my bed (Ps. 63:6); those who escape will remember me among the nations (Ezek. 6:9); I remembered the Lord (Jonah 2:7).

● Reminders

j This day will be a memorial for you (Exod. 12:14); remember this day (Exod. 13:3); it shall be a reminder on your forehead (Exod. 13:9); Aaron will bear their names on his shoulders as a memorial (Exod. 28:12); as also on the breastpiece (Exod. 28:29); the tassels are a reminder of the Lord's commands (Num. 15:39–40); the trumpets a memorial before God (Num. 10:10); these stones are a memorial for Israel (Josh. 4:7).

k Memorial portion: of the grain offering (Lev. 2:2, 9, 16; 5:12; 6:15); of the bread (Lev. 24:7); everywhere I cause my name to be remembered (Exod. 20:24).

l The sacrifices are a reminder of sins (Heb. 10:3).

m Wherever the gospel is preached, what she has done will be told in memory of her (Matt. 26:13; Mark 14:9); the righteous will be remembered for ever (Ps. 112:6).

n I have written boldly to remind you (Rom. 15:15); remind them of these things (2 Tim. 2:14); Timothy will remind you of my ways in Christ (1 Cor. 4:17); I stir up your mind by a reminder

(2 Pet. 3:1); I have said these things that you may remember (John 16:4).

- **Remember!** *o* Remember Lot's wife (Luke 17:32); remember what God did to Miriam (Deut. 24:9); do not forget about Amalek (Deut. 25:17–19); Joseph asked the butler to remember him (Gen. 40:14); he asked us to remember the poor (Gal. 2:10); do you not remember the leftovers you gathered? (Matt. 16:9; Mark 8:18–19).

p Remember the former days (Heb. 10:32); remember what you have received (Rev. 3:3); remember the words of the apostles (Jude 17).

- **People remembering** *q* The memory of the righteous is a blessing (Prov. 10:7); do not slay them lest my people forget (Ps. 59:11); we wept when we remembered Zion (Ps. 137:1); Jerusalem remembers the precious things from days gone by (Lam. 1:7).

r Joseph remembered his dreams (Gen. 42:9); Peter remembered Jesus' word (Matt. 26:75); you will remember your ways (Ezek. 16:63; 20:43); you will remember your evil ways (Ezek. 36:31).

506 Forgetfulness

- **No remembrance** *a* There is no remembrance of former things (Eccles. 1:11); no lasting remembrance of wise or fools (Eccles. 2:16); I am forgotten like a dead man (Ps. 31:12).

- **God forgetting** *b* God has forgotten (Ps. 10:11); the Lord has forgotten me (Isa. 49:14); I will forget your children (Hos. 4:6); I am like the dead whom you remember no more (Ps. 88:5); why have you forgotten me? (Ps. 42:9); will you forget me for ever? (Ps. 13:1); why do you forget us for ever? (Lam. 5:20).

c Do not remember the sins of my youth (Ps. 25:7); their sins I will remember no more (Heb. 8:12; 10:17); I will not remember your sins (Isa. 43:25).

d None of his sins will be remembered (Ezek. 33:16); none of his righteous deeds will be remembered (Ezek. 33:13).

- **Forgetting God** *e* Do not forget the Lord (Deut. 6:12; 8:11, 14); they forgot the Lord (1 Sam. 12:9; Jer. 3:21); they forgot God their Saviour (Ps. 106:21); they did not remember the Lord (Judg. 8:34); you have forgotten God (Isa. 17:10; 51:13); you who forget God (Ps. 50:22); they forgot me (Hos. 13:6); you have forgotten me (Jer. 13:25; Ezek. 22:12; 23:35); she forgot me (Hos. 2:13); you did not remember me (Isa. 57:11); my people have forgotten me (Jer. 2:32; 18:15); those who forget God will perish (Job 8:13).

f They did not remember your wonderful deeds (Neh. 9:17); they forgot his deeds (Ps. 78:11); they soon forgot his works (Ps. 106:13); they did not remember his power (Ps. 78:42); our fathers did not remember your lovingkindness (Ps. 106:7); you did not remember the days of your youth (Ezek. 16:22, 43).

- **Blotting out** *g* I will blot out the memory of Amalek (Exod. 17:14); I would have removed the memory of Israel (Deut. 32:26); their very memory has perished (Ps. 9:6); the Lord will cut off the memory of evildoers (Ps. 34:16); may he cut off their memory (Ps. 109:15); you will not be remembered (Ezek. 21:32); let us wipe out Israel that their name not be remembered (Ps. 83:4).

Blot out name, see **561z.**

- **Forgetting people**

h The butler forgot Joseph (Gen. 40:23); Joash did not remember Jehoiada's kindness (2 Chr. 24:22); no one remembered the poor man who delivered the city (Eccles. 9:15); your lovers have forgotten you (Jer. 30:14); forget your people and your father's house (Ps. 45:10).

- **Forgetting things**

i Stay with Laban until Esau forgets (Gen. 27:45); have you forgotten the wickedness of your father? (Jer. 44:9).

j He has forgotten he was cleansed from his old sins (2 Pet. 1:9); he forgets what his face is like (Jas. 1:24); if I forget Jerusalem, let my right hand forget (Ps. 137:5).

k God has made me forget my trouble (Gen. 41:51); let him drink and forget his trouble (Prov. 31:7); forgetting what lies behind (Phil. 3:13).

l They had forgotten to bring any bread (Matt. 16:5; Mark 8:14); I forget to eat my bread (Ps. 102:4).

507 Expectation

- **Waiting for God**

a Wait for the Lord (Ps. 27:14; 37:34); wait patiently for him (Ps. 37:7).

b I wait for you (Ps. 25:21); for you I wait all day (Ps. 25:5); I wait for the Lord more than watchmen wait for the morning (Ps. 130:5–6); I wait for God my Saviour (Mic. 7:7); I wait patiently for the Lord (Ps. 40:1); I wait in silence for God (Ps. 62:1, 5); we wait for you (Isa. 26:8; 33:2).

c Those who wait for the Lord renew their strength (Isa. 40:31); those who wait for the Lord will inherit the land (Ps. 37:9); blessed are those who wait for him (Isa. 30:18); may those who wait for you not be ashamed through me (Ps. 69:6); this is our God for whom we have waited (Isa. 25:9); the Lord is good to those who wait for him (Lam. 3:25–6).

- **Waiting for the second coming**

d We wait for: a Saviour from heaven (Phil. 3:20); the revealing of the Lord Jesus (1 Cor. 1:7); the appearing of our God and Saviour (Titus 2:13); his Son from heaven (1 Thess. 1:10); the mercy of our Lord Jesus (Jude 21); the redemption of our bodies (Rom. 8:23–5).

e Be like men waiting for their master (Luke 12:36); the creation waits for the sons of God to be revealed (Rom. 8:19).

- **People waiting**

f Saul was told to wait seven days for Samuel (1 Sam. 10:8; 13:8); David would wait until word came (2 Sam. 15:28).

508 Lack of expectation

● Unexpected

a The coming of the Son of man will be unexpected (Matt. 24:37–41; Luke 12:40); at an hour you do not think (Matt. 24:44); lest the day come unexpectedly like a trap (Luke 21:34–5); the master will come on a day the slave does not expect (Matt. 24:50; Luke 12:46).

509 Disappointment

● Not disappointed

a He who believes in him will not be disappointed (Rom. 9:33; 10:11).

510 Foresight

● The elect foreknown

a Chosen according to the foreknowledge of God (1 Pet. 1:2); those whom he foreknew he also predestined (Rom. 8:29); God has not rejected those he foreknew (Rom. 11:2).

● Christ foreknown

b Christ was foreknown before the foundation of the world (1 Pet. 1:20).

511 Prediction

● Predicting Christ

a The Spirit predicted the sufferings of Christ (1 Pet. 1:11); God foretold by the prophets that Christ would suffer (Acts 3:18); they killed those who predicted the coming of the Righteous One (Acts 7:52).

● Predicting the future

b I have told you in advance (Matt. 24:25; Mark 13:23; John 13:19; 14:29); Agabus predicted the famine (Acts 11:28).
Knowing the future, see **124k**.

c No one knows what will be (Eccles. 10:14).

Section seven: Creative thought

512 Supposition
Opinion, see **451**.

513 Imagination
Dreams, see **438s**.

4.2: Communication of ideas

Section one: Nature of ideas communicated

514 Meaning

● Significance   *a* What do these things mean? (Ezek. 24:19).

515 Lack of meaning

● Meaningless   *a* They honour me with their lips but their heart is far from me (Isa. 29:13; Matt. 15:8; Mark 7:6); you are near to their lips but far from their heart (Jer. 12:2); in prayer do not use meaningless babbling (Matt. 6:7).

         b The women's words seemed like nonsense (Luke 24:11); avoid empty chatter (1 Tim. 6:20; 2 Tim. 2:16).

516 Intelligibility

● Need for un-   *a* Hear and understand! (Matt. 15:10); let the reader understand
derstanding   (Matt. 24:15; Mark 13:14); what I do now you will understand later (John 13:7).

         b The one who hears the word and understands it bears fruit (Matt. 13:23); have you understood? (Matt. 13:51); do you understand what you are reading? (Acts 8:30); how will you understand all the parables? (Mark 4:13); what they had not heard they will understand (Isa. 52:15).

         c Men who understood the times (1 Chr. 12:32).

● God has un-   *d* God understands all their works (Ps. 33:15); they were amazed
derstanding   at Jesus' understanding (Luke 2:47).

● God gives un-   *e* The breath of the Almighty gives a man understanding (Job
derstanding   32:8); the Lord will give you understanding (2 Tim. 2:7); those who seek the Lord understand all (Prov. 28:5); give me understanding that I might live (Ps. 119:144); the unfolding of your word gives understanding (Ps. 119:130).

● Understanding   *f* Give me understanding to know your testimonies (Ps. 119:125);
God's word   open my eyes to see wonders in your law (Ps. 119:18); make me understand the way of your precepts (Ps. 119:27); give me understanding to keep your law (Ps. 119:34); give me understanding according to your word (Ps. 119:169); he opened their minds to understand the scriptures (Luke 24:45); they celebrated because they had understood the words (Neh. 8:12); they understood he was speaking about them (Matt. 21:45).

● Conveying   *g* Unless you speak intelligible words, how will the message be
the message   understood? (1 Cor. 14:9); I write nothing but what you can understand (2 Cor. 1:13).

● Eyes opened   *h* Your eyes will be opened, knowing good and evil (Gen. 3:5); their eyes were opened and they knew they were naked (Gen. 3:7); Elisha asked the Lord to open the servant's eyes (2 Kgs.

6:17); their eyes were opened through the breaking of bread (Luke 24:31); the eyes of those who see will not be blinded (Isa. 32:3); the eyes of your hearts being enlightened (Eph. 1:18). **Eyes seeing**, see **438**.

517 Unintelligibility

● Understanding mysteries

a The peace of God passes all understanding (Phil. 4:7); the love of Christ passes knowledge (Eph. 3:19); how inscrutable are his ways! (Rom. 11:33); when I tried to understand this it was hard (Ps. 73:16); there are four things I do not understand (Prov. 30:18–19).

b I do not understand my actions (Rom. 7:15).

● Understanding the message

c No one understands (Rom. 3:11); they will see and hear but never understand (Isa. 6:9; Matt. 13:13–14; Mark 4:12; Luke 8:10; Acts 28:26); he has shut their hearts so that they cannot understand (Isa. 44:18); some hear the word but do not understand it (Matt. 13:19); the natural man cannot understand the things of the Spirit (1 Cor. 2:14); Paul wrote some things hard to understand (2 Pet. 3:16).

d The disciples did not understand (Matt. 16:8–11; Mark 9:32; Luke 9:45; 18:34; John 12:16; 20:9); are you still without understanding? (Matt. 15:16; Mark 8:17); they did not understand about the loaves (Mark 6:52); Jesus' parents did not understand the saying (Luke 2:50); the Israelites did not understand (Acts 7:25); none of the rulers understood this mystery (1 Cor. 2:8); they did not understand (John 10:6).

e It is hard to explain because you are dull of hearing (Heb. 5:11); having eyes, do you not see? (Mark 8:18); do you not understand? (Mark 8:21); are you a teacher of Israel yet you do not understand? (John 3:10); they want to be teachers of the law though they do not understand (1 Tim. 1:7); why do you not understand what I say? (John 8:43). **Unintelligible language**, see **557***b*.

518 Ambiguity

● Half-hearted

a I hate half-hearted men (Ps. 119:113).

519 Metaphor: figure of speech

● Using parables

a Is he not a maker of parables? (Ezek. 20:49); through the prophets I gave parables (Hos. 12:10).

● Jesus using parables

b Jesus told them many things in parables (Matt. 13:3; Mark 4:2); he began to speak to them in parables (Mark 12:1); Jesus spoke to them again in parables (Matt. 22:1); he spoke to them in a parable (Mark 3:23); what parable shall we use for the kingdom of God? (Mark 4:30); when Jesus had finished these parables (Matt. 13:53); I have said these things in figures (John 16:25).

c Why speak to them in parables? (Matt. 13:10–13); I will open my mouth in parables (Ps. 78:2; Matt. 13:34–5); to those outside everything is in parables (Mark 4:11; Luke 8:10); he did not speak to them without a parable (Mark 4:33–4); they asked him about the parables (Mark 4:10); how will you understand all the parables? (Mark 4:13).

● Jesus'
parables

d Parable of the: blind leading the blind (Matt. 15:14; Luke 6:39); drag-net (Matt. 13:47–50); fig tree (Matt. 24:32–33; Mark 13:28; Luke 21:29–31); fig tree without fruit (Luke 13:6–8); good Samaritan (Luke 10:30–7); good shepherd (John 10:1–5); guests choosing places (Luke 14:7–11); houses on rock and sand (Matt. 7:24–7; Luke 6:48–9); importunate neighbour (Luke 11:5–8); invitations to the feast (Matt. 22:2–14; Luke 14:16–24); king settling accounts (Matt. 18:23–34); labourers in the vineyard (Matt. 20:1–16); lamp and lampstand (Luke 8:16); leaven (Matt. 13:33); lost coin (Luke 15:8–10); lost sheep (Luke 15:3–7; Matt. 18:12–14); master returning from the wedding feast (Luke 12:36–40); mustard seed (Matt. 13:31–2; Mark 4:31–2; Luke 13:18–19); patched garments (Luke 5:36); pearl (Matt. 13:45–6); Pharisee and tax collector (Luke 18:9–14); prodigal son (Luke 15:11–32); rich fool (Luke 12:16–21); rented vineyard (Matt. 21:33–41; Mark 12:1–12; Luke 20:9–13); rich man and Lazarus (Luke 16:19–31); sheep and goats (Matt. 25:31–46); sower (Matt. 13:3–9; Mark 4:3–9; Luke 8:4–8); sprouting seed (Mark 4:26–9); talents (Matt. 25:14–30); ten minas (Luke 19:11–27); ten virgins (Matt. 25:1–13); treasure (Matt. 13:44); two debtors (Luke 7:41–3); two sons (Matt. 21:28–32); unjust judge (Luke 18:1–8); unjust steward (Luke 16:1–9); wheat and tares (Matt. 13:24–30, 36–43); wineskins (Luke 5:37–8).

● Various
parables

e Jotham's parable of the trees choosing a king (Judg. 9:8–15); Nathan's parable of the poor man's ewe lamb (2 Sam. 12:1–4); Jehoash's parable of the thorn bush and the cedar (2 Kgs. 14:9; 2 Chr. 25:18); parable of the vineyard (Isa. 5:1–7); parable of the two eagles and the vine (Ezek. 17:2–10); parable of the cedar (Ezek. 17:22–4); parable of Oholah and Oholibah (Ezek. 23:2–45); parable of the boiling pot (Ezek. 24:3–14).

520 Interpretation

● Interpreting
dreams

a No one could interpret the dreams (Gen. 41:8; Dan. 4:6–7); Joseph interpreted the dreams of the butler and baker (Gen. 40:8–19; 41:11–13); of Pharaoh (Gen. 41:15–32); Gideon heard the dream and its interpretation (Judg. 7:15); Daniel interpreted Nebuchadnezzar's dreams (Dan. 2:16, 24–45; 4:18–26); Daniel interpreted the inscription (Dan. 5:17–28).

Dreams interpreted, see **438***w*.

b Tell the dream and we will show the interpretation (Dan. 2:4); tell me the interpretation (Dan. 4:9); anyone who can interpret this writing will be clothed in purple (Dan. 5:7); the wise men could not interpret the inscription (Dan. 5:8); a bystander told me the interpretation (Dan. 7:16).

● Interpreting language

c Joseph used an interpreter (Gen. 42:23); the gift of interpretation (1 Cor. 12:10; 14:26); not all interpret (1 Cor. 12:30); interpretation is necessary when one speaks in tongues (1 Cor. 14:5, 27–28); pray to be able to interpret (1 Cor. 14:13).

● Explanation

d They could interpret the appearance of the sky, but could not interpret the present time (Matt. 16:3; Luke 12:56).

e The Levites gave the meaning of the Law (Neh. 8:7–8); explain to us the parable (Matt. 13:36); he explained to them the Scriptures concerning himself (Luke 24:27, 32); they explained the way of God more accurately (Acts 18:26).

f Explain the parable (Matt. 15:15); he explained the parables privately to his disciples (Mark 4:34).

g The Son has explained the Father (John 1:18).

h No Scripture is a matter of private interpretation (2 Pet. 1:20).

521 Misinterpretation
Not understand, see **517**.

Section two: Modes of communication

522 Manifestation

● Manifest to God

a Everything is uncovered before God's eyes (Heb. 4:13); Sheol lies open before God, how much more men's hearts (Prov. 15:11).

● God manifest

b What is to be known about God is evident to men (Rom. 1:19–20); Jesus Christ was placarded as crucified (Gal. 3:1).

● Things manifest

c Both sins and good deeds are evident (1 Tim. 5:24–5); you did it in secret but I will do it openly (2 Sam. 12:12); nothing is hidden from the sun's heat (Ps. 19:6); when the wheat sprang up the tares were apparent (Matt. 13:26).

d Sanballat sent an open letter (Neh. 6:5); I have always spoken openly (John 18:20).

e It is useless to spread a net in the bird's sight (Prov. 1:17).

f The disciples pointed out the buildings of the temple (Matt. 24:1).

523 Hiding oneself

● God hiding

a Do not hide your face from me (Ps. 27:9; 69:17; 102:2; 143:7); why do you hide your face? (Job 13:24; Ps. 44:24; 88:14); why do you hide in times of trouble (Ps. 10:1).

b I will hide my face from them (Deut. 31:17–18; 32:20); he will hide his face from them (Mic. 3:4); I hid my face from them (Ezek. 39:23, 24); I hid my face from you for a moment (Isa. 54:8); you hid your face (Ps. 30:7); you have hidden your face from us (Isa. 64:7); I have hidden my face from this city (Jer. 33:5); the Lord is hiding his face from Israel (Isa. 8:17); God has withdrawn from them (Hos. 5:6); you are a God who hides yourself (Isa. 45:15); how long will you hide your face? (Ps. 13:1); will you hide yourself for ever, O Lord? (Ps. 89:46); you hide your face and they are dismayed (Ps. 104:29); your sins have hidden his face from you (Isa. 59:2).

c Hide your face from my sins (Ps. 51:9); Cain would be hidden from God's face (Gen. 4:14).

d I will not hide my face from them any more (Ezek. 39:29).

● Hiding from God

e Adam and Eve hid from the Lord (Gen. 3:8, 10); Moses hid his face (Exod. 3:6); Daniel's companions ran to hide themselves (Dan. 10:7); hide in the dust from the fear of the Lord (Isa. 2:10); hide until wrath is past (Isa. 26:20); they hid in the caves and among the rocks (Rev. 6:15); can a man hide so that I cannot see him? (Jer. 23:24).

f Then I will not hide from your face (Job 13:20).

● Hiding from people

g The spies hid themselves in the hill country (Josh. 2:16); five kings hid in a cave (Josh. 10:16–17); Israel hid in caves and pits (1 Sam. 13:6); the Benjaminites hid in the vineyards (Judg. 21:20); the king thought the Arameans were hiding (2 Kgs. 7:12).

h Jotham hid himself (Judg. 9:5); Saul hid among the baggage (1 Sam. 10:22); David hid from Saul (1 Sam. 19:2; 26:1; Ps. 54:t); David hid himself in the field (1 Sam. 20:5, 19, 24); find out about his hiding places (1 Sam. 23:23); he will have hidden himself in some cave (2 Sam. 17:9); hide by the brook Cherith (1 Kgs. 17:3); go hide yourself (Jer. 36:19); Jesus hid himself (John 8:59; 12:36).

i The wicked man lurks to catch the innocent (Ps. 10:8–9).

j A prudent man sees danger and hides himself (Prov. 22:3; 27:12); when the wicked rise, men hide themselves (Prov. 28:28).

k You will go into an inner room to hide yourself (1 Kgs. 22:25; 2 Chr. 18:24); one from whom men hide their face (Isa. 53:3); the people stole into the city like those who flee ashamed (2 Sam. 19:3); Elizabeth hid herself for five months (Luke 1:24).

Avoiding, see **620**; **acting in secret**, see **530***d*.

524 Information

● Reporting events

a The servant told Isaac all he had done (Gen. 24:66); Rebekah was told what Esau said (Gen. 27:42); Joseph brought a bad report about his brethren (Gen. 37:2); all Ruth did was told to Boaz (Ruth 2:11); a servant told Abigail (1 Sam. 25:14); afraid to tell David the child was dead (2 Sam. 12:18); the slaves informed their master (Matt. 18:31); the guards reported what had happened to the chief priests (Matt. 28:11).

- Reporting
statements

  b Samson told his wife and she told the men (Judg. 14:17); they told David what Nabal said (1 Sam. 25:12); Samuel told Eli all that God said (1 Sam. 3:18).

- Reporting
and Jesus

  c The herdsmen told what Jesus had done to the demoniacs (Matt. 8:33); the herdsmen reported what had happened (Mark 5:14); John's disciples reported these things to him (Luke 7:18); tell John what you have seen and heard (Luke 7:22); the disciples told Jesus all they had done and taught (Mark 6:30); go tell his disciples and Peter (Mark 16:7); tell his disciples that he has risen (Matt. 28:7); Mary Magdalene told those who had been with him (Mark 16:10); the women reported these things to the disciples (Luke 24:9–10); two walking in the country reported seeing Jesus (Mark 16:13).

- Giving vital
information

  d David was told Saul was coming (1 Sam. 23:25); Saul was told where David was (1 Sam. 19:19; 23:7, 13, 19; 24:1; 26:1; Ps. 54:t); Doeg told Saul about David (1 Sam. 22:9–10, 22; Ps. 52:t); Saul was told that David had fled (1 Sam. 27:4); a lad told Absalom (2 Sam. 17:18); they went and told David (2 Sam. 17:21); David would wait until word came (2 Sam. 15:28); a man told Joab about Absalom (2 Sam. 18:19); Ahimaaz wanted to tell David about Absalom (2 Sam. 18:19); they told David what Rizpah had done (2 Sam. 21:11); they told the old prophet what the man of God had done (1 Kgs. 13:11); the Lord had told Ahijah that Jeroboam's wife was coming (1 Kgs. 14:5); Ahab told Jezebel what Elijah had done (1 Kgs. 19:1); Naaman told his master what the girl said (2 Kgs. 5:4); Elisha told the king of Israel where the Arameans would be (2 Kgs. 6:9–12); the lepers told the people in the city (2 Kgs. 7:9–10); the enemies were told that the wall was built (Neh. 6:1).

  e Jonathan told David all he found out (1 Sam. 19:3, 7; 20:12–13); whatever you hear, tell to the priests (2 Sam. 15:35); Gehazi told the king all that Elisha had done (2 Kgs. 8:4–5); the Jews who lived near told us ten times (Neh. 4:12); Mordecai gave information about the plot (Esther 2:22); they told Haman about Mordecai (Esther 3:4).

- Reporting
conflicts

  f A fugitive told Abraham about Lot's capture (Gen. 14:13); Abimelech was told about the bandits (Judg. 9:25); the man told the city the news of the battle (1 Sam. 4:13); David was to bring back news (1 Sam. 17:18); David told Samuel all that had happened (1 Sam. 19:18); Abiathar told David that Saul killed the priests (1 Sam. 22:21).

525 Concealment

- God's things
concealed

  a Shall I hide from Abraham what I am going to do? (Gen. 18:17); the word of the Lord was not yet revealed to him (1 Sam. 3:7); the Lord has hidden it from me (2 Kgs. 4:27); it is the glory of God to conceal a matter (Prov. 25:2); you hid these things from the wise and revealed them to babes (Matt. 11:25; Luke 10:21); the mystery hidden for ages in God (Eph. 3:9).

b Do not hide from me what God said (1 Sam. 3:17); if our gospel is veiled, it is veiled to those who are perishing (2 Cor. 4:3); the things that make for peace are hidden from you (Luke 19:42).

● Sealed matters

c Seal up the vision (Dan. 8:26); seal up the book (Dan. 12:4); these words are sealed up until the end (Dan. 12:9); seal up what the seven thunders said (Rev. 10:4).

● Jesus concealing

d Jesus would not let the demons say who he was (Mark 1:34; 3:12; Luke 4:41); he warned the cured leper not to tell anyone (Matt. 8:4; Mark 1:44; Luke 5:14); also the blind men (Matt. 9:30); also Jairus and his wife (Mark 5:43; Luke 8:56); also the sick who were healed (Matt. 12:16; Mark 8:26) and those who saw it (Mark 7:36); he warned his disciples not to say he was the Christ (Matt. 16:20; Mark 8:30; Luke 9:21); not to tell anyone about the transfiguration (Matt. 17:9; Mark 9:9); which they did not (Luke 9:36); Jesus did not want anyone to know he was in a house (Mark 7:24); or in the area (Mark 9:30); Jesus would not tell them by what authority he acted (Matt. 21:27; Mark 11:33; Luke 20:8).

● Hiding people

e Moses' mother hid him for three months (Exod. 2:2; Heb. 11:23); she has hidden her son (2 Kgs. 6:29); Joash was hidden for six years (2 Kgs. 11:2–3; 2 Chr. 22:11–12); Rahab hid the spies (Josh. 2:4, 6; 6:17, 25); Obadiah hid a hundred prophets (1 Kgs. 18:4, 13); hide the outcasts! (Isa. 16:3–4); perhaps you will be hidden on the day of the Lord's anger (Zeph. 2:3); they called on mountains and rocks to hide them (Rev. 6:16).

● God hiding people

f In trouble he will hide me in his tent (Ps. 27:5); you hide them in the secret place of your presence (Ps. 31:20); in his quiver he hid me (Isa. 49:2); God hid Jeremiah and Baruch (Jer. 36:26).

g Your life is hid with Christ in God (Col. 3:3).

● Hiding things

h Achan hid the things in his tent (Josh. 7:21–2); the lepers hid valuables (2 Kgs. 7:8); he hid his talent in the ground (Matt. 25:18, 25); he kept his mina in a handkerchief (Luke 19:20); hide the waistcloth in a crevice of rock (Jer. 13:4).

● Not telling

i Better an open rebuke than concealed love (Prov. 27:5).

j Samson did not tell his parents about the lion (Judg. 14:16); Saul did not tell his uncle about the kingship (1 Sam. 10:16); we are keeping quiet on a day of good news (2 Kgs. 7:9); why should my father hide this from me? (1 Sam. 20:2); Saul does not want Jonathan to know this (1 Sam. 20:3); no one tells me when my son makes a covenant (1 Sam. 22:8); you have not told me the riddle (Judg. 14:16).

k Abigail did not tell Nabal (1 Sam. 25:19, 36); Jonathan did not tell Saul (1 Sam. 14:1); Nehemiah did not tell anyone (Neh. 2:12, 16); Esther did not make her people known (Esther 2:10, 20); the women said nothing to anyone (Mark 16:8).

l Let it not be known that a woman came here (Ruth 3:14); tell it not in Gath (2 Sam. 1:20; Mic. 1:10); let no one tell it in Jezreel (2 Kgs. 9:15); do not let anyone know about this matter (1 Sam. 21:2; Jer. 38:24); do not tell anyone (Acts 23:22).

m Do not curse the king even in private (Eccles. 10:20); a prudent man conceals his knowledge (Prov. 12:23); he who is trustworthy keeps a secret (Prov. 11:13).

Secret, see **530**, **keep silent**, see **582**.

● Hiding the truth

n Woe to those who hide their plans from the Lord (Isa. 29:15); men suppress the truth (Rom. 1:18).

o He who conceals his transgressions will not prosper (Prov. 28:13); he who conceals hatred has lying lips (Prov. 10:18).

526 Disclosure

● Disclosure in general

a Nothing is concealed which will not be revealed (Matt. 10:26; Mark 4:22; Luke 8:17; 12:2); a bird will make the matter known (Eccles. 10:20); no one lights a lamp and hides it (Matt. 5:15; Mark 4:21; Luke 8:16; 11:33); God will bring to light the things hidden in darkness (1 Cor. 4:5); what you hear whispered in darkness, proclaim in the light (Matt. 10:27); a city on a hill cannot be hid (Matt. 5:14); do not seal up the words of this book (Rev. 22:10).

Preaching, see **528**.

b The secret things belong to the Lord but the things revealed belong to us (Deut. 29:29); I will utter things hidden from the foundation of the world (Matt. 13:35; cf. Ps. 78:2).

● God making himself known

c God made known his ways to Moses (Ps. 103:7); you have begun to show me your goodness (Deut. 3:24); I revealed myself to the house of your fathers (1 Sam. 2:27); at the proper time he manifested his word (Titus 1:3); the Lord revealed himself to Samuel (1 Sam. 3:21).

d The glory of the Lord will be revealed (Isa. 40:5); God will make himself known to the Egyptians (Isa. 19:21).

e The Lord has revealed his salvation (Ps. 98:2); he has made known the power of his works (Ps. 111:6); in the gospel the righteousness of God is revealed (Rom. 1:18).

● God making mysteries known

f If God wanted to kill us he would not have shown us these things (Judg. 13:23); God had revealed Saul's coming to Samuel (1 Sam. 9:15); God revealed to Simeon that he would see the Christ (Luke 2:26).

g There is a God who reveals mysteries (Dan. 2:28, 29); the mystery was revealed to Daniel in a vision of the night (Dan. 2:19); God reveals mysteries out of darkness (Job 12:22); God reveals hidden things (Dan. 2:22); I will show you great and unknown things (Jer. 33:3); the mystery now made known (Rom. 16:25–6; Eph. 3:3–5); God does nothing without revealing it to the prophets (Amos 3:7); he made known the mystery of his will (Eph. 1:9); he made known among the Gentiles the riches of this mystery (Col. 1:27); it has been given to you to know the mysteries of the kingdom (Matt. 13:11; Mark 4:11; Luke 8:10); you have revealed these things to babes (Matt. 11:25; Luke 10:21); my Father revealed it to you (Matt. 16:17); God has revealed them to us (1 Cor. 2:10); to make known the mystery of the gospel (Eph. 6:19); that God may give you a spirit of wisdom and revelation (Eph. 1:17); I went up by revelation (Gal. 2:2).

h The thoughts of many hearts will be revealed (Luke 2:35).

- Making God known

i No one knows the Father except those to whom the Son reveals him (Matt. 11:27; Luke 10:22); everything I heard from my Father I have made known (John 15:15); I made known your name to them (John 17:6, 26); the only begotten God has made the Father known (John 1:18).

j In all your ways acknowledge him (Prov. 3:6).

- Making God's deeds known

k Make known God's deeds among the peoples (1 Chr. 16:8; Ps. 105:1; Isa. 12:4); they will speak of your deeds (Ps. 145:6); they will make known your deeds (Ps. 145:11–12); I have made your faithfulness known (Ps. 40:9–10); this was that the works of God might be displayed in him (John 9:3); they reported all that God had done (Acts 14:27); he proclaimed it freely and spread the news (Mark 1:45); the news of Jesus' healings went into all the land (Matt. 9:26, 31); salvation to be revealed in the last time (1 Pet. 1:5).

- Making Jesus known

l You are going to disclose yourself to us, and not to the world? (John 14:22); show yourself to the world (John 7:4).

m Christ was revealed in these last times (1 Pet. 1:20); John came so that Christ might be revealed (John 1:31); he showed them his hands and side (John 20:20); God revealed his Son in me (Gal. 1:15–16); the Spirit will make known the things of Christ (John 16:14); revelation of Jesus Christ (Gal. 1:12; 1 Pet. 1:7, 13; Rev. 1:1); you wait for the revealing of our Lord Jesus Christ (1 Cor. 1:7); when Christ is revealed, you will be revealed with him (Col. 3:4).

- Acknowledging Jesus

n Every tongue will confess that Jesus is Lord (Phil. 2:11); if you confess with your mouth that Jesus is Lord (Rom. 10:9); everyone who acknowledges me before men, I will acknowledge before my Father (Matt. 10:32; Luke 12:8); announce to your family what the Lord has done for you (Mark 5:19).

- God's people revealed

o The creation longs for the revealing of the sons of God (Rom. 8:19); when Christ is revealed, you will be revealed with him (Col. 3:4).

- Confessing sins

p The guilty person must confess his sin (Lev. 5:5; Num. 5:7); only acknowedge your iniquity (Jer. 3:13); Aaron had to confess the sins of the Israelites (Lev. 16:21); as Nehemiah did (Neh. 1:6); the people confessing their sins (Lev. 26:40; Ezra 10:11; Neh.

9:2); Achan had to confess his sin (Josh. 7:19–21); tell me what you have done (1 Sam. 14:43).

q I will confess my transgressions (Ps. 32:5); I confess my iniquity (Ps. 38:18); he who confesses will find mercy (Prov. 28:13).

r Confessing their sins, they were baptised by John (Matt. 3:6; Mark 1:5); the Ephesians confessed their deeds (Acts 19:18); confess your sins to each other (Jas. 5:16); if we confess our sins he will forgive us (1 John 1:9).

s The secrets of his heart are disclosed (1 Cor. 14:25).

● People revealed

t Joseph made himself known to his brethren (Acts 7:13); I will show you the man you seek (Judg. 4:22); Jonathan showed himself to the Philistines (1 Sam. 14:8, 11); reveal yourself to Ahab (1 Kgs. 18:1, 15); Esther had declared her link with Mordecai (Esther 8:1); he does not come to the light lest his deeds be exposed (John 3:20); the man of sin will be revealed (2 Thess. 2:6).

● People revealing

u The thing is known (Exod. 2:14); my father does nothing without disclosing it to me (1 Sam. 20:2); there is nothing hidden from the king (2 Sam. 18:13).

v Show us the entrance to the city (Judg. 1:24–5); do not hide anything from me (2 Sam. 14:18); make known to me my dream (Dan. 2:5–6, 9); Hezekiah showed the Babylonians all he had (2 Kgs. 20:13; Isa. 39:2).

527 Disguising

● Disguise

a The adulterer disguises his face (Job 24:15).

b Those who disguised themselves: Jacob (Gen. 27:15–23); Tamar (Gen. 38:14); Joseph (Gen. 42:7); Saul (1 Sam. 28:8); Jeroboam's wife (1 Kgs. 14:2); a prophet (1 Kgs. 20:38); the king of Israel in battle (1 Kgs. 22:30; 2 Chr. 18:29); king Josiah (2 Chr. 35:22); wolves in sheep's clothing (Matt. 7:15); false apostles as apostles of Christ (2 Cor. 11:13); Satan as an angel of light (2 Cor. 11:14).

● Ambush

c They set an ambush behind Ai (Josh. 8:2–9, 12–21); the men of Shechem set an ambush against Abimelech (Judg. 9:25); Abimelech set an ambush for the men of Shechem (Judg. 9:32–5, 43); Israel set an ambush against Gibeah (Judg. 20:29–38); Saul set an ambush against Amalek (1 Sam. 15:5); Jeroboam had set an ambush behind Judah (2 Chr. 13:13); the Lord set ambushes against the enemy (2 Chr. 20:22); they have set an ambush against us (Ps. 59:3); prepare ambushes against Babylon (Jer. 51:12).

d They lay in wait for Samson all night (Judg. 16:2); men lying in wait for Samson (Judg. 16:9, 12); David lies in ambush against me (1 Sam. 22:8, 13); the Jews wanted to set an ambush for Paul (Acts 23:21; 25:3).

e Let us ambush the innocent (Prov. 1:11); the words of the wicked lie in wait for blood (Prov. 12:6); do not lie in wait against the righteous (Prov. 24:15).

528 Publication

● Preachers

a The words of the Preacher (Eccles. 1:1); I the Preacher have been king (Eccles. 1:12).

b John the Baptist preached (Matt. 3:1; Mark 1:4); Noah, a preacher of righteousness (2 Pet. 2:5); Philip the evangelist (Acts 21:8).

● Preachers sent out

c The apostles were sent out to preach (Matt. 10:7; Mark 3:14; 6:12; Luke 9:2); go and preach the kingdom of God (Luke 9:60); they preached the gospel and healed (Luke 9:6); this gospel must be preached to all nations (Matt. 24:14; Mark 13:10); preach the gospel to all creation (Mark 16:15); repentance and forgiveness should be preached to all nations (Luke 24:47); he commanded us to preach to the people (Acts 10:42).

d Christ did not send me to baptise but to preach the gospel (1 Cor. 1:17); woe to me if I do not preach the gospel (1 Cor. 9:16); to preach among the Gentiles the riches of Christ (Eph. 3:8); to preach Christ among the Gentiles (Gal. 1:16); that by me the message be proclaimed to all the Gentiles (2 Tim. 4:17); my ambition has been to preach the gospel where Christ was unknown (Rom. 15:20); God called us to preach the gospel to them (Acts 16:10).

● Preachers preaching

e The Lord has anointed me to preach good news to the poor (Isa. 61:1; Luke 4:18); good news is preached to the poor (Matt. 11:5; Luke 7:22); they will declare my glory among the nations (Isa. 66:19); I have proclaimed righteousness in the great congregation (Ps. 40:9).

f Jesus began to preach (Matt. 4:17); Jesus preached the good news of the kingdom in Galilee (Matt. 4:23; Mark 1:14); in all the towns (Matt. 9:35; Luke 8:1); I must preach the good news in other towns also (Mark 1:38; Luke 4:43); the kingdom of God is preached (Luke 16:16); Christ preached to the spirits in prison (1 Pet. 3:19); the gospel was preached to the dead (1 Pet. 4:6).

g They went out and preached everywhere (Mark 16:20); they never stopped preaching the good news (Acts 5:42); those scattered preached the message (Acts 8:4); they continued to preach the gospel (Acts 14:7); Paul preached the kingdom of God (Acts 28:31); many women proclaim the good news (Ps. 68:11).

h He who persecuted us is now preaching the faith (Gal. 1:23); I have not hesitated to proclaim the whole purpose of God (Acts 20:27); I have fully preached the gospel (Rom. 15:19).

● The gospel preached

i Wherever the gospel is preached, what she has done will be told (Matt. 26:13; Mark 14:9).

j The scripture preached the gospel beforehand to Abraham (Gal. 3:8); day to day pours forth speech (Ps. 19:2); the gospel was proclaimed in all creation (Col. 1:23); the word of the Lord has sounded forth from you (1 Thess. 1:8).

Preaching the kingdom, see **733***h*.

● Preach!

k Preach the word (2 Tim. 4:2); do the work of an evangelist (2 Tim. 4:5); he gave some as evangelists (Eph. 4:11); how can they hear without a preacher? (Rom. 10:14); feet shod with the preparation of the gospel of peace (Eph. 6:15).

● Preaching Christ

l Christ is proclaimed (Phil. 1:18); him we proclaim (Col. 1:28); we do not preach ourselves but Christ as Lord (2 Cor. 4:5); Philip preached Jesus to him (Acts 8:35); he was preached among the nations (1 Tim. 3:16); we proclaim the mystery of Christ (Col. 4:3); in the Lord's supper you proclaim the Lord's death (1 Cor. 11:26).

Christ preached, see **357***ac*.

● Proclaiming edicts

m They proclaimed that the levy should be brought (2 Chr. 24:9); proclaiming that the king delights to honour him (Esther 6:9, 11); a copy of the edict was published (Esther 3:14).

● Spreading stories

n The more he told them not to tell anyone, the more they proclaimed it (Mark 7:36); the report of him spread throughout Syria (Matt. 4:24); news of him spread everywhere (Mark 1:28); this story spread among the Jews (Matt. 28:15).

529 News

● The word of God

a The word of the Lord abides for ever (1 Pet. 1:25); my words will not pass away (Matt. 24:35); the word of the Lord is tested (2 Sam. 22:31; Ps. 18:30); the word of the Lord is upright (Ps. 33:4); the words of the Lord are pure (Ps. 12:6); is not my word like a hammer? (Jer. 23:29); in praise of the word of God (Ps. 19:7–11; Ps. 119:1–176).

b The sword of the Spirit, which is the word of God (Eph. 6:17); the word of God is living and active (Heb. 4:12); my word will accomplish what I purpose (Isa. 55:11).

c Man lives by every word from the mouth of God (Deut. 8:3; Matt. 4:4); the word of the Lord was rare (1 Sam. 3:1); your words were found and I ate them (Jer. 15:16); God's word was on my tongue (2 Sam. 23:2).

d The worlds were made by the word of God (Ps. 33:6; Heb. 11:3; 2 Pet. 3:5); he spoke and it was done (Ps. 33:9); in the beginning was the Word (John 1:1); the Word of life (1 John 1:1); his name is the Word of God (Rev. 19:13).

● God's word through people

e The word of the Lord came through Jehu (1 Kgs. 16:1, 7); the word of the Lord was with Elisha (2 Kgs. 3:12); I have a message from God for you (Judg. 3:20; 1 Sam. 9:27); what the Lord says I will speak (1 Kgs. 22:14; 2 Chr. 18:13); 'oracle of the Lord' is not to be used (Jer. 23:33–8).

f The word of the Lord came to: Gad (2 Sam. 24:11; 1 Chr. 21:9); the prophet (1 Kgs. 13:20); Elijah (1 Kgs. 17:2, 8; 19:9; 21:17,

28); Jacob (1 Kgs. 18:31); Isaiah (2 Kgs. 20:4); Jeremiah (Jer. 1:2); John (Luke 3:2); Nathan (2 Sam. 7:4; 1 Chr. 17:3); Shemaiah (2 Chr. 11:2; 12:7).

- Receiving God's word

g Let the word of Christ dwell in you (Col. 3:16); receive the implanted word which can save your souls (Jas. 1:21); born again of imperishable seed, the living and abiding word of God (1 Pet. 1:23); he gave us birth by the word of truth (Jas. 1:18); you received God's message not at the word of men but as the word of God (1 Thess. 2:13); the word of his grace is able to build you up (Acts 20:32); a workman correctly handling the word of truth (2 Tim. 2:15).

Hearing the word, see **455m**.

- Progress of God's word

h The seed is the word of God (Luke 8:11); the sower sows the word (Mark 4:14); they spoke the word of God boldly (Acts 4:29, 31); the word of God had to be spoken to you first (Acts 13:46); the word of God continued to grow (Acts 12:24); that the word of the Lord may speed on (2 Thess. 3:1).

- Good news

i Good news makes the bones fat (Prov. 15:30); good news is like cold water to the thirsty (Prov. 25:25).

j He thought Saul's death was good news (2 Sam. 4:10); the Philistines sent the good news to their idols and people (1 Chr. 10:9).

k This is a day of good news (2 Kgs. 7:9); a man running alone brings good news (2 Sam. 18:25, 26); Ahimaaz is a good man and brings good news (2 Sam. 18:27); you are a valiant man and bring good news (1 Kgs. 1:42); Zion, herald of good news (Isa. 40:9); the feet of him who brings good news (Isa. 52:7; Nahum 1:15; Rom. 10:15).

- The gospel

l I bring you good news of great joy (Luke 2:10); the beginning of the gospel of Jesus Christ (Mark 1:1); the word of truth, the gospel (Col. 1:5); I am not ashamed of the gospel (Rom. 1:16); the gospel promised before hand through the prophets (Rom. 1:1–2); the terms of the gospel (1 Cor. 15:1–7); preaching the good news of the kingdom (Matt. 4:23); the gospel I preached is not man-made (Gal. 1:11); I set before them the gospel I preach (Gal. 2:2); the glorious gospel of the blessed God (1 Tim. 1:11); the message of reconciliation (2 Cor. 5:19).

m An angel with an eternal gospel to preach (Rev. 14:6).

The gospel preached, see **528i**.

- Rumour

n David was told that all his sons were dead (2 Sam. 13:30); he will hear a rumour and return home (2 Kgs. 19:7; Isa. 37:7); it is reported (Neh. 6:6).

- Messengers

o A faithful messenger is like the cold of snow at harvest time (Prov. 25:13).

p Gideon sent messengers to summon others to war (Judg. 6:35); Jabesh-gilead sent messengers throughout Israel (1 Sam. 11:3–4); a messenger came to David (2 Sam. 15:13); send news by Ahimaaz and Jonathan (2 Sam. 15:36); as Hushai did (2 Sam. 17:15–21); you are not the one to carry news today (2 Sam. 18:20); the Cushite was sent to David (2 Sam. 18:21); Ahimaaz ran after (2 Sam. 18:22–3); Hathach the eunuch used as a messenger (Esther 4:5–6, 9–10).

q Messengers sent by: Jacob to Esau (Gen. 32:3); Jephthah to Ammon (Judg. 11:12, 14); Israel to Edom (Judg. 11:17); Joab to Abner (2 Sam. 3:26); Hiram to David (2 Sam. 5:11); David to Bathsheba (2 Sam. 11:4); Joab to David (2 Sam. 11:19, 22–3; 12:27); Benhadad to Ahab (1 Kgs. 20:2); the king to Elisha (2 Kgs. 6:32–3); Amaziah to Joash (2 Kgs. 14:8); Ahaz to Tiglath-pileser (2 Kgs. 16:7).

● Messengers
of the Lord

r Malachi—'my messenger' (Mal. 1:1); I will send my messenger, the messenger of the covenant (Mal. 3:1); I send my messenger before you (Matt. 11:10; Luke 7:27); he sent messengers ahead of him (Luke 9:52); a priest is a messenger of the Lord (Mal. 2:7).

530 Secret

● God in secret

a The secret things belong to the Lord our God (Deut. 29:29); your Father who sees in secret (Matt. 6:4, 6, 18); your Father who is in secret (Matt. 6:6, 18).

● God's mystery

b The secret of the Lord is with those who fear him (Ps. 25:14); I proclaim hidden things which you have not known (Isa. 48:6); the secret of the kingdom of God (Mark 4:11); the mystery of the gospel (Eph. 6:19); the mystery of Christ (Eph. 3:4; Col. 4:3); God's mystery, which is Christ (Col. 2:2); the mystery of the faith (1 Tim. 3:9); the mystery of godliness (1 Tim. 3:16).

c The mystery hidden for ages but now made known (Col. 1:26); to you it has been given to know the secrets of the kingdom (Matt. 13:11); the mystery was made known by revelation (Eph. 3:3); we speak God's wisdom in a mystery (1 Cor. 2:7); the mystery of God is completed (Rev. 10:7).

Understanding mysteries, see **517a**; **God making mysteries known**, see **526f.**

● Acting in secret

d Why flee secretly? (Gen. 31:27); you did it in secret (2 Sam. 12:12).

e Threshing wheat in the wine press (Judg. 6:11).

f Do not let your left hand know what your right hand is doing (Matt. 6:3); Jesus went up to the feast secretly (John 7:10).

g Mystery: Babylon the Great (Rev. 17:5); the mystery of lawlessness is at work (2 Thess. 2:7); the shameful things done by them in secret (Eph. 5:12); Israel did things secretly which were not right (2 Kgs. 17:9); see what the elders of Israel are doing in the dark (Ezek. 8:12); bread eaten in secret is pleasant (Prov. 9:17).

h A secret message for king Eglon (Judg. 3:19); Joab spoke with

Abner privately (2 Sam. 3:27); the king questioned Jeremiah secretly (Jer. 37:17); Herod called the magi secretly (Matt. 2:7).

i Joseph wanted to divorce Mary secretly (Matt. 1:19).
Concealing, see **525**.

- Riddles

j Samson's riddle (Judg. 14:12–18); propound a riddle (Ezek. 17:2).

531 Communications

See **528**.

532 Affirmation

- Swearing oaths

a When a man swears an oath in this temple (1 Kgs. 8:31; 2 Chr. 6:22); if someone takes an oath thoughtlessly (Lev. 5:4); if someone has lied and sworn falsely (Lev. 6:3).

b You shall swear by the name of the Lord (Deut. 6:13; 10:20); if they swear by my name (Jer. 12:16); he who swears will swear by the God of truth (Isa. 65:16); he who has not sworn deceitfully (Ps. 24:4).

c The woman must swear with the oath of the curse (Num. 5:21).

d If one swears, whether by the temple, its gold, the altar or the sacrifice, it is binding (Matt. 23:16–22).

e They swear falsely (Jer. 5:2); those who swear by the Lord but not in truth (Isa. 48:1); they taught my people to swear by Baal (Jer. 12:16).

- Not swearing

f Do not swear falsely (Lev. 19:12); do not swear at all, by anything (Matt. 5:34–6; Jas. 5:12); let your Yes be Yes and your No be No (Matt. 5:37; Jas. 5:12).

- People who swore

g Abraham swore to Abimelech (Gen. 21:23–4, 31); the servant swore to Abraham (Gen. 24:3, 9, 37); Joseph swore to Jacob (Gen. 47:31); Jonathan and David swore to each other (1 Sam. 20:42; 2 Sam. 21:7); David gave his oath to Saul (1 Sam. 24:21–22); David promised Shimei on oath that he would not die (2 Sam. 19:23; 1 Kgs. 2:8); Ahab made people swear Elijah was not with them (1 Kgs. 18:10); Peter swore that he did not know Jesus (Matt. 26:74; Mark 14:71); Herod promised his daughter with an oath (Matt. 14:7, 9; Mark 6:23).

h Abraham swore he would take nothing from the king of Sodom (Gen. 14:22); the Jews bound themselves by an oath to kill Paul (Acts 23:12).

i Esau swore away his birthright to Jacob (Gen. 25:33); Joseph swore to his father that he would not be buried in Egypt (Gen. 47:29–31; 50:5).

j Jacob swore an oath with Laban (Gen. 31:53); Joseph made the Israelites swear an oath (Gen. 50:25; Exod. 13:19); the spies swore to Rahab (Josh. 2:12); Israel swore to the Gibeonites (Josh. 9:15, 18–20); David had sworn to Bathsheba (1 Kgs. 1:13, 17, 29–30); many Jews were bound by oath to Tobiah (Neh. 6:18).

k Ezra bound Israel with an oath (Ezra 10:5); the men of Israel had taken an oath (Judg. 21:1); Saul bound the people by oath not to eat (1 Sam. 14:24); Nehemiah made the priests swear an oath (Neh. 5:12); Nehemiah made the people swear not to intermarry (Neh. 13:25); a curse and an oath to walk in God's law (Neh. 10:29).

l Swear that you will not kill me (Judg. 15:12; 1 Sam. 30:15); let Solomon swear not to kill me (1 Kgs. 1:51).

m May God do so to me and more also (Ruth 1:17; 1 Sam. 14:44; 2 Sam. 3:9, 35; 19:13; 1 Kgs. 2:23; 19:2; 20:10; 2 Kgs. 6:31); may God do so to you and more also (1 Sam. 3:17).

n I have sworn to keep your ordinances (Ps. 119:106); they made an oath to the Lord with a loud voice and trumpets (2 Chr. 15:14); the angel swore by the Creator of all (Rev. 10:6).

● God swearing oaths

o God swore to the patriarchs that he would multiply their descendants (Exod. 32:13); God promised to confirm the oath (Gen. 26:3); God confirmed his promise with an oath (Heb. 6:16–17); God swore by himself to bless Abraham (Gen. 22:16–17; Heb. 6:13–14); the oath which he swore to Abraham (Luke 1:73); the Lord has sworn by himself (Jer. 51:14); I have sworn by myself (Isa. 45:23); I have sworn by my holiness (Ps. 89:35); the Lord has sworn by his right hand (Isa. 62:8); God kept his oath to bring Israel out of Egypt (Deut. 7:8); God swore to make David king (2 Sam. 3:9); God swore to David that one of his descendants would reign (Ps. 132:11–12; Acts 2:30); the Lord has sworn, 'You are a priest for ever' (Ps. 110:4); Christ was made a priest by an oath (Heb. 7:20–1).

p God swore to give the land (Gen. 24:7; 50:24; Exod. 6:8; 13:5, 11; 32:13; 33:1; Deut. 1:8, 35; 6:10, 18, 23; 7:13; 8:1; 10:11; 11:9, 21; 26:3; 28:11; 30:20; 31:7, 20; 34:4; Josh. 1:6; 5:6; 21:43; Ezek. 20:5–6).

q The Lord has sworn war against Amalek (Exod. 17:16); I swore in my anger they would not enter my rest (Ps. 95:11); God swore to make them fall in the wilderness (Ps. 106:26).

● Adjuring

r If someone hears an adjuration (Lev. 5:1); he hears the adjuration but says nothing (Prov. 29:24); I adjure you to tell us whether you are the Christ (Matt. 26:63); I adjure you to have this letter read (1 Thess. 5:27).

● Making vows

s I will fulfil my vows (Ps. 22:25; 61:8; 66:13; 116:14, 18); a vow must be fulfilled (Num. 30:2; Deut. 23:23; Matt. 5:33); pay your vows to the Most High (Ps. 50:14); make your vows to the Lord and fulfil them (Ps. 76:11); perform your vows (Judg. 11:35–6); better not vow than vow and not repay (Eccles. 5:5); do not delay in fulfilling a vow (Deut. 23:21; Eccles. 5:4); that which I have vowed I will pay (Jonah 2:9).

t Do not make vows rashly (Prov. 20:25); vows made by a dependant woman may be countermanded (Num. 30:3–16); what you would have gained from me is under a vow [corban] (Matt. 15:5; Mark 7:11).

u A deformed animal is unacceptable in fulfilment of a vow (Lev. 22:23); valuation of things vowed (Lev. 27:2–33).

v The vow of the Nazirite (Num. 6:1–21).

- People who made vows

w Jacob made a vow to God at Bethel (Gen. 28:20; 31:13); Jephthah swore to sacrifice the first to greet him (Judg. 11:30–1, 35); Hannah vowed to give her son to the Lord (1 Sam. 1:11); Saul vowed not to kill David (1 Sam. 19:6); Jonathan made David vow again (1 Sam. 20:17); Saul vowed that no punishment would come to her (1 Sam. 28:10); Absalom had vowed to worship at Hebron (2 Sam. 15:7–8); David vowed to find a dwelling for God (Ps. 132:2–5); Paul had his hair cut because of a vow (Acts 18:18); four men were under a vow (Acts 21:23).

x Israel vowed to destroy the Canaanites (Num. 21:2); Israel took an oath about those who did not come to fight (Judg. 21:5); they had sworn not to give wives to Benjamin (Judg. 21:18).

Vowing to fast, see **946n**.

533 Negation

- God denying
- Denying Christ

a God cannot deny himself (2 Tim. 2:13).

b Peter would deny Christ three times (Matt. 26:34; Mark 14:30, 72; Luke 22:34; John 13:38); as he did (Matt. 26:70–5; Mark 14:68–71; Luke 22:57–61; John 18:17, 25–7); I will not deny you (Matt. 26:35; Mark 14:31); whoever denies me before men, I will deny before my Father (Matt. 10:33; Luke 12:9); denying the Master who bought them (2 Pet. 2:1); they deny him by their deeds (Titus 1:16).

c You denied the holy and righteous one (Acts 3:14); if we deny him, he will deny us (2 Tim. 2:12); they deny our only Master and Lord (Jude 4); no one who denies the Son has the Father (1 John 2:23); the antichrist denies the Father and the Son (1 John 2:22).

d You have a little strength and have not denied my name (Rev. 3:8); you did not deny my faith (Rev. 2:13).

e Whoever does not provide for his family has denied the faith (1 Tim. 5:8).

- Denying oneself

f Whoever would come after me must deny himself (Matt. 16:24; Mark 8:34; Luke 9:23).

- Contradicting

g Sarah denied that she laughed (Gen. 18:15); this will never happen to you! (Matt. 16:22); the Jews contradicted what Paul said (Acts 13:45).

534 Teaching

- Teaching God

a Who has taught God? (Isa. 40:14); shall anyone teach God knowledge? (Job 21:22).

- God teaching

b Whom will he teach knowledge? (Isa. 28:9); God teaches man knowledge (Ps. 94:10); happy is the man whom you teach (Ps. 94:12); his God teaches him (Isa. 28:26); God teaches us more than the beasts and birds (Job 35:11); all your children will be taught by the Lord (Isa. 54:13); you have taught me from my youth (Ps. 71:17); you have taught me (Ps. 119:102); I taught Ephraim to walk (Hos. 11:3).

c He will teach us his ways (Isa. 2:3; Mic. 4:2); he instructs sinners in his ways (Ps. 25:8); he will instruct him in the way (Ps. 25:12); I will teach you in the way you should go (Ps. 32:8); God teaches the humble his way (Ps. 25:9); receive instruction from God's mouth (Job 22:22).

d Teach me to do your will (Ps. 143:10); teach me your way, O Lord (Ps. 25:4–5; 27:11; 86:11); teach me the way I should go (Ps. 143:8); teach them the good way to walk (1 Kgs. 8:36; 2 Chr. 6:27); teach me good discernment (Ps. 119:66); let the man of God teach us how to bring up the boy (Judg. 13:8).

e He trains my hands for battle (2 Sam. 22:35; Ps. 18:34; 144:1); you are taught by God to love one another (1 Thess. 4:9).

● The Spirit teaching

f You gave your Spirit to instruct them (Neh. 9:20); the Holy Spirit will teach you all things (John 14:26); you have no need for anyone to teach you because the anointing teaches you (1 John 2:27); they shall all be taught by God (John 6:45).

● Scripture teaching

g These things were written for our instruction (1 Cor. 10:11); all scripture is profitable for teaching (2 Tim. 3:16).

h Teach me your statutes (Ps. 119:12, 26, 33, 64, 68, 124, 135); you teach me your statutes (Ps. 119:171); teach me your ordinances (Ps. 119:108).

● Jesus teaching

i Jesus taught in the temple (Matt. 21:23; 26:55; Mark 14:49; Luke 19:47; 21:37; Luke 20:1; John 7:14; 8:2, 20); teaching in the towns and villages (Matt. 9:35; 11:1; Mark 6:6; Luke 13:22); teaching large crowds (Mark 2:13; 6:34; 10:1); from a boat (Mark 4:1; Luke 5:3); in synagogues (Matt. 4:23; 9:35; 13:54; Mark 1:21; 6:2; Luke 4:15–16, 31–3; 6:6; 13:10); I always taught in synagogues or the temple (John 18:20); he taught his disciples (Matt. 5:1–2); he was teaching his disciples about his sufferings (Mark 9:31); teach us to pray (Luke 11:1); people were amazed at his teaching (Matt. 7:28; Mark 11:18; Luke 4:32); when he was teaching, God's power was present to heal (Luke 5:17); what Jesus began to do and to teach (Acts 1:1).

● Teach the way of God

j Teach them the statutes (Exod. 18:20; Lev. 10:11); Israel to be taught 'The Bow' lament (2 Sam. 1:18).

k Keep my teaching as the apple of your eye (Prov. 7:2); the teaching of the wise is a fountain of life (Prov. 13:14); to receive instruction in wise behaviour (Prov. 1:3); whoever practises and teaches will be called great (Matt. 5:19); we know you teach the way of God in truth (Matt. 22:16; Mark 12:14; Luke 20:21).

- **People who taught**

l Joseph taught the elders wisdom (Ps. 105:22); God inspired Bezalel to teach (Exod. 35:34); Levi teaches God's ordinances to Jacob (Deut. 33:10); Samuel would instruct them in the way that was good (1 Sam. 12:23); Jehoiada instructed Joash (2 Kgs. 12:2); the officials and priests taught throughout Judah (2 Chr. 17:9); let one of the priests teach them (2 Kgs. 17:27–8); priests are to teach the difference between holy and profane (Ezek. 44:23); Ezra taught the law (Ezra 7:10, 25); Job had instructed many (Job 4:3); the Levites taught all Israel (2 Chr. 35:3); the scribes and Pharisees sit in Moses' seat (Matt. 23:2).

m Let my teaching fall like rain (Deut. 32:2); I will teach transgressors your ways (Ps. 51:13); the Jew thought himself a teacher of the immature (Rom. 2:20); you who teach, do you not teach yourself? (Rom. 2:21).

- **Nurture**

n Sons I have reared (Isa. 1:2); Pharaoh's daughter brought up Moses as her son (Acts 7:21).

o Teach these words to your children (Deut. 4:9; 6:7; 11:19); he commanded our fathers to teach them to their children (Ps. 78:5); train a child in the way he should go (Prov. 22:6); bring your children up in the instruction of the Lord (Eph. 6:4).

- **Teaching in the church**

p They devoted themselves to the apostles' teaching (Acts 2:42); the apostles taught the people (Acts 5:21); Barnabas and Paul taught great numbers (Acts 11:26); they and others taught the word (Acts 15:35); Paul taught the word of God in Corinth for 18 months (Acts 18:11); Paul had taught them in public and in private (Acts 20:20); you have known my teaching (2 Tim. 3:10).

q Teach them to observe all I have commanded you (Matt. 28:20); teach these things (1 Tim. 4:11); entrust these things to faithful men who will be able to teach others also (2 Tim. 2:2); older women should train younger ones (Titus 2:4); use your gift in teaching (Rom. 12:7).

r I do not permit a woman to teach (1 Tim. 2:12).

s Elders who labour at teaching deserve a double stipend (1 Tim. 5:17); attend to teaching (1 Tim. 4:13).

t Speak the things fitting to sound doctrine (Titus 2:1); show purity in doctrine (Titus 2:7); that they may adorn the doctrine of God (Titus 2:10).

u You need teaching the elementary principles over again (Heb. 5:12); let us leave the elementary teaching (Heb. 6:1).
Doctrine, see **452**.

- **People teaching**

v Moses was taught all the wisdom of Egypt (Acts 7:22); teach me and I will be silent (Job 6:24).

w Bodily training is only a little value (1 Tim. 4:8); Chananiah gave instruction in singing (1 Chr. 15:22).

535 Misteaching

● Heresies

a Blown to and fro by every wind of doctrine (Eph. 4:14); many are teaching things they ought not to teach (Titus 1:11); you have some who hold the teachings of Balaam (Rev. 2:14); the teaching of the Nicolaitans (Rev. 2:15); beware of the teaching of the Pharisees and Sadducees (Matt. 16:12); teaching as doctrines the traditions of men (Matt. 15:9; Mark 7:7).

b Instruct some not to teach strange doctrines (1 Tim. 1:3); bringing destructive heresies (2 Pet. 2:1).

536 Learning

● Learning from God

a Ezra determined to study the law of the Lord (Ezra 7:10); let a woman learn in silence (1 Tim. 2:11); take my yoke and learn from me (Matt. 11:29); you did not so learn Christ (Eph. 4:20).

● Fruitless learning

b Always learning but never coming to a knowledge of the truth (2 Tim. 3:7).

537 Teacher

● About teachers

a They want to be teachers of the law, but are ignorant (1 Tim. 1:7); they love being called Rabbi (Matt. 23:7); are you a teacher and do not understand? (John 3:10); I have more insight than my teachers (Ps. 119:99).

b A disciple is not above his teacher (Matt. 10:24–5; Luke 6:40); do not be called Rabbi, for you have one Teacher (Matt. 23:8); do not be called teacher, for the Christ is your only Teacher (Matt. 23:10).

c They will accumulate teachers after their own lusts (2 Tim. 4:3); for many days Israel was without a teaching priest (2 Chr. 15:3).

● Specific teachers

d Jehiel was teacher of the king's sons (1 Chr. 27:32); a teacher called Gamaliel (Acts 5:34).

● Jesus the teacher

e You call me Teacher and Lord (John 13:13); hail, Rabbi! (Matt. 26:49); the Teacher says, 'My time is at hand' (Matt. 26:18); Mary called out Rabboni! meaning Teacher (John 20:16).

● Teachers in the church

f God appointed teachers in the church (1 Cor. 12:28); he gave some pastors and teachers (Eph. 4:11); in the church there were prophets and teachers (Acts 13:1); you ought by this time to be teachers (Heb. 5:12); the Lord's servant should be an able teacher (2 Tim. 2:24); as must elders (1 Tim. 3:2); not many of you should be teachers (Jas. 3:1); let him who is taught share with him who teaches (Gal. 6:6).

538 Learner

● Disciples

a Jesus called his twelve disciples (Matt. 10:1; Mark 6:7; Luke 6:13); his disciples came to him (Matt. 5:1); Jesus took the twelve aside (Matt. 20:17); Jesus spoke to his disciples (Luke 6:20); Joseph of Arimathea was a disciple (Matt. 27:57); but secretly, for fear of the Jews (John 19:38).

b The disciples wanted to send the crowds away (Matt. 14:15); the disciples wanted to send the woman away (Matt. 15:23).
Chosen disciples, see **605e; apostles**, see **754a.**

● True disciples

c If you remain in my word you are truly my disciples (John 8:31); Jesus called his disciples his mother and brothers (Matt. 12:49); whoever does not hate his father and mother cannot be my disciple (Luke 14:26); whoever does not give up all he has cannot be my disciple (Luke 14:33); why do the disciples of John fast but not your disciples? (Matt. 9:14; Mark 2:18; Luke 5:33); we are Moses' disciples (John 9:28).

● Making disciples

d Make disciples of all nations (Matt. 28:19).

539 School

● School

a Paul discussed in the school of Tyrannus (Acts 19:9).

540 Truthfulness

● Truthful

a God does not lie (Titus 1:2).

b Speak the truth to one another (Zech. 8:16; Eph. 4:25); speaking the truth in love (Eph. 4:15); we speak in sincerity before God (2 Cor. 2:17); by manifestation of the truth we commend ourselves to everyone's conscience (2 Cor. 4:2).

c All that John said about this man was true (John 10:41); no lie was in their mouth (Rev. 14:5); have I become your enemy by telling you the truth? (Gal. 4:16).
The truth, see **494.**

541 Untruthfulness

● God and lying

a The Lord hates lying lips (Prov. 12:22); the Lord hates a lying tongue (Prov. 6:17); you destroy those who speak falsehood (Ps. 5:6); Ananias lied not to men but to the Holy Spirit (Acts 5:3–4); you have not lied to men but to God (Acts 5:4).

b God is not a man to lie (Num. 23:19; 1 Sam. 15:29); it is impossible for God to lie (Heb. 6:18); I will not lie to David (Ps. 89:35); God put a lying spirit in the mouths of the prophets (1 Kgs. 22:22, 23; 2 Chr. 18:21–2).

● Making God a liar

c He who does not believe God has made him a liar (1 John 5:10); if we say we have not sinned, we make him a liar (1 John 1:10); the lying pen of scribes has made the law a lie (Jer. 8:8).

● People lying

d You love falsehood (Ps. 52:3); we have made falsehood our refuge (Isa. 28:15); their lies have led them astray (Amos 2:4); Satan filled Ananias' heart to lie (Acts 5:3).

e They use their tongues like a bow to shoot lies (Jer. 9:3); they speak lies against me (Hos. 7:13); you have spoken falsehood and seen lies (Ezek. 13:8); you smear with lies (Job 13:4); they speak against me with lying tongues (Ps. 109:2); they have taught their tongue to speak lies (Jer. 9:5–6); your lips have spoken falsehood (Isa. 59:3); there is nothing reliable in their mouth (Ps. 5:9); they speak peace with evil in their hearts (Ps. 28:3); his speech was smoother than butter but war was in his heart (Ps. 55:21).

f The Israelites have lied (Josh. 7:11); Delilah said Samson lied to her (Judg. 16:10); Samson lied to Delilah three times (Judg. 16:15); David told Achish he raided Judah (1 Sam. 27:10).

g You are inventing these reports (Neh. 6:8).

Deceiving, see **542**.

- **Prophesying lies**

h They are prophesying lies (Jer. 27:16); they said Jeremiah was lying (Jer. 43:2); the old prophet was lying (1 Kgs. 13:18).

Prophesying deceit, see **542***j*.

- **Avoid lying**

i Do not lie to one another (Lev. 19:11; Col. 3:9); do not lie to me (2 Kgs. 4:16, 28); do not be arrogant and lie against the truth (Jas. 3:14); lying speech is not fitting for a prince (Prov. 17:7); save me from lying lips (Ps. 120:2); no lie was found in their mouth (Rev. 14:5); the remnant of Israel will tell no lies (Zeph. 3:13).

- **Pretending**

j Israel pretended to be beaten (Josh. 8:15); the Gibeonites pretended to be from a far country to deceive Joshua (Josh. 9:3–13, 22); David pretended to be mad (1 Sam. 21:13; Ps. 34:t); Amnon pretended to be ill (2 Sam. 13:5); the wise woman of Tekoa pretended to be in mourning (2 Sam. 14:2); Jeroboam's wife pretended to be someone else (1 Kgs. 14:5, 6); one pretends to be rich but has nothing, and vice versa (Prov. 13:7); for a pretence they offer long prayers (Mark 12:40); pretending to lay out anchors from the bow (Acts 27:30).

Mislead, see **495**; **hypocrities**, see **545***e*.

542 Deception

- **Laws about deceit**

a The law concerning a man who deceives his neighbour (Lev. 6:2); the law concerning a man who finds something and lies about it (Lev. 6:3).

- **God and deceit**

b Do not let your God deceive you (2 Kgs. 19:10; Isa. 37:10); Lord, you deceived me and I was deceived (Jer. 20:7); you have utterly deceived this people (Jer. 4:10); God sends them a delusion (2 Thess. 2:11).

c Will you deceive God? (Job 13:9); they deceived him and lied to him (Ps. 78:36); will you plead deceitfully for God? (Job 13:7).

- **Jesus and deceit**

d There was no deceit in his mouth (Isa. 53:9; 1 Pet. 2:22); they called Jesus a deceiver (Matt. 27:63); he deceives the people (John 7:12).

- **Men deceive**

e Impostors will go from bad to worse (2 Tim. 3:13); evil men and impostors, deceiving and deceived (2 Tim. 3:13); many deceivers have gone out into the world (2 John 7); you are full of deceit and fraud (Acts 13:10); filled with deceit (Rom. 1:29); they deceive the hearts of the unsuspecting (Rom. 16:18); bread gained by deceit is sweet at first (Prov. 20:17).

f See that no one deceives you (Mark 13:5); see that no one takes you captive through deception (Col. 2:8).

- **Deceitful tongues**

g They devise deceitful words (Ps. 35:20); his words are deceit (Ps. 36:3); his mouth is full of curses and deceit (Ps. 10:7); deceitful tongue! (Ps. 52:4); their tongue speaks with deceit (Jer. 9:8); they deceive with their tongues (Rom. 3:13).

- **Deceiving oneself**

h The heart is deceitful above all things (Jer. 17:9); from the heart comes deceit (Mark 7:22); let no one deceive himself (1 Cor. 3:18); do not deceive yourselves (Jer. 37:9); do not be deceived (Jas. 1:16); deceiving themselves (Gal. 6:3; Jas. 1:22); if anyone deceives his own heart, his religion is in vain (Jas. 1:26); if we say we have no sin, we deceive ourselves (1 John 1:8); if we say we have fellowship with him when we do not, we lie (1 John 1:6).

i Beware lest your hearts be deceived (Deut. 11:16); sin deceived me (Rom. 7:11); the pride of your hearts has deceived you (Jer. 49:16; Obad. 3); hardened by the deceitfulness of sin (Heb. 3:13); the deceitfulness of riches chokes the word (Matt. 13:22; Mark 4:19).

- **Prophesying deceit**

j False prophets will deceive many (Matt. 24:11); do not let the prophets deceive you (Jer. 29:8).

Prophesying lies, see **541***h*; **false prophets**, see **579***al*.

- **Those who deceived**

k Jacob deceived Isaac (Gen. 27:11–24, 35); and Laban (Gen. 31:20, 26); Jacob was deceived over Rachel (Gen. 29:25); Jacob's sons deceived the men of Shechem (Gen. 34:13); Zebul sent deceitful messengers to Abimelech (Judg. 9:31); Michal deceived her father with an idol (1 Sam. 19:13, 17); why have you deceived me? you are Saul! (1 Sam. 28:12); Abner came to deceive you (2 Sam. 3:25); Zibah deceived Mephibosheth (2 Sam. 19:26); Pharaoh acted deceitfully (Exod. 8:29); do not let Hezekiah deceive you (2 Kgs. 18:29); the wise men tricked Herod (Matt. 2:16); an Israelite in whom is no guile (John 1:47).

l The men of Shechem dealt treacherously with Abimelech (Judg. 9:23); treachery, Ahaziah! (2 Kgs. 9:23).

Misleading, see **495**.

- **Avoid deceit**

m Once we were deceived (Titus 3:3); do not be deceived (Gal. 6:7); let no one deceive you (Eph. 5:6; 2 Thess. 2:3; 1 John 3:7); that no one delude you with plausible arguments (Col. 2:4); keep me from deception and lies (Prov. 30:8).

n Blessed is the man in whose spirit there is no deceit (Ps. 32:2); he who practises deceit shall not dwell in my house (Ps. 101:7); keep your lips from speaking deceit (Ps. 34:13; 1 Pet. 3:10); do not deceive with your lips (Prov. 24:28); put away from you a deceitful mouth (Prov. 4:24); put aside all guile (1 Pet. 2:1); let love be without hypocrisy (Rom. 12:9).

o Our exhortation is not from deceit (1 Thess. 2:3); as deceivers and yet we are true (2 Cor. 6:8).

● Satan and
deceit

p The serpent deceived me and I ate (Gen. 3:13); the woman was deceived (1 Tim. 2:14); the serpent deceived Eve by its craftiness (2 Cor. 11:3).

q Satan will go out to deceive the nations (Rev. 20:8); Satan deceives the whole world (Rev. 12:9); deceitful spirits (1 Tim. 4:1).

● God trapping

r The Lord will become a snare and a trap (Isa. 8:14); I set a snare for you (Jer. 50:24); I will spread my net over him and he will be caught in my snare (Ezek. 12:13; 17:20); I will spread my net over you (Ezek. 32:3); I will spread my net over them (Hos. 7:12); he spread a net for my feet (Lam. 1:13); an evil man is ensnared in his transgression (Prov. 29:6); the wicked is ensnared and trapped (Job 18:8–10); therefore snares surround you (Job 22:10); does a trap spring up when it has caught nothing? (Amos 3:5).

s Lest that day come on you suddenly like a trap (Luke 21:34).

● Man trapping

t How long will this man be a snare to us? (Exod. 10:7); Saul wanted Michal to be a snare for David (1 Sam. 18:21); the woman whose heart is a snare and a trap (Eccles. 7:26).

u Why lay a snare for my life? (1 Sam. 28:9); the survivors of the nations will be a snare and a trap for you (Josh. 23:13); the Chaldeans catch them in their net (Hab. 1:15–17).

v They hid a net for me (Ps. 35:7; 57:6); everyone hunts his brother with a net (Mic. 7:2); they brought us into the net (Ps. 66:11); the proud have set a net and snares for me (Ps. 140:5); you have been a snare at Mizpah, a net on Tabor (Hos. 5:1); they have hidden a trap for me (Ps. 142:3); those who seek my life lay snares (Ps. 38:12); the wicked have laid a snare for me (Ps. 119:110); they have dug a pit and laid snares for me (Jer. 18:22); they talk of laying snares secretly (Ps. 64:5); wicked men set a trap to catch men (Jer. 5:26).

w Keep me from the snares of the wicked (Ps. 141:9); he will deliver you from the snare (Ps. 91:3); the snare is broken and we have escaped (Ps. 124:7).

x They plotted to arrest Jesus by stealth (Matt. 26:4); Pharisees and Herodians tried to trap him in his talk (Mark 12:13); they planned to trap him in his talk (Matt. 22:15).

● Evil trapping

y Their gods will be a snare to you (Exod. 23:33; Judg. 2:3); the ephod was a snare for Gideon (Judg. 8:27); idolatry became a snare to them (Ps. 106:36); wanting to be rich is a snare (1 Tim. 6:9); the snares of death (2 Sam. 22:6; Ps. 18:5); they may escape from the snare of the devil (2 Tim. 2:26).

● Fishing

z Peter and Andrew casting their net into the sea (Matt. 4:18); James and John mending their nets (Matt. 4:21); washing nets (Luke 5:2); let down your nets for a catch (Luke 5:4); fishing with a hook (Matt. 17:27); I am going fishing (John 21:3).
Hunting, see **619a**; **fishermen**, see **686c**.

543 Untruth

● Lies

    a No lie comes from the truth (1 John 2:21); the devil is the father of lies (John 8:44).

    b They exchanged the truth about God for a lie (Rom. 1:25); the leaven of the Pharisees is hypocrisy (Luke 12:1); within you are full of hypocrisy (Matt. 23:28).
Mislead, see **495**; **tell lies**, see **541**.

● Myths

    c Have nothing to do with silly myths (1 Tim. 4:7); not to pay heed to myths (1 Tim. 1:4); not paying heed to Jewish myths (Titus 1:14); they will turn aside to myths (2 Tim. 4:4); we did not follow cleverly devised myths (2 Pet. 1:16).

544 Dupe
Fool, see **501**.

545 Deceiver

● Men are
liars

    a Men speak lies to one another (Ps. 12:2); all men are liars (Ps. 116:11); let God be true though every man a liar (Rom. 3:4); they delight in lies (Ps. 62:4); Cretans are always liars (Titus 1:12); aliens who speak lies (Ps. 144:7–8, 11); they have lied about the Lord (Jer. 5:12); the arrogant besmear me with lies (Ps. 119:69); they persecute me with a lie (Ps. 119:86).

    b He who claims to love God yet hates his brother is a liar (1 John 4:20); he who denies that Jesus is the Christ is a liar (1 John 2:22); he who says he knows him but does not keep his commands is a liar (1 John 2:4); the hypocrisy of liars with seared consciences (1 Tim. 4:2).

    c When the devil lies, he speaks from his own, for he is a liar and the father of lies (John 8:44).
Telling lies, see **541**; **lies**, see **543***a*.

● The end
of liars

    d The law is for liars (1 Tim. 1:10); the mouths of liars will be stopped (Ps. 63:11); liars will end in the lake of fire (Rev. 21:8); all who love lying will be outside the city (Rev. 22:15).

● Hypocrites

    e Hypocrites sound a trumpet when they give alms (Matt. 6:2); hypocrites love to pray on street corners (Matt. 6:5); hypocrites look gloomy when they fast (Matt. 6:16).

    f Knowing their hypocrisy (Mark 12:15); you hypocrites! (Matt. 7:5; 15:7; 22:18; Mark 7:6; Luke 6:42; 12:56; 13:15); scribes and Pharisees, hypocrites! (Matt. 23:13, 14, 15, 23, 25, 27, 29); the Jews joined Peter in his hypocrisy (Gal. 2:13); give him a place with the hypocrites (Matt. 24:51).

● False people

    g False Christs and false prophets will arise (Matt. 24:24; Mark 13:22); false prophets (2 Pet. 2:1; 1 John 4:1); false apostles (2 Cor. 11:13); false brethren (2 Cor. 11:26; Gal. 2:4); false teachers (2 Pet. 2:1).
False Christs, see **357***ad*; **false apostles**, see **754***d*.

546 Exaggeration

Overestimate, see **482**.

Section three: Means of communicating ideas

---

547 Indication

- Signs in the heavens

a Lights in the sky will be signs to mark the seasons (Gen. 1:14); the rainbow would be the sign of the covenant (Gen. 9:13); there will be great signs from heaven (Luke 21:11); a sign appeared in heaven (Rev. 12:1, 3).
Stars as signs, see **321***k*.

- Ceremonies as signs

b The feast of unleavened bread would be a sign (Exod. 13:9); as would the consecration of the firstborn (Exod. 13:16); and the Sabbath (Exod. 31:13, 17; Ezek. 20:12, 20).

- Signs for guidance

c The servant asked for a sign to indicate the right girl (Gen. 24:13–14, 43–4); this will be the sign that I have sent you (Exod. 3:12); give me a sign that it is you speaking to me (Judg. 6:17); the sign of the fleece (Judg. 6:36–40); when these signs take place (1 Sam. 10:7); this will be the sign that the Lord has given them into our hands (1 Sam. 14:10); what is the sign? (Isa. 38:22); this will be the sign for you (1 Sam. 2:34; 2 Kgs. 19:29; Isa. 37:30; 38:7); show me a sign of good (Ps. 86:17).

- Signs to convince

d Signs for Moses to perform (Exod. 4:1–9, 17, 28, 30); God did great signs (Josh. 24:17); the sign that God had sent Moses (Num. 16:28–30); the signs God did (Deut. 11:2–7); the blood shall be a sign for you (Exod. 12:13); keep Aaron's rod as a sign (Num. 17:10); unbelief despite all the signs (Num. 14:11); the sign, the altar would be split apart (1 Kgs. 13:3); what will be the sign that the Lord will heal me? (2 Kgs. 20:8–11); the Lord gave Hezekiah a sign (2 Chr. 32:24); this will be the sign to you (Jer. 44:29).

e I am a sign to you (Ezek. 12:11); Ezekiel will be a sign to you (Ezek. 24:24); I have made you a sign to the people (Ezek. 12:6); Jonah was a sign to the men of Nineveh (Luke 11:30); the Son of man will be a sign to this generation (Luke 11:30).

- Signs of the Christ

f The sign of Immanuel (Isa. 7:11–16); the sign will be the baby wrapped in cloths (Luke 2:12); they asked Jesus for a sign (Matt. 12:38; 16:1; Mark 8:11; Luke 11:16; John 2:18); what sign do you do? (John 6:30); Herod wanted to see a sign (Luke 23:8); a sign that will be spoken against (Luke 2:34); the betrayer used a kiss as the sign (Matt. 26:48; Mark 14:44); unless I see in his hands the print of the nails (John 20:25).

g Jesus was attested by wonders and signs (Acts 2:22); Jesus performed the first of his signs (John 2:11); the second sign (John 4:54); the sign of the feeding of the 5000 (John 6:14); he had done this sign (John 12:18); no one can do these signs unless God is with him (John 3:2); how can a sinner perform such signs? (John 9:16).

h Those who saw his signs believed (John 2:23); though he performed many signs, they did not believe (John 12:37); the crowds followed him because they saw the signs he did (John 6:2); not because you saw signs but because you ate the bread (John 6:26).

i Will the Christ do more signs than this? (John 7:31); this man performs many signs (John 11:47); Jesus did many other signs (John 20:30).

● Signs of Christ's return

j What will be the sign of your coming? (Matt. 24:3); what will be the sign that these things are about to happen? (Mark 13:4; Luke 21:7); there will be signs in sun, moon and stars (Luke 21:25); signs on the earth, blood, fire and smoke (Acts 2:19); the sign of the Son of man in the sky (Matt. 24:30); you cannot discern the signs of the times (Matt. 16:3).

● Signs and wonders

k Moses performed wonders and signs (Acts 7:36); God confirmed the word with the signs that followed (Mark 16:20); the Lord bore witness to his word with signs and wonders (Acts 14:3); God bore witness with signs and wonders (Heb. 2:4); many signs and wonders were done through the apostles (Acts 2:43; 5:12); Paul and Barnabas recounted the signs and wonders God had done through them (Acts 15:12); signs and wonders, the signs of a true apostle (2 Cor. 12:12); signs and wonders in the power of the Spirit (Rom. 15:19).

l Grant that signs and wonders take place in the name of Jesus (Acts 4:30); a noteworthy sign has been done through them (Acts 4:16); Stephen performed great wonders and signs (Acts 6:8); they saw the signs Philip performed (Acts 8:6); Simon saw signs and great miracles performed (Acts 8:13).

m These signs will follow those who believe (Mark 16:17); tongues are a sign for unbelievers, prophecy for believers (1 Cor. 14:22); not being afraid of them is a sign to them of destruction (Phil. 1:28).

n The beast performed great signs (Rev. 13:13–14); the three unclean spirits perform signs (Rev. 16:14); the false prophet who performed the signs (Rev. 19:20).

Miracles, see **864**.

● Asking for a sign

o Abraham's servant asked for a sign (Gen. 24:14, 43–4); give me a sign that it is you speaking to me (Judg. 6:17); Gideon asked for signs on the fleece (Judg. 6:36–9); a wicked and adulterous generation asks for a sign (Matt. 12:39; 16:4); the Jews require signs (1 Cor. 1:22); what sign do you perform? (John 2:18; 6:30); unless you see signs and wonders you will not believe (John 4:48).

● No signs

p John did no sign (John 10:41); no sign will be given to this generation (Mark 8:12); no sign will be given except the sign of Jonah (Matt. 12:39; 16:4; Luke 11:29).

● Marks on people
   q A mark on all those who mourn over Jerusalem (Ezek. 9:4); you were sealed with the Holy Spirit (2 Cor. 1:22; Eph. 1:13; 4:30); an angel with the seal of God (Rev. 7:2); seal the servants of God on their foreheads (Rev. 7:3); to harm only people without the seal of God on their foreheads (Rev. 9:4).

   r Memorial bands between your eyes (Exod. 13:9, 16).

   s The Lord put a mark on Cain (Gen. 4:15); the mark of the beast on the right hand or forehead (Rev. 13:16–17; 14:9; 16:2; 20:4).

● Boundary marks
   t Do not move a boundary mark (Deut. 19:14; Prov. 22:28; 23:10); cursed is he who moves his neighbour's boundary mark (Deut. 27:17); some remove landmarks (Job 24:2); the princes of Judah are like those who remove a boundary mark (Hos. 5:10).
Borders of land, see **236a**.

   u Set up road signs (Jer. 31:21); make a signpost (Ezek. 21:19).

● Signalling
   v Two silver trumpets for signalling (Num. 10:2–10).

   w A column of smoke was the signal (Judg. 20:38).

● Gesturing
   x Zacharias made signs to them (Luke 1:22); they made signs to Zacharias (Luke 1:62); Peter gestured to the disciple lying by Jesus (John 13:24); Peter motioned with his hand for them to be quiet (Acts 12:17); Alexander motioned with his hand (Acts 19:33); Paul motioned with his hand (Acts 13:16; 21:40; 26:1); the governor nodded for Paul to speak (Acts 24:10).

● Winking
   y The wicked man winks and points (Prov. 6:13); he who winks the eye causes trouble (Prov. 10:10); he who winks the eye plans perverse things (Prov. 16:30).

● Whistling
   z God will whistle for a distant nation (Isa. 5:26); God will whistle for the fly in Egypt (Isa. 7:18).

● Banners
   aa Tribes camping by their banners (Num. 2:2, 34); the banner of Judah (Num. 2:3; 10:14); of Reuben (Num. 2:10; 10:18); of Ephraim (Num. 2:18; 10:22); of Dan (Num. 2:25; 10:25); in the name of our God we will set up our banners (Ps. 20:5).

   ab The Lord is my banner (Exod. 17:15); you have given a banner to those who fear you (Ps. 60:4); his banner over me is love (S. of S. 2:4).

   ac He will lift up an ensign to the nations (Isa. 5:26; 11:12; 49:22); lift up a standard over the peoples (Isa. 62:10); raise a standard towards Zion (Jer. 4:6); lift up an ensign on a bare hill (Isa. 13:2); lift up a standard (Jer. 50:2; 51:27); lift up a standard against the walls of Babylon (Jer. 51:12); the root of Jesse will stand as an ensign (Isa. 11:10); you will be left like a banner on a hill top (Isa. 30:17).

   ad The enemy set up their own signs for signs (Ps. 74:4); how long must I see the standard? (Jer. 4:21); when a standard is raised on the mountains (Isa. 18:3).

548 Record

● Monuments
   a Jacob set up a pillar at Bethel (Gen. 28:18; 31:13; 35:14); and at

Mizpah (Gen. 31:45); and near Bethlehem (Gen. 35:20); Moses set up twelve stone pillars (Exod. 24:4); Saul set up a monument to himself (1 Sam. 15:12); Absalom had set up a pillar as a monument to himself (2 Sam. 18:18); you adorn the monuments of the righteous (Matt. 23:29).

b Set up large stones coated with plaster on Mount Ebal (Deut. 27:2–4, 8).

Stones as monuments, see **344***f*.

- Tablets

c Moses was given two tablets of stone (Exod. 24:12; 31:18; Deut. 4:13; 5:22; 9:9–11); which he threw down (Exod. 32:15–19; Deut. 9:17); hew two stone tablets like the first (Exod. 34:1, 4; Deut. 10:1–5); put into the ark (Deut. 10:5); nothing in the ark except the two stone tablets (1 Kgs. 8:9; 2 Chr. 5:10).

- Bills of divorce

d He who divorces his wife must give her a certificate of divorce (Deut. 24:1; Matt. 5:31; 19:7; Mark 10:4); I gave faithless Israel her certificate of divorce (Jer. 3:8); where is your mother's certificate of divorce? (Isa. 50:1).

- Names written in heaven

e Rejoice that your names are written in heaven (Luke 10:20); whose names are written in heaven (Heb. 12:23); when the Lord registers the peoples he will record who was born in Zion (Ps. 87:6); everyone recorded for life in Jerusalem (Isa. 4:3).

Book of life, see **589***l*.

- Written records

f Shemaiah recorded the divisions of priests (1 Chr. 24:6).

Historical records, see **589***b*; **register**, see **589***e*.

549 Recorder

- Recorder

a Jehoshaphat was recorder (2 Sam. 8:16; 20:24; 1 Kgs. 4:3; 1 Chr. 18:15); Joah the recorder (Isa. 36:3); Josiah sent Joah the recorder (2 Chr. 34:8).

550 Obliteration

Name blotted out, see **561***z*.

551 Representation

- Drawing

a Jerusalem drawn on a brick (Ezek. 4:1).

552 Misrepresentation

Lying, see **541**; **false witness**, see **466***t*.

553 Painting

- Painting

a Oholibah saw Chaldeans painted on the wall (Ezek. 23:14).

554 Sculpture

- Sculpting

a Aaron carved the calf (Exod. 32:4); Bezalel was skilled in carving wood (Exod. 35:33).

b The king cast them in the clay ground (1 Kgs. 7:46; 2 Chr. 4:17).

● Sculpture
for God

c The walls of the temple were carved with cherubim, palm trees and flowers (1 Kgs. 6:29, 32, 35); palm trees and chains (2 Chr. 3:5); cherubim on the walls (2 Chr. 3:7); gourds and flowers (1 Kgs. 6:18); two cherubim were carved (1 Kgs. 6:23–8; 2 Chr. 3:10–13); flowers on the lampstand (2 Chr. 4:21); pomegranates on the capitals (1 Kgs. 7:18, 20, 42; 2 Kgs. 25:17; 2 Chr. 3:16; 4:13; Jer. 52:22–3); lilies at the top of the pillars (1 Kgs. 7:22); gourds round the 'sea' (1 Kgs. 7:24); the 'sea' standing on 12 oxen (1 Kgs. 7:25, 44; 2 Chr. 4:4, 15; Jer. 52:20); oxen around the 'sea' (2 Chr. 4:3); lions, oxen and cherubim around the stands (1 Kgs. 7:29); cherubim, lions and palm trees on the stands (1 Kgs. 7:36); palm trees (Ezek. 40:16, 22, 31, 34, 37; 41:26); carved with cherubim and palm trees (Ezek. 41:18–20, 25).

d The carved work was smashed with hatchets and hammers (Ps. 74:6).

● Various
sculptures

e Lions on the steps of the throne (1 Kgs. 10:19–20; 2 Chr. 9:19); a graven image and a molten image (Judg. 17:3, 4; 18:14, 17); five golden tumours and five golden mice (1 Sam. 6:4–5, 11, 17–18); animals and creeping things and idols carved round the wall (Ezek. 8:10); every man in his room of images (Ezek. 8:12).

f Nebuchadnezzar saw in his dream a large statue (Dan. 2:31). **Images**, see **982c**.

555 Engraving. Printing
See **586o**.

556 Artist
Sculptors, see **554a**; **skilled people**, see **696e**.

557 Language

● Languages
of the earth

a All the earth had one language (Gen. 11:1, 6); God confused their language (Gen. 11:7, 9); the nations were separated according to their languages (Gen. 10:5, 20, 31); confuse and divide their tongues (Ps. 55:9); there are many languages in the world (1 Cor. 14:10); they heard them speak in their own languages (Acts 2:6, 8–11).

b When Israel went forth from a people of a strange language (Ps. 114:1); a nation of unknown language will swoop on you (Deut. 28:49); a nation whose language you do not understand (Jer. 5:15); through foreign languages God will speak to this people (Isa. 28:11; 1 Cor. 14:21).

c You will no longer see a people with unintelligible language (Isa. 33:19); you are not sent to a people of unintelligible language (Ezek. 3:5–6).

● Particular
languages

d Five cities in Egypt will speak the language of Canaan (Isa. 19:18); they were taught the language of the Chaldeans (Dan.

1:4); half of them spoke the language of Ashdod, and none could speak the language of Judah (Neh. 13:24).

e Messages were sent to every people in their own language (Esther 1:22; 3:12; 8:9); the Assyrians called out in Hebrew (2 Chr. 32:18); please speak in Aramaic, not Hebrew (2 Kgs. 18:26; Isa. 36:11); the letter was written in Aramaic (Ezra 4:7); the inscription was in Hebrew, Latin and Greek (John 19:20); Paul spoke to them in Hebrew (Acts 21:40; 22:2); Christ spoke to Paul in Hebrew (Acts 26:14); they spoke in the Lycaonian language (Acts 14:11); do you know Greek? (Acts 21:37); dispute between the Hebrews and Hellenists in the church (Acts 6:1).

- Speaking in tongues

f They will speak in new tongues (Mark 16:17); they spoke in other languages (Acts 2:4); they heard them speaking in tongues and exalting God (Acts 10:46); they spoke in tongues and prophesied (Acts 19:6); the gift of speaking in tongues (1 Cor. 12:10, 28).

g The one who speaks in a tongue speaks to God, not men (1 Cor. 14:2); the one who speaks in a tongue edifies himself (1 Cor. 14:4); I wish you all spoke in tongues (1 Cor. 14:5); I speak in tongues more than you all (1 Cor. 14:18).

h If I come speaking in tongues, how do I benefit you? (1 Cor. 14:6); if all speak in tongues, will they not say you are mad? (1 Cor. 14:23); the one who prophesies is greater than he who speaks in tongues unless he interprets (1 Cor. 14:5); if I pray in a tongue my spirit prays, not my mind (1 Cor. 14:14).

i Not all speak in tongues (1 Cor. 12:30); if I speak with the tongues of men and angels (1 Cor. 13:1); tongues, prophecy and knowledge will cease (1 Cor. 13:8).

j Let each one have a tongue etc. (1 Cor. 14:26); do not forbid speaking in tongues (1 Cor. 14:39); let him who speaks in tongues pray for an interpretation (1 Cor. 14:13); two or three may speak in tongues if someone interprets (1 Cor. 14:27).
Interpreting language, see **520c**.

558 Letter

- Letters of the alphabet

a To every province in its own script (Esther 1:22; 3:12; 8:9); write it in ordinary characters (Isa. 8:1); see with what large letters I am writing (Gal. 6:11).

- Acrostics

b Acrostic chapters using the letters of the alphabet (Ps. 25:1–22; 34:1–22; 37:1–40; 119:1–176; 145:1–21; Lam. 1:1–22; 2:1–22; 3:1–66; 4:1–22).

559 Word

Message, see **529**.

560 Neology

561 Nomenclature

● Name of God   *a* The name of God is I AM (Exod. 3:13–15); by my name the Lord [Jahweh] I did not make myself known (Exod. 6:3); Yahweh is his name (Exod. 15:3); I am the Lord, that is my name (Isa. 42:8); this glorious and awesome name (Deut. 28:58); his name is wonderful (Judg. 13:18); the ark of God, which is called by the name of the Lord (2 Sam. 6:2; 1 Chr. 13:6); you made a name for yourself (Dan. 9:15).

b The God of Abraham, Isaac and Jacob, this is my name for ever (Exod. 3:15).

● Proclaiming   *c* Everywhere I cause my name to be remembered (Exod. 20:24);
God's name   I have raised you up that my name might be proclaimed in all the earth (Exod. 9:16); God proclaimed his name, the Lord, before Moses (Exod. 33:19; 34:5); I will proclaim the name of the Lord (Deut. 32:3); what will you do for your great name? (Josh. 7:9).

● Called by   *d* You are called by the name of the Lord (Deut. 28:10); we are
God's name   called by your name (Jer. 14:9); they will put my name on the sons of Israel (Num. 6:27); I will write on him the name of my God (Rev. 3:12).

e Keep them in your name which you gave me (John 17:11); blessed is he who comes in the name of the Lord (Matt. 21:9; 23:39; Mark 11:9; Luke 13:35; 19:38; John 12:13).

f We will walk in the name of the Lord our God (Mic. 4:5); in his name they will walk (Zech. 10:12); the name of the Lord is a strong tower (Prov. 18:10); I come against you in the name of the Lord (1 Sam. 17:45).

● A place for   *g* The place chosen as a dwelling for his name (Deut. 12:5, 11, 21;
God's name   14:23–5; 16:2, 6, 11; 26:2; 1 Kgs. 14:21; 1 Chr. 22:19; 2 Chr. 6:6, 20; 12:13; Neh. 1:9); I have consecrated this house by putting my name there for ever (1 Kgs. 9:3; 2 Chr. 7:16); in this house I will put my name (2 Chr. 33:7); the God who has made his name dwell there (Ezra 6:12); in Jerusalem will I put my name (2 Kgs. 21:4, 7; 2 Chr. 2:4); Jerusalem, where I chose to put my name (1 Kgs. 11:36); I have chosen Jerusalem for my name (2 Chr. 6:6); the city called by your name (Dan. 9:18); your city and your people are called by your name (Dan. 9:18); I am working evil in the city called by my name (Jer. 25:29); Shiloh, where I made my name dwell at first (Jer. 7:12).

● What is   *h* What is your name? (Gen. 32:29; Judg. 13:17); why ask my
God's name?   name? (Judg. 13:18); what is his name or his son's name? (Prov. 30:4); he did not tell me his name (Judg. 13:6).

● Profaning   *i* Do not take the name of the Lord in vain (Exod. 20:7; Deut.
God's name   5:11); do not profane the name of the Lord (Lev. 18:21); whoever blasphemes the name of the Lord must be put to death (Lev. 24:11, 16); I acted so that my name would not be profaned (Ezek. 20:9, 14, 22); I had concern for my name which they had

profaned (Ezek. 36:20–1, 22–3); never again shall my name be invoked by Jews in Egypt (Jer. 44:26).

j Profaning God's name by: swearing falsely (Lev. 19:12); giving children to Molech (Lev. 20:3); being unholy priests (Lev. 21:6; 22:2, 32).

● The name of Christ

k The man named the Branch (Zech. 6:12); the Lord our righteousness (Jer. 23:6); his name will be Wonderful Counsellor, Mighty God, Everlasting Father, Prince of Peace (Isa. 9:6); his name is the Word of God (Rev. 19:13); he will be called a Nazarene (Matt. 2:23); you shall name him Jesus (Matt. 1:21, 25; Luke 1:31; 2:21); by the name of Jesus Christ this man stands healed (Acts 4:10); there is no other name by which we must be saved (Acts 4:12); God has given him the name above all names (Phil. 2:9–10); he has a name written which no one knows but himself (Rev. 19:12).

l He is my chosen instrument to carry my name to the Gentiles (Acts 9:15); the disciples were first called Christians (Acts 11:26); you want to make me a Christian (Acts 26:28); suffering as a Christian (1 Pet. 4:16); do all in the name of the Lord Jesus (Col. 3:17); everyone who names the name of the Lord must depart from wickedness (2 Tim. 2:19); they went out for the sake of the name (3 John 7); his name will be on their foreheads (Rev. 22:4).

m Many will come in my name (Matt. 24:5; Mark 13:6); in what name have you done this? (Acts 4:7).

● God naming

n God called the light day and the darkness night (Gen. 1:5); God called the expanse heaven (Gen. 1:8); God called the dry land earth and the gathering of waters seas (Gen. 1:10); God names all the stars (Ps. 147:4); God named them Man (Gen. 5:2).

o He will be called John (Luke 1:13, 60, 63); call him Isaac (Gen. 17:19; 21:3); Lo-ruhamah—No pity (Hos. 1:6); Lo-ammi—Not my people (Hos. 1:9); Ammi—My people (Hos. 2:1); Ruhamah—Pitied (Hos. 2:1).

● Man naming

p The man named all the living creatures (Gen. 2:19–20); man names woman (Gen. 2:23).

q May they be called by my name (Gen. 48:16); let us be called by your name (Isa. 4:1); they were going to call him Zacharias after his father (Luke 1:59); none of your relatives is called John (Luke 1:61).

r People named: Asher—happy (Gen. 30:13); Benjamin—son of right hand (Gen. 35:18); Benoni—son of my sorrow (Gen. 35:18); Beriah—misfortune (1 Chr. 7:23); Dan—judge (Gen. 30:6); Eliezer—God is my help (Exod. 18:4); Ephraim—fruitful (Gen. 41:52); Eve—life (Gen. 3:20); Gad—fortune (Gen. 30:11); Gershom—sojourner (Exod. 2:22; 18:3); Ishmael—God hears (Gen. 16:15); Issachar—reward (Gen. 30:18); Jerubaal—let Baal contend (Judg. 6:32); Joseph—adds (Gen. 30:24);

Judah—praise (Gen. 29:35); Levi—joined (Gen. 29:34); Manasseh—forgetting (Gen. 41:51); Mara—bitter (Ruth 1:20); Naphtali—wrestling (Gen. 30:8); Perez—breach (Gen. 38:29); Reuben—see! a son (Gen. 29:32); Samuel—asked of God (1 Sam. 1:20); Simeon—hearing (Gen. 29:33); Zebulun—dwelling (Gen. 30:20).

● **Man naming places**

 s Cain named the city Enoch after his son (Gen. 4:17); lest the city be called by my name (2 Sam. 12:28); Isaac called the wells what his father had named them (Gen. 26:18); Abraham called the placed Beersheba (Gen. 21:31); Isaac called the well Shibah (Gen. 26:33); Jacob called the place Bethel (Gen. 28:19; 35:15); Mara—bitter (Exod. 15:23); manna—what is it? (Exod. 16:15, 31).

 t Pillars named Jachin and Boaz (1 Kgs. 7:21; 2 Chr. 3:17); Absalom named the pillar after himself (2 Sam. 18:18).

 u Hormah—destruction (Num. 21:3; Judg. 1:17); Bochim—weepers (Judg. 2:5); Cabul—as good as nothing (1 Kgs. 9:13); Ebenezer—stone of help (1 Sam. 7:12); Baal-perazim—Lord of breaking through (2 Sam. 5:20; 1 Chr. 14:11); Perez-uzzah—breaking through on Uzzah (2 Sam. 6:8; 1 Chr. 13:11); Beracah—blessing (2 Chr. 20:26); Golgotha—place of a skull (Matt. 27:33; Mark 15:22).

● **God renaming**

 v You will be called by a new name (Isa. 62:2); my servants will be called by a different name (Isa. 65:15); I will give him a new name (Rev. 2:17).

 w Your name will be no more Abram but Abraham (Gen. 17:5; Neh. 9:7); no more Sarai but Sarah (Gen. 17:15); no more Jacob, but Israel (Gen. 32:28; 35:10; 1 Kgs. 18:31; 2 Kgs. 17:34).

 x Jesus gave Simon the name Peter (Mark 3:16); Jesus named James and John Sons of Thunder (Mark 3:17).

● **Man renaming**

 y Joseph renamed Zaphenath-Paneah (Gen. 41:45); Naomi renamed Marah—bitter (Ruth 1:20); Eliakim renamed Jehoiakim (2 Kgs. 23:34; 2 Chr. 36:4); Mattaniah renamed Zedekiah (2 Kgs. 24:17); Passhur renamed Terror on every side (Jer. 20:3); Daniel, Hananiah, Mishael and Azariah renamed Belteshazzar, Shadrach, Meshach and Abednego (Dan. 1:7); Joseph renamed Barnabas—son of encouragement (Acts 4:36); the names of the cities were changed (Num. 32:38, 42).

● **Name blotted out**

 z Levirate marriage so that the name not be blotted out (Deut. 25:6); the Lord will blot out his name (Deut. 29:20); swear to me that you will not destroy my name (1 Sam. 24:21); they will leave my husband neither name nor remnant (2 Sam. 14:7); the Lord did not say that he would blot out the name of Israel (2 Kgs. 14:27).

 aa May their name be blotted out (Ps. 109:13); that his name be remembered no more (Jer. 11:19); you will leave your name for a curse (Isa. 65:15).

Blot out memory, see **506g**.

● Various
names

ab The name of the demons was Legion (Mark 5:9; Luke 8:30).

ac The names of the sons of Israel engraved upon stones (Exod. 28:9–11, 21; 39:6, 14); Aaron bore the stones before the Lord (Exod. 28:12, 29); names of heads of tribes written on the rods (Num. 17:2); the shepherd calls his sheep by name (John 10:3). **Repute**, see **866**.

562 Misnomer

563 Phrase

564 Grammar
Language, see **557**.

565 Solecism

566 Style

567 Perspicuity
Intelligible, see **516**.

568 Imperspicuity
Not understanding, see **517**; **unintelligible language**, see **557b**.

569 Conciseness

● Briefly

a I have written to you briefly (Heb. 13:22; 1 Pet. 5:12).

570 Diffuseness
Wordy, see **581**.

571 Vigour

● Vigorously

a Hebrew women are vigorous and give birth quickly (Exod. 1:19); whatever you do, do it with all your might (Eccles. 9:10).

572 Feebleness
Weak, see **163**.

573 Plainness

● Plain
speaking

a He was stating the matter plainly (Mark 8:32); no one was speaking openly of him (John 7:13); if you are the Christ, tell us plainly (John 10:24); Jesus said to them plainly (John 11:14); I will tell you plainly of the Father (John 16:25); now you are speaking plainly (John 16:29).

b We use great boldness in our speech (2 Cor. 3:12).

574 Ornament

Eloquence, see **579***as*.

575 Elegance

Eloquence, see **579***as*.

576 Inelegance

Speech defect, see **580**.

577 Voice

● Voices

a The voice is the voice of Jacob (Gen. 27:22); Saul recognised David's voice (1 Sam. 26:17); your voice is sweet (S. of S. 2:14); the voice of joy and gladness, of bridegroom and bride (Jer. 33:11).

b My sheep hear my voice (John 10:27); the sheep hear and know his voice (John 10:3–4); they do not know the voice of strangers (John 10:5).

● God's voice

c Moses heard a voice from between the cherubim (Num. 7:89); after the fire, a still small voice (1 Kgs. 19:12); God speaks with a mighty voice (Ps. 68:33); the voice of the Lord like the sound of many waters (Ezek. 43:2); his voice was like the sound of many waters (Rev. 1:15); the cherubim's wings sounded like the voice of the Lord (Ezek. 1:24; 10:5); a voice like a trumpet (Rev. 1:10; 4:1); the power of the voice of the Lord (Ps. 29:3–9); the Lord will roar from on high (Jer. 25:30); a voice came from heaven (Matt. 3:17; John 12:28–30).

● Shout

d Jesus cried out with a loud voice (Matt. 27:46, 50; Mark 15:34, 37; Luke 23:46).

e Joshua heard the people shout (Exod. 32:17); not the cry of victory or defeat (Exod. 32:18); all the city shouted (1 Sam. 4:13); the prophets of Baal shouted (1 Kgs. 18:28); the demoniac shouted out (Mark 1:23; 5:5; Luke 4:33).

f When the ark came into the camp, the Israelites raised a great shout (1 Sam. 4:5–6); the people shouted, 'Long live the king!' (1 Sam. 10:24).

g Shout to the Lord with a voice of joy (Ps. 47:1); praising the Lord with a very loud voice (2 Chr. 20:19); the people shouted for joy when they praised the Lord (Ezra 3:11–13); the Levites cried to the Lord with a loud voice (Neh. 9:4); they made an oath to the Lord with shouting (2 Chr. 15:14); if they kept quiet, the stones would cry out (Luke 19:40).

h My servant will not quarrel or shout out (Matt. 12:19).

● Battle cry

i Around Jericho, all the people shouted (Josh. 6:5, 16, 20); Gideon's men shouted (Judg. 7:20); shouting the war cry (1 Sam. 17:20; 2 Chr. 13:15).

● Hailing

j Jotham shouted from the top of Mount Gerizim (Judg. 9:7); David shouted from a distant mountain (1 Sam. 26:13–14);

Goliath shouted to Israel (1 Sam. 17:8); Micah and his men shouted to the Danites (Judg. 18:23); the Rabshakeh cried with a loud voice (2 Kgs. 18:28); wisdom calls out (Prov. 8:1); wisdom shouts in the streets (Prov. 1:20); a voice says 'Shout!' (Isa. 40:6).

● Cry of distress

k God remembers the cry of the afflicted (Ps. 9:12); your brother's blood cries out from the ground (Gen. 4:10).

l I screamed (Gen. 39:14–15, 18); a woman attacked in a city should cry out (Deut. 22:23–4); the witch cried out (1 Sam. 28:12); David wailed with a loud voice (2 Sam. 19:4); they wept with a loud voice (Ezra 3:12).

Outcry, see **924***n*.

578 Voicelessness

● Dumb

a God makes man dumb (Exod. 4:11); I will make you dumb (Ezek. 3:26); Zacharias was struck dumb (Luke 1:20–2); a demonised dumb man ws brought to him (Matt. 9:32); a dumb spirit (Mark 9:17).

b The dumb spoke (Matt. 9:33; 12:22; 15:31; Mark 7:35; Luke 11:14); he makes the dumb speak (Mark 7:37); the tongue of the dumb will sing for joy (Isa. 35:6); you will be dumb no longer (Ezek. 24:27); I was no longer dumb (Ezek. 33:22).

c Idols have mouths but cannot speak (Ps. 115:5, 7; 135:16); they cannot speak (Jer. 10:5); you were led astray to dumb idols (1 Cor. 12:2).

● Silenced

d The wicked are silenced in darkness (1 Sam. 2:9); these men must be silenced (Titus 1:11); by doing right you will silence foolish men (1 Pet. 2:15); the law speaks that every mouth may be closed (Rom. 3:19).

e Ishbosheth could not answer Abner (2 Sam. 3:11); the man was speechless (Matt. 22:12); Jesus had silenced the Sadduccees (Matt. 22:34); no one could answer him a word (Matt. 22:46); kings will shut their mouths because of him (Isa. 52:15); they could not reply (Neh. 5:8; Luke 14:6); they had nothing to say (Acts 4:14).

f Do not speak any more of this matter (Deut. 3:26); Jesus told the unclean spirit to be silent (Mark 1:25; Luke 4:35); he heard things a man is not permitted to speak (2 Cor. 12:4).

g Paul's companions stood speechless (Acts 9:7).

h Be silent! (Judg. 3:19; 18:19); they commanded the apostles not to speak in the name of Jesus (Acts 4:17–18; 5:28, 40); they told the blind men to be quiet (Matt. 20:31; Mark 10:48; Luke 18:39); Paul motioned to them to be quiet (Acts 12:17); the town clerk quieted the crowd (Acts 19:35).

Keep silent, see **582**.

● Under one's breath

i Hannah was praying without a sound (1 Sam, 1:12–13); David's servants were whispering (2 Sam. 12:19).

- **Without speech**

j There is no speech nor words (Ps. 19:3).

579 Speech

- **Faculty of speech**

a Life and death are in the power of the tongue (Prov. 18:21); from the fulness of the heart the mouth speaks (Matt. 12:34–6; Luke 6:45); there is a time to speak (Eccles. 3:7); with the mouth a man confesses and is saved (Rom. 10:10).

b Zacharias' tongue was loosed and he could speak (Luke 1:64); the dumb spoke (Matt. 9:33; 12:22; 15:31; Mark 7:35; Luke 11:14); he makes the dumb speak (Mark 7:37).

c The Lord opened the mouth of the donkey (Num. 22:28); a dumb donkey spoke (2 Pet. 2:16).

- **Beware of your speech**

d The tongue is a small member, but boasts great things (Jas. 3:5); the tongue is a fire, a world of evil (Jas. 3:6); a restless evil, full of deadly poison (Jas. 3:8); trying to catch him in what he said (Matt. 22:15; Luke 11:54); he who guards his tongue guards his life (Prov. 13:3); Lord, set a guard over my mouth (Ps. 141:3); let no unwholesome talk come out of your mouth (Eph. 4:29).

e If you have been snared by your own words (Prov. 6:2); men shall render account for every careless word (Matt. 12:36); by your words you will be acquitted or condemned (Matt. 12:37); a fool's lips bring strife (Prov. 18:6).

- **Not speech alone**

f This people honours me with their lips (Isa. 29:13; Matt. 15:8; Mark 7:6); the Pharisees say but do not do (Matt. 23:3); let us not love in word but in deed (1 John 3:18); our gospel did not come to you in word only (1 Thess. 1:5).

- **Curbing speech**

g There is more hope for a fool than for a man hasty in speech (Prov. 29:20); when words abound, sin is not wanting (Prov. 10:19); be slow to speak (Jas. 1:19); if anyone does not bridle his tongue his religion is vain (Jas. 1:26); who can refrain from speaking? (Job 4:2).

- **Good speech**

h The mouth of the righteous is a fountain of life (Prov. 10:11); a healing tongue is a tree of life (Prov. 15:4); the tongue of the wise brings healing (Prov. 12:18); lips of knowledge are more precious than gold (Prov. 20:15); a word fitly spoken is like apples of gold (Prov. 25:11).

i Abel, though dead, still speaks (Heb. 11:4); the blood which speaks better things than that of Abel (Heb. 12:24).

- **Evil speech**

j The wicked sharpen their tongues like a sword (Ps. 64:3); rash speaking is like sword thrusts (Prov. 12:18); they make their tongues sharp as a serpent's (Ps. 140:3); let us attack him with our tongue (Jer. 18:18); the tongue that speaks great things (Ps. 12:3–4); the lips of an adulteress drip honey (Prov. 5:3); the mouth of an adulteress is a deep pit (Prov. 22:14); their throat is an open grave (Ps. 5:9; Rom. 3:13); the words of a son of Belial are like scorching fire (Prov. 16:27); you will be hidden from the scourge of the tongue (Job 5:21).

- Reading

k Read this law before the people (Deut. 31:11); Joshua read all the law (Josh. 8:34); Shaphan read the book of the law before Josiah (2 Kgs. 22:10; 2 Chr. 34:18); the king must read the law (Deut. 17:19); Josiah read it to all the people (2 Kgs. 23:2; 2 Chr. 34:30); Ezra read the book of the law before the people (Neh. 8:1–3, 18); the book of the law was read (Neh. 9:3; 13:1); Baruch read from the scroll (Jer. 36:6, 8, 10, 15); Jehudi read the scroll to the king (Jer. 36:21, 23); Zephaniah had to read the scroll in Babylon (Jer. 51:61–3); the eunuch was reading Isaiah (Acts 8:28, 30); reading the law and the prophets (Acts 13:15); Moses is read in the synagogues every sabbath (Acts 15:21); the prophets are read every sabbath (Acts 13:27); blessed is he who reads the words of this prophecy (Rev. 1:3); attend to the public reading of Scripture (1 Tim. 4:13); Jesus stood up to read (Luke 4:16).

l Have you not read? (Matt. 12:3, 5; 19:4; 21:42; 22:31; Mark 2:25; 12:10; Luke 6:3).

m The book of the chronicles was read to the king (Esther 6:1); letters were read out (Ezra 4:18, 23); I cannot read (Isa. 29:12).

- Reading letters

n Zephaniah read the letter to Jeremiah (Jer. 29:29); they read the letter to the congregation (Acts 15:31); when this letter is read, read it to the Laodiceans also (Col. 4:16); have this letter read to all the brethren (1 Thess. 5:27).

- God speaking

o I have spoken to you from heaven (Exod. 20:22); God spoke to Moses at the tent of meeting (Exod. 33:9, 11); let not God speak to us lest we die (Exod. 20:19); God speaks once or twice, but no one notices (Job 33:14–16); God has spoken to us in his Son (Heb. 1:2).

p I have spoken openly to the world (John 18:20); the words you gave me I gave them (John 17:8); no man ever spoke like this man (John 7:46); speak the word and my servant will be healed (Matt. 8:8; Luke 7:7); he whom God has sent speaks the word of God (John 3:34).

- Speaking as from God

q I will be with your mouth and teach you what to say (Exod. 4:12, 15); you will be as my mouth (Jer. 15:19); I have put my words in your mouth (Isa. 51:16; Jer. 1:9); my Spirit and my words will not depart from your mouth (Isa. 59:21); the Lord has given me the tongue of those who are taught (Isa. 50:4); the law will be in your mouth (Exod. 13:9); I must speak the word God puts in my mouth (Num. 22:38; 23:12, 26; 24:13; 1 Kgs. 22:14; 2 Chr. 18:13); I am making my words in your mouth a fire (Jer. 5:14); whoever speaks, as the utterances of God (1 Pet. 4:11); what to say will be given you (Matt. 10:19); the Holy Spirit will teach you what to say (Luke 12:12); it is not you speaking, but the Holy Spirit (Matt. 10:20; Mark 13:11); I will give you words that no one can withstand (Luke 21:15); speaking to the Gentiles that they may be saved (1 Thess. 2:16).

Speaking by the Spirit, see **965aa**.

● God sending prophets

r I sent my servants the prophets (Jer. 7:25; 44:4); the Lord has sent you all his servants the prophets (Jer. 25:4); I raised up some of your sons to be prophets (Amos 2:11); I will send you prophets and wise men and scribes (Matt. 23:34); I will send prophets and apostles (Luke 11:49); God spoke to our forefathers by the prophets (Heb. 1:1); as he spoke by the mouth of his holy prophets (Luke 1:70); I speak to prophets in visions (Num. 12:6); I have hewn them by the prophets (Hos. 6:5).

s By a prophet the Lord brought Israel from Egypt (Hos. 12:13); when the Israelites cried to the Lord, he sent a prophet (Judg. 6:8); a man of God came to Eli (1 Sam. 2:27); God was angry with Amaziah and sent a prophet (2 Chr. 25:15); God sent Amos to prophesy (Amos 7:14–15); the Lord sent prophets to bring the people back to him (2 Chr. 24:19); the Lord warned Israel through the prophets (2 Kgs. 17:13); I have appointed you a prophet to the nations (Jer. 1:5); the Lord sent me to prophesy (Jer. 26:12); I will send you Elijah the prophet (Mal. 4:5).

Anointing prophets, see **357i**.

● Prophesying

t Would that all the Lord's people were prophets! (Num. 11:29); a prophet was called a seer (1 Sam. 9:9); do not despise prophesyings (1 Thess. 5:20); David provided for regular prophesying (1 Chr. 25:1–3); the sons of Asaph to prophesy by music (1 Chr. 25:1–3); to prophesy in thanks and praise to the Lord (1 Chr. 25:3).

u God has spoken, who can but prophesy? (Amos 3:8); prophesy to the dry bones (Ezek. 37:4); the prophets enquired about Christ (1 Pet. 1:10–11); of him all the prophets bear witness (Acts 10:43); the prophets and the law prophesied until John (Matt. 11:13); you must prophesy about many peoples (Rev. 10:11); the two witnesses will prophesy (Rev. 11:3, 10).

Prediction, see **511**; **writing the prophets**, see **586c**.

● Hindered prophecy

v They commanded the prophets not to prophesy (Jer. 11:21; Amos 2:12; Mic. 2:6); do not prophesy at Bethel (Amos 7:13); they tell the prophets not to prophesy truth (Isa. 30:10); have we made you a royal adviser? (2 Chr. 25:16); has the Lord only spoken through Moses? (Num. 12:2); if I say I will not speak any more in his name (Jer. 20:9).

w This is how they persecuted the prophets (Matt. 5:12); so their fathers did to the prophets (Luke 6:23, 26); a prophet is not without honour except in his home town (Matt. 13:57; Mark 6:4; John 4:44).

Killing prophets, see **362ao**.

x The prophets were an example of patience (Jas. 5:10); do not harm my prophets (1 Chr. 16:22; Ps. 105:15); Jezebel destroyed the prophets of the Lord (1 Kgs. 18:4); that I may avenge the blood of my servants the prophets (2 Kgs. 9:7); the blood of all the prophets will be on this generation (Luke 11:50–1).

y God did not answer Saul by prophets (1 Sam. 28:6, 15); there is no longer any prophet (Ps. 74:9); he closed your eyes, the prophets (Isa. 29:10); prophets will be forbidden to prophesy (Zech. 13:3–5).

● Prophets
  of the Lord

z Prophets: Abraham (Gen. 20:7); Agabus (Acts 21:10); Ahijah (1 Kgs. 11:29; 12:15; 14:2–3; 2 Chr. 9:29); Daniel (Matt. 24:15); David (Acts 2:30); Elijah (1 Kgs. 18:36; 2 Chr. 21:12); Elisha (2 Kgs. 3:11; 5:3, 8, 13); Enoch (Jude 14); Gad (1 Sam. 22:5; 2 Sam. 24:11); Habakkuk (Hab. 1:1; 3:1); Haggai (Ezra 5:1; 6:14; Hag. 1:1); Iddo (2 Chr. 12:15; 13:22); Isaiah (2 Kgs. 19:2; 2 Chr. 26:22; Isa. 37:2; Matt. 3:3; 4:14; 8:17; 12:17; 13:14; 15:7; Mark 1:2; 7:6; John 1:23; 12:38; Acts 8:28, 30; 28:25); Jehu (1 Kgs. 16:7); Jeremiah (2 Chr. 36:12; Dan. 9:2; Matt. 2:17; 27:9); Joel (Acts 2:16); Jonah (Matt. 12:39; Luke 11:29–30); Micah of Moresheth (Jer. 26:18); Micaiah (1 Kgs. 22:7–9; 2 Chr. 18:6–8); Nathan (2 Sam. 12:1–15; 1 Kgs. 1:10, 22–3, 32, 34, 38, 44–5; 2 Chr. 9:29; 29:25; Ps. 51:t); Oded (2 Chr. 28:9); Samuel (1 Sam. 3:20; 9:6; Acts 3:24; 13:20); Shemaiah the man of God (1 Kgs. 12:22; 2 Chr. 12:5, 15); Uriah son of Shemaiah (Jer. 26:20); Zechariah (2 Chr. 24:20–1; Ezra 5:1; 6:14; Zech. 1:1; Matt. 23:35; Luke 11:51); an old prophet of Bethel (1 Kgs. 13:11); a prophet (1 Kgs. 20:13, 22); a man of God from Judah (1 Kgs. 13:1–3); a man of God (1 Kgs. 20:28).

aa Prophetesses: Miriam (Exod. 15:20); Huldah (2 Kgs. 22:14; 2 Chr. 34:22); Anna (Luke 2:36); Philip's four daughters (Acts 21:9).

ab No prophet has arisen like Moses (Deut. 34:10); Aaron would be Moses' prophet (Exod. 7:1); the seventy elders prophesied (Num. 11:25); Eldad and Medad prophesied in the camp (Num. 11:26–7); Saul prophesied (1 Sam. 10:5; 19:23–4); and his men (1 Sam. 19:20–4); is Saul also among the prophets? (1 Sam. 10:11–12); Eliezer prophesied against Jehoshaphat (2 Chr. 20:37); John was more than a prophet (Matt. 11:9; Luke 7:26); you will be called prophet of the Most High (Luke 1:76); the people considered John a prophet (Matt. 14:5; 21:26; Mark 11:32; Luke 20:6); Zacharias prophesied (Luke 1:67); Caiaphas prophesied (John 11:51).

ac Moses and Elijah appeared to them (Matt. 17:3–4; Mark 9:4; Luke 9:30); he is calling for Elijah (Matt. 27:47; Mark 15:35); let us see whether Elijah will come and save him (Matt. 27:49; Mark 15:36).

ad One of the sons of the prophets (1 Kgs. 20:35); 50 sons of the prophets (2 Kgs. 2:7).

Seers, see **438***ae*; **believing the prophets,** see **485***ad*.

● Jesus the
prophet

ae The Lord will raise up for you a prophet like me (Deut. 18:15, 18; Acts 3:22; 7:37); this is Jesus, the prophet (Matt. 21:11); a great prophet has arisen (Luke 7:16); I can see you are a prophet (John 4:19); the people considered him a prophet (Matt. 21:46); are you the Prophet? (John 1:21); this is the Prophet who is to come into the world (John 6:14; 7:40); he is a prophet (John 9:17); a prophet, mighty in word and deed (Luke 24:19).

af A prophet does not come from Galilee (John 7:52); if this man were a prophet (Luke 7:39); no prophet is accepted in his home town (Luke 4:24); prophesy! who hit you? (Matt. 26:68; Mark 14:65; Luke 22:64).

● Prophecy in
the church

ag Your sons and your daughters will prophesy (Joel 2:28; Acts 2:17–18); God appointed prophets in the church (1 Cor. 12:28–9; Eph. 4:11); built on the foundation of apostles and prophets (Eph. 2:20); the mystery now revealed to his apostles and prophets (Eph. 3:5); the gift of prophecy (1 Cor. 12:10); not all are prophets (1 Cor. 12:29).

ah Earnestly desire to prophesy (1 Cor. 14:1, 39); prophecy is a sign for believers (1 Cor. 14:22); if all prophesy, the unbeliever is called to acount (1 Cor. 14:24); two or three prophets may speak (1 Cor. 14:29); he who receives a prophet as a prophet will receive a prophet's reward (Matt. 10:41); in the church there were prophets and teachers (Acts 13:1); prophets came from Jerusalem to Antioch (Acts 11:27); the prophecies made about Timothy (1 Tim. 1:18); a gift bestowed on Timothy by prophetic utterance (1 Tim. 4:14).

ai If I have the gift of prophecy and have not love (1 Cor. 13:2); the use of prophecy in the church (1 Cor. 14:3–5); you can all prophesy in turn (1 Cor. 14:31); the spirits of prophets are subject to the prophets (1 Cor. 14:32); be keen to prophesy (1 Cor. 14:39); they spoke in tongues and prophesied (Acts 19:6); prophecy should be according to one's faith (Rom. 12:6); the testimony of Jesus is the spirit of prophecy (Rev. 19:10); we prophesy in part (1 Cor. 13:9); prophecy will cease (1 Cor. 13:8).

● Wicked
prophets

aj The prophets are prophesying lies (Jer. 5:31; 14:14; 27:10, 14, 16); prophets who teach lies (Isa. 9:15); the Lord has not sent you (Jer. 28:15); I have not sent them (Jer. 29:9); I did not send them, but they ran; I did not speak to them yet they prophesied (Jer. 23:21); Shemaiah has prophesied though I did not send him (Jer. 29:31); the prophets speak visions of their own minds (Jer. 23:16); they prophesy from their own inspiration (Ezek. 13:2–5); your prophets have seen false and deceptive visions (Jer. 14:14); where are the prophets who said the king of Babylon would not come? (Jer. 37:19); you have appointed prophets to proclaim your kingship (Neh. 6:7).

ak Both prophet and priest are polluted (Jer. 23:11); from the prophets of Jerusalem has gone forth pollution (Jer. 23:15); the prophets committed adultery (Jer. 23:14; 29:23); her prophets are faithless (Zeph. 3:4).

● False prophets

al Beware of false prophets (Matt. 7:15); false prophets will arise (Matt. 24:11, 24; Mark 13:22; 2 Pet. 2:1); many false prophets have gone out into the world (1 John 4:1); did we not prophesy in your name? (Matt. 7:22); a prophet leading people astray must not be followed (Deut. 13:1–3; 18:20); false prophets denounced (Jer. 23:9–40; Mic. 3:5–7); Ahab and Zedekiah prophesied falsely (Jer. 29:21); a false prophet called Bar-Jesus (Acts 13:6); Jezebel calls herself a prophetess (Rev. 2:20).

Prophesying lies, see **541***h*; **prophesying deceit**, see **542***j*.

● Prophets of other gods

am 450 prophets of Baal (1 Kgs. 18:19, 22); Elijah killed the prophets of Baal (1 Kgs. 18:40); summon the prophets of Baal (2 Kgs. 10:19); 400 prophets of the Asherah (1 Kgs. 18:19); four hundred prophets, not of the Lord (1 Kgs. 22:6–7; 2 Chr. 18:5–6); 400 prophets urged them to battle (1 Kgs. 22:6); go to the prophets of your father and mother (2 Kgs. 3:13); a Cretan prophet (Titus 1:12).

an The prophets prophesied by Baal (Jer. 2:8); the prophets of Samaria prophesied by Baal (Jer. 23:13).

● Eloquence

ao Sweet speech increases persuasiveness (Prov. 16:21); pleasant words are a honeycomb (Prov. 16:24).

ap Moses had never been eloquent (Exod. 4:10; 6:12, 30); Aaron could speak well (Exod. 4:14); he will be your mouth (Exod. 4:16); Paul came not with eloquence (1 Cor. 2:1); or with persuasive words (1 Cor. 2:4); Apollos was eloquent (Acts 18:24); the kingdom of God is not words but power (1 Cor. 4:20).

580 Speech defect

● Accent

a The Gileadites could not say Shibboleth (Judg. 12:6); your speech gives you away (Matt. 26:73).

● Impediment

b A man with an impediment in his speech (Mark 7:32).

581 Talkativeness

● Too many words

a Is there no end to windy words? (Job 16:3); shall a multitude of words go unanswered? (Job 11:2).

● Wordy folly

b The more words, the more vanity (Eccles. 6:11); a fool multiplies words (Eccles. 10:14); a fool's voice comes with many words (Eccles. 5:3); should a wise man answer with windy words? (Job 15:2); he who opens wide his lips comes to ruin (Prov. 13:3); Job multiplies words without knowledge (Job 35:16).

● Eager to speak

c My tongue is the pen of a ready writer (Ps. 45:1).

d They think they will be heard for their many words (Matt. 6:7).

582 Not speaking

● Silence is wise

a He who restrains is lips is wise (Prov. 10:19); a man of understanding keeps silent (Prov. 11:12); he who curbs his words has knowledge (Prov. 17:27); a silent fool is considered wise (Prov. 17:28); be silent and let that be your wisdom (Job 13:5); he who guards his tongue guards his soul from evil (Prov. 21:23); there is a time to be silent (Eccles. 3:7); the prudent keeps silent at such a time (Amos 5:13); if you have been foolish, put your hand on your mouth (Prov. 30:32).

- Silent before God

b Let your words be few before God (Eccles. 5:2); be silent before the Lord (Zeph. 1:7); my heart waits in silence for God (Ps. 62:1, 5).

Silenced, see **578d**.

- God keeping silent

c These things you did and I kept silence (Ps. 50:21); will you keep silence? (Isa. 64:12); why are you silent when the wicked swallows up the righteous? (Hab. 1:13); he will be silent in his love (Zeph. 3:17).

d Do not be silent to me (Ps. 28:1); O God, do not be silent (Ps. 83:1; 109:1); for Zion's sake I will not keep silent (Isa. 62:1).

- Christ silent

e God's servant will not cry out (Isa. 42:2; Matt. 12:19); he did not open his mouth (Isa. 53:7; Acts 8:32); Jesus kept silent (Matt. 15:23; 26:63; 27:12, 14; Mark 14:61; 15:5; Luke 23:9; John 19:9).

- Silent under provocation

f If we were to be made slaves, I would have kept quiet (Esther 7:4); I do not open my mouth (Ps. 38:13–14); I muzzled my mouth before the wicked (Ps. 39:1–2); Job's friends did not speak for seven days (Job 2:13).

- Those who kept quiet

g Jacob kept quiet until his sons returned (Gen. 34:5); Saul said nothing that day (1 Sam. 20:26); Aaron kept silent (Lev. 10:3); be silent until told to shout (Josh. 6:10); none of the people answered Saul (1 Sam. 14:39); Absalom told Tamar to keep silent (2 Sam. 13:20); Absalom did not speak to Amnon (2 Sam. 13:22); the people did not answer Elijah (1 Kgs. 18:21); the people did not answer the Assyrians (2 Kgs. 18:36; Isa. 36:21); the Pharisees kept silent (Mark 3:4; Luke 14:4); the scribes were silenced (Luke 20:26); the disciples kept silent (Mark 9:34); they listened in silence (Acts 15:12); when they heard him speak in Hebrew they were quieter (Acts 22:2); the princes stopped talking before Job (Job 29:9–10); they kept silent for my counsel (Job 29:21).

- Being silent

h Be silent while I speak (Job 13:13).

i If there is no interpreter, the speaker in tongues should keep silent (1 Cor. 14:28); if a revelation comes to another, let the first prophet be silent (1 Cor. 14:30).

j Let women keep silent in the churches (1 Cor. 14:34–5); women are to be quiet (1 Tim. 2:12); let a woman learn in silence (1 Tim. 2:11).

Be silent!, see **578h**.

- Unduly quiet

k If you remain silent, help will come from elsewhere (Esther 4:14); when I kept silent, my body wasted away (Ps. 32:3); I will not be quiet (Job 7:11); open my lips that my mouth may praise you (Ps. 51:15).

  l If one hears an adjuration but does not speak (Lev. 5:1).

● Not speaking   *m* Do not even speak of other gods (Exod. 23:13).
of evil   **Not tell**, see **525*i***.

583 Allocution
Greeting, see **884**.

584 Conversation
● Conversing   *a* Moses and Elijah talking with him (Matt. 17:3; Mark 9:4); they discussed what they might do with Jesus (Luke 6:11); they discussed which of them might betray him (Luke 22:23); they discussed what had happened (Luke 24:14–15).

585 Soliloquy

586 Writing
● Writing   *a* The first tablets of stone were engraved with God's writing
the law   (Exod. 32:15–16; Deut. 5:22); written with the finger of God (Exod. 31:18); the second set were God's writing (Exod. 34:1; Deut. 10:2–4); but in Moses' hand (Exod. 34:27–8); Joshua wrote this in the book of the law of God (Josh. 24:26); the ministry of death, in letters engraved on stone (2 Cor. 3:7); the law was to be written on plastered stones on Mount Ebal (Deut. 27:3); Joshua wrote on the stones a copy of the law (Josh. 8:32).

  b Moses wrote down the law (Exod. 24:4; Deut. 31:9, 24); the king was to write a copy of the law for himself (Deut. 17:18); Samuel wrote out the ordinances of the kingdom (1 Sam. 10:25).

● Writing the   *c* Write it on a tablet and a scroll (Isa. 30:8); write the vision of
prophets   tablets (Hab. 2:2); a writing of Hezekiah (Isa. 38:9); Jeremiah had to write his prophecy on a scroll (Jer. 36:2); Baruch wrote at Jeremiah's dictation (Jer. 36:4; 45:1); did you write at his dictation? (Jer. 36:17–18); Jeremiah wrote it again (Jer. 36:28, 32).

● Scripture   *d* What is written in the law of Moses (1 Kgs. 2:3); as it is written
says   in the law of Moses (2 Chr. 23:18); what is written in the law? (Luke 10:26).

  e Thus it is written by the prophet (Matt. 2:5); thus it is written (Luke 24:46); it is written (Matt. 4:4, 6, 7, 10; 21:13; Luke 2:23; 4:4, 8, 10; 19:46; Acts 23:5; Gal. 3:10, 13); as it is written (Acts 15:15; Rom. 2:24); as it is written in the book of the prophets (Acts 7:42); the scripture says (1 Tim. 5:18); it was written not just for his sake but for ours (Rom. 4:23–4); everything written in the past was written for our sake (Rom. 15:4).

  f They did to Elijah as it was written of him (Mark 9:13); how is it written of the Son of man? (Mark 9:12); the Son of man goes as it is written of him (Matt. 26:24; Mark 14:21); everything written about the Son of man will be fulfilled (Luke 18:31).

g We have found the one about whom Moses wrote in the law (John 1:45); Moses wrote about me (John 5:46).

- **Writing the New Testament**

h These have been written that you may believe (John 20:31); these things we write that our joy may be complete (1 John 1:4).

i Write what you have seen (Rev. 1:11, 19); if everything about Jesus was written, the world could not contain the books (John 21:25); it seemed good for me to write an account (Luke 1:3).

j Paul wrote in his own handwriting (1 Cor. 16:21; Col. 4:18; 2 Thess. 3:17; Philem. 19); with large letters (Gal. 6:11); Peter wrote by Silvanus (1 Pet. 5:12); the letter was written by Tertius (Rom. 16:22).

Paul's letters, see **588d**.

k I do not wish to write with pen and ink (2 John 12; 3 John 13).

- **Signatures**

l Here is my signature (Job 31:35); I signed and sealed the deed (Jer. 32:10); King Darius signed the document (Dan. 6:9, 10).

- **Written matter**

m Write on a scroll that the Amalekites are to be wiped out (Exod. 17:14); write down this song and teach the Israelites (Deut. 31:19); a written survey of the land (Josh. 18:4); writing the names of the leaders of Succoth (Judg. 8:14).

Bills of divorce, see **548d**.

n Jesus wrote on the ground with his finger (John 8:6, 8); Zacharias wrote, 'His name is John' (Luke 1:63); writing on two sticks (Ezek. 37:16–17); what I have written, I have written (John 19:22).

- **Engraving**

o Engraving the names of Israel on two onyx stones (Exod. 28:9–11; 39:6); on twelve stones (Exod. 28:21; 39:14).

p 'Holy to the Lord' was to be engraved on a gold plate (Exod. 28:36; 39:30); oh that my words were engraved with an iron stylus and lead (Job 19:24).

q I have engraved you on the palms of my hands (Isa. 49:16); the sin of Judah is written with an iron pen, engraved with a diamond (Jer. 17:1).

- **Writing on hearts**

r The law written in our hearts (Jer. 31:33; Heb. 8:10); the work of the law is written on their hearts (Rom. 2:15); a letter written by the Spirit on human hearts (2 Cor. 3:3).

s I will write on him the name of my God (Rev. 3:12); his name and his Father's name written on their foreheads (Rev. 14:1).

- **Judgements written**

- **Secretaries**

t Fingers wrote on the plaster of the wall (Dan. 5:5); curses written down and washed off into the water of bitterness (Num. 5:23).

u Those who were secretaries [scribes]: Elihoreph and Ahijah (1 Kgs. 4:3); Ezra (Neh. 12:36); Jeiel (2 Chr. 26:11); Jonathan, David's uncle (1 Chr. 27:32); Seraiah (2 Sam. 8:17); Shavsha (1 Chr. 18:16); Shebna (Isa. 36:3); Shemaiah (1 Chr. 24:6); Sheva (2 Sam. 20:25).

v The captain's scribe (2 Kgs. 25:19); the families of scribes (1 Chr. 2:55); Ezra was a scribe skilled in the law of Moses (Ezra 7:6, 11, 12, 21); the man with a writing case at his side (Ezek. 9:2); some of the Levites were scribes (2 Chr. 34:13); the scribes were summoned (Esther 3:12; 8:9).

w Herod gathered the scribes (Matt. 2:4); the scribes and Pharisees sit on Moses' seat (Matt. 23:2); I send you prophets and wise men and scribes (Matt. 23:34); why do the scribes say Elijah comes first? (Matt. 17:10); beware of the scribes (Matt. 12:38; Luke 20:46).

● Jesus and the scribes

x He taught with authority, not as the scribes (Matt. 7:29); a scribe offered to follow him (Matt. 8:19); every scribe trained for the kingdom of heaven (Matt. 13:52).

y The scribes said he blasphemed (Matt. 9:3); scribes from Jerusalem said he was possessed by Beelzebub (Mark 3:22); the scribes questioned how a man could forgive sins (Mark 2:6–7); the chief priests and scribes were indignant (Matt. 21:15); he must suffer from the elders, chief priests and scribes (Matt. 16:21); he will be delivered to the chief priests and scribes (Matt. 20:18).

587 Print

588 Correspondence

● Letters written

a David wrote to Joab (2 Sam. 11:14); Huram wrote a letter to Solomon (2 Chr. 2:11); a letter from Elijah (2 Chr. 21:12); Jezebel wrote letters in Ahab's name (1 Kgs. 21:8); the king of Aram sent a letter to the king of Israel (2 Kgs. 5:5); Jehu wrote letters (2 Kgs. 10:1, 6); Hezekiah sent letters to all Israel (2 Chr. 30:1, 6); Sennacherib wrote letters insulting the Lord (2 Chr. 32:17); the king of Babylon sent Hezekiah letters (Isa. 39:1); Hezekiah spread the letter before the Lord (2 Kgs. 19:14; Isa. 37:14); Berodach-baladan sent letters to Hezekiah (2 Kgs. 20:12).

b The enemies of Judah sent a letter to Artaxerxes (Ezra 4:6–16); Atraxerxes sent a reply (Ezra 4:17–22); Tattenai sent a letter to Darius (Ezra 5:6–17); Nehemiah carried letters to the governors (Neh. 2:7, 8, 9); Sanballat sent his servant with an open letter (Neh. 6:5); many letters went to and from Tobiah (Neh. 6:17); Tobiah sent letters to frighten me (Neh. 6:19); Jeremiah sent a letter to all the exiles (Jer. 29:1); letters sent out to every province (Esther 1:22; 3:12; 8:8–17); Esther and Mordecai sent letters to the Jews (Esther 9:20; 9:29–31); Shelemaiah sent letters to those in Jerusalem (Jer. 29:25); Darius wrote to all people (Dan. 6:25).

c Paul asked for letters to Damascus (Acts 9:2; 22:5); a letter from Claudius Lysias to Felix (Acts 23:25–30).

● Paul's
letters

d As our brother Paul wrote to you (2 Pet. 3:15); Paul's letters contain some things hard to understand (2 Pet. 3:16); his letters are weighty (2 Cor. 10:10); have this letter read to all the brethren (1 Thess. 5:27); see this letter is read by the Laodiceans, and read the letter from Laodicea (Col. 4:16); do not be shaken by a letter supposed to be from us (2 Thess. 2:2).

e I wrote to you with many tears (2 Cor. 2:3–4); I caused you sorrow by my letter (2 Cor. 7:8); I do not want to appear to frighten you by my letters (2 Cor. 10:9); hold fast to the traditions whether taught by word of mouth or letter (2 Thess. 2:15).

● Letters to
churches

f A letter sent to the church at Antioch (Acts 15:23–9); I will give letters to the men carrying your gift (1 Cor. 16:3); do we need letters of recommendation? (2 Cor. 3:1); the brethren sent to the disciples to welcome Apollos (Acts 18:27); you are a letter from Christ written on human hearts (2 Cor. 3:2–3); this is my second letter to you (2 Pet. 3:1); I wrote to the church (3 John 9).

g The letter to the church of: Ephesus (Rev. 2:1–7); Smyrna (Rev. 2:8–11); Pergamum (Rev. 2:12–17); Thyatira (Rev. 2:18–29); Sardis (Rev. 3:1–6); Philadelphia (Rev. 3:7–13); Laodicea (Rev. 3:14–22).

Reading letters, see **579***n*.

589 Book

● Books in
general

a The deaf will hear the words of a book (Isa. 29:18); like the words of a sealed book (Isa. 29:11).

● Historical
records

b The book of the generations of Adam (Gen. 5:1); the book of the Wars of the Lord (Num. 21:14); the book of Jashar (Josh. 10:13; 2 Sam. 1:18); the book of the Chronicles of the Kings of Israel (1 Kgs. 14:19; 15:31; 16:5, 14, 20, 27; 22:39; 2 Kgs. 1:18; 10:34; 13:8, 12; 14:15, 28; 15:11, 15, 21, 26, 31); the book of the Chronicles of the Kings of Judah (1 Kgs. 14:29; 15:7, 23; 22:45; 2 Kgs. 8:23; 12:19; 14:18; 15:6, 36; 16:19; 20:20; 21:17, 25; 23:28; 24:5); the book of the Kings of Judah and Israel (2 Chr. 16:11; 25:26; 27:7; 28:26; 32:32; 35:27; 36:8); the book of the Kings of Israel (1 Chr. 9:1; 2 Chr. 20:34); the book of the Kings (2 Chr. 24:27); the records of the kings of Israel (2 Chr. 33:18); the records of the seers (2 Chr. 33:19); the records of Nathan, Iddo *et al.* (1 Chr. 29:29; 2 Chr. 9:29; 12:15; 13:22); the book of the deeds of Solomon (1 Kgs. 11:41); the book of the Chronicles of the Kings of Media and Persia (Esther 2:23; 6:1; 10:2).

c Write this in a book, that I will blot out Amalek (Exod. 17:14); the prophet Isaiah has written about Uzziah (2 Chr. 26:22); the deeds of Hezekiah are written in the vision of Isaiah the prophet (2 Chr. 32:32).

d Search in the record books (Ezra 4:15); search was made in the house of the books (Ezra 6:1); a scroll was found in Ecbatana

(Ezra 6:2); the customs for Purim were written in the book (Esther 9:32); many have compiled narratives (Luke 1:1).

Books registering people

e The number was not entered in David's chronicles (1 Chr. 27:24); the Levites were registered in the book of the Chronicles (Neh. 12:23); the book of the genealogy of returned exiles (Neh. 7:5); false prophets will not be written in the register of Israel (Ezek. 13:9).

Book of the covenant

f Moses read the book of the covenant (Exod. 24:7); as did Josiah (2 Kgs. 23:2).

Book of the law

g Moses wrote the law in a book (Deut. 31:24); Joshua wrote this in the book of the law of God (Josh. 24:26); the book of the law of Moses (Josh. 8:31, 34; Neh. 8:1); the book of Moses (2 Chr. 35:12; Ezra 6:18; Neh. 13:1); take this book of the law (Deut. 31:26); this book of the law shall not depart out of your mouth (Josh. 1:8); Hezekiah found the book of the law in the temple (2 Kgs. 22:8–10; 2 Chr. 34:14–16); they had the book of the law of the Lord (2 Chr. 17:9); every curse written in this book of the law (Deut. 29:20–1, 27).

h They wrote the ordinances of the kingdom in a book (1 Sam. 10:25).

Law, see 953.

Books of scripture

i Write the words I have spoken in a book (Jer. 30:2); in a scroll (Jer. 36:2, 32); Baruch wrote these words in a book (Jer. 45:1); everything written in this book, which Jeremiah prophesied (Jer. 25:13); Jeremiah wrote on a scroll all that would befall Babylon (Jer. 51:60); the scroll of the prophet Isaiah (Luke 4:17); oh, that my words were written in a book! (Job 19:23); I observed in the books the years for Jerusalem (Dan. 9:2); that the writings of the prophets might be fulfilled (Matt. 26:56); as it is written in the book of the prophets (Acts 7:42).

j They are written in Lamentations (2 Chr. 35:25); the book of the genealogy of Jesus Christ (Matt. 1:1).

Books in prophecy

k A book in the hand of the one on the throne (Rev. 5:1); a scroll written on both sides (Ezek. 2:9–3:3); a little book in the angel's hand (Rev. 10:2); take the book from the angel (Rev. 10:8–10); a flying scroll (Zech. 5:1–2).

God's book

l Seek and read in the book of the Lord (Isa. 34:16); blot me out of your book (Exod. 32:32); whoever has sinned I will blot them out of my book (Exod. 32:33); may they be blotted out of the book of life (Ps. 69:28); a book of remembrance for those who fear the Lord (Mal. 3:16); everyone found written in the book will be saved (Dan. 12:1); fellow-workers whose names are in the book of life (Phil. 4:3); I will not rub out his name from the book of life (Rev. 3:5); names written in the book of life of the Lamb that was slain from the foundation of the world (Rev. 13:8; 17:8); another book was opened, the book of life (Rev. 20:12); if anyone's name was not found written in the book of life (Rev.

20:15); only those whose names are written in the Lamb's book of life (Rev. 21:27); those enrolled in heaven (Heb. 12:23); the days ordained for me were written in your book (Ps. 139:16); are my tears not in your book? (Ps. 56:8).

Opening the scroll, see **263***ai*.

● Various
books

m Of the writing of books there is no end (Eccles. 12:12); the world could not contain all the books (John 21:25).

n At the judgement the books were opened (Dan. 7:10; Rev. 20:12).

o Books of magic were burned (Acts 19:19).

p Bring the books, especially the parchments (2 Tim. 4:13).

590 Description

● Inscription

a The inscription Mene, Mene, Tekel, Upharsin (Dan. 5:25); whose likeness and inscription are these? (Matt. 22:20; Mark 12:16; Luke 20:24); there was an inscription above the cross (Luke 23:38; John 19:19).

591 Dissertation

592 Compendium

593 Poetry. Prose

594 Drama. Ballet

Hypocrites [play actors], see **545***e*.

Class five: Volition: the exercise of the will

5.1: Individual volition

Section one: Volition in general

---

595 Will

● God's will

a This is God's will, that I should raise up those he has given me (John 6:39); by his will he gave birth to us by the word of truth (Jas. 1:18); those born not of the will of the flesh nor of the will of man but of God (John 1:13); this is the will of God, your sanctification (1 Thess. 4:3); it is not God's will that one little one perish (Matt. 18:14); in everything give thanks, for this is God's will (1 Thess. 5:18); God is at work in you both to will and to work (Phil. 2:13).

b Paul, an apostle by the will of God (1 Cor. 1:1; 2 Cor. 1:1; Eph. 1:1; Col. 1:1); I will return if God wills (Acts 18:21).

c By your will all things were created (Rev. 4:11); he works all things according to the counsel of his will (Eph. 1:11); God does according to his will (Dan. 4:35); who can resist his will? (Rom. 9:19).

● Knowing God's will

d Prove what the will of God is (Rom. 12:2); prove what the will of the Lord is (Eph. 5:17); filled with the knowledge of his will (Col. 1:9); if you know his will (Rom. 2:18); the mystery of his will (Eph. 1:9).

● Not my will but God's

e Not as I will, but as you will (Matt. 26:39; Mark 14:36; Luke 22:42); I do not seek my own will, but the will of the Father (John 5:30); I came not to do my own will, but the will of him who sent me (John 6:38); my food is to do the will of him who sent me (John 4:34); those born not of the will of the flesh or the will of man, but of God (John 1:13); Christ delivers us according to the will of God the Father (Gal. 1:4).

● God's will be done

f The Lord's will be done (Acts 21:14); your will be done (Matt. 6:10; 26:42); doing the will of God from the heart (Eph. 6:6); suffering according to the will of God (1 Pet. 4:19); if the Lord wills we shall do this and that (Jas. 4:15).

● Doing God's will

g If any man is willing to do his will, he will know of the teaching (John 7:17); he who does the will of God abides for ever (1 John 2:17).

h Which son did the will of his father? (Matt. 21:31).

596 Necessity

● Necessary

a Only a few things are necessary, or only one (Luke 10:42); it was necessary for the Christ to suffer (Luke 24:26); for me to remain in the flesh is more necessary for you (Phil. 1:24).

● Destiny   *b* You who set a table for Fortune and Destiny (Isa. 65:11).

597 Willingness

● God
willing

a If you are willing, you can make me clean (Matt. 8:2; Mark 1:40; Luke 5:12); I am willing! (Matt. 8:3; Mark 1:41; Luke 5:13); God is willing for all men to be saved (1 Tim. 2:4); if the Lord wills we will live and do this or that (Jas. 4:15).
God's will, see **595a**.

● People
willing

b Rebekah was willing to go (Gen. 24:58); some volunteered to live in Jerusalem (Neh. 11:2).

c The spirit is willing but the flesh is weak (Matt. 26:41; Mark 14:38); your people will volunteer freely in the day of your power (Ps. 110:3).

598 Unwillingness

● God
unwilling

a It is not your Father's will that one of these little ones should perish (Matt. 18:14); the Lord does not willingly afflict men (Lam. 3:33).

b Jesus would not drink the wine mixed with gall (Matt. 27:34).

● People
unwilling

c What if the woman is unwilling to come back here? (Gen. 24:5, 8); the man who is unwilling to take his brother's wife (Deut. 25:7); Herod was unwilling to refuse her (Mark 6:26); the judge was unwilling (Luke 18:4); they will bring you where you do not want to go (John 21:18).

d The Levite was unwilling to spend the night there (Judg. 19:10); they were not willing to strike the priests (1 Sam. 22:17); David was unwilling to bring the ark of the Lord in (2 Sam. 6:10).

e I would have gathered you and you would not (Matt. 23:37; Luke 13:34); they would not come to the wedding feast (Matt. 22:3); the son said, 'I will not' (Matt. 21:29).

599 Resolution

● God resolute

a I will not change my mind (Jer. 4:28); the Lord has sworn and will not change his mind (Ps. 110:4; Heb. 7:21).

● Wholehearted

b They helped David with an undivided heart (1 Chr. 12:33); Hezekiah did everything with all his heart (2 Chr. 31:21); the priests and Levites were to devote themselves to the law of the Lord (2 Chr. 31:4).

● Purposeful

c He set his face to go to Jerusalem (Luke 9:51); I have set my face like a flint (Isa. 50:7).

d Be steadfast, unmoveable (1 Cor. 15:58).

600 Perseverance

● Standing firm

a Continue in the faith, stable and steadfast (Col. 1:23); stand against the devil's wiles (Eph. 6:11–14); resist the devil, standing firm in the faith (1 Pet. 5:9); stand firm in the faith (1 Cor. 16:13; 2 Cor. 1:24); we must hold fast our confidence (Heb. 3:6, 14); realize the full assurance of hope until the end (Heb. 6:11); stand firm in the teaching (2 Thess. 2:15); stand firm in one spirit (Phil. 1:27); stand firm in the Lord (Phil. 4:1); persevering in tribulation (Rom. 12:12); hold fast our confession (Heb. 4:14); hold fast the confession of our hope (Heb. 10:23).

b We boast of your perseverance (2 Thess. 1:4); you have endured (Rev. 2:3).

- Enduring to the end

c Love endures all things (1 Cor. 13:7); he who endures to the end will be saved (Matt. 10:22; 24:13; Mark 13:13); by your endurance you will gain your lives (Luke 21:19); if we endure we shall reign with him (2 Tim. 2:11); they bear fruit with perseverance (Luke 8:15); he who keeps my works to the end (Rev. 2:26); I want to complete my course and ministry (Acts 20:24).

d We commend ourselves by much endurance (2 Cor. 6:4); we endure all things (1 Cor. 9:12); I endure all things for the sake of the elect (2 Tim. 2:10); when persecuted we endure (1 Cor. 4:12); I know your perseverance (Rev. 2:19); here is the perseverance of the saints (Rev. 13:10; 14:12); the endurance of Job (Jas. 5:11).

e God gives perseverance (Rom. 15:5); may the Lord direct your hearts into the steadfastness of Christ (2 Thess. 3:5).

f Blessed is the man who perseveres under trial (Jas. 1:12); we count those blessed who endured (Jas. 5:11); the testing of your faith produces endurance (Jas. 1:3); tribulation produces perseverance (Rom. 5:3).

g Endure hardship (2 Tim. 4:5); you have need of endurance (Heb. 10:36); pursue perseverance (1 Tim. 6:11); add to self-control perseverance (2 Pet. 1:6).

- Persisting

h Because of his friend's persistence he will give him what he needs (Luke 11:8); the unjust judge will be worn out by the widow's persistence (Luke 18:5).

- God enduring

i You bore with them for many years (Neh. 9:30).

601 Irresolution

- Double-minded

a A double-minded man, unstable in all his ways (Jas. 1:8); purify your hearts, you double-minded (Jas. 4:8); how long will you limp between two opinions? (1 Kgs. 18:21).

- Yes and no

b Was I vacillating? (2 Cor. 1:17); Christ Jesus is not yes and no (2 Cor. 1:19).

602 Obstinacy

- Obstinate foreigners

a Pharaoh's heart was hardened (Exod. 7:13, 14, 22; 8:19; 9:7); Pharaoh hardened his heart (Exod. 8:15, 32; 9:34); why harden your hearts as Pharaoh did? (1 Sam. 6:6).

● Obstinate
Israel

b The Israelites were a stiff-necked people (Exod. 32:9; 33:3, 5; 34:9; Deut. 9:6, 13; 2 Kgs. 17:14; Neh. 9:16, 17, 29); Zedekiah was stiff-necked and hardened his heart (2 Chr. 36:13); they stiffened their neck (Jer. 17:23; 19:15); they made their hearts like flint (Zech. 7:12); you stiff-necked people (Acts 7:51).

c I know that you are obstinate (Isa. 48:4); a disobedient and obstinate people (Rom. 10:21); a stubborn generation (Ps. 78:8); stubborn children (Ezek. 2:4); Israel is like a stubborn heifer (Hos. 4:16); this people has a stubborn heart (Jer. 5:23); they walked in the stubbornness of their own heart (Jer. 11:8); do not look at the stubbornness of this people (Deut. 9:27); listen to me, you stubborn of heart (Isa. 46:12); we will act according to our stubbornness (Jer. 18:12).

d Divorce was permitted because of their hardness of heart (Matt. 19:8; Mark 10:5).

● Avoid obstinacy

e Do not be stiff-necked (Deut. 10:16; 2 Chr. 30:8); do not harden your hearts (Ps. 95:8; Heb. 3:8, 15; 4:7).

f An elder must not be self-willed (Titus 1:7).

● Consequences
of obstinacy

g A man stiff-necked after much reproof will suddenly be broken (Prov. 29:1); because of your stubborn, unrepentant heart you store up wrath (Rom. 2:5); Jesus reproached them for their hardness of heart (Mark 16:14); Gentiles are ignorant because of their hardness of heart (Eph. 4:18).

● God
hardening

h The Lord hardened Pharaoh's heart (Exod. 4:21; 7:3; 9:12; 10:1, 20, 27; 11:10; 14:4, 8); I will harden the heart of the Egyptians (Exod. 14:17); the Lord made Sihon's heart obstinate (Deut. 2:30); the Lord hardened the hearts of the Canaanites (Josh. 11:20); why do you harden our heart? (Isa. 63:17); he hardens their heart (John 12:40); he hardens whom he will (Rom. 9:18); the rest were hardened (Rom. 11:7); I gave them over to their stubbornness (Ps. 81:12); a hardening has come on part of Israel (Rom. 11:25).

i I have made your face as hard as theirs (Ezek. 3:8–9).

603 Change of mind

● God changing
his mind

a God is not man, that he should change his mind (Num. 23:19); God does not change his mind like a man (1 Sam. 15:29); the Son of God was not Yes and No (2 Cor. 1:19).

b God changed his mind (Exod. 32:14; Amos 7:3, 6; Jonah 3:9, 10); if the nation turns from evil, I will repent of the evil (Jer. 18:8); the Lord will repent of the evil he pronounced (Jer. 26:13); the Lord repented of the evil he pronounced (Jer. 26:19); if it does evil, I will repent of the good (Jer. 18:10).

● People
changing
their minds

c The Egyptians changed their minds (Exod. 14:5); lest the people change their minds when they see war (Exod. 13:17).

d He changed his mind and went to work (Matt. 21:29); you did not change your minds and believe John (Matt. 21:32).

- Change of allegiance

e Which of you is for the king of Israel? (2 Kgs. 6:11); you are going over to the Chaldeans (Jer. 37:13–14); I fear the Jews who have deserted to the Chaldeans (Jer. 38:19); my friend has lifted up his heel against me (Ps. 41:9).

- Backsliding

f Why has this people turned away in perpetual apostasy? (Jer. 8:5); our backslidings are many (Jer. 14:7); those who have turned back from following the Lord (Zeph. 1:6).

g You will all fall away this night (Matt. 26:31; Mark 14:27); even if all fall away, I will not (Matt. 26:33; Mark 14:29); many will fall away (Matt. 24:10); when persecution comes he falls away (Matt. 13:21; Mark 4:17).

h The day of the Lord will be preceded by apostasy (2 Thess. 2:3); in the last days some will fall away from the faith (1 Tim. 4:1); an unbelieving heart to fall away from the living God (Heb. 3:12);

i No one who puts his hand to the plough and looks back is fit for the kingdom (Luke 9:62); if they fall away it is impossible to bring them to repentance (Heb. 6:4–7).

j I will heal their backsliding (Hos. 14:4).
   Turning away, see **282**.

604 Caprice
Fickle, see **152*b***.

605 Choice

- God choosing

a Blessed is the man you choose (Ps. 65:4); many are called but few chosen (Matt. 22:14); the Lord has set apart the godly for himself (Ps. 4:3).

b God chose: Abraham (Gen. 18:19; Neh. 9:7); Bezalel (Exod. 31:2); the priests (Deut. 18:5; 21:5; 1 Sam. 2:28); Saul (1 Sam. 10:24); David (1 Sam. 16:1; 2 Sam. 6:21; 1 Kgs. 8:16; 1 Chr. 28:4; 2 Chr. 6:6; Ps. 78:70); Solomon (1 Chr. 28:5); Judah (Ps. 78:68); Zion (Ps. 132:13); the temple (2 Chr. 7:12, 16).

c God will bring near whom he will choose (Num. 16:5, 7); the rod of the one I choose will sprout (Num. 17:5); the Lord has chosen you Levites to minister (2 Chr. 29:11); the Lord chose the Levites to carry the ark (1 Chr. 15:2); your king shall be the one God chooses (Deut. 17:15).

- Chosen son

d I have chosen him to be my son (1 Chr. 28:6); this is my Son, my chosen one (Luke 9:35); my servant, my chosen one (Isa. 42:1; 43:10; Matt. 12:18); the Holy One of Israel has chosen you (Isa. 49:7).

- Chosen disciples

e Jesus chose twelve disciples (Luke 6:13); you did not choose me but I chose you (John 15:16); I have chosen you out of the world (John 15:19); I know the ones I have chosen (John 13:18); I chose you and one of you is a devil (John 6:70); show which of these two you have chosen (Acts 1:24).

f Paul is my chosen instrument (Acts 9:15); chosen in him before the foundation of the world (Eph. 1:4); we know he chose you (1 Thess. 1:4); God chose you for salvation (2 Thess. 2:13); God chose the poor to be rich in faith (Jas. 2:5); make your calling and election sure (2 Pet. 1:10); those with him are called, chosen and faithful (Rev. 17:14); God's purpose in choosing (Rom. 9:11); God made a choice among you (Acts 15:7); God has chosen the weak and foolish things (1 Cor. 1:27–8); a remnant chosen by grace (Rom. 11:5); God's elect ones (Col. 3:12; 1 Pet. 1:1).

g For the sake of the elect the days have been shortened (Matt. 24:22; Mark 13:20); misleading, if possible, even the elect (Matt. 24:24); I endure all things for the sake of the elect (2 Tim. 2:10); angels will gather his elect (Matt. 24:31; Mark 13:27).

● Chosen people

h God chose Israel (Deut. 4:37; 7:6; 10:15); you only have I chosen (Amos 3:2); Israel, my chosen one (Isa. 45:4); the God of Israel chose our fathers (Acts 13:17); sons of Jacob, his chosen ones (1 Chr. 16:13); the day I chose Israel (Ezek. 20:5); the Lord will again choose Israel (Isa. 14:1).

i You are a chosen race (1 Pet. 2:9).

● God choosing a place

j God choosing a place for his name (Deut. 12:5, 11, 14, 21, 26; 14:23–5; 16:2, 6–7; 17:8, 10; 18:6; 26:2; 31:11; Josh. 9:27; 2 Kgs. 21:7; 2 Chr. 12:13; Neh. 1:9).

k The city you have chosen (1 Kgs. 8:48); Jerusalem which I have chosen (1 Kgs. 11:13, 32, 36); I have chosen Jerusalem for my name (2 Chr. 6:6); the city the Lord chose (1 Kgs. 14:21); the Lord will again choose Jerusalem (Zech. 1:17; 2:12).

l He chooses our inheritance for us (Ps. 47:4).

● Choosing in judgement

m God selected down to Achan (Josh. 7:14–18); selecting down to Saul (1 Sam. 10:20–1); selecting down to Jonathan (1 Sam. 14:40–2).

● People choosing

n Choose this day whom you will serve (Josh. 24:15); choose life (Deut. 30:15–20); I have chosen the faithful way (Ps. 119:30); I have chosen your precepts (Ps. 119:173); I will follow the one the Lord and this people have chosen (2 Sam. 16:18); choose one of these three things (2 Sam. 24:12; 1 Chr. 21:10); multitudes in the valley of decision (Joel 3:14).

o Moses chose able men (Exod. 18:21, 25); choose a man for single combat (1 Sam. 17:8).

p Lot chose the valley of Jordan (Gen. 13:11); Jeremiah could choose whether to go or stay in the land (Jer. 40:4).

● Deciding by lots

q The lot is cast into the lap, but the decision is from the Lord (Prov. 16:33); the lot puts an end to disputes (Prov. 18:18).

r Casting lots: over the two goats (Lev. 16:8); for tribal allocations (Num. 26:55; 33:54; Josh. 18:6–11; 19:1, 10, 17, 24, 32, 40;

Ezek. 45:1; 47:22; 48:29); for towns for the Levites (Josh. 21:4); for attackers of Benjamin (Judg. 20:9); for who had broken the oath (1 Sam. 14:41–2); for divisions of the priests (1 Chr. 24:5); for divisions of the Levites (1 Chr. 24:31); for duties of the musicians (1 Chr. 25:8); for gates for the gatekeepers (1 Chr. 26:13); for people to bring firewood (Neh. 10:34); for who should live in Jerusalem (Neh. 11:1); for a day and month to destroy the Jews (Esther 3:7; 9:24, 26); for my people (Joel 3:3); over Jerusalem (Obad. 11); to decide the troublemaker (Jonah 1:7); for the priest to burn incense (Luke 1:9); for a replacement for Judas (Acts 1:26); for Jesus' garments (Ps. 22:18; Matt. 27:35; Mark 15:24; Luke 23:34; John 19:24).

s Urim and Thummim (Exod. 28:30; Lev. 8:8; Deut. 33:8; Ezra 2:63; Neh. 7:65); the judgement of the Urim (Num. 27:21); God did not answer Saul by Urim (1 Sam. 28:6).

t The king of Babylon consults omens to choose the way (Ezek. 21:21–2).

606 Absence of choice
See **601**.

607 Rejection

- God rejecting Israel

a Do not forsake us (Jer. 14:9); the Lord rejected Israel (Deut. 32:19; 2 Kgs. 17:20; Ps. 78:59; 108:11); because you have forsaken the Lord, he has forsaken you (2 Chr. 24:20); the Lord has rejected this generation (Jer. 7:29); you have rejected us (Ps. 44:9; 60:1, 10; 74:1); he rejected the tent of Joseph (Ps. 78:67); the Lord has forsaken the land (Ezek. 8:12); you have rejected your anointed one (Ps. 89:38); reject silver, because the Lord has rejected them (Jer. 6:30).

b I will reject this temple (1 Kgs. 9:7; 2 Chr. 7:20); the Lord has rejected his altar (Lam. 2:7); I will reject Jerusalem and this temple (2 Kgs. 23:27); I reject you as my priests (Hos. 4:6).

c Will the Lord reject us for ever? (Ps. 77:7); have you utterly rejected Judah? (Jer. 14:19); for a brief moment I forsook you (Isa. 54:7); the rejection of the Jews led to the reconciliation of the world (Rom. 11:15).

- God rejecting individuals

d Do not cast me from your presence (Ps. 51:11); do not cast me off in old age (Ps. 71:9, 18); why have you rejected me? (Ps. 43:2; 88:14); God has forsaken him (Ps. 71:11).

e Afterwards Esau was rejected (Heb. 12:17).

Driven from God's presence, see **300***m*.

- God not rejecting

f God will not reject a blameless man (Job 8:20); I will not reject them (Lev. 26:44); the Lord will not reject for ever (Lam. 3:31); God has not rejected his people (Rom. 11:1–2); you will no longer be called 'Forsaken' (Isa. 62:4); a city not forsaken (Isa. 62:12).

- Rejecting God

g You have rejected your God who saves you (1 Sam. 10:19); you have forsaken the Lord (2 Chr. 13:11; Jer. 2:17); you have forsaken me (Jer. 5:19; 15:6); they have forsaken me (2 Chr. 34:25; Jer. 1:16); for you who forsake the Lord (Isa. 65:11); they have rejected me as king (1 Sam. 8:7); our fathers have forsaken him (2 Chr. 29:6); your fathers have forsaken me (Jer. 16:11); your children have forsaken me (Jer. 5:7); the Pharisees and lawyers rejected God's purpose for themselves (Luke 7:30).

h They abandoned the temple (2 Chr. 24:18); he abandoned the law of the Lord (2 Chr. 12:1); they rejected his statutes and covenant (2 Kgs. 17:15); they have forsaken his commandments (2 Kgs. 17:16); we have forsaken your commandments (Ezra 9:10); they have forsaken my law (Jer. 9:13); they have rejected the word of the Lord (Jer. 8:9); you have abandoned your first love (Rev. 2:4).

i Those who forsake the Lord will perish (Isa. 1:28); it is evil and bitter to forsake the Lord (Jer. 2:19); a few Arameans defeated them because they had forsaken the Lord (2 Chr. 24:24); Pekah slew men of Judah because they had forsaken the Lord (2 Chr. 28:6).

j Because you rejected him, he has rejected you (1 Sam. 15:23, 26); you have forsaken me so I have forsaken you (2 Chr. 12:5). **Avoiding God**, see **620p**; **abandoning God**, see **621h**.

- Rejecting Jesus

k He was despised and rejected by men (Isa. 53:3); the Son of Man must be rejected (Mark 8:31; Luke 9:22); they asked Jesus to leave them (Matt. 8:34; Mark 5:17; Luke 8:37); the stone which the builders rejected (Matt. 21:42; Mark 12:10; Luke 20:17; Acts 4:11; 1 Pet. 2:7); a living stone rejected by men (1 Pet. 2:4); rejected by this generation (Luke 17:25); he who rejects me has one who judges him (John 12:48).

- Rejecting foreign gods

l They put away the foreign gods (Judg. 10:6).

- Jettisoning goods

m There is a time to throw away (Eccles. 3:6); the Arameans had thrown their equipment away (2 Kgs. 7:15); they jettisoned the cargo (Acts 27:18); they threw the ship's tackle overboard (Acts 27:19); they threw the wheat into the sea (Acts 27:38).

608 Predetermination

- Predestined plan

a The peoples did whatever your hand predestined to occur (Acts 4:28); God prepared our good works beforehand (Eph. 2:10); delivered up by the predetermined plan and foreknowledge of God (Acts 2:23).

b A man's lifespan is predetermined (Job 14:5).

- Predestined people

c Whom he knew, he also predestined to become conformed to the image of his Son (Rom. 8:29); whom he predestined, these he also called (Rom. 8:30); the hidden wisdom which God predestined (1 Cor. 2:7); he predestined us to adoption (Eph. 1:5);

predestined according to his purpose (Eph. 1:11); names written in the book of life before the foundation of the world (Rev. 17:8).

d Vessels of mercy prepared beforehand for glory (Rom. 9:23); God has not destined us for wrath but to obtain salvation (1 Thess. 5:9); vessels of wrath intended for destruction (Rom. 9:22).

● Men pre-determining

e Absalom determined this beforehand (2 Sam. 13:32).

609 Spontaneity
Unpremeditated, see **618**.

610 Habit
Custom, see **127c**.

611 Weaning

● Wean

a The day Isaac was weaned (Gen. 21:8); Samuel stayed with his mother until he was weaned (1 Sam. 1:22–4); Tahpenes weaned Genubath in Pharaoh's house (1 Kgs. 11:20).

b My soul is like a weaned child (Ps. 131:2); will he teach those just weaned? (Isa. 28:9).

612 Motive

● Exhortation

a Lot strongly urged the angels (Gen. 19:3); the angels urged Lot (Gen. 19:15); his servants urged him to eat (1 Sam. 28:23); Absalom urged the king to send Amnon (2 Sam. 13:27).

b The chief priests persuaded the crowds (Matt. 27:20); the chief priests incited the crowd to ask for Barabbas (Mark 15:11).

c Use your gift in exhortation (Rom. 12:8); stirring up one another to love and good works (Heb. 10:24); knowing the fear of the Lord, we persuade men (2 Cor. 5:11); Paul was persuading Jews and Greeks (Acts 18:4).

● Enticing

d Sweet speech increases persuasiveness (Prov. 16:21); wisdom adds persuasiveness to the lips (Prov. 16:23); with patience a ruler may be persuaded (Prov. 25:15).

e Entice your husband to tell us the riddle (Judg. 14:15); entice him to see where his strength lies (Judg. 16:5); who will entice Ahab? (1 Kgs. 22:20–2; 2 Chr. 18:19–21).

f If sinners entice you, do not consent (Prov. 1:10); the harlot entices him (Prov. 7:21); a man of violence entices his neighbour (Prov. 16:29); Baruch is inciting you (Jer. 43:3).

● Bribery

g A bribe is a magic charm for its owner (Prov. 17:8); a man's gift makes room for him (Prov. 18:16); a gift in secret averts anger (Prov. 21:14); everyone loves a bribe (Isa. 1:23); you take bribes (Amos 5:12).

h A bribe corrupts the heart (Eccles. 7:7); the right hand of the wicked is full of bribes (Ps. 26:10); a wicked man receives a bribe

(Prov. 17:23); they acquit the guilty for a bribe (Isa. 5:23); leaders give judgement for a bribe (Mic. 3:11); the prince and the judge ask for a bribe (Mic. 7:3); cursed is he who accepts a bribe to kill (Deut. 27:25); they have taken bribes to shed blood (Ezek. 22:12).

i Samuel's sons took bribes (1 Sam. 8:3); the priests bribed the soldiers (Matt. 28:12); Felix hoped Paul would give him a bribe (Acts 24:26).

● Avoiding bribes

j Do not accept a bribe (Exod. 23:8; Deut. 16:19); he who hates bribes will live (Prov. 15:27); he does not take a bribe against the innocent (Ps. 15:5); from whom have I taken a bribe? (1 Sam. 12:3); he who shakes his hands lest they hold a bribe (Isa. 33:15); have I asked you to offer a bribe? (Job 6:22).

● Bribing God

k There is no bribery with God (2 Chr. 19:7).

● Temptation

l Jezebel incited Ahab to do evil (1 Kgs. 21:25); Satan moved David to number Israel (1 Chr. 21:1).

m No temptation has taken you except what is common to man (1 Cor. 10:13); come together again lest Satan tempt you (1 Cor. 7:5); do not lead us into temptation (Matt. 6:13; Luke 11:4); pray that you might not enter into temptation (Matt. 26:41; Mark 14:38; Luke 22:40, 46); look to yourself lest you also be tempted (Gal. 6:1).

n Let no one say he is tempted by God (Jas. 1:13); each one is tempted by his own lust (Jas. 1:14); the seduction of riches (Matt. 13:22).

o I was afraid the tempter might have tempted you (1 Thess. 3:5); this persuasion was not from him who calls you (Gal. 5:8). **Testing**, see **461**.

● Jesus' temptation

p Jesus was tempted by the devil (Matt. 4:1; Mark 1:13; Luke 4:2); we have a high priest who has been tempted in every way (Heb. 4:15); since he was tempted, he is able to help those are tempted (Heb. 2:18).

613 Dissuasion
See **612**.

614 Pretext

● Excuses

a They began to make excuses (Luke 14:18).

615 Good
See **644**.

616 Evil
See **645**.

Section two: Prospective volition

617 Intention

● God's
purposes

a You meant evil but God meant it for good (Gen. 50:20); in accord with God's eternal purpose (Eph. 3:11); the Pharisees and lawyers rejected God's purpose for themselves (Luke 7:30).
Plan, see **623**.

● Man's
purposes

b The one who sins high-handedly is to be cut off (Num. 15:30).

c The word of God is able to discern the intentions of the heart (Heb. 4:12); Assyria does not intend so (Isa. 10:7).

618 Nondesign. Gamble

● Unintentional

a Sinning unintentionally (Lev. 4:2, 22, 27; 5:15, 18; Num. 15:24, 27, 29).

b Instructions concerning one who kills another unintentionally (Exod. 21:13; Num. 35:11, 15, 22–3; Deut. 4:42; 19:4; Josh. 20:3, 9).
By chance, see **159**.

619 Pursuit

● Hunting

a Nimrod was a mighty hunter (Gen. 10:9); Esau became a skilful hunter (Gen. 25:27; 27:3); fishermen will fish for them and hunters will hunt for them (Jer. 16:16).
Fishing, see **542z**.

b My enemies hunt me down like a bird (Lam. 3:52).

● Pursuing
people

c You will pursue your enemies (Lev. 26:7); five of you will chase 100 and 100 chase 10 000 (Lev. 26:8); one puts to flight 1000 (Josh. 23:10).

d Pursue your enemies! (Josh. 10:19); I pursued my enemies (2 Sam. 22:38; Ps. 18:37); Abraham pursued the kings (Gen. 14:14, 15); Judah pursuing Adoni-bezek (Judg. 1:6); pursue the Moabites! (Judg. 3:28); Barak pursuing Sisera (Judg. 4:16, 22); faint yet pursuing (Judg. 8:4); they pursued the Midianites (Judg. 7:25); Abimelech chased Gaal (Judg. 9:40); they pursued the Philistines (1 Sam. 7:11; 14:22; 17:52); David pursued the raiding party (1 Sam. 30:8); Asa pursued the Ethiopians (2 Chr. 14:13).

e Joab restrained them from pursuing Israel (2 Sam. 18:16).
Tired in pursuit, see **684c**.

● Being
pursued

f How could one chase 1000 and two put 10 000 to flight unless the Lord had given them up (Deut. 32:30); 1000 will flee from one (Isa. 30:17).

g In pride the wicked pursue (Ps. 10:2); the enemy said 'I will pursue!' (Exod. 15:9); our pursuers were swifter than eagles (Lam. 4:19); Laban pursued Jacob (Gen. 31:23, 36); Pharaoh pursued the Israelites (Exod. 14:4, 8, 23); the Amorites chased you like bees (Deut. 1:44); men pursued the spies (Josh. 2:7); the men of Ai pursued the Israelites (Josh. 7:5; 8:16); Saul pursued by chariots and horsemen (2 Sam. 1:6); the Philistines pursued Saul and his sons (1 Chr. 10:2); the Chaldeans pursued the king (2 Kgs. 25:5; Jer. 52:8).

h Saul pursued David (1 Sam. 23:25–28); why do you pursue me? (1 Sam. 26:18); Asahel pursued Abner (2 Sam. 2:19); Joab and Abishai pursued Abner (2 Sam. 2:24); Absalom should pursue David (2 Sam. 17:1); Joab's men pursued Sheba (2 Sam. 20:6, 7, 10, 13).

i How long will you pursue your brothers? (2 Sam. 2:26); your pursuers will be swift (Isa. 30:16).

- **God pursuing**
j You have pursued us (Lam. 3:43); you will pursue them (Lam. 3:66).

- **Pursuing good**
k Pursue righteousness, faith, love and peace (2 Tim. 2:22); pursue peace with all men (Heb. 12:14); pursue peace (1 Pet. 3:11).

620 Avoidance

- **Fleeing**
a May your enemies flee (Num. 10:35).

b They will flee when no one pursues (Lev. 26:36–7); the wicked flee when no one pursues (Prov. 28:1); three months fleeing from your enemies? (2 Sam. 24:13; 1 Chr. 21:12); the hireling sees the wolf and flees (John 10:12–13); flight will perish from the swift (Amos 2:14).

c He who flees from the report of disaster will fall into a pit (Isa. 24:18); those who see me flee from me (Ps. 31:11).
Tired in flight, see **684***d*.

- **Peoples who fled**
d Those who fled: the kings of Sodom and Gomorrah (Gen. 14:10); the five kings (Josh. 10:16); Adoni-bezek (Judg. 1:6); Sisera (Judg. 4:15, 17); Midian (Judg. 7:21; 8:12); the Philistines (1 Sam. 14:22; 19:8); the Arameans and Ammonites (2 Sam. 10:13–14, 18; 1 Chr. 19:14, 15, 18); Benhadad (1 Kgs. 20:30); Moab (2 Kgs. 3:24); the Arameans (1 Kgs. 20:20, 30; 2 Kgs. 7:7); the Ethiopians (2 Chr. 14:12); the fugitives of Moab (Isa. 15:5); Nineveh (Nahum 2:8).

e The Benjaminites put to flight the citizens of Gath (1 Chr. 8:13); Edom have fled from the sword and bow (Isa. 21:15); a sound of fugitives from Babylon (Jer. 50:28).

- **Israel fleeing**
f The people fled from the Philistines (1 Sam. 31:1; 2 Sam. 23:11; 1 Chr. 10:1); the men of war fled from Jerusalem (2 Kgs. 25:4); Judah fled from Israel (2 Chr. 25:22); all your rulers have fled (Isa. 22:3); every city flees (Jer. 4:29).

g Joshua pretended to flee (Josh. 8:5–6, 15); Israel fled to draw Benjamin out (Judg. 20:32); everyone with David will flee (2 Sam. 17:2); if we flee, they will not care about us (2 Sam. 18:3).

h People in Thebez fled into the tower (Judg. 9:51); you are fugitives from Ephraim, you Gileadites (Judg. 12:4); 600 Benjaminites fled (Judg. 20:47); the Israelites fled to their tents (1 Sam. 4:10; 2 Sam. 18:17; 19:8; 2 Kgs. 8:21); Judah fled to their tents (2 Kgs. 14:12); the Israelites fled from the battle (1 Sam. 4:17; 2 Sam. 1:4); they abandoned their homes and fled (1 Sam. 31:7; 1 Chr. 10:7); like those ashamed who flee in battle (2 Sam. 19:3).

● **Individuals fleeing**

i Those who fled from people: Hagar from Sarah (Gen. 16:6, 8); Lot from Sodom (Gen. 19:17–20); Jacob from Esau (Gen. 27:43); from Laban (Gen. 31:21); Joseph from Potiphar's wife (Gen. 39:12); Moses from Pharaoh (Exod. 2:15; Acts 7:29); Jotham from Abimelech (Judg. 9:21); Gaal from Abimelech (Judg. 9:40); Jephthah from his brothers (Judg. 11:3); David from Saul (1 Sam. 19:10, 12, 18; 21:10; 27:4; Ps. 57:t); Absalom from David (2 Sam. 13:34, 37–8); David from Absalom (2 Sam. 19:9; 1 Kgs. 2:7); David and his men from Absalom (2 Sam. 15:14); Jeroboam from Solomon (1 Kgs. 11:40; 12:2; 2 Chr. 10:2); Elijah from Jezebel (1 Kgs. 19:3); Ahaziah from Jehu (2 Kgs. 9:27); Uriah the prophet from Jehoiakin (Jer. 26:21).

j Two of Shimei's slaves ran away (1 Kgs. 2:39); Rezon had fled from his master (1 Kgs. 11:23).

k Those who fled: Mephibosheth's nurse (2 Sam. 4:4); the king's sons (2 Sam. 13:29); Hadad to Egypt (1 Kgs. 11:17); Rehoboam to Jerusalem (1 Kgs. 12:18; 2 Chr. 10:18); the prophet (2 Kgs. 9:10); Amaziah (2 Kgs. 14:19); the people to Egypt (2 Kgs. 25:26); Zedekiah and his men (Jer. 39:4); the herdsmen (Matt. 8:33; Mark 5:14); the disciples (Matt. 26:56; Mark 14:50); a naked man (Mark 14:52); the women from the tomb (Mark 16:8); Paul and Barnabas to Lystra (Acts 14:6); the woman into the wilderness (Rev. 12:6).

l Jesus dodged their grasp (John 10:39).

● **Manslayers fleeing**

m The cities of refuge to which the manslayer could flee (Exod. 21:13; Num. 35:6, 11–34; Deut. 4:42; 19:3–4); a man burdened with another's blood will be fugitive until death (Prov. 28:17).

● **Flee!**

n Flee! (2 Kgs. 9:3; Jer. 48:6; 49:30); flee from Babylon (Isa. 48:20; Jer. 50:8; 51:6; Zech. 2:6–7); flee to Egypt (Matt. 2:13); flee like a bird to the mountain (Ps. 11:1); should a man like me flee? (Neh. 6:11).

o Let those in Judea flee to the mountains (Matt. 24:16; Mark 13:14; Luke 21:21); when they persecute you, flee to the next town (Matt. 10:23); pray that your flight will not be in winter or on the Sabbath (Matt. 24:20); flee from Jerusalem (Jer. 6:1).

● **Avoiding God**

p Jonah ran away from the Lord (Jonah 1:3, 10); where can I flee from your presence? (Ps. 139:7).

q Who warned you to flee from the wrath to come? (Matt. 3:7; Luke 3:7); earth and sky fled from his presence (Rev. 20:11). **Rejecting God**, see **607g**; **abandoning God**, see **621h**.

- Avoiding
  evil

r Flee from youthful lusts (2 Tim. 2:22); flee immorality (1 Cor. 6:18); flee from idolatry (1 Cor. 10:14); abstain from every kind of evil (1 Thess. 5:22); flee from these things (1 Tim. 6:11); abstain from iniquity (2 Tim. 2:19).

- Leaving
  others
  alone

s Do not associate with a hot-tempered man (Prov. 22:24); keep away from those who cause divisions (Rom. 16:17); keep away from every brother living in idleness (2 Thess. 3:6); do not associate with those who do not obey these intructions (2 Thess. 3:14); have nothing to do with these people (2 Tim. 3:5); leave them alone (Matt. 15:14; 19:14); get away from all that belongs to these wicked men (Num. 16:26).
Have no dealings, see **10e**.

t Leave us alone to serve the Egyptians (Exod. 14:12); leave him alone and let him curse (2 Sam. 16:11); leave us alone (Job 21:14); leave me alone (Job 7:16, 19; 10:20); do not bother me (Luke 11:7); turn your gaze from me (Ps. 39:13); turn from him that he may rest (Job 14:6); leave me alone for two months (Judg. 11:37); leave her alone (2 Kgs. 4:27; Mark 14:6; John 12:7); have nothing to do with that righteous man (Matt. 27:19); leave this work on the temple alone (Ezra 6:7); leave these men alone (Acts 5:38); they left the bones of the man of God alone (2 Kgs. 23:18); let it alone this year also (Luke 13:8).

u Resist the devil and he will flee from you (Jas. 4:7).

621 Relinquishment

- God
  abandoning
  people

a God will abandon them in the wilderness (Num. 32:15); I will forsake them (Deut. 31:17); unless the Lord had given them up (Deut. 32:30).

b You have abandoned your people (Isa. 2:6); you abandoned them to their enemies (Neh. 9:28); he abandoned the tent at Shiloh (Ps. 78:60); I have forsaken my house (Jer. 12:7); why do you forsake us so long? (Lam. 5:20); Zion said, 'The Lord has forsaken me' (Isa. 49:14); the Lord has abandoned us (Judg. 6:13); I will abandon the remnant of my inheritance (2 Kgs. 21:14); he will give Israel up (1 Kgs. 14:16); how can I give you up? (Hos. 11:8).

c He leaves the 99 to search for the one (Matt. 18:12; Luke 15:4).

- God
  abandoning
  individuals

d Samson did not know that the Lord had left him (Judg. 16:20); he has rejected you from being king (1 Sam. 15:23); the Spirit of God left Saul (1 Sam. 16:14); I have rejected Eliab (1 Sam. 16:7).

e My God, why have you forsaken me? (Ps. 22:1; Matt. 27:46; Mark 15:34); God has forsaken him (Ps. 71:11).

- Not abandoned
  by God

f Do not forsake me (Ps. 27:9; 38:21; 119:8); I am old yet have I not seen the righteous forsaken (Ps. 37:25); the Lord does not forsake his godly ones (Ps. 37:28).

g I will not leave you (Gen. 28:15); I will not forsake my people (1 Kgs. 6:13); the Lord will not abandon his people (Ps. 94:14);

Israel and Judah have not been forsaken by God (Jer. 51:5); God will never leave you or forsake you (Deut. 31:6, 8; Josh. 1:5; 1 Chr. 28:20; Heb. 13:5); may he not leave us nor forsake us (1 Kgs. 8:57); I will not forsake them (Isa. 41:17); you did not forsake them (Neh. 9:17, 19, 31); we are persecuted but not forsaken (2 Cor. 4:9); I will not leave you as orphans (John 14:18).

● Abandoning God

h If you forsake him, he will harm you (Josh. 24:20); if you forsake him, he will forsake you (1 Chr. 28:9; 2 Chr. 15:2); because you have rejected him he has rejected you (1 Sam. 15:23); if you forsake my statutes (2 Chr. 7:19); far be it from us to forsake the Lord! (Josh. 24:16).

i They forsook the Lord (Judg. 2:12; 10:6, 10, 13; 1 Kgs. 9:9; 2 Chr. 7:22); they have forsaken the Lord (Isa. 1:4; Jer. 19:4); they have forsaken me (2 Kgs. 22:17); they have forsaken the spring of living water (Jer. 2:13; 17:13); he forsook the God who made him (Deut. 32:15); Amon forsook the Lord (2 Kgs. 21:22); Jehoram forsook the Lord (2 Chr. 21:10).

j You are deserting him who called you (Gal. 1:6)

k You have forsaken the Lord's commandments (1 Kgs. 18:18); the wicked forsake your law (Ps. 119:53); they have forsaken your covenant (1 Kgs. 19:10, 14).

Rejecting God, see **607g**; **avoiding God**, see **620p**.

● Abandoning for God

l Go forth from your country, your kin and your home (Gen. 12:1); Ruth left her parents and her land (Ruth 2:11); put away the foreign gods (Josh. 24:23).

m They left their nets (Matt. 4:20; Mark 1:18); they left the boat and their father (Matt. 4:22; Mark 1:20); Matthew left everything and followed him (Luke 5:28); we have left everything (Matt. 19:27; Mark 10:28–9; Luke 18:28–9); whoever does not forsake everything cannot be my disciple (Luke 14:33); they left everything and followed him (Luke 5:11).

n He who leaves his family for Christ will gain a new family (Matt. 19:29; Mark 10:29–30; Luke 18:29–30);

o Let the wicked forsake his way (Isa. 55:7).

● Abandoning people

p For this reason a man will leave his father and mother (Gen. 2:24; Matt. 19:5; Mark 10:7; Eph. 5:31).

q Treating people as outcasts by shaking dust off one's feet (Matt. 10:14; Mark 6:11; Luke 9:5; 10:11; Acts 13:51); shaking out one's garments (Neh. 5:13; Acts 18:6; 22:23).

r Do not forsake your friend (Prov. 27:10); woe to the shepherd who deserts the flock (Zech. 11:17).

s Everyone has deserted me (2 Tim. 1:15); John Mark left them in Pamphylia (Acts 13:13; 15:38); Demas has deserted me (2 Tim. 4:10); at my first defence everyone deserted me (2 Tim. 4:16); Paul agreed to be left behind in Athens (1 Thess. 3:1).

t The devil left him (Matt. 4:11).

Leaving, see **296c**.

● Abandoning in haste

u The Philistines abandoned their idols (2 Sam. 5:21; 1 Chr. 14:12); the woman left her water pot (John 4:28); Bartimaeus threw aside his cloak (Mark 10:50).

● Animals abandoning

v The ostrich abandons her eggs (Job 39:14); the doe abandons her newborn calf for lack of grass (Jer. 14:5).

622 Business

See **686**.

623 Plan

● God's plans

a No plan of yours can be thwarted (Job 42:2); the Lord has planned and who can annul it? (Isa. 14:27); the plans of the Lord stand for ever (Ps. 33:11); I will accomplish all my purpose (Isa. 46:10); God planned it long ago (2 Kgs. 19:25; Isa. 22:11; 25:1; 37:26); the Lord planned it (Isa. 23:9).

b Hear the Lord's plan against Edom (Jer. 49:20); against Babylon (Jer. 50:45); I know the plans I have for you, plans for welfare (Jer. 29:11); God has planned to destroy you (2 Chr. 25:16); they do not understand the Lord's purpose (Mic. 4:12).

Intention, see **617**.

● Man's plans

c Man plans his way but the Lord directs his steps (Prov. 16:9); the plans are man's but the answer is the Lord's (Prov. 16:1); man plans much, but the Lord's purposes will stand (Prov. 19:21); whatever you devise against the Lord, he will put a stop to it (Nahum 1:9).

d Man was made upright, but seeks many devices (Eccles. 7:29); woe to those who carry out a plan, but not mine (Isa. 30:1); you will devise an evil plan (Ezek. 38:10); one who plots evil against the Lord (Nahum 1:11); the wicked plots against the righteous (Ps. 37:12); he plans wickedness on his bed (Ps. 36:4); the Lord hates hearts that devise wicked plans (Prov. 6:18); God frustrates the plots of the cunning (Job 5:12).

e David gave Solomon the plans for the temple (1 Chr. 28:11–12).

● Conspiracies

f Do not call conspiracy what this people call conspiracy (Isa. 8:12); they plot against your people (Ps. 83:3); Amos has conspired against you (Amos 7:10).

g Those who conspired: Ahimelech against Saul (1 Sam. 22:13); Absalom against David (2 Sam. 15:12); Baasha against Nadab (1 Kgs. 15:27); Zimri against Elah (1 Kgs. 16:9, 16); Jehu against Joram (2 Kgs. 9:14; 10:9); his servants against Joash (2 Kgs. 12:20; 2 Chr. 24:25, 26); people against Amaziah (2 Kgs. 14:19; 2 Chr. 25:27); Shallum against Zechariah (2 Kgs. 15:10, 15); Joash against Zechariah (2 Chr. 24:21); Pekah against Pekahiah (2 Kgs. 15:25); Hoshea against Pekah (2 Kgs. 15:30); Hoshea against Salmaneser (2 Kgs. 17:4); his servants against Amon (2 Kgs. 21:23; 2 Chr. 33:24–5); Sanballat etc. against Jerusalem (Neh. 4:8); the Jews against Paul (Acts 20:3).

h Ahithophel was one of the conspirators (2 Sam. 15:31).

i They plotted to kill Joseph (Gen. 37:18); they plotted to kill Jeremiah (Jer. 11:19); let us make plots against Jeremiah (Jer. 18:18); the Jews plotted how to kill Jesus (Matt. 12:14; 26:4; 27:1; Mark 3:6); they plotted how to kill Paul (Acts 9:23–4; 23:12–15, 20–1, 30).

j We are not ignorant of Satan's schemes (2 Cor. 2:11).

624 Way

● God's ways

a God's way is perfect (2 Sam. 22:31; Ps. 18:30); the ways of the Lord are right (Hos. 14:9); just and true are your ways (Rev. 15:3); my ways are not your ways (Isa. 55:8); my ways are right but yours are not (Ezek. 18:25, 29); as the heavens are higher than the earth, so are God's ways than our ways (Isa. 55:9); your way was through the sea (Ps. 77:19); build up a highway for him who rides through the deserts (Ps. 68:4).

A way prepared, see **669a**.

b Teach me your ways (Exod. 33:13; Ps. 86:11); that he may teach us his ways (Isa. 2:3; Mic. 4:2); that your way may be known on earth (Ps. 67:2); God made known his ways to Moses (Ps. 103:7); you know the way I am going (John 14:4–5); they have not known my ways (Ps. 95:10; Heb. 3:10).

c The way of the Lord is not right (Ezek. 18:25, 29; 33:17, 20).

● Man's ways

d The ways of a man are before the Lord (Prov. 5:21); there is a way which seems right to a man but it ends in death (Prov. 14:12; 16:25); every man's way is right in his own eyes (Prov. 21:2); do not walk in the way of evil men (Prov. 4:14); the way of the wicked ends in ruin (Ps. 1:6); the way of the wicked is like darkness (Prov. 4:19); the way of the wicked is an abomination to the Lord (Prov. 15:9); let the wicked forsake his way (Isa. 55:7); keep your feet from their path (Prov. 1:15); the old path which wicked men have trod (Job 22:15); they are walking in bypaths, not on the highway (Jer. 18:15).

● The right way

e Commit your way to the Lord (Ps. 37:5); all my ways are before you (Ps. 119:168); a man's way is ordained by the Lord (Prov. 20:24); a man's way is not in himself (Jer. 10:23); make straight paths for your feet (Heb. 12:13); he will make your paths straight (Prov. 3:6).

f I am the way (John 14:6); ask for the ancient paths, where the good way is (Jer. 6:16); this is the way, walk in it (Isa. 30:21).

g The path of the righteous is like the dawn (Prov. 4:18); the path of the upright is a highway (Prov. 15:19); the Lord knows the way of the righteous (Ps. 1:6).

● Paths

h We will go by the highway (Num. 21:22; Deut. 2:27); the highways were deserted (Judg. 5:6); they spread garments on the road (Matt. 21:8; Mark 11:8; Luke 19:36); go to the road from Jerusalem to Gaza (Acts 8:26).

i You made the depths of the sea a pathway for the redeemed (Isa. 51:10); there will be a highway from Assyria (Isa. 11:16; 19:23); a highway will be there called the Way of Holiness (Isa. 35:8); in the desert prepare a highway for our God (Isa. 40:3; Matt. 3:3; Mark 1:3; Luke 3:4; John 1:23); the Lord who made a way through the sea (Isa. 43:16); is making a highway in the wilderness (Isa. 43:19); my highways will be raised up (Isa. 49:11); build up the highway (Isa. 57:14; 62:10); consider the road by which you went into exile (Jer. 31:21); they will ask the way to Zion (Jer. 50:5).

Straight paths, see **249a**.

j Some seed fell by the path (Matt. 13:4, 19; Mark 4:4, 15; Luke 8:5, 12); they went into the streets and gathered all they could (Matt. 22:9, 10).

● Pavements

k Ahaz removed the covered way into the temple (2 Kgs. 16:18); the judgement seat at a place called The Pavement (John 19:13).

l Under God's feet there appeared to be a pavement of sapphire (Exod. 24:10); the street of the city was pure gold (Rev. 21:21); a mosaic pavement (Esther 1:6).

● The Way

m 'The Way' (Acts 9:2; 19:9, 23; 22:4; 24:14, 22).

625 Middle way
Moderation, see **177**.

626 Circuit
See **314**.

627 Requirement

● God's needs

a God is not served by human hands as though he needed anything (Acts 17:25); what does the Lord require of you? (Deut. 10:12; Mic. 6:8).

b The Lord has need of it (Matt. 21:3; Mark 11:3; Luke 19:31, 34). **Needful**, see **596a**.

● Man's needs

c What do I lack? (Matt. 19:20); one thing you lack (Mark 10:21; Luke 18:22); the eye cannot say it has no need of the hand (1 Cor. 12:21).

Lack of water, see **342e**.

628 Instrumentality
Tool, see **630**.

629 Means
Remedy, see **658**.

630 Tool

● Literal tools

a Tubal-cain forged tools of bronze and iron (Gen. 4:22); pierce his ear with an awl (Exod. 21:6); the axe-head fell into the water (2 Kgs. 6:5); sharpening ploughshares, mattocks, axes and hoes (1 Sam. 13:20–1); a sharp sickle (Rev. 14:14, 17).

b David made the Ammonites work with saws and iron axes (2 Sam. 12:31; 1 Chr. 20:3); costly stones, sawed with saws (1 Kgs. 7:9).

c No tool used on the altar (Exod. 20:25; Deut. 27:5); no iron tool was heard at the site when the temple was being built (1 Kgs. 6:7).

Temple utensils, see **194g**.

● Metaphorical
tools

d Does the axe or saw boast over the one who uses them? (Isa. 10:15); do not present your limbs to sin as tools of wickedness (Rom. 6:13).

e Is not my word like a hammer? (Jer. 23:29); the hammer of the whole earth is broken (Jer. 50:23).

631 Materials

● Materials
in general

a Materials were to be given for making the tabernacle (Exod. 25:3–7; 35:5–9); and they were (Exod. 35:22–8); the amounts of materials used for the tabernacle (Exod. 38:21–31); gifts of materials for the tabernacle (Exod. 35:21–9); materials for the temple (1 Chr. 22:3–4, 14; 29:2).

b That day will show what materials have been used to build on the foundation, gold, silver, precious stones, wood, hay, stubble (1 Cor. 3:12–13).

● Wood
and stone

c The bricks and sycamore have fallen but we will rebuild with stone and cedar (Isa. 9:10); what use is the wood of the vine? (Ezek. 15:2–6).

d Timber for Solomon's palace and the temple (1 Kgs. 5:6–10; 9:11; 2 Chr. 2:3, 8–9); one course of timbers (Ezra 6:4); timber for gates of the city (Neh. 2:8); Hiram sent cedar for David's house (2 Sam. 5:11); he made cedar as plentiful as sycamore (1 Kgs. 10:27; 2 Chr. 1:15; 9:27); cedar wood from Lebanon (Ezra 3:7); almug wood from Ophir (1 Kgs. 10:11–12); algum trees (2 Chr. 9:10–11).

e Planks of fir from Senir (Ezek. 27:5); a cedar of Lebanon for a mast (Ezek. 27:5); oars from oaks of Bashan (Ezek. 27:6); decks of Cyprus pine inlaid with ivory (Ezek. 27:6).

f They were no gods but only wood and stone (2 Kgs. 19:18).

● Metals
and ivory

g Objects of gold, silver, bronze, iron, tin, lead passed through the fire (Num. 31:22–23); David took much bronze from Hadadezer (2 Sam. 8:8; 1 Chr. 18:8); Hadoram brought gold, silver and bronze articles (1 Chr. 18:10); David took gold and silver from the nations (1 Chr. 18:11).

h Hiram sent Solomon 120 talents of gold (1 Kgs. 9:14); they brought 420 talents of gold from Ophir (1 Kgs. 9:28); 450 talents of gold from Ophir (2 Chr. 8:18); the Queen of Sheba brought much gold (1 Kgs. 10:2; 2 Chr. 9:1); 120 talents (1 Kgs. 10:10; 2 Chr. 9:9); 666 talents in one year (1 Kgs. 10:14; 2 Chr. 9:13); Jehoshaphat built ships to go to Ophir for gold (1 Kgs. 22:48); silver, iron, tin and lead were exchanged for goods (Ezek. 27:12).

i David gave 3000 talents of gold and 7000 of silver for the temple (1 Chr. 29:4); the leaders gave 5000 talents of gold, 10 000 of silver, 18 000 of brass and 100 000 of iron (1 Chr. 29:7).

j Silver was not esteemed in Solomon's time (1 Kgs. 10:21; 2 Chr. 9:20); he made silver and gold as common as stones (1 Kgs. 10:27; 2 Chr. 1:15; 9:27); gold instead of bronze, silver instead of iron, bronze instead of wood, iron instead of stones (Isa. 60:17).

k The ships brought gold, silver and ivory (1 Kgs. 10:22; 2 Chr. 9:21); ivory tusks and ebony were traded (Ezek. 27:15); Solomon built a throne of ivory (1 Kgs. 10:18; 2 Chr. 9:17).

l The head of gold, chost of silver, belly of bronze, legs of iron, feet of iron and clay (Dan. 2:32–3); his feet were like burnished bronze (Rev. 1:15; 2:18); vessels of gold, silver and earthenware (2 Tim. 2:20).

Minerals, see **359**.

● Bricks and tar

m They used bricks for stone and tar for mortar (Gen. 11:3); the valley of Siddim was full of tar pits (Gen. 14:10); basket covered with tar and pitch (Exod. 2:3); streams turned into pitch (Isa. 34:9).

n Hard labour with mortar and bricks (Exod. 1:14); no straw to make bricks (Exod. 5:7–18); David set the Ammonites to making bricks (2 Sam. 12:31); take a brick and draw Jerusalem on it (Ezek. 4:1).

● Cloth

o Pharaoh clothed Joseph in fine linen (Gen. 41:42); I clothed you with linen and silk (Ezek. 16:10, 13); a rich man dressed in purple and fine linen (Luke 16:19); the great city clothed in fine linen (Rev. 18:16); the bride was clothed in fine linen, which is the righteous deeds of the saints (Rev. 19:8); the armies of heaven clothed in fine linen (Rev. 19:14); a sail of linen from Egypt (Ezek. 27:7).

p Linen for: hangings of the court (Exod. 27:9, 18; 38:9, 16); the tunics and turban (Exod. 28:39; 39:27–8); caps and breeches (Exod. 39:28).

q Linen and blue, purple and scarlet material for: the tabernacle (Exod. 25:4; 35:6, 23, 25, 35; 38:23); the curtains (Exod. 26:1; 36:8); the veil (Exod. 26:31; 36:35); the screen (Exod. 26:36; 36:37); the gateway (Exod. 27:16; 38:18); the holy garments (Exod. 28:5); the ephod (Exod. 28:6; 39:2–3); the woven band (Exod. 28:8; 39:5, 29); the breastpiece (Exod. 28:15; 39:8).

632 Store

● Stores of
food

a Joseph stored up the food of Egypt (Gen. 41:35, 48–9); storage cities (1 Kgs. 9:19; 2 Chr. 8:4, 6); overseeing the king's store-houses (1 Chr. 27:25); people appointed over the storehouses (Neh. 12:44); Hezekiah made storehouses for produce (2 Chr. 32:28); storehouses for the temple (1 Chr. 28:11, 12; 2 Chr. 8:15); Rehoboam put stores of food in the fortresses (2 Chr. 11:11).

b The Lord will bless your barns (Deut. 28:8); your barns will be filled with plenty (Prov. 3:10); let our garners be full (Ps. 144:13).

c Keep an omer of manna (Exod. 16:32–4).

● Storing
treasure
on earth

d Do not store up treasure on earth (Matt. 6:19); but in heaven (Matt. 6:20); I will demolish my barns and build bigger ones (Luke 12:18).

Stocking weapons, see **723*h*; treasure house**, see **799*c*.

● God's
storehouses

e God's storehouses of snow and hail (Job 38:22); he gathers the deeps in storehouses (Ps. 33:7).

f Gather the wheat into my barn (Matt. 13:30); he will gather the wheat into his barn (Luke 3:17).

633 Provision

● God providing

a God richly supplies us with everything to enjoy (1 Tim. 6:17); God will equip you with everything good to do his will (Heb. 13:21); the provision of the Spirit (Phil. 1:19); his divine power has given us everything pertaining to life and godliness (2 Pet. 1:3); the Lord will provide a lamb (Gen. 22:8, 14).

b God provided for his people in the wilderness (Ps. 105:40–1); you provided for them in the wilderness (Neh. 9:21); you provided for the poor (Ps. 68:10).

God providing water, see **339*k*; God providing rivers**, see **350*g*.

● People
providing

c Joseph promised to provide for his relatives in Egypt (Gen. 45:11); I will provide (Gen. 50:21); if any one will not provide for his family, he has denied the faith (1 Tim. 5:4, 8).

d Barzillai provided for the king (2 Sam. 19:32); Rehoboam provided abundant food for his sons (2 Chr. 11:23); twelve governors provided for the king for each month (1 Kgs. 4:7, 27–8).

e The land could not support both: Abraham and Lot (Gen. 13:6); Jacob and Esau (Gen. 36:7).

Providing food, see **301*l*; man providing a meal**, see **301*r*; man providing water**, see **339*q*.

634 Waste

● Wasting
goods

a Why this waste of perfume? (Matt. 26:8–9; Mark 14:4); the unjust steward was squandering his master's possessions (Luke

435

16:1); he who goes with harlots wastes his wealth (Prov. 29:3); the younger son squandered his property (Luke 15:13).

● Wasting time

b I will not waste time (2 Sam. 18:14).

635 Sufficiency

● Plenty of food

a God give you abundance of grain and wine (Gen. 27:28); Esau had plenty (Gen. 33:9); so had Jacob (Gen. 33:11); seven years of plenty (Gen. 41:29); grain like the sand of the sea (Gen. 41:49); you will eat the fat of the land (Gen. 45:18); in Egypt we ate bread to the full (Exod. 16:3); you brought us from a land flowing with milk and honey (Num. 16:13); rivers flowing with honey and curds (Job 20:17); more gladness than when their grain and wine abound (Ps. 4:7).

b He who tills his land will have plenty of bread (Prov. 12:11).

● Plenty in the wilderness

c These forty years you have not lacked anything (Deut. 2:7); what have you lacked? (1 Kgs. 11:22); they did not thirst when he led them through the deserts (Isa. 48:21); he who gathered little had no lack (Exod. 16:18; 2 Cor. 8:15).

● Plenty in the land

d A land flowing with milk and honey (Exod. 3:8, 17; 13:5; 33:3; Lev. 20:24; Num. 13:27; 14:8; 16:14; Deut. 6:3; 11:9; 26:9, 15; 27:3; 31:20; Josh. 5:6; Jer. 11:5; 32:22; Ezek. 20:6, 15); a land where there is no lack (Judg. 18:10); you will eat and be satisfied (Deut. 6:11; 11:15); you will lack nothing (Deut. 8:9); plenty of food (Lev. 26:5, 10); the bounty of the land for Joseph (Deut. 33:13–16); the abundance of the seas (Deut. 33:19); they ate, drank and rejoiced (1 Kgs. 4:20); the priests had plenty to eat and to spare (2 Chr. 31:10); they ate, were filled and grew fat (Neh. 9:25); you crown the year with your bounty (Ps. 65:11); I will bless Zion's provisions (Ps. 132:15); you will be satisfied with Jerusalem's consoling breasts (Isa. 66:11); in famine they will have abundance (Ps. 37:19).

e You did not serve the Lord with joy for your abundance (Deut. 28:47).

● Plenty for the poor

f He fills the hungry with good things (Ps. 107:9; Luke 1:53); those who were hungry cease to hunger (1 Sam. 2:5); the poor will eat and be satisfied (Ps. 22:26); I will satisfy her poor with bread (Ps. 132:15); the widow's flour and oil will not run out until rain comes (1 Kgs. 17:14, 16); the oil flowed until all the vessels were full (2 Kgs. 4:5–6); all the people ate and were satisfied (Matt. 14:20; 15:37; Mark 6:42; 8:8; Luke 9:17; John 6:12); he who gives to the poor will not want (Prov. 28:27).

● Plenty through God

g You satisfy the desire of every living thing (Ps. 145:16); he fulfils the desire of all who fear him (Ps. 145:19); those who fear him lack nothing (Ps. 34:9); the Lord does not let the righteous hunger (Prov. 10:3); the righteous has enough to eat (Prov. 13:25); I will send you grain and you will be satisfied (Joel 2:19); there will be overflowing threshing floors and vats (Joel 2:24); you will have plenty to eat (Joel 2:26); they will not hunger nor thirst (Isa. 49:10); I shall not want (Ps. 23:1); my cup overflows (Ps. 23:5); the abundance of the sea will be turned to you (Isa. 60:5). **Desires satisfied in God**, see **859c**.

h Whoever drinks the water I give will never thirst (John 4:14); he who believes in me will never hunger or thirst (John 6:35); those who hunger and thirst after righteousness will be satisfied (Matt. 5:6); you do not lack any gift (1 Cor. 1:7); God is able to make all grace abound to you (2 Cor. 9:8); God will supply all your needs according to his riches in Christ (Phil. 4:19); good measure, pressed down, shaken together, running over (Luke 6:38); they will never again hunger or thirst (Rev. 7:16).

i There was no needy person among them (Acts 4:34); your abundance will supply their need (2 Cor. 8:14); I know how to face abundance and want (Phil. 4:12); as you abound in everything, abound in giving too (2 Cor. 8:7). **Fruitfulness**, see **171**.

● Enough!

j Enough! (2 Sam. 24:16; 1 Chr. 21:15; Luke 22:38); a sated man loathes honey (Prov. 27:7).

636 Insufficiency

● Particular shortages

a Famine in the time of: Abraham (Gen. 12:10); Isaac (Gen. 26:1); Joseph (Gen. 41:27–36, 50–7; 42:5; 43:1; 45:6, 11; 47:4, 13, 20; Ps. 105:16; Acts 7:11); the judges (Ruth 1:1); David (2 Sam. 21:1); Elijah (1 Kgs. 18:2; Luke 4:25); Elisha (2 Kgs. 4:38; 6:25; 7:4; 8:1); Zedekiah (2 Kgs. 25:3; Jer. 52:6); Nehemiah (Neh. 5:3); the prodigal son (Luke 15:14); Claudius (Acts 11:28).

b There is no food (Num. 21:5); only a handful of flour and a little oil (1 Kgs. 17:12); Jeremiah will die in the famine (Jer. 38:9); the doe abandons her newborn calf for lack of grass (Jer. 14:5–6); children faint from hunger (Lam. 2:19); better those slain by the sword than those slain with hunger (Lam. 4:9); our skin is like an oven from the heat of famine (Lam. 5:10); there was shortage before a start was made on the temple (Hag. 2:16–17); I gave you cleanness of teeth and lack of bread (Amos 4:6).

c The wine failed (John 2:3).

● Shortage anticipated

d David was given the option of three years of famine (1 Chr. 21:12); seven years (2 Sam. 24:13); God's judgement will include lack of all things (Deut. 28:48); the staff of bread broken (Lev. 26:26; Ps. 105:16; Ezek. 4:16; 5:16; 14:13); the Lord will remove the supply of bread and water (Isa. 3:1); they shall be wasted by famine (Deut. 32:24); I will send famine against Jerusalem (Ezek. 14:21); I will kill your root with famine (Isa. 14:30); give their children over to famine (Jer. 18:21); the invading nation will eat up everything (Deut. 28:51); those who were full have hired themselves out for bread (1 Sam. 2:5); they are hungry and not satisfied (Isa. 9:20); they will eat but not have enough (Hos. 4:10); you will eat but not be satisfied (Mic. 6:14); threshing floor and wine press will not feed them (Hos. 9:2); their honourable men die of hunger (Isa. 5:13); those who are gaunt from want and famine (Job 30:3).

Failing rivers, see **350j**.

e May Joab's house always have someone who lacks bread (2 Sam. 3:29).

Hunger, see **859g**.

f There will be famine in the last days (Matt. 24:7; Mark 13:8; Luke 21:11); my servants will eat but you will hunger (Isa. 65:13); you will die with hunger and thirst (2 Chr. 32:11); those who are well-fed now will be hungry (Luke 6:25); those who are intended for famine, let them go to famine (Jer. 15:2); famine will follow close after you to Egypt (Jer. 42:16); famine, sword and pestilence will come (Jer. 14:12–16); to kill with sword and famine (Rev. 6:8).

- Help in famine

g When famine comes and your people pray (1 Kgs. 8:37; 2 Chr. 6:28; 20:9); famine will not separate us from the love of Christ (Rom. 8:35); in famine God will redeem you from death (Job 5:20); he will keep them alive in famine (Ps. 33:19).

h Better the little of the righteous than the abundance of the wicked (Ps. 37:16); I know how to face abundance and want (Phil. 4:12); if a brother or sister is without food (Jas. 2:15).

- No more famine

i They will no longer be subject to famine (Ezek. 34:29; 36:29); no longer the disgrace of famine (Ezek. 36:30).

- Shortage other than food

j The women were not sufficient for the Benjaminites (Judg. 21:14); the dust of Samaria will not suffice for my people (1 Kgs. 20:10); men will be scarcer than gold (Isa. 13:12); there will not be enough oil for us and you (Matt. 25:9).

k There will be a famine of hearing the Lord's word (Amos 8:11).

Insatiable, see **859v**.

- Empty-handed

l You will not go empty-handed (Exod. 3:21); none will come before me empty-handed (Exod. 23:15; Deut. 16:16); do not send away a slave empty-handed (Deut. 15:13).

m You would have sent me away empty-handed (Gen. 31:42); do not go to your mother-in-law empty-handed (Ruth 3:17); do not send the ark back empty (1 Sam. 6:3); he has sent the rich away empty-handed (Luke 1:53).

637 Excess

- More than enough
- Surplus

a The people brought more than enough for the tabernacle (Exod. 36:5–7); I have had enough of burnt offerings (Isa. 1:11).

b Luxury does not befit a fool (Prov. 19:10); they contributed from their surplus (Mark 12:44; Luke 21:4); those who gathered much had nothing over (Exod. 16:18; 2 Cor. 8:15).

c It is superfluous for me to write to you (2 Cor. 9:1).

638 Importance

• God is great

a The Lord is greater than all gods (Exod. 18:11; 2 Chr. 2:5); great is the Lord (1 Chr. 16:25); he that is in you is greater than he that is in the world (1 John 4:4); he who comes from heaven is above all (John 3:31); he should have the preeminence (Col. 1:18).

• Great things

b The great commandment (Matt. 22:36–8; Mark 12:28); I am doing a great work (Neh. 6:3); which is greater, the gold or the temple? (Matt. 23:17); which is greater, the offering or the altar? (Matt. 23:19).

• Greatness of man

c Man is worth more than: many sparrows (Matt. 10:31; Luke 12:7); the birds (Luke 12:24); a sheep (Matt. 12:12).

d Samuel set Saul at the head of those invited (1 Sam. 9:22); Simon claimed to be someone great (Acts 8:9); do you seek great things for yourself? (Jer. 45:5).

e See how great Melchizedek is (Heb. 7:4); you are worth 10 000 of us (2 Sam. 18:3); Job was the greatest of the men of the east (Job 1:3).

Superior, see **34**; **greatest in the kingdom**, see **733***o*.

639 Unimportance

• I am nothing

a Who am I? (Exod. 3:11; 2 Sam. 7:18; 1 Chr. 17:16; 29:14; 2 Chr. 2:6); who am I to be the king's son-in-law? (1 Sam. 18:18); a dead dog like me? (2 Sam. 9:8); who are you pursuing? a dead dog, one flea? (1 Sam. 24:14); I am dust and ashes (Gen. 18:27); my family is least in Benjamin (1 Sam. 9:21); though you were little in your own eyes (1 Sam. 15:17); if I have not love I am nothing (1 Cor. 13:2, 3).

b God has chosen the things that are not (1 Cor. 1:28).

• Unimportant people

c Who is Abimelech? (Judg. 9:28, 38); who is this uncircumcised Philistine? (1 Sam. 17:26); who is David? (1 Sam. 25:10); your servants are nothing to you (2 Sam. 19:6).

d All the nations are as nothing before him (Isa. 40:17); all the inhabitants of the earth are as nothing (Dan. 4:35); he brings princes to nought (Isa. 40:23–4); Egypt will be the lowliest of nations (Ezek. 29:14–15).

Least in the kingdom, see **733***n*.

• Unimportant things

e Does not this temple seem as nothing in comparison? (Hag. 2:3); Bethlehem is by no means least (Matt. 2:6); the least commandment (Matt. 5:19).

Inferior, see **35**.

640 Usefulness

• Useful people

a You will be neither useless nor unfruitful (2 Pet. 1:8); a vessel useful for the master (2 Tim. 2:21); what benefit is it to God if you are righteous? (Job 22:2–3).

b Onesimus—'Useful' (Philem. 10); now Onesimus is useful to you and me (Philem. 11); Mark is useful to me (2 Tim. 4:11).

● Useful
things

c All scripture is profitable for correction etc. (2 Tim. 3:16); it is expedient that one man die (John 11:50; 18:14); it is to your advantage that I go away (John 16:7).

641 Uselessness

● Useless
endeavour

a Vanity, vanity, everything is vanity (Eccles. 1:2; 12:8); all is vanity (Eccles. 3:19); all comes to vanity (Eccles. 11:8); vanity, chasing after wind (Eccles. 1:14, 17; 2:11, 17, 26; 4:4, 16; 6:9); this too is vanity (Eccles. 2:1, 15, 19, 21, 23; 4:8; 5:10; 6:2; 7:6; 8:10, 14); vanity under the sun (Eccles. 4:7); they followed vanity and became vain (2 Kgs. 17:15); the more words, the more vanity (Eccles. 6:11); the Lord knows that the thoughts of the wise are futile (1 Cor. 3:20); the creation was subjected to futility (Rom. 8:20).

● In vain

b If Christ is not raised, our preaching is in vain (1 Cor. 15:14); if righteousness is by the law, then Christ died in vain (Gal. 2:21); your faith is in vain (1 Cor. 15:17); lest the cross of Christ should be made void (1 Cor. 1:17); in vain do they worship me (Matt. 15:9; Mark 7:7); if anyone does not bridle his tongue his religion is vain (Jas. 1:26); in vain I have kept my heart pure (Ps. 73:13).

c Egypt's help is worthless (Isa. 30:7); lest our labour should be in vain (1 Thess. 3:5); they will not labour in vain (Isa. 65:23); for fear I was running in vain (Gal. 2:2); I may have laboured over you in vain (Gal. 4:11); I have laboured in vain (Isa. 49:4).

d Did you suffer so much in vain? (Gal. 3:4); I did not run in vain or labour in vain (Phil. 2:16); I box, not as one beating the air (1 Cor. 9:26); your labour is not in vain in the Lord (1 Cor. 15:58); our coming to you was not in vain (1 Thess. 2:1); do not receive the grace of God in vain (2 Cor. 6:1).

● Useless
things

e Not all things are profitable (1 Cor. 6:12; 10:23); tasteless salt is good for nothing (Matt. 5:13; Luke 14:34–5); tares among the wheat (Matt. 13:25–30, 36–42); controversies are unprofitable (Titus 3:9); do not turn aside after futile, profitless things (1 Sam. 12:21); bring no more useless offerings (Isa. 1:13).

f Cities called Cabul—as good as nothing (1 Kgs. 9:13); the waistcloth was worthless (Jer. 13:7); that we may sell the refuse of the wheat (Amos 8:6).

g Silver was not esteemed in Solomon's day (1 Kgs. 10:21; 2 Chr. 9:20); take away dross from silver (Prov. 25:4); your silver has become dross (Isa. 1:22); reject silver (Jer. 6:30).

h An idol is nothing in the world (1 Cor. 8:4); you are nothing (Isa. 41:24).

i For Christ I count all things as dung (Phil. 3:8); his house made a refuse heap (Ezra 6:11); there is much rubbish (Neh. 4:10).
Dung, see **302***f;* **light as chaff**, see **323***d;* **dung for fuel**, see **385***f;* **weapons are useless**, see **723***r.*

- Useless
  people

j We have become the scum of the earth (1 Cor. 4:13); you have made us offscouring and refuse (Lam. 3:45); the house of Israel has become dross to me (Ezek. 22:18–19); formerly Onesimus was useless to you (Philem. 11).

k Gentiles walk in the futility of their minds (Eph. 4:17); they are worthless for any good deed (Titus 1:16); they went after worthless things and became worthless (Jer. 2:5); they twisted like a deceitful bow (Ps. 78:57); the tares are the sons of the evil one (Matt. 13:38).

642 Good policy
Utility, see **640**.

643 Inexpedience
Harmful, see **645**.

644 Goodness

- God is good

a No one is good except God (Matt. 19:17; Mark 10:18; Luke 18:19); taste and see that the Lord is good (Ps. 34:8); the Lord is good (Ps. 100:5; 135:3; Nahum 1:7); he is good (Ps. 136:1); I will make my goodness pass before you (Exod. 33:19); how great is your goodness! (Ps. 31:19).

- God does
  good

b God saw that what he had made was good (Gen. 1:4, 10, 12, 18, 21, 25); it was very good (Gen. 1:31).

c The Lord has promised good to Israel (Num. 10:29); I have purposed to do good to Jerusalem and Judah (Zech. 8:15); I am bringing on them all the good I promised (Jer. 32:42); God is good to Israel (Ps. 73:1); you are good and do good (Ps. 119:68); the Lord is good to all (Ps. 145:9); God sends sun and rain on all (Matt. 5:45); do good, Lord, to those who are good (Ps. 125:4); I will repent of the good I intended (Jer. 18:10); my words do good to him who walks uprightly (Mic. 2:7); in all things God works for good to those who love him (Rom. 8:28); you meant evil but God meant it for good (Gen. 50:20); no good thing does he withhold from them who walk uprightly (Ps. 84:11); surely goodness and mercy shall follow me (Ps. 23:6); apart from you I have no good thing (Ps. 16:2); he has done all things well (Mark 7:37).

- Doing good

d Do good! (Ps. 37:3, 27); Jesus went about doing good (Acts 10:38); Mordecai worked for the good of his people (Esther 10:3); do not withhold good from those to whom it is due (Prov. 3:27); do good to your enemies (Luke 6:35); let us do good to all men (Gal. 6:10); he who does good is of God (3 John 11); she has done a good thing to me (Matt. 26:10); Dorcas was always doing good (Acts 9:36); the good wife does her husband good (Prov. 31:12).

e Do good to those who hate you (Luke 6:27); even sinners so good to those who do good to them (Luke 6:33); is it lawful on the sabbath to do good or to harm? (Luke 6:9).

- Good fruit

f The fruit of the Spirit is goodness (Gal. 5:22); a good tree bears good fruit (Matt. 7:17); a good tree does not bear bad fruit nor vice versa (Matt. 7:18; Luke 6:43); make the tree good and its fruit good (Matt. 12:33).

g Did you not sow good seed? (Matt. 13:27); the good seed are the sons of the kingdom (Matt. 13:38)

- Good people

h Your daughter-in-law is better than seven sons (Ruth 4:15); am I not better to you than ten sons? (1 Sam. 1:8); good teacher (Mark 10:17).

- Good things

i An exceedingly good land (Num. 14:7); my life was precious in your eyes (1 Sam. 26:21); may my life be valued in the Lord's eyes (1 Sam. 26:24); a basket of good figs (Jer. 24:2, 5); it is good for us to be here (Matt. 17:4; Mark 9:5); the old is good (Luke 5:39).

j Prophesy good like all the other prophets (1 Kgs. 22:13; 2 Chr. 18:12); if you utter what is precious rather than what is worthless (Jer. 15:19).

- Nothing good

k Nothing good dwells in me (Rom. 7:18); how can you do good who are accustomed to do evil? (Jer. 13:23).

645 Badness

- Not good

a It is not good for the man to be alone (Gen. 2:18); Ahithophel's advice is not good (2 Sam. 17:7).

- Calamity

b I will raise up evil from your own household (2 Sam. 12:11); the Lord brought evil on Absalom (2 Sam. 17:14); I will bring evil in his son's days (1 Kgs. 21:29); this evil is from the Lord (2 Kgs. 6:33); I am bringing evil on this place (2 Kgs. 22:16; 2 Chr. 34:24); I brought all this evil on this place (Jer. 32:42); I will set my eyes against them for evil and not for good (Amos 9:4); I purposed to do evil to you (Zech. 8:14).

c Shall we accept good from God and not accept evil? (Job 2:10); Job expected good but evil came (Job 30:26); God causes peace and creates calamity (Isa. 45:7); does evil befall a city and the Lord has not done it? (Amos 3:6).

- Bad things

d A basket of very bad figs (Jer. 24:2, 8; 29:17); a bad tree produces bad fruit (Matt. 7:17); a good tree does not produce bad fruit nor vice versa (Matt. 7:18); make the tree bad and its fruit bad (Matt. 12:33).

e Micaiah only prophesies evil (1 Kgs. 22:8, 18; 2 Chr. 18:7, 17).

- Doing harm

f The Egyptians ill-treated us (Num. 20:15); Alexander the coppersmith did me much harm (2 Tim. 4:14); he has returned evil for good (1 Sam. 25:21).

g Afraid David would do himself harm (2 Sam. 12:18).

h I have not harmed them (Num. 16:15); nothing will harm you (Luke 10:19); love does no wrong to anyone (Rom. 13:10).

Stones for harming, see **344k**.

● No evil

i No evil will befall you (Ps. 91:10); they will not hurt or destroy in my holy mountain (Isa. 11:9; 65:25).

646 Perfection

● God is
perfect

a Your heavenly Father is perfect (Matt. 5:48); the law of the Lord is perfect (Ps. 19:7); God's way is perfect (2 Sam. 22:31; Ps. 18:30); his work is perfect (Deut. 32:4); with those who are complete you show yourself complete (2 Sam. 22:26; Ps. 18:25).

● Christ made
perfect

b The author of salvation was made perfect through suffering (Heb. 2:10); having been made perfect (Heb. 5:9); a Son, made perfect for ever (Heb. 7:28).

● Perfect
sacrifices

c The animals for sacrifice must be without defect (Exod. 12:5; Lev. 9:2, 3; 14:10; 22:19–25; Num. 28:19, 31; 29:2, 8, 13, 17, 20, 23, 26, 29, 32, 36); male or female without defect (Lev. 3:1, 6); female without defect (Lev. 4:28, 32; Num. 6:14; 19:2); male without defect (Lev. 1:3, 10; 4:23; 23:12, 18; Num. 6:14; 28:3, 9); a bull without defect (Lev. 4:3); a ram without defect (Lev. 5:15, 18; 6:6; Num. 6:14); as of a lamb without blemish (1 Pet. 1:19); he offered himself without blemish to God (Heb. 9:14).

● Being made
perfect

d God makes my way perfect (Ps. 18:32); the spirits of just men made perfect (Heb. 12:23); without us they should not be made perfect (Heb. 11:40); if you want to be perfect (Matt. 19:21); be perfect as your heavenly Father is (Matt. 5:48); that you may be perfect (Jas. 1:4); not that I am already perfect (Phil. 3:12); when the perfect comes the imperfect disappears (1 Cor. 13:10); by one offering he has perfected those who are sanctified (Heb. 10:14); presenting the church without spot or blemish (Eph. 5:27).

e The king of Tyre had the seal of perfection (Ezek. 28:12); perfect in beauty (Ezek. 27:3, 4, 11; 28:12); there was no defect in Absalom (2 Sam. 14:25); Nebuchadnezzar sought youths without a defect (Dan. 1:4); there is no blemish in you (S. of S. 4:7); if anyone does not make a mistake in speech he is perfect (Jas. 3:2).

Perfection limited, see **647c**.

647 Imperfection

● Blemished
creatures

a Jacob took every speckled and spotted animal (Gen. 30:32–3, 39–40; 31:8–12); an animal with a blemish or defect was not to be sacrificed (Lev. 22:20–5; Deut. 15:21; 17:1); cursed be he who offers a blemished animal (Mal. 1:14).

● Blemished
people

b No one with a defect could act as priest (Lev. 21:17–21); his appearance was marred (Isa. 52:14); gifts are offered which cannot make the conscience perfect (Heb. 9:9).

● Perfection
limited

c There is a limit to all perfection (Ps. 119:96); the law made nothing perfect (Heb. 7:19); the law cannot perfect those who draw near (Heb. 10:1).

648 Cleanness

● Washing
face

a Joseph washed his face (Gen. 43:31); Ruth washed and anointed herself (Ruth 3:3); as did David (2 Sam. 12:20); when you fast, anoint your head and wash your face (Matt. 6:17).

● Washing
hands

b The elders shall wash their hands (Deut. 21:6); Pilate washed his hands (Matt. 27:24).

c Moses, Aaron and sons washed hands and feet (Exod. 30:19–21; 40:31–2); wash your hands and purify your hearts (Jas. 4:8); he who has clean hands and a pure heart (Ps. 24:4); though I wash my hands with snow and lye (Job 9:30); though you wash with lye and use much soap (Jer. 2:22).

d The disciples did not wash before they ate (Matt. 15:2; Mark 7:2–5); Jesus did not wash before he ate (Luke 11:38).

● Washing
feet

e Water to wash their feet (Gen. 24:32); Joseph's brothers washed their feet (Gen. 43:24); as did the Levite and his concubine (Judg. 19:21); Abraham offered to have the men's feet washed (Gen. 18:4); Lot offered to have the men wash their own feet (Gen. 19:2); the woman washed Jesus' feet with her tears (Luke 7:38, 44); Jesus washed the disciples' feet (John 13:5–10, 14); an enrolled widow should have washed the saints' feet (1 Tim. 5:10); I am a maid to wash your feet (1 Sam. 25:41); go home and wash your feet (2 Sam. 11:8); I had washed my feet (S. of S. 5:3).

● Bathing

f Pharaoh's daughter went to bathe in the Nile (Exod. 2:5); David saw Bathsheba bathing (2 Sam. 11:2); I bathed you (Ezek. 16:9); he who has bathed only needs to wash his feet (John 13:10); the jailer washed their wounds (Acts 16:33).

g The high priest had to bathe (Lev. 16:4, 24); helpers bathing (Lev. 16:26, 28); bathing for ritual cleansing (Lev. 15:5, 6, 7, 10, 11, 13, 16, 18, 21, 22, 27; 17:15–16; 22:6; Num. 19:7, 8, 19).

h Naaman washed himself in Jordan seven times (2 Kgs. 5:10, 14); wash in the pool of Siloam (John 9:7, 11, 15).

● Shaving

i The Nazirite must shave off his hair at his dedication (Num. 6:18–19); or after defilement (Num. 6:9); Levites must shave their whole bodies (Num. 8:7); shaving heads on completion of a vow (Acts 21:24); a cleansed leper must shave (Lev. 14:8, 9); the woman must shave her head and pare her nails (Deut. 21:12).

j Joseph shaved (Gen. 41:14); Samson's hair was shaved off (Judg. 16:19); half of each man's beard was shaved off (2 Sam. 10:4; 1 Chr. 19:4); the king of Assyria will be the razor to shave your head and legs (Isa. 7:20); Ezekiel had to shave off his hair and beard (Ezek. 5:1); Job shaved his head (Job 1:20).

k Priests must not shave their heads (Lev. 21:5; Ezek. 44:20); the

Nazirite must not shave (Num. 6:5; Judg. 13:5; 16:17); Samuel's head would not be shaved (1 Sam. 1:11); do not shave your forehead (Deut. 14:1).

● Clean clothes

l The people had to wash their clothes (Exod. 19:10, 14); as had the Levites (Num. 8:7); wash clothes splashed with blood (Lev. 6:27); washing clothes for ritual cleansing (Lev. 11:25, 28, 40; 13:6, 34; 14:8; 15:5–8, 10–11, 13, 22, 27; 16:28; 17:15; Num. 8:21; 19:7, 8, 10, 19, 21; 31:24); he washes his garments in wine (Gen. 49:11).

m Jacob told his household to purify themselves and change their clothes (Gen. 35:2); Joseph changed his clothes (Gen. 41:14); David changed his clothes (2 Sam. 12:20).

n You have a few who have not soiled their clothes (Rev. 3:4).

o He is like fuller's soap (Mal. 3:2); clothes whiter than any laundryman could whiten them (Mark 9:3).

p The heavens and the earth will wear out and be changed like a garment (Ps. 102:25–6; Heb. 1:10–12).

● Ritual cleanliness

q According to the law, all things are cleansed with blood (Heb. 9:22).

r What God has cleansed, do not call common (Acts 10:15; 11:9); no man should be called common or unclean (Acts 10:28); nothing is unclean of itself (Rom. 14:14); all things are clean (Rom. 14:20); Jesus declared all foods clean (Mark 7:19); give what is within for alms and all is clean (Luke 11:41); cleansing their hearts by faith (Acts 15:9).

● Cleansing things

s A clean place outside the camp (Lev. 4:12); the temple was purified (2 Chr. 29:15); washing parts of the sacrifice (Exod. 29:17; Lev. 1:9, 13; 8:21; 9:14); where the burnt offering was to be washed (Ezek. 40:38); scouring and rinsing bronze vessels (Lev. 6:28); cleansing of utensils (Matt. 23:25; Mark 7:4; Luke 11:39–41); a sacrifice to cleanse the leprous house (Lev. 14:49); they washed the chariot (1 Kgs. 22:38); they cleansed the rooms Tobiah had had (Neh. 13:9).

t I will wipe Jerusalem like a dish (2 Kgs. 21:13); fishermen washing their nets (Luke 5:2).

● Means of purifying

u A bronze laver for washing (Exod. 30:18; 31:9; 38:8; 39:39; 40:7); the laver anointed (Exod. 30:28; 40:11); the laver set up (Exod. 40:30); ten basins for washing (1 Kgs. 7:38, 43; 2 Chr. 4:6, 14); Ahaz removed the lavers from the stands (2 Kgs. 16:17); six stone jars for purification (John 2:6); John's disciples argued with a Jew over purification (John 3:25).

v Moab is my washbasin (Ps. 60:8; 108:9).

The 'sea', see **343*p***; **purifying by fire**, see **381*n***.

● Cleansing people

w Priest pronouncing a person clean (Lev. 13:6, 13, 17, 23, 28, 34, 37); cleansing from bodily discharges (Lev. 15:5–30); instructions about washings (Heb. 6:2).

x Moses to wash Aaron and his sons (Exod. 29:4; 40:12; Lev. 8:6);

the priests and Levites purified themselves (Ezra 6:20; Neh. 12:30); the Levites had to purify themselves (Neh. 13:22); the Levites were cleansed (Num. 8:6); he will purify the sons of Levi (Mal. 3:3); purify yourself with the four men (Acts 21:24).

● Cleansing lepers

y Cleansing a leper (Lev. 14:2–32); his leprosy was cleansed (Matt. 8:3); cleanse the lepers (Matt. 10:8); lepers are cleansed (Matt. 11:5).

● Clean animals

z Lists of clean and unclean animals (Lev. 11:2–47; Deut. 14:3–21); chewing the cud a criterion for clean animals (Lev. 11:3); seven pairs of every clean animal (Gen. 7:2, 8); clean animals sacrificed (Gen. 8:20).

● Cleansing of sin

aa Wash me from my sin (Ps. 51:2); cleanse me with hyssop and I shall be clean (Ps. 51:7); the Lord will wash away the filth of the daughters of Zion (Isa. 4:4); I will sprinkle clean water on you and you will be clean (Ezek. 36:25).

ab The day of atonement to cleanse from sin (Lev. 16:30); the Levites purified themselves from sin (Num. 8:21); purifying after war- fare (Num. 31:19–24); a fountain will be opened to cleanse sin (Zech. 13:1); the blood of Christ cleanses our consciences (Heb. 9:14); the blood of Jesus purifies us from all sin (1 John 1:7); they have washed their robes in the blood of the Lamb (Rev. 7:14).

ac The washing of regeneration (Titus 3:5); our hearts sprinkled from an evil conscience and our bodies washed with pure water (Heb. 10:22); you are clean through the word I have spoken (John 15:3); you were washed, you were sanctified (1 Cor. 6:11); Christ cleansed the church by the washing of water with the word (Eph. 5:26).

Atonement, see **941**.

● Be clean from sin

ad Wash yourselves (Isa. 1:16); wash your heart from evil (Jer. 4:14); be baptized and wash away your sins (Acts 22:16); let us cleanse ourselves from every defilement of flesh and spirit (2 Cor. 7:1); if a man cleanses himself from these things he will be a vessel for honour (2 Tim. 2:21); blessed are those who wash their robes (Rev. 22:14); everyone who has this hope in him purifies himself (1 John 3:3); true religion is to keep yourself unspotted from the world (Jas. 1:27).

● Sieving

ae He will shake the nations in a sieve (Isa. 30:28); I will shake Jacob as in a sieve (Amos 9:9); Satan has demanded to have you all to sieve you like wheat (Luke 22:31).

649 Uncleanness

● Making unclean

a He defiled my sanctuary (Lev. 20:3; Num. 19:13); they have defiled your holy temple (Ps. 79:1); he has defiled this holy place (Acts 21:28); he who regards the blood of the covenant as unclean (Heb. 10:29).

b Jerusalem sinned and so became unclean (Lam. 1:8); Jerusalem has become an unclean thing (Lam. 1:17); they became unclean by their deeds (Ps. 106:39); what comes out of a man makes him unclean (Matt. 15:11; Mark 7:15, 20–3); put aside all filthiness (Jas. 1:21).

c Do not pollute the land by bloodshed (Num. 35:33); the earth is polluted by its inhabitants (Isa. 24:5); the land became defiled (Lev. 18:27).

d These dreamers defile the flesh (Jude 8); to eat with unclean hands does not defile anyone (Matt. 15:20).

- **Touching the unclean**

e Do not touch what is unclean (2 Cor. 6:17); if any one touches what is unclean he becomes unclean (Lev. 5:2); unclean through having killed in war (Num. 31:19).

f Becoming unclean by touching: human uncleanness (Lev. 5:3); a dead body (Num. 19:11; 31:19); unclean animals (Lev. 11:24–8, 31–8); the carcass of a clean animal which dies (Lev. 11:39; 17:15).

g Do not eat anything unclean (Judg. 13:4, 7, 14).

- **Unclean people**

h A woman who gives birth is unclean (Lev. 12:2–5); a leper is unclean (Lev. 13:3, 44–5); discharges from the body make people unclean (Lev. 15:2–33); an unclean person touching food defiles it (Hag. 2:13); the disciples ate food with unclean hands (Mark 7:2).

i I am a man of unclean lips (Isa. 6:5); at the New Moon David must be unclean (1 Sam. 20:26); we have all become like one unclean (Isa. 64:6); how long will you be unclean? (Jer. 13:27).

- **Uncleanness not allowed**

j A priest must not become unclean except for a close relative (Lev. 21:1); and the high priest not at all (Lev. 21:11); a priest must not serve whilst unclean (Lev. 22:3); no unclean priest may eat of the offerings (Lev. 22:4–6); I have not removed the tithe whilst unclean (Deut. 26:14); a Nazirite must not become unclean (Num. 6:6–7).

- **Restrictions on the unclean**

k Anyone unclean must be sent out of the camp (Num. 5:2; Deut. 23:10); a priest pronouncing the leper unclean (Lev. 13:8, 11, 15, 20, 22, 25, 27, 30, 44); the leper must shout, 'Unclean!' (Lev. 13:45); priest and prophet shouted, 'Unclean!' (Lam. 4:15).

l If any one is unclean he must eat the Passover on another day (Num. 9:6–10); Hezekiah prayed for those who were unclean yet ate the Passover (2 Chr. 30:19); the Jews did not want to be unclean and unable to eat the Passover (John 18:28).

- **Unclean animals**

m Clean and unclean: land animals (Lev. 11:2–8; Deut. 14:4–8); fish (Lev. 11:9–12; Deut. 14:9–10); birds (Lev. 11:13–19; Deut. 14:11–20); insects (Lev. 11:20–3; Deut. 14:19); reptiles and rodents (Lev. 11:29–31).

n Two of every unclean animal (Gen. 7:2, 9); valuation of unclean animals (Lev. 27:11–12); redeeming unclean animals (Lev. 27:27); Peter had never eaten anything unclean (Acts 10:14–15;

11:8–9); meat touching anything unclean must not be eaten (Lev. 7:19); you offered defiled food on my altar (Mal. 1:7).

● Unclean
things

o A garment with leprosy is unclean (Lev. 13:51); as is a leprous house (Lev. 14:36); if your land is unclean (Josh. 22:19); the land you are entering is an unclean land (Ezra 9:11).

p Mephibosheth had not washed his clothes (2 Sam. 19:24).

q Who can bring a clean thing from an unclean? (Job 14:4); a sow after washing returns to the mud (2 Pet. 2:22).

650 Health

● Health
promoted

a The Lord will remove sickness from you (Exod. 23:25; Deut. 7:15); I will not give you any of the Egyptians' diseases (Exod. 15:26; Deut. 7:15); no one will say they are sick (Isa. 33:24).

● Health
achieved

b Faith has given him this wholeness (Acts 3:16); my words are health to all their body (Prov. 4:22).

c I pray you may be in good health (3 John 2); those who are well do not need a doctor (Matt. 9:12; Mark 2:17; Luke 5:31).

651 Ill health. Disease

● Illness

a There is no health in me because of my sin (Ps. 38:3–8); if God's people disobey he will bring on them diseases (Lev. 26:16; Deut. 28:21–2, 27, 35, 59–61; 29:22; 32:24); this is why many of you are weak and ill (1 Cor. 11:30); from head to toe the whole body is sick (Isa. 1:5–6); they will die of deadly diseases (Jer. 16:4).

b If anyone is ill he should call for the elders of the church (Jas. 5:14); the Lord sustains him on his sickbed (Ps. 41:3); I was sick and you visited me (Matt. 25:36); I was sick and you did not visit me (Matt. 25:43); when did we see you sick? (Matt. 25:39, 44); he carried our sicknesses (Isa. 53:4; Matt. 8:17).

c This sickness is so that the Son of God may be glorified (John 11:4); that the works of God might be shown in the blind man (John 9:3).

● Particular
diseases

d The plague of boils (Exod. 9:9); Job had painful sores (Job 2:7); those with the mark of the beast had painful sores (Rev. 16:2); my flesh is clothed with maggots and scabs (Job 7:5).

e The Lord struck the Philistines with tumours (1 Sam. 5:6, 9, 12); five golden tumours (1 Sam. 6:4–5, 11, 17); lest God bring pestilence (Exod. 5:3); pestilence on livestock (Exod. 9:1–7).

f He gave them what they asked but sent a wasting disease (Ps. 106:15); God will send a wasting disease among his warriors (Isa. 10:16); their talk will spread like gangrene (2 Tim. 2:17).

● People who
were ill

g Joseph heard that his father was ill (Gen. 48:1); Michal said David was ill (1 Sam. 19:14); Nabal's heart was like a stone within him (1 Sam. 25:37); the Egyptian fell ill (1 Sam. 30:13); the Lord struck Bathsheba's child with an illness (2 Sam. 12:15); Elisha had the illness from which he died (2 Kgs. 13:14); Daniel was ill for several days (Dan. 8:27).

h Those who fell ill: Abijah (1 Kgs. 14:1); the son of the woman of Zarephath (1 Kgs. 17:17); Benhadad king of Aram (2 Kgs. 8:7); Hezekiah (2 Kgs. 20:1; 2 Chr. 32:24; Isa. 38:1); Lazarus, but not to death (John 11:1–4).

i Paul left Trophimus ill at Miletus (2 Tim. 4:20); Epaphroditus had been sick, near to death (Phil. 2:26–7); Timothy's frequent ailments (1 Tim. 5:23); Paul first preached the gospel to the Galatians through illness (Gal. 4:13).

j They brought to him all who were sick (Matt. 4:24; Mark 6:55); many invalids at the pool of Bethesda (John 5:3); they carried the sick out into the streets (Acts 5:15).

● People with specified ailments

k The Lord struck Jehoram with a disease of his bowels (2 Chr. 21:15, 18); a woman bled for twelve years (Mark 5:25; Luke 8:43); Peter's mother-in-law had fever (Matt. 8:14; Mark 1:30; Luke 4:38); a man with dropsy (Luke 14:2); Publius' father had fever and dysentery (Acts 28:8).

l The centurion's servant was paralyzed (Matt. 8:6); a paralytic (Matt. 9:2; Mark 2:3; Luke 5:18); Aeneas was paralyzed (Acts 9:33); Asa was diseased in his feet (1 Kgs. 15:23; 2 Chr. 16:12); a lame man at Lystra (Acts 14:8); my son is moon-struck [epileptic] (Matt. 17:15); a leper (Matt. 8:2; Mark 1:40); Simon the leper (Matt. 26:6; Mark 14:3).

● Leprosy

m Instructions over leprosy (Lev. 13:2–59; 14:2–57; Num. 5:2; Deut. 24:8); priests with leprosy may not each of the offerings (Lev. 22:4).

n Naaman was a leper (2 Kgs. 5:1); Naaman's leprosy was on Gehazi (2 Kgs. 5:27); there were many lepers in Israel (Luke 4:27); four men with leprosy (2 Kgs. 7:3); Uzziah was leprous (2 Kgs. 15:5; 2 Chr. 26:19–21); Jesus with a leper (Matt. 8:2; Luke 5:12); the ten lepers (Luke 17:12); Moses' hand was leprous (Exod. 4:6); Miriam was leprous (Num. 12:10; Deut. 24:9).

o May Joab's house never be without a leper (2 Sam. 3:29).

p A garment with leprosy (Lev. 13:47–58).

652 Salubrity
See **650**.

653 Insalubrity
See **651**.

654 Improvement

● People improved

a Trying to refine the people like silver (Jer. 6:29–30); I will smelt away your dross (Isa. 1:25); I will refine and assay them (Jer. 9:7); I have refined you but not like silver (Isa. 48:10); he will refine the sons of Levi (Mal. 3:3).

● Things
improved

b He enquired the hour when his son began to get better (John 4:52); that all may see your progress (1 Tim. 4:15).

c The Lord's words are like silver refined seven times (Ps. 12:6); your word is well refined (Ps. 119:140).

d Felix carried out reforms (Acts 24:2).

e The last deeds are more than the first (Rev. 2:19).

655 Deterioration

● From bad
to worse

a The last state is worse than the first (Matt. 12:45; Luke 11:26; 2 Pet. 2:20); evil men will go from bad to worse (2 Tim. 3:13); the woman was no better but rather worse (Mark 5:26); the last deception will be worse than the first (Matt. 27:64).

b The people have corrupted themselves (Exod. 32:7); you have fallen from grace (Gal. 5:4).

● Things
wearing
out

c Moth and rust destroy (Matt. 6:19); during forty years in the desert your clothes did not wear out (Deut. 8:4; 29:5; Neh. 9:21); the Gibeonites wore worn-out clothes (Josh. 9:4–5, 13); water wears away stones (Job 14:19).

d The heavens and earth will wear out like a garment (Ps. 102:26; Isa. 51:6).

Rot, see **51***b*.

● People
wearing
out

e They will all wear out and be moth-eaten like a garment (Isa. 50:9); the moth will eat them like a garment (Isa. 51:8); you will wear yourself out (Exod. 18:18).

● Wounds

f The law on injuries (Exod. 21:12–27); these wounds I received in the house of my friends (Zech. 13:6); your wound is incurable (Jer. 30:12; Nahum 3:19); my wound is incurable (Jer. 10:19).

g God wounds but he binds up (Job 5:18); God wounds me without cause (Job 9:17); strike all he has (Job 1:11); strike his flesh and bones (Job 2:5); blows that wound cleanse away evil (Prov. 20:30); faithful are the wounds of a friend (Prov. 27:6); by his wounds you were healed (1 Pet. 2:24).

h He was wounded for our transgressions (Isa. 53:5); he will bruise your head and you will bruise his heel (Gen. 3:15); a fatal wound which was healed (Rev. 13:3, 12).

● People
wounded

i Lamech killed a man for wounding him (Gen. 4:23); Gideon promised to tear their flesh with briers (Judg. 8:7); a woman dropped a millstone on Abimelech's head (Judg. 9:53); they gouged out Samson's eyes (Judg. 16:21); Nahash wanted to gouge out every right eye (1 Sam. 11:2); the king of Israel was wounded (1 Kgs. 22:34; 2 Chr. 18:33); Ahaziah fell through the lattice and injured himself (2 Kgs. 1:2); Joram was wounded (2 Kgs. 8:28; 2 Chr. 22:5); Ahaziah was wounded (2 Kgs. 9:27); Peter cut off the slave's ear (Matt. 26:51; Mark 14:47; Luke 22:50; John 18:10); the horses' tails wounded like snakes (Rev. 9:19).

j A prophet asked another to wound him (1 Kgs. 20:35–7); the man cut himself with stones (Mark 5:5); they fled naked and wounded (Acts 19:16).

● Piercing   *k* Pierce his ear with an awl (Exod. 21:6; Deut. 15:17); Phinehas transfixed the man and woman with a spear (Num. 25:8); Saul was wounded by the archers (1 Sam. 31:3; 1 Chr. 10:3); Joab pierced Absalom (2 Sam. 18:14); archers wounded Josiah (2 Chr. 35:23); a staff of crushed reed will pierce your hand (2 Kgs. 18:21); through love of money some have pierced themselves (1 Tim. 6:10).

l They pierced my hands and feet (Ps. 22:16); they will look on him they pierced (Zech. 12:10; John 19:37); those who pierced him (Rev. 1:7); a soldier pierced his side (John 19:34); he showed them his hands and his side (John 20:20).

m I bear in my body the marks of Jesus (Gal. 6:17).

● Lameness   *n* Jacob's hip was wrenched (Gen. 32:25); Jacob limped (Gen. 32:31); that the lame joint may not be dislocated (Heb. 12:13); Mephibosheth was lame in both feet (2 Sam. 4:4; 9:3, 13); I am lame (2 Sam. 19:26); a man lame from birth (Acts 3:2); it is better to enter life lame or crippled (Matt. 18:8); invite the lame (Luke 14:13, 21).

o Lame men could not serve as priests (Lev. 21:18–19); the blind and the lame could defend Jerusalem (2 Sam. 5:6, 8).

p David hamstrung chariot horses (2 Sam. 8:4; 1 Chr. 18:4); hamstring their horses (Josh. 11:6, 9).

q I was feet to the lame (Job 29:15); the lame will leap like a deer (Isa. 35:6); the lame walk (Matt. 11:5); the lame came to him and he healed them (Matt. 15:30–1; 21:14); the lame man healed (Acts 3:2–10).

656 Restoration

● Resurrection   *a* Instruction about the resurrection of the dead (Heb. 6:2); they proclaimed in Jesus the resurrection of the dead (Acts 4:2); Paul was preaching 'Jesus' and 'Resurrection' (Acts 17:18); by a man came resurrection (1 Cor. 15:21); in the resurrection they are children of the resurrection (Luke 20:35–6).

● Are the dead raised?   *b* They discussed what rising from the dead meant (Mark 9:10); the Sadducees say there is no resurrection (Matt. 22:23; Mark 12:18; Luke 20:27; Acts 23:8); if a man dies, will he live again? (Job 14:14); a tree cut down will sprout again (Job 14:7–9); can these bones live? (Ezek. 37:3); why should it be thought incredible that God raises the dead? (Acts 26:8); when they heard of the resurrection of the dead, some mocked (Acts 17:32); if there is no resurrection then Christ has not been raised (1 Cor. 15:13, 16).

● The dead are raised   *c* Abraham reckoned that God could raise the dead (Heb. 11:19); your dead will live (Isa. 26:19); Moses showed that the dead are raised (Luke 20:37); we trust in God who raises the dead (2 Cor.

1:9); God gives life to the dead (Rom. 4:17); you will not abandon me to Sheol (Ps. 16:10); as a Pharisee, Paul is on trial concerning the resurrection of the dead (Acts 23:6; 24:21); I hope in God that there will be a resurrection of both righteous and wicked (Acts 24:15); this is the first resurrection (Rev. 20:5); the sea, death and Hades gave up the dead in them (Rev. 20:13).

d   Some said the resurrection has already happened (2 Tim. 2:18).

- Resurrection of Christ

e   Moses said that Christ would suffer and be the first to rise (Acts 26:23); Christ had to suffer and rise again (Acts 17:3); David spoke of the resurrection of Christ (Acts 2:31); on the third day he would be raised (Matt. 16:21; 17:23; 20:19; 27:63; Mark 8:31; 9:31; 10:34; Luke 9:22; 18:33; 24:46); tell no one until he is risen from the dead (Matt. 17:9; Mark 9:9); they did not yet understand the scripture that he must rise (John 20:9); after I have risen I will go into Galilee (Matt. 26:32; Mark 14:28).

- Christ is risen

f   He has risen (Matt. 28:6–7; Mark 16:6; Luke 24:6); the Lord has risen indeed! (Luke 24:34); Jesus Christ, risen from the dead (2 Tim. 2:8); Christ has risen, the firstfruits of those who slept (1 Cor. 15:20); the firstborn of the dead (Rev. 1:5); who died and came to life (Rev. 2:8).

g   God raised him from the dead (Acts 2:24, 32; 3:15, 26; 4:10; 5:30; 10:40; 13:30, 34; Rom. 4:24; 6:4; 1 Cor. 15:12–21; 2 Cor. 4:14; Gal. 1:1; 1 Pet. 1:21); his Son whom he raised from the dead (1 Thess. 1:10); God brought from the dead the great Shepherd (Heb. 13:20); God fulfilled the promise in raising Jesus (Acts 13:33); there is no need to bring Christ up from the dead (Rom. 10:7); Christ Jesus died and was raised (Rom. 8:34); he was raised on the third day (1 Cor. 15:4).

h   Declared the Son of God by his resurrection (Rom. 1:4); God bore witness to him by raising him from the dead (Acts 17:31); I was dead and now I am alive for evermore (Rev. 1:18); with power the apostles bore witness to his resurrection (Acts 4:33).

- His resurrection for us

i   God works in us with the power which raised Christ from the dead (Eph. 1:20); that I may know the power of his resurrection (Phil. 3:10); you were raised with him in baptism by faith in God who raised him (Col. 2:12); born again through the resurrection of Christ (1 Pet. 1:3); he was raised for our justification (Rom. 4:25); he died and rose again for them (2 Cor. 5:15); if you believe God raised him you will be saved (Rom. 10:9).

- Our resurrection

j   We have been raised with Christ (Col. 3:1); he raised us up with Christ (Eph. 2:6); arise from the dead and Christ will shine on you (Eph. 5:14); he will also raise us with Jesus (2 Cor. 4:14); he who raised Christ from the dead will give life to your mortal bodies (Rom. 8:11); God raised Christ and will raise us also (1 Cor. 6:14); we will be united with him in his resurrection (Rom. 6:5); as Jesus died and rose, so God will bring those who have fallen asleep (1 Thess. 4:14).

k Lazarus will rise in the resurrection (John 11:24); I will raise him up at the last day (John 6:40, 44, 54); all in the tombs will hear his voice and come forth (John 5:28–9); many will awake, some to eternal life, others to eternal contempt (Dan. 12:2); the resurrection of the just (Luke 14:14); those who sleep in the dust of the earth will awake (Dan. 12:2); I am the resurrection and the life (John 11:25); as the Father raises the dead, so the Son gives life (John 5:21, 25); the dead in Christ will rise first (1 Thess. 4:16); that I may attain the resurrection from the dead (Phil. 3:11).

l How are the dead raised? (1 Cor. 15:35); the dead will be raised imperishable (1 Cor. 15:52); the sons of the resurrection cannot die any more (Luke 20:36); the resurrection of life and the resurrection of judgement (John 5:29).

● People raised   m Women received their dead raised to life (Heb. 11:35); I will open your graves and bring you out (Ezek. 37:12–13); the bodies of many saints were raised to life (Matt. 27:52); this is John the Baptist risen from the dead (Matt. 14:2; Mark 6:14, 16; Luke 9:7); they will not be persuaded if someone rises from the dead (Luke 16:31); Elijah prayed and the boy revived (1 Kgs. 17:21–3); the man whose body touched Elisha's bones revived (2 Kgs. 13:21).

n Can I bring the child back to life again? (2 Sam. 12:23); the dead are raised (Matt. 11:5; Luke 7:22); raise the dead (Matt. 10:8); your brother will rise (John 11:23).

o Those who were raised: the Shunammite's son (2 Kgs. 4:33–7; 8:5); the widow of Nain's son (Luke 7:11–16); Jairus' daughter (Matt. 9:23–5; Mark 5:38–43; Luke 8:49–56); Lazarus (John 11:43–4; 12:1, 9, 17); Tabitha (Acts 9:36–42); Eutychus (Acts 20:10, 12).

p What will the acceptance of the Jews be but life from the dead? (Rom. 11:15).

q Allowed to give breath to the image of the beast (Rev. 13:15).

● God heals   r There is a time to heal (Eccles. 3:3); the Lord heals all your diseases (Ps. 103:3); I will heal you (2 Kgs. 20:5); I wound and I heal (Deut. 32:39); God wounds and heals (Job 5:18); God will strike and heal (Isa. 19:22); I will heal them (Jer. 33:6); the Lord will heal the wounds of his people (Isa. 30:26); God heals the broken-hearted (Ps. 147:3).

s I cried to you and you healed me (Ps. 30:2); he sent out his word and healed them (Ps. 107:20).

t The sun of righteousness will rise with healing in its wings (Mal. 4:2); I will heal their backsliding (Hos. 14:4); by his scourging we are healed (Isa. 53:5); their leaves are for healing (Ezek. 47:12); the leaves of the tree are for the healing of the nations (Rev. 22:2); fear of the Lord will be healing to your body (Prov. 3:8).

God healing sorrow, see **825i**.

● People
healed

u Will I recover from my illness? (2 Kgs. 1:2; 8:7–10); you will surely recover (2 Kgs. 8:10, 14).

v Abraham prayed and God healed Abimelech's household (Gen. 20:17); Moses' leprous hand was healed (Exod. 4:7); Moses prayed for God to heal Miriam (Num. 12:13); the king's hand was restored (1 Kgs. 13:6); the prophet would cure him of his leprosy (2 Kgs. 5:3); cure Naaman of his leprosy (2 Kgs. 5:6); he was clean from his leprosy (2 Kgs. 5:14); no leper was healed except Naaman (Luke 4:27); Hezekiah prayed for healing (Isa. 38:16); stay in camp until healed of circumcision (Josh. 5:8); Ahaziah went to Jezreel to recuperate (2 Chr. 22:6); Joram was convalescing in Jezreel (2 Kgs. 8:29; 9:15).

w A mortal wound which was healed (Rev. 13:3, 12).

Means of healing, see **658, blind healed**, see **439p; prayer for healing**, see **761s**.

● Jesus
healing

x Jesus healed all who were ill (Matt. 4:23–4; 8:16; 9:35; 12:15; 14:14, 36; 15:30; 19:2; 21:14; Mark 1:32–4; 3:10; Luke 4:40; 5:17; 6:18; 9:11); all who touched his cloak were healed (Mark 6:56); Jesus healed all who were oppressed by the devil (Acts 10:38); crowds came to be healed (Luke 5:15; 6:18); Jesus healed a few sick people (Mark 6:5); tell John the sick are healed (Matt. 11:5; Luke 7:21–2); he makes the deaf hear and the dumb speak (Mark 7:37); I will come and heal him (Matt. 8:7); I cast out demons and cure today and tomorrow (Luke 13:32); Jesus Christ heals you (Acts 9:34); by his wounds you were healed (1 Pet. 2:24).

y Physician, heal yourself! (Luke 4:23); come and be healed on working days (Luke 13:14); is it lawful to heal on the sabbath? (Matt. 12:10; Luke 14:3); they watched him heal on the sabbath (Mark 3:2; Luke 6:7).

● Those Jesus
healed

z Jesus healed: the leper (Matt. 8:2–3; Mark 1:40–2; Luke 5:12–14); ten lepers (Luke 17:12–19); the man with the withered hand (Matt. 12:13; Mark 3:5; Luke 6:10); the centurion's servant (Matt. 8:13; Luke 7:2–10); Peter's mother-in-law (Matt. 8:15; Mark 1:31; Luke 4:39); the ruler's daughter (Matt. 9:18, 25; Mark 5:23, 41–2; Luke 8:41, 54–5); a dumb demoniac (Matt. 9:33; Luke 11:14); a blind and dumb demoniac (Matt. 12:22); a deaf man with a speech impediment (Mark 7:32–5); the Canaanite woman's daughter (Matt. 15:28; Mark 7:30); a demoniac in the synagogue (Luke 4:35); the Gadarene demoniac (Matt. 8:28–34; Mark 5:8–20; Luke 8:29–35); the blind (Matt. 9:29–30; 20:34; Mark 8:22–6; 10:46–52; Luke 18:35–43; John 9:1–7); an invalid (John 5:8–9); the widow's son (Luke 7:14–15); a woman bent over (Luke 13:13); the woman with the flow of blood (Matt. 9:22; Mark 5:29; Luke 8:44); several women (Luke 8:2); an official's son (John 4:47–53); the paralytic (Matt. 9:2–7; Mark

2:5–12; Luke 5:18–25); the epileptic boy (Matt. 17:18; Mark 9:25–7; Luke 9:42); the man with dropsy (Luke 14:4); the slave's ear (Luke 22:51).

Cleansing lepers, see **648y**.

- Healing in the name of Jesus

aa He gave them authority to heal diseases (Matt. 10:1; Luke 9:1); the gift of healings (1 Cor. 12:9, 28, 30); they will lay hands on the sick and they will recover (Mark 16:18); the prayer of faith will heal the sick (Jas. 5:15); pray for one another that you may be healed (Jas. 5:16); he sent them out to heal (Luke 9:2); heal the sick (Matt. 10:8; Luke 10:9); stretch out your hand to heal! (Acts 4:30); those troubled with unclean spirits were cured (Luke 6:18); they preached the gospel and healed (Luke 9:6); they anointed the sick with oil and healed them (Mark 6:13); all were healed (Acts 5:16); many were healed (Acts 8:7); handkerchiefs and aprons from Paul were used to heal the sick (Acts 19:12); all the people on the island came to be cured (Acts 28:9).

ab Those who were healed: the lame man (Acts 3:1–10); blind Paul (Acts 9:17–18; 22:13); a cripple in Lystra (Acts 14:8–10); Publius' father and the rest of the sick (Acts 28:8–9).

- No healing

ac Why is there no healing for my people? (Jer. 8:22); they have healed my people superficially (Jer. 6:14; 8:11); Assyria cannot heal you (Hos. 5:13).

- Repairing

ad Repairing the altar (1 Kgs. 18:30; 2 Chr. 15:8); repairing the temple (2 Kgs. 12:5; 22:5–6; 2 Chr. 24:4, 27; 34:8); Hezekiah repaired the doors of the temple (2 Chr. 29:3); repairing the wall (2 Chr. 32:5; Neh. 3:1–32); they will repair the ruined cities (Isa. 61:4); the repairer of the breech, the restorer of streets to dwell in (Isa. 58:12); mending nets (Matt. 4:21; Mark 1:19); patching garments (Matt. 9:16; Mark 2:21; Luke 5:36).

- Restoring property

ae Abraham brought back the goods taken by the kings (Gen. 14:16); David recovered all that was taken (1 Sam. 30:18); David would restore Saul's land to Mephibosheth (2 Sam. 9:7).

- Reinstating people

af Pharaoh would restore his butler (Gen. 40:13, 21); the king did not bring back his banished son (2 Sam. 14:13); bring back Absalom (2 Sam. 14:21); if the Lord brings me back (2 Sam. 15:8); the Lord may bring me back (2 Sam. 15:25); Israel will restore my father's kingdom to me (2 Sam. 16:3); why are you silent about bringing the king back? (2 Sam. 19:10); why are you last to bring the king back? (2 Sam. 19:11–12); I will bring back all the people to you (2 Sam. 17:3); trying to restore the kingdom to Rehoboam (1 Kgs. 12:21); the Lord restored the fortunes of Job (Job 42:10); Nebuchadnezzar was re-established in his kingdom (Dan. 4:36).

- Restoring nations

ag Restore us! (Ps. 80:3, 7, 19; 85:4); revive us again (Ps. 85:6); restore our fortunes! (Ps. 14:7; 53:6; 126:4); God would restore their fortunes (Deut. 30:3; Jer. 32:44); restore to her all that was hers (2 Kgs. 8:6); the Lord will restore the splendour of Jacob

(Nahum 2:2); Elijah restores all things (Matt. 17:11; Mark 9:12); the time for the restoration of all things (Acts 3:21); will you now restore the kingdom to Israel? (Acts 1:6); restoration of Israel promised (Jer. 33:6–13).

ah I will restore the fortunes of: the Ammonites (Jer. 49:6); Elam (Jer. 49:39); Egypt (Ezek. 29:14); Israel (Hos. 6:11–7:1); Jacob (Jer. 30:18; Ezek. 39:25); Judah (Zeph. 2:7); Judah and Jerusalem (Joel 3:1; Zeph. 3:20); Moab (Jer. 48:47).

ai I will restore the captivity of: Sodom, Samaria and Jerusalem (Ezek. 16:53); of Israel (Amos 9:14).

aj The Lord will recover the remnant of his people from the lands (Isa. 11:11); I will bring them back to their inheritance (Jer. 12:15); I will restore them to their land (Jer. 16:15; 24:6; 30:3); I will hear from heaven and heal their land (2 Chr. 7:14).

ak The service of the temple was restored (2 Chr. 29:35); you restored the fortunes of Jacob (Ps. 85:1); to bring Jacob back to him (Isa. 49:5).

al Revive your work (Hab. 3:2); restore us to you that we may be restored (Lam. 5:21).

- Restoring sinners

am He will bring back many to the Lord (Luke 1:16); Jehoshaphat brought people back to the Lord (2 Chr. 19:4); restore the sinner gently (Gal. 6:1); if one wanders from the truth and someone brings him back (Jas. 5:19).

an The law of the Lord restores the soul (Ps. 19:7).
Sinners saved, see **938k**.

657 Relapse

658 Remedy

- God as doctor

a I, the Lord, am your healer (Exod. 15:26); those who are well do not need a doctor (Matt. 9:12; Mark 2:17; Luke 5:31); doctor, heal yourself! (Luke 4:23).

- Human doctors

b Asa sought help from doctors, not the Lord (2 Chr. 16:12); you are worthless physicians (Job 13:4); is there no physician in Gilead? (Jer. 8:22); the woman had suffered much from many doctors (Mark 5:26; Luke 8:43); Luke, the beloved doctor (Col. 4:14); the Hebrew midwives (Exod. 1:15).

- Medicines

c There is no medicine to cure you (Jer. 30:13); in vain you have used many medicines (Jer. 46:11).

d A poultice of figs (2 Kgs. 20:7; Isa. 38:21); flour counteracted the poisonous gourds (2 Kgs. 4:41).

e Anointing the sick with oil (Mark 6:13; Jas. 5:14); pouring oil and wine on wounds (Luke 10:34); not pressed out nor bandaged nor softened with oil (Isa. 1:6); Pharaoh's arm has not been bound with a bandage (Ezek. 30:21); making clay with saliva to put on a man's eyes (John 9:6, 11, 15); the jailer washed their wounds (Acts 16:33).

f Is there no balm in Gilead? (Jer. 8:22); go up to Gilead and get balm (Jer. 46:11); buy salve to put on your eyes (Rev. 3:18); drink a little wine for your stomach's sake (1 Tim. 5:23).

g A cheerful heart is good medicine (Prov. 17:22).

659 Bane

● Plagues

a The Lord struck Pharaoh with plagues because of Sarah (Gen. 12:17); the plagues in Egypt (Exod. 7:14–12:32); now I send all my plagues (Exod. 9:14); one plague more (Exod. 11:1); these are the gods who struck the Egyptians with plagues (1 Sam. 4:8); the plague which the Lord will send on the attackers of Jerusalem (Zech. 14:12); and a similar plague on the animals (Zech. 14:15); God struck the Israelites with a plague (Num. 11:33; 31:16; Josh. 22:17; 2 Sam. 24:15; 2 Chr. 21:14; Ps. 106:29); I send a plague on you as on Egypt (Amos 4:10); if there is pestilence (1 Kgs. 8:37; 2 Chr. 6:28; 7:13; 20:9); the plague has started (Num. 16:46); three days of plague? (2 Sam. 24:13; 1 Chr. 21:12); if I send a plague on the land (Ezek. 14:19); I will strike them with a plague (Num. 14:12); the plague was stopped (Num. 25:8; 2 Sam. 24:25); lest plague strike the Israelites (Num. 8:19).

b The seven last plagues (Rev. 15:1); her plagues will overtake her in one day (Rev. 18:8).

● Poisons and pests

c There were poisonous gourds in the stew (2 Kgs. 4:39–40); his food is changed to cobra's venom within him (Job 20:14, 16); the Lord has given us poisonous water to drink (Jer. 8:14); I will give them poisonous water to drink (Jer. 9:15; 23:15).

d A root bearing poison and wormwood (Deut. 29:18); the tongue is full of poison (Jas. 3:8); viper's poison is under their lips (Ps. 140:3; Rom. 3:13); their grapes are poisonous (Deut. 32:32–3); they have venom like a serpent (Ps. 58:4).

Snakes and scorpions, see **365o**.

e We have found this man to be a pestilence (Acts 24:5).

660 Safety

● Safety through God

a You alone make me dwell in safety (Ps. 4:8); Israel lives in security (Deut. 33:28); Judah and Israel lived in safety (1 Kgs. 4:25); the eye of God was on the Jew (Ezra 5:5); like hovering birds the Lord will protect Jerusalem (Isa. 31:5); I will set him in safety (Ps. 12:5); protect him from this generation (Ps. 12:7); guard my soul (Ps. 25:20); protect my life (Ps. 64:1); he will strengthen and protect you (2 Thess. 3:3); unless the Lord guards the city the watchman keeps awake in vain (Ps. 127:1); they will be secure in their land (Ezek. 34:27).

b Keep them from the evil one (John 17:15); I guarded them (John 17:12); his angels will guard you (Ps. 91:11).

c The peace of God will guard your hearts and minds (Phil. 4:7).

d Guard through the Holy Spirit what has been entrusted (2 Tim.

1:14); he is able to guard what I have committed to him (2 Tim. 1:12).

Refuge, see **662**.

● Safeguarding
 e Wisdom is a protection as money is (Eccles. 7:12); a woman protects a man! (Jer. 31:22).

 f Bring your animals and people in to safety (Exod. 9:19); not even the altar will be a sanctuary for a crafty killer (Exod. 21:14).

 g The men were a wall to us by day and night (1 Sam. 25:16); I will make you my bodyguard for life (1 Sam. 28:2); David set Benaiah over the guard (2 Sam. 23:23); the king charged you to protect Absalom (2 Sam. 18:12); the temple guards guarding the king's son Joash (2 Kgs. 11:8; 2 Chr. 23:7).

 h Men to guard the mouth of the cave (Josh. 10:18); the tomb was made secure (Matt. 27:64–6).

 i Asher's locks will be iron and bronze (Deut. 33:25).

661 Danger

● Risking
 a Zebulun and Naphtali risked their lives (Judg. 5:18); Gideon risked his life for them (Judg. 9:17); I took my life in my hands (Judg. 12:3; 1 Sam. 28:21); David took his life in his hands (1 Sam. 19:5); the mighty men risked their lives to bring David water (2 Sam. 23:17; 1 Chr. 11:19); we get our bread at the risk of our lives (Lam. 5:9); Paul and Barnabas risked their lives for the Lord Jesus (Acts 15:26); Prisca and Aquila risked their lives for Paul (Rom. 16:4); as did Epaphroditus (Phil. 2:30); they did not love their lives even to death (Rev. 12:11).

● In danger
 b Place Uriah in the thick of the battle (2 Sam. 11:15); in danger from robbers, countrymen, Gentiles etc. (2 Cor. 11:26); the voyage was now dangerous (Acts 27:9); do not think that in the palace you will escape (Esther 4:13).

 c Danger will not separate us from the love of Christ (Rom. 8:35); why are we in danger every hour? (1 Cor. 15:30).

● Unguarded
 d Ai was left unguarded (Josh. 8:17); their protection is removed (Num. 14:9).

662 Refuge. Safeguard

● Refuge in God
 a God is a refuge (Ps. 62:8; 71:7); blessed are all who take refuge in him (Ps. 2:12); he delivers them because they take refuge in him (Ps. 37:40); I take refuge in God (Ps. 7:1; 11:1; 16:1; 31:1; 57:1; 71:1; 94:22; 141:8; 143:9; 144:2); my refuge is God (Ps. 62:7); I have made the Lord my refuge (Ps. 73:28); my God in whom I take refuge (2 Sam. 22:3; Ps. 18:2); you are my refuge (Jer. 17:17); let all who take refuge in you be glad (Ps. 5:11); none who take refuge in him will be condemned (Ps. 34:22); he who takes refuge in me will inherit the land (Isa. 57:13); better to take refuge in the Lord than trust in man (Ps. 118:8–9); we have fled for refuge (Heb. 6:18).

b The Lord is the refuge of the poor (Ps. 14:6; Isa. 25:4); God is our refuge and strength (Ps. 46:1); you are my refuge (Ps. 59:16; 61:3; 142:5); a refuge (Ps. 61:3; 91:2; 119:114; Joel 3:16; Nahum 1:7); a rock of refuge (Ps. 71:3; 94:22); my hiding place (Ps. 32:7).

Safety, see **660**.

● Refuge under God's wings

c Under God's wings you have sought refuge (Ruth 2:12); taking refuge in the shadow of your wings (Ps. 36:7; 61:4); under his wings you will seek refuge (Ps. 91:2–4); in the shadow of your wings I sing (Ps. 63:7).

● God is a fortress

d God is my fortress (2 Sam. 22:2, 33); you are my fortress (Ps. 31:3; 91:2); a fortress and stronghold (Ps. 9:9; 18:2; 59:9, 16; 91:2; 144:2; Jer. 16:19; Joel 3:16); God is a stronghold (Ps. 48:3; 62:2, 6); the God of Jacob is our stronghold (Ps. 46:11); the way of the Lord is a stronghold (Prov. 10:29).

● Other refuge

e There will be a refuge and a shelter (Isa. 4:6); the king and princes will be like a refuge from the wind (Isa. 32:2).

f They take refuge in Pharaoh (Isa. 30:2–3).

● Sanctuary of refuge

g Those clutching the horns of the altar: Adonijah (1 Kgs. 1:50–1); Joab (1 Kgs. 2:28).

h The Lord will become a sanctuary (Isa. 8:14).

Cities of refuge, see **184***ae*.

● Shields

i The shield of Saul, not anointed with oil (2 Sam. 1:21); David took Hadadezer's gold shields (2 Sam. 8:7; 1 Chr. 18:7); 300 shields of beaten gold (1 Kgs. 10:17; 2 Chr. 9:16); 200 large shields of beaten gold (1 Kgs. 10:16; 2 Chr. 9:15); all taken away by Shishak (1 Kgs. 14:26; 2 Chr. 12:9); Rehoboam made shields of bronze (1 Kgs. 14:27; 2 Chr. 12:10); Uzziah prepared shields, helmets and armour (2 Chr. 26:14); Hezekiah provided many shields (2 Chr. 32:5); 1000 shields hung on the tower of David (S. of S. 4:4).

j God is a shield (Gen. 15:1; 2 Sam. 22:3, 31; Ps. 3:3; 18:2, 30; 84:11; 119:114; 144:2); the Lord is a shield (Prov. 2:7; 30:5); the Lord is my shield (Ps. 28:7); he is our help and shield (Ps. 33:20; 115:9, 10, 11); the shield of faith (Eph. 6:16); the shield of your salvation (2 Sam. 22:36; Ps. 18:35); his faithfulness is a shield (Ps. 91:4); you surround the righteous with favour like a shield (Ps. 5:12).

● Helmets

k Goliath wore a bronze helmet (1 Sam. 17:5); Saul put a bronze helmet on David (1 Sam. 17:38); the helmet of salvation (Eph. 6:17); as a helmet the hope of salvation (1 Thess. 5:8); a helmet of salvation on his head (Isa. 59:17).

● Hiding holes

l The Israelites made shelters in caves and strongholds (Judg. 6:2); the stronghold of the cave of Adullam (1 Sam. 22:1); the strongholds of Engedi (1 Sam. 23:29); David went down to the stronghold (2 Sam. 5:17).

663 Pitfall: source of danger
See **661**.

664 Warning

● Warning
the people

a Warn the people not to break though (Exod. 19:21); I warned your fathers when I brought them up from Egypt (Jer. 11:7).

b Ezekiel was made a watchman to warn the people (Ezek. 3:17–21; 33:7–9); the watchman has to give warning (Ezek. 33:2–6); sounding an alarm on the silver trumpets (Num. 10:5–9).

Trumpets for warning, see **414h**.

c Samuel had to warn the people about kings (1 Sam. 8:9); Elisha warned the king of Israel about the Arameans (2 Kgs. 6:10); kings of the earth, be warned (Ps. 2:10); the Lord warned Israel and Judah through the prophets (2 Kgs. 17:13); these things were written down as examples for us (1 Cor. 10:6, 11).

● Warning
individuals

d The magi were warned in a dream (Matt. 2:12); Joseph was warned in a dream (Matt. 2:22); the rich man wanted someone to warn his five brothers (Luke 16:28); by your words I am warned (Ps. 19:11).

e Warn those who are unruly (1 Thess. 5:14); warn him as a brother (2 Thess. 3:15); shun a factious man after two warnings (Titus 3:10); you are able to admonish one another (Rom. 15:14); I write to admonish you (1 Cor. 4:14).

f They warned them not to speak about Jesus (Acts 4:17–21); Jesus warned them not to make him known (Matt. 12:16).

g The disciples warned Paul not to go to Jerusalem (Acts 21:4, 11).

h God made Sodom and Gomorrah an example (2 Pet. 2:6; Jude 7).

Warnings about quarrels, see **709a**.

665 Danger signal
See **664**.

666 Preservation

● God keeping

a I will keep you (Gen. 28:15, 20); the Lord is your keeper (Ps. 121:5); he will keep you from all evil (Ps. 121:7); the Lord bless and keep you (Num. 6:24); he who keeps you will not sleep (Ps. 121:3–4); he preserves the way of his saints (Prov. 2:8).

667 Escape

● Escaping
from people

a If Esau attacks one group the other may escape (Gen. 32:8); Ehud escaped (Judg. 3:26); Jotham escaped from Abimelech (Judg. 9:21); David escaped from Saul's spear (1 Sam. 18:11; 19:10); David escaped from Keilah (1 Sam. 23:13); Abiathar escaped the slaughter (1 Sam. 22:20); the Rock of Escape (1 Sam. 23:28); David escaped to the land of the Philistines (1 Sam. 27:1); flee, or no one will escape from Absalom (2 Sam. 15:14); in Jerusalem there will be those who escape (Joel 2:32); let no one escape (2 Kgs. 9:15); the sailors tried to escape from the ship (Acts 27:30); pray that you will have strength to escape these things (Luke 21:36); how will you escape being sentenced to hell? (Matt. 23:33).

b The man escaped from the battle line (1 Sam. 4:16); 400 men escaped on camels (1 Sam. 30:17); Israel escaped from under the hand of the Arameans (2 Kgs. 13:5).

c Do not hand back an escaped slave (Deut. 23:15); many servants are breaking away from their masters (1 Sam. 25:10).
Run away, see **620.**

- Escaping
evil

d I have escaped by the skin of my teeth (Job 19:20); they may escape from the devil (2 Tim. 2:26); how shall we escape if we ignore this great salvation? (Heb. 2:3); how shall we escape if we turn from him who speaks from heaven? (Heb. 12:25).

- Escaping
through
God

e We have escaped like a bird from a snare (Ps. 124:7); oh, for wings like a dove, to fly away! (Ps. 55:6); by faith they escaped the edge of the sword (Heb. 11:34); with the temptation God will provide the way of escape (1 Cor. 10:13).

668 Deliverance

- Deliverance
is of God

a Deliverance is from the Lord (Ps. 3:8; Jonah 2:9); God is a God of deliverance (Ps. 68:20); salvation to our God (Rev. 7:10; 19:1).

b The Lord has become my salvation (Exod. 15:2; Isa. 12:2); the Lord is my light and my salvation (Ps. 27:1); the Lord is my deliverer (2 Sam. 22:2); you are my deliverer (Ps. 40:17); O Lord, my salvation (Ps. 38:22); God of our salvation (Ps. 65:5); he has become my salvation (Ps. 118:14, 21); a righteous God and a saviour (Isa. 45:21); I rejoice in God my Saviour (Luke 1:47); there is no saviour besides me (Isa. 43:11).

- Deliver us!

c Save us, O God! (1 Chr. 16:35); save us, Lord! (Matt. 8:25); save me! (Matt. 14:30); Hosanna! [save, Lord!] (Matt. 21:9, 15; Mark 11:9, 10; John 12:13); rescue me (Ps. 31:2).

d Deliver me from Esau (Gen. 32:11); deliver us from his hand (2 Kgs. 19:19); save me from all who pursue me (Ps. 7:1); deliver me from evildoers (Ps. 59:2); deliver me from my foes (Ps. 69:14); deliver me from Aram and Israel (2 Kgs. 16:7); deliver me out of the hand of the wicked (Ps. 71:4); rescue me from evil men (Ps. 140:1); pray that we may be delivered from evil men (2 Thess. 3:2); deliver us from evil (Matt. 6:13); save me from all my transgressions (Ps. 39:8).

- A Saviour

e A Saviour, Christ the Lord (Luke 2:11); this is the Saviour of the world (John 4:42); a Saviour, Jesus (Acts 13:23); Christ is the Saviour of the body (Eph. 5:23); God is the Saviour of all men (1 Tim. 4:10); the Father sent the Son to be the Saviour of the world (1 John 4:14); I did not come to judge but to save (John 12:47); not to destroy but to save (Luke 9:56); the Son of Man came to seek and to save (Luke 19:10); there is no other name by which we may be saved (Acts 4:12); God sent the Son that the world might be saved (John 3:17); Jesus who saves us from the wrath to come (1 Thess. 1:10); your king comes with salvation (Zech. 9:9); the source of eternal salvation (Heb. 5:9); my eyes have seen your salvation (Luke 2:30); he will appear a second time for salvation (Heb. 9:28).

● Can God save?

f Many say God will not deliver me (Ps. 3:2); let God deliver him (Ps. 22:8; Matt. 27:43); do not believe Hezekiah that the Lord can deliver you (2 Kgs. 18:32); how can the Lord deliver Jerusalem? (2 Kgs. 18:35); what god can deliver you out of my hands? (Dan. 3:15); has your God been able to deliver you from the lions? (Dan. 6:20); our God is able to save us (Dan. 3:17); God will deliver us (2 Cor. 1:10); no other god can save like this (Dan. 3:29); salvation is impossible with men but possible with God (Luke 18:26–7); the Lord is not limited in saving by many or by few (1 Sam. 14:6); the Lord does not save by sword or spear (1 Sam. 17:47); shall I say, 'Save me from this hour'? (John 12:27).

Hard to be saved, see **700c**.

● God delivers from enemies

g God saved them from their enemies (Judg. 2:18; 1 Sam. 12:11; 2 Sam. 18:19, 31; Ps. 18:48); he delivers them from the wicked (Ps. 97:10); you gave them deliverers [messiahs] (Neh. 9:27); I delivered you from the nations (Judg. 10:11–12); he delivered me from my strong enemy (2 Sam. 22:18; Ps. 18:17).

h The Lord will deliver me from this Philistine (1 Sam. 17:37); may the Lord deliver me from your hand (1 Sam. 24:15); he will pluck my feet out of the net (Ps. 25:15); you will pull me out of the net (Ps. 31:4); I am saved from my enemies (2 Sam. 22:4; Ps. 18:3); when the Lord delivered him from all his enemies (2 Sam. 22:1; Ps. 18:t); the Lord rescued me from persecutions (2 Tim. 3:11); the Lord rescued me from Herod (Acts 12:11); the Lord will deliver you from all your enemies (2 Kgs. 17:39); the Lord will rescue me from every evil (2 Tim. 4:18); this will turn out for my deliverance (Phil. 1:19).

i I have come down to deliver them from the Egyptians (Exod. 3:8); stand still and see the salvation of the Lord (Exod. 14:13); the Lord saved Israel from the Egyptians (Exod. 14:30); the Lord had saved them (Exod. 18:8); a people saved by the Lord (Deut. 33:29); I delivered you from the hand of Saul (2 Sam. 12:7); I will deliver you from the king of Assyria (2 Kgs. 20:6); the Lord saved Hezekiah from the Assyrians (2 Chr. 32:22).

● God delivers from sin and death

j He will save his people from their sins (Matt. 1:21); Christ gave himself for our sins to rescue us from this evil age (Gal. 1:4); Christ Jesus came into the world to save sinners (1 Tim. 1:15);

God saved us and called us with a holy calling (2 Tim. 1:9); he saved us by the washing of regeneration (Titus 3:5); now is the day of salvation (2 Cor. 6:2).

k You have delivered my soul from death (Ps. 56:13; 86:13; 116:8); who will save me from this body of death? (Rom. 7:24–5).

● God saves the needy

l He will deliver the needy (Ps. 72:12); I was brought low and he saved me (Ps. 116:6); he delivers the soul of the needy (Jer. 20:13); you save an afflicted people (2 Sam. 22:28; Ps. 18:27); you were like a brand plucked from the burning (Amos 4:11); is this not a brand plucked from the fire? (Zech. 3:2); who then can be saved? (Matt. 19:25; Mark 10:26).

● God saves those who turn to him

m I will save you because you trust in me (Jer. 39:18); he who believes and is baptised will be saved (Mark 16:16); believe in the Lord Jesus and you will be saved (Acts 16:31); the angel of the Lord delivers those who fear him (Ps. 34:7); you save those who take refuge in you from their foes (Ps. 17:7); the Lord knows how to rescue the godly from trials (2 Pet. 2:9); call upon me and I will deliver you (Ps. 50:15); whoever calls on the name of the Lord will be saved (Acts 2:21; Rom. 10:13); I call to God and he saves me (Ps. 55:16); I lift up the cup of salvation and call on the name of the Lord (Ps. 116:13).

n He who endures to the end will be saved (Matt. 10:22; 24:13; Mark 13:13).

● God saves because of love

o Save me because of your steadfast love (Ps. 6:4); because he loves me I will rescue him (Ps. 91:14–15); he rescued me because he delighted in me (Ps. 18:19); he saved them for his name's sake (Ps. 106:8).

● God wants to save all

p The ends of the earth have seen the salvation of our God (Ps. 98:2–3); turn to me and be saved, all the ends of the earth (Isa. 45:22); I will save my people from the east and the west (Zech. 8:7); God our Saviour wants all men to be saved (1 Tim. 2:3–4); all Israel will be saved (Rom. 11:26).

● God saves his people

q I will defend this city and save it (2 Kgs. 19:34); God will save Zion (Ps. 69:35); the Lord delivered Israel (1 Sam. 14:23); you went out to save your people (Hab. 3:13); those who proclaim salvation to Zion (Isa. 52:7); you will call your walls Salvation (Isa. 60:18); on Mount Zion will be deliverance (Obad. 17); Oh that the salvation of Israel would come from Zion! (Ps. 53:6); you have not delivered your people at all (Exod. 5:23).

● The salvation of God

r God has destined us for salvation (1 Thess. 5:9); the helmet of salvation (Eph. 6:17; 1 Thess. 5:8); you receive the salvation of your souls (1 Pet. 1:9); the grace of God that brings salvation (Titus 2:11); he has raised up a horn of salvation for us (Luke 1:69–71); that the elect may obtain salvation (2 Tim. 2:10); the Scriptures are able to make you wise to salvation (2 Tim. 3:15); by grace you are saved through faith (Eph. 2:5, 8); if you confess

Jesus as Lord and believe God raised him you will be saved (Rom. 10:9–10); the message of salvation has been sent to us (Acts 13:26); he will speak words by which you will be saved (Acts 11:14); things that accompany salvation (Heb. 6:9); what must I do to be saved? (Acts 16:30); the gospel by which you are saved (1 Cor. 15:2); salvation is nearer now than when we first believed (Rom. 13:11); salvation to be revealed in the last time (1 Pet. 1:5).

● Save others
s Deliver those being led away to death (Prov. 24:11); deliver the one who has been robbed (Jer. 22:3); how do you know whether you will save your husband? (1 Cor. 7:16); he who turns a sinner from his way will save his soul (Jas. 5:20).

● People saving others
t Reuben tried to rescue Joseph (Gen. 37:21); Joseph saved the Egyptians' lives (Gen. 47:25); Moses rescued Reuel's daughters (Exod. 2:17, 19); the Lord raised up deliverers: Othniel (Judg. 3:9); Ehud (Judg. 3:15); Shamgar saved Israel (Judg. 3:31); Gideon was told to save Israel (Judg. 6:14); Tola rose to save Israel (Judg. 10:1); Samson would begin to deliver Israel (Judg. 13:5); Jabesh Gilead would be delivered (1 Sam. 11:9); Jonathan brought great deliverance (1 Sam. 14:45); the people rescued Jonathan (1 Sam. 14:45); David rescued his two wives (1 Sam. 30:18); the Lord gave a deliverer to Israel (2 Kgs. 13:5); Moses was sent to be a deliverer (Acts 7:25, 35); your servants have saved your life and everyone else's (2 Sam. 19:5).

u He will deliver you from the Philistines (1 Sam. 7:3); pray that he will deliver us from the Philistines (1 Sam. 7:8); Saul will deliver them from the Philistines (1 Sam. 9:16); how can this man save us? (1 Sam. 10:27); by David I will save Israel from the Philistines (2 Sam. 3:18); David delivered Keilah from the Philistines (1 Sam. 23:5); the king has saved us from our enemies (2 Sam. 19:9).

v God sent Joseph in order to save lives (Gen. 45:5, 7; 50:20); he saved them by the hand of Jeroboam (2 Kgs. 14:27); Hezekiah will not be able to deliver you (2 Kgs. 18:29); a poor man delivered a city by wisdom (Eccles. 9:15).

● Saved by various things
w Has any nation's god delivered them? (2 Kgs. 18:33; 2 Chr. 32:13–15, 17); silver and gold cannot deliver them (Zeph. 1:18).

● Saving oneself
x Noah, Daniel and Job would only save themselves (Ezek. 14:14, 20); save yourself! (Matt. 27:40; Mark 15:30; Luke 23:35, 37, 39); he cannot save himself (Matt. 27:42; Mark 15:31); save yourselves from this perverse generation (Acts 2:40); a king is not saved by his large army nor a warrior by his great strength (Ps. 33:16).

669 Preparation

● A way prepared
a I send my messenger to prepare the way (Mal. 3:1; Matt. 11:10; Mark 1:2; Luke 7:27); prepare the way of the Lord (Isa. 40:3;

Matt. 3:3; Mark 1:3; Luke 3:4; John 1:23); you will prepare the way for him (Luke 1:76).

● A people prepared

b Make ready a people prepared for the Lord (Luke 1:17); prepare to meet your God (Amos 4:12); vessels of mercy prepared beforehand for glory (Rom. 9:23).

c That the man of God may be equipped for every good work (2 Tim. 3:17); the equipping of the saints for service (Eph. 4:12); be dressed in readiness with your lamps burning (Luke 12:35); be ready in season and out of season (2 Tim. 4:2); be ready, for he is coming when you least expect (Matt. 24:44); be ready (Luke 12:40); his bride has made herself ready (Rev. 19:7).

d The Corinthians needed to be prepared for giving (2 Cor. 9:2–4); I am ready to go to prison and death (Luke 22:33); I am ready to die for the Lord Jesus (Acts 21:13).

● A place prepared

e The places are for those for whom they have been prepared (Matt. 20:23; Mark 10:40); I go to prepare a place for you (John 14:2); what neither eye has seen nor ear heard, God has prepared (1 Cor. 2:9); inherit the kingdom prepared for you from the foundation of the world (Matt. 25:34).

● Preparing to build

f David prepared for building the temple (1 Chr. 22:5); the stones for the temple were prepared at the quarry (1 Kgs. 6:7); they made Joram's chariot ready (2 Kgs. 9:21).

● Preparing for action

g Uzziah prepared weapons (2 Chr. 26:14); get your baggage ready for exile (Jer. 46:19); prepare your work in the field and afterward build your house (Prov. 24:27); now take purse, bag and sword (Luke 22:36).

h Gird up your loins like a man (Job 38:3; 40:7); gird up your loins (2 Kgs. 4:29; 9:1); gird up your loins and speak to them (Jer. 1:17); gird up your minds (1 Pet. 1:13).

i The fields are ripe for harvest (John 4:35); feet shod with the preparation of the gospel (Eph. 6:15).

Saddling animals, see **267*m*.**

● Preparing food

j The disciples made preparations for the Passover in the upper room (Matt. 26:17–19; Mark 14:12–16; Luke 22:8–13); it was the day of preparation, the day before the Sabbath (Mark 15:42; Luke 23:54; John 19:31, 42); the day of Preparation for the passover (John 19:14); the day after the day of Preparation (Matt. 27:62).

k Prepare provisions (Josh. 1:11); I have prepared my dinner (Matt. 22:4); preparing food for Peter (Acts 10:10); the wedding is ready (Matt. 22:8); come, for everything is now ready (Luke 14:17).

● Preparing for burial

l The women prepared spices and perfumes (Luke 23:56); she has prepared my body for burial (Matt. 26:12).

● Preparing to travel

m The Passover had to be eaten by those prepared to travel (Exod. 12:11).

670 Unpreparedness

● Unprepared   *a* Gideon attacked the Midianites when they were unsuspecting (Judg. 8:11).

b Altars of uncut stones (Exod. 20:25; Deut. 27:5; Josh. 8:31).

c Do not think beforehand what to say (Matt. 10:19–20; Luke 12:11–12; 21:14–15).

● Not equipped   *d* Those sent out had to take no extra equipment (Matt. 10:9–10; Mark 6:8–9; Luke 9:3; 10:4); when I sent you out without purse, bag or sandals, did you lack anything? (Luke 22:35); the foolish virgins took no oil with them (Matt. 25:3).

671 Attempt

Attempting to kill, see **362***k*.

672 Undertaking

Work, see **676**.

673 Use

Useful, see **640**.

674 Nonuse

Useless, see **641**.

675 Misuse

Doing harm, see **645***f*.

Section three: Voluntary action

---

676 Action

● God's works   *a* His work is perfect (Deut. 32:4); great are the works of the Lord (Ps. 111:2); the Lord has done great things (Joel 2:21); the Lord has done great things for us (Ps. 126:2, 3); how awesome are your deeds! (Ps. 66:3, 5); I act and who can hinder it? (Isa. 43:13); Jesus, a prophet mighty in deed and word (Luke 24:19); my Father is working and I work (John 5:17).

b Let your work be manifest to us (Ps. 90:16); let them know that you have done it (Ps. 109:27); see the works of the Lord (Ps. 46:8); the elders who had seen God's deeds (Josh. 24:31; Judg. 2:7); this is the Lord's doing (Ps. 118:23).

c Do as you have said (2 Sam. 7:25).

● God's work   *d* Of Israel it will be said, See what God has done! (Num. 23:23);
in us   the Father living in me does his works (John 14:10); we are God's workmanship (Eph. 2:10); you have performed for us all our works (Isa. 26:12); God works in you to will and to work (Phil. 2:13); establish the work of our hands (Ps. 90:17); the Lord has done great things for us (Ps. 126:2–3); tell them how much the

Lord has done for you (Mark 5:19; Luke 8:39); he told how much Jesus had done for him (Mark 5:20; Luke 8:39).

● Works of the law

e The man who does them shall live (Lev. 18:5; Neh. 9:29; Ezek. 20:11, 13, 21; Rom. 10:5; Gal. 3:12); not the hearers of the law but the doers will be justified (Rom. 2:13); they did not pursue righteousness by faith but as if it were based on works (Rom. 9:32); do this and you will live (Luke 10:28).

● Repaid for deeds

f He will reward every man according to his deeds (Matt. 16:27); he will render to every one according to his deeds (Prov. 24:12; Rom. 2:6; Rev. 22:12); he pays a man according to his work (Job 34:11); each one will receive according to what he has done (2 Cor. 5:10); the dead were judged according to their deeds (Rev. 20:13).

● Doing God's works

g What shall we do to do the works of God? (John 6:28); brothers, what shall we do? (Acts 2:37); what must I do to be saved? (Acts 16:30); what shall I do? (Acts 22:10); what must I do to inherit eternal life? (Matt. 19:16; Mark 10:17; Luke 10:25; 18:18); he who hears my words and does them (Matt. 7:24; Luke 6:47).

● Grace not works

h By grace you are saved, not by works (Eph. 2:8–9); not by righteous deeds which we have done (Titus 3:5); not according to our works (2 Tim. 1:9); by the works of the law no one is justified (Rom. 3:20; Gal. 2:16); justified by faith apart from works of the law (Rom. 3:28); to him who does not work but believes (Rom. 4:4–5).

i The one who enters God's rest rests from his own works (Heb. 4:10); repentance from dead works (Heb. 6:1).

j God's choice is not because of works (Rom. 9:11–12); a remnant chosen by grace, not works (Rom. 11:5–6); did you receive the Spirit by the works of the law? (Gal. 3:2).

● Works of grace

k I know your deeds (Rev. 2:2, 19; 3:1, 8, 15); by their deeds they deny God (Titus 1:16); good deeds which God prepared for us to do (Eph. 2:10); God works in us what is pleasing to him (Heb. 13:21); command them to be rich in good deeds (1 Tim. 6:18); careful to devote themselves to good deeds (Titus 3:8, 14); women should be decked with good deeds (1 Tim. 2:9–10); they may see your good deeds and glorify God (Matt. 5:16; 1 Pet. 2:12); deeds wrought in God (John 3:21); always abounding in the work of the Lord (1 Cor. 15:58); we remember your work of faith and labour of love (1 Thess. 1:3); a believer will do the works I do, and greater (John 14:12).

l What use is faith without works? (Jas. 2:14); faith without works is dead (Jas. 2:17, 20, 26); I will show you my faith by my works (Jas. 2:18); was not Abraham justified by works? (Jas. 2:21); faith was working with his works (Jas. 2:22); Rahab was justified by works (Jas. 2:25); if a man will not work he shall not eat (2 Thess. 3:10).

m Work out your own salvation (Phil. 2:12); blessed is the servant whom his master finds so doing (Matt. 24:46; Luke 12:43).

● Bad deeds   *n* The deeds of the flesh (Gal. 5:19–21); the unfruitful works of darkness (Eph. 5:11); I do not do what I want, but what I hate (Rom. 7:15–25).

677 Inaction

● No work on feast days

a No work to be done on: the sabbath (Exod. 20:9–10; Deut. 5:14); days one and seven of the Passover (Exod. 12:16; Num. 28:18, 25; Deut. 16:8); the Day of Atonement (Lev. 16:29; 23:28, 30–2; Num. 29:7); the Feast of Weeks (Num. 28:26); the Feast of Trumpets (Num. 29:1); the Feast of Booths (Lev. 23:36; Num. 29:12, 35).

Sabbath rest, see **683**.

● Lack of activity

b A land and cities on which you have not laboured (Deut. 6:10–11; Josh. 24:13); they hear your words but do not do them (Ezek. 33:31).

Idleness, see **679h**.

c Sit still, my daughter (Ruth 3:18).

d 'The Lord will not do either good or evil' (Zeph. 1:12).

678 Activity

● Sleeplessness

a My sleep fled from me (Gen. 31:40); the king could not sleep (Esther 6:1; Dan. 6:18); I lie awake (Ps. 102:7); at night his mind does not rest (Eccles. 2:23); the full stomach of the rich does not let him sleep (Eccles. 5:12).

b I will not sleep until I find a dwelling for God (Ps. 132:3–4); no one in their army slumbers or sleeps (Isa. 5:27); give your eyes no sleep until you are delivered from the pledge (Prov. 6:4); they cannot sleep unless they do evil (Prov. 4:16).

c We commend ourselves in sleeplessness (2 Cor. 6:5); through many a sleepless night (2 Cor. 11:27).

d God neither slumbers nor sleeps (Ps. 121:3–4).

● Waking up

e Awake, Lord! (Ps. 35:23; 44:23; 59:5); awake, arm of the Lord! (Isa. 51:9); the Lord awoke (Ps. 78:65); perhaps Baal is asleep and needs to be awakened (1 Kgs. 18:27).

f Awake, Deborah! (Judg. 5:12); awake, Zion! (Isa. 52:1); rouse yourself, Jerusalem! (Isa. 51:17); awake, sleeper! (Eph. 5:14); wake up! (Rev. 3:2); it is time for you to wake from sleep (Rom. 13:11).

g Samson woke up (Judg. 16:20); morning by morning he awakens me (Isa. 50:4); the captain woke Jonah up (Jonah 1:6); they woke Jesus up (Matt. 8:25; Mark 4:38; Luke 8:24); I am going to wake Lazarus out of sleep (John 11:11); when the jailer woke up (Acts 16:27).

● Industriousness

h The hand of the diligent makes rich (Prov. 10:4); the hand of the diligent will rule (Prov. 12:24); she does not eat the bread of idleness (Prov. 31:27); Solomon saw that Jeroboam was industrious (1 Kgs. 11:28).

679 Inactivity

● Sleeping

a The sleep of a labourer is sweet (Eccles. 5:12); I lay down and slept (Ps. 3:5); in peace I will lie down and sleep (Ps. 4:8); my sleep was pleasant to me (Jer. 31:26); your sleep will be sweet (Prov. 3:24); I was asleep but my heart was awake (S. of S. 5:2).

b God put Adam into a deep sleep (Gen. 2:21); Abraham fell into a deep sleep (Gen. 15:12); the Lord has poured on you a spirit of deep sleep (Isa. 29:10); God gives sleep to his beloved (Ps. 127:2).

c Jacob fell asleep at Bethel (Gen. 28:11); Delilah made Samson sleep on her knees (Judg. 16:19); Saul lay asleep in the camp (1 Sam. 26:7); the Lord put them into a deep sleep (1 Sam. 26:12); I fell into a deep sleep (Dan. 8:18; 10:9); Jonah fell into a deep sleep (Jonah 1:5–6); Jesus was asleep in the stern (Matt. 8:24; Mark 4:38; Luke 8:23); Peter and the others were overcome with sleep (Luke 9:32); the disciples were sleeping (Matt. 26:40, 43; Mark 14:37, 40; Luke 22:45); are you still sleeping? (Matt. 26:45); his disciples stole him while we were sleeping (Matt. 28:13); Peter was sleeping between two soldiers (Acts 12:6); perhaps Baal is asleep (1 Kgs. 18:27).

d While men were asleep his enemy sowed tares (Matt. 13:25); when the bridegroom was delayed they slept (Matt. 25:5); whether awake or asleep we live with him (1 Thess. 5:10).

● Sleep of death

e Eutychus fell into a deep sleep (Acts 20:9); the girl is not dead but sleeping (Matt. 9:24; Mark 5:39; Luke 8:52); Lazarus' death referred to as sleep (John 11:11–13); David fell asleep (Acts 13:36); many have fallen asleep (1 Cor. 11:30); those who sleep in Jesus (1 Thess. 4:14); the firstfruits of those who slept (1 Cor. 15:20); we shall not all sleep (1 Cor. 15:51).

● Do not sleep

f Watch, lest he find you asleep (Mark 13:36); let us not sleep as others do (1 Thess. 5:6); those who sleep, sleep at night (1 Thess. 5:7); Uriah did not sleep at home (2 Sam. 11:9, 13).
Not sleep, see **678a**.

● Sleep instead of work

g Do not love sleep lest you come to poverty (Prov. 20:13); a little sleep, a little slumber (Prov. 6:10; 24:33); he who sleeps in harvest brings shame (Prov. 10:5); laziness casts into a deep sleep (Prov. 19:15).

● Idleness

h The sluggard: craves and gets nothing (Prov. 13:4); says there is a lion outside (Prov. 22:13; 26:13); turns on his bed like a door on its hinges (Prov. 26:14); buries his hand in the dish (Prov. 19:24; 26:15); does not plough in autumn (Prov. 20:4).

i The desire of the sluggard kills him (Prov. 21:25); the way of the sluggard is overgrown with thorns (Prov. 15:19); go to the ant, you sluggard (Prov. 6:6); how long will you lie, sluggard? (Prov. 6:9); the sluggard's field is neglected (Prov. 24:30–4).

j Through idleness the roof sags (Eccles. 10:18); the lazy will be put to forced labour (Prov. 12:24); he who is slack in his work is brother to him who destroys (Prov. 18:9); the fool folds his hands and eats his own flesh (Eccles. 4:5).

k Pharaoh said the Israelites were lazy (Exod. 5:8, 17); some among you are idle (2 Thess. 3:11); Cretans are lazy gluttons (Titus 1:12); younger widows become idle (1 Tim. 5:13); people standing idle (Matt. 20:3); why stand here idle all day? (Matt. 20:6); you lazy slave! (Matt. 25:26).

680 Haste

- Hurrying others on

a The Egyptians urged them to leave in haste (Exod. 12:33); hurry! (1 Sam. 9:12; 20:38); quick, lest he overtake us (2 Sam. 15:14); they brought Haman in haste to the banquet (Esther 6:14); hastening the coming of the day of God (2 Pet. 3:12).

- Acting hurriedly

b I hastened to keep your commandments (Ps. 119:60); let him hasten his work that we may see it (Isa. 5:19).

c The people hurried across Jordan (Josh. 4:10); Shimei hurried to meet King David (2 Sam. 19:16); as did Ziba (2 Sam. 19:17); Rehoboam mounted his chariot hastily (1 Kgs. 12:18; 2 Chr. 10:18); the king went in hast to the lions' den (Dan. 6:19); Paul was hurrying to be in Jerusalem for Pentecost (Acts 20:16).

d He who makes haste errs (Prov. 19:2); you will not go out in haste (Isa. 52:12).

Running, see **277c**; **Hasty**, see **857a**.

681 Leisure

Rest, see **683**.

682 Exertion

- Working hard

a Through toil you will eat (Gen. 3:17); by the sweat of your brow (Gen. 3:19); man has to labour on earth (Job 7:1); a man goes to work to labour until evening (Ps. 104:23); there is profit in all labour (Prov. 14:23); a man with no dependants gets no end to his toil (Eccles. 4:8).

b Noah will give us rest in our toil (Gen. 5:29); Jacob's toil for Laban (Gen. 31:42).

c By hard work we must help the weak (Acts 20:35); to this end I toil (Col. 1:29); you remember our toil, working night and day (1 Thess. 2:9); we toiled night and day (2 Thess. 3:8); we toiled, working with our hands (1 Cor. 4:12); I laboured more than them (1 Cor. 15:10); in far more labours (2 Cor. 11:23); we toil and strive because we set our hope on the living God (1 Tim. 4:10).

d Bowed down with hard labour (Ps. 107:12); come to me, you who labour and are heavy-laden (Matt. 11:28); the lilies of the field do not toil or spin (Matt. 6:28).

● Forced labour

e Issachar submits to forced labour (Gen. 49:15); conquered people will be subject to forced labour (Deut. 20:11); the Gibeonites became slaves, hewers of wood and drawers of water (Josh. 9:21–7); the Canaanites were put to forced labour (Josh. 16:10; 17:13; Judg. 1:28, 30, 33, 35); David put the Ammonites to forced labour (2 Sam. 12:31); Solomon levied forced labourers (1 Kgs. 5:13; 9:15, 21); Solomon made the Canaanites forced labourers (2 Chr. 8:8); Adoram [Adoniram / Hadoram] was over the forced labour (2 Sam. 20:24; 1 Kgs. 4:6; 5:14; 12:18; 2 Chr. 10:18); Jeroboam was over the forced labour (1 Kgs. 11:28).

683 Repose

● Sabbath instituted

a On the seventh day God rested (Gen. 2:2–3; Exod. 20:11; 31:17; Heb. 4:4); a day of rest, a holy sabbath (Exod. 16:23); a sabbath of rest (Exod. 31:15; 35:2–3); on the sabbath they rested (Exod. 16:30; Luke 23:56); on the seventh day you shall rest (Exod. 34:21; Lev. 23:3); you shall not do any work (Exod. 20:10; 23:12); every sabbath two lambs as a burnt offering (Num. 28:9–10); you made known to them your sabbath (Neh. 9:14); I gave them my sabbaths as a sign (Ezek. 20:12).

b It is lawful to do good on the sabbath (Matt. 12:12); the sabbath was made for man, not man for the sabbath (Mark 2:27); the Son of Man is Lord of the sabbath (Matt. 12:8; Mark 2:28; Luke 6:5).

c The Day of Atonement was a day of sabbath rest (Lev. 16:31).

● Sabbath observed

d Observe the sabbath day (Exod. 20:8; Exod. 31:13; Lev. 19:3, 30; 26:2; Deut. 5:12); blessed is the man who keeps the sabbath (Isa. 56:2); sanctify my sabbaths (Ezek. 20:20); if you call the sabbath a delight (Isa. 58:13); a song for the sabbath (Ps. 92:t).

e No manna on the sabbath (Exod. 16:25–9); pray that your flight may not be on the sabbath (Matt. 24:20).

f Do not carry a load on the sabbath (Jer. 17:21–2, 24, 27); we will not buy from them on the sabbath (Neh. 10:31); the bodies were not to remain on the cross on the sabbath (John 19:31); the day of Preparation was the day before the sabbath (Mark 15:42); after the sabbath women came to the tomb (Matt. 28:1; Mark 16:1).

● On the sabbath

g On the sabbath they went to the synagogue (Matt. 12:9–10; Luke 4:16; Acts 13:14); on the sabbath he taught in the synagogue (Mark 1:21; 6:2; Luke 4:31–3; 6:6; 13:10); Paul reasoned in the synagogues every sabbath (Acts 18:4); Moses is read in the synagogues every sabbath (Acts 15:21); they went through the grainfields on the sabbath (Matt. 12:1; Luke 6:1).

● Sabbath violated

h They profaned my sabbaths (Ezek. 20:13, 16, 21, 24; 23:38); you have profaned my sabbaths (Ezek. 22:8); why are you profaning the sabbath? (Neh. 13:17–18); when will the sabbath be over that we may trade? (Amos 8:5).

i A man gathered wood on the sabbath (Num. 15:32); men trod winepresses on the sabbath (Neh. 13:15); men of Tyre sold fish on the sabbath (Neh. 13:16).

● Sabbath in question

j Your disciples are doing what is unlawful on the sabbath (Matt. 12:2; Mark 2:24; Luke 6:2); on the sabbath the priests break the sabbath (Matt. 12:5); it is unlawful to carry your mat on the sabbath (John 5:10); do not come to be healed on the sabbath (Luke 13:14); is it lawful to heal on the sabbath? (Matt. 12:10; Luke 14:3); they watched him to see if he would heal on the sabbath (Mark 3:2; Luke 6:7); Jesus healed on the sabbath (John 5:9, 16; 9:14); is it lawful to do good or to harm on the sabbath? (Mark 3:4; Luke 6:9); you do good to livestock on the sabbath (Matt. 12:11; Luke 13:15; 14:5); you circumcise on the sabbath, so why not heal? (John 7:22–3).

● Sabbatical year

k The sabbatical year (Exod. 23:10–11; Deut. 15:1–18); at the end of seven years, at the remission of debts (Deut. 31:10); we will observe the seventh year (Neh. 10:31).

l The land must observe a sabbath (Lev. 25:2); when the land is desolate it will enjoy its sabbaths (Lev. 26:34, 43); the land enjoyed its sabbaths (2 Chr. 36:21).

● God giving rest

m My presence will go with you and I will give you rest (Exod. 33:14); God has given rest to his people (1 Kgs. 8:56); return to your rest, my soul (Ps. 116:7); this is rest, give rest to the weary (Isa. 28:12); come to me, all who are weary, and I will give you rest (Matt. 11:28).

n Come away and rest (Mark 6:31); you will find rest for your souls (Jer. 6:16; Matt. 11:29); in returning and rest you will be saved (Isa. 30:15); we who believe enter that rest (Heb. 4:3); there remains a Sabbath rest for the people of God (Heb. 4:9–10); the Spirit of the Lord gave them rest (Isa. 63:14).

o They shall never enter my rest (Ps. 95:11; Heb. 3:11, 18; 4:3, 5); if Joshua had given them rest, God would not have spoken of another day (Heb. 4:8).

p Arise to your resting place, O God (2 Chr. 6:41).
Rest from war, see 717*i*.

● Rest in death

q I would have been at rest in death (Job 3:13); there the weary are at rest (Job 3:17).

● Taking rest

r Noah will give us rest (Gen. 5:29); rest yourselves under the tree (Gen. 18:4); Ishbosheth taking his midday rest (2 Sam. 4:5).

● Those at ease

s Woe to those who are at ease in Zion (Amos 6:1); Moab has been at ease from his youth (Jer. 48:11); go up against a nation at ease (Jer. 49:31); I, Nebuchadnezzar, was at ease in my house (Dan. 4:4).

● No rest

t The dove found no resting-place (Gen. 8:9); among the nations you will find no rest (Deut. 28:65); take no rest and give him no rest (Isa. 62:6–7); I had no rest in my spirit (2 Cor. 2:13); our flesh had no rest (2 Cor. 7:5); the unclean spirit seeks rest and does not find it (Matt. 12:43).

684 Fatigue

● Tired out

a If you ran with men on foot and they wearied you (Jer. 12:5); I am weary with holding it in (Jer. 6:11); Moses' hands grew heavy (Exod. 17:12); the strength of the burden bearers is failing (Neh. 4:10); Eleazar struck the Philistines till his hand was weary (2 Sam. 23:10); David became exhausted fighting the Philistines (2 Sam. 21:15); lest the crowd faint on the way home (Matt. 15:32; Mark 8:3).

b Jesus was tired from his journey (John 4:6); you were tired out by the length of your journey (Isa. 57:10).

● Tired in pursuit

c Gideon and his men were exhausted yet pursuing (Judg. 8:4); the people were weary pursuing the Philistines (1 Sam. 14:28, 31); some of David's men were too exhausted to continue the pursuit (1 Sam. 30:10).

● Tired in flight

d David and his men arrived exhausted (2 Sam. 16:14); wine for those who are faint (2 Sam. 16:2); attack him when he is tired and weak (2 Sam. 17:2); the people are hungry and tired (2 Sam. 17:29)

● Fatigue and God

e The Lord does not grow weary or tired (Isa. 40:28); you have wearied the Lord (Mal. 2:17); you have wearied me with your iniquities (Isa. 43:24).

f You have been weary of me (Isa. 43:22); how have I wearied you? (Mic. 6:3).

● Do not grow weary

g Do not grow weary in doing good (2 Thess. 3:13); consider him, lest you grow weary (Heb. 12:3); they will walk and run and not get tired (Isa. 40:31); you have not grown weary (Rev. 2:3).

685 Refreshment

● Refreshed

a On the seventh day God was refreshed (Exod. 31:17).

b That times of refreshing may come from the Lord (Acts 3:19); I will refresh the weary (Jer. 31:25).

c Jonathan's eyes brightened after the honey (1 Sam. 14:27, 29); Saul was refreshed by David's playing (1 Sam. 16:23); come home with me and refresh yourself (1 Kgs. 13:7).

d Onesiphorus often refreshed me (2 Tim. 1:16); the hearts of the saints have been refreshed (Philem. 7); refresh my heart (Philem. 20); they have refreshed my spirit (1 Cor. 16:18).

686 Worker

● Workers

a Pray that the Lord of the harvest will sent out workers (Matt. 9:38; Luke 10:2); hiring workers for his vineyard (Matt. 20:1); be a workman who does not need to be ashamed (2 Tim. 2:15).

● Occupations

b What is your occupation? (Gen. 46:33; 47:3).

c I will send for many fishermen (Jer. 16:16); fishermen will stand

473

there (Ezek. 47:10); Simon and Andrew were fishermen (Matt. 4:18; Mark 1:16); I will make you fishers of men (Matt. 4:19; Mark 1:17; Luke 5:10).

d The king of Egypt's butler (Gen. 40:1–23); Nehemiah was cupbearer to the king (Neh. 1:11); Shebra the steward (Isa. 22:15); Joanna the wife of Herod's steward Chuza (Luke 8:3); the king of Egypt's baker (Gen. 40:1–23); Solomon's waiters and cupbearers (1 Kgs. 10:5).

e The king will take your daughters as perfumers (1 Sam. 8:13); Hananiah of the perfumers (Neh. 3:8).

f Carpenters and stonemasons sent by Hiram (2 Sam. 5:11; 1 Chr. 14:1); carpenters, builders, masons and stonecutters (2 Kgs. 12:11–12; 22:6; 1 Chr. 22:15; 2 Chr. 24:12; 34:10–11); David used stonecutters (1 Chr. 22:2); masons and carpenters (Ezra 3:7); is not this the carpenter? (Mark 6:3); is not this the carpenter's son? (Matt. 13:55); she thought Jesus was the gardener (John 20:15).

g Tubal-cain forged implements (Gen. 4:22); Israel had no blacksmith (1 Sam. 13:19); craftsmen and smiths were taken into exile (2 Kgs. 24:14, 16); four smiths to cast down the horns (Zech. 1:20–1); the goldsmiths (Neh. 3:32); Uzziel of the goldsmiths (Neh. 3:8); she gave the silver to a silversmith (Judg. 17:4); Demetrius the silversmith (Acts 19:24); Alexander the coppersmith (2 Tim. 4:14).

h They were tentmakers (Acts 18:3); linen workers (1 Chr. 4:21); potters (1 Chr. 4:23); lesson from the potter (Jer. 18:1–6); the potter (Rom. 9:21); Simon the tanner (Acts 9:43; 10:6, 32). **Gatekeepers**, see **264i**; **shepherds, herdsmen**, see **369a**; **farmers**, see **370f**.

687 Workshop

688 Conduct

● Manner of life

a Put away your former way of life (Eph. 4:22); conduct yourselves in a manner worthy of the gospel (Phil. 1:27); how one ought to conduct himself in the church (1 Tim. 3:15); whoever says he abides in him should live as he lived (1 John 2:6); as you received Christ, so walk in him (Col. 2:6).

689 Management

● Guiding

a Bits in horses' mouths direct their whole bodies (Jas. 3:3); ships are guided by a small rudder (Jas. 3:4); the integrity of the upright guides them (Prov. 11:3); blind guides! (Matt. 15:14; 23:16, 24); the blind leading the blind (Matt. 15:14; Luke 6:39).

b The Egyptian led them to the Amalekites' camp (1 Sam. 30:15–16); Paul was led by the hand (Acts 9:8; 22:11).

c The gift of administrations (1 Cor. 12:28).

● God guiding

d You will guide me (Ps. 31:3); let your good Spirit lead me (Ps. 143:10); lead me in the everlasting way (Ps. 139:24); lead me in your truth (Ps. 25:5); the Lord will guide you continually (Isa. 58:11); with your counsel you will guide me (Ps. 73:24); I will lead the blind by a way they do not know (Isa. 42:16); he will lead them to springs of water (Isa. 49:10); I led them with cords of love (Hos. 11:4); I lead you in the way you should go (Isa. 48:17); the Lord directs his steps (Prov. 16:9); the Lord has guided me (Gen. 24:27, 48); however far away I go, your hand leads me (Ps. 139:10); you led them to your holy habitation (Exod. 15:13); the pillar of cloud to guide them (Neh. 9:12, 19); he leads me in the paths of righteousness (Ps. 23:3).

e The Lord turns the king's heart where he will (Prov. 21:1).
God leading the way, see **283***a*; **signs for guidance**, see **547***c*.

● The Spirit guiding

f Jesus was led by the Spirit into the wilderness (Matt. 4:1; Luke 4:1); all who are led by the Spirit of God are sons of God (Rom. 8:14).
Going before, see **283**; **led by the Spirit**, see **965***ae*.

690 Director

● Human guides

a Ithamar directed the Gershonites (Num. 4:28; 7:8); and the Merarites (Num. 4:33; 7:8).

● The law our guide

b The law was our guide to lead us to Christ (Gal. 3:24).
Judges of Israel, see **957***f*.

691 Advice

● Need for advice

a Listen to advice (Prov. 19:20); a wise man listens to advice (Prov. 12:15); those who take advice have wisdom (Prov. 13:10); what king goes to war without first taking counsel? (Luke 14:31); wage war with wise guidance (Prov. 20:18; 24:6).

b In many counsellors there is safety (Prov. 11:14); with many counsellors plans succeed (Prov. 15:22).

● Advising God
● God's advice

c Who has been counsellor to the Lord? (Isa. 40:13; Rom. 11:34).

d You guide me with your counsel (Ps. 73:24); your testimonies are my counsellors (Ps. 119:24); his name will be called wonderful counsellor (Isa. 9:6); great in counsel (Jer. 32:19).

e His advice was like consulting God (2 Sam. 16:23).

f They spurned the counsel of the Most High (Ps. 107:11); they did not wait for his counsel (Ps. 106:13); you ignored Wisdom's counsel (Prov. 1:25); they would not accept Wisdom's counsel (Prov. 1:30).

● Counsellors

g Ahithophel: was a counsellor (1 Chr. 27:33); David's counsellor, sent for by Absalom (2 Sam. 15:12); David prayed for his counsel to be foolish (2 Sam. 15:31); thwart his advice (2 Sam. 15:34; 17:14); gave his advice (2 Sam. 16:20–1); his advice is not good (2 Sam. 17:7); he has counselled against you (2 Sam. 17:21); when he saw his advice was not followed (2 Sam. 17:23).

h Jethro advised Moses (Exod. 18:19); Jonathan, David's uncle, was a counsellor (1 Chr. 27:32); Jehoiada and Abiathar succeeded Ahithophel (1 Chr. 27:34); five of the king's advisors (2 Kgs. 25:19); the people of the land hired counsellors (Ezra 4:5); Artaxerxes had seven counsellors (Ezra 7:14).

i Have we made you a royal counsellor? (2 Chr. 25:16).

j Ahaziah's mother was his counsellor to do evil (2 Chr. 22:3–4).

● Man's counsel

k Let me give you advice (1 Kgs. 1:12); 'ask advice at Abel' (2 Sam. 20:18).

l The counsel of Hushai (2 Sam. 17:11–14); the advice of Hushai is better (2 Sam. 17:14); David consulted with the captains (1 Chr. 13:1); Rehoboam sought counsel from the elders (1 Kgs. 12:6–8; 2 Chr. 10:6); and from the young men (1 Kgs. 12:9; 2 Chr. 10:8); Rehoboam rejected the elders' advice (1 Kgs. 12:13; 2 Chr. 10:8); Jeroboam consulted (1 Kgs. 12:28); the king of Aram conferred with his servants (2 Kgs. 6:8); let us take counsel together (Neh. 6:7).

m The Pharisees took counsel how to trap him in his talk (Matt. 22:15); the chief priests and elders took counsel how to kill Jesus (Matt. 27:1); the chief priests and elders took counsel together (Matt. 28:12); the Pharisees and Herodians took counsel how to destroy him (Mark 3:6).

● Lack of counsel

n There is no counsellor among them (Isa. 41:28); Pharaoh's counsellors give stupid counsel (Isa. 19:11); an old and foolish king who will no long take advice (Eccles. 4:13).

o God thwarts the advice of the cunning (Job 5:13); happy the man who does not walk in the counsel of the wicked (Ps. 1:1).

692 Council

● Councils of men

a The council assembled (Luke 22:66; Acts 5:21; 22:30); Joseph of Arimathea was a member of the council (Mark 15:43; Luke 23:50); the chief priests and Pharisees held a council (John 11:47).

b They will deliver you up to the councils (Matt. 10:17; Mark 13:9); they brought Stephen before the council (Acts 6:12); asking for Paul to be brought to the council (Acts 23:15, 20); I brought this man to their council (Acts 23:28); they sent them out of the council (Acts 4:15; 5:34).

c The chief priests and the council sought testimony against Jesus (Mark 14:55); sought false evidence against Jesus (Matt. 26:59).

● The Lord's council

d Who has stood in the council of the Lord? (Jer. 23:18, 22).

693 Precept

Proverb, see **496**.

694 Skill

Skilled people, see **696**.

695 Unskilfulness

● Inexperienced

a Solomon was young and inexperienced (1 Chr. 22:5; 29:1); I do not know how to speak (Jer. 1:6).

696 Proficient person

● Skilled
people

a Do you see a man skilled in his work? (Prov. 22:29); idols are the work of skilled men (Jer. 10:9).

b In all skilled people God has put skill (Exod. 31:6; 36:1, 2).

c The Scripture makes the man of God proficient (2 Tim. 3:17).

d They are skilled in evil (Jer. 4:22).

● Particular
skilled
people

e Skilled people had to make the priests' garments (Exod. 28:3, 6, 15); and the tabernacle (Exod. 35:10, 30–5); Bezalel was an expert craftsman (Exod. 31:2–5); send me a man skilled in working with many materials (2 Chr. 2:7); Huram-Abi was a skilled man (2 Chr. 2:13); no one knows how to cut timber like the Sidonians (1 Kgs. 5:6; 2 Chr. 2:8); Hiram was skilled in working with bronze (1 Kgs. 7:14).

697 Bungler

Failure, see **728**.

698 Cunning

● Crafty ones

a The serpent was more crafty than any beast of the field (Gen. 3:1); David is very cunning (1 Sam. 23:22).

● Acting
craftily

b Killing a man craftily (Exod. 21:14); the Gibeonites acted craftily (Josh. 9:4); Jehu did it in cunning (2 Kgs. 10:19); when Herod saw he had been tricked by the wise men (Matt. 2:16).

699 Artlessness

Single-hearted, see **44**.

Section four: Antagonism

---

700 Difficulty

● Hard tasks

a The task is too heavy for you (Exod. 18:18); if a case is too difficult (Deut. 17:8); it was hard for Amnon to do anything to Tamar (2 Sam. 13:2); what you ask is too difficult (Dan. 2:11).

b The chariots met difficulty (Exod. 14:25); we sailed slowly and with difficulty (Acts 27:7); in the last days there will be difficult times (2 Tim. 3:1); I will hedge up your way with thorns (Hos. 2:6).

Impossible, see **470**.

● Hard to be saved	*c* It is hard for a rich man to enter the kingdom (Matt. 19:23; Mark 10:23; Luke 18:24); how hard it is to enter the kingdom (Mark 10:24); it is difficult for the righteous to be saved (1 Pet. 4:18).
	d This is a difficult saying (John 6:60).

701 Facility

● Easy for God	*a* Is anything too hard for the Lord? (Gen. 18:14); is anything too hard for me? (Jer. 32:27); will it be difficult in my sight? (Zech. 8:6); nothing is too hard for you (Jer. 32:17).
● Easy for people	*b* The people of the land are bread for us (Num. 14:9); the inhabitants of the land have melted away (Josh. 2:24).
	c Which is easier, to say 'Your sins are forgiven' or 'Arise' (Matt. 9:5; Mark 2:9; Luke 5:23); easier for a camel to go through the eye of a needle (Matt. 19:24; Mark 10:25).
● Easy burdens	*d* Lighten the heavy yoke (1 Kgs. 12:4, 9, 10; 2 Chr. 10:4, 9, 10); my yoke is easy and my burden light (Matt. 11:30); this commandment is not too difficult for you (Deut. 30:11).

702 Hindrance

● Beware of hindrances	*a* Watch out for those who cause divisions and hindrances (Rom. 16:17); I have said these things to you that you may not be stumbled (John 16:1).
● Do not hinder	*b* You are stopping the people working (Exod. 5:5); do not delay me (Gen. 24:56).
	c Do not put a stumbling block before the blind (Lev. 19:14); determine not to put an obstacle or stumbling block in a brother's way (Rom. 14:13); let the children come to me and do not hinder them (Matt. 19:14; Mark 10:14; Luke 18:16); why do you truble the woman? (Matt. 26:10); do not cause anyone to stumble (1 Cor. 10:32); we do not cause anyone to stumble (2 Cor. 6:3); take care your liberty does not become a stumbling block to the weak (1 Cor. 8:9); remove every obstacle from the people's way (Isa. 57:14); it is not good to do anything which makes your brother stumble (Rom. 14:21); if food makes my brother stumble I will never eat meat again (1 Cor. 8:13); lest we give offence (Matt. 17:27).
● Woe to hinderers	*d* Woe to the world for stumbling blocks! (Matt. 18:7); woe to the one through whom stumbling blocks come (Luke 17:1); whoever causes one of these little ones to stumble (Matt. 18:6; Mark 9:42); they will extract from his kingdom all stumbling blocks (Matt. 13:41).
● Hindrance to God's work	*e* Discouraging Israel from possessing the land (Num. 32:7, 9); the people of the land discouraged Judah (Ezra 4:4).
	f Christ crucified was a stumbling block to the Jews (1 Cor. 1:23); it I preach circumcision the stumbling block of the cross is removed (Gal. 5:11); you are a stumbling block to me (Matt. 16:23).

g Israel stumbled over the stone of stumbling (Rom. 9:32–3); they took offense at him (Matt. 13:57; Mark 6:3); the Pharisees were offended (Matt. 15:12); does this causes you to stumble? (John 6:61); blessed is he who is not stumbled over me (Matt. 11:6; Luke 7:23); they stumble because they are disobedient (1 Pet. 2:8).

h Let us lay aside every hindrance (Heb. 12:1); if your hand or foot causes you to stumble, cut it off (Matt. 18:8); if your eye causes you to stumble, pluck it out (Matt. 18:9); who hindered you from obeying the truth? (Gal. 5:7); Paul had been hindered from coming to Rome (Rom. 1:13; 15:22); the Jews hinder us from speaking to the Gentiles (1 Thess. 2:16); Satan hindered us (1 Thess. 2:18); the wind was contrary (Matt. 14:24; Acts 27:4).

i We do not cause a hindrance to the gospel (1 Cor. 9:12); in him who loves there is no cause for stumbling (1 John 2:10); give honour to your wife so that your prayers are not hindered (1 Pet. 3:7).

- Hindering the enemy

j Thwart the counsel of Ahithophel (2 Sam. 15:34); God ordained that Ahithophel's advice should be thwarted (2 Sam. 17:14); I am setting stumbling-blocks before this people (Jer. 6:21); God had frustrated their plan (Neh. 4:15); Jeremiah is discouraging the soldiers (Jer. 38:4).

703 Aid

- God, help!

a Be a help against Judah's enemies! (Deut. 33:7); rise up and help me! (Ps. 35:2); be my helper! (Ps. 30:10); give us help against the enemy (Ps. 60:11); make haste to help me (Ps. 70:1, 5; 71:12); may he send you help from the sanctuary (Ps. 20:2); I call for help but you do not listen (Hab. 1:2); if the Lord does not help, how can I? (2 Kgs. 6:27).

- God helping

b God helps you (Gen. 49:25; 1 Chr. 12:18); Eliezer, God was my help (Exod. 18:4); God is my helper (Ps. 54:4); the Lord is my helper (Heb. 13:6); the Lord is your shield of help (Deut. 33:29); he is their help and shield (Ps. 33:20; 115:9, 10, 11); a very present help in trouble (Ps. 46:1); our help is in the name of the Lord (Ps. 124:8); Ebenezer, this far has the Lord helped us (1 Sam. 7:12); the Lord helped David wherever he went (2 Sam. 8:6; 1 Chr. 18:6, 13); he has helped his servant Israel (Luke 1:54); you are the helper of the orphan (Ps. 10:14); my help is from the Lord (Ps. 121:2); your help made me great (2 Sam. 22:36; Ps. 18:35); the Lord helped me (Ps. 118:13); with us is the Lord to help us (2 Chr. 32:8); Christ is able to help those who are tempted (Heb. 2:18); the Spirit helps us in our weakness (Rom. 8:26); we have an advocate with the Father (1 John 2:1); if the Lord had not been my help (Ps. 94:17).

c God helped the Levites to carry the ark (1 Chr. 15:26); the wall had been built with the help of God (Neh. 6:16); God helped

Uzziah against his enemies (2 Chr. 26:7); Jehoshaphat cried out and the Lord helped him (2 Chr. 18:31).

d The hand of God was on them [to help] (Ezra 7:6, 9, 28; 8:18, 22, 31; Neh. 2:8, 18).

● Alongside to help

e The Father will give you another helper (John 14:16); the helper, the Holy Spirit, whom the Father will send (John 14:26); the helper whom I will send from the Father (John 15:26); I will send the helper to you (John 16:7).

f We have a helper with the Father, Jesus Christ the righteous (1 John 2:1).

● People help

g No animal was a helper suitable for man (Gen. 2:20); God made a helper suitable for man (Gen. 2:18).

h Help your brothers fight (Josh. 1:14); let us help the one being defeated (2 Sam. 10:11; 1 Chr. 19:12); you help us from the city (2 Sam. 18:3); the Gibeonites sent for Joshua to help them (Josh. 10:6); people were coming to help David (1 Chr. 12:20–2); David commanded the leaders to help Solomon (1 Chr. 22:17); they helped Adonijah (1 Kgs. 1:7); help, O king! (2 Kgs. 6:26); the Levites were to assist the priests (1 Chr. 23:28); Ahaz sent to the king of Assyria for help (2 Chr. 28:16); help your enemy (Exod. 23:5); if you come in peace to help me (1 Chr. 12:17).

i The disciples wanted to help the brethren in Judea (Acts 11:29); help Phoebe, for she has helped many (Rom. 16:2); help these women (Phil. 4:3); help Zenas and Apollos (Titus 3:13); we ought to help such people (3 John 8); come to Macedonia and help us (Acts 16:9); the gift of helps (1 Cor. 12:28); tell my sister to help me (Luke 10:40).

j Meroz did not help the Lord against the mighty (Judg. 5:23); he who is not with me is against me (Matt. 12:30).

k Should you help the wicked? (2 Chr. 19:2); help me attack Gibeon (Josh. 10:4); Horam helped Lachish (Josh. 10:33).

704 Opposition

● God opposing

a You will know God's opposition (Num. 14:34); the hand of the Lord was against Israel (Judg. 2:15); if you rebel, his hand will be against you (1 Sam. 12:15); the face of the Lord is against those who do evil (Ps. 34:16; 1 Pet. 3:12).

b The Lord is against: Edom (Ezek. 35:3); Gog (Ezek. 38:3; 39:1); Nineveh (Nahum 2:13; 3:5); Pharaoh king of Egypt (Ezek. 29:3, 10); Sidon (Ezek. 28:22); the shepherds (Ezek. 34:10); Tyre (Ezek. 26:3).

c I have set my face against Jerusalem (Jer. 21:10; Ezek. 15:7); I will set my face against the idolater (Ezek. 14:8); I am against you (Jer. 21:13; Ezek. 5:8; 13:8; 21:3); I will stretch out my hand against Judah (Zeph. 1:4); the word of the Lord is against the land of Hadrach (Zech. 9:1).

- Opposing God

   d If you are hostile to God, he will be hostile to you (Lev. 26:27–8, 40–1); you are against me (Hos. 13:9); you may be fighting against God (Acts 5:39); he who opposes a ruler opposes God (Rom. 13:2); the wicked man acts in opposition to God (Job 15:25–6); the mind set on the flesh is hostile to God (Rom. 8:7); once you were hostile to God (Col. 1:21).

   e He who is not with me is against me (Matt. 12:30; Luke 11:23); I should oppose the name of Jesus (Acts 26:9); consider him who endured such hostility from sinful men (Heb. 12:3); the Pharisees were very hostile (Luke 11:53).

- Opposing people

   f Only Jonathan and Jahzeiah opposed this (Ezra 10:15); Elymas the sorceror opposed them (Acts 13:8); as Jannes and Jambres opposed Moses, so these people oppose the truth (2 Tim. 3:8); Alexander strongly opposed our teaching (2 Tim. 4:15); we told you the gospel amid much opposition (1 Thess. 2:2).

   g Believers will be handed over by their families for execution (Matt. 10:21; Mark 13:12; Luke 21:16); division will be caused within families (Matt. 10:35; Luke 12:52).

   h Be hostile to the Midianites for they have been hostile to you (Num. 25:17–18).

   i Paul opposed Peter to his face (Gal. 2:11).

   j Ishmael would be against everyone and everyone against him (Gen. 16:12); the Jews are hostile to all men (1 Thess. 2:15); the Philistines feared David would turn against them in battle (1 Sam. 29:4).

   k If God be for us, who is against us? (Rom. 8:31).
      Enmity, see **881**.

- Meeting opposition

   l All these things are against me (Gen. 42:36).
      Wind in opposition, see **352o**.

705 Opponent

- God as enemy

   a The angel of the Lord stood in the road as Balaam's adversary (Num. 22:22, 32); the Lord has become your enemy (1 Sam. 28:16); God turned and became their enemy (Isa. 63:10); God counts me as an enemy (Job 19:11; 33:10); God has bent his bow like an enemy (Lam. 2:4); the Lord has become like an enemy (Lam. 2:5); I will be an enemy to your enemies (Exod. 23:22).

- Enemies of God

   b Many live as enemies of the cross of Christ (Phil. 3:18); while we were enemies to God we were reconciled (Rom. 5:10); whoever is a friend of the world is an enemy of God (Jas. 4:4); you have given opportunity to the enemies of the Lord (2 Sam. 12:14); why do you consider me your enemy? (Job 13:24).

   c Satan—'Adversary' (Matt. 4:10); many antichrists have appeared (1 John 2:18); this is the spirit of antichrist (1 John 4:3); this is the antichrist who denies Father and Son (1 John 2:22); this is the deceiver and antichrist (2 John 7); those who hate you have become my enemies (Ps. 139:22).

d A door for service has opened and there are many adversaries (1 Cor. 16:9); they are enemies of the gospel for your sake (Rom. 11:28); you enemy of all righteousness! (Acts 13:10); his enemy sowed tares (Matt. 13:25); an enemy has done this (Matt. 13:28); the enemy is the devil (Matt. 13:39); you are an adversary [Satan] to me (2 Sam. 19:22); get behind me, Satan! (Matt. 16:23; Mark 8:33).

e May all the Lord's enemies perish! (Judg. 5:31); your enemies will perish (Ps. 92:9); the last enemy to be destroyed in death (1 Cor. 15:26).

● Enemies
of people

f How my enemies have increased! (Ps. 3:1); my enemies are many (Ps. 25:19).

g Saul was David's enemy (1 Sam. 18:29); the Lord raised up adversaries against Solomon (1 Kgs. 11:14, 23, 25); the Lord raises up adversaries against them (Isa. 9:11); an enemy will loot your fortresses (Amos 3:11); the enemies of Judah heard of the rebuilding of the temple (Ezra 4:1); this wicked Haman is the enemy (Esther 7:6); your adversary the devil is like a roaring lion (1 Pet. 5:8).

h A man's enemies will be from his own family (Mic. 7:6; Matt. 10:36).

i Have you found me, my enemy? (1 Kgs. 21:20); have I become your enemy by telling you the truth? (Gal. 4:16); do not regard him as an enemy (2 Thess. 3:15).

j He delivered me from my enemies (2 Sam. 22:18; Ps. 18:17); deliverance from our enemies (Luke 1:71).

k Hate your enemy (Matt. 5:43); love your enemies (Matt. 5:44; Luke 6:27); help your enemy (Exod. 23:4, 5); if your enemy is hungry, feed him (Prov. 25:21).

706 Cooperation

● God for us

a God is for me (Ps. 56:9; 118:6, 7); I am for you (Ezek. 36:9); if it had not been the Lord who was on our side (Ps. 124:1); if God be for us, who can be against us? (Rom. 8:31).

● For God

b Whoever is for the Lord (Exod. 32:26); can wicked rulers be allied to you? (Ps. 94:20).

● For people

c We are with you, David (1 Chr. 12:18); who is on my side? (2 Kgs. 9:32).

d Whoever is not against us is for us (Mark 9:40); whoever is not against you is for you (Luke 9:50); are you for us or for our enemies? (Josh. 5:13).

e The Tekoite nobles did not support the rebuilding (Neh. 3:5).

707 Co-worker

● Fellow-worker

a We are the fellow-workers of God (1 Cor. 3:9).

708 Party

● Factions	*a* Factions are deeds of the flesh (Gal. 5:20).
● Pharisees and Sadducees	*b* Pharisees and Sadducees coming for baptism (Matt. 3:7); the Council was part Sadducees, part Pharisees (Acts 23:6).
	c The Pharisees and Sadducees tested him by asking for a sign (Matt. 16:1; Mark 8:11); the chief priests and Pharisees understood he meant them (Matt. 21:45); the chief priests and the Pharisees asked Pilate to set a guard (Matt. 27:62).
	d Beware of the leaven of the Pharisees and Sadducees (Matt. 16:6, 11–12).
● Sadducees	*e* The Sadducees say there is no resurrection (Matt. 22:23; Mark 12:18; Luke 20:27); nor an angel nor a spirit (Acts 23:8); when the Pharisees heard he had silenced the Sadducees (Matt. 22:34); the priests and Sadducees came on them (Acts 4:1); the high priest rose up and his associates, the Sadducees (Acts 5:17).
● Pharisees	*f* The Pharisees acknowledge angels and spirits (Acts 23:8); the scribes and Pharisees sit on Moses' seat (Matt. 23:2); the Pharisees fast (Matt. 9:14; Mark 2:18); how the Pharisee prayed with himself (Luke 18:11–12); the Pharisees and lawyers rejected God's purpose for them (Luke 7:30); the Pharisees were lovers of money (Luke 16:14).
	g Beware of the leaven of the Pharisees and of Herod (Mark 8:15); woe to you, scribes and Pharisees, hypocrites! (Matt. 23:13, 14, 15, 23, 25, 27, 29); you blind Pharisee! (Matt. 23:26).
	h The Pharisees plotted against Jesus (Matt. 12:14); the Pharisees wanted to trap him in his words (Matt. 22:15; Mark 12:13); the Pharisees took counsel with the Herodians (Mark 3:6); Pharisees warned him that Herod wanted to kill him (Luke 13:31).
	i A Pharisee called Nicodemus (John 3:1); a Pharisee called Gamaliel (Acts 5:34); a Pharisee invited him to a meal (Luke 7:36; 11:37; 14:1); I am a Pharisee, a son of Pharisees (Acts 23:6); Paul had lived as a Pharisee (Acts 26:5); as to the law, a Pharisee (Phil. 3:5); unless your righteousness exceeds that of the scribes and Pharisees (Matt. 5:20); some of the party of the Pharisees who believed (Acts 15:5).
● Pharisees displeased	*j* The Pharisees accused the disciples over the sabbath (Matt. 12:2; Mark 2:24; Luke 6:2); Pharisees told him to rebuke his disciples (Luke 19:39); scribes of the Pharisees asked why he ate with sinners (Mark 2:16; Luke 15:2); Pharisees and scribes came to ask about hand-washing (Matt. 15:1–2); Pharisees tested him about divorce (Matt. 19:3; Mark 10:2); scribes and Pharisees watched to see whether he would heal on the sabbath (Luke 6:7); Pharisees and teachers of the law were present when he taught (Luke 5:17); the Pharisees and scribes gathered round him (Mark 7:1); scribes and Pharisees wanted to see a sign (Matt. 12:38; Mark 8:11); questioners had been sent by the Pharisees (John 1:24); they brought the man who had been born blind to the

Pharisees (John 9:13); the Pharisees said he cast out demons by the prince of demons (Matt. 9:34; 12:24); the Pharisees were offended (Matt. 15:12).

● Christians

k Paul was called a ringleader of the sect of the Nazarenes (Acts 24:5); the Way, which they call a sect (Acts 24:14); this sect (Acts 28:22); suffering as a Christian (1 Pet. 4:16).

● Circumcision party

l Those of the circumcision (Acts 11:2; Titus 1:10); the circumcision party—the concision (Gal. 2:12; Phil. 3:2–3); fellow-workers from the circumcision (Col. 4:11).

● Zealots etc.

m Simon the Zealot (Matt. 10:4; Luke 6:15; Acts 1:13); 4000 men of the Assassins (Acts 21:38).

709 Dissension

● Warnings about quarrels

a Disputes and dissensions are deeds of the flesh (Gal. 5:20); every fool will quarrel (Prov. 20:3); foolish controversies produce quarrels (2 Tim. 2:23); out of controversies arises strife (1 Tim. 6:4).

b Stop the quarrel before it breaks out (Prov. 17:14); avoid disputes about the law (Titus 3:9); disputes about words (1 Tim. 6:4); warn them not to dispute about words (2 Tim. 2:14); the Lord's servant must not be quarrelsome (2 Tim. 2:24); watch those who cause dissensions (Rom. 16:17).

c Woe to him who argues with his Maker (Isa. 45:9).
Discuss, see **475***b*.

● Strife

d What causes conflicts among you? (Jas. 4:1); filled with strife (Rom. 1:29); strife is a deed of the flesh (Gal. 5:20); not in strife or jealousy (Rom. 13:13); the wicked man spreads strife (Prov. 6:14); a greedy man stirs up strife (Prov. 28:25); the Lord hates those who spread strife among brothers (Prov. 6:19).

● Quarrelsome wives

e Rather than live with a quarrelsome wife it is better to live on a housetop (Prov. 21:9; 25:24); better to live in a desert (Prov. 21:19); a quarrelsome wife is like constant dripping on a day of rain (Prov. 27:15).

● Cases of quarreling

f Abraham's herdsmen quarrelled with Lot's (Gen. 13:7); the herdsmen of Gerar quarrelled with Isaac's herdsmen (Gen. 26:20); don't quarrel on the way! (Gen. 45:24); everyone was arguing about the king (2 Sam. 19:9).

g The Israelites quarrelled with Moses about water (Exod. 17:2, 7; Num. 20:3); they quarrelled with the Lord (Num. 20:13).

h An argument arose as to who was the greatest (Luke 9:46; 22:24); Paul and Barnabas had great dissension with the circumcisers (Acts 15:2); if anyone is contentious, we have no other practice (1 Cor. 11:16).

i The Pharisees argued with Jesus (Mark 8:11); scribes arguing with his disciples (Mark 9:14); what are you arguing about with them? (Mark 9:16); a scribe heard them arguing (Mark 12:28); some argued with Stephen (Acts 6:9).

       j Paul and Barnabas had a sharp disagreement (Acts 15:39); a dissension arose between the Pharisees and Sadducees (Acts 23:7); the Jews were at variance among themselves (Acts 28:25).

       k I fear there may be quarrelling (2 Cor. 12:20); I hear there are quarrels among you (1 Cor. 1:11).

       l My servant will not quarrel (Matt. 12:19).

● Inconsistent   *m* Their testimony was not consistent (Mark 14:56, 59).

710 Concord

● Agreeing for good
   a David was a man after God's own heart (1 Sam. 13:14; Acts 13:22).

   b If two agree about anything they ask (Matt. 18:19); be like-minded (2 Cor. 13:11; Phil. 2:2); live in harmony (1 Pet. 3:8); I exhort you all to agree with one another (1 Cor. 1:10); may God grant you to be of the same mind (Rom. 15:5); I urge Euodia and Syntyche to agree in the Lord (Phil. 4:2); to glorify God with one accord (Rom. 15:6); the labourers agreed on a denarius a day (Matt. 20:2, 13).

   c Lovingkindness and truth have met, justice and peace have kissed (Ps. 85:10).

● Agreeing for evil
   d Ananias and Sapphira agreed to test the Spirit (Acts 5:9); they have one opinion (Rev. 17:17).

   e Joseph had not agreed with the council's action (Luke 23:51).

711 Defiance

● Defying
   a Goliath defied the armies of Israel (1 Sam. 17:10, 25, 26, 36).

   b Who has defied God with impunity? (Job 9:4).

712 Attack

● The nations attacked
   a If a city will not make peace, besiege it (Deut. 20:12); how to conduct a siege (Deut. 20:19–20); a small city besieged and saved by wisdom (Eccles. 9:14–15); God besieges my tent (Job 19:12).

   b Through God I can attack a troop (2 Sam. 22:30; Ps. 18:29); attack the Midianites (Num. 25:17); I give my daughter to the man who attacks Kiriath Sepher (Josh. 15:16; Judg. 1:12); Jonathan attacked the Philistines (1 Sam. 13:3–4); attack the Philistines (1 Sam. 23:2); shall I attack the Philistines? (2 Sam. 5:19); they were encamped against Gibbethon of the Philistines (1 Kgs. 16:15); Joab besieged Rabbah of the Ammonites (2 Sam. 11:1; 12:26–9); the kings of Israel and Judah attacked Ramoth-gilead (1 Kgs. 22:29; 2 Chr. 18:2–3, 28); Jehoram attacked Edom by night (2 Kgs. 8:21); siege walls against Tyre (Ezek. 26:8); the king of the north will besiege a fortified city (Dan. 11:15).
Ships for attacking, see **275g**.

● Nations
attacking
Israel

c You will be besieged (Deut. 28:52); if their enemies besiege them (1 Kgs. 8:37); Gad, raiders will raid him (Gen. 49:19); the archers attacked Joseph (Gen. 49:22–3).

d Nahash besieged Jabesh-gilead (1 Sam. 11:1); Benhadad attacked Israel (1 Kgs. 15:20); Samaria besieged (1 Kgs. 20:1; 2 Kgs. 6:24; 17:5); the Arameans attacked Israel (1 Kgs. 20:26); Shalmaneser besieged Samaria (2 Kgs. 18:9); Dothan was surrounded (2 Kgs. 6:14); Pul, king of Assyria, came against Israel (2 Kgs. 15:19–20); Sennacherib was besieging Lachish (2 Chr. 32:9).

e The Amalekites attacked the Israelites (Exod. 17:8); the king of Arad attacked the Israelites (Num. 21:1); let us attack Gibeon (Josh. 10:4–5); Sennacherib attacked the cities of Judah (2 Kgs. 18:13; Isa. 36:1); the Arameans came against Joash (2 Chr. 24:23); Zerah the Ethiopian came against Judah (2 Chr. 14:9); the Edomites attacked Judah (2 Chr. 28:17); the Philistines and Arabs invaded Judah (2 Chr. 21:16–17).

f The nations have invaded your inheritance (Ps. 79:1); I am bringing a nation from afar against you (Jer. 5:15); a great army will advance against my people Israel (Ezek. 38:8–9, 16); siege is laid against us (Mic. 5:1).

● Attacks on
Jerusalem

g Sishak king of Egypt attacked Jerusalem (1 Kgs. 14:25; 2 Chr. 12:2); the Lord sent Rezin king of Aram and Pekah king of Israel against Jerusalem (2 Kgs. 15:37; 16:5); Assyria besieging Jerusalem (2 Kgs. 18:17; 2 Chr. 32:1–2); the king of Assyria will not besiege Jerusalem (2 Kgs. 19:32–3); the king of Babylon besieged Jerusalem (2 Kgs. 24:10–11; 25:1–2; Jer. 32:2; 39:1; 52:4–5; Ezek. 24:2; Dan. 1:1); prophecies concerning the siege of Jerusalem (Isa. 29:1–3; Jer. 4:16; 6:4–6; Ezek. 4:2–3; Luke 19:43; 21:20); the kingdoms of the north will set their thrones round Jerusalem (Jer. 1:15); the siege mounds have reached the city (Jer. 32:24); horsemen took up position at the gates (Isa. 22:7); the omens are for besieging Jerusalem (Ezek. 21:22).

h The Chaldeans lifted the siege of Jerusalem (Jer. 37:5).

● Israelites
attacking
Israelites

i Abimelech camped against Thebez (Judg. 9:50); Saul went to besiege Keilah (1 Sam. 23:8); Joab besieged Sheba (2 Sam. 20:15); Baasha attacked Judah (1 Kgs. 15:17; 2 Chr. 16:1); they besieged Tirzah (1 Kgs. 16:17); Jehoash king of Israel attacked Amaziah king of Judah (2 Kgs. 14:11; 2 Chr. 25:21); Baasha king of Israel went up against Judah (2 Chr. 16:1); Pekah fought against Judah (2 Chr. 28:5–8).

● Attacked
by evil

j The wicked have drawn sword and bent the bow (Ps. 37:14); though a host camp against me (Ps. 27:3).

713 Defence

● Defending

a The Lord will plead the case of the poor (Prov. 22:23; 23:11);

defend the rights of the poor and needy (Prov. 31:9); I will defend Jerusalem (Isa. 37:35; 38:6).

b The three mighty men defended the plot of barley (1 Chr. 11:14).

● Fortified cities

c Are the cities open or fortified? (Num. 13:19); the cities are fortified and very large (Num. 13:28); Baasha fortified Ramah (1 Kgs. 15:17; 2 Chr. 16:1); fortified cities in Judah and Benjamin (2 Chr. 11:10); he strengthened their defences (2 Chr. 11:11); he placed troops in all the fortified cities of Judah (2 Chr. 17:2).

Refuge, see **662a**.

714 Retaliation

See **804m**.

715 Resistance

● Resisting

a Resist the devil and he will flee from you (Jas. 4:7); resist the devil, firm in your faith (1 Pet. 5:9); you have not yet resisted to blood (Heb. 12:4).

b You always resist the Holy Spirit (Acts 7:51).

● Not resisting

c Do not resist one who is evil (Matt. 5:39); the righteous man does not resist you (Jas. 5:6).

d They could not stand before their enemies (Josh. 7:12–13; Judg. 2:14).

716 Contention

● God fights for you

a The Lord fights for you (Exod. 14:14, 25; Deut. 1:30; 3:22; 20:4; Josh. 23:3, 10); the Lord fights our battles (2 Chr. 32:8); our God fights for us (Neh. 4:20); the Lord fought for Israel (Josh. 10:14, 42); the Lord will fight against those nations (Zech. 14:3); the Lord struck down the Ethiopians (2 Chr. 14:12); the battle is God's (1 Sam. 17:47; 2 Chr. 20:15); you need not fight (2 Chr. 20:17); Lord, fight against those who fight me (Ps. 35:1).

● God fighting you

b The Lord will fight against you (Jer. 21:5); I will contend with you (Jer. 2:9); I will fight against them with the sword of my mouth (Rev. 2:16); God fought against them (Isa. 63:10); my spirit will not strive with man for ever (Gen. 6:3); a man wrestled with Jacob (Gen. 32:24); the stars in heaven fought against Sisera (Judg. 5:20).

● Fighting God

c Israel, you have striven with God and men (Gen. 32:28); he strove with God (Hos. 12:3–4); do not fight against the Lord (2 Chr. 13:12).

● Fighting enemies

d Joshua fought the Amalekites (Exod. 17:9–10); Saul fought Moab, Ammon, Edom, Zobah, the Philistines and the Amalekites (1 Sam. 14:47–8); David raided the Geshurites etc. (1 Sam. 27:8); David fought the Amalekites (1 Sam. 30:17); the Amorites fought Israel (Num. 21:23); Ai went out to join battle with Israel (Josh. 8:14); Dan fought Leshem (Josh. 19:47);

Jerubaal—let Baal contend (Judg. 6:31–2); Judah and Simeon fought the Canaanites (Judg. 1:1–3); Israel fought the Philistines (1 Sam. 4:1; 17:1); Joab fought the Arameans (2 Sam. 10:12–13; 1 Chr. 19:13–14); David and his men fought the Philistines (2 Sam. 21:15); fight for your families (Neh. 4:14).

e Who will begin the fight? (Judg. 1:1; 10:18; 20:18); they wanted a king to fight their battles (1 Sam. 8:20); you are fighting the Lord's battles (1 Sam. 25:28); fight the Lord's battles (1 Sam. 18:17); on the seventh day battle was joined (1 Kgs. 20:29).
Trumpets for battle, see **414*i*.**

- Enemies fighting

f Ammonites fighting Israel (Judg. 11:4); Sihon fought Israel (Judg. 11:20); the Philistines fought Israel (1 Sam. 7:10; 28:1; 31:1; 1 Chr. 10:1); the Philistines are fighting Keilah (1 Sam. 23:1); come, for the Philstines are raiding (1 Sam. 23:27); the Amalekites raided Ziklag (1 Sam. 30:1); only fight with the king of Israel (1 Kgs. 22:31–2; 2 Chr. 18:30–1); the king of Assyria was fighting Libnah (2 Kgs. 19:8); Rezin and Pekah fought Jerusalem (Isa. 7:1); the Babylonians, Chaldeans and Assyrians will come against you (Ezek. 23:23–4); our enemies conspired to fight against Jerusalem (Neh. 4:8).

g Increase your army and come out (Judg. 9:29); rise up for battle (Jer. 49:14); go out and fight (Judg. 9:38); single combat to decide a battle (1 Sam. 17:8–10); I will go and fight him (1 Sam. 17:32).

- Fighting one another

h The children struggled within her (Gen. 25:22); two Hebrews fighting (Exod. 2:13); Dathan *et al.* contended against Moses, Aaron and the Lord (Num. 26:9); Abner and Joab's young men fought (2 Sam. 2:16–17); the citizens of Shechem fought Abimelech (Judg. 9:39); the Gileadites fought the men of Ephraim (Judg. 12:4); the men of Israel fought the Benjaminites (Judg. 20:20); fight for your master's house (2 Kgs. 10:3); do not fight your brothers (2 Chr. 11:4); Amaziah challenged Jehoash to a fight (2 Chr. 25:17); David told Achish he raided Judah (1 Sam. 27:10); Johanan fought against Ishmael (Jer. 41:11); they will fight against you but not overcome you (Jer. 1:19).

i The Philistines fought one another (1 Sam. 14:20); Ammon and Moab destroyed Mount Seir and one another (2 Chr. 20:23).

j Shall we strike with the sword? (Luke 22:49); if my kingdom were of this world, my servants would be fighting (John 18:36).
Israelites attacking Israelites, see **712*i*; civil war**, see **718*g*.**

- Fight for the faith

k Contend for the faith (Phil. 1:27; Jude 3); fight the good fight (1 Tim. 1:18; 6:12); I have fought the good fight (2 Tim. 4:7); I fought with wild beasts at Ephesus (1 Cor. 15:32); strive to enter by the narrow door (Luke 13:24).

- Run the race

l Let us run the race before us (Heb. 12:1); in a race only one receives the prize (1 Cor. 9:24); an athlete must compete according to the rules (2 Tim. 2:5).

- Wrestling

m A man wrestled with Jacob (Gen. 32:24); with great wrestlings I have wrestled with my sister (Gen. 30:8); we do not wrestle against flesh and blood (Eph. 6:12).

717 Peace

- God of peace

a The Lord is Peace (Judg. 6:24); peace in heaven (Luke 19:38); God is not a God of disorder but of peace (1 Cor. 14:33); the God of peace (Rom. 15:33; 16:20; 2 Cor. 13:11; Phil. 4:9; Heb. 13:20); the Lord of peace (2 Thess. 3:16); his name will be Prince of Peace (Isa. 9:6); there is a time for peace (Eccles. 3:8).

- Peace of God

b I will give you peace in the land (Lev. 26:6); I give Phinehas my covenant of peace (Num. 25:12–13); the Lord will bless his people with peace (Ps. 29:11); all her paths are peace (Prov. 3:17); peace be on Israel (Ps. 125:5; 128:6); peace to you (Phil. 1:2; 1 Thess. 1:1; 1 Pet. 1:2; 2 Pet. 1:2; 3 John 14; Jude 2); peace be with you (John 20:19, 21, 26).

c Peace from God (Eph. 1:2; 6:23; Col. 1:2; 2 Thess. 1:2; 1 Tim. 1:2; 2 Tim. 1:2; Titus 1:4; 2 John 3; Rev. 1:4); may the Lord of peace give you peace (2 Thess. 3:16); be at peace with God (Job 22:21); the peace of God (Phil. 4:7); he preached peace to those far away and to those near (Eph. 2:17); this one will be our peace (Mic. 5:5); he is our peace (Eph. 2:14); peace to you and your house (1 Sam. 25:6); peace to you and peace to him who helps you (1 Chr. 12:18).

d The good news of peace (Acts 10:36); we have peace with God (Rom. 5:1); peace to all who are in Christ (1 Pet. 5:14); my peace I give you (John 14:27); in me you have peace (John 16:33); let the peace of Christ rule in your hearts (Col. 3:15).

- Live in peace

e Great peace have they who love your law (Ps. 119:165); if you had obeyed your peace would have been like a river (Isa. 48:18); the effect of righteousness will be peace (Isa. 32:17–18); you will keep in perfect peace him who trusts in you (Isa. 26:3); the mind set on the Spirit is life and peace (Rom. 8:6); the kingdom of God is peace in the Holy Spirit (Rom. 14:17); the fruit of the Spirit is peace (Gal. 5:22); may God fill you with joy and peace in believing (Rom. 15:13).

f As far as possible, be at peace with all men (Rom. 12:18); preserving the unity of the Spirit in the bond of peace (Eph. 4:3); be at peace with one another (Mark 9:50; 1 Thess. 5:13); live in peace and the God of love and peace will be with you (2 Cor. 13:11); God has called us to peace (1 Cor. 7:15); peace and mercy be on all who walk by this rule (Gal. 6:16); be diligent to be found by him in peace (2 Pet. 3:14); pursue peace (2 Tim. 2:22; Heb. 12:14); seek peace and pursue it (1 Pet. 3:11); the wisdom from above is peaceable (Jas. 3:17); pray for kings, that we may have a quiet life (1 Tim. 2:2).

● Men of
peace

g Solomon would be a man of peace (1 Chr. 22:9); Melchizedek was king of peace (Heb. 7:2); Jacob was a quiet man (Gen. 25:27); through Felix they had much peace (Acts 24:2).

h The people in Laish were quiet and secure (Judg. 18:7, 27); David sent away Abner in peace (2 Sam. 3:21–3).

● Time of
peace

i He makes peace in your borders (Ps. 147:14); there will be no end to peace (Isa. 9:7); the land had rest from war (Josh. 11:23; 14:15); the whole earth is at rest (Isa. 14:7); rest from their enemies (Josh. 23:1); the Lord gave them rest (Josh. 21:44; 22:4; 2 Sam. 7:1); I will give you rest from your enemies (2 Sam. 7:11); until the Lord gives them rest (Josh. 1:15); in this place I will give peace (Hag. 2:9); her warfare has ended (Isa. 40:2); the land had peace (Judg. 3:11, 30; 5:31; 8:28; 2 Chr. 14:1); Solomon had peace on all sides (1 Kgs. 4:24; 5:4); no one was at war with Asa, for the Lord gave him rest (2 Chr. 14:6); the Lord gave them rest (1 Chr. 22:18; 23:25; 2 Chr. 15:15); there was no more war (2 Chr. 15:19); the kingdom was at peace (2 Chr. 20:30); there was peace between Israel and the Amorites (1 Sam. 7:14); peace between Hiram and Solomon (1 Kgs. 5:12); there will be peace in my lifetime (2 Kgs. 20:19; Isa. 39:8); the church had peace (Acts 9:31).

● No peace

j There is no peace for the wicked (Isa. 48:22; 57:21); never seek the peace of Ammon or Moab (Deut. 23:6); they have not known the way of peace (Isa. 59:8; Rom. 3:17); they seek peace but there will be none (Ezek. 7:25); there was no peace in those days (2 Chr. 15:5); if you only knew the things that make for peace! (Luke 19:42).

k The prophets prophesy peace falsely (Jer. 14:13); 'peace', when there is no peace (Jer. 6:14; 8:11; Ezek. 13:10, 16); they cry 'Peace!' when fed (Mic. 3:5); they prophesy peace to those who despise the Lord (Jer. 23:17); when a prophet prophesies peace and it comes to pass you will know (Jer. 28:9); when they say 'Peace and security' destruction will come (1 Thess. 5:3); Jesus did not come to bring peace (Matt. 10:34; Luke 12:51). **Making peace**, see **719**; **Peace offering**, see **981***v*.

718 War

● Principles
of war

a There is a time for war (Eccles. 3:8); by wise guidance you can wage war (Prov. 24:6); in war God will redeem you from the power of the sword (Job 5:20); though war rise against me I will be confident (Ps. 27:3); the war was of God (1 Chr. 5:22); evil men continually stir up wars (Ps. 140:2).

b When the people see war they might change their minds (Exod. 13:17); lest in war they join our enemies (Exod. 1:10); when you go to war, do not be afraid (Deut. 20:1); when you hear of wars, do not be afraid (Matt. 24:6; Mark 13:7; Luke 21:9); when your people go to war and they pray (1 Kgs. 8:44; 2 Chr. 6:34).

c When you go to war, keep the camp clean (Deut. 23:9–14).

d We do not wage war according to the flesh (2 Cor. 10:3).

● Ready
for war

e What king goes to war without first considering? (Luke 14:31); in the spring kings go to war but David did not (2 Sam. 11:1; 1 Chr. 20:1); shall your brethren go to war and you sit here? (Num. 32:6); prepare for war! (Joel 3:9); he trains my hands for war (2 Sam. 22:35; Ps. 18:34; 144:1); I am for peace, but they are for war (Ps. 120:7); David was a man of warfare (2 Sam. 17:8); so could not build the temple (1 Kgs. 5:3; 1 Chr. 28:3).

f If the trumpet makes an unclear sound, who will prepare for war? (1 Cor. 14:8); the sound of the trumpet, the alarm and war (Jer. 4:19).

● Civil war

g Civil war in Israel (Josh. 22:12); Benjamin went to battle against Israel (Judg. 20:14); war between the houses of Saul and David (2 Sam. 3:1, 6); Rehoboam was about to make war with Israel (1 Kgs. 12:21; 2 Chr. 11:1); war between Rehoboam and Jeroboam (1 Kgs. 14:30; 15:6; 2 Chr. 12:15); war between Abijam [Abijah] and Jeroboam (1 Kgs. 15:7; 2 Chr. 13:2); war between Asa and Baasha (1 Kgs. 15:16, 32); Egyptians will fight Egyptians (Isa. 19:2); the rider on the red horse caused civil war (Rev. 6:4).

Fighting one another, see **716h**.

● Various
wars

h Four kings went to war against five (Gen. 14:1–2, 8–9); Og king of Bashan went to battle against Israel (Num. 21:33; Deut. 3:1); the Canaanites made war on Israel (Josh. 9:2); Moab and Ammon made war on Jehoshaphat (2 Chr. 20:1); Aram warred against Israel (2 Kgs. 6:8); Rezin of Aram and Pekah of Israel made war on Jerusalem (2 Kgs. 16:5); from now on you will have wars (2 Chr. 16:9).

i The Lord will war against Amalek (Exod. 17:16); Joshua waged war a long time with the kings (Josh. 11:18); war against the Philistines (1 Sam. 14:52; 28:15; 2 Sam. 21:18; 1 Chr. 20:4); Ahaziah and Joram made war against Hazael (2 Kgs. 8:28; 2 Chr. 22:5); the Reubenites made war on the Hagrites (1 Chr. 5:10, 18–20); Neco making war on Carchemish (2 Chr. 35:20); Uzziah made war against the Philistines (2 Chr. 26:6).

j Nation will rise against nation (Luke 21:10); the horn waged war against the saints (Dan. 7:21); the beast waged war against the saints (Rev. 13:7); the kings gathered for battle at Armageddon (Rev. 16:14, 16); they waged war against the rider and his army (Rev. 19:19); there was war in heaven (Rev. 12:7).

k In righteousness he wages war (Rev. 19:11).

Attack, see **712**.

719 Pacification

● God gives
peace

a He makes wars cease (Ps. 46:9); I will break the bow, sword and war from the land (Hos. 2:18); he makes even his enemies at peace with him (Prov. 16:7); the Lord give you peace (Num. 6:26); he speaks peace to his people (Ps. 85:8); let them make peace with me (Isa. 27:5); on earth peace to men (Luke 2:14); they will never again learn war (Isa. 2:4; Mic. 4:3).

b Pray for the peace of Jerusalem (Ps. 122:6); may peace be within you (Ps. 122:8); I will extend peace to her like a river (Isa. 66:12); peace to those far and near (Isa. 57:19).

● Peace through Christ

c God was in Christ reconciling the world to himself (2 Cor. 5:18–20); through Christ God reconciles all things to himself (Col. 1:20); reconciled through Christ's death (Rom. 5:10–11; Col. 1:22).

d He is our peace, who made both one (Eph. 2:14); he reconciles Jew and Gentile in one body through the cross (Eph. 2:16). **Peace with God**, see **717c**.

● People seeking peace

e Blessed are the peacemakers (Matt. 5:9); we have been given the ministry of reconciliation (2 Cor. 5:18–19); a greeting of peace to the house (Matt. 10:12–13; Luke 10:5–6); if a man of peace is there your peace will rest on him (Luke 10:6).

f Pursue what makes for peace (Rom. 14:19); pursue peace with all men (Heb. 12:14); shall the sword devour for ever? (2 Sam. 2:26); make it your ambition to lead a quiet life (1 Thess. 4:11); righteousness is sown in peace by those who make peace (Jas. 3:18); they will beat their swords into ploughshares (Isa. 2:4; Mic. 4:3).

● People making peace

g Jacob sought to pacify Esau with his present (Gen. 32:20); Moses wanted to bring peace (Acts 7:26); the Gibeonites made peace with Israel (Josh. 10:1, 4); no city made peace except Gibeon (Josh. 11:19); Jonathan reconciled David to Saul (1 Sam. 19:4–7); Joab reconciled David to Absalom (2 Sam. 14:1–24); make your peace with me (Isa. 36:16); the people of Sidon sued for peace (Acts 12:20).

h The Levite went to reconcile his concubine to him (Judg. 19:3); go and be reconciled with your brother (Matt. 5:24); be reconciled with your accuser (Matt. 5:25; Luke 12:58).

i Moses offered peace to Sihon (Deut. 2:26); when you attack a city, offer terms of peace (Deut. 20:10); he will ask for terms of peace (Luke 14:32); they made peace with the Benjaminites (Judg. 21:13); the kings made peace with Israel (2 Sam. 10:19; 1 Chr. 19:19); Jehoshaphat made peace with the king of Israel (1 Kgs. 22:44); make your peace with me (2 Kgs. 18:31). **Rest from war**, see **717i**.

720 Mediation

● Mediator with God

a If one man sins against another, God will mediate (1 Sam. 2:25); if only there were an arbitrator between God and man (Job 9:33); God sought for a man to stand in the gap (Ezek. 22:30); Moses stood in the breach (Ps. 106:23); there is one mediator between

God and man (1 Tim. 2:5); Jesus is the mediator of a new covenant (Heb. 8:6; 9:15; 12:24).

b The law was mediated by angels (Acts 7:53; Gal. 3:19); if there is an angel as mediator (Job 33:23).

● Mediator between men

c The wise woman of Tekoa mediated between Absalom and David (2 Sam. 14:1–20); no one is deputed to listen to you on behalf of the king (2 Sam. 15:3).

721 Submission

● Submit to God

a We should submit to the Father of spirits (Heb. 12:9); submit yourselves to God (Jas. 4:7); the church submits to Christ (Eph. 5:24).

● Submit to others

b Submit yourselves to one another (Eph. 5:21); submit to such men (1 Cor. 16:16); servants, be submissive to your masters (1 Pet. 2:18); submit to your leaders (Heb. 13:17); the younger should be submissive to their elders (1 Pet. 5:5).

c Hagar had to submit to her mistress (Gen. 16:9); wives, be submissive to your husbands (Eph. 5:22–4; Col. 3:18; Titus 2:5; 1 Pet. 3:1); a woman should learn in submission (1 Cor. 14:34–5; 1 Tim. 2:11); holy women in the past were submissive to their husbands (1 Pet. 3:5).

Slavery, see **745***e*.

722 Combatant. Army. Navy. Air Force

● God as a warrior

a The Lord is a warrior (Exod. 15:3); the Lord will go forth like a warrior (Isa. 42:13); the Lord of hosts, the God of the armies of Israel (1 Sam. 17:45); the Lord is with me like a warrior (Jer. 20:11); the Lord at the head of his army (Joel 2:11); the commander of the army of the Lord (Josh. 5:14); the Lord is mustering an army for battle (Isa. 13:4).

● Warriors

b By your sword you shall live (Gen. 27:40); Makir was a man of war (Josh. 17:1); Jephthah was a mighty warrior (Judg. 11:1); Kish was a mighty man of valour (1 Sam. 9:1); Goliath was a champion (1 Sam. 17:4); Goliath was a warrior from his youth (1 Sam. 17:33); David was a warrior, a mighty man (1 Sam. 16:18); David and his men were mighty men (2 Sam. 17:8, 10); David could not build the temple because he was a man of war (1 Chr. 28:3); Jeroboam was a valiant warrior (1 Kgs. 11:28); Asa had an army of brave warriors (2 Chr. 14:8).

● Mighty men

c David's mighty men (2 Sam. 23:8–39; 1 Chr. 11:10–47; 12:1–22); Benaiah had charge of the 30 (1 Chr. 27:6); the mighty men did not follow Adonijah (1 Kgs. 1:8); and were not invited (1 Kgs. 1:10); 60 mighty men, expert in war (S. of S. 3:7–8).

● Officers

d Saul set David over the men of war (1 Sam. 18:5); Saul made him commander of a thousand (1 Sam. 18:13); Abner was commander of Saul's army (2 Sam. 2:8); Joab was over the army (2 Sam. 8:16; 20:23; 1 Kgs. 1:19; 1 Chr. 11:6; 18:15; 27:34);

Absalom set Amasa over the army in place of Joab (2 Sam. 17:25; 19:13); Benaiah was over the Cherethites and Pelethites (2 Sam. 8:18; 20:23; 1 Chr. 18:17); Benaiah was over the army (1 Kgs. 2:35; 4:4); Joab, Abishai and Ittai were over thirds of David's army (2 Sam. 18:2); commanders of thousands and hundreds (2 Sam. 18:1); Abishai became commander of the 30 (2 Sam. 23:19); Naaman was captain of the army of Aram (2 Kgs. 5:1); Shophach commanded Hadadezer's army (1 Chr. 19:16, 18).

- Centurions
  e A centurion whose servant was paralysed (Matt. 8:5–6); a centurion's slave was ill (Luke 7:2); a centurion called Cornelius (Acts 10:1, 22); a centurion named Julius (Acts 27:1).

- Chiliarchs
  f Lysias, the chiliarch of the Roman cohort (Acts 21:31–7; 22:24, 26–9; 23:10, 15–19, 22; 24:7, 22).

- Armies
  g A king is not saved by a big army (Ps. 33:16); awesome as an army with banners (S. of S. 6:4, 10); locusts have no king but march in rank (Prov. 30:27); God's great army of locusts (Joel 2:5, 8).

  h Saul chose 3000 men for a standing army (1 Sam. 13:2); the army of Judah (2 Chr. 17:14–19); all Israel were mustered (2 Kgs. 3:6); David put garrisons in Damascus (2 Sam. 8:6); and in Edom (2 Sam. 8:14; 1 Chr. 18:13); Uzziah had a prepared army (2 Chr. 26:11); an army of 307 500 (2 Chr. 26:13); the garrison of the Philistines was in Bethlehem (2 Sam. 23:14).

  i The Israelites went in battle array (Exod. 13:18); Israel drew up in battle array against the Philistines (1 Sam. 17:2, 21); an army surrounded Dothan (2 Kgs. 6:14, 15).

  j The armies of heaven (1 Kgs. 22:19; 2 Chr. 18:18; Rev. 19:14); the Father would send Jesus more than twelve legions of angels (Matt. 26:53).

- Soldiers
  k Men 20 and up able to go to war (Num. 1:3, 20–45; 26:2); a man newly married shall not go to war (Deut. 24:5).

  l A census was taken of men able to serve in the army (Num. 1:3); armed men from Gilead must fight beyond the Jordan (Num. 32:20; Deut. 3:18); Saul enlisted any mighty man he saw (1 Sam. 14:52); the men of war came to make David king (1 Chr. 12:23–38); Amaziah hired soldiers from Israel (2 Chr. 25:6); the Cherethites and Pelethites accompanied them (1 Kgs. 1:38, 44).

  m 12 000 armed men to fight Midian (Num. 31:5); 600 armed men of Dan (Judg. 18:11, 16, 17); 400 000 soldiers fought the Benjaminites (Judg. 20:2, 17); 26 000 Benjaminites who drew sword (Judg. 20:15); Ahithophel wanted to choose 12 000 men (2 Sam. 17:1); 180 000 men of Judah and Benjamin (1 Kgs. 12:21); 400 000 men for Abijah against 800 000 for Jeroboam (2 Chr. 13:3); 232 young men and 7000 of Israel (1 Kgs. 20:15); 200 soldiers, 70 cavalry and 200 spearmen to guard Paul (Acts 23:23); a captain of 50 with his 50 (2 Kgs. 1:9, 11, 13).

n The governor's soldiers mocked Jesus (Matt. 27:27–31; Mark 15:16–20).

o A good soldier of Jesus Christ (2 Tim. 2:3–4); soldiers asked, 'What shall we do?' (Luke 3:14); who serves as a soldier at his own expense? (1 Cor. 9:7); Epaphroditus, my fellow-soldier (Phil. 2:25); Archippus our fellow-soldier (Philem. 2).

723 Weapons

● Weapons of God

a A flaming sword at the garden of Eden (Gen. 3:24); the commander of the Lord's army with a drawn sword (Josh. 5:13); the angel with his sword drawn (Num. 22:23, 31; 1 Chr. 21:16); a sword for the Lord and Gideon! (Judg. 7:20); rest, sword of the Lord! (Jer. 47:6).

b The Lord has brought out weapons and wrath from his armoury (Jer. 50:25); Assyria, the rod of God's anger (Isa. 10:5); Babylon is his war-club (Jer. 51:20); Israel is like a faulty bow (Hos. 7:16).

c Six men with shattering weapons to slay at God's command (Ezek. 9:2); a sword against God's people (Ezek. 21:9–12); a sword is drawn for slaughter (Ezek. 21:28).

d Christ has a sharp two-edged sword (Rev. 1:16; 2:12); gird your sword on your thigh (Ps. 45:3); out of his mouth comes a sharp sword (Rev. 19:15); the sword of the Spirit, which is the word of God (Eph. 6:17); the word of God is sharper than a two-edged sword (Heb. 4:12).

● Weapons of the Christian

e The weapons of righteousness (2 Cor. 6:7); weapons with divine power (2 Cor. 10:4); a two-edged sword in their hands (Ps. 149:6); let him who has no sword sell his mantle and buy one (Luke 22:36).

f Put on the armour of light (Rom. 13:12); put on the full armour of God (Eph. 6:11–17); put on the breastplate of faith etc. (1 Thess. 5:8); righteousness as a breastplate (Isa. 59:17); wisdom is better than weapons of war (Eccles. 9:18).

g Take the helmet of salvation (Eph. 6:17); as a helmet the hope of salvation (1 Thess. 5:8).

● Stocking weapons

h The king will have people make his weapons (1 Sam. 8:12); the Philistines did not want Israel to make weapons (1 Sam. 13:19).

i Rehoboam put shields and spears in every city (2 Chr. 11:12); Uzziah prepared spears (2 Chr. 26:14); Hezekiah provided many weapons and shields (2 Chr. 32:5); beat ploughshares into swords and pruning hooks into spears (Joel 3:10); here are two swords—enough! (Luke 22:38).

● Literal weapons

j Goliath wore bronze scale armour weighing 5000 shekels (1 Sam. 17:5); bronze greaves on his legs (1 Sam. 17:6); Saul's armour was too heavy for David (1 Sam. 17:38–9); Jonathan gave David his armour (1 Sam. 18:4); David put Goliath's weapons in his tent (1 Sam. 17:54); they put Saul's armour in the house of their gods (1 Chr. 10:10).

k Take your quiver and your bow (Gen. 27:3); gird on your swords (Exod. 32:27); Joab had a dagger at his waist (2 Sam. 20:8); Samson used the jaw-bone of a donkey (Judg. 15:15).

l Ehud had a two-edged sword (Judg. 3:16); Goliath's sword (1 Sam. 17:51; 21:9; 22:10, 13); they all girded on their swords (1 Sam. 25:13); the Field of Sword-edges (2 Sam. 2:16); bring me a sword (1 Kgs. 3:24).

m Nehemiah stationed armed men by the wall (Neh. 4:13); half of the people carried arms (Neh. 4:16, 21); a weapon in one hand and a load in the other (Neh. 4:17).

n The crowd armed with swords and clubs (Matt. 26:47, 55; Mark 14:43; Luke 22:52); they carried weapons (John 18:3); have you come with swords and clubs to arrest me? (Mark 14:48).
Weapons for fuel, see **385g**.

● Spears and javelins

o Joshua held out his javelin towards Ai (Josh. 8:18); Goliath had a bronze javelin (1 Sam. 17:6); the shaft of his spear was like a weaver's beam (1 Sam. 17:7; 2 Sam. 21:19; 1 Chr. 11:23; 20:5); you come to me with a sword, a spear and a javelin (1 Sam. 17:45); Saul's spear was stuck in the ground (1 Sam. 26:7); they took Saul's spear (1 Sam. 26:11–12, 16, 22); Jehoiada gave them the shields and spears which had been David's (2 Kgs. 11:10–11; 2 Chr. 23:9).

p Joab pierced Absalom with three spears (2 Sam. 18:14); Abishai killed 300 with his spear (2 Sam. 23:18); Benaiah snatched the Egyptian's spear and killed him with it (2 Sam. 23:21).
Missiles, see **287**; **shields**, see **662i**; **helmets**, see **662k**.

● Armour bearers

q Abimelech was killed by his armour bearer (Judg. 9:54); Jonathan's armour bearer (1 Sam. 14:1); David became Saul's armour bearer (1 Sam. 16:21); Goliath had a shield bearer (1 Sam. 17:7, 41); Saul's armour bearer was afraid to kill him (1 Sam. 31:4; 1 Chr. 10:4); ten men who carried Joab's armour (2 Sam. 18:15); Joab's armour bearers (2 Sam. 23:37).

● Weapons are useless

r No weapon will succeed against you (Isa. 54:17); weapons are useless against the crocodile (Job 41:26–9).

s Not by your sword or your bow (Josh. 24:12); the Lord does not deliver by sword or spear (1 Sam. 17:47); swords into ploughshares and spears into pruning hooks (Isa. 2:4; Mic. 4:3).

● Lacking weapons

t Lack of arms in Israel (Judg. 5:8; 1 Sam. 13:22); David had no sword (1 Sam. 17:50); David was without weapons (1 Sam. 21:8); how have the weapons of war perished! (2 Sam. 1:27).

724 Arena

● Theatre

a They rushed together into the theatre (Acts 19:29).

Section five: Results of action

725 **Completion**

● God's work
finished

a God finished his work of creation (Gen. 2:1–2; Heb. 4:3); I have finished the work you gave me to do (John 17:4); it is finished! (John 19:30); Jesus, knowing that all was accomplished (John 19:28); Christ sat down on the right hand of God [his work finished] (Heb. 8:1; 10:12); the Lord will complete what concerns me (Ps. 138:8); he who began a good work in you will complete it (Phil. 1:6); it is done! (Rev. 16:17).

● God's words
fulfilled

b The Lord did what he had promised to Abraham (Gen. 18:19; 21:1; Neh. 9:8); convinced that God had power to do what he promised (Rom. 4:21); every one of God's promises was fulfilled (Josh. 21:45; 23:14); that the Lord may fulfil his promise (1 Kgs. 2:4); the word of the Lord about Eli was fulfilled (1 Kgs. 2:27); the Lord has fulfilled his word (1 Kgs. 8:20); God fulfilled to Solomon what he promised to David (1 Kgs. 6:12; 8:15, 24; 2 Chr. 6:4, 10, 15); has he spoken and will he not do it? (Num. 23:19); my words will be fulfilled in their time (Luke 1:20); blessed is she who believed that there would be a fulfilment (Luke 1:45); that Jesus' word might be fulfilled (John 18:32); the mystery of God will be completed (Rev. 10:7); do as you have said (1 Chr. 17:23).

c Who speaks and it comes to pass unless the Lord commanded it? (Lam. 3:37); whatever word I speak will be performed (Ezek. 12:25); God did not let any of Samuel's words fall to the ground (1 Sam. 3:19); all Samuel said came true (1 Sam. 9:6); the days approach and the fulfilment of every vision (Ezek. 12:23).

d The word fulfilled which was spoken to: Ahijah (1 Kgs. 15:29); Jehu (1 Kgs. 16:12; 2 Kgs. 15:12); Joshua (1 Kgs. 16:34); Elijah (2 Kgs. 1:17; 9:36; 10:10); Jonah (2 Kgs. 14:25); Jeremiah (2 Chr. 36:21, 22; Ezra 1:1).

● The scriptures
fulfilled

e The scriptures must be fulfilled (Matt. 26:54, 56; Mark 14:49; Luke 4:21; 18:31; 24:44; John 19:28; Acts 1:16); what is written about me must be fulfilled (Luke 22:37); Jesus came to fulfil the Law and the Prophets (Matt. 5:17); not a jot or tittle will pass from the law till all is fulfilled (Matt. 5:18); I will not eat it until it is fulfilled (Luke 22:16); that the scripture may be fulfilled (John 13:18; 15:25; 17:12; 19:24, 28, 36); that what was spoken through the prophet might be fulfilled (Matt. 1:22; 2:15, 17, 23; 4:14; 8:17; 12:17; 13:35; 21:4; 27:9; John 12:38); the scripture was fulfilled (Mark 15:28); John is the one spoken of by Isaiah (Matt. 3:3); God fulfilled the words of the prophets (Acts 3:18); the people fulfilled the words of the prophets (Acts 13:27); days of vengeance, that everything written might be fulfilled (Luke 21:22).

f He who loves his neighbour has fulfilled the law (Rom. 13:8);

love fulfils the law (Rom. 13:10); that the requirement of the law might be fulfilled in us (Rom. 8:4).

● Completing work

g Complete the quota of bricks (Exod. 5:13–18); the tabernacle was completed (Exod. 39:32); the temple was finished (1 Kgs. 6:38; 7:51; 2 Chr. 5:1; 7:11; 8:16); Hiram finished all his work in the temple (1 Kgs. 7:40); Zerubbabel will complete the temple (Zech. 4:9); the rebuilt temple finished (Ezra 6:14–15); the wall of Jerusalem was completed (Neh. 6:15).

h Tell Archippus to complete his work in the Lord (Col. 4:17); that I may finish my course (Acts 20:24); I have finished the race (2 Tim. 4:7).

i Fill up the measure of your fathers! (Matt. 23:32).

● Vows fulfilled

j Vows must be fulfilled (Num. 30:2–15); fulfil your vows (Matt. 5:33).

726 Non-completion

● Incomplete works

a I have not found your works completed (Rev. 3:2); Joab began the count but did not finish (1 Chr. 27:24); if he is not able to finish the tower (Luke 14:29–30).

b The iniquity of the Amorite is not yet complete (Gen. 15:16).

● Unfulfilled word

c If a prophet's word does not happen, it is not from the Lord (Deut. 18:22); the days lengthen and every vision comes to nothing (Ezek. 12:22).

727 Success

● God victorious

a Victory belongs to the Lord (Prov. 21:31); God defeats your enemies (Deut. 23:14; 33:29); the Lord routed Sisera (Judg. 4:15); God routed Jeroboam (2 Chr. 13:15); the Lord thundered so that the Philistines were routed (1 Sam. 7:10); may your enemies be scattered (Num. 10:35); God will tread down our enemies (Ps. 60:12; 108:13); the Lord will prevail over his enemies (Isa. 42:13); do not let men prevail against you (2 Chr. 14:11).

● Success through God

b Abraham's servant prayed for success (Gen. 24:12, 42); grant me success this day (Neh. 1:11); the God of heaven will give us success (Neh. 2:20); keep the law that you may have success (Josh. 1:7, 8; 1 Kgs. 2:3; 1 Chr. 22:13); the Lord be with you that you may be successful (1 Chr. 22:11); God was with Joseph so he was successful (Gen. 39:2, 23); David always prospered, for God was with him (1 Sam. 18:14); wherever Hezekiah went he prospered (2 Kgs. 18:7).

Good hand of God, see **703***d*.

● Victory over enemies

c A wise man brings down the stronghold of the mighty (Prov. 21:22); victory over enemies through God (2 Sam. 22:38–43; Ps. 18:37–42); by faith they conquered kingdoms (Heb. 11:33); I will crush his enemies before him (Ps. 89:23); the Lord had given victory to Aram through Naaman (2 Kgs. 5:1); the Lord gave victory through Shammah (2 Sam. 23:12); Judah conquered because they relied on the Lord (2 Chr. 13:18); God commands victories for Jacob (Ps. 44:4); David defeated his enemies when the Lord broke out against them (2 Sam. 5:20; 1 Chr. 14:11); the Lord will cause your enemies to be defeated (Deut. 28:7); seed possessing the gate of their enemies (Gen. 22:17; 24:60); we will overcome (Num. 13:30); you will defeat the Arameans at Aphek (2 Kgs. 13:17).

d Defeating: Midian (Judg. 6:16); Og (Deut. 1:4; 29:7); Sihon (Deut. 4:46; 29:7); the Amorites (Num. 21:24; Deut. 1:4; Josh. 2:10); the Amalekites (1 Sam. 15:7); Hadadezer (2 Sam. 8:3, 9; 1 Chr. 18:3); Ammon, Moab and Mount Seir (2 Chr. 20:22).

e The Amorites had defeated Moab (Num. 21:26–30); Abimelech took Thebez (Judg. 9:50); the Gileadites defeated Ephraim (Judg. 12:4).

f Chedorlaomer defeated the Rephaim (Gen. 14:5); they conquered the country of the Amalekites (Gen. 14:7); Abraham defeated the kings (Gen. 14:15); Nebuchadnezzar defeated Pharaoh Neco (Jer. 46:2).

g Joshua overcame Amalek (Exod. 17:13); Joshua defeated Horam (Josh. 10:33); Gideon routed Zeba and Zalmunna (Judg. 8:12); David defeated the Philistines (2 Sam. 8:1; 1 Chr. 18:1); and the Moabites (2 Sam. 8:2; 1 Chr. 18:2); Hezekiah defeated the Philistines (2 Kgs. 18:8).

h My enemies fell under my feet (2 Sam. 22:39; Ps. 18:38); my enemies stumbled and fell (Ps. 27:2); David's enemies were put under his feet (1 Kgs. 5:3).

Death overcome, see **361***aw*.

• Given into their hands

i God gave into their hands: their enemies (Gen. 14:20; Josh. 21:44); the people of the land (Deut. 7:2; 31:5; Josh. 11:8); the Canaanites (Num. 21:3; Judg. 1:2, 4; Neh. 9:24); Og (Num. 21:34; Deut. 3:2–3); Sihon (Deut. 2:24, 30–3, 36; Judg. 11:21); Jericho (Josh. 6:2, 16); Ai (Josh. 8:1, 18); the kings (Deut. 7:24; Josh. 10:8, 19; 11:6); the Canaanite towns (Josh. 10:30, 32); the Amalekites (Josh. 24:8; 1 Sam. 30:23); Moab (Judg. 3:28); Sisera (Judg. 4:7); Midian (Judg. 7:9, 14, 15); Oreb and Zeeb (Judg. 8:3); Ammon (Judg. 11:32); the Benjaminites (Judg. 20:28); the Philistines (1 Sam. 14:12; 23:4; 1 Chr. 14:10); the Arameans (1 Kgs. 20:13, 28).

j Will you give them into our hands? (1 Sam. 14:37); I will give them into your hands (2 Sam. 5:19); the Lord will give you into my hands (1 Sam. 17:46, 47); if you give the Ammonites into my hand (Judg. 11:30); the Lord gave the Ammonites into my hand (Judg. 12:3); our god has given Samson into our hands (Judg. 16:23–4); the Lord gave Saul into David's hands (1 Sam. 24:4, 10, 18; 26:8, 23); God has delivered David into my hand (1 Sam. 23:7); God did not deliver David into Saul's hands

(1 Sam. 23:14); God has delivered up the rebels (2 Sam. 18:28); the Lord will give Ramoth-gilead into the king's hand (1 Kgs. 22:6, 12, 15; 2 Chr. 18:5, 11, 14); the Lord will give the Moabites into your hand (2 Kgs. 3:18); the Lord delivered Jehoiakim into Nebuchadnezzar's hand (Dan. 1:2).

Pursuing enemies, see **619c**.

- Jesus overcoming

k I have overcome the world (John 16:33); he triumphed over authorities in the cross (Col. 2:15); the Lamb will overcome them (Rev. 17:14); his enemies will become his footstool (Ps. 110:1; Matt. 22:44; Mark 12:36; Luke 20:42–3; Acts 2:34–5; Heb. 1:13; 10:13); he must reign until his enemies are put under his feet (1 Cor. 15:25).

- Overcoming through Jesus

l The power of Hades will not overcome the church (Matt. 16:18); we are more than conquerors through him who loved us (Rom. 8:37); he gives us the victory through our Lord Jesus Christ (1 Cor. 15:57); God leads us in triumph in Christ (2 Cor. 2:14); death is swallowed up in victory (1 Cor. 15:54–5); God will soon crush Satan under your feet (Rom. 16:20); you have overcome the evil one (1 John 2:13, 14); they overcame him by the blood of the Lamb (Rev. 12:11); everyone born of God overcomes the world by faith (1 John 5:4–5); those victorious over the beast (Rev. 15:2); overcome evil with good (Rom. 12:21).

m Promises to those who overcome (Rev. 2:7, 11, 17, 26; 3:5, 12, 21); he who overcomes will be God's son (Rev. 21:7).

- Various victories

n The rider on the white horse went out conquering and to conquer (Rev. 6:2).

728 Failure

- Prospect of defeat

a You will be defeated before your enemies (Lev. 26:17; Num. 14:42; Deut. 28:25); when Israel have been defeated by an enemy (1 Kgs. 8:33; 2 Chr. 6:24).

b Three months being defeated by your enemies? (2 Sam. 24:13; 1 Chr. 21:12).

c It is defeat for you to go to law with one another (1 Cor. 6:7).

- Defeat of Israel

d Israel were defeated by the Amalekites and Canaanites (Num. 14:45); the Lord delivered Israel into the hands of the Philistines (Judg. 13:1; 1 Sam. 28:19); the Lord is giving these three kings into the hand of Moab (2 Kgs. 3:10, 13); the Israelites were defeated (1 Sam. 4:10); the Lord delivered Ahaz into the hands of the king of Aram (2 Chr. 28:5); the Lord gave them into the hands of Hazael (2 Kgs. 13:3); he handed them over to the nations (Ps. 106:41); Jerusalem will be handed over to the king of Babylon (Jer. 38:3); Israel were routed by the men of Ai (Josh. 7:4); Israel has been routed by their enemies (Josh. 7:8).

- Defeat of Judah

e The Lord delivered Judah into the hands of the Arameans (2 Chr. 24:24); I will deliver them into the hand of Nebuchadnezzar (Jer. 21:7); I will give this city into the hand of the king of Babylon

(Jer. 32:3–5; 34:2); the Lord gave them into the hand of Nebuchadnezzar (Ezra 5:12); I will give you into the hands of those you hate (Ezek. 23:28); you delivered them into the hands of their oppressors (Neh. 9:27); into the hands of the people of the land (Neh. 9:30); we have been given into the hands of the kings of the lands (Ezra 9:7); he delivered his people to the sword (Ps. 78:62).

● Defeated by their fellows

f Israel were beaten by Benjamin (Judg. 20:21, 25); Israel were defeated by David's men (2 Sam. 2:17; 18:7); Judah was routed by Israel (2 Kgs. 14:12; 2 Chr. 25:22).

● Defeat of others

g The kings defeated by the Israelites (Josh. 12:1–24).

h I will give Pharaoh Hophra into the hand of his enemies (Jer. 44:30); I will give Egypt into the hand of Nebuchadnezzar (Jer. 46:26).

729 Trophy

Booty, see **790**.

730 Prosperity

● The righteous prosper

a He who fears the Lord will prosper (Ps. 25:13); prosperity rewards the righteous (Prov. 13:21); whatever he does, he prospers (Ps. 1:3); the humble will delight in prosperity (Ps. 37:11); prosperity for those who hear and serve God (Job 36:11).

b May prosperity be in your towers! (Ps. 122:7).

● The wicked prosper

c The wicked prosper (Ps. 10:5); I saw the prosperity of the wicked (Ps. 73:3); the wicked spend their days in prosperity (Job 21:13); robbers prosper (Job 12:6).

d Why does the way of the wicked prosper? (Jer. 12:1); do not fret over him who prospers (Ps. 37:7).

Prosperity of the wicked, see **938***j*.

731 Adversity

See **735**.

732 Averageness

See **30**.

5.2 Social volition

733 Authority

- Rule of God

a The Lord reigns (1 Chr. 16:31; Ps. 93:1; 96:10; 97:1; 99:1; Rev. 19:6); your God reigns (Isa. 52:7); the kingdom is the Lord's (1 Chr. 29:11; Obad. 21); the Lord sits enthroned (Ps. 103:19; Isa. 6:1; 40:22); enthroned above the cherubim (2 Kgs. 19:15; 1 Chr. 13:6; Ps. 99:1); enthroned in the heavens (Ps. 123:1); the Lord will rule over you (Judg. 8:23); God rules over Jacob (Ps. 59:13); the Lord will reign on Mount Zion (Isa. 24:23; Mic. 4:7); he rules over all the kingdoms (2 Chr. 20:6); the Lord rules over the nations (Ps. 22:28); men are in the hand of God (Eccles. 9:1); God rules over mankind (Dan. 4:17, 25, 32; 5:21); Heaven rules (Dan. 4:26); the Father has fixed times by his own authority (Acts 1:7).

- Everlasting rule

b The Lord reigns for ever (Exod. 15:18; Ps. 9:7; 66:7; 146:10; Lam. 5:19; Rev. 11:15); his kingdom is an everlasting kingdom (Dan. 4:3); an eternal dominion (Dan. 4:34); enthroned for ever (Ps. 29:10).

- Kingdom of God / heaven

c The kingdom of God is not food and drink but righteousness, peace and joy in the Holy Spirit (Rom. 14:17); the kingdom of God does not consists of words but of power (1 Cor. 4:20); a kingdom which cannot be shaken (Heb. 12:28); the kingdom of heaven suffers violence (Matt. 11:12).

- People of the kingdom

d The good seed are the sons of the kingdom (Matt. 13:38); the righteous will shine in the kingdom of their Father (Matt. 13:43); the kingdom of God belongs to such as these (Luke 18:16); every scribe trained for the kingdom of heaven (Matt. 13:52); eunuchs for the sake of the kingdom of heaven (Matt. 19:12); those who have left things for the sake of the kingdom of God (Luke 18:29).

e Are you at this time restoring the kingdom to Israel? (Acts 1:6).

- Waiting for the kingdom

f The kingdom of God [/heaven] is near (Matt. 3:2; 4:17; 10:7; Mark 1:15; Luke 10:9, 11; 21:31); they thought the kingdom of God would appear immediately (Luke 19:11); Joseph of Arimathea was waiting for the kingdom of God (Mark 15:43; Luke 23:51); the kingdom of God is among you (Luke 17:20–1); the kingdom of God has come upon you (Matt. 12:28; Luke 11:20); some will not taste death until they see the kingdom come (Matt. 16:28; Mark 9:1; Luke 9:27); after his resurrection he spoke of the kingdom of God (Acts 1:3).

- Secrets of the kingdom

g To you it has been given to know the secrets of the kingdom of God (Matt. 13:11; Mark 4:11; Luke 8:10).

- Preaching the kingdom

h Jesus was preaching the good news of the kingdom (Matt. 4:23; 9:35); preaching the kingdom of God (Luke 8:1); he spoke to them of the kingdom of God (Luke 9:11); he sent them to preach the kingdom of God and to heal (Luke 9:2); go and preach the kingdom of God (Luke 9:60); the kingdom of God is preached (Luke 16:16); this gospel of the kingdom will be preached in all the world (Matt. 24:14); Philip preached the good news of the kingdom of God (Acts 8:12); Paul testified to the kingdom of God (Acts 28:23).

● Parables of the kingdom

 i How shall we represent the kingdom of God? (Mark 4:30); the kingdom of God likened to: the seed sown (Matt. 13:19); a man sowing seed (Matt. 13:24; Mark 4:26); mustard seed (Matt. 13:31; Luke 13:18–19); a king settling accounts (Matt. 18:23); a landowner hiring men (Matt. 20:1); a king giving a wedding feast (Matt. 22:2); ten virgins (Matt. 25:1).
Parables, see **519**.

● Seeking the kingdom

 j Your kingdom come (Matt. 6:10; Luke 11:2); seek first God's kingdom (Matt. 6:33; Luke 12:31).

● Given the kingdom

 k The kingdom of God belongs to the poor in spirit (Matt. 5:3); to the poor (Luke 6:20); God chose the poor to be heirs of the kingdom (Jas. 2:5); the kingdom belongs to those persecuted for righteousness (Matt. 5:10); to the childlike (Matt. 19:14; Mark 10:14); the kingdom prepared for you from the creation (Matt. 25:34); your Father's pleasure is to give you the kingdom (Luke 12:32); I give you a kingdom (Luke 22:29); he has brought us into the kingdom of his dear son (Col. 1:13); entrance into the eternal kingdom of our Lord and Saviour (2 Pet. 1:11); the Lord will save me for his heavenly kingdom (2 Tim. 4:18).

 l God calls you into his own kingdom (1 Thess. 2:12).

● Worthy of the kingdom

 m That you may be worthy of the kingdom of God (2 Thess. 1:5); no one who looks back is fit for the kingdom of God (Luke 9:62).

● Least in the kingdom

 n Whoever annuls the least commandment is least in the kingdom of heaven (Matt. 5:19); the least in the kingdom of heaven is greater than John (Matt. 11:11; Luke 7:28).

● Greatest in the kingdom

 o Who is the greatest in the kingdom of heaven? (Matt. 18:1); whoever humbles himself like a child is the greatest (Matt. 18:4); whoever keeps the least commandment is great in the kingdom of heaven (Matt. 5:19).

● The kingdom entered

 p Unless one is born again he cannot see the kingdom of God (John 3:3); unless one is born of water and the Spirit he cannot enter the kingdom of God (John 3:5); unless your righteousness exceeds you will not enter the kingdom of heaven (Matt. 5:20); unless you become like children you will not enter the kingdom (Matt. 18:3; Mark 10:15; Luke 18:17); not everyone who says 'Lord' will enter (Matt. 7:21).

 q How hard it is to enter the kingdom of God! (Mark 10:24); it is hard for the rich to enter the kingdom (Matt. 19:23, 24; Mark 10:23, 25; Luke 18:24, 25); harlots enter the kingdom of God before you (Matt. 21:31); through many tribulations we must enter the kingdom of God (Acts 14:22); you are not far from the kingdom of God (Mark 12:34).

Entering the kingdom, see **297i**.

r I give you the keys of the kingdom of heaven (Matt. 16:19); you shut the kingdom of heaven against men (Matt. 23:13).

● Bereft of the kingdom

s Those who will not inherit the kingdom of God: the unrighteous (1 Cor. 6:9–10); those who do the deeds of the flesh (Gal. 5:21); the immoral or covetous (Eph. 5:5); flesh and blood (1 Cor. 15:50).

t The kingdom of God will be taken away from you (Matt. 21:43).

Shutting the kingdom, see **264l**.

● The kingdom coming

u He hands over the kingdom to God the Father (1 Cor. 15:24); the kingdom of the world has become the kingdom of our Lord and of his Christ (Rev. 11:15); you have begun to reign (Rev. 11:17).

v Eating with the patriarchs in the kingdom of God (Matt. 8:11; Luke 13:28–9); blessed are those who will eat in the kingdom of God (Luke 14:15); I will not eat or drink until I do so with you in the kingdom of God (Matt. 26:29; Luke 22:16, 18).

● Kingdom of the Son

w A king will rule in righteousness (Isa. 32:1); a son who was to rule the nations (Rev. 12:5); rule in the midst of your enemies! (Ps. 110:2); in love and faithfulness a descendant of David will reign (Isa. 16:5); blessed is the kingdom of our father David (Mark 11:10); the Father gave him a kingdom (Luke 22:29); remember me when you come in your kingdom (Luke 23:42); the Son of man was given dominion and a kingdom (Dan. 7:14); a man went into a far country to receive a kingdom (Luke 19:12); God will give him the throne of his father David (Luke 1:32–3); he will rule from sea to sea (Ps. 72:8; Zech. 9:10); your kingdom is an everlasting kingdom (Ps. 145:13); a kingdom which will never be destroyed (Dan. 2:44); his kingdom will never end (Luke 1:33); the government will rest upon his shoulders (Isa. 9:6); of the increase of his government there will be no end (Isa. 9:7).

x The Father gave all things into his hands (John 13:3); the authority of Christ has come (Rev. 12:10); he must reign until all enemies are put under his feet (1 Cor. 15:25); your throne, O God, is for ever (Ps. 45:6); when the Son of man sits on his glorious throne (Matt. 19:28; 25:31); my kingdom is not of this world (John 18:36).

y We do not want this man to rule over us (Luke 19:14).

● Authority of the Son

z By what authority are you doing these things? (Matt. 21:23; Mark 11:28; Luke 20:2); neither will I tell you by what authority I do these things (Matt. 21:27; Mark 11:33; Luke 20:8).

aa Jesus taught with authority (Matt. 7:29; Mark 1:22; Luke 4:32); with authority he commands evil spirits (Mark 1:27; Luke 4:36); given all authority in heaven and on earth (Matt. 28:18); the Father gave the Son authority to judge (John 5:27); authority to firgive sins (Matt. 9:6; Mark 2:10; Luke 5:24); authority to grant eternal life (John 17:2); authority to rule the nations (Rev. 2:27); raised far above all rule and authority (Eph. 1:21); the Son of 'man is Lord of the sabbath (Matt. 12:8; Mark 2:28; Luke 6:5); they glorified God who had given such authority to men (Matt. 9:8).

● Authority delegated to people

ab Man was to rule all living things (Gen. 1:26, 28); to subdue the earth (Gen. 1:28); God appointed man over all creation (Ps. 8:6–8; Heb. 2:7–8).

ac Your husband will rule over you (Gen. 3:16); every man should be master in his own house (Esther 1:22); a wise servant will rule over a shameful son (Prov. 17:2); rule over ten cities (Luke 19:17); rule over five cities (Luke 19:19).

ad By Wisdom kings rule (Prov. 8:15); God removes kings and sets up kings (Dan. 2:21); I gave you a king and took him away (Hos. 13:11); the God of heaven has given you the kingdom (Dan. 2:37); the Most High decides who should rule (Dan. 4:17, 25, 32; 5:21); God gave Nebuchadnezzar sovereignty (Dan. 5:18); I have authority to release you or cricify you (John 19:10); you would have no authority unless you were given it from above (John 19:11); there is no authority except from God (Rom. 13:1); I also am a man under authority (Matt. 8:9; Luke 7:8); the king who observes the law will rule for a long time (Deut. 17:20); when someone rules in righteousness he is like the light of sunshine (2 Sam. 23:3–4).

ae The word of the king is supreme (Eccles. 8:4); the king made Joseph ruler (Ps. 105:21).

Ruling over Israel, see **741m**.

● Authority to disciples

af Moses put some of his authority on Joshua (Num. 27:20).

ag He gave his disciples authority over evil spirits (Matt. 10:1; Mark 3:15; 6:7; Luke 9:1); I have given you authority over snakes and the enemy (Luke 10:19); the authority the Lord gave me for building up (2 Cor. 10:8; 13:10); I will give the overcomer authority over the nations (Rev. 2:26); you will rule over many nations but none will rule over you (Deut. 15:6); they will reign on the earth (Rev. 5:10); they will reign with him 1000 years (Rev. 20:6); they reigned with Christ 1000 years (Rev. 20:4); I will put you in charge of many things (Matt. 25:21, 23); if we endure we will reign with him (2 Tim. 2:12); they will reign in life through Jesus Christ (Rom. 5:17); you will sit on 12 thrones (Matt. 19:28); the overcomer will sit with him on his throne (Rev. 3:21); they will reign for ever (Rev. 22:5); the saints of the Most High will possess the kingdom for ever (Dan. 7:18).

ah An elder must keep his children under control (1 Tim. 3:4); as must deacons (1 Tim. 3:12); a woman should have authority on her head (1 Cor. 11:10).

- The wicked ruling
  ai When the wicked rule people groan (Prov. 29:2); the sceptre of wickedness will not rest on the land of the righteous (Ps. 125:3); other lords besides you have ruled over us (Isa. 26:13); all Job has is in Satan's hands (Job 1:12; 2:6).

- Sin ruling
  aj Sin desires you, but you must master it (Gen. 4:7); do not let sin reign in your mortal bodies (Rom. 6:12); sin shall not rule over you (Rom. 6:14); do not let iniquity rule over me (Ps. 119:133); as sin reigned, so grace might reign (Rom. 5:21); I will not be mastered by anything (1 Cor. 6:12).

- Unsatisfactory rulers
  ak Children would rule over them (Isa. 3:4); woe to the land whose king is a boy (Eccles. 10:16); women rule over them (Isa. 3:12); I do not permit a woman to have authority over a man (1 Tim. 2:12); those who hated them ruled over them (Ps. 106:41); you have a cloak, you be our ruler! (Isa. 3:6–7); slaves rule over us (Lam. 5:8); the Philistines ruled over Israel (Judg. 14:4; 15:11).

  al The four beasts are four kingdoms (Dan. 7:17, 23); four kingdoms in succession (Dan. 2:37–40); the dragon gave the beast his authority (Rev. 13:2); the beast exercised authority for 42 months (Rev. 13:5); authority over all peoples and nations (Rev. 13:7); the ten kings give their authority to the beast (Rev. 17:13).

- Lording it
  am Do you want to Lord it over us? (Num. 16:13); the rulers of the Gentiles lord it over them (Matt. 20:25; Mark 10:42; Luke 22:25); do not lord it over the flock (1 Pet. 5:3); we do not lord it over your faith (2 Cor. 1:24).
  The rich lording it, see **800*m***.

- Rule in nature
  an Lights to govern day and night (Gen. 1:18); the greater light to govern the day and the lesser light to govern the night (Gen. 1:16); the sun to rule by day (Ps. 136:8); the moon and stars to rule by night (Ps. 136:9).

734 Anarchy

- No king
  a There was no king in Israel (Judg. 18:1; 19:1); so everyone did what was right in his own eyes (Judg. 17:6; 21:25); there was no king in Edom (1 Kgs. 22:47); Israel will have no king for many days (Hos. 3:4); we have no king (Hos. 10:3); is there no king among you? (Mic. 4:9).

- Not ruled
  b The ant has no chief or ruler (Prov. 6:7); locusts have no king (Prov. 30:27); you make men like fish without a ruler (Hab. 1:14).

  c We have become like those you have never ruled (Isa. 63:19).

735 Severity

- Strictness
  a Consider the severity of God (Rom. 11:22); I knew you to be a hard man (Matt. 25:24; Luke 19:21); God disciplines you as a man his son (Deut. 8:5).

  b My punishment is unbearable (Gen. 4:13); God's hand was

heavy on the Philistines (1 Sam. 5:6–12); you have become cruel to me (Job 30:21).

● Oppression

c Do not oppress your neighbour (Lev. 19:13); do not rule harshly over an Israelite (Lev. 25:43, 46, 53); the compassion of the wicked is cruel (Prov. 12:10); I saw the oppressions done under the sun (Eccles. 4:1); redeem me from the oppression of man (Ps. 119:134).

d Sarah ill-treated Hagar (Gen. 16:6); Joseph spoke harshly to his brothers (Gen. 42:30); the words of Judah were fiercer than those of Israel (2 Sam. 19:43); Solomon was to deal harshly with Joab (1 Kgs. 2:6); and with Shimei (1 Kgs. 2:9); Rehoboam spoke harshly to the people (1 Kgs. 12:10–11, 13–14; 2 Chr. 10:10–11, 13–14); Asa oppressed some of the people (2 Chr. 16:10).

e Slave drivers oppressed the Israelites (Exod. 1:11); the Egyptians treated us harshly (Deut. 26:6); the more they were oppressed, the more they multiplied (Exod. 1:12); make the work harder (Exod. 5:9); they did not listen to Moses because of the cruel bondage (Exod. 6:9); Sisera cruelly oppressed the Israelites (Judg. 4:3); their enemies oppressed them (Ps. 106:42); your father made our yoke hard (1 Kgs. 12:4, 14; 2 Chr. 10:4, 10, 14); with harshness you have ruled the sheep (Ezek. 34:4); Israel has been persecuted from youth (Ps. 129:1–3); you will have nothing but oppression (Deut. 28:33); servants should be submissive even to harsh masters (1 Pet. 2:18).

● Persecuting

f They will persecute you (Luke 21:12); a hundred times more, with persecutions (Mark 10:30); if they persecute me, they will persecute you (John 15:20); which prophet did your fathers not persecute? (Acts 7:52); so they persecuted the prophets (Matt. 5:12); you will persecute them from town to town (Matt. 23:34); the one born according to the flesh persecutes the one of the Spirit (Gal. 4:29); the dragon persecuted the woman (Rev. 12:13).

g Why do you persecute me? (Acts 9:4, 5; 22:7, 8; 26:14, 15); I persecuted the church (Acts 22:4; 1 Cor. 15:9; Gal. 1:13; Phil. 3:6); I was once a persecutor (1 Tim. 1:13); persecution arose against the church (Acts 8:1); the Jews stirred up persecution (Acts 13:50; 14:5).

h God persecutes me (Job 30:21); why do you persecute me as God does? (Job 19:22).

● Persecuted

i See how my enemies persecute me (Ps. 9:13); I am persecuted without a cause (Ps. 119:86, 161); many are my persecutors (Ps. 119:157).

j We told you we would be afflicted (1 Thess. 3:4); all who would live godly will be persecuted (2 Tim. 3:12); if I preach circumcision, why am I still persecuted? (Gal. 5:11); persecuted for the cross of Christ (Gal. 6:12).

k Blessed are you when people persecute you (Matt. 5:10–11); when persecution comes he falls away (Matt. 13:21; Mark 4:17);

your perseverance in persecutions (2 Thess. 1:4); pray for those who persecute you (Matt. 5:44); bless those who persecute you (Rom. 12:14); when persecuted, we endure (1 Cor. 4:12); we are persecuted but not forsaken (2 Cor. 4:9); when they persecute you in one town, flee to the next (Matt. 10:23).

Persecution from synagogues, see **192r**.

736 Leniency

● Soft treatment

a Deal gently with Absalom (2 Sam. 18:5); his father never pained him by asking what he did (1 Kgs. 1:6); he who pampers a slave will find him his heir (Prov. 29:21).

● Less punishment

b The slave who sins in ignorance will be punished less severely (Luke 12:48); it will be more tolerable for Tyre and Sidon (Matt. 11:22); it will be more tolerable for Sodom (Matt. 11:24).

Gentle, see **177**.

737 Command

● God's orders

a At the Lord's command they camped and set out (Num. 9:18, 23).

b If the Lord has told him to curse David (2 Sam. 16:10); the Lord had commanded that Ahithophel's counsel be thwarted (2 Sam. 17:14); the Lord told me to destroy this country (2 Kgs. 18:25); the Lord has commanded his sword to attack Ashkelon (Jer. 47:7); the Lord commanded this through his prophets (2 Chr. 29:25).

● The king's orders

c I will give orders concerning you (2 Sam. 14:8); David ordered them to deal gently with Absalom (2 Sam. 18:5); we heard the king charge you to protect Absalom (2 Sam. 18:12); David charged Solomon (1 Kgs. 2:1–9); David charged Solomon to build the temple (1 Chr. 22:6).

d Who issued a decree to rebuild this house? (Ezra 5:3, 9); King Cyrus issued a decree to rebuild the temple (2 Chr. 36:22–3; Ezra 1:1–4; 5:13, 17; 6:3–5); Artaxerxes' decree (Ezra 7:11–26); an edict from Ahasuerus (Esther 1:19–20); an edict to destroy the Jews (Esther 3:9–15; 4:8); a decree from Caesar Augustus for a census (Luke 2:1).

● Command-ments

e Which is the greatest commandment? (Matt. 22:36–40; Mark 12:28–31); whoever annuls the least commandment (Matt. 5:19).

Keeping the commandments, see **739g**.

● Commands of Jesus

f Jesus gave orders by the Holy Spirit to the apostles (Acts 1:2); what I am writing is a command from the Lord (1 Cor. 14:37); this is my commandment, that you love one another (John 15:12, 17); a new commandment, that you love one another (John 13:34); not a new commandment but an old one (1 John 2:7–8; 2 John 5); this is his command, to believe and to love (1 John

3:23); the commands we gave you by the Lord Jesus (1 Thess. 4:2).

Keeping Jesus' commands, see **739k**.

g He charged the leper not to tell anyone (Matt. 8:4; Mark 1:43–4); he ordered them not to tell anyone he was the Christ (Matt. 16:20); he ordered them not to tell anyone about the vision (Matt. 17:9).

h He cast out the demons with a word (Matt. 8:16); he charged unclean spirits not to make him known (Mark 3:12).

Commandment, see **953**.

● Summoning

i God called to: man (Gen. 3:9); Abraham (Gen. 22:11, 15); Moses (Exod. 3:4); Samuel (1 Sam. 3:4–10).

j Saul summoned Ahimelech (1 Sam. 22:11); Absalom summoned Joab (2 Sam. 14:29, 32); Absalom summoned Hushai (2 Sam. 17:5); David summoned Bathsheba (1 Kgs. 1:28); David summoned Zadok, Nathan and Benaiah (1 Kgs. 1:32); call the Shunammite woman (2 Kgs. 4:12, 15, 36); rise, he is calling you! (Mark 10:49).

● Called by God

k From the womb the Lord called me (Isa. 49:1); out of Egypt I called my son (Hos. 11:1; Matt. 2:15); you will call and I will answer you (Job 14:15).

l The king called those who were invited (Matt. 22:3); call them to the wedding feast (Matt. 22:9); many are called but few chosen (Matt. 22:14); I did not come to call the righteous but sinners (Matt. 9:13; Mark 2:17; Luke 5:32).

m Those whom he predestined he called and those he called he justified (Rom. 8:30); called according to his purpose (Rom. 8:28); not because of works but of God's call (Rom. 9:11); God calls you into his own kingdom (1 Thess. 2:12); the promise is for all whom the Lord will call (Acts 2:39).

n The gifts and calling of God are irrevocable (Rom. 11:29); confirm your calling and election (2 Pet. 1:10); those with him are called and chosen and faithful (Rev. 17:14).

o God called me through his grace (Gal. 1:15); he called you so as to obtain the glory of our Lord (2 Thess. 2:14); he has called us with a holy calling (2 Tim. 1:9); brethren who share in a heavenly calling (Heb. 3:1); the hope of his calling (Eph. 1:18).

p To those who are the called (1 Cor. 1:24; Jude 1); you are the called of Jesus Christ (Rom. 1:6).

738 Disobedience

● Disobedient children

a A rebellious son must be stoned to death (Deut. 21:18–21); an elder must not have disobedient children (Titus 1:6); disobedient to parents (Rom. 1:30; 2 Tim. 3:2).

● Rebellion against men

b The kings rebelled against Chedorlaomer (Gen. 14:4); Absalom's conspiracy against David (2 Sam. 15:7–12); Jeroboam rebelled against Solomon (1 Kgs. 11:26; 2 Chr. 13:6); Israel rebelled against the house of David (1 Kgs. 12:19; 2 Chr. 10:19); Moab rebelled against Israel (2 Kgs. 1:1; 3:5); Edom rebelled against Judah (2 Kgs. 8:20, 22; 2 Chr. 21:8, 10); Libnah revolted against Judah (2 Kgs. 8:22; 2 Chr. 21:10); Hezekiah rebelled against the king of Assyria (2 Kgs. 18:7); Jehoiakim rebelled against Nebuchadnezzar (2 Kgs. 24:1); as did Zedekiah (2 Kgs. 24:20; 2 Chr. 36:13; Ezek. 17:15)).

c This is a rebellious city (Ezra 4:12, 15; Zeph. 3:1); with rebellion and sedition (Ezra 4:19); the Jews are planning to rebel (Neh. 6:6); Barabbas committed insurrection (Mark 15:7; Luke 23:19, 25).

d Vashti disobeyed Ahasuerus (Esther 1:15); why are you transgressing the king's command? (Esther 3:3).

• Rebellion against God

e Do not rebel against the angel (Exod. 23:21); do not rebel against the Lord (Num. 14:9; Josh. 22:19); rebellion is like the sin of divination (1 Sam. 15:23).

f They rebelled in being unwilling to go up (Deut. 1:26; 9:23); they rebelled in going up (Num. 14:41; Deut. 1:43); they rebelled in not throwing away their idols (Ezek. 20:8); Moses and Aaron did not obey God's command (Num. 20:24; 27:14); they disobeyed in the desert (Num. 14:22; Deut. 9:7; Heb. 3:16–18); they rebelled against him in the wilderness (Ps. 78:40); our fathers rebelled at the Red Sea (Ps. 106:7); they disobeyed in the land (Judg. 2:2); they have rebelled against me (Hos. 7:13).

g I know how rebellious you are (Deut. 31:27); a rebellious people (Ps. 78:8; Isa. 30:9; 65:2; Ezek. 2:3; 12:2; Rom. 10:21); rebellious from the day I knew you (Deut. 9:24); I raised up children but they rebelled (Isa. 1:2); they became disobedient and rebelled against you (Neh. 9:26); they rebelled against the Most High (Ps. 78:17); they rebelled against God's Spirit (Ps. 106:33); they rebelled and grieved his Holy Spirit (Isa. 63:10); prisoners because they rebelled against God (Ps. 107:11).

h None of you keep the law (John 7:19).

• Results of disobedience

i The disastrous consequences of disobedience (Lev. 26:14–39; Deut. 30:17–18); woe to the rebellious children (Isa. 30:1).

j You will be destroyed through disobedience (Deut. 28:45); if you rebel, the Lord will be against you (1 Sam. 12:15); if you do not obey, curses will come upon you (Deut. 28:15); because you did not obey, the Lord has done this (1 Sam. 28:18); because you disobeyed the Lord you will not be buried in the family grave (1 Kgs. 13:21–2); if you rebel you will be devoured by the sword (Isa. 1:20); Israel was exiled through disobedience (2 Kgs. 18:11–12); those who were disobedient would not enter his rest (Heb. 3:18; 4:6).

• Disobedience of sin

k Many become sinners through the disobedience of the one (Rom. 5:19); once we also were disobedient (Titus 3:3); the sons of disobedience (Eph. 2:2; 5:6) *l* He who does not obey the Son shall not see life (John 3:36); those who do not obey the truth but obey unrighteousness (Rom. 2:8); those who do not obey the gospel (2 Thess. 1:8); God has hemmed them all in to disobedience (Rom. 11:32); you were once disobedient to God (Rom. 11:30); we are ready to punish all disobedience (2 Cor. 10:6); lest any fall through disobedience (Heb. 4:11).

739 Obedience

● Obey!

a Obey my voice (Jer. 7:23); why say 'Lord' and do not do what I say? (Luke 6:46); not everyone who says 'Lord' but he who does the will of my Father (Matt. 7:21); he who hears my words and does them is like a wise man (Matt. 7:24); whoever does the will of my Father is my brother (Matt. 12:50; Mark 3:35; Luke 8:21); if you know these things, happy are you if you do them (John 13:17); as obedient children (1 Pet. 1:14); remind them to be obedient (Titus 3:1); whatever he says to you, do it (John 2:5).

● We obey

b All God has said we will do (Exod. 19:8; 24:3); whatever God says we will do it (Jer. 42:5–6, 20); I do what the Father commanded (John 14:31); I have kept my Father's commandments (John 15:10); I come to do your will (Ps. 40:8; Heb. 10:7); my food is to do the will of him who sent me (John 4:34); not disobedient to the heavenly vision (Acts 26:19).

c Is it right to obey you rather than God? (Acts 4:19); we must obey God rather than men (Acts 5:29).

● Those who obeyed

d Abraham obeyed God (Gen. 22:18; 26:5; Heb. 11:8); Noah did all that God commanded (Gen. 6:22; 7:5); through one man's obedience many are made righteous (Rom. 5:19); Christ was obedient to death (Phil. 2:8); though a son, he learned obedience by what he suffered (Heb. 5:8).

e The obedience of faith (Rom. 1:5; 16:26); obedience to your confession of the gospel (2 Cor. 9:13); taking every thought captive to obey Christ (2 Cor. 10:5); obedience to Jesus Christ (1 Pet. 1:2); the source of salvation to all who obey him (Heb. 5:9); you were obedient to the teaching (Rom. 6:17); the obedience of the Gentiles (Rom. 15:18); even wind and wave obey him (Matt. 8:27; Luke 8:25); evil spirits obeyed Jesus (Mark 1:27).

f Angels obeying the voice of God (Ps. 103:20).

● Keeping the commandments

g Keep the commandments (Deut. 8:6; 10:13; 11:1, 8, 32; 13:4, 18; 15:5; 26:16; 27:1, 10; 28:9, 13, 58; 29:9, 29; 30:8, 10, 16; 31:12; 32:46; Josh. 1:7; 22:5; 23:6; 1 Kgs. 2:3; 3:14; 6:12; 8:61; 9:4; 11:38; 2 Kgs. 17:13, 37; 21:8; 1 Chr. 22:12; 2 Chr. 14:4; 33:8; Ps. 78:7; Matt. 19:17–19); may God incline our hearts to keep the commandments (1 Kgs. 8:58).

h I have carried out the Lord's commands (1 Sam. 15:13); I have kept the ways of the Lord (2 Sam. 22:22–3; Ps. 18:21–2); I have not departed from his commands (Job 23:12); I observe your testimonies (Ps. 119:22); David kept my commands (1 Kgs. 11:34; 14:8; 15:5); Hezekiah kept the commandments (2 Kgs. 18:6); they kept his statutes (Ps. 99:7).

i Converted Gentiles must observe the law of Moses (Acts 15:5); they would see that Paul kept the law (Acts 21:24); circumcison is only of value if you keep the law (Rom. 2:25); what matters is keeping the commandments (1 Cor. 7:19); that they might keep his laws (Ps. 105:45; 119:4).

j Be doers of the word (Jas. 1:22); blessed are those who hear the word of God and do it (Luke 11:28); happy are those who keep his testimonies (Ps. 119:2); the wise of heart take commands (Prov. 10:8).

● Keeping Jesus' commands

k Teaching them to observe all that I have commanded you (Matt. 28:20); you are my friends if you do what I command you (John 15:14); if you love me, you will keep my commandments (John 14:15); if anyone loves me he will keep my word (John 14:23–4); he who has my commandments and keeps them is the one who loves me (John 14:21); if you keep my Father's commandments you will abide in my love (John 15:10); we know that we know him if we keep his commandments (1 John 2:3); this is love, that we walk according to his commands (2 John 6); this is the love of God, that we keep his commandments (1 John 5:3).

Doing God's works, see **676g**.

● Blessings of obedience

l Obeying God's commands brings blessing (Lev. 26:3–10; Deut. 6:24; 28:1–2; 30:2, 9–10; 1 Chr. 28:8); if you do all I command I will establish your throne (1 Chr. 28:7; 2 Chr. 7:17–18); if you paid attention to my commands your peace would be like a river (Isa. 48:18); God gives the Holy Spirit to those who obey him (Acts 5:32); those who obey the law are righteous (Deut. 6:25; Rom. 2:13); to obey is better than sacrifice (1 Sam. 15:22).

● Obeying people

m As we obeyed Moses, we will obey you (Josh. 1:17); obey the Pharisees (Matt. 23:3); Jesus was obedient to Mary and Joseph (Luke 2:51); children, obey your parents (Eph. 6:1; Col. 3:20); slaves, obey your masters (Eph. 6:5; Col. 3:22); Titus remembers your obedience (2 Cor. 7:15).

740 Compulsion

● Outward compulsion

a If any one forces you to go one mile, go two (Matt. 5:41); Simon of Cyrene was forced to bear Christ's cross (Matt. 27:32; Mark 15:21; Luke 23:26); compel them to come in (Luke 14:23); they were going to make Jesus king by force (John 6:15).

● Inner compulsion

b I am under compulsion to preach the gospel (1 Cor. 9:16).

● No compulsion

c There was no compulsion over drinking (Esther 1:8); giving should not be by compulsion (2 Cor. 9:7); tend the flock of God, not under compulsion but willingly (1 Pet. 5:2); why compel Gentiles to live like Jews? (Gal. 2:14).

741 **Master**

● God is King

a The Lord is king (Ps. 10:16); you are my king (Ps. 44:4); God is the king of all the earth (Ps. 47:2, 7; Zech. 14:9); the king of glory (Ps. 24:7–10); you are my king (Ps. 74:12); the Lord is our king (Isa. 33:22); the King eternal (1 Tim. 1:17); your eyes will see the king in his beauty (Isa. 33:17); Jerusalem is the city of the great King (Matt. 5:35); with wrath I will be king over you (Ezek. 20:33).

b The shout of a king is among them (Num. 23:21); they have rejected me as king (1 Sam. 8:7); the Lord was your king (1 Sam. 12:12).

● Christ is Lord

c A ruler will come out of Jacob (Num. 24:17, 19); from Judah will come a ruler over Israel (Mic. 5:2; Matt. 2:6); my servant David will be king over them for ever (Ezek. 37:24–5); king of the Jews (Matt. 2:2; 27:11, 29, 37; Mark 15:2, 9, 12, 18, 26; Luke 23:3, 38; John 18:33; 19:19, 21); king of Israel (John 1:49; 12:13); the righteous Branch will reign as king (Jer. 23:5); are you a king? (John 18:37); behold, your king! (John 19:14–15); your king is coming to you riding on a donkey (Matt. 21:5; John 12:15); saying he is Christ, a king (Luke 23:2); everyone who makes himself a king opposes Caesar (John 19:12); saying there is another king, Jesus (Acts 17:7); if you are the king of the Jews, save yourself (Luke 23:37); let the Christ, the king of Israel, come down from the cross (Mark 15:32); I have installed my king on Zion (Ps. 2:6).

d It is the Lord! (John 21:7); Jesus Christ is lord of all (Acts 10:36); Christ is Lord both of the dead and the living (Rom. 14:9); the head of every man is Christ (1 Cor. 11:3); reverence Christ as Lord (1 Pet. 3:15); lord of lords and king of kings (Rev. 17:14); Christ is the head of the church (Eph. 1:22; 4:15; 5:23; Col. 1:18; 2:19); head over every authority (Col. 2:10); David calls him Lord (Matt. 22:43–5; Mark 12:36–7; Luke 20:42–4).

e Christ, the ruler of the kings of the earth (Rev. 1:5); the only Sovereign (1 Tim. 6:15); king of kings and lord of lords (1 Tim. 6:15; Rev. 19:16); the same Lord is Lord of all (Rom. 10:12).

● Jesus is my Lord

f If you confess with your mouth that Jesus is Lord (Rom. 10:9); no one can say, 'Jesus is Lord' except by the Holy Spirit (1 Cor. 12:3); we do not preach ourselves but Christ Jesus as Lord (2 Cor. 4:5); every tongue will confess that Jesus Christ is Lord (Phil. 2:11).

g Not everyone who says, 'Lord, Lord' will enter (Matt. 7:21); why call me Lord and do not do what I say? (Luke 6:46).

● Earthly
kings

h Prayer should be made for kings (1 Tim. 2:2); submit yourselves to the king (1 Pet. 2:13); give to Caesar what is Caesar's (Matt. 22:21; Mark 12:17).

i The wrath of a king is a messenger of death (Prov. 16:14); in the light of a king's face is life (Prov. 16:15)

j A king who rules in justice disperses evil with his eyes (Prov. 20:8); a wise king winnows the wicked (Prov. 20:26); it is an abomination for kings to do evil (Prov. 16:12).

● Making
kings

k Making kings: Abimelech (Judg. 9:6, 18); Saul (1 Sam. 9:16; 11:15; 12:1); David (2 Sam. 2:4, 7; 3:17, 21; 1 Chr. 12:31, 38); Ish-Bosheth (2 Sam. 2:9); Solomon (1 Chr. 23:1); Rehoboam (1 Kgs. 12:1; 2 Chr. 10:1); Ahaziah (2 Chr. 22:1); select the best of Ahab's sons and make him king (2 Kgs. 10:3); the king's son shall reign (2 Chr. 23:3); it is said that you are to be their king (Neh. 6:6).

l They made kings, but not by me (Hos. 8:4); 'give me a king and princes' (Hos. 13:10); they were going to make Jesus king by force (John 6:15).

Anointing kings, see **357*e***; **death of kings**, see **361*af***; **killing rulers**, see **362*w***.

● Kings of Israel
and Judah

m Kings will come from Israel (Gen. 35:11); his king shall be higher than Agag (Num. 24:7); they asked for a king (Acts 13:21); appoint a king over us like all the nations (Deut. 17:14–16; 1 Sam. 8:5–6, 19–20; 10:19; 12:12); tell them what a king will do (1 Sam. 8:9–18); appoint a king for them (1 Sam. 8:22); the Lord has set a king over you (1 Sam. 12:13); this one will rule my people (1 Sam. 9:17).

n Rule over us (Judg. 8:22–3); should 70 men rule over you or one? (Judg. 9:2); the trees went forth to anoint a king (Judg. 9:8).

o David was to be king (1 Sam. 16:1; 23:17; 24:20; 2 Sam. 5:2; 6:21; 7:8; 1 Chr. 17:7; 28:4; Acts 13:22); when God makes you king (1 Sam. 25:30); the Lord had established David as king (2 Sam. 5:12; 1 Chr. 14:2); David the king (Matt. 1:6).

p Say Absalom is king (2 Sam. 15:10); the Lord has given the kingdom to Absalom (2 Sam. 16:8); Adonijah seems to be king (1 Kgs. 1:5, 11, 18, 24–5); all Israel expected Adonijah to be king (1 Kgs. 2:15); who shall reign after you? (1 Kgs. 1:20); God chose Solomon to be king (1 Chr. 28:5); Solomon shall be king (1 Kgs. 1:13, 17, 30, 35); Solomon ruled (1 Kgs. 2:12; 4:1; 1 Chr. 29:28); David has made Solomon king (1 Kgs. 1:43); the kingdom was his from the Lord (1 Kgs. 2:15); because the Lord loves Israel he has made Solomon king (1 Kgs. 10:9).

q The rule shall not depart from Judah until Shiloh comes (Gen. 49:10); Solomon's kingdom was established (1 Kgs. 2:46); I will establish his kingdom (2 Sam. 7:12); for ever (2 Sam. 7:13, 16; 1 Kgs. 9:5; 1 Chr. 28:7); David's dynasty would last for ever (2 Sam. 7:16; 2 Chr. 13:5; Ps. 89:4, 29, 36; 132:12); you will not lack a descendant ruling Israel (1 Kgs. 2:4; 8:25; 2 Chr. 6:16; 7:18; Jer. 33:17, 21); Jeroboam would rule over all he wanted (1 Kgs. 11:37); I made you leader over Israel (1 Kgs. 14:7; 16:2); Jehu's sons of the fourth generation would rule Israel (2 Kgs. 10:30; 15:12).

r The Lord has appointed another as ruler (1 Sam. 13:14); God would not establish Saul's kingdom for ever (1 Sam. 13:13); whilst David lives, your kingship is insecure (1 Sam. 20:31); today Israel will restore my father's kingdom to me (2 Sam. 16:3); Abner threatened to transfer the kingdom to David (2 Sam. 3:10); David reigned in Saul's place (2 Sam. 16:8); God tore the kingdom away from Saul (1 Sam. 15:28; 28:17); and from Solomon (1 Kgs. 11:11, 31); the Lord will raise up a king of Israel who will cut off the house of Jeroboam (1 Kgs. 14:14).

● Rulers of Israel

s Those who reigned over Israel: Jeroboam (1 Kgs. 12:20; 2 Kgs. 17:21); Nadab (1 Kgs. 14:20; 15:25); Baasha (1 Kgs. 15:28, 33); Elah (1 Kgs. 16:6, 8); Zimri (1 Kgs. 16:10, 15); Omri (1 Kgs. 16:16, 22–3); Tibni [over half Israel] (1 Kgs. 16:21); Ahab (1 Kgs. 16:28–9); Ahaziah (1 Kgs. 22:40, 51); Jehoram (2 Kgs. 1:17; 3:1); Jehu (2 Kgs. 10:36); Jehoahaz (2 Kgs. 10:35; 13:1); Joash (2 Kgs. 13:9, 10); Jeroboam (2 Kgs. 13:13; 14:16, 23); Zechariah (2 Kgs. 14:29; 15:8); Shallum (2 Kgs. 15:10, 13); Menahem (2 Kgs. 15:14, 17); Pekahiah (2 Kgs. 15:22, 23); Pekah (2 Kgs. 15:25, 27); Hoshea (2 Kgs. 15:30; 17:1).

● Rulers of Judah

t Those who reigned over Judah: Rehoboam (1 Kgs. 11:43; 12:17; 2 Chr. 9:31; 10:17); Abijam [Abijah] (1 Kgs. 14:31; 15:1; 2 Chr. 12:16; 13:1); Asa (1 Kgs. 15:8, 9; 2 Chr. 14:1); Jehoshaphat (1 Kgs. 15:24; 22:41; 2 Chr. 17:1); Jehoram (1 Kgs. 22:50; 2 Kgs. 8:16; 2 Chr. 21:1); Ahaziah (2 Kgs. 8:25; 9:29); Athaliah (2 Kgs. 11:3); Joash (2 Kgs. 11:12); Amaziah (2 Kgs. 12:21; 14:1; 2 Chr. 24:27; 25:1); Uzziah [Azariah] (2 Kgs. 14:21; 15:1; 2 Chr. 26:1); Jotham (2 Kgs. 15:7, 32; 2 Chr. 26:23; 27:1); Ahaz (2 Kgs. 15:38; 16:1; 2 Chr. 27:9; 28:1); Hezekiah (2 Kgs. 16:20; 18:1; 2 Chr. 28:27; 29:1); Manasseh (2 Kgs. 20:21; 21:1; 2 Chr. 32:33; 33:1); Amon (2 Kgs. 21:18; 2 Chr. 33:20, 21); Josiah (2 Kgs. 21:24, 26; 22:1; 2 Chr. 33:25; 34:1); Jehoahaz [Shallum] (2 Kgs. 23:30, 31; 2 Chr. 36:1; Jer. 22:11); Jehoiakim [Eliakim] (2 Kgs. 23:34; 2 Chr. 36:4); Jehoiachin (2 Kgs. 24:6; 2 Chr. 36:8); Zedekiah [Mattaniah] (2 Kgs. 24:17, 18; 2 Chr. 36:10; Jer. 37:1).

● Rulers of the Gentiles

u Melchizedek king of Salem (Gen. 14:18; Heb. 7:1, 2); the kings of Edom (Gen. 36:31–43; 2 Kgs. 8:20; 1 Chr. 1:43–54; 2 Chr. 21:8); kings of the Canaanites (Num. 21:1; 33:40; Josh. 12:1–24); Hazael becoming king of Aram (2 Kgs. 8:13, 15); Benhadad son of Hazael (2 Kgs. 13:24); Hanun became king of Ammon (2 Sam. 10:1; 1 Chr. 19:1); Esarhaddon became king of Assyria (2 Kgs. 19:37; Isa. 37:38); Evil-merodach became king of Babylon (2 Kgs. 25:27); taunt against the king of Babylon (Isa. 14:4–23); Artaxerxes, king of kings (Ezra 7:12); Ahasuerus reigned over 127 provinces (Esther 1:1); Darius become king (Dan. 5:31); Caesar Augustus (Luke 2:1); Tiberius Caesar (Luke 3:1); Aretas king of Damascus (2 Cor. 11:32).

v Herod the Great (Matt. 2:1–8, 16; Luke 1:5); Archelaus (Matt. 2:22); Herod Antipas the tetrarch of Galilee (Matt. 14:1–10; Mark 6:14–28; Luke 3:1, 19; 9:7–9; 13:31–2; 23:7–12; Acts 4:27); Herod the king (Acts 12:1–3, 19–23); Agrippa (Acts 25:13–26; 26:1, 26–32); Philip tetrarch of Ituraea (Luke 3:1); Lysanias tetrarch of Abilene (Luke 3:1); Quirinius was governor of Syria (Luke 2:2).

w Rulers were gathered together against the Lord (Acts 4:26); kings will come to the brightness of your rising (Isa. 60:3); you will be brought before governors and kings (Matt. 10:18; Mark 13:9; Luke 21:12).

x Three kings will appear in Persia (Dan. 11:2–3); the ram and goat represent kings (Dan. 8:20–1); the seven hills and ten horns are kings (Rev. 17:9–12).

● Earthly masters

y Masters, do not threaten (Eph. 6:9); masters, show justice (Col. 4:1).

z Be master of your brothers (Gen. 27:29); I made him your master (Gen. 27:37); Joseph was governor of Egypt (Gen. 42:6; 45:26); God has made me lord of all Egypt (Gen. 45:8–9).

aa The 12 heads, one from each tribe (Num. 1:4–16, 44; 13:3–16); they made an offering (Num. 7:2–88); they apportioned the land (Num. 34:18–28); the officials of Solomon (1 Kgs. 4:2–6); 12 prefects (1 Kgs. 4:7–19); the leaders of Israel (1 Chr. 27:1–34); the heads of families (Ezra 8:1–14); the 70 elders (Num. 11:24).

ab Leaders of thousands, hundreds, fifties, tens (Exod. 18:21, 25; Deut. 1:15); the officers are to appoint army commanders (Deut. 20:9); 550 chief officers (1 Kgs. 9:23); 250 chief officers (2 Chr. 8:10).

ac Choose a leader and return to Egypt (Num. 14:4); the one to begin the fight will be head over Gilead (Judg. 10:18); be our leader to fight the Ammonites (Judg. 11:6, 8–11); David became their leader (1 Sam. 22:2).

742 Servant

● Serving God

a Serve the Lord (Deut. 10:12; Josh. 24:14); Israel served the Lord while Joshua was living (Josh. 24:31); we are servants of God (Ezra 5:11); I am your servant (Ps. 116:16; 119:125; 143:12); all things are your servants (Ps. 119:91); it is vain to serve God (Mal. 3:14); to serve him without fear (Luke 1:74); he is not served by human hands (Acts 17:25); they serve God day and night (Rev. 7:15); his servants will serve him (Rev. 22:3); I am the handmaid of the Lord (Luke 1:38); make me your hired servant (Luke 15:19).

b I have found David my servant (Ps. 89:20); Moses was faithful as a servant (Heb. 3:5); slaves of God (Rom. 6:22).

c Samuel ministered before the Lord (1 Sam. 2:11); the service of the house of the Lord was re-established (2 Chr. 29:35).

d They worshipped and served the creature rather than the Creator (Rom. 1:25).

● Servants of people

e Do not oppress a poor hireling (Deut. 24:14–15); Hagar was Sarah's Egyptian maidservant (Gen. 16:1); a maidservant went to tell Jonathan and Ahimaz (2 Sam. 17:17); Joseph attended the butler and baker (Gen. 40:4); David served Saul (1 Sam. 16:22); Elisha was Elijah's servant (1 Kgs. 19:21; 2 Kgs. 3:11).

f If you will be a servant to these people, they will be your servants (1 Kgs. 12:7; 2 Chr. 10:7); as I served your father, I will serve you (2 Sam. 16:19).

● Deacons

g Requirements for deacons (1 Tim. 3:8–13); to the elders and deacons (Phil. 1:1); Phoebe was a deacon of the church at Cenchrea (Rom. 16:1).

● Servants of Christ

h Paul, a slave of Christ Jesus (Rom. 1:1); the free man is Christ's slave (1 Cor. 7:22); slaves of righteousness (Rom. 6:18, 19).

i Servants of Christ (1 Cor. 4:1; Phil. 1:1); serving the Lord Christ (Col. 3:24); if any one serves me, let him follow me (John 12:26); Paul and Apollos are servants through whom you believed (1 Cor. 3:5).

j Ourselves your servants for Jesus' sake (2 Cor. 4:5); whoever would be great must be your servant (Matt. 20:26–7; 23:11; Mark 9:35; 10:43–4; Luke 22:26); we are unworthy servants (Luke 17:10); I was made a minister [servant] (Eph. 3:7; Col. 1:23, 25); the priestly service of the gospel (Rom. 15:16).

● Christ the Servant

k The Son of Man came not to be served but to serve (Matt. 20:28; Mark 10:45); I am among you as one who serves (Luke 22:27); their master will gird himself and wait on them (Luke 12:37); Christ became a servant to the circumcision (Rom. 15:8); behold, my servant (Matt. 12:18; Phil. 2:7); Israel, the servant of the Lord (Isa. 41:8–9; 42:1; 44:21; 49:3, 5, 6; 52:13); my servant, the Branch (Zech. 3:8).

● Slaves

l Slaves should be subject to their masters (Titus 2:9); slaves should honour their masters (1 Tim. 6:1); a slave is not above his master (Matt. 10:24; John 13:16; 15:20); which of you will tell his slave to eat and drink first? (Luke 17:7–8); slaves of priests may eat the sacrifices (Lev. 22:11).

m If I have despised the rights of my slaves (Job 31:13); do not slander a slave to his master (Prov. 30:10).

n The slave is Christ's free man (1 Cor. 7:22); in Christ there is neither slave nor free (Gal. 3:28; Col. 3:11); I do not call you slaves (John 15:15); you are no longer a slave but a son (Gal. 4:7).

o I bought male and female slaves (Eccles. 2:7); I have seen slaves riding and princes walking (Eccles. 10:7).

p Abraham's chief slave (Gen. 24:2); remember you were slaves in Egypt (Deut. 5:15; 6:21; 15:15; 16:12; 24:18, 22); we will be Pharaoh's slaves (Gen. 47:25); they would be slaves for four hundred years (Gen. 15:13; Acts 7:6); Israel came out of the land of slavery (Exod. 13:3, 14; 20:2; Deut. 6:12; 8:14; 13:5, 10; Judg. 6:8; Jer. 34:13); is Israel a slave? (Jer. 2:14); you will be the king's slaves (1 Sam. 8:17); you will serve your enemies (Deut. 28:48); they will become Shishak's slaves (2 Chr. 12:8); you will offer yourselves as slaves (Deut. 28:68); we are slaves (Ezra 9:9; Neh. 9:36).

Slavery, see **745e**.

● Serving people

q The king will make many serve him (1 Sam. 8:11–16); the older will serve the younger (Gen. 25:23; Rom. 9:12); no one can serve two masters (Matt. 6:24; Luke 16:13).

r I know your service (Rev. 2:19); they devoted themselves to serving the saints (1 Cor. 16:15); through love serve one another (Gal. 5:13); use your gift in serving one another (1 Pet. 4:10).

s Angels came and served him (Matt. 4:11); Peter's mother-in-law rose and served him (Matt. 8:15; Mark 1:31; Luke 4:39); women who ministered to him in Galilee (Mark 15:41).

743 Badge of rule

● God's throne

a God sits on his holy throne (Ps. 47:8); something like a throne above a platform (Ezek. 1:26); heaven is God's throne (Matt. 5:34); he who swears by heaven swears by God's throne (Matt. 23:22); Jerusalem will be called the Throne of the Lord (Jer. 3:17); a glorious throne set on high is the place of our sanctuary (Jer. 17:12); this is the place of my throne (Ezek. 43:7); a throne of sapphire (Ezek. 10:1); his throne was flaming (Dan. 7:9); I saw the Lord sitting on his throne (1 Kgs. 22:19; 2 Chr. 18:18); there was a throne in heaven (Rev. 4:2); let us draw near to the throne of grace (Heb. 4:16); a great white throne (Rev. 20:11); I will set my throne in Elam (Jer. 49:38).

● Christ's throne

b When the Son of man sits on his glorious throne (Matt. 19:28; 25:31); the throne of God and of the Lamb will be in the city (Rev. 22:3); the river flowing from the throne of God and of the Lamb (Rev. 22:1); your throne is for ever (Heb. 1:8).

● Various thrones

c Solomon has taken his seat on the throne (1 Kgs. 1:46); Solomon made a great throne (1 Kgs. 10:18; 2 Chr. 9:17); the kings were sitting on their thrones (1 Kgs. 22:10; 2 Chr. 18:9); they set Joash on the throne (2 Kgs. 11:19; 2 Chr. 23:20); Ahasuerus sat on his throne (Esther 1:2; 5:1); Nebuchadnezzar will set his throne over these stones (Jer. 43:10); you will sit on 12 thrones (Matt. 19:28;

Luke 22:30); the elders on 24 thrones (Rev. 4:4); Satan's throne (Rev. 2:13); a bowl was poured on the throne of the beast (Rev. 16:10).

- Crowns for Christ

d They put a crown of thorns on Jesus' head (Matt. 27:29; Mark 15:17; John 19:2); on his head are many crowns (Rev. 19:12).

- Priest's crown

e A plate of pure gold (Exod. 28:36); the holy crown (Exod. 29:6); the plate of the holy crown (Exod. 39:30); make a crown and set it on the head of Joshua the high priest (Zech. 6:11).

- Crowns for people

f You set a crown of fine gold on the king's head (Ps. 21:3); the Amalekite took Saul's crown and armlet (2 Sam. 1:10); David took the crown of the king of Rabbah (2 Sam. 12:30; 1 Chr. 20:2); they put the crown on Joash (2 Kgs. 11:12; 2 Chr. 23:11); the king put a crown on Esther's head (Esther 2:17); a golden crown on his head (Rev. 14:14).

g Mordecai had a gold crown (Esther 8:15); the proud crown of the drunkards of Ephraim (Isa. 28:1, 3).

- Crowns on creatures

h A crown for the king's horse (Esther 6:8); on the heads were seven diadems (Rev. 12:3); on its horns were ten diadems (Rev. 13:1); the locusts had golden crowns (Rev. 9:7).

- Crowns for God's people

i The Lord will become a crown of glory for his people (Isa. 28:5); the crown of righteousness is laid up for me (2 Tim. 4:8); the crown of life (Jas. 1:12; Rev. 2:10); the crown of glory (1 Pet. 5:4); lest any one take your crown (Rev. 3:11); 24 elders with golden crowns (Rev. 4:4); they cast their crowns before the throne (Rev. 4:10); a crown was given to the rider (Rev. 6:2); the woman had a crown of 12 stars (Rev. 12:1).

j Who is our hope and joy and crown but you? (1 Thess. 2:19); my joy and crown (Phil. 4:1); you will be a crown in the hand of your God (Isa. 62:3).

- Signet rings

k Judah's signet ring given to Tamar (Gen. 38:18, 25); Pharaoh gave Joseph his signet ring (Gen. 41:42); Jezebel sealed the letters with Ahab's seal (1 Kgs. 21:8); the king gave his signet ring to Haman (Esther 3:10, 12); then to Mordecai (Esther 8:2, 8, 10); the stone was sealed with a signet ring (Dan. 6:17); I will make Zerubbabel like my signet ring (Hag. 2:23); even if Jehoiachin were a signet ring (Jer. 22:24); put a ring on his finger (Luke 15:22).

- Sceptre

l A sceptre will rise from Israel (Num. 24:17); unless the king extends the golden sceptre (Esther 4:11); the king held out the gold sceptre to Esther (Esther 5:2; 8:4); the righteous sceptre is the sceptre of your kingdom (Heb. 1:8).

- Gold chains

m Pharaoh put a gold chain round Joseph's neck (Gen. 41:42). **Royal robes**, see **228o**.

744 Freedom

See **746**.

745 Subjection

● Subject
to people

a We do not yet see everything subject to man (Heb. 2:8); put your feet on their necks (Josh. 10:24); he subdues people under us (Ps. 47:3).

b Be subject to rulers and authorities (Rom. 13:1, 5; Titus 3:1; 1 Pet. 2:13); I make myself a slave to all men (1 Cor. 9:19).

c The Israelites were subject to Eglon (Judg. 3:14); Hoshea became a servant of Shalmaneser (2 Kgs. 17:3); Jehoiakim was Nebuchadnezzar's servant for three years (2 Kgs. 24:1).

d The Moabites became subject to David (2 Sam. 8:2); the Arameans became subject to him (2 Sam. 8:6); these countries were subject to Solomon (1 Kgs. 4:21).

● The law
on slavery

e The law on slavery (Exod. 21:2; Lev. 25:39–55; Deut. 15:12); do not enslave your brother (Lev. 25:39–43).

● Enslaved

f Do not become slaves of men (1 Cor. 7:23); do not hand back an escaped slave (Deut. 23:15).

g The men of Israel intended to make slaves of the people of Judah (2 Chr. 28:10); Solomon did not enslave Israelites (1 Kgs. 9:22; 2 Chr. 8:9); they turned around and took back their slaves (Jer. 34:11, 16); our sons and daughters are being forced into slavery (Neh. 5:5); if we were to be made slaves I would have kept quiet (Esther 7:4); Joseph was sold as a slave (Ps. 105:17); Israel will make slaves of the aliens (Isa. 14:2); may Canaan be his brothers' slave (Gen. 9:25, 27); Joseph's brothers contemplated being his slaves (Gen. 43:18; 44:9, 17, 33; 50:18).

h Lest you be slaves to the Hebrews (1 Sam. 4:9).
Slaves, see **742***l*.

● Subject
to Christ

i Angels, authorities and powers are subjected to Christ (1 Pet. 3:22); he is able to subject all things to himself (Phil. 3:21); he has put all things under his feet (Ps. 8:6; 1 Cor. 15:27; Eph. 1:22); you have led captives (Ps. 68:18).

● Subject
to God

j The Son will be subject to God (1 Cor. 15:28); the Son can do nothing of himself (John 5:19, 30); I have come not to do my own will (John 6:38); I do not speak from myself (John 12:49; 14:10).

k I would quickly subdue their enemies (Ps. 81:14); till I make your enemies your footstool (Ps. 110:1).

● Subject
to evil

l We were in slavery to the elemental principles of the world (Gal. 4:3); through fear of death they were in lifelong bondage (Heb. 2:15).

m Everyone who sins is a slave to sin (John 8:34); a slave to sin (Rom. 6:17); what overcomes a man enslaves him (2 Pet. 2:19); you are slaves of the one you obey, whether sin or obedience (Rom. 6:16); once we were in slavery to various lusts (Titus 3:3); no longer slaves to sin (Rom. 6:6).

n Hagar bearing children for slavery (Gal. 4:22–31); the present Jerusalem is in slavery with her children (Gal. 4:25); you desire to be enslaved once more (Gal. 4:9); false brethren bringing us into bondage (Gal. 2:4); do not take on a yoke of slavery (Gal. 5:1); we have not received a spirit of bondage (Rom. 8:15).

● Taming
    o Every kind of animal has been tamed by man (Jas. 3:7); no one can tame the tongue (Jas. 3:8).

746 Liberation

● God releasing captives
    a The Lord sent me to proclaim release to the captives (Isa. 61:1; Luke 4:18); to bring prisoners out of the prison (Isa. 42:7); the Lord releases those condemned to death (Ps. 102:20); God shattered their yoke (Isa. 9:4; Jer. 30:8); when I break the bars of their yoke (Ezek. 34:27); I will break his yoke from off you (Nahum 1:13); God leads out the prisoners (Ps. 68:6); four men loosed in the fiery furnace (Dan. 3:25); God breaks their bonds (Ps. 107:14, 16); God loosens the bond of kings (Job 12:18); you have loosed my bonds (Ps. 116:16); God sets the prisoners free (Ps. 146:7); I will set your captives free (Zech. 9:11).

    b Bring me out of prison! (Ps. 142:7); Peter's chains fell off (Acts 12:7); everyone's chains were unfastened (Acts 16:26); the angel opened the prison doors and brought them out (Acts 5:19); the angel brought Peter out of the prison (Acts 12:7–10); I will walk at liberty for I seek your precepts (Ps. 119:45).

● Freeing Israel
    c Let my people go (Exod. 5:1; 7:16; 8:1, 20; 9:1, 13; 10:3); let my son go (Exod. 4:23); let them go (Exod. 6:11; 7:2); I will deliver you from their bondage (Exod. 6:6); I have come down to free them (Acts 7:34); I broke the bars of your yoke (Lev. 26:13); I brought you out of the land of bondage (Deut. 5:6).

    d When the Lord brought back the captives of Zion (Ps. 126:1); I broke the yoke of the king of Babylon (Jer. 28:2); I broke your yoke and burst your bonds (Jer. 2:20).

● Men releasing captives
    e The king set Joseph free (Ps. 105:20); Jeremiah was freed from his chains (Jer. 40:4); return your captive brethren (2 Chr. 28:11); the fast I choose is to break every yoke (Isa. 58:6).

    f It was the governor's custom to release a prisoner (Matt. 27:15; Mark 15:6; Luke 23:17; John 18:39); whom do you want me to release? (Matt. 27:17); do you want me to release the king of the Jews? (Mark 15:9); Pilate tried to release Jesus (John 19:12); I will punish him and release him (Luke 23:16, 22); release Barabbas! (Luke 23:18); Barabbas was released (Matt. 27:26; Mark 15:11, 15; Luke 23:25); Paul and Silas were to be released from prison (Acts 16:35–7); Jehoiachin was released from prison (2 Kgs. 25:27; Jer. 52:31); Timothy has been released (Heb. 13:23); Paul could have been set free if he had not appealed (Acts 26:32); you have released the man devoted to destruction (1 Kgs. 20:42).

    g You will break your brother's yoke from your neck (Gen. 27:40).

● Freeing
servants

h In the seventh year the Hebrew slave must go free (Exod. 21:2; Deut. 15:12; Jer. 34:14); a wounded slave must go free (Exod. 21:26–7); a slave must be released in the year of Jubilee (Lev. 25:54); Hebrew slaves had to be set free (Jer. 34:8–10, 15).

i If you can become free, do so (1 Cor. 7:21); hired men released at the Jubilee (Lev. 25:40–1).

j I will not go out free (Exod. 21:5); a female slave shall not go free like males (Exod. 21:7).

● Freedom
from law

k If her husband dies, the woman is free from the law of marriage (Rom. 7:2, 3); free to be married to whom she wishes (1 Cor. 7:39); released from the law (Rom. 7:6).

l Do not use your freedom as an opportunity for the flesh (Gal. 5:13); do not use your freedom as a cover for evil (1 Pet. 2:16); the law of liberty (Jas. 1:25); act as those to be judged by the law of liberty (Jas. 2:12).

No compulsion, see **740c**.

● Freedom
through
Christ

m If the Son sets you free you will be free indeed (John 8:36); the truth shall make you free (John 8:32); freed from sin (Rom. 6:18); he who has died is freed from sin (Rom. 6:7); set free from the principle of sin and death (Rom. 8:2); everyone who believes is freed from all things (Acts 13:39); he has freed us from our sins by his blood (Rev. 1:5).

n Jesus released a woman bound by Satan (Luke 13:12, 16); Lazarus was to be loosed (John 11:44).

o Where the Spirit of the Lord is, there is freedom (2 Cor. 3:17); for freedom Christ has set us free (Gal. 5:1); if the Son makes you free you shall be free indeed (John 8:36); Jerusalem above is free (Gal. 4:26); we are children of the free woman (Gal. 4:22–31); am I not free? (1 Cor. 9:1); the word of God is not imprisoned (2 Tim. 2:9).

p Whatever you loose on earth will be loosed in heaven (Matt. 16:19; 18:18); the creation will be released from bondage (Rom. 8:21).

● Animals
released

q Let the live bird go free (Lev. 14:7, 53); the goat released in the wilderness (Lev. 16:22); untie the donkey and the colt (Matt. 21:2; Mark 11:2, 4–5; Luke 19:30, 33).

● Freedom
and evil

r At the end of the 1000 years Satan will be released from prison (Rev. 20:7); the four angels were released (Rev. 9:14–15).

s They promise freedom, though they are slaves of corruption (2 Pet. 2:19); let us break their fetters and bonds from us! (Ps. 2:3); I proclaim a release to sword, pestilence and famine (Jer. 34:17).

● Things
released

t Untie her hair (Num. 5:18); I am not worthy to loose his sandals (Mark 1:7; Acts 13:25).

747 Restraint

● Imprisoned

a God imprisons and there is no release (Job 12:14); you put my feet in the stocks (Job 13:27).

b Those imprisoned: Joseph (Gen. 39:20); the butler and baker (Gen. 40:3); Joseph's brothers (Gen. 42:17); Simeon (Gen. 42:19); Micaiah (1 Kgs. 22:27; 2 Chr. 18:26); Hoshea (2 Kgs. 17:4); a seer (2 Chr. 16:10); Jeremiah in the court of the guard (Jer. 32:2; 33:1); Jeremiah (Jer. 37:15); John the Baptist (Matt. 4:12; 14:3; Mark 1:14; 6:17; Luke 3:20); Peter and John (Acts 4:3); the apostles (Acts 5:18); Paul and Silas (Acts 16:23).

c Pharaoh Neco imprisoned Jehoahaz (2 Kgs. 23:33).

● Believers
imprisoned

d We commend ourselves in imprisonment (2 Cor. 6:5); in far more imprisonments (2 Cor. 11:23); in my imprisonment (Phil. 1:7, 17); an ambassador in chains (Eph. 6:20); my imprisonment in Christ (Phil. 1:13); remember my imprisonment (Col. 4:18); the mystery of Christ, for which I was imprisoned (Col. 4:3).

e Some were chained and imprisoned (Heb. 11:36); you will be thrown into prison (Matt. 5:25); I was in prison and you came to me (Matt. 25:36); when did we see you in prison? (Matt. 25:39, 44); you sympathised with the prisoners (Heb. 10:34); remember those in prison as if in prison with them (Heb. 13:3); I was in prison and you did not visit me (Matt. 25:43).

f Paul imprisoned men and women (Acts 8:3; 22:4); Paul imprisoned many of the saints (Acts 26:10); Paul imprisoned and beat believers (Acts 22:19); Herod arrested Peter (Acts 12:3); the devil will imprison some of you (Rev. 2:10); he had his fellow-servant imprisoned (Matt. 18:30).

Prison, see **748**.

● Taken
captive

g Let those intended for captivity go into captivity (Jer. 15:2; 43:11); if anyone is to be taken captive, to captivity he will go (Rev. 13:10).

h You will be taken captive (Ezek. 21:24); your sons and daughters will be taken captive (Deut. 28:41); when your people are taken captive (1 Kgs. 8:46); they will be taken captive (Isa. 28:13); those who took Israel and Judah captive hold them fast (Jer. 50:33).

i Those taken captive: Lot (Gen. 14:12, 14); the Kenites (Num. 24:22); the king of Ai (Josh. 8:23); Agag (1 Sam. 15:8); the women of Ziklag (1 Sam. 30:2); a young girl from Israel (2 Kgs. 5:2); Jehoiachin (2 Kgs. 24:12); Zedekiah (2 Kgs. 25:6); Judah (2 Kgs. 25:21; Jer. 52:27); the Lord's flock (Jer. 13:17); our children and wives (2 Chr. 29:9).

j The Canaanite king took some Israelites captive (Num. 21:1); Joash captured Amaziah (2 Kgs. 14:13; 2 Chr. 25:23); Edom took some of Judah captive (2 Chr. 28:17); Israel took 200 000 of Judah captive (2 Chr. 28:8).

k Would you kill those you have taken captive? (2 Kgs. 6:22).

● Arrest

l When they arrest you, do not be anxious what to say (Mark 13:11).

m They seized Jeremiah (Jer. 26:8); Jeremiah was arrested (Jer. 37:13, 14); the Philistines seized David in Gath (Ps. 56:t).

n Jesus' family sought to seize him, saying he was mad (Mark 3:21); they looked for a way to arrest Jesus (Matt. 21:46; Mark 12:12; Luke 20:19; John 7:30, 44; 11:57); they sent temple guards to arrest him (John 7:32); they tried to seize him (John 10:39); they plotted to arrest him by stealth (Matt. 26:4); they arrested him (Matt. 26:50; Mark 14:46; Luke 22:54; John 18:12); Paul went to Damascus in order to arrest believers (Acts 9:14); Herod arrested some of the church (Acts 12:1); Herod arrested Peter (Acts 12:3).

● Binding

o Abraham bound Isaac (Gen. 22:9); Joseph was shackled (Ps. 105:18); Samson was bound with new ropes (Judg. 15:10, 12, 13; 16:11–12); with seven fresh cords (Judg. 16:7); that we may bind him (Judg. 16:5); how may you be bound? (Judg. 16:6, 10, 13); with bronze shackles (Judg. 16:21); Manasseh was bound with bronze shackles (2 Chr. 33:11); as was Zedekiah (2 Kgs. 25:7; Jer. 39:7; 52:11); and Jehoiakim (2 Chr. 36:6); Jeremiah was put in the stocks (Jer. 20:2); the demoniac was chained (Mark 5:4; Luke 8:29); prisoners in iron chains (Ps. 107:10); Ezekiel would be tied with ropes (Ezek. 3:25); ropes on Ezekiel so he could not turn (Ezek. 4:8); Shadrach, Meshach and Abednego were tied up (Dan. 3:20, 24); Lazarus was bound hand and foot (John 11:44); bind him hand and foot (Matt. 22:13); to put every madman who prophesies into the stocks (Jer. 29:26); they bound Jesus and led him away (Mark 15:1).

p Whatever you bind on earth will be bound in heaven (Matt. 16:19; 18:18); unless he first binds the strong man (Matt. 12:29; Mark 3:27; Luke 11:22); to bind their kings with chains and fetters (Ps. 149:8).

q He ties his donkey to the vine (Gen. 49:11); bind the sacrifice to the horns of the altar (Ps. 118:27).

r Make a yoke and put it on your neck (Jer. 27:2); yokes of iron made (Jer. 28:13–14).

s Abner was not bound when he died (2 Sam. 3:34).

● Believers bound

t They bound Jesus (Matt. 27:2); Paul and Silas were put in the stocks (Acts 16:24); Paul was chained (Acts 21:33; 2 Tim. 2:9); Paul took believers bound to Jerusalem (Acts 9:2); Paul would be bound in Jerusalem (Acts 21:11); Peter was bound with chains (Acts 12:6); Paul was tied up with the thongs (Acts 22:25).

● Spiritual restraint

u Take my yoke upon you (Matt. 11:29); my yoke is easy (Matt. 11:30); why put a yoke on the disciples which we ourselves could not bear? (Acts 15:10); before faith came we were in custody under the law (Gal. 3:23).

v You know what restrains the man of sin now (2 Thess. 2:6).

● People restraining	w Joab restrained them from pursuing Israel (2 Sam. 18:16); I will not let you go unless you bless me (Gen. 32:26).
	x Do not muzzle an ox which is threshing (Deut. 25:4; 1 Cor. 9:9; 1 Tim. 5:18).

748 Prison

● Prison

a The house of Jonathan was made the prison (Jer. 37:15, 20); Christ preached to the spirits in prison (1 Pet. 3:19). **Imprisoned**, see **747**.

● Hooks etc.

b I will put my hook in your nose and my bridle in your lips (2 Kgs. 19:28; Isa. 37:29); they brought him with hooks to Egypt (Ezek. 19:4); they put him in a cage with hooks and brought him to Babylon (Ezek. 19:9); I will put hooks in your jaws (Ezek. 29:4; 38:4); they will take you away with meat hooks and fish hooks (Amos 4:2–3).

c We put bits in horses' mouths (Jas. 3:3)

749 Keeper

● Guardian

a Am I my brother's keeper? (Gen. 4:9).

b Guard this man (1 Kgs. 20:39); soldiers guarding Peter (Acts 12:4).

750 Prisoner

● Prisoners

a Jeconiah the prisoner (1 Chr. 3:17); a well-known prisoner called Barabbas (Matt. 27:16).

b Joash took hostages (2 Kgs. 14:14; 2 Chr. 25:24).

● Prisoners for Christ

c The prisoner of Christ (Eph. 3:1; Philem. 1, 9); the prisoner of the Lord (Eph. 4:1); Andronicus and Junias, my fellow-prisoners (Rom. 16:7); Aristarchus my fellow-prisoner (Col. 4:10); Epaphras, my fellow-prisoner in Christ (Philem. 23).

d When he ascended, he led a host of captives (Eph. 4:8).

751 Commission: vicarious authority

● God commissioning

a God sent Moses and Aaron (Ps. 105:26); I have appointed you over the nations (Jer. 1:10).

b Aaron and his sons were ordained as priests (Exod. 28:41; 29:9, 29, 35; Lev. 8:2–36); no one takes this honour to himself, but is called by God (Heb. 5:4); God commisioned Bezalel (Exod. 31:2; 35:30); and Oholiab (Exod. 31:6); let the Lord appoint a leader for the community (Num. 27:16); I will commission Joshua (Deut. 31:14).

c The twelve apostles were appointed (Matt. 10:1–4; Mark 3:14–19); the Lord appointed 70 others and sent them two by two (Luke 10:1); God appointed first apostles, second prophets (1 Cor. 12:28); I was appointed an apostle (2 Tim. 1:11); we have received grace and apostleship (Rom. 1:5).

● Man com-
missioning

d Jethro taught Moses how to delegate responsibility (Exod. 18:19–22); the king has commissioned me (1 Sam. 21:2); oh, that they would make me a judge! (2 Sam. 15:4).

e Set apart Barnabas and Paul for the work (Acts 13:2); Paul and Barnabas appointed elders (Acts 14:23); appoint elders in every town (Titus 1:5).

f Paul went to Damascus with the commission of the high priests (Acts 26:12).

g You are the seal of my apostleship (1 Cor. 9:2); God has set his seal on his Son (John 6:27).

Hands laid on to commission, see **378v**.

● Entrusting

h Potiphar entrusted everything to Joseph (Gen. 39:4); as did the keeper of the prison (Gen. 39:22); and Pharaoh (Gen. 41:41); Solomon put Jeroboam in charge of the forced labour (1 Kgs. 11:28); a man entrusted his property to his servants (Matt. 25:14); who has the master put in charge to feed his household? (Matt. 24:45); he will put him in charge of all (Luke 12:44).

● Sending
people

i I am sending you to Pharaoh (Exod. 3:10); please send someone else (Exod. 4:13); here am I, send me! (Isa. 6:8); the ones the Lord has sent throughout the earth (Zech. 1:10); the Lord sent Nathan to David (2 Sam. 12:1, 25); the Lord has sent me and his Spirit (Isa. 48:16).

j I did not send the prophets (Jer. 23:21).

k Jesus sent out the 12 apostles (Matt. 10:5; Mark 6:7); I send you out as sheep among wolves (Matt. 10:16; Luke 10:3); these people know that you sent me (John 17:25); that the world may know that you sent me (John 17:23); as the Father sent me, so I send you (John 20:21); as you sent me into the world, I have sent them (John 17:18); pray the Lord of the harvest to send out workers (Matt. 9:38); there was a man sent from God, named John (John 1:6); how shall they preach unless they are sent? (Rom. 10:15); send us into the pigs (Mark 5:12).

l It pleased the king to send me (Neh. 2:5–6).

752 Abrogation

● Depose

a He has put down the mighty from their thrones (Luke 1:52); he has rejected you from being king (1 Sam. 15:23, 26); sovereignty has been taken from you (Dan. 4:31); his dominion will be taken away (Dan. 7:26); I will depose you from your office (Isa. 22:19).

b Asa removed Maacah from being queen mother (1 Kgs. 15:13; 2 Chr. 15:16); the king of Egypt dethroned Jehoahaz (2 Chr. 36:3); Vashti would no longer be queen (Esther 1:19); Nebuchadnezzar was deposed (Dan. 5:20); Jeroboam prevented the Levites from serving as priests (2 Chr. 11:14; 13:9); danger that Artemis may be deposed (Acts 19:27).

Deposed priests, see **986t**.

● Cancel

c Let Haman's letters be countermanded (Esther 8:5).

d I have not come to abolish the law (Matt. 5:17); nothing will pass from the law until all is fulfilled (Matt. 5:18); the laws of the Medes and Persians cannot be repealed (Esther 1:19; Dan. 6:8); the king's decree may not be revoked (Esther 8:8); whoever annuls the least commandment will be least in the Kingom (Matt. 5:19).

e You nullify the word of God for the sake of your traditions (Matt. 15:6; Mark 7:9, 13); do we nullify the law by faith? (Rom. 3:31); the law does not invalidate the covenant (Gal. 3:17).

f The former commandment is set aside (Heb. 7:18); if those of the law are heirs, the promise is void (Rom. 4:14); I do not nullify the grace of God (Gal. 2:21); he cancelled the bill of debt (Col. 2:14).

Cancelling debts, see **803***e*.

g A woman's vows may be annulled by her father (Num. 30:3–5); or her husband (Num. 30:6–15).

h Your covenant with death will be cancelled (Isa. 28:18).

Marriage annulled, see **896**.

753 Resignation

754 Nominee

- Apostles

a Jesus, the apostle and high priest (Heb. 3:1); God appointed in the church first apostles (1 Cor. 12:28–9); he gave some as apostles (Eph. 4:11); built on the foundation of apostles and prophets (Eph. 2:20); the mystery now revealed to his apostles and prophets (Eph. 3:5); the signs of a true apostle, perseverance and signs and wonders (2 Cor. 12:12).

b Jesus chose twelve whom he named apostles (Luke 6:13); we might have used authority as apostles of Christ (1 Thess. 2:6); the foundations have the names of the 12 apostles (Rev. 21:14); God has exhibited us apostles last of all (1 Cor. 4:9); those who were apostles before me (Gal. 1:17).

- Particular apostles

c Matthias was numbered with the eleven apostles (Acts 1:26); Paul was called as an apostle (Rom. 1:1; 1 Cor. 1:1); Paul, an apostle (Gal. 1:1; Eph. 1:1; Col. 1:1; 1 Tim. 1:1; 2 Tim. 1:1; Titus 1:1); for this I was appointed an apostle (1 Tim. 2:7; 2 Tim. 1:11); am I not an apostle? (1 Cor. 9:1–2); the least of the apostles (1 Cor. 15:9); you are the seal of my apostleship (1 Cor. 9:2); Peter, an apostle of Jesus Christ (1 Pet. 1:1; 2 Pet. 1:1); Andronicus and Junias, of note among the apostles (Rom. 16:7); these brethren are the apostles of the churches (2 Cor. 8:23).

- False apostles

d False apostles, disguising themselves as apostles (2 Cor. 11:13); you test those who call themselves apostles but are not (Rev. 2:2); I am not inferior to these superlative apostles (2 Cor. 11:5; 12:11).

● Ambassadors *e* We are ambassadors for Christ (2 Cor. 5:20); I am an ambassador in chains (Eph. 6:20).

755 Deputy
Delegating authority, see **733***ab*.

Section two: Special social volition

---

756 Permission

● Permitting *a* Do not grant the desires of the wicked (Ps. 140:8); Jesus gave the spirits permission to enter the pigs (Mark 5:13; Luke 8:32); let it be so for the moment (Matt. 3:15); permit me first to bury my father (Matt. 8:21); this we will do if God permits (Heb. 6:3).

757 Prohibition

● God forbidding *a* God commanded them not to eat of the tree (Gen. 3:11).

b God did not allow Laban to harm Jacob (Gen. 31:7); God would not let Balaam go (Num. 22:12–13); he did not permit anyone to oppress them (1 Chr. 16:21; Ps. 105:14).

c The Holy Spirit prevented them from preaching in Asia (Acts 16:6); the Spirit of Jesus did not allow them to enter Bithynia (Acts 16:7).

● Christ forbidding *d* He would not permit the demons to speak (Mark 1:34); he did not allow any to follow him except Peter, James and John (Mark 5:37; Luke 8:51); he would not allow people to carry anything through the temple (Mark 11:16).

● People forbidding *e* Moses, my lord, stop them! (Num. 11:28); do not let anyone enter the temple (2 Chr. 23:6); make these men stop work (Ezra 4:21); they did not stop them (Ezra 5:5).

f Pharaoh will not let you go (Exod. 3:19); Edom would not let them pass through (Num. 20:21); nor would Sihon (Num. 21:23); the Amorites would not allow the Danites into the valley (Judg. 1:34).

g John tried to stop Jesus from being baptised (Matt. 3:14); we forbade him because he was not following us (Mark 9:38–9; Luke 9:49); men who forbid marriage (1 Tim. 4:3).

758 Consent

● Concession *a* I say this by way of concession, not command (1 Cor. 7:6).

759 Offer

● Offer *a* I offer you three things (2 Sam. 24:12; 1 Chr. 21:10).

760 Refusal

● Refusing
people

a David refused to eat (2 Sam. 12:17); Amnon refused to eat (2 Sam. 13:9); do not listen or consent (1 Kgs. 20:8–9); the man refused to strike the prophet (1 Kgs. 20:35); Elisha refused a present from Naaman (2 Kgs. 5:16).

b Queen Vashti refused to come (Esther 1:12); I did not refuse him (1 Kgs. 20:7).

c Let husband and wife not refuse one another (1 Cor. 7:5).

● Refusing
God

d See that you do not refuse him who speaks (Heb. 12:25); oh, no, my lords! (Gen. 19:18).

761 Request

● Prayer

a My house shall be called a house of prayer for all nations (Isa. 56:7; Matt. 21:13; Mark 11:17; Luke 19:46); may my prayer be like incense (Ps. 141:2); golden bowls full of incense which are the prayers of the saints (Rev. 5:8); incense with the prayers of the saints (Rev. 8:3–4).

Incense and prayer, see **396***d*.

● Pray!

b Call on me in the day of trouble (Ps. 50:15); call to me and I will answer you (Jer. 33:3).

c They ought always to pray (Luke 18:1); pray constantly (1 Thess. 5:17); men should pray, lifting up holy hands (1 Tim. 2:8); devote yourselves to prayer (Col. 4:2); prayer should be made for everyone (1 Tim. 2:1); in everything, by prayer and supplication, make known your requests to God (Phil. 4:6); be engaged in prayer (Rom. 12:12); pray at all times in the Spirit (Eph. 6:18); pray in the Holy Spirit (Jude 20); you do not have because you do not ask (Jas. 4:2); if anyone is suffering, let him pray (Jas. 5:13).

● How to pray

d Teach us how to pray (Luke 11:1); we do not know how to pray, but the Spirit helps us (Rom. 8:26); do not pray to be seen by men (Matt. 6:5–6); for appearance they make long prayers (Mark 12:40); do not pray repetitiously like the heathen (Matt. 6:7); praying in tongues (1 Cor. 14:14); I will pray with my spirit and also with my mind (1 Cor. 14:15); direct your heart and put away sin (Job 11:13–14).

e 'Our Father' (Matt. 6:9–13; Luke 11:2–4); Cornelius prayed to God continually (Acts 10:2); abstinence to devote oneself to prayer (1 Cor. 7:5); prayer and fasting (Matt. 17:21; Acts 13:3; 14:23); when you pray, forgive (Mark 11:25); if two agree in what they ask, it shall be done (Matt. 18:19); this kind comes out only by prayer (Mark 9:29); the prayer of faith will save the sick (Jas. 5:14–15); when you pray, believe that you have received (Mark 11:24); how shall they call on him in whom they do not believe? (Rom. 10:14); be sober for your prayers (1 Pet. 4:7); be considerate with your wives lest your prayers be hindered (1 Pet. 3:7).

Prayer and fasting, see **946g**.

● Where to pray

f Elisha shut the door and prayed (2 Kgs. 4:33); go to your room and pray in secret (Matt. 6:6); the Pharisee and the tax-collector went to the temple to pray (Luke 18:10–13); Peter prayed on the roof (Acts 10:9); a place of prayer at the riverside (Acts 16:13).

● When to pray

g In the morning I will pray (Ps. 5:3); evening, morning and noon I meditate (Ps. 55:17); Daniel prayed three times a day (Dan. 6:10, 13); going up to the temple at the ninth hour, the hour of prayer (Acts 3:1); Cornelius prayed at the ninth hour (Acts 10:30); the people were praying at the hour of incense (Luke 1:10).

● Jesus praying

h During Jesus' earthly life he prayed (Heb. 5:7); he prayed at his baptism (Luke 3:21); at the transfiguration (Luke 9:28–9); in the hills (Matt. 14:23; Mark 6:46; Luke 6:12); in solitary places (Mark 1:35; Luke 5:16; 9:18); at Gethsemane (Matt. 26:36, 39, 42, 44; Mark 14:32, 35, 39; Luke 22:41–5); in another place (Luke 11:1).

i He prayed for Simon, that his faith may not fail (Luke 22:32); he interceded for the transgressors (Isa. 53:12); he always lives to intercede for them (Heb. 7:25); I do not say I will ask the Father on your behalf (John 16:26); Jesus' prayer (John 17:1–25); I will ask the Father and he will give you the Advocate (John 14:16); God will give you whatever you ask (John 11:22); Christ intercedes for us (Rom. 8:34); the Spirit makes intercession for the saints (Rom. 8:26–7).

● Praying for sinners

j Pray for those who harm you (Luke 6:28); pray for those who persecute you (Matt. 5:44); pray for a brother who sins (1 John 5:16).

k Abraham prayed for Sodom (Gen. 18:23–32); Abraham prayed for Abimelech (Gen. 20:7, 17); Moses prayed for Pharaoh (Exod. 8:8, 12, 28, 29–31; 9:28, 29; 10:17–18); Moses asked God not to destroy the people (Exod. 32:11–13, 31–2; Num. 11:2; Deut. 9:18–19, 25–9); Moses prayed for Miriam to be healed (Num. 12:13); ask the Lord to remove the snakes (Num. 21:7); Moses prayed for Aaron (Deut. 9:20); the man of God prayed for Jeroboam (1 Kgs. 13:6); Job prayed for his friends (Job 42:8–9); Peter prayed for Simon (Acts 8:24).

● Praying for the righteous

l Isaac prayed for his wife because she was barren (Gen. 25:21); the Israelites won whilst Moses held up his hands (Exod. 17:11–12); David prayed for Bathsheba's child (2 Sam. 12:16); Peter prayed for dead Tabitha (Acts 9:40); they prayed for Peter in prison (Acts 12:5, 12).

m They prayed and laid hands on them to commission them (Acts 6:6; 13:3); Peter and John prayed for them to receive the Holy Spirit (Acts 8:15).

● I pray for you

n I remember you in my prayers (Rom. 1:9–10; Eph. 1:16; Phil. 1:3–4; 2 Tim. 1:3); we have not stopped praying for you (Col.

1:9); I would sin against the Lord if I stopped praying for you (1 Sam. 12:23); we thank God when we pray for you (Col. 1:3; 1 Thess. 1:2; Philem. 4); night and day we pray we may see you again (1 Thess. 3:10); praying for their spiritual maturity (Eph. 3:14–19; Col. 1:9–12); we pray that God may count you worthy of his calling (2 Thess. 1:11); praying that you may stand mature (Col. 4:12); he knelt and prayed with them (Acts 20:36; 21:5).

● Pray for us

o Samuel prayed to God for them (1 Sam. 7:5, 9); do not cease to cry to the Lord for us (1 Sam. 7:8; 12:19); pray to the Lord for us (Jer. 37:3); Esther asked the Jews to fast (Esther 4:16); Daniel asked his friends to pray (Dan. 2:17–18); pray for us (1 Thess. 5:25; 2 Thess. 3:1; Heb. 13:18); help us by your prayers (2 Cor. 1:11); pray to God for me (Rom. 15:30); pray for the remnant that is left (2 Kgs. 19:4; Jer. 42:2); through your prayers I will be delivered (Phil. 1:19); I hope to be freed through your prayers (Philem. 22).

● Crying to God
for help

p Those who prayed: Abraham's servant for success (Gen. 24:12); Jacob when Esau drew near (Gen. 32:9); the Israelites when the Egyptians drew near (Exod. 14:10); Israel (Judg. 4:3; 6:6–7; 10:10; 1 Sam. 12:8, 10); Samson, for strength (Judg. 16:28); the Philistines (1 Sam. 5:12); David, about Ahithophel (2 Sam. 15:31); Hezekiah when threatened by Sennacherib (2 Kgs. 19:14–19; Isa. 37:15–20); Jehoahaz entreated the Lord's favour (2 Kgs. 13:4); Judah when ambushed (2 Chr. 13:14); Asa before the battle (2 Chr. 14:11); Jehoshaphat in battle (2 Chr. 18:31); Jehoshaphat before the battle (2 Chr. 20:5–12); Hezekiah when besieged (2 Chr. 32:20); Manasseh in prison (2 Chr. 33:12–13, 18, 19); Nehemiah about Israel (Neh. 1:4–11); Nehemiah before the king (Neh. 2:4); Nehemiah, and set a guard (Neh. 4:9); the sailors, about to throw Jonah in the sea (Jonah 1:14); Jonah, from the belly of the fish (Jonah 2:1); Jonah, for death (Jonah 4:2–3); Habakkuk (Hab. 3:1); the believers when threatened (Acts 4:24–30); Paul and Silas in prison (Acts 16:25).

q You will cry out because of your king (1 Sam. 8:18); I cried out to God for help (Ps. 77:1); in my distress I called on the Lord (2 Sam. 22:7; Ps. 18:6; 118:5); they cried to you in their trouble (Ps. 107:6, 13, 28); when they cried to you you heard them (Neh. 9:27); the Egyptians will cry to the Lord (Isa. 19:20); I call to the Lord and I am saved (2 Sam. 22:4; Ps. 18:3); I cried to the Lord (Ps. 3:4); my prayer is to you (Ps. 69:13).

Asking for a sign, see **547o**.

● Praying
about needs

r Moses cried to the Lord about the bitter water (Exod. 15:25); about the lack of water (Exod. 17:4); Manoah prayed for the angel to return (Judg. 13:8); Hannah prayed for a child (1 Sam. 1:10–17); one thing have I asked of the Lord (Ps. 27:4); Samuel prayed about their request for a king (1 Sam. 8:6); David's prayer for God to confirm his word (2 Sam. 7:18–29; 1 Chr. 17:16–17);

David's prayer for the temple to be built (1 Chr. 29:10–20); a prayer of David (Ps. 17:t); Solomon's prayer of dedication of the temple (1 Kgs. 8:22–54; 2 Chr. 6:14–42); Elijah prayed for God to reveal himself (1 Kgs. 18:36–7); Elijah prayed for rain (1 Kgs. 18:42–4); open his eyes! (2 Kgs. 6:17); open their eyes! (2 Kgs. 6:20); blind this people! (2 Kgs. 6:18); Jeremiah's prayer on buying the field (Jer. 32:16–25); Ezra prayed in shame over Israel (Ezra 9:6–10:1); praying for a safe journey (Ezra 8:21, 23); Daniel prayed about the desolation of Jerusalem (Dan. 9:3–19); pray for the welfare of the city to which you are exiled (Jer. 29:7); let them pray for the life of the king (Ezra 6:10); let them pray for him continually (Ps. 72:15); Paul prayed God to remove the thorn in the flesh (2 Cor. 12:8); pray that you will not fall into temptation (Luke 22:40, 46); pray that you will escape what is going to happen (Luke 21:36); pray that your flight will not be in winter or on the sabbath (Matt. 24:20).

● Praying for healing

   s Hezekiah cried to the Lord when mortally ill (2 Kgs. 20:2; 2 Chr. 32:24; Isa. 38:2–3); Elijah praying for the child's healing (1 Kgs. 17:21); Peter prayed for Tabitha (Acts 9:40); Paul prayed and laid hands on Publius' father (Acts 28:8).

● Calling on God

   t Men began to call on the name of the Lord (Gen. 4:26); as Abraham did (Gen. 12:8; 13:4; 21:33); and Isaac (Gen. 26:25); everyone who calls on the name of the Lord will be saved (Joel 2:32; Acts 2:21; Rom. 10:13); Elijah called to the Lord (1 Kgs. 17:20); you call on the name of your god and I will call on mine (1 Kgs. 18:24); call upon his name! (1 Chr. 16:8); David called to the Lord (1 Chr. 21:26); I called on the name of the Lord (Ps. 116:4); I will call on the name of the Lord (Ps. 116:13, 17); Naaman thought Elisha would call on the name of the Lord (2 Kgs. 5:11); repent and pray (Acts 8:22); blind Saul was praying (Acts 9:11); those who call on the name of our Lord Jesus (1 Cor. 1:2).

● Praying for God's kingdom

   u Pray the Lord of the harvest to send out labourers (Matt. 9:38; Luke 10:2); they devoted themselves to prayer (Acts 1:14; 2:42; 6:4); they prayed when choosing a replacement apostle (Acts 1:24); my prayer for the Israelites is that they be saved (Rom. 10:1).

● Begging Jesus

   v The demons begged him to send them into the pigs (Matt. 8:31; Mark 5:12; Luke 8:31–2); the demons begged him not to send them out of the country (Mark 5:10); the city begged him to depart (Matt. 8:34); they begged Jesus to leave their region (Mark 5:17).

   w They begged to be able to touch the fringe of his garment (Matt. 14:36); the man begged to accompany Jesus (Mark 5:18); Zebedee's wife made request for her sons (Matt. 20:20–1).

● Not praying

   x Do not pray for this people (Jer. 7:16; 11:14; 14:11); anyone who prays will be thrown into the den of lions (Dan. 6:7, 12); none of them calls on me (Hos. 7:7).

● **Hear prayer!**

y Hear the prayers of your people (1 Kgs. 8:29–30; 2 Chr. 6:20–1); if your people pray, hear! (1 Kgs. 8:33–4, 35–6, 38–9, 44–5, 47–9, 52; 2 Chr. 6:22–3, 24–5, 26–7, 28–30); hear the foreigner's prayer (1 Kgs. 8:42–3; 2 Chr. 6:32–3); may God grant your petition! (1 Sam. 1:17); may the Lord fulfil all your petitions (Ps. 20:5); hear my prayer (2 Chr. 6:19; Ps. 39:12).

Hear our prayer!, see **455a**.

● **God answers prayer**

z You will pray and he will hear (Job 22:27); you will pray to me and I will listen to you (Jer. 29:12).

God hears prayer, see **455c**.

aa The Lord has granted my prayer (1 Sam. 1:27); God answered prayer for the land (2 Sam. 21:14; 24:25); he answered their prayers because they trusted in him (1 Chr. 5:20); God is attentive to the prayers of the righteous (Ps. 34:15; 1 Pet. 3:12); your prayers have been heard (Luke 1:13; Acts 10:4).

ab Because you prayed I have heard you (2 Kgs. 19:20); I have heard your prayer (2 Kgs. 20:5); your prayer has been heard (Acts 10:31); God granted Jabez what he requested (1 Chr. 4:10).

ac Ask and it will be given you (Matt. 7:7; Luke 11:9; Jas. 1:5); God gives to all men liberally (Jas. 1:5); ask for what you want me to give you (1 Kgs. 3:5; 2 Chr. 1:7).

ad Whatever you ask in my name, I will do it (John 14:13–14); whatever you ask in my name, the Father will give you (John 15:16; 16:23); ask what you wish and it will be given you (John 15:7); we receive from him whatever we ask (1 John 3:22); if we ask anything according to his will, he hears us (1 John 5:14–15); the prayer of a righteous man accomplishes much (Jas. 5:16–18); whatever you ask in prayer, believing, you will receive (Matt. 21:22).

God heeding, see **455h**; **God answering**, see **460a**.

● **Prayer not answered**

ae The Lord will not answer you (1 Sam. 8:18); when you pray I will hide my eyes from you (Isa. 1:15); he shuts out my prayer (Lam. 3:8); you wrapped yourself in a cloud so no prayer can pass through (Lam. 3:44).

af If anyone will not listen to the law, even his prayer is an abomination (Prov. 28:9); you ask and do not receive because you ask amiss (Jas. 4:3); if I regard iniquity in my heart the Lord will not hear me (Ps. 66:18); the Lord does not answer because of man's pride (Job 35:12).

ag When Moab comes to pray he will not prevail (Isa. 16:12); let his prayer become sin (Ps. 109:7).

God not heeding, see **456a**; **not answering**, see **460j**.

● **Praying to other gods**

ah Cry to the gods you have chosen (Judg. 10:14); praying to a graven image (Isa. 44:17); praying to a god who cannot save (Isa.

45:20); they called on the name of Baal (1 Kgs. 18:26–9); each cried to his god (Jonah 1:5).

● Begging

ai Your descendants will beg for money and bread (1 Sam. 2:36); may his children beg (Ps. 109:10); the blind man used to sit and beg (John 9:8); a blind beggar called Bartimaeus (Mark 10:46); the blind man sat begging (Luke 18:35); the lame man begged for money (Acts 3:2–3, 10); the poor use supplications (Prov. 18:23).

aj I have not seen the righteous begging bread (Ps. 37:25); I am ashamed to beg (Luke 16:3).

● Requesting from people

ak Requesting gold and silver items (Exod. 11:2; 12:35); Gideon asked for the gold earrings (Judg. 8:24).

al Achsah asked her father for a field (Josh. 15:18; Judg. 1:14); the woman appealed to the king for her house and land (2 Kgs. 8:5); David asked for a gift from Nabal (1 Sam. 25:8); Adonijah requested Abishag as wife (1 Kgs. 2:16–17, 20–1); Nehemiah requested leave from the king (Neh. 13:6); Esther was to beg the king for mercy (Esther 4:8); my life and my people are my request (Esther 7:3); Esther implored the king again (Esther 8:3); Daniel made request of Nebuchadnezar for his friends (Dan. 2:49); ask me for whatever you want and I will give it (Matt. 14:7; Mark 6:22–3); the crowd made their request to Pilate (Mark 15:8); Nicodemus asked for the body of Jesus (Matt. 27:58).

am If your son asks for a loaf or a fish (Matt. 7:9–10; Luke 11:11–12).

an We appeal to you on Christ's behalf to be reconciled (2 Cor. 5:20); they begged to be allowed to contribute (2 Cor. 8:4).

ao Ask what I shall do for you (2 Kgs. 2:9); Queen Esther, what is your request? (Esther 5:3, 6; 7:2; 9:12); Paul appealed to Caesar (Acts 25:11–12, 21, 25; 26:32; 28:19).

● Inviting

ap Absalom invited the king's sons to the sheep shearing (2 Sam. 13:23); Absalom invited 200 men from Jerusalem (2 Sam. 15:11); Adonijah invited the king's sons (1 Kgs. 1:9, 19, 25); a man of Macedonia begging them to come (Acts 16:9).

762 Deprecation: negative request

763 Petitioner
See **761**.

Section three: Conditional social volition

764 Promise

● God's promises

a None of God's good promises have failed (Josh. 21:45; 1 Kgs. 8:56); the promises of God are Yes in Christ (2 Cor. 1:20); what

God had promised he was able to do (Rom. 4:21); God promised the gospel through the scriptures (Rom. 1:2).

b The first commandment with a promise (Eph. 6:2).

- **Promise to Abraham**

c The promise to Abraham (Rom. 4:13); God granted the inheritance to Abraham by promise (Gal. 3:18); Abraham patiently endured and obtained the promise (Heb. 6:15); the promises were to Abraham and his seed (Gal. 3:16); one son was born through promise (Gal. 4:23); the promise made to the fathers (Acts 13:32; 26:6); to Israel belong the promises (Rom. 9:4); Christ came to confirm the promise made to the fathers (Rom. 15:8).

d You are children of promise (Gal. 4:28); the children of the promise are reckoned as the seed (Rom. 9:8); the Gentiles share in the promise (Eph. 3:6).

- **Promise of eternal life**

e God promised eternal life ages ago (Titus 1:2); this is his promise, eternal life (1 John 2:25); great and precious promises to become partakers of God's nature (2 Pet. 1:4); having these promises (2 Cor. 7:1).

f Where is the coming he promised? (2 Pet. 3:4); none of them received what was promised (Heb. 11:39); those who through faith and patience inherit the promises (Heb. 6:12).

- **Promise of the Holy Spirit**

g I send the promise of my Father (Luke 24:49); they had to wait for what the Father had promised (Acts 1:4); Jesus received from the Father the promised Holy Spirit (Acts 2:33); the promise is for you (Acts 2:39); the Holy Spirit of promise (Eph. 1:13); the promise of the Spirit through faith (Gal. 3:14).

765 Covenant

- **Covenant with Noah**

a God made a covenant with Noah (Gen. 6:18; 9:9–11); the rainbow being the sign (Gen. 9:13).

- **Covenant with the patriarchs**

b The Lord made a covenant with Abraham (Gen. 15:18); God made an everlasting covenant with Abraham (Gen. 17:2, 7); the sign being circumcision (Gen. 17:9–14); the covenant of circumcision (Acts 7:8); the holy covenant sworn to Abraham (Luke 1:72–3); the Lord was kind to them because of his covenant with Abraham (2 Kgs. 13:23); a covenant to give his descendants the land (Exod. 6:4; Neh. 9:8); God made an everlasting covenant with Isaac (Gen. 17:19, 21); you are heirs of the covenant God made with your fathers (Acts 3:25); theirs are the covenants (Rom. 9:4); the law 430 years later does not annul the covenant (Gal. 3:17).

- **Covenant at Sinai**

c I am making a covenant with you (Exod. 34:10, 27); the Lord made a covenant with us at Horeb (Deut. 5:2); the Lord made a covenant with Israel (2 Kgs. 17:35); I made a covenant with your fathers (Jer. 34:13); I entered into a covenant with you (Ezek. 16:8); my covenant with Levi was life and peace (Mal. 2:4–5); one covenant is from Mount Sinai (Gal. 4:24).

d He declared his covenant, the ten commandments (Deut. 4:13); the words of the covenant, the ten commandments (Exod. 34:28); the ark containing the covenant (1 Kgs. 8:21); the book of the covenant (Exod. 24:7; 2 Chr. 34:30); they gave the king a copy of the covenant (2 Kgs. 11:12; 2 Chr. 23:11).

e This is the blood of the covenant (Exod. 24:8; Heb. 9:20); because of the blood of my covenant with you (Zech. 9:11); the first covenant was not ratified without blood (Heb. 9:18–20).

f Do not omit the salt of the covenant of your God from grain offerings (Lev. 2:13); a covenant of salt (2 Chr. 13:5); it is an everlasting covenant of salt (Num. 18:19).

g When reading the old covenant the veil remains (2 Cor. 3:14). **Ark of the covenant**, see **194a; blood of the covenant**, see **335o; book of the covenant**, see **589f; breaking the covenant**, see **769a; keeping covenant**, see **768b**.

● Later
covenants

h Covenant made in the land of Moab (Deut. 29:1, 12).

i God made a covenant of peace with Phinehas (Num. 25:12); God made an everlasting covenant with David (2 Sam. 23:5; Ps. 89:3, 28; Jer. 33:21); the kingdom given to David by a covenant of salt (2 Chr. 13:5); the covenant the Lord made with David (2 Chr. 21:7); I will make an everlasting covenant (Isa. 55:3; 61:8; Jer. 32:40; Ezek. 16:60; 37:26).

j Joshua made a covenant with the people (Josh. 24:25); Jephthah spoke all his words before the Lord (Judg. 11:11); Jehoiada made a covenant with the temple guards (2 Kgs. 11:4; 2 Chr. 23:1); and between the Lord, the king and the people (2 Kgs. 11:17; 2 Chr. 23:3, 16); Josiah renewed the covenant (2 Kgs. 23:3; 2 Chr. 34:31–2); they made a covenant to seek the Lord (2 Chr. 15:12); Hezekiah wanted to make a covenant with the Lord (2 Chr. 29:10); let us make a covenant to send away these women (Ezra 10:3); the people made a binding agreement to follow the law of God (Neh. 9:38; 10:29).

k Gather those who have made a covenant with me by sacrifice (Ps. 50:5).

● New
covenant

l If the first covenant had been faultless there would have been no need for another (Heb. 8:7); he made the first covenant obsolete (Heb. 8:13); he is the mediator of a new covenant (Heb. 9:15; 12:24); I have given you as a covenant to the people (Isa. 42:6; 49:8); they will join themselves to the Lord in an everlasting covenant (Jer. 50:5); I will make a covenant of peace with them (Ezek. 34:25); I will make a covenant with them and abolish war (Hos. 2:18).

m This cup is the new covenant in my blood (Luke 22:20; 1 Cor. 11:25); this is my blood of the covenant (Matt. 26:28; Mark 14:24); the blood of the covenant (Heb. 10:29; 13:20); this is my covenant, when I remove their sins (Rom. 11:27); I will make a new covenant with the house of Israel (Jer. 31:31; Heb. 8:8–13); servants of a new covenant (2 Cor. 3:6); a better covenant (Heb. 7:22; 8:6); this is my covenant, my Spirit will not depart from you (Isa. 59:21).

● Agreements between people

n Those who made a covenant: Abraham and Abimelech (Gen. 21:27); Isaac and Abimelech (Gen. 26:28); Jacob and Laban (Gen. 31:44); Jonathan and David (1 Sam. 18:3; 20:8, 16, 23; 23:18); David and the people (2 Sam. 5:3; 1 Chr. 11:3); the king of Babylon and Zedekiah (Ezek. 17:13–14).

o Abner was to make a covenant between the people and David (2 Sam. 3:21); Zedekiah made a covenant with the people to release slaves (Jer. 34:8).

p Hiram and Solomon made a covenant (1 Kgs. 5:12); Asa called for a treaty with Ben-Hadad (1 Kgs. 15:19; 2 Chr. 16:3); Ahab made a treaty with Ben-Hadad (1 Kgs. 20:34); Abner made a treaty with David (2 Sam. 3:12–13); Jehoshaphat made an alliance with Ahaziah (2 Chr. 20:35, 37); the peoples make a covenant against you (Ps. 83:5); he will make a strong covenant with many for one week (Dan. 9:27).

● Covenants with evil

q Do not make a covenant with these people or their gods (Exod. 23:32; 34:12, 15; Deut. 7:2; Judg. 2:2); Israel made a covenant with the Gibeonites (Josh. 9:6, 11, 15; 2 Sam. 21:2); the men of Jabesh Gilead asked for a covenant with Nahash the Ammonite (1 Sam. 11:1).

r Will the crocodile make a covenant with you? (Job 41:4); I made a covenant with my eyes (Job 31:1); we have made a covenant with death (Isa. 28:15); your covenant with death will be cancelled (Isa. 28:18).

● Last will and testament

s No one annuls a man's will once it has been ratified (Gal. 3:15).

766 Conditions

Multiplied conditionally, see **104h**.

767 Security

● Laws about pledges

a Do not take a widow's cloak as a pledge (Deut. 24:17); or a millstone (Deut. 24:6); do not go into your neighbour's house to get a pledge (Deut. 24:10–11); return the pledge by sunset (Exod. 22:26; Deut. 24:12); if a man restores a pledge (Ezek. 18:7, 16; 33:15); if he does not restore a pledge (Ezek. 18:12).

● Pledges given

b Judah's daughter-in-law asked for a pledge (Gen. 38:17); they took security from Jason (Acts 17:9).

● Avoid giving pledges

c Do not give pledges (Prov. 22:26–7); a senseless man gives a pledge (Prov. 17:18); he who gives surety for a stranger will suffer for it (Prov. 11:15); if you have given a pledge for a stranger (Prov. 6:1); take the garment of one who goes surety for a stranger (Prov. 20:16; 27:13).

● Pledges abused

d You have taken pledges needlessly (Job 22:6); some take the widow's ox in pledge (Job 24:3); they take a pledge against the poor (Job 24:9); they lie beside altars on garments taken in pledge (Amos 2:8).

● Guarantee

e Judah guaranteed Benjamin's safety (Gen. 43:9; 44:32); the beloved of the Lord dwells in safety (Deut. 33:12).

f We are given the Spirit as a pledge (2 Cor. 1:22; 5:5; Eph. 1:14).

g The title deed signed and sealed (Jer. 32:10–14, 16).

768 Observance

● Keeping passover

a A night to be observed by all Israelites (Exod. 12:42).

● Keeping covenant

b Keep my covenant (Exod. 19:5); do not forget the covenant (Deut. 4:23; 2 Kgs. 17:38); to those who keep his covenant (Ps. 25:10).

● God keeps covenant

c Have regard to the covenant! (Ps. 74:20); I will keep my covenant with you (Lev. 26:9); God keeps covenant (Neh. 1:5; 9:32); God confirms the covenant by giving you wealth (Deut. 8:18); God remembers his covenant (Exod. 2:24; 6:5; Lev. 26:42, 45; 1 Chr. 16:15–18; Ps. 105:8–11; 106:45; 111:5); he keeps his covenant of love (Deut. 7:9, 12; 1 Kgs. 8:23; 2 Chr. 6:14); I will never break my covenant (Judg. 2:1); my covenant will not be moved (Isa. 54:10); if you can break my covenant with day and night then my covenant with David will be broken (Jer. 33:20–1, 25).

Keeping the commandments, see **739g**.

769 Nonobservance

● Breaking the covenant

a Breaking the covenant (Gen. 17:14; Ezek. 16:59); you have not kept my covenant (1 Kgs. 11:11); Israel and Judah have broken my covenant (Jer. 11:10); my covenant which they broke (Jer. 31:32); they forsook the covenant of the Lord their God (Jer. 22:9); like Adam they broke the covenant (Hos. 6:7).

b They broke the covenant (Deut. 31:16; Hos. 8:1); they did not continue in my covenant (Heb. 8:9); they abandoned the covenant (Deut. 29:25); they rejected the covenant (2 Kgs. 17:15); they violated the covenant (Josh. 7:11, 15; 23:16; Judg. 2:20); they did not keep the covenant (Ps. 78:10).

c Cursed is the one who does not obey the covenant (Jer. 11:3); the adulteress forgets the covenant of her God (Prov. 2:17).

● Breaking treaties

d Break your treaty with Baasha (1 Kgs. 15:19; 2 Chr. 16:3); Zedekiah broke covenant with the king of Babylon (Ezek. 17:15–19).

● Not keeping
  passover

    e Whoever does not keep the passover will be cut off (Num. 9:13).

770 Compromise

Section four: Possessive relations

---

771 Acquisition

● Inheriting

    a Daughters can inherit (Num. 27:4–11; Josh. 17:3–6); Job's daughters inherited with their brothers (Job 42:15).

    b A wise servant will share the inheritance (Prov. 17:2). **Inheritance**, see **777**; **heir**, see **776**.

● Inheriting
  the land

    c The land will be inherited by: those who wait for the Lord (Ps. 37:9, 34); the humble (Ps. 37:11); those blessed by him (Ps. 37:22); the righteous (Ps. 37:29); him who takes refuge in me (Isa. 57:13); his seed (Ps. 25:13).

    d Take possession of the land (Num. 13:30; 21:35; Josh. 18:3); Israel took possession of the land of the Amorites (Num. 21:24–5).

● Taking
  possession

    e They took possession of houses full of good things (Neh. 9:25); they took possession of the fruit of the peoples' toil (Ps. 105:44); woe to those who add house to house and field to field (Isa. 5:8).

    f Why has Molech taken possession of Gad? (Jer. 49:1).

    g Their property will be ours (Gen. 34:23); let us possess the pastures of God (Ps. 83:12); all that belongs to Mephibosheth is yours (2 Sam. 16:4).

● Gain

    h What does a man gain from his toil? (Eccles. 1:3; 3:9); what gain do we have if we pray to God? (Job 21:15); what do I gain by not sinning? (Job 35:3); what shall it profit a man if he gains the whole world? (Matt. 16:26; Mark 8:36; Luke 9:25).

    i They think godliness is a means of gain (1 Tim. 6:5); an elder should not seek shameful gain (Titus 1:7); shepherding the flock not for shameful gain (1 Pet. 5:2); teaching for the sake of shameful gain (Titus 1:11); choose men who hate unjust gain (Exod. 18:21).

    j Every one is greedy for gain (Jer. 6:13; 8:10); ill-gotten gains do not profit (Prov. 10:2); wealth gained hastily will dwindle (Prov. 13:11); gain by violence leads to loss of life (Prov. 1:19); a people who cannot profit them (Isa. 30:5, 6).

    k The one with five talents made five more (Matt. 25:16, 20); the one with two talents made two more (Matt. 25:17, 22); your mina made ten minas more (Luke 19:16); your mina made five minas more (Luke 19:18); you who reckon on getting a profit (Jas. 4:13).

    l The gain from wisdom is better than from silver (Prov. 3:14); I am the Lord who teaches you to profit (Isa. 48:17); to die is gain (Phil. 1:21).

● Winning
people

m I am a slave to all that I might win the more (1 Cor. 9:19–22); if he listens, you have gained your brother (Matt. 18:15).

772 Loss

● Loss in
general

a Whoever does not have will lose what he has (Matt. 25:29; Mark 4:25; Luke 8:18; 19:26); if anyone's work is burned up, he will suffer loss (1 Cor. 3:15).

b Restore lost things which you have found (Deut. 22:3).

● Losing things

c Jacob bore the loss due to wild beasts (Gen. 31:39); earning wages to put into a bag with holes (Hag. 1:6); the donkeys of Kish were lost (1 Sam. 9:3, 20); nothing was missing from the spoil (1 Sam. 30:19).

d The voyage will be with great loss (Acts 27:10).

● Bereavement

e If I am bereaved, I am bereaved (Gen. 43:14); Naomi was bereaved of husband and sons (Ruth 1:5); loss of children and widowhood in one day (Isa. 47:9).
Orphans, see **779a**; **being widowed**, see **896m**.

f David will be like a bear bereaved (2 Sam. 17:8); I will be like a bear robbed of her cubs (Hos. 13:8); better meeting a she-bear robbed of her cubs than a fool (Prov. 17:12).

g Why should one tribe be missing from Israel? (Judg. 21:3, 6); I will bereave them till none is left (Hos. 9:12).

h I will not know the loss of my children (Isa. 47:8); I have not lost one of those you gave me (John 18:9).

● Losing
one's life

i He who would save his life will lose it but whoever loses his life will gain it (Matt. 10:39; 16:25; Mark 8:35; Luke 9:24; 17:33); he who loves his life will lose it (John 12:25); to gain the whole world and forfeit your soul (Matt. 16:26; Mark 8:36; Luke 9:25); whatever was gain I consider loss for the sake of Christ, for whom I have lost all things (Phil. 3:7–8).

● Seeking
the lost

j The Son of Man came to seek and save the lost (Luke 19:10); the lost sheep of the house of Israel (Matt. 10:6; 15:24); he goes to find the sheep which was lost (Luke 15:4); if a woman loses one coin (Luke 15:8); rejoice with me, I have found what was lost (Luke 15:6, 9); he was lost and is found (Luke 15:24, 32); this is his will, that I lose nothing of what he has given me (John 6:39).

773 Possession

● Possessing
in general

a He who has will be given more (Matt. 25:29; Mark 4:25; Luke 8:18; 19:26).

● God
possessing

b All the earth is mine (Exod. 19:5); the land belongs permanently to God (Lev. 25:23); everything under heaven is mine (Job 41:11); the mountains are his (Ps. 95:4); the sea is his (Ps. 95:5).

c The firstborn are mine (Num. 3:12–13); the Levites are mine (Num. 8:14, 16); Gilead is mine and Manasseh is mine (Ps. 60:7;

108:8); you possess all the nations (Ps. 82:8); all souls are mine (Ezek. 18:4).

d I have called you by name, you are mine (Isa. 43:1); I am the Lord's (Isa. 44:5).

e All that the Father has is mine (John 16:15); all that are mine are yours and yours are mine (John 17:10); whether we live or die we are the Lord's (Rom. 14:8); you are Christ's and Christ is God's (1 Cor. 3:23).

God's possession, see **777***f*.

● Possessing through God

f The house of Jacob will possess their possessions (Obad. 17); all things are yours and you are Christ's and Christ is God's (1 Cor. 3:22–3); as having nothing yet possessing all things (2 Cor. 6:10); if you have not been faithful with another's, who will give you your own? (Luke 16:12).

● Man possessing

g My beloved is mine and I am his (S. of S. 2:16); I am my beloved's and he is mine (S. of S. 6:3); I am my beloved's (S. of S. 7:10).

h The daughters, children and flocks are mine (Gen. 31:43); your most beautiful wives and children are mine (1 Kgs. 20:3); I am yours and all that I have (1 Kgs. 20:4); Ephraim and Manasseh are mine as Reuben and Simeon are mine (Gen. 48:5); you said, these two lands will be mine (Ezek. 35:10).

i The one this people has chosen, his will I be (2 Sam. 16:18).

Taking possession, see **771***e*.

● The devil possessing

j All this has been delivered to me (Luke 4:6).

774 Nonownership

● No earthly inheritance

a God gave Abraham no inheritance in the land (Acts 7:5); there was no inheritance for the priests (Num. 18:20); or the Levites (Num. 18:24; 26:62; Josh. 13:14, 33; 14:3–4; 18:7).

b Jephthah was denied an inheritance (Judg. 11:7).

c As having nothing, yet possessing all things (2 Cor. 6:10).

● No heavenly inheritance

d You have no portion in the Lord (Josh. 22:25); the wicked will not inherit the kingdom of God (1 Cor. 6:9); no immoral or covetous man can inherit the kingdom (Eph. 5:5); flesh and blood cannot inherit the kingdom of God (1 Cor. 15:50).

e These people are not the Lord's (Jer. 5:10).

775 Joint possession

● Sharing material things

a Do we have any share in our father's house? (Gen. 31:14); we have no share in David (2 Sam. 20:1; 1 Kgs. 12:16; 2 Chr. 10:16); you have no portion in Jerusalem (Neh. 2:20).

b Those who believed had all things in common (Acts 2:44; 4:32).

● Sharing in Christ

c The cup and the bread are a sharing in the blood and body of Christ (1 Cor. 10:16); we are partakers in Christ (Heb. 3:14); the

Gentiles share in the promise of Christ (Eph. 3:6); I John share with you the tribulation and the kingdom (Rev. 1:9).

d Those who became partakers of the Holy Spirit (Heb. 6:4); a partaker of the glory to be revealed (1 Pet. 5:1); partakers of the divine nature (2 Pet. 1:4).

● Sharing evil

e He who greets him shares in his evil deeds (2 John 11).

776 Possessor

● Heirs of men

a The heir of my house is Eliezer (Gen. 15:2–4); your own son will be your heir (Gen. 15:3–4); Ishmael would not be heir along with Isaac (Gen. 21:10); they will kill the heir (2 Sam. 14:7).

● Heirs of God

b This is the heir (Matt. 21:38; Mark 12:7; Luke 20:14); God appointed his Son heir of all things (Heb. 1:2).

c Heirs of God and fellow-heirs with Christ (Rom. 8:17); if a son, then an heir (Gal. 4:7); heirs according to the hope of eternal life (Titus 3:7); heirs according to the promise (Gal. 3:29); while the heir is a child he is no better off than a slave (Gal. 4:1).

777 Property

● Owning property

a The law on property rights (Exod. 22:1–4).

b A man's life does not consist in the abundance of his possessions (Luke 12:15); the rich fool built bigger barns to store his goods (Luke 12:18); you accepted the seizure of your goods, knowing you have a better possession (Heb. 10:34).

c The field was made over to Abraham as his possession (Gen. 23:18).

d They will come out with many possessions (Gen. 15:14).

● Owning God

e God is my portion for ever (Ps. 73:26); you are my portion (Ps. 142:5); O Lord, you are my portion (Ps. 16:5; 119:57); the Lord is my portion (Lam. 3:24).

● God's possession

f You will be my special possession among the nations (Exod. 19:5); a people for his own possession (Deut. 4:20; 7:6); God's special possession (Deut. 14:2; 26:18; Ps. 135:4; 1 Pet. 2:9); his inheritance (Deut. 4:20; 9:26, 29; 32:9; 1 Kgs. 8:53; Ps. 33:12; 78:71; Jer. 10:16); Israel, my inheritance (Isa. 19:25); take us as your possession (Exod. 34:9); they will be mine when I make up my own possession (Mal. 3:17).

g The riches of the glory of his inheritance in the saints (Eph. 1:18). **God possessing**, see **773***b*.

● The land an inheritance

h The land was divided for an inheritance (Num. 26:53); the land you gave us for an inheritance (2 Chr. 20:11); the land on which Caleb's foot trod was to be his inheritance (Josh. 14:9); the Israelites gave Joshua an inheritance (Josh. 19:49); our inheritance is east of Jordan (Num. 32:19).
The land inherited, see **184***e*.

i I will not give you the inheritance of my fathers (1 Kgs. 21:3).

● Priestly
inheritance

j The priests' offerings are their inheritance (Deut. 18:1; Josh. 13:14); the priesthood is their inheritance (Josh. 18:7).

k The Lord is the inheritance of Levi (Deut. 10:9; 18:2; Josh. 13:33; Ezek. 44:28); I am your inheritance (Num. 18:20); the Lord is their inheritance (Josh. 13:33).

● Inheriting
property

l A good man leaves an inheritance for his children's children (Prov. 13:22); house and wealth are inherited from fathers (Prov. 19:14).

Dividing inheritance, see **783d**.

● Inheriting
from God

m You have given me the inheritance of those who fear your name (Ps. 61:5); their inheritance will last for ever (Ps. 37:18); the meek will inherit the earth (Matt. 5:5); I will give you the nations as your inheritance (Ps. 2:8); that they may obtain an inheritance (Acts 26:18); we have obtained an inheritance in Christ (Eph. 1:11); an imperishable inheritance in heaven (1 Pet. 1:4).

n Come, inherit the kingdom prepared for you (Matt. 25:34); he has qualified us to share the inheritance of the saints (Col. 1:12); what shall I do to inherit eternal life? (Mark 10:17; Luke 10:25; 18:18); the word of God is able to give you the inheritance (Acts 20:32).

o We have no inheritance in the son of Jesse (2 Sam. 20:1; 1 Kgs. 12:16; 2 Chr. 10:16).

p This is the inheritance of a wicked man from God (Job 27:13).

Inheriting, see **771a**.

● Baggage

q Prepare baggage for exile (Ezek. 12:3–7).

r David left his things with the baggage keeper (1 Sam. 17:22); 200 men stayed with the baggage (1 Sam. 25:13); those who stay with the baggage have the same share as those in the battle (1 Sam. 30:24).

778 Retention

● Keeping
things

a There is a time to keep (Eccles. 3:6); Ananias kept back a part of the price (Acts 5:2).

779 Nonretention

● Orphans

a We have become orphans (Lam. 5:3); Esther had neither father nor mother (Esther 2:7).

b Let his children be fatherless (Ps. 109:9).

● Help the
orphans

c Give the tithe to the fatherless (Deut. 26:12–13); use the tithe to feed the orphan (Deut. 14:29); invite the orphan to the Feast of Booths (Deut. 16:14); leave the forgotten sheaf and gleanings for the fatherless (Deut. 24:19–21); defend the orphan (Isa. 1:17); true religion is to visit orphans and widows (Jas. 1:27).

d I delivered the orphan (Job 29:12); if the orphan has not shared my morsel (Job 31:17).

- God helps
  orphans

e The Lord supports the fatherless (Ps. 146:9); you are the helper of the orphan (Ps. 10:14); God is a father of the fatherless (Ps. 68:5); in you the orphan finds mercy (Hos. 14:3).

- Oppressing
  orphans

f Do not oppress widows or orphans (Exod. 22:22–4); God judges for orphans and widows (Deut. 10:18); do not pervert the justice due to the fatherless (Deut. 24:17; 27:19).

g You have broken the strength of orphans (Job 22:9); some drive away orphans' donkeys (Job 24:3); evildoers murder widows and orphans (Ps. 94:6); they do not defend the orphan (Isa. 1:23).

h If I have lifted up my hand against the orphan (Job 31:21).

780 Transfer (of property)

- Bequeathing

a A man who has toiled leaves a legacy to those who have not (Eccles. 2:21); I must leave it to the man who comes after me (Eccles. 2:18).

b Slaves may be bequeathed (Lev. 25:46).

781 Giving

- Giving in
  general

a The leech has two daughters, 'Give, give!' (Prov. 30:15); give to him who asks you (Matt. 5:42; Luke 6:30); give and it will be given you (Luke 6:38); it is more blessed to give than to receive (Acts 20:35); God loves a cheerful giver (2 Cor. 9:7); you know how to give good gifts to your children (Matt. 7:11; Luke 11:13).

b Give as God has blessed (Deut. 15:14; 16:17).

- God giving
  to the Son

c All things have been handed over to me by my Father (Matt. 11:27; Luke 10:22); the Father has given all things into the Son's hands (John 3:35; 13:3).

d All that the Father gives to me will come to me (John 6:37); you have given them to me (John 17:2, 6, 9, 24); of all that you have given to me I should lose none (John 6:39); of those you gave me I did not lose one (John 18:9).

- God giving
  freely

e God gives generously to all (Jas. 1:5); your Father in heaven gives good gifts (Matt. 7:11); every good and perfect gift is from the Father (Jas. 1:17); all God had given to David (2 Sam. 12:8); the Lord has much more to give you (2 Chr. 25:9); he gives to all life and breath and all things (Acts 17:25); he gives to the poor (2 Cor. 9:9); he who did not spare his own Son will with him freely give us all things (Rom. 8:32).

f The Lord gave and the Lord has taken away (Job 1:21); he gave them what they asked but sent a disease (Ps. 106:15).

- The gifts
  of God

g If you knew the gift of God (John 4:10); God so loved the world that he gave his only son (John 3:16); thanks be to God for his inexpressible gift (2 Cor. 9:15).

h The gift of God is eternal life (Rom. 6:23); being saved is the gift of God (Eph. 2:8); the gift is not like the transgression (Rom. 5:15); the gifts of God are irrevocable (Rom. 11:29); I was made a servant according to God's gift (Eph. 3:7).

i To you it is given to know the secrets of the kingdom (Matt. 13:11; Luke 8:10); to you has been given the secret of the kingdom (Mark 4:11).

j Your Father gives the Holy Spirit (Luke 11:13); you will receive the gift of the Holy Spirit (Acts 2:38); God who gives his Holy Spirit (1 Thess. 4:8); God gave us the Spirit as a pledge (2 Cor. 1:22; 5:5); God gave the same gift to them as to us (Acts 11:17); God gives the Holy Spirit to those who obey him (Acts 5:32).
God gives food, see **301*u***; **God gives life**, see **360*i***; **God gives light**, see **417*i***; **God gives wisdom**, see **498*k***; **God gives understanding**, see **516*e***; **God gives rest**, see **683*m***; **God gives peace**, see **719*a***; **God gives wealth**, see **800*a***; **God gives repentance**, see **939*c***.

● God giving words

k What to say will be given you (Matt. 10:19; Luke 12:11–12); I will give you words of wisdom (Luke 21:15).

● To whom it is given

l Only those to whom it is given can accept this (Matt. 19:11); a man can only receive what has been given him from heaven (John 3:27); to him who has will more be given (Matt. 13:12; 25:29; Mark 4:24–5; Luke 8:18; 19:26); from him who is given much will much be required (Luke 12:48).
The land given, see **184*a***.

● Spiritual gifts

m When he ascended he gave gifts to men (Eph. 4:8); concerning spiritual gifts (1 Cor. 12:1–31); we have different gifts (Rom. 12:6); every one has his own gift from God (1 Cor. 7:7); do not neglect the spiritual gift within you (1 Tim. 4:14); rekindle the gift of God (2 Tim. 1:6); whoever has a gift should use it in serving (1 Pet. 4:10); there are various gifts but the same Spirit (1 Cor. 12:4); gifts of the Holy Spirit (Heb. 2:4); you are not lacking in any gift (1 Cor. 1:7); I long to impart some spiritual gift to you (Rom. 1:11).
The gift of the Spirit, see **965*t***.

● Giving to God

n Who has given to God that God should repay him? (Rom. 11:35); what shall I render to the Lord? (Ps. 116:12); give to God what is God's (Matt. 22:21; Mark 12:17; Luke 20:25); everything comes from you and from your hand we have given to you (1 Chr. 29:14, 16); when you ascended you received gifts from men (Ps. 68:18).

o Kings will bring you gifts (Ps. 68:29); gifts will be brought to the Lord by a tall people (Isa. 18:7); they brought gifts of gold, incense and myrrh (Matt. 2:11).

● Giving for the sanctuary

p The Israelites were to make a contribution of materials (Exod. 25:2; 35:5, 21); a freewill offering (Exod. 35:29); the tribal leaders made an offering (Num. 7:2); David and the leaders gave materials for the temple (1 Chr. 29:3–9); Asa dedicated gifts to God (2 Chr. 15:18); the heads of families gave offerings for the temple (Ezra 2:68).

q The crowd put money in the treasury (Mark 12:41; Luke 21:1);

some gave of their wealth, but the widow put in all she had (Mark 12:44; Luke 21:4).

- **Giving sacrifices**

  r Hezekiah gave 1000 bulls and 7000 sheep (2 Chr. 30:24); the princes gave 1000 bulls and 10 000 sheep (2 Chr. 30:24); Josiah gave 30 000 from the flock and 3000 bulls (2 Chr. 35:7); the officers gave 2600 from the flock and 300 bulls (2 Chr. 35:8); officers of the Levites gave 5000 from the flock and 500 bulls (2 Chr. 35:9); everything needed for sacrifices is to be given to them (Ezra 6:9–10); the prince will provide the offerings (Ezek. 45:17).

- **Giving the firstborn**

  s Give the firstborn of your sons to me (Exod. 22:29); Samuel was given to the Lord (1 Sam. 1:11); shall I give my firstborn for my transgression? (Mic. 6:7).

- **Giving oneself**

  t The people offered themselves willingly (Judg. 5:2); they gave themselves first to the Lord, then to us (2 Cor. 8:5); into your hand I commit my spirit (Ps. 31:5).

- **Giving to the poor**

  u If I give away all I have and have not love (1 Cor. 13:3); the righteous is gracious and gives (Ps. 37:21); he who gives to the poor will not want (Prov. 28:27); your alms have been remembered before God (Acts 10:31).

  v When you give alms, do not sound a trumpet (Matt. 6:2–4); use your gift when giving (Rom. 12:8); sell your possessions and give to the poor (Matt. 19:21; Mark 10:21; Luke 12:33; 18:22); freely you have received, freely give (Matt. 10:8); contribute to the needs of the saints (Rom. 12:13); let the former thief work so that he can give (Eph. 4:28).

  w Such as I have I give you (Acts 3:6); I give half my possessions to the poor (Luke 19:8); Cornelius gave alms (Acts 10:2); Macedonia and Achaia made a contribution to the poor saints (Rom. 15:26; 1 Cor. 16:1); Macedonia gave beyond their means (2 Cor. 8:3); those returning to Jerusalem were supported with gifts (Ezra 1:4, 6); I came to give alms to my nation (Acts 24:17); no church except you shared with me in giving and receiving (Phil. 4:15); the perfume could have been sold and given to the poor (Matt. 26:9; Mark 14:5; John 12:5).

- **Giving to others**

  x Give to Caesar the things that are Caesar's (Matt. 22:21; Mark 12:17; Luke 20:25); send lambs as tribute to the ruler (Isa. 16:1).

  y Pharaoh gave to Abraham (Gen. 12:16); Abimelech gave livestock to Abraham (Gen. 20:14); as Abraham did to Abimelech (Gen. 21:27); Jacob chose a gift for Esau (Gen. 32:13); and for the ruler of Egypt (Gen. 43:11); the brothers gave their gifts (Gen. 43:25–6); Saul wondered what to give to Samuel (1 Sam. 9:7); David gave a present to the elders of Judah (1 Sam. 30:26); David sent a present for Uriah (2 Sam. 11:8); the Queen of Sheba gave Solomon gold and spices (1 Kgs. 10:10); Solomon gave the Queen of Sheba all she desired (1 Kgs. 10:13; 2 Chr. 9:12); gifts were brought to Solomon (1 Kgs. 10:25; 2 Chr. 9:24); Elisha would not accept a gift from Naaman (2 Kgs. 5:15); Hazael took a gift of forty camel-loads to Elisha (2 Kgs. 8:9); Ahaz sent a gift to the king of Assyria (2 Kgs. 16:8); Berodach-baladan sent gifts to Hezekiah (2 Kgs. 20:12); many brought gifts to Hezekiah (2 Chr. 32:23).

z Abraham gave Isaac all he had (Gen. 24:36; 25:5); he gave gifts to the sons of his concubines (Gen. 25:6); Jehoshaphat gave his sons gifts (2 Chr. 21:3); Herod promised to give her whatever she asked (Matt. 14:7).

782 Receiving

● God receiving

a If God wanted to kill us, he would not have received an offering (Judg. 13:23); let my words and thoughts be acceptable (Ps. 19:14); may he find your offerings acceptable! (Ps. 20:3).

● Receiving from God

b Whoever has forsaken for Christ will receive a hundredfold (Matt. 19:29; Mark 10:29–30).

c Receive the Holy Spirit (John 20:22); you shall receive power when the Holy Spirit has come (Acts 1:8); did you receive the Holy Spirit when you believed? (Acts 19:2); did you receive the Spirit by works or by faith? (Gal. 3:2).

d The Gentiles had received the word of God (Acts 11:1); the Bereans receive the word eagerly (Acts 17:11); as you received Christ, so walk in him (Col. 2:6); of his fulness we have all received (John 1:16); what do you have that you did not receive? (1 Cor. 4:7).

● Receiving from man

e Abraham would take nothing from the king of Sodom (Gen. 14:22–4); Elisha would take nothing from Naaman (2 Kgs. 5:16).

783 Apportionment

● Dividing out land

a Apportioning the land (Num. 26:53–6; 34:13–29; Ezek. 47:13–23; 48:29); when you divide the land by lot (Ezek. 45:1); apportioning this land among the nine tribes (Josh. 13:7; 14:1–2); divide the land into seven portions (Josh. 18:5); they finished dividing the land (Josh. 19:51); I have apportioned the nations in the land (Josh. 23:4); he apportioned an inheritance for them (Ps. 78:55); I will portion out Shechem and Succoth (Ps. 60:6; 108:7); God has apportioned the land to the wild animals (Isa. 34:17).

● Dividing plunder

b Divide the booty (Num. 31:27); all share alike in the plunder (1 Sam. 30:22–5).

c Jesus' garments were divided by casting lots (Matt. 27:35; Mark 15:24; Luke 23:34; John 19:23–4); they divided my garments between them (Ps. 22:18).

● Dividing inheritance

d Tell my brother to divide the inheritance with me (Luke 12:13); the father divided his goods between his two sons (Luke 15:12).

● Dividing food

e The priests had an allowance from Pharaoh (Gen. 47:22); Jehoiachin had a regular allowance every day (2 Kgs. 25:30); David distributed food to the people (1 Chr. 16:3); Jesus and the disciples distributed the food (Matt. 14:19; 15:36).

f The offerings are for the priests as their allotment (Num. 18:8); Aaron and his sons' portion (Exod. 29:28); the portions were distributed to the priests (2 Chr. 31:15); the Levites will receive equal portions (Deut. 18:8); Kore apportioned offerings to the Lord (2 Chr. 31:14).

● Sharing

g Do not neglect to do good and share (Heb. 13:16); the one with two tunics or food should share with him who has none (Luke 3:11); the proceeds of sales were distributed to those in need (Acts 2:45; 4:35); he who is taught must share with his teacher (Gal. 6:6).

h Spiritual gifts are distributed by the Spirit (1 Cor. 12:11); gifts of the Holy Spirit distributed according to his will (Heb. 2:4).

● Apportioning carcasses

i The Levite sent out parts of the concubine (Judg. 19:29); Saul sent out parts of the yoke of oxen (1 Sam. 11:7).

784 Lending

● Lend!

a Do not just lend to those from whom you hope to receive (Luke 6:34); lend, expecting nothing (Luke 6:35); lend generously to the poor (Deut. 15:8); do not refuse one who wants to borrow (Matt. 5:42); the righteous is gracious and lends (Ps. 37:26); it is well with the man who is gracious and lends (Ps. 112:5); lend me three loaves (Luke 11:5).

● Lending to the Lord

b Samuel was lent to the Lord (1 Sam. 1:28; 2:20); he who is kind to the poor lends to the Lord (Prov. 19:17).

● Lending to others

c You will lend to many nations but not borrow (Deut. 15:6; 28:12); if you lend, do not charge interest (Exod. 22:25); if you lend to your neighbour, do not enter his house to get his pledge (Deut. 24:10); in the seventh year the item loaned shall be released (Deut. 15:2–3).

d We are lending them money and grain (Neh. 5:10).

e I have neither lent nor borrowed yet everyone curses me (Jer. 15:10).

● Being lent

f The alien will lend to you, and not you to him (Deut. 28:44). **Borrowing**, see **785**.

● Leasing

g Solomon let out his vineyard to keepers (S. of S. 8:11); a landowner let his vineyard to vine-growers (Matt. 21:33; Mark 12:1; Luke 20:9); he will let the vineyard to others (Matt. 21:41).

785 Borrowing

● Principles of borrowing

a You will lend to many nations but not borrow (Deut. 15:6; 28:12); the wicked borrow and do not repay (Ps. 37:21); the borrower becomes a slave to the lender (Prov. 22:7); if borrowed property is damaged (Exod. 22:14); give to him who wants to borrow (Matt. 5:42).

● Things
borrowed

b Borrow as many vessels as you can (2 Kgs. 4:3); a borrowed axe-head (2 Kgs. 6:5); we borrowed money to pay the king's tax (Neh. 5:4).
Lending, see **784**.

786 Taking

● Taking people

a They brought back Lot (Gen. 14:16); took away Dinah (Gen. 34:26); you will be captured (Jer. 34:3); Zedekiah was taken (Jer. 39:5; 52:9).

b Catching wives from those dancing (Judg. 21:21, 23); you have taken my husband (Gen. 30:15); they took Jehoram's sons and wives (2 Chr. 21:17); some of your sons will be taken away to Babylon (Isa. 39:7).

c No one can take them out of my hand (John 10:28, 29).

d Enoch was no more because God took him (Gen. 5:24); the Lord is going to take your master from you today (2 Kgs. 2:3, 5); when the bridegroom is taken away they will fast (Matt. 9:15; Mark 2:20); they have taken the Lord away (John 20:2, 13); one will be taken and the other left (Matt. 24:40, 41; Luke 17:34, 35, 36).
Kidnapping, see **788a**.

● Taking
property

e The Lord gave and the Lord has taken away (Job 1:21).

f Jacob has taken all our father's property (Gen. 31:1); the Israelites plundered the Egyptians (Exod. 3:22; 12:36); the Philistines were plundering (1 Sam. 23:1); taking possession of Naboth's vineyard (1 Kgs. 21:15–16, 18); you murdered a man and seized his goods (1 Kgs. 21:19); the Midianites took all the produce of the land (Judg. 6:3–5); my servants will take whatever they want (1 Kgs. 20:6); he has seized a house he did not build (Job 20:19); can the prey be taken from the mighty man? (Isa. 49:24–5); the Sabeans took Job's oxen and donkeys (Job 1:14–15); the Chaldeans took Job's camels (Job 1:17); take the mina from him and give it to the one with ten minas (Luke 19:24).

g The ark was captured (1 Sam. 4:11, 17); David captured 1000 chariots (2 Sam. 8:4; 1 Chr. 18:4).

h Jacob took birthright and blessing (Gen. 27:36).
Stealing, see **788**.

● Taking temple
treasures

i All the things in the temple were carried off to Babylon (2 Kgs. 20:17; 25:13–15; 2 Chr. 36:7, 18; Isa. 39:6; Jer. 52:17–19); Shishak carried off temple treasures to Egypt (1 Kgs. 14:26; 2 Chr. 12:9); Ahaz took some things from the temple to give to the king of Assyria (2 Chr. 28:21); Nebuchadnezzar took away all the treasure of the temple (2 Kgs. 24:13).

● Capturing
cities

j David captured the stronghold of Zion (1 Chr. 11:5); David captured Jerusalem (2 Sam. 5:6–9); Joab and David captured Rabbah (2 Sam. 12:26–9); Pharaoh captured Gezer (1 Kgs. 9:16); David took Gath from the Philistines (1 Chr. 18:1); Solomon captured Hamath-zobah (2 Chr. 8:3); Abijah took cities from Jeroboam (2 Chr. 13:19); the Philistines had captured cities (2 Chr. 28:18); Hazael captured Gath (2 Kgs. 12:17); Jehoash took cities back from the Arameans (2 Kgs. 13:25); Tiglath-pileser captured cities of Israel (2 Kgs. 15:29); Rezin recovered Elath for Aram (2 Kgs. 16:6); the king of Assyria captured Damascus (2 Kgs. 16:9); and Samaria (2 Kgs. 17:6; 18:10); Sennacherib took the cities of Judah (2 Kgs. 18:13); Jerusalem will be captured (Zech. 14:2); Jerusalem was captured (Jer. 39:1); they captured cities from the Canaanites (Neh. 9:25).

● Taking away the things of God

k From him who has not, what he has will be taken away (Matt. 13:12; 25:29; Mark 4:25; Luke 8:18; 19:26); Satan takes away the word (Matt. 13:19; Mark 4:15; Luke 8:12).

l I will tear the kingdom from Solomon (1 Kgs. 11:11–13, 31); the Romans will take away our place and our nation (John 11:48); I will remove your lampstand from its place (Rev. 2:5); the kingdom of God will be taken from you (Matt. 21:43).

● Taking away sin

m The goat of removal [scapegoat] (Lev. 16:8, 10, 20–2).
Atonement, see **941**.

● Grasping

n Jacob grasped Esau's heel (Gen. 25:26); is he not rightly named Jacob? (Gen. 27:36); grasp the snake by the tail (Exod. 4:4); if a wife seizes her husband's assailant by the private parts (Deut. 25:11); Amnon seized Tamar (2 Sam. 13:11); she clasped Elisha's feet (2 Kgs. 4:27); I held him and would not let him go (S. of S. 3:4); ten men will grasp the garment of a Jew (Zech. 8:23); he seized his fellow-slave and began to choke him (Matt. 18:28); do not hold on to me (John 20:17).
Touch, see **378**.

787 Restitution

● Law of restitution

a Restitution for violation of property (Exod. 22:1–15); for stealing an animal (2 Sam. 12:6); a sinner must make restitution (Lev. 5:16; 6:4–5; 22:14; Num. 5:7); paying for loss of time (Exod. 21:19); a thief must repay sevenfold (Prov. 6:31).

b Restitution made by owner of: a dangerous pit (Exod. 21:34); a dangerous ox (Exod. 21:36).

● Actual restitution

c If a man gives back what he took by robbery (Ezek. 33:15); what I did not steal must I now restore? (Ps. 69:4); I will pay back for the years the locust has eaten (Joel 2:25).

d Give back Gilead to Ammon (Judg. 11:13); Zacchaeus was prepared to make restitution (Luke 19:8).

788 Stealing

● Kidnapping

a The law is for kidnappers (1 Tim. 1:10); a kidnapper must be executed (Exod. 21:16; Deut. 24:7); the Amalekites had taken the women captive (1 Sam. 30:2–3).

b Joseph was kidnapped (Gen. 40:15); why have Judah stolen the king? (2 Sam. 19:41).

● Stealing property

c Regulations concerning the theft of property (Exod. 22:1–13); from the heart comes theft (Matt. 15:19; Mark 7:21); inside they are full of robbery (Matt. 23:25; Luke 11:39).

d Do not steal (Exod. 20:15; Lev. 19:11; Deut. 5:19; Matt. 19:18; Mark 10:19; Luke 18:20; Rom. 13:9); do not rob your neighbour (Lev. 19:13); I hate robbery (Isa. 61:8); woe to him who gets evil gain (Hab. 2:9); do not take money by force (Luke 3:14); you who preach against stealing, do you steal? (Rom. 2:21); will you steal and murder? (Jer. 7:9); if he commits robbery (Ezek. 18:12); let him who stole steal no more (Eph. 4:28); not pilfering (Titus 2:10); do not defraud (Mark 10:19); he who robs father and mother (Prov. 28:24); lest I be needy and steal (Prov. 30:9).

e Let no one defraud his brother in this matter (1 Thess. 4:6); stolen water is sweet (Prov. 9:17).

f They have stolen and deceived (Josh. 7:11); they robbed all who passed by (Judg. 9:25); I am against the prophets who steal my words from one another (Jer. 23:30); they did not repent of their thefts (Rev. 9:21).

g Guilt offering for theft (Lev. 6:2–7).

● No stealing

h How could we steal silver and gold? (Gen. 44:8); whose ox or donkey have I stolen? (1 Sam. 12:3); the shepherds did not miss anything when they were with us (1 Sam. 25:7, 15, 21); if he does not commit robbery (Ezek. 18:7, 16); what I did not steal must I now restore? (Ps. 69:4).

i Treasure in heaven, where no thief comes (Luke 12:33).

● Being robbed

j Do not store up treasure on earth where thieves break in and steal (Matt. 6:19); from him who takes from you do not ask them again (Luke 6:30); why not rather suffer robbery? (1 Cor. 6:7); whoever takes your coat, give him your shirt too (Matt. 5:40; Luke 6:29); you took joyfully the plundering of your goods (Heb. 10:34).

k You will be robbed with none to save (Deut. 28:29).

● Stealing the body

l His disciples might steal the body (Matt. 27:64); as others said they did (Matt. 28:13).

● Robbing gods

m Rachel stole the household gods (Gen. 31:19, 32); why steal my gods? (Gen. 31:30); they took the image, teraphim and ephod (Judg. 18:17–18, 20); you have stolen the gods I made, and the priest (Judg. 18:24); do you rob temples? (Rom. 2:22).

● Robbing God

n You rob God (Mal. 3:8); you rob your brethren (1 Cor. 6:8); I robbed other churches, taking pay from them (2 Cor. 11:8).

789 Thief

● Nature of thieves

a He who climbs in another way is a thief and a robber (John 10:1); all who came before me were thieves and robbers (John 10:8); the thief comes only to steal, kill and destroy (John 10:10).

b When you see a thief you consort with him (Ps. 50:18); do not associate with a 'brother' who is a swindler (1 Cor. 5:11); let none of you suffer as a thief (1 Pet. 4:15); thieves will not inherit the kingdom of God (1 Cor. 6:10); in danger from robbers (2 Cor. 11:26).

c A thief is not despised who steals through hunger (Prov. 6:30).

d You made my house a den of robbers (Jer. 7:11; Matt. 21:13; Mark 11:17; Luke 19:46).

Stealing, see **788**.

● Actual thieves

e Judas was a thief (John 12:6); Barabbas was a robber (John 18:40); two thieves were crucified with Jesus (Matt. 27:38; Mark 15:27); a man fell among robbers (Luke 10:30).

● The Lord as a thief

f The day of the Lord will come like a thief in the night (1 Thess. 5:2, 4; 2 Pet. 3:10); I come like a thief (Rev. 3:3; 16:15); if the householder had known when the thief was coming (Matt. 24:43; Luke 12:39).

g Have you come with swords and clubs to arrest me like a thief? (Matt. 26:55; Mark 14:48).

790 Booty

● Concerning booty

a Regulations concerning the taking of plunder (Deut. 20:14); apportioning booty (Num. 31:26–54); divide the plunder with your brothers (Josh. 22:8); all share in the booty (1 Sam. 30:22–5); better to be of humble spirit than to divide the spoil with the proud (Prov. 16:19).

Dividing plunder, see **783*b***.

b He will divide the spoil with the strong (Isa. 53:12); I rejoice at your word as one who finds great spoil (Ps. 119:162); they will rejoice like those who divide the spoil (Isa. 9:3).

c He will have his life as booty (Jer. 21:9); you will have your life as booty (Jer. 39:18; 45:5).

● The peoples plundering

d They took goods and food from Sodom and Gomorrah (Gen. 14:11); the Amalekites took spoil from Ziklag (1 Sam. 30:16); to the spoil! (2 Kgs. 3:23); plunder silver and gold! (Nahum 2:9).

e Our wives and children will be taken as plunder (Num. 14:3, 31); they will become plunder and spoil to their enemies (2 Kgs. 21:14).

f Sisera is delayed, dividing the spoils (Judg. 5:30).

g The Jews' possessions to be taken as booty (Esther 3:13); Maher-Shalal-Hash-Baz—the spoil hastes, the prey speeds (Isa. 8:1, 3); I will give your wealth as booty (Jer. 15:13; 17:3); this people have become spoil (Isa. 42:22, 24).

h I will give Egypt to Nebuchadnezzar as spoil (Ezek. 29:19); spoil was sent to the king of Damascus (2 Chr. 24:23); their camels and cattle will be booty (Jer. 49:32).

● Israel plundering

i Israel took the plunder from: Shechem (Gen. 34:27–9); Midian (Num. 31:9, 11–12); Sihon (Deut. 2:35); Bashan (Deut. 3:7); Ai

(Josh. 8:2, 27); the cities of the land (Josh. 11:14); the Philistines (1 Sam. 17:53); the Hagrites (1 Chr. 5:21); Rabbah (2 Sam. 12:30; 1 Chr. 20:2); the camp of the Arameans (2 Kgs. 7:16); the Ethiopians (2 Chr. 14:13); Ammon, Moab and Mount Seir (2 Chr. 20:25); Gerar (2 Chr. 14:14–15); Judah (2 Chr. 28:8; 2 Chr. 25:13).

j David's men brought much plunder from a raid (2 Sam. 3:22); David took plunder from his raids (1 Sam. 27:9); this is David's spoil (1 Sam. 30:20).

k Spoil dedicated to the Lord (2 Sam. 8:11–12); some plunder was given for the repair of the temple (1 Chr. 26:27).

l The Jews were given the right to plunder their enemies (Esther 8:11); they did not touch the plunder (Esther 9:10, 15, 16).

m Let us take spoil by night (1 Sam. 14:36); we will fill our houses with spoil (Prov. 1:13); they rushed on the spoil (1 Sam. 14:32; 15:19); take someone else's spoil (2 Sam. 2:21); women at home divide the spoil (Ps. 68:12).

● Plundering the strong man

n Bind the strong man and you can plunder his house (Matt. 12:29; Mark 3:27).

791 Trade

● Trading

a Trade with us (Gen. 34:10); let them trade here (Gen. 34:21).

b They gave their animals and land in exchange for food (Gen. 47:16–20); horses and chariots imported and exported (1 Kgs. 10:29; 2 Chr. 1:16–17); Tarshish traded with Tyre (Ezek. 27:12); Ahab would have exchanged a vineyard for Naboth's (1 Kgs. 21:2, 6); the one with five talents traded with them (Matt. 25:16); trade with these till I return (Luke 19:13).

Ships for trading, see **275*e***; **trader**, see **794**; **mourning loss of trade**, see **836*ah***.

● Trading for a soul

c What will one give in exchange for his soul? (Matt. 16:26; Mark 8:37).

792 Purchase

● Buying things

a Houses, fields and vineyards will again be bought (Jer. 32:15); fields will be bought in this land (Jer. 32:43–4); she considers a field and buys it (Prov. 31:16); those who buy should live as if they had no possessions (1 Cor. 7:30); we did not buy land (Neh. 5:16); we will not buy on the sabbath day (Neh. 10:31); no one could buy or sell without the mark of the beast (Rev. 13:17).

b The buyer says it is bad, but boasts of the bargain (Prov. 20:14); let not the buyer rejoice nor the seller mourn (Ezek. 7:12).

● Actual purchases

c Abraham bought the field at Machpelah (Gen. 23:8–16); the tomb Abraham purchased in Shechem (Acts 7:16); Jacob bought a plot of ground near Shechem (Gen. 33:19; Josh. 24:32); Joseph bought all the land of Egypt for Pharaoh (Gen. 47:20); buying Araunah's [Ornan's] threshing floor (2 Sam. 24:21–4; 1 Chr.

21:22–5); Omri bought the hill of Samaria (1 Kgs. 16:24); Ahab wanted to buy Naboth's vineyard (1 Kgs. 21:2, 6); Jeremiah bought the field at Anathoth (Jer. 32:7–15, 25); they bought the potter's field (Matt. 27:7).

d All the earth came to buy grain (Gen. 41:57); go buy some food in Egypt (Gen. 42:2; 43:2); buy food and water on the way (Deut. 2:6, 28); send them away to buy food (Mark 6:36); go to the dealers and buy oil (Matt. 25:9); the centurion had bought his citizenship (Acts 22:28).

- Buying people

e Potiphar bought Joseph (Gen. 39:1); Hosea bought his wife (Hos. 3:2).

f No one will buy you (Deut. 28:68).

Selling people, see **793*f*.**

- Hiring people

g Abimelech hired worthless men (Judg. 9:4); the Ammonites hired the Arameans (2 Sam. 10:6); Israel must have hired other kings (2 Kgs. 7:6); the people of the land hired counsellors (Ezra 4:5); Tobiah and Sanballat had hired him (Neh. 6:12–13); the Moabites hired Balaam (Neh. 13:2); Ephraim has hired lovers (Hos. 8:9–10); a landowner hiring workers for his vineyard (Matt. 20:1); the hireling flees (John 10:12–13).

- About redeeming

h Every firstborn offspring is to be redeemed (Exod. 13:13; 34:20; Num. 18:15–16); a female slave is to be redeemed (Exod. 21:8); the owner of a bull which kills may be redeemed (Exod. 21:30); the excess firstborn Israelites were redeemed (Num. 3:46–8); redeeming an Israelite slave (Lev. 25:48–52).

i Redemption for land (Lev. 25:24–6); in a town, right of redemption for one year (Lev. 25:29–30); Levites have permanent right of redemption (Lev. 25:32–3).

j A ransom is not to be accepted for a murderer (Num. 35:31–2); or for someone under a ban (Lev. 27:29); no one can redeem another's soul from death (Ps. 49:7–9).

k A jealous husband will not accept a ransom (Prov. 6:35); the rich man's wealth is his ransom (Prov. 13:8); the wicked is a ransom for the righteous (Prov. 21:18).

- Actual redeeming

l Redeeming Naomi's field and Ruth (Ruth 4:3–9); we redeemed our brethren who were sold to the nations (Neh. 5:8); Jeremiah redeeming his uncle's field (Jer. 32:7–15).

m Boaz was a kinsman-redeemer (Ruth 3:9); a close one (Ruth 2:20); though there is a closer (Ruth 3:12–13); the Lord has not left you without a kinsman-redeemer (Ruth 4:14).

- God redeeming his people

n Redeem Israel! (Ps. 25:22); Israel was the people God redeemed (Exod. 6:6; 15:13; 1 Chr. 17:21; Neh. 1:10; Ps. 74:2); the Lord redeemed you from the house of slavery (Deut. 7:8; 15:15); God bought his people (Exod. 15:16); the Lord redeemed you from Egypt (Deut. 24:18; 2 Sam. 7:23); I have given Egypt as your ransom (Isa. 43:3); the Lord will redeem Israel from their sins (Ps. 130:8); return to me, for I have redeemed you (Isa. 44:22);

the Lord has ransomed Jacob (Jer. 31:11); I would redeem them (Hos. 7:13); I would ransom them from the power of Sheol (Hos. 13:14).

o They will call them the redeemed of the Lord (Isa. 62:12); those whom the Lord redeemed (Ps. 107:2); the redeemed of the Lord will return (Isa. 35:10; 51:11).

p The angel who redeemed me from all evil (Gen. 48:16); God will redeem me from the power of Sheol (Ps. 49:15); you have ransomed me (Ps. 31:5); I have found a ransom (Job 33:24).

● Redemption in Christ

q You will be redeemed without money (Isa. 52:3); redeemed not with silver or gold but with the blood of Christ (1 Pet. 1:18–19); you have been bought with a price (1 Cor. 6:20; 7:23); with your blood you purchased men for God (Rev. 5:9); the church of God which he purchased with his own blood (Acts 20:28); in him we have redemption through his blood (Eph. 1:7); he gave himself as a ransom for all (1 Tim. 2:6); to give his life a ransom for many (Matt. 20:28; Mark 10:45).

r God has redeemed his people (Luke 1:68); Anna spoke of Jesus to all who were looking for the redemption of Jerusalem (Luke 2:38); we hoped he would be the one to redeem Israel (Luke 24:21); Christ Jesus is made to us redemption (1 Cor. 1:30); in him we have redemption, the forgiveness of sins (Col. 1:14); the 144 000 have been purchased from among men (Rev. 14:4); I know that my redeemer lives (Job 19:25); eternal redemption (Heb. 9:12).

s He redeemed us from lawlessness (Titus 2:14); Christ redeemed us from the curse of the law (Gal. 3:13); that he might redeem those under the law (Gal. 4:5); justified through the redemption in Christ Jesus (Rom. 3:24).

t Denying the master who bought them (2 Pet. 2:1).

● Purchasing God's gift

u Buy wine and milk without money (Isa. 55:1); buy truth and do not sell it (Prov. 23:23); I counsel you to buy from me gold, garments and eyesalve (Rev. 3:18).

v Wisdom cannot be bought with gold (Job 28:15); you thought to buy the gift of God with money (Acts 8:20).

w He sells all that he has and buys that field (Matt. 13:44); he sold all that he had and bought that pearl (Matt. 13:46).

793 Sale

● Concerning selling

a Selling should be according to the years before the Jubilee (Lev. 25:14–16, 50–2); a blessing is on the head of him who sells grain (Prov. 11:26); she makes linen garments and sells them (Prov. 31:24).

● Selling things

b Ephron sold the cave of Machpelah to Abraham (Gen. 23:9); Ornan sold the threshing floor to David (1 Chr. 21:22); Barnabas sold his field (Acts 4:37); Ananias sold some property (Acts 5:1).

c Joseph sold grain to the Egyptians (Gen. 41:56); the widow sold the oil to pay her debts (2 Kgs. 4:7); men of Tyre sold fish on the sabbath (Neh. 13:16); he threw out those who were selling in the temple (Luke 19:45).

d Sell your possessions and give alms (Luke 12:33); sell all you have and give to the poor (Matt. 19:21; Mark 10:21); those owning land or houses would sell them (Acts 4:34).

e Esau sold his birthright for a single meal (Gen. 25:31–4; Heb. 12:16).

● Selling people

f You may not sell a captive woman whom you married (Deut. 21:14).

g Laban had sold his daughters (Gen. 31:15); Joseph's brothers sold him (Gen. 37:27–8); Joseph was sold into Egypt (Acts 7:9); Joseph was sold to Potiphar (Gen. 37:36; 39:1); I am Joseph whom you sold (Gen. 45:4); Joseph was sold as a slave (Ps. 105:17); would you sell your brethren? (Neh. 5:8); they sell a girl for wine (Joel 3:3); they sell the righteous for silver (Amos 2:6).

h Tyre's sons and daughters will be sold to the Sabeans (Joel 3:8); his lord ordered him to be sold (Matt. 18:25).

● Sold to enemies

i How could one chase a thousand unless their rock had sold them? (Deut. 32:30); he sold them into the hands of their enemies (Judg. 2:14; 3:8; 4:2; 10:7; 1 Sam. 12:9); you have sold yourself to do evil (1 Kgs. 21:20, 25); I am carnal, sold under sin (Rom. 7:14).

794 Merchant

● Wicked traders

a Merchants and traders camped outside Jerusalem (Neh. 13:20); he found some selling animals, and moneychangers (John 2:14); he overturned the tables of the money-changers and the seats of those selling pigeons (Matt. 21:12; Mark 11:15; John 2:15).

● Peddling God's word

b We are not peddlers of God's word (2 Cor. 2:17).

795 Merchandise

● Merchandise

a The merchandise of Tyre (Ezek. 27:12–24); the merchandise of Babylon (Rev. 18:12–13); the merchandise of Egypt and Ethiopia will be yours (Isa. 45:14).

796 Market

● Market place

a When they come from the market place they wash before eating (Mark 7:4); they love salutations in the market place (Matt. 23:7; Mark 12:38; Luke 20:46).

● The temple a market

b Do not make my Father's house a house of merchandise (John 2:16).

797 Money

● About money

a Money is a protection as wisdom is (Eccles. 7:12); money is the answer to everything (Eccles. 10:19); if I have put my trust in gold (Job 31:24); the silver is mine and the gold is mine (Hag. 2:8).

b A shekel is 20 gerahs (Lev. 27:25; Num. 3:47); the two-drachma tax (Matt. 17:24); a stater (Matt. 17:27); a denarius (Matt. 20:2, 9, 10, 13).

Silver and gold, see **631g**.

- **Transfer of money**

c Abimelech gave Abraham 1000 pieces of silver (Gen. 20:16); Joseph gave Benjamin 300 pieces of silver (Gen. 45:22); Joseph gathered in all the money in Egypt (Gen. 47:14–15); Achan coveted 200 silver shekels and a wedge of gold (Josh. 7:21).

d Exchange the tithe for money (Deut. 14:25).

e Talents of money were apportioned (Matt. 25:15); ten minas given to each (Luke 19:13); they brought him a denarius (Matt. 22:19; Mark 12:15; Luke 20:24); the good Samaritan gave two denarii (Luke 10:35).

f The silver was returned to Joseph's brothers (Gen. 42:25, 27, 28, 35; 43:12, 18, 21–3; 44:1, 2, 8).

g The Israelites were to ask the Egyptians for articles of silver and gold (Exod. 3:22; 11:2; 12:35); give me your silver and gold (1 Kgs. 20:3, 5); each one gave Job a qesita (Job 42:11).

h May gold of Sheba be given to him (Ps. 72:15); they will bring gold and frankincense (Isa. 60:6); they gave gold, frankincense and myrrh (Matt. 2:11).

- **Money for the temple**

i Money for the guilt offering and sin offering were for the priests (2 Kgs. 12:16); silver and gold to buy offerings (Ezra 7:15–18).

j Collect all the money for the temple (2 Kgs. 12:4; 2 Chr. 24:5); they counted the money in the chest (2 Kgs. 12:10); they collected much money (2 Chr. 24:11); the widow put in two copper coins which make a penny (Mark 12:42); this money was paid to the workmen (2 Kgs. 22:4–6; 2 Chr. 34:9–11; Ezra 3:7).

k The temple treasures were carried off by the king of Egypt (1 Kgs. 14:26); by Jehoash king of Israel (2 Kgs. 14:14; 2 Chr. 25:24); temple treasures used as gifts to foreign kings (1 Kgs. 15:18; 2 Kgs. 12:18; 16:8; 18:15, 16; 2 Chr. 16:2).

l David dedicated articles of silver, gold and bronze to the Lord (2 Sam. 8:10–11); the silver and gold were brought into the temple (1 Kgs. 15:15); Ezra weighed out the silver and gold (Ezra 8:25–30); gifts of gold, silver and priests' garments for the temple (Neh. 7:70–2).

- **Love of money**

m Whoever loves money will not be satisfied with money (Eccles. 5:10); men will be lovers of money (2 Tim. 3:2); the love of money is the root of all evil (1 Tim. 6:10); you cannot serve God and Mammon (Luke 16:13); the Pharisees loved money (Luke 16:14); Balaam loved the wages of unrighteousness (2 Pet. 2:15).

n Be free from the love of money (Heb. 13:5); an elder must be free from love of money (1 Tim. 3:3); get rid of your gold and the Almighty will be your gold and silver (Job 22:24–5). **Loving money**, see **887***ah*.

- Accumulating money

o I accumulated silver and gold (Eccles. 2:8); though the wicked heaps up silver, the innocent will divide it (Job 27:16–17).

p I have no silver or gold (Acts 3:6); do not take money (Matt. 10:9; Mark 6:8; Luke 9:3; 10:4); we are not concerned for silver or gold (2 Sam. 21:4).

- Money's deficiencies

q Neither silver nor gold will be able to deliver them (Zeph. 1:18); silver and gold cannot deliver them and will be thrown away (Ezek. 7:19); you were not redeemed with silver and gold (1 Pet. 1:18); Simon offered them money for power to confer the Holy Spirit (Acts 8:18–19).

- Alternatives to money

r Wisdom is more profitable than silver or gold (Prov. 3:14); wisdom's fruit is better than gold or silver (Prov. 8:19); wisdom is much better than gold or silver (Prov. 16:16); a good name is better than silver or gold (Prov. 22:1); choose my instruction rather than silver or gold (Prov. 8:10); the Lord's words are better than much gold (Ps. 19:10); I love your commandments more than fine gold (Ps. 119:127); I counsel you to buy gold refined in the fire (Rev. 3:18); I will come forth as gold (Job 23:10).

798 Treasurer

- Treasurers

a Levites were keepers of the treasures of the temple (1 Chr. 26:20–8); Mithredath the treasurer (Ezra 1:8); Judas had the money-box (John 13:29); the Ethiopian eunuch had charge of all the queen's treasure (Acts 8:27); Erastus was the city treasurer (Rom. 16:23).

799 Treasury

- Money box

a A money chest was made for the upkeep of the temple (2 Kgs. 12:9; 2 Chr. 24:8); putting money in the treasury (Mark 12:41).

b We will have one purse (Prov. 1:14); Judas had the money box (John 12:6).

- Treasure house

c Hezekiah made treasuries for his wealth (2 Chr. 32:27); Hezekiah showed the Babylonians his treasure-house (2 Kgs. 20:13, 15); he said these things in the treasury (John 8:20).

d Gifts put in the treasuries of the temple (2 Chr. 5:1); it is not right to put the money in the treasury (Matt. 27:6).

e Why did you not put my money in the bank? (Luke 19:23).

- Heart's treasure

f The good man brings good out of his treasure and the evil man evil (Matt. 12:35).

800 Wealth

- God gives wealth

a God gives you the power to make wealth (Deut. 8:18); the Lord makes poor and rich (1 Sam. 2:7); riches and honour come from you (1 Chr. 29:12); wealth and riches are in the house of the man who fears the Lord (Ps. 112:3).

b I will give you riches and honour (2 Chr. 1:12); God gave Hezekiah great wealth (2 Chr. 32:29); a man to whom God has given wealth (Eccles. 5:19; 6:2).

● Wisdom gives wealth

c Wisdom gives riches and honour (Prov. 3:16); riches and honour are with me (Prov. 8:18); wisdom fills the treasuries of those who love her (Prov. 8:21); the crown of the wise is their riches (Prov. 14:24); by your wisdom you have acquired wealth (Ezek. 28:4).

● People giving wealth

d Lest you should say you have made Abraham rich (Gen. 14:23); merchants grew rich by Babylon's wealth (Rev. 18:3, 19).

● Various sources of wealth

e Much wealth is in the house of the righteous (Prov. 15:6); the blessing of the Lord makes rich (Prov. 10:22); riches are a reward for humility and fear of the Lord (Prov. 22:4); the hand of the diligent makes rich (Prov. 10:4).

● Wealthy people

f Those who were wealthy: Abraham (Gen. 13:2; 24:35); Isaac (Gen. 26:13); Jacob (Gen. 30:43; 32:5); Jacob and Esau (Gen. 36:7); Boaz (Ruth 2:1); Nabal (1 Sam. 25:2); Barzillai (2 Sam. 19:32); Solomon (1 Kgs. 3:13; 10:7, 23; 2 Chr. 1:11–12; 9:22); Jehoshaphat (2 Chr. 17:5; 18:1); Hezekiah (2 Chr. 32:27); Ahasuerus (Esther 1:4); Haman (Esther 5:11); Job (Job 1:3); Ephraim (Hos. 12:8); the rich young ruler (Matt. 19:22; Mark 10:22; Luke 18:23); Zacchaeus (Luke 19:2); Joseph of Arimathea (Matt. 27:57).

● Getting rich

g The king must not accumulate silver and gold (Deut. 17:17); Solomon did not ask for riches (1 Kgs. 3:11); do not lay up treasures on earth (Matt. 6:19).

h Jacob took all Laban's wealth (Gen. 31:1); the wealth God took away from our father belongs to us (Gen. 31:16); the king will grant riches to the man who kills Goliath (1 Sam. 17:25).

i Balak offered to make Balaam rich (Num. 22:17–18); may you become rich and famous (Ruth 4:11); there is no end to their treasures (Isa. 2:7).

j The wealth of the nations will come to you (Isa. 60:5); you will eat the wealth of nations (Isa. 61:6); they will bring you the wealth of the nations (Isa. 60:11); the wealth of the surrounding nations will be collected (Zech. 14:14).

k The wicked increase in riches (Ps. 73:12); violent men get riches (Prov. 11:16); a fortune unjustly made will flee (Jer. 17:11); he who gains wealth by interest will lose it (Prov. 28:8); do not toil to gain wealth (Prov. 23:4); he who hastens to get rich will not go unpunished (Prov. 28:20).

Money, see **797**.

● Attitude towards wealth

l A rich man's wealth is his fortified city (Prov. 18:11); he saw the rich giving to the treasury (Luke 21:1); the rich man's wealth is his fortress (Prov. 10:15); the deceitfulness of riches chokes the word (Matt. 13:22; Mark 4:19; Luke 8:14); woe to you rich, for you have received your comfort (Luke 6:24); weep and wail, you rich (Jas. 5:1); the rich man will fade away (Jas. 1:10–11); do not be afraid when a man grows rich (Ps. 49:16); I am rich, I have need of nothing (Rev. 3:17); those who want to get rich fall into a temptation and a snare (1 Tim. 6:9); let not a rich man boast of his riches (Jer. 9:23); direct the rich not to be conceited (1 Tim. 6:17); if I rejoiced because I was wealthy (Job 31:25).

● The rich lording it

m The rich oppress you (Jas. 2:6); the rich rule over the poor (Prov. 22:7); many people love the rich (Prov. 14:20); do not be partial to the rich man (Jas. 2:2–3); parable of the rich man and poor man (2 Sam. 12:1–4).

● Drawbacks to riches

n It is hard for the rich to enter the kingdom of God (Matt. 19:23; Mark 10:23; Luke 18:24); a rich man ended up in hell (Luke 16:19–23); he has sent the rich away empty-handed (Luke 1:53); you cannot serve God and mammon (Matt. 6:24); if riches increase, do not set your heart on them (Ps. 62:10); he who hoards treasure for himself but is not rich toward God (Luke 12:21); riches do not profit in the day of wrath (Prov. 11:4).

o Wealth takes wings and flies away (Prov. 23:5); riches do not last for ever (Prov. 27:24); they leave their wealth to others (Ps. 49:10).

● Right use of wealth

p Honour the Lord with your wealth (Prov. 3:9); many rich people gave large amounts (Mark 12:41); make friends by means of unrighteous mammon (Luke 16:9); wealth brings friends (Prov. 19:4).

● True treasure

q I delight in your testimonies as much as in riches (Ps. 119:14); your law is better than thousands of gold and silver pieces (Ps. 119:72); search for wisdom as for hidden treasure (Prov. 2:4).

r Where your treasure is, there will your heart be also (Matt. 6:21; Luke 12:34); lay up treasure in heaven (Matt. 6:20); you will have treasure in heaven (Matt. 19:21; Mark 10:21; Luke 12:33; 18:22); true riches (Luke 16:11); rich in good works (1 Tim. 6:18); God chose the poor to be rich in faith (Jas. 2:5); the reproach of Christ considered greater riches than all the treasures of Egypt (Heb. 11:26); the man who is not rich toward God (Luke 12:21).

s You are enriched in Christ (1 Cor. 1:5); though he was rich, he became poor that we might be rich (2 Cor. 8:9); you will be enriched in every way (2 Cor. 9:11); the treasures of wisdom and knowledge are hidden in Christ (Col. 2:3); the treasure of a good foundation for the future (1 Tim. 6:19); the kingdom of heaven is like treasure hidden in a field (Matt. 13:44); to preach the unsearchable riches of Christ (Eph. 3:8); riches in glory in Christ Jesus (Phil. 4:19); if their transgression be riches for the Gentiles (Rom. 11:12).

t The riches of the glory of his inheritance (Eph. 1:18); the depth of the riches of the wisdom and knowledge of God (Rom. 11:33).

801 Poverty

● Being poor

a There will be no poor among you if you obey (Deut. 15:4); there will always be poor people (Deut. 15:11; Matt. 26:11; Mark 14:7; John 12:8); the poverty of the poor is their ruin (Prov. 10:15). **Nakedness and poverty**, see **229f**.

b The Lord sends poverty and wealth (1 Sam. 2:7); give me neither poverty nor riches (Prov. 30:8); better to be poor than a liar (Prov. 19:22); though he was rich, yet for your sake he became poor (2 Cor. 8:9).

c A poor man loses his friends (Prov. 19:4, 7); a poor man is hated by his brothers (Prov. 19:7); the poor man is disliked even by his neighbour (Prov. 14:20); these are only the poor who are foolish (Jer. 5:4).

d If he cannot afford a lamb (Lev. 5:7; 12:8); if he cannot afford pigeons (Lev. 5:11); if he is poor (Lev. 14:21).

e Did you invite us to make us poor? (Judg. 14:15).

● Avoiding poverty

f Do not love sleep lest you come to poverty (Prov. 20:13); poverty will come on you like an armed man (Prov. 6:11; 24:34); a negligent hand causes poverty (Prov. 10:4); he who loves pleasure will become poor (Prov. 21:17); the drunkard and the glutton will come to poverty (Prov. 23:21).

● God helps the poor

g The Lord maintains justice for the poor (Ps. 140:12); God exalts the poor and needy (1 Sam. 2:8); God saves the poor (Job 5:15); God stands at the right hand of the needy to save him (Ps. 109:31); God lifts the poor from the dust (Ps. 113:7); God provided for the poor (Ps. 68:10); he raises the needy out of affliction (Ps. 107:41). **Plenty for the poor**, see **635f**.

● Helping the poor

h He who is kind to the poor lends to the Lord (Prov. 19:17).

i Support a poor man (Lev. 25:35); leave gleanings for the poor and alien (Lev. 19:10; 23:22; Deut. 24:19–21); do not be stingy with the poor (Deut. 15:7–8); the Levite, alien, orphan and widow will eat the tithe (Deut. 14:28–9; 26:11–12); bring the homeless poor into your house (Isa. 58:7); when you give a feast, invite the poor (Luke 14:13); bring in the poor (Luke 14:21); send portions to those who have nothing (Neh. 8:10, 12); we should continue to remember the poor (Gal. 2:10); this perfume could have been sold and the money given to the poor (John 12:5); they thought Jesus was saying to give something to the poor (John 13:29); visit orphans and widows in their tribulation (Jas. 1:27).

j I delivered the poor (Job 29:12–13); he delivers the needy (Ps. 72:12–14); he gives to the poor (Ps. 112:9; 2 Cor. 9:9); may he defend the cause of the poor (Ps. 72:4); the righteous knows the rights of the poor (Prov. 29:7); the poor have good news preached to them (Matt. 11:5; Luke 7:22); anointed to preach the gospel to the poor (Luke 4:18).

● Not helping the poor

k He who oppresses the poor insults his Maker (Prov. 14:31); he who mocks the poor insults his Maker (Prov. 17:5); he who oppresses the poor will come to poverty (Prov. 22:16); a poor man who oppresses the poor is like driving rain (Prov. 28:3); what do you mean by grinding the face of the poor? (Isa. 3:15); you trample on the poor (Amos 5:11; 8:4); do not rob the poor because he is poor (Prov. 22:22).

l If I have kept the poor from their desire (Job 31:16); if he oppresses the poor and needy (Ezek. 18:12).

m Sodom's sin was that she did not help the poor and needy (Ezek. 16:49); they do not defend the rights of the poor (Jer. 5:28); he has oppressed the poor (Job 20:19); the poor are victimised and left helpless (Job 24:4–8); you cows of Bashan oppress the poor (Amos 4:1); you have insulted the poor man (Jas. 2:6).

n Do not be partial to a poor man (Exod. 23:3).

Not helping the poor, see **458***a*; **orphan**, see **779**; **widow**, see **896**; **alien**, see **59**; **Levite**, see **986**.

● Poor people

o David was a poor man (1 Sam. 18:23); parable of a rich man and a poor man (2 Sam. 12:1–4); I am poor and needy (Ps. 40:17; 86:1; 109:22); the poorest of the land were left to tend the vines (Jer. 39:10; 52:16); only the poorest people were left (2 Kgs. 24:14); a poor widow (Mark 12:42; Luke 21:2–3); the poor man Lazarus was laid at the rich man's gate (Luke 16:20).

● Poor yet rich

p She out of her poverty put in all she had (Mark 12:44; Luke 21:4); their poverty overflowed in liberality (2 Cor. 8:2); God has chosen the poor to be rich in faith (Jas. 2:5); as poor yet making many rich (2 Cor. 6:10); that you through his poverty might be made rich (2 Cor. 8:9); I know your poverty but you are rich! (Rev. 2:9); you say you are rich, but you do not realise you are poor (Rev. 3:17); we are homeless (1 Cor. 4:11).

q Better the little of the righteous than the wealth of the wicked (Ps. 37:16); better a poor man who walks in integrity than the perverse (Prov. 19:1; 28:6).

r Blessed are you poor (Luke 6:20); blessed are the poor in spirit (Matt. 5:3).

802 Credit

Lending, see **784**.

803 Debt

● Being in debt

a Owe no man anything except to love one another (Rom. 13:8).

b I am a debtor to Greeks and barbarians (Rom. 1:14); we are debtors, but not to the flesh (Rom. 8:12); the Gentiles are indebted to minister to the Jerusalem church (Rom. 15:27).

● People in debt

c Anyone in debt joined David (1 Sam. 22:2); a prophet's widow was in debt (2 Kgs. 4:1–7); a man owed 10 000 talents (Matt. 18:24); a fellow-servant owed him 100 denarii (Matt. 18:28); the parable of the two debtors, one owing 500 denarii, the other 50 (Luke 7:41–3); how much do you owe my master? (Luke 16:5, 7).

d We are mortgaging our fields (Neh. 5:3).

- Cancelling debts

e At the end of every seven years you are to cancel debts (Deut. 15:1); we will remit debts (Neh. 10:31).

f Forgive us our debts as we forgive our debtors (Matt. 6:12); God cancelled the bill of debt (Col. 2:14).

g If he owes you anything, charge it to me (Philem. 18).
Remission of debts, see 909*q*.

- Charging interest

h Do not charge your brother interest (Exod. 22:25; Lev. 25:36; Deut. 23:19–20; Neh. 5:7, 10); he who increases wealth by interest will lose it (Prov. 28:8); he does not put out his money at interest (Ps. 15:5); if he does not lend money at interest (Ezek. 18:8, 17).

i If he lends for interest (Ezek. 18:13); you have taken interest (Ezek. 22:12).

j I would have received my money with interest (Matt. 25:27; Luke 19:23).

804 Payment

- Paying wages

a Pay a hired man before sunset (Lev. 19:13; Deut. 24:15); the labourer deserves his wages (Luke 10:7); wages are not a favour but a right (Rom. 4:4); pay them their wages (Matt. 20:8); those who preach the gospel should receive payment (1 Cor. 9:7–14); elders who rule well deserve a double stipend (1 Tim. 5:17–18); you have withheld pay for your workmen (Jas. 5:4).

b Name your wages (Gen. 29:15; 30:28); be content with your wages (Luke 3:14); Jacob paid for a wife by tending sheep (Hos. 12:12); Laban changed my wages ten times (Gen. 31:7, 41); nurse this baby and I will pay you your wages (Exod. 2:9); Micah offered ten pieces of silver a year (Judg. 17:10); they paid the workmen who worked in the temple (2 Kgs. 12:11–12; 2 Chr. 24:12); Solomon would pay Hiram's servants wages (1 Kgs. 5:6); the men's expenses are to be paid from the royal treasury (Ezra 6:8); a landowner agreed to pay a denarius a day (Matt. 20:2–10); they agreed to pay Judas money (Luke 22:5); thirty shekels of silver as wages (Zech. 11:12); the wages of a prostitute are not to be offered to God (Deut. 23:18); from a prostitute's earnings she gathered them and to a prostitute's earnings they will return (Mic. 1:7); I will give Egypt as wages to Nebuchadnezzar (Ezek. 29:19–20).

c Preachers should get their living from the gospel (1 Cor. 9:14); he who reaps receives wages (John 4:36); your Father will repay you (Matt. 6:4, 6, 18).

d The wages of sin is death (Rom. 6:23); the wages of the righteous is life (Prov. 10:16); the income of the wicked is punishment (Prov. 10:16).

● Paying tribute

e A tax of booty for the Lord (Num. 31:28–47); let the kings of the isles bring tribute (Ps. 72:10).

f Tribute sent by Ehud to Eglon (Judg. 3:15); all brought tribute to Solomon (1 Kgs. 4:21); the king of Moab paid lambs and wool as tribute (2 Kgs. 3:4); the Moabites brought tribute to David (1 Chr. 18:2); tribute was brought to the kings of Israel (Ezra 4:20); Hoshea paid Shalmaneser tribute (2 Kgs. 17:3); the king of Assyria imposed on Hezekiah 300 talents of silver and 30 of gold (2 Kgs. 18:14); Pharaoh Neco imposed tribute on Judah (2 Kgs. 23:33); the Arameans paid tribute to David (1 Chr. 18:6); Philistines brought Jehoshaphat tribute (2 Chr. 17:11); the Ammonites brought Uzziah tribute (2 Chr. 26:8); the Ammonites paid Jotham tribute (2 Chr. 27:5); if this city is built, no more tax or duty will be paid (Ezra 4:13); the priests should not pay tax or tribute (Ezra 7:24); Ahasuerus imposed tribute throughout his empire (Esther 10:1).

● Paying tax

g In a census, every Israelite is to pay half a shekel (Exod. 30:13, 15; 38:26); the levy of Moses (2 Chr. 24:9); one third of a shekel per year for the temple service (Neh. 10:32); Menahem exacted 50 shekels from every rich man (2 Kgs. 15:20); Jehoiakim taxed the land to pay Pharaoh Neco (2 Kgs. 23:35); former governors made the people pay 40 shekels of silver (Neh. 5:15); Jesus paid the two-drachma tax (Matt. 17:24–7); is it right to pay taxes to Caesar? (Matt. 22:17; Mark 12:14–15; Luke 20:22); he opposes paying taxes to Caesar (Luke 23:2); from whom do kings collect tax? (Matt. 17:25); pay tax to whom it is due (Rom. 13:6–7).

h Matthew [Levi] sitting in the tax office (Matt. 9:9; Mark 2:14; Luke 5:27); Matthew the taxman (Matt. 10:3); a chief taxman called Zaccheus (Luke 19:2); tax collectors came to be baptised (Luke 3:12).

● Settling up

i A king wanted to settle accounts (Matt. 18:23); the master came to settle accounts (Matt. 25:19); be patient and I will repay you (Matt. 18:26, 29); you will not get out till you have paid the last coin (Matt. 5:26; Luke 12:59); do not invite your friends lest they repay you (Luke 14:12).

● Requiting

j Requite them for their deeds (Ps. 28:4); according to their deeds, so he will repay (Isa. 59:18); repay them seven times the reproach with which they reproached you (Ps. 79:12); may the Lord repay the evildoer for his evil (2 Sam. 3:39); give her back double for her deeds (Rev. 18:6).

k He has brought back their sins upon them (Ps. 94:23); you will see the recompense of the wicked (Ps. 91:8); God will repay with affliction those who afflict you (2 Thess. 1:6); the Lord will repay him according to his deeds (2 Tim. 4:14); God will repay everyone for his works (Matt. 16:27); he will render to every one according to his deeds (Rom. 2:6); we will be recompensed for what we have done, good or bad (2 Cor. 5:10); whatever good anyone does, he will receive back from the Lord (Eph. 6:8); you will be repaid at the resurrection of the just (Luke 14:14); if the righteous is paid back, how much more the sinner? (Prov. 11:31); suffering harm as the wages of doing harm (2 Pet. 2:13); I will give each of you according to his deeds (Rev. 2:23).

l God has paid me back for what I did (Judg. 1:7); God repaid the wickedness of Abimelech (Judg. 9:56); the Lord will repay Joab for the blood he shed (1 Kgs. 2:32); the Lord will return your evil on your own head (1 Kgs. 2:44); I will repay (Isa. 65:6).

Repaid for deeds, see **676***f*; **Rewarding**, see **962**.

● Repaying evil for evil

m Do not repay evil for evil (Rom. 12:17; 1 Thess. 5:15); do not repay insult with insult (1 Pet. 3:9); do not resist one who is evil but turn the other cheek (Matt. 5:39); what if Joseph pays us back for the wrongs we did? (Gen. 50:15); as they did to me, so I did to them (Judg. 15:11); I will do to him as he has done to me (Prov. 24:29); happy is he who repays you as you have done to us (Ps. 137:8); raise me up that I may repay them (Ps. 41:10).

● Repaying evil for good

n Why have you repaid evil for good? (Gen. 44:4); they repay me evil for good (Ps. 35:12; 38:20; 109:5); he who repays evil for good will not have evil leave his house (Prov. 17:13); should good be repaid with evil? (Jer. 18:20).

o The Lord will repay everyone for his righteousness (1 Sam. 26:23); perhaps the Lord will repay me with good for the cursing I receive (2 Sam. 16:12).

Reward for works, see **962***b*.

805 Nonpayment

● Not paying

a If I have eaten fruit from the land without payment (Job 31:39); we did not eat anyone's bread without paying (2 Thess. 3:8).

806 Expenditure

● Spending

a I will gladly spend and be spent for you (2 Cor. 12:15).

807 Receipt

Receiving, see **782**; **income**, see **804**.

808 Accounts

● Account

a They did not require an account from the workmen (2 Kgs. 12:15; 22:7).

809 Price

● Price of a person

a The precious sons of Zion, worth as much as gold (Lam. 4:2); are you not worth much more than the birds? (Matt. 6:26); of more value than many sparrows (Matt. 10:31); of more value than a sheep (Matt. 12:12); the worth of a good wife exceeds jewels (Prov. 31:10).

b Valuation of a person (Lev. 27:1–8); 50 shekels for a male aged 20 to 60 (Lev. 27:3); 30 shekels for a female aged 20 to 60 (Lev. 27:4); 20 shekels for a male aged 5 to 20 (Lev. 27:5); 10 shekels for a female aged 5 to 20 (Lev. 27:5); 15 shekels for a male over 60 (Lev. 27:7); 10 shekels for a female over 60 (Lev. 27:7).

c Five shekels a head for ransoming the firstborn (Num. 3:46–7; Num. 18:16); 30 shekels of silver for the death of a slave (Exod. 21:32); 30 shekels of silver paid to Zechariah and thrown to the potter (Zech. 11:12–13).

d A kid for a prostitute (Gen. 38:17, 20); I bought her for 15 shekels of silver and a homer and a half of barley (Hos. 3:2); they sell a girl for wine (Joel 3:3); they sell the needy for a pair of sandals (Amos 2:6; 8:6).

e They paid 30 pieces of silver for Jesus (Matt. 26:15; 27:3, 9); they promised Judas money (Mark 14:11; Luke 22:5); Joseph was sold for 20 pieces of silver (Gen. 37:28); warriors of Israel hired for 100 talents of silver (2 Chr. 25:6, 9).

Man's value, see **371*e***; **ransoming**, see **792*h***.

- Fine as penalty

f A talent of silver as fine for losing a prisoner (1 Kgs. 20:39).

- Dowry

g Pay a dowry (Exod. 22:16–17); 50 shekels of silver as a bride-price (Deut. 22:29); ask what you will as a bridal price (Gen. 34:12); as bridal price, 100 Philistine foreskins (1 Sam. 18:25; 2 Sam. 3:14); Pharaoh gave Gezer as dowry (1 Kgs. 9:16).

- Price of sparrows

h Are not two sparrows sold for an assarion? (Matt. 10:29); are not five sparrows sold for two assarions? (Luke 12:6).

- Price of property

i Valuation of property (Lev. 27:9–25); the cost of building the temple to be met from the royal treasury (Ezra 6:4, 8).

j Ephron set the price of the field at 400 shekels (Gen. 23:15–16); a piece of land bought for 100 qesitas (Gen. 33:19; Josh. 24:32); David paid 600 gold shekels for Ornan's threshing floor (1 Chr. 21:25); David paid 50 shekels for the threshing floor (2 Sam. 24:24); Samaria bought for two talents of silver (1 Kgs. 16:24); the field at Anathoth bought for 17 shekels of silver (Jer. 32:9); Peter asked Sapphira the price of the land (Acts 5:8).

k A chariot imported for 600 shekels of silver (1 Kgs. 10:29; 2 Chr. 1:17); a horse imported for 150 shekels of silver (1 Kgs. 10:29; 2 Chr. 1:17); this perfume might have been sold for more than 300 denarii (Mark 14:5); why was this perfume not sold for 300 denarii? (John 12:5); the price of the books of magic was 50 000 pieces of silver (Acts 19:19).

l The price of wisdom is beyond gold and pearls (Job 28:15–19).

- Price of food

m A donkey's head for 80 shekels and dove's dung for five shekels (2 Kgs. 6:25); a measure of flour for a shekel and two measures of barley for a shekel (2 Kgs. 7:1, 16, 18); a measure of wheat for a denarius and three measures of barley for a denarius (Rev. 6:6); shall we spend 200 denarii on bread? (Mark 6:37); 200 denarii would not be enough (John 6:7); 1000 shekels of silver for the fruit (S. of S. 8:11–12).

● Fee

n The elders of Moab and Midian took with them the fee for divination (Num. 22:7); the 1100 pieces of silver stolen (Judg. 17:2); 200 pieces of silver to make an image (Judg. 17:4); two thirds of a shekel for sharpening tools (1 Sam. 13:21); they gave Abimelech 70 pieces of silver (Judg. 9:4); the Philistine rulers offered Delilah 1100 pieces of silver each (Judg. 16:5); they brought the money in their hands (Judg. 16:18); a quarter of a shekel to give Samuel (1 Sam. 9:8); Joab would have given ten pieces of silver for the killing of Absalom (2 Sam. 18:11); if you gave me 1000 pieces of silver I would not harm Absalom (2 Sam. 18:12); Naaman took ten talents of silver and 6000 shekels of gold (2 Kgs. 5:5); Gehazi accepted two talents of silver (2 Kgs. 5:22–3); 1000 talents of silver to buy off the king of Assyria (2 Kgs. 15:19); to hire mercenaries (1 Chr. 19:6); a denarius a day (Matt. 20:2); the exact sum Haman was paying for the destruction of the Jews (Esther 4:7); Haman would pay 10 000 talents of silver (Esther 3:9); Jonah paid the fare (Jonah 1:3); the money paid to Judas was blood money (Matt. 27:6); the widow put in two copper coins (Luke 21:2).

o No one builds a tower without first considering the cost (Luke 14:28).

810 Discount

Cheapness, see 812.

811 Dearness

● Expensive

a The dearness of a donkey's head and dove's dung in Samaria (2 Kgs. 6:25); very expensive perfume (Matt. 26:7; Mark 14:3); the perfume could have been sold for a high price (Matt. 26:9).

● Precious
  to God

b Redemption from death is costly (Ps. 49:8); the death of his saints is costly to the Lord (Ps. 116:15).

812 Cheapness

● Inexpensive

a The cheapness of flour and barley in Samaria (2 Kgs. 7:1, 16, 18); buy wine and milk without price (Isa. 55:1).

b Two sparrows are sold for an assarion (Matt. 10:29); five sold for two (Luke 12:6).

● Free of
  charge

c She shall go out for nothing (Exod. 21:11); you sell your people cheaply (Ps. 44:12).

d I will not offer burnt offerings which cost nothing (2 Sam. 24:24; 1 Chr. 21:24); Paul preached the gospel to the Corinthians free of charge (1 Cor. 9:18; 2 Cor. 11:7); freely you received, freely give (Matt. 10:8); I will give the water of life without cost (Rev. 21:6); come and take the water of life without cost (Rev. 22:17).

813 Liberality

● Generosity

a God has given freely to the poor (Ps. 112:9).

b Give generously to the poor (Deut. 15:8, 10–11); direct the rich to be generous (1 Tim. 6:18); give liberally to the freed slave (Deut. 15:14); the righteous gives and does not hold back (Prov. 21:26).

c The generous man will prosper (Prov. 11:25); he who is generous will be blessed (Prov. 22:9); their joy and poverty overflowed in liberality (2 Cor. 8:2); you will be enriched to all generosity (2 Cor. 9:11); he who sows bountifully will reap bountifully (2 Cor. 9:6); many seek the favour of the generous (Prov. 19:6).

● Hospitality

d Show hospitality to strangers, for some have entertained angels unawares (Heb. 13:2); an elder must be hospitable (1 Tim. 3:2; Titus 1:8); be hospitable (Rom. 12:13; 1 Pet. 4:9); I opened my doors to the sojourner (Job 31:32); if she has shown hospitality to strangers (1 Tim. 5:10).

e Those who gave hospitality: Abraham to the angels (Gen. 18:1–7); Lot to the two angels (Gen. 19:1–3); Laban to Abraham's servant (Gen. 24:31–3); Reuel to Moses (Exod. 2:20–1); the concubine's father to the Levite (Judg. 19:4–9); the old man of Ephraim to the Levite (Judg. 19:16–21).

● Inhospitable

f No one took them in (Judg. 19:15, 18).

814 Economy

815 Prodigality

816 Parsimony

● Stingy people

a One withholds what is due yet suffers want (Prov. 11:24); a man with evil eye hastens after wealth (Prov. 28:22).

● Do not be stingy

b Do not close your hand towards your poor brother (Deut. 15:7, 9); do not eat the bread of an evil-eyed man (Prov. 23:6); is your eye evil because I am good? (Matt. 20:15).

Class six: Emotion, religion and morality

817 Affections

- Affection

a David longed for Absalom (2 Sam. 13:39; 14:1); I long for you with all the affection of Christ (Phil. 1:8); if there is any affection (Phil. 2:1).

b Absalom stole away the hearts of Israel (2 Sam. 15:6); the hearts of Israel are with Absalom (2 Sam. 15:13).

818 Feeling

- Zeal

a Passion makes the bones rot (Prov. 14:30).

b I have been very zealous for the Lord (1 Kgs. 19:10, 14); my zeal consumes me because they forget your words (Ps. 119:139); the zeal of the Lord will do this (2 Kgs. 19:31; Isa. 9:7; 37:32); zeal for your house has consumed me (Ps. 69:9; John 2:17); do not be lacking in zeal (Rom. 12:11); see what eagerness this godly sorrow has produced (2 Cor. 7:11); your zeal has stirred up most of them (2 Cor. 9:2); did not our hearts burn within us? (Luke 24:32).

c A people zealous for good deeds (Titus 2:14); who will harm you if you are zealous for what is right? (1 Pet. 3:13).

d Apollos was fervent in spirit (Acts 18:25); Paul was zealous for God (Acts 22:3); a zeal for God but not according to knowledge (Rom. 10:2); I was zealous for the traditions (Gal. 1:14); as to zeal, a persecutor of the church (Phil. 3:6).
Zealot, see **708m**.

- Emotion

e Joseph was deeply moved over his brother (Gen. 43:30); David was deeply moved (2 Sam. 18:33); Jesus wept (John 11:35); they were pierced in their hearts (Acts 2:37).
Weeping through emotion, see **836m**.

819 Sensibility
Feeling, see **818**.

820 Insensibility
Unconcerned, see **860a**.

821 Excitement

- Exciting

a Do not stir up love until it please (S. of S. 2:7; 3:5; 8:4); you have aroused my heart (S. of S. 4:9).

b All the city was stirred (Matt. 21:10).

822 Excitability

Zeal, see **818***a*.

823 Inexcitability

● Patience
    a Love is patient and kind (1 Cor. 13:4); the fruit of the Spirit is patience (Gal. 5:22).

    b The one who is slow to anger has great understanding (Prov. 14:29); he who is slow to anger is better than the mighty (Prov. 16:32); discretion makes a man slow to anger (Prov. 19:11); he who restrains his words and has a cool spirit (Prov. 17:27); patience is better than pride (Eccles. 7:8).

    c Put on patience (Col. 3:12); be patient with everyone (1 Thess. 5:14); walk with patience and forbearance in love (Eph. 4:2); be quick to listen, slow to speak, slow to anger (Jas. 1:19).

    d Be patient until the Lord's coming (Jas. 5:7); consider the Lord's patience as salvation (2 Pet. 3:15).

    e Abraham patiently endured and obtained the promise (Heb. 6:15); the prophets are an example of patience in the face of suffering (Jas. 5:10); you have heard of the patience of Job (Jas. 5:11); those who through faith and patience inherit the promises (Heb. 6:12); we commend ourselves in patience (2 Cor. 6:6).

● God's
  patience
    f God is slow to anger (Neh. 9:17; Ps. 103:8; 145:8; Joel 2:13; Jonah 4:2; Nahum 1:3); God endured with patience the vessels of wrath (Rom. 9:22); the Lord is patient towards you (2 Pet. 3:9); in me Christ demonstrated his patience (1 Tim. 1:16); the riches of his forbearance and longsuffering (Rom. 2:4); be patient and I will pay everything (Matt. 18:26, 29).

● Self-control
    g If they do not have self-control, let them marry (1 Cor. 7:9); competitors in the games exercise self-control (1 Cor. 9:25); the fruit of the Spirit is self-control (Gal. 5:23); Paul spoke about righteousness, self-control and judgement (Acts 24:25); add to knowledge self-control (2 Pet. 1:6).

Section two: Personal emotion

824 Joy

● Rejoicing
    a Rejoice always (1 Thess. 5:16); rejoice in hope (Rom. 12:12); we write this that our joy may be complete (1 John 1:4); rejoice with those who rejoice (Rom. 12:15).

    b Love does not rejoice in wrong but rejoices in the truth (1 Cor. 13:6).

    c Those who rejoice should live as though they did not (1 Cor. 7:30).

● God
  rejoicing
    d God will rejoice over you (Isa. 62:5; Zeph. 3:17); I will rejoice over Jerusalem and be glad in my people (Isa. 65:19).

    e Rejoicing over the lost sheep which is found (Matt. 18:13; Luke

15:5); over the lost coin (Luke 15:9); over a sinner who repents (Luke 15:7, 10); over a son brought from death to life (Luke 15:24, 32).

● Christ
rejoicing

f God has anointed you with the oil of gladness (Ps. 45:7; Heb. 1:9); for the joy set before he him endured the cross (Heb. 12:2); I have told you this that my joy may be in you and your joy may be full (John 15:11); my joy is now full (John 3:29); that they may have my joy fulfilled (John 17:13); enter into the joy of your master (Matt. 25:21, 23).

● Rejoicing
in the Lord

g Let the righteous rejoice in the Lord (Ps. 32:11; 33:1; 64:10; 68:3; 97:12); rejoice in the Lord (Joel 2:23; Phil. 3:1; 4:4); the needy will rejoice in the Lord (Isa. 29:19); let those who seek the Lord rejoice (1 Chr. 16:10; Ps. 70:4); my heart rejoices in the Lord (1 Sam. 2:1); I rejoice in God my Saviour (Luke 1:47); the king will rejoice in God (Ps. 63:11); the joy of the Lord is your strength (Neh. 8:10); shout for joy to the Lord (Ps. 81:1; 100:1); sing for joy to the Lord (Ps. 95:1; 98:4–6).

h Happy the people whose God is the Lord (Ps. 144:15); happy the man who takes refuge in him (Ps. 2:12); let Israel rejoice in their King (Ps. 149:2); God my exceeding joy (Ps. 43:4); in your presence is fulness of joy (Ps. 16:11); you make him joyful in your presence (Ps. 21:6); you put gladness into my heart more than when their grain and wine abound (Ps. 4:7); I was glad to go to the house of the Lord (Ps. 122:1); satisfy us with your lovingkindness that we may rejoice all our lives (Ps. 90:14).

i Let all creation rejoice for the Lord comes (1 Chr. 16:31; Ps. 96:11–13; 98:7–9); the trees of the forest will sing for joy for the Lord comes (1 Chr. 16:33); the Lord led forth his people with joy (Ps. 105:43); you will go out with joy (Isa. 55:12).

j You did not serve the Lord with joy (Deut. 28:47).

● Rejoicing in
right living

k Happy the man who does not follow sinners (Ps. 1:1); happy are those who observe justice (Ps. 106:3); happy is the man who fears the Lord (Ps. 112:1; 128:1); they rejoiced because they had given willingly (1 Chr. 29:9); make me hear joy and gladness (Ps. 51:8); nothing better than that a man enjoy his work (Eccles. 3:22).

l Happy those who dash your little ones (Ps. 137:9).

● Rejoicing
over justice

m When the righteous increase the people rejoice (Prov. 29:2); when the wicked perish there are shouts of joy (Prov. 11:10); do not rejoice when your enemy falls (Prov. 24:17–18); heaven and earth will shout for joy over Babylon (Jer. 51:48).

● Rejoicing in
God's word

n I rejoice at your word (Ps. 119:162); the precepts of the Lord give joy to the heart (Ps. 19:8); your testimonies are the joy of my heart (Ps. 119:111); your words were the joy of my heart (Jer. 15:16); your commandments are my delight (Ps. 119:143); one immediately receives the word with joy (Matt. 13:20; Mark 4:16;

Luke 8:13); happy are those who walk in the law of the Lord (Ps. 119:1).

● Rejoicing in God's works

o They were joyful for all God had done (1 Kgs. 8:66; 2 Chr. 7:10); Hezekiah and the people rejoiced at what God had done (2 Chr. 29:36); they shouted for joy when the foundation of the temple was laid (Ezra 3:12); they rejoiced because God had given them great joy (Neh. 12:43); the Lord had caused them to rejoice (Ezra 6:22); happy he whose help is the God of Jacob (Ps. 146:5); God richly supplies us with everything to enjoy (1 Tim. 6:17).

p Jethro rejoiced over God's goodness to Israel (Exod. 18:9); shout for joy, daughter of Zion (Zeph. 3:14; Zech. 9:9).

q They rejoiced when Solomon became king (1 Kgs. 1:40); when Joash became king (2 Kgs. 11:14); happy are your servants! (1 Kgs. 10:8; 2 Chr. 9:7); the Lord had caused them to rejoice over their enemies (2 Chr. 20:27); for the Jews it was a time of joy (Esther 8:16); the king rejoices in the victory of the Lord (Ps. 21:1); they rejoiced with Elizabeth over God's mercy (Luke 1:58).

● Rejoicing in Jerusalem

r There was great joy in Jerusalem for what had happened (2 Chr. 30:25–6); joy and gladness will be found in Zion (Isa. 51:3); I create Jerusalem a rejoicing (Isa. 65:18–19); Zion is the joy of the whole earth (Ps. 48:2); rejoice with Jerusalem (Isa. 66:10); on the height of Zion I will turn their mourning into joy (Jer. 31:12–13).

s Is this the city called a joy to all the earth? (Lam. 2:15).

● Rejoicing in salvation

t The fruit of the Spirit is joy (Gal. 5:22); shout for joy, barren one (Isa. 54:1); shout for joy for the Lord has redeemed us (Isa. 44:22–3); the kingdom of God is joy in the Holy Spirit (Rom. 14:17); rejoice that your names are written in heaven (Luke 10:20).

u When they saw the star, they rejoiced (Matt. 2:10); the baby in Elizabeth's womb leaped for joy (Luke 1:44); Abraham rejoiced that he was to see my day (John 8:56); they went from the tomb in fear and great joy (Matt. 28:8); they returned with great joy (Luke 24:52); many would rejoice at John's birth (Luke 1:14).

v My soul will rejoice in the Lord and his salvation (Ps. 35:9); the ransomed of the Lord will return with everlasting joy on their heads (Isa. 35:10; 51:11); you have increased their joy (Isa. 9:3).

w They rejoiced to hear of the conversion of the Gentiles (Acts 15:3); we rejoice before God because of you (1 Thess. 3:9); the jailer rejoiced, believing in God (Acts 16:34); there was much rejoicing in Samaria (Acts 8:8); the eunuch went on his way rejoicing (Acts 8:39); the disciples were filled with joy and with the Holy Spirit (Acts 13:52); restore to me the joy of your salvation (Ps. 51:12).

x Your sorrow will be turned to joy (John 16:20); no one will take your joy from you (John 16:22); we rejoice in God through our

Lord Jesus (Rom. 5:11); we rejoice in hope of the glory of God (Rom. 5:2); ask and you will receive, that your joy may be full (John 16:24); joy unspeakable and full of glory (1 Pet. 1:8); in this salvation you rejoice (1 Pet. 1:6).

y May God fill you with all joy and peace in believing (Rom. 15:13).

- Eating, drinking and rejoicing

z Eat your good things and rejoice before the Lord (Deut. 12:7, 12, 18; 14:26; 16:11; 26:11); eat and be joyful! (1 Kgs. 21:7); they were eating, drinking and rejoicing (1 Kgs. 4:20; 1 Chr. 12:40); be joyful at the Feast of Tabernacles (Deut. 16:14). **Eat, drink and be merry**, see **301i**.

- Rejoicing in trial

aa Rejoice when you are persecuted (Matt. 5:12; Luke 6:23); rejoice as you share the sufferings of Christ (1 Pet. 4:13); count it all joy when you face testings (Jas. 1:2); rejoicing that they were found worthy to suffer (Acts 5:41); you took joyfully the plundering of your goods (Heb. 10:34); God gives songs in the night (Job 35:10); though all fails, yet I will rejoice in the Lord (Hab. 3:17–18).

- Lack of rejoicing

ab The end of joy may be grief (Prov. 14:13); gaiety ceases (Isa. 24:8).

825 Suffering

- Sorrow

a Sorrow is better than laughter (Eccles. 7:3).

- God suffering

b God could not bear Israel's misery (Judg. 10:16); in all their affliction he was afflicted (Isa. 63:9).

- God's people suffering

c I am lonely and afflicted (Ps. 25:16–18); woe is me! (Ps. 120:5); many are the afflictions of the righteous (Ps. 34:19); a prayer of the afflicted (Ps. 102:t).

d The Lord has added sorrow to my pain (Jer. 45:3); is any suffering like my suffering? (Lam. 1:12); why is my pain unending? (Jer. 15:18); her soul is troubled (2 Kgs. 4:27); the heart knows its own bitterness (Prov. 14:10).

e The thing distressed Abraham (Gen. 21:11); Rachel in severe labour (Gen. 35:16–17); son of my sorrow (Gen. 35:18); Samuel was distressed over Saul (1 Sam. 15:11).

f The Israelites groaned in their slavery (Exod. 2:23); I have heard their groaning (Exod. 6:5); the Lord saw how all the Israelites were suffering (2 Kgs. 14:26); you saw the affliction of our fathers in Egypt (Neh. 9:9).

g In distress and sorrow I called on the Lord (Ps. 116:3–4); in my distress I called on the Lord (Ps. 118:5); is anyone suffering? let him pray (Jas. 5:13).

- Suffering of the ungodly

h Many are the sorrows of the wicked (Ps. 32:10); the enemies of Israel were displeased (Neh. 2:10); on the third day they were sore (Gen. 34:25).

- God healing
  sorrow

i God heals the broken-hearted (Ps. 147:3); he has anointed me to bind up the broken-hearted (Isa. 61:1); the Lord saves the broken-hearted (Ps. 34:18).

- Suffering
  of Christ

j A man of sorrows and acquainted with grief (Isa. 53:3); he bore our griefs (Isa. 53:4); grieved to the point of death (Matt. 26:37–8; Mark 14:33–4); ought not the Christ to have suffered? (Luke 24:26); Christ had to suffer and rise (Luke 24:46; Acts 17:3; 26:23); he must suffer many things from the elders and the chief priests (Matt. 16:21; Mark 8:31; Luke 9:22); the Son of man will suffer at their hands (Matt. 17:12); he must suffer many things (Luke 17:25); he learned obedience by what he suffered (Heb. 5:8); he was made perfect through suffering (Heb. 2:10); the prophets predicted the sufferings of Christ (Acts 3:18; 1 Pet. 1:11); Christ suffered for you (1 Pet. 2:21); Christ suffered in the flesh (1 Pet. 4:1).

Christ suffering, see **357z**.

- Suffering
  with Christ

k Christ suffered leaving us an example (1 Pet. 2:21); the sufferings of Christ abound for us (2 Cor. 1:5); since Christ suffered, arm yourselves with the same mind (1 Pet. 4:1); you share in the sufferings of Christ (1 Pet. 4:13); the fellowship of his sufferings (Phil. 3:10); I fill up what is lacking in Christ's afflictions (Col. 1:24); we suffer with him that we may be glorified with him (Rom. 8:17).

- Suffering
  of Christ's
  disciples

l Endure hardship, evangelize (2 Tim. 4:5); endure hardship as a soldier of Christ (2 Tim. 2:3); join me in suffering for the gospel (2 Tim. 1:8); if one limb suffers, all suffer (1 Cor. 12:26).

m How much he must suffer for my name's sake (Acts 9:16); it is given to you not only to believe on Christ but also to suffer for him (Phil. 1:29); he who would be a disciple must take up his cross (Matt. 10:38; 16:24; Mark 8:34; Luke 14:27); daily (Luke 9:23); we were destined for affliction (1 Thess. 3:3).

n What we suffered in Asia (2 Cor. 1:8); in Philippi (1 Thess. 2:2); in Antioch, Iconium and Lystra (2 Tim. 3:11); I suffer because I teach the gospel (2 Tim. 1:11–12); we were afflicted on all sides (2 Cor. 7:5); you received the word in much tribulation (1 Thess. 1:6); you endured the same sufferings (1 Thess. 2:14); you endured much suffering (Heb. 10:32).

o We glory in tribulations (Rom. 5:3); we commend ourselves in afflictions (2 Cor. 6:4); we are afflicted but not crushed (2 Cor. 4:8); momentary light affliction (2 Cor. 4:17); you share in our suffering (2 Cor. 1:7).

p For a little while you may have to suffer (1 Pet. 1:6); you should suffer for doing right, not for doing wrong (1 Pet. 2:19–20; 3:14, 17); suffer as a Christian (1 Pet. 4:15–17); suffer according to God's will (1 Pet. 4:19); after you have suffered a little, God will strengthen you (1 Pet. 5:10).

● Various
suffering

q Jabez—born in pain (1 Chr. 4:9).

r The present sufferings are not worth comparing with the glory to come (Rom. 8:18); we groan, waiting for our redemption (Rom. 8:23); the creation groans in travail (Rom. 8:22).

s God is just to afflict those who afflict you (2 Thess. 1:6).

● Anxiety

t Anxiety weighs the heart down (Prov. 12:25); anxiety chokes the word (Mark 4:19); when anxious thoughts are many (Ps. 94:19); eat and drink with trembling and anxiety (Ezek. 12:18–19).

u Mary was worried about many things (Luke 10:41); my anxiety for the churches (2 Cor. 11:28–9); I am in labour until Christ is formed in you (Gal. 4:19).

● Do not be
anxious

v Do not fret over evildoers (Ps. 37:1, 7); do not fret as it only leads to wrongdoing (Ps. 37:8).

w Be anxious for nothing (Phil. 4:6); do not be anxious for to-morrow (Matt. 6:34); do not be anxious about what to say in your defence (Matt. 10:19; Mark 13:11; Luke 12:11); do not worry about what to eat or drink (Matt. 6:25–31; Luke 12:22–9); who by being anxious can add a cubit to his life? (Matt. 6:27; Luke 12:25); the worries of this life choke the word (Matt. 13:22; Luke 8:14); do not be weighed down by the worries of life (Luke 21:34); do not let your heart be troubled (John 14:1); do not be anxious (Luke 12:29); I want you to be free from anxiety (1 Cor. 7:32); cast your anxiety on him (1 Pet. 5:7).

826 Pleasurableness

● God's
pleasure

a God does whatever he pleases (Ps. 115:3; 135:6); you have done what you pleased (Jonah 1:14); this was well-pleasing in your sight (Matt. 11:26; Luke 10:21); Wisdom was daily his delight (Prov. 8:30); it pleased the Lord to crush him (Isa. 53:10).

b God's delight: a just weight (Prov. 11:1); those who act faithfully (Prov. 12:22); the blameless (Prov. 11:20); the prayer of the upright (Prov. 15:8).

c God does not delight in the strength of a horse or a man's legs (Ps. 147:10); God takes no pleasure in the death of the wicked (Ezek. 18:23, 32; 33:11).

● Christ
pleasing
God

d This is my Son with whom I am well pleased (Matt. 3:17; 17:5; Mark 1:11; Luke 3:22); my beloved in whom I am well pleased (Matt. 12:18; 2 Pet. 1:17); I always do the things that please him (John 8:29); even Christ did not please himself (Rom. 15:3); let God deliver him if he delights in him (Matt. 27:43).

● God pleased
with people

e The Lord takes pleasure in his people (Ps. 149:4); Wisdom delighted in the sons of men (Prov. 8:31); if the Lord is pleased with us, he will give us the land (Num. 14:8); God is pleased to give you the kingdom (Luke 12:32); God took pleasure in David to make him king (1 Chr. 28:4); he delighted in me (2 Sam. 22:20; Ps. 18:19); God took pleasure in Solomon to make him king (2 Chr. 9:8); the Lord delights in you (Isa. 62:4); Enoch pleased God (Heb. 11:5); by this I know you are pleased with me (Ps. 41:11); Samuel grew in favour with God and man (1 Sam. 2:26).

f Finding favour in God's eyes: Noah (Gen. 6:8); Abraham (Gen. 19:19); Moses (Exod. 33:12, 13, 16, 17; 34:9; Num. 11:11, 15); Gideon (Judg. 6:17); David (2 Sam. 15:25; Acts 7:46).

g Those who are in the flesh cannot please God (Rom. 8:8); if God says 'I have no delight in you' (2 Sam. 15:26); with most of them God was not pleased (1 Cor. 10:5).

● Doing what pleases God

h Learn what is pleasing to the Lord (Eph. 5:10); how you ought to live and please God (1 Thess. 4:1); we do what pleases him (1 John 3:22); to please the Lord in every way (Col. 1:10); the unmarried man is concerned to please the Lord (1 Cor. 7:32); whether home or away, we want to please him (2 Cor. 5:9); a soldier wants to please the one who enlisted him (2 Tim. 2:4); may God work in you what is pleasing in his sight (Heb. 13:21).

i Without faith it is impossible to please him (Heb. 11:6); not pleasing men but God (1 Thess. 2:4); it pleased God that Solomon asked this (1 Kgs. 3:10); children, obey your parents, for this is pleasing to the Lord (Col. 3:20); your sacrifice was well-pleasing to God (Phil. 4:18); has the Lord as much delight in sacrifice as in obeying? (1 Sam. 15:22); you had no pleasure in burnt offerings (Heb. 10:6, 8).

● Pleasure in God

j Delight yourself in the Lord (Ps. 37:4); then you will take delight in the Lord (Isa. 58:14); they drink from your river of delights (Ps. 36:8); they delight to know my ways (Isa. 58:2); will the godless take delight in the Almighty? (Job 27:10).

● Pleasure in God's law

k He delights in the law of the Lord (Ps. 1:2); I delight in your law (Ps. 119:70, 77, 92, 174); I delight in your commandments (Ps. 119:35, 47); I delight in your statutes (Ps. 119:16); I delight in the way of your testimonies (Ps. 119:14); your testimonies are my delight (Ps. 119:24); happy the man who delights in his commandments (Ps. 112:1).

● Pleasing people

l It please Pharaoh and his servants (Gen. 45:16); these words pleased Phinehas and the leaders (Josh. 22:30); and Israel (Josh. 22:33); the plan pleased Absalom (2 Sam. 17:4); this word pleased the king (Esther 1:21); you would be pleased if Absalom were alive and we dead (2 Sam. 19:6).

m Everything David did pleased the people (2 Sam. 3:36); the king delights in you (1 Sam. 18:22); Jonathan delighted in David (1 Sam. 19:1); Esther pleased the king (Esther 2:9); the daughter of Herodias pleased Herod (Matt. 14:6; Mark 6:22); the married person is concerned to please the partner (1 Cor. 7:33, 34); if I were trying to please men I would not be a slave of Christ (Gal. 1:10).

n I please all men (1 Cor. 10:33); let each of us please his neighbour for his good (Rom. 15:2).

Pleasing men, see **371r**.

o The cities in Galilee did not please Hiram (1 Kgs. 9:12).

● Finding favour with people

p Finding favour in the sight of others: Abraham and the visitors (Gen. 18:3); Laban and Jacob (Gen. 30:27); Jacob and Esau (Gen. 32:5; 33:8, 10, 15); Shechem and Jacob's sons (Gen. 34:11); Joseph and Potiphar (Gen. 39:4); Joseph and the jailer (Gen. 39:21); Joseph and Pharaoh (Acts 7:10); the Egyptians and Joseph (Gen. 47:25); Jacob and Joseph (Gen. 47:29); Joseph and Pharaoh (Gen. 50:4); Israel and the Egyptians (Exod. 3:21; 11:3; 12:36); Reuben, Gad and Moses (Num. 32:5); a wife and her husband (Deut. 24:1); Ruth and someone kind (Ruth 2:2); Ruth and Boaz (Ruth 2:10, 13); Hannah and Eli (1 Sam. 1:18); David and Saul (1 Sam. 16:22); David and Jonathan (1 Sam. 20:3, 29); David's men and Nabal (1 Sam. 25:8); David and Achish (1 Sam. 27:5); Joab and David (2 Sam. 14:22); Ziba and David (2 Sam. 16:4); Hadad and Pharaoh (1 Kgs. 11:19); Esther and everyone (Esther 2:15); Esther and the king (Esther 2:17; 5:2); Daniel and the commander (Dan. 1:9).

● Pleasures

q The trees in the garden were pleasing to the eye (Gen. 2:9); the woman saw that the fruit was pleasing to the eye (Gen. 3:6); Issachar saw that the land was pleasant (Gen. 49:15); the pleasures of sin (Heb. 11:25).

r Your pleasures wage war in your members (Jas. 4:1); you have lived a life of pleasure (Jas. 5:5); men will be lovers of pleasure rather than lovers of God (2 Tim. 3:4); in slavery to pleasures (Titus 3:3).

s They took pleasure in wickedness (2 Thess. 2:12).

Pleasure seeking, see **837a**.

827 Painfulness

● Trouble for the world

a Man is born for trouble (Job 5:7); man's life is full of trouble (Job 14:1); pain in childbirth was greatly increased (Gen. 3:16); those who marry will have trouble (1 Cor. 7:28).

b A time of distress unknown since the beginning of the world (Dan. 12:1; Matt. 24:21; Mark 13:19); this is a day of distress (2 Kgs. 19:3; Isa. 37:3); great distress in the land (Luke 21:23); I will keep you from the hour of trial which is coming on the whole world (Rev. 3:10); they have come out of the great tribulation (Rev. 7:14).

c There will be weeping and gnashing of teeth (Matt. 13:42, 50; 22:13; 24:51; 25:30; Luke 13:28); there will be tribulation for every one who does evil (Rom. 2:9); it will be more bearable for Sodom and Gomorrah than for them (Matt. 10:15; 11:24; Luke 10:12); more bearable for Tyre and Sidon (Matt. 11:22; Luke 10:14).

d Is it you, you troubler of Israel? (1 Kgs. 18:17); you have troubled Israel (1 Kgs. 18:18); these two prophets had tormented those who dwell on the earth (Rev. 11:10); the men who have disturbed the world have come here (Acts 17:6).

● God troubling his people

e I will afflict the seed of David (1 Kgs. 11:39); you have made your people experience hardship (Ps. 60:3); why have you brought trouble on this people? (Exod. 5:22); the Almighty has dealt bitterly with me (Ruth 1:20).

● Others troubling God's people

f O afflicted ones! (Isa. 54:11); the Egyptians made their lives bitter (Exod. 1:14); Achor—trouble (Josh. 7:24); why trouble us? the Lord will trouble you (Josh. 7:25); a sword will pierce your own soul (Luke 2:35); shall trouble, hardship or persecution separate us from the love of Christ? (Rom. 8:35); do not be surprised at the fiery trial (1 Pet. 4:12); through many tribulations we must enter the kingdom of God (Acts 14:22); persevere in tribulation (Rom. 12:12); some were tortured (Heb. 11:35).

g Paul lists his afflictions (2 Cor. 11:23–7); his thorn in the flesh (2 Cor. 12:7); I bear in my body the marks of Jesus (Gal. 6:17).

● Discipline

h Whoever loves discipline loves knowledge (Prov. 12:1); he who loves his son is careful to discipline him (Prov. 13:24); discipline your son (Prov. 19:18; 29:17); discipline will remove folly from the heart (Prov. 22:15); do not withhold discipline from a child (Prov. 23:13); a wise son takes his father's discipline (Prov. 13:1).

Rebuke as discipline, see **925*h***.

● God's discipline

i Do not reject the Lord's discipline (Job 5:17; Prov. 3:11–12; Heb. 12:5–6); happy is the man you discipline (Ps. 94:12); when he sins, I will correct him with the rod (2 Sam. 7:14); the master handed over the slave to the torturers (Matt. 18:34); no discipline seems joyful but rather painful (Heb. 12:11); when we are judged, we are disciplined by the Lord (1 Cor. 11:32); the Lord has disciplined me severely (Ps. 118:18); before I was afflicted I went astray (Ps. 119:67); it was good for me to be afflicted (Ps. 119:71); in faithfulness you have afflicted me (Ps. 119:75); he does not willingly afflict the sons of men (Lam. 3:33).

God disciplining, see **924*c***.

● Lack of discipline

j His father had never pained him by challenging what he did (1 Kgs. 1:6); you hate discipline (Ps. 50:17); poverty and shame come to him who ignores discipline (Prov. 13:18).

● Annoying people

k There are four unbearable things (Prov. 30:21–3); a lazy man is like vinegar or smoke to him who sends him (Prov. 10:26); Esau's wives brought grief to Isaac and Rebekah (Gen. 26:35); Delilah nagged Samson to death (Judg. 16:16); Hannah's rival provoked her (1 Sam. 1:6); the Ammonites had become odious to David (2 Sam. 10:6); David had become odious to the Israelites (1 Sam. 27:12); the inhabitants of the land will become pricks in your eyes and thorns in your sides (Num. 33:55); a whip on your sides and thorns in your eyes (Josh. 23:13); lest she wear me out by continually coming (Luke 18:5).

l Simeon and Levi brought trouble on Jacob (Gen. 34:30); the butler and baker offended the king of Egypt (Gen. 40:1); the request for a king displeased Samuel (1 Sam. 8:6); why have you disturbed me? (1 Sam. 28:15).

● Grieving God

m David's census displeased God (1 Chr. 21:7); they rebelled and grieved his Holy Spirit (Isa. 63:10); do not grieve the Holy Spirit (Eph. 4:30).

● Troubling Satan

n Do not torment us! (Matt. 8:29; Mark 5:7; Luke 8:28).

828 Content

● Be content!

a Be content with your wages (Luke 3:14); be content with what you have (Heb. 13:5).

● Contentment

b I have learned to be content in all circumstances (Phil. 4:11); I am well-pleased with weakness, insults etc. (2 Cor. 12:10); godliness with contentment is great gain (1 Tim. 6:6); if we have food and clothing we will be content (1 Tim. 6:8).

829 Discontent

● Grumbling

a The Israelites complained against Moses (Exod. 15:24; 17:3); against Moses and Aaron (Exod. 16:2; Num. 14:2; 16:41); who is Aaron that you grumble at him? (Num. 16:11); they grumbled against their leaders (Josh. 9:18); they grumbled in their tents (Deut. 1:27; Ps. 106:25); they complained about their hardships (Num. 11:1); I will reduce the grumblings of the Israelites against you (Num. 17:5); they grumbled against the Lord (Exod. 16:7, 8, 9; Num. 14:27); I have heard their grumbling (Exod. 16:12).

b If the menfolk complain (Judg. 21:22).

c The workmen grumbled at the landowner (Matt. 20:11); the Pharisees and scribes grumbled at Jesus receiving sinners (Luke 15:2); they grumbled at Jesus going to Zaccheus' house (Luke 19:7); the Hellenists complained against the Hebrews (Acts 6:1); the Pharisees grumbled at the disciples (Luke 5:30).

d These men are grumblers, finding fault (Jude 16); we played and you did not dance, we sang a dirge and you did not mourn (Matt. 11:17; Luke 7:32); men will be irreconcilable (2 Tim. 3:3).

e Do all things without grumbling (Phil. 2:14); do not complain against one another (Jas. 5:9); do not grumble as some of them did (1 Cor. 10:10).

● Dissatisfaction

f All this does me no good when I see Mordecai (Esther 5:13); the eye is not satisfied with seeing nor the ear with hearing (Eccles. 1:8).

830 Regret

● Regretting

a The Lord was sorry that he had made man (Gen. 6:6, 7); God regretted that he made Saul king (1 Sam. 15:11, 35).

b The people were very sorry for Benjamin (Judg. 21:15).

c Judas was filled with remorse (Matt. 27:3).

d Jehoram went without anyone regretting it (2 Chr. 21:20).
Mourning in regret, see **836z**.

● Alas!

e Woe to you, Chorazin and Bethsaida (Matt. 11:21; Luke 10:13); woe to the world for stumbling blocks (Matt. 18:7); woe to that man by whom they come (Matt. 18:7; Luke 17:1); woe to that man (Matt. 26:24; Mark 14:21; Luke 22:22); woe to those who are pregnant in those days (Matt. 24:19; Mark 13:17; Luke 21:23).

f Woe to those who are rich (Luke 6:24); woe to those who are full (Luke 6:25); woe to you who laugh now (Luke 6:25); woe to you when all speak well of you (Luke 6:26).

g Woe to you, scribes and Pharisees (Matt. 23:13, 14, 15, 23, 25, 27, 29); woe to you, Pharisees (Luke 11:42, 43, 44); woe to you, lawyers (Luke 11:46, 47, 52); woe to you, blind guides (Matt. 23:16).
Woe to hinderers, see **702d**.

● The three woes

h Woe, woe, woe because of the last three trumpet blasts (Rev. 8:13); the first woe is past, two more to come (Rev. 9:12); the second woe is past, the third comes quickly (Rev. 11:14).

831 Comfort

● God comforting

a Your anger turned away and you comforted me (Isa. 12:1); comfort my people, says your God (Isa. 40:1); the Lord has comforted his people (Isa. 49:13; 52:9); the Lord will again comfort Zion (Zech. 1:17); the God of all comfort comforts us so that we can comfort others (2 Cor. 1:3–5); God comforted us (2 Cor. 7:6–7); I am the one who comforts you (Isa. 51:12).

b As one whom his mother comforts, so will I comfort you (Isa. 66:13); the Lord will comfort Zion (Isa. 51:3); God will wipe away every tear (Isa. 25:8; Rev. 7:17; 21:4).

c God has sent me to comfort those who mourn (Isa. 61:2); Simeon was looking for the consolation of Israel (Luke 2:25); blessed are those who mourn for they shall be comforted (Matt. 5:4); Lazarus received bad things and now he is comforted (Luke 16:25); you share in our comfort (2 Cor. 1:7); the church was walking in the comfort of the Holy Spirit (Acts 9:31); eternal comfort (2 Thess. 2:16); God is just to give relief to those afflicted (2 Thess. 1:7).

d May your lovingkindness comfort me (Ps. 119:76); may he comfort you (2 Thess. 2:17); are the consolations of God too small for you? (Job 15:11); in anxiety your consolations cheer me (Ps. 94:19); my comfort is that you have revived me (Ps. 119:50).

The Comforter, see **703***e*.

● Human
comfort

e The rich receive their comfort now (Luke 6:24); how will you comfort me with vanity? (Job 21:34); Job was as one who comforts mourners (Job 29:25); comfort one another with these words (1 Thess. 4:18).

f Ephraim's kin came to comfort him (1 Chr. 7:22); David sent to console Hanun on his father's death (2 Sam. 10:2; 1 Chr. 19:2); David comforted Bathsheba (2 Sam. 12:24); Job's friends came to comfort him (Job 2:11); Job's relatives comforted him (Job 42:11); many Jews came to comfort Martha and Mary (John 11:19); Tychicus will comfort your hearts (Eph. 6:22); I have had much comfort from your love (Philem. 7).

g Isaac was comforted after his mother's death (Gen. 24:67); David was comforted about Amnon (2 Sam. 13:39); they were greatly comforted about Eutychus (Acts 20:12); we were comforted about you (1 Thess. 3:7).

h Wine cheers God and man (Judg. 9:13).

● No comfort

i Storm-tossed and not comforted (Isa. 54:11); I looked for comforters and there were none (Ps. 69:20); there is none to comfort (Lam. 1:2, 9, 16, 17, 21); the oppressed had no one to comfort them (Eccles. 4:1).

j Jacob would not be comforted (Gen. 37:35); my soul refused to be comforted (Ps. 77:2); do not try to comfort me (Isa. 22:4); Rachel refuses to be comforted for her children (Jer. 31:15; Matt. 2:18).

k Miserable comforters! (Job 16:2).

832 Aggravation

Deterioration, see **655**.

833 Cheerfulness

● Cheerful

a A glad heart makes a cheerful face (Prov. 15:13); a cheerful heart has a continual feast (Prov. 15:15); a cheerful heart is a good medicine (Prov. 17:22); is anyone cheerful? let him sing praise (Jas. 5:13).

● Acting
cheerfully

b God loves a cheerful giver (2 Cor. 9:7); Agag came cheerfully (1 Sam. 15:32).

834 Sadness

● Sad

a He who sings songs to a heavy heart is like vinegar on soda (Prov. 25:20); my life is spent with sorrow (Ps. 31:10); why do you despair, O my soul? (Ps. 42:5, 11; 43:5).

b The Israelites did not listen because of their depression (Exod. 6:9).

c Joseph saw that the butler and baker were sad (Gen. 40:6–7);

Amnon was continually depressed (2 Sam. 13:4); Nehemiah was sad before the king (Neh. 2:1–3); Herod was grieved about John (Mark 6:26); the king was sad at the request (Matt. 14:9).

d Do not be dismayed by them lest I dismay you before them (Jer. 1:17).

● Godly
sorrow

e God was sorry that he made man and it grieved him (Gen. 6:6–7); Jesus was grieved at their hardness of heart (Mark 3:5); Jesus was grieved to the point of death (Matt. 26:38; Mark 14:34).

f As sorrowful yet always rejoicing (2 Cor. 6:10); those who weep now shall laugh (Luke 6:21); godly sorrow produced repentance (2 Cor. 7:9–11); a broken and a contrite heart you will not despise (Ps. 51:17); out of the depths I cry to you (Ps. 130:1).

● Disciples'
sorrow

g The disciples were very sad (Matt. 17:23); grieved that one of them would betray him (Matt. 26:22; Mark 14:19); sorrow has filled your heart (John 16:6); the rich young man went away grieved (Matt. 19:22; Mark 10:22; Luke 18:23).

h Paul grieved about his countrymen (Rom. 9:2); in anguish of heart I wrote to you (2 Cor. 2:4); if I make you sad, who is there to make me glad? (2 Cor. 2:2); if your brother is grieved by your food, you are not walking in love (Rom. 14:15).

835 Signs of joy

● Laughter

a There is a time to laugh (Eccles. 3:4); I said laughter was mad (Eccles. 2:2); the laughter of fools is like the crackling of thorns (Eccles. 7:6); woe to you who laugh now (Luke 6:25).

b Abraham laughed (Gen. 17:17); call him Isaac—he laughs (Gen. 17:19; 21:3); Sarah laughed (Gen. 18:12–15); God has made laughter for me (Gen. 21:6); God will fill your mouth with laughter (Job 8:21); you who weep will laugh (Luke 6:21).

● Dancing

c There is a time to dance (Eccles. 3:4); our dancing has been turned to mourning (Lam. 5:15); we played the flute and you did not dance (Matt. 11:17; Luke 7:32); the elder brother heard music and dancing (Luke 15:25).

d With tambourines and dancing: Miriam (Exod. 15:20); Jephthah's daughter (Judg. 11:34).

e The daughters of Shiloh dancing (Judg. 21:21, 23); the women came out singing and dancing (1 Sam. 18:6); David danced before the Lord (2 Sam. 6:14, 16; 1 Chr. 15:29); praise his name with dancing (Ps. 149:3).

f Moses saw the calf and the dancing (Exod. 32:19); the daughter of Herodias danced (Matt. 14:6; Mark 6:22).

836 Lamentation

● Concerning
mourning

a There is a time to mourn (Eccles. 3:4); better to go to the house of mourning than to the house of feasting (Eccles. 7:2, 4).

b The scroll contained words of mourning and lamentation (Ezek. 2:10); groan before them (Ezek. 21:6–7).

Fasting in mourning, see **946*l***.

● Instruction
about
mourning

c Blessed are those who mourn (Matt. 5:4); blessed are you who weep now (Luke 6:21); weeping may last for a night but joy comes in the morning (Ps. 30:5); those who sow in tears will reap in joy (Ps. 126:5).

d Weep with those who weep (Rom. 12:15); pretend to be a mourner (2 Sam. 14:2).

e Those who weep should live as if they did not (1 Cor. 7:30).

f Mourn and weep, you sinners (Jas. 4:9); wail, you rich, weep for the miseries that are coming (Jas. 5:1); those who laugh now will weep (Luke 6:25); weep for yourselves and your children (Luke 23:28).

● Tearing
clothes
in grief

g Those who tore their clothes in grief: Reuben (Gen. 37:29); Jacob (Gen. 37:34); Joseph's brothers (Gen. 44:13); Joshua and Caleb (Num. 14:6); Joshua (Josh. 7:6); Jephthah (Judg. 11:35); a man from Saul's camp (2 Sam. 1:2); David and his men (2 Sam. 1:11); Tamar (2 Sam. 13:19); David (2 Sam. 13:31); Hushai the Arkite (2 Sam. 15:32); Ahab (1 Kgs. 21:27); Eliakim, Shebra and Asaph (2 Kgs. 18:37; Isa. 36:22); Hezekiah (2 Kgs. 19:1; Isa. 37:1); Josiah (2 Kgs. 22:11; 2 Chr. 34:19); Ezra (Ezra 9:3); Mordecai (Esther 4:1); Job (Job 1:20); Job's comforters (Job 2:12); the high priest (Matt. 26:65); Barnabas and Paul (Acts 14:14).

h The leper must wear torn clothes (Lev. 13:45); a man ran with his clothes torn and dust on his head (1 Sam. 4:12); David commanded Joab and his people to tear their clothes and put on sackcloth (2 Sam. 3:31); you have torn your clothes and wept before me (2 Kgs. 22:19); because you tore your clothes and wept I have heard you (2 Chr. 34:27).

i The high priest must not tear his clothes (Lev. 10:6; 21:10); tear your heart and not your clothes (Joel 2:13).

Tearing clothes in anger, see **891*t***.

● Wearing
sackcloth

j Those who wore sackcloth: the king of Israel (2 Kgs. 6:30); David and the elders (1 Chr. 21:16); the Israelites (Neh. 9:1); Mordecai (Esther 4:1); Hezekiah (2 Kgs. 19:1; Isa. 37:1); Job (Job 16:15); Moab (Isa. 15:2–3); Daniel (Dan. 9:3).

k Put on sackcloth and mourn (2 Sam. 3:31; Isa. 22:12; Joel 1:13); put on sackcloth, lament and wail (Jer. 4:8); prophecy that sackcloth would be worn (Jer. 48:37; Ezek. 7:18); when they were sick, my clothing was sackcloth (Ps. 35:13–14).

● Ashes/dust
on head

l Tamar put ashes on her head (2 Sam. 13:19); as did Mordecai (Esther 4:1); Hushai the Arkite had dust on his head (2 Sam. 15:32); as did Job's comforters (Job 2:12); and the Israelites (Neh. 9:1); a man from the camp (1 Sam. 4:12; 2 Sam. 1:2).

● Weeping
through
emotion

m Those who wept on meeting; Jacob (Gen. 29:11); Esau and Jacob (Gen. 33:4); Saul (1 Sam. 24:16).

Emotion, see **818*e***.

n Joseph wept (Gen. 42:24; 43:30; 45:2, 14, 15; 46:29; 50:1, 17).

● Mourning after
a death

o Mourners go about the streets (Eccles. 12:5); the captive woman shall mourn her parents one month (Deut. 21:13).

p Mourning for a spouse: Abraham for Sarah (Gen. 23:2); Judah for his wife (Gen. 38:12); Bathsheba for Uriah (2 Sam. 11:26).

q Jacob mourned for Joseph (Gen. 37:34–5); Joseph mourned for Jacob (Gen. 50:1); as did the Egyptians (Gen. 50:3–4, 10–11); the Egyptians wailed over the firstborn (Exod. 11:6; 12:30); David's household mourned for Amnon (2 Sam. 13:36); David wept for Absalom (2 Sam. 18:33–19:1); Ephraim mourned for his sons (1 Chr. 7:22); they mourned over Jairus' daughter (Mark 5:38–9; Luke 8:52).

r Israel mourned for Aaron (Num. 20:29); and for Moses (Deut. 34:8); and for Samuel (1 Sam. 25:1); and for Abijam son of Jeroboam (1 Kgs. 14:13, 18); David mourned for Saul and Jonathan (2 Sam. 1:12); weep over Saul (2 Sam. 1:24); David wept for Abner (2 Sam. 3:32); the prophet mourned for the man of God from Judah (1 Kgs. 13:29–30); all Judah mourned Josiah (2 Chr. 35:24); they would mourn for Zedekiah (Jer. 34:5); the women mourned for Tammuz (Ezek. 8:14); Jesus wept for Lazarus (John 11:35); lamentation over Stephen (Acts 8:2).

s David made a lament for Saul and Jonathan (2 Sam. 1:17); as Jeremiah did for Josiah (2 Chr. 35:25); I would weep night and day for the slain of my people (Jer. 9:1); Rachel weeping for her children (Jer. 31:15; Matt. 2:18).

t The disciples mourned for Jesus (Mark 16:10); Mary wept outside the tomb (John 20:11); you will weep and lament (John 16:20).

u They mourned and wailed for Jesus (Luke 23:27); they beat their breasts (Luke 23:48); all nations will mourn (Matt. 24:30); they will look on him they have pierced and mourn for him (Zech. 12:10; Rev. 1:7).

● Mourning
over God

v The people mourned because God would not go with them (Exod. 33:4); they mourned because they could not go up (Num. 14:39; Deut. 1:45); Israel wept before the Lord when Benjamin beat them (Judg. 20:23, 26); they wept before the Lord because Benjamin was cut off (Judg. 21:2).

w The assembly wept over the worship of Baal of Peor (Num. 25:6); the people wept over the angel's rebuke (Judg. 2:4–5); the people of Israel mourned after the Lord (1 Sam. 7:2); the people wept bitterly (Ezra 10:1); Ezra was mourning over the unfaithfulness of the exiles (Ezra 10:6); the people wept when they heard the book of the law (Neh. 8:9); my eyes stream with tears because they do not keep your law (Ps. 119:136); I water my couch with tears (Ps. 6:6); Israel and Judah will go in tears to seek the Lord (Jer. 50:4); you weep because the Lord does not accept your sacrifices (Mal. 2:13).

x A mark on the foreheads of those who groan over the abominations (Ezek. 9:4).

y Christ prayed with loud crying and tears (Heb. 5:7).

● Mourning in regret

z The people wept for tasty food (Num. 11:4, 10); Samuel mourned over Saul (1 Sam. 15:35–16:1); David mourned over Absalom (2 Sam. 13:37); the king of Israel wept to see Elisha ill (2 Kgs. 13:14); there will be weeping and gnashing of teeth (Matt. 8:12); Peter wept after denying Jesus (Mark 14:72).

● Mourning catastrophe

aa The people wept over the fate of Gibeah (1 Sam. 11:4); Elisha wept over what Hazael would do (2 Kgs. 8:11–12); mourning when the Jews heard the edict (Esther 4:3); Haman covered his head and mourned (Esther 6:12).

ab Jephthah's daughter bewailed her virginity (Judg. 11:37–8); Samson's wife wept before him (Judg. 14:16, 17); Hezekiah wept because he was due to die (2 Kgs. 20:3); the people of Israel wept over their situation (Num. 14:1); wail, you shepherds, for your day of slaughter has come (Jer. 25:34); I will turn your festivals into mourning (Amos 8:10); there is wailing in the streets (Amos 5:16–17); mourning the plague of locusts (Joel 1:8–13).

● Mourning oppression

ac Why do I go mourning, oppressed by the enemy? (Ps. 42:9; 43:2); put my tears in your bottle (Ps. 56:8); you fed them with the bread of tears (Ps. 80:5); Ariel will lament and mourn (Isa. 29:2).

● Mourning parting

ad Naomi, Ruth and Orpah wept at parting (Ruth 1:9); David and Jonathan wept at parting (1 Sam. 20:41); Paltiel wept over his wife Michal (2 Sam. 3:16); the people wept over David's exile (2 Sam. 15:23); as did David (2 Sam. 15:30); mourn for him who goes into exile (Jer. 22:10); grieving that they would not see Paul again (Acts 20:37–8); why weep and break my heart? (Acts 21:13).

● Personal mourning

ae Esau wept on losing the blessing (Gen. 27:38); Hannah wept and would not eat (1 Sam. 1:7–8); Hannah wept before the Lord (1 Sam. 1:10); David and his men wept over their families (1 Sam. 30:4); mourn as for an only son (Jer. 6:26); Peter wept bitterly after his denial of Christ (Matt. 26:75; Luke 22:62); the woman wept and wet Jesus' feet with her tears (Luke 7:38); you should rather have mourned (1 Cor. 5:2).

af The baby was crying (Exod. 2:6).

● Mourning over Israel

ag Some wept when the foundation of the temple was laid (Ezra 3:12); Nehemiah mourned at the fate of Jerusalem (Neh. 1:4); Jesus wept over Jerusalem (Luke 19:41); call for the mourning women to wail Zion's disaster (Jer. 9:17–20); 80 men with beards shaved, clothes torn and bodies gashed (Jer. 41:5); Judah and Jerusalem mourn the drought (Jer. 14:2); we wept when we remembered Zion (Ps. 137:1); I must mourn for Judah (Mic. 1:8); a lamentation for the princes of Israel (Ezek. 19:1–14); a lament

for Israel (Amos 5:1–3); I had been mourning for three weeks (Dan. 10:2); Paul's grief over his kinsmen, the Israelites (Rom. 9:2–4).

- Mourning loss of trade

ah Mariners will weep over Tyre (Ezek. 26:17–18; 27:30–2); Egypt will be in enguish over Tyre's downfall (Isa. 23:5); lamentation over Tyre (Ezek. 27:2); lamentation over the king of Tyre (Ezek. 28:12–19); lamentation over Egypt (Ezek. 30:2–19); lamentaion over Pharaoh (Ezek. 32:2–16); wail, ships of Tarshish (Isa. 23:1, 14); they will weep over Babylon (Rev. 18:9, 11, 15, 19); the fishermen of the Nile will mourn (Isa. 19:8).

- Not mourning

ai I have not eaten the tithe whilst mourning (Deut. 26:14); do not enter a house of mourning or lament (Jer. 16:5); do not mourn when your wife dies (Ezek. 24:16); do not uncover your heads or tear your clothes (Lev. 10:6); do not mourn the dead (Jer. 22:10); they will not be lamented or buried (Jer. 16:4, 6); they will not lament for Jehoiakim (Jer. 22:18); their widows did not weep (Ps. 78:64); you will not mourn (Ezek. 24:23); we wailed and you did not mourn (Matt. 11:17; Luke 7:32); they have not grieved over the ruin of Joseph (Amos 6:6).

aj Those who mourn are lifted to safety (Job 5:11); you will weep no more (Isa. 30:19); to comfort all who mourn (Isa. 61:2–3); the voice of weeping will no more be heard in her (Isa. 65:19).

ak Can wedding guests mourn when the bridegroom is with them? (Matt. 9:15); do not weep (Luke 7:13); that you may not grieve like those without hope (1 Thess. 4:13); you have turned mourning into dancing (Ps. 30:11).

Weeping and gnashing of teeth, see **827c**.

837 Amusement

- Pleasure seeking

a Pleasure also proved to be futile (Eccles. 2:1); I did not refuse any pleasure (Eccles. 2:10); what does pleasure accomplish? (Eccles. 2:2); he who loves pleasure will become a poor man (Prov. 21:17).

Pleasures, see **826q**.

- Playing

b Sarah saw Ishmael playing (Gen. 21:9); boys and girls playing in the streets of Jerusalem (Zech. 8:5); they rose up to play (Exod. 32:6; 1 Cor. 10:7); let the young men make sport (2 Sam. 2:14); will you play with the crocodile as with a bird? (Job 41:5); doing wrong is like sport to a fool (Prov. 10:23); wisdom is like sport to a man of understanding (Prov. 10:23).

- Making fun

c Bring out Samson to amuse us (Judg. 16:25); lest these uncircumcised make fun of me (1 Sam. 31:4).

Joke, see **839**; **mocking**, see **851**.

838 Tedium

839 Wit

● Jokes

a Lot's sons-in-law thought he was joking (Gen. 19:14); a man who deceives as a joke is like a madman (Prov. 26:18–19).
Making fun, see **837c**.

● Dirty jokes

b Dirty jokes are not fitting (Eph. 5:4).

840 Dullness

841 Beauty

● Lovely things

a He has made everything beautiful in its time (Eccles. 3:11); whatever is lovely, think about it (Phil. 4:8).

b Trees pleasing to the sight (Gen. 2:9); the tree was a delight to the eyes (Gen. 3:6).

c Mount Zion is beautiful in elevation (Ps. 48:2); she became very beautiful (Ezek. 16:13–14); Zion, the perfection of beauty (Ps. 50:2); is this the city which was called the perfection of beauty? (Lam. 2:15).

d The temple was adorned with beautiful stones (Luke 21:5); garments for glory and beauty (Exod. 28:2, 40).

e Tyre, perfect in beauty (Ezek. 27:3–4, 11; 28:12); your heart was proud because of your beauty (Ezek. 28:17); Egypt, whom do you surpass in beauty? (Ezek. 32:19).

f Whitewashed tombs appear beautiful outwardly (Matt. 23:27).

● Lovely women

g When you see a beautiful woman among the captives (Deut. 21:11); a beautiful woman without discretion is like a gold ring in a pig's snout (Prov. 11:22); charm is deceitful, beauty is vain (Prov. 31:30).

h Beautiful women: Sarah (Gen. 12:11, 14); Rebekah (Gen. 24:16; 26:7); Rachel (Gen. 29:17); Abigail (1 Sam. 25:3); Bathsheba (2 Sam. 11:2); Tamar (2 Sam. 13:1); Absalom's daughter Tamar (2 Sam. 14:27); Abishag (1 Kgs. 1:4); Queen Vashti (Esther 1:11); Esther (Esther 2:7); Job's daughters (Job 42:15); the beloved (S. of S. 1:15; 4:1, 7; 6:4; 7:6).

i The sons of God saw that the daughters of men were beautiful (Gen. 6:2); your most beautiful wives and children are mine (1 Kgs. 20:3); a search was made for beautiful young virgins (Esther 2:2); is not her younger sister more beautiful? (Judg. 15:2); the king will desire your beauty (Ps. 45:11); most beautiful of women (S. of S. 1:8).

j Do not desire her beauty (Prov. 6:25).

● Handsome men

k Handsome men: Joseph (Gen. 39:6); Saul (1 Sam. 9:2); David (1 Sam. 16:12); Absalom (2 Sam. 14:25); Adonijah (1 Kgs. 1:6); the lover (S. of S. 5:10, 16).

l When she saw he was a fair child (Exod. 2:2); Moses was a beautiful child (Heb. 11:23); the king brought youths who were good-looking (Dan. 1:4); you are fairer than the sons of men (Ps. 45:2).

● God's beauty   *m* The Branch of the Lord will be beautiful and glorious (Isa. 4:2); the Lord will be a beautiful crown (Isa. 28:5); your eyes will see the King in his beauty (Isa. 33:17); to behold the beauty of the Lord (Ps. 27:4).

● Beauty of God's   *n* How beautiful are your tents, Jacob (Num. 24:5); how beautiful
people   are the feet of those who bring good news (Rom. 10:15).

842 Ugliness

843 Beautification

● Cosmetics   *a* The women had cosmetics given to them (Esther 2:3, 9, 12); Jezebel painted her eyes and adorned her head (2 Kgs. 9:30); you painted your eyes (Ezek. 23:40); though you enlarge your eyes with paint (Jer. 4:30); in vain you beautify yourself (Jer. 4:30). **Cosmetic anointing, see 357r.**

844 Ornamentation

● Provision of   *a* Abraham's servant took a gold ring and two gold bracelets (Gen.
jewellery   24:22, 47); and gold and silver jewellery (Gen. 24:53); Laban saw the ring and bracelets (Gen. 24:30); the crown contained a precious stone (2 Sam. 12:30; 1 Chr. 20:2); the Queen of Sheba brought precious stones (1 Kgs. 10:2, 10; 2 Chr. 9:1, 9); precious stones brought from Ophir (1 Kgs. 10:11; 2 Chr. 9:10); each one gave Job a gold ring (Job 42:11); we will make you ornaments of gold (S. of S. 1:11); I will lay your stones in antimony and sapphires (Isa. 54:11–12); I adorned you with ornaments (Ezek. 16:11–13); whoever reads the writing will have a chain of gold for his neck (Dan. 5:7, 16); Daniel was given a chain of gold (Dan. 5:29); wisdom will put a garland on your head (Prov. 4:9).

b Do not cast pearls before swine (Matt. 7:6).

● Wearing   *c* Saul put gold ornaments on you (2 Sam. 1:24); your cheeks are
jewellery   lovely with ornaments (S. of S. 1:10); as a bride adorns herself with jewels (Isa. 61:10); though you deck yourself with ornaments of gold (Jer. 4:30); every precious stone was your covering (Ezek. 28:13); the great harlot was adorned with jewels (Rev. 17:4; 18:16).

d Aaron used their gold ear-rings to make the calf (Exod. 32:2); Gideon used gold ear-rings to make an ephod (Judg. 8:24–7); Gideon took the ornaments off the camels (Judg. 8:21).

e Can a maid forget her ornaments? (Jer. 2:32).

● Removing   *f* Jacob buried the ear-rings (Gen. 35:4); the Israelites took off
jewellery   their ornaments at Mount Horeb (Exod. 33:4–6); the Lord will take away all their finery (Isa. 3:18–23).

● Jewellery   *g* They brought gold jewellery to the Lord as an offering (Exod.
and God   35:22); jewellery from the war as an offering (Num. 31:50–4); onyx stones and stones for setting (Exod. 25:7; 35:9, 27).

h The names of the sons of Israel were engraved on precious stones

(Exod. 28:9–12, 17–21; 39:6–7, 10–14); his people are as the jewels of a crown (Zech. 9:16).

i A pavement of sapphire (Exod. 24:10); the one on the throne was like a jasper and a sardius (Rev. 4:3); a rainbow like an emerald (Rev. 4:3).

j Precious stones given for the temple (1 Chr. 29:8); the temple adorned with precious stones (2 Chr. 3:6); the new Jerusalem shone like a precious stone (Rev. 21:11); the foundations were adorned with precious stones (Rev. 21:19–20).

k Parable of the pearl of great price (Matt. 13:45–6); the gates were 12 pearls (Rev. 21:21).

● Embroidery

l Embroidered dyed material as spoil (Judg. 5:30); cherubim embroidered on the veil (2 Chr. 3:14).

● Internal adornment

m Your adornment should not be external but internal (1 Pet. 3:3–4); women should not adorn themselves with gold or pearls (1 Tim. 2:9); wisdom is more precious than jewels (Prov. 3:15; 8:11); a wise reprover is like a gold ornament (Prov. 25:12).

n They should adorn the doctrine (Titus 2:10).

845 Blemish
Defect, see **647**.

846 Good taste

847 Bad taste

848 Fashion. Etiquette
Tradition, see **127***c*.

849 Ridiculousness

850 Affectation

851 Ridicule

● Mocking people

a He who mocks the poor insults his Maker (Prov. 17:5); fools mock at guilt (Prov. 14:9); the eye that mocks parents will be plucked out (Prov. 30:17).

b Ishmael mocked Isaac (Gen. 21:9); lest we become a laughing-stock (Gen. 38:23); the people of Ephraim mocked the couriers from Judah (2 Chr. 30:10); they mocked God's messengers (2 Chr. 36:16); our enemies mocked us (Neh. 2:19); Sanballat mocked the Jews (Neh. 4:1); the Chaldeans scoff at kings (Hab. 1:10); we are mocked by those around us (Ps. 79:4); our enemies laugh among themselves (Ps. 80:6); those near and far will mock you (Ezek. 22:5).

c Elijah mocked the prophets of Baal (1 Kgs. 18:27); youths mocked Elisha (2 Kgs. 2:23); the virgin daughter of Zion has mocked you (2 Kgs. 19:21); Wisdom will laugh at your calamity (Prov. 1:26); the righteous will laugh at him (Ps. 52:6).

d Those younger than I mock me (Job 30:1); all who see me mock me (Ps. 22:7); everyone mocks me (Jer. 20:7); mockers are with me (Job 17:2); I have become a laughingstock to all the people (Lam. 3:14); I am a joke to my friends (Job 12:4).

e In the last days there will be scoffers (2 Pet. 3:3; Jude 18); happy the man who does not sit in the seat of scoffers (Ps. 1:1); they mocked at Pentecost (Acts 2:13); some were mocked and scourged (Heb. 11:36).

Making fun, see **837c**.

● Mocking
Jesus

f When Jesus said the girl was not dead they laughed at him (Matt. 9:24; Mark 5:40; Luke 8:53); they will mock the Son of Man (Matt. 20:19; Mark 10:34; Luke 18:32); they ridiculed and mocked him (Matt. 27:29, 31; Mark 15:20; Luke 22:63); the chief priests mocked him (Matt. 27:41; Mark 15:31); the soldiers mocked him (Luke 23:11, 36); the Pharisees scoffed at him (Luke 16:14).

g When they heard of the resurrection, some mocked (Acts 17:32).

● Mocking
and God

h God is not mocked (Gal. 6:7); the Lord laughs at the wicked (Ps. 2:4; 37:13; 59:8); he scoffs at the scoffers (Prov. 3:35).

Despise, see **922**.

852 Hope

● Concerning
hope

a Love hopes all things (1 Cor. 13:7); faith, hope and love remain (1 Cor. 13:13); hope that is seen is not hope (Rom. 8:24–5); hope deferred makes the heart sick (Prov. 13:12); character produces hope (Rom. 5:4).

● The hope
of Israel

b Israel, hope in the Lord (Ps. 130:7; 131:3); for the hope of Israel I am chained (Acts 28:20); the valley of Achor will be a door of hope (Hos. 2:15).

● Hope in
Christ

c Christ in you, the hope of glory (Col. 1:27); Christ Jesus, our hope (1 Tim. 1:1).

d Be joyful in hope (Rom. 12:12); the God of hope fill you with joy and peace so that you may overflow with hope (Rom. 15:13); that you might know what is the hope of his calling (Eph. 1:18); by faith we wait for the hope of righteousness (Gal. 5:5); this hope is an anchor of the soul (Heb. 6:19); in his name will the Gentiles hope (Matt. 12:21); the hope laid up for you in heaven (Col. 1:5); your steadfastness of hope (1 Thess. 1:3); looking for the blessed hope (Titus 2:13); a better hope through which we draw near to God (Heb. 7:19).

e If for this life only we have hope, we are pitiable (1 Cor. 15:19).

853 Hopelessness

● Despairing

a I despaired of the fruit of my toil (Eccles. 2:20); we despaired of life itself (2 Cor. 1:8); perplexed but not despairing (2 Cor. 4:8).

- Without
  hope

b That you may not grieve like others without hope (1 Thess. 4:13); you were without hope (Eph. 2:12).

854 Fear

- Fear God!

a Fear God (Eccles. 5:7; 12:13; 1 Pet. 2:17; Rev. 14:7); fear the Lord (Deut. 6:13, 24; 10:12, 20; 13:4; 31:12–13; Josh. 4:24; 24:14; 1 Sam. 12:14, 24; 2 Kgs. 17:36, 39; Ps. 34:9; Prov. 3:7; 24:21); stand in awe of the Lord (2 Chr. 19:7); act in the fear of the Lord (2 Chr. 19:9); serve the Lord with fear (Ps. 2:11); the Lord is the one you are to fear (Isa. 8:13); fear him who can destroy body and soul in hell (Matt. 10:28; Luke 12:5); who will not fear you, O Lord? (Rev. 15:4); tremble before him, all the earth (1 Chr. 16:30; Ps. 114:7); let all the earth fear the Lord (Ps. 33:8); let all the ends of the earth fear him (Ps. 67:7); God is feared in the council of the holy ones (Ps. 89:7); oh, that they would fear me! (Deut. 5:29); work out your salvation with fear and trembling (Phil. 2:12); live in the fear of the Lord always (Prov. 23:17); walk in the fear of God (Neh. 5:9); do you not fear me? (Jer. 5:22); since you call on an impartial Father, live your lives in fear (1 Pet. 1:17); let us fear lest any fail to enter his rest (Heb. 4:1); fear, lest God not spare you (Rom. 11:20–1).

- God is to be
  feared

b The Lord is an awesome God (Deut. 7:21; 10:17); the Lord is to be feared (Ps. 47:2); he is to be feared above all gods (1 Chr. 16:25; Ps. 96:4); who would not fear you? (Jer. 10:7); the Fear of his father Isaac (Gen. 31:53); he is feared by the kings of the earth (Ps. 76:12); it is a terrifying thing to fall into the hands of the living God (Heb. 10:31); I am going to do a fearful thing (Exod. 34:10).

- The fear of
  the Lord

c The fear of the Lord is wisdom (Job 28:28); the fear of the Lord is the beginning of wisdom (Ps. 111:10; Prov. 9:10); the fear of the Lord teaches one wisdom (Prov. 15:33); the fear of the Lord is the beginning of knowledge (Prov. 1:7).

d The fear of the Lord lengthens life (Prov. 10:27); the fear of the Lord is a fountain of life (Prov. 14:27); the fear of the Lord leads to life (Prov. 19:23); the fear of the Lord is his treasure (Isa. 33:6); in the fear of the Lord there is security (Prov. 14:26); to fear the Lord is to hate evil (Prov. 8:13); the fear of the Lord will keep you from sinning (Exod. 20:20); he who walks in uprightness fears the Lord (Prov. 14:2).

- Fearing God

e Blessed are those who fear the Lord (Ps. 112:1; 128:1, 4); the one who fears God is acceptable to him (Acts 10:35); now I know that you fear God (Gen. 22:12); I fear God (Gen. 42:18); the midwives feared God (Exod. 1:17, 21); Obadiah feared the Lord (1 Kgs. 18:3); men who fear God (Exod. 18:21); the people feared the Lord and Samuel (1 Sam. 12:18); that they may fear you (1 Kgs. 8:40; 2 Chr. 6:31); that all peoples may fear you (1 Kgs. 8:43); everyone who trembled at the word of the God of

Israel (Ezra 9:4); my heart stands in awe at your word (Ps. 119:161); servants of Pharaoh who feared the word of the Lord (Exod. 9:20); the church went on in the fear of the Lord (Acts 9:31).

f Those who feared God: Nehemiah (Neh. 5:15); Hanani (Neh. 7:2); Job (Job 1:1, 8; 2:3); Cornelius (Acts 10:2).

g I will put the fear of me in their hearts (Jer. 32:40); men fear God (Job 37:24); then all men will fear (Ps. 64:9); they will fear the Lord from west to east (Isa. 59:19).

● Results of the fear of God

h A woman who fears the Lord is to be praised (Prov. 31:30); those who feared the Lord talked with one another (Mal. 3:16); knowing the fear of the Lord, we persuade men (2 Cor. 5:11); fear fell on all and the name of the Lord Jesus was magnified (Acts 19:17).

i His salvation is near to those who fear him (Ps. 85:9); he will bless those who fear him (Ps. 115:13); by the fear of the Lord a man avoids evil (Prov. 16:6); your word is for the fear of you (Ps. 119:38); God will instruct the one who fears him (Ps. 25:12); there is forgiveness that you may be feared (Ps. 130:4); it will be well for those who fear God (Eccles. 8:12); his mercy is on those who fear him (Luke 1:50); he will delight in the fear of the Lord (Isa. 11:3); does Job fear God for nothing? (Job 1:9).

● Frightened of God

j Adam was afraid because he was naked (Gen. 3:10); Sarah was afraid because she had laughed (Gen. 18:15); how awesome is this place! (Gen. 28:17); my flesh creeps for fear of you (Ps. 119:120); the terrors of God are arrayed against me (Job 6:4); will not his majesty terrify you? (Job 13:11); at the day of the Lord men will be terrified (Isa. 13:6–8); God will terrify them by his anger (Ps. 2:5); Assyria will be terrified at the voice of the Lord (Isa. 30:31); before the terror of the Lord (Isa. 2:19, 21); do not be a terror to me (Jer. 17:17); stop terrifying me with your dread (Job 13:21).

k Terror and darkness fell on Abraham (Gen. 15:12); the terror of God fell on the towns round about (Gen. 35:5; 2 Chr. 14:14); the terror of the Lord fell on the people (1 Sam. 11:7); the fear of the Lord fell on the kingdoms around (2 Chr. 17:10; 20:29); the peoples tremble (Exod. 15:14–16); I will send my terror ahead of you (Exod. 23:27); fear came on all nearby (Luke 1:65).

l Moses was afraid to look at God (Exod. 3:6); the people feared the Lord (Exod. 14:31); the people were afraid at Mount Sinai (Exod. 19:16; 20:18; Deut. 5:5); Moses was full of fear and trembling (Heb. 12:21); the Philistines were afraid (1 Sam. 4:7); David was afraid of the Lord that day (2 Sam. 6:9; 1 Chr. 13:12); the kings were panic-stricken (Ps. 48:5–6); the sailors feared the Lord (Jonah 1:16); the shepherds were frightened (Luke 2:9); the ends of the earth tremble (Isa. 41:5); Herod was troubled at the news of Christ's birth (Matt. 2:3); Felix was afraid (Acts 24:25); fear when Ananias and Sapphira died (Acts 5:5, 11).

● Afraid of
angels

m David was terrified by the sword of the angel of the Lord (1 Chr. 21:30); Zecharias was afraid when he saw the angel (Luke 1:12); the guards were afraid of the angel of the Lord (Matt. 28:4); the women were afraid seeing angels at the resurrection (Matt. 28:8; Mark 16:8).

● Fearing
God's word

n I will look to the one who trembles at my word (Isa. 66:2); you who tremble at my word (Isa. 66:5); the king was not afraid of the scroll (Jer. 36:24).

● Fear of
Jesus

o The chief priests were afraid of Jesus (Mark 11:18); they were afraid when the widow's son was raised (Luke 7:16); they were afraid when they saw the demoniac healed (Mark 5:15; Luke 8:35, 37); they were afraid when they saw the paralytic walking (Luke 5:26); the woman who was healed was afraid (Mark 5:33); Pilate was the more afraid (John 19:8).

p The disciples were afraid: to ask (Luke 9:45); when Jesus stilled the wind and sea (Mark 4:41); at the transfiguration (Matt. 17:6; Mark 9:6); when Jesus appeared (Luke 24:37); seeing Jesus walking on the lake (Matt. 14:26; Mark 6:50; John 6:19).

● No fear
of God

q There is no fear of God here (Gen. 20:11); Amalek did not fear God (Deut. 25:18); there is no fear of God before their eyes (Ps. 36:1; Rom. 3:18); they do not fear God (Ps. 55:19); you still do not fear the Lord (Exod. 9:30); they did not choose the fear of the Lord (Prov. 1:29); you do away with the fear of God (Job 15:4); do you not fear God? (Luke 23:40); there was a judge who did not fear God (Luke 18:2, 4).

● Fear of the
consequences

r Among the nations the Lord will give you a trembling heart (Deut. 28:65); what I fear befalls me (Job 3:25); what the wicked fears will come on him (Prov. 10:24); I will appoint terror for you (Lev. 26:16); they will eat their food in anxiety (Ezek. 12:19); all Israel will hear and will be afraid (Deut. 13:11); men are afraid of terrors in the way (Eccles. 12:5); Passhur renamed Terror on every side (Jer. 20:3); terror on every side (Ps. 31:13; Jer. 46:5; 49:29; Lam. 2:22).

s The fear of death (Heb. 2:15); Saul was afraid because of Samuel's words (1 Sam. 28:20); Elijah was afraid for his life (1 Kgs. 19:3); Moses was afraid (Exod. 2:14); we are afraid here in Judah (1 Sam. 23:3).

t Jether was afraid to fall on Zebah and Zalmunna (Judg. 8:20); Saul's armour bearer was afraid to kill him (1 Sam. 31:4; 1 Chr. 10:4).

u Men will faint with fear (Luke 21:26); Isaac trembled violently (Gen. 27:33); the Benjaminites were terrified by the impending disaster (Judg. 20:41); Eli feared for the ark (1 Sam. 4:13); the people feared the oath (1 Sam. 14:26); Adonijah's guests were terrified (1 Kgs. 1:49); the disciples were afraid when Jesus was going to Jerusalem (Mark 10:32); Peter was afraid when he saw the wind (Matt. 14:30); the soldiers were afraid at the crucifixion (Matt. 27:54); the commander was afraid because he had bound a Roman citizen (Acts 22:29); fear fell on those who saw the witnesses come to life (Rev. 11:11); conflicts without and fears within (2 Cor. 7:5); I was with you in weakness and fear (1 Cor. 2:3).

v He who does evil has reason to fear (Rom. 13:3–4); when I am afraid I will put my trust in you (Ps. 56:3).

Fear of death, see **361l**.

● Fearing God's people

w The beasts of the earth would fear Noah's descendants (Gen. 9:2).

x Abimelech's men were very frightened (Gen. 20:8); the Egyptians were in dread of the Israelites (Exod. 1:12; Ps. 105:38); the sons of Esau will fear you (Deut. 2:4); all nations would fear them (Deut. 2:25; 11:25; 28:10); a fear of you has fallen on us (Josh. 2:9); we feared for our lives (Josh. 9:24); Adonizedek was afraid (Josh. 10:2); Moab was terrified (Num. 22:3); the fear of David fell on all lands (1 Chr. 14:17); fear of the Jews fell on them (Esther 8:17; 9:2); the land of Judah will be a terror to Egypt (Isa. 19:17).

● Fear of enemies

y The Israelites were afraid of the Philistines (1 Sam. 7:7; 13:7); of Goliath (1 Sam. 17:11, 24); David was afraid of Achish (1 Sam. 21:12); Saul was afraid of the Philistine army (1 Sam. 28:5); even the lion-hearted will fear (2 Sam. 17:10); they were afraid of the Chaldeans (Jer. 41:18); the Assyrians used the language of Judah to frighten them (2 Chr. 32:18); they were afraid of the Chaldeans (2 Kgs. 25:26); Jehoshaphat was afraid (2 Chr. 20:3).

z Whoever is afraid may go home (Deut. 20:8; Judg. 7:3); if you are afraid to attack, go down into the camp (Judg. 7:10); the people of the land made the men of Judah afraid (Ezra 4:4); they were terrified of the people of the land (Ezra 3:3); he was hired so that I might be frightened (Neh. 6:13); they were trying to frighten us (Neh. 6:9, 13, 14); Tobiah sent letters to frighten me (Neh. 6:19).

aa The disciples were afraid of Paul (Acts 9:26); Peter was afraid of the circumcision party (Gal. 2:12).

ab No one spoke openly for fear of the Jews (John 7:13); his parents were afraid of the Jews (John 9:22); a secret disciple for fear of the Jews (John 19:38); doors locked for fear of the Jews (John 20:19).

● Fear of men

ac The fear of man brings a snare (Prov. 29:25); who are you to be afraid of mortal man? (Isa. 51:12); render fear to those to whom fear is due (Rom. 13:7).

ad Isaac was afraid to admit that Rebekah was his wife (Gen. 26:7); the Israelites were afraid of the Egyptians (Exod. 14:10); Gideon was afraid of his family (Judg. 6:27); Saul was afraid of the people (1 Sam. 15:24); as was Herod (Matt. 14:5); Joseph was afraid to settle in Judea (Matt. 2:22); I fear the Jews who have deserted (Jer. 38:19); the Jews feared the people, who said John was a prophet (Matt. 21:26; Mark 11:32); they wanted to arrest Jesus but were afraid of the people (Matt. 21:46; Mark 12:12; Luke 20:19; 22:2); they brought the apostles out without force because they feared the people (Acts 5:26); they were afraid when they heard that they were Romans (Acts 16:38).

● Fear of an individual

ae Jacob was afraid of Laban (Gen. 31:31); Jacob was afraid of Esau (Gen. 32:7, 11); Joseph's brothers were afraid of him (Gen. 42:28, 35; 43:18; 45:3); the Israelites were afraid to come near Moses (Exod. 34:30); Samuel was afraid to tell Eli (1 Sam. 3:15); people feared the Lord and Samuel (1 Sam. 12:18); the elders trembled before Samuel (1 Sam. 16:4); Saul was afraid of David (1 Sam. 18:12, 29); Ishbosheth was afraid of Abner (2 Sam. 3:11); they were afraid to tell David the child was dead (2 Sam. 12:18); when Israel heard the judgement they feared the king (1 Kgs. 3:28); Haman was terrified before the king and queen (Esther 7:6); the people were afraid of Mordecai (Esther 9:3); Herod feared John (Mark 6:20).

● Do not fear men

af Do not be afraid of any man (Deut. 1:17); do not be scared by your opponents (Phil. 1:28); do not be afraid of the people of the land (Num. 14:9; Deut. 1:29; 3:22; 7:18, 21; 31:6; Josh. 10:8; 11:6); do not be afraid of Og (Num. 21:34; Deut. 3:2); do not be afraid of the Chaldeans (2 Kgs. 25:24); do not be afraid of fellow Israelites (2 Kgs. 1:15; Jer. 1:8; Ezek. 2:6; 3:9); do not be afraid of your enemies (Deut. 20:1, 3; 2 Chr. 20:15, 17; Neh. 4:14; Matt. 10:26); do not fear those who kill the body (Matt. 10:28; Luke 12:4).

ag Jael told Sisera not to be afraid (Judg. 4:18); Saul told the witch not to be afraid (1 Sam. 28:13); do not be afraid [of Saul] (1 Sam. 22:23; 23:17).

● Do not fear

ah Do not be afraid (Gen. 35:17; 43:23; 50:19, 21; 1 Sam. 4:20; 12:20; 2 Sam. 9:7; Isa. 7:4; 40:9; 44:2; Jer. 30:10; Lam. 3:57; Dan. 10:12, 19; Zeph. 3:16; Matt. 17:7; 24:6; 28:5, 10; Luke 1:13, 30; 2:10; 5:10; 12:32; John 14:27; Rev. 1:17); do not fear what they fear (Isa. 8:12; 1 Pet. 3:14); do not fear signs in the heavens (Jer. 10:2); do not fear when you hear of wars (Mark 13:7); do not fear what you will soon suffer (Rev. 2:10); do not be afraid or dismayed (Deut. 1:21; 31:8; Josh. 1:9; 8:1; 10:25; 1 Chr. 28:20); do not be afraid of what you have heard (2 Kgs. 19:6; Isa. 37:6).

ai Do not fear because God will undertake (Gen. 15:1; 21:17; 46:3; Exod. 14:15; 20:20; Judg. 6:23; 2 Kgs. 6:16; 2 Chr. 32:7; Prov. 3:25–6; Acts 27:24); do not be afraid for I am with you (Gen. 26:24; Isa. 41:10; 43:5; Jer. 42:11; 46:28; Acts 18:9–10); for I will help you (Isa. 41:14); for I have redeemed you (Isa. 43:1); for your God will come (Isa. 35:4); do not be afraid for you will not be ashamed (Isa. 54:4); for I will save you (Jer. 46:27); it is I, do not be afraid (Matt. 14:27; Mark 6:50; John 6:20); do not be afraid, only believe (Mark 5:36; Luke 8:50).

Anxiety, see **825v**.

855 Courage

● Boldness

a Be strong and courageous (Deut. 31:6, 7, 23; Josh. 1:6, 9, 18; 10:25; 2 Sam. 10:12; 13:28; 1 Chr. 22:13; 2 Chr. 32:7); be strong and brave (2 Sam. 2:7); be strong and take courage (Ps. 31:24); be of good courage and act (Ezra 10:4); be men, Philistines (1 Sam. 4:9); let us not lose heart (Gal. 6:9); do not lose heart at my tribulations (Eph. 3:13).

b The righteous are bold as a lion (Prov. 28:1); he will not fear bad news (Ps. 112:7); we do not lose heart (2 Cor. 4:1, 16); they spoke the word of God boldly (Acts 4:31).

● Encouraging

c God gives encouragement (Rom. 15:5); the Lord caused the king of Assyria to encourage them (Ezra 6:22).

d Jonathan strengthened David's hand in God (1 Sam. 23:16); Hezekiah spoke encouragingly to the Levites (2 Chr. 30:22); Hezekiah encouraged the officers (2 Chr. 32:6–7); Barnabas encouraged them to go on (Acts 11:23); they encouraged the disciples (Acts 14:22; 15:32).

e Encourage Joshua (Deut. 3:28); encourage Joab (2 Sam. 11:25); encourage one another (1 Thess. 5:11); daily (Heb. 3:13); encourage and reprove with all authority (Titus 2:15); the brethren have been encouraged to speak the word (Phil. 1:14).

f Take courage, my son! (Matt. 9:2); take courage, my daughter! (Matt. 9:22); be of good courage, for I believe God (Acts 27:25); when Paul saw the believers he took courage (Acts 28:15); Barnabas—'son of encouragement' (Acts 4:36); if there is any encouragement in Christ (Phil. 2:1).

g You encouraged the wicked (Ezek. 13:22); they encourage one another in making idols (Isa. 41:6–7).

● I will not fear

h I will not be afraid (Ps. 56:4, 11; Heb. 13:6); I will trust and not be afraid (Isa. 12:2); I will not be afraid of tens of thousands (Ps. 3:6); I will fear no evil (Ps. 23:4); you will not fear the terror by night (Ps. 91:5); the Lord is my light, whom shall I fear? (Ps. 27:1); God has not given us a spirit of timidity (2 Tim. 1:7); we have not received a spirit of bondage to fear (Rom. 8:15); perfect love casts out fear (1 John 4:18); he delivered me from all my fears (Ps. 34:4).

i You will not be afraid (Prov. 3:24); you will not be afraid of arrow or pestilence (Ps. 91:5–6).

j We are not those who shrink back (Heb. 10:38–9); we will not fear though the earth change (Ps. 46:2).

Do not fear, see **854***ah*.

856 Cowardice

• Cowards

a Cowards will go to the lake of fire (Rev. 21:8); why are you cowardly, men of little faith? (Matt. 8:26).

b No one dared join them (Acts 5:13).

• Losing courage

c The hearts of the kings melted (Josh. 5:1); our hearts melted (Josh. 2:11); the hearts of the Israelites melted (Josh. 7:5; 14:8); Ish-Bosheth lost courage (2 Sam. 4:1).

857 Rashness

• Do not be rash

a Men will be reckless (2 Tim. 3:4); there is more hope for a fool than for one hasty in his words (Prov. 29:20); every one who is hasty comes to poverty (Prov. 21:5); do not be hasty in word before God (Eccles. 5:2); do not lay hands on anyone hastily (1 Tim. 5:22).

• Rash action

b They became impatient (Num. 21:4); Moses spoke rashly (Ps. 106:33); is the Spirit of the Lord impatient? (Mic. 2:7).

858 Caution

See **457**.

859 Desire

• Desire for God

a My soul thirsts for God (Ps. 42:2; 63:1; 143:6); my soul yearns for the courts of the Lord (Ps. 84:2); at night my soul longs for you (Isa. 26:9); there is nothing on earth that I desire but you (Ps. 73:25); your name and your memory are our desire (Isa. 26:8); many desired to see and hear what you do (Matt. 13:17; Luke 10:24).

• Desire for God's word

b I long for your: ordinances (Ps. 119:20); precepts (Ps. 119:40); commandments (Ps. 119:131); salvation (Ps. 119:174).

• Desires satisfied in God

c The Lord will fulfil all my desires (2 Sam. 23:5); he will give you the desires of your heart (Ps. 37:4); may he grant your heart's desire! (Ps. 20:4); you have given him his heart's desire (Ps. 21:2); the desire of the righteous will be granted (Prov. 10:24); the desire of the righteous ends in good (Prov. 11:23).

d Come, every one who thirsts (Isa. 55:1); if any one thirsts, let him come to me and drink (John 7:37); to him who thirsts I will give the water of life without cost (Rev. 21:6); whoever is thirsty, let him come (Rev. 22:17); whoever drinks the water I give will never thirst again (John 4:14); give me this water so I will not be thirsty (John 4:15).

e Blessed are those who hunger and thirst for righteousness (Matt. 5:6); blessed are you who hunger now, for you will be filled (Luke 6:21); he who comes to me will not hunger or thirst (John 6:35); he has filled the hungry with good things (Luke 1:53);

those who were hungry cease to hunger (1 Sam. 2:5); earnestly desire spiritual gifts (1 Cor. 12:31; 14:1).

f What do you want me to do for you? (Matt. 20:32; Luke 18:41); do you want to be healed? (John 5:6).

- Physical hunger

g If I were hungry I would not tell you (Ps. 50:12); I was hungry (Matt. 25:35, 42); when did we see you hungry? (Matt. 25:37, 44).

h A man's appetite is not satisfied (Eccles. 6:7); a worker's appetite works for him (Prov. 16:26); these men serve their own appetites (Rom. 16:18); an idle man will suffer hunger (Prov. 19:15); those who are full now will be hungry (Luke 6:25); like hungry and thirsty men unsatisfied by dreams (Isa. 29:8); do not desire the ruler's delicacies (Prov. 23:3).

i If they were disobedient they would know hunger and thirst (Deut. 28:48); descendants of the wicked will go hungry (Job 27:14); God caused you to hunger (Deut. 8:3); when they are hungry they will curse the king and their God (Isa. 8:21); if your enemy is hungry, give him food (Prov. 25:21; Rom. 12:20).

j The Lord will not let the righteous go hungry (Prov. 10:3); we apostles hunger and thirst (1 Cor. 4:11); we commend ourselves in hunger (2 Cor. 6:5); one is hungry and another is drunk (1 Cor. 11:21); if anyone is hungry let him eat at home (1 Cor. 11:34).

- Hungry people

k Esau was famished (Gen. 25:29–30); the people were hungry and thirsty in the wilderness (2 Sam. 17:29); they were hungry and thirsty (Ps. 107:5); what David did when he was hungry (Matt. 12:3; Mark 2:25; Luke 6:3); after Jesus fasted he was hungry (Matt. 4:2; Luke 4:2); on his way to Jerusalem he was hungry (Matt. 21:18; Mark 11:12); Jesus did not want to send the crowd home hungry (Matt. 15:32; Mark 8:3); Paul had known hunger and thirst (2 Cor. 11:27); David longed for water (1 Chr. 11:17); Peter was hungry (Acts 10:10).

- Physical thirst

l The people were thirsty (Exod. 17:3); they are parched with thirst (Isa. 5:13); Sisera was thirsty (Judg. 4:19); Samson was thirsty (Judg. 15:18); when you are thirsty, drink from the water jars (Ruth 2:9); David longed for water from the well at Bethlehem (2 Sam. 23:15; 1 Chr. 11:17); if your enemy is thirsty give him a drink (Prov. 25:21; Rom. 12:20); the baby's tongue cleaves to the roof of its mouth with thirst (Lam. 4:4); as the deer longs for water (Ps. 42:1); whoever drinks this water will thirst again (John 4:13).

m Jesus was thirsty (John 19:28); I was thirsty (Matt. 25:35, 42); when did we see you thirsty? (Matt. 25:37, 44).

Drought, see **342**.

- Sexual desire

n Woman's desire will be for her husband (Gen. 3:16); I am my beloved's and his desire is for me (S. of S. 7:10).

o You burn with lust under every green tree (Isa. 57:5); you are like a wild donkey in heat (Jer. 2:24); like well-fed lusty stallions

(Jer. 5:8); Oholah lusted after her lovers (Ezek. 23:5, 7, 9, 12, 16, 20); he who looks at a woman lustfully has committed adultery (Matt. 5:28); I made a covenant with my eyes, so how could I look at a maid? (Job 31:1); not in the lusts of passion like the Gentiles (1 Thess. 4:5); younger widows feel sensual desires (1 Tim. 5:11); better to marry than to burn (1 Cor. 7:9).

p Potiphar's wife desired Joseph (Gen. 39:7); Amnon desired Tamar (2 Sam. 13:1, 4, 15); men burning with passion for men (Rom. 1:27).

- Greed

q Greed, which is idolatry (Col. 3:5); his greed is wide as Sheol (Hab. 2:5); greed should not even be named (Eph. 5:3); consider your members dead to greed (Col. 3:5); gentiles practice impurity with greed (Eph. 4:19); filled with greed (Rom. 1:29).

r The rabble were greedy for food (Num. 11:4); their god is the belly (Phil. 3:19); Kibroth-hattaavah—graves of greed (Num. 11:34); they had a craving in the wilderness (Ps. 106:14); why look with greedy eye at the sacrifices? (1 Sam. 2:29).

s Fleshly lusts war against the soul (1 Pet. 2:11); the corruption that is in the world through lust (2 Pet. 1:4).

t We never came with a pretext for greed (1 Thess. 2:5); those who are Christ's have crucified the flesh with its passions and desires (Gal. 5:24).

u We formerly followed the lusts of our flesh (Eph. 2:3); the lust of the flesh and the lust of the eyes (1 John 2:16); the world and its lust is passing away (1 John 2:17).

- Insatiable

v Sheol and Abaddon are never satisfied, nor a man's eyes (Prov. 27:20); Sheol, the barren womb, earth and fire are never satisfied (Prov. 30:15–16).

- Coveting

w Do not covet (Exod. 20:17; Deut. 5:21; Rom. 7:7; 13:9); do not covet things under the ban (Josh. 6:18); beware of all covetousness (Luke 12:15); from the heart come covetings (Mark 7:22); sin produced in me all kinds of coveting (Rom. 7:8); they covet fields and seize them (Mic. 2:2).

x The covetous will not inherit the kingdom (1 Cor. 6:10; Eph. 5:5); do not associate with a 'brother' who is covetous (1 Cor. 5:11); Achan coveted things (Josh. 7:21).

y I have not coveted any one's silver, gold or clothes (Acts 20:33); no one will covet your land when you go to the feast (Exod. 34:24).

- Evil desires

z One is tempted when enticed by his own desire (Jas. 1:14); we should not lust for evil things as they did (1 Cor. 10:6); whatever my eyes desired I did not refuse them (Eccles. 2:10); you desire and do not have (Jas. 4:2); sinful desires were awakened by the law (Rom. 7:5); they entice by fleshly desires (2 Pet. 2:18); flee youthful passions (2 Tim. 2:22).

aa Sin's desire is for you (Gen. 4:7).

- Right desires

ab I have earnestly desired to eat this passover with you (Luke

22:15); I have longed to come to you (Rom. 15:23); we eagerly desired to see you (1 Thess. 2:17); I long to see you (Rom. 1:11; 2 Tim. 1:4); longing to see us as we long to see you (1 Thess. 3:6).

ac What do you want me to do for you? (Matt. 20:21, 32; Mark 10:36, 51); my heart's desire for Israel is that they be saved (Rom. 10:1).

ad Every one whose heart moves him is to contribute (Exod. 25:2). **Satisfying desires**, see **635g**.

860 Indifference

● Unconcerned   *a* They will not care about us (2 Sam. 18:3); do you not care if we perish? (Mark 4:38); Gallio was not concerned (Acts 18:17); what is that to us? (Matt. 27:4).

b Do not take it to heart (2 Sam. 13:20).

● Lukewarm   *c* You are lukewarm, neither cold nor hot (Rev. 3:15–16).

861 Dislike
See **888**.

862 Fastidiousness
Discrimination, see **463**.

863 Satiety
See **637**.

864 Wonder

● God performs   *a* Who is like God, working wonders? (Exod. 15:11); God does
miracles   countless wonders (Job 5:9); he performs signs and wonders (Dan. 6:27); I will show you miracles (Mic. 7:15); consider the wonders of God (Job 37:14); remember the marvels he has done (1 Chr. 16:12); I will remember your wonders of old (Ps. 77:11); I will tell of all your wonders (Ps. 9:1); you are the God who works wonders (Ps. 77:14); God alone works wonders (Ps. 72:18; 136:4); many are the wonders you have done (Ps. 40:5); he who works miracles among you (Gal. 3:5); where are all his miracles? (Judg. 6:13).

b God performed signs among the Egyptians (Exod. 10:1); I will strike Egypt with my wonders (Exod. 3:20); his wonders were multiplied in Egypt (Exod. 11:9); I will multiply my signs and wonders (Exod. 7:3); he sent signs and wonders upon Egypt (Deut. 6:22; 26:8; 29:3; Ps. 135:9); he did wonders in Egypt (Ps. 78:12, 43; 106:21–2); signs and wonders against Pharaoh (Neh. 9:10); he did wonders in driving out the nations (Exod. 34:10–11; 1 Chr. 17:21); tomorrow the Lord will do wonders among you (Josh. 3:5); perhaps the Lord will do wonderful things for us (Jer. 21:2); I will declare the signs and wonders which God has done

(Dan. 4:2); I will show wonders in heaven and on earth (Joel 2:30; Acts 2:19); the curses will be a sign and wonder (Deut. 28:46).

- **Jesus' miracles**
  c If the signs had been performed in Tyre and Sidon they would have repented (Luke 10:13); if the miracles had been done in Tyre and Sidon they would have repented (Matt. 11:21); if the miracles had been done in Sodom it would have remained (Matt. 11:23); many people saw the signs he did and believed (John 2:23); no one could do these signs if God were not with him (John 3:2); Jesus did many other signs in the presence of his disciples (John 20:30); Jesus was attested by God by miracles, wonders and signs (Acts 2:22); they praised God for all the miracles they had seen (Luke 19:37); Jesus could not do many miracles there because of their unbelief (Matt. 13:58; Mark 6:5).

  d Where did this man get these deeds of power? (Matt. 13:54; Mark 6:2); it must be John, resurrected, and so able to work miracles (Matt. 14:2).

  Signs of the Christ, see **547***f*.

- **Performing miracles**
  e The gift of miracles (1 Cor. 12:10, 28–9); no one who does a miracle in my name can soon speak evil of me (Mark 9:39).

  f Moses performed miracles in Egypt (Exod. 7:9; Ps. 105:27; Acts 7:36); perform all the wonders (Exod. 4:21); I and my children are for signs and wonders (Isa. 8:18).

  g Many wonders and signs were done by the apostles (Acts 2:43; 5:12); an outstanding miracle has taken place (Acts 4:16); may signs and wonders take place though the name of Jesus (Acts 4:30); Stephen did wonders and signs (Acts 6:8); Simon was amazed at the signs and miracles (Acts 8:13); the Lord confirmed the word by signs and wonders (Acts 14:3); God did extraordinary miracles by Paul (Acts 19:11); Barnabas and Paul related the signs and wonders God had done (Acts 15:12); what Christ has done through me by the power of signs and wonders (Rom. 15:18–19); the marks of a true apostle, signs, wonders and miracles (2 Cor. 12:12); God bore witness by signs and wonders (Heb. 2:4).

  Signs and wonders, see **547***k*.

- **False miracles**
  h If a false prophet shows a sign or wonder (Deut. 13:1–2); false Christs and false prophets will show great signs and wonders (Matt. 24:24; Mark 13:22); the lawless one will come with signs and wonders (2 Thess. 2:9); did we not perform miracles in your name? (Matt. 7:22).

- **Amazed by God**
  i This is the Lord's doing and it is marvellous in our eyes (Matt. 21:42; Mark 12:11).

  j His name is wonderful (Judg. 13:18).

- **Amazed by Jesus**
  k Many were astonished at him (Isa. 52:14); they were amazed at his understanding (Luke 2:47); astonished that the wind stopped (Mark 6:51); amazed to see him (Mark 9:15; Luke 2:48); amazed

to see he was talking to a woman (John 4:27); amazed that he was going to Jerusalem (Mark 10:32); amazed that he did not wash before eating (Luke 11:38); Pilate was amazed that he said nothing (Matt. 27:14; Mark 15:5).

l They were amazed at Jesus' teaching (Matt. 7:28; 13:54; 19:25; 22:22, 33; Mark 1:22; 6:2; 10:24, 26; 11:18; 12:17; Luke 4:32; 20:26; John 7:15).

● Jesus amazed

m Jesus marvelled at their unbelief (Mark 6:6); Jesus marvelled at the centurion's faith (Matt. 8:10; Luke 7:9).

● Amazed by people

n Joseph's brothers were astonished at the portions served to them (Gen. 43:33); Jacob was stunned to hear that Joseph was ruler of Egypt (Gen. 45:26).

o I am amazed that you are turning from the gospel (Gal. 1:6).

p They were amazed at Zacharias (Luke 1:63); Jesus' parents marvelled at what the shepherds said (Luke 2:18); they were amazed at Simeon's words (Luke 2:33).

q The Lord is coming to be marvelled at in those who have believed (2 Thess. 1:10).

● Amazed by miracles

r They were amazed by healings (Matt. 9:33; 12:23; 15:31; Mark 2:12; 5:20, 42; 7:37; Luke 4:36; 5:26; 8:56; 9:43; 11:14; John 7:21; Acts 3:10–11).

s Amazed at the fig tree withering (Matt. 21:20); amazed at his authority over demons (Mark 1:27); amazed at the catch of fishes (Luke 5:9); greater works will he show him that you may marvel (John 5:20).

t Amazed to see the angel (Mark 16:5, 8); amazed at the empty tomb (Luke 24:12); some women amazed us (Luke 24:22); amazed to see him risen (Luke 24:41).

u Amazed at Pentecost (Acts 2:7, 12); amazed that the Spirit fell on the Gentiles (Acts 10:45); amazed at miracles (Acts 8:13); amazed that Paul had believed (Acts 9:21); amazed that Peter was freed (Acts 12:16).

v The whole earth was amazed by the beast (Rev. 13:3).

● Amazed by teaching

w The proconsul was amazed at the teaching (Acts 13:12).

865 Lack of wonder

Unconcerned, see **860a**.

866 Repute

● Glory

a The priests' clothes were for glory and beauty (Exod. 28:2, 40); the house of God will be magnificent (1 Chr. 22:5); the latter glory of this house will be greater than the former (Hag. 2:9); glorious things are spoken of Zion (Ps. 87:3).

b They were to be a people for renown, praise and glory (Jer. 13:11); you are our glory and joy (1 Thess. 2:20).

c The devil offered Jesus all kingdoms and their glory (Matt. 4:8;

Luke 4:5–6); the glory of kings and nations will be brought into the new Jerusalem (Rev. 21:24, 26).

d Woman is the glory of man (1 Cor. 11:7); a woman's long hair is her glory (1 Cor. 11:15).

The glory of God

e The glory of the Lord appeared in the cloud (Exod. 16:10; 24:16; Num. 16:42); filling the tabernacle (Exod. 40:34); the glory of the Lord filled the temple (1 Kgs. 8:11; 2 Chr. 5:14; 7:1–3; Ezek. 43:5; 44:4); the glory of the Lord appeared to all the people (Lev. 9:6, 23; Num. 14:10; 16:19); appeared to Moses and Aaron (Num. 20:6); the glory of the God of Israel came from the east (Ezek. 43:2); glory like a consuming fire (Exod. 24:17); the glory of the Lord shone about them (Luke 2:9).

f To God be the glory for ever! (Rom. 11:36; 16:27; 1 Tim. 1:17); I will be honoured through Pharaoh (Exod. 14:4, 17, 18); I do not give my glory to another (Isa. 42:8; 48:11); you made a name for yourself (Neh. 9:10); glorify your name (John 12:28); how majestic is your name in all the earth! (Ps. 8:1, 9).

God is exalted

g Be exalted above the heavens (Ps. 57:5, 11; 108:5); his glory is above earth and heavens (Ps. 148:13); I will be exalted (Isa. 33:10); the Lord is exalted (Exod. 15:21; Ps. 47:9; Isa. 5:16; 33:5); the Lord alone will be exalted (Isa. 2:11, 17); he is exalted above the peoples (Ps. 99:2); the Lord is high above all nations (Ps. 113:4); you are exalted for ever (Ps. 92:8); you are exalted far above all gods (Ps. 97:9).

God's glory exhibited

h Tell of his glory among the nations (1 Chr. 16:24); ascribe glory to the Lord (1 Chr. 16:28, 29; Ps. 29:1–2); in his temple everything says, 'Glory!' (Ps. 29:9).

i Show me your glory (Exod. 33:18); the heavens are telling the glory of God (Ps. 19:1); all the earth will be filled with the glory of God (Num. 14:21); they will see the glory of our God (Isa. 35:2).

Glorifying God

j Those who honour me I will honour (1 Sam. 2:30); do all for the glory of God (1 Cor. 10:31); glorify God in your body (1 Cor. 6:20); everyone whom I have created for my glory (Isa. 43:7); I glorified you on earth (John 17:4); by what kind of death he would glorify God (John 21:19); that in everything God may be glorified through Jesus Christ (1 Pet. 4:11); confessing Jesus is Lord, to the glory of God the Father (Phil. 2:11); with one accord glorify the God and Father of our Lord (Rom. 15:6).

k God in whose hand is your breath you have not glorified (Dan. 5:23); Herod did not give God the glory (Acts 12:23); they did not honour him as God (Rom. 1:21).

The glory of the Son

l We saw his glory, the glory of the only begotten of the Father (John 1:14); the Son is the radiance of God's glory (Heb. 1:3); Isaiah saw his glory and spoke of him (John 12:41); Jesus manifested his glory (John 2:11); worthy of more honour than Moses (Heb. 3:3).

m I do not seek my glory (John 8:50); if I glorify myself, my glory is nothing (John 8:54).

n Glorify your Son (John 17:1, 5); my Father glorifies me (John 8:54); Jesus was not yet glorified (John 7:39); the hour has come for the Son of man to be glorified (John 12:23); now is the Son of man glorified (John 13:31); God has glorified his servant Jesus (Acts 3:13).

o It was necessary for him to suffer and enter his glory (Luke 24:26); the suffering of Christ and the glory following (1 Pet. 1:11); crowned with glory and honour because he suffered and died (Heb. 2:9); he was obedient to death, therefore God exalted him (Phil. 2:9); God exalted him to his own right hand (Acts 5:31); the Spirit will glorify Christ (John 16:14).

p All should honour the Son as they honour the Father (John 5:23); that Christ shall be exalted in my body (Phil. 1:20); this sickness is for the Son of God to be glorified (John 11:4).

q The Son of man will come with great power and glory (Matt. 24:30; Mark 13:26; Luke 21:27); when the Son of man comes in his glory (Luke 9:26).

- Glory through Christ

r That you may acquire the glory of our Lord (2 Thess. 2:14); vessels for honour (Rom. 9:21; 2 Tim. 2:20, 21); vessels of mercy prepared beforehand for glory (Rom. 9:23); that the elect may obtain salvation and eternal glory (2 Tim. 2:10); I gave them the glory you gave me (John 17:22); we will be glorified with Christ (Rom. 8:17); if anyone serves me, the Father will honour him (John 12:26); the glory to be revealed to us (Rom. 8:18); those whom he justified he also glorified (Rom. 8:30); an eternal weight of glory beyond all comparison (2 Cor. 4:17); you will receive the crown of glory (1 Pet. 5:4); the ministry of the Spirit has more glory than the ministry of condemnation (2 Cor. 3:7–11).

- Famous men

s Man is crowned with glory and honour (Heb. 2:7); they were mighty men of renown (Gen. 6:4); let us make a name for ourselves (Gen. 11:4); David's name was esteemed (1 Sam. 18:30); David made a name for himself (2 Sam. 8:13); the fame of David spread (1 Chr. 14:17); Solomon's fame was known all around (1 Kgs. 4:31); the Queen of Sheba heard of the fame of Solomon (2 Chr. 9:1); Naaman was highly respected (2 Kgs. 5:1); Jabez was more honourable than his brothers (1 Chr. 4:9); Jehoshaphat had riches and honour (2 Chr. 17:5; 18:1); Uzziah's fame reached afar (2 Chr. 26:8, 15); Hezekiah had riches and honour (2 Chr. 32:27); Mordecai's fame spread abroad (Esther 9:4); those who were of high reputation in the church (Gal. 2:6, 9).

t Moses and Elijah appeared in glory (Luke 9:30–1).

- Honour due

u Honour your father and mother (Exod. 20:12; Deut. 5:16; Matt. 15:4; 19:19; Mark 7:10; Luke 18:20; Eph. 6:2); a son honours his father and a servant his master (Mal. 1:6); I honour my Father (John 8:49).

v Pay honour to whom it is due (Rom. 13:7); honour the king (1 Pet. 2:17); outdo one another in showing honour (Rom. 12:10); man is crowned with glory and honour (Ps. 8:5).

w Honour is not fitting for a fool (Prov. 26:1); honouring a fool is like binding a stone in a sling (Prov. 26:8).

● Seeking honour

x The scribes and Pharisees love places of honour in synagogues and at feasts (Matt. 23:6; Mark 12:39; Luke 11:43; 20:46); Jesus saw how they chose places of honour for themselves (Luke 14:7–10); do not give alms in order to be honoured by men (Matt. 6:2); nor did we seek glory from men (1 Thess. 2:6).

y It is not glory to seek one's own glory (Prov. 25:27); you exalt yourself (Exod. 9:17); why exalt yourself? (Num. 16:3); the king will exalt himself above every god (Dan. 11:36; 2 Thess. 2:4).

● Source of honour

z Wisdom gives riches and honour (Prov. 3:16); wisdom will honour you (Prov. 4:8); riches and honour are with Wisdom (Prov. 8:18); a gracious woman gets honour (Prov. 11:16).

aa Riches and honour come from God (1 Chr. 29:12); God brings low and exalts the poor and needy (1 Sam. 2:7); splendour and majesty you place on him (Ps. 21:5); I will give you riches and honour (2 Chr. 1:12); I will make your name great (Gen. 12:2; 2 Sam. 7:9; 1 Chr. 17:8); I will honour them (Jer. 30:19); the Lord has glorified you (Isa. 55:5); God exalted Joshua in the eyes of Israel (Josh. 3:7; 4:14); God gave Solomon honour (1 Kgs. 3:13; 1 Chr. 29:25).

● Honouring

ab The honour will not be yours, but a woman's (Judg. 4:9); honour me before the people (1 Sam. 15:30); all women will honour their husbands (Esther 1:20).

ac Do not honour yourself (Prov. 25:6); if you have been foolish, exalting yourself (Prov. 30:32).
Give honour, see **923**.

● Good reputation

ad The disciples were held in honour by all the people (Acts 2:47; 5:13); an elder must have a good reputation with those outside (1 Tim. 3:7); we commend ourselves in honour and dishonour (2 Cor. 6:8); may you become rich and famous (Ruth 4:11).

ae A good name is better than riches (Prov. 22:1); better than perfume (Eccles. 7:1); the glory has departed from Israel (1 Sam. 4:21–2).

af Whatever is of good repute, think of it (Phil. 4:8).

867 Disrepute

● Dishonour

a By breaking the law you dishonour God (Rom. 2:23).

b Only at home is a prophet without honour (Matt. 13:57; Mark 6:4; Luke 4:24; John 4:44).

c A vessel for dishonourable use (Rom. 9:21); vessels for honour and dishonour (2 Tim. 2:20); apostles are without honour (1 Cor.

4:10); less honourable members are given more honour (1 Cor. 12:23); the body is sown in dishonour and raised in glory (1 Cor. 15:43).

d A man praying or prophesying with head covered dishonours his head (1 Cor. 11:4); a woman praying or prophesying with head uncovered dishonours her head (1 Cor. 11:5).

● Losing honour

e God has stripped my honour from me (Job 19:9); the glory of Moab will be brought down (Isa. 16:14); the glory of Jacob will be brought low (Isa. 17:4).

● Disgrace

f Shechem had done a disgraceful thing (Gen. 34:7); giving our sister to the uncircumcised would be a disgrace (Gen. 34:14); impurity, the dishonouring of their bodies (Rom. 1:24). **Shame**, see **872n**.

868 Nobility

Master, see **741**.

869 Commonalty

● Ordinary people

a Let the lowly brother glory in his exaltation (Jas. 1:9).

b We have this treasure in earthenware vessels (2 Cor. 4:7).

870 Title

Honour, see **866**.

871 Pride

● Nature of pride

a In pride the wicked pursue the afflicted (Ps. 10:2); evildoers speak arrogantly (Ps. 94:4); their mouths speak proudly (Ps. 17:10); bold and arrogant, they are not afraid to slander (2 Pet. 2:10); the pride of your heart has deceived you (Obad. 3); from the heart comes pride (Mark 7:22); they are insolent, arrogant (Rom. 1:30); men will be arrogant (2 Tim. 3:2); conceited (2 Tim. 3:4); he is conceited (1 Tim. 6:4).

b Arrogance is like idolatry (1 Sam. 15:23); love is not arrogant (1 Cor. 13:4); knowledge puffs up but love builds up (1 Cor. 8:1); when pride comes, disgrace follows (Prov. 11:2); haughty eyes and a proud heart are sin (Prov. 21:4); 'scoffer' is the name of the proud man (Prov. 21:24).

c The proud are an abomination to the Lord (Prov. 16:5).

● Do not be proud

d Do not think of yourself more highly than you ought (Rom. 12:3); if anyone thinks he is something when he is nothing (Gal. 6:3); do nothing out of vain conceit (Phil. 2:3); do not let arrogance come from your mouth (1 Sam. 2:3); do not be arrogant towards the branches (Rom. 11:18); do not be conceited (Rom. 11:20); do not become arrogant (1 Cor. 4:6); do not be arrogant and lie against the truth (Jas. 3:14); not a new convert, lest he become conceited (1 Tim. 3:6).

e I was envious of the arrogant (Ps. 73:3).

- **Proud people**

f You rebelled and in arrogance marched to the hill country (Deut. 1:43); our fathers acted arrogantly (Neh. 9:16, 29); you have defeated Edom and now you are proud (2 Kgs. 14:10; 2 Chr. 25:19); when Uzziah became strong, he became proud (2 Chr. 26:16); Hezekiah's heart was proud (2 Chr. 32:25); Zedekiah did not humble himself (2 Chr. 36:12); some of you have become arrogant (1 Cor. 4:18); we have heard of the pride of Moab (Isa. 16:6; Jer. 48:29); Diotrephes loves to be first (3 John 9); you have become arrogant (1 Cor. 5:2).

g The pride of Israel witness against him (Hos. 5:5; 7:10).
Humbling and exalting, see **872h**.

- **Pride and externals**

h When riches increase, your heart will become proud (Deut. 8:14); charge those who are rich not to be proud (1 Tim. 6:17); Sodom was arrogant and did not help the poor (Ezek. 16:49); because of your wealth, your heart has become proud (Ezek. 28:5); the women of Zion are proud in their finery (Isa. 3:16); your heart was proud because of your beauty (Ezek. 28:17); those who pride themselves on appearance and not on the Lord (2 Cor. 5:12).

- **Fate of the proud**

i The proud, God knows from afar (Ps. 138:6); I hate pride and arrogance (Prov. 8:13); I loathe the pride of Jacob (Amos 6:8); your eyes are on the haughty to bring them low (2 Sam. 22:28); those who walk in pride he is able to humble (Dan. 4:37); he has scattered the proud (Luke 1:51); God opposes the proud (Jas. 4:6; 1 Pet. 5:5); God will abase the proud (Isa. 2:12); the Lord hates haughty eyes (Prov. 6:17); you abase haughty eyes (Ps. 18:27); you rebuke the arrogant (Ps. 119:21); the Lord tears down the house of the proud (Prov. 15:25); because the tree [Egypt] was proud, it was cut down (Ezek. 31:10–12); the Lord will punish the arrogance of Assyria (Isa. 10:12); I will destroy the pride of Judah and Jerusalem (Jer. 13:9); you will no more be proud on my holy mountain (Zeph. 3:11).

j Pride goes before a fall (Prov. 16:18; 18:12); a man's pride brings him low (Prov. 29:23); when he was proud he was deposed (Dan. 5:20); I will break your pride of power (Lev. 26:19).

872 Humility. Humiliation

- **Lowliness**

a With the humble is wisdom (Prov. 11:2); humility goes before honour (Prov. 15:33; 18:12); the humble will inherit the land (Ps. 37:11); blessed are the meek, for they will inherit the earth (Matt. 5:5); the humble will receive honour (Prov. 29:23).

b Insistence on humility (Col. 2:18, 23).

- **Be humble!**

c Live with humility and gentleness (Eph. 4:2); in humility reckon others better than yourselves (Phil. 2:3); put on humility (Col. 3:12); be clothed with humility (1 Pet. 5:5); humble yourselves under the mighty hand of God (1 Pet. 5:6); walk humbly with your God (Mic. 6:8); do not be haughty, but associate with the lowly (Rom. 12:16); in humility accept the implanted word (Jas. 1:21); at a feast, take the lowest place (Luke 14:10); better is a humble man than one who honours himself (Prov. 12:9); better to be of humble spirit than to divide spoil with the proud (Prov. 16:19).

Modest clothes, see **228h**.

● God and
the humble

d The Lord is on high yet regards the lowly (Ps. 138:6); I dwell with the lowly and contrite in spirit (Isa. 57:15); I look to him who is humble and contrite (Isa. 66:2); God gives grace to the humble (Jas. 4:6; 1 Pet. 5:5); God teaches the humble his way (Ps. 25:9); I will leave among you the humble and lowly (Zeph. 3:12); he has regarded the humble state of his maidservant (Luke 1:48).

● God humbling
people

e God led you these forty years to humble you (Deut. 8:2, 3); he fed you manna to humble you (Deut. 8:16); God humbled Judah (2 Chr. 28:19).

f The arrogance of man will be brought low (Isa. 2:11, 17); I will humble the haughtiness of the ruthless (Isa. 13:11); the Lord will lay low the pride of Moab (Isa. 25:11); he brings low those who dwell on high (Isa. 26:5).

g God makes counsellors walk barefoot (Job 12:17); God makes priests walk barefoot (Job 12:19); man is humbled (Isa. 5:15).

● Humbling
and exalting

h Whoever exalts himself will be humbled and whoever humbles himself will be exalted (Matt. 23:12; Luke 14:11; 18:14); he humbles and he exalts (1 Sam. 2:7); he has brought down rulers and exalted the humble (Luke 1:52); humble yourselves and he will exalt you (Jas. 4:10; 1 Pet. 5:6).

● Humbling
oneself

i Humble yourselves on the Day of Atonement (Lev. 16:29; 23:27, 29, 32); humble yourself and importune your neighbour (Prov. 6:3); if my people humble themselves and pray (2 Chr. 7:14); whoever humbles himself like this child is the greatest (Matt. 18:4); humbling ourselves before God (Ezra 8:21).

j David would be humble in his own eyes (2 Sam. 6:22); Rehoboam and the princes humbled themselves (2 Chr. 12:6–7); when he humbled himself, the Lord's anger turned away (2 Chr. 12:12); Ahab humbled himself (1 Kgs. 21:29); because you humbled yourself, I have heard you (2 Kgs. 22:19; 2 Chr. 34:27); since they humbled themselves, I will not destroy them (2 Chr. 12:7); some men of Israel humbled themselves and went up to Jerusalem (2 Chr. 30:11); Hezekiah humbled the pride of his heart (2 Chr. 32:26); Manasseh humbled himself (2 Chr. 33:12).

k How long will you refuse to humble yourself (Exod. 10:3); you, Belshazzar, have not humbled yourself (Dan. 5:22); Amon did not humble himself (2 Chr. 33:23).

● Christ humbled
himself

l Jesus was made temporarily lower than the angels (Heb. 2:7, 9); he emptied himself (Phil. 2:7); I am gentle and lowly of heart (Matt. 11:29).

- Humble
  people

m Moses was more humble than anyone else (Num. 12:3); my heart is not proud (Ps. 131:1); I served the Lord with all humility (Acts 20:19); he must increase but I must decrease (John 3:30).

- Shame

n Where could I rid myself of my shame? (2 Sam. 13:13); you have covered your servants' faces with shame (2 Sam. 19:5); with shame you take the lowest place (Luke 14:9); the things of which you are now ashamed (Rom. 6:21); long hair is a disgrace for a man (1 Cor. 11:14); I am ashamed to beg (Luke 16:3).
Nakedness and shame, see **229***a*.

o The servants were humiliated by Hanun (2 Sam. 10:5; 1 Chr. 19:5); they stole into the city like those humiliated (2 Sam. 19:3); the priests and Levites were ashamed of themselves (2 Chr. 30:15); if her father spat in her face she would be in shame seven days (Num. 12:14); I was ashamed to ask the king for soldiers (Ezra 8:22); I am too ashamed to lift up my face to you (Ezra 9:6); shame belongs to us (Dan. 9:7, 8); you chose David to your own shame (1 Sam. 20:30).

p They will be ashamed because of their sacrifices (Hos. 4:19); you will be ashamed of the oaks (Isa. 1:29); the seers will be ashamed (Mic. 3:7); Moab will be ashamed of Chemosh (Jer. 48:13); the protection of Pharaoh will be your shame (Isa. 30:3–5); your mother will be ashamed (Jer. 50:12); they shall be ashamed (Ps. 109:28); my enemies will be ashamed (Ps. 6:10).

q If anyone is ashamed of me, the Son of Man will be ashamed of him (Mark 8:38; Luke 9:26).

r They rejoiced that they were counted worthy of suffering shame (Acts 5:41).
Disgrace, see **867***f*.

- Shaming

s Nahash wanted to bring reproach on all Israel (1 Sam. 11:2); you have covered David with shame (Ps. 89:45); I will bring on you everlasting shame (Jer. 23:40); describe the temple that they may be ashamed of their sins (Ezek. 43:10); as thief is shamed when caught, Israel will be shamed (Jer. 2:26); those who make graven images will be put to shame (Isa. 44:9–11; 45:16); lest I be put to shame by your unpreparedness (2 Cor. 9:4).

t Let the wicked be put to shame (Ps. 31:17; 119:78); let my enemies be ashamed (Ps. 35:26; 71:13); that those who hate me may be ashamed (Ps. 86:17); may those who seek my life be put to shame (Ps. 35:4; 40:14–15; 70:2); may all who hate Zion be put to shame (Ps. 129:5); let them be ashamed (Ps. 83:17); let them be clothed with shame (Ps. 109:29); I will clothe his enemies with shame (Ps. 132:18); those who hate you will be clothed with shame (Job 8:22); those who oppose us will be ashamed (Titus 2:8); that those who revile you may be put to shame (1 Pet. 3:16); have nothing to do with him that he may be ashamed (2 Thess. 3:14); those who seek my hurt are put to shame (Ps. 71:24); God chose the foolish and weak things to shame the wise and strong (1 Cor. 1:27).

● Not ashamed

u I do not write these things to shame you (1 Cor. 4:14); Joseph did not want to put Mary to shame (Matt. 1:19); I will not be put to shame (Phil. 1:20).

v Do not let me be ashamed (Ps. 25:2, 20; 31:1, 17; 71:1; 119:31, 80, 116); my people will never be put to shame (Joel 2:26); they will not be ashamed (Ps. 37:19; 127:5); Jacob will no longer be ashamed (Isa. 29:22); no one who waits for you will be ashamed (Ps. 25:3); then I will not be ashamed (Ps. 119:6, 46); you will not be put to shame to all eternity (Isa. 45:17).

w Adam and his wife were naked yet not ashamed (Gen. 2:25); their faces were not ashamed (Ps. 34:5).

x He endured the cross, despising the shame (Heb. 12:2); God is not ashamed to be called their God (Heb. 11:16); Jesus is not ashamed to call them brothers (Heb. 2:11).

y I am not ashamed (2 Tim. 1:12); I am not ashamed of the gospel (Rom. 1:16); do not be ashamed to testify (2 Tim. 1:8); a workman who does not need to be ashamed (2 Tim. 2:15); may those who seek you not be put to shame (Ps. 69:6).

z They were not ashamed of their conduct (Jer. 6:15); you refused to be ashamed (Jer. 3:3); they were not ashamed of the abominations (Jer. 8:12).

aa Onesiphorus was not ashamed of my chains (2 Tim. 1:16).

● Removing shame

ab What shall be for the one who takes away reproach from Israel? (1 Sam. 17:26); take away our reproach (Isa. 4:1); let us rebuild that we may not be a reproach (Neh. 2:17).

873 Vanity

Useless, see **641a**; **pride**, see **871**.

874 Modesty

Humility, see **872**.

875 Ostentation. Formality

● For appearance sake

a Do not practise your religion to be seen by men (Matt. 6:1, 2, 5, 16); the Pharisees do everything to be seen by men (Matt. 23:5); for appearance they offer long prayers (Mark 12:40; Luke 20:47).

● Pomp

b Agrippa and Bernice came with great pomp (Acts 25:23).

876 Celebration

● Feasts

a Feast for Isaac's weaning (Gen. 21:8); Isaac made a feast for Abimelech (Gen. 26:30); Pharaoh made a birthday feast (Gen. 40:20); Joseph summoned his brothers to a feast (Gen. 43:16, 31–4); Nabal was having a feast (1 Sam. 25:36); the Amalekites were eating, drinking and dancing (1 Sam. 30:16); David made a feast for Abner (2 Sam. 3:20); Solomon gave a feast for his servants (1 Kgs. 3:15); each son held a feast in turn (Job 1:4); his sons and daughters were eating and drinking together (Job 1:13, 18).

b Laban made a wedding feast (Gen. 29:22); Samson gave a wedding feast (Judg. 14:10); a king who gave a wedding feast (Matt. 22:2).

c Kill the fatted calf and let us eat and be merry (Luke 15:23).

d Do not go into a house of feasting (Jer. 16:8); when you give a feast, do not invite your friends (Luke 14:12–14).

Banquet, see **882***f.*

● Feasting in the kingdom

e Feasting in the kingdom of God (Matt. 8:11; Luke 13:29; 14:15); you will eat and drink at my table in my kingdom (Luke 22:30); blessed are those called to the marriage supper of the Lamb (Rev. 19:9); God will prepare a rich feast for all (Isa. 25:6).

● Celebrating

f All Israel were celebrating (2 Sam. 6:5); I will celebrate before the Lord (2 Sam. 6:21); celebrating victory over their enemies (Esther 9:17–22, 27–8).

● Dedication

g Dedicating the temple (1 Kgs. 8:63; 2 Chr. 7:5; Ezra 6:16–17; Ps. 30:t); dedicating the altar (Num. 7:10–11, 84, 88; 2 Chr. 7:9); dedicating the wall (Neh. 12:27); dedicating the image (Dan. 3:2–3).

877 Boasting

● Those who boast

a Men will be boastful (2 Tim. 3:2); they are boastful (Rom. 1:30); your boasting is not good (1 Cor. 5:6); the circumcisers want to boast in your flesh (Gal. 6:13).

b Those who boast of their riches (Ps. 49:6); you who boast in the law (Rom. 2:23); a man who boasts of non-existent gifts is like clouds without rain (Prov. 25:14); is not this great Babylon which I have made? (Dan. 4:30); the horn had a mouth uttering great things (Dan. 7:8, 20).

c Paul boasted that he made the gospel free of charge (1 Cor. 9:15–16; 2 Cor. 11:10); let me boast of my endeavours (2 Cor. 11:17–18); if I boast too much of our authority (2 Cor. 10:8); we will not boast beyond our limit (2 Cor. 10:13, 15); I will boast of my weakness (2 Cor. 11:30; 12:1, 5, 9).

● Do not boast

d Do not boast (1 Sam. 2:3; Ps. 75:4); let us not be boastful (Gal. 5:26); do not boast of wisdom, strength or riches (Jer. 9:23–4); let no one boast about men (1 Cor. 3:21).

e Why do you boast of evil? (Ps. 52:1); do not boast about tomorrow (Prov. 27:1); boasting about future success is evil (Jas. 4:16); too many soldiers, lest Israel boast (Judg. 7:2); let not him who puts on his armour boast like him who takes it off (1 Kgs. 20:11).

● Boasting
excluded

f Boasting is excluded by the principle of faith (Rom. 3:27); no one may boast before God (1 Cor. 1:29); the boastful will not stand before you (Ps. 5:5); why boast, as if you have something you did not receive? (1 Cor. 4:7); where is now your boasting? (Judg. 9:38); Abraham has no reason to boast before God (Rom. 4:2); salvation is not of works, lest any one should boast (Eph. 2:9).

● Boasting
in God

g Let him who boasts, boast in the Lord (Jer. 9:23–4; 1 Cor. 1:31; 2 Cor. 10:17); I will boast in the Lord (Ps. 34:2); in God we boast (Ps. 44:8); we will boast in the name of the Lord (Ps. 20:7); I boast in things regarding God (Rom. 15:17); if you are a Jew and boast of God (Rom. 2:17).

h We glory in Christ Jesus (Phil. 3:3); I will not boast except in the cross (Gal. 6:14).

878 Insolence
Arrogance, see **871**.

879 Servility
Subjection, see **745**.

Section three: Interpersonal emotion

880 Friendship

● Friends

a There is a friend who sticks closer than a brother (Prov. 18:24); a friend loves at all times (Prov. 17:17); the despairing man should have kindness from his friend (Job 6:14).

● Friends
of God

b The friendship of God (Job 29:4); my Father, the friend of my youth (Jer. 3:4).

c Abraham your friend (2 Chr. 20:7); Abraham my friend (Isa. 41:8); Abraham was called the friend of God (Jas. 2:23); God spoke to Moses as to a friend (Exod. 33:11).

● Human
friendship

d Hiram was a friend of David (1 Kgs. 5:1); Hushai was David's friend (2 Sam. 16:16; 1 Chr. 27:33); Amnon's friend Jonadab (2 Sam. 13:3); Zabud, Solomon's friend (1 Kgs. 4:5); Herod and Pilate became friends (Luke 23:12); Job's three friends (Job 2:11); Paul went to his friends (Acts 27:3); Jesus called his disciples friends (John 15:14–15); a friend of taxmen and sinners (Matt. 11:19; Luke 7:34); Paul's friends ministered to him (Acts 24:23).

e He who loves purity will have the king as his friend (Prov. 22:11).

● Friends
failing

f Friends desert a poor man (Prov. 19:4, 7); you have taken lover and friend from me (Ps. 88:8, 18); friends and relatives have forgotten (Job 19:13–14); my close friend has lifted up his heel against me (Ps. 41:9); my familiar friend reproaches me (Ps.

55:12–13); in return for my love they accuse me (Ps. 109:4); all her friends have dealt treacherously (Lam. 1:2); friend, why are you here? (Matt. 26:50).

Friendship and money

g Friendship of the world is hostility to God (Jas. 4:4); wealth brings many friends (Prov. 19:4); everyone is a friend to him who gives gifts (Prov. 19:6); make friends by means of unrighteous mammon (Luke 16:9).

881 Enmity

• Enmity between people

a Enmity is a deed of the flesh (Gal. 5:20); the enmity which Christ abolished (Eph. 2:15–16).

• Enmity with the devil

b Enmity between the serpent and the woman (Gen. 3:15).
Enemy, see **705**.

882 Sociality

• Eating together

a Be careful when you sit down to eat with a ruler (Prov. 23:1).

b Melchizedek brought bread and wine (Gen. 14:18); Isaac ate and drank with Abimelech and Phicol (Gen. 26:30); they ate by the heap of witness (Gen. 31:46); you will eat with me today (1 Sam. 9:19); you set me among those who eat at your table (2 Sam. 19:28); let them eat at your table (1 Kgs. 2:7); the man of God ate and drank with the prophet (1 Kgs. 13:19); the king and Haman sat down to drink (Esther 3:15).

c Jesus ate with tax-collectors and sinners (Matt. 9:10–11; Mark 2:15–17; Luke 5:29–30; Luke 15:2); he has gone to be the guest of a sinner (Luke 19:7); Peter used to eat with Gentiles (Gal. 2:12); you ate with the uncircumcised (Acts 11:3).

d A Pharisee invited him to a meal (Luke 7:36; 11:37); he went in to eat in the house of a Pharisee (Luke 14:1); they made him a dinner in Bethany (John 12:2); they ate and drank with Jesus after he rose (Acts 10:41); I will come in and eat with him (Rev. 3:20).

e He who eats my bread has lifted his heel against me (John 13:18); he who dips his hand in the dish with me will betray me (Matt. 26:23; Mark 14:18–20; Luke 22:21); while they were eating together Ishmael killed Gedaliah (Jer. 41:1–2).

• Banquets

f Ahasuerus gave a banquet (Esther 1:3, 5); Queen Vashti gave a banquet for the women (Esther 1:9); the king gave a banquet for Esther (Esther 2:18); may the king and Haman come to the banquet (Esther 5:4, 8); Esther invites no one to the banquet but the king and me (Esther 5:12); they brought Haman to the banquet (Esther 6:14); he brought me to the banqueting hall (S. of S. 2:4); Belshazzar gave a feast for his nobles (Dan. 5:1); Herod gave a banquet on his birthday (Mark 6:21); a man gave a big dinner (Luke 14:16); they love the places of honour at banquets (Matt. 23:6; Mark 12:39; Luke 20:46).
Feasts, see **876a**.

- Visiting

g Dinah went to visit (Gen. 34:1); let me see the king's face (2 Sam. 14:32); I intended to visit you (2 Cor. 1:15–16).

h God has visited his people (Luke 7:16); they did not recognise the day of their visitation (Luke 19:44).

- Saying goodbye

i One man wanted first to say goodbye to those at home (Luke 9:61).

j Moses said goodbye to Jethro (Exod. 18:27).

883 Unsociability. Seclusion

- No dealings

a Egyptians would not eat bread with Hebrews (Gen. 43:32); Jews have no dealings with Samaritans (John 4:9).

b Absalom did not see the king (2 Sam. 14:24, 28).

c The man of God was commanded not to eat or drink there (1 Kgs. 13:8–9, 15–18); do not associate with them (1 Kgs. 11:2); do not associate with immoral people (1 Cor. 5:9); do not associate with those who disobey this letter (2 Thess. 3:14); do not even eat with a disorderly 'brother' (1 Cor. 5:11).
Do not greet, see **884***h*.

- Isolation

d Withdraw from Uriah (2 Sam. 11:15); David will not spend the night with the people (2 Sam. 17:8); you would have stood aloof (2 Sam. 18:13); my loved ones stand aloof (Ps. 38:11); you stood aloof from the destruction of Jerusalem (Obad. 11).

e Jesus withdrew to a lonely place (Matt. 14:13; Luke 4:42); Jesus withdrew into the hills by himself (John 6:15); Jesus went out to a lonely place and prayed (Mark 1:35; Luke 5:16); Jesus withdrew into Galilee (Matt. 4:12); Jesus withdrew from there (Matt. 12:15; 15:21; Mark 3:7); he left them and went away (Matt. 16:4; 21:17); Jesus and the disciples withdrew by themselves (Mark 6:31–2; Luke 9:10); Jesus took the man aside (Mark 7:33); he took the blind man out of the village (Mark 8:23).

f Paul withdrew and took the disciples away (Acts 19:9); Peter withdrew from the Gentiles (Gal. 2:12).

g Paul went into Arabia (Gal. 1:17).

884 Courtesy

- Who to greet

a If you greet only your brothers, what do you do more than others? (Matt. 5:47); they love salutations in the market place (Matt. 23:7; Mark 12:38; Luke 11:43).
Welcoming people, see **299***a*.

b As you enter the house, greet it (Matt. 10:12).

- How to greet

c Greet one another with a holy kiss (Rom. 16:16; 1 Cor. 16:20; 2 Cor. 13:12; 1 Thess. 5:26); with a kiss of love (1 Pet. 5:14).

- Spoken greetings

d Boaz greeted his reapers (Ruth 2:4); greet Nabal in my name (1 Sam. 25:5); Tou sent Hadoram to greet David (1 Chr. 18:10); hail, favoured one! (Luke 1:28); she pondered what kind of greeting this was (Luke 1:29); Mary greeted Elizabeth and the baby leaped (Luke 1:40–1, 44); Judas said, 'Hail, Rabbi' (Matt.

26:49); hail, king of the Jews! (Mark 15:18); Jesus met them and greeted them (Matt. 28:9).

● Written greetings

e Everyone with me sends you greetings (Phil. 4:21; Titus 3:15); as do the churches in Asia (1 Cor. 16:19); all the saints (2 Cor. 13:13; Phil. 4:22); those from Italy (Heb. 13:24); she who is in Babylon (1 Pet. 5:13); Aquila and Prisca (1 Cor. 16:19); all the churches (Rom. 16:16); Epaphras *et al.* (Philem. 23–4); Aristarchus *et al.* (Col. 4:10–14); Eubulus (2 Tim. 4:21).

f The children of your elect sister greet you (2 John 13); the friends greet you (3 John 14); greetings from sundry people (Rom. 16:21–3).

g Greet Prisca and Aquila (2 Tim. 4:19); all the saints (Phil. 4:21; Heb. 13:24); the friends (3 John 14); greet those who love us (Titus 3:15); greetings to sundry people (Rom. 16:3–15; Col. 4:15).

● Do not greet

h Anyone who greets him shares in his evil work (2 John 10–11).

i Greet no one on the way (Luke 10:4); neither greet nor return a greeting (2 Kgs. 4:29).

885 Discourtesy

Not welcoming people, see **299***f*; **contempt**, see **922**.

886 Congratulation

Celebration, see **876**.

887 Love

● Love in general

a The characteristics of love (1 Cor. 13:4–7); there is a time for love (Eccles. 3:8); love is strong as death (S. of S. 8:6); love covers all transgressions (Prov. 10:12; 1 Pet. 4:8); love is the fulfilment of the law (Rom. 13:10); many waters cannot quench love (S. of S. 8:7); love never fails (1 Cor. 13:8); perfect love casts out fear (1 John 4:18); knowledge puffs up but love builds up (1 Cor. 8:1); better a meal of vegetables where love is (Prov. 15:17); faith, hope and love remain, but the greatest is love (1 Cor. 13:13); if I have not love I am nothing (1 Cor. 13:1–3); greater love has no one than this, that one lay down his life for his friends (John 15:13).

● Aim at love

b Over all things put on love (Col. 3:14); make love your aim (1 Cor. 14:1); the aim of this command is love (1 Tim. 1:5); do everything in love (1 Cor. 16:14); this I pray, that your love may abound (Phil. 1:9); may the Lord cause your love to increase (1 Thess. 3:12); let love be sincere (Rom. 12:9); pursue love (1 Tim. 6:11; 2 Tim. 2:22); let us love in deed and truth (1 John 3:18).

● God's love

c God is love (1 John 4:8, 16); the God of love and peace (2 Cor. 13:11); love is from God (1 John 4:7); he will be silent in his love (Zeph. 3:17); the love of God be with you (2 Cor. 13:14); may the Lord direct your hearts to the love of God (2 Thess. 3:5); this is love, not that we loved God but that he loved us (1 John 4:10).

● Love between
Father and Son

d The Father loves the Son (John 3:35; 5:20); you loved me before the creation of the world (John 17:24); the Father loves me because I lay down my life (John 10:17); the Beloved (Eph. 1:6); my beloved in whom I am well-pleased (Matt. 12:18); my beloved Son (Matt. 3:17; 17:5; Mark 9:7; Luke 3:22); he had a beloved son (Mark 12:6); I will send my beloved son (Luke 20:13); as the Father loved me, so have I loved you (John 15:9); that the love you have for me may be in them (John 17:26).

e I have kept the Father's commandments and remain in his love (John 15:10); that the world may know that I love the Father (John 14:31).

● God's love
for people

f God loves you (Deut. 23:5); the Lord loved your fathers (Deut. 4:37; 10:15); the Lord did not love you because of your numbers (Deut. 7:7); it was because the Lord loved you (Deut. 7:8); the Lord loved Solomon (2 Sam. 12:24; Neh. 13:26); Jacob I loved but Esau I hated (Mal. 1:2–3; Rom. 9:13); the Lord loved Israel for ever (1 Kgs. 10:9); when Israel was a child I loved him (Hos. 11:1); the Lord loves his people (2 Chr. 2:11); Israel are beloved for the sake of their forefathers (Rom. 11:28); beloved of the Lord (Deut. 33:12; 2 Sam. 12:25); love her as the Lord loves the Israelites (Hos. 3:1); the Lord loves the gates of Zion (Ps. 87:2); the Lord loves the righteous (Ps. 37:28; 146:8); I loved you with an everlasting love (Jer. 31:3).

g The Lord shows love to thousands (Exod. 20:6); her who was not beloved I will call beloved (Rom. 9:25); God loves aliens (Deut. 10:18).

h He whom the Lord loves he reproves (Prov. 3:12; Heb. 12:6); keep yourselves in the love of God (Jude 21).

● God's love
in Christ

i God so loved the world that he gave his Son (John 3:16); the Father himself loves you (John 16:27); he who loves me will be loved by my Father (John 14:21); the love of God has been poured into our hearts (Rom. 5:5); God shows his love in that Christ died for us (Rom. 5:8); you being rooted and grounded in love (Eph. 3:17); this is love, not that we loved God, but that he loved us (1 John 4:9–10); God, because of his great love, raised us with Christ (Eph. 2:4–5); when the love of God our Saviour appeared, he saved us (Titus 3:4–5); what manner of love the Father has bestowed upon us (1 John 3:1); nothing can separate us from the love of God in Christ (Rom. 8:35–9); more than conquerors through him who loved us (Rom. 8:37); those beloved of God (Rom. 1:7).

● Christ's love

j Jesus loved the rich young ruler (Mark 10:21); Jesus loved Martha, Mary and Lazarus (John 11:5); he whom you love is sick (John 11:3); see how he loved him! (John 11:36); the disciple whom Jesus loved (John 13:23; 19:26; 20:2; 21:7, 20); the Son of God who loved me (Gal. 2:20); Christ loved us and gave himself up for us (Eph. 5:2); by this we know love, that he laid down his life for us (1 John 3:16); I will love him (John 14:21); to know the love of Christ which surpasses knowledge (Eph. 3:18–19); having loved his own, he loved them to the end (John 13:1); Christ loved the church and gave himself up for her (Eph. 5:25).

k The love of Christ constrains us (2 Cor. 5:14).

● Loving God

l Love the Lord your God (Deut. 6:5; 10:12; 11:1, 13, 22; 13:3; 30:6, 16, 20; Josh. 22:5; 23:11; Matt. 22:37; Mark 12:30; Luke 10:27); love the Lord, all his saints! (Ps. 31:23); to love him with all the heart (Mark 12:33); because he loves me I will deliver him (Ps. 91:14); if anyone loves God he is known by him (1 Cor. 8:3).

m I love you, O Lord (Ps. 18:1); I love the Lord because he hears me (Ps. 116:1); not seeing him, you love him (1 Pet. 1:8); I love your house, O Lord (Ps. 26:8); Solomon loved the Lord (1 Kgs. 3:3).

n Showing lovingkindness to those who love me (Exod. 20:6); he who loves me will keep my word (John 14:23); whoever keeps his word, in him the love of God is made perfect (1 John 2:5); if you love me, keep my commandments (John 14:15); this is the love of God, that we keep his commandments (1 John 5:3); this is love, that we walk according to his commandments (2 John 6); if you keep my commandments you will remain in my love (John 15:10); by this we know that we love the children of God, when we love God (1 John 5:2).

o What God has promised for those that love him (1 Cor. 2:9); God has promised a crown of life to those who love him (Jas. 1:12); God promised the kingdom to those who love him (Jas. 2:5); grace be with all who love our Lord (Eph. 6:24).

p Simon, do you love me? (John 21:15–17); he who is forgiven much loves much (Luke 7:42–3, 47); he who loves father or mother more than me is not worthy of me (Matt. 10:37).

● Not loving God

q The love of many will grow cold (Matt. 24:12); you do not have the love of God in your hearts (John 5:42); if God were your Father you would love me (John 8:42); men will be lovers of pleasure rather than lovers of God (2 Tim. 3:4); if anyone does not love the Lord let him be accursed (1 Cor. 16:22).

● Loving God's word

r I love your: commandments (Ps. 119:47, 48); law (Ps. 119:97, 113, 163); testimonies (Ps. 119:119, 167); word (Ps. 119:140); precepts (Ps. 119:159).

s Those who love your law have great peace (Ps. 119:165).

● Love your neighbour

t Love your neighbour as yourself (Lev. 19:18; Matt. 19:19; 22:39; Mark 12:31; Luke 10:27); the law is summed up as 'love your neighbour as yourself' (Rom. 13:9; Gal. 5:14); he who loves his neighbour has fulfilled the law (Rom. 13:8); love aliens

(Deut. 10:19); love an alien as yourself (Lev. 19:34); the royal law to love your neighbour as yourself (Jas. 2:8).

u Love your neighbour and hate your enemies (Matt. 5:43); love your enemies (Matt. 5:44; Luke 6:27); do not only love those who love you, even sinners love those who love them (Matt. 5:46; Luke 6:32).

- Loving yourself

v He who gets wisdom loves himself (Prov. 19:8); men will be lovers of self (2 Tim. 3:2).

- Love one another

w We love because he first loved us (1 John 4:19); if God so loved us, we ought to love one another (1 John 4:11); a new commandment to love one another as I have loved you (John 13:34; 15:12, 17); this is his commandment, that we love one another (1 John 3:23; 2 John 5); by this will all know that you are my disciples (John 13:35); he who loves God should love his brother also (1 John 4:21).

x Be devoted to one another in brotherly love (Rom. 12:10); love one another fervently (1 Pet. 1:22; 4:8); love the brotherhood (1 Pet. 2:17); let brotherly love continue (Heb. 13:1); let us love one another (1 John 3:11; 4:7).

y Everyone who loves is born of God (1 John 4:7); if we love each other, God lives in us (1 John 4:12); he who loves his brother remains in the light (1 John 2:10); the fruit of the Spirit is love (Gal. 5:22); God has given us a spirit of love (2 Tim. 1:7); the breastplate of faith and love (1 Thess. 5:8).

z Your love for all the saints (Eph. 1:15; Col. 1:4); your love in the Spirit (Col. 1:8); about brotherly love we do not need to write to you (1 Thess. 4:9–10); I have joy and comfort in your love (Philem. 7); we had come to love you (1 Thess. 2:8); we commend ourselves in genuine love (2 Cor. 6:6); we know we have passed from death to life because we love the brethren (1 John 3:14); we thank God for your love (Philem. 5); your love for one another is growing (2 Thess. 1:3); add to brotherly kindness love (2 Pet. 1:7); reaffirm your love for the one who did wrong (2 Cor. 2:8).

- Love of man and woman

aa Husbands, love your wives (Eph. 5:25, 28, 33; Col. 3:19); they should teach young women to love their husbands and children (Titus 2:4); be intoxicated with your wife's love (Prov. 5:19); enjoy life with the wife you love (Eccles. 9:9); your love is better than wine (S. of S. 1:2; 4:10); we will extol your love more than wine (S. of S. 1:4); I am faint with love (S. of S. 2:5; 5:8); I will give you my love (S. of S. 7:12); let us take our fill of love till morning (Prov. 7:18).

ab Isaac loved Rebekah (Gen. 24:67); Jacob loved Rachel (Gen. 29:18); more than Leah (Gen. 29:30); surely my husband will love me now (Gen. 29:32); Shechem loved Dinah (Gen. 34:3); Samson loved Delilah (Judg. 16:4); Michal loved David (1 Sam. 18:20, 28); Ammon loved Tamar (2 Sam. 13:1, 4); Solomon loved many foreign women (1 Kgs. 11:1); two wives, one loved and one hated (Deut. 21:15); how can you say, 'I love you'? (Judg. 16:15).

ac Do not stir up love until it please (S. of S. 2:7; 3:5; 8:4).

● Love between people

ad Your only son whom you love (Gen. 22:2); Isaac loved Esau but Rebekah loved Jacob (Gen. 25:28); Israel loved Joseph more than his other sons (Gen. 37:3); Jacob loved Benjamin (Gen. 44:20).

ae Ruth loved Naomi (Ruth 4:15); Saul loved David (1 Sam. 16:21); all Israel loved David (1 Sam. 18:16, 22); Jonathan loved David (1 Sam. 18:1, 3; 20:17); your love for me was more than the love of women (2 Sam. 1:26); my love be with you all (1 Cor. 16:24).

af You love those who hate you and hate those who love you (2 Sam. 19:6); should you love those who hate the Lord? (2 Chr. 19:2).

Favourite, see **890**.

● Loving evil

ag You who hate good and love evil (Mic. 3:2); do not love the world (1 John 2:15); Demas has loved this present world (2 Tim. 4:10); men loved darkness rather than light (John 3:19).

● Loving money

ah Whoever loves money will not be satisfied with money (Eccles. 5:10); men will be lovers of money (2 Tim. 3:2); the love of money is the root of all evil (1 Tim. 6:10); the Pharisees loved money (Luke 16:14); Balaam loved the wages of unrighteousness (2 Pet. 2:15).

ai Be free from the love of money (Heb. 13:5); an elder must be free from love of money (1 Tim. 3:3).

Love of money, see **797***m*.

● Lack of love

aj They are unloving (Rom. 1:31); men will be unloving (2 Tim. 3:3); you have abandoned your first love (Rev. 2:4); Leah was not loved (Gen. 29:31); I will love them no more (Hos. 9:15).

ak If your brother is hurt by what you eat, you are not walking in love (Rom. 14:15); he who does not love his brother is not of God (1 John 3:10); he who does not love is not of God (1 John 4:8).

888 Hatred

● Hating

a There is a time to hate (Eccles. 3:8); hatred stirs up strife (Prov. 10:12); he who hates hides it with his lips (Prov. 26:24–6).

Lack of love, see **887***aj*.

● God hating

b Because of these customs God abhorred them (Lev. 20:23); I will loathe you (Lev. 26:30); whoever does these things is detestable to the Lord (Deut. 18:12); the Lord detests those who wear clothing of the opposite sex (Deut. 22:5); the Lord hates him that loves violence (Ps. 11:5); I hate the pride of Jacob (Amos 6:8); I hate false oaths (Zech. 8:17); seven things are detestable to the Lord (Prov. 6:16); you hate the deeds of the Nicolaitans, which

I also hate (Rev. 2:6); Jacob I loved but Esau I hated (Mal. 1:2–3; Rom. 9:13); God abhorred his heritage (Ps. 106:40); I hate your feasts and offerings (Isa. 1:13–14).

c The Lord detests the earnings of prostitutes (Deut. 23:18); the Lord detests different weights and measures (Deut. 25:16); unclean animals are detestable (Lev. 11:10, 11, 41–3); graven images are an abomination (Deut. 7:25–6); they put their abominations in the house called by my name (Jer. 32:34).

d Because God hates us he brought us out of Egypt (Deut. 1:27).

● Hating God

e Haters of God (Rom. 1:30); God will repay those who hate him with destruction (Deut. 7:10); punishing those who hate me (Exod. 20:5); let those who hate him flee before him (Ps. 68:1); he who hates me hates my Father (John 15:23); do I not hate those who hate you? (Ps. 139:21); evildoers hate the light (John 3:20); the world hates me because I testify against it (John 7:7); the man's citizens hated him (Luke 19:14).

f Once we were hateful and hating (Titus 3:3); all who hate Wisdom love death (Prov. 8:36).

● Hating evil

g The fear of the Lord is to hate evil (Prov. 8:13); let those who love the Lord hate evil (Ps. 97:10); hate what is evil (Rom. 12:9); I hate every false way (Ps. 119:104, 128); I hate falsehood (Ps. 119:163); I hate the work of those who fall away (Ps. 101:3); you love righteousness and hate evil (Ps. 45:7).

● Hating life

h I hated life (Eccles. 2:17); I hated all my work (Eccles. 2:18); they hated all kinds of food (Ps. 107:18); his life loathes food (Job 33:20); he who hates his life in this world will keep it (John 12:25).

● Hating good

i You who hate good and love evil (Mic. 3:2); men will be haters of good (2 Tim. 3:3).

● Hating the righteous

j They hate him who speaks the truth (Amos 5:10); God turned the Egyptians' heart to hate his people (Ps. 105:25).

k All men will hate you because of me (Matt. 10:22; 24:9; Mark 13:13; Luke 21:17); blessed are you when men hate you (Luke 6:22); if the world hates you, it hated me first (John 15:18–19); the world has hated them (John 17:14); do not be surprised if the world hates you (1 John 3:13).

l Do good to those who hate you (Luke 6:27); those who hate you will be clothed with shame (Job 8:22).

● Hating without a cause

m Many hate me wrongfully (Ps. 38:19); those who hate me without a cause are more than the hairs of my head (Ps. 69:4); they hated me without a cause (John 15:25).

● Hating one another

n Do not hate your brother (Lev. 19:17); he who hates his brother is in darkness (1 John 2:9, 11); he who hates his brother is a murderer (1 John 3:15); one who hates his neighbour and kills him (Deut. 19:11); love your neighbour and hate your enemy (Matt. 5:43).

o You will make yourself odious to your father (2 Sam. 16:21); the

Ammonites saw they had made themselves odious to David (1 Chr. 19:6); I am loathsome to my wife and brothers (Job 19:17); many will betray and hate each other (Matt. 24:10).

p He who does not hate father, mother etc. cannot be my disciple (Luke 14:26).

● **Those who hated**

q You hate me (Gen. 26:27; Judg. 14:16); I thought you hated her (Judg. 15:2); his brothers hated Joseph (Gen. 37:4, 8); shepherds are detestable to the Egyptians (Gen. 46:34); the sacrifices would be detestable to the Egyptians (Exod. 8:26); they hated Jephthah (Judg. 11:7); Amnon hated Tamar (2 Sam. 13:15); Absalom hated Amnon (2 Sam. 13:22); you hate those who love you (2 Sam. 19:6); Rezon hated Israel (1 Kgs. 11:25); I hate Micaiah because he prophesies evil (1 Kgs. 22:8; 2 Chr. 18:7).

r The king's command was abhorrent to Joab (1 Chr. 21:6).

s The beast and the ten horns will hate the harlot (Rev. 17:16).

t They will loathe themselves for what them have done (Ezek. 6:9).

Enmity, see **881**; **anger**, see **891**.

● **Not hating**

u Killing unintentionally one you did not hate (Deut. 4:42; 19:4, 6; Josh. 20:5).

889 Endearment

● **Kissing**

a Let him kiss me with the kisses of his mouth (S. of S. 1:2); if I met you outside I would kiss you (S. of S. 8:1); the father kissed the prodigal (Luke 15:20); let me kiss my father and mother (1 Kgs. 19:20); the elders kissed Paul (Acts 20:37); greet one another with a holy kiss (Rom. 16:16; 1 Cor. 16:20; 2 Cor. 13:12; 1 Thess. 5:26); greet one another with a kiss of love (1 Pet. 5:14).

b Jacob kissed Isaac (Gen. 27:26–7); Jacob kissed Rachel (Gen. 29:11); Laban kissed Jacob (Gen. 29:13); Laban kissed his children (Gen. 31:55); Esau embraced and kissed Jacob (Gen. 33:4); Joseph kissed his brothers (Gen. 45:15); Joseph fell on Jacob's neck (Gen. 46:29); Israel kissed and embraced Joseph's children (Gen. 48:10); Joseph kissed his dead father (Gen. 50:1); Aaron kissed Moses (Exod. 4:27); Moses kissed Jethro (Exod. 18:7); Naomi kissed her daughters-in-law (Ruth 1:9); Orpah kissed Naomi (Ruth 1:14); Jonathan and David kissed each other (1 Sam. 20:41); David kissed Absalom (2 Sam. 14:33); Absalom would kiss those about to prostrate themselves (2 Sam. 15:5); David kissed Barzillai (2 Sam. 19:39); Joab kissed Amasa (2 Sam. 20:9).

c A right answer is a kiss on the lips (Prov. 24:26); justice and peace have kissed (Ps. 85:10).

● **Evil kissing**

d Every mouth that has not kissed Baal (1 Kgs. 19:18); the harlot kisses him (Prov. 7:13); the kisses of an enemy are profuse (Prov. 27:6).

● **Kissing Jesus**

e Judas came to kiss Jesus (Luke 22:47); the one I kiss is the man

(Matt. 26:48–9; Mark 14:44–5); do you betray the Son of Man with a kiss? (Luke 22:48).

f This woman has not stopped kissing my feet (Luke 7:45); she kissed his feet (Luke 7:38); kiss the Son, lest he be angry (Ps. 2:12).

● Embracing

g A time to embrace and a time to refrain from embracing (Eccles. 3:5); Abimelech saw Isaac caressing his wife Rebekah (Gen. 26:8); let his right hand embrace me (S. of S. 2:6).

890 Darling. Favourite

● Favourite

a Isaac loved Esau but Rebekah loved Jacob (Gen. 25:28); Jacob loved Rachel more than Leah (Gen. 29:30); Israel loved Joseph more than all his sons (Gen. 37:3); the king loved Esther more than all the women (Esther 2:17); she is her mother's favourite (S. of S. 6:9).

891 Anger

● God's anger

a The law brings wrath (Rom. 4:15).

b The Lord is angry with all nations (Isa. 34:2); the nations were angry, and your wrath has come (Rev. 11:18).

c In anger put down the peoples (Ps. 56:7); destroy my foes in wrath (Ps. 59:13); pour out your indignation on them (Ps. 69:24); the earth shook because God was angry (2 Sam. 22:8; Ps. 18:7); your anger consumed them like chaff (Exod. 15:7); you did not execute his anger on Amalek (1 Sam. 28:18); God was angry that Balaam went (Num. 22:22).

d The day of God's wrath (Zeph. 2:2; Rom. 2:5); the day of his anger (Lam. 2:1); my anger will be poured out on this place (2 Chr. 34:25); hide us from the wrath of the Lamb! (Rev. 6:16); the winepress of the wrath of God (Isa. 63:1–6; Rev. 14:19; 19:15); fleeing from the wrath to come (Luke 3:7).

e The cup of God's anger (Isa. 51:22); the cup of the wine of wrath (Jer. 25:15; Rev. 16:19).

f The wrath of God is against all wickedness of men (Rom. 1:18); for those who follow evil there will be wrath and anger (Rom. 2:8); vessels of wrath prepared for destruction (Rom. 9:22); we were by nature children of wrath (Eph. 2:3); God's wrath comes on the disobedient (Eph. 5:6); because of these things, God's wrath is coming (Col. 3:6); the wrath of God has come upon them (1 Thess. 2:16); the wrath of God remains on him (John 3:36).

● Will God be angry?

g Will you be angry for ever? (Ps. 79:5; 85:5); would you not be angry? (Ezra 9:14); if you are angry with them (1 Kgs. 8:46; 2 Chr. 6:36); how long will you be angry with the prayer of your people? (Ps. 80:4); why this outburst of anger? (Deut. 29:24); why does your anger smoke against your sheep? (Ps. 74:1).

● God will be angry

h If you rebel today, tomorrow the Lord will be angry with all Israel (Josh. 22:18)4; if you serve other gods, the Lord will be angry (Deut. 7:4; 11:16–17; 29:27); on that day I will be angry with them (Deut. 31:17); my wrath will be on you when you go to Egypt (Jer. 42:18); I will pour out my wrath on them (Hos. 5:10).

i Leave me alone that my anger may burn against them (Exod. 32:10); his anger was aroused (Num. 11:1, 10); will you be angry with the whole assembly? (Num. 16:22); I feared the anger of the Lord (Deut. 9:19); the Lord did not turn from his fierce anger (2 Kgs. 23:26).

● God angry with his people

j The Lord's anger burned against his people (Isa. 5:25); his anger is not turned away (Isa. 5:25; 9:12, 17, 21; 10:4); I was angry with that generation (Heb. 3:10); I was angry with my people (Isa. 47:6); the Lord's anger was against Judah (2 Chr. 29:8); my anger was poured out on Judah and Jerusalem (Jer. 44:6); the anger of God rose against them (Ps. 78:31); the Lord was very angry with your fathers (Zech. 1:2).

k When the Lord heard what you said, he was angry (Deut. 1:34); the anger of the Lord burned against Israel (Num. 12:9; 25:3; 32:10, 13–14; Judg. 2:20; 3:8; 10:7; 2 Sam. 24:1; 2 Kgs. 13:3; 17:18; Ps. 78:21; 106:40); my wrath burns against this place (2 Kgs. 22:17); the Lord's anger burned against Israel because of Achan (Josh. 7:1, 26); wrath fell on the whole congregation (Josh. 22:20); wrath came against Israel (2 Kgs. 3:27; 1 Chr. 27:24); great wrath burns against us (2 Kgs. 22:13); Assyria, the rod of my anger (Isa. 10:5).

l You made the Lord angry (Deut. 9:22); they provoked the Lord to anger (Judg. 2:12; 2 Kgs. 21:15; Ps. 106:29, 32); Ahaziah provoked the Lord to anger (1 Kgs. 22:53); our fathers angered the God of heaven (Ezra 5:12).

● God angry with individuals

m The Lord's anger against Moses (Exod. 4:14; Deut. 3:26; 4:21); the Lord's anger broke out against Uzzah (2 Sam. 6:7–8; 1 Chr. 13:10); the Lord was angry with Solomon (1 Kgs. 11:9); God was angry with Job's friends (Job 42:7); God tears me in his anger (Job 16:9); I eat ashes because of your great wrath (Ps. 102:9–10).

● Speed of God's anger

n God is slow to anger (Exod. 34:6; Ps. 86:15; 103:8; 145:8; Joel 2:13); his anger lasts for a moment, but his favour is for a lifetime (Ps. 30:5); in a little while my anger will be spent (Isa. 10:25).

o His anger is quickly kindled (Ps. 2:12).

● God turning from anger

p I have sworn not to be angry with you (Isa. 54:9); will he be angry for ever? (Jer. 3:5); I will not always be angry (Isa. 57:16); we are saved from God's wrath (Rom. 5:9); God did not appoint us to wrath but to salvation (1 Thess. 5:9).

● Jesus' anger

q Jesus looked round at them with anger (Mark 3:5); Jesus was indignant at the disciples (Mark 10:14).

● Angry with God

r I know your raging against me (2 Kgs. 19:27–8); the fool rages against the Lord (Prov. 19:3).

- Acceptable anger

s The wrath of men shall praise you (Ps. 76:10); be angry and sin not (Eph. 4:26; cf. Ps. 4:4).

- Tearing clothes in anger

t Those who tore their clothes: the king of Israel (2 Kgs. 5:7, 8); Athaliah (2 Kgs. 11:14); the high priest (Matt. 26:65).

- Anger of people

u A king's wrath is like a lion's roar (Prov. 19:12; 20:2); a king's wrath is like messengers of death (Prov. 16:14); if a ruler's anger rises against you (Eccles. 10:4); wise men turn away from anger (Prov. 29:8); anger is in the heart of fools (Eccles. 7:9); the wicked will see it and be angry (Ps. 112:10).

- Angry people

v Cain was angry about his sacrifices (Gen. 4:5–6); Jacob's sons were furious about Shechem (Gen. 34:7); cursed be their anger (Gen. 49:7); Saul was angry about Jabesh-gilead (1 Sam. 11:6); Saul was angry about David's success (1 Sam. 18:8); if Saul is very angry (1 Sam. 20:7); David was angry at Perez-uzzah (2 Sam. 6:8); David was angry at Nathan's story (2 Sam. 12:5); David was angry about Amnon (2 Sam. 13:21); why are you angry? (2 Sam. 19:42); Ahab was sullen and angry (1 Kgs. 20:43; 21:4); Naaman went away angry (2 Kgs. 5:11); the troops from Ephraim were furious to be sent home (2 Chr. 25:10); Sanballat was angry that the wall was being rebuilt (Neh. 4:1, 7); Nehemiah was angry (Neh. 5:6); Jonah was angry (Jonah 4:1, 4).

- People angry with others

w Esau bore a grudge against Jacob (Gen. 27:41); Jacob was angry with Laban (Gen. 31:36); Potiphar was angry with Joseph (Gen. 39:19); Pharaoh was angry with his butler and baker (Gen. 40:2); what if Joseph holds a grudge against us? (Gen. 50:15); Moses was angry with Pharaoh (Exod. 11:8); with the people (Exod. 16:20; 32:19); with Aaron's sons (Lev. 10:16); with Korah and his followers (Num. 16:15); with the officers (Num. 31:14); Balaam was angry with his donkey (Num. 22:27); Balak was angry with Balaam (Num. 24:10); Eliab was angry with David (1 Sam. 17:28); Saul was angry with Jonathan (1 Sam. 20:30); Jonathan was very angry with his father (1 Sam. 20:34); the commanders were angry with Achish (1 Sam. 29:4); Asa was angry with the seer (2 Chr. 16:10); Uzziah was enraged with the priest (2 Chr. 26:19); King Ahasuerus was furious with Queen Vashti (Esther 1:12); Ahasuerus rose in anger (Esther 7:7); Haman was filled with rage against Mordecai (Esther 3:5; 5:9); Herodias bore a grudge against John (Mark 6:19).

x The ten were indignant with James and John (Matt. 20:24; Mark 10:41); they were furious with Stephen (Acts 7:54); the prodigal's older brother was angry (Luke 15:28).

- Angry with Jesus

y The people in the synagogue were furious with Jesus (Luke 4:28); they were angry because he healed on the Sabbath (Luke 6:11; 13:14); the priests were indignant (Matt. 21:15); they were infuriated (Acts 5:33); why are you angry with me for healing on the Sabbath? (John 7:23).

● Avoid anger   *z* Cease from anger (Ps. 37:8); get rid of anger (Eph. 4:31; Col. 3:8); be slow to anger (Jas. 1:19); the anger of man does not work the righteousness of God (Jas. 1:20); outbursts of anger are deeds of the flesh (Gal. 5:20); everyone who is angry with his brother will be liable to judgement (Matt. 5:22); an elder must not be quick-tempered (Titus 1:7).

aa Fathers, do not provoke your children to anger (Eph. 6:4; Col. 3:21).

892 Quick temper

● Quick-   *a* A man of quick temper acts foolishly (Prov. 14:17); a hasty
tempered   temper exalts folly (Prov. 14:29); a fool loses his temper (Prov. 29:11); a hot-tempered man abounds in transgression (Prov. 29:22); a hot-tempered man stirs up strife (Prov. 15:18); do not associate with a hot-tempered man (Prov. 22:24).

● Fierce men   *b* Fierce men may fall on you (Judg. 18:25); David and his men are fierce (2 Sam. 17:8).
Violence, see **176**.

● Irritable   *c* Love is not irritable (1 Cor. 13:5).

893 Sullenness

● Sulking   *a* Ahab was sullen and angry (1 Kgs. 20:43; 21:4).

894 Marriage

● Marriage   *a* Do we not have a right to take a believer as wife? (1 Cor. 9:5).
allowed

b I counsel younger widows to marry (1 Tim. 5:14); marriage to a captive woman is permitted (Deut. 21:11); take wives and have children in exile (Jer. 29:6).

● Marriage   *c* Some forbid marriage (1 Tim. 4:3); you must not marry in this
discouraged   place (Jer. 16:2).

d It is better not to marry (Matt. 19:10); it is good for a man not to marry (1 Cor. 7:1); those who marry will have troubles (1 Cor. 7:28); married people are concerned about their partners (1 Cor. 7:33–4); he who marries does right but he who does not marry does better (1 Cor. 7:38); those who have wives should live as though they had none (1 Cor. 7:29).

● Marriage   *e* A man must not marry his father's wife (Deut. 22:30); must not
controlled   marry a woman and her sister (Lev. 18:18); or a woman and her mother (Lev. 20:14); someone has his father's wife (1 Cor. 5:1); it is not lawful for you to have your brother's wife (Matt. 14:4; Mark 6:18); a daughter who inherits must marry within her clan (Num. 36:2–12).

f A woman divorced twice must not re-marry her first husband (Deut. 24:4); priests must not marry prostitutes or divorcees (Lev. 21:7, 13–14); priests must not marry divorcees or widows of non-priests (Ezek. 44:22); he who marries a divorced woman commits adultery (Matt. 5:32).

g An elder must be the husband of one wife (1 Tim. 3:2; Titus 1:6); as must be a deacon (1 Tim. 3:12); an enrolled widow should have been the wife of one man (1 Tim. 5:9); a widow is free to marry but only in the Lord (1 Cor. 7:39).

h A married woman is bound to her husband as long as he lives (Rom. 7:2; 1 Cor. 7:39); if a slave comes with a wife, she may be released with him (Exod. 21:3); if given a wife, the wife and children belong to the master (Exod. 21:4).

Quarrelsome wives, see **709***e*.

• Marriage duties

i Do not break faith with the wife of your youth (Mal. 2:14–15); the husband and wife should fulfil their duty to each other (1 Cor. 7:3–5); let marriage be held in honour and the marriage bed be undefiled (Heb. 13:4).

j Husbands, love your wives (Eph. 5:25; Col. 3:19); be considerate to your wives (1 Pet. 3:7); a husband may annul his wife's vows (Num. 30:6–15).

k Wives, be subject to your husbands (Eph. 5:22; Col. 3:18; 1 Pet. 3:1); women may look with contempt on their husbands (Esther 1:17); all women will give honour to their husbands (Esther 1:20); teach wives to love their husbands (Titus 2:4).

• Levirate marriage

l The husband's brother must marry the widow (Deut. 25:5; Matt. 22:24; Mark 12:19; Luke 20:28); raise up children for your brother (Gen. 38:8); raising up the name of the dead man (Ruth 4:5, 10).

• Marriage blessings

m An excellent wife is her husband's crown (Prov. 12:4); your wife will be like a fruitful vine (Ps. 128:3); a prudent wife is from the Lord (Prov. 19:14); description of an excellent wife (Prov. 31:10–31).

n He who finds a wife finds a good thing (Prov. 18:22); may you rejoice in the wife of your youth (Prov. 5:15–20).

o A man recently married must not go to war (Deut. 24:5).

• Punishments affecting marriage

p You will be betrothed to a woman, but another will rape her (Deut. 28:30); another will lie with your wives in broad daylight (2 Sam. 12:11).

q You will die for taking a married woman (Gen. 20:3).

• Marriage no more

r At the resurrection, whose wife will she be? (Matt. 22:28; Mark 12:23; Luke 20:33); at the resurrection they will not marry (Matt. 22:30; Mark 12:25; Luke 20:35).

s In the days of Noah they were marrying and giving in marriage until the flood came (Matt. 24:38; Luke 17:27).

• Multiple marriages

t A king must not take many wives (Deut. 17:17); if a man has two wives, one loved and one not (Deut. 21:15–17); on taking a second wife, marriage rights must not be reduced (Exod. 21:10).

u Lamech married two women (Gen. 4:19); Sarah gave Hagar to Abraham as wife (Gen. 16:3); Esau married two Hittite women

(Gen. 26:34); plus a woman of Ishmael (Gen. 28:9); Jacob married Leah (Gen. 29:21–5); Rachel (Gen. 29:28–30); Bilhah (Gen. 30:4); and Zilpah (Gen. 30:9); Gideon had many wives (Judg. 8:30); Elkanah had two wives (1 Sam. 1:2); David married Abigail (1 Sam. 25:39–42); and Ahinoam (1 Sam. 25:43); David took more concubines and wives (2 Sam. 5:13; 1 Chr. 14:3); David married Bathsheba (2 Sam. 11:27; 12:9); give me my wife Michal (2 Sam. 3:13–15); Solomon had 700 wives (1 Kgs. 11:3); Rehoboam married Mahalath and Maacah (2 Chr. 11:18–21); Rehoboam had 18 wives and 60 concubines (2 Chr. 11:21); Rehoboam sought many wives for his sons (2 Chr. 11:23); Abijah took 14 wives (2 Chr. 13:21); Jehoiada took two wives for Joash (2 Chr. 24:3).

● Transferring
wives

v Samson's wife was given to his friend (Judg. 14:20; 15:2, 6); David's wife Michal given to Palti (1 Sam. 25:44); I gave your master's wives into your bosom (2 Sam. 12:8); Absalom went in to his father's concubines (2 Sam. 16:21–2); Adonijah wanted Abishag as his wife (1 Kgs. 2:17, 21–2); your most beautiful wives are mine (1 Kgs. 20:3); give me your wives and children (1 Kgs. 20:5); Jehoram's wives and children were taken (2 Chr. 21:17).

● Intermarriage

w Do not intermarry with them (Exod. 34:16; Deut. 7:3; Josh. 23:12; Ezra 9:12); shall we intermarry with the peoples? (Judg. 14:3; Ezra 9:14); they intermarried with them (Judg. 3:6; Ezra 9:1–2; 10:44); we have been unfaithful to God by marrying foreign women (Ezra 10:2); they had married foreign women (Neh. 13:23, 27); you have married foreign wives (Ezra 10:10); lists of those who had married foreign wives (Ezra 10:18–44); Jews were linked to Tobiah by marriage (Neh. 6:18); we promise not to intermarry with them (Neh. 10:30).

x The sons of God married the daughters of men (Gen. 6:2); an Egyptian wife for Ishmael (Gen. 21:21); do not take a wife from the Canaanites (Gen. 24:3, 4, 37); if Jacob takes a wife from the women of the land (Gen. 27:46); do not marry a Canaanite woman (Gen. 28:1, 2, 6–9); Esau married Canaanites (Gen. 36:2); Shechem wanted Dinah as his wife (Gen. 34:4); intermarry with us (Gen. 34:9); let us intermarry with them (Gen. 34:21); Joseph married Asenath (Gen. 41:45); Moses married Zipporah (Exod. 2:21); Moses had married a Cushite (Num. 12:1); Samson married a Philistine woman (Judg. 14:1–3); Naomi's sons married Moabite women (Ruth 1:4); Judah has married the daughter of a foreign god (Mal. 2:11).

● Wives for
Benjamin

y No one will give his daughter in marriage to a Benjaminite (Judg. 21:1); how shall we provide wives? (Judg. 21:7, 16); seize a wife from the girls of Shiloh (Judg. 21:21).

● Actual
marriages

z Isaac married Rebekah (Gen. 24:67); Abraham took another wife (Gen. 25:1); Israel worked for a wife (Hos. 12:12); Judah took a wife for Er (Gen. 38:6); Saul offered his daughter Merab to David in marriage (1 Sam. 18:17); but she was given to Adriel instead (1 Sam. 18:19); Solomon married Pharaoh's daughter (1 Kgs. 3:1; 7:8; 2 Chr. 8:11); Pharaoh gave Hadad his wife's sister in marriage (1 Kgs. 11:19); Ahab married Jezebel (1 Kgs. 16:31); Jehoshaphat allied himself with Ahab by marriage (2 Chr. 18:1); Jehoram married Ahab's daughter (2 Kgs. 8:18; 2 Chr. 21:6); Joseph married Mary (Matt. 1:24); there was a wedding at Cana in Galilee (John 2:1); call your husband (John 4:16).

aa Caleb gave his daughter in marriage to the one who took Kiriath-sepher (Josh. 15:16–17; Judg. 1:12–13); the king will give his daughter in marriage to the man who kills Goliath (1 Sam. 17:25); Saul gave David his daughter Michal in marriage on payment of 100 Philistine foreskins (1 Sam. 18:27).

● Betrothal

ab An engaged man should return from war (Deut. 20:7); Mary was pledged in marriage to Joseph (Matt. 1:18; Luke 1:27; 2:5); you will be betrothed to a woman, but another will rape her (Deut. 28:30).

● Marriage to God

ac Your Maker is your husband (Isa. 54:5); the Lord will take delight in you and your land will be married (Isa. 62:4); you will call me 'my husband' (Hos. 2:16).

ad I remember how as a bride you loved me (Jer. 2:2); I was a husband to them (Jer. 31:32); return, for I am your husband (Jer. 3:14); I betrothed you to one husband, to Christ (2 Cor. 11:2); I will betroth you to me in righteousness (Hos. 2:19–20).

ae A king prepared a wedding feast for his son (Matt. 22:2); the marriage of the Lamb has come (Rev. 19:7); blessed are those invited to the wedding supper of the Lamb (Rev. 19:9); I will show you the wife of the Lamb (Rev. 21:9); new Jerusalem as a bride adorned for her husband (Rev. 21:2).

● Marriage as a picture

af The sun like a bridegroom (Ps. 19:4–5).
Wedding garments, see **228***p*.

895 Celibacy

● Virginity

a Proof of a woman's virginity on marriage (Deut. 22:13–21); virgin princesses wore a long-sleeved robe (2 Sam. 13:18); the high priest must marry a virgin (Lev. 21:13, 14); spare those women who have not known man (Num. 31:18).

b Lot's daughters had never had relations with a man (Gen. 19:8); take my virgin daughter (Judg. 19:24); Rebekah was a virgin (Gen. 24:16); Jephthah's daughter would remain a virgin (Judg. 11:37–9); 400 young virgins (Judg. 21:12); Tamar was a virgin (2 Sam. 13:2); they sought a virgin to keep David warm (1 Kgs. 1:2); beautiful young virgins were sought for Ahasuerus (Esther 2:2).

c Mary was a virgin (Luke 1:27, 34); a virgin shall conceive (Isa. 7:14; Matt. 1:23); Philip had four virgin daughters (Acts 21:9).

d Paul wanted to present them to Christ as a pure virgin (2 Cor. 11:2).

e The virgin daughter of Zion (2 Kgs. 19:21); the parable of the ten virgins (Matt. 25:1–12).

● Chastity

f Do not go near a woman (Exod. 19:15); they have not been defiled by women for they are virgins (Rev. 14:4).

g Judah did not know Tamar again (Gen. 38:26); they may eat holy bread if they have kept themselves from women (1 Sam. 21:4).

● Unmarried

h Paul's opinion on the unmarried (1 Cor. 7:25–35); the unmarried person is concerned with the things of the Lord (1 Cor. 7:32, 34); regulations on the marriage of a virgin (1 Cor. 7:36–8); it is good for them to remain unmarried like me (1 Cor. 7:8); if you are unmarried, do not seek for a wife (1 Cor. 7:27).

i Men who forbid marriage (1 Tim. 4:3).

Eunuchs, see **172*h***.

896 Divorce. Widowhood

● Avoid divorce

a I hate divorce, says the Lord (Mal. 2:16); a man cannot divorce a woman he seized (Deut. 22:28–9); a husband must not divorce his wife (1 Cor. 7:11); a wife should not leave her husband (1 Cor. 7:10); a believer must not divorce an unbelieving spouse willing to live with the believer (1 Cor. 7:12–13); if you are bound to a wife, do not seek to be released (1 Cor. 7:27).

Divorce and adultery, see **951*h***.

● Divorce permitted

b Is it lawful for a man to divorce his wife? (Matt. 19:3; Mark 10:2); he who divorces his wife must give her a certificate of divorce (Deut. 24:1; Matt. 5:31; 19:7; Mark 10:4); Moses permitted you to divorce your wives because your hearts were hard (Matt. 19:8; Mark 10:5); he who divorces his wife, except for unchastity, makes her an adulteress (Matt. 5:32).

Bills of divorce, see **548*d***.

● Divorcees

c He who divorces his wife and marries another commits adultery (Matt. 19:9; Mark 10:11; Luke 16:18); if a wife leaves her husband she should remain single or be reconciled (1 Cor. 7:11); if she divorces her husband and marries another, she commits adultery (Mark 10:12); he who marries a divorced woman commits adultery (Matt. 5:32; Luke 16:18); if a divorced wife returns to her former husband (Jer. 3:1); a woman who leaves her husband should remain unmarried (1 Cor. 7:11); a priest must not marry a divorcee (Lev. 21:7, 14).

d A divorcee's vow will stand (Num. 30:9); a priest's daughter divorced may eat the offerings (Lev. 22:13).

● Actual divorces

e Shaharaim sent away his two wives (1 Chr. 8:8); separate yourselves from these foreign wives (Ezra 10:11); they promised to put away their foreign wives (Ezra 10:19); Joseph wanted to divorce Mary privately (Matt. 1:19); send away all these women (Ezra 10:3).

● Divorce from the Lord

   f I gave faithless Israel her certificate of divorce (Jer. 3:8); where is your mother's certfificate of divorce? (Isa. 50:1).

● Widowhood

   g A widow's vow will stand (Num. 30:9); a priest's daughter widowed may eat the offerings (Lev. 22:13); rules for enrolling widows (1 Tim. 5:3–16); the high priest must not marry a widow (Lev. 21:14); a poor widow (Mark 12:42–3; Luke 21:2–3).

   h When you buy the land you acquire the dead man's widow (Ruth 4:5).

● Helping widows

   i God judges for orphans and widows (Deut. 10:18); the Lord supports the widow (Ps. 146:9); God maintains the widow's boundary (Prov. 15:25); let your widows trust in me (Jer. 49:11).

   j Do not pervert the justice due to a widow (Deut. 27:19); a widow kept coming to the judge (Luke 18:3); plead for the widow (Isa. 1:17); do not take a widow's garment in pledge (Deut. 24:17).

   k Do not take advantage of a widow (Exod. 22:22); give the tithe to the widow (Deut. 14:29; 26:12–13); invite the widow to the Feast of Booths (Deut. 16:14); leave a forgotten sheaf and gleanings for the widow (Deut. 24:19); true religion is to visit orphans and widows (Jas. 1:27); I made the widow's heart sing for joy (Job 29:13).

● Oppressing widows

   l Evildoers murder widows and orphans (Ps. 94:6); you have sent widows away empty (Job 22:9); you devour widows' houses (Matt. 23:14; Mark 12:40; Luke 20:47); some take the widow's ox in pledge (Job 24:3); the widow's plea is neglected (Isa. 1:23); if I have neglected the widow (Job 31:16).

● Being widowed

   m In a single day widowhood will come (Isa. 47:9); let their wives become widows (Jer. 18:21); let his wife be a widow (Ps. 109:9); I will not sit as a widow (Isa. 47:8); I am not a widow (Rev. 18:7). **Bereavement**, see **772e**.

● Actual widows

   n Tamar was to live as a widow (Gen. 38:11); Abigail the widow of Nabal (1 Sam. 27:3; 30:5; 2 Sam. 2:2; 3:3); Uriah's widow (2 Sam. 12:15); I am a widow (2 Sam. 14:5); the ten concubines lived as widows (2 Sam. 20:3); a widow looked after Elijah (1 Kgs. 17:9–16); the widow of one of the prophets (2 Kgs. 4:1); there were many widows in Israel (Luke 4:25).

897 Benevolence

● Blessing

   a The lesser is blessed by the greater (Heb. 7:7).

● God's blessing

   b The blessing of the Lord makes rich (Prov. 10:22); I will give showers of blessing (Ezek. 34:26).

   c May God Almighty bless you (Gen. 28:3); may he bless the boys (Gen. 48:16); the Lord bless you (Judg. 17:2; 1 Sam. 23:21; 2 Sam. 2:5); may you be blessed by the Lord (Ps. 115:15); I will not let you go unless you bless me (Gen. 32:26); with your blessing may my house be blessed for ever (2 Sam. 7:29).

d The Lord blesses his people with peace (Ps. 29:11); he will bless your bread and water (Exod. 23:25); the Lord bless you and keep you (Num. 6:23–6); may God be gracious to us and bless us (Ps. 67:1); blessed are those who dwell in your house (Ps. 84:4); blessed are those whose strength is in you (Ps. 84:5); he will bless those who fear the Lord (Ps. 115:13); God blesses you with all blessings (Gen. 49:25).

● Those blessed by God

e God blessed the seventh day (Gen. 2:3; Exod. 20:11); God blessed sea creatures and birds (Gen. 1:22).

f God blessed mankind (Gen. 1:28; 5:2); God blessed Noah and his sons (Gen. 9:1); I will bless Ishmael (Gen. 17:20); the Lord had blessed Abraham (Gen. 24:1, 35); God blessed Isaac (Gen. 25:11; 26:12, 29); stay in this land and I will bless you (Gen. 26:3); the man blessed Jacob (Gen. 32:29); Naphtali, full of the blessing of the Lord (Deut. 33:23); God blessed Jacob (Gen. 48:3); God blessed Samson (Judg. 13:24); the Lord blessed Obed-Edom (2 Sam. 6:11, 12; 1 Chr. 13:14).

g I will bless Sarah (Gen. 17:16); Jael was most blessed among women (Judg. 5:24); Mary was blessed among women (Luke 1:42); all generations will call me blessed (Luke 1:48).

● God's people blessed

h You will be blessed above all peoples (Deut. 7:14); the beatitudes (Matt. 5:3–12; Luke 6:20–3); they may curse, but you will bless (Ps. 109:28); do not put a curse on this people, for they are blessed (Num. 22:12); I brought you to curse and you have blessed them (Num. 23:11); he has blessed and I cannot change it (Num. 23:20); it pleased the Lord to bless Israel (Num. 24:1); you have blessed and it will be blessed for ever (1 Chr. 17:27).

● Blessing and curse

i I am setting before you a blessing and a curse (Deut. 11:26; 30:19); blessing if you heed the commandments (Deut. 11:27); you will place the blessing on Mount Gerizim (Deut. 11:29); these shall stand on Mount Gerizim to bless the people (Deut. 27:12); these blessings will come upon you if you obey the Lord (Deut. 28:2–6); Joshua read the blessings and the curses (Josh. 8:34).

● Blessing through God's people

j I will bless those who bless you (Gen. 12:3); may those who bless you be blessed (Gen. 27:29; Num. 24:9); all nations will be blessed through you (Gen. 12:2–3; 18:18; 22:17–18; 26:4; 28:14; Ps. 72:17; Acts 3:25); Israel will be a blessing in the midst of the earth (Isa. 19:24–5); the Lord blessed Laban because of Jacob (Gen. 30:27, 30); the Lord blessed Potiphar because of Joseph (Gen. 39:5); may he give you the blessing of Abraham (Gen. 28:4).

● God's loving-kindness

k God's lovingkindness endures for ever (1 Chr. 16:34, 41; 2 Chr. 5:13; 7:3, 6; 20:21; Ps. 106:1; 107:1; 118:1–4, 29; 136:1–26); his lovingkindness to Israel endures for ever (Ezra 3:11); his lovingkindness is from everlasting to everlasting (Ps. 103:17).

l Lovingkindness is yours, O Lord (Ps. 62:12); your lovingkindness is better than life (Ps. 63:3); consider the lovingkindness of the Lord (Ps. 107:43); I will sing of the lovingkindness of the Lord for ever (Ps. 89:1); your lovingkindness is great (Ps. 108:4); lovingkindness and truth go before you (Ps. 89:14); lovingkindness and truth have met together (Ps. 85:10); your lovingkindness reaches to the heavens (Ps. 36:5); as high as the heavens, so great is his lovingkindness (Ps. 103:11).

● Lovingkind-   *m*   Lovingkindness will surround the one who trusts in the Lord (Ps.
ness to men   32:10); with the kind you show yourself kind (2 Sam. 22:26; Ps. 18:25); you have magnified your lovingkindness in saving my life (Gen. 19:19); show lovingkindness to my master Abraham (Gen. 24:12); he has not forsaken his lovingkindness toward my master (Gen. 24:27); I am unworthy of all the lovingkindness you have shown me (Gen. 32:10); the Lord showed Joseph lovingkindness (Gen. 39:21); in your lovingkindness you led the people you redeemed (Exod. 15:13); you showed great kindness to David (1 Kgs. 3:6); he crowns you with lovingkindness (Ps. 103:4); the Lord was gracious to them (2 Kgs. 13:23).

● God's favour   *n*   The Lord has shown his favour (Luke 1:25); you have found favour with God (Luke 1:28, 30); may the favour of the Lord our God be on us (Ps. 90:17); he who finds Wisdom obtains favour from the Lord (Prov. 8:35); he who finds a wife obtains favour from the Lord (Prov. 18:22).
Finding favour in God's eyes, see **826*f***; **face shining on**, see **417*l*.**

           o   His mercies are very great (1 Chr. 21:13); the Lord is gracious and compassionate (2 Chr. 30:9); the Most High is kind to the ungrateful and wicked (Luke 6:35); if favour is shown to the wicked he does not learn righteousness (Isa. 26:10).

● Grace through   *p*   The grace of the Lord Jesus be with you (1 Cor. 16:23; Gal. 6:18;
Christ   Phil. 4:23; 1 Thess. 5:28; 2 Thess. 3:18; Philem. 25); grace be with you (2 Tim. 4:22; Titus 3:15; Heb. 13:25); the grace of the Lord Jesus be with God's people (Rev. 22:21); grace and peace to you (2 Cor. 1:2; Phil. 1:2; Col. 1:2; 1 Thess. 1:1; 2 Thess. 1:2; Titus 1:4; Philem. 3; 1 Pet. 1:2; 2 Pet. 1:2); grace, mercy and peace (1 Tim. 1:2; 2 Tim. 1:2; 2 John 3); the grace of our Lord Jesus Christ, the love of God and the fellowship of the Holy Spirit (2 Cor. 13:14); grace be with those who love our Lord Jesus (Eph. 6:24); the manifold grace of God (1 Pet. 4:10).

           q   Grace and truth came through Jesus Christ (John 1:14, 17); from his fulness we all received, grace upon grace (John 1:16); through the grace of the Lord Jesus we must be saved (Acts 15:11); you know the grace of our Lord Jesus Christ (2 Cor. 8:9); the grace which he bestowed on us in the Beloved (Eph. 1:6); the riches of his kindness and forbearance (Rom. 2:4); this grace was given us in Christ from all eternity (2 Tim. 1:9); in coming ages he will show the riches of his kindness to us (Eph. 2:7); the grace of our Lord was poured out on me (1 Tim. 1:14); by the grace of God I am what I am (1 Cor. 15:10); my grace is sufficient (2 Cor. 12:9).

r By grace you have been saved (Eph. 2:5, 8); where sin increased, grace abounded (Rom. 5:20); that grace might reign (Rom. 5:21); see that no one misses the grace of God (Heb. 12:15); this is the true grace of God (1 Pet. 5:12); a remnant chosen by grace, not works (Rom. 11:5–6); we are not under law but under grace (Rom. 6:14); God's kindness, if you remain in his kindness (Rom. 11:22).

Grace not works, see **676*h***.

s God has blessed us with every spiritual blessing in Christ (Eph. 1:3); he lifted his hands and blessed them (Luke 24:50).

- Kindness between people

t Bless those who persecute you (Rom. 12:14); bless those who curse you (Luke 6:28); when reviled we bless (1 Cor. 4:12); the fruit of the Spirit is kindness (Gal. 5:22); a gracious woman gets honour (Prov. 11:16).

- People blessing

u Her children rise and bless her (Prov. 31:28); he who blesses with a loud voice early in the morning will be reckoned as a curse (Prov. 27:14).

v Melchizedek blessed Abraham (Gen. 14:19); they blessed Rebekah (Gen. 24:60); Isaac blessed Jacob (Gen. 27:27; 28:1; Heb. 11:20); intending to bless Esau (Gen. 27:4, 7, 10); bless me also! (Gen. 27:34; Exod. 12:32); we bless you in the name of the Lord (Ps. 129:8); Laban blessed his grandchildren and daughters (Gen. 31:55); Jacob blessed Pharaoh (Gen. 47:10); Jacob blessed Joseph's sons (Gen. 48:9, 20; Heb. 11:21); Jacob blessed Joseph (Gen. 48:15); and all his sons (Gen. 49:28); Joshua blessed Caleb (Josh. 14:13); Joshua blessed the two and a half tribes (Josh. 22:6); Eli blessed Elkanah (1 Sam. 2:20); David blessed Barzillai (2 Sam. 19:39).

w Blessing the people: Moses (Exod. 39:43; Deut. 33:1); Aaron (Lev. 9:22); Moses and Aaron (Lev. 9:23); David (2 Sam. 6:18); Solomon (1 Kgs. 8:14, 55; 2 Chr. 6:3).

x Show me the kindness I have shown you (Gen. 21:23); if you are going to show lovingkindness and truth, tell me (Gen. 24:49); David showed kindness to Mephibosheth (2 Sam. 9:1, 7); is this your kindness to your friend? (2 Sam. 16:17); show kindness to the sons of Barzillai (1 Kgs. 2:7); Evil-merodach spoke kindly to Jehoiachin (2 Kgs. 25:28).

Finding favour in people's eyes, see **826*p***.

898 Malevolence

- Malice

a Men will be brutal (2 Tim. 3:3); filled with malice (Rom. 1:29); put away malice (Eph. 4:31); Nabal was churlish (1 Sam. 25:3).

899 Curse

● Principles
of cursing

a Anyone who curses father or mother must be put to death (Exod. 21:17; Lev. 20:9); whoever curses his parents, his lamp will go out (Prov. 20:20); do not curse the deaf (Lev. 19:14); do not curse the king even in private (Eccles. 10:20); a curse without cause does not alight (Prov. 26:2); bless those who curse you (Luke 6:28).

● God cursing

b God cursed the serpent (Gen. 3:14); cursed is the ground (Gen. 3:17); never again will I curse the ground (Gen. 8:21); the Lord's curse is on the house of the wicked (Prov. 3:33); I will curse your blessings (Mal. 2:2); a curse devours the earth (Isa. 24:6); your curse will be on them (Lam. 3:65).

c Cain was under a curse (Gen. 4:11); cursed be Canaan (Gen. 9:25); Eli's sons brought a curse on themselves (1 Sam. 3:13); I could wish that I were accursed (Rom. 9:3).

● The curse
of the law

d I am setting before you a blessing and a curse (Deut. 11:26); the curse if you disobey (Deut. 11:28); the curse set on Mount Ebal (Deut. 11:29); these tribes shall stand on Mount Ebal for the curse (Deut. 27:13–26); if you do not obey, these curses will come on you (Deut. 28:15–20); Joshua read the blessings and the curses (Josh. 8:34).

e Cursed be he who does not do the law (Deut. 27:26); a curse and an oath to walk in God's law (Neh. 10:29); cursed is he who does not heed the words of this covenant (Jer. 11:3); cursed be he who offers a blemished animal (Mal. 1:14); you are cursed for robbing me (Mal. 3:9); those under the law are under a curse (Gal. 3:10); he who is hanged is accursed by God (Deut. 21:23; Gal. 3:13); every curse in the book (Deut. 29:20, 27; 2 Chr. 34:24); the curses will be turned on your enemies (Deut. 30:7).

f The priest puts the woman under the curse of the oath (Num. 5:21); the priest writes these curses on a scroll (Num. 5:23); the water of bitterness which brings a curse (Num. 5:19); the flying scroll is the curse over the land (Zech. 5:3).

g Christ redeemed us from the curse of the law (Gal. 3:13); there will no longer be any curse (Rev. 22:3).

● Cursing
God

h Do not curse God or a ruler of your people (Exod. 22:28); he blasphemed the Name and cursed (Lev. 24:11); if anyone curses his God he will bear his sin (Lev. 24:15); testify that he has cursed both God and the king (1 Kgs. 21:10, 13); no one speaking by the Spirit of God can say 'Jesus is cursed' (1 Cor. 12:3).

i Satan predicted that Job would curse God (Job 1:11; 2:5); his wife told him to curse God (Job 2:9); perhaps my sons have cursed God (Job 1:5); when they are hungry they will curse the king and their God (Isa. 8:21); they cursed God because of the plague of hail (Rev. 16:21).

● Cursing
Israel

j Balak summoned Balaam to curse you (Josh. 24:9); Moab hired Balaam to curse them (Neh. 13:2); curse Israel for me (Num.

22:11, 17; 23:7, 13; Deut. 23:4); do not curse them and do not bless them (Num. 23:25); God turned the curse into a blessing (Deut. 23:5; Josh. 24:9–10; Neh. 13:2).

k Whoever curses you I will curse (Gen. 12:3); cursed be those who curse you (Gen. 27:29; Num. 24:9); put a curse on these people, for those you curse are cursed (Num. 22:6); how can I curse whose whom God has not cursed? (Num. 23:8).

- Ungodly cursing

l They bless with their mouths, but in their hearts they curse (Ps. 62:4); with the tongue we curse men (Jas. 3:9); from the same mouth come blessing and cursing (Jas. 3:10); their mouth is full of curses and bitterness (Rom. 3:14); my enemies use my name for a curse (Ps. 102:8); I have not lent or borrowed but everyone curses me (Jer. 15:10); he loved cursing, so it came on him (Ps. 109:17); you know you have often cursed others (Eccles. 7:21–2); they ate, drank and cursed Abimelech (Judg. 9:27); Goliath cursed David by his gods (1 Sam. 17:43).

- Cursing the ungodly

m Cursed be the one who gives a wife to Benjamin (Judg. 21:18); cursed be the man who rebuilds Jericho (Josh. 6:26); curse Meroz because they did not help the Lord (Judg. 5:23); cursed be he who is negligent in the Lord's work (Jer. 48:10); the curse of Jotham came on them (Judg. 9:57); cursed be any one who eats before evening (1 Sam. 14:24, 28); Elisha called down a curse on the youths (2 Kgs. 2:24); Shiméi cursed David (2 Sam. 16:5–9, 13; 1 Kgs. 2:8); perhaps the Lord told him to curse (2 Sam. 16:10, 11); he cursed the Lord's anointed (2 Sam. 19:21); Nehemiah called down curses on those who married foreign women (Neh. 13:25).

n If anyone preaches a different gospel, let him be cursed (Gal. 1:8–9); if anyone does not love the Lord, let him be accursed (1 Cor. 16:22).

o You will become a curse (Jer. 42:18); they will use their names as a curse (Jer. 29:22).

- Cursing oneself

p I will bring a curse on myself rather than a blessing (Gen. 27:12); your curse be on me (Gen. 27:13); Peter called down a curse on himself (Matt. 26:74; Mark 14:71).

q Let my shoulder fall from the socket (Job 31:22); let me sow and another eat (Job 31:8); may my wife grind for another (Job 31:10); let briars grow instead of wheat (Job 31:40); let the enemy pursue me (Ps. 7:5).

r The Jews bound themselves with a curse to kill Paul (Acts 23:21).

- Cursing things

s Job cursed the day of his birth (Job 3:1); the fig tree you cursed has withered (Mark 11:21).

900 Threat

- Threats

a The Danites threatened Micah with death (Judg. 18:25); Paul was breathing out threats and murder against the disciples (Acts 9:1); Lord, note their threats (Acts 4:29).

● Not threat-
ening

b Masters, do not threaten your slaves (Eph. 6:9); Jesus did not threaten (1 Pet. 2:23).

901 Philanthropy
Benevolence, see **897**.

902 Misanthropy
Malevolence, see **898**.

903 Benefactor
People blessing, see **897***u*.

904 Evildoer
See **938**.

905 Pity

● Be merciful!

a Be merciful to me, O Lord (Ps. 6:2; 31:9); God have mercy on me, a sinner! (Luke 18:13); Daniel urged his friends to plead for mercy from God (Dan. 2:18).

b Son of David, have mercy! (Matt. 9:27; 15:22; 20:30–1; Mark 10:47, 48; Luke 18:38, 39); Jesus, have mercy! (Luke 17:13); lord, have mercy on my son! (Matt. 17:15).

● God shows
mercy

c God is merciful (Deut. 4:31; Ps. 116:5); God is rich in mercy (Eph. 2:4); his mercy is great (2 Sam. 24:14); your Father is merciful (Luke 6:36); the Father of mercies (2 Cor. 1:3); the Lord is merciful and forgiving (Dan. 9:9); we make requests because of your great mercy (Dan. 9:18); God has mercy on whom he will have mercy (Exod. 33:19; Rom. 9:15, 18); God shows lovingkindness to thousands (Deut. 5:10); God will have mercy on all (Rom. 11:32); the Lord will show you mercy (Deut. 13:17); vessels of mercy (Rom. 9:23); his mercy is on generations of those who fear him (Luke 1:50).

d The Lord is compassionate and gracious (Exod. 34:6; Ps. 103:8; 111:4; 145:8; Joel 2:13; Jas. 5:11); you are a kind and compassionate God (Neh. 9:31); as a father has compassion on his children, so the Lord has compassion (Ps. 103:13); the Lord will have compassion (Lam. 3:32); the Lord waits to have compassion on you (Isa. 30:18); his compassions are new every morning (Lam. 3:22–3); all my compassion is aroused (Hos. 11:8); God had compassion (Judg. 2:18); the Lord will have compassion on his servants (Deut. 32:36); I will have compassion on all the children of Israel (Ezek. 39:25); I will not take my lovingkindness from him (2 Sam. 7:15); should I not have compassion on Nineveh? (Jonah 4:11); the father had compassion for the prodigal (Luke 15:20); that slave's master felt compassion for him (Matt. 18:27); Ruhamah—pitied (Hos. 2:1).

● Jesus has compassion

e Jesus had compassion on the crowds (Matt. 9:36; 14:14; 15:32; Mark 6:34; 8:2); Jesus was filled with compassion for the leper (Mark 1:41); Jesus had compassion on the widow of Nain (Luke 7:13); moved with compassion, he touched the blind men (Matt. 20:34).

● Receiving mercy

f Tell your family how the Lord has had mercy on you (Mark 5:19); he has remembered to be merciful to Abraham (Luke 1:54–5); I was shown mercy because I acted in ignorance (1 Tim. 1:13); once you had not received mercy, but now you have (1 Pet. 2:10); let us approach the throne of grace that we may find mercy (Heb. 4:16).

g Mercy, peace and love to you (Jude 2).

● Need for mercy

h Blessed are the merciful, for they shall receive mercy (Matt. 5:7); I desire mercy, not sacrifice (Matt. 9:13; 12:7; cf. Hos. 6:6); you should have had mercy on your fellow-servant (Matt. 18:33); clothe yourselves with compassion (Col. 3:12); be merciful as your Father is merciful (Luke 6:36); be kind, tender-hearted, forgiving (Eph. 4:32); use your gift in showing mercy with cheerfulness (Rom. 12:8); mercy triumphs over judgement (Jas. 2:13).

● People showing mercy

i Pharaoh's daughter had pity on the baby (Exod. 2:6); you have had compassion on me (1 Sam. 23:21); Esther had to plead for mercy (Esther 4:8); we have heard that the kings of Israel are merciful (1 Kgs. 20:31); the mother of the child was deeply stirred over her son (1 Kgs. 3:26); the Samaritan had compassion (Luke 10:33).

j No one is sorry for me (1 Sam. 22:8).

906 Pitilessness

● God without mercy

a Show them no mercy (Deut. 7:2); judgement without mercy will be shown to him who is not merciful (Jas. 2:13).

b How long will you withhold mercy from Jerusalem? (Zech. 1:12); Lo-ruhamah—I will no longer have pity (Hos. 1:6); I will no longer have pity on the inhabitants of the land (Zech. 11:6); I will not have pity (Jer. 13:14; Ezek. 7:4; 8:18; 9:10); their Maker will not have compassion on them (Isa. 27:11).

● People without mercy

c People are unmerciful (Rom. 1:31); they are cruel and have no mercy (Jer. 6:23); the Medes will have no mercy (Isa. 13:18); you did not show mercy to my people (Isa. 47:6); he must pay four times over, because he had no pity (2 Sam. 12:6); if anyone sees his brother in need and closes his heart (1 John 3:17); we saw his distress but we would not listen (Gen. 42:21).

d If I rejoiced at my enemy's destruction (Job 31:29).

907 Gratitude

● Give thanks to God

a Give thanks to the Lord (1 Chr. 16:8, 34; Ps. 97:12; 100:4; 105:1; 107:1, 8, 15, 21, 31; 118:1, 29; 136:1–3; Isa. 12:4); give thanks to the God of heaven (Ps. 136:26); be thankful (Col. 3:15); give thanks in everything (1 Thess. 5:18); by prayer and supplication with thanksgiving (Phil. 4:6).

b Come before him with thanksgiving (Ps. 95:2); offer a sacrifice of thanksgiving (Ps. 50:14; 107:22).

c It is good to give thanks to the Lord (Ps. 92:1); thanksgiving will please the Lord better than an ox (Ps. 69:30–1); he who offers a sacrifice of thanksgiving honours me (Ps. 50:23).

● Giving thanks to God

d I will give thanks to the Lord (2 Sam. 22:50; Ps. 9:1; 18:49; 86:12; 108:3; 111:1; 118:21; 119:7; 138:1; 139:14; Isa. 12:1); I will give thanks because of his righteousness (Ps. 7:17); I will give thanks in the great congregation (Ps. 35:18); I will offer a sacrifice of thanksgiving (Ps. 116:17); I will sacrifice to you with the voice of thanksgiving (Jonah 2:9); we give thanks to you (Ps. 75:1).

e The righteous will give thanks (Ps. 140:13); all kings will give thanks to you (Ps. 138:4); all your works will give thanks to you (Ps. 145:10); Mattaniah led the thanksgiving (Neh. 11:17; 12:8); Levites appointed to give thanks before the Lord (1 Chr. 16:4, 7, 41).

f The fruit of lips which give thanks to his name (Heb. 13:15); giving thanks to the Father (Eph. 5:20; Col. 1:12; 3:17); no dirty jokes, but rather thanksgiving (Eph. 5:4); an offering by way of thanksgiving (Lev. 7:12); the Levites every morning were to thank and praise the Lord (1 Chr. 23:30); prayer with thanksgiving (Col. 4:2); overflowing with thanksgiving (Col. 2:7).

g Thanks be to God! (Rom. 7:25; 1 Cor. 15:57; 2 Cor. 2:14; 8:16).

● Thanks for Jesus

h Thanks be to God for his inexpressible gift! (2 Cor. 9:15); Anna gave thanks to God for Jesus (Luke 2:38).

● Thanks for food

i Jesus gave thanks and broke the loaves (Matt. 14:19; 15:36; 26:26; Mark 6:41; 8:6–7; 14:22–3; Luke 9:16; 22:19; 24:30; John 6:11; 1 Cor. 11:24); he took a cup and gave thanks (Luke 22:17); Paul gave thanks and broke bread (Acts 27:35); if I eat with thankfulness, why am I slandered? (1 Cor. 10:30); those who eat or do not eat give thanks to God (Rom. 14:6); nothing is to be rejected if it is received with thanksgiving (1 Tim. 4:3–4).

● Thanks for benefits

j The Samaritan leper returned to give thanks (Luke 17:16); let us be grateful for receiving an unshakeable kingdom (Heb. 12:28).

k That grace to many people may cause thanksgiving to abound (2 Cor. 4:15); liberality causes thanksgiving to God (2 Cor. 9:11–12).

l They were thankful to Felix (Acts 24:3); he does not thank the slave for obeying (Luke 17:9).

● Thanks for people	*m* I thank my God for you (Rom. 1:8; 1 Cor. 1:4); what thanks can we render to God for you? (1 Thess. 3:9); I do not cease to give thanks for you (Eph. 1:16); I thank my God on every remembrance of you (Phil. 1:3); we give thanks to God as we pray for you (Col. 1:3; 1 Thess. 1:2; 2 Tim. 1:3; Philem. 4); we should always give thanks to God for you (2 Thess. 1:3; 2:13); Paul thanked God for the brothers meeting him (Acts 28:15).

908 Ingratitude

● Ungrateful	*a* Men will be ungrateful (2 Tim. 3:2); they neither glorified God nor gave thanks (Rom. 1:21); no one returned to give thanks or to give glory to God but the foreigner (Luke 17:15–18); God is kind to the ungrateful (Luke 6:35).

909 Forgiveness

● A forgiving God	*a* God forgives wickedness (Exod. 34:7); the Lord forgives sin and rebellion (Num. 14:18); you forgive our transgressions (Ps. 65:3); you are a forgiving God (Neh. 9:17; Ps. 99:8); you are kind and forgiving (Ps. 86:5); with you there is forgiveness (Ps. 130:4); the Lord forgives all your sins (Ps. 103:3); I am he who blots out your transgressions (Isa. 43:25); he is faithful to forgive our sins (1 John 1:9); our God will freely pardon (Isa. 55:7); who is a God like you, forgiving sin? (Mic. 7:18).
● God will forgive	*b* I will forgive their wickedness and will remember their sins no more (Jer. 31:34; Heb. 8:12; 10:17); I will pardon their iniquities (Jer. 33:8); I will forgive their sin and heal their land (2 Chr. 7:14); I will forgive the remnant (Jer. 50:20); the sins of those who dwell in Zion will be forgiven (Isa. 33:24); bloodguilt will be forgiven (Deut. 21:8); perhaps the Lord will forgive you (Acts 8:22); when I forgive you all you have done (Ezek. 16:63).
	c My covenant when I take away their sins (Rom. 11:27); blessed is he whose transgressions are forgiven (Ps. 32:1; Rom. 4:7–8); knowledge of salvation through the forgiveness of their sins (Luke 1:77); forgiveness of sins will be preached to all nations (Luke 24:47); everyone who believes receives forgiveness of sins (Acts 10:43); the forgiveness of sins is proclaimed (Acts 13:38); that they may receive forgiveness of sins (Acts 26:18); speaking against the Son of man will be forgiven (Matt. 12:32); if the sick person has sinned, he will be forgiven (Jas. 5:15); if you forgive anyone's sins, they are forgiven (John 20:23).
	d If there is one who does justice, I will pardon Jerusalem (Jer. 5:1); if they hear, I will forgive (Jer. 36:3).
● God, forgive!	*e* Forgive their sin (Exod. 32:32; Num. 14:19); hear and forgive (2 Chr. 6:25, 27, 39); forgive our wickedness (Exod. 34:9); when you hear, forgive (1 Kgs. 8:30; 2 Chr. 6:21); forgive the sin of your people (1 Kgs. 8:34, 36, 50); forgive and act (1 Kgs. 8:39); may the good Lord pardon everyone who seeks God (2 Chr.

30:18–19); forgive my iniquity, though it is great (Ps. 25:11); pass over my iniquity (1 Chr. 21:8); blot out my iniquities (Ps. 51:9); blot out my transgressions (Ps. 51:1); forgive us our debts as we forgive (Matt. 6:12); may the Lord forgive your servant (2 Kgs. 5:18); Father, forgive them (Luke 23:34); Lord, do not hold this sin against them (Acts 7:60).

● God has forgiven

f The Lord has taken away your sin (2 Sam. 12:13); you forgave the guilt of my sin (Ps. 32:5); you forgave the iniquity of your people (Ps. 85:2); God forgave their iniquity (Ps. 78:38); I have forgiven them (Num. 14:20); God was not counting their trespasses against them (2 Cor. 5:19); your sins are forgiven (Matt. 9:2; Mark 2:5; Luke 5:20, 23; 7:48); her sins are forgiven, for she loved much (Luke 7:47); your sins have been forgiven for his name's sake (1 John 2:12); he forgave us our sins (Col. 2:13).

● Sins removed far away

g So far he has removed our transgressions from us (Ps. 103:12); I have swept away your sins like the morning mist (Isa. 44:22); you have cast all my sins behind your back (Isa. 38:17).

● God not forgiving

h The angel will not forgive (Exod. 23:21); God will never forgive one whose heart turns away (Deut. 29:20); God will not forgive your rebellion and your sins (Josh. 24:19); this iniquity will not be forgiven you (Isa. 22:14); the Lord would not forgive (2 Kgs. 24:4); blasphemy against the Spirit will not be forgiven (Matt. 12:31–2; Mark 3:28–9; Luke 12:10); if you do not forgive, your Father will not forgive you (Matt. 6:15); lest they turn and be forgiven (Mark 4:12).

i Why do you not forgive me? (Job 7:21); you have not forgiven us (Lam. 3:42).

j Do not forgive them (Neh. 4:5; Isa. 2:9; Jer. 18:23); do not forgive the sins of their parents (Ps. 109:14).

● Forgiveness by atonement

k The priest will make atonement and they will be forgiven (Lev. 4:20, 26, 31, 35; 5:13; 6:7; 19:22; Num. 15:25, 26, 28).

l In him we have redemption, the forgiveness of sins (Eph. 1:7; Col. 1:14); my blood, poured out for many for the forgiveness of sins (Matt. 26:28); without the shedding of blood there is no forgiveness (Heb. 9:22); where sins have been forgiven, there is no more sacrifice (Heb. 10:18).

● Forgiveness by repentance

m A baptism of repentance for the forgiveness of sins (Mark 1:4; Luke 3:3); repent, that your sins may be forgiven (Acts 2:38); repent, that your sins may be blotted out (Acts 3:19); he gives repentance and forgiveness of sins to Israel (Acts 5:31).

● Who forgives sins?

n Who is this who forgives sins? (Luke 7:49); who can forgive sins but God? (Mark 2:7; Luke 5:21); the Son of Man has authority to forgive sins (Mark 2:10; Luke 5:24).

● Man forgiving

o He who covers a transgression seeks love (Prov. 17:9).

p Joseph was asked to forgive his brothers (Gen. 50:17); Abigail asked David to forgive Nabal (1 Sam. 25:28); Pharaoh asked

Moses for forgiveness (Exod. 10:17); pardon my sin (1 Sam. 15:25).

q At the end of seven years, a year of remission of debts (Deut. 15:1, 9; 31:10); the master took pity on him and cancelled the debt (Matt. 18:27); the money-lender cancelled their debts (Luke 7:42).

● Forgive one another

r Shall I forgive my brother as many as seven times? (Matt. 18:21–2); if your brother sins and repents seven times in a day, forgive him (Luke 17:3–4); you must forgive your brother from the heart (Matt. 18:35); forgive and you will be forgiven (Matt. 6:14–15; Mark 11:25; Luke 6:37; 11:4); forgive one another, as God in Christ forgave you (Eph. 4:32; Col. 3:13); you ought to forgive and comfort him (2 Cor. 2:7).

s Whoever you forgive, I forgive also (2 Cor. 2:10).

910 Revenge

● God avenges

a Vengeance is mine; I will repay (Deut. 32:35; Rom. 12:19; Heb. 10:30); the Lord is a God of retribution (Jer. 51:56); the God who avenges (Ps. 94:1); an avenger of wrongdoing (Ps. 99:8); I will avenge myself on my enemies (Isa. 1:24); I will take vengeance (Isa. 47:3; Jer. 51:11; Ezek. 25:14); he will come with vengeance (Isa. 35:4); they will know I am the Lord, when I take vengeance (Ezek. 25:17); the Lord is a jealous and avenging God (Nahum 1:2); he put on garments of vengeance for clothing (Isa. 59:17); to execute vengeance on the nations (Ps. 149:7); taking vengeance on the disobedient (2 Thess. 1:8).

b The Lord has a day of vengeance (Isa. 34:8); the day of vengeance was in my heart (Isa. 63:4); these are days of vengeance (Luke 21:22).

c God avenges bloodshed (Ps. 9:12); he will avenge the blood of his servants (Deut. 32:43; 2 Kgs. 9:7; Ps. 79:10; Rev. 19:2); how long before you avenge our blood? (Rev. 6:10); I will avenge their blood (Joel 3:21).

d May the Lord see and avenge (2 Chr. 24:22); may the Lord avenge me on you, but I will not harm you (1 Sam. 24:12); let me see your vengeance on them (Jer. 11:20; 20:12); God performs vengeance for me (2 Sam. 22:48; Ps. 18:47); the Lord has avenged you on your enemies (Judg. 11:36); the Lord has avenged the king (2 Sam. 4:8).

● Man avenging

e The avenger of blood shall put the murderer to death (Num. 35:19–21); the avenger of blood might pursue him (Deut. 19:6); so the avenger of blood will not destroy (2 Sam. 14:11).

f An eye for an eye (Deut. 19:21; Matt. 5:38); Samson wanted to take revenge (Judg. 15:7); avenged for my two eyes (Judg. 16:28).

g Take vengeance on the Midianites (Num. 31:2); the Jews were to avenge themselves (Esther 8:13); Moses took vengeance for the oppressed (Acts 7:24); Edom took revenge on the house of Judah and became guilty (Ezek. 25:12); the Philistines took revenge in malice (Ezek. 25:15).

h If anyone kills Cain, he will suffer vengeance seven times (Gen. 4:15); if Cain is avenged seven times, then Lamech seventy-seven times (Gen. 4:24).

● Do not avenge yourselves

i Do not seek revenge (Lev. 19:18); do not avenge yourselves (Rom. 12:19); do not say, 'I will repay evil' (Prov. 20:22); never repay evil for evil (Rom. 12:17; 1 Pet. 3:9); the Lord has restrained you from taking your own revenge (1 Sam. 25:26, 31, 33).

j Cities of refuge from the avenger (Num. 35:12; Josh. 20:3, 5, 9).

911 Jealousy

● Jealousy in general

a Jealousy enrages a man (Prov. 6:34); jealousy is hard as Sheol (S. of S. 8:6); who can stand before jealousy? (Prov. 27:4). **Envious**, see **912**.

● God is jealous

b The Lord is a jealous God (Exod. 20:5; Deut. 4:24; 5:9; 6:15; Josh. 24:19); the Lord, whose name is Jealous, is a jealous God (Exod. 34:14); the Lord is a jealous and avenging God (Nahum 1:2).

c I will be jealous for my holy name (Ezek. 39:25); the Lord will be jealous for his land (Joel 2:18); I am very jealous for Jerusalem (Zech. 1:14; 8:2); he yearns jealously over the Spirit in us (Jas. 4:5).

d They made him jealous with their foreign gods (Deut. 32:16, 21; Ps. 78:58); they provoked the Lord to jealousy (1 Kgs. 14:22); the image of jealousy which provokes to jealousy (Ezek. 8:3); do we make the Lord jealous? (1 Cor. 10:22).

e Phinehas was jealous with my jealousy (Num. 25:11, 13).

● Making Israel jealous

f I will make you jealous by what is not a nation (Deut. 32:21; Rom. 10:19); Paul wanted to make the Jews jealous (Rom. 11:14); salvation has come to the Gentiles to make Israel jealous (Rom. 11:11).

g The Sadducees were filled with jealousy (Acts 5:17); the Jews were jealous (Acts 13:45; 17:5).

● Jealous for people

h I am jealous for you with a godly jealousy (2 Cor. 11:2); regulations concerning a jealous husband (Num. 5:11–31).

● Jealous of people

i Rachel was jealous of Leah (Gen. 30:1); his brothers were jealous of Joseph (Gen. 37:11; Acts 7:9); Saul looked on David with suspicion (1 Sam. 18:9).

● Avoiding jealousy

j Since there is jealousy among you, are you not worldly? (1 Cor. 3:3); I fear there may be strife and jealousy (2 Cor. 12:20); jealousy is a deed of the flesh (Gal. 5:20).

k Love is not jealous (1 Cor. 13:4); not in strife and jealousy (Rom. 13:13).

l Ephraim and Judah will no longer be jealous of one another (Isa. 11:13)

912 Envy

● Nature
of envy

a All achievement springs from envy (Eccles. 4:4); envy and selfish ambition are of the devil (Jas. 3:14, 16); envy is a deed of the flesh (Gal. 5:21); from the heart comes envy (Mark 7:22); filled with envy (Rom. 1:29); you are envious and cannot obtain, so you fight (Jas. 4:2).
Jealous, see **911**.

● Avoid envy

b Put aside all envy (1 Pet. 2:1); do not envy one another (Gal. 5:26); do not let your heart envy sinners (Prov. 23:17); do not envy the wicked (Ps. 37:1; Prov. 24:1, 19); do not envy a violent man (Prov. 3:31).

● Those who
envied

c The Philistines envied Isaac (Gen. 26:14); the people grew envious of Moses (Ps. 106:16); it was out of envy that Jesus was handed over to Pilate (Matt. 27:18; Mark 15:10); some preach Christ out of envy and selfish ambition (Phil. 1:15–17).

d I was envious of the arrogant (Ps. 73:3); we once spent our days in malice and envy (Titus 3:3).

Section four: Morality

913 Righteousness

● God is
righteous

a God is just (Neh. 9:33; 2 Thess. 1:6); the Lord is righteous (Ps. 11:7; 119:137; 129:4; 145:17; Lam. 1:18; Zeph. 3:5); all his ways are just (Deut. 32:4); just and the justifier of him who believes (Rom. 3:26); the Lord is a God of justice (Isa. 30:18); the Lord is known by his justice (Ps. 9:16); God is not unjust (Heb. 6:10); with God there is no injustice (2 Chr. 19:7); righteousness and justice are the foundation of God's throne (Ps. 89:14; 97:2); his righteousness endures for ever (Ps. 112:3, 9; 2 Cor. 9:9).

b You are righteous (Ezra 9:15; Jer. 12:1); righteousness belongs to you (Dan. 9:7); your righteousness is everlasting (Ps. 119:142); your righteousness is like great mountains (Ps. 36:6).

● Christ is
righteous

c Jesus Christ the righteous (1 John 2:1); as he is righteous, so every one who does right is born of him (1 John 2:29); the one who does righteousness is righteous as he is righteous (1 John 3:7); you loved righteousness (Ps. 45:7).

● Declaring that
God is just

d My tongue will speak of your righteousness (Ps. 35:28; 71:15, 24); they will proclaim his righteousness (Ps. 22:31); I will ascribe justice to my Maker (Job 36:3); the heavens declare his righteousness (Ps. 97:6); will you deny that I am just? (Job 40:8).

● God loves
right

e The Lord loves justice (Ps. 11:7; 99:4; Isa. 61:8); the Lord loves righteousness and justice (Ps. 33:5); he looked for justice and righteousness (Isa. 5:7); if you are righteous, what do you give to him? (Job 35:7).

● God does
what is right

f Will not the Judge of all the earth do right? (Gen. 18:25); he will not do violence to justice (Job 37:23); the Lord executes justice for the oppressed (Ps. 103:6; 146:7); God's righteous judgement (2 Thess. 1:5); just and true are your judgements (Rev. 16:5, 7); he will not falter till he establishes justice (Isa. 42:4); he will bring justice to the nations (Isa. 42:1).

g What nation has statutes so righteous? (Deut. 4:8); your testimonies are righteous for ever (Ps. 119:144); the Lord will cause righteousness to sprout (Isa. 61:11).

h The Holy Spirit will convict the world of righteousness (John 16:8, 10); Paul spoke of righteousness, self-control and judgement (Acts 24:25).

● Do right!

i Justice, justice shall you pursue (Deut. 16:20); pursue righteousness (1 Tim. 6:11; 2 Tim. 2:22); administer justice every morning (Jer. 21:12); let justice flow like a river, righteousness like a stream (Amos 5:24); administer true justice (Zech. 7:9); do justice and righteousness (Jer. 22:3); do not deny justice to the poor (Exod. 23:6); do not deprive the alien or fatherless of justice (Deut. 24:17); perform justice for the needy (Ps. 82:3); I will make justice the measuring-line and righteousness the plumb-line (Isa. 28:17); should you not know justice? (Mic. 3:1); what does the Lord require of you but to act justly (Mic. 6:8); sow for yourselves in righteousness (Hos. 10:12); masters, show justice (Col. 4:1).

j He has made you king to maintain justice and righteousness (1 Kgs. 10:9); maintain justice and do what is right (Isa. 56:1); seek good, not evil (Amos 5:14); stop doing wrong, learn to do right! (Isa. 1:16–17); walk before me and be blameless (Gen. 17:1).

k Your righteousness must exceed that of the Pharisees (Matt. 5:20); thus it becomes us to fulfil all righteousness (Matt. 3:15).

l The kingdom of God is a matter of righteousness (Rom. 14:17); created like God in true righteousness (Eph. 4:24); happy are those who observe justice (Ps. 106:3); filled with the fruit of righteousness (Phil. 1:11); to live upright lives (Titus 2:12); he will increase the harvest of your righteousness (2 Cor. 9:10); blessed are those who hunger for righteousness (Matt. 5:6).

m A robe of righteousness (Isa. 61:10); righteousness as a breastplate (Isa. 59:17); the breastplate of righteousness (Eph. 6:14).

n Fine linen stands for the righteous deeds of the saints (Rev. 19:8).

o Scripture is profitable for training in righteousness (2 Tim. 3:16).

p Woe to those who call evil good and good evil (Isa. 5:20); do not be too righteous (Eccles. 7:16).

● Doing right

q If you do what is right, will you not be accepted? (Gen. 4:7); to keep the way of the Lord by doing what is right and just (Gen. 18:19); David did what was just and right (2 Sam. 8:15; 1 Chr. 18:14); your claims are good and right (2 Sam. 15:3); you are more righteous than I (1 Sam. 24:17); in him something good towards God was found (1 Kgs. 14:13); Job did not sin (Job 1:22; 2:10); John came in the way of righteousness (Matt. 21:32).

r Kings who did what was right in the eyes of the Lord: David (1 Kgs. 15:5); Asa (1 Kgs. 15:11; 2 Chr. 14:2); Jehoshaphat (1 Kgs. 22:43; 2 Chr. 20:32); Joash (2 Kgs. 12:2; 2 Chr. 24:2); Amaziah (2 Kgs. 14:3; 2 Chr. 25:2); Azariah [Uzziah] (2 Kgs. 15:3; 2 Chr. 26:4); Jotham (2 Kgs. 15:34; 2 Chr. 27:2); Hezekiah (2 Kgs. 18:3; 2 Chr. 29:2); Josiah (2 Kgs. 22:2; 2 Chr. 34:2).

● Right by obedience

s If we obey all the law, that will be our righteousness (Deut. 6:25); his intervention was credited to Phinehas as righteousness (Ps. 106:31).

● Our own righteousness

t Doing what is right in one's own eyes (Deut. 12:8; Judg. 17:6; 21:25); Jesus told a parable to those who trusted in their own righteousness (Luke 18:9); can man be more righteous than God? (Job 4:17); how can man born of woman be righteous? (Job 15:14; 25:4–6); all our righteousnesses are as filthy rags (Isa. 64:6).

u They sought to establish their own righteousness, and did not submit to God's (Rom. 10:3); they did not pursue righteousness by faith but as if it were based on works (Rom. 9:30–2); Job was righteous in his own eyes (Job 32:1; 33:9; 34:5); not having a righteousness of my own based on law (Phil. 3:9).

● Right by faith

v Abraham believed God and it was reckoned to him as righteousness (Gen. 15:6; Rom. 4:3, 5, 9, 22; Gal. 3:6; Jas. 2:23); a righteousness from God, by faith (Rom. 3:21–2; Phil. 3:9); the righteousness of faith (Rom. 4:13); righteousness reckoned to all who believe (Rom. 4:11); by faith we wait for the hope of righteousness (Gal. 5:5); God credits righteousness apart from works (Rom. 4:6, 24); righteousness for all who believe (Rom. 10:4); righteousness by faith (Rom. 9:30; Heb. 11:7); the righteous by faith shall live (Hab. 2:4; Rom. 1:17; Gal. 3:11; Heb. 10:38).

w The dispensation of righteousness (2 Cor. 3:9); the crown of righteousness (2 Tim. 4:8).

● Christ our righteousness

x Christ has become our righteousness (1 Cor. 1:30); the righteousness of God is revealed in the gospel (Rom. 1:17); we become the righteousness of God in him (2 Cor. 5:21); a righteous branch for David (Jer. 23:5; 33:15); the Lord our righteousness (Jer. 23:6; 33:16); Melchizedek, king of righteousness (Heb. 7:2); lead me in your righteousness (Ps. 5:8); seek first his righteousness (Matt. 6:33).

● The righteous people

y You will be called the City of Righteousness (Isa. 1:26); Zion will be redeemed with justice, her penitent ones with righteousness (Isa. 1:27); he will fill Zion with justice and righteousness (Isa. 33:5); justice will dwell in the desert and righteousness in the fertile field (Isa. 32:16); I will betroth you to me in righteousness and justice (Hos. 2:19); where were the righteous destroyed? (Job 4:7).

z Discipline yields the peaceful fruit of righteousness (Heb. 12:11); the fruit of righteousness is sown in peace (Jas. 3:18). **Good people**, see **937**.

● Distinctives of righteousness

aa When the righteous prosper, the city rejoices (Prov. 11:10); righteousness exalts a nation (Prov. 14:34); righteousness delivers from death (Prov. 10:2; 11:4); better a little with righteousness than much gain with injustice (Prov. 16:8); the fruit of righteousness will be peace (Isa. 32:17).

ab The tree of the knowledge of good and evil (Gen. 2:9); you will be like God, knowing good and evil (Gen. 3:5); the man has become like us, knowing good and evil (Gen. 3:22).

ac What fellowship has righteousness with lawlessness? (2 Cor. 6:14).

914 Wrong

● Nature of sin

a All unrighteousness is sin (1 John 5:17); there is a sin to death and a sin not to death (1 John 5:16–17); haughty eyes and a proud heart are sin (Prov. 21:4); to know the right thing and not to do it is sin (Jas. 4:17); I would sin if I ceased to pray for you (1 Sam. 12:23); sin is a disgrace to a people (Prov. 14:34).

b Woe to those who call evil good and good evil* (Isa. 5:20); the devil has sinned from the beginning (1 John 3:8).

● Is God unjust?

c God has wronged me (Job 19:6); God has denied me justice (Job 27:2); the way of the Lord is not just (Ezek. 18:25; 33:17); there is no justice (Job 19:7); is God unjust in bringing his wrath upon us? (Rom. 3:5); does God pervert justice? (Job 8:3).

d Far be it from God to do evil (Job 34:10); God will not do evil (Job 34:12); there is no injustice in God (Rom. 9:14); what wrong did your fathers find in me? (Jer. 2:5).

● God's attitude to sin

e If I have sinned, what do I do to you? (Job 7:20); if you sin, how does that affect him? (Job 35:6); if I sinned, you would be watching me (Job 10:14); you have set our secret sins in the light of your presence (Ps. 90:8); you are not a God who takes pleasure in evil (Ps. 5:4); the Lord was displeased that there was no justice (Isa. 59:15); against you only have I sinned (Ps. 51:4).

f The Holy Spirit will convict the world of sin because they do not believe (John 16:8–9).

● The entrance of sin

g Your first forefather sinned (Isa. 43:27); through one man sin entered the world (Rom. 5:12).

h Through the commandment sin might become sinful beyond measure (Rom. 7:13); before the law, sin was in the world (Rom. 5:13); this is wickedness (Zech. 5:8).

i You were blameless until iniquity was found in you (Ezek. 28:15).

● All have
sinned

j There is no one who does not sin (1 Kgs. 8:46; 2 Chr. 6:36); there is no righteous man who never sins (Eccles. 7:20); there is none righteous (Rom. 3:10–12); there is no one who does good (Ps. 14:3; 53:3); no one is righteous before you (Ps. 143:2); Jews and Gentiles are all under sin (Rom. 3:9); all have sinned and fall short of the glory of God (Rom. 3:23); all men are shut up under sin (Gal. 3:22); you, being evil (Matt. 7:11; Luke 11:13).

● Thoroughly
sinful

k Sin reigned in death (Rom. 5:21); their feet rush into sin (Isa. 59:7); evil things come out of the heart of man (Matt. 15:18–19); men are filled with every kind of wickedness (Rom. 1:29–31); the wickedness of man was great, every thought being evil (Gen. 6:5); man's thoughts are evil from youth (Gen. 8:21); I was conceived and born in sin (Ps. 51:5); all flesh was corrupt (Gen. 6:12); the works of the flesh are plain (Gal. 5:19–21); my sins are more than the hairs of my head (Ps. 40:12); if you kept a record of sins, who could stand? (Ps. 130:3).

● Hidden sins

l The sins of some men are obvious, the sins of others not so (1 Tim. 5:24); who can discern his errors? forgive my hidden faults (Ps. 19:12); be sure your sin will find you out (Num. 32:23); he who is unrighteous in little is unrighteous in much (Luke 16:10).

● Removing
sin

m He appeared to take away sins and in him there is no sin (1 John 3:5); he who knew no sin God made to be sin for us (2 Cor. 5:21); he was wounded for our transgressions (Isa. 53:5); the Lord has laid on him the iniquity of us all (Isa. 53:6); he will bear their iniquities (Isa. 53:11); he bore the sin of many (Isa. 53:12).

n Though your sins are as scarlet they shall be as white as snow (Isa. 1:18); I will remove the sin of this land in a single day (Zech. 3:9).

o The sin offering when anyone sins unintentionally (Lev. 4:2); if the anointed priest sins (Lev. 4:3); if the whole community sins unintentionally (Lev. 4:13); when a leader sins unintentionally (Lev. 4:22); if a member of the community sins unintentionally (Lev. 4:27).

Sin offering, see **981x**.

● Avoiding
sin

p God has come that you may not sin (Exod. 20:20); stop sinning (1 Cor. 15:34); your word have I hid in my heart that I might not sin (Ps. 119:11); renounce your sins by doing what is right (Dan. 4:27); I write this that you may not sin (1 John 2:1).

q Do not be too wicked (Eccles. 7:17).

● Continuing
in sin

r No one who abides in him continues to sin (1 John 3:6); no one born of God goes on sinning (1 John 3:9; 5:18); shall we continue in sin that grace may abound? (Rom. 6:1); shall we sin because we are not under law but under grace? (Rom. 6:15); if we are found to be sinners, is Christ a minister of sin? (Gal. 2:17); if we sin after we received the knowledge of the truth, there is no sacrifice for sins (Heb. 10:26); he who does not do right is not a child of God (1 John 3:10); 'let us do evil that good may come' (Rom. 3:8); the wicked will continue to be wicked (Dan. 12:10); let him who does wrong continue to do wrong (Rev. 22:11); go to Bethel and sin (Amos 4:4).

● Results
of sin

s They suffered affliction because of their iniquities (Ps. 107:17); my sin is ever before me (Ps. 51:3); your iniquities have separated you and your God (Isa. 59:2); God drove out the people of the land because of their wickedness (Deut. 9:4–5); Israel was exiled because they had sinned (2 Kgs. 17:7); wickedness overthrows the sinner (Prov. 13:6); those who plough evil reap it (Job 4:8); Sheol snatches away those who have sinned (Job 24:19); the wages of sin is death (Rom. 6:23); everyone who commits sin is a slave of sin (John 8:34); he who sins without law will perish without law (Rom. 2:12).

t If Christ is not risen, you are still in your sins (1 Cor. 15:17).

u If anyone sins defiantly he must be cut off (Num. 15:30); if your brother sins, reprove him privately (Matt. 18:15); if a man sins against the Lord, who will intercede for him? (1 Sam. 2:25).

v Cursed is the man who withholds justice (Deut. 27:19); woe to those who deny justice to the innocent (Isa. 5:23; 29:21); woe to him who builds his palace by unrighteousness (Jer. 22:13).

Death due to sin, see **361***t*.

● Evil kings

w Kings who did evil in the eyes of the Lord: Ahab (1 Kgs. 16:30); Ahaz (2 Kgs. 16:2; 2 Chr. 28:1); Ahaziah of Israel (1 Kgs. 22:52); Ahaziah of Judah (2 Kgs. 8:27; 2 Chr. 22:4); Amon (2 Kgs. 21:20; 2 Chr. 33:22); Baasha (1 Kgs. 15:34; 16:7, 13); Hoshea (2 Kgs. 17:2); Jehoahaz of Israel (2 Kgs. 13:2); Jehoahaz of Judah (2 Kgs. 23:32); Jehoash (2 Kgs. 13:11); Jehoiachin (2 Kgs. 24:9; 2 Chr. 36:9); Jehoiakim (2 Kgs. 23:37; 2 Chr. 36:5); Jehoram (2 Kgs. 8:18; 2 Chr. 21:6); Jeroboam (1 Kgs. 14:9, 16; 15:30, 34; 2 Kgs. 14:24); Joram (2 Kgs. 3:2); Menahem (2 Kgs. 15:18); Manasseh (2 Kgs. 21:2; 2 Chr. 33:2); Nadab (1 Kgs. 15:26); Omri (1 Kgs. 16:25); Pekah (2 Kgs. 15:28); Pekahiah (2 Kgs. 15:24); Rehoboam (2 Chr. 12:14); Solomon (1 Kgs. 11:6); Zechariah (2 Kgs. 15:9); Zedekiah (2 Kgs. 24:19; 2 Chr. 36:12; Jer. 52:2); Zimri (1 Kgs. 16:19).

● Following
evil

x Walking in the way of Jeroboam (1 Kgs. 16:2, 7, 19, 26, 31; 22:52; 2 Kgs. 3:3; 10:29, 31; 13:2, 11; 14:24; 15:9, 18, 24, 28; 17:22); they did not turn away from the sins of Jeroboam (2 Kgs. 13:6; 15:9, 18, 24, 28); Jeroboam committed a great sin (2 Kgs. 17:21); Jeroboam made Israel sin (2 Kgs. 23:15).

y Walking in the way of the kings of Israel (2 Chr. 21:13; 28:2); walking in the way of the house of Ahab (2 Chr. 21:13; 22:3–4); following the abominations of the nations whom the Lord dispossessed (1 Kgs. 14:24; 2 Kgs. 16:3; 17:8, 11; 21:2, 9; 2 Chr. 28:3; 33:2, 9); did not Solomon sin in these ways? (Neh. 13:26).

<table>
<tr><td>● Those who
sinned</td><td>z</td><td>David sinned in the matter of Uriah the Hittite (1 Kgs. 15:5); Abijah committed all the sins of his father (1 Kgs. 15:3); Ahab sold himself to do evil (1 Kgs. 21:25); Baasha caused Israel to sin (1 Kgs. 16:2, 13); Judah did wrong in the eyes of the Lord (1 Kgs. 14:22); the Israelites did evil in the eyes of the Lord (Judg. 3:7, 12; 4:1; 6:1; 10:6; 13:1); you have committed a great sin (Exod. 32:30); the sins of the house of Israel (Mic. 1:5); lie on your left side for the sin of the house of Israel (Ezek. 4:4); lie on your right side for the sin of the house of Judah (Ezek. 4:6); the people turned to ways even more corrupt than their fathers (Judg. 2:19); he who delivered me up has the greater sin (John 19:11).</td></tr>
</table>

aa For three sins and for four: of Damascus (Amos 1:3); of Gaza (Amos 1:6); of Tyre (Amos 1:9); of Ammon (Amos 1:13); of Moab (Amos 2:1); of Judah (Amos 2:4); of Israel (Amos 2:6).

ab The sin of Sodom and Gomorrah is grievous (Gen. 18:20); the sin of the Amorites is not yet complete (Gen. 15:16); Pharaoh sinned again (Exod. 9:34); is not your wickedness great? (Job 22:5); in your hearts you devise injustice (Ps. 58:2); wounding their weak conscience you sin against Christ (1 Cor. 8:12).

● We have
sinned

ac We sinned when we spoke against the Lord (Num. 21:7); we have sinned (Deut. 1:41; 1 Sam. 7:6; 12:10; Ps. 106:6; Dan. 9:5).

ad I have sinned, said by: Pharaoh (Exod. 9:27; 10:16); Balaam (Num. 22:34); Saul (1 Sam. 15:24, 30; 26:21); David (2 Sam. 12:13; 24:10; 1 Chr. 21:8); Shimei (2 Sam. 19:20); the prodigal son (Luke 15:18, 21); Judas (Matt. 27:4).

● What sin?

ae What is my crime? (Gen. 31:36; 1 Sam. 20:1); what wrong am I guilty of? (1 Sam. 26:18); show me how I have erred (Job 6:24); make my sin known to me (Job 13:23); is there any wickedness on my lips? (Job 6:30); how could I do such a thing and sin against God? (Gen. 39:9); if I have denied justice to my servants (Job 31:13); who sinned, this man or his parents? (John 9:2).

af What crime has he committed? (Matt. 27:23; Mark 15:14); declare to my people their sins (Isa. 58:1).

● The man
of sin

ag The man of sin will be revealed (2 Thess. 2:3).

915 Dueness

● God is worthy

a God is worthy to receive honour (Rev. 4:11).

b Who is worthy to break the seals? (Rev. 5:2–3); you are worthy to take the scroll (Rev. 5:9); worthy is the Lamb! (Rev. 5:12).

● Worthy people

c When you enter a town, ask who is worthy in it (Matt. 10:11); he is worthy for you to do this (Luke 7:4).

● Being worthy

d Live a life worthy of your calling (Eph. 4:1); that God may count you worthy of your calling (2 Thess. 1:11); worthy of the gospel (Phil. 1:27); worthy of the Lord (Col. 1:10); live lives worthy of God who calls you (1 Thess. 2:12); worthy of the kingdom of

God (2 Thess. 1:5); they rejoiced that they were worthy to suffer shame (Acts 5:41); not that we are worthy in ourselves; our worth is from God (2 Cor. 3:5); they are worthy (Rev. 3:4).

Worthy of the kingdom, see **733***m*.

● Due rights

e If you dealt with Gideon as he deserved (Judg. 9:16); a workman deserves his food (Matt. 10:10); the workman is worthy of his wages (1 Tim. 5:18); render to all what is due (Rom. 13:7); render to Caesar the things that are Caesar's and to God the things that are God's (Matt. 22:21; Mark 12:17; Luke 20:25).

● Due return

f We are receiving our just deserts (Luke 23:41); he deserves death (Matt. 26:66).

g From him who has been given much, much will be demanded (Luke 12:48).

● What is fitting

h It is fitting for us to fulfil all righteousness (Matt. 3:15); it was fitting for God to perfect Christ through suffering (Heb. 2:10); it was fitting for us to have such a high priest (Heb. 7:26).

i All things are proper but not all are useful (1 Cor. 6:12; 10:23); all things are proper but I will not be mastered by any (1 Cor. 6:12).

j Is it right to pay taxes to Caesar? (Matt. 22:17; Mark 12:14; Luke 20:22); is it right to heal on the sabbath? (Matt. 12:10; Luke 14:3); is it proper on the sabbath to heal or to kill? (Mark 3:4; Luke 6:9); is it proper for a man to divorce his wife? (Matt. 19:3; Mark 10:2); is it not proper for me to do what I want with my own? (Matt. 20:15).

916 Unbdueness

● People unworthy

a I am unworthy of all the kindness you have shown (Gen. 32:10); his sandals I am not worthy to untie (Matt. 3:11; Mark 1:7; Luke 3:16; John 1:27; Acts 13:25); I am not worthy for you to enter my house (Matt. 8:8; Luke 7:6–7); I am no longer worthy to be called your son (Luke 15:19, 21); those who were invited were not worthy (Matt. 22:8); no one who looks back is fit for the kingdom (Luke 9:62); you judge yourselves unworthy of eternal life (Acts 13:46); whoever loves relatives more than me is not worthy of me (Matt. 10:37); he who does not take up his cross and follow me is not worthy of me (Matt. 10:38); the world was not worthy of them (Heb. 11:38).

b No one was worthy to open the book (Rev. 5:3–4); we are unworthy slaves (Luke 17:10).

● Unfitting action

c To eat on such a day would not have been fitting (Lev. 10:19–20); your disciples are doing what is not proper on a sabbath (Matt. 12:2; Mark 2:24; Luke 6:2); it is not proper for you to carry your bed on the sabbath (John 5:10); David ate the bread of the Presence, which was not proper (Matt. 12:4; Mark 2:26; Luke 6:4); it is not right for you to have your brother's wife (Matt. 14:4; Mark 6:18); it is not right to put the money in the treasury (Matt. 27:6); you have done to me what ought not to be done (Gen. 20:9).

d Whoever eats the bread or drinks the cup of the Lord in an unworthy manner (1 Cor. 11:27).

e Do not give what is holy to dogs or pearls to swine (Matt. 7:6); honour is not fitting for a fool (Prov. 26:1).

● Evil without cause

f Let us ambush the innocent without cause (Prov. 1:11); I have done nothing to deserve being imprisoned (Gen. 40:15); why kill David without a cause? (1 Sam. 19:5; 20:32); they attack me without a cause (Ps. 109:3); they hate me without a cause (Ps. 35:19; John 15:25); those who hate me without a cause are more than the hairs of my head (Ps. 69:4); righteous men who get what the wicked deserve and vice versa (Eccles. 8:14).

g Satan incited God against Job without a cause (Job 2:3); God wounds me without cause (Job 9:17).

h A curse without cause does not alight (Prov. 26:2).

917 Duty

● Good conscience

a A good conscience (1 Tim. 1:5, 19; 3:9); I have lived my life in all good conscience (Acts 23:1); I try to keep a clear conscience (Acts 24:16); I serve God with a clear conscience (2 Tim. 1:3); we are sure we have a good conscience (Heb. 13:18); keep a good conscience (1 Pet. 3:16); the spirit of man is the lamp of the Lord (Prov. 20:27).

b Do not eat, for the sake of conscience (1 Cor. 10:28–9); be subject to rulers for conscience sake (Rom. 13:5); commending ourselves to every one's conscience (2 Cor. 4:2).

● Cleansing the conscience

c The blood of Christ cleanses the conscience (Heb. 9:14); our hearts sprinkled from an evil conscience (Heb. 10:22); an appeal to God for a good conscience (1 Pet. 3:21).

d Gifts are offered which cannot perfect the conscience (Heb. 9:9).

● Bad conscience

e David's heart smote him (1 Sam. 24:5); some eat food as offered to an idol and their weak conscience is defiled (1 Cor. 8:7); someone's weak conscience may be emboldened to eat food sacrificed to idols (1 Cor. 8:10); by wounding their weak consciences you sin aganst Christ (1 Cor. 8:12).

f Some have rejected conscience (1 Tim. 1:19); consciences seared as with an iron (1 Tim. 4:2); their minds and consciences are defiled (Titus 1:15).

● Knowing right and wrong

g The tree of the knowledge of good and evil (Gen. 2:9, 17; 3:3–7); the man has become like one of us, knowing good and evil (Gen. 3:22); their conscience bearing witness (Rom. 2:15).

918 Undutifulness

Negligence, see **458**.

919 Exemption

● Spared   *a* Spare my family (Josh. 2:13); Joshua spared Rahab and her family (Josh. 6:17, 25); they spared the man and his family (Judg. 1:25); they spared the Midianite women (Num. 31:9, 15); spare those who are virgins (Num. 31:18); Saul spared Agag and the best of the animals (1 Sam. 15:9, 15); the king spared Mephibosheth (2 Sam. 21:7); you spared the one devoted to destruction (1 Kgs. 20:42); will you be spared? (2 Kgs. 19:11); if the king extends the gold sceptre and spares her life (Esther 4:11; 5:2); I spared them (Ezek. 20:17); it was to spare you that I did not come (2 Cor. 1:23).

                   b You will be free from this oath (Gen. 24:8).

● Not sparing   *c* You did not withhold your son (Gen. 22:12, 16); he who did not spare his own son (Rom. 8:32).

                   d If God did not spare the natural branches, neither will he spare you (Rom. 11:21); if God did not spare the angels who sinned (2 Pet. 2:4); if God did not spare the ancient world (2 Pet. 2:5).

● Pass over   *e* I will pass over you (Exod. 12:13); God passed over their houses and spared them (Exod. 12:27); God passed over former sins (Rom. 3:25).

                   Passover, see **988*o***.

● Exempt   *f* He will exempt his father's house from taxes (1 Sam. 17:25); the sons are exempt (Matt. 17:26); my master let Naaman off lightly (2 Kgs. 5:20).

920 Respect

● Respect   *a* Respect your God (Lev. 19:32); have reverence for my sanctuary for God   (Lev. 26:2); they will respect my son (Matt. 21:37; Mark 12:6).

● Respect   *b* Honour your father and mother (Exod. 20:12; Lev. 19:3; Deut. for people   5:16; Matt. 15:4; Mark 7:10; 10:19; Eph. 6:2); honour men like Epaphroditus (Phil. 2:29); respect those who are over you in the Lord (1 Thess. 5:12); husbands, treat your wives with honour (1 Pet. 3:7); let the wife respect her husband (Eph. 5:33); those who have believing masters should not be disrespectful to them (1 Tim. 6:2); show respect for the elderly (Lev. 19:32).

                   Honour, see **966*u***.

● Winning   *c* Win the respect of outsiders (1 Thess. 4:12). respect

921 Disrespect

● Insulting God   *a* Sennacherib wrote letters insulting the Lord (2 Chr. 32:17); you have insulted the Holy One of Israel (2 Kgs. 19:22; Isa. 37:23); they insulted Jesus (Matt. 27:39, 44; Mark 15:29, 32); the man who has trampled under foot the Son of God and insulted the Spirit of grace (Heb. 10:29); the insults of those who insult you fall on me (Ps. 69:9).

- Insulted
  for God
- Insulting
  people

- No respect
- Reviling

b Blessed are you if you are reviled for the name of Christ (1 Pet. 4:14); blessed are you when you are insulted (Matt. 5:11).

c Cursed is he who dishonours his father or mother (Deut. 27:16); Nabal hurled insults at David's servants (1 Sam. 25:14); do you dare to insult God's high priest? (Acts 23:4); teacher, you insult us also (Luke 11:45).

d A judge who did not respect man (Luke 18:2, 4).

e Do not associate with a 'brother' who is a reviler (1 Cor. 5:11); revilers will not inherit the kingdom of God (1 Cor. 6:10); when reviled, he did not revile back (1 Pet. 2:23).

922 Contempt

- Despising
  God

a They have treated the Lord with contempt (Num. 16:30); those who despise me will be disdained (1 Sam. 2:30); you have despised me (2 Sam. 12:10).

b The Son of man will be treated with contempt (Mark 9:12).

- Despising
  God's
  things

c He who despises the word will suffer (Prov. 13:13); you have despised the Lord's word (2 Sam. 12:9).

d The man who shows contempt for the judge or the priest must be put to death (Deut. 17:12); they treated the Lord's offering with contempt (1 Sam. 2:17); you have despised my holy things (Ezek. 22:8).

- God
  despising

e God pours contempt on nobles (Job 12:21); he endured the cross, depising the shame (Heb. 12:2).

f He has not despised my affliction (Ps. 22:24).

- Despising
  people

g Hagar despised her mistress (Gen. 16:4); here are the people you despised (Judg. 9:38); they despised Saul (1 Sam. 10:27); Michal despised David in her heart (2 Sam. 6:16; 1 Chr. 15:29); women will despise their husbands (Esther 1:17); those who trusted in their own righteousness and despised others (Luke 18:9).

h The virgin daughter of Israel despises you (2 Kgs. 19:21; Isa. 37:22); the revilings of Moab (Zeph. 2:8).

i I despise my life (Job 9:21); he who ignores discipline despises himself (Prov. 15:32).

j Let him who eats not despise him who does not (Rom. 14:3).

- Despising
  things

k Esau despised his birthright (Gen. 25:34); they despised the pleasant land (Ps. 106:24); who has despised the day of small things? (Zech. 4:10); do not treat prophecies with contempt (1 Thess. 5:20).

- Those who
  are despised

l Hear us, for we are despised (Neh. 4:4); we have endured much contempt (Ps. 123:3); I am the contempt of my neighbours (Ps. 31:11); I am lowly and despised (Ps. 119:141); I endure scorn for your sake (Ps. 69:7–10); the arrogant deride me (Ps. 119:51); the one despised by the nations (Isa. 49:7); despised by the people (Ps. 22:6).

m God has chosen those who are despised (1 Cor. 1:28).

- Do not
  despise
n Do not look down on one of these little ones (Matt. 18:10); do not let anyone despise you (1 Tim. 4:12; Titus 2:15); the one who eats should not despise the one who does not (Rom. 14:3); why do you look down on your brother? (Rom. 14:10); let no one despise Timothy (1 Cor. 16:11).
Mocking, see **851**.

923 Approval

- Praise to
  God is fitting
a Great is the Lord and worthy of praise (Ps. 145:3); the Lord is worthy of praise (2 Sam. 22:4); he is your praise (Deut. 10:21); from the lips of children you have ordained praise (Ps. 8:2; Matt. 21:16); it is good to praise the Lord (Ps. 92:1); everywhere the name of the Lord is to be praised (Ps. 113:3); the heavens praise your wonders (Ps. 89:5).

b You are enthroned on the praises of Israel (Ps. 22:3).

c Will the dead praise you? (Ps. 88:10–11); will the dust praise you? (Ps. 30:9); in Sheol who can praise you? (Ps. 6:5).

- Praise God!
d Praise the Lord! (Ps. 106:1, 48; 111:1; 112:1; 113:1, 9; 115:18; 116:19; 117:1, 2; 135:1, 3, 21; 146:1; 147:1, 12, 20; 148:1–4, 14; 149:1, 9; 150:1–6); bless the Lord! (Ps. 103:1, 2, 20, 21, 22; 104:1, 35; 134:1; 135:19–21); praise God in his sanctuary (Ps. 150:1); offer to God a sacrifice of praise (Heb. 13:15); praise the Lord your God (1 Chr. 29:20); sing to the Lord, praise his name (Ps. 96:2); sing praises to God (Ps. 47:6); praise the Lord from the heavens (Ps. 148:1).

- Those
  praising God
e Levites were appointed to give praise before the ark (1 Chr. 16:4); the Levites took their places to praise the Lord (Ezra 3:10); the Levites sang praises with joy (2 Chr. 29:30); the Levites praised the Lord with a very loud voice (2 Chr. 20:19).

f Jehoshaphat appointed those to praise God before the army (2 Chr. 20:21); Ezra blessed the Lord (Neh. 8:6); the heavenly host praising God (Luke 2:13); the disciples praised God for the great works they had seen (Luke 19:37).

- I will praise
  you
g I will praise you, O Lord (Ps. 9:2; Ps. 145:1–2); I will praise the Lord who counsels me (Ps. 16:7); I praise you, Father (Matt. 11:25); in the congregation I will praise you (Ps. 22:22); I will extol the Lord at all times (Ps. 34:1); I will praise you among the nations (Ps. 57:9); I will praise God's name in song (Ps. 69:30); I will sing praise to you (Ps. 101:1); in the great throng I will praise him (Ps. 109:30); I will praise you with all my heart (Ps. 138:1); I will praise the Lord while I live (Ps. 146:2); he is my God and I will praise him (Exod. 15:2); my lips will shout for joy when I sing praise to you (Ps. 71:23); this time I will praise the Lord (Gen. 29:35); he put a new song into my mouth, praise to our God (Ps. 40:3); my soul magnifies the Lord (Luke 1:46); we will sing and praise your might (Ps. 21:13).

- Praising God
h Blessed be the Lord! (1 Kgs. 1:48; 8:15; 10:9; 1 Chr. 16:36;

2 Chr. 9:8; Ps. 41:13; 89:52; 106:48; 124:6); blessed be the name of the Lord (Job 1:21; Ps. 113:2); blessed be my rock (2 Sam. 22:47; Ps. 18:46; 144:1); blessing God in the valley of Beracah (2 Chr. 20:26).

i They praised the God of Israel (Matt. 15:31); walking and leaping and praising God (Acts 3:8).

j With the tongue we both praise God and curse men (Jas. 3:9).

- Praise be to God

k To our God and Father be glory (Phil. 4:20); to him be glory in the church (Eph. 3:21); to the only God and Saviour be glory (Jude 25); you are worthy to receive glory, honour and power (Rev. 4:9–11); to him who sits on the throne and to the Lamb be praise, honour, glory and power (Rev. 5:13); praise and glory be to our God (Rev. 7:12); ascribe to the Lord glory and strength (1 Chr. 16:28); glory to God in the highest (Luke 2:14).

l Blessed be the Lord God (Gen. 9:26; 24:27; Exod. 18:10; Ruth 4:14; 1 Sam. 25:32, 39; 1 Kgs. 8:56; 1 Chr. 29:10; Ezra 7:27; Ps. 72:18; Luke 1:68); blessed be the name of God (Dan. 2:20); blessed be your glorious name (Neh. 9:5); blessed be the God and Father (Eph. 1:3; 1 Pet. 1:3); not to us but to your name be glory (Ps. 115:1).

- Praise God for his benefits

m Praise the Lord your God for the good land (Deut. 8:10); that the people offered themselves willingly, praise the Lord (Judg. 5:2); bless the Lord and forget not all his benefits (Ps. 103:2).

- Showing forth his praise

n That we might be to the praise of his glory (Eph. 1:12); that you may declare the praises of him who called you out of darkness (1 Pet. 2:9).

o We pray that the name of the Lord Jesus may be glorified in you (2 Thess. 1:12); you will be for praise, fame and honour (Deut. 26:19); when he comes to be glorified in his saints (2 Thess. 1:10).

p That men may see your good deeds and glorify your Father in heaven (Matt. 5:16); they saw Jesus healing and glorified God (Matt. 15:31); the fruit of righteousness is to the glory of God (Phil. 1:11).

- Judah—praise

q Named Judah—praise (Gen. 29:35); Judah, your brothers will praise you (Gen. 49:8); one who is a Jew inwardly has praise from God (Rom. 2:29).

- People commended by God

r The men of old were commended for their faith (Heb. 11:2, 39); it is not he one who commends himself who is approved, but the one the Lord commends (2 Cor. 10:18); we speak as men approved by God (1 Thess. 2:4); show yourself approved to God (2 Tim. 2:15); food will not commend us to God (1 Cor. 8:8).

- People commended by people

s The man fell to the ground to pay David honour (2 Sam. 1:2); Abishai was the most honoured of the 30 (2 Sam. 23:19); Benaiah had a name like that of the three (2 Sam. 23:22); honoured among the 30 (2 Sam. 23:23); why do you honour your sons more than me? (1 Sam. 2:29); what honour has been given to

Mordecai for this? (Esther 6:3); what should be done for the man the king delights to honour? (Esther 6:6–9); whom can the king want to honour but me? (Esther 6:6); her husband praises her (Prov. 31:28–9); the master commended the dishonest steward (Luke 16:8); he who serves Christ like this is approved by men (Rom. 14:18); I commend to you our sister Phoebe (Rom. 16:1).

t Woe to you when all men speak well of you (Luke 6:26); the Jews spoke highly of Tobiah (Neh. 6:19); do we need letters of recommendation to you or from you? (2 Cor. 3:1); Mordecai would not pay honour to Haman (Esther 3:2).

Honour, see **866**.

- Commending oneself

u Let another praise you, not your own mouth (Prov. 27:2); it is not he one who commends himself who is approved, but the one the Lord commends (2 Cor. 10:18); we are not commending ourselves to you again (2 Cor. 5:12); we do not compare ourselves with those who commend themselves (2 Cor. 10:12).

v We commend ourselves in every way by the hardships we endure (2 Cor. 6:4); we commend ourselves to everyone's conscience (2 Cor. 4:2).

- Things approved

w You approve what your forefathers did (Luke 11:48); they not only do such things, but approve those who practise them (Rom. 1:32); Paul approved of Stephen's death (Acts 8:1; 22:20); he cast his vote to kill believers (Acts 26:10); that you may approve the things which are excellent (Phil. 1:10).

924 **Disapproval**

- God reproaching

a He who rebukes the nations, will he not rebuke? (Ps. 94:10); he reproved kings for their sake (1 Chr. 16:21; Ps. 105:14); last night God rebuked you (Gen. 31:42); do not rebuke me in your anger (Ps. 38:1); I will bring on you everlasting reproach (Jer. 23:40).

b He rebuked the Red Sea and it dried up (Ps. 106:9).

- God disciplining

c He whom the Lord loves he reproves (Prov. 3:12); those whom I love I reprove and discipline (Rev. 3:19); happy is the man whom God reproves (Job 5:17); correct me, O Lord, but with justice (Jer. 10:24).

d They spurned Wisdom's reproof (Prov. 1:25, 30).

- Jesus rebuking

e Jesus turned and rebuked the disciples (Luke 9:55); Jesus rebuked the eleven for their lack of faith (Mark 16:14); Jesus rebuked the wind and waters (Matt. 8:26; Mark 4:39; Luke 8:24); Jesus rebuked evil spirits (Mark 1:25; 9:25; Luke 4:35, 41; 9:42); Jesus rebuked him and the demon came out (Matt. 17:18); he rebuked the fever (Luke 4:39); Jesus reproached the cities (Matt. 11:20); teacher, rebuke your disciples (Luke 19:39); Jesus rebuked Peter (Mark 8:33).

- Reproaching God

f Let him who reproves God answer him! (Job 40:2); the reproaches of those who reproached you fell on me (Rom. 15:3); let us go out to him, bearing his reproach (Heb. 13:13); Moses considered the reproach of Christ greater riches than the treasures of Egypt (Heb. 11:26); Peter rebuked Jesus (Matt. 16:22; Mark 8:32).

● God's people reproached

g You have made us a reproach to our neighbours (Ps. 44:13); today I have rolled away the reproach of Egypt from you (Josh. 5:9); this sect is spoken against everywhere (Acts 28:22); do not fear the reproach of man (Isa. 51:7); blessed are you when men revile you (Luke 6:22); when reviled, we bless (1 Cor. 4:12).

● Rebuke as discipline

h Elders who sin are to be rebuked publicly (1 Tim. 5:20); rebuke them sharply (Titus 1:13); do not rebuke an older man harshly (1 Tim. 5:1); rebuke a wise man and he will love you (Prov. 9:8–9); if your brother sins, reprove him (Matt. 18:15; Luke 17:3); reprove, rebuke (2 Tim. 4:2); all Scripture is profitable for reproof (2 Tim. 3:16).

Discipline, see **827*h***.

i Eli did not rebuke his sons (1 Sam. 3:13).

Lack of discipline, see **827*j***.

● Rebuking people

j A rebuke goes deeper into a wise man than blows into a fool (Prov. 17:10); he who rebukes will find more favour than he who flatters (Prov. 28:23); better the rebuke of a wise man than the song of fools (Eccles. 7:5); he who reproves a scoffer is insulted (Prov. 9:7–8).

k I reprimanded the officials (Neh. 13:11); I reprimanded the nobles (Neh. 13:17); I reprimanded people profaning the sabbath (Neh. 13:15); I reprimanded those who married foreigners (Neh. 13:25); John reproved Herod (Luke 3:19).

l The Ephraimites criticised Gideon (Judg. 8:1); the disciples rebuked those bringing children to Jesus (Matt. 19:13; Mark 10:13; Luke 18:15); they rebuked the woman who poured perfume on Jesus' head (Mark 14:5).

m We want to avoid criticism in administering this gift (2 Cor. 8:20).

Slander, see **926**.

● Outcry

n The outcry against Sodom and Gomorrah is great (Gen. 18:20–1; 19:13); the cry of the poor came before God (Job 34:28); there was an outcry against their brethren (Neh. 5:1); the outcry of your labourers has reached the Lord's ears (Jas. 5:4); he looked for righteousness but behold a cry (Isa. 5:7).

925 Flattery

● Flatterers

a They flatter with their tongue (Ps. 5:9); with flattering lips (Ps. 12:2–3); a flattering mouth works ruin (Prov. 26:28); with smooth and flattering speech they deceive (Rom. 16:18); flattering to gain advantage (Jude 16); he who flatters his neighbour spreads a net (Prov. 29:5).

● Avoiding flattery	*b* I do not know how to flatter (Job 32:21–2); we never came with flattering speech (1 Thess. 2:5); he who rebukes will find more favour than he who flatters (Prov. 28:23).

926 Calumny

● Slandering	*a* From the heart comes slander (Matt. 15:19; Mark 7:22); a slanderer separates close friends (Prov. 16:28); with his mouth the godless destroys his neighbour (Prov. 11:9); he who spreads slander is a fool (Prov. 10:18); you slander your own brother (Ps. 50:20); my enemies speak evil of me (Ps. 41:5).
	b Miriam and Aaron spoke against Moses (Num. 12:1); the people spoke against God and Moses (Num. 21:5, 7); Ziba slandered Mephibosheth (2 Sam. 19:27); some spoke evil of the Way (Acts 19:9).
	c The name of God is blasphemed among the heathen (Rom. 2:24); the way of truth will be maligned (2 Pet. 2:2); reviling angels (2 Pet. 2:10; Jude 8); reviling without knowledge (2 Pet. 2:12; Jude 10); they are gossips, slanderers (Rom. 1:29–30); men will be slanderers (2 Tim. 3:3).
	d The devil—'slanderer' (Matt. 4:1).
● Being slandered	*e* Wicked men have opened their mouths against me (Ps. 109:2).
	f Blessed are you when you are slandered (Matt. 5:11); they malign you for not sharing in dissipation (1 Pet. 4:4); when slandered we conciliate (1 Cor. 4:13); we commend ourselves by bad report and good report (2 Cor. 6:8).
● Avoiding being slandered	*g* Give the enemy no opportunity for slander (1 Tim. 5:14); that they may be ashamed of their slander (1 Pet. 3:16); no one performing a miracle in my name can then speak evil of me (Mark 9:39).
	h No one spoke against the Israelites (Josh. 10:21); not a dog will growl against Israel (Exod. 11:7).
● Do not slander	*i* Do not spread slander (Lev. 19:16); why were you not afraid to speak against Moses? (Num. 12:8); slander no one (Titus 3:2); do not slander one another (Jas. 4:11); he who speaks evil of parents must die (Matt. 15:4); do not speak evil of a ruler (Acts 23:5); put away slander (Eph. 4:31; Col. 3:8; 1 Pet. 2:1); I fear there may be gossip (2 Cor. 12:20); deacons must not be double-tongued (1 Tim. 3:8); women must not be slanderers (1 Tim. 3:11; Titus 2:3); they become gossips and busybodies (1 Tim. 5:13); he does not slander (Ps. 15:3).
	j Are not the rich slandering the name you belong to? (Jas. 2:7); do not associate with a gossip (Prov. 20:19); I will destroy him who slanders in secret (Ps. 101:5).

927 Vindication

- God
  vindicates

a God has vindicated me (Gen. 30:6); vindicate me, O Lord (Ps. 7:8; 26:1; 43:1; 54:1); he who vindicates me is near (Isa. 50:8); it is God who justifies (Rom. 8:33); the Lord will vindicate his people (Deut. 32:36; Ps. 135:14); will not God vindicate his elect? (Luke 18:7); their vindication is from me (Isa. 54:17); the Lord has brought our vindication (Jer. 51:10); he will bring forth your righteousness as the light (Ps. 37:6); he shall receive righteousness from God (Ps. 24:5); he was vindicated in the Spirit (1 Tim. 3:16); the Lord has upheld my cause against Nabal (1 Sam. 25:39); you have upheld my right and my cause (Ps. 9:4).

- Justified
  by grace

b They are justified freely by his grace (Rom. 3:24; Titus 3:7); by his knowledge my servant will justify many (Isa. 53:11); justified by his blood (Rom. 5:9); the result of one act of righteousness was justification bringing life for all (Rom. 5:16, 18); he was raised for our justification (Rom. 4:25); those he called he also justified (Rom. 8:30); you were justified (1 Cor. 6:11); he is just and the justifier of him who believes (Rom. 3:26); God justifies the ungodly (Rom. 4:5); this man went home justified rather than the other (Luke 18:14).

c A man is not justified by works of the law but by faith (Gal. 2:16); justified by faith apart from works of the law (Rom. 3:28); justified by faith (Rom. 5:1; Gal. 3:24); God justifies both circumcised and uncircumcised by faith (Rom. 3:30).

d Wisdom is vindicated by her children (Luke 7:35).

- Justified by
  works

e Abraham was justified by works (Jas. 2:21); as was Rahab (Jas. 2:25); a man is justified by works and not by faith alone (Jas. 2:24).

f By the works of the law no one will be justified (Rom. 3:20); in seeking to be justified by the law you are severed from Christ (Gal. 5:4); if Abraham was justified by works, he has something to boast about (Rom. 4:2).

- Man
  vindicates

g It is your vindication (Gen. 20:16).

h You are those who justify yourselves (Luke 16:15); the lawyer wished to vindicate himself (Luke 10:29).

928 Accusation

- Rules about
  accusations

a Do not accuse a man for no reason (Prov. 3:30); do not receive an accusation against an elder except on the evidence of two or three witnesses (1 Tim. 5:19).

b If your brother has something against you, leave your gift (Matt. 5:23).

- Accusing
  God

c Job did not accuse God (Job 1:22).

- God and
scripture
accuse

d The Lord is bringing a charge against Israel (Mic. 6:2); your accuser is Moses (John 5:45); why does he still find fault? (Rom. 9:19).

- Satan
accuses

e Satan stood to accuse the high priest (Zech. 3:1); the accuser of the brethren, who accuses them day and night (Rev. 12:10).

- Accusing
Jesus

f They looked for a reason to accuse Jesus (Matt. 12:10; Mark 3:2; Luke 6:7; John 8:6); what charges are you bringing? (John 18:29); the chief priests accused him (Matt. 27:12; Mark 15:3; Luke 23:2, 10); above the head was the charge (Matt. 27:37); the charge read, 'The king of the Jews' (Mark 15:26).

- Accusing
angels

g Even angels do not bring slanderous accusations against angelic beings (2 Pet. 2:11; Jude 9).

- Accusing
men

h They tried to find grounds to accuse Daniel (Dan. 6:4–5); let them bring charges against these men (Acts 19:38); there was no charge against Paul deserving death or imprisonment (Acts 23:29); they brought their charges against Paul (Acts 24:1; 25:2); they brought many serious charges which they could not prove (Acts 25:7); Felix had no charge to write about (Acts 25:27).

i Abner was accused over a woman (2 Sam. 3:7–8); no accusation was lodged against the people of Judah (Ezra 4:6).

j If all prophesy, an unbeliever is called to account (1 Cor. 14:24); their thoughts accuse or excuse them (Rom. 2:15).

929 Faithfulness

- God is
faithful

a God is faithful (1 Cor. 1:9; 10:13; 2 Thess. 3:3); the faithful God (Deut. 7:9); God keeps faith for ever (Ps. 146:6); the one who calls you is faithful (1 Thess. 5:24); he who promised is faithful (Heb. 10:23); great is your faithfulness (Lam. 3:23); Sarah believed him faithful who had promised (Heb. 11:11); if we are faithless, he remains faithful (2 Tim. 2:13); you acted faithfully while we did wrong (Neh. 9:33); the Lord is upright (Ps. 92:15); he is faithful to forgive our sins (1 John 1:9).

- Jesus is
faithful

b Jesus was faithful to the one who appointed him (Heb. 3:2); the rider is called Faithful and True (Rev. 19:11).

- Faithful
people

c We are honest men (Gen. 42:31); Moses was faithful in all God's house (Num. 12:7); the workmen acted with complete honesty (2 Kgs. 12:15); Achish found no fault in David (1 Sam. 29:3, 6–9); what have you found against me? (1 Sam. 29:8); who is as faithful as David? (1 Sam. 22:14); if Adonijah is worthy he will not die (1 Kgs. 1:52); if you walk before me in integrity and uprightness as David did (1 Kgs. 9:4); Asa was blameless all his days (2 Chr. 15:17); Job was blameless and upright (Job 1:1, 8; 2:3); Zechariah and Elizabeth were upright in the sight of God (Luke 1:6); Simeon was righteous (Luke 2:25); the Bereans were more noble than the Thessalonians (Acts 17:11).

d The Lord has dealt with me according to my righteousness

(2 Sam. 22:21; Ps. 18:20); Christ considered me faithful (1 Tim. 1:12).

e Noah was a righteous man (Gen. 6:9; 7:1); Lot was a righteous man (2 Pet. 2:7); she is more righteous than I (Gen. 38:26).

● Need to be faithful

f God made man upright (Eccles. 7:29); the fruit of the Spirit is faithfulness (Gal. 5:22).

g Be blameless before the Lord (Deut. 18:13); it is required that stewards must prove faithful (1 Cor. 4:2); an overseer must be above reproach (1 Tim. 3:2; Titus 1:6, 7); be faithful even to death (Rev. 2:10); the upright will live in the land (Prov. 2:21).

h He who does right is righteous as he is righteous (1 John 3:7).

i You have been faithful in a few things (Matt. 25:21, 23); you have been faithful in a very little (Luke 19:17); he who is faithful in a little is faithful also in much (Luke 16:10).

j If you can find one person who deals honestly, I will forgive this city (Jer. 5:1); there is no faithfulness in the land (Hos. 4:1); many a man proclaims his own loyalty (Prov. 20:6).
Innocence, see **935**.

930 Unfaithfulness

● Unfaithful

a The Israelites acted unfaithfully (Josh. 7:1); how could you break faith with God? (Josh. 22:16); they were unfaithful to the Lord (2 Chr. 12:2; 30:7); they acted treacherously against God (1 Chr. 5:25); as a faithless wife leaves her husband, so you have been faithless to me (Jer. 3:20); Judah exiled for their unfaithfulness (1 Chr. 9:1); if we are faithless, he remains faithful (2 Tim. 2:13); they are untrustworthy (Rom. 1:31).

b If I had acted treacherously against Absalom's life (2 Sam. 18:13); treason! (2 Kgs. 11:14; 2 Chr. 23:13).

● Cheating

c Your father has cheated me (Gen. 31:7); if anyone cheats his neighbour (Lev. 6:2); whom have I cheated? (1 Sam. 12:3–4); if I have cheated anyone, I will repay it fourfold (Luke 19:8).

931 Unselfishness

● Unselfish

a None of us lives or dies for himself (Rom. 14:7); even Christ did not please himself (Rom. 15:3).

932 Selfishness

● Selfish people

a People will be lovers of self (2 Tim. 3:2); everyone looks to his own things (Phil. 2:21); he who speaks from himself seeks his own glory (John 7:18).

b If you have selfish ambition (Jas. 3:14); where there is selfish ambition there is disorder (Jas. 3:16).
Self, see **80**.

● Do not be selfish

c Let no one seek his own things (1 Cor. 10:24); not looking to one's own things (Phil. 2:4); those who live should no longer live for themselves (2 Cor. 5:15); do nothing through selfishness (Phil. 2:3); we ought not merely to please ourselves (Rom. 15:1).

d Love does not seek its own (1 Cor. 13:5).

Not acting alone, see **88r**.

933 Virtue

● Character

a Perseverance produces character (Rom. 5:4).

Faithfulness, see **929**.

934 Wickedness

See **914**.

935 Innocence

● Need for innocence

a Who may walk in your sanctuary? he whose walk is blameless (Ps. 15:2); blessed are those whose ways are blameless (Ps. 119:1); be wise as serpents and innocent as doves (Matt. 10:16); be wise as to good, innocent as to evil (Rom. 16:19); make every effort to be found spotless and blameless (2 Pet. 3:14).

b You will be blameless on the day of our Lord Jesus (1 Cor. 1:8); God is able to make you stand blameless (Jude 24); sincere and blameless until the day of Christ (Phil. 1:10); you will be blameless when our Lord Jesus comes (1 Thess. 3:13); that the church should be holy and blameless (Eph. 5:27); he has chosen us to be holy and blameless (Eph. 1:4); blameless and innocent (Phil. 2:15); to present you holy and blameless (Col. 1:22).

● Plea of innocence

c Lord, will you destroy an innocent nation? (Gen. 20:4–5); who, being innocent, has ever perished? (Job 4:7); God does not reject a blameless man (Job 8:20); as you know, I am not guilty (Job 10:7); I wash my hands in innocence (Ps. 26:6); I am innocent (Dan. 6:22).

d I am innocent of the blood of Abner (2 Sam. 3:28); I was blameless (2 Sam. 22:24; Ps. 18:23); God will know that I am blameless (Job 31:6); I am free from guilt (Job 33:9); I am innocent (Job 34:5); I am pure in your sight (Job 11:4); I lead a blameless life (Ps. 26:11); though you test me, you will find nothing (Ps. 17:3); I am not guilty of wrongdoing (1 Sam. 24:11); the king is guiltless (2 Sam. 14:9); the 200 men went innocently (2 Sam. 15:11); I am innocent of this man's blood (Matt. 27:24); as to righteousness under the law, blameless (Phil. 3:6).

e You show yourself to be innocent (2 Cor. 7:11).

f An adulteress says she has done no wrong (Prov. 30:20); yet you say, 'I am innocent' (Jer. 2:35).

● Innocence of Jesus

g This man has done nothing wrong (Luke 23:41); he committed no sin (1 Pet. 2:22); tempted in every way, yet without sin (Heb. 4:15); such a high priest, innocent, undefiled (Heb. 7:26); which of you convicts me of sin? (John 8:46); I find no guilt in this man

(Luke 23:4, 14–15, 22; John 18:38; 19:4, 6); surely this man was righteous (Luke 23:47).

● Innocence
of Paul

h I am innocent of the blood of all men (Acts 20:26); I have done nothing wrong (Acts 25:8); we find nothing wrong in this man (Acts 23:9); he has done nothing deserving death (Acts 25:25); this man is not doing anything deserving death or imprisonment (Acts 26:31); there were no grounds for putting me to death (Acts 28:18).

● Innocent?

i All a man's ways seem innocent to him, but the Lord weighs motives (Prov. 16:2); if anyone is without sin let him cast the first stone (John 8:7); if we say we have not sinned we deceive ourselves (1 John 1:8, 10); if I had not come and spoken to them, they would not have had sin (John 15:22, 24).

936 Guilt

● Found
guilty

a We are guilty (Gen. 42:21); I am already found guilty (Job 9:29); the king is as one guilty (2 Sam. 14:13);bloodguilt for killing the Gibeonites (2 Sam. 21:1); my guilt has overwhelmed me (Ps. 38:4); you have become guilty (Ezek. 22:4); whoever keeps the whole law but breaks one point is guilty of all (Jas. 2:10); mankind is without excuse (Rom. 1:20).

b You would have brought guilt upon us (Gen. 26:10); may my Lord not hold me guilty (2 Sam. 19:19).

● Incurring
guilt

c Ways of becoming guilty (Lev. 5:1–5, 15, 17, 19); bloodguilt if blood is not offered (Lev. 17:4).

d Aaron will bear the guilt of the holy things (Exod. 28:38; Num. 18:1–2); that the priests may not incur guilt (Exod. 28:43); the Levites will bear the punishment for their iniquity (Ezek. 44:10–12).

e David was conscience-stricken for cutting Saul's robe (1 Sam. 24:5); for counting the fighting men (2 Sam. 24:10).

f Do not bring prisoners in here to add to our guilt (2 Chr. 28:13); if you put me to death you will bring innocent blood on yourselves (Jer. 26:15).

g Guilty of the body and blood of the Lord (1 Cor. 11:27).

h No bloodguilt for killing a thief in the dark (Exod. 22:2–3).

● Removal
of guilt

i Deliver me from bloodguilt (Ps. 51:14); the guilt of Eli's house will never be atoned for (1 Sam. 3:14).
Guilt offering, see **981***ad*.

937 Good person

● The righteous

a Tell the righteous it will be well with them (Isa. 3:10); he who receives a righteous man as a rithteous man will receive a righteous man's reward (Matt. 10:41).

b Noah, Daniel and Job would only deliver themselves by their righteousness (Ezek. 14:14–20); Joseph, Mary's husband, was a righteous men (Matt. 1:19); Herod knew John was a righteous man (Mark 6:20); some said Jesus was a good man (John 7:12); Joseph of Arimathea was a good man (Luke 23:50).

● The good
perishing

c The godly person has perished from the earth (Mic. 7:2); the righteous man perishes and no one takes it to heart (Isa. 57:1).

938 Bad person

● Wicked
people

a The earth was corrupt (Gen. 6:11, 12); the men of Sodom were wicked (Gen. 13:13); Judah's firstborn was wicked (Gen. 38:7; 1 Chr. 2:3); what Onan did was wicked (Gen. 38:10); this is a wicked generation (Luke 11:29); from the wicked comes wickedness (1 Sam. 24:13).

b God has made even the wicked for the day of evil (Prov. 16:4).

c Abimelech hired worthless men (Judg. 9:4); worthless men gathered to Jephthah (Judg. 11:3).

d Sons of Belial: cause trouble (Prov. 6:12–15); hand them over (Judg. 20:13); Eli's sons (1 Sam. 2:12); some despised Saul (1 Sam. 10:27); Nabal (1 Sam. 25:17, 25); among David's men (1 Sam. 30:22); David was called such (2 Sam. 16:7); Sheba (2 Sam. 20:1); two as false witnesses (1 Kgs. 21:9, 13); gathered round Jeroboam (2 Chr. 13:7).

e How can you who are evil say anything good? (Matt. 12:34); you who are evil (Matt. 7:11; Luke 11:13); you were born in sin, and would you teach us? (John 9:34).

● Ways of the
wicked

f Do not even the tax collectors love those who love them? (Matt. 5:46); even sinners love those who love them (Luke 6:32); even sinners do good to those who do good to them (Luke 6:33); even sinners lend to sinners (Luke 6:34); do not even pagans greet their brethren? (Matt. 5:47).

g Blessed is the man who does not walk in the counsel of the wicked (Ps. 1:1).

● Judgement on
the wicked

h The wicked man's portion from God (Job 20:29; 27:13); the wicked man is in pain all his life (Job 15:20–4); tell the wicked it will go badly for them (Isa. 3:11); the wicked will not stand in the judgement (Ps. 1:4–6); a little while and the wicked will be no more (Ps. 37:9–10); the wicked will perish (Ps. 37:20); evil men are all to be cast aside like thorns (2 Sam. 23:6); the lamp of the wicked will be snuffed out (Job 18:5).

i Do you think these were worse sinners than all the others? (Luke 13:2, 4).

● Prosperity of
the wicked

j Why do the wicked live on? (Job 21:7–13); how often is the lamp of the wicked snuffed out? (Job 21:17); the wicked goes to his end unpunished (Job 21:30–3); I saw the prosperity of the wicked (Ps. 73:3–9); why does the way of the wicked prosper? (Jer. 12:1); why are you silent when the wicked swallow up those more righteous? (Hab. 1:13).

● Sinners
saved

k Tax collectors and prostitutes enter the kingdom of God ahead of you (Matt. 21:31); I have not come to call the righteous, but sinners (Matt. 9:13; Mark 2:17; Luke 5:32); the tax collectors and sinners were gathering round to hear him (Luke 15:1); Jesus ate with tax collectors and sinners (Matt. 9:10–11; Mark 2:15–17); a friend of tax collectors and sinners (Matt. 11:19; Luke 7:34); Christ Jesus came into the world to save sinners, of whom I am chief (1 Tim. 1:15–16); depart from me, for I am a sinful man (Luke 5:8); a woman who was a sinner (Luke 7:37); if he were a prophet he would know that this woman is a sinner (Luke 7:39).

l God be merciful to me, the sinner (Luke 18:13).

m We know that this man is a sinner (John 9:24–5).

Restoring sinners, see **656*am***.

939 Penitence

● Repent!

a Turn from your evil ways! (Ezek. 33:11); if my people will turn from their wicked ways (2 Chr. 7:14); if they repent (1 Kgs. 8:47); change your ways and your actions (Jer. 7:3, 5); repent and live! (Ezek. 18:32).

b Repent, for the kingdom of heaven is at hand (Matt. 3:2; 4:17); repent and believe the gospel (Mark 1:15); they preached that men should repent (Mark 6:12); repentance and forgiveness should be preached (Luke 24:47); unless you repent you will all likewise perish (Luke 13:3, 5); the angels of God rejoice over one sinner who repents (Luke 15:7, 10); stop sinning or something worse will happen to you (John 5:14); go and sin no more (John 8:11); repent and turn to God (Acts 3:19); repent and do the first works (Rev. 2:5); remember what you have heard, keep it and repent (Rev. 3:3); repent of this wickedness (Acts 8:22); repent, or I will come (Rev. 2:16); be zealous and repent (Rev. 3:19); he commands all people everywhere to repent (Acts 17:30); they must turn to God in repentance (Acts 20:21; 26:20); repentance from dead works (Heb. 6:1).

● God gives repentance

c God gives repentance to Israel (Acts 5:31); God has granted to the Gentiles repentance unto life (Acts 11:18); God may grant them repentance (2 Tim. 2:25); God's kindness leads you to repentance (Rom. 2:4); he is willing that all should come to repentance (2 Pet. 3:9).

● Signs of repentance

d I repent in dust and ashes (Job 42:6); a baptism of repentance (Matt. 3:11; Mark 1:4; Luke 3:3; Acts 13:24; 19:4); repent and be baptised (Acts 2:38).

e Bring forth fruit fitting repentance (Matt. 3:8; Luke 3:8); perform deeds fitting repentance (Acts 26:20).

f If the miracles had been done, they would have repented (Luke 10:13); Tyre and Sidon would have repented long ago (Matt. 11:21); Nineveh repented at the preaching of Jonah (Matt. 12:41); godly sorrow produces repentance (2 Cor. 7:9–10).

940 Impenitence

● Unrepentant   *a*   A stubborn, unrepentant heart (Rom. 2:5).

                     b   Jesus upbraided the cities because they did not repent (Matt. 11:20); the rest of mankind did not repent (Rev. 9:20–1); they refused to repent (Rev. 16:9, 11); I gave her time to repent but she will not (Rev. 2:21).

● No repentance   *c*   It is impossible to restore to repentance some who have fallen away (Heb. 6:6); those who have sinned and not repented (2 Cor. 12:21); Esau found no place for repentance (Heb. 12:17).

941 Atonement

● Day of   *a*   Regulations for the Day of Atonement (Lev. 16:1–34; 23:26–32;
   atonement   Num. 29:7–11); start of the year of Jubilee (Lev. 25:9).

                     b   On this day atonement will be made for you (Lev. 16:30); the high priest enters the Holy of Holies every year with blood not his own (Heb. 9:7, 25); the 'fast' was already past (Acts 27:9).

● Priests   *c*   The priest makes atonement (Lev. 4:20, 26, 31, 35; 5:6, 10, 13,
   atoning   16, 18; 6:7; 7:7; 9:7; 10:17; 12:7, 8; 14:18–20, 29–31, 53; 15:15, 30; 16:16–18, 24, 32–4; 19:22; Num. 6:11; 15:25, 28); Aaron's descendants make atonement for Israel (1 Chr. 6:49); the priests made atonement for all Israel (2 Chr. 29:24).

                     d   The high priest makes atonement for himself (Lev. 16:6, 11, 17, 24); the Levites make atonement (Num. 8:19); making atonement for the Levites (Num. 8:12, 21).

                     e   The place of propitiation [the mercy seat] (Heb. 9:5).
                         Mercy seat, see **226*l*.**

● Atoning by   *f*   The burnt offering will make atonement (Lev. 1:4; Num. 28:30);
   sacrifices   the sin offering to make atonement (Num. 28:22; 29:5, 11; Neh. 10:33); making atonement for the altar (Ezek. 43:26).

                     g   Blood to make atonement: on the altar (Lev. 17:11); of the sin offering (Lev. 16:27); on the horns of the incense altar (Exod. 30:10); round the altar of burnt offering (Lev. 8:15).

                     h   The ram of atonement (Num. 5:8); atonement cannot be made except by the blood of the one who shed blood (Num. 35:33).

                     i   It is impossible for the blood of bulls and goats to take away sins (Heb. 10:4).
                         Bearing sin, see **273*i*; taking away sin**, see **786*m*.**

● Various   *j*   Aaron offered incense to make atonement (Num. 16:46–7); the
   atoning   half-shekel tax to make atonement (Exod. 30:15–16); an offering of jewellery to make atonement (Num. 31:50).

                     k   Perhaps I can make atonement for your sin (Exod. 32:30); atone for your people (Deut. 21:8); Phinehas made atonement with his spear (Num. 25:13); how can I make atonement? (2 Sam. 21:3); through love and faithfulness sin is atoned for (Prov. 16:6); your sin is atoned for (Isa. 6:7); by exile Jacob's iniquity will be atoned for (Isa. 27:9); seventy sevens are decreed to atone for wickedness (Dan. 9:24).

l The sin of Eli's house will never be atoned for (1 Sam. 3:14).

● Jesus'
atonement

m The Lamb of God who takes away the sin of the world (John 1:29); Christ died for our sins in accordance with the scriptures (1 Cor. 15:3); God displayed him as a propitiation in his blood (Rom. 3:25); we have redemption through his blood (Eph. 1:7); after he had made purification for sins, he sat down (Heb. 1:3); that he might make atonement for the sins of the people (Heb. 2:17); he is the propitiation for our sins (1 John 2:2; 4:10); he appeared to take away sins (1 John 3:5).
Cleansing of sin, see **648***aa*.

942 Temperance

Gentleness, see **177**; **sobriety**, see **948**.

943 Intemperance

● Self-
indulgence

a A man without self-control is like a city broken into (Prov. 25:28); inside they are full of robbery and self-indulgence (Matt. 23:25); men will be without self-control (2 Tim. 3:3).

944 Sensualism

● Sensual

a These things are no use against fleshly indulgence (Col. 2:23).

945 Asceticism

● Ascetic

a Severe treatment of the body (Col. 2:23).

946 Fasting

● How
to fast

a Instructions for times of fasting and mourning (Esther 9:31); is not this the kind of fasting I have chosen? (Isa. 58:5–7); when you fast, do not look gloomy but anoint your head (Matt. 6:16–18).

b On the day of fasting, you do as you please (Isa. 58:3); when you fasted, was it for me? (Zech. 7:5); you fast to quarrel and fight (Isa. 58:4).

● Who will
fast

c How is it that John's disciples fast but your do not? (Matt. 9:14; Mark 2:18; Luke 5:33); on that day they will fast (Matt. 9:15; Mark 2:20; Luke 5:35).

● Fasting
regularly

d Anna fasted and prayed (Luke 2:37); John came neither eating nor drinking (Matt. 11:18; Luke 7:33); the Pharisee fasted twice a week (Luke 18:12).

e Fasting in the fifth and seventh months (Zech. 7:3, 5); the fasts of the fourth, fifth, seventh and tenth month will become joy (Zech. 8:19).

● Fasting
for long
periods

f Moses did not eat or drink for 40 days (Deut. 9:9); and for another 40 days (Deut. 9:18); Elijah did not eat or drink for 40 days (1 Kgs. 19:8); Jesus fasted for 40 days (Matt. 4:2; Luke 4:2); my knees are weak from fasting (Ps. 109:24).

● Prayer and fasting

g They fasted and confessed their sin (1 Sam. 7:6); Ahab fasted (1 Kgs. 21:27); the men of Israel fasted and presented burnt offerings (Judg. 20:26); David pleaded with God for the child and fasted (2 Sam. 12:16, 17, 21, 22); I, Daniel, ate no choice food (Dan. 10:3); we fasted and prayed to our God (Ezra 8:21, 23); gather all the Jews and fast for me (Esther 4:16); the Jews mourned and fasted (Esther 4:3); Nehemiah was fasting and praying (Neh. 1:4); fasting and in sackcloth to confess their sins (Neh. 9:1); prayer and supplication with fasting (Dan. 9:3).

h Jehoshaphat proclaimed a fast to enquire of the Lord (2 Chr. 20:3); proclaim a fast (1 Kgs. 21:9, 12); declare a holy fast, call a sacred assembly (Joel 1:14; 2:15); the men of Nineveh declared a fast and put on sackcloth (Jonah 3:5); they proclaimed a fast before the Lord (Jer. 36:9).

i While they were ministering to the Lord and fasting (Acts 13:2); prayer and fasting (Matt. 17:21; Mark 9:29) they fasted and prayed and laid their hands on them (Acts 13:3); with prayer and fasting they committed the elders to the Lord (Acts 14:23).

● Pointless fasting

j Now the child is dead, why should I fast? (2 Sam. 12:23); why have we fasted and you did not see it? (Isa. 58:3); when they fast I will not listen (Jer. 14:12).

● Going without food

k Saul had eaten nothing all that day (1 Sam. 28:20); the Egyptian had not eaten nor drunk for three days (1 Sam. 30:12); Ahab would not eat (1 Kgs. 21:4–5); the king spent the night without eating (Dan. 6:18); I will not eat the passover until it is fulfilled (Luke 22:16); Paul did not eat or drink for three days (Acts 9:9); they had gone a long time without food (Acts 27:21); for fourteen days you have not eaten anything (Acts 27:33).

● Fasting in mourning

l Hannah wept and would not eat (1 Sam. 1:7–8); Jonathan ate nothing that day (1 Sam. 20:34); I was reproached for weeping and fasting (Ps. 69:10).

m The men of Israel fasted seven days, mourning Saul (1 Sam. 31:13; 1 Chr. 10:12); they fasted until evening for Saul and Jonathan (2 Sam. 1:12); he ate no food and drank no water, mourning over their unfaithfulness (Ezra 10:6).

● Vowing to fast

n David took an oath not to eat before the sun set (2 Sam. 3:35); cursed be the man who eats food before evening (1 Sam. 14:24, 28); they vowed not to eat or drink until they had killed Paul (Acts 23:12, 14, 21).

947 Gluttony

● Gluttons

a Our son is a glutton and a drunkard (Deut. 21:20); they called Jesus a glutton and a drunkard (Matt. 11:19; Luke 7:34); Cretans are lazy gluttons (Titus 1:12).

● Avoid gluttons

b Do not be with gluttonous eaters of meat (Prov. 23:20–1); a companion of gluttons shames his father (Prov. 28:7).

948 Sobriety

● Drinking
no wine

a Aaron and his sons were not to drink wine or other fermented drink (Lev. 10:9); no priest is to drink wine when he enters the inner court (Ezek. 44:21).

b A Nazirite must not consume anything from the vine (Num. 6:3–4, 20); Samson's mother had to drink no wine or liquor (Judg. 13:4, 7, 14); the Rechabites do not drink wine (Jer. 35:14); John the Baptist had to drink no wine (Luke 1:15).

c I will not drink of the fruit of the vine (Matt. 26:29; Mark 14:25; Luke 22:18); he would not drink the wine mixed with gall (Matt. 27:34); he would not drink the wine mixed with myrrh (Mark 15:23).

● Not too
much wine

d Deacons must not take much wine (1 Tim. 3:8); an overseer must not be given to much wine (1 Tim. 3:3; Titus 1:7); older women must not be addicted to much wine (Titus 2:3); do not join those who drink too much wine (Prov. 23:20–1).
Avoiding alcohol, see **949***a*.

● Not drunk

e Hannah was not drunk (1 Sam. 1:15); in the morning when he had sobered up (1 Sam. 25:37).
Drunkenness, see **949**.

949 Drunkenness. Drug-taking

● Avoiding
alcohol

a Wine is a mocker and beer a brawler (Prov. 20:1); wine is treacherous (Hab. 2:5); do not gaze at wine when it is red (Prov. 23:29–35); not in carousing and drunkenness (Rom. 13:13); they no longer drink wine with singing (Isa. 24:9).

b It is not for kings to drink wine or crave beer (Prov. 31:4); woe to those who rise early to run after drink (Isa. 5:11); woe to those who are heroes at drinking wine (Isa. 5:22); wail, all you drinkers of wine! (Joel 1:5).

● Use of wine

c The vine would not leave its wine, which cheers God and men, to reign (Judg. 9:13); wine to make man's heart glad (Ps. 104:15); wine gladdens life (Eccles. 10:19); wine to make him forget his trouble (Prov. 31:6–7); take a little wine for the sake of your stomach (1 Tim. 5:23); I investigated wine (Eccles. 2:3).

● Provision
of wine

d Squeezing grapes into Pharaoh's cup (Gen. 40:11); Nehemiah served wine to the king (Neh. 2:1); wine was plentiful (Esther 1:7); every jug will be filled with wine (Jer. 13:12); water into wine (John 2:3–10).

● Love and
wine

e I would give you spiced wine (S. of S. 8:2); your mouth is like best wine (S. of S. 7:9); your love is better than wine (S. of S. 1:2; 4:10); we will extol your love more than wine (S. of S. 1:4).

● Do not
get drunk

f Those who get drunk, get drunk at night (1 Thess. 5:7); drunkenness and carousing are deeds of the flesh (Gal. 5:21); be careful lest your hearts be weighed down with dissipation, drunkenness and anxiety (Luke 21:34); put your wine from you (1 Sam. 1:14);

do not be drunk with wine but be filled with the Spirit (Eph. 5:18).

g Priests and prophets stagger from beer (Isa. 28:7); woe to the land whose princes feast in the morning (Eccles. 10:16–17); princes sick with the heat of wine (Hos. 7:5); woe to the pride of Ephraim's drunkards (Isa. 28:1, 3); let us drink our fill of beer! (Isa. 56:12); he begins to beat his fellow-servants and to eat and drink with drunkards (Matt. 24:49; Luke 12:45).

h Do not associate with a 'brother' who is a drunkard (1 Cor. 5:11); drunkards will not inherit the kingdom of God (1 Cor. 6:10); let the time that is past suffice for drunkenness (1 Pet. 4:3).

● Drunken people

i Noah drank wine and became drunk (Gen. 9:21); Eli thought Hannah was drunk (1 Sam. 1:13–14); Nabab was very drunk (1 Sam. 25:36); when Amnon is merry with wine (2 Sam. 13:28); Elah was getting drunk (1 Kgs. 16:9); Benhadad and the kings were getting drunk (1 Kgs. 20:12, 16); Ahasuerus was merry with wine (Esther 1:10); one is hungry and another is drunk (1 Cor. 11:21).

j I am the song of the drunkards (Ps. 69:12); they reeled like drunken men (Ps. 107:27); 'I will preach of wine and strong drink' (Mic. 2:11).

● Making others drunk

k Lot's daughters made their father drunk (Gen. 19:32–5); David made Uriah drunk (2 Sam. 11:13); give the Rechabites wine to drink (Jer. 35:2–6); you made the Nazirites drink wine (Amos 2:12); woe to those who make others drunk to look at their nakedness (Hab. 2:15).

● Accused of drunkenness

l Our son is a glutton and a drunkard (Deut. 21:20); they said Jesus was a glutton and a drunkard (Matt. 11:19; Luke 7:34); they have had too much wine (Acts 2:13); these men are not drunk (Acts 2:15).

● The cup of Jesus

m Can you drink the cup I drink? (Matt. 20:22–3; Mark 10:38); let this cup pass from me (Matt. 26:39; Mark 14:36); shall I not drink the cup? (John 18:11).

n New wine (Matt. 9:17; Mark 2:22).

● God making drunk

o In the hand of the Lord is a cup full of foaming wine (Ps. 75:8); drink the cup in the Lord's hand (Hab. 2:16); the cup of reeling, the bowl of my anger (Isa. 51:22; Jer. 25:15–26); you who have drunk the cup of his wrath (Isa. 51:17); I will make Jerusalem a cup which causes reeling to the people around (Zech. 12:2); if those who did not deserve to drink the cup must drink it (Jer. 49:12).

p Drink and be drunk (Jer. 25:27–8); be drunk, but not from wine (Isa. 29:9); I will fill with drunkenness all who live in this land (Jer. 13:13); I will make her priests and wise men drunk (Jer. 51:57); you will be drunk, O daughter of Edom (Lam. 4:21); make Moab drunk (Jer. 48:26); Nineveh will also be drunk (Nahum 3:11).

q The wine of the wrath of God (Rev. 14:10; 16:19); you who are drunk, but not with new wine (Isa. 51:21); you gave us wine that made us reel (Ps. 60:3); they will become drunk with their own blood (Isa. 49:26).

● Evil making drunk

r Babylon made the whole earth drunk (Jer. 51:7; Rev. 14:8); the wine of the passion of her immorality (Rev. 18:3); the woman was drunk with the blood of the saints (Rev. 17:6); drunk with the wine of her immorality (Rev. 17:2).

s My belly is like wine about to burst (Job 32:19).

950 Purity

● God is pure

a To the pure you show yourself pure (2 Sam. 22:27; Ps. 18:26); your eyes are too pure to look on evil (Hab. 1:13); the wisdom from above is pure (Jas. 3:17); the Lord's words are pure words (Ps. 12:6).

● Pure in heart

b Create in me a pure heart (Ps. 51:10); how can a young man keep his way pure? (Ps. 119:9); who can say, 'I have kept my heart pure' (Prov. 20:9).

c Blessed are the pure in heart (Matt. 5:8); that you may become blameless and pure (Phil. 2:15); we commend ourselves in purity (2 Cor. 6:6); to the pure all things are pure (Titus 1:15).
Singleness of heart, see **44**.

d All the ways of a man are pure in his own eyes (Prov. 16:2); those who are pure in their own eyes (Prov. 30:12); in vain have I kept my heart pure (Ps. 73:13).

● Pure things

e Whatever is pure, think about it (Phil. 4:8).

951 Impurity

● About immorality

a From the heart comes fornication (Matt. 15:19; Mark 7:21); immorality and impurity are deeds of the flesh (Gal. 5:19).

b The immoral will end in the lake of fire (Rev. 21:8); God will judge fornicators and adulterers (Heb. 13:4); nothing impure will enter the city (Rev. 21:27); fornicators will not inherit the kingdom of God (1 Cor. 6:9); outside are fornicators (Rev. 22:15); no immoral man has any inheritance in the kingdom of Christ (Eph. 5:5); our exhortation is not from uncleanness (1 Thess. 2:3).

c If a man lies with a virgin not pledged to be married (Exod. 22:16).
Death penalty for sexual sin, see **963r**.

● They committed immorality

d The men of Israel played the harlot with Moabite women (Num. 25:1); a stumbling block before Israel to commit immorality (Rev. 2:14); God gave them over to impurity (Rom. 1:24); they change the grace of God into licentiousness (Jude 4); Sodom and Gomorrah indulged in gross immorality (Jude 7); he whom you now have is not your husband (John 4:18); they indulge in every kind of impurity (Eph. 4:19); Jezebel teaches my servants to commit immorality (Rev. 2:20); they did not repent of their immorality (Rev. 9:21).

- Avoid immorality

e They should abstain from fornication (Acts 15:20, 29; 21:25); not in sexual promiscuity (Rom. 13:13); flee immorality (1 Cor. 6:18); we should not commit immorality (1 Cor. 10:8); that you abstain from sexual immorality (1 Thess. 4:3); do not let immorality even be named (Eph. 5:3); God did not call us to be impure (1 Thess. 4:7); see that no one is immoral (Heb. 12:16); the body is not for immorality (1 Cor. 6:13); reckon your members dead to immorality *etc.* (Col. 3:5); I wrote to you not to associate with immoral people (1 Cor. 5:9–11); some in the church who have not repented of immorality (2 Cor. 12:21).

- About adultery

f From the heart come adulteries (Matt. 15:19; Mark 7:21); anyone who looks at a woman lustfully has already committed adultery (Matt. 5:28); adulterers will not inherit the kingdom of God (1 Cor. 6:9); the adulterer waits for twilight (Job 24:15); an adulterer destroys himself (Prov. 6:32).

g Sex with your neighbour's wife is forbidden (Lev. 18:20); if he defiles his neighbour's wife (Ezek. 18:11); if he does not defile his neighbour's wife (Ezek. 18:6, 15); if a man is found lying with a married woman, both shall die (Deut. 22:22); an adulteress must be put to death (Lev. 20:10); if a man lies with a virgin pledged to be married, both shall die (Deut. 22:23–5); if with a slave girl promised to another (Lev. 19:20); if a man's wife sleeps with another and it is hidden from him (Num. 5:12–14).

- Divorce and adultery

h Anyone divorcing his wife, except for unchastity, makes her commit adultery, and anyone marrying a divorced woman commits adultery (Matt. 5:32; 19:9); if either husband or wife divorces and remarries, they commit adultery (Mark 10:11–12; Luke 16:18); if she belongs to another man she will be called an adulteress (Rom. 7:3).

- They committed adultery

i They committed adultery (Jer. 5:7); they are all adulterers (Hos. 7:4); they commit adultery and live a lie (Jer. 23:14); they brought in a woman caught in adultery (John 8:3); the Levite's concubine played the harlot against him (Judg. 19:2); with eyes full of adultery (2 Pet. 2:14); stolen water is sweet (Prov. 9:17); take a wife of adultery (Hos. 1:2); you who forbid adultery, do you commit adultery? (Rom. 2:22); will you steal, murder and commit adultery? (Jer. 7:9); you are friendly with adulterers (Ps. 50:18).

- The adulteress

j It will save you from the adulteress (Prov. 2:16; 6:24; 7:5); description of the adulteress (Prov. 5:3–23; 6:24–35); the mouth of an adulteress is a deep pit (Prov. 22:14); why embrace the bosom of a stranger? (Prov. 5:20); an adulteress says she has done no wrong (Prov. 30:20).

- Avoid adultery

k Do not commit adultery (Exod. 20:14; Deut. 5:18; Matt. 5:27; 19:18; Mark 10:19; Luke 18:20; Rom. 13:9; Jas. 2:11); no one who lies with another man's wife will go unpunished (Prov. 6:29); let her remove the adulterous look from her face (Hos. 2:2); if I have lurked at my neigbour's door (Job 31:9).

● Adultery to God

l Like a woman unfaithful to her husband, so you have been unfaithful to me (Jer. 3:20); they committed adultery with their idols (Ezek. 23:37); the land is guilty of adultery in departing from the Lord (Hos. 1:2); you have been unfaithful to your God (Hos. 9:1); Judah committed adultery with stones and trees (Jer. 3:9); all of them are adulterers (Jer. 9:2); you adulterers! (Jas. 4:4); you adulterous wife! (Ezek. 16:32); an evil and adulterous generation (Matt. 12:39; 16:4; Mark 8:38).

m The inhabitants of the earth were intoxicated with the wine of her adultery (Rev. 17:2); she held a golden cup filled with the filth of her adulteries (Rev. 17:4); all nations have drunk the wine of her adulteries (Rev. 18:3).

● Bestiality

n Cursed is he who lies with an animal (Deut. 27:21); whoever lies with an animal shall be put to death (Exod. 22:19); you shall not have intercourse with an animal (Lev. 18:23); if a man or woman has intercourse with an animal, both shall be killed (Lev. 20:15–16).

● Homo-sexuality

o You shall not lie with a male as one lies with a female (Lev. 18:22); if a man lies with a man as one lies with a woman, both shall be put to death (Lev. 20:13); male prostitutes are an abomination (Deut. 23:18); God gave them over to the shameful lusts of homosexual relations (Rom. 1:26–7); neither the effeminate nor homosexuals will inherit the kingdom of God (1 Cor. 6:9); the law is for the immoral, homosexuals (1 Tim. 1:10).

p Bring out the men that we may have relations with them (Gen. 19:5; Judg. 19:22); Sodom and Gomorrah practised homosexuality (Jude 7).

● Incest

q Cursed be he who lies with his father's wife (Deut. 27:20); Reuben lay with his father's concubine (Gen. 35:22); you went up to your father's bed (Gen. 49:4; 1 Chr. 5:1); Absalom went in to his father's concubines (2 Sam. 16:22); father and son use the same girl (Amos 2:7); they have uncovered their father's nakedness (Ezek. 22:10); sexual immorality of a kind unknown to pagans: a man has his father's wife (1 Cor. 5:1).

r Cursed is the man who lies with his sister (Deut. 27:22); cursed is the man who lies with his mother-in-law (Deut. 27:23); sexual intercourse with a close relative is forbidden (Lev. 18:6–18; 20:11–12, 17, 19–21; Ezek. 22:11).

● Prostitutes

s Description of the prostitute (Prov. 7:6–27); a prostitute is a deep pit (Prov. 23:27); harlots enter the kingdom of God before you (Matt. 21:31).

t Judah thought Tamar was a prostitute (Gen. 38:15, 21–2); Rahab the prostitute (Josh. 2:1; 6:22; Heb. 11:31; Jas. 2:25); Jephthah's mother was a prostitute (Judg. 11:1); two prostitutes came before Solomon (1 Kgs. 3:16); harlots bathed in the pool of Samaria (1 Kgs. 22:38); your wife will be a harlot in the city (Amos 7:17).

● Going with prostitutes

u They thronged to the houses of the prostitutes (Jer. 5:7); he who goes with harlots wastes his wealth (Prov. 29:3); this son has devoured your wealth with harlots (Luke 15:30); Samson went in to a prostitute in Gaza (Judg. 16:1); I will not punish your daughters when they turn to prostitution because the men consort with harlots (Hos. 4:14).

● Avoid prostitution

v Do not make your daughter a prostitute (Lev. 19:29); if a priest's daughter becomes a prostitute, she must be burned (Lev. 21:9); a priest is not to marry a prostitute (Lev. 21:7, 14); the sons of Israel shall not be cult prostitutes (Deut. 23:17); the earnings of a male or female prostitute are not to be brought into the Lord's house (Deut. 23:18); should he treat our sister like a prostitute? (Gen. 34:31); shall I take the limbs of Christ and make them limbs of a prostitute? (1 Cor. 6:15).

● Male prostitutes

w There were male prostitutes in the land (1 Kgs. 14:24); Asa removed them (1 Kgs. 15:12); Jehoshaphat expelled the male cult prostitutes (1 Kgs. 22:46); Josiah tore down the quarters of the male shrine prostitutes (2 Kgs. 23:7); the earnings of a male or female prostitute are not to be brought into the Lord's house (Deut. 23:18).

● Prostitution to other gods

x A spirit of harlotry (Hos. 4:12; 5:4); when they prostituted themselves to their gods (Exod. 34:15–16); they prostituted themselves to other gods (Judg. 2:17; 1 Chr. 5:25); they prostituted themselves to the Baals (Judg. 8:33); they prostituted themselves by worshipping the ephod (Judg. 8:27); harlotry with idols (Ezek. 16:17–21, 35–6); they played the harlot in their acts (Ps. 106:39); Oholah and Oholibah played the harlot (Ezek. 23:3–19); the faithful city has become a harlot (Isa. 1:21); under every green tree you lay as a harlot (Jer. 2:20); as Israel did also (Jer. 3:6); Ephraim, you have played the harlot (Hos. 5:3); Judah was a harlot also (Jer. 3:8).

● Nations as prostitutes

y Tyre will return to her hire as a prostitute (Isa. 23:17); you have lived as a prostitute with many lovers (Jer. 3:1); Babylon, the mother of prostitutes (Rev. 17:5); the great harlot (Rev. 17:1); you prostituted yourself with every passer-by (Ezek. 16:15–22, 25–6, 28–9); a harlot who paid rather than charged (Ezek. 16:33–4).

● Rape

z If a man rapes a girl pledged to be married (Deut. 22:25); a virgin not pledged to be married (Deut. 22:28–9); you will be betrothed to a woman and another will rape her (Deut. 28:30).

aa Shechem raped Dinah (Gen. 34:2, 5); rape my virgin daughters (Gen. 19:8); rape my virgin daughter and his concubine (Judg. 19:24); they raped the man's concubine (Judg. 19:25; 20:5); Amnon raped Tamar (2 Sam. 13:12–14, 32); women have been ravished in Zion (Lam. 5:11); the women of Jerusalem will be raped (Zech. 14:2); their wives will be raped (Isa. 13:16); will he even assault the queen? (Esther 7:8).

952 Libertine

● Specific concubines

a Concubines of: Abraham (Gen. 22:24; 25:6; 1 Chr. 1:32); Eliphaz son of Esau (Gen. 36:12); Gideon (Judg. 8:31); a Levite (Judg. 19:1–29); Manasseh (1 Chr. 7:14).

b Bilhah, Jacob's concubine (Gen. 35:22); Maacah, Caleb's concubine (1 Chr. 2:48); Rizpah, Saul's concubine (2 Sam. 3:7).

● Numbers of concubines

c I got many concubines—man's delight (Eccles. 2:8); David took more concubines (2 Sam. 5:13); David left ten concubines to keep the house (2 Sam. 15:16); Absalom went in to them (2 Sam. 16:21, 22); David shut them up like widows (2 Sam. 20:3); the sons of David's concubines (1 Chr. 3:9); Solomon had 300 concubines (1 Kgs. 11:3); Rehoboam had 60 concubines (2 Chr. 11:21); 80 concubines (S. of S. 6:8); the eunuch in charge of the king's concubines (Esther 2:14).

Prostitutes, see **951***s*.

953 Legality

● The law given

a Moses wrote this law (Deut. 31:9, 24); Moses charged us with the law (Deut. 33:4); the book of the law of Moses (Josh. 8:31, 34); the law of Moses (1 Kgs. 2:3); the law was given through Moses (John 1:17); you gave them laws through Moses (Neh. 9:14); Moses gave you the law (John 7:19); I will give you the tablets of stone with the law and commands (Exod. 24:12); I gave them my statutes and ordinances (Ezek. 20:11); theirs is the receiving of the law (Rom. 9:4); he wrote on the tablets the Ten Commandments (Exod. 34:28; Deut. 10:4); hear now the decrees and the laws (Deut. 4:1); take this book of the law and place it beside the ark (Deut. 31:26); I have found the book of the law (2 Kgs. 22:8); the law written in the book (2 Kgs. 23:24); he established the law in Israel (Ps. 78:5); the law will go out from Zion (Isa. 2:3; Mic. 4:2); a law will go forth from me (Isa. 51:4).

b The laws of the Jews are different (Esther 3:8).

● Excellent law

c The law of the Lord is perfect (Ps. 19:7); what other nation has such righteous decrees? (Deut. 4:8); you gave them regulations and laws that are just and right (Neh. 9:13); to the law and to the testimony! (Isa. 8:20).

● Written in the law

d As it is written in the law of Moses (2 Kgs. 14:6; 2 Chr. 23:18; 25:4; Ezra 3:2; Dan. 9:13); as it is written in the law of the Lord (2 Chr. 31:3).

● Copying the law

e Joshua copied on stones the law of Moses (Josh. 8:32); the king must write a copy of the law (Deut. 17:18).

● The law proclaimed

f The law of the Lord is to be on your lips (Exod. 13:9); teach them the decrees and the laws (Exod. 18:20); do not let this Book of the Law depart out of your mouth (Josh. 1:8); the law and the prophets were preached until John (Luke 16:16).

- **Taking the law to heart**

g His delight is in the law of the Lord (Ps. 1:2); the law of his God is in his heart (Ps. 37:31); your law is within my heart (Ps. 40:8); I will put my laws in their minds and write them on their hearts (Jer. 31:33; Heb. 8:10; 10:16); remember the law of Moses (Mal. 4:4).

- **Studying the law**

h Ezra determined to study the law of the Lord (Ezra 7:10); Ezra was a scribe skilled in the law of Moses (Ezra 7:6); Ezra read from the book of the law of Moses (Neh. 8:1–3).

Pleasure in God's law, see **826k**.

- **Purpose of the law**

i What was the purpose of the law? It was added because of transgressions (Gal. 3:19); the law was added so that the trespass might increase (Rom. 5:20); the law is a shadow of good things to come (Heb. 10:1); the law is not for the righteous but for lawbreakers (1 Tim. 1:9); the law was our schoolteacher to bring us to Christ (Gal. 3:24).

j The law is spiritual (Rom. 7:14); the law is not sin (Rom. 7:7); the law is holy (Rom. 7:12); the law is good (Rom. 7:16; 1 Tim. 1:8); I agree with the law (Rom. 7:16, 22).

- **Effect of the law**

k The law brings wrath (Rom. 4:15); anyone who rejected the law of Moses died without mercy (Heb. 10:28); the letter kills (2 Cor. 3:6).

l Sinful passions were awakened by the law (Rom. 7:5); I would not have known coveting except through the law (Rom. 7:7–8); apart from the law sin is dead (Rom. 7:8); the power of sin is the law (1 Cor. 15:56).

- **Blessing not through the law**

m No one will be justified by works of the law (Rom. 3:20; Gal. 2:16); if righteousness was through the law, Christ died in vain (Gal. 2:21); if a law could bring life, righteousness would be by the law (Gal. 3:21); I gave them bad statutes by which they could not live (Ezek. 20:25); the law made nothing perfect (Heb. 7:19); it was not through the law that Abraham received the promise (Rom. 4:13); did you receive the Spirit by works of law? (Gal. 3:2); does God work miracles among you because you keep the law? (Gal. 3:5).

- **Under the law**

n You who want to be under the law (Gal. 4:21); if you receive circumcision you are obliged to keep the whole law (Gal. 5:3); the Jew relied on the law (Rom. 2:17–18); Jesus was born under the law (Gal. 4:4); the law has authority over a man only while he lives (Rom. 7:1).

o All who rely on the law are under a curse (Gal. 3:10); those who sin under the law will be judged by the law (Rom. 2:12).

The curse of the law, see **899d**.

p Though not under the law, Paul became as under the law to win others (1 Cor. 9:20).

Works of the law, see **676e**.

• Without
the law

q Where there is no law there is no transgression (Rom. 4:15); sin is not reckoned where there is no law (Rom. 5:13); those who do not have the law show that the requirements of the law are written on their hearts (Rom. 2:14–15); all who have sinned without law will perish without law (Rom. 2:12).

r You are not under the law but under grace (Rom. 6:14); if you are led by the Spirit you are not under the law (Gal. 5:18); released from the law (Rom. 7:6); we died to the law (Rom. 7:4); Christ is the end of the law (Rom. 10:4); there is no law against the fruit of the Spirit (Gal. 5:23).

s Paul became as without law to win others (1 Cor. 9:21).

• Fulfilling
the law

t God commanded you to follow these decrees and laws (Deut. 26:16); you know the commandments (Mark 10:19; Luke 18:20).

u Which is the greatest commandment? (Mark 12:28); the law is fulfilled by loving your neighbour (Gal. 5:14).

v Jesus did not come to abolish the law but to fulfil it (Matt. 5:17); Christ was born under the law (Gal. 4:4); Jesus abolished the enmity, the law (Eph. 2:15).

w We establish the law through faith (Rom. 3:31); the law is fulfilled in us (Rom. 8:4); I will put my Spirit in you and cause you to walk in my statutes (Ezek. 36:27); he who loves has fulfilled the law (Rom. 13:8); love fulfils the law (Rom. 13:10).

• Rejecting
the law

x What right have you to recite my laws? (Ps. 50:16); they have rejected the law of the Lord (Isa. 5:24); her priests have done violence to my law (Ezek. 22:26); you have neglected the more important matters of the law (Matt. 23:23); the law is no more (Lam. 2:9).

• The law
of Christ

y I am under the law of Christ (1 Cor. 9:21); fulfil the law of Christ (Gal. 6:2); the law of liberty (Jas. 2:12).

Commandment, see **737*e***.

• Human law

z Woe to those who enact unjust decrees (Isa. 10:1).

954 Illegality

• Lawlessness

a Sin is lawlessness (1 John 3:4); lawlessness will increase (Matt. 24:12); inwardly you are full of lawlessness (Matt. 23:28); the man of lawlessness will be revealed (2 Thess. 2:3); the mystery of lawlessness (2 Thess. 2:7); the lawless one will be revealed (2 Thess. 2:8–9); they will gather out of his kingdom all lawlessness (Matt. 13:41).

b He was reckoned with the lawless (Isa. 53:12; Mark 15:28; Luke 22:37).

Without law, see **953*q***.

• Breaking
God's law

c They disobeyed the law (Neh. 9:16; Isa. 24:5; Jer. 9:13; Acts 7:53); Judah did not keep the commandments (2 Kgs. 17:19); our fathers have not observed everything in this book (2 Chr. 34:21); we have not kept your law (Neh. 1:7; 9:34); they have not kept his statutes (Amos 2:4); the law is ignored (Hab. 1:4); they cast your law behind their backs (Neh. 9:26); why do you transgress God's commandments for the sake of your tradition? (Matt. 15:3); the Samaritans do not keep the commandments (2 Kgs. 17:34); whoever does not keep the law is to be executed (Ezra 7:26); if his children forsake my law (Ps. 89:30–1); whoever breaks one part of the law is guilty of all (Jas. 2:10–11).

d The priests break the sabbath and are innocent (Matt. 12:5).

● Breaking man's law

e Why do you transgress the tradition of the elders? (Matt. 15:2); they proclaim customs which it is not lawful for Romans to accept (Acts 16:21); this man persuades people to worship God contrary to the law (Acts 18:13).

f They do not observe the king's laws (Esther 3:8).

● Illegitimate

g If God does not discipline you, you are illegitimate children (Heb. 12:8); the illegitimate may not enter the assembly (Deut. 23:1); they have borne illegitimate children (Hos. 5:7).

955 Jurisdiction

Authority, see **733**.

956 Tribunal

● Judgement seat

a Pilate was on the judgement seat (Matt. 27:19; John 19:13); they brought Paul before the judgement seat (Acts 18:12); Gallio sat on the judgement seat (Acts 18:12–17).

b We must all stand before the judgement seat of God (Rom. 14:10); of Christ (2 Cor. 5:10).

957 Magistrate

● God the Judge

a Shall not the Judge of all the earth do right? (Gen. 18:25); rise up, Judge of the earth! (Ps. 94:2); let the Lord, the Judge, decide (Judg. 11:27); God is a righteous judge (Ps. 7:11); God himself is judge (Ps. 50:6); you have come to God, the judge of all men (Heb. 12:23); the Lord is our Judge (Isa. 33:22); God is a judge for widows (Ps. 68:5); there is one lawgiver and judge (Jas. 4:12); the judge is at the door (Jas. 5:9).

b Jesus is the one God has appointed as judge of the living and the dead (Acts 10:42); who made me a judge over you? (Luke 12:14).

c The parable of the unjust judge (Luke 18:2).

● Human judges

d Have them serve as judges (Exod. 18:22); appoint judges and officials (Deut. 16:18); six thousand Levites were to be officials and judges (1 Chr. 23:4); Jehoshaphat appointed judges (2 Chr. 19:5–7, 8–11); Ezra, appoint magistrates and judges (Ezra 7:25).

e The Lord raised up judges (Judg. 2:16); he gave them judges (Acts 13:20); the day I commanded judges to be over Israel (2 Sam. 7:11; 1 Chr. 17:10); in the days of the judges (Ruth 1:1;

2 Kgs. 23:22); the Lord sent Jerubbaal and Barak and Jephthah and Samuel (1 Sam. 12:11).

f Judges: Othniel (Judg. 3:9–11); Ehud (Judg. 3:15–30); Shamgar (Judg. 3:31); Deborah (Judg. 4:4–24); Gideon (Judg. 6:11–8:32); Abimelech (Judg. 9:1–57); Tola (Judg. 10:1–2); Jair (Judg. 10:3–5); Jephthah (Judg. 11:1–7); Ibzan (Judg. 12:8–10); Elon (Judg. 12:11–12); Abdon (Judg. 12:13–15); Samson (Judg. 13:24–16:31); Eli (1 Sam. 1:9–4:18); Samuel (1 Sam. 7:6, 15–17); Samuel's sons (1 Sam. 8:1).

g Moses took his seat to serve as judge (Exod. 18:13); who made you ruler and judge? (Exod. 2:14; Acts 7:27, 35); that our king may judge us (1 Sam. 8:20); if only I were made judge! (2 Sam. 15:4).

Judging, see **480**.

958 Lawyer

● Lawyers

a A lawyer tested him (Matt. 22:35; Luke 10:25); the Pharisees and lawyers rejected God's purpose for them (Luke 7:30); Jesus spoke to the lawyers and Pharisees (Luke 14:3); a lawyer said he insulted them also (Luke 11:45); woe to you, lawyers! (Luke 11:46, 52); help Zenas the lawyer (Titus 3:13).

959 Litigation

● God suing

a Do not bring your servant into judgement (Ps. 143:2); God will bring to judgement both the righteous and the wicked (Eccles. 3:17); the wicked will not stand in the judgement (Ps. 1:5); for all these things God will bring you to judgement (Eccles. 11:9); whoever is angry with his brother will be subject to judgement (Matt. 5:22).

● Suing God

b I would argue my case with God (Job 13:3); anyone bringing a dispute against God could not hope to win (Job 9:3).

● Man suing man

c When men have a dispute, they are to take it to court (Deut. 25:1); any one with a dispute went to the king for judgement (2 Sam. 15:2); if anyone wants to sue you and take your tunic, let him have your cloak as well (Matt. 5:40); make friends with your accuser before it comes to court (Matt. 5:25; Luke 12:57–9); brother goes to law against brother (1 Cor. 6:1–6); the rich drag you into court (Jas. 2:6).

960 Acquittal

● Acquitting the just

a Justify the righteous (1 Kgs. 8:32; 2 Chr. 6:23); by your words you will be justified or condemned (Matt. 12:37).

● Acquitting the guilty

b Acquitting the guilty is what the Lord detests (Prov. 17:15); he who tells the wicked they are innocent will be cursed (Prov. 24:24).

c Can a man be in the right before God? (Job 9:2).

Vindication, see **927**.

961 Condemnation

Condemning Jesus

a They will condemn the Son of Man to death (Matt. 20:18; Mark 10:33); they all condemned him as worthy of death (Mark 14:64).

Condemning the wicked

b God did not send his Son to condemn the world (John 3:17); whoever does not believe is condemned already (John 3:18); all will be condemned who have not believed the truth (2 Thess. 2:12); God, sending his Son, condemned sin in the flesh (Rom. 8:3); the result of one trespass was condemnation for all (Rom. 5:16, 18); the word I spoke will condemn him at the last day (John 12:48); their condemnation has long been hanging over them (2 Pet. 2:3); the men of Nineveh and the Queen of the South will condemn this generation (Matt. 12:41–2; Luke 11:31–2); they will receive greater condemnation (Mark 12:40); you will receive the greater condemnation (Matt. 23:14; Luke 20:47); the prince of this world stands condemned (John 16:11); he who eats and drinks unworthily brings judgement on himself (1 Cor. 11:29); when he is tried, let him be found guilty (Ps. 109:7); the Lord will by no means clear the guilty (Nahum 1:3).

c Noah by faith condemned the world (Heb. 11:7); the Holy Spirit will convict the world (John 16:8); whoever does not believe will be condemned (Mark 16:16).

d The ministry of condemnation (2 Cor. 3:9).

Hands laid on to condemn, see **378***aa*.

Condemning the innocent

e They condemn the innocent to death (Ps. 94:21); condemning the innocent is an abomination to the Lord (Prov. 17:15); you would not have condemned the innocent (Matt. 12:7); when Judas saw Jesus was condemned (Matt. 27:3).

Condemning ourselves

f Your own mouth condemns you (Job 15:6); in judging another, you condemn yourself (Rom. 2:1); blessed is he who does not condemn himself in what he approves (Rom. 14:22); if our hearts condemn us, God is greater than our hearts (1 John 3:20).

Condemning others

g Do not condemn and you will not be condemned (Matt. 7:1–2; Luke 6:37); does our law judge a man without first hearing him? (John 7:51); does no one condemn you? Nor do I condemn you (John 8:10–11).

No condemnation

h The Lord helps me, who is to condemn me? (Isa. 50:9); it is God who justifies, who is he that condemns? (Rom. 8:33–4); no one who takes refuges in him will be condemned (Ps. 34:22); there is no condemnation for those who are in Christ (Rom. 8:1); the Lord will not let them be condemned (Ps. 37:33); I do not say this to condemn you (2 Cor. 7:3).

Being condemned

i I know you will not acquit me (Job 9:28); do not condemn me (Job 10:2); by your words you will be justified or condemned (Matt. 12:37).

962 Reward

● Reward
from God

a I am your shield; your reward will be very great (Gen. 15:1); the Lord has rewarded me for my righteousness (2 Sam. 22:21; Ps. 18:20); surely there is a reward for the righteous (Ps. 58:11); my reward is with my God (Isa. 49:4); his reward is with him (Isa. 40:10; 62:11); children are a reward from the Lord (Ps. 127:3); the time has come for rewarding your servants the prophets (Rev. 11:18).

● Reward
for works

b God will reward everyone according to what he has done (Ps. 62:12; Rom. 2:6); each will receive a reward according to his work (1 Cor. 3:8); there is reward for your work (2 Chr. 15:7); my reward is with me and I will give to everyone according to what he has done (Rev. 22:12); if what he has built survives, he will receive his reward (1 Cor. 3:14); work as to the Lord and you will receive the inheritance as a reward (Col. 3:24); in keeping God's word there is great reward (Ps. 19:11); the reward for humility and fear of the Lord (Prov. 22:4).

c God has rewarded me for giving my maidservant to my husband (Gen. 30:18); may the Lord reward your work (Ruth 2:12); may the Lord reward you well for the way you treated me (1 Sam. 24:19); he who gives a cup of water will not lose his reward (Matt. 10:42; Mark 9:41); whoever receives a prophet as a prophet will receive a prophet's reward (Matt. 10:41); when persecuted, great is your reward in heaven (Matt. 5:12; Luke 6:23); do good and your reward will be great (Luke 6:35); pray in secret and your Father will reward you (Matt. 6:6); your confidence has great reward (Heb. 10:35).

d Run in such a way as to get the prize (1 Cor. 9:24); take heed to yourselves that you may receive a full reward (2 John 8); Moses was looking to the reward (Heb. 11:26); the prize of the upward call of God (Phil. 3:14).

● Men
rewarding

e Come home with me and I will reward you (1 Kgs. 13:7).

● No reward

f You will have no reward from your Father in heaven (Matt. 6:1); if you love those who love you, what reward will you have? (Matt. 5:46); they have received their reward (Matt. 6:2, 5, 16); the Lord has kept you from being rewarded (Num. 24:11).

● Paul's reward

g Paul's reward is to make the gospel free of charge (1 Cor. 9:18).

963 Punishment

● God punishing

a I will punish them for their sin (Exod. 32:34); he does not leave the guilty unpunished (Exod. 34:7); I will punish you for your sins seven times over (Lev. 26:18); I will choose their punishments (Isa. 66:4); visiting the sins of the fathers on the children (Exod. 20:5; Num. 14:18); on the wicked he will rain coals and sulphur (Ps. 11:6); I will punish their sin with the rod (Ps. 89:32); the wicked will not go unpunished (Prov. 11:21); God knows how to keep the unrighteous under punishment (2 Pet. 2:9); the Lord will punish the powers in heaven and the kings on earth (Isa. 24:21); the Lord is coming to punish the people of the earth for their sins (Isa. 26:21); the Lord will punish men for all such sins (1 Thess. 4:6); they receive the penalty of their straying (Rom. 1:27).

b I will punish the Amalekites (1 Sam. 15:2); the Lord will punish Leviathan (Isa. 27:1); the Lord will punish Assyria (Isa. 10:12); will you go unpunished? (Jer. 25:29); you will not go unpunished (Jer. 25:29); now comes the reckoning for his blood (Gen. 42:22).

c God punished Israel (1 Chr. 21:7); the Lord will punish Jacob according to his deeds (Hos. 12:2); you only have I chosen, therefore I will punish you for all your sins (Amos 3:2); I will punish the house of Jehu (Hos. 1:4); my punishment is more than I can bear (Gen. 4:13).

- Graded punishment

d He who knew his master's will will receive a severe beating (Luke 12:47); one who did not know will receive a light beating (Luke 12:48); how much more severe punishment for him who tramples the Son of God (Heb. 10:29).

Less punishment, see **736***b*.

- Final punishment

e Described as eternal fire (Matt. 18:8; 25:41; Jude 7; Rev. 14:10–11; 19:3); eternal destruction (2 Thess. 1:9); torment for ever (Rev. 14:11; 20:10); eternal chains in the lower darkness (Jude 6, 13); eternal judgement (Heb. 6:2); their worm will not die, nor will their fire be quenched (Isa. 66:24; Mark 9:48); its smoke will go up for ever (Isa. 34:10).

f This is intended for the fallen angels (Matt. 25:41; Jude 6; Rev. 20:10); shared by the rebellious (Jude 13); those led into sin (Matt. 18:8); the uncaring (Matt. 25:41, 46); Babylon (Rev. 19:3); those who worship the beast (Rev. 14:11); those who do not obey the gospel (2 Thess. 1:9); those who blaspheme the Holy Spirit (Mark 3:29); the cowardly, faithless, polluted, murderers, fornicators, sorcerors, idolators and liars (Rev. 21:8).

g These will go away to eternal punishment (Matt. 25:46); how will you escape being condemned to hell? (Matt. 23:33).

- Judicial punishment

h God sends governors to punish evildoers (1 Pet. 2:14); rulers do not bear the sword for nothing (Rom. 13:4); when the scoffer is punished the simple becomes wise (Prov. 21:11).

i If a man beats his slave to death he is to be punished (Exod. 21:20); the elders shall take the man and punish him (Deut. 22:18); the offender must be fined (Exod. 21:22); whoever does not obey the law must be punished by death, banishment, confiscation or imprisonment (Ezra 7:26); life for life, eye for eye, tooth for tooth (Exod. 21:23–5; Deut. 19:21; Lev. 24:19–20; Matt. 5:38).

Corporal punishment, see **279***b*; **death as punishment**, see **361***z*.

● Fines

j A man causing miscarriage shall be fined (Exod. 21:22); the king of Egypt fined them 100 talents of silver and one talent of gold (2 Chr. 36:3); you will not go out until you have paid the last penny (Matt. 5:26).

Fine as penalty, see **809***f*.

● Death penalty for killing

k Whoever sheds man's blood, by man shall his blood be shed (Gen. 9:6); I will require your lifeblood (Gen. 9:5); he who kills a man shall be put to death (Exod. 21:12; Num. 35:30); he who takes the life of another human being must be put to death (Lev. 24:17); the murderer shall be put to death by the avenger of blood (Num. 35:16–19); hand over the guilty son to be put to death (2 Sam. 14:7); six executioners drew near (Ezek. 9:2).

l Whoever kills Cain will meet sevenfold vengeance (Gen. 4:15); death penalty if anyone harmed Isaac or his wife (Gen. 26:11); under the Romans the Jews could not execute anyone (John 18:31).

● Death penalty for violence

m The death penalty for cursing one's parents (Exod. 21:17; Lev. 20:9; Matt. 15:4; Mark 7:10); for striking one's parents (Exod. 21:15); for a rebellious son (Deut. 21:18–21); for one who shows contempt for judge or priest (Deut. 17:12); for kidnapping (Exod. 21:16; Deut. 24:7); for the owner of an ox that kills (Exod. 21:29); for sinning defiantly (Num. 15:30); better he were drowned in the sea (Matt. 18:6).

n Death penalty for coming in to the king unbidden (Esther 4:11).

● Death penalty for profanity

o The death penalty for desecrating the sabbath (Exod. 31:14, 15; 35:2; Num. 15:32–6); for not being circumcised (Gen. 17:14); for not observing the Day of Atonement (Lev. 23:29–30); for not observing the Passover (Num. 9:13); for eating yeast at Passover time (Exod. 12:15, 19); for not purifying oneself after touching a dead body (Num. 19:13, 20); for eating offerings whilst unclean (Lev. 7:20–1; 22:3); for eating the fat of the offering (Lev. 7:25); for eating blood (Lev. 7:26–7; 17:10); for eating a peace offering on the third day (Lev. 19:8); for using holy anointing oil (Exod. 30:33); for making sacred incense illegally (Exod. 30:38); for making a sacrifice other than at the Tent of Meeting (Lev. 17:4, 9); for coming near the sactuary illegally (Num. 18:7); for cursing the Lord's anointed (2 Sam. 19:21).

● Death penalty for heresy

p The death penalty for blaspheming God's name (Lev. 24:10–16); for urging people to worship other gods (Deut. 13:1–15); for worshipping other gods (Exod. 22:20); for serving other gods (Deut. 17:2–7); for giving one's children to Molech (Lev. 20:2, 5); for turning to mediums and spirits (Lev. 20:6); for being a medium or spiritist (Lev. 20:27); for not seeking the Lord (2 Chr. 15:13); the leaders were to be executed for linking themselves to Baal of Peor (Num. 25:4–5).

q Jeremiah deserves the death penalty (Jer. 26:11); this man has done nothing deserving death (Luke 23:15).

● Death penalty for sexual sin

r The death penalty for adultery (Gen. 38:24; Lev. 20:10; Deut. 22:22; John 8:5); for sexual relations with a betrothed woman (Deut. 22:23–4); with a near relative (Lev. 20:11, 12, 14, 17); with an animal (Lev. 20:15–16); with a menstruating woman (Lev. 20:18); for homosexuality (Lev. 20:13); for promiscuity before marriage (Deut. 22:21); for following the abominations of the nations (Lev. 18:29).

s Those who do these things are worthy of death (Rom. 1:32); he who goes in to his neighbour's wife will not go unpunished (Prov. 6:29).

964 Means of punishment

● Beating with a rod

a A rod is for the back of fools (Prov. 26:3); the rod and reproof give wisdom (Prov. 29:15); he who spares the rod hates his son (Prov. 13:24); beat him with the rod and save him from Sheol (Prov. 23:13–14); shall I come to you with a rod? (1 Cor. 4:21).

b Assyria, the rod of my anger (Isa. 10:5); God will strike Assyria with the rod (Isa. 30:31–2).

Beating, see **279**.

● Gallows

c The two officials were hanged on a gallows (Esther 2:23); a gallows 50 cubits high (Esther 5:14; 7:9).

● Crucifixion

d Take up the cross (Matt. 10:38; 16:24; Mark 8:34; Luke 9:23; 14:27); Jesus carrying his own cross (John 19:17); carrying Jesus' cross (Matt. 27:32; Mark 15:21; Luke 23:26); he endured the cross (Heb. 12:2).

e Our bill of debt was nailed to the cross (Col. 2:14); he bore our sins in his own body on the tree (1 Pet. 2:24); reconciled to God through the cross (Eph. 2:16); no boasting except in the cross (Gal. 6:14).

f The message of the cross is foolishness to those who are perishing (1 Cor. 1:18); the stumbling block of the cross (Gal. 5:11); that they may not be persecuted for the cross of Christ (Gal. 6:12); enemies of the cross of Christ (Phil. 3:18).

Section five: Religion

965 Deity

● Character of God

a God is spirit (John 4:24); God is light (1 John 1:5); God is love (1 John 4:8, 16); your heavenly Father is perfect (Matt. 5:48); his godhead is seen in what is made (Rom. 1:20); he is not the God of the dead but of the living (Matt. 22:32; Mark 12:27; Luke 20:38); a figure like a man ... the likeness of the glory of the Lord (Ezek. 1:26–8); he is not a man like me (Job 9:32); do you see as man sees? (Job 10:4); are your years man's? (Job 10:5); I am God and not man (Hos. 11:9).

God as fire, see **381**; **God is light**, see **417***b*.

b The Lord is God (Josh. 22:34; 1 Kgs. 18:39; Ps. 118:27); the Lord is God in heaven and earth (Josh. 2:11); the Lord of all the earth (Josh. 3:13); Lord of heaven and earth (Matt. 11:25); the Lord is the true God (Jer. 10:10).

God is unique, see **21***a*; **the Trinity**, see **93***a*.

● God
Almighty

c I am God Almighty (Gen. 17:1; 35:11); the Lord, the eternal God (Gen. 21:33); wonderful Counsellor, mighty God, everlasting Father, Prince of peace (Isa. 9:6).

d The Lord is the great King above all gods (Ps. 95:3); our Lord is greater than all gods (Ps. 135:5); your God is the God of gods and Lord of kings (Dan. 2:47); God of gods and Lord of lords (Deut. 10:17); the god who answers by fire, he is God (1 Kgs. 18:24).

God is great, see **34***a*.

● God of
his people

e I will be their God (Gen. 17:8; Exod. 29:45; Ezek. 11:20; 14:11; Zech. 8:8; 2 Cor. 6:16; Heb. 8:10); I am the Lord your God (Isa. 41:13; Ezek. 20:5, 19); I will be his God (Rev. 21:7); to be God to you (Gen. 17:7); I am your God (Isa. 41:10; Ezek. 34:31); you have become their God (2 Sam. 7:24; 1 Chr. 17:22); I will be your God (Exod. 6:7; Lev. 26:12; Ezek. 36:28); I brought you out of Egypt to be your God (Lev. 22:33; 25:38; Num. 15:41); to be your God (Deut. 29:13); the Lord is your God (Deut. 26:17); the Lord is our God (Josh. 24:18; 2 Chr. 13:10); this God is our God (Ps. 48:14); this is our God (Isa. 25:9); he is our God (Ps. 95:7); if he will look after me, the Lord will be my God (Gen. 28:21–1); your God will be my God (Ruth 1:16); you are my God (Ps. 31:14; 63:1; 118:28; 140:6; 143:10; Isa. 25:1); this is my God (Exod. 15:2); from my mother's womb you have been my God (Ps. 22:10); God is not ashamed to be called their God (Heb. 11:16).

f The God of Abraham and Isaac (Gen. 28:13); God of Abraham, Isaac and Jacob (Exod. 3:15, 16; Matt. 22:32; Mark 12:26; Luke 20:37; Acts 7:32); the God of both Jews and Gentiles (Rom. 3:29); the God of the spirits of all flesh (Num. 16:22; 27:16).

God's people, see **371***ac*.

● The Father

g There is but one God, the Father, and one Lord, Jesus Christ (1 Cor. 8:6); the Father from which every family is named (Eph. 3:14–15).

God our Father, see **169***q*.

● The Son

h The Word was God (John 1:1); the only begotten God (John 1:18); of the Son he says, 'Your throne, O God, is for ever' (Heb. 1:8); Christ is God over all, blessed for ever (Rom. 9:5); our great God and Saviour, Jesus Christ (Titus 2:13); he was in the form of God (Phil. 2:6); my Lord and my God! (John 20:28); he called

God his Father, making himself equal with God (John 5:18); God has made this Jesus Lord and Christ (Acts 2:36); the fulness of God dwells in him (Col. 2:9); I know who you are, the Holy One of God (Mark 1:24; Luke 4:34).

i Jesus, Son of the Most High God! (Mark 5:7); he claimed to be the Son of God (John 19:7); surely he was the Son of God (Mark 15:39); the gospel of Jesus Christ, the Son of God (Mark 1:1); you are the Christ, the Son of God (Matt. 16:16; Luke 9:20; John 11:27); we have found the Christ (John 1:41); could this be the Christ? (John 4:29); are you the Christ, the Son of the Blessed? (Mark 14:61); I am the Christ (Mark 14:62; John 4:26).

j Whose son is the Christ? (Matt. 22:42); is the Christ the son of David? (Mark 12:35); no one will know where the Christ comes from (John 7:27); he had come from God and was returning to God (John 13:3).

Anointed Christ, see **357*u***; **Christ's life**, see **360*h***; **death of Christ**, see **361*ai***; **human nature of Christ**, see **371*g***.

● Nature of the Spirit

k The Spirit of truth (John 14:17; 15:26; 16:13); the Spirit of his Son (Gal. 4:6); the Spirit of your Father (Matt. 10:20); the Spirit of God hovering over the waters (Gen. 1:2); the seven spirits of God (Rev. 1:4; 3:1; 4:5; 5:6).

● The Spirit on Christ

l The Spirit descended on Jesus like a dove (Matt. 3:16; Mark 1:10; Luke 3:22; John 1:32, 33); Jesus returned in the power of the Spirit (Luke 4:14); full of the Holy Spirit (Luke 4:1); the Spirit of the Lord will rest on him (Isa. 11:2); the Spirit of the Lord is upon me (Isa. 61:1; Luke 4:18); I will put my Spirit in him (Matt. 12:18); I have put my Spirit upon him (Isa. 42:1); to him God gives the Spirit without limit (John 3:34); God anointed Jesus of Nazareth with the Holy Spirit (Acts 10:38); if I drive out demons by the Spirit of God (Matt. 12:28); by the finger of God (Luke 11:20); Jesus gave orders to the apostles by the Holy Spirit (Acts 1:2).

● The Spirit on people

m The Spirit of God upon: Joseph (Gen. 41:38); Balaam (Num. 24:2); Joshua (Num. 27:18); Othniel (Judg. 3:10); Gideon (Judg. 6:34); Jephthah (Judg. 11:29); Samson (Judg. 13:25; 14:6, 19; 15:14); Saul (1 Sam. 10:6, 10; 11:6; 19:23); David (1 Sam. 16:13); the messengers of Saul (1 Sam. 19:20); Amasai (1 Chr. 12:18); Azariah (2 Chr. 15:1); Jahaziel (2 Chr. 20:14); Zechariah (2 Chr. 24:20); Simeon (Luke 2:25).

n The Spirit of the Lord fell on me (Ezek. 11:5); I was in the Spirit on the Lord's day (Rev. 1:10).

o My Spirit shall not always strive with man (Gen. 6:3); how did the Spirit pass from me to you? (1 Kgs. 22:24; 2 Chr. 18:23); the Spirit will carry you somewhere else (1 Kgs. 18:12); maybe the Spirit has taken him up and thrown him down (2 Kgs. 2:16).

p I will take of the Spirit that is on you and put the Spirit on them

(Num. 11:17, 25, 29); I will put my Spirit in you (Ezek. 36:27; 37:14).

● Filled with the Spirit

q Those filled with the Holy Spirit: Bezalel (Exod. 31:3; 35:31); John, from his mother's womb (Luke 1:15); Elizabeth (Luke 1:41); Zacharias (Luke 1:67); Jesus (Luke 4:1); the disciples in Jerusalem (Acts 2:4; 4:31); Peter (Acts 4:8); Stephen (Acts 6:5; 7:55); Paul (Acts 9:17; 13:9); Barnabas (Acts 11:24); the disciples in Antioch of Pisidia (Acts 13:52).

r He has sent me that you may be filled with the Holy Spirit (Acts 9:17); be filled with the Spirit (Eph. 5:18); the seven men should be full of the Spirit (Acts 6:3).

● The Spirit poured out

s I will pour out my Spirit on your offspring (Isa. 44:3); I will pour out my Spirit on you (Prov. 1:23); I will pour out my Spirit on the house of Israel (Ezek. 39:29); I will pour out my Spirit on all flesh (Joel 2:28–9; Acts 2:17–18); until the Spirit is poured on us from on high (Isa. 32:15); the Holy Spirit was poured out on the Gentiles (Acts 10:44–6); the Holy Spirit poured out on us abundantly (Titus 3:6); where is he who put his Holy Spirit in the midst of them? (Isa. 63:11); the Holy Spirit who lives within us (2 Tim. 1:14).

Promise of the Holy Spirit, see **764*g***.

● The gift of the Spirit

t Those who believed in him were to receive the Spirit (John 7:39); the Father will give you a Comforter to be with you for ever, the Spirit of truth (John 14:16–17); if I go I will send him to you (John 16:7); the Spirit had not been given as Jesus was not yet glorified (John 7:39).

u He has received from the Father the promised Holy Spirit and poured forth what you see and hear (Acts 2:33); the Father sends the Holy Spirit in my name (John 14:26); the Spirit was given at the laying on of the apostles' hands (Acts 8:15–18); when Paul laid hands on them the Holy Spirit came on them (Acts 19:6); receive the Holy Spirit (John 20:22); they received the Holy Spirit just as we have (Acts 10:47; 11:15; 15:8); did you receive the Holy Spirit when you believed? (Acts 19:2); did you receive the Spirit by law or by believing? (Gal. 3:2); we receive the promise of the Spirit by faith (Gal. 3:14); you will receive the gift of the Holy Spirit (Acts 2:38); the Father gives the Holy Spirit to those who ask him (Luke 11:13); God who gives his Holy Spirit (1 Thess. 4:8); God has given us the Spirit as a deposit (2 Cor. 1:22; 5:5).

Spiritual gifts, see **781*m***.

● Sealed with the Spirit

v Sealed with the Holy Spirit as a pledge (2 Cor. 1:22; Eph. 1:13–14); do not grieve the Holy Spirit by whom you were sealed (Eph. 4:30).

● Baptism in the Spirit

w He will baptise you with the Holy Spirit (Matt. 3:11; Mark 1:8; Luke 3:16; John 1:33; Acts 1:5; 11:16); by one Spirit we were all baptised and all drink of one Spirit (1 Cor. 12:13).

- The power
  of the Spirit

  x Not by might nor by power but by my Spirit (Zech. 4:6); you will receive power when the Holy Spirit has come on you (Acts 1:8); signs and wonders in the power of the Spirit (Rom. 15:19); demonstration of the Spirit and of power (1 Cor. 2:4); abound in hope by the power of the Holy Spirit (Rom. 15:13).

- Activity of
  the Spirit

  y The Spirit of God has made me (Job 33:4); the Spirit set me on my feet (Ezek. 2:2; 3:24); the Spirit lifted me up (Ezek. 3:12, 14; 8:3; 11:1, 24; 43:5); the Spirit of the Lord caught up Philip (Acts 8:39).

  z God's love is poured into our hearts by the Holy Spirit (Rom. 5:5); the kingdom of God is righteousness, peace and joy in the Holy Spirit (Rom. 14:17).

- Speaking by
  the Spirit

  aa The Spirit of God spoke through me (2 Sam. 23:2); my Spirit and my words will not depart from your mouth (Isa. 59:21); the Holy Spirit will teach you what to say (Luke 12:12); it is not you who speak but the Spirit (Matt. 10:20; Mark 13:11); you admonished them by your Spirit (Neh. 9:30); the Holy Spirit spoke rightly through Isaiah the prophet (Acts 28:25); we are witnesses and so is the Holy Spirit (Acts 5:32); the Spirit and the bride say 'Come' (Rev. 22:17); no one can say 'Jesus is Lord' except by the Spirit (1 Cor. 12:3); no one speaking by the Spirit says 'Jesus is cursed' (1 Cor. 12:3).

- Taught by
  the Spirit

  ab The Spirit searches the depths of God (1 Cor. 2:10–11); we have received the Spirit of God that we might understand what God has given us (1 Cor. 2:12); the mystery made known to apostles and prophets by the Spirit (Eph. 3:5); you gave your Spirit to teach them (Neh. 9:20); we know that he lives in us, because of the Spirit (1 John 3:24; 4:13); the Spirit bears witness with our spirits (Rom. 8:16).

- Life by
  the Spirit

  ac We have rebirth and renewal by the Holy Spirit (Titus 3:5); the Spirit gives life (2 Cor. 3:6); we commend ourselves in the Holy Spirit (2 Cor. 6:6); you are a letter written not with ink but with the Spirit (2 Cor. 3:3).

- Living by
  the Spirit

  ad Living according to the Spirit (Rom. 8:4–11; Gal. 5:16); if we live by the Spirit let us walk by the Spirit (Gal. 5:25); he who sows to the Spirit will reap eternal life (Gal. 6:8); those who are of the Spirit set their minds on the things of the Spirit (Rom. 8:5); the fruit of the Spirit (Gal. 5:22–3); the gifts of the Spirit (1 Cor. 12:4–11); all these are the work of the one Spirit (1 Cor. 12:11).

- Led by
  the Spirit

  ae Let your good Spirit lead me (Ps. 143:10); led by the Spirit (Rom. 8:14; Gal. 5:18); he brought me out by the Spirit of the Lord (Ezek. 37:1); the Spirit led Jesus out into the wilderness (Matt. 4:1); the Spirit drove Jesus out into the wilderness (Mark 1:12); the Lord has sent me and his Spirit (Isa. 48:16).

- Pregnant by
  the Spirit

  af Mary was with child by the Holy Spirit (Matt. 1:18); that which is conceived in her is of the Holy Spirit (Matt. 1:20); the Holy Spirit will come upon you (Luke 1:35).

- **Without God**   *ag* The Spirit of the Lord had departed from Saul (1 Sam. 16:14); do not take your Holy Spirit from me (Ps. 51:11); do not quench the Spirit (1 Thess. 5:19).

   ah If anyone does not have the Spirit of Christ he does not belong to him (Rom. 8:9); they follow their instincts, men without the Spirit (Jude 19); you were without God in the world (Eph. 2:12); a natural man does not accept the things of the Spirit (1 Cor. 2:14); blasphemy against the Spirit will not be forgiven (Matt. 12:32; Mark 3:29; Luke 12:10).

966 Deities in general

- **Many 'gods'**   *a* There are many 'gods' and many 'lords' (1 Cor. 8:5); you were slaves to what are no gods (Gal. 4:8); you have as many gods as cities (Jer. 2:28; 11:13); you are gods (Ps. 82:6; John 10:34–5).

   b The Lord is greater than all other gods (Exod. 18:11); the gods of the people are idols (1 Chr. 16:26; Ps. 96:5); can a man make gods for himself? such are no gods (Jer. 16:20); the gods who did not make heaven and earth will perish from heaven and earth (Jer. 10:11).

- **No other gods**   *c* You shall have no other gods before me (Exod. 20:3, 23; Deut. 5:7); you shall have no foreign god among you (Ps. 81:9); do not enquire after their gods (Deut. 12:30); do not invoke the names of other gods (Exod. 23:13; Josh. 23:7); do not follow other gods (Deut. 6:14; 8:19; 13:1–3; 28:14); foreign wives will cause you to follow other gods (Deut. 7:4); a curse if you follow other gods (Deut. 11:28); death penalty for following other gods (Deut. 17:2–7).

- **Do not worship other gods**   *d* Do not worship any other god (Exod. 34:14; Deut. 5:9; 2 Kgs. 17:35); do not go after other gods (1 Kgs. 11:10; Jer. 25:6); do not fear other gods (2 Kgs. 17:38); do not worship their gods (Exod. 23:24); do not worship things the Lord has allotted to the nations (Deut. 4:19); you may be enticed to worship other gods (Deut. 11:16); let us go and worship other gods (Deut. 13:6, 13); any one whose heart turns away to worship the gods of the nations (Deut. 29:18); anyone who has worshipped other gods (Deut. 17:3); they will teach you the detestable things they do in worshipping their gods (Deut. 20:18); there you will worship other gods (Deut. 28:36, 64).

   e He who sacrifices to another god shall be put to death (Exod. 22:20); if you bow down to other gods and worship them you will be destroyed (Deut. 30:17); if you serve other gods and bow down to them (Josh. 23:16; 1 Kgs. 9:6; 2 Chr. 7:19).

   f Put away your foreign gods (Gen. 35:2, 4); throw away the gods your forefathers worshipped (Josh. 24:14); rid yourselves of the foreign gods (1 Sam. 7:3); they put away the foreign gods (Judg. 10:16); Nebuchadnezzar will burn the temples of the gods of Egypt (Jer. 43:12–13).

● Serving
other gods

g They will soon prostitute themselves to the gods of the land (Deut. 31:16); they will serve other gods (Deut. 31:20).

h Your forefathers worshipped other gods (Josh. 24:2); they worshipped other gods (Deut. 29:26; 2 Kgs. 17:7); they served the gods of the peoples (Judg. 2:12; 3:6); they served other gods (Judg. 2:19; 10:6, 10, 13; 1 Sam. 8:8; 1 Kgs. 9:9); you have served foreign gods (Jer. 5:19); they worshipped and served other gods (2 Chr. 7:22; Jer. 22:9); they burned incense to other gods (2 Chr. 34:25); they have sacrificed to other gods (Jer. 1:16); they followed other gods (Jer. 16:11); Solomon's wives turned his heart after other gods (1 Kgs. 11:4); and sacrificed to their gods (1 Kgs. 11:8); they feared the Lord and served their own gods (2 Kgs. 17:33, 41); you plant slips of an alien god (Isa. 17:10); their gods are gods of the hills (1 Kgs. 20:23); teach the people what the god of that land requires (2 Kgs. 17:26–7); 'advocating foreign gods' because he preached Jesus and Resurrection (Acts 17:18).

Bowing to false gods, see **311*l*; prophets of other gods**, see **579*am*; praying to other gods**, see **761*ah*; robbing gods**, see **788*m*; prostitution to other gods**, see **951*x*.

● No help in
other gods

i The Lord executed judgement on their gods (Num. 33:4); did their gods deliver them? (2 Kgs. 19:12–13; Isa. 36:18–20; 37:12); they will cry to the gods to whom they burned incense (Jer. 11:12); let those gods help you! (Deut. 32:37–8); if Baal is a god, let him defend himself (Judg. 6:31); when they chose new gods, war came to the city gates (Judg. 5:8); the sorrows of those will increase who run after other gods (Ps. 16:4).

● Hand-made
gods

j Rachel stole her father's household gods (Gen. 31:19, 30, 32); you have stolen the gods I made (Judg. 18:24); make us gods (Exod. 32:1, 23); they made a god of gold (Exod. 32:31); every people still made gods of their own (2 Kgs. 17:29); he brought back the gods of the people of Seir (2 Chr. 25:14); they praised the gods of silver and gold (Dan. 5:4, 23); they were not gods but only wood and stone (2 Kgs. 19:18; Isa. 37:19); saying that gods made with hands are no gods (Acts 19:26).

● Men as gods

k You will be like God (Gen. 3:5); man has become like one of us (Gen. 3:22).

l The gods have come down in human form (Acts 14:11); they said Paul was a god (Acts 28:6); the king of Tyre said he was a god (Ezek. 28:2, 9); the voice of a god and not man! (Acts 12:22); their might is their god (Hab. 1:11).

m You will be like God to Aaron (Exod. 4:16); I have made you like God to Pharaoh (Exod. 7:1).

n God judges in the midst of the gods (Ps. 82:1); I said, 'You are gods' (Ps. 82:6; John 10:34–5); do you speak righteousness, O gods? (Ps. 58:1).

967 Pagan gods

• Serving Baal	*a*	Baals and Ashtaroth (Judg. 2:13; Judg. 10:6; 1 Sam. 12:10); Baals and Asheroth (Judg. 3:7); they played the harlot with Baals and made Baal-berith their god (Judg. 8:33; 9:4); Ahaziah served Baal (1 Kgs. 22:53); enquire of Baal-zebub (2 Kgs. 1:2, 3, 6, 16).
	b	Do not set up a pillar [for Baal] (Deut. 16:22); Ahaz made molten images for the Baals (2 Chr. 28:2); Manasseh made altars for Baal (2 Kgs. 21:3; 2 Chr. 33:3); altars to burn incense to Baal (Jer. 11:13); sacrifices to Baal (Jer. 11:17); the vessels made for Baal (2 Kgs. 23:4); the holy things of the temple had been used for the Baals (2 Chr. 24:7).
	c	High places of Baal (Num. 22:41; Jer. 32:35); they worshipped Baal (Judg. 2:11; 2 Kgs. 17:16); Israelites were linked with Baal of Peor (Num. 25:3, 5; Ps. 106:28).
• Followers of Baal	*d*	450 prophets of Baal (1 Kgs. 18:19, 22); summon the prophets and priests of Baal (2 Kgs. 10:19); sanctify an assembly for Baal (2 Kgs. 10:20); all the worshippers of Baal came (2 Kgs. 10:20); the house of Baal was filled (2 Kgs. 10:21); Ahab served Baal (1 Kgs. 16:31–2; 18:18); Ahab served Baal a little but Jehu will serve him much (2 Kgs. 10:18).
• Destroying Baal	*e*	Gideon demolished the altar of Baal (Judg. 6:25–32); they removed the Baals (1 Sam. 7:4); Jehoram put away the pillar of Baal (2 Kgs. 3:2); they tore down the house of Baal and killed Mattan the priest of Baal (2 Kgs. 11:18; 2 Chr. 23:17); they tore down the altars of Baal before Josiah (2 Chr. 34:4).
• Serving Asherah / Astarte	*f*	Ashtoreth goddess of the Sidonians (1 Kgs. 11:5, 33); do not set up an Asherah (Deut. 16:21).
	g	Baals and Ashtaroth (Judg. 2:11, 13; Judg. 10:6, 10; 1 Sam. 12:10); Baals and Asheroth (Judg. 3:7); they made their Asherim (1 Kgs. 14:15, 23; 2 Kgs. 17:10, 16); an image as an Asherah (1 Kgs. 15:13); Ahab made an Asherah (1 Kgs. 16:33); they served the Asherim and the idols (2 Chr. 24:18); 400 prophets of the Asherah (1 Kgs. 18:19); the Asherah remained in Samaria (2 Kgs. 13:6); Manasseh made an Asherah (2 Kgs. 21:3, 7; 2 Chr. 33:3, 19); the vessels made for Asherah (2 Kgs. 23:4); weaving hangings for the Asherah (2 Kgs. 23:7).
	h	Making cakes for the queen of heaven (Jer. 7:18); burning sacrifices to the queen of heaven (Jer. 44:17–19, 25).
• Destroying Asherah / Astarte	*i*	Gideon demolished the Asherah (Judg. 6:25–32); they removed the Ashtaroth (1 Sam. 7:4); Asa cut down the Asherim (2 Chr. 14:3; 15:16); Jehoshaphat removed the Asherim (2 Chr. 17:6; 19:3); Hezekiah cut down the Asherah (2 Kgs. 18:4; 2 Chr. 31:1); the Asherah removed from the house of the Lord (2 Kgs. 23:6); Joash cut down the Asherim (2 Kgs. 23:14; 2 Chr. 34:3, 4); and burned the Asherah (2 Kgs. 23:15).
	j	I will root out the Asherim from among you (Mic. 5:14); they will not look to the Asherim (Isa. 17:8).

- Chemosh

k Chemosh god of Ammon (Judg. 11:24); Moabites worshipped Chemosh (Num. 21:29); Chemosh the abomination of Moab (1 Kgs. 11:7, 33; 2 Kgs. 23:13); Moab will be ashamed of Chemosh (Jer. 48:13).

- Dagon

l Dagon god of the Philistines (Judg. 16:23; 1 Sam. 5:2–5); they put Saul's head in the house of Dagon (1 Chr. 10:10).

- Molech /
  Milcom

m Milcom the abomination of the Ammonites (1 Kgs. 11:5, 33; 2 Kgs. 23:13); Molech the abomination of the Ammonites (1 Kgs. 11:7); making children pass through the fire for Molech (2 Kgs. 23:10; Jer. 32:35); do not give your children to Molech (Lev. 18:21; 20:2–5); Milcom will go into exile (Jer. 49:3); you took up the tent of Moloch (Acts 7:43).

- Bel

n Bel bows down, Nebo stoops (Isa. 46:1), Bel has been shamed, Marduk shattered (Jer. 50:2); I will punish Bel in Babylon (Jer. 51:44).

- National
  deities

o Nisroch god of the king of Assyria (2 Kgs. 19:37); Naaman bowing in the house of Rimmon (2 Kgs. 5:18); the men of Babylon made Succoth-benoth, the men of Cuth made Negal and the men of Hamath made Ashima (2 Kgs. 17:30); the Avvites made Nibhaz and Tartak (2 Kgs. 17:31); Sepharvites burned their children to Adrammelech and Anammelech, the gods of Sepharvaim (2 Kgs. 17:31).

p Do not worship the gods of the Amorites (Judg. 6:10); the people bowed down before the gods of Moab (Num. 25:2); Ahaz offered sacrifices to the gods of Damascus (2 Chr. 28:23); on the altar from Damascus (2 Kgs. 16:12–13, 15).

- Various
  deities

q Vessels for the host of heaven (2 Kgs. 23:4); Demetrius made silver shrines of Artemis (Acts 19:24); the great goddess Artemis (Acts 19:27, 35); great is Artemis of the Ephesians! (Acts 19:28, 34); the star of the god Rephan (Acts 7:43); sacrificing to goats (Lev. 17:7; 2 Chr. 11:15); you carried Sakkuth and Kaiwan, your images (Amos 5:26).

r The god of this world (2 Cor. 4:4); the man of sin sets himself up as being God (2 Thess. 2:4).

s They called Barnabas Zeus and Paul Hermes (Acts 14:12).

968 Angel

- Nature
  of angels

a Are not angels ministering spirits? (Heb. 1:14); he will give his angels charge of you (Ps. 91:11; Matt. 4:6; Luke 4:10); he makes his angels winds (Heb. 1:7); angels are fellow-servants with the brethren (Rev. 19:10; 22:9); angels are more powerful than men (2 Pet. 2:11); angels are not to be worshipped (Col. 2:18; Rev. 19:10; 22:8–9); if there is an angel as mediator (Job 33:23).

b The Son is much higher than the angels (Heb. 1:4); all angels worship him (Heb. 1:6); he did not subject to angels the world to come (Heb. 2:5); not even angels know (Matt. 24:36; Mark 13:32); things angels desire to look into (1 Pet. 1:12); we shall judge angels (1 Cor. 6:3); he is not concerned with angels (Heb. 2:16); Jesus was made for a little while lower than the angels (Heb. 2:7, 9).

c At the resurrection people are like angels (Matt. 22:30; Mark 12:25; Luke 20:36); his face was like an angel's (Acts 6:15); you received me like an angel of God (Gal. 4:14); some entertained angels unawares (Heb. 13:2); men ate the food of angels (Ps. 78:25).

d Bless the Lord, you his angels (Ps. 103:20); at the creation the sons of God shouted for joy (Job 38:7); joy in the presence of the angels of God (Luke 15:10).

e Sadducees say there is no angel (Acts 23:8); suppose an angel has spoken to him? (Acts 23:9).

Evil angels, see **969***q*; **worshipping angels**, see **981***al*.

- **Angels in heaven**

f You have come to thousands of angels (Heb. 12:22); their angels in heaven always behold the face of my Father (Matt. 18:10); the sons of God came to present themselves before the Lord (Job 1:6; 2:1); the Lord Jesus will be revealed from heaven with his mighty angels (2 Thess. 1:7).

- **The angel of the Lord**

g The angel of the Lord dealing with: Hagar (Gen. 16:7; 21:17); Abraham (Gen. 22:11); Moses (Exod. 3:2); Israel's army (Exod. 14:19); Balaam (Num. 22:22–6); the Israelites (Judg. 2:1); Gideon (Judg. 6:11); Manoah and his wife (Judg. 13:3, 6, 9, 16, 21); Elijah (2 Kgs. 1:15); David (1 Chr. 21:16); Zechariah the prophet (Zech. 1:12); Zechariah the priest (Luke 1:11); Joseph (Matt. 1:20; 2:13, 19).

h The angel stretched out his hand to destroy Jerusalem (2 Sam. 24:16; 1 Chr. 21:15); an angel of the Lord killed 185 000 Assyrians (2 Kgs. 19:35); all the Assyrian warriors (2 Chr. 32:21); the angel of the Lord pursuing them (Ps. 35:5, 6).

i The angel of the Lord camps round those who fear him (Ps. 34:7); the angel of His presence saved them (Isa. 63:9)

j The king is like the angel of God (2 Sam. 19:27).

- **Angels and the law**

k Angels were involved in the giving of the law (Acts 7:53; Gal. 3:19); the angel spoke to Moses on Mount Sinai (Acts 7:38); the word spoken through angels (Heb. 2:2).

- **Angels before Jesus' birth**

l God will send his angel before you (Gen. 24:7, 40); I am sending an angel ahead of you (Exod. 23:20); I will send an angel before you (Exod. 32:34; 33:2); God sent an angel and brought us out of Egypt (Num. 20:16); my God sent an angel and shut the mouths of the lions (Dan. 6:22); God sent the angel Gabriel to Mary (Luke 1:26); the angels of God met Jacob (Gen. 32:1); an angel fed Elijah (1 Kgs. 19:5, 7).

m The angels of God were ascending and descending the stairway (Gen. 28:12); may the angel who redeemed me bless the lads (Gen. 48:16).

● Angels
and Jesus

n An angel of the Lord appeared to the shepherds (Luke 2:9); the angels of God ascending and descending on the Son of man (John 1:51); angels attended Jesus (Matt. 4:11; Mark 1:13); he will give his angels charge over you (Ps. 91:11; Matt. 4:6; Luke 4:10); an angel strengthened him (Luke 22:43); some said an angel had spoken to him (John 12:29); would my Father not send more than 12 legions of angels? (Matt. 26:53); he was seen by angels (1 Tim. 3:16); even angels long to look into these things (1 Pet. 1:12); myriads and myriads of angels praising Jesus (Rev. 5:11–12).

o There were two angels seated where Jesus' body had been (John 20:12); an angel of the Lord rolled away the stone (Matt. 28:2–7); a vision of angels (Luke 24:23); men with white clothes at the resurrection (Mark 16:5–7; Luke 24:4–7); at the ascension (Acts 1:10).

● Angels and
the church

p An angel of the Lord opened the prison (Acts 5:19); an angel directed Philip (Acts 8:26); Cornelius saw an angel in a vision (Acts 10:3, 22, 30; 11:13); an angel released Peter (Acts 12:7–10); now I know the Lord sent his angel and rescued me (Acts 12:11); an angel of the Lord struck Herod (Acts 12:23); an angel appeared to Paul (Acts 27:23–4).

q We have become a spectacle to angels and men (1 Cor. 4:9); women should have authority on their heads because of the angels (1 Cor. 11:10); if an angel from heaven should preach a different gospel (Gal. 1:8); the seven stars are the angels of the seven churches (Rev. 1:20).

● Angels at
the end

r Four angels holding back the winds (Rev. 7:1); an angel having the seal of God (Rev. 7:2); seven angels with seven trumpets (Rev. 8:2, 6); an angel clothed in a cloud (Rev. 10:1); an angel flying in mid-heaven (Rev. 14:6, 8, 9); seven angels with seven plagues (Rev. 15:6); an angel coming from heaven with great authority (Rev. 18:1).

s He will send his angels to gather the elect (Matt. 24:31; Mark 13:27); the reapers are angels (Matt. 13:39, 41); the angels will separate the wicked from the righteous (Matt. 13:49); he will be denied before the angels of God (Luke 12:9).

t The Son of man will come with his angels (Matt. 16:27; 25:31; Mark 8:38); in the glory of the angels (Luke 9:26); the Lord will descend with the voice of the archangel (1 Thess. 4:16).

● Cherubim

u Cherubim were placed on the east side of Eden (Gen. 3:24); cherubim were depicted in the tabernacle (Exod. 25:18; 26:1, 31; 37:7–9; Num. 7:89); in the temple (1 Kgs. 6:23; 2 Chr. 3:10; Ezek. 41:18, 25); the cherubim of glory overshadowing the mercy seat (Heb. 9:5); God is enthroned on the cherubim (2 Sam. 6:2; 2 Kgs. 19:15; 1 Chr. 13:6; Ps. 80:1); the chariot of the cherubim (1 Chr. 28:18; Ezek. 1:5–12; 10:9–17); whirling wheels under the cherubim (Ezek. 10:2); the ark under the wings of the cherubim (1 Kgs. 8:6–7; 2 Chr. 5:7–8); the glory of the Lord went up from the cherubim (Ezek. 9:3).

v The living creatures were cherubim (Ezek. 10:20–2); the cherubim were standing in the temple (Ezek. 10:3–8); each had the face of a cherub (Ezek. 10:14).

Cherubim's wings, see **271***e*.

- Seraphs

w Seraphs in the temple (Isa. 6:2); God rode on a seraph (2 Sam. 22:11; Ps. 18:10).

- Named angels

x The man Gabriel (Dan. 8:16; 9:21); I am Gabriel (Luke 1:19); Michael, one of the chief princes (Dan. 10:13); Michael, your prince (Dan. 10:21); Michael the great prince (Dan. 12:1); Michael the archangel (Jude 9); Michael and his angels (Rev. 12:7).

969 Devil

- Nature of the devil

a The dragon, that ancient serpent, who is the devil, or Satan (Rev. 12:9; 20:2); Beelzebul the prince of demons (Matt. 12:24, 27); the ruler of the world (John 12:31; 14:30; 16:11); the god of this world (2 Cor. 4:4); the prince of the power of the air (Eph. 2:2).

b He who does what is sinful is of the devil, because the devil has sinned from the beginning (1 John 3:8); the devil had the power of death (Heb. 2:14).

c Satan appeared before God (Job 1:6; 2:1); the devils believe that God is one – and tremble (Jas. 2:19); if Satan is divided against himself, how can his kingdom stand? (Matt. 12:26; Mark 3:26; Luke 11:18); how can Satan cast out Satan? (Mark 3:23); what agreement has Christ with Belial? (2 Cor. 6:15).

- Activity of the devil

d The serpent was more crafty than any other wild animal (Gen. 3:1); the serpent deceived Eve by its craftiness (2 Cor. 11:3); Satan disguises himself as an angel of light (2 Cor. 11:14); Jesus tempted by the devil (Matt. 4:1; Mark 1:13; Luke 4:2).

e Condemnation of the devil (1 Tim. 3:6); reproach and snare of the devil (1 Tim. 3:7); the snare of the devil (2 Tim. 2:26).

f There is no truth in him (John 8:44); he is a liar and the father of lies (John 8:44); Satan filled Ananias' heart to lie to the Holy Spirit (Acts 5:3).

g The god of this world has blinded their minds (2 Cor. 4:4); the evil one snatches away the seed (Matt. 13:19); Satan takes away the word (Mark 4:15; Luke 8:12).

h Satan has bound this woman for 18 years (Luke 13:16); we wanted to come but Satan hindered us (1 Thess. 2:18); the thorn in the flesh was a messenger of Satan (2 Cor. 12:7).

i The enemy who sows the weeds is the devil (Matt. 13:39); your enemy the devil prowls round like a roaring lion (1 Pet. 5:8); the devil has come down to the earth in great wrath (Rev. 12:12); Satan accusing Joshua (Zech. 3:1); he accuses the brethren day and night (Rev. 12:10).

j Satan urged David to number Israel (1 Chr. 21:1); the devil put it into Judas' heart to betray Jesus (John 13:2); Satan entered Judas (Luke 22:3; John 13:27); one of you is a devil (John 6:70).

k That Satan may gain no advantage, for we are not ignorant of his devices (2 Cor. 2:11).

● Following the devil

l The whole world is under the control of the evil one (1 John 5:19); you live where Satan's throne is (Rev. 2:13); the synagogue of Satan (Rev. 2:9; 3:9); the Gentiles sacrifice to demons, not to God (1 Cor. 10:20); some have turned away to follow Satan (1 Tim. 5:15).

Worshipping the devil, see **981***am*.

m You cannot drink the cup of the Lord and the cup of demons (1 Cor. 10:21).

● Children of the devil

n You son of the devil! (Acts 13:10); sons of the evil one (Matt. 13:38); you are of your father the devil (John 8:44).

● Evil spirits

o Evil spirits like frogs came out of the mouths of the dragon, the beast and the false prophet (Rev. 16:13); the unclean spirit wanders, seeking rest (Matt. 12:43; Luke 11:24); you deaf and dumb spirit! (Mark 9:25).

p They sacrificed to demons (Deut. 32:17); they did not turn from worshipping demons (Rev. 9:20); deceitful spirits and doctrines of demons (1 Tim. 4:1); God sent an evil spirit between Abimelech and the men of Shechem (Judg. 9:23); an evil spirit from the Lord came on Saul (1 Sam. 16:14–15, 23; 18:10; 19:9).

● Evil angels

q Satan disguises himself as an angel of light (2 Cor. 11:14); angels cannot separate us from the love of God (Rom. 8:38–9); promoting the worship of angels (Col. 2:18).

r God did not spare angels who sinned (2 Pet. 2:4); angels are kept in bonds for judgement (Jude 6); release the four angels bound at the Euphrates (Rev. 9:14); Satan's angels were thrown down with him (Rev. 12:9); the angel of the abyss is king over them, Abaddon or Apollyon (Rev. 9:11).

● Principalities and powers

s Principalities and powers were created through Christ (Col. 1:16); the rulers of spiritual wickedness (Eph. 6:12); our struggle is against principalities and powers (Eph. 6:12); principalities cannot separate us from the love of God (Rom. 8:38–9); he disarmed principalities and powers (Col. 2:15); angels, authorities and powers are subject to Christ (1 Pet. 3:22); the wisdom of God made known to the principalities and powers in the heavenlies (Eph. 3:10).

t The prince of this world (John 14:30); the prince of the power of the air (Eph. 2:2); the prince of the kingdom of Persia withstood Gabriel (Dan. 10:13, 20); the prince of Greece is coming (Dan. 10:20).

● Demonised

u A man in the synagogue was possessed by an unclean spirit (Mark 1:23, 26; Luke 4:33); Gadarene demoniacs from the tombs (Matt. 8:28; Mark 5:2; Luke 8:27); a man who was demon-possessed and dumb (Matt. 9:32); a boy possessed by a spirit (Matt. 17:18; Mark 9:17; Luke 9:39); the Canaanite woman's daughter was demonised (Matt. 15:22; Mark 7:25); demon-possessed, blind and dumb (Matt. 12:22); a sickness due to a spirit (Luke 13:11).

Demons entering, see **297n**.

- Accused of being demonised

v They said Jesus had an evil spirit (Matt. 11:18; Mark 3:30); they said he was possessed by Beelzebul (Mark 3:22); you are demon-possessed (John 7:20; 8:52); are we not right in saying you are a Samaritan and demon-possessed? (John 8:48); he is demon-possessed and mad (John 10:20); it is by the prince of demons that he drives out demons (Matt. 9:34; 12:24, 27; Mark 3:22; Luke 11:15); they called the master of the house Beelzebul (Matt. 10:25).

w You say John the Baptist has a demon (Luke 7:33).

- God's authority over the devil

x The Lord cursed the serpent (Gen. 3:14); he commands evil spirits and they obey him (Mark 1:27; Luke 4:36); he would not permit the demons to speak (Mark 1:34); unclean spirits fell down before him (Mark 3:11); angels, authorities and powers are subject to Christ (1 Pet. 3:22); I saw Satan fall from heaven (Luke 10:18).

y Seven demons were cast out of Mary Magdalene (Luke 8:2); a girl with a spirit of divination (Acts 16:16); they brought him many who were demonised (Matt. 8:16); demons came out of many (Luke 4:41); those troubled with unclean spirits were healed (Luke 6:18); Jesus healed all who were oppressed by the devil (Acts 10:38).

z The ruler of this world is judged (John 16:11); the ruler of this world will be cast out (John 12:31).

Casting out demons, see **300a**.

- Disciples' authority over the devil

aa He gave the disciples authority over unclean spirits (Matt. 10:1; Mark 6:7; Luke 9:1); I have given you authority over all the power of the enemy (Luke 10:19); cast out demons (Matt. 10:8); even the demons are subject to us (Luke 10:17); young men, you have overcome the evil one (1 John 2:13, 14); turn them from the authority of Satan to God (Acts 26:18); resist the devil and he will flee from you (Jas. 4:7); do not give the devil a foothold (Eph. 4:27); stand against the wiles of the devil (Eph. 6:11); the God of peace will soon crush Satan under your feet (Rom. 16:20).

- Handing over to the devil

ab Hand him over to Satan for the destruction of the flesh (1 Cor. 5:5); Hymenaeus and Alexander, whom I have handed over to Satan (1 Tim. 1:20).

970 Ghost

- Ghosts

a The spirits of the dead greet the king of Babylon (Isa. 14:9); your voice will come from the ground like that of a ghost (Isa. 29:4).

b They thought Jesus was a ghost (Matt. 14:26; Mark 6:49; Luke 24:37); a ghost does not have flesh and bones (Luke 24:39).

971 Heaven

● God in
heaven

a Our God is in the heavens (Ps. 115:3); God is in heaven and you on earth (Eccles. 5:2); our Father in heaven (Matt. 6:9); look down from heaven, your dwelling-place (Deut. 26:15); if I ascend to heaven, you are there (Ps. 139:8); whom have I in heaven but you? (Ps. 73:25); the highest heavens belong to the Lord (Ps. 115:16); the highest heaven cannot contain God (1 Kgs. 8:27; 2 Chr. 2:6; 6:18); heaven is my throne (Isa. 66:1; Acts 7:49); the Lord is on his heavenly throne (Ps. 11:4); do not swear by heaven, for it is God's throne (Matt. 5:34).

b God's will is done in heaven (Matt. 6:10); joy in heaven (Luke 15:7); silence in heaven for half an hour (Rev. 8:1).

● Open heaven

c The heavens were opened and the Holy Spirit descended (Matt. 3:16; Luke 3:21–2); you will see the heavens opened (John 1:51); an open door in heaven (Rev. 4:1); I saw heaven opened (Rev. 19:11).

Heaven opened, see **263***ag*.

● Jesus and
heaven

d How will you believe if I tell you heavenly things? (John 3:12); he who comes from heaven is above all (John 3:31); the bread which comes down from heaven (John 6:33, 41, 42, 50, 51); no one has ascended to heaven but he who descended from heaven (John 3:13).

e Christ entered not a man-made sanctuary but heaven itself (Heb. 9:24); we have a great high priest who has passed through the heavens (Heb. 4:14); Jesus has gone into heaven (1 Pet. 3:22).

● Heaven
for us

f God blessed us in the heavenlies (Eph. 1:3); God seated us in the heavenlies (Eph. 2:6); our citizenship is in heaven (Phil. 3:20); the Lord will save me for his heavenly kingdom (2 Tim. 4:18); an inheritance reserved in heaven for you (1 Pet. 1:4); the church of the firstborn enrolled in heaven (Heb. 12:23); they desire a better country, a heavenly one (Heb. 11:16); set your minds on things above, not on things on earth (Col. 3:1–2); whatever you bind or loose on earth will be done in heaven (Matt. 16:19; 18:18).

g You will have treasure in heaven (Matt. 19:21; Mark 10:21; Luke 18:22); lay up treasure in heaven (Matt. 6:20; Luke 12:33); great is your reward in heaven (Luke 6:23).

h I know a man in Christ who was caught up to the third heaven (2 Cor. 12:2); to paradise (2 Cor. 12:4).

i Afterwards you will take me to glory (Ps. 73:24); the beggar died and the angels carried him to Abraham's bosom (Luke 16:22); today you will be with me in paradise (Luke 23:43); eating of the tree of life in the paradise of God (Rev. 2:7); new Jerusalem comes down out of heaven (Rev. 3:12; 21:2, 10).

Going up to heaven, see **308***a*; coming down from heaven, see **309***e*; kingdom of heaven, see **733***c*.

972 Hell

● Hell of fire

a It is better to lose one limb than for your whole body to be thrown into hell (Matt. 5:29, 30; 18:8, 9; Mark 9:43, 45, 47–8); fear him who can destroy soul and body in hell (Matt. 10:28); fear him who has authority to cast into hell (Luke 12:5); the rich man was in torment in hades (Luke 16:23); guilty enough for the hell of fire (Matt. 5:22); how will you escape being sentenced to hell? (Matt. 23:33); thrown into the fiery furnace (Matt. 13:42, 50); God cast angels into hell (2 Pet. 2:4).

b You make him twice as much a son of hell (Matt. 23:15); the tongue is set on fire by hell (Jas. 3:6).

Second death, see **361***at*; **fire of hell**, see **381***ab*.

● Bottomless pit

c The demons entreated him not to command them to depart into the abyss (Luke 8:31); God consigned angels to pits of darkness (2 Pet. 2:4); lest I be like those who go down to the pit (Ps. 28:1); the abyss was opened with a key (Rev. 9:1–2); the angel of the abyss is king over them (Rev. 9:11); the beast that comes up out of the abyss (Rev. 11:7; 17:8); the angel sealed the devil in the abyss (Rev. 20:1–3).

d Who will descend into the abyss? (Rom. 10:7).

Hades, Sheol, see **361**.

973 Religion

● Religious

a Religion with unbridled tongue is worthless (Jas. 1:26); pure religion is to visit the needy (Jas. 1:27); having a form of religion but denying the power of it (2 Tim. 3:5).

b I see that you are very religious (Acts 17:22); some disagreement about their own religion (Acts 25:19).

● Judaism

c My former life in Judaism (Gal. 1:13); I advanced in Judaism (Gal. 1:14).

974 Irreligion

● Uncircumcised

a Those born in the wilderness had not been circumcised (Josh. 5:5, 7); all the nations are uncircumcised (Jer. 9:26).

b We cannot give in marriage to the uncircumcised (Gen. 34:14); this uncircumcised Philistine (1 Sam. 17:26, 36); lest these uncircumcised make sport of me (1 Sam. 31:4); Paul was entrusted with the gospel to the uncircumcised (Gal. 2:7).

c Israel are uncircumcised in heart (Jer. 9:26); uncircumcised in heart and ears (Acts 7:51); Gentiles, the 'uncircumcision' (Eph. 2:11); you were dead in the uncircumcision of your flesh (Col. 2:13).

d If the uncircumcised man keeps the law he will be regarded as circumcised (Rom. 2:26); Abraham was justified while uncircumcised (Rom. 4:10); the uncircumcised will no more come into you (Isa. 52:1).

● The world without God

e You are not of this world (John 15:19); the world has not known you (John 17:25); they are not of the world as I am not (John 17:16); all that is in the world is not of the Father (1 John 2:16); I have overcome the world (John 16:33).

f The world hates you as it hated me (John 15:18–19); do not love the world (1 John 2:15); friendship of the world is enmity with God (Jas. 4:4); if anyone loves the world, love of the Father is not in him (1 John 2:15); Demas has loved this present world (2 Tim. 4:10).

975 Scriptures

● Authority of the scriptures

a The scriptures cannot be broken (John 10:35); your testimonies are very sure (Ps. 93:5); all scripture is God-breathed and profitable (2 Tim. 3:16); no scripture is of private interpretation (2 Pet. 1:20); believing everything in the law and the prophets (Acts 24:14); speaking only what the prophets and Moses said (Acts 26:22); they have Moses and the prophets (Luke 16:29).

b Men moved by the Holy Spirit spoke from God (2 Pet. 1:21); as the Holy Spirit says (Heb. 3:7).

The scriptures fulfilled, see **725e.**

● Jesus and the scriptures

c The scriptures bear witness to me (John 5:39); Moses wrote of me (John 5:46); we have found him of whom Moses and the prophets wrote (John 1:45).

d I did not come to abolish the law and the prophets, but to fulfil (Matt. 5:17); treat men as you want to be treated, for this is the law and the prophets (Matt. 7:12); the law and the prophets depend on these two commandments (Matt. 22:40).

e He opened their minds to understand the scriptures (Luke 24:45); he explained in all the scriptures the things concerning himself (Luke 24:27); Paul spoke about Jesus from the law of Moses and the prophets (Acts 28:23); Christ died and rose according to the scriptures (1 Cor. 15:3–4).

● The gospel in the scriptures

f The gospel was promised in the holy scriptures (Rom. 1:2); the gospel is made known by the scriptures of the prophets (Rom. 16:26); the law and the prophets testify of righteousness through faith (Rom. 3:21–2).

● Use of the scriptures

g These things were written in earlier times so that through the encouragement of the scriptures we might have hope (Rom. 15:4).

h They were entrusted with the oracles of God (Rom. 3:2); from a child you have known the scriptures (2 Tim. 3:15); Apollos was powerful in the scriptures (Acts 18:24); you do not perceive the scriptures nor the power of God (Matt. 22:29; Mark 12:24).

i Moses is read in the synagogues every sabbath (Acts 15:21);

after the reading of the law and the prophets (Acts 13:15); the Bereans examined the scriptures daily (Acts 17:11).

The word of God, see **529***a*; **scripture**, see **586***a*; **books of scripture**, see **589***i*; **the law**, see **953***a*.

976 Orthodoxy
Sound doctrine, see **452***a*.

977 Heterodoxy
Unsound doctrine, see **452***c*.

978 Sectarianism
See **708**.

979 Holiness

- God is holy

a He is a holy God (Josh. 24:19); holy is he! (Ps. 99:3, 5); who can stand before this holy God? (1 Sam. 6:20); the Lord our God is holy (Ps. 99:9); holy, holy, holy is the Lord Almighty (Isa. 6:3; Rev. 4:8); the Holy One of Israel (Isa. 37:23); I will show myself holy (Lev. 10:3); he showed himself holy among them (Num. 20:13); the Spirit of holiness (Rom. 1:4); the Lord Almighty is the one you are to regard as holy (Isa. 8:13).

b There is no one holy like the Lord (1 Sam. 2:2); you alone are holy (Rev. 15:4); who is like you, majestic in holiness? (Exod. 15:11).

c His name is holy (Isa. 57:15; Luke 1:49); they will keep my name holy (Isa. 29:23); hallowed be your name (Matt. 6:9; Luke 11:2); I will be sanctified among Israel (Lev. 22:32); you did not sanctify me (Deut. 32:51).

- Be holy for I am holy

d Be holy because I am holy (Lev. 11:44–45; 19:2; 20:7, 26; 1 Pet. 1:15–16); priests are to be considered holy because I, the Lord, who makes you holy, am holy (Lev. 21:6–8); holiness befits your house (Ps. 93:5); worship the Lord in holy adornment (1 Chr. 16:29).

e I am the Lord who sanctifies you (Lev. 20:8; 21:15, 23; 22:16, 32; Ezek. 20:12).

- Holy people

f Israel was holy to the Lord (Jer. 2:3); a people holy to the Lord (Exod. 22:31; Deut. 7:6; 14:2, 21; 26:19; 28:9); a holy people (Exod. 19:6; Deut. 14:2, 21; 26:19; 28:9; Isa. 62:12; 1 Pet. 2:9); that we should be holy and blameless before him (Eph. 1:4); the temple of God is holy, which temple you are (1 Cor. 3:17); those left in Zion will be called holy (Isa. 4:3); all the congregation is holy (Num. 16:3); he whom the Lord chooses is holy (Num. 16:7); this is a holy man of God (2 Kgs. 4:9).

g The Nazirite will be holy to the Lord (Num. 6:5, 8); that we might serve him in holiness (Luke 1:74–5); perfecting holness in the fear of God (2 Cor. 7:1); he disciplines us that we may share his holiness (Heb. 12:10).

h Do not come near, for I am holier than you (Isa. 65:5); those who sanctify themselves to eat pork and mice (Isa. 66:17).

● Consecrating people

i Consecrate to me every firstborn male (Exod. 13:2; Luke 2:23); consecrate the people (Exod. 19:10, 14; Num. 11:18; Josh. 3:5; 7:13); consecrate yourselves (1 Chr. 15:12); before you were born I consecrated you (Jer. 1:5); the priests were consecrated (Exod. 28:41; 29:1, 21; Lev. 8:12–13); you have been set apart to the Lord today (Exod. 32:29); Aaron and his descendants were set apart (1 Chr. 23:13); the priests consecrated themselves (Exod. 19:22; 1 Chr. 15:14; 2 Chr. 5:11; 29:5); Job sanctified his children (Job 1:5).

● Saints

j The saints possessed the kingdom (Dan. 7:22); he will wear down the saints of the Most High (Dan. 7:25); many bodies of the saints were raised (Matt. 27:52).

k Called saints (Rom. 1:7; 1 Cor. 1:2); to all the saints (2 Cor. 1:1; Eph. 1:1; Phil. 1:1; Col. 1:2); the churches of the saints (1 Cor. 14:33); you are fellow-citizens with the saints (Eph. 2:19); as is fitting among saints (Eph. 5:3); the mystery revealed to the saints (Col. 1:26); the faith delivered to the saints (Jude 3); we share in the inheritance of the saints (Col. 1:12); God's inheritance in the saints (Eph. 1:18); the prayers of the saints (Rev. 5:8; 8:3, 4); perseverance of the saints (Rev. 13:10; 14:12; 18:24); the blood of the saints (Rev. 16:6; 17:6); fine linen is the righteous deeds of the saints (Rev. 19:8); the reward for prophets and saints (Rev. 11:18); greet all the saints (Rom. 16:15; Heb. 13:24); all the saints greet you (2 Cor. 13:13; Phil. 4:22).

l The harm he did to your saints in Jerusalem (Acts 9:13); I imprisoned many of the saints (Acts 26:10); I am the least of the saints (Eph. 3:8); why go to law before the unrighteous and not before the saints? (1 Cor. 6:1); the saints will judge the world (1 Cor. 6:2); making war on the saints (Rev. 13:7; 20:9); the coming of our Lord Jesus with his saints (1 Thess. 3:13); when he comes to be glorified in his saints (2 Thess. 1:10).

● Saints served

m The collection for the saints (1 Cor. 16:1); the support of the saints (2 Cor. 8:4); service to the saints (2 Cor. 9:1; Heb. 6:10); they have devoted themselves to serve the saints (1 Cor. 16:15); supplying the needs of the saints (2 Cor. 9:12); for equipping the saints (Eph. 4:12); your love for all the saints (Eph. 1:15; Col. 1:4; Philem. 5); you have refreshed the hearts of the saints (Philem. 7); washing the saints' feet (1 Tim. 5:10); that my service may be acceptable to the saints (Rom. 15:31); pray for all the saints (Eph. 6:18); the Spirit intercedes for the saints (Rom. 8:27).

● Sanctification in Christ

n I sanctify myself that they may be sanctified (John 17:19); sanctify them by the truth (John 17:17); Christ sanctified the church (Eph. 5:26); he has reconciled you to present you holy in his sight (Col. 1:22); the unbelieving husband is sanctified through his wife (1 Cor. 7:14).

o Those sanctified by faith in me (Acts 26:18); those sanctified in Christ Jesus (1 Cor. 1:2); you were sanctified (1 Cor. 6:11).

p This is God's will, your sanctification (1 Thess. 4:3); chosen through the sanctification of the Spirit (1 Pet. 1:2); may God sanctify you wholly (1 Thess. 5:23); without holiness no one will see the Lord (Heb. 12:14); you ought to live holy and godly lives (2 Pet. 3:11); we have conducted ourselves in holiness from God (2 Cor. 1:12).

q Christ is made to us sanctification (1 Cor. 1:30); sanctification by the Spirit (2 Thess. 2:13); presenting your limbs as slaves to righteousness produces sanctification (Rom. 6:19, 22).

- Consecrating things

r The tent of meeting, altar and priests will be consecrated by my glory (Exod. 29:43–4); the tabernacle and its contents were consecrated (Exod. 30:29; 40:9; Lev. 8:10); the holy place (Lev. 16:2, 3, 16, 17, 20, 23, 27); the altar was consecrated (Exod. 29:36–7; 40:10).

s I have consecrated this house by putting my name there for ever (1 Kgs. 9:3).

- Holy things

t God sanctified the seventh day (Gen. 2:3; Exod. 20:11); the sabbath is holy (Exod. 31:14, 15).

u The ram of ordination was holy (Exod. 29:33, 34); all who touch the offerings become holy (Lev. 6:18, 27); holiness is not imparted by touching holy things (Hag. 2:12).

v The silver, gold, bronze and iron from Jericho were sacred to the Lord (Josh. 6:19); David dedicated gold, silver and bronze to the Lord (2 Sam. 8:11; 1 Chr. 18:11); the censers of Nadab's company became holy (Num. 16:38).

w HOLY TO THE LORD: engraved on a plate (Exod. 28:36; 39:30); on the bells of the horses (Zech. 14:20).

x Holy ground (Exod. 3:5; Josh. 5:15; Acts 7:33); the holy place (Heb. 9:2); a holy portion of land for the Lord (Ezek. 45:1; 48:10–20); boil the ram in a holy place (Exod. 29:31); they have built a sanctuary for your name (2 Chr. 20:8); the valley of corpses and ashes will be holy to the Lord (Jer. 31:40); the holy way (Isa. 35:8); holy chambers (Ezek. 42:13).

y Do not give dogs what is holy (Matt. 7:6).

Carrying holy things, see **273a**; **looking at holy things**, see **441a**.

- Most holy things

z The most holy place [holy of holies] (Exod. 26:34; Ezek. 41:4; Heb. 9:3); the veil separates between the holy and the most holy (Exod. 26:33).

aa Things that were most holy: the temple area (Ezek. 43:12); the bronze altar (Exod. 29:37; 40:10); the altar of incense (Exod. 30:10); the furniture of the tabernacle (Exod. 30:29; Num. 4:4,

19); the incense (Exod. 30:36); the grain offering (Lev. 2:3, 10; 10:12); the bread of the Presence (Lev. 24:9); the sacrifices (Lev. 6:17, 25, 29; 7:1, 6; 10:17; 14:13; 24:9; Num. 18:9, 10; Ezek. 42:13); things under a ban of destruction (Lev. 27:28).

ab The Kohathites were to take care of the most holy things (Num. 4:4).

● Godliness

ac Training in godliness (1 Tim. 4:7–8); they think godliness is gain (1 Tim. 6:5); godliness is great gain with contentment (1 Tim. 6:6); all who live godly will be persecuted (2 Tim. 3:12).

980 Impiety

● Lack of holiness

a There were many who had not consecrated themselves (2 Chr. 30:18); men will be unholy (2 Tim. 3:2).

● Blasphemy

b He will speak against the God of gods (Dan. 11:36); the beast opened his mouth to blaspheme God (Rev. 13:6); blasphemous names on the beast's heads (Rev. 13:1); the scarlet beast was covered with blasphemous names (Rev. 17:3).

c They said Jesus was blaspheming (Matt. 9:3; Mark 2:7; Luke 5:21; John 10:33, 36); he has spoken blasphemy! (Matt. 26:65; Mark 14:64); we have heard Stephen speak blasphemy against Moses and against God (Acts 6:11); he tried to profane the temple (Acts 24:6).

d Blasphemy against the Spirit will not be forgiven (Matt. 12:31; Mark 3:29; Luke 12:10); speaking against the Son of man will be forgiven (Matt. 12:32; Luke 12:30).

e Paul tried to force the believers to blaspheme (Acts 26:11); I was formerly a blasphemer (1 Tim. 1:13); you have given the Lord's enemies occasion to blaspheme (2 Sam. 12:14).

f I delivered them to Satan that they may be taught not to blaspheme (1 Tim. 1:20).

● Misusing God's name

g Do not take God's name in vain (Exod. 20:7; Deut. 5:11).

981 Worship

● Worship God!

a Worship God (Rev. 19:10; 22:9); let us worship and bow down (Ps. 95:6); worship the Lord your God (Matt. 4:10; Luke 4:8); worship the Lord in holiness (Ps. 96:9); worship the Lord in holy adornment (1 Chr. 16:29); bring an offering and come into his courts (Ps. 96:8).

● How to worship

b The Father seeks those who will worship him in spirit and truth (John 4:23); we are the circumcision who worship by the Spirit of God (Phil. 3:3); you say Jerusalem is where one should worship (John 4:20); if they go up to Jerusalem to worship (1 Kgs. 12:27); all nations will come and worship before you (Ps. 86:9).

c In vain do they worship me (Matt. 15:9).

- Worship
  of God

d You will serve God on this mountain (Exod. 3:12); let my son go that he may serve me (Exod. 4:23); let my people go that they may serve me (Exod. 7:16; 8:1, 20; 9:1, 13; 10:3, 7); serve the Lord as you have requested (Exod. 12:31).

e The people bowed down and worshipped (Exod. 4:31; 12:27); you are to worship at a distance (Exod. 24:1); the people stood and worshipped, each at the entrance to his tent (Exod. 33:10); the angels, elders and living creatures fell on their faces and worshipped (Rev. 7:11).

- Individuals
  who
  worshipped

f We will worship and return (Gen. 22:5); the man bowed down and worshipped the Lord (Gen. 24:26, 48); Israel worshipped, leaning on his staff (Gen. 47:31); Gideon worshipped God (Judg. 7:15); David went into the house of the Lord and worshipped (2 Sam. 12:20); Hezekiah bowed down and worshipped (2 Chr. 29:29); Job fell to the ground and worshipped (Job 1:20); an unbeliever will fall down and worship God (1 Cor. 14:25); I went up to Jerusalem to worship (Acts 24:11); I worship the God of our fathers (Acts 24:14).

- Worshipping
  Jesus

g We saw his star in the east and have come to worship him (Matt. 2:2); tell me that I may go and worship him (Matt. 2:8); they bowed down and worshipped him (Matt. 2:11); they worshipped him (Matt. 14:33); they clasped his feet and worshipped him (Matt. 28:9); they worshipped him, but some doubted (Matt. 28:17); let all God's angels worship him (Heb. 1:6); the man born blind worshipped Jesus (John 9:38).

- Sacrificial
  offerings

h Cain brought fruit and Abel brought firstlings (Gen. 4:3–4); by faith Abel offered a better sacrifice (Heb. 11:4); Jacob offered a sacrifice (Gen. 31:54); Israel offered sacrifices (Gen. 46:1); let us take a three–day journey into the desert to offer sacrifices (Exod. 3:18; 5:3); I will let your people go to offer sacrifices (Exod. 8:8); sacrifice to your God here in the land (Exod. 8:25); Balak sacrificed cattle and sheep (Num. 22:40); Elkanah went to sacrifice to the Lord in Shiloh (1 Sam. 1:3, 21); Samuel went to sacrifice (1 Sam. 9:12; 16:2–5); our family are observing a sacrifice (1 Sam. 20:29); every six steps he sacrificed a bull and a calf (2 Sam. 6:13); Absalom offered sacrifices (2 Sam. 15:12); Adonijah sacrificed sheep, cattle and calves (1 Kgs. 1:9, 19, 25); Solomon offered sacrifices before the ark (1 Kgs. 3:15); they offered innumerable sacrifices (1 Kgs. 8:5); Solomon offered 22 000 oxen and 120 000 sheep (1 Kgs. 8:62–3; 2 Chr. 7:5); Judah sacrificed 700 oxen and 7000 sheep (2 Chr. 15:11); Solomon offered sacrifices on the high places (1 Kgs. 3:3–4); two sac- rifices but no fire to be used (1 Kgs. 18:23); Elisha sacrificed the oxen (1 Kgs. 19:21).

i You have not brought me your sacrifices (Isa. 43:23–4). **Wave offering**, see **317a**; **blood of sacrifices**, see **335m**; **oil on sacrifices**, see **357o**; **fat of the sacrifices**, see **357ai**; **aroma of** sacrifices, see **396*h***; **perfect sacrifices**, see **646*c***; **giving sacrifices**, see **781*r***; **atoning by sacrifices**, see **941*f*.

● Regulating
sacrifices

j The types of sacrificial offerings listed (Lev. 7:37); sacrifices must be offered at the tent of meeting (Lev. 17:3–9); at the place the Lord chooses (Deut. 12:6, 11, 13–14); on the Lord's altar (Deut. 12:27; 27:6); blow the trumpets over your sacrifices (Num. 10:10); every grain offering, sin offering and guilt offering was for the priests (Num. 18:9); the sin offering should have been eaten (Lev. 10:16–19); Aaron's descendants made offering on the altars (1 Chr. 6:49); money from burnt offerings and sin offerings was for the priests (2 Kgs. 12:16).

k The altar was for witness, not for burnt offerings (Josh. 22:23, 26–9).

● Burnt
offering

l The law of burnt offerings (Lev. 1:3–17; 6:8–13); bring your burnt offerings to the place God shall choose (Deut. 12:6); they are to offer all the burnt offerings (1 Chr. 23:31); offering the burnt offering with song (2 Chr. 29:27–8).

m Two lambs as a daily burnt offering, morning and evening (Exod. 29:38–42; Num. 28:3–8, 23–4, 31; 29:6, 11, 16, 19, 22, 25, 28, 31, 34, 38; 1 Chr. 16:40; 2 Chr. 2:4; 8:13; 13:11; 31:3; Ezra 3:3); continual burnt offerings were made all the days of Jehoiada (2 Chr. 24:14); the continual burnt offering (Neh. 10:33); each morning (Ezek. 46:13–15); he will abolish the daily sacrifice (Dan. 11:31; 12:11); the continual burnt offering was taken away (Dan. 8:11–12); may my prayer be as the evening offering (Ps. 141:2).

n Each sabbath two extra lambs (Num. 28:9–10; 2 Chr. 8:13; 31:3); siz lambs and a ram on the sabbath (Ezek. 46:4); a burnt offering at the start of every month (Num. 28:11–14; 29:6; 2 Chr. 8:13; 31:3); new moon (Neh. 10:33); they presented the regular burnt offerings (Ezra 3:4–6); burnt offerings at Passover (Num. 28:17–24; 2 Chr. 8:13); at firstfruits (Lev. 23:12); at the Feast of Weeks (Lev. 23:18; Num. 28:27–31; 2 Chr. 8:13); for the seventh month (Num. 29:2–4, 13); for the Day of Atonement (Num. 29:8–10; Lev. 16:3, 5, 24); for the Feast of Booths (Num. 29:13–39; 2 Chr. 8:13); for ordaining priests (Exod. 29:18, 25; Lev. 8:18–21); for ordaining the Levites (Num. 8:12); for the Nazirite (Num. 6:14, 16).

o A burnt offering for cleansing: a woman after giving birth (Lev. 12:6–8); a leper (Lev. 14:19–20, 22, 31); from a discharge (Lev. 15:14–15, 29–30); from defilement (Num. 6:11); from unintentional sin (Num. 15:24); present the offering Moses commanded (Matt. 8:4; Mark 1:44; Luke 5:14).

p Those who offer burnt offerings: Noah (Gen. 8:20); Abraham offering Isaac (Gen. 22:2, 3, 6, 7–8); the ram instead (Gen. 22:13); Jethro (Exod. 18:12); Moses (Exod. 24:5); Aaron (Exod. 32:6; Lev. 9:2, 12–14); the Israelites (Lev. 9:3, 16; Judg. 20:26;

21:4); the leaders (Num. 7:15, 21, 27, 33, 39, 45, 51, 57, 63, 69, 75, 81, 87); Balaam (Num. 23:1–3, 6, 15, 17); Joshua (Josh. 8:31); Gideon (Judg. 6:26); Jephthah (Judg. 11:31); Manoah (Judg. 13:16, 23); the men of Beth-shemesh (1 Sam. 6:14–15); Samuel (1 Sam. 7:9–10; 10:8); Saul (1 Sam. 13:9–10, 12); David (2 Sam. 6:13, 17–18; 1 Chr. 16:1–2); the assembly (2 Chr. 29:32); the returned exiles (Ezra 8:35); Job's friends (Job 42:8); the prince (Ezek. 46:4–7).

q Solomon offered 1000 burnt offerings (2 Chr. 1:6); Solomon offered daily burnt offerings (2 Chr. 8:12–13).

- **Cereal offerings and libations**

r Instructions on the cereal offering (Lev. 2:1–16; 6:14–18); cereal offerings from the priest (Lev. 6:20–3; 9:4, 17); cereal offerings belong to the priests (Lev. 7:9–10; 10:12–13; Num. 18:9); cereal offerings for Firstfruits (Lev. 23:13); at the Feast of Weeks (Lev. 23:16; Num. 28:26); the continual cereal offering (Num. 4:16); a cereal offering of jealousy (Num. 5:15, 18, 25–6); cereal offerings from the leaders (Num. 7:13, 19, 25, 31, 37, 43, 49, 55, 61, 67, 73, 79).

s Cereal offering and libations as part of other offerings (Exod. 29:40–1; 40:29; Lev. 14:10, 20, 21, 31; 23:13, 18; Num. 6:15, 17; 7:87; 8:8; 15:4–10, 24; 28:3–8, 9, 11–15, 19–24, 27–31; 29:2–3, 6, 8–11, 13–39; Judg. 13:19, 23).

t Jacob poured a drink offering on the pillar (Gen. 35:14); I am being poured out like a drink offering (Phil. 2:17; 2 Tim. 4:6).

u There is no cereal offering or libation (Joel 1:9, 13); perhaps he will leave a cereal offering and libation (Joel 2:14).

- **Peace offerings**

v Instructions on the peace offering (Lev. 3:1–17; 7:11–21, 29–34); the fat of the peace offerings to be burnt (Lev. 6:12); a portion of peace offerings to be eaten by the priests (Exod. 29:28; Lev. 10:14); to be eaten by those offering it (Lev. 19:5–8); peace offering at the Feast of Weeks (Lev. 23:19); presented by the Nazirite (Num. 6:14, 17–18).

w Young men sacrificed peace offerings (Exod. 24:5); the Israelites brought peace offerings (Exod. 32:6); peace offerings of the people (Lev. 9:4, 18, 22; Judg. 20:26; 21:4; 1 Sam. 11:15); of the leaders (Num. 7:17, 23, 29, 35, 41, 47, 53, 59, 65, 71, 77, 83, 88); of Joshua (Josh. 8:31); of Samuel (1 Sam. 10:8); of Saul (1 Sam. 13:9); of David (2 Sam. 6:17–18; 1 Chr. 16:1–2).

- **Sin offering**

x Regulations for the sin offering (Lev. 4:1–35; 5:6–13; 6:24–30).

y A sin offering: at the start of every month (Num. 28:15; 29:11); at the Passover (Num. 28:22); at the seventh month (Num. 29:5, 11, 16, 19, 22, 25, 28, 31, 34, 38); when consecrating priests (Exod. 29:10–14, 36; Lev. 8:2, 14–17; 9:2, 7–8, 10); for cleansing the Levites (Num. 8:8, 12); for the people (Lev. 9:3, 15); on the Day of Atonement (Lev. 16:3, 5–6, 9, 11, 15, 25, 27); at the Feast of Weeks (Lev. 23:19); by the Nazirite (Num. 6:14–16); making atonement for the incense altar (Exod. 30:10); for cleansing the altar (Ezek. 43:19–27); for cleansing a priest (Ezek. 44:27); for the dedication of the temple (Ezra 6:17).

z A sin offering for cleansing: a woman after giving birth (Lev. 12:6, 8); a leper (Lev. 14:19, 22, 31); from a discharge (Lev. 15:15, 30); from defilement (Num. 6:11); from unintentional sin (Num. 15:24–5, 27).

aa Present the offering Moses commanded (Matt. 8:4; Mark 1:44; Luke 5:14); a pair of turtledoves or two young pigeons (Luke 2:24).

ab Sin offerings from the leaders (Num. 7:16, 22, 28, 34, 40, 46, 52, 58, 64, 70, 76, 82, 87); seven bulls, rams, lambs and goats for a sin offering (2 Chr. 29:21).

● Christ the
sin offering

ac God sent his own Son to be a sin offering (Rom. 8:3); the high priest offers sacrifices for his own sins as well as for the sins of the people (Heb. 5:3); which Christ does not; he offered himself as a sacrifice for sins once for all (Heb. 7:27); Christ was once offered to take away sins (Heb. 9:28; 10:12); Christ gave himself for us, a sacrifice to God (Eph. 5:2); the offering of the body of Jesus Christ (Heb. 10:10).

● Guilt
offering

ad Instructions on the guilt offering (Lev. 7:1–7); guilt offerings belong to the priests (Num. 18:9); a ram for their guilt (Ezra 10:19).

ae Guilt offering for sin (Lev. 5:6, 7, 15–16, 18–19; 6:6–7; 19:21–2); for a cleansed leper (Lev. 14:12–14, 17, 25, 28); for a defiled Nazirite (Num. 6:12); the Philistines gave a guilt offering with the ark (1 Sam. 6:3–4, 8, 17).

af The suffering servant will be a guilt offering (Isa. 53:10).

● Human
sacrifices

ag Offer your son Isaac as a burnt offering (Gen. 22:2); by faith Abraham offered Isaac as a sacrifice (Heb. 11:17); shall I give my firstborn for my transgression? (Mic. 6:7).

ah Jephthah offered up his daughter as a burnt offering (Judg. 11:31–9); the king of Moab sacrificed his son on the city wall (2 Kgs. 3:27); you sacrificed your sons and daughters as food to the idols (Ezek. 16:20); Ahaz made his son pass through the fire (2 Kgs. 16:3; 2 Chr. 28:3); they made their children pass through the fire (2 Kgs. 17:17; Jer. 7:31; Ezek. 20:26); as Manasseh did (2 Kgs. 21:6); making them pass through the fire for Molech (2 Kgs. 23:10; Jer. 32:35); they burned their sons in the fire to Baal (Jer. 19:5); they burned their children in the fire to the gods of Sepharvaim (2 Kgs. 17:31); they slaughtered their children for their idols (Ezek. 23:39); they sacrificed sons and daughters to demons (Ps. 106:37–8); Pilate mixed their blood with their sacrifices (Luke 13:1).

ai God's great sacrifice, for birds and beasts to eat men (Ezek. 39:17–20).

● Worshipping
men etc.

aj They worshipped the creature rather than the creator (Rom. 1:25); Nebuchadnezzar made an offering with incense to Daniel

(Dan. 2:46); the crowd wanted to offer sacrifices to Barnabas and Paul (Acts 14:13); Cornelius tried to worship Peter (Acts 10:25–6).

ak They sacrifice to their net (Hab. 1:16).

Worshipping the universe, see **321***j*.

● Worshipping angels

al I fell down to worship at the feet of the angel (Rev. 19:10; 22:8–9); worship of angels (Col. 2:18).

● Worshipping the devil

am All this I will give you if you will bow down and worship me (Matt. 4:9; Luke 4:7); men worshipped the dragon and the beast (Rev. 13:4); all inhabitants of the earth will worship the beast (Rev. 13:8, 12); if anyone worships the beast (Rev. 14:9); they had not worshipped the beast (Rev. 20:4).

Worshipping on the high places, see **209***ac*; **worshipping other gods**, see **966***d*.

● Enough of sacrifices

an Sacrifice and offering you did not desire (Ps. 40:6; Heb. 10:5–6); you do not delight in sacrifice (Ps. 51:16); you took no pleasure in burnt offering (Heb. 10:6, 8); shall I come before him with burnt offerings? (Mic. 6:6–7); I do not reprove you for your sacrifices (Ps. 50:8); I have no need of a bull from your stall (Ps. 50:9); I have more than enough of burnt offerings (Isa. 1:11–13); he who kills an ox is like he who kills a man (Isa. 66:3); add your burnt offerings to the sacrifices and eat the meat (Jer. 7:21–3).

ao Your sacrifices are not acceptable to me (Jer. 6:20); I will not accept your offerings (Amos 5:22); I will accept no offering from your hands (Mal. 1:10); God no longer regards your offering (Mal. 2:13); the Lord detests the sacrifice of the wicked (Prov. 15:8); the sacrifice of the wicked is detestable (Prov. 21:27); listen rather than offer the sacrifice of fools (Eccles. 5:1); leave your offering and be reconciled with your brother (Matt. 5:23–4).

ap Where there is forgiveness there is no longer any offering for sin (Heb. 10:18); if we sin wilfully there no longer remains a sacrifice for sins (Heb. 10:26).

● Right sacrifices

aq Offer right sacrifices and trust in the Lord (Ps. 4:5); you will delight in right sacrifices (Ps. 51:19).

ar The sacrifices of God are a broken spirit (Ps. 51:17); to do what is right and just is more acceptable to the Lord than sacrifice (Prov. 21:3); has the Lord as great delight in sacrifice as in obedience? (1 Sam. 15:22); I desire compassion more than sacrifice (Matt. 9:13; 12:7); to obey is better than sacrifice (1 Sam. 15:22); I desire steadfast love and the knowledge of God, not sacrifice (Hos. 6:6); to love God and one's neighbour is more than all sacrifices (Mark 12:33); to do good and to share are sacrifices which please God (Heb. 13:16).

as Offer a sacrifice of thanksgiving (Ps. 50:14); he who offers a sacrifice of thanksgiving honours me (Ps. 50:23); bring a sacrifice of praise and thanksgiving (Heb. 13:15).

at Present your bodies as living sacrifices (Rom. 12:1); offering spiritual sacrifices acceptable to God (1 Pet. 2:5); priestly service that the offering of the Gentiles might be acceptable (Rom. 15:16).

982 Idolatry

● Nature of idolatry

a Idolaters have no knowledge (Isa. 45:20); they exchanged the glory of God for an image (Ps. 106:20; Rom. 1:23); idolatry is a deed of the flesh (Gal. 5:20).

b The covetous are idolaters (Eph. 5:5); greed is idolatry (Col. 3:5); disobedience is as idolatry (1 Sam. 15:23); you who abhor idols, do you rob temples? (Rom. 2:22).

● Idols are hand-made

c He nails down an idol so that it will not topple (Isa. 41:7); of what value is an idol, since man has carved it? (Hab. 2:18–19); he says man-made gods are no gods at all (Acts 19:26); their idols are silver and gold, made by the hands of men (Ps. 115:4–8; 135:15–18); with silver and gold they make idols (Hos. 8:4); we should not think that God is like silver and gold an image made by man (Acts 17:29); the idol is made of materials by men (Isa. 40:19–20; 44:12–17; 46:6; Jer. 10:3–5, 8–9); craftsmen encouraging one another in making an idol (Isa. 41:6–7).
Man-made gods, see **966***j*.

● Idols are useless

d You have seen their idols (Deut. 29:17); their idols are borne by beasts of burden (Isa. 46:1–2); all who make idols are nothing and the things they treasure are worthless (Isa. 44:9–10); their molten images are empty wind (Isa. 41:29); his images are false with no breath in them (Jer. 51:17); you were led astray to dumb idols (1 Cor. 12:2); they can do no harm, nor can they do good (Jer. 10:3–5); the idols of Egypt tremble before the Lord (Isa. 19:1); the idols will utterly vanish (Isa. 2:18).
Trusting in idols, see **485***ak*.

● Shun idolatry

e Do not make idols (Exod. 20:4; 34:17; Lev. 19:4; 26:1; Deut. 4:16, 23; 5:8); do not make for yourselves gods of silver and gold (Exod. 20:23).

f Do not worship idols (Exod. 20:5); turn away from your idols (Ezek. 14:6); do not defile yourself with the idols of Egypt (Ezek. 20:7); keep yourselves from idols (1 John 5:21); do not be idolaters as they were (1 Cor. 10:7); flee from idolatry (1 Cor. 10:14); what has the temple of God to do with idols? (2 Cor. 6:16); how you turned to God from idols (1 Thess. 1:9).

g Do not associate with a 'brother' who is an idolater (1 Cor. 5:11).

● Food offered to idols

h Instructions concerning food offered to idols (1 Cor. 8:1–13; 10:14–33); Gentiles warned to abstain from food sacrificed to idols (Acts 15:20, 29; 21:25).

i The Israelites ate food offered to idols (Rev. 2:14); eating sacrifices to other gods (Exod. 34:15; Num. 25:2); idolaters, sitting down to eat and drink (Exod. 32:6; 1 Cor. 10:7); teaching God's servants to eat food offered to idols (Rev. 2:14, 20).

● Idolatry
at Sinai

j Aaron made an idol in the form of a calf (Exod. 32:4); make us gods to go before us (Acts 7:40); they made a molten image (Deut. 9:12); a molten calf (Deut. 9:16; Neh. 9:18); they made a calf in Horeb (Ps. 106:19).

● Idolatry in
Samaria

k Jeroboam made two golden calves (1 Kgs. 12:28–9; 2 Chr. 13:8); the worship of the golden calves at Bethel and Dan (2 Kgs. 10:29); you have made for yourselves other gods, idols made of metal (1 Kgs. 14:9); they made molten images and two calves (2 Kgs. 17:16); Jeroboam appointed priests for the goat and calf idols he had made (2 Chr. 11:15); he has rejected your calf, Samaria (Hos. 8:5–6); Samaria fears for the calf of Beth-aven (Hos. 10:5); Samaria and her idols (Isa. 10:10–11).

● Jews and
idolatry

l Gideon made an ephod of gold (Judg. 8:27); Micah made an ephod and teraphim (Judg. 17:3–5; 18:14); they took the image, teraphim and ephod (Judg. 18:17–18, 20); the Danites set up the graven image (Judg. 18:30–1); Michal put teraphim in her bed (1 Sam. 19:13, 16).

m Ahab followed idols (1 Kgs. 21:26); Manasseh put the image he had made in God's temple (2 Kgs. 21:7; 2 Chr. 33:7, 19); Amon served idols (2 Kgs. 21:21; 2 Chr. 33:22).

n The elders of Israel, each at the shrine of his own idol (Ezek. 8:12); these men have set up their idols in their hearts (Ezek. 14:3, 4, 7); they consult a wooden idol (Hos. 4:12); they make idols for themselves from their silver (Hos. 13:2); they worshipped idols (2 Kgs. 17:12); their land is full of idols (Isa. 2:8); my people burn incense to worthless idols (Jer. 18:15); Molech and Rephan, the idols you made to worship (Acts 7:42–3); there you will worship man-made gods of wood and stone (Deut. 4:28); they served the idols of the peoples (Ps. 106:36).

● Gentiles
and idolatry

o King Nebuchadnezzar made an image of gold (Dan. 3:1); you must worship the image of gold (Dan. 3:5); they neither serve your gods nor worship the image of gold (Dan. 3:12, 14); we will not serve your gods (Dan. 3:18); they set up an image in honour of the beast (Rev. 13:14); Paul was distressed to see Athens full of idols (Acts 17:16).

● God and
idolatry

p They made him jealous with their graven images (Ps. 78:58); I saw the idol of jealousy (Ezek. 8:5); lest you should say your idol has done it (Isa. 48:5).

● Destroying
idols

q The images of their gods you are to burn in the fire (Deut. 7:25); Asa removed the idols (1 Kgs. 15:12; 2 Chr. 15:8); Hezekiah broke in pieces the bronze snake Moses had made (2 Kgs. 18:4); Josiah removed the horses that the kings of Judah had dedicated to the sun (2 Kgs. 23:11); and the teraphim and idols (2 Kgs. 23:24); Manasseh removed the idol (2 Chr. 33:15); Josiah removed all the detestable idols (2 Chr. 34:3).

r The Philistines abandoned their idols (2 Sam. 5:21); men will throw away their idols of silver and gold (Isa. 2:20); then you will defile your idols (Isa. 30:22); every one of you will reject the idols your hands have made (Isa. 31:7); the images of Babylon's gods are shattered (Isa. 21:9); I will destroy the idols of Egypt (Ezek. 30:13); I will cut off the names of idols from the land (Zech. 13:2).

Burning idols, see **381h**.

● Fate of idolaters

s I will put your corpses on the corpses of your idols (Lev. 26:30); all who worship images are put to shame (Ps. 97:7); those who trust in idols will be put to shame (Isa. 42:17); all makers of idols will be put to shame (Isa. 45:16); let idolaters be ashamed (Ps. 97:7); cursed is the man who carves an image or casts an idol (Deut. 27:15); I hate those who cling to worthless idols (Ps. 31:6).

t Idolaters will not inherit the kingdom of God (1 Cor. 6:9); idolaters will end in the lake of fire (Rev. 21:8); idolaters will be outside the city (Rev. 22:15); let the time that is past suffice for idolatries (1 Pet. 4:3); they did not repent of their idolatry (Rev. 9:20).

983 Sorcery

● Nature of sorcery

a Sorcery is a deed of the flesh (Gal. 5:20); rebellion is as the sin of divination (1 Sam. 15:23).

b Sorcerers will end in the lake of fire (Rev. 21:8); outside the city (Rev. 22:15).

● Avoid sorcery

c Do not allow a sorceress to live (Exod. 22:18); do not practise divination or sorcery (Lev. 19:26; Deut. 18:10, 14); woe to the women who sew magic charms on their wrists (Ezek. 13:18).

d How can there be peace as long as the witchcraft of Jezebel abounds? (2 Kgs. 9:22).

● Practice of sorcery

e I have learned by divination that the Lord has blessed me through you (Gen. 30:27); is not this the cup my master uses for divination? (Gen. 44:5); do you not know I can find things out by divination? (Gen. 44:15); the Egyptian magicians did the same by their secret arts (Exod. 7:11); Balaam the diviner (Josh. 13:22); they practised divination and enchantments (2 Kgs. 17:17); Manasseh practised sorcery and divination (2 Kgs. 21:6; 2 Chr. 33:6); the king of Babylon will seek an omen (Ezek. 21:21); they practise' divination like the Philistines (Isa. 2:6); Simon had practised sorcery in Samaria (Acts 8:9); a girl with a spirit of divination (Acts 16:16); many who had practiced magic burnt their books (Acts 19:19).

f The Philistines called for priests and diviners (1 Sam. 6:2–9); the king summoned the magicians, enchanters, sorcerors and astrologers (Dan. 2:2); magi from the east (Matt. 2:1, 7).

g The nations practice witchcraft (Deut. 18:14); nations were deceived by the sorcery of Babylon (Rev. 18:23); they did not repent of their sorceries (Rev. 9:21); in spite of your sorceries and spells (Isa. 47:9); let your astrologers save you (Isa. 47:13); your spells and sorceries just might succeed (Isa. 47:12).

h Who has bewitched you? (Gal. 3:1).

- Sorcery
ineffective

i There is no sorcery against Jacob, no divination against Israel (Num. 23:23); Balaam did not resort to sorcery as at other times (Num. 24:1); I will cut off sorceries and fortune-telling (Mic. 5:12).

j God makes fools of diviners (Isa. 44:25); I will be a swift witness against the sorcerers (Mal. 3:5).

984 Occultism

- Practice of
spiritism

a The Egyptians will consult the spirits of the dead, the mediums and spiritists (Isa. 19:3); Saul calling up the dead through a medium (1 Sam. 28:7–14); Saul asked counsel of a medium (1 Chr. 10:13); Manasseh dealt with mediums and spiritists (2 Kgs. 21:6; 2 Chr. 33:6); they ate sacrifices offered to the dead (Ps. 106:28).

- Avoid
spiritism

b Do not turn to mediums or seek out spiritists (Lev. 19:31; 20:6); mediums and spiritists are to be stoned (Lev. 20:27); let no one be a medium or spiritist or consult the dead (Deut. 18:11); why consult the dead on behalf of the living? (Isa. 8:19).

- Avoiding
spiritism

c I have not offered the tithe to the dead (Deut. 26:14); Saul had expelled the mediums and spiritists (1 Sam. 28:3, 9); Josiah got rid of the mediums and spiritists (2 Kgs. 23:24).

985 The church

- The church
universal

a On this rock I will build my church (Matt. 16:18); the church of the firstborn (Heb. 12:23); Christ is the head of the church (Eph. 1:22; 5:23; Col. 1:18); his body, the church (Col. 1:24); Christ loved the church and gave himself up for her (Eph. 5:25–7, 29); I speak about Christ and the church (Eph. 5:32); the church of God which he obtained with his own blood (Acts 20:28); the wisdom of God made known to principalities through the church (Eph. 3:10); God has appointed in the church apostles etc. (1 Cor. 12:28); to him be glory in the church (Eph. 3:21).
The church as Christ's body, see **319f**.

b Fear came on the whole church (Acts 5:11); persecution arose against the church (Acts 8:1); I persecuted the church of God (1 Cor. 15:9; Gal. 1:13); persecutor of the church (Phil. 3:6); Paul laid the church waste (Acts 8:3); the church throughout Judea, Galilee and Samaria had peace (Acts 9:31); prayer was made by the church (Acts 12:5); if someone refuses to listen to the church (Matt. 18:17); do you despise the church of God? (1 Cor. 11:22); give no offense to the church of God (1 Cor. 10:32).

- The local
church

c They appointed elders in every church (Acts 14:23); call for the elders of the church (Jas. 5:14); Paul strengthened the churches

(Acts 15:41); the churches were strengthened (Acts 16:5); concern for all the churches (2 Cor. 11:28); if a man cannot manage his own household, how can he care for the church of God? (1 Tim. 3:5); the household of God, the church of the living God (1 Tim. 3:15); when you come together as a church (1 Cor. 11:18); edifying the church (1 Cor. 14:4, 5, 12); in the church I would rather speak five words with my mind (1 Cor. 14:19); let the women keep silence in the churches (1 Cor. 14:34, 35); let the church not be burdened (1 Tim. 5:16).

d The churches of God have no other practice (1 Cor. 11:16); as I teach in every church (1 Cor. 4:17; 7:17); as in all the churches (1 Cor. 14:33); as I directed the churches of Galatia (1 Cor. 16:1). **Prophecy in the church**, see **579ag**.

- **Local churches**

e The church in Jerusalem (Acts 11:22; 15:4, 22); the church in Antioch (Acts 11:26; 13:1; 14:27; 15:3); the church in Caesarea (Acts 18:22); the church in Cenchrea (Rom. 16:1); to the church of God at Corinth (1 Cor. 1:2; 2 Cor. 1:1); to the churches of Galatia (Gal. 1:2); to the church of the Thessalonians (1 Thess. 1:1; 2 Thess. 1:1); the grace of God in the churches of Macedonia (2 Cor. 8:1); the church of the Laodiceans (Col. 4:16); the churches of the Gentiles (Rom. 16:4); the churches in Judea (Gal. 1:22; 1 Thess. 2:14); the seven churches in Asia (Rev. 1:4, 11); the seven lampstands are the seven churches (Rev. 1:20).

f Letter to the church in: Ephesus (Rev. 2:1–7); Smyrna (Rev. 2:8–11); Pergamum (Rev. 2:12–17); Thyatira (Rev. 2:18–29); Sardis (Rev. 3:1–6); Philadelphia (Rev. 3:7–13); Laodicea (Rev. 3:14–22).
Letters to churches, see **588f**.

g Paul greeted the church (Acts 18:22); the church in their house (Rom. 16:5; 1 Cor. 16:19); to the church in your house (Philem. 2); the church in her house (Col. 4:15).

986 Priests and elders

- **Priests**

a Regulations for the priests (Lev. 21:1–24; Ezek. 44:15–31); a priest must not defile himself by going near a dead body (Lev. 21:1; Ezek. 44:25).
Anointing priests, see **357d**; **killing priests**, see **362am**; **priestly inheritance**, see **777j**.

- **Aaronic priesthood**

b Aaron and his sons will serve me as priests (Exod. 28:1, 3); the sons of Aaron are serving as priests (2 Chr. 13:10); the priests, the sons of Aaron, are to burn incense (2 Chr. 26:18); they were given the priesthood (Num. 18:7); a covenant of perpetual priesthood (Num. 25:13); the consecration of the priests (Exod. 29:1; 40:13, 15); Aaron's sons, the anointed priests (Num. 3:3); Aaron's sons make atonement (1 Chr. 6:49); Korah and others sought the priesthood (Num. 16:10).

● Work of
the priests

c The Lord has chosen you to minister (2 Chr. 29:11); the priests were to blow the trumpets (Num. 10:8); the priest to address the people going to war (Deut. 20:2–4); the priests carried the ark (Josh. 3:3, 14, 17; 4:10, 16, 18); priests collect the tithe (Heb. 7:5); priests were given tax of the booty (Num. 31:28–9, 41); a teaching priest (2 Chr. 15:3); show yourselve to the priests (Luke 17:14).

● Particular
priests

d Those who were priests: Hophni and Phineas (1 Sam. 1:3); Zadok and Ahimelech [Abimelech] (2 Sam. 8:17; 1 Chr. 18:16); Zadok and Abiathar (2 Sam. 20:25; 1 Kgs. 4:4; 1 Chr. 15:11); Ira the Jairite, a priest to David (2 Sam. 20:26); Zadok the priest (1 Kgs. 1:8, 26, 32, 34, 38, 44–5; 2:35; 1 Chr. 16:39); Abiathar the priest (1 Kgs. 1:7, 19, 25, 42; 2:22, 26–7); Zabud the king's friend (1 Kgs. 4:5); Urijah the priest (2 Kgs. 16:10–11); Zephaniah the second priest (2 Kgs. 25:18); Eleazar and Ithamar (1 Chr. 24:2); Azariah the priest (2 Chr. 26:17); Ezra the priest (Ezra 7:11, 12, 21); Jeremiah (Jer. 1:1); Passhur (Jer. 20:1); Zephaniah (Jer. 21:1); Ezekiel the priest (Ezek. 1:3); Zacharias (Luke 1:5); Sceva (Acts 19:14).

e Let one of the priests teach them (2 Kgs. 17:27–8); 12 of the leading priests (Ezra 8:24); Moses and Aaron were among his priests (Ps. 99:6); many of the priests were obedient to the faith (Acts 6:7).

Sacrifices as food for the priests, see **301***aa*.

● Faithful
priests

f I will raise up for myself a faithful priest (1 Sam. 2:35); may your priests be clothed with salvation (2 Chr. 6:41); with righteousness (Ps. 132:9); I will clothe her priests with salvation (Ps. 132:16).

g Zadok, Abiathar and the Levites brought the ark (2 Sam. 15:24); Zadok and Abiathar were for David (2 Sam. 15:35–6); the priests and Levites sided with Rehoboam (2 Chr. 11:13); the priests and Levites who returned with Zerubbabel (Neh. 12:1–8).

● High priest

h Regulations for the high priest (Lev. 21:10–15); Aaron was to bear the guilt of the priesthood (Num. 18:1); every high priest is selected to offer gifts and sacrifices (Heb. 5:1; 8:3); only the high priest entered the inner chamber (Heb. 9:7).

i Aaron the priest (Exod. 31:10; 35:19; 38:21; 39:41; Lev. 1:7; 13:2); the priest who is anointed and ordained (Lev. 16:32); the high priest (Lev. 21:10); the anointed priest (Lev. 4:16).

j If the anointed priest sins (Lev. 4:3, 5); manslayers remain in the city of refuge until the death of the high priest (Num. 35:25, 28, 32; Josh. 20:6).

● Particular
high priests

k Those who were high priests: Eleazar (Num. 20:26–8); Eli (1 Sam. 1:9); Ahimelech (1 Sam. 21:1); Azariah served as high priest in Solomon's temple (1 Chr. 6:10); Abiathar, then Zadok (1 Kgs. 2:35); Azariah son of Zadok (1 Kgs. 4:2); Hilkiah (2 Kgs. 22:4; 23:4; 2 Chr. 34:9); Seraiah (2 Kgs. 25:18; Jer.

52:24); Zadok anointed as priest (1 Chr. 29:22); Amariah (2 Chr. 19:11); Jehoiada (2 Chr. 24:6); Azariah of the house of Zadok (2 Chr. 31:10); Eliashib the high priest (Neh. 3:1, 20; 12:10–11; 13:4, 28); Joshua son of Jehozadak (Hag. 2:2); Joshua the high priest (Zech. 3:1); Caiaphas (Matt. 26:3, 57; John 11:49; 18:13, 24); Annas and Caiaphas (Luke 3:2; Acts 4:6); Ananias (Acts 24:1).

l They led Jesus away to the high priest (Mark 14:53); the high priest questioned Jesus (Mark 14:60); the high priest rose up and his associates, the Sadducees (Acts 5:17); would you revile God's high priest? (Acts 23:4).

m The Lord has made Zephaniah high priest instead of Jehoiada (Jer. 29:26).

● High-priestly family

n Herod gathered the chief priests (Matt. 2:4); he must suffer many things from the chief priests (Matt. 16:21; Luke 9:22); he will be delivered to the chief priests (Matt. 20:18).

o Judas went to the chief priests (Matt. 26:14); a mob from the chief priests and elders (Matt. 26:47); all of the high-priestly family (Acts 4:6).

p The chief priests: were indignant (Matt. 21:15); asked him of his authority (Matt. 21:23; Mark 11:27–8); plotted to kill him (Matt. 26:3; 27:1; Mark 11:18; 14:1; Luke 19:47; 22:2); planned to kill Lazarus also (John 12:10); accused Jesus (Matt. 27:12; Mark 15:3; Luke 23:10); persuaded the crowds (Matt. 27:20; Mark 15:11); mocked him (Matt. 27:41; Mark 15:31); asked Pilate to set a guard (Matt. 27:62–4); took counsel together (Matt. 28:12).

● Non-Levitical priests

q Melchizedek was priest of God most high (Gen. 14:18; Heb. 7:1); Potipherah priest of On (Gen. 41:45, 50; 46:20); the land of the Egyptian priests was not bought (Gen. 47:22, 26); Reuel [Jethro] priest of Midian (Exod. 2:16; 3:1; 18:1).

r Micah made his own son a priest (Judg. 17:5); Jeroboam appointed priests from all sorts of people (1 Kgs. 12:31; 13:33; 2 Chr. 11:15); you drive out the priests of the Lord and made your own priests (2 Chr. 13:9); Josiah will sacrifice the priests of the high places (1 Kgs. 13:2); as he did (2 Kgs. 23:20); idolatrous priests who burned incense to other gods (2 Kgs. 23:5); Mattan the priest of Baal (2 Kgs. 11:18); Amaziah, priest of Bethel (Amos 7:10).

● Deficiencies of priests

s The priests rule by their own authority (Jer. 5:31); both prophet and priest are polluted (Jer. 23:11); her priests profane what is sacred (Zeph. 3:4); the life of a priest ought to preserve knowledge (Mal. 2:7); the priest and Levite passed by on the other side (Luke 10:31–2).

● Deposed priests

t The priests were slaughtered (1 Sam. 22:17–19, 21); Solomon removed Abiathar from the priesthood (1 Kgs. 2:27); the Lord has made Zephaniah high priest instead of Jehoiada (Jer. 29:26).

● A priest for
ever

   u You are a priest for ever after the order of Melchizedek (Ps. 110:4; Heb. 5:6, 10; 6:20; 7:11, 17); a priest for ever (Heb. 7:3, 21); he has permanent priesthood (Heb. 7:24); the man called the Branch will be a priest on his throne (Zech. 6:13).

● A great
high priest

   v Jesus, the apostle and high priest of our confession (Heb. 3:1); we have a great high priest (Heb. 4:14); a great high priest over the house of God (Heb. 10:21); we have a high priest who has been tempted, yet without sin (Heb. 4:15); if perfection was attained by the Levitical priesthood, why was there need for another priest? (Heb. 7:11); the law appoints weak men as high priests, but the oath appoints the Son (Heb. 7:28); Christ did not glorify himself to become high priest (Heb. 5:5).

   w I will raise up a faithful priest (1 Sam. 2:35); a merciful and faithful high priest (Heb. 2:17); a priest of the good things to come (Heb. 9:11); we have a high priest who sat down in heaven (Heb. 8:1); it was fitting that we should have such a high priest (Heb. 7:26).

● Kingdom
of priests

   x You will be called priests of the Lord (Isa. 61:6); he has made us a kingdom and priests (Rev. 1:6; 5:10); a kingdom of priests (Exod. 19:6); a royal priesthood (1 Pet. 2:9); a holy priesthood (1 Pet. 2:5); they will be priests of God and of Christ (Rev. 20:6); the priestly service of the gospel (Rom. 15:16).

● Levites

   y Levites: belong to God (Num. 8:14, 16); given to Aaron and his sons (Num. 3:9; 8:19; 18:6); joined to the priests (Num. 18:2, 4); set apart for special duties (Deut. 10:8–9); to have charge of the tabernacle (Num. 1:50–3; 3:6–8); to camp around the tabernacle (Num. 1:53; 2:17); were not numbered (Num. 1:47–9); have no inheritance (Deut. 18:1); have permanent right of redemption on their houses (Lev. 25:32–3); have charge of the temple (Ezek. 44:14); will not serve as priests (Ezek. 44:13).

   z Do not neglect the Levite (Deut. 12:19; 14:27); invite Levites to the Feast of Booths (Deut. 16:14).

  aa Levites given: food (Deut. 14:29); firstfruits (Deut. 26:11); tax of the booty (Num. 31:30, 47); the tithe (Deut. 26:12–13; Neh. 10:37–8).

  ab The Levites arose and consecrated themselves (2 Chr. 29:12–15); Ezra did not find any Levites (Ezra 8:15); Levites were sent for and came (Ezra 8:16–20); he will refine the sons of Levi (Mal. 3:3).

  ac The Levite became his priest (Judg. 17:12–13; 18:4); be a father and a priest to me (Judg. 17:10); to us (Judg. 18:19); is it better to be a priest to one man or to a tribe? (Judg. 18:19); you have stolen the priest (Judg. 18:24).

  ad A Levite passed by on the other side (Luke 10:32).

● Elders

  ae Gather the elders of Israel (Exod. 3:16); they gathered all the elders of Israel (Exod. 4:29; 12:21); 70 of the elders of Israel

(Exod. 24:1, 9; Num. 11:16, 24–5); Joshua went up with the elders of Israel (Josh. 8:10).

af He must suffer many things from the elders (Matt. 16:21); the high priests and elders asked him of his authority (Matt. 21:23).

ag Appoint elders in every town (Titus 1:5); they appointed elders in every church (Acts 14:23); the apostles and elders met to consider this matter (Acts 15:6); Paul called together the elders of the church (Acts 20:17); the overseers in Philippi (Phil. 1:1); 24 elders (Rev. 4:4, 10; 5:8; 11:16).

ah Requirements for elders [overseers] (1 Tim. 3:1–7; Titus 1:6–9); elders who rule well should be given double honour (1 Tim. 5:17–18); accusations against elders (1 Tim. 5:19–20); let the sick one call for the elders of the church (Jas. 5:14); to the elders I appeal as a fellow-elder (1 Pet. 5:1–3).

987 Laity

God's people, see **371***ac*.

988 Ritual

● Festivals in general

a Three times a year you are to celebrate a festival (Exod. 23:14; 2 Chr. 8:13); three times a year, for the feasts of Unleavened Bread, Weeks and Booths (Deut. 16:16); these are my appointed feasts (Lev. 23:2); the appointed feasts (Ezek. 46:9, 11); your appointed feasts (Num. 10:10); the fixed festivals (2 Chr. 31:3; Ezra 3:5); Zion, city of our appointed feasts (Isa. 33:20); no one comes to Zion's appointed feasts (Lam. 1:4); Jesus went up to Jerusalem for a feast of the Jews (John 5:1); let no one judge you with regard to a festival, New Moon or sabbath (Col. 2:16); let my people go that they may hold a festival to me (Exod. 5:1); we are to celebrate a festival to the Lord (Exod. 10:9); a feast of the Lord in Shiloh (Judg. 21:19).

Ceremonies as signs, see **547***b*.

b I hate your festivals (Amos 5:21).

● Passover

c The regulations for the passover (Exod. 12:43–9); the Lord's passover (Exod. 12:11–13, 27); the passover begins on the fourteenth day of the first month (Lev. 23:5; Num. 28:16; Ezek. 45:21); those who are unclean may eat it in the second month (Num. 9:9–12).

d Celebrate the feast of Unleavened Bread (Exod. 12:17; 23:15; 34:18); for generations to come you shall celebrate it as a festival to the Lord (Exod. 12:14); celebrate the passover (Deut. 16:1; Num. 9:2; 2 Kgs. 23:21); when you enter the land, observe this ceremony (Exod. 12:25; 13:5).

Not keeping passover, see **769***e*.

● Passover celebrated

e By faith Moses kept the passover (Heb. 11:28); at Gilgal the Israelites celebrated the passover (Josh. 5:10); Hezekiah sent invitations to celebrate the passover (2 Chr. 30:1); a crowd assembled to celebrate the feast of Unleavened Bread (2 Chr. 30:13); they continued for a further seven days (2 Chr. 30:23); Josiah celebrated the passover (2 Chr. 35:1, 16); the exiles celebrated the passover (Ezra 6:19).

f When Jesus was twelve he went up to the feast of the passover (Luke 2:41–3); when it was about time for the passover, Jesus went up to Jerusalem (John 2:13); the feast of the passover was near (John 6:4); it was almost time for the passover (John 11:55); six days before the passover (John 12:1); it was just before the passover (John 13:1); the passover was two days away (Matt. 26:2; Mark 14:1); the feast of Unleavened Bread was approaching (Luke 22:1); on the first day of the feast of Unleavened Bread the disciples made preparations (Matt. 26:17; Mark 14:12; Luke 22:7–8); I have eagerly desired to eat this passover with you (Luke 22:15); not during the feast, or the people may riot (Matt. 26:5; Mark 14:2); at the feast the governor's custom was to release a prisoner (Matt. 27:17; Mark 15:6; Luke 23:17; John 18:39); if they were defiled they could not eat the passover (John 18:28); Herod arrested Peter during the feast of Unleavened Bread (Acts 12:3); we sailed from Philippi after the feast of Unleavened Bread (Acts 20:6).

g Christ our passover has been sacrificed (1 Cor. 5:7–8); the passover fulfilled in the kingdom of God (Luke 22:16).

● Feast of weeks (Pentecost)

h Celebrate the feast of harvest with the firstfruits (Exod. 23:16; Lev. 23:9–14); celebrate the feast of weeks with the firstfruits of the wheat harvest (Exod. 34:22); count off fifty days to the day after the seventh sabbath (Lev. 23:15–16); on the day of firstfruits during the feast of weeks (Num. 28:26); celebrate the feast of weeks (Deut. 16:10); when the day of Pentecost came (Acts 2:1); Paul tried to reach Jerusalem by Pentecost (Acts 20:16); I shall stay in Ephesus until Pentecost (1 Cor. 16:8).

● Feast of booths (tabernacles)

i Celebrate the feast of ingathering at the end of the year (Exod. 23:16); on the fifteenth day of the seventh month is the feast of tabernacles (Lev. 23:33–6, 39–43; Num. 29:12–38; Deut. 16:13–15); the feast in the seventh month (1 Kgs. 8:2, 65; 2 Chr. 5:3); they celebrated the feast of tabernacles (Ezra 3:4; Neh. 8:14–18); the nations will go up to Jerusalem to celebrate the feast of tabernacles (Zech. 14:16–19); the feast of tabernacles was near (John 7:2); at the end of every seven years at the feast of booths (Deut. 31:10); I will make you live in tents, as at the festival (Hos. 12:9).

● Year of Jubilee

j The fiftieth year will be a year of Jubilee (Lev. 25:8–12); when the year of Jubilee comes (Num. 36:4); the year of liberty (Ezek. 46:17).

● Feast of trumpets

k On the first day of the seventh month is the feast of Trumpets (Lev. 23:24–5; Num. 29:1–6).

● Various
festivals

l Tomorrow is the New Moon festival (1 Sam. 20:5); it is not the New Moon or sabbath (2 Kgs. 4:23); the fourteenth and fifteenth days of the month Adar were to be celebrated annually (Esther 9:21); Solomon observed the festival [of dedication of the temple] (2 Chr. 7:8–10); dedication of the rebuilt temple (Ezra 6:16); the feast of Dedication at Jerusalem (John 10:22). **Day of Atonement**, see **941a; sabbath**, see **683a.**

● Circumcision

m Every male shall be circumcised (Gen. 17:10–14); circumcised on the eighth day (Lev. 12:3); he gave him the covenant of circumcision (Acts 7:8); Moses gave you circumcision (John 7:22); a slave may eat the passover after he has been circumcised (Exod. 12:44); an alien who wants to celebrate the passover must have his males circumcised (Exod. 12:48); circumcision is permitted on the sabbath (John 7:22–3).

● Circumcision
performed

n Abraham circumcised every male in his household (Gen. 17:23); those who were circumcised: Isaac (Gen. 21:4; Acts 7:8); the men of Shechem (Gen. 34:15–24); Moses' son (Exod. 4:25–6); the Israelites at Gilgal (Josh. 5:2, 7–8); John the Baptist (Luke 1:59); Jesus (Luke 2:21); Timothy (Acts 16:3); Paul (Phil. 3:5).

● Is circumcision
necessary?

o Unless you are circumcised you canot be saved (Acts 15:1); the Gentiles must be circumcised (Acts 15:5); not even Titus was compelled to be circumcised (Gal. 2:3); if you let yourselves be circumcised, Christ will be of no value to you (Gal. 5:2–3); those who want to make a good impression compel you to be circumcised (Gal. 6:12); many deceivers, especially the circumcision party (Titus 1:10); circumcision is only of value if you keep the law (Rom. 2:25–7); those who are circumcised do not keep the law (Gal. 6:13); if I preach circumcision the stumbling block of the cross is removed (Gal. 5:11); Paul was said to teach Jews to forsake circumcision (Acts 21:21).

p Whether you are circumcised or uncircumcised, do not try to alter it (1 Cor. 7:18); neither circumcision nor uncircumcision is anything (1 Cor. 7:19; Gal. 5:6; 6:15); is this blessedness only for the circumcised? (Rom. 4:9); Abraham was the father of the circumcised and uncircumcised who believe (Rom. 4:11–12); there is no distinction between circumcised and uncircumcised (Col. 3:11); God justifies both circumcised and uncircumcised through faith (Rom. 3:30).

● True
circumcision

q The Lord will circumcise your hearts (Deut. 30:6); circumcise your hearts (Deut. 10:16; Jer. 4:4); in him you were circumcised, not done by men (Col. 2:11); I will punish all who are circumcised only in the flesh (Jer. 9:25–6); circumcision is of the heart, not external (Rom. 2:28–9); we are the true circumcision (Phil. 3:3).

● Baptism into
Moses

r Our fathers were all baptised into Moses (1 Cor. 10:2).

● John
baptising

s John the baptiser (Matt. 3:1; 17:13); confessing their sins, they were baptised by John (Matt. 3:6); John was baptising (John 3:23) John preached a baptism of repentance for forgiveness (Mark 1:4; Luke 3:3; Acts 13:24); beginning at the baptism of John (Acts 1:22); John's baptism (Acts 10:37); I baptise you with water (Matt. 3:11; Mark 1:8; Luke 3:16; John 1:26); why do you baptise if you are not the Christ? (John 1:25); was John's baptism from heaven or from men? (Matt. 21:25; Mark 11:30; Luke 20:4); I came baptising in water that he might be manifested (John 1:31); he went to the place where John had baptised (John 10:40).

● Baptised by
John

t Apollos knew only the baptism of John (Acts 18:25); the disciples in Ephesus knew only John's baptism (Acts 19:3–4); the people had been baptised by John (Luke 7:29); tax-collectors came to be baptised (Luke 3:12); Pharisees and Saducees coming for baptism (Matt. 3:7); the Pharisees and scribes had not been baptised by John (Luke 7:30).

● Jesus'
baptism

u Jesus came to be baptised by John (Matt. 3:13; Mark 1:9; Luke 3:21); John tried to prevent Jesus being baptised (Matt. 3:14).

v Can you drink the cup I drink or be baptised with the baptism I undergo? (Mark 10:38); I have a baptism to undergo (Luke 12:50).

● Christian
baptism

w Jesus is baptising and everyone is going to him (John 3:22, 26; John 4:1); though it was not Jesus who baptised, but his disciples (John 4:2); make disciples, baptising them in the name of Father, Son and Spirit (Matt. 28:19); they were baptised in the name of the Lord Jesus (Acts 19:5); repent and be baptised (Acts 2:38); those who received the message were baptised (Acts 2:41); the Samaritans were baptised (Acts 8:12); the Ethiopian eunuch was baptised (Acts 8:36, 38); rise, be baptised and wash away your sins (Acts 22:16); Saul got up and was baptised (Acts 9:18); who can forbid these people being baptised with water since they have received the Holy Spirit? (Acts 10:47); Cornelius and his friends were baptised in the name of Jesus Christ (Acts 10:48); the Philippian jailer was baptised (Acts 16:33); Lydia and her household were baptised (Acts 16:15); many Corinthians believed and were baptised (Acts 18:8).

Baptism with water, see **339t**.

● Baptised
into Christ

x We were baptised into his death (Rom. 6:3–4); buried with him in baptism (Col. 2:12); by one Spirit we were all baptised into one body (1 Cor. 12:13); you who have been baptised into Christ have put on Christ (Gal. 3:27); were you baptised in the name of Paul? (1 Cor. 1:13–16); this water symbolises baptism that now saves you (1 Pet. 3:21); he who believes and is baptised will be saved (Mark 16:16); one Lord, one faith, one baptism (Eph. 4:5).

● Baptised with
the Spirit

y He will baptise you with the Holy Spirit (Mark 1:8; Acts 11:16); and fire (Matt. 3:11; Luke 3:16); he is the one who will baptise with the Holy Spirit (John 1:33); you will be baptised with the Holy Spirit (Acts 1:5; 11:16); by one Spirit we were all baptised and all drink of one Spirit (1 Cor. 12:13).

Baptism in the Spirit, see **965w**.

● Baptised for the dead   *z* What will those do who are baptised for the dead? (1 Cor. 15:29).

989 Priests' garments

● Holy garments   *a* Holy garments for glory and for beauty (Exod. 28:2, 40); making the garments (Exod. 31:10; 35:19; 39:1, 41); putting on the garments (Lev. 8:7–9; 16:4, 32); put the holy garments on Aaron (Exod. 40:13); Aaron's garment shall be for his sons after him (Exod. 29:29); strip Aaron of his garments and put them on Eleazar his son (Num. 20:26, 28); Aaron's sons clothed (Lev. 8:13); changing their holy garments (Ezek. 42:14; 44:19).

b Clothed in linen, not wool (Ezek. 44:17).

● Breastpiece   *c* The breastpiece (Exod. 25:7; 28:4, 15–30; 29:5; 35:9, 27; 39:8–21).

● Ephods   *d* The ephod (Exod. 25:7; 28:4, 6–14; 29:5; 35:9, 27; 39:2–7); Ahijah was wearing an ephod (1 Sam. 14:3); Abiathar fled with an ephod in his hand (1 Sam. 23:6, 9); ephod used to enquire of God (1 Sam. 30:7–8); David wore a linen ephod (2 Sam. 6:14).

e The robe of the ephod (Exod. 28:4, 31–5; 29:5; 39:22–6).

● Tunics   *f* The tunic (Exod. 28:4, 39; 29:5); tunics for Aaron's sons (Exod. 28:40; 29:8; 39:27).

● Turban and caps   *g* The turban (Exod. 28:4, 37, 39; 29:6; 39:28); caps for Aaron's sons (Exod. 28:40; 29:9; 39:28).

● Priests' girdles   *h* The girdle (Exod. 28:4, 39; 39:29); girdles for Aaron's sons (Exod. 28:40; 29:9).

● Undergarments   *i* Linen undergarments (Exod. 28:42; 39:28; Lev. 6:10; 16:4; Ezek. 44:18);

990 Temple

● Altars in general   *a* Make an altar of earth (Exod. 20:24); not an altar of cut stone (Exod. 20:25); no steps to the altar (Exod. 20:26); build an altar at Bethel (Gen. 35:1); build an altar on mount Ebal (Deut. 27:5); build an altar to the Lord your God (Judg. 6:26); build an altar on the threshing-floor of Araunah the Jebusite (2 Sam. 24:18; 1 Chr. 21:18).

● Altar of burnt offering   *b* Build an altar of acacia wood (Exod. 27:1); building the altar of burnt offering (Exod. 31:9; 35:16; 38:1; 40:6); the bronze altar (Exod. 39:39); purify the altar by making atonement for it (Exod. 29:36–7); the altar set up (Exod. 40:29; Ezra 3:3); anointed (Exod. 30:28; 40:10; Lev. 8:11); dedication of the altar (Num. 7:10–11); Gershonites looked after the altar (Num. 3:26); censers beaten into plates for the altar (Num. 16:38–9); the altar of burnt offering was at Gibeon (1 Chr. 21:29); this is the altar of burnt offering for Israel (1 Chr. 22:1); the bronze altar was there (2 Chr. 1:5, 6); Solomon made a bronze altar (2 Chr. 4:1); the exiles began to build the altar (Ezra 3:2); these are the measurements of the altar (Ezek. 43:13).

c Adonijah took hold of the horns of the altar (1 Kgs. 1:50–3); as did Joab (1 Kgs. 2:28); the bronze altar was too small for all the offerings (1 Kgs. 8:64; 2 Chr. 7:7); the bronze altar was removed from in front of the temple (2 Kgs. 16:14); the altar of burnt offering was cleansed (2 Chr. 29:18).

● Altar of incense

d Make an altar of acacia wood for burning incense (Exod. 30:1); the golden altar (Exod. 39:38; 40:5; 1 Kgs. 7:48; 2 Chr. 4:19; Rev. 9:13); the altar of incense (Heb. 9:4); making the altar of incense (Exod. 31:8; 35:15; 37:25); the altar of incense set up (Exod. 40:26); anointed (Exod. 30:27); atoned for (Lev. 16:18–19); the Kohathites looked after (Num. 3:31); gold for the altar of incense (1 Chr. 28:18); incense on the altar (Rev. 8:3–5); Uzziah entered the temple to burn incense on the altar of incense (2 Chr. 26:16); an angel near the altar of incense (Luke 1:11).

● Who built altars

e Those who built altars: Noah (Gen. 8:20); Abraham (Gen. 12:7, 8; 13:4, 18; 22:9); Isaac (Gen. 26:25); Jacob (Gen. 33:20; 35:3, 7); Moses (Exod. 17:15; 24:4); Aaron (Exod. 32:5); Balak for Balaam (Num. 23:1); Joshua (Josh. 8:30); the two and a half tribes (Josh. 22:10); Gideon (Judg. 6:24); Israelites (Judg. 21:4); Samuel (1 Sam. 7:17); Saul (1 Sam. 14:35); David (2 Sam. 24:25; 1 Chr. 21:26); Elijah (1 Kgs. 18:32).

● Various altars

f Do not build another altar (Josh. 22:16, 19); an altar for witness, not for sacrifice (Josh. 22:23, 26–9); there will be an altar to the Lord in Egypt (Isa. 19:19); Manasseh made altars for Baal (2 Kgs. 21:3); and to the host of heaven (2 Kgs. 21:4–5); Ahab set up an altar for Baal in the temple of Baal (1 Kgs. 16:32); King Ahaz copied an altar in Damascus (2 Kgs. 16:10–11); Ahaz made altars all over Jerusalem (2 Chr. 28:24); you have as many altars as streets (Jer. 11:13); Ephraim multiplied altars for sinning (Hos. 8:11); the more fruit, the more altars he built (Hos. 10:1).

● Destroying altars

g Break down their altars (Deut. 7:5); tear down your father's altar to Baal (Judg. 6:25); altar, altar, hear the word of the Lord (1 Kgs. 13:1–3); Asa removed the foreign altars (2 Chr. 14:3); they removed the altars and incense altars (2 Chr. 30:14; 31:1); isn't he the one whose altars Hezekiah removed? (2 Kgs. 18:22; 2 Chr. 32:12; Isa. 36:7); Manasseh removed the altars (2 Chr. 33:15); Josiah destroyed the altars Manasseh had made (2 Kgs. 23:12); and the altar at Bethel (2 Kgs. 23:15); altar stones will be pulverised (Isa. 27:9).

h They have torn down your altars (1 Kgs. 19:10, 14; Rom. 11:3).

- Heavenly altar

i We have an altar from which those who minister at the tabernacle have no right to eat (Heb. 13:10); under the altar were the souls of those martyred (Rev. 6:9).

- The tent of meeting

j Moses pitched a tent and called it the tent of meeting (Exod. 33:7); light in the tent of meeting (Exod. 27:21); the Israelites are to camp round the tent of meeting (Num. 2:2, 17).

- The tabernacle

k Make a sanctuary for me (Exod. 25:8); make this tabernacle according to the pattern I will show you (Exod. 25:9); to make the Tent of Meeting (Exod. 31:7); skilled men made the tabernacle (Exod. 35:10–11; 36:8); setting up the tabernacle (Exod. 40:2, 17–33); anointing it (Exod. 30:26; Lev. 8:10); have reverence for my sanctuary (Lev. 19:30); appoint Levites to be in charge of the tabernacle (Num. 1:50); the Gershonites were responsible for the tent and its coverings (Num. 3:25–6; 4:21–8; 10:17); the Kohathites were responsible for the furniture (Num. 3:27–32; 4:1–20; 10:21); the Merarites were responsible for the frames (Num. 3:36–7; 4:29–33; 10:17).

l The tabernacle erected (Num. 9:15; 10:21); taken down (Num. 10:17); our forefathers had the tabernacle of testimony in the wilderness (Acts 7:44); a tabernacle was set up (Heb. 9:2); the house of God was in Shiloh (Judg. 18:31); bringing offerings to the house of the Lord in Shiloh (Jer. 41:5); Solomon went to God's tent of meeting at Gibeon (2 Chr. 1:3).

m The true tent which God pitched (Heb. 8:2).

- Solomon's temple

n I intend to build a temple for the name of the Lord (1 Kgs. 5:5); he began to build the temple (1 Kgs. 6:1); I have built a magnificent temple, a place for you to dwell for ever (1 Kgs. 8:13); they have built a sanctuary for your name (2 Chr. 20:8); Hezekiah went up to the temple of the Lord (2 Kgs. 19:1, 14); the Levites helped Aaron's descendants in the service of the temple (1 Chr. 23:28).

The ark in the temple, see **194d**; **money for the temple**, see **797i**.

o Stand in the court of the Lord's house (Jer. 26:2).

- Desecrating the temple

p Manasseh put an Asherah pole in the temple (2 Kgs. 21:7); Manasseh built foreign altars in the temple (2 Chr. 33:4); Josiah had all the articles made for Baal and Asherah removed from the temple (2 Kgs. 23:4); he tried to desecrate the temple (Acts 24:6).

The temple a market, see **796b**.

- The temple entered

q David entered the house of God (Matt. 12:4; Mark 2:26; Luke 6:4); Uzziah entered the temple to burn incense (2 Chr. 26:16); Zacharias was chosen by lot to enter the temple (Luke 1:9); Simeon came into the temple in the Spirit (Luke 2:27); I always taught in the synagogue and in the temple (John 18:20).

r Jesus entered the temple (Matt. 21:12, 23; Mark 11:11, 15; Luke 19:45; John 2:14; 8:2); they found boy Jesus in the temple (Luke 2:46); he was walking in the temple (Mark 11:27; John 10:23).

s The disciples were continually in the temple, praising God (Luke 24:53); they met in the temple day by day (Acts 2:46); Peter and John went up to the temple at the ninth hour (Acts 3:1); they entered the temple at daybreak and taught (Acts 5:21); Jews from Asia saw Paul in the temple (Acts 21:27).

Opening the temple, see **263***ah*; **shutting temple doors**, see **264***f*; **entering the temple**, see **297***e*.

t The man of lawlessness takes his seat in the temple of God (2 Thess. 2:4).

● The temple destroyed

u I will make this house like Shiloh (Jer. 26:6, 9); I will do to the house called by my name as I did to Shiloh (Jer. 7:14); this house will become a desolation (Jer. 22:5); I am about to profane my sanctuary (Ezek. 24:21).

v The temple was burned (2 Kgs. 25:9; Jer. 52:13); our holy temple has been burned with fire (Isa. 64:11); pagan nations entered her sanctuary (Lam. 1:10); they entered my temple to profane it (Ezek. 23:39); they have defiled your temple (Ps. 79:1); you said Aha! over my sanctuary when it was desecrated (Ezek. 25:3); your house is left to you desolate (Matt. 23:38).

Taking temple treasures, see **786***i*.

● Rebuilding the temple

w Cyrus' order to rebuild the temple (2 Chr. 36:23; Ezra 1:2–3; 6:3–5); the foundation laid (Ezra 3:10–11); the building stopped (Ezra 4:24); the building resumed (Ezra 5:2–5); the house of the great God is being built (Ezra 5:8); building completed (Ezra 6:14–15); enemies heard they were rebuilding (Ezra 4:1); let us meet in the house of God, inside the temple (Neh. 6:10).

x Destroy this temple and in three days I will raise it up (John 2:19); I can destroy this temple and rebuild it in three days (Matt. 26:61; Mark 14:58); you who would destroy the temple and rebuild it in three days (Matt. 27:40; Mark 15:29).

● Status of the temple

y Do not trust in deceptive words, saying, The temple of the Lord! (Jer. 7:4); whoever swears by the temple, it is nothing (Matt. 23:16); has this house become a den of robbers? (Jer. 7:11; Matt. 21:13; Mark 11:17; Luke 19:46); the Lord you seek will suddenly come to his temple (Mal. 3:1); Jesus stood on the pinnacle of the temple (Matt. 4:5; Luke 4:9); the disciples pointed out the temple buildings to Jesus (Matt. 24:1; Mark 13:1); the temple was beautifully adorned (Luke 21:5); zeal for your house will consume me (John 2:17).

● The perfect temple

z Ezekiel's vision of the temple being measured (Ezek. 40:5–44:31); measure the temple of God (Rev. 11:1); my sanctuary will be in their midst for ever (Ezek. 37:26, 28).

aa The mountain of the Lord's house will be as chief among the mountains (Isa. 2:2); where is the house you will build for me? (Isa. 66:1); God is in his temple (Hab. 2:20); Christ went through the perfect tabernacle which is not man-made (Heb. 9:11); God's temple in heaven was opened (Rev. 11:19); in heaven the temple was opened, the tabernacle of testimony (Rev. 15:5); I saw no temple, because the Lord God Almighty and the Lamb are its temple (Rev. 21:22).

● The living
temple

ab The temple of his body (John 2:21); something greater than the temple is here (Matt. 12:6); you are God's temple and God's Spirit lives in you (1 Cor. 3:16); your body is a temple of the Holy Spirit (1 Cor. 6:19); we are the temple of the living God (2 Cor. 6:16); the whole building is growing into a holy temple (Eph. 2:21); I will make him a pillar in the temple of my God (Rev. 3:12).

● Holy of holies

ac He built the holy of holies (2 Chr. 3:8); within the temple was an inner sanctuary, the holy of holies (1 Kgs. 6:16, 19–20); the priests brought the ark to its place in the holy of holies (1 Kgs. 8:6); the ark was brought to the holy of holies (2 Chr. 5:7); doors for the holy of holies (2 Chr. 4:22); in the holy district will be the sanctuary, the holy of holies (Ezek. 45:3); behind the second curtain was a room called the holy of holies (Heb. 9:3); the veil separated the holy place from the holy of holies (Exod. 26:33).

ad Christ entered the holy of holies once for all by his own blood (Heb. 9:12); our hope enters the inner sanctuary where Jesus entered for us (Heb. 6:19–20); we have confidence to enter the holy place through the veil (Heb. 10:20).

● Foreign
temples

ae The ark was carried into Dagon's temple (1 Sam. 5:2); the temple of El-berith (Judg. 9:46); Micah had a shrine (Judg. 17:5); Demetrius made silver shrines of Artemis (Acts 19:24).

The ark of the covenant, see 194a; mercy seat, see 226*l*.

Index of Bible references

Note

Numbers refer to categories and italic letters to paragraphs within those categories, e.g. 68*b*. Superscripts indicate that a verse is referred to several times from the same paragraph, e.g. 365a^2.

6:15	195a	**9:10**	365d	**12:13**	11d	**15:16**	148n 726b
6:16	194u 263a 264a	**9:11**	350a	**12:14**	841h		914ab
6:17	165o 350a	**9:12**	250c	**12:16**	781y	**15:17**	305b 381p
6:18	765a	**9:13**	355a 547a 765a	**12:17**	659a		417c 418b
6:19	90o 360b 365d	**9:15**	505c	**12:19**	11d		420d
	372a	**9:16**	355a	**13:1**	89o	**15:18**	183e 184a
6:20	77a³	**9:18**	169h	**13:2**	800f		350p 765b
6:21	301l	**9:20**	370k	**13:3**	148n	**15:19**	371v
6:22	739d	**9:21**	229j 949i	**13:4**	761t 990e	**16:1**	172a 742e
7:1	297a 929e	**9:23**	226a 439g	**13:6**	633e	**16:2**	172e
7:2	90o 99c 372a	**9:25**	745g 899c	**13:7**	369b 709f	**16:3**	894u
	648z 649n	**9:26**	923l	**13:8**	11h	**16:4**	167g 922g
7:4	110r 350z	**9:27**	197a 745g	**13:9**	46am	**16:5**	480c
	362bj	**9:29**	131j	**13:10**	341a	**16:6**	620i 735d
7:5	739d	**10:1**	169a 169g	**13:11**	281n 605p	**16:7**	339d 968g
7:6	131g 350a	**10:5**	46ai 557a	**13:12**	184av	**16:8**	187b 620i
7:7	297a	**10:9**	619a	**13:13**	938a	**16:9**	148e 721c
7:8	90o 648z	**10:20**	557a	**13:14**	183e 281u	**16:10**	104c
7:9	90o 372a 649n	**10:25**	46ai	**13:15**	184a	**16:11**	455d
7:11	131g	**10:30**	281n	**13:16**	104c	**16:12**	84a 281n
7:12	350z	**10:31**	557a	**13:17**	267e		365be 704j
7:13	297a	**10:32**	46ai	**13:18**	366s 990e	**16:13**	438c
7:14	77a	**11:1**	557a	**14:1**	718h	**16:14**	339d 339e
7:15	90o	**11:2**	281n	**14:4**	110z 738b	**16:15**	561r
7:16	264e 372a	**11:3**	381n 631m	**14:5**	727f	**16:16**	131h
7:17	110r	**11:4**	164p 209al	**14:7**	727f	**17:1**	13a 89g 131g
7:18	323a		866s	**14:8**	718h		160a 913j 965c
7:20	209f	**11:6**	469c 557a	**14:10**	255b 309c	**17:2**	104b 765b
7:21	361ag 365d	**11:7**	557a		620d 631m	**17:3**	311f
7:23	41h 362bj	**11:8**	75a 145a	**14:11**	790d	**17:4**	169p
7:24	110s	**11:9**	184az 557a	**14:12**	747i	**17:5**	104b 561w
8:1	37c 352g 505c	**11:10**	131h 169a 169g	**14:13**	366s 524f	**17:6**	104b²
8:4	209t	**11:12**	131h	**14:14**	619d 747i	**17:7**	115k 765b 965e
8:6	110r 263b	**11:14**	131h	**14:15**	46al 129h 619d	**17:8**	115i 184a 965e
8:7	365al	**11:16**	131h		727f	**17:9**	765b
8:9	148e 683t	**11:18**	131h	**14:16**	656ae 786a	**17:10**	372c 988m
8:10	110o	**11:20**	131h	**14:18**	184af 741u	**17:12**	131f
8:11	366c	**11:22**	131h		882b 986q	**17:14**	769a 963o
8:12	110o	**11:24**	131h	**14:19**	164a 897v	**17:15**	561w
8:13	342b	**11:26**	131h	**14:20**	102f 727i	**17:16**	897g
8:16	298a	**11:27**	169g	**14:22**	164a 532h 782e	**17:17**	131g² 131h
8:17	171a	**11:30**	172a	**14:23**	800d		167i 311f 835b
8:20	648z 981p 990e	**11:31**	298b	**15:1**	438aa 662j	**17:19**	115k 561o
8:21	362bj 396h	**11:32**	131j 361ad		854ai 962a		765b 835b
	899b 914k	**12:1**	11j 184d 298b	**15:2**	172a 776a	**17:20**	104j 897f
8:22	115h 128a 128n		621l	**15:3**	776a	**17:21**	765b
	129a 141a	**12:2**	104b 866aa	**15:5**	104c	**17:23**	372c 988n
	370s 379a 380a		897j	**15:6**	480t 485s 913v	**17:24**	131g
9:1	171a 897f	**12:3**	371ai 897j 899k	**15:7**	13a 184a 304a	**17:25**	131g
9:2	365c² 371a²	**12:4**	89o 131g	**15:8**	473a	**18:1**	263e 366s 379a
	854w	**12:6**	366s	**15:10**	92a		445a 813e
9:3	301a 365c	**12:7**	184a 990e	**15:11**	300ab 365ak	**18:2**	93b 311a
9:4	335b 335g 360a	**12:8**	281t 761t 990e	**15:12**	418j 679b 854k	**18:3**	305a 826p
9:5	335b 963k	**12:9**	267a 281k	**15:13**	59u 110ag 742p	**18:4**	648e 683r
9:6	18a 371a 963k	**12:10**	184m 636a	**15:14**	480e 777d	**18:5**	301r
9:7	171a	**12:11**	841h	**15:15**	133g 361n	**18:9**	187a
9:9	765a	**12:12**	362h			**18:10**	167i 415a

18:11 133g 172a
18:12 835b
18:14 701a
18:15 533g 854j
18:17 525a
18:18 897j
18:19 605b 725b 913q
18:20 914ab 924n
18:23 362bc 761k
18:24 99r
18:25 480h 913f 957a
18:26 99r
18:27 639a
18:28 99r
18:29 99r
18:30 99q
18:31 99p
18:32 99k
19:1 129b 263l 813e
19:2 128b 648e
19:3 301r 612a
19:5 951p
19:8 895b 951aa
19:9 59e 480o
19:10 264e 288a
19:11 439i
19:12 304a
19:13 165o 924n
19:14 839a
19:15 612a
19:16 136e 288a 304a
19:17 209j 238f 439g 620i
19:18 760d
19:19 209j 826f 897m
19:20 184av 196e
19:22 161a 184av 196e
19:23 128f
19:24 184av 381v 385h
19:26 238f 282d 388a
19:27 128b
19:28 383b 388e 438n
19:29 304a 505c
19:30 209j 255f
19:31 45i 133g
19:32 45f 949k
19:36 167f
20:1 281k
20:2 11d
20:3 361z 438u 894q
20:4 362bi 935c
20:5 11d
20:6 378r
20:7 361z 579z 761k
20:8 128b 854x

20:9 916c
20:11 362h 854q
20:12 11d
20:14 781y
20:16 797c 927g
20:17 171c 656v 761k
20:18 172a
21:1 725b
21:2 133g 167i
21:3 561o 835b
21:4 131f 988n
21:5 131g 131h 133g
21:6 835b
21:7 133g 171c 301o
21:8 611a 876a
21:9 837b 851b
21:10 300v 776a
21:11 825e
21:12 170h
21:13 104j
21:14 128b 172w 300v 301l
21:15 342e
21:16 439g
21:17 455g 854ai 968g
21:18 104j
21:19 339d 438a
21:20 89h 287e
21:21 172u 894x
21:22 89h
21:23 532g 897x
21:25 339d
21:27 765n 781y
21:28 99c
21:30 466b
21:31 532g 561s
21:33 115b 370i 761t 965c
22:1 461b
22:2 88h 170h 209r 887ad 981p 981ag
22:3 128b 365bd 385a 981p
22:5 365bd 981f
22:6 381af 385a 981p
22:7 981p
22:8 633a
22:9 747o 990e
22:10 362af
22:11 737i 968g
22:12 88h 854e 919c
22:13 150a 254a 981p
22:14 633a
22:15 737i

22:16 88h 532o 919c
22:17 $104c^2$ 727c 897j
22:18 371ai 739d
22:20 169a
22:24 952a
23:1 131j
23:2 361ad 836p
23:4 59u 364e
23:8 235q 792c
23:9 255d 793b
23:15 809j
23:18 777c
24:1 133g 897f
24:2 742p
24:3 532g 894x
24:4 11e 894x
24:5 148m 598c
24:7 184a 304a 532p 968l
24:8 598c 919b
24:9 378b 532g
24:10 365bb
24:11 129b 304d 311q 339e
24:12 727b 761p 897m
24:13 304d 547c
24:14 339q 339r 547o
24:16 841h 895b
24:17 339q
24:19 339r
24:22 844a
24:23 13j 192ag
24:26 311f 981f
24:27 689d 897m 923l
24:30 844a
24:31 813e
24:32 648e
24:33 301r
24:35 800f 897f
24:36 133g 781z
24:37 532g 894x
24:38 11e
24:40 968l
24:42 727b
24:43 304d 339q 547c 547o
24:44 339r
24:45 304d 339q
24:46 339r
24:47 13j 844a
24:48 311f 689d 981f
24:49 897x
24:52 311f
24:53 228x 844a
24:55 136f
24:56 702b

24:58 597b
24:60 104a 727c 897v
24:63 129b 449i
24:65 13j 226f
24:66 524a
24:67 831g 887ab 894z
25:1 169a 894z
25:5 781z
25:6 281n 300v 781z 952a
25:7 131j
25:8 133g 361ad
25:9 255d 364e 364l
25:11 897f
25:12 169a 169g
25:16 99m
25:17 131j 361ad
25:19 169g
25:20 131g
25:21 167i 172a 761l
25:22 459a 716h
25:23 90n 130i 162h 742q
25:24 90b
25:25 259a 431a
25:26 131g 300ad 786n
25:27 192t 619a 717g
25:28 887ad 890a
25:29 859k
25:30 431a
25:31 119d 793e
25:33 532i
25:34 119d 301r 922k
26:1 636a
26:2 184d
26:3 184a 532o 897f
26:4 104c 897j
26:5 739d
26:7 11d 362h 841h 854ad
26:8 889g
26:9 11d
26:10 936b
26:11 963l
26:12 99t 370i 897f
26:13 800f
26:14 912c
26:15 264k 339d
26:16 300z
26:18 339d 561s
26:19 339d
26:20 709f
26:22 171g 183a
26:24 13a 104b 445a 854ai

26:25	339*d* 761*t* 990*e*
26:27	300*z* 888*q*
26:28	89*h* 765*n*
26:29	897*f*
26:30	876*a* 882*b*
26:31	128*b*
26:32	339*e*
26:33	561*s*
26:34	131*g* 894*u*
26:35	827*k*
27:1	133*g* 439*a*
27:2	361*m* 491*z*
27:3	287*e* 619*a* 723*k*
27:4	301*ah* 390*a* 897*v*
27:5	415*a*
27:7	301*ah* 390*a* 897*v*
27:9	301*ah* 390*a*
27:10	897*v*
27:11	258*a* 259*a* 542*k*
27:12	899*p*
27:13	899*p*
27:14	301*ah* 390*a*
27:15	228*m* 527*b*
27:16	226*t*
27:17	390*a*
27:18	13*j*
27:19	13*o* 119*d*
27:20	135*a*
27:22	378*a* 577*a*
27:23	491*s*
27:26	889*b*
27:27	394*a* 396*k* 897*v*
27:28	341*e* 635*a*
27:29	311*b* 741*z* 897*j* 899*k*
27:31	390*a*
27:32	13*j* 13*o* 119*d*
27:33	854*u*
27:34	897*v*
27:35	542*k*
27:36	300*ad* 786*h* 786*n*
27:37	741*z*
27:38	836*ae*
27:39	172*o* 342*f*
27:40	722*b* 746*g*
27:41	362*ac* 891*w*
27:42	524*a*
27:43	620*i*
27:45	506*i*
27:46	894*x*
28:1	894*x* 897*v*
28:2	11*e* 894*x*
28:3	104*a* 897*c*
28:4	184*f* 897*j*

28:6	894*x*
28:9	894*u*
28:11	129*b* 344*f* 679*c*
28:12	308*f* 308*m* 438*u* 968*m*
28:13	13*a* 184*a* 965*f*
28:14	104*c* 183*e* 281*u* 371*ai* 897*j*
28:15	89*h* 621*g* 666*a*
28:16	189*a* 491*i*
28:17	192*g* 854*j*
28:18	128*b* 344*f* 357*l* 548*a*
28:19	561*s*
28:20	89*h* 228*v* 301*x* 532*w* 666*a*
28:21	965*e*
28:22	102*b* 192*g*
29:1	281*m* 369*a*
29:2	339*d* 339*r* 344*i*
29:4	187*b*
29:5	490*x*
29:6	8*a*
29:11	836*m* 889*b*
29:12	11*b*
29:13	889*b*
29:14	11*a*
29:15	804*b*
29:17	438*i* 841*h*
29:18	110*y* 887*ab*
29:20	110*y* 114*q*
29:21	45*i* 894*u*
29:22	876*b*
29:23	45*e* 150*b*
29:25	13*o* 542*k*
29:26	119*c* 127*c*
29:27	110*o* 110*y*
29:28	894*u*
29:30	45*e* 110*y* 887*ab* 890*a*
29:31	167*i* 172*a* 887*aj*
29:32	438*c* 561*r* 887*ab*
29:33	561*r*
29:34	561*r*
29:35	561*r* 923*g* 923*q*
30:1	172*a* 361*p* 911*i*
30:2	172*e*
30:3	45*e*
30:4	167*i* 894*u*
30:6	561*r* 927*a*
30:8	561*r* 716*m*
30:9	894*u*
30:10	167*i*
30:11	561*r*
30:13	561*r*

30:14	366*i* 370*t*
30:15	786*b*
30:16	45*e*
30:17	167*i*
30:18	561*r* 962*c*
30:20	561*r*
30:22	505*c*
30:23	167*i*
30:24	38*e* 561*r*
30:25	148*n*
30:27	826*p* 897*j* 983*e*
30:28	804*b*
30:30	36*e* 897*j*
30:31	369*a*
30:32	647*a*
30:36	199*d*
30:37	437*a*
30:39	45*g* 647*a*
30:41	45*g*
30:43	800*f*
31:1	786*f* 800*h*
31:3	148*n* 184*d*
31:5	89*h*
31:7	757*b* 804*b* 930*c*
31:8	647*a*
31:10	45*g* 438*u*
31:13	184*d* 357*l* 532*w* 548*a*
31:14	775*a*
31:15	59*v* 793*g*
31:16	800*h*
31:17	365*bb*
31:19	369*e* 788*m* 966*j*
31:20	542*k*
31:21	620*i*
31:23	619*g*
31:24	438*u*
31:26	542*k*
31:27	412*a* 530*d*
31:30	788*m* 966*j*
31:31	854*ae*
31:32	362*s* 491*z* 788*m* 966*j*
31:34	459*ae*
31:35	302*d*
31:36	619*g* 891*w* 914*ae*
31:38	110*aa* 172*m*
31:39	772*c*
31:40	379*a* 380*c* 678*a*
31:41	110*y* 110*aa* 804*b*
31:42	636*m* 682*b* 924*a*
31:43	773*h*
31:44	466*b* 765*n*
31:45	344*h* 548*a*

31:46	209*z* 882*b*
31:48	466*b*
31:49	457*b*
31:50	466*b*
31:52	305*a*
31:53	480*c* 532*j* 854*b*
31:54	301*z* 981*h*
31:55	128*b* 889*b* 897*v*
32:1	968*l*
32:2	74*l*
32:3	529*q*
32:5	800*f* 826*p*
32:6	74*m*
32:7	92*d* 854*ae*
32:8	667*a*
32:9	761*p*
32:10	90*t* 897*m* 916*a*
32:11	668*d* 854*ae*
32:12	104*c*
32:13	781*y*
32:17	459*o*
32:20	719*g*
32:22	222*a*
32:24	88*n* 716*b* 716*m*
32:25	378*b* 655*n*
32:26	747*w* 897*c*
32:28	561*w* 716*c*
32:29	561*h* 897*f*
32:30	200*a* 438*d*
32:31	655*n*
32:32	127*d* 301*ap* 378*b*
33:1	74*m*
33:3	311*a*
33:4	836*m* 889*b*
33:8	826*p*
33:9	635*a*
33:10	438*d* 826*p*
33:11	635*a*
33:13	163*b*
33:15	826*p*
33:17	192*y*
33:19	792*c* 809*j*
33:20	990*e*
34:1	882*g*
34:2	951*aa*
34:3	887*ab*
34:4	894*x*
34:5	582*g* 951*aa*
34:7	867*f* 891*v*
34:9	894*x*
34:10	791*a*
34:11	826*p*
34:12	809*g*
34:13	542*k*
34:14	867*f* 974*b*
34:15	372*c* 988*n*

34:21 791*a* 894*x*
34:22 372*c*
34:23 771*g*
34:24 372*c*
34:25 362*ax* 372*f*
825*h*
34:26 786*a*
34:27 790*i*
34:30 105*a* 827*l*
34:31 951*v*
35:1 192*g* 445*a* 990*d*
35:2 648*m* 966*f*
35:3 89*h* 990*e*
35:4 366*s* 844*f* 966*f*
35:5 854*k*
35:7 445*a* 990*e*
35:8 301*o* 361*ae*
364*l* 366*s*
35:9 445*a*
35:10 561*w*
35:11 13*a* 104*d* 160*a*
171*a* 741*m*
965*c*
35:12 184*a*
35:14 357*l* 548*a* 981*t*
35:15 192*g* 561*s*
35:16 167*i* 825*e*
35:17 854*ah*
35:18 241*d* 361*ad*
561*r*² 825*e*
35:19 184*ao* 364*l*
35:20 548*a*
35:22 45*f* 99*m* 169*a*
951*q* 952*b*
35:28 131*j*
35:29 133*g* 361*ad*
364*l*
36:1 169*a* 169*g*
36:2 894*x*
36:6 272*i*
36:7 633*e* 800*f*
36:9 169*g*
36:12 952*a*
36:20 169*a*
36:31 741*u*
37:1 184*d*
37:2 131*g* 169*g* 369*a*
524*a*
37:3 228*m* 887*ad*
890*a*
37:4 888*q*
37:5 438*u*
37:7 311*a* 370*t*
37:8 888*q*
37:9 311*a* 321*l*
37:10 311*a*
37:11 911*i*

37:12 369*a*
37:14 8*a*
37:15 459*af*
37:16 187*b*
37:18 199*e* 362*ac*
623*i*
37:19 438*u*
37:20 255*b*
37:21 668*t*
37:23 229*l*
37:25 268*d* 365*bb*
396*m*
37:27 793*g*
37:28 809*e*
37:29 836*g*
37:31 228*m* 335*d*
37:33 365*e*
37:34 836*g* 836*q*
37:35 361*m* 831*j*
37:36 793*g*
38:2 45*e*
38:3 167*f*
38:6 894*z*
38:7 362*be* 938*a*
38:8 45*e* 894*l*
38:9 302*c*
38:10 362*be* 938*a*
38:11 896*n*
38:12 361*ae* 369*e*
836*p*
38:14 527*b*
38:15 951*t*
38:16 45*f*
38:17 767*b* 809*d*
38:18 167*f* 218*b* 743*k*
38:20 809*d*
38:21 187*a* 951*t*
38:23 851*b*
38:24 167*f* 963*r*
38:25 218*b* 743*k*
38:26 895*g* 929*e*
38:27 90*b*
38:28 431*b*
38:29 263*x* 561*r*
38:30 431*b*
39:1 184*m* 792*e* 793*g*
39:2 89*h* 727*b*
39:3 89*h*
39:4 751*h* 826*p*
39:5 897*j*
39:6 841*k*
39:7 45*i* 859*p*
39:9 914*ae*
39:10 45*i*
39:12 45*i* 229*q* 620*i*
39:14 45*i* 577*l*
39:15 229*q*

39:18 577*l*
39:19 891*w*
39:20 747*b*
39:21 89*h* 826*p* 897*m*
39:22 751*h*
39:23 89*h* 727*b*
40:1 686*d*² 827*l*
40:2 891*w*
40:3 747*b*
40:4 742*e*
40:5 438*u*
40:6 834*c*
40:8 438*w* 520*a*
40:9 366*k*
40:10 93*c*
40:11 949*d*
40:12 93*c* 110*l* 438*w*
40:13 310*j* 656*af*
40:14 505*o*
40:15 788*b* 916*f*
40:16 93*c* 301*ai*
40:17 365*ak*
40:18 93*c* 110*l* 438*w*
40:19 217*b* 310*j*
40:20 141*f* 310*j* 876*a*
40:21 656*af*
40:22 217*b*
40:23 506*h*
41:1 99*c* 350*q* 438*u*
41:2 195*d* 365*az*
41:3 196*d*
41:4 195*d*
41:5 195*d*
41:6 196*d* 352*k*
41:8 500*e* 520*a*
41:11 520*a*
41:12 438*w*
41:13 217*b*
41:14 648*j* 648*m*
41:15 438*w* 520*a*
41:16 438*w* 460*c*
41:18 195*d*
41:19 196*d*
41:20 195*d*
41:22 195*d*
41:23 196*d* 352*k*
41:24 195*d*
41:25 438*w*
41:26 110*y*
41:27 196*d*² 352*k*
636*a*
41:29 635*a*
41:32 91*e*
41:33 500*c*
41:34 102*j*
41:35 632*a*
41:38 965*m*

41:39 500*c*
41:41 751*h*
41:42 228*m* 631*o*
743*k* 743*m*
41:43 274*d*
41:45 561*y* 894*x* 986*q*
41:46 131*g*
41:47 171*j*
41:48 632*a*
41:49 465*d* 635*a*
41:50 636*a* 986*q*
41:51 506*k* 561*r*
41:52 171*o* 561*r*
41:56 793*c*
41:57 792*d*
42:2 792*d*
42:3 99*k*
42:5 636*a*
42:6 311*a* 741*z*
42:7 527*b*
42:8 491*s*
42:9 459*q* 505*r*
42:15 461*h*
42:17 110*l* 747*b*
42:18 854*e*
42:19 747*b*
42:21 456*h* 906*c* 936*a*
42:22 180*c* 963*b*
42:23 520*c*
42:24 836*n*
42:25 194*s* 797*f*
42:27 194*s* 797*f*
42:28 797*f* 854*ae*
42:30 459*q* 735*d*
42:31 929*c*
42:34 459*q*
42:35 194*s* 797*f*
854*ae*
42:36 704*l*
42:37 362*s*
42:38 361*m*
43:1 636*a*
43:2 792*d*
43:7 459*o*
43:9 767*e*
43:11 301*ai* 392*a*
396*m* 781*y*
43:12 91*c* 194*s* 797*f*
43:14 772*e*
43:15 91*c*
43:16 876*a*
43:18 194*s* 745*g* 797*f*
854*ae*
43:21 194*s* 797*f*
43:23 854*ah*
43:24 648*e*
43:25 781*y*

43:26	311*a*	**46:32**	369*a*	**49:15**	682*e* 826*q*	
43:28	311*a*	**46:33**	686*b*	**49:16**	480*o*	
43:30	818*e* 836*n*	**46:34**	888*q*	**49:17**	365*q*	
43:31	648*a* 876*a*	**47:2**	99*a*	**49:19**	712*c*	

43:26 311*a*
43:28 311*a*
43:30 818*e* 836*n*
43:31 648*a* 876*a*
43:32 883*a*
43:33 73*a* 119*c* 864*n*
43:34 99*a*
44:1 194*s* 797*f*
44:2 194*l* 797*f*
44:4 804*n*
44:5 983*e*
44:8 194*s* 788*h* 797*f*
44:9 362*s* 745*g*
44:11 194*s*
44:12 73*a*
44:13 836*g*
44:14 311*a*
44:15 983*e*
44:17 745*g*
44:18 28*f*
44:20 41*h* 887*ad*
44:29 361*m*
44:31 361*m*
44:32 767*e*
44:33 150*a* 745*g*
45:1 300*aa*
45:2 836*n*
45:3 13*o* 854*ae*
45:4 13*o* 200*h* 793*g*
45:5 668*v*
45:6 636*a*
45:7 41*l* 668*v*
45:8 741*z*
45:11 633*c* 636*a*
45:14 836*n*
45:15 836*n* 889*b*
45:16 826*l*
45:18 635*a*
45:19 274*i*
45:21 274*i*
45:22 99*a* 228*x* 797*c*
45:23 365*bd*
45:24 709*f*
45:26 360*b* 741*z* 864*n*
45:27 274*i*
45:28 360*b*
46:1 981*h*
46:2 438*s*
46:3 104*b* 184*m* 854*ai*
46:4 364*b*
46:5 274*i*
46:8 169*b*
46:20 986*q*
46:27 99*s*
46:29 274*d* 836*n* 889*b*
46:30 360*b* 361*q*

46:32 369*a*
46:33 686*b*
46:34 888*q*
47:2 99*a*
47:3 369*a* 686*b*
47:4 636*a*
47:9 114*d* 131*g*
47:10 897*v*
47:12 301*l*
47:13 636*a*
47:14 797*c*
47:15 301*c*
47:16 365*az* 791*b*
47:20 184*n* 636*a* 792*c*
47:22 783*e* 986*q*
47:23 370*i*
47:24 102*j*
47:25 668*t* 742*p* 826*p*
47:26 102*j* 986*q*
47:27 104*e*
47:28 131*j*
47:29 364*f* 378*b* 532*i* 826*p*
47:30 364*e*
47:31 218*x* 532*g* 981*f*
48:1 651*g*
48:2 218*x*
48:3 160*a* 445*a* 897*f*
48:4 104*b*² 115*i* 184*a*
48:5 170*h* 773*h*
48:7 184*ao* 364*l*
48:8 13*j*
48:9 897*v*
48:10 439*a* 889*b*
48:12 311*a*
48:13 241*c*
48:14 119*d* 222*j*
48:15 369*k* 897*v*
48:16 104*a* 561*q* 792*p* 897*c* 968*m*
48:19 104*d* 132*a*
48:20 897*v*
48:21 89*d* 184*d* 361*m*
48:22 119*d*
49:1 124*l*
49:3 119*d*
49:4 152*c* 951*q*
49:5 176*a*
49:7 75*f* 891*v*
49:8 311*a* 923*q*
49:9 365*af*
49:10 741*q*
49:11 648*l* 747*q*
49:13 275*a*
49:14 365*be*

49:15 682*e* 826*q*
49:16 480*o*
49:17 365*q*
49:19 712*c*
49:21 365*x*
49:22 366*k* 712*c*
49:24 344*w* 369*k*
49:25 703*b* 897*d*
49:27 365*w*
49:28 897*v*
49:29 255*d* 361*m* 364*e*
49:31 255*d*
49:33 218*x* 361*ad*
50:1 836*n* 836*q* 889*b*
50:2 364*b*
50:3 110*r* 836*q*
50:4 826*p*
50:5 361*m* 364*e* 532*i*
50:10 370*z* 836*q*
50:13 255*d* 364*e* 364*l*
50:15 804*m* 891*w*
50:17 836*n* 909*p*
50:18 745*g*
50:19 28*b* 854*ah*
50:20 617*a* 644*c* 668*v*
50:21 633*c* 854*ah*
50:22 131*j*
50:24 184*b* 361*m* 532*p*
50:25 363*f* 532*j*
50:26 131*j* 361*ad* 364*b*

Exodus

1:1 170*h*
1:5 99*s*
1:7 104*e*
1:8 491*r*
1:10 498*r* 718*b*
1:11 164*p* 735*e*
1:12 104*e* 735*e* 854*x*
1:14 631*n* 827*f*
1:15 658*b*
1:16 167*e* 362*al* 372*f*
1:17 854*e*
1:19 167*e* 571*a*
1:20 104*e*
1:21 170*g* 854*e*
1:22 362*al* 372*f*
2:2 167*i* 525*e* 841*l*
2:3 194*s* 226*p* 631*m*
2:4 441*b*
2:5 648*f*
2:6 836*af* 905*i*
2:7 301*o*
2:9 301*o* 804*b*

2:10 170*k* 304*e* 339*v*
2:11 279*d*
2:12 362*af*
2:13 716*h*
2:14 362*af* 526*u* 854*s* 957*g*
2:15 339*d* 362*l* 620*i*
2:16 339*r* 986*q*
2:17 300*z* 668*t*
2:18 135*a*
2:19 668*t*
2:20 813*e*
2:21 894*x*
2:22 59*u* 561*r*
2:23 825*f*
2:24 455*h* 505*c* 768*c*
3:1 172*u* 209*k* 281*r* 369*a* 986*q*
3:2 366*o* 381*p* 968*g*
3:4 737*i*
3:5 229*p* 979*x*
3:6 13*a* 523*e* 854*l*
3:7 455*h*
3:8 184*d* 371*v* 635*d* 668*i*
3:10 304*e* 751*i*
3:11 639*a*
3:12 89*d* 209*k* 547*c* 981*d*
3:13 561*a*
3:14 1*a*
3:15 561*b* 965*f*
3:16 965*f* 986*ae*
3:17 371*v* 635*d*
3:18 981*h*
3:19 757*f*
3:20 864*b*
3:21 636*l* 826*p*
3:22 228*x* 786*f* 797*g*
4:1 486*n* 547*d*
4:2 218*a*
4:3 365*o*
4:4 786*n*
4:5 485*g*
4:6 53*f* 651*n*
4:7 656*v*
4:9 335*k* 339*h*
4:10 579*ap*
4:11 164*k* 416*a* 438*a* 439*i* 578*a*
4:12 579*q*
4:13 150*b* 751*i*
4:14 579*ap* 891*m*
4:15 579*q*
4:16 579*ap* 966*m*
4:17 218*a* 547*d*
4:19 362*l*

4:20	218a 365bd	**7:13**	456e 602a	**9:28**	761k	**12:22**	223d 263f 298c
4:21	602h 864f	**7:14**	602a 659a	**9:29**	321g 761k		335l 366g
4:22	119a 170s	**7:15**	218a 350q	**9:30**	854q	**12:23**	168b 305b
4:23	119e 362bi 746c	**7:16**	746c 981d	**9:31**	165o 366h		305d 335l
	981d	**7:17**	335k 339h 490n	**9:34**	602a 914ab	**12:24**	115i
4:24	362be	**7:18**	365av	**10:1**	602h 864b	**12:25**	988d
4:25	46c 256e 988n	**7:21**	365av	**10:2**	170b 490n	**12:26**	170b 459i
4:26	335d	**7:22**	456e 500e	**10:3**	746c 872k 981d	**12:27**	311f 362bi
4:27	209k 889b		602a	**10:4**	365j		919e 981e 988c
4:28	547d	**8:1**	365m 746c	**10:7**	165o 542t 981d	**12:29**	119e 129l 362bi
4:29	986ae		981d	**10:9**	988a	**12:30**	836q
4:30	547d	**8:3**	218y	**10:11**	300z 372e	**12:31**	300z 981d
4:31	311f 485g 981e	**8:5**	218a	**10:13**	218a 352k	**12:32**	897v
5:1	746c 988a	**8:7**	500e	**10:14**	104w	**12:33**	361aa 680a
5:2	13b 491e	**8:8**	761k 981h	**10:15**	418b	**12:34**	323i
5:3	362bg 651e	**8:9**	124a	**10:16**	914ad	**12:35**	228x 761ak
	981h	**8:10**	21b	**10:17**	761k 909p		797g
5:5	702b	**8:12**	761k	**10:19**	352k	**12:36**	786f 826p
5:7	631n	**8:14**	397a	**10:20**	602h	**12:37**	99v
5:8	37b 679k	**8:15**	456e 602a	**10:21**	218a 418i	**12:38**	43c
5:9	735e	**8:16**	218a 332a 365i	**10:22**	110l	**12:39**	323i 381m
5:13	725g	**8:18**	500e	**10:23**	417i	**12:40**	110ag
5:14	279d	**8:19**	53p 378s 456e	**10:24**	365az	**12:42**	768a
5:17	679k		602a	**10:27**	602h	**12:43**	59i 988c
5:21	480c	**8:20**	128b 350q 365i	**10:28**	300z 439h	**12:44**	988m
5:22	827e		746c 981d	**11:1**	300z 659a	**12:46**	46i
5:23	668q	**8:22**	15b	**11:2**	761ak 797g	**12:48**	59i 372c 988m
6:1	160b	**8:23**	46aq	**11:3**	826p	**12:49**	28g
6:2	13a	**8:24**	165o	**11:4**	129l	**12:51**	304a
6:3	561a	**8:25**	981h	**11:5**	119e	**13:2**	119a 979i
6:4	184b 765b	**8:26**	888q	**11:6**	836q	**13:3**	160b 323i 505j
6:5	768c 825f	**8:28**	199c 761k	**11:7**	15b 365bk 409a		742p
6:6	13a 160b 322m	**8:29**	542k 761k		926h	**13:4**	108e
	746c 792n	**8:32**	602a	**11:8**	891w	**13:5**	371v 532p 635d
6:7	322m 371ac	**9:1**	651e 746c 981d	**11:9**	456e 864b		988d
	490n 965e	**9:4**	15b	**11:10**	602h	**13:6**	110o 323i
6:8	184d 532p	**9:5**	124a	**12:2**	68e 108e	**13:8**	170b
6:9	456f 735e 834b	**9:6**	365az	**12:3**	108e	**13:9**	53d 160b 237b
6:11	746c	**9:7**	602a	**12:4**	12a 85a 105b		304a 505j
6:12	456e 456f	**9:8**	332e		301z		547b 547r
	579ap	**9:9**	651d	**12:5**	372g 646c		579q 953f
6:14	169b	**9:10**	332e	**12:6**	108e 129d	**13:11**	184d 532p
6:15	169b	**9:11**	500e		362bn	**13:12**	119a 372c
6:16	131j 169b	**9:12**	456e 602h	**12:7**	263f 335l	**13:13**	792h
6:18	131j	**9:13**	128b 746c 981d	**12:8**	301z 323i 381m	**13:14**	160b 304a 459i
6:20	131j 169b	**9:14**	21b 659a		391a		742p
6:29	13a	**9:15**	362bi	**12:10**	41a 381ai	**13:15**	119e 362bi
6:30	579ap	**9:16**	160c 561c	**12:11**	669m 988c		372c
7:1	579ab 966m	**9:17**	866y	**12:12**	13a 119e 362bi	**13:16**	53d 160b 237b
7:2	746c	**9:18**	350af	**12:13**	335l 547d 919e		304a 547b 547r
7:3	602h 864b	**9:19**	660f	**12:14**	115i 505j 988d	**13:17**	172u 603c 718b
7:4	304a 456e	**9:20**	854e	**12:15**	110o 323i 963o	**13:18**	343i 722i
7:5	490n	**9:21**	456e	**12:16**	74k 677a	**13:19**	363f 532j
7:7	131g^2	**9:23**	218a 350af 381p	**12:17**	304a 988d	**13:21**	267a 283a
7:9	218a 365o 864f	**9:24**	381p	**12:18**	108e^2 323i		355c 381q 417i
7:11	500e 983e	**9:25**	165o	**12:19**	963o	**14:2**	343i
7:12	165u	**9:27**	914ad	**12:21**	986ae		

14:4	490*n* 602*h* 619*g* 866*f*	**15:26** 455*l* 650*a* 658*a*	**18:7** 311*a* 889*b*	**20:14** 951*k*
14:5	603*c*	**15:27** 339*d* 366*n*	**18:8** 668*i*	**20:15** 788*d*
14:6	274*a*	**16:1** 108*f* 172*w*	**18:9** 824*p*	**20:16** 466*t*
14:8	602*h* 619*g*	**16:2** 829*a*	**18:10** 923*l*	**20:17** 859*w*
14:9	274*a* 343*i*	**16:3** 361*s* 635*a*	**18:11** 638*a* 966*b*	**20:18** 176*k* 199*d*
14:10	761*p* 854*ad*	**16:4** 301*ae* 461*c*	**18:12** 301*z* 981*p*	388*e* 414*g* 854*l*
14:11	361*p* 364*f*	**16:5** 91*b*	**18:13** 480*m* 957*g*	**20:19** 361*aa* 579*o*
14:12	620*t*	**16:6** 129*c* 490*o*	**18:15** 459*b*	**20:20** 461*d* 854*d*
14:13	439*h* 668*i*	**16:7** 128*e* 829*a*	**18:16** 480*m*	854*ai* 914*p*
14:14	716*a*	**16:8** 128*e* 129*c* 829*a*	**18:18** 655*e* 700*a*	**20:21** 199*d* 355*d*
14:15	146*e* 854*ai*	**16:9** 829*a*	**18:19** 691*h* 751*d*	**20:22** 579*o*
14:16	46*l* 218*a* 342*a* 343*i*	**16:10** 355*e* 866*e*	**18:20** 534*j* 953*f*	**20:23** 966*c* 982*e*
14:17	602*h* 866*f*	**16:12** 128*e* 129*c* 490*n* 829*a*	**18:21** 494*h* 605*o* 741*ab* 771*i* 854*e*	**20:24** 505*k* 561*c* 990*d*
14:18	490*n* 866*f*	**16:13** 128*e* 129*c* 341*e* 365*am*	**18:22** 480*m* 957*d*	**20:25** 46*k* 630*c* 670*b* 990*d*
14:19	238*d* 355*c* 968*g*		**18:25** 605*o* 741*ab*	**20:26** 229*e* 308*d* 990*d*
14:20	417*i*	**16:15** 13*l* 301*ae* 491*aa* 561*s*	**18:26** 480*m*	**21:2** 110*y* 745*e* 746*h*
14:21	46*l* 342*a* 352*g*	**16:16** 12*a* 26*a* 85*a*	**18:27** 882*j*	**21:3** 894*h*
14:22	241*f*	**16:17** 32*a* 33*a*	**19:1** 108*g* 172*w*	**21:4** 170*c* 894*h*
14:23	274*a* 619*g*	**16:18** 28*j* 32*a* 33*a* 635*c* 637*b*	**19:2** 209*k*	**21:5** 746*j*
14:24	128*g* 441*g*		**19:3** 308*c*	**21:6** 263*f* 415*g* 630*a* 655*k*
14:25	315*a* 700*b* 716*a*	**16:19** 41*b*	**19:4** 273*l*	**21:7** 373*g* 746*j*
14:26	218*a* 343*i*	**16:20** 51*a* 891*w*	**19:5** 768*b* 773*b* 777*f*	**21:8** 792*h*
14:28	274*a* 361*ag*	**16:21** 337*a*	**19:6** 979*f* 986*x*	**21:10** 37*a* 228*w* 301*c* 894*t*
14:29	241*f* 342*a*	**16:22** 26*a* 91*b*	**19:8** 739*b*	**21:11** 812*c*
14:30	668*i*	**16:23** 41*b* 381*m* 683*a*	**19:9** 355*e* 485*ad*	**21:12** 279*a* 362*d* 655*f* 963*k*
14:31	160*c* 485*g* 485*ad* 854*l*	**16:24** 51*a*	**19:10** 648*l* 979*i*	**21:13** 362*d* 618*b* 620*m*
15:1	412*c*	**16:25** 683*e*	**19:11** 309*e*	**21:14** 660*f* 698*b*
15:2	162*b* 668*b* 923*g* 965*e*	**16:30** 683*a*	**19:12** 235*s* 378*d*	**21:15** 169*n* 279*a* 963*m*
15:3	561*a* 722*a*	**16:31** 301*ae* 386*a* 392*a* 561*s*	**19:13** 287*a* 414*g*	**21:16** 788*a* 963*m*
15:4	274*a* 361*ag*	**16:32** 194*a* 632*c*	**19:14** 648*l* 979*i*	**21:17** 169*n* 899*a* 963*m*
15:6	160*b* 241*a*	**16:33** 194*i*	**19:15** 895*f*	**21:18** 279*a*
15:7	891*c*	**16:35** 110*ac*	**19:16** 176*k* 355*d* 414*g* 854*l*	**21:19** 457*k* 787*a*
15:8	209*aa* 339*w*	**16:36** 465*c*		**21:20** 279*a* 963*i*
15:9	619*g*	**17:1** 267*a* 342*e*	**19:18** 176*f* 381*p*	**21:22** 172*k* 279*a* 963*i* 963*j*
15:10	322*j* 352*g*	**17:2** 461*f* 709*g*	**19:19** 176*k* 414*g*	**21:23** 28*o* 963*i*
15:11	21*a* 21*b* 864*a* 979*b*	**17:3** 829*a* 859*l*	**19:20** 308*c* 309*e*	**21:24** 53*c* 256*n* 438*m*
15:12	165*u*	**17:4** 761*r*	**19:21** 438*d* 664*a*	**21:26** 438*m* 746*h*
15:13	192*a* 689*d* 792*n* 897*m*	**17:5** 218*a*	**19:22** 979*i*	**21:27** 256*n*
15:14	854*k*	**17:6** 279*m* 339*k* 344*q*	**19:23** 235*s*	**21:28** 362*bp* 365*aw* 365*ay*
15:16	266*c* 792*n*	**17:7** 89*d* 461*f* 709*g*	**20:2** 13*a* 304*a* 742*p*	**21:29** 963*m*
15:17	192*a* 209*x*	**17:8** 712*e*	**20:3** 966*c*	**21:30** 792*h*
15:18	115*g* 733*b*	**17:9** 218*a* 716*d*	**20:4** 18*j* 982*e*	**21:32** 809*c*
15:19	274*a* 342*a*	**17:11** 761*l*	**20:5** 169*x* 888*e* 911*b* 963*a* 982*f*	**21:33** 255*a*
15:20	414*b* 579*aa* 835*d*	**17:12** 218*ah* 344*t* 684*a*	**20:6** 887*g* 887*n*	**21:34** 787*b*
15:21	412*c* 866*g*	**17:13** 727*g*	**20:7** 561*i* 980*g*	**21:35** 92*a* 362*bp*
15:22	172*w* 342*e*	**17:14** 165*o* 506*g* 586*m* 589*c*	**20:8** 683*d*	**21:36** 787*b*
15:23	339*h* 391*c* 561*s*	**17:15** 547*ab* 990*e*	**20:9** 677*a*	**22:1** 777*a* 787*a* 788*c*
15:24	301*c* 829*a*	**17:16** 532*q* 718*i*	**20:10** 683*a*	**22:2** 362*a* 936*h*
15:25	366*v* 392*h* 461*d* 761*r*	**18:1** 304*a* 986*q*	**20:11** 110*n* 164*a* 683*a* 897*e* 979*t*	
		18:3 59*u* 561*r*	**20:12** 113*c* 113*d* 169*i* 184*a* 866*u* 920*b*	
		18:4 561*r* 703*b*	**20:13** 362*a*	
		18:5 209*k*		

30:10   254*h* 335*m*
       941*g* 979*aa*
       981*y*
30:12   86*d*
30:13   465*b* 804*g*
30:14   131*c*
30:15   28*i* 804*g* 941*j*
30:18   648*u*
30:19   648*c*
30:21   361*aa*
30:22   357*c* 396*a*
30:23   26*b*
30:26   194*a* 357*m*
       466*i* 990*k*
30:27   990*c*
30:28   648*u* 990*a*
30:29   378*d* 420*f* 979*r*
       979*aa*
30:30   357*d*
30:33   963*o*
30:34   26*b* 396*b*
30:36   979*aa*
30:38   963*o*
31:2   605*b* 696*e* 751*b*
31:3   54*i* 965*q*
31:6   696*b* 751*b*
31:7   194*a* 226*l* 466*i*
       990*k*
31:8   218*ae* 420*f* 990*c*
31:9   648*u* 990*a*
31:10   986*i* 989*a*
31:11   357*c* 396*b*
31:13   547*b* 683*d*
31:14   963*o* 979*t*
31:15   683*a* 963*o* 979*t*
31:17   110*n* 164*a*
       547*b* 683*a*
       685*a*
31:18   53*p* 90*q* 378*s*
       466*i* 548*c* 586*a*
32:1   136*e* 491*v* 966*j*
32:2   844*d*
32:4   304*b* 554*a* 982*j*
32:5   990*e*
32:6   128*b* 837*b* 981*p*
       981*w* 982*i*
32:7   304*a* 655*b*
32:9   602*b*
32:10   104*j* 165*r* 891*i*
32:11   160*b* 304*a* 761*k*
32:12   362*bh*
32:13   104*c* 184*a*
       505*a* 532*o*
       532*p*
32:14   603*b*
32:15   90*q* 466*i* 548*c*
       586*a*

32:17   577*e*
32:18   412*a* 577*e*
32:19   46*m* 835*f* 891*w*
32:20   301*ar* 332*f*
       381*h*
32:23   491*v* 966*j*
32:25   61*a*
32:26   74*f* 263*o* 706*b*
32:27   362*ad* 723*k*
32:29   979*i*
32:30   914*z* 941*k*
32:31   761*k* 966*j*
32:32   165*v* 589*l* 909*e*
32:33   165*v* 589*l*
32:34   963*a* 968*l*
33:1   184*d* 532*p*
33:2   300*h* 371*v* 968*l*
33:3   190*b* 602*b* 635*d*
33:4   836*v* 844*f*
33:5   602*b*
33:7   223*e* 459*w* 990*j*
33:9   355*c* 579*o*
33:10   441*b* 981*e*
33:11   200*a* 579*o* 880*c*
33:12   826*f*
33:13   371*ac* 490*r*
       624*b* 826*f*
33:14   89*a* 683*m*
33:16   15*b* 826*f*
33:17   826*f*
33:18   866*i*
33:19   561*c* 644*a* 905*c*
33:20   438*e*
33:22   46*k* 226*a*
33:23   238*a*
34:1   90*q* 548*c* 586*a*
34:2   209*k* 308*c*
34:4   90*q* 548*c*
34:5   309*e* 355*e* 561*c*
34:6   494*f* 891*n* 905*d*
34:7   169*x* 909*a* 963*a*
34:8   311*f*
34:9   89*a* 602*b* 777*f*
       826*f* 909*e*
34:10   765*c* 854*b* 864*b*
34:11   300*h* 371*v*
34:12   765*q*
34:13   165*j*
34:14   911*b* 966*d*
34:15   765*q* 951*x* 982*i*
34:16   894*w*
34:17   982*e*
34:18   108*e* 110*o* 988*d*
34:19   119*a*
34:20   792*h*
34:21   683*a*
34:22   171*l* 988*h*

34:23   94*a* 141*c*
34:24   183*a* 300*h* 859*y*
34:25   41*a* 323*j*
34:26   132*l* 169*aj* 171*l*
       335*a* 381*m*
34:27   586*a* 765*c*
34:28   110*r* 765*d* 953*a*
34:29   90*q* 417*q* 466*i*
34:30   199*d* 854*ae*
34:33   226*f* 421*f*
34:35   417*q* 421*f*
35:2   683*a* 963*o*
35:3   381*am*
35:5   631*a* 781*p*
35:6   435*f* 631*q*
35:7   226*v* 431*c*
35:8   357*a* 357*c* 396*a*
       396*b*
35:9   844*g* 989*c* 989*d*
35:10   696*e* 990*k*
35:12   194*a* 421*d*
35:13   189*d* 301*aa*
35:14   357*a* 420*f*
35:15   396*b* 990*c*
35:16   990*a*
35:19   986*i* 989*a*
35:21   631*a* 781*p*
35:22   631*a* 844*g*
35:23   226*v* 431*c* 435*f*
       631*q*
35:25   222*k* 435*f* 631*q*
35:27   844*g* 989*c* 989*d*
35:28   357*a* 357*c* 396*b*
35:29   781*p*
35:30   696*e* 751*b*
35:31   54*i* 498*k* 965*q*
35:33   554*a*
35:34   534*l*
35:35   435*f* 631*q*
36:1   696*b*
36:2   696*b*
36:5   637*a*
36:8   421*a* 435*f* 631*q*
       990*k*
36:9   195*a*
36:11   250*b* 435*d*
36:13   47*a*
36:14   421*a*
36:15   195*a*
36:17   250*b*
36:18   47*a*
36:20   207*a*
36:21   195*a*
36:22   47*c*
36:24   255*m*
36:31   47*c*
36:34   226*q*^{2}

36:35   421*d* 435*f* 631*q*
36:36   218*n* 226*q*
       255*m*
36:37   421*a* 435*f* 631*q*
36:38   218*n* 226*q*
       255*m*
37:1   194*a* 195*a*
37:2   226*q*
37:3   250*a*
37:4   218*i* 226*q*
37:6   195*a* 226*l*
37:7   968*u*
37:9   226*m* 237*f* 271*c*
37:10   195*a* 218*ae*
37:11   226*q*
37:13   250*a*
37:14   218*i*
37:15   226*q*
37:16   194*g*
37:17   420*f*
37:18   99*f*
37:25   28*n* 195*a* 990*c*
37:26   226*q* 254*h*
37:28   226*q*
37:29   357*c* 396*b*
38:1   990*a*
38:2   226*r* 254*g*
38:3   194*g*
38:5   250*a*
38:6   218*i* 226*r*
38:7   250*a* 255*o*
38:8   442*a* 648*u*
38:9   195*a* 235*a* 421*b*
       631*p*
38:10   218*n* 255*m*
38:16   631*p*
38:18   421*b* 435*f* 631*q*
38:20   47*b*
38:21   631*a* 986*i*
38:23   435*f* 631*q*
38:24   26*c*
38:25   86*b*
38:26   99*v* 131*c* 804*g*
38:27   255*m*
38:30   255*m*
38:31   47*b*
39:1   435*f* 989*a*
39:2   435*f* 631*q* 989*d*
39:3   208*b* 435*f*
39:5   435*f* 631*q*
39:6   561*ac* 586*o*
       844*h*
39:8   435*f* 631*q* 989*c*
39:9   28*n*
39:10   844*h*
39:14   99*n* 561*ac* 586*o*
39:16   250*a*

39:19 250*a*	**40:33** 235*a* 421*b*^{2}	**4:17** 99*g* 335*m*	**6:20** 357*d* 981*r*
39:22 435*a* 989*e*	**40:34** 355*d* 866*e*	**4:18** 254*h*	**6:21** 357*o* 396*h*
39:23 47*d*	**40:36** 296*a* 355*f*	**4:19** 357*ai*	**6:23** 301*ab*
39:24 435*f*	**40:37** 355*f*	**4:20** 909*k* 941*c*	**6:24** 981*x*
39:25 414*a*	**40:38** 355*d* 381*q*	**4:21** 223*e*	**6:25** 979*aa*
39:27 631*p* 989*f*		**4:22** 618*a* 914*o*	**6:26** 301*ab*
39:28 631*p* 989*g*^{2}	**Leviticus**	**4:23** 372*g* 646*c*	**6:27** 335*n* 648*l* 979*u*
989*i*	**1:3** 263*d* 372*g* 646*c*	**4:24** 378*t*	**6:28** 194*n* 648*s*
39:29 435*f* 631*q* 989*h*	981*l*	**4:25** 254*g*	**6:29** 301*ac* 372*e*
39:30 586*p* 743*e* 979*w*	**1:4** 378*t* 941*f*	**4:26** 357*ai* 909*k* 941*c*	979*aa*
39:31 208*a* 435*d*	**1:5** 335*m*	**4:27** 618*a* 914*o*	**6:30** 301*ab*
39:32 725*g*	**1:6** 229*v*	**4:28** 373*l* 646*c*	**7:1** 979*aa* 981*ad*
39:33 47*c* 207*a* 218*n*	**1:7** 381*af* 385*a* 986*i*	**4:29** 378*t*	**7:2** 335*m*
255*m*	**1:9** 396*h* 648*s*	**4:30** 254*g*	**7:3** 357*ai*
39:34 226*n* 226*v*	**1:10** 372*g* 646*c*	**4:31** 357*ai* 909*k* 941*c*	**7:4** 53*t*
421*d* 431*c*	**1:11** 335*m*	**4:32** 373*l* 646*c*	**7:6** 301*ab* 301*ac*
39:35 194*a* 218*i* 226*l*	**1:13** 648*s*	**4:33** 378*t*	372*e* 979*aa*
466*i*	**1:15** 335*m*^{2}	**4:34** 254*g*	**7:7** 941*c*
39:36 189*d* 218*ae*	**2:1** 357*o* 396*b* 981*r*	**4:35** 357*ai* 909*k* 941*c*	**7:8** 226*u*
301*aa*	**2:2** 505*k*	**5:1** 466*a* 532*r* 582*l*	**7:9** 981*r*
39:37 357*a* 420*f*	**2:3** 301*ab* 979*aa*	936*c*	**7:11** 981*v*
39:38 357*c* 396*b*	**2:4** 323*j* 357*o*	**5:2** 378*e* 649*e*	**7:12** 323*j* 357*o* 907*f*
421*a* 990*c*	**2:9** 505*k*	**5:3** 649*f*	**7:13** 323*f*
39:39 648*u* 990*a*	**2:10** 301*ab* 979*aa*	**5:4** 450*a* 532*a*	**7:14** 301*ab*
39:40 47*b* 218*n* 255*m*	**2:11** 323*j* 392*d*	**5:5** 526*p*	**7:15** 41*a*
421*b*^{2}	**2:12** 171*l*	**5:6** 373*l* 941*c* 981*x*	**7:17** 381*ai*
39:41 986*i* 989*a*	**2:13** 388*b* 765*f*	981*ae*	**7:19** 649*n*
39:43 897*w*	**2:14** 381*m*	**5:7** 801*d* 981*ae*	**7:20** 963*o*
40:2 108*e* 990*k*	**2:15** 357*o* 396*b*	**5:10** 941*c*	**7:23** 357*af*
40:3 194*a*^{2} 421*d*^{2}	**2:16** 505*k*	**5:11** 357*p* 396*b* 801*d*	**7:24** 357*af*
466*i*	**3:1** 372*h* 646*c* 981*v*	**5:12** 505*k*	**7:25** 963*o*
40:4 218*ae* 420*f*	**3:2** 335*m* 378*t*	**5:13** 301*ab* 909*k*	**7:26** 335*g* 963*o*
40:5 421*d* 466*i* 990*c*	**3:3** 357*ai*	941*c*	**7:29** 981*v*
40:6 990*a*	**3:4** 53*t*	**5:15** 618*a* 646*c* 936*c*	**7:30** 317*a* 357*ai*
40:7 648*u*	**3:6** 372*h* 646*c*	981*ae*	**7:32** 301*ab*
40:8 235*a*	**3:8** 335*m* 378*t*	**5:16** 102*i* 787*a* 941*c*	**7:33** 357*ai*
40:9 357*m* 979*r*	**3:9** 357*ai*	**5:17** 491*w* 936*c*	**7:37** 981*j*
40:10 979*r* 979*aa*	**3:10** 53*t*	**5:18** 618*a* 646*c* 941*c*	**8:2** 323*j* 751*b* 981*y*
990*a*	**3:11** 301*aa*	981*ae*	**8:6** 648*x*
40:11 648*u*	**3:13** 335*m* 378*t*	**5:19** 936*c*	**8:7** 989*a*
40:12 648*x*	**3:14** 357*ai*	**6:2** 542*a* 788*g* 930*c*	**8:8** 605*s*
40:13 357*d* 986*b* 989*a*	**3:15** 53*t*	**6:3** 532*a* 542*a*	**8:10** 357*m* 979*r* 990*k*
40:15 115*i* 986*b*	**3:16** 357*af*	**6:4** 787*a*	**8:11** 99*g* 357*m* 990*a*
40:17 108*e* 990*k*	**3:17** 335*g* 357*af*	**6:5** 102*i*	**8:12** 357*d* 979*i*
40:19 226*n*	**4:1** 981*x*	**6:6** 646*c* 981*ae*	**8:13** 989*a*
40:20 226*l* 466*i*	**4:2** 618*a* 914*o*	**6:7** 909*k* 941*c*	**8:14** 378*t* 981*y*
40:21 194*a*^{2} 421*d*	**4:3** 646*c* 914*o* 986*j*	**6:8** 981*l*	**8:15** 254*g* 335*m* 941*g*
466*i*	**4:4** 378*t*	**6:10** 989*i*	**8:16** 53*t* 357*ai*
40:22 218*ae*	**4:5** 986*j*	**6:11** 381*ah*	**8:17** 223*e*
40:23 301*aa*	**4:6** 99*g* 335*m*	**6:12** 357*ai* 981*v*	**8:18** 378*t* 981*n*
40:24 420*f*	**4:7** 254*h*	**6:13** 381*af*	**8:21** 396*h* 648*s*
40:26 990*c*	**4:8** 357*ai*	**6:14** 981*r*	**8:22** 378*t*
40:27 396*b*	**4:9** 53*t*	**6:15** 357*o* 396*b* 505*k*	**8:23** 53*o* 241*e* 335*m*
40:28 421*a*	**4:12** 223*e* 648*s*	**6:16** 301*ab* 323*j*	415*g*
40:29 981*s* 990*a*	**4:13** 914*o*	**6:17** 323*j* 979*aa*	**8:25** 53*t* 357*ai*
40:30 648*u*	**4:15** 378*t*	**6:18** 301*ac* 372*e*	**8:26** 323*j*
40:31 648*c*	**4:16** 986*i*	979*u*	**8:27** 317*a*

8:28	396*h*	**11:33**	46*o*	**14:7**	335*m* 746*q*	**15:27**	648*g* 648*l*
8:29	317*a*	**11:35**	46*o*	**14:8**	110*o* 648*i* 648*l*	**15:29**	981*o*
8:30	335*m* 357*d*	**11:36**	363*o*	**14:9**	648*i*	**15:30**	941*c* 981*z*
8:31	301*ab*	**11:39**	649*f*	**14:10**	373*l* 646*c* 981*s*	**15:33**	45*j*
8:32	41*a* 381*ai*	**11:40**	648*l*	**14:12**	317*a* 981*ae*	**16:1**	361*z* 941*a*
8:33	110*o*	**11:41**	888*c*	**14:13**	301*ab* 979*aa*	**16:2**	226*m* 355*e*
9:2	646*c* 981*p* 981*y*	**11:42**	53*n* 311*u*	**14:14**	53*o* 241*e* 335*m*		361*aa* 445*a*
9:3	646*c* 981*p* 981*y*	**11:44**	979*d*		415*g*		979*r*
9:4	357*o* 981*r* 981*w*	**11:47**	15*a*	**14:16**	99*g* 357*q*	**16:3**	297*a* 979*r* 981*n*
9:6	866*e*	**12:2**	110*o* 167*d* 372*c*	**14:17**	53*o* 241*e* 357*j*		981*y*
9:7	941*c* 981*y*		649*h*		415*g* 981*ae*	**16:4**	648*g* 989*a* 989*i*
9:9	254*g* 335*m*^{2}	**12:3**	131*f* 988*m*	**14:18**	213*e* 941*c*	**16:5**	372*g* 981*n* 981*y*
9:10	53*t* 357*ai* 981*y*	**12:5**	373*g*	**14:19**	981*o* 981*z*	**16:6**	941*d*
9:11	223*e*	**12:6**	981*o* 981*z*	**14:20**	981*s*	**16:8**	605*r* 786*m*
9:12	335*m* 981*p*	**12:7**	302*e* 941*c*	**14:21**	317*a* 801*d* 981*s*	**16:9**	981*y*
9:14	648*s*	**12:8**	801*d* 941*c* 981*z*	**14:22**	981*o* 981*z*	**16:10**	172*v* 786*m*
9:15	981*y*	**13:2**	651*m* 986*i*	**14:24**	317*a*	**16:11**	941*d* 981*y*
9:16	981*p*	**13:3**	427*d* 438*q* 649*h*	**14:25**	241*e* 335*m*	**16:12**	381*af* 396*b*
9:17	981*r*	**13:4**	110*o* 427*d*		415*g* 981*ae*	**16:13**	355*g* 361*aa*
9:18	335*m* 981*w*	**13:5**	110*o*	**14:27**	99*g* 357*q*	**16:14**	99*g* 226*l* 335*m*
9:19	53*t* 357*ai*	**13:6**	648*l* 648*w*	**14:28**	53*o* 241*e* 357*j*	**16:15**	226*l* 981*y*
9:21	317*a*	**13:7**	197*b*		415*g* 981*ae*	**16:16**	941*c* 979*r*
9:22	897*w* 981*w*	**13:8**	649*k*	**14:29**	213*e* 941*c*	**16:17**	941*d* 979*r*
9:23	866*e* 897*w*	**13:10**	427*d*	**14:31**	981*o* 981*s* 981*z*	**16:18**	254*h* 990*c*
9:24	381*t*	**13:11**	649*k*	**14:33**	192*ae*	**16:19**	99*g*
10:1	381*af*	**13:13**	648*w*	**14:36**	438*q* 649*o*	**16:20**	786*m* 979*r*
10:2	361*z* 381*t*	**13:15**	649*k*	**14:38**	110*o*	**16:21**	172*v* 187*e* 378*t*
10:3	582*g* 979*a*	**13:17**	648*w*	**14:39**	438*q*		526*p*
10:4	223*f*	**13:20**	427*d* 649*k*	**14:44**	438*q*	**16:22**	273*i* 746*q*
10:5	273*g*	**13:21**	110*o* 427*d*	**14:48**	438*q*	**16:23**	229*o* 979*r*
10:6	259*h* 836*i* 836*ai*	**13:22**	197*b* 649*k*	**14:49**	366*g* 431*b* 648*s*	**16:24**	648*g* 941*c*
10:7	357*d*	**13:23**	648*w*	**14:50**	350*f*		941*d* 981*n*
10:9	948*a*	**13:25**	427*d* 649*k*	**14:51**	335*m* 366*g*	**16:25**	981*y*
10:10	15*a*	**13:26**	110*o* 427*d*		431*b*	**16:26**	648*g*
10:11	534*j*	**13:27**	197*b* 649*k*	**14:53**	746*q* 941*c*	**16:27**	223*e* 941*g* 979*r*
10:12	301*ac* 979*aa*	**13:28**	648*w*	**15:2**	302*a* 649*h*		981*y*
	981*r*	**13:30**	649*k*	**15:4**	218*v*	**16:28**	648*g* 648*l*
10:14	301*ac* 981*v*	**13:31**	110*o*	**15:5**	648*g* 648*l* 648*w*	**16:29**	108*k* 677*a* 872*i*
10:15	317*c*	**13:33**	110*o*	**15:6**	218*v* 648*g*	**16:30**	648*ab* 941*b*
10:16	381*aj* 891*w*	**13:34**	648*l* 648*w*	**15:7**	378*e* 648*g*	**16:31**	683*c*
	981*j*	**13:35**	197*b*	**15:8**	302*a*	**16:32**	941*c* 986*i*
10:17	941*c* 979*aa*	**13:37**	648*w*	**15:9**	218*v*		989*a*
10:19	916*c*	**13:40**	229*u*	**15:10**	648*g* 648*l*	**17:3**	335*b* 362*bn*
11:2	648*z* 649*m*	**13:44**	649*h* 649*k*	**15:11**	378*e* 648*g*		981*j*
11:3	46*j* 301*aj* 648*z*	**13:45**	226*f* 259*d* 649*k*	**15:12**	46*o*	**17:4**	936*c* 963*o*
11:8	363*o*		836*h*	**15:13**	110*o* 648*g* 648*l*	**17:6**	357*ai* 396*h*
11:9	53*s* 226*w* 649*m*	**13:46**	88*l* 223*e*	**15:14**	981*o*	**17:7**	967*q*
11:10	888*c*	**13:47**	228*k* 651*p*	**15:15**	941*c* 981*z*	**17:9**	963*o*
11:11	363*o* 888*c*	**13:50**	110*o* 438*q*	**15:16**	302*c* 648*g*	**17:10**	335*g* 963*o*
11:13	649*m*	**13:51**	197*b* 649*o*	**15:18**	45*j* 648*g*	**17:11**	335*b* 335*m*
11:20	311*u* 649*m*	**13:54**	110*o*	**15:19**	302*d*		360*a* 941*g*
11:21	312*c*	**14:2**	648*y* 651*m*	**15:20**	218*v*	**17:13**	335*b*
11:24	363*o* 649*f*	**14:3**	438*q*	**15:21**	648*g*	**17:14**	335*g* 360*a*
11:25	648*l*	**14:4**	366*g* 431*b*	**15:22**	648*g* 648*l*	**17:15**	301*ap* 363*o*
11:28	648*l*	**14:5**	350*f*	**15:24**	45*j*^{2} 110*o*		648*g* 648*l* 649*f*
11:29	365*n* 649*m*	**14:6**	335*m* 366*g*	**15:25**	302*e*	**18:3**	20*g*
11:31	363*o* 649*f*		431*b*	**15:26**	218*v*	**18:5**	676*e*

27:1 809b	3:13 119a	4:31 207a 218n 255n 273a	7:15 981p
27:2 532u	3:15 86e 131c 372d	4:33 690a	7:16 981ab
27:3 131c 372c 809b	3:17 169b	4:34 86e 131d	7:17 981w
27:4 373g 809b	3:21 281v	4:38 86e 131d	7:19 194h 357o 981r
27:5 131c 809b²	3:22 86e 131c	4:42 86e 131d	7:20 396b
27:7 809b²	3:23 281s	4:46 86e	7:21 981p
27:9 809i	3:25 226o 421a 990k	5:2 300u 302a 649k 651m	7:22 981ab
27:10 150c	3:26 235b 421b 990a	5:3 192e 372a	7:23 981w
27:11 649n	3:27 169b 990k	5:7 102i 526p 787a	7:25 194h 357o 981r
27:13 102i	3:28 86e 131c	5:8 941h	7:26 396b
27:14 192ab	3:29 281l	5:9 301ab	7:27 981p
27:15 102i	3:31 194a 218ae 420f 421d 990c	5:11 911h	7:28 981ab
27:16 235p	3:33 169b	5:12 951g	7:29 981w
27:19 102i	3:34 86e 131c	5:15 357p 396b 981r	7:31 194h 357o 981r
27:25 797b	3:35 281b	5:17 332a 339u	7:32 396b
27:26 119a	3:36 218n 255n 990k	5:18 259d 339i 391c 746t 981r	7:33 981p
27:27 102i 649n	3:37 47b	5:19 899f	7:34 981ab
27:28 165w 979aa	3:38 281p 361ab	5:21 36d 224e 532c 899f	7:35 981w
27:29 165w 792j	3:39 86e 131c	5:22 36d 488c	7:37 194h 357o 981r
27:30 102b	3:40 86b 119a 131c 150a 372d	5:23 301ar 391c 586t 899f	7:38 396b
27:31 102i	3:46 792h 809c	5:25 981r	7:39 981p
27:32 102b	3:47 797b	5:27 36d 172e 224e 391c	7:40 981ab
27:33 150c	4:1 990k	6:1 46ag 532v	7:41 981w
	4:2 86e 131d	6:3 948b	7:43 194h 357o 981r
Numbers	4:3 131d	6:5 259j 648k 979g	7:44 396b
1:1 108f	4:4 979aa 979ab	6:6 363b 649j	7:45 981p
1:2 86b 372d	4:5 194a 226n² 421d 466i	6:8 979g	7:46 981ab
1:3 131c² 722k 722l	4:6 218i 226v 435b	6:9 648i	7:47 981w
1:4 741aa	4:7 189d 194j 218ae 301aa 435b	6:11 941c 981o 981z	7:49 194h 357o 981r
1:18 108f 131c²	4:8 218i 226v 431c	6:12 981ae	7:50 396b
1:20 131c 722k	4:9 435b	6:14 373l 646c³ 981n 981v 981y	7:51 981p
1:44 741aa	4:10 218j 226v	6:15 357o 981s	7:52 981ab
1:46 99v	4:11 218i 226v 435b	6:16 981n	7:53 981w
1:47 86e 986y	4:12 218j 226v 435b	6:17 981s 981v	7:55 194h 357o 981r
1:50 986y 990k	4:13 436a	6:18 259i 648i	7:56 396b
1:51 361ab	4:14 218i 226v	6:19 317a	7:57 981p
1:53 986y	4:15 273a 361aa 378d	6:20 948b	7:58 981ab
2:1 65c	4:16 357a 357c 396b 981r	6:23 897d	7:59 981w
2:2 192w 547aa 990j	4:18 361aa	6:24 666a	7:61 194h 357o 981r
2:3 281p 281v 547aa	4:19 979aa	6:25 417d 417l	7:62 396b
2:10 281l 547aa	4:20 441a	6:26 719a	7:63 981p
2:17 986y 990j	4:21 990k	6:27 561d	7:64 981ab
2:18 281s 547aa	4:22 86e 131d	7:1 357m	7:65 981w
2:25 281b 547aa	4:23 131d	7:2 741aa 781p	7:67 194h 357o 981r
2:32 99v	4:24 273a	7:3 274i	7:68 396b
2:34 547aa	4:25 226v 421a	7:8 690a²	7:69 981p
3:1 169g	4:26 421b	7:9 273a	7:70 981ab
3:2 169b	4:28 690a	7:10 876g 990a	7:71 981w
3:3 986b	4:29 86e 131d 990k	7:13 194h 357o 981r	7:73 194h 357o 981r
3:4 172b 361z 381af	4:30 131d	7:14 396b	7:74 396b
3:6 986y			7:75 981p
3:9 986y			7:76 981ab
3:10 361ab			7:77 981w
3:12 119a 773c			7:79 194h 357o 981r
			7:80 396b
			7:81 981p
			7:82 981ab

18:11	301*ac*	**21:5**	301*ae* 342*e*	**23:11**	897*h*	**26:55**	605*r*
18:13	171*l*		361*p* 636*b*	**23:12**	579*q*	**26:57**	86*e*
18:15	119*a* 792*h*		926*b*	**23:13**	899*j*	**26:61**	361*z* 381*af*
18:16	809*c*	**21:6**	361*z* 365*o*	**23:14**	99*c*	**26:62**	131*c* 774*a*
18:17	335*m* 357*ai*	**21:7**	761*k* 914*ac*	**23:15**	981*p*	**26:63**	86*b*
	396*h*		926*b*	**23:17**	981*p*	**26:65**	41*h* 361*z*
18:19	115*k* 301*ab*	**21:8**	365*p*	**23:19**	371*b* 541*b*	**27:1**	170*i*
	388*b* 765*f*	**21:9**	438*o*		603*a* 725*b*	**27:2**	263*d*
18:20	774*a* 777*k*	**21:10**	267*a*	**23:20**	897*h*	**27:3**	172*b*
18:21	102*d*	**21:13**	236*b*	**23:21**	89*a* 741*b*	**27:4**	771*a*
18:22	361*ab*	**21:14**	589*b*	**23:22**	162*c* 304*a*	**27:12**	184*c* 209*t*
18:24	301*ab* 774*a*	**21:16**	339*k*	**23:23**	676*d* 983*i*	**27:13**	361*ad*
18:26	102*d*	**21:17**	339*d*	**23:24**	335*j* 365*af*	**27:14**	172*w* 738*f*
18:30	301*ab* 301*ad*	**21:22**	305*c* 339*s* 624*h*	**23:25**	899*j*	**27:16**	320*b* 751*b* 965*f*
19:2	126*a* 431*e* 646*c*	**21:23**	716*d* 757*f*	**23:26**	579*q*	**27:17**	283*d* 369*j*
19:4	99*g* 335*m*	**21:24**	184*p* 727*d* 771*d*	**23:29**	99*c*	**27:18**	378*v* 965*m*
19:6	366*g* 431*c*	**21:25**	184*aa*	**24:1**	897*h* 983*i*	**27:20**	733*af*
19:7	648*g* 648*l*	**21:26**	184*p* 727*e*	**24:2**	192*w* 965*m*	**27:21**	459*c* 605*s*
19:8	648*g* 648*l*	**21:29**	165*o* 967*k*	**24:4**	438*d*	**27:23**	378*v*
19:9	339*u* 381*ah*	**21:32**	459*q*	**24:5**	192*v* 841*n*	**28:2**	301*aa* 396*h*
19:10	648*l*	**21:33**	718*h*	**24:6**	350*i* 370*c*	**28:3**	141*e* 372*g* 646*c*
19:11	110*o* 363*b* 649*f*	**21:34**	727*i* 854*af*	**24:7**	339*k* 350*i* 741*m*		981*m* 981*s*
19:13	339*u* 649*a* 963*o*	**21:35**	362*ax* 771*d*	**24:8**	162*c* 304*a*	**28:4**	128*i*
19:14	110*o* 363*a*	**22:3**	104*g* 854*x*	**24:9**	365*af* 897*j* 899*k*	**28:5**	357*o*
19:15	194*w*	**22:6**	300*l* 899*k*	**24:10**	891*w*	**28:8**	129*d* 396*h*
19:16	110*o* 363*b*	**22:7**	809*n*	**24:11**	962*f*	**28:9**	141*e* 372*g* 646*c*
19:17	339*u* 381*ah*	**22:8**	459*a*	**24:13**	579*q*		683*a* 981*n* 981*s*
19:18	366*g*	**22:9**	13*j*	**24:17**	165*o* 321*k*	**28:11**	141*e* 981*n* 981*s*
19:19	648*g* 648*l*	**22:11**	300*l* 899*j*		741*c* 743*l*	**28:13**	396*h*
19:20	963*o*	**22:12**	757*b* 897*h*	**24:19**	165*o* 741*c*	**28:15**	372*g* 981*y*
19:21	648*l*	**22:17**	800*i* 899*j*	**24:20**	165*o* 371*x*	**28:16**	108*e* 988*c*
20:1	172*w* 361*ad*	**22:19**	459*a*		438*ad*	**28:17**	108*e* 110*o* 323*i*
20:2	342*e*	**22:20**	89*o*	**24:21**	153*v*		981*n*
20:3	361*s* 709*g*	**22:22**	365*bd* 705*a*	**24:22**	747*i*	**28:18**	677*a*
20:4	361*p*		891*c* 968*g*	**24:24**	275*g*	**28:19**	372*g* 646*c* 981*s*
20:5	342*e*	**22:23**	279*e* 723*a*	**25:1**	951*d*	**28:22**	372*g* 941*f* 981*y*
20:6	311*g* 866*e*	**22:24**	206*a*	**25:2**	967*p* 982*i*	**28:23**	981*m*
20:8	218*a* 339*k* 344*q*	**22:25**	279*e*	**25:3**	891*k* 967*c*	**28:24**	396*h*
20:11	279*m* 344*q*	**22:26**	206*a* 241*f*	**25:4**	963*p*	**28:25**	677*a*
20:12	184*h*² 486*f*	**22:27**	279*e* 311*aa*	**25:5**	967*c*	**28:26**	677*a* 981*r* 988*h*
20:13	709*g* 979*a*		891*w*	**25:6**	836*w*	**28:27**	372*g* 981*n* 981*s*
20:15	645*f*	**22:28**	579*c*	**25:8**	655*k* 659*a*	**28:30**	372*g* 941*f*
20:16	304*a* 968*l*	**22:31**	311*f* 438*a* 723*a*	**25:11**	911*e*	**28:31**	646*c* 981*m*
20:17	249*c* 305*c* 339*s*	**22:32**	279*e* 705*a*	**25:12**	717*b* 765*i*	**29:1**	108*k* 414*l* 677*a*
20:18	305*c*	**22:33**	362*be*	**25:13**	115*i* 911*e* 941*k*		988*k*
20:19	339*s*	**22:34**	914*ad*		986*b*	**29:2**	396*h* 646*c* 981*n*
20:21	757*f*	**22:35**	89*o*	**25:17**	704*h* 712*b*		981*s*
20:22	209*t*	**22:38**	579*q*	**26:2**	86*b* 131*c* 722*k*	**29:5**	941*f* 981*y*
20:24	184*h* 361*ad*	**22:40**	981*h*	**26:4**	131*c* 169*b*	**29:6**	396*h* 981*m*
	738*f*	**22:41**	209*ac* 967*c*	**26:9**	716*h*		981*n* 981*s*
20:26	229*l* 986*k* 989*a*	**23:1**	99*c* 981*p* 990*e*	**26:10**	165*u* 263*s*	**29:7**	108*k* 677*a* 941*a*
20:28	229*l* 989*a*	**23:4**	99*c*	**26:11**	170*d*	**29:8**	396*h* 646*c* 981*n*
20:29	836*r*	**23:6**	981*p*	**26:19**	362*be*		981*s*
21:1	712*e* 741*u* 747*j*	**23:7**	899*j*	**26:33**	172*b*	**29:11**	941*f* 981*m*
21:2	165*q* 532*x*	**23:8**	899*k*	**26:51**	99*v*		981*y*²
21:3	561*u* 727*i*	**23:9**	46*aq*	**26:53**	12*a* 85*a* 777*h*	**29:12**	108*k* 677*a* 988*i*
21:4	857*b*	**23:10**	104*e* 361*am*		783*a*		

29:13 396h 646c 981n² 981s	**32:13** 110ac 891k	**35:16** 362d 963k	**2:8** 172w
29:16 981m 981y	**32:15** 621a	**35:19** 910e	**2:9** 184r
29:17 646c	**32:16** 184aa 369d	**35:22** 362d 618b	**2:10** 195h
29:19 981m 981y	**32:19** 281o 777h	**35:25** 357d 361ac 986j	**2:13** 222a 350t
29:20 646c	**32:20** 722l		**2:14** 110ab
29:22 981m 981y	**32:21** 222d	**35:28** 148f 361ac 986j	**2:15** 361z
29:23 646c	**32:23** 914l	**35:30** 90d 466a 963k	**2:18** 222a 236b
29:25 981m 981y	**32:24** 184aa 369d	**35:31** 792j	**2:19** 184r
29:26 646c	**32:27** 222d	**35:32** 361ac 986j	**2:20** 195h
29:28 981m 981y	**32:29** 184p 222d	**35:33** 335b 649c 941h	**2:24** 727i
29:29 646c	**32:32** 222d	**35:34** 89a 192e	**2:25** 854x
29:31 981m 981y	**32:34** 184aa	**36:2** 170i 894e	**2:26** 172w 719i
29:32 646c	**32:38** 561y	**36:4** 988j	**2:27** 249c 305c 624h
29:34 981m 981y	**32:42** 561y		**2:28** 792d
29:35 677a	**33:1** 267a	**Deuteronomy**	**2:29** 184a 222b
29:36 396h 646c	**33:3** 108e	**1:2** 209u	**2:30** 602h 727i
29:38 981m 981y	**33:4** 119e 966i	**1:3** 108o	**2:34** 362ax
30:2 532s 725j	**33:8** 343i	**1:4** 727d²	**2:35** 790i
30:3 373h 532t 752g	**33:9** 339d 366n	**1:6** 209k²	**2:36** 727i
30:6 373h 752g 894j	**33:10** 343i	**1:7** 350p	**3:1** 718h
30:9 896d 896g	**33:11** 172w	**1:8** 184b 532p	**3:2** 727i 854af
31:2 361n 371y 910g	**33:14** 342e	**1:9** 322l	**3:3** 362ax
31:4 99v	**33:15** 172w	**1:10** 104e	**3:4** 184aa
31:5 722m	**33:16** 364f	**1:11** 104a	**3:7** 790i
31:6 414h	**33:36** 172w	**1:12** 322l	**3:12** 184p² 371ah
31:7 362az 372f	**33:37** 209t	**1:13** 500c	**3:15** 184p
31:9 373c 790i 919a	**33:38** 108i 361ad	**1:15** 500c 741ab	**3:16** 236c
31:10 381e	**33:39** 131j	**1:17** 480d 481b 854af	**3:17** 209u 343k 343n
31:11 790i	**33:40** 741u		**3:18** 184a 722l
31:14 891w	**33:48** 209v	**1:19** 209k	**3:22** 716a 854af
31:15 373c 919a	**33:52** 165j 209ag 300i	**1:21** 184a 854ah	**3:24** 21b 526c
31:16 659a	**33:54** 12a 85a 605r	**1:22** 459q	**3:25** 184h 222c
31:17 45c 362az 372f 373c	**33:55** 300j 827k	**1:23** 99m	**3:26** 578f 891m
	33:56 28p	**1:25** 171k 184c	**3:27** 209u 281u
31:18 373c 895a 919a	**34:1** 184c	**1:26** 738f	**3:28** 184a 283d 855e
31:19 110o 648ab 649e 649f	**34:2** 236c	**1:27** 304b 829a 888d	**4:1** 184a 184g 360n 953a
	34:3 172w 281k 343n	**1:28** 195g	
31:22 381k 631g	**34:5** 343m	**1:29** 854af	**4:2** 38a 39a
31:23 339u	**34:6** 281r	**1:30** 716a	**4:3** 362bf
31:24 648l	**34:7** 209u 281d	**1:31** 273l	**4:6** 498l
31:26 790a	**34:10** 281o	**1:32** 486d	**4:7** 21e 200a
31:27 783b	**34:11** 343k	**1:33** 192w 283a 355e 381q	**4:8** 913g 953c
31:28 102k 804e 986c	**34:12** 343n		**4:9** 534o
31:30 102k 986aa	**34:13** 783a	**1:34** 891k	**4:10** 209k
31:41 986c	**34:14** 184p 371ah	**1:35** 184h 532p	**4:11** 381p
31:47 986aa	**34:18** 99m 741aa	**1:39** 184f	**4:12** 381q 438e
31:49 86a 190g	**35:1** 184ae	**1:41** 483a 914ac	**4:13** 90q 548c 765d
31:50 844g 941j	**35:4** 199j	**1:42** 190b	**4:15** 438e
32:1 369b 371ah	**35:6** 99b 99r 620m	**1:43** 738f 871f	**4:16** 18j 982e
32:5 184p 826p	**35:8** 12a 85a	**1:44** 365k 619g	**4:19** 321j 966d
32:6 718e	**35:11** 362d 618b 620m	**1:45** 456b 836v	**4:20** 304a 383c 777f²
32:7 702e		**2:1** 209u	**4:21** 222c 891m
32:8 459q	**35:12** 910j	**2:3** 209k	**4:23** 768b 982e
32:9 702e	**35:13** 99b	**2:4** 854x	**4:24** 381o 911b
32:10 891k	**35:14** 93d	**2:5** 184r	**4:26** 361z
32:11 131e	**35:15** 362d 618b	**2:6** 792d	**4:27** 75c 105c
		2:7 110ac 635c	

32:39 21*c* 362*bc* 656*r*
32:40 310*i*
32:41 256*c*
32:43 59*n* 910*c*
32:46 739*g*
32:47 113*c* 222*b*
32:49 184*i* 209*t* 438*n*
32:50 361*ad*
32:51 172*w* 979*c*
32:52 184*h* 184*i* 199*e*
33:1 897*w*
33:2 209*k*
33:4 953*a*
33:6 104*a*
33:7 703*a*
33:8 605*s*
33:10 534*l*
33:12 767*e* 887*f*
33:13 635*d*
33:16 366*o*
33:17 160*h*
33:19 343*c* 635*d*
33:20 365*af*
33:22 365*af*
33:23 897*f*
33:24 357*b*
33:25 660*i*
33:26 21*b*
33:27 165*l* 192*k* 210*a*
300*h*
33:28 660*a*
33:29 21*e* 668*i* 703*b*
727*a*
34:1 184*c* 209*u* 438*n*
34:2 343*m*
34:4 532*p*
34:5 361*ad*
34:6 364*l* 491*v*
34:7 131*j* 162*f*
34:8 836*r*
34:9 378*w* 500*c*
34:10 200*a* 579*ab*

Joshua

1:1 361*ad*
1:2 222*b*
1:3 183*e* 267*e*
1:4 183*e* 343*m*
1:5 89*h* 160*i* 621*g*
1:6 162*l* 532*p* 855*a*
1:7 162*l* 249*c* 727*b*
739*g*
1:8 449*h* 589*g* 727*b*
953*f*
1:9 89*h* 162*l* 854*ah*
855*a*
1:11 222*b* 669*k*

1:12 371*ah*
1:13 184*p*
1:14 222*d* 703*h*
1:15 184*p* 717*i*
1:17 739*m*
1:18 162*l* 855*a*
2:1 459*q* 951*t*
2:4 525*e*
2:5 264*g*
2:6 213*k* 226*a* 525*e*
2:7 222*f* 264*g* 619*g*
2:8 213*k*
2:9 184*a* 854*x*
2:10 342*a* 727*d*
2:11 856*c* 965*b*
2:12 532*j*
2:13 919*a*
2:15 208*c* 235*e* 263*c*
311*n*
2:16 110*l* 523*g*
2:18 208*c* 431*b*
2:19 180*b* 180*c* 223*d*
2:21 208*c* 431*b*
2:22 110*l* 459*af*
2:24 184*a* 701*b*
3:1 222*b*
3:3 194*b* 986*c*
3:4 126*c* 199*j*
3:5 864*b* 979*i*
3:6 194*b* 222*b* 283*b*
3:7 89*h* 866*aa*
3:8 269*f* 350*l*
3:10 89*a* 371*v*
3:11 194*b* 222*b* 283*b*
3:12 99*m*
3:13 209*aa* 342*a*
350*l* 965*b*
3:14 283*b* 986*c*
3:15 269*f* 350*l*
3:16 209*aa*
3:17 342*a* 986*c*
4:1 222*b*
4:2 99*m* 99*n*
4:3 344*f*
4:6 459*i*
4:7 505*j*
4:10 222*b* 680*c* 986*c*
4:12 371*ah*
4:13 99*v*
4:14 866*aa*
4:16 986*c*
4:18 350*l* 986*c*
4:19 108*e*
4:20 344*f*
4:21 459*i*
4:22 222*b* 342*a*
4:23 342*a*

4:24 160*b* 854*a*
5:1 342*a* 371*v* 856*c*
5:2 256*e* 988*n*
5:4 361*z*
5:5 974*a*
5:6 110*ac* 361*z*
439*h* 532*p*
635*d*
5:7 974*a* 988*n*
5:8 656*v*
5:9 315*e* 924*g*
5:10 108*e* 988*e*
5:11 301*ae* 323*i*
5:12 145*e*
5:13 706*d* 723*a*
5:14 311*g* 722*a*
5:15 229*p* 979*x*
6:1 184*au* 264*g*
6:2 727*i*
6:3 267*d* 314*a*
6:4 99*f* 99*g* 194*b*
414*a* 414*j* 414*o*
6:5 309*d* 577*i*
6:6 99*f* 194*b* 414*a*
414*o*
6:8 194*b* 414*a* 414*j*
414*o*
6:10 582*g*
6:12 194*b*
6:13 99*f* 414*a* 414*j*
414*o*
6:15 99*g* 128*b*
6:16 414*j* 577*i* 727*i*
6:17 165*w* 525*e* 919*a*
6:18 859*w*
6:19 359*a* 979*v*
6:20 184*au* 235*k*
309*d* 414*j* 577*i*
6:21 362*ay*
6:22 304*c* 951*t*
6:24 359*a* 381*e*
6:25 525*e* 919*a*
6:26 119*f* 132*c* 164*p*
184*au* 214*c*
264*c* 899*m*
6:27 89*h*
7:1 165*w* 891*k* 930*a*
7:2 459*q*
7:3 105*f* 483*a*
7:4 728*d*
7:5 619*g* 856*c*
7:6 311*g* 836*g*
7:7 222*b*
7:8 728*d*
7:9 561*c*
7:10 308*i*
7:11 541*f* 769*b* 788*f*

7:12 165*w* 715*d*
7:13 979*i*
7:14 605*m*
7:15 381*i* 769*b*
7:16 128*b*
7:19 526*p*
7:21 228*n* 525*h* 797*c*
859*x*
7:24 827*f*
7:25 344*n* 381*i* 827*f*
7:26 209*z* 891*k*
8:1 727*i* 854*ah*
8:2 527*c* 790*i*
8:5 620*g*
8:8 381*e*
8:9 281*r*
8:10 74*f* 128*b* 986*ae*
8:11 255*j* 281*d*
8:12 281*r* 527*c*
8:13 255*j*
8:14 128*b* 491*ab*
716*d*
8:15 541*j* 620*g*
8:16 619*g*
8:17 661*d*
8:18 723*o* 727*i*
8:19 381*e*
8:20 388*e*
8:22 362*ay*
8:23 747*i*
8:24 362*ay*
8:25 99*v*
8:27 790*i*
8:28 381*e*
8:29 129*e* 209*z* 217*b*
8:30 209*u* 990*e*
8:31 589*g* 670*b* 953*a*
981*p* 981*w*
8:32 586*a* 953*e*
8:33 209*u*^{2}
8:34 579*k* 589*g* 897*i*
899*d* 953*a*
9:2 718*h*
9:3 541*j*
9:4 194*r* 655*c* 698*b*
9:6 199*a* 765*q*
9:9 199*a*
9:11 765*q*
9:13 655*c*
9:14 459*e*
9:15 532*j* 765*q*
9:16 200*i*
9:17 184*aa*
9:18 532*j* 829*a*
9:21 339*q* 385*c* 682*e*
9:22 199*a* 200*i* 541*j*
9:23 339*q* 385*c*

9:24 362*az* 854*x*	**12:10** 184*af*	**17:11** 184*ad*	**22:5** 739*g* 887*l*
9:27 339*q* 385*c* 605*j*	**13:1** 41*s* 133*g*	**17:12** 161*e*	**22:6** 897*v*
10:1 184*af* 719*g*	**13:3** 99*a* 371*v*	**17:13** 300*j* 682*e*	**22:7** 92*e*
10:2 854*x*	**13:5** 209*u*	**17:14** 104*f*	**22:8** 790*a*
10:4 703*k* 712*e* 719*g*	**13:6** 300*h*	**17:16** 274*b*	**22:10** 990*e*
10:5 371*v*	**13:7** 783*a*	**17:18** 274*b* 300*i*	**22:12** 718*g*
10:6 703*h*	**13:8** 184*p*	**18:1** 192*i*	**22:16** 282*b* 930*a* 990*f*
10:8 727*i* 854*af*	**13:11** 209*u*	**18:3** 771*d*	**22:17** 659*a*
10:9 116*a* 129*i*	**13:13** 300*j*	**18:4** 93*b* 586*m*	**22:18** 282*b* 891*h*
10:10 362*bi*	**13:14** 774*a* 777*j*	**18:5** 783*a*	**22:19** 192*h* 649*o*
10:11 350*af*	**13:15** 184*q*	**18:6** 605*r*	738*e* 990*f*
10:12 266*a* 321*q*	**13:21** 362*az*	**18:7** 184*p* 774*a* 777*j*	**22:20** 891*k*
10:13 589*b*	**13:22** 362*af* 983*e*	**18:11** 184*q* 236*d*	**22:22** 490*i*
10:14 455*g* 716*a*	**13:23** 350*m*	**18:16** 184*af*	**22:23** 282*b* 981*k* 990*f*
10:16 255*g* 523*g* 620*d*	**13:24** 184*q*	**18:19** 343*n* 350*m*	**22:24** 10*a*
10:18 315*c* 344*i* 660*h*	**13:27** 343*k* 350*m*	**18:21** 184*ad*	**22:25** 236*b* 350*n* 774*d*
10:19 238*e* 619*d* 727*i*	**13:29** 184*q*	**18:28** 184*af*	**22:26** 981*k* 990*f*
10:20 362*ax*	**13:33** 774*a* 777*k*^{2}	**19:1** 184*q* 224*h* 605*r*	**22:27** 466*b*
10:21 926*h*	**14:1** 783*a*	**19:2** 184*ad*	**22:30** 826*l*
10:22 263*ab* 304*c*	**14:3** 184*p* 774*a*	**19:9** 224*h*	**22:31** 89*a*
10:24 745*a*	**14:4** 184*ae*	**19:10** 184*q* 236*d* 605*r*	**22:33** 826*l*
10:25 162*l* 854*ah*	**14:7** 131*g* 459*q*	**19:15** 184*ad*	**22:34** 466*b* 965*b*
855*a*	**14:8** 856*c*	**19:17** 184*q* 605*r*	**23:1** 133*g* 717*i*
10:26 217*b* 362*x*	**14:9** 267*e* 777*h*	**19:22** 184*ad* 350*m*	**23:3** 716*a*
10:27 129*e* 255*e* 344*i*	**14:10** 131*g*	**19:24** 236*d* 605*r*	**23:4** 343*m* 350*n*
10:28 362*ay*	**14:11** 162*f*	**19:25** 184*q*	783*a*
10:30 362*ay* 727*i*	**14:12** 89*d* 195*g* 300*i*	**19:30** 184*ad*	**23:5** 300*h* 300*i*
10:32 362*ay* 727*i*	**14:13** 184*aa* 897*v*	**19:32** 184*q* 236*d* 605*r*	**23:6** 249*c* 739*g*
10:33 362*ay* 703*k*	**14:15** 195*g* 717*i*	**19:33** 366*s*	**23:7** 966*c*
727*g*	**15:1** 172*w* 184*q* 236*c*	**19:34** 350*m*	**23:8** 48*a*
10:35 362*ay*	236*d*	**19:35** 184*ad*	**23:9** 161*h* 300*h*
10:37 362*ay*	**15:2** 343*n*	**19:40** 184*q* 605*r*	**23:10** 619*c* 716*a*
10:39 362*ay*	**15:4** 350*t*	**19:41** 184*ad*	**23:11** 887*l*
10:40 362*ax*	**15:5** 343*n* 350*m*	**19:47** 716*d*	**23:12** 894*w*
10:42 716*a*	**15:8** 184*af*	**19:49** 777*h*	**23:13** 300*k* 542*u* 827*k*
11:3 371*v*	**15:9** 209*u*	**19:50** 184*aa*	**23:14** 361*m* 725*b*
11:4 104*r* 274*b*	**15:10** 209*u*^{2}	**19:51** 263*d* 783*a*	**23:15** 362*bg*
11:6 381*e* 655*p* 727*i*	**15:11** 209*u*	**20:2** 184*ae*	**23:16** 362*bg* 769*b*
854*af*	**15:12** 343*m*	**20:3** 618*b* 910*j*	966*e*
11:7 116*a* 350*u*	**15:13** 184*aa* 195*g*	**20:5** 888*u* 910*j*	**24:1** 74*f*
11:8 362*ax* 727*i*	**15:14** 300*i*	**20:6** 148*f* 986*j*	**24:2** 125*e* 350*p* 966*h*
11:9 381*e* 655*p*	**15:16** 712*b* 894*aa*	**20:7** 184*ae*	**24:3** 104*e*
11:11 362*ay* 381*e*	**15:18** 235*q* 761*al*	**20:9** 618*b* 910*j*	**24:4** 209*u*
11:12 362*ax*^{2}	**15:19** 339*q*	**21:2** 184*ae*	**24:5** 304*a*
11:13 209*ab* 381*e*	**15:21** 184*ad*	**21:4** 184*ad* 605*r*	**24:6** 343*i*
11:14 362*ax* 790*i*	**15:47** 343*m* 350*t*	**21:5** 184*ad*	**24:7** 172*u* 418*i* 441*j*
11:17 209*u*^{2}	**15:63** 161*e* 184*af*	**21:6** 184*ad*	**24:8** 184*p* 727*i*
11:18 718*i*	300*j* 371*v*	**21:7** 184*ad*	**24:9** 899*j*^{2}
11:19 719*g*	**16:1** 184*q* 350*m*	**21:13** 184*ad*	**24:11** 222*b* 371*v*
11:20 362*bd* 602*h*	**16:5** 184*q* 236*d*	**21:20** 184*ad*	**24:12** 300*h* 365*k* 723*s*
11:21 195*g* 362*ax*	**16:7** 350*m*	**21:27** 184*ad*	**24:13** 184*c* 370*m*
11:22 41*i*	**16:8** 350*t*	**21:34** 184*ad*	370*q* 677*b*
11:23 717*i*	**16:9** 184*ad*	**21:43** 184*a* 532*p*	**24:14** 742*a* 854*a* 966*f*
12:1 209*u* 728*g* 741*u*	**16:10** 300*j* 682*e*	**21:44** 717*i* 727*i*	**24:15** 605*n*
12:2 184*p* 236*b* 350*t*	**17:1** 184*p* 722*b*	**21:45** 725*b* 764*a*	**24:16** 621*h*
12:3 209*u* 343*k* 343*n*	**17:3** 170*i* 771*a*	**22:1** 371*ah*	**24:17** 304*a* 547*d*
12:5 209*u*	**17:7** 184*q* 236*d*	**22:4** 717*i*	**24:18** 300*h* 965*e*

24:19	161g 909h	2:12	304a 621i 891l	4:15	620d 727a	6:26	385b 981p 990d
	911b 979a		966h	4:16	619d	6:27	129f 854ad
24:20	621h	2:13	967a 967g	4:17	620d	6:31	716d 966i
24:22	466g	2:14	715d 793i	4:18	226a 854ag	6:32	561r
24:23	621l	2:15	704a	4:19	335a 859l	6:34	414f 965m
24:25	765j	2:16	957e	4:20	190n	6:35	529p
24:26	344f 586a 589g	2:17	456j 951x	4:21	47b 256f 303a	6:36	226u 547c 547o
24:27	466b	2:18	89h 668g 905d		362af	6:37	341f
24:29	131j 361ad	2:19	361ac 914z	4:22	526t 619d	6:39	341f
24:30	209u 364l		966h	5:1	412c	7:1	209v 339d
24:31	490o 676b 742a	2:20	769b 891k	5:2	283d 781t 923m	7:2	104t 877e
24:32	363f 364l 792c	2:21	300k	5:4	176g 350z	7:3	209u 854z
	809j	2:22	461c	5:5	176g 209k	7:4	104t 461b
24:33	361ad 364l	2:23	300k	5:6	190m 624h	7:5	301f
		3:1	461c	5:7	169ac	7:6	99t
Judges		3:3	371v	5:8	723t 966i	7:8	414j
1:1	68h 361ad 459a	3:4	461c	5:11	263o	7:9	727i
	716d 716e	3:6	894w 966h	5:12	678f	7:10	415a 854z
1:2	727i	3:7	914z 967a 967g	5:16	266d	7:12	104r 104w
1:3	89q	3:8	110y 793i 891k	5:18	661a		365bb
1:4	727i	3:9	668t 957f	5:20	321d 716b	7:13	301bb 438u
1:6	46b 53q 619d	3:10	965m	5:21	350s	7:14	727i
	620d	3:11	110ac 717i	5:22	365bg	7:15	520a 727i 981f
1:7	46b 53q 804l	3:12	914z	5:23	703j 899m	7:16	95e 194m 414j
1:8	184af 381f	3:13	184aa	5:24	897g		420d
1:10	184aa	3:14	110z 745c	5:25	335a	7:17	20e
1:12	712b 894aa	3:15	242a 668t 804f	5:26	47b 256f 303a	7:18	414j
1:14	235q 761al		957f		362af	7:19	46o 108q 194m
1:15	339q	3:16	90s 723l	5:28	136e 263b		414j
1:17	89q 165q 561u	3:17	195e	5:30	373d 425a 790f	7:20	420d 577i 723a
1:19	161e 274b 300j	3:19	344h 530h 578h		844l	7:21	620d
1:20	93b 195g 300i	3:20	380d 529e	5:31	110ac 321d	7:22	362ai 414j
1:21	161e 184af 300j	3:21	224f 303a 362x		705a 717i	7:24	350n
1:22	89h	3:22	302g	6:1	110y 914z	7:25	344h 363j 370l
1:23	459q	3:23	264e	6:2	255g 662l		619d
1:24	263i 526v	3:24	302f	6:3	786f	8:1	924l
1:25	919a	3:26	344h 667a	6:4	165aa	8:2	41g
1:26	164p	3:27	414f	6:5	104r 365bb	8:3	727i
1:27	300j	3:28	222d 350n 619d	6:6	761p	8:4	619d 684c
1:28	682e		727i	6:8	304a 579s 742p	8:5	301s
1:30	682e	3:29	362au	6:10	967p	8:7	256k 370aa 655i
1:33	682e	3:30	110af 717i	6:11	366s 370z 530e	8:9	165f 209al
1:34	757f	3:31	256f 362au 668t		957f 968g	8:11	670a
1:35	682e		957f	6:12	89h	8:12	620d 727g
1:36	236c	4:1	914z	6:13	621b 864a	8:14	99s 459o 586m
2:1	184d 304a 768c	4:2	793i	6:14	668t	8:16	256k 370aa
	968g	4:3	110aa 274b	6:15	132b 163g	8:17	165f 209al
2:2	165j 738f 765q		735e 761p	6:16	89h 727d		362aj
2:3	300k 542y	4:4	957f	6:17	547c 547o 826f	8:18	18f
2:4	836w	4:6	209u	6:18	296d	8:19	11b
2:5	561u	4:7	727i	6:19	301r	8:20	119b 130k 362x
2:7	676b	4:8	89q	6:21	218b 381t 446a		854t
2:8	131j 361ad	4:9	373k 866ab	6:22	361ab 438d	8:21	844d
2:9	364l	4:11	366s	6:23	854ai	8:22	741n
2:10	491e	4:12	209u	6:24	717a 990e	8:23	733a
2:11	967c 967g	4:13	274b	6:25	165j 967e 967i	8:24	761ak 844d
		4:14	209u		990g	8:26	228n 322a 436c

8:27	542y 951x 982l	**9:51**	209al 213k
8:28	110ac 310j 717i		620h
8:30	99s 894u	**9:52**	381e
8:31	952a	**9:53**	344k 363g 373k
8:32	133g 361ad		655i
	364l	**9:54**	362af 723q
8:33	951x 967a	**9:55**	148k
8:34	506e	**9:56**	99s 362ac 804l
9:1	957f	**9:57**	899m
9:2	11a 99s 741n	**10:1**	668t 957f
9:4	792g 809n 938c	**10:2**	110aa 361ad
	967a		364l
9:5	41h 99s 132b	**10:3**	110aa 957f
	344k 362ac	**10:4**	99q 184aa
	523h		365bd
9:6	218t 366s 741k	**10:5**	361ad 364l
9:7	209t 209u 455d	**10:6**	607l 621i 914z
	455r 577j		966h 967a
9:8	357e 366l 366u		967g
	519e 741n	**10:7**	793i 891k
9:9	357a	**10:8**	110z
9:10	366r	**10:9**	222e
9:11	392f	**10:10**	621i 761p 966h
9:12	366j		967g
9:13	831h 949c	**10:11**	668g
9:15	256k 381i	**10:13**	621i 966h
9:16	494h 915e	**10:14**	761ah
9:17	661a	**10:16**	825b 966f
9:18	99s 362ac 741k	**10:18**	68h 716e 741ac
9:19	494h	**11:1**	722b 951t 957f
9:20	381i	**11:2**	300v
9:21	620i 667a	**11:3**	620i 938c
9:22	110v	**11:4**	716f
9:23	542l 969p	**11:6**	741ac
9:24	99s 362ac	**11:7**	300v 774b 888q
9:25	524f 527c 788f	**11:8**	741ac
9:26	485ai	**11:11**	765j
9:27	370l 899l	**11:12**	10a 529q
9:28	639c	**11:13**	184p 787d
9:29	716g	**11:14**	529q
9:31	542k	**11:17**	305c 529q
9:32	129h 527c	**11:18**	236b
9:33	128b	**11:19**	305c
9:34	129h	**11:20**	486o 716f
9:36	18g 418d	**11:21**	184p 727i
9:38	639c 716g 877f	**11:23**	300h
	922g	**11:24**	967k
9:39	716h	**11:26**	110ag
9:40	619d 620i	**11:27**	957a
9:41	300v	**11:28**	456i
9:43	362aj 527c	**11:29**	965m
9:45	165f 388a	**11:30**	532w 727j
9:46	194t 209al	**11:31**	295c 981p
	990ae		981ah
9:48	209u 366c	**11:32**	727i
9:49	194t 362aj 381e	**11:33**	362az
9:50	712i 727e		

11:34	88h 170i 295c	**14:10**	127c 876b
	412a 835d	**14:12**	228x 530j
11:35	532s 532w 836g	**14:14**	162m 301ak
11:36	910d		392f
11:37	110s 620t	**14:15**	381i 612e 801e
	836ab 895b	**14:16**	525j² 836ab
11:39	127c		888q
12:1	190f 381i	**14:17**	524b 836ab
12:3	661a 727j	**14:18**	162m 365ab
12:4	620h 716h 727e		365ba 370g
12:5	222d 350n 463b		392g
12:6	362aj 580a	**14:19**	228x 362au
12:7	110y 361ad		965m
	364l	**14:20**	894v
12:8	957f	**15:1**	45i
12:9	99q 110y	**15:2**	841i 888q 894v
12:10	361ad 364l	**15:4**	365t 381j
12:11	110z 957f	**15:6**	381i 894v
12:12	361ad 364l	**15:7**	910f
12:13	957f	**15:8**	46k 344t 362az
12:14	99r 110y 365bd	**15:10**	747o
12:15	361ad 364l	**15:11**	46k 344t 733ak
13:1	110ac 728d		804m
	914z	**15:12**	272c 532l 747o
13:2	172a	**15:13**	126b 208c 747o
13:3	167i 968g	**15:14**	46w 965m
13:4	649g 948b	**15:15**	363g 723k
13:5	46ag 130b 648k	**15:16**	362au
	668t	**15:18**	859l
13:6	187b 561h 968g	**15:19**	46m 339k
13:7	130b 167i 649g	**15:20**	110aa
	948b	**16:1**	951u
13:8	534d 761r	**16:2**	527d
13:9	455g 968g	**16:3**	129l 264h 273c
13:11	13m	**16:4**	887ab
13:14	649g 948b	**16:5**	162g 612e 747o
13:15	301r		809n
13:16	968g 981p	**16:6**	747o
13:17	561h	**16:7**	99f 208c 341i
13:18	561a 561h 864j		747o
13:19	981s	**16:9**	46w 527d
13:20	308f 311f	**16:10**	541f 747o
	381ag	**16:11**	126b 208c 747o
13:21	968g	**16:12**	46w 527d
13:22	361ab 438d	**16:13**	99f 222k 259g
13:23	526f 782a 981p		747o
	981s	**16:15**	541f 887ab
13:24	167i 897f 957f	**16:16**	827k
13:25	965m	**16:17**	46ag 163c
14:1	894x		259g 648k
14:3	894w	**16:18**	809n
14:4	733ak	**16:19**	99f 163c 259g
14:5	365ac		648j 679c
14:6	46a 365ad	**16:20**	621d 678g
	965m	**16:21**	332g 438m
14:8	363o 392a		439k 655i 747o
14:9	392a	**16:22**	36c 259g

16:23 727*j* 967*l*	**19:22** 279*p* 951*p*	**Ruth**	**4:16** 301*o*
16:25 837*c*	**19:24** 895*b* 951*aa*	**1:1** 184*ao* 188*i*	**4:18** 169*b*
16:26 218*o* 378*g*	**19:25** 951*aa*	636*a* 957*e*	
16:27 54*b* 213*k*	**19:26** 309*c*	**1:4** 894*x*	**1 Samuel**
16:28 162*c* 438*m*	**19:29** 46*a* 99*n* 363*k*	**1:5** 772*e*	**1:2** 172*a* 894*u*
761*p* 910*f*	783*i*	**1:6** 148*l* 301*x*	**1:3** 981*h* 986*d*
16:29 218*o*	**20:1** 74*f*	**1:8** 148*h*	**1:5** 91*a* 172*e*
16:30 361*q* 362*ae*	**20:2** 722*m*	**1:9** 836*ad* 889*b*	**1:6** 827*k*
362*av*	**20:5** 951*aa*	**1:11** 148*h*	**1:7** 836*ae* 946*l*
16:31 110*aa* 364*l*	**20:6** 46*a* 363*k*	**1:12** 167*f*	**1:8** 170*j* 644*h*
17:2 809*n* 897*c*	**20:9** 605*r*	**1:14** 48*b* 889*b*	**1:9** 957*f* 986*k*
17:3 554*e* 982*l*	**20:10** 102*g* 301*m*	**1:15** 148*h*	**1:10** 761*r* 836*ae*
17:4 554*e* 686*g* 809*n*	**20:11** 45*m*	**1:16** 89*r* 371*ad* 965*e*	**1:11** 46*ag* 170*g* 532*w*
17:5 986*r* 990*ae*	**20:13** 272*a* 456*j* 938*d*	**1:17** 361*r* 364*a* 532*m*	648*k* 781*s*
17:6 734*a* 913*t*	**20:14** 718*g*	**1:19** 13*m* 184*ao*	**1:12** 578*i*
17:7 184*ao*	**20:15** 722*m*	**1:20** 391*d* 561*r* 561*y*	**1:13** 949*i*
17:9 184*ao*	**20:16** 242*a* 287*b*	827*e*	**1:14** 949*f*
17:10 169*v* 228*x*	**20:17** 722*m*	**1:21** 54*e*	**1:15** 948*e*
804*b* 986*ac*	**20:18** 68*h* 716*e*	**1:22** 148*l* 184*ao* 370*t*	**1:17** 761*y*
17:12 986*ac*	**20:20** 716*h*	**2:1** 800*f*	**1:18** 826*p*
18:1 734*a*	**20:21** 728*f*	**2:2** 41*g* 826*p*	**1:19** 45*e* 128*b* 148*l*
18:2 459*q*	**20:23** 459*a* 836*v*	**2:4** 89*d* 884*d*	**1:20** 167*f* 561*r*
18:4 986*ac*	**20:25** 728*f*	**2:5** 13*j*	**1:21** 981*h*
18:5 459*b*	**20:26** 836*v* 946*g*	**2:8** 89*p*	**1:22** 611*a*
18:7 717*h*	981*p* 981*w*	**2:9** 859*l*	**1:23** 153*f*
18:9 184*c*	**20:27** 194*b* 459*a*	**2:10** 311*a* 826*p*	**1:24** 192*i*
18:10 635*d*	**20:28** 727*i*	**2:11** 524*a* 621*l*	**1:26** 13*p*
18:11 722*m*	**20:29** 527*c*	**2:12** 271*d* 662*c* 962*c*	**1:27** 761*aa*
18:14 554*e* 982*l*	**20:32** 620*g*	**2:13** 826*p*	**1:28** 784*b*
18:15 8*a*	**20:35** 362*bf*	**2:14** 301*l*	**2:1** 824*g*
18:16 722*m*	**20:38** 381*e* 388*e* 547*w*	**2:17** 465*d*	**2:2** 344*w* 979*b*
18:17 554*e* 722*m*	**20:41** 854*u*	**2:19** 187*b*	**2:3** 480*d* 490*e* 871*d*
788*m* 982*l*	**20:42** 362*aj*	**2:20** 792*m*	877*d*
18:19 169*v* 578*h*	**20:47** 41*i* 344*h* 620*h*	**2:23** 89*p*	**2:4** 162*h*
986*ac*²	**20:48** 381*e*	**3:2** 370*z*	**2:5** 171*c* 635*f* 636*d*
18:20 788*m* 982*l*	**21:1** 532*k* 894*y*	**3:3** 357*r* 648*a*	859*e*
18:23 577*j*	**21:2** 836*v*	**3:4** 229*n* 311*aa*	**2:6** 360*i* 362*bc*
18:24 788*m* 966*j*	**21:3** 190*g* 772*g*	**3:7** 229*n* 311*aa*	**2:7** 800*a* 801*b*
986*ac*	**21:4** 981*p* 981*w* 990*e*	**3:9** 13*j* 226*a* 792*m*	866*aa* 872*h*
18:25 892*b* 900*a*	**21:5** 532*x*	**3:12** 792*m*	**2:8** 164*b* 801*g*
18:27 362*az* 381*e*	**21:6** 190*g* 772*g*	**3:14** 525*l*	**2:9** 162*n* 578*d*
717*h*	**21:7** 894*y*	**3:15** 301*l* 465*d*	**2:10** 162*c* 480*e*
18:28 164*p*	**21:9** 86*c*	**3:17** 465*d* 636*m*	**2:11** 148*l* 742*c*
18:30 982*l*	**21:10** 362*aj*	**3:18** 677*c*	**2:12** 491*e* 938*d*
18:31 192*i* 990*l*	**21:12** 895*b*	**4:1** 263*l* 311*v*	**2:13** 256*e*
19:1 184*ao* 734*a*	**21:13** 344*h* 719*i*	**4:2** 99*k*	**2:15** 357*af*
952*a*	**21:14** 636*j*	**4:3** 235*q* 792*l*	**2:16** 176*a*
19:2 184*ao* 951*i*	**21:15** 46*ai* 830*b*	**4:5** 894*l* 896*h*	**2:17** 922*d*
19:3 365*bd* 719*h*	**21:16** 894*y*	**4:7** 229*p*	**2:18** 228*q*
19:4 813*e*	**21:18** 532*x* 899*m*	**4:9** 466*d*	**2:19** 228*x*
19:10 184*af* 365*bd*	**21:19** 988*a*	**4:10** 894*l*	**2:20** 148*l* 784*b* 897*v*
598*d*	**21:20** 523*g*	**4:11** 466*d* 800*i*	**2:21** 36*a* 167*f*
19:12 59*y*	**21:21** 786*b* 835*e* 894*y*	866*ad*	**2:22** 45*f* 133*g* 263*d*
19:15 813*f*	**21:22** 829*b*	**4:13** 45*e* 167*i*	**2:25** 362*be* 456*j*
19:16 813*e*	**21:23** 148*k* 164*p*	**4:14** 792*m* 923*l*	720*a* 914*u*
19:18 184*ao* 813*f*	786*b* 835*e*	**4:15** 133*f* 170*j* 644*h*	**2:26** 36*a* 826*e*
19:21 648*e*	**21:25** 734*a* 913*t*	887*ae*	**2:27** 526*c* 579*s*

2:28	301*ab* 396*c* 605*b*
2:29	859*r* 923*s*
2:30	115*j* 866*j* 922*a*
2:31	133*e*
2:33	114*g* 361*z*
2:34	361*ae* 547*c*
2:35	986*f* 986*w*
2:36	311*b* 761*ai*
3:1	140*a* 438*ac* 529*c*
3:2	439*a*
3:3	420*g*
3:4	737*i*
3:7	491*e* 525*a*
3:9	455*k*
3:11	415*i*
3:13	899*c* 924*i*
3:14	936*i* 941*l*
3:15	263*ah* 854*ae*
3:17	525*b* 532*m*
3:18	524*b*
3:19	36*a* 89*h* 725*c*
3:20	579*z*
3:21	526*c*
4:1	716*d*
4:2	362*ak*
4:3	194*b*
4:4	311*ag*
4:5	577*f*
4:7	854*l*
4:8	659*a*
4:9	162*l* 745*h* 855*a*
4:10	362*ak* 620*h* 728*d*
4:11	194*b* 361*ae* 786*g*
4:12	277*c* 836*h* 836*l*
4:13	524*f* 577*e* 854*u*
4:15	131*j* 439*a*
4:16	667*b*
4:17	194*b* 361*ae* 620*h* 786*g*
4:18	110*ac* 133*g* 309*c* 322*i* 361*ad*
4:19	167*j*
4:20	456*l* 854*ah*
4:21	194*b* 866*ae*
5:1	194*b*
5:2	967*l* 990*ae*
5:3	128*b* 309*c*
5:4	46*b* 309*c*
5:5	127*d* 267*h*
5:6	651*e* 735*b*
5:9	651*e*
5:10	361*ab*

5:11	300*ac*
5:12	651*e* 761*p*
6:1	110*s* 194*b*
6:2	983*f*
6:3	636*m* 981*ae*
6:4	99*a* 365*n* 554*e* 651*e*
6:5	18*j*
6:6	602*a*
6:7	126*a* 126*b* 132*l* 169*aj* 274*i* 365*az*
6:8	194*i* 981*ae*
6:9	159*a* 463*a*
6:10	132*l* 169*aj*
6:11	194*i* 365*n* 554*e* 651*e*
6:12	249*c* 409*b*
6:13	370*t*
6:14	344*t* 385*b* 981*p*
6:15	194*i* 344*t*
6:17	99*a* 554*e* 651*e* 981*ae*
6:18	344*t* 365*n*
6:19	194*b* 362*bf* 441*a*
6:20	979*a*
7:1	194*b* 457*l*
7:2	110*aa* 836*w*
7:3	148*b* 668*u* 966*f*
7:4	967*e* 967*i*
7:5	74*f* 761*o*
7:6	350*w* 914*ac* 946*g* 957*f*
7:7	854*y*
7:8	668*u* 761*o*
7:9	132*l* 761*o* 981*p*
7:10	176*k* 716*f* 727*a*
7:11	619*d*
7:12	199*i* 344*h* 561*u* 703*b*
7:14	184*aa* 717*i*
7:15	480*n* 957*f*
7:16	314*b*
7:17	192*ac* 990*e*
8:1	133*g* 957*f*
8:3	612*i*
8:5	18*k* 133*g* 741*m*
8:6	761*r* 827*l*
8:7	607*g* 741*b*
8:8	304*a* 966*h*
8:9	664*c* 741*m*
8:11	274*e* 742*q*
8:12	370*g* 723*h*
8:13	686*e*
8:14	235*q*
8:15	102*f*

8:17	102*f* 742*p*
8:18	761*q* 761*ae*
8:19	456*j* 741*m*
8:20	18*k* 716*e* 957*g*
8:22	148*h* 741*m*
9:1	722*b*
9:2	195*f* 841*k*
9:3	459*ae* 772*c*
9:5	148*h*
9:6	579*z* 725*c*
9:7	781*y*
9:8	809*n*
9:9	438*ae* 579*t*
9:11	304*d*
9:12	209*ac* 680*a* 981*h*
9:15	526*f*
9:16	357*f* 668*u* 741*k*
9:17	13*p* 741*m*
9:18	187*b*
9:19	882*b*
9:20	484*a* 772*c*
9:21	196*e* 639*a*
9:22	638*d*
9:23	301*r*
9:26	213*k*
9:27	529*e*
10:1	357*f*
10:2	484*a*
10:3	366*s*
10:4	301*m*
10:5	209*ac* 414*b* 579*ab*
10:6	147*a* 965*m*
10:7	89*h* 547*c*
10:8	110*o* 507*f* 981*p* 981*w*
10:10	965*m*
10:11	579*ab*
10:12	496*c*
10:14	459*ae*
10:16	484*a* 525*j*
10:17	74*f*
10:19	607*g* 741*m*
10:20	605*m*
10:21	190*f*
10:22	459*b* 523*h*
10:23	195*f*
10:24	21*h* 360*c* 577*f* 605*b*
10:25	148*h* 586*b* 589*h*
10:27	668*u* 922*g* 938*d*
11:1	712*d* 765*q*
11:2	438*m* 655*i* 872*s*
11:3	529*p*
11:4	836*aa*
11:6	891*v* 965*m*

11:7	46*a* 783*i* 854*k*
11:8	86*c*
11:9	379*a* 668*t*
11:11	362*av*
11:15	741*k* 981*w*
12:1	741*k*
12:2	133*g*
12:3	466*d* 612*j* 788*h* 930*c*
12:5	466*k*
12:6	304*a*
12:8	304*a* 761*p*
12:9	506*e* 793*i*
12:10	761*p* 914*ac* 967*a* 967*g*
12:11	668*g* 957*e*
12:12	741*b* 741*m*
12:13	741*m*
12:14	854*a*
12:15	704*a* 738*j*
12:17	176*k* 350*ac* 370*t*
12:18	854*e* 854*ae*
12:19	761*o*
12:20	282*c* 854*ah*
12:21	641*e*
12:23	534*l* 761*n* 914*a*
12:24	854*a*
13:2	148*h* 722*h*
13:3	414*f* 712*b*
13:5	104*r*
13:6	255*g* 523*g*
13:7	222*d* 854*y*
13:8	110*o* 507*f*
13:9	981*p* 981*w*
13:11	75*e*
13:12	981*p*
13:13	499*f* 741*r*
13:14	710*a* 741*r*
13:15	86*c* 99*t*
13:19	686*g* 723*h*
13:20	256*a* 630*a*
13:21	809*n*
13:22	723*t*
14:1	525*k* 723*q*
14:2	99*t* 366*n*
14:3	491*ac* 989*d*
14:4	209*w*
14:6	105*e* 668*f*
14:7	89*q*
14:8	526*t*
14:10	289*a* 547*c*
14:11	298*a* 526*t*
14:12	289*a* 727*i*
14:13	308*j* 362*az*
14:15	176*f* 318*d*
14:17	86*a* 190*f*

14:18 194*b* 459*c*	**15:26** 607*j* 752*a*	**17:32** 716*g*	**19:1** 362*m* 826*m*
14:19 61*b*	**15:27** 46*t*	**17:33** 130*g* 130*k* 722*b*	**19:2** 523*h*
14:20 61*b* 362*ai* 716*i*	**15:28** 46*t* 741*r*	**17:34** 365*y* 365*ad*	**19:3** 524*e*
14:22 619*d* 620*d*	**15:29** 371*b* 541*b* 603*a*	369*a*	**19:4** 719*g*
14:23 668*q*	**15:30** 866*ab* 914*ad*	**17:35** 362*bo*	**19:5** 362*q* 661*a* 916*f*
14:24 532*k* 899*m*	**15:32** 391*f* 833*b*	**17:36** 360*g* 711*a* 974*b*	**19:6** 532*w*
946*n*	**15:33** 172*f* 362*x*	**17:37** 668*h*	**19:7** 524*e*
14:25 366*q* 392*a*	**15:35** 830*a* 836*z*	**17:38** 662*k* 723*j*	**19:8** 362*at* 620*d*
14:26 854*u*	**16:1** 357*e* 605*b* 741*o*	**17:40** 99*a* 194*s* 218*b*	**19:9** 413*c* 969*p*
14:27 218*b* 392*a* 438*i*	**16:2** 362*i* 981*h*	287*b* 344*l*	**19:10** 362*m* 620*i* 667*a*
685*c*	**16:3** 357*f*	**17:41** 723*q*	**19:11** 362*m*
14:28 684*c* 899*m*	**16:4** 184*ao* 854*ae*	**17:42** 431*a*	**19:12** 263*c* 311*n* 620*i*
946*n*	**16:7** 195*f* 223*a* 224*b*	**17:43** 218*b* 365*bl* 899*l*	**19:13** 218*y* 542*k* 982*l*
14:29 392*a* 438*i* 685*c*	371*n* 445*f* 621*d*	**17:44** 363*n*	**19:14** 651*g*
14:31 362*az* 684*c*	**16:10** 99*j*	**17:45** 561*f* 722*a* 723*o*	**19:15** 362*m*
14:32 335*g* 790*m*	**16:11** 132*b* 369*a*	**17:46** 46*f* 363*j* 363*n*	**19:16** 982*l*
14:33 344*k* 362*bn*	**16:12** 13*p* 357*f* 431*a*	727*j*	**19:17** 362*q* 542*k*
14:35 990*e*	438*i* 841*k*	**17:47** 668*f* 716*a* 723*s*	**19:18** 524*f* 620*i*
14:36 129*h* 459*a*	**16:13** 965*m*	727*j*	**19:19** 524*d*
790*m*	**16:14** 190*c* 621*d*	**17:48** 277*c*	**19:20** 579*ab* 965*m*
14:37 460*j* 727*j*	965*ag* 969*p*	**17:49** 287*b* 344*l* 362*y*	**19:22** 187*a*
14:38 459*p*	**16:16** 413*c*	**17:50** 344*l* 723*t*	**19:23** 579*ab* 965*m*
14:39 362*l* 582*g*	**16:18** 89*h* 413*c* 722*b*	**17:51** 46*f* 363*j* 723*l*	**19:24** 229*k*
14:40 605*m*	**16:19** 369*a*	**17:52** 362*az* 619*d*	**20:1** 362*i* 914*ae*
14:41 605*r*	**16:20** 301*l*	**17:53** 790*i*	**20:2** 525*j* 526*u*
14:43 218*b* 362*l* 392*a*	**16:21** 723*q* 887*ae*	**17:54** 363*j* 723*j*	**20:3** 525*j* 826*p*
526*p*	**16:22** 742*e* 826*p*	**17:55** 13*j*	**20:5** 108*c* 523*h* 988*l*
14:44 361*z* 532*m*	**16:23** 413*c* 685*c* 969*p*	**17:57** 363*j*	**20:6** 190*f*
14:45 259*k* 668*r*[2]	**17:1** 716*d*	**18:1** 887*ae*	**20:7** 891*v*
14:46 148*k*	**17:2** 722*i*	**18:3** 765*n* 887*ae*	**20:8** 362*t* 765*n*
14:47 716*d*	**17:3** 209*w*	**18:4** 228*x* 229*o* 723*j*	**20:11** 235*q*
14:52 718*i* 722*l*	**17:4** 195*i* 722*b*	**18:5** 722*d*	**20:12** 524*e*
15:1 357*f*	**17:5** 322*c* 662*k* 723*j*	**18:6** 412*a* 835*e*	**20:13** 89*h*[2]
15:2 371*y* 963*b*	**17:6** 723*j* 723*o*	**18:7** 104*p* 362*e*	**20:16** 765*n*
15:3 362*aw*	**17:7** 218*k* 322*c* 723*o*	**18:8** 891*v*	**20:17** 532*w* 887*ae*
15:4 86*b*	723*q*	**18:9** 911*i*	**20:18** 108*c* 190*f* 190*o*
15:5 527*c*	**17:8** 577*j* 605*o* 716*g*	**18:10** 413*c* 969*p*	**20:19** 344*h* 523*h*
15:6 46*ar*	**17:10** 711*a*	**18:11** 287*d* 362*m*	**20:20** 287*e*
15:7 727*d*	**17:11** 854*y*	667*a*	**20:21** 200*j*
15:8 362*aw* 747*i*	**17:12** 99*j* 133*g* 184*ao*	**18:12** 89*h* 190*c* 854*ae*	**20:22** 199*g*
15:9 365*ax* 919*a*	**17:14** 132*b*	**18:13** 722*d*	**20:23** 466*k* 765*n*
15:11 282*d* 825*e* 830*a*	**17:15** 369*a*	**18:14** 89*h* 727*b*	**20:24** 108*c* 523*h*
15:12 128*b* 548*a*	**17:16** 110*r*	**18:16** 887*ae*	**20:25** 190*o*
15:13 739*h*	**17:17** 301*l*	**18:17** 362*m* 716*e* 894*z*	**20:26** 582*g* 649*i*
15:14 409*b*	**17:18** 524*f*	**18:18** 639*a*	**20:27** 190*o*
15:15 919*a*	**17:19** 255*j*	**18:19** 894*z*	**20:29** 826*p* 981*h*
15:17 357*f* 639*a*	**17:20** 128*b* 369*d* 577*i*	**18:20** 887*ab*	**20:30** 872*o* 891*w*
15:18 362*aw*	**17:21** 722*i*	**18:21** 362*m* 542*t*	**20:31** 362*m* 741*r*
15:19 790*m*	**17:22** 277*c* 777*r*	**18:22** 826*m* 887*ae*	**20:32** 362*q* 916*f*
15:22 455*l* 739*l* 826*i*	**17:24** 854*y*	**18:23** 801*o*	**20:33** 287*d*
981*ar*[2]	**17:25** 711*a* 800*h*	**18:25** 99*t* 167*a* 362*m*	**20:34** 891*w* 946*l*
15:23 607*j* 621*d* 621*h*	894*aa* 919*f*	809*g*	**20:35** 132*d* 235*q*
738*e* 752*a*	**17:26** 360*g* 639*c*	**18:27** 99*t* 167*a* 362*at*	**20:36** 287*e*
871*b* 982*b*	711*a* 872*ab*	894*aa*	**20:37** 199*g*
983*a*	974*b*	**18:28** 89*h* 887*ab*	**20:38** 680*a*
15:24 854*ad* 914*ad*	**17:28** 369*d* 891*w*	**18:29** 705*g* 854*ae*	**20:39** 491*ac*
15:25 89*o* 909*p*	**17:29** 459*h*	**18:30** 866*s*	

20:41	311*a* 836*ad* 889*b*	**23:21**	897*c* 905*i*	**25:31**	362*q* 910*i*	**28:9**	542*u* 984*c*

20:41 311*a* 836*ad* 889*b*
20:42 466*k* 532*g*
21:1 88*n* 986*k*
21:2 525*l* 751*d*
21:3 301*l*
21:4 301*ac* 895*g*
21:6 189*d*
21:7 369*d*
21:8 723*t*
21:9 21*m* 723*l*
21:10 620*i*
21:11 104*p* 362*e*
21:12 854*y*
21:13 302*o* 503*c* 541*j*
22:1 255*g* 662*l*
22:2 741*ac* 803*c*
22:3 59*s* 169*i*
22:5 366*q* 579*z*
22:6 366*n*
22:7 370*m*
22:8 525*j* 527*d* 905*j*
22:9 524*d*
22:10 301*l* 459*b* 723*l*
22:11 737*j*
22:13 301*l* 459*b* 527*d* 623*g* 723*l*
22:14 929*c*
22:15 459*b* 491*ac*
22:16 362*am*
22:17 362*am* 598*d* 986*t*
22:20 667*a*
22:21 362*am* 524*f* 986*t*
22:22 524*d*
22:23 89*p* 362*m* 854*ag*
23:1 716*f* 786*f*
23:2 459*a* 712*b*
23:3 854*s*
23:4 459*a* 727*i*
23:5 362*at* 668*u*
23:6 989*d*
23:7 264*g* 524*d* 727*j*
23:8 712*i*
23:9 459*c* 989*d*
23:10 459*a*
23:11 272*c*
23:13 524*d* 667*a*
23:14 172*x* 459*af* 727*j*
23:15 172*x* 362*m*
23:16 162*c* 855*d*
23:17 741*o* 854*ag*
23:18 765*n*
23:19 524*d*
23:20 272*c*

23:21 897*c* 905*i*
23:22 459*af* 698*a*
23:23 523*h*
23:24 172*x*
23:25 524*d* 619*h*
23:26 209*w*
23:27 716*f*
23:28 344*h* 667*a*
23:29 662*l*
24:1 172*x* 524*d*
24:2 344*h*
24:3 255*g* 302*f*
24:4 46*t* 727*j*
24:5 917*e* 936*e*
24:6 357*g*
24:8 311*a*
24:10 357*g* 727*j*
24:11 46*t* 362*m* 935*d*
24:12 480*c* 910*d*
24:13 496*c* 938*a*
24:14 365*h* 365*bl* 639*a*
24:15 480*c* 668*h*
24:16 836*m*
24:17 913*q*
24:18 727*j*
24:19 962*c*
24:20 741*o*
24:21 532*g* 561*z*
25:1 172*x* 361*ad* 364*l* 836*r*
25:2 369*e* 800*f*
25:3 500*c* 841*h* 898*a*
25:4 369*e*
25:5 884*d*
25:6 717*c*
25:7 369*e* 788*h*
25:8 761*al* 826*p*
25:10 639*c* 667*c*
25:11 491*r*
25:12 524*b*
25:13 723*l* 777*r*
25:14 524*a* 921*c*
25:15 788*h*
25:16 235*f* 660*g*
25:17 938*d*
25:18 301*l*
25:19 525*k*
25:20 267*j* 365*bd*
25:21 645*f* 788*h*
25:22 302*j* 372*f*
25:23 311*d*
25:25 501*f* 938*d*
25:26 362*q* 910*i*
25:28 716*e* 909*p*
25:29 287*c* 360*c*
25:30 741*o*

25:31 362*q* 910*i*
25:32 923*l*
25:33 362*q* 910*i*
25:34 302*j* 372*f*
25:35 455*r*
25:36 525*k* 876*a* 949*i*
25:37 651*g* 948*e*
25:38 362*be*
25:39 280*d* 894*u* 923*l* 927*a*
25:41 648*e*
25:42 267*j* 365*bd*
25:43 894*u*
25:44 894*v*
26:1 523*h* 524*d*
26:2 172*x*
26:3 209*v*
26:4 459*q*
26:5 192*x*
26:6 89*q*
26:7 679*c* 723*o*
26:8 727*j*
26:9 357*g*
26:10 362*be*
26:11 339*g* 357*g* 723*o*
26:12 679*c*
26:13 209*w* 577*j*
26:14 13*j*
26:16 339*g* 723*o*
26:17 577*a*
26:18 619*h* 914*ae*
26:19 300*m*
26:20 365*h* 365*am*
26:21 499*f* 644*i* 914*ad*
26:22 723*o*
26:23 727*j* 804*o*
26:24 644*i*
27:1 362*i* 667*a*
27:2 59*s*
27:3 896*n*
27:4 524*d* 620*i*
27:5 184*aa* 826*p*
27:7 110*t*
27:8 716*d*
27:9 362*ax* 790*j*
27:10 541*f* 716*h*
27:11 362*ax*
27:12 485*ai* 827*k*
28:1 89*q* 716*f*
28:2 660*g*
28:3 361*ad* 364*l* 984*c*
28:5 854*y*
28:6 438*s* 459*a* 460*j* 579*y* 605*s*
28:7 984*a*
28:8 129*f* 228*z* 527*b*

28:9 542*u* 984*c*
28:10 532*w*
28:12 542*k* 577*l*
28:13 854*ag*
28:14 133*h* 226*a* 311*a*
28:15 190*c* 438*s* 460*j* 579*y* 718*i* 827*l*
28:16 190*c* 705*a*
28:17 46*t* 741*r*
28:18 738*j* 891*c*
28:19 89*r* 728*d*
28:20 163*c* 301*r* 309*c* 854*s* 946*k*
28:21 661*a*
28:23 218*x* 612*a*
29:2 89*q*
29:3 929*c*
29:4 148*h* 704*j* 891*w*
29:5 104*p* 362*e*
29:6 929*c*
29:7 148*h*
29:8 929*c*
29:10 128*b* 148*h*
30:1 381*e* 716*f*
30:2 747*i* 788*a*
30:3 381*e*
30:4 836*ae*
30:5 896*n*
30:6 162*c* 362*m* 391*d*
30:7 459*c* 989*d*
30:8 619*d*
30:10 350*t* 684*c*
30:11 301*r*
30:12 946*k*
30:13 651*g*
30:14 381*e*
30:15 532*l* 689*b*
30:16 790*d* 876*a*
30:17 362*at* 365*bb* 667*b* 716*d*
30:18 656*ae* 668*t*
30:19 772*c*
30:20 790*j*
30:21 350*t*
30:22 783*b* 790*a* 938*d*
30:23 727*i*
30:24 777*r*
30:25 127*c*
30:26 781*y*
31:1 620*f* 716*f*
31:2 362*af*
31:3 287*f* 655*k*
31:4 362*t* 362*ae* 723*q* 837*c* 854*t* 974*b*
31:5 362*ae*

31:6	361*ad* 361*af*	**2:22**	362*af*	**5:6**	184*af* 297*c*	**7:23**	21*e* 371*ad* 792*n*
31:7	184*aa* 620*h*	**2:23**	224*f* 266*c* 279*l*		439*o* 655*o* 786*j*	**7:24**	115*i* 371*ac*
31:8	229*l*	**2:24**	172*w* 209*v* 619*h*	**5:8**	351*a* 439*o* 496*c*		965*e*
31:9	46*f* 363*j*	**2:26**	619*i* 719*f*		655*o*	**7:25**	676*c*
31:10	363*k*	**2:28**	414*k*	**5:9**	164*p*	**7:29**	897*c*
31:11	364*l*	**2:29**	129*i*	**5:10**	89*h* 160*i*	**8:1**	727*g*
31:12	381*i*	**2:31**	362*aj*	**5:11**	164*u* 529*q* 631*d*	**8:2**	95*e* 362*av* 465*h*
31:13	946*m*	**2:32**	129*i*		686*f*		727*g* 745*d*
		3:1	162*h* 163*c* 718*g*	**5:12**	741*o*	**8:3**	350*p* 727*d*
2 Samuel		**3:2**	169*b*	**5:13**	169*b* 894*u* 952*c*	**8:4**	274*c* 655*p* 786*g*
1:2	311*d* 836*g* 836*l*	**3:3**	896*n*	**5:17**	357*f* 662*l*	**8:5**	362*au*
	923*s*	**3:6**	718*g*	**5:19**	459*a* 712*b* 727*j*	**8:6**	703*b* 722*h* 745*d*
1:4	361*ad* 361*af*	**3:7**	45*f* 928*i* 952*b*	**5:20**	176*d* 561*u* 727*c*	**8:7**	662*i*
	620*h*	**3:9**	532*m* 532*o*	**5:21**	621*u* 982*r*	**8:8**	631*g*
1:6	209*u* 619*g*	**3:10**	272*b* 741*r*	**5:23**	314*a* 366*n* 459*a*	**8:9**	727*d*
1:8	13*j*	**3:11**	578*e* 854*ae*	**5:24**	415*d*	**8:10**	797*l*
1:9	362*t*	**3:12**	765*p*	**5:25**	362*at*	**8:11**	790*k* 979*v*
1:10	362*x* 743*f*	**3:13**	894*u*	**6:2**	194*c* 561*a* 968*u*	**8:13**	255*j* 362*au* 866*s*
1:11	836*g*	**3:14**	809*g*	**6:3**	126*b* 274*i*	**8:14**	722*h*
1:12	836*r* 946*m*	**3:16**	148*h* 836*ad*	**6:5**	414*b* 876*f*	**8:15**	913*q*
1:13	59*s*	**3:17**	741*k*	**6:6**	370*z* 378*d*	**8:16**	549*a* 722*d*
1:14	357*g*	**3:18**	668*u*	**6:7**	176*d* 362*be*	**8:17**	586*u* 986*d*
1:15	362*ah*	**3:20**	876*a*		891*m*	**8:18**	722*d*
1:16	180*b* 357*g* 466*g*	**3:21**	717*h* 741*k* 765*o*	**6:8**	561*u* 891*v*	**9:1**	41*h* 897*x*
1:17	836*s*	**3:22**	790*j*	**6:9**	854*l*	**9:2**	13*m*
1:18	287*h* 534*j* 589*b*	**3:25**	459*q* 542*k*	**6:10**	194*b* 194*c* 598*d*	**9:3**	655*n*
1:19	309*b*	**3:26**	339*e* 491*ac*	**6:11**	110*s* 897*f*	**9:4**	187*a*
1:20	525*l*		529*q*	**6:12**	194*c* 897*f*	**9:6**	311*d*
1:21	209*u* 342*c* 357*n*	**3:27**	224*f* 279*l* 362*af*	**6:13**	981*h* 981*p*	**9:7**	301*l* 656*ae*
	662*i*		530*h*	**6:14**	835*e* 989*d*		854*ah* 897*x*
1:22	362*e*	**3:28**	180*d* 935*d*	**6:15**	414*c*	**9:8**	639*a*
1:23	89*r* 162*f* 277*a*	**3:29**	302*b* 636*e* 651*o*	**6:16**	835*e* 922*g*	**9:10**	301*l* 370*g*
	365*ag* 365*as*	**3:30**	362*af*^{2}	**6:17**	192*t* 981*p* 981*w*	**9:13**	655*n*
1:24	228*m* 431*d* 836*r*	**3:31**	836*h* 836*k*	**6:18**	897*w*	**10:1**	361*af* 741*u*
	844*c*	**3:32**	364*l* 836*r*	**6:19**	301*l*	**10:2**	831*f*
1:25	309*b*	**3:33**	501*h*	**6:20**	229*p*	**10:3**	459*q*
1:26	887*ae*	**3:34**	747*s*	**6:21**	605*b* 741*o* 876*f*	**10:4**	92*b* 229*d* 259*l*
1:27	309*b* 723*t*	**3:35**	532*m* 946*n*	**6:22**	872*j*		648*j*
2:1	184*aa*	**3:36**	826*m*	**6:23**	172*a*	**10:5**	36*c* 259*l* 872*o*
2:2	896*n*	**3:39**	163*c* 357*f* 804*j*	**7:1**	192*aa* 717*i*	**10:6**	792*g* 827*k*
2:3	184*aa*	**4:1**	856*c*	**7:2**	192*d* 192*t*	**10:11**	703*h*
2:4	357*f* 364*l* 741*k*	**4:4**	131*g* 309*c* 620*k*		192*aa* 194*b*	**10:12**	162*l* 716*d* 855*a*
2:5	897*c*		655*u*	**7:3**	89*h*	**10:13**	620*d*
2:7	357*f* 741*k* 855*a*	**4:5**	379*a* 683*r*	**7:4**	529*f*	**10:16**	350*p*
2:8	722*d*	**4:6**	224*f* 362*w*	**7:5**	192*d*	**10:17**	222*e*
2:9	741*k*	**4:7**	46*f* 218*x* 363*j*	**7:6**	192*t*	**10:18**	362*at* 620*d*
2:10	110*u* 131*g*	**4:8**	910*d*	**7:8**	369*d* 741*o*	**10:19**	719*i*
2:11	110*y*	**4:10**	362*ah* 529*j*	**7:9**	89*h* 866*aa*	**11:1**	128*m* 712*b*
2:13	346*a*	**4:11**	180*d* 218*x*	**7:10**	153*o*		718*e*
2:14	837*b*	**4:12**	46*b* 217*b* 346*a*	**7:11**	717*i* 957*e*	**11:2**	129*b* 218*x* 648*f*
2:15	99*m*		362*af* 363*j*	**7:12**	361*n* 741*q*		841*h*
2:16	716*h* 723*l*		363*k* 364*l*	**7:13**	115*j* 192*d* 741*q*	**11:3**	13*o*
2:17	728*f*	**5:1**	11*a*	**7:14**	169*s* 827*i*	**11:4**	45*f* 529*q*
2:18	277*a*	**5:2**	369*f* 741*o*	**7:15**	905*d*	**11:5**	167*g*
2:19	249*c* 619*h*	**5:3**	357*f* 765*n*	**7:16**	115*j* 741*q*^{2}	**11:7**	8*a*
2:20	13*m*	**5:4**	110*ac* 131*g*	**7:18**	639*a* 761*r*	**11:8**	148*i* 648*e* 781*y*
2:21	249*c* 282*h* 790*m*	**5:5**	110*y* 110*ab*	**7:22**	21*b*	**11:9**	679*f*

11:11	45*i* 192*t* 194*b* 301*k*	**13:4**	834*c* 859*p* 887*ab*
11:13	679*f* 949*k*	**13:5**	301*r* 541*j*
11:14	588*a*	**13:8**	381*m*
11:15	362*s* 661*b* 883*d*	**13:9**	300*aa* 760*a*
11:17	362*af*	**13:11**	45*i* 786*n*
11:19	529*q*	**13:12**	127*g* 499*f* 951*aa*
11:20	200*j* 235*e* 287*g*		
11:21	344*k* 362*af*	**13:13**	501*h* 872*n*
11:22	529*q*	**13:14**	45*f* 162*f* 456*h*
11:24	235*e* 287*g* 362*af*	**13:15**	300*aa* 859*p* 888*q*
11:25	361*q* 855*e*	**13:16**	456*h*
11:26	836*p*	**13:17**	264*e* 300*aa*
11:27	167*j* 894*u*	**13:18**	228*p* 264*e* 895*a*
12:1	519*e* 579*z* 751*i* 800*m* 801*o*	**13:19**	836*g* 836*l*
		13:20	165*ab* 582*g* 860*b*
12:3	365*bn*	**13:21**	891*v*
12:4	301*r*	**13:22**	582*g* 888*q*
12:5	361*z* 891*v*	**13:23**	369*e* 761*ap*
12:6	97*a* 787*a* 906*c*	**13:25**	322*l*
12:7	13*q* 357*f* 668*i*	**13:27**	612*a*
12:8	781*e* 894*v*	**13:28**	362*ac* 855*a* 949*i*
12:9	362*af* 894*u* 922*c*		
12:10	362*j* 922*a*	**13:29**	267*j* 620*k*
12:11	45*i* 645*b* 894*p*	**13:30**	529*n*
12:12	522*c* 530*d*	**13:31**	311*h* 836*g*
12:13	361*w* 909*f* 914*ad*	**13:32**	608*e* 951*aa*
		13:34	457*h* 620*i*
12:14	361*o* 705*b* 980*e*	**13:36**	836*q*
12:15	651*g* 896*n*	**13:37**	620*i* 836*z*
12:16	311*h* 459*a* 761*l* 946*g*	**13:39**	817*a* 831*g*
		14:1	719*g* 720*c* 817*a*
12:17	310*b* 760*a* 946*g*	**14:2**	228*i* 357*s* 500*c* 541*j* 836*d*
12:18	361*ae* 524*a* 645*g* 854*ae*		
		14:4	311*d*
12:19	361*ae* 578*i*	**14:5**	896*n*
12:20	301*e* 357*r* 648*a* 648*m* 981*f*	**14:6**	362*ac*
		14:7	41*l* 272*a* 561*z* 776*a* 963*k*
12:21	301*e* 946*g*		
12:22	946*g*	**14:8**	148*h* 737*c*
12:23	361*o* 656*n* 946*j*	**14:9**	935*d*
12:24	45*f* 167*i* 831*f* 887*f*	**14:11**	259*k* 910*e*
		14:13	656*af* 936*a*
12:25	751*i* 887*f*	**14:14**	350*w* 361*f*
12:26	184*aa* 712*b* 786*j*	**14:17**	89*d*
		14:18	526*v*
12:27	339*y* 529*q*	**14:20**	500*c*
12:28	561*s*	**14:21**	656*af*
12:30	322*a* 743*f* 790*i* 844*a*	**14:22**	311*d* 826*p*
		14:24	883*b*
12:31	630*b* 631*n* 682*e*	**14:25**	646*e* 841*k*
13:1	841*h* 859*p* 887*ab*	**14:26**	259*i* 322*c*
		14:27	841*h*
13:2	700*a* 895*b*	**14:28**	110*u* 883*b*
13:3	500*c* 880*d*	**14:29**	737*j*

14:30	381*j*	**16:13**	287*b* 332*b* 344*l* 899*m*
14:32	362*t* 737*j* 882*g*		
14:33	311*d* 889*b*	**16:14**	684*d*
15:1	99*r* 274*c*	**16:16**	360*c* 880*d*
15:2	128*b* 263*o* 959*c*	**16:17**	897*x*
15:3	720*c* 913*q*	**16:18**	89*s* 605*n* 773*i*
15:4	751*d* 957*g*	**16:19**	742*f*
15:5	311*a* 889*b*	**16:20**	691*g*
15:6	817*b*	**16:21**	45*f* 162*j* 888*o* 894*v* 952*c*
15:7	532*w* 738*b*		
15:8	656*af*	**16:22**	192*u* 213*k* 441*b* 951*q* 952*c*
15:10	414*m* 459*q* 741*p*		
		16:23	459*b* 691*e*
15:11	491*ac* 761*ap* 935*d*	**17:1**	619*h* 722*m*
		17:2	362*m* 620*g* 684*d*
15:12	623*g* 691*g* 981*h*		
15:13	529*p* 817*b*	**17:3**	656*af*
15:14	362*j* 620*i* 667*a* 680*a*	**17:4**	826*l*
		17:5	737*j*
15:16	99*k* 457*l* 952*c*	**17:7**	645*a* 691*g*
15:18	99*t* 305*a*	**17:8**	365*z* 718*e* 722*b* 772*f* 883*d* 892*b*
15:19	59*t* 148*i*		
15:20	268*b*	**17:9**	255*g* 362*j* 523*h*
15:21	89*r*	**17:10**	722*b* 854*y*
15:23	350*t* 836*ad*	**17:11**	74*g* 104*e* 691*l*
15:24	194*c* 986*g*	**17:12**	341*h* 362*j*
15:25	656*af* 826*f*	**17:13**	184*ab* 208*c* 288*b*
15:26	826*g*		
15:27	438*ae*	**17:14**	645*b* 691*g* 691*l* 702*j* 737*b*
15:28	222*f* 507*f* 524*d*		
15:29	194*c*	**17:15**	529*p*
15:30	209*q* 226*f* 836*ad*	**17:16**	129*g* 222*f* 362*j*
		17:17	297*c* 742*e*
15:31	499*i* 623*h* 691*g* 761*p*	**17:18**	339*d* 524*d*
		17:19	226*h* 301*ai* 491*ac*
15:32	213*a* 836*g* 836*l*		
15:33	322*l*	**17:20**	148*k* 187*a* 222*f* 459*af* 484*c*
15:34	691*g* 702*j*		
15:35	524*e* 986*g*	**17:21**	222*f* 524*d* 691*g*
15:36	529*p*	**17:22**	222*e*
15:37	297*c*	**17:23**	60*c* 148*l* 217*d* 267*m* 362*ae* 364*l* 691*g*
16:1	213*a* 301*l* 365*bd*		
		17:24	222*e*
16:2	267*j* 684*d*	**17:25**	45*e* 722*d*
16:3	656*af* 741*r*	**17:26**	192*x*
16:4	311*d* 771*g* 826*p*	**17:27**	301*l*
16:5	899*m*	**17:28**	194*l* 218*w*
16:6	287*b* 344*l*	**17:29**	684*d* 859*k*
16:7	362*f* 938*d*	**18:1**	86*a* 722*d*
16:8	150*b* 280*e* 741*p* 741*r*	**18:2**	89*s* 95*e* 722*d*
		18:3	92*c* 620*g* 638*e* 703*h* 860*a*
16:9	46*f* 365*bl*		
16:10	10*a* 737*b* 899*m*	**18:4**	263*o*
16:11	362*m* 620*t* 899*m*	**18:5**	415*d* 736*a* 737*c*
		18:6	366*q*
16:12	804*o*		

18:7 362*ak* 728*f*	**19:26** 267*m* 542*k*	**21:15** 684*a* 716*d*	**22:50** 59*n* 412*c* 907*d*
18:8 366*q*	655*n*	**21:16** 195*i* 322*c*	**22:51** 209*an* 357*h*
18:9 217*e* 267*j* 366*s*	**19:27** 926*b* 968*j*	362*m* 362*y*	**23:1** 69*j* 357*g* 413*f*
18:11 228*x* 362*s* 809*n*	**19:28** 361*p* 882*b*	**21:17** 420*k*	**23:2** 529*c* 965*aa*
18:12 415*d* 660*g*	**19:29** 92*e*	**21:18** 195*i* 362*y* 718*i*	**23:3** 344*w* 733*ad*
737*c* 809*n*	**19:31** 222*e*	**21:19** 218*k* 362*y* 723*o*	**23:4** 350*ae* 417*p*
18:13 526*u* 883*d* 930*b*	**19:32** 131*g* 133*g*	**21:20** 53*r* 99*b* 195*i*	**23:5** 765*i* 859*c*
18:14 93*c* 362*w* 634*b*	633*d* 800*f*	**21:21** 362*y*	**23:6** 256*k* 938*h*
655*k* 723*p*	**19:33** 222*f*	**22:1** 412*c* 668*h*	**23:7** 378*f* 381*u*
18:15 723*q*	**19:35** 131*g* 133*g* 322*l*	**22:2** 344*w* 662*d*	**23:8** 160*i* 362*e* 722*c*
18:16 414*k* 619*e* 747*w*	387*b* 416*a*	668*b*	**23:9** 93*b*
18:17 209*z* 255*b* 364*l*	**19:36** 222*e*	**22:3** 162*b* 344*w*	**23:10** 48*d* 229*l* 684*a*
620*h*	**19:37** 361*q* 364*f*	662*a* 662*j*	**23:11** 366*h* 620*f*
18:18 548*a* 561*t*	**19:39** 222*e* 889*b* 897*v*	**22:4** 668*h* 761*q* 923*a*	**23:12** 727*c*
18:19 524*d*² 668*g*	**19:40** 89*s*	**22:5** 361*l*	**23:13** 93*b* 99*q* 255*g*
18:20 529*p*	**19:41** 222*e* 788*b*	**22:6** 361*m* 542*y*	255*j* 370*s*
18:21 277*c* 529*p*	**19:42** 11*b* 891*v*	**22:7** 455*e* 761*q*	**23:14** 184*ao* 722*h*
18:22 277*c* 529*p*	**19:43** 99*k* 735*d*	**22:8** 176*f* 891*c*	**23:15** 263*i* 339*d* 859*l*
18:23 277*d*	**20:1** 148*j* 414*f* 775*a*	**22:9** 381*o*	**23:16** 176*d* 263*i* 304*d*
18:24 263*n* 277*c*	777*o* 938*d*	**22:10** 309*e* 418*h*	350*w*
311*v* 457*h*	**20:2** 284*h*	**22:11** 267*o* 352*m*	**23:17** 335*g* 661*a*
18:25 88*n* 529*k*	**20:3** 45*h* 99*k* 148*l*	968*w*	**23:18** 362*e* 723*p*
18:26 88*n* 277*c* 529*k*	896*n* 952*c*	**22:12** 355*e* 418*h*	**23:19** 93*b* 722*d* 923*s*
18:27 277*c* 529*k*	**20:4** 74*g* 110*l*	**22:13** 381*t* 417*c*	**23:20** 255*b* 350*ai*
18:28 311*d* 727*j*	**20:5** 136*e*	**22:14** 176*k*	362*bo* 365*ad*
18:29 8*a* 61*a* 491*ac*	**20:6** 619*h*	**22:15** 176*k* 287*i*	380*c*
18:30 266*c*	**20:7** 619*h*	**22:16** 214*a* 343*a*	**23:21** 723*p*
18:31 668*g*	**20:8** 344*t* 723*k*	**22:17** 304*e* 339*v*	**23:22** 93*b* 923*s*
18:32 8*a* 18*h*	**20:9** 8*b* 259*l* 889*b*	**22:18** 668*g* 705*j*	**23:23** 660*g* 923*s*
18:33 361*s* 818*e* 836*q*	**20:10** 224*f* 362*af* 619*h*	**22:19** 218*ai*	**23:37** 723*q*
19:3 523*k* 620*h* 872*o*	**20:11** 284*h*	**22:20** 183*a* 826*e*	**23:39** 99*q*
19:4 226*f* 577*l*	**20:12** 226*d* 335*d* 363*d*	**22:21** 929*d* 962*a*	**24:1** 86*b* 891*k*
19:5 668*t* 872*n*	**20:13** 619*h*	**22:22** 739*h*	**24:3** 38*e* 104*c*
19:6 639*c* 826*l* 887*af*	**20:15** 209*ab* 235*l* 712*i*	**22:24** 935*d*	**24:5** 222*e*
888*q*	**20:16** 500*c*	**22:26** 646*a* 897*m*	**24:8** 110*s*
19:7 75*e* 308*i*	**20:17** 13*m*	**22:27** 246*a* 950*a*	**24:9** 99*v*
19:8 74*g* 263*l* 311*v*	**20:18** 496*c* 691*k*	**22:28** 311*r* 668*l* 871*i*	**24:10** 499*f* 914*ad*
620*h*	**20:19** 165*f* 169*ai*	**22:29** 417*j* 420*i*	936*e*
19:9 620*i* 668*u* 709*f*	**20:21** 272*a* 363*j*	**22:30** 312*a* 712*b*	**24:11** 438*af* 529*f* 579*z*
19:10 357*f* 656*af*	**20:22** 46*f* 148*k* 414*k*	**22:31** 529*a* 624*a*	**24:12** 93*c* 605*n* 759*a*
19:11 136*f* 656*af*	**20:23** 722*d*²	646*a* 662*j*	**24:13** 110*l* 110*s* 110*v*
19:12 11*a*	**20:24** 549*a* 682*e*	**22:32** 21*a* 344*w*	620*b* 636*d*
19:13 11*a* 532*m* 722*d*	**20:25** 586*u* 986*d*	**22:33** 662*d*	659*a* 728*b*
19:14 148*g*	**20:26** 986*d*	**22:34** 153*i*	**24:14** 371*q* 905*c*
19:15 350*n*	**21:1** 110*v* 362*av*	**22:35** 287*e* 534*e* 718*e*	**24:15** 99*v* 659*a*
19:16 680*c*	459*a* 636*a*	**22:36** 177*a* 662*j* 703*b*	**24:16** 165*b* 184*af*
19:17 680*c*	936*a*	**22:37** 153*i*	370*z* 635*j* 968*h*
19:18 222*e* 311*d*	**21:2** 765*q*	**22:38** 619*d* 727*c*	**24:17** 438*d*
19:19 936*b*	**21:3** 941*k*	**22:39** 727*h*	**24:18** 370*z* 990*d*
19:20 68*i* 914*ad*	**21:4** 362*q* 797*p*	**22:40** 228*af*	**24:20** 311*d*
19:21 357*h* 899*m*	**21:6** 99*d* 217*b* 362*s*	**22:42** 460*j*	**24:21** 792*c*
963*o*	**21:7** 532*g* 919*a*	**22:43** 332*h*	**24:22** 385*b*
19:22 10*a* 362*q* 705*d*	**21:9** 217*b* 370*t*	**22:44** 59*o*	**24:24** 809*j* 812*d*
19:23 532*g*	**21:10** 226*h* 365*ak*	**22:47** 344*w* 360*g*	**24:25** 659*a* 761*aa*
19:24 53*k* 259*l* 649*p*	**21:11** 524*d*	923*h*	990*e*
19:25 89*t*	**21:12** 217*b* 363*f*	**22:48** 910*d*	
	21:14 364*l* 761*aa*	**22:49** 176*e* 310*f*	

1 Kings

1:1	133g 380c
1:2	381an 895b
1:4	45h 841h
1:5	274c 741p
1:6	459p 736a 827j 841k
1:7	703h 986d
1:8	722c 986d
1:9	344h 761ap 981h
1:10	579z 722c
1:11	491ac 741p
1:12	691k
1:13	532j 741p
1:14	466e
1:15	133g
1:16	311d
1:17	532j 741p
1:18	491ac 741p
1:19	722d 761ap 981h 986d
1:20	455t 741p
1:21	361n
1:22	579z
1:23	311d
1:24	741p
1:25	360c 761ap 981h 986d
1:26	986d
1:28	737j
1:29	532j
1:30	741p
1:31	311d 360c
1:32	579z 737j 986d
1:33	267j
1:34	357f 360c 414m 579z 986d
1:35	741p
1:36	488c
1:37	89h
1:38	267j 579z 722l 986d
1:39	357f 360c 414m
1:40	176f 412a 824q
1:41	412a 415d
1:42	529k 986d
1:43	741p
1:44	267j 579z 722l 986d
1:45	357f
1:46	743c
1:48	438n 923h
1:49	854u
1:50	662g 990b
1:51	532l
1:52	259k 929c
1:53	311a
2:1	361af 737c
2:2	162l 361m
2:3	586d 727b 739g 953a
2:4	725b 741q
2:5	362f
2:6	362n 498n 735d
2:7	620i 882b 897x
2:8	532g 899m
2:9	362n 735d
2:10	361af 364l
2:11	110ac
2:12	741p
2:15	741p^2
2:16	761al
2:17	894v
2:19	241c 311a
2:20	761al
2:21	894v
2:22	986d
2:23	532m
2:24	362ag
2:26	194c 361u 986d
2:27	725b 986t
2:28	662g 990b
2:30	298c 362ag
2:32	491ac 804l
2:34	364l
2:35	722d 986d 986k
2:36	192ac 298d
2:39	620j
2:40	267m 459af
2:44	804l
2:46	362ag 741q
3:1	164u 235i 894z
3:2	209ac
3:3	209ac 396f 887m 981h
3:4	209ac
3:5	438t 761ac
3:6	897m
3:7	132g 499e
3:8	104e
3:9	455k 463a 480n 500d
3:10	826i
3:11	113g 800g
3:12	21h 500d
3:13	800f 866aa
3:14	113c 739g
3:15	194d 438s 876a 981h
3:16	951t
3:17	167f
3:19	361ae 362u
3:20	150b
3:21	13j
3:24	723l
3:25	92a
3:26	905i
3:28	500d 854ae
4:1	741p
4:2	741aa 986k
4:3	549a 586u
4:4	722d 986d
4:5	880d 986d
4:6	682e
4:7	99n 633d 741aa
4:13	184aa 235g
4:19	184p
4:20	104e 635d 824z
4:21	350p 745d 804f
4:22	301l
4:24	717i
4:25	366j 366r 370o 660a
4:26	274c 365bg
4:27	633d
4:28	301aj
4:29	26d 500d
4:30	281m 306a
4:31	866s
4:32	413f 496b
4:33	365a 366a
4:34	289b 500d
5:1	880d
5:3	164y 718e 727h
5:4	717i
5:5	164z 990n
5:6	46z 631d 696e 804b
5:7	500d
5:9	301l 343o
5:12	500d 717i 765p
5:13	682e
5:14	141b 682e
5:17	214d 344r
6:1	108f 164z 990n
6:2	195a
6:4	263a
6:5	194t
6:6	303b
6:7	344r 630c 669f
6:8	308m
6:9	226s
6:10	195b
6:12	725b 739g
6:13	192e 621g
6:15	226s 235i
6:16	990ac
6:17	195a
6:18	554c
6:19	194d 990ac
6:20	28l 226q 226s
6:22	226q
6:23	195a 554c 968u
6:27	271c
6:28	226q
6:29	554c
6:30	226q
6:31	264a
6:32	226q 554c
6:33	263f
6:34	264a
6:35	554c
6:36	344r
6:37	108f 214d
6:38	108l 110y 725g
7:1	110z 164u
7:2	192aa 195a
7:3	194t 218o
7:4	263a
7:5	263a 263f
7:6	194t 195a 218o
7:7	194t 226s 480n
7:8	894z
7:9	344r 630b
7:10	195b 344r
7:14	696e
7:15	195a 218p
7:16	195a 213b
7:17	222n
7:18	554c
7:20	554c
7:21	561t
7:22	554c
7:23	195a 250d 343p
7:24	554c
7:25	99n 281v 554c
7:26	195c 205a 234b
7:27	99k 195a 218g
7:29	554c
7:30	218g 315b
7:31	28n 195a
7:32	195a 315b
7:34	218g
7:36	554c
7:37	28k
7:38	99k 195a 195c 648u
7:39	343p
7:40	194g 725g
7:41	213b 218p 222n
7:42	554c
7:43	99k 218g 648u
7:44	99n 343p 554c
7:45	194g
7:46	344c 348a 554b
7:47	322h

7:48 189d 218ae
      301aa 990c
7:49 99k 420h
7:50 194g 315f
7:51 725g
8:1   74g 194d
8:2   108k 988i
8:3   194d
8:5   104w 981h
8:6   226m 271c
      968u 990ac
8:7   218i
8:9   190o 194f 548c
8:10 355d
8:11 866e
8:12 192b 355e
8:13 192a 990n
8:14 897w
8:15 725b 923h
8:16 304a 605b
8:17 164y
8:19 164z
8:20 725b
8:21 194d 304a 765d
8:22 761r
8:23 21b 768c
8:24 725b
8:25 741q
8:27 192b 971a
8:28 455b
8:29 455a 761y
8:30 909e
8:31 532a
8:32 280c 960a
8:33 455a 728a 761y
8:34 184k 909e
8:35 342c 455a 761y
8:36 350ab 534d
      909e
8:37 365j 636g 659a
      712c
8:38 455a 761y
8:39 490i 909e
8:40 854e
8:41 59m
8:42 455a 761y
8:43 490n 854e
8:44 455a 718b 761y
8:46 188a 747h 891g
      914j
8:47 455a 761y 939a
8:48 184a 184aj
      188a 192d
      605k
8:50 909e
8:51 304a 383c
8:52 455a 761y

8:53 46aq 304a 777f
8:54 53e 311e
8:55 897w
8:56 683m 764a 923l
8:57 89d 621g
8:58 739g
8:60 21c 490n
8:61 739g
8:62 981h
8:63 876g
8:64 196e 235c 990b
8:65 110o 988i
8:66 824o
9:2   445a
9:3   455c 561g 979s
9:4   739g 929c
9:5   153q 741q
9:6   966e
9:7   188a 300n 496d
      607b
9:8   165g
9:9   304a 621i 966h
9:10 164u
9:11 184aa 631d
9:12 826o
9:13 561u 641f
9:14 322b 631h
9:15 682e
9:16 362av 381e
      786j 809g
9:17 164q
9:19 274e 632a
9:20 371v
9:21 682e
9:22 745g
9:23 741ab
9:24 164s 164u
9:25 94a
9:26 275a
9:27 270a
9:28 322b 631h
10:1 459j 461h
10:2 396m 631h
      844a
10:3 460i
10:4 192aa 500d
10:5 301m 308m
      686d
10:7 486n 500d 800f
10:8 824q
10:9 741p 887f 913j
      923h
10:10 396m 631h
      781y 844a
10:11 631d 844a
10:12 414a
10:13 148l 781y

10:14 322b 631h
10:16 322a 662i
10:17 192aa 322a
       662i
10:18 226q 631k 743c
10:19 308m 554e
10:20 21m
10:21 194l 631j 641g
10:22 110v 275e
       365an 631k
10:23 500d 800f
10:24 459af 500d
10:25 781y
10:26 274c 274e
10:27 631d 631j
10:28 365bg
10:29 274c 791b
       809k^2
11:1   59ah 887ab
11:2   883c
11:3   894u 952c
11:4   282g 966h
11:5   967f 967m
11:6   914w
11:7   209ae 967k
       967m
11:8   396f 966h
11:9   91e 891m
11:10 966d
11:11 741r 769a 786l
11:12 136c
11:13 371ah 605k
11:14 705g
11:15 362ax 364m
       372f
11:17 620k
11:19 826p 894z
11:20 611a
11:21 148g 361af
11:22 635c
11:23 620j 705g
11:25 705g 888q
11:26 738b
11:27 164s 264n
11:28 678h 682e
       722b 751h
11:29 126b 228n 579z
11:30 46t 99n
11:31 99k 741r 786l
11:32 605k
11:33 967f 967k 967m
11:34 739h
11:35 99k
11:36 420k 561g 605k
11:37 741q
11:38 739g
11:39 827e

11:40 362n 620i
11:41 589b
11:42 110ac
11:43 361af 364l 741t
12:1   741k
12:2   620i
12:4   323c 701d 735e
12:5   110l
12:6   691l
12:7   742f
12:9   323c 691l 701d
12:10 323c 701d 735d
12:11 279c 322k 365s
12:13 691l 735d
12:14 279c 322k 365s
       735e
12:15 456h 579z
12:16 46aj 148j 456h
       775a 777o
12:17 371ah 741t
12:18 274d 362af
       620k 680c 682e
12:19 738b
12:20 371ah 741s
12:21 74g 656af 718g
       722m
12:22 579z
12:24 11h 148h
12:25 164q
12:27 362h 981b
12:28 304b 691l 982k
12:31 209ae 986r
12:32 108l 209af
12:33 108l 396f
13:1   396f 579z 990g
13:2   170h 363h 381h
       986r
13:3   46m 381h 547d
13:4   342k
13:5   46m 381h
13:6   656v 761k
13:7   685c 962e
13:8   883c
13:9   148h
13:11 524d 579z
13:13 267m
13:14 13m 366s
13:15 883c
13:18 541h
13:19 882b
13:20 529f
13:21 738j
13:22 364l
13:23 267m
13:24 362bq 363d
       365ac
13:28 363d

13:29 363*d* 364*l* 836*r*
13:30 364*f*
13:31 364*f*
13:32 209*ae*
13:33 209*af* 986*r*
13:34 165*r*
14:1 651*h*
14:2 527*b* 579*z*
14:3 301*ai* 392*a*
14:4 133*g* 439*a*
14:5 524*d* 541*j*
14:6 415*d* 541*j*
14:7 741*q*
14:8 46*aj* 739*h*
14:9 914*w* 982*k*
14:10 372*f*
14:11 301*ak* 363*m*
14:12 148*h* 361*o*
       361*ad*
14:13 364*l* 836*r* 913*q*
14:14 741*r*
14:15 75*c* 176*c* 188*a*
       279*h* 350*p*
       967*g*
14:16 621*b* 914*w*
14:17 361*ad*
14:18 364*l* 836*r*
14:19 589*b*
14:20 110*aa* 361*af*
       741*s*
14:21 110*z* 131*i* 561*g*
       605*k*
14:22 911*d* 914*z*
14:23 209*ae* 218*u*
       967*g*
14:24 914*y* 951*w*
14:25 712*g*
14:26 662*i* 786*i* 797*k*
14:27 263*e* 662*i*
14:29 589*b*
14:30 718*g*
14:31 361*af* 364*l* 741*t*
15:1 741*t*
15:2 110*v*
15:3 914*z*
15:4 420*k*
15:5 739*h* 913*r* 914*z*
15:6 718*g*
15:7 589*b* 718*g*
15:8 361*af* 364*l* 741*t*
15:9 741*t*
15:10 110*ac*
15:11 913*r*
15:12 951*w* 982*q*
15:13 165*k* 350*t* 381*h*
       752*b* 967*g*
15:14 209*ac*

15:15 797*l*
15:16 718*g*
15:17 264*n* 712*i* 713*c*
15:18 797*k*
15:19 765*p* 769*d*
15:20 455*t* 712*d*
15:21 145*a*
15:22 164*q* 273*c*
15:23 589*b* 651*l*
15:24 361*af* 364*l* 741*t*
15:25 110*u* 741*s*
15:26 914*w*
15:27 362*w* 623*g*
15:28 362*w* 741*s*
15:29 362*z* 725*d*
15:30 914*w*
15:31 589*b*
15:32 718*g*
15:33 110*aa* 741*s*
15:34 914*w*[2]
16:1 529*e*
16:2 741*q* 914*x* 914*z*
16:3 165*r*
16:4 301*ak* 363*m*
16:5 589*b*
16:6 361*af* 364*l* 741*s*
16:7 529*e* 579*z* 914*w*
       914*x*
16:8 110*u* 741*s*
16:9 623*g* 949*i*
16:10 362*w* 741*s*
16:11 362*z* 372*f*
16:12 725*d*
16:13 914*w* 914*z*
16:14 589*b*
16:15 110*o* 712*b* 741*s*
16:16 623*g* 741*s*
16:17 712*i*
16:18 362*ae* 381*i*
16:19 914*w* 914*x*
16:20 589*b*
16:21 46*aj* 741*s*
16:22 361*af* 741*s*
16:23 110*z*
16:24 164*q* 184*s* 209*v*
       792*c* 809*j*
16:25 914*w*
16:26 914*x*
16:27 589*b*
16:28 361*af* 364*l* 741*s*
16:29 110*aa*
16:30 914*w*
16:31 894*z* 914*x* 967*d*
16:32 990*f*
16:33 967*g*

16:34 119*f* 132*c* 164*p*
       184*au* 214*c*
       264*c* 725*d*
17:1 342*c* 350*ad*
17:2 529*f*
17:3 350*t* 523*h*
17:4 301*x* 365*al*
17:5 350*t*
17:6 365*al*
17:7 342*c* 342*e*
17:8 529*f*
17:9 301*x* 896*n*
17:10 385*a*
17:12 361*q* 385*a* 636*b*
17:13 301*r*
17:14 635*f*
17:16 635*f*
17:17 651*h*
17:18 10*a* 362*n*
17:19 273*g*
17:20 362*be* 761*t*
17:21 378*i* 656*m* 761*s*
17:22 455*g*
17:24 494*d*
18:1 350*ab* 526*t*
18:2 636*a*
18:3 854*e*
18:4 255*g* 301*l*
       362*ao* 525*e*
       579*x*
18:5 301*aj* 366*d*
18:7 13*m*[2] 311*a* 490*y*
18:9 362*h*
18:10 459*af* 532*g*
18:12 362*h* 965*o*
18:13 255*g* 301*l*
       362*ao* 525*e*
18:14 362*h*
18:15 526*t*
18:17 827*d*
18:18 621*k* 827*d* 967*d*
18:19 74*g* 579*am*[2]
       967*d* 967*g*
18:20 209*u*
18:21 582*g* 601*a*
18:22 41*h* 88*j* 579*am*
       967*d*
18:23 981*h*
18:24 381*t* 460*c* 761*t*
       965*d*
18:26 312*a* 460*m*
       761*ah*
18:27 108*u* 678*e*
       679*c* 851*c*
18:28 46*g* 335*f* 577*e*
18:29 456*l* 460*m*
18:30 656*ad*

18:31 99*n* 529*f* 561*w*
18:32 262*a* 990*e*
18:33 350*w*
18:36 579*z* 761*r*
18:38 381*t*
18:39 311*g* 965*b*
18:40 362*ap* 579*am*
18:41 350*ab*
18:42 311*f* 761*r*
18:43 99*g*
18:44 196*e* 274*d* 355*a*
18:45 321*n* 350*ab*
       355*a*
18:46 277*d*
19:1 362*ap* 524*d*
19:2 362*ao* 532*m*
19:3 620*i* 854*s*
19:4 172*u* 361*s* 366*n*
19:5 301*x* 968*l*
19:7 968*l*
19:8 110*r* 209*k* 946*f*
19:9 255*g* 529*f*
19:10 41*h* 88*j* 362*ao*[2]
       621*k* 818*b*
       990*h*
19:11 176*i* 352*h*
19:12 381*r* 577*c*
19:13 226*f*
19:14 41*h* 88*j* 362*ao*[2]
       621*k* 818*b*
       990*h*
19:15 357*f*
19:16 357*f* 357*i*
19:17 362*j*
19:18 41*m* 99*u* 311*l*
       889*d*
19:19 226*a* 370*g*
19:20 169*i* 889*a*
19:21 385*b* 742*e* 981*h*
20:1 712*d*
20:2 529*q*
20:3 773*h* 797*g* 841*i*
       894*v*
20:4 773*h*
20:5 797*g* 894*v*
20:6 786*f*
20:7 760*b*
20:8 760*a*
20:10 332*a* 532*m* 636*j*
20:11 877*e*
20:12 949*i*
20:13 104*r* 490*n* 579*z*
       727*i*
20:14 68*h*
20:15 722*m*
20:16 949*i*
20:18 360*f*

20:20	620d
20:21	274b 362au
20:22	108d 162l 579z
20:23	209g 348a 966h
20:25	348a
20:26	108d 712d
20:27	104r 105a
20:28	209g 490n 579z 727i
20:29	362au 716e
20:30	235l 620d²
20:31	208c 228l 905i
20:32	11b 360b
20:33	274d
20:34	184aa 765p
20:35	279d 579ad 655j 760a
20:36	362bq 365ac
20:37	279d
20:38	226f 527b
20:39	28o 749b 809f
20:40	190f
20:41	490y
20:42	28o 746f 919a
20:43	891v 893a
21:1	370n
21:2	791b 792c
21:3	777i
21:4	891v 946k 893a
21:6	791b 792c
21:7	824z
21:8	588a 743k
21:9	938d 946h
21:10	362af 466v 899h
21:12	946h
21:13	362af 466v 899h 938d
21:14	362af
21:15	786f
21:17	529f
21:18	786f
21:19	301ak 335d 362af 786f
21:20	705i 793i
21:21	372f
21:23	301ak 363m
21:24	301ak 363m
21:25	612l 793i 914z
21:26	982m
21:27	836g 946g
21:28	529f
21:29	136c 645b 872j
22:4	89s
22:5	459b
22:6	579am² 727j
22:7	579z

22:8	645e 888q
22:10	228o 370z 743c
22:11	160h
22:12	727j
22:13	644j
22:14	529e 579q
22:15	727j
22:16	494e
22:17	75g 148g 369j
22:18	645e
22:19	722j 743a
22:20	612e
22:22	541b
22:23	541b
22:24	279d 965o
22:25	523k
22:27	301ar 747b
22:29	712b
22:30	228o 527b
22:31	716f
22:34	159a 287f 655i
22:35	274d 335d 361af
22:36	148j
22:37	361af 364l
22:38	301ak 335d 648s 951t
22:39	164q 184aa 589b
22:40	361af 741s
22:41	741t
22:42	110aa 131i
22:43	209ac 913r
22:44	719i
22:45	589b
22:46	951w
22:47	734a
22:48	165y 275e 631h
22:49	89s
22:50	361af 364l 741t
22:51	110u 741s
22:52	914w 914x
22:53	891l 967a

2 Kings

1:1	738b
1:2	309c 459f 655i 656u 967a
1:3	190a 967a
1:4	361n
1:6	190a 361n 459f 967a
1:8	13o 228j 259a 259b
1:9	309g 722m
1:10	381t
1:11	309g 722m

1:12	381t
1:13	311a 722m
1:14	381t
1:15	854af 968g
1:16	190a 361n 459f 967a
1:17	361af 725d 741s
1:18	589b
2:1	310d 352m
2:2	89r
2:3	786d
2:4	89r
2:5	786d
2:6	89r
2:7	579ad
2:8	46l 228e 279o 342a
2:9	91a 320b 761ao
2:10	438o
2:11	274f 352m 361au 381t
2:12	46t 274f
2:13	228e
2:14	46l 190a 279o
2:15	311a 320b
2:16	459af 965o
2:19	172o 339h
2:20	126b 388a
2:23	132f 229u 851c
2:24	362bq 365y 899m
3:1	110z 741s
3:2	218u 914w 967e
3:3	914x
3:4	259n 369a 804f
3:5	738b
3:6	722h
3:7	89s
3:8	172w
3:9	342e
3:10	728d
3:11	459b 579z 742e
3:12	529e
3:13	10a 579am 728d
3:15	413c
3:16	262a
3:17	339k 350ad 352j
3:18	727j
3:19	46z 342i 344m 366p
3:20	339k
3:22	128b 335k 431f
3:23	362ai 790d
3:24	362au 620d

3:25	46z 287b 342i 344m 366p
3:27	119g 891k 981ah
4:1	803c 896n
4:2	357a
4:3	194l 785b
4:4	264e 350x
4:5	635f
4:7	793c
4:9	979f
4:10	194t 218w 218af 420h
4:12	737j
4:14	133g 172b
4:15	263e 737j
4:16	170g 541i
4:17	167g
4:18	370t
4:19	213f
4:20	311w 361ae
4:21	311o
4:23	108c 988l
4:24	267i 267m 277h
4:25	209u
4:26	8b
4:27	53k 300aa 525a 620t 786n 825d
4:28	541i
4:29	218b 669h 884i
4:30	89r
4:31	218b
4:33	264e 656o 761f
4:34	378i
4:35	99g 302s 438a
4:36	737j
4:37	311a
4:38	301s 636a
4:39	366g 659c
4:41	301ai 658d
4:42	99t 301l 301t
4:43	41c
5:1	651n 722d 727c 866s
5:2	132d 747i
5:3	579z 656v
5:4	524d
5:5	588a 809n
5:6	656v
5:7	360i 362bc 891t
5:8	579z 891t
5:9	263e 274b
5:10	99g 648h
5:11	317d 761t 891v
5:12	350s
5:13	579z
5:14	99g 648h 656v

5:15 781*y*	**7:19** 441*j* 470*c*	**9:31** 8*b* 362*w*	**12:2** 534*l* 913*r*
5:16 760*a* 782*e*	**7:20** 279*q*	**9:32** 706*c*	**12:3** 209*ac*
5:17 344*b*	**8:1** 110*y* 636*a*	**9:33** 311*p* 335*f*	**12:4** 797*j*
5:18 909*e* 967*o*	**8:2** 110*y*	**9:34** 364*l*	**12:5** 656*ad*
5:20 919*f*	**8:3** 148*l*	**9:35** 363*d*	**12:9** 799*a*
5:21 8*b* 284*h*	**8:4** 524*e*	**9:36** 301*ak* 363*m*	**12:10** 86*h* 797*j*
5:22 809*n*	**8:5** 656*o* 761*al*	725*d*	**12:11** 686*f* 804*b*
5:26 138*a*	**8:6** 656*ag*	**9:37** 363*d*	**12:13** 194*g*
5:27 427*d* 651*n*	**8:7** 651*h* 656*u*	**10:1** 99*s* 588*a*	**12:15** 808*a* 929*c*
6:1 196*e*	**8:8** 459*b*	**10:3** 716*h* 741*k*	**12:16** 797*i* 981*j*
6:2 218*l*	**8:9** 781*y*	**10:6** 46*f* 99*s* 363*j*	**12:17** 786*j*
6:3 89*r*	**8:10** 361*o* 656*u*	588*a*	**12:18** 797*k*
6:4 46*z*	**8:11** 836*aa*	**10:7** 362*aa*	**12:19** 589*b*
6:5 630*a* 785*b*	**8:12** 167*h* 362*j*	**10:8** 209*aa*	**12:20** 362*w* 623*g*
6:6 218*b* 323*a*	**8:13** 365*bl* 741*u*	**10:9** 623*g*	**12:21** 364*l* 741*t*
6:8 691*l* 718*h*	**8:14** 656*u*	**10:10** 725*d*	**13:1** 110*z* 741*s*
6:9 524*d*	**8:15** 362*u* 362*x* 741*u*	**10:11** 362*z*	**13:2** 914*w* 914*x*
6:10 664*c*	**8:16** 741*t*	**10:14** 362*z*	**13:3** 728*d* 891*k*
6:11 603*e*	**8:17** 110*y* 131*i*	**10:16** 274*d*	**13:4** 455*g* 761*p*
6:14 274*b* 712*d* 722*i*	**8:18** 894*z* 914*w*	**10:17** 362*z*	**13:5** 667*b* 668*t*
6:15 274*b* 722*i*	**8:19** 420*k*	**10:18** 967*d*	**13:6** 914*x* 967*g*
6:16 89*e* 854*ai*	**8:20** 129*h* 738*b* 741*u*	**10:19** 362*an* 579*am*	**13:7** 274*c* 332*h*
6:17 274*f* 438*a* 516*h*	**8:21** 620*h* 712*b*	698*b* 967*d*	**13:8** 589*b*
761*r*	**8:22** 738*b*^{2}	**10:20** 967*d*^{2}	**13:9** 361*af* 741*s*
6:18 439*i* 761*r*	**8:23** 589*b*	**10:21** 967*d*	**13:10** 110*z* 741*s*
6:20 438*a* 761*r*	**8:24** 361*af*	**10:22** 228*x*	**13:11** 914*w* 914*x*
6:21 362*n*	**8:25** 741*t*	**10:24** 28*o*	**13:12** 589*b*
6:22 301*r* 362*q* 747*k*	**8:26** 110*t* 131*i*	**10:26** 165*k* 218*u* 381*h*	**13:13** 361*af* 364*l* 741*s*
6:24 712*d*	**8:27** 914*w*	**10:27** 302*f*	**13:14** 274*f* 651*g* 836*z*
6:25 26*a* 213*g* 302*h*	**8:28** 89*s* 655*i* 718*i*	**10:29** 914*x* 982*k*	**13:15** 287*e*
636*a* 809*m*	**8:29** 656*v*	**10:30** 741*q*	**13:17** 287*i* 727*c*
811*a*	**9:1** 669*h*	**10:31** 456*f* 914*x*	**13:18** 94*c* 279*m*
6:26 703*h*	**9:3** 357*f* 620*n*	**10:32** 198*a*	**13:19** 94*c*
6:27 703*a*	**9:6** 357*f*	**10:33** 184*p*	**13:20** 361*ad* 364*l*
6:28 301*at*	**9:7** 579*x* 910*c*	**10:34** 589*b*	**13:21** 363*f* 364*f* 656*m*
6:29 525*e*	**9:8** 372*f*	**10:35** 361*af* 741*s*	**13:23** 300*n* 765*b*
6:30 228*l* 836*j*	**9:10** 301*ak* 363*m*	**10:36** 110*aa* 741*s*	897*m*
6:31 362*ao* 532*m*	620*k*	**11:1** 362*aa*	**13:24** 361*af* 741*u*
6:32 362*ao* 529*q*	**9:11** 8*b* 503*c*	**11:2** 525*e*	**13:25** 94*c* 786*j*
6:33 165*r* 645*b*	**9:12** 357*f*	**11:3** 110*y* 741*t*	**14:1** 741*t*
7:1 26*a* 809*m* 812*a*	**9:13** 226*i* 414*m*	**11:4** 765*j*	**14:2** 110*aa* 131*i*
7:2 441*j* 470*c*	**9:14** 623*g*	**11:5** 95*e*	**14:3** 913*r*
7:3 651*n*	**9:15** 525*l* 656*v* 667*a*	**11:8** 660*g*	**14:4** 209*ac*
7:4 361*q* 636*a*	**9:16** 274*d*	**11:10** 723*o*	**14:5** 362*ah*
7:5 190*n*	**9:17** 8*b* 267*k* 457*h*	**11:12** 357*f* 360*c* 741*t*	**14:6** 169*y* 362*q* 953*d*
7:6 415*d* 792*g*	**9:18** 8*b*	743*f* 765*d*	**14:7** 362*au*
7:7 620*d*	**9:19** 8*b*	**11:14** 218*p* 414*m*	**14:8** 200*h* 529*q*
7:8 525*h*	**9:20** 267*i*	824*q* 891*t* 930*b*	**14:9** 366*u* 519*e*
7:9 524*d* 525*j* 529*k*	**9:21** 274*d* 669*f*	**11:15** 362*r*	**14:10** 871*f*
7:10 190*n*	**9:22** 8*b* 983*d*	**11:16** 362*w*	**14:11** 456*i* 712*i*
7:12 523*g*	**9:23** 542*l*	**11:17** 371*ac* 765*j*	**14:12** 620*h* 728*f*
7:14 274*d*	**9:24** 287*f* 362*w*	**11:18** 165*k* 362*an*	**14:13** 235*m* 747*j*
7:15 607*m*	**9:25** 235*q*	967*e* 986*r*	**14:14** 750*b* 797*k*
7:16 26*a* 790*i* 809*m*	**9:27** 362*w* 620*i* 655*i*	**11:19** 743*c*	**14:15** 589*b*
812*a*	**9:28** 364*l*	**11:20** 362*w*	**14:16** 361*af* 364*l* 741*s*
7:17 279*q*	**9:29** 741*t*	**11:21** 131*g* 131*i*	**14:18** 589*b*
7:18 26*a* 809*m* 812*a*	**9:30** 263*b* 843*a*	**12:1** 110*ac*	**14:19** 362*w* 620*k* 623*g*

11:17 339d 859k 859l
11:18 304d 350w
11:19 335g 661a
11:20 99q 362e
11:21 93b
11:22 255b 350ai
362bo 365ad
380c
11:23 195i 218k 362y
723o
11:24 93b
11:25 99q
12:1 722c
12:2 242a 287b
12:8 365x 365ag
12:15 222d
12:17 703h
12:18 703b 706c
717c 965m
12:19 300z
12:20 703h
12:23 86a 722l
12:31 741k
12:32 516c
12:33 599b
12:38 741k
12:39 301l
12:40 824z
13:1 691l
13:3 194c
13:5 74g
13:6 561a 733a 968u
13:7 126b 274i
13:8 412a
13:9 370z 378d
13:10 362be 891m
13:11 176d 561u
13:12 854l
13:13 194b
13:14 897f
14:1 164u 686f
14:2 741o
14:3 894u
14:8 357f
14:9 255j
14:10 459a 727i
14:11 176d 561u 727c
14:12 381h 621u
14:14 314a 366n 459a
14:17 854x 866s
15:1 164u 192t 194b
15:2 273a 605c
15:3 74g 194c
15:11 986d
15:12 194c 979i
15:13 176d 459e
15:14 979i

15:15 218i 273a
15:16 413a 413d
15:19 413d
15:22 534w
15:23 264i
15:24 264i
15:25 194c
15:26 703c
15:27 228q
15:29 263c 312a
835e 922g
16:1 192t 194b 981p
981w
16:3 301l 783e
16:4 907e 923e
16:5 413d
16:7 907e
16:8 526k 761t 907a
16:9 412e
16:10 459aa 824g
16:11 459s
16:12 505g 864a
16:13 605h
16:15 505g 768c
16:18 184a
16:19 105a
16:20 268a
16:21 757b 924a
16:22 357k 579x
16:23 412c
16:24 866h
16:25 638a 854b
16:26 164a 966b
16:28 866h 923k
16:29 866h 979d 981a
16:30 153c 854a
16:31 733a 824i
16:32 343b
16:33 366q 480e 824i
16:34 897k 907a
16:35 74c 668c
16:36 488c 923h
16:37 194c
16:38 264i
16:39 986d
16:40 981m
16:41 897k 907e
16:42 413d
16:43 148k
17:1 192d 192t
192aa 194b
17:2 89h
17:3 529f
17:4 192d
17:7 369d 741o
17:8 866aa
17:9 153o

17:10 957e
17:11 153q
17:13 169s
17:16 639a 761r
17:18 490i
17:20 21b
17:21 21e 792n 864b
17:22 371ac 965e
17:23 725b
17:24 153q
17:27 897h
18:1 727g 786j
18:2 727g 804f
18:3 350p 727d
18:4 274c 655p 786g
18:5 362at
18:6 703b 804f
18:7 662i
18:8 218p 343p 631g
18:10 631g 884d
18:11 631g 979v
18:13 703b 722h
18:14 913q
18:15 549a 722d
18:16 586u 986d
18:17 722d
19:1 361af 741u
19:2 831f
19:3 459q
19:4 92b 229d 259l
648j
19:5 36c 259l 872o
19:6 809n 888o
19:7 274b
19:12 703h
19:13 162l 716d
19:14 620d
19:15 620d
19:16 350p 722d
19:17 74g 222d
19:18 362at 620d
722d
19:19 719i
20:1 128m 718e
20:2 322a 743f 790i
844a
20:3 630b
20:4 195i 362y 718i
20:5 195i 218k 362y
723o
20:6 99b 195i
20:7 362y
21:1 86b 612l 969j
21:3 38e 104c
21:5 99v
21:6 888r
21:7 827m 963c

21:8 499f 909e
914ad
21:9 438af 529f
21:10 93c 605n 759a
21:12 110l 110s 110v
620b 636d
659a 728b
21:13 371q 897o
21:14 99v
21:15 165b 184af
370z 635j 968h
21:16 311g 723a 836j
968g
21:18 370z 990d
21:20 370z
21:21 311d
21:22 792c 793b
21:23 385b
21:24 812d
21:25 809j
21:26 381t 761t 990e
21:27 226j
21:29 209ac 990a
21:30 459a 854m
22:1 192d 990a
22:2 59j 344r 686f
22:3 322h 631a
22:5 130k 669f 695a
866a
22:6 164z 737c
22:8 164y 362e
22:9 164z 717g
22:10 153q 169s 192d
22:11 89d 727b
22:12 498k 739g
22:13 162l 727b 855a
22:14 322h 631a
22:15 686f
22:16 89d 322h
22:17 703h
22:18 89d 717i
22:19 164z 194d 459s
561g
23:1 133g 741k
23:3 86e 131d
23:4 957d
23:5 264i 413d
23:7 169b
23:11 172d
23:13 396c 979i
23:17 172d
23:22 172b
23:24 131c
23:25 192j 717i
23:26 273a
23:27 131c
23:28 703h 990n

23:29	189d 465a
23:30	907f
23:31	981l
24:1	169b
24:2	172b 361z 986d
24:3	53x
24:4	99p
24:5	605r
24:6	548f 586u
24:20	169b
24:28	172b
24:31	605r
25:1	413d 579t²
25:3	579t
25:6	413d
25:8	605r
25:9	99p
26:1	53y 169b 264i
26:10	119d
26:13	605r
26:20	798a
26:21	169b
26:27	790k
26:29	223d
26:32	371ah
27:1	53y 86b 99m 741aa
27:6	99q 722c
27:16	371ah
27:23	104c 131c
27:24	86c 589e 726a 891k
27:25	632a
27:26	370f
27:27	370n
27:28	357a 370q
27:29	369c
27:32	537d 586u 691h
27:33	691g 880d
27:34	691h 722d
28:2	164y 194d 218ac
28:3	164y 718e 722b
28:4	605b 741o 826e
28:5	605b 741p
28:6	164z 169s 605d
28:7	153q 739l 741q
28:8	184g 739l
28:9	447a 459y 459ac 490r 621h
28:10	162l 164z
28:11	194t 623e 632a
28:12	632a
28:13	53x 194g
28:14	322a
28:16	218ae

28:18	274f 968u 990c
28:20	89h 162l 621g 854ah
28:21	53x
29:1	130k 695a
29:2	631a
29:3	781p
29:4	226q 631i
29:7	631i
29:8	844j
29:9	824k
29:10	761r 923l
29:11	160c 733a
29:12	160c 800a 866aa
29:14	639a 781n
29:15	59w 114c
29:16	781n
29:17	447a 461a
29:20	311f 923d
29:22	301z 357d 357f 986k
29:25	866aa
29:27	110y 110ab 110ac
29:28	361af 741p
29:29	589b

2 Chronicles

1:1	89h 153q
1:3	209ac 990l
1:4	194c
1:5	990a
1:6	981q 990a
1:7	445a 761ac
1:9	104c
1:10	500d
1:11	113g 800f
1:12	21h 500d 800b 866aa
1:14	274c
1:15	631d 631j
1:16	365bg 791b
1:17	274c 809k²
2:1	164z
2:3	631d
2:4	189d 396c 561g 981m
2:5	638a
2:6	192b 639a 971a
2:7	696e
2:8	631d 696e
2:10	301l
2:11	588a 887f
2:12	164a
2:13	696e
2:15	301l

2:16	343o
2:17	59j 86b
3:1	164z 209r 370z
3:2	108f
3:3	195a 214d
3:4	226q
3:5	554c
3:6	844j
3:7	554c
3:8	28l 195a 990ac
3:9	322a
3:10	226q 554c 968u
3:11	195a 271c
3:14	421e 435f 844l
3:15	218p
3:16	554c
3:17	561t
4:1	28n 195a 990a
4:2	195a 343p
4:3	554c
4:4	99n 281v 554c
4:5	195c 205a 234b
4:6	99k 343p 648u
4:7	99k 420h
4:8	99k 194g 218ae
4:9	226r 235c 264a
4:10	343p
4:11	194g
4:12	213b 218p 222n
4:13	554c
4:14	218g 648u
4:15	99n 343p 554c
4:16	194g
4:17	344c 554b
4:18	322h
4:19	189d 218ae 990c
4:20	420h
4:21	554c
4:22	264a 990ac
5:1	725g 799d
5:2	194d
5:3	108k 988i
5:4	273a
5:6	104w
5:7	271c 968u 990ac
5:9	218i
5:10	190o 194f 548c
5:11	979i
5:12	413d
5:13	355d 897k
5:14	866e
6:1	355e
6:2	192d
6:3	897w
6:4	725b

6:5	304a
6:6	561g² 605b 605k
6:7	164y
6:9	164z
6:10	725b
6:11	194d
6:12	53e
6:13	218h
6:14	21b 761r 768c
6:15	725b
6:16	741q
6:18	192b 971a
6:19	761y
6:20	455a 561g 761y
6:21	455a 909e
6:22	532a 761y
6:23	280c 455a 960a
6:24	728a 761y
6:25	184k 455a 909e
6:26	342c 761y
6:27	350ab 455a 534d 909e
6:28	365j 636g 659a 761y
6:30	455a
6:31	854e
6:32	59m 761y
6:33	455a 490n
6:34	718b
6:35	455a
6:36	188a 891g 914j
6:37	188a
6:39	455a 909e
6:40	455a
6:41	192d 683p 986f
7:1	381t 866e
7:2	297e
7:3	311f 897k
7:5	876g 981h
7:6	414a 897k
7:7	196e 235c 990b
7:8	110o 988l
7:9	876g
7:10	108k 824o
7:11	725g
7:12	445a 605b
7:13	342c 365j 659a
7:14	459u 656aj 872i 909b 939a
7:15	455c
7:16	455c 561g 605b
7:17	739l
7:18	741q
7:19	621h 966e
7:20	300n 496d 607b
7:22	304a 621i 966h

8:1 164*u*	**10:9** 323*c* 701*d*	**13:11** 189*d* 218*ae*	**16:9** 441*f* 718*h*
8:2 164*q*	**10:10** 323*c* 701*d* 735*d* 735*e*	420*g* 607*g* 981*m*	**16:10** 735*d* 747*b* 891*w*
8:3 786*j*	**10:11** 279*c* 322*k* 365*s*	**13:12** 89*d* 414*h* 716*c*	**16:11** 589*b*
8:4 632*a*	**10:13** 735*d*	**13:13** 527*c*	**16:12** 53*k* 651*l* 658*b*
8:6 274*e* 632*a*	**10:14** 279*c* 322*k* 365*s* 735*e*	**13:14** 414*h* 761*p*	**16:13** 110*ac* 361*af*
8:7 371*v*	**10:15** 456*h*	**13:15** 577*i* 727*a*	**16:14** 364*l* 381*l* 396*n*
8:8 682*e*	**10:16** 148*j* 456*h* 775*a* 777*o*	**13:17** 362*aj*	**17:1** 741*t*
8:9 745*g*	**10:17** 371*ah* 741*t*	**13:18** 485*k* 727*c*	**17:2** 713*c*
8:10 741*ab*	**10:18** 274*d* 362*af* 620*k* 680*c* 682*e*	**13:19** 786*j*	**17:3** 89*h*
8:11 894*z*	**10:19** 738*b*	**13:20** 362*be*	**17:4** 459*w*
8:12 981*q*	**11:1** 718*g*	**13:21** 894*u*	**17:5** 153*q* 800*f* 866*s*
8:13 94*a* 981*m* 981*n*^{5} 988*a*	**11:2** 529*f*	**13:22** 579*z* 589*b*	**17:6** 209*ah* 967*i*
8:14 53*x* 53*y*	**11:4** 716*h*	**14:1** 361*af* 364*l* 717*i* 741*t*	**17:9** 534*l* 589*g*
8:15 632*a*	**11:5** 164*q*	**14:2** 913*r*	**17:10** 854*k*
8:16 725*g*	**11:10** 713*c*	**14:3** 165*k* 209*ah* 218*u* 967*i* 990*g*	**17:11** 804*f*
8:17 234*c*	**11:11** 632*a* 713*c*	**14:4** 459*s* 739*g*	**17:12** 164*q*
8:18 270*a* 275*a* 631*h*	**11:12** 723*i*	**14:5** 209*ah* 396*g*	**17:14** 722*h*
9:1 396*m* 459*j* 461*h* 631*h* 844*a* 866*s*	**11:13** 986*g*	**14:6** 164*q* 717*i*	**18:1** 800*f* 866*s* 894*z*
9:2 460*i*	**11:14** 752*b*	**14:7** 184*g*	**18:2** 712*b*
9:3 192*aa* 500*d*	**11:15** 967*q* 982*k* 986*r*	**14:8** 722*b*	**18:4** 459*b*
9:4 308*m*	**11:16** 459*x*	**14:9** 712*e*	**18:5** 579*am* 727*j*
9:6 500*d*	**11:18** 894*u*	**14:11** 21*b* 485*e* 727*a* 761*p*	**18:6** 579*z*
9:7 824*q*	**11:21** 894*u* 952*c*	**14:12** 620*d* 716*a*	**18:7** 645*e* 888*q*
9:8 826*e* 923*h*	**11:23** 498*m* 633*d* 894*u*	**14:13** 619*d* 790*i*	**18:9** 228*o* 370*z* 743*c*
9:9 396*m* 631*h* 844*a*	**12:1** 607*h*	**14:14** 790*i* 854*k*	**18:10** 160*h*
9:10 631*d* 844*a*	**12:2** 712*g* 930*a*	**15:1** 965*m*	**18:11** 727*j*
9:11 308*m* 414*a*	**12:3** 104*r* 274*b*	**15:2** 89*d* 459*y* 621*h*	**18:12** 644*j*
9:12 148*l* 781*y*	**12:5** 579*z* 607*j*	**15:3** 537*c* 986*c*	**18:13** 529*e* 579*q*
9:13 631*h*	**12:6** 872*j*	**15:4** 459*y*	**18:14** 727*j*
9:15 322*a* 662*i*	**12:7** 529*f* 872*j*	**15:5** 717*j*	**18:15** 494*e*
9:16 192*aa* 322*a* 662*i*	**12:8** 742*p*	**15:7** 162*l* 962*b*	**18:16** 75*g* 148*g* 369*j*
9:17 226*q* 631*k* 743*c*	**12:9** 662*i* 786*i*	**15:8** 165*k* 656*ad* 982*q*	**18:17** 645*e*
9:18 308*m*	**12:10** 662*i*	**15:9** 89*h*	**18:18** 722*j* 743*a*
9:19 21*m* 554*e*	**12:12** 872*j*	**15:10** 108*g*	**18:19** 612*e*
9:20 194*l* 631*j* 641*g*	**12:13** 110*z* 131*g* 561*g* 605*j*	**15:11** 981*h*	**18:21** 541*b*
9:21 365*an* 631*k*	**12:14** 914*w*	**15:12** 459*w* 765*j*	**18:23** 279*d* 965*o*
9:22 500*d* 800*f*	**12:15** 438*af* 579*z*^{2} 589*b* 718*g*	**15:13** 963*p*	**18:24** 523*k*
9:23 459*af*	**12:16** 361*af* 364*l* 741*t*	**15:14** 414*c* 532*n* 577*g*	**18:26** 301*ar* 747*b*
9:24 781*y*	**13:1** 741*t*	**15:15** 459*y* 717*i*	**18:28** 712*b*
9:25 274*c*	**13:2** 110*v* 718*g*	**15:16** 165*k* 381*h* 752*b* 967*i*	**18:29** 228*o* 527*b*
9:26 350*p*	**13:3** 68*h* 722*m*	**15:17** 209*ac* 929*c*	**18:30** 716*f*
9:27 631*d* 631*j*	**13:4** 209*t*	**15:18** 781*p*	**18:31** 703*c* 761*p*
9:28 365*bg*	**13:5** 388*b* 741*q* 765*f* 765*i*	**15:19** 717*i*	**18:33** 159*a* 287*f* 655*i*
9:29 438*af* 579*z*^{2} 589*b*	**13:6** 738*b*	**16:1** 264*n* 712*i*^{2} 713*c*	**18:34** 274*d* 361*af*
9:30 110*ac*	**13:7** 130*k* 938*d*	**16:2** 797*k*	**19:2** 703*k* 887*af*
9:31 361*af* 741*t*	**13:8** 982*k*	**16:3** 765*p* 769*d*	**19:3** 459*w* 967*i*
10:1 741*k*	**13:9** 752*b* 986*r*	**16:4** 455*t*	**19:4** 656*am*
10:2 620*i*	**13:10** 965*e* 986*b*	**16:5** 145*a*	**19:5** 957*d*
10:4 323*c* 701*d* 735*e*		**16:6** 273*c*	**19:6** 89*h* 480*n*
10:5 110*l*		**16:7** 438*af* 485*ai*	**19:7** 612*k* 854*a* 913*a*
10:6 691*l*		**16:8** 485*k*	**19:8** 957*d*
10:7 742*f*			**19:9** 854*a*
10:8 691*l*^{2}			**19:11** 986*k*
			20:1 718*h*
			20:2 104*r*
			20:3 459*w* 854*y* 946*h*

20:5 761*p*	**22:3** 691*j* 914*y*	**25:1** 110*aa* 131*i*	**27:3** 235*i* 264*c*
20:6 160*c* 733*a*	**22:4** 914*w*	741*t*	**27:4** 164*q* 209*ak*
20:7 184*a* 300*h* 880*c*	**22:5** 655*i* 718*i*	**25:2** 913*r*	**27:5** 804*f*
20:8 979*x* 990*n*	**22:6** 656*v*	**25:3** 362*ah*	**27:7** 589*b*
20:9 455*a* 636*g* 659*a*	**22:7** 357*g*	**25:4** 169*y* 362*q* 953*d*	**27:8** 110*z* 131*i*
20:11 300*l* 777*h*	**22:8** 362*aj*	**25:5** 86*b* 131*c*	**27:9** 361*af* 364*l* 741*t*
20:12 163*g* 441*l* 480*c*	**22:9** 362*w* 364*l*	**25:6** 722*l* 809*e*	**28:1** 110*z* 131*i* 741*t*
491*z*	459*w*	**25:7** 190*b*	914*w*
20:14 965*m*	**22:10** 362*aa*	**25:8** 162*l*	**28:2** 914*y* 967*b*
20:15 716*a* 854*af*	**22:11** 525*e*	**25:9** 781*e* 809*e*	**28:3** 255*j* 381*ak*
20:16 172*w*	**22:12** 110*y*	**25:10** 300*z* 891*v*	396*f* 914*y*
20:17 89*d* 716*a* 854*af*	**23:1** 765*j*	**25:11** 255*j* 362*av*	981*ah*
20:18 311*f*	**23:3** 741*k* 765*j*	**25:12** 311*p*	**28:4** 209*ac* 366*m*
20:19 577*g* 923*e*	**23:4** 95*e*	**25:13** 362*aj* 790*i*	**28:5** 188*d* 712*i* 728*d*
20:20 128*b* 485*d*	**23:6** 757*e*	**25:14** 966*j*	**28:6** 362*aj* 607*i*
485*ad*	**23:7** 660*g*	**25:15** 579*s*	**28:7** 362*aj*
20:21 228*q* 413*a*	**23:9** 723*o*	**25:16** 579*v* 623*b* 691*i*	**28:8** 747*j* 790*i*
897*k* 923*f*	**23:11** 357*f* 360*c* 466*j*	**25:17** 716*h*	**28:9** 579*z*
20:22 527*c* 727*d*	743*f* 765*d*	**25:18** 366*u* 519*e*	**28:10** 745*g*
20:23 716*i*	**23:12** 415*d*	**25:19** 871*f*	**28:11** 746*e*
20:24 363*e*	**23:13** 218*p* 414*m*	**25:20** 456*i*	**28:13** 936*f*
20:25 110*l* 790*i*	930*b*	**25:21** 712*i*	**28:15** 228*w* 301*s* 357*r*
20:26 255*j* 561*u* 923*h*	**23:14** 362*r*	**25:22** 620*f* 728*f*	**28:16** 703*h*
20:27 824*q*	**23:15** 362*w*	**25:23** 235*m* 747*j*	**28:17** 712*e* 747*j*
20:28 414*b*	**23:16** 765*j*	**25:24** 750*b* 797*k*	**28:18** 786*j*
20:29 854*k*	**23:17** 165*k* 967*e*	**25:26** 589*b*	**28:19** 872*e*
20:30 717*i*	**23:18** 586*d* 953*d*	**25:27** 362*w* 623*g*	**28:21** 786*i*
20:31 110*aa* 131*i*	**23:19** 264*i*	**25:28** 364*l*	**28:23** 967*p*
20:32 913*r*	**23:20** 743*c*	**26:1** 131*i* 741*t*	**28:24** 194*k* 264*f* 990*f*
20:33 209*ac*	**23:21** 362*w*	**26:2** 164*q*	**28:25** 209*ae*
20:34 589*b*	**24:1** 110*ac* 131*g*	**26:3** 110*ad* 131*i*	**28:26** 589*b*
20:35 765*p*	**24:2** 913*r*	**26:4** 913*r*	**28:27** 361*af* 364*l* 741*t*
20:36 275*e*	**24:3** 894*u*	**26:5** 438*aa* 459*aa*	**29:1** 110*aa* 131*g*
20:37 165*y* 579*ab*	**24:4** 656*ad*	**26:6** 164*q* 165*q* 718*i*	741*t*
765*p*	**24:5** 136*e* 797*j*	**26:7** 703*c*	**29:2** 913*r*
21:1 361*af* 364*l* 741*t*	**24:6** 986*k*	**26:8** 804*f* 866*s*	**29:3** 263*ah* 656*ad*
21:3 119*c* 781*z*	**24:7** 967*b*	**26:9** 209*ak*	**29:5** 979*i*
21:4 362*ac*	**24:8** 799*a*	**26:10** 209*ak* 339*f*	**29:6** 607*g*
21:5 110*y* 131*g*	**24:9** 528*m* 804*g*	369*a* 370*f* 370*g*	**29:7** 264*f* 418*p*
21:6 894*z* 914*w*	**24:11** 797*j*	**26:11** 586*u* 722*h*	**29:8** 891*j*
21:7 420*k* 765*i*	**24:12** 686*f* 804*b*	**26:13** 722*h*	**29:9** 362*ak* 747*i*
21:8 738*b* 741*u*	**24:14** 194*g* 981*m*	**26:14** 287*b* 662*i* 669*g*	**29:10** 765*j*
21:9 362*au*	**24:15** 131*j* 133*g*	723*i*	**29:11** 605*c* 986*c*
21:10 621*i* 738*b*^{2}	**24:16** 364*l*	**26:15** 287*b* 866*s*	**29:12** 986*ab*
21:11 209*ae*	**24:17** 455*t*	**26:16** 162*n* 297*e*	**29:15** 648*s*
21:12 579*z* 588*a*	**24:18** 607*h* 967*g*	396*e* 871*f*	**29:16** 255*j*
21:13 362*ac* 914*y*^{2}	**24:19** 456*f* 579*s*	990*c* 990*q*	**29:17** 108*e*
21:14 659*a*	**24:20** 579*z* 607*a* 965*m*	**26:17** 986*d*	**29:18** 218*ae* 990*b*
21:15 651*k*	**24:21** 362*ao* 623*g*	**26:18** 300*o* 986*b*	**29:20** 128*b*
21:16 712*e*	**24:22** 506*h* 910*d*	**26:19** 237*d* 651*n*	**29:21** 99*c* 981*ab*
21:17 786*b* 894*v*	**24:23** 712*e* 790*h*	891*w*	**29:22** 335*m*
21:18 651*k*	**24:24** 105*f* 607*i* 728*e*	**26:20** 237*d* 300*o*	**29:23** 378*t*
21:19 377*a* 381*l*	**24:25** 362*w* 364*l* 623*g*	**26:21** 46*ad*	**29:24** 941*c*
21:20 110*y* 131*g* 364*l*	**24:26** 623*g*	**26:22** 579*z* 589*c*	**29:25** 413*d* 438*af*
830*d*	**24:27** 589*b* 656*ad*	**26:23** 361*af* 364*l* 741*t*	579*z* 737*b*
22:1 741*k*	741*t*	**27:1** 110*z* 131*i* 741*t*	**29:27** 981*l*
22:2 110*t* 131*g*		**27:2** 297*e* 913*r*	**29:29** 311*f* 981*f*

29:30 923e	**32:18** 557e 854y	**34:9** 797j 986k	**36:22** 725d 737d
29:32 981p	**32:19** 16d	**34:10** 686f	**36:23** 164aa 990w
29:34 105d 229v	**32:20** 761p	**34:12** 413d	
29:35 656ak 742c	**32:21** 362x 362bi	**34:13** 264i 586v	**Ezra**
29:36 116a 824o	968h	**34:14** 589g	**1:1** 725d 737d
30:1 588a 988e	**32:22** 668i	**34:18** 579k	**1:2** 164aa 990w
30:2 108f	**32:23** 781y	**34:19** 836g	**1:4** 781w
30:3 105d	**32:24** 547d 651h 761s	**34:21** 459b 954c	**1:6** 781w
30:6 148c 588a	**32:25** 871f	**34:22** 579aa	**1:8** 86h 798a
30:7 930a	**32:26** 872j	**34:24** 165b 645b 899e	**1:9** 194k
30:8 602e	**32:27** 799c 800f 866s	**34:25** 607g 891d 966h	**1:11** 148p
30:9 148b 897o	**32:28** 632a	**34:27** 455f 836h 872j	**2:1** 148p 188d
30:10 851b	**32:29** 164q 800b	**34:28** 361n	**2:2** 86c
30:11 872j	**32:30** 351a	**34:30** 579k 765d	**2:59** 169c
30:12 45m	**32:31** 461d	**34:31** 765j	**2:63** 301aw 605s
30:13 108f 988e	**32:32** 438aa 589b	**35:1** 108e 988e	**2:65** 413a
30:14 165k 350t 990g	589c	**35:3** 194d 273a 534l	**2:66** 365ax
30:15 108f 872o	**32:33** 361af 364l 741t	**35:4** 53x	**2:68** 781p
30:16 335m	**33:1** 110ad 131i 741t	**35:7** 781r	**3:2** 953d 990a
30:18 909e 980a	**33:2** 914w 914y	**35:8** 781r	**3:3** 854z 981m 990a
30:19 649l	**33:3** 209ae 321j	**35:9** 781r	**3:4** 981n 988i
30:20 455g	967b 967g	**35:10** 53x	**3:5** 988a
30:21 110o 412d	**33:4** 990p	**35:11** 229v 335m	**3:6** 108k
30:22 110o 855d	**33:5** 321j	**35:12** 589g	**3:7** 343o 631d 686f
30:23 110o 988e	**33:6** 255j 381ak	**35:15** 264i 413a	797j
30:24 781r^2	983e 984a	**35:16** 988e	**3:8** 131c
30:25 824r	**33:7** 561g 982m	**35:17** 110o	**3:10** 214d 414b 923e
30:26 21l	**33:8** 188a 739g	**35:18** 21l	990w
31:1 165k 209ah	**33:9** 495c 914y	**35:20** 718i	**3:11** 412c 577g 897k
218u 967i 990g	**33:10** 456e	**35:21** 10a	**3:12** 577l 824o 836ag
31:2 53x	**33:11** 188f 747o	**35:22** 527b	**4:1** 705g 990w
31:3 953d 981m	**33:12** 761p 872j	**35:23** 655k	**4:2** 164aa 459v
981n^2 988a	**33:13** 148p 490n	**35:24** 274d 361af	**4:3** 10a
31:4 102d 301ab	**33:14** 235i^2 264d	364l 836r	**4:4** 702e 854z
599b	**33:15** 165k 982q 990g	**35:25** 589j 836s	**4:5** 691h 792g
31:6 209aa	**33:17** 209ac	**35:27** 589b	**4:6** 588b 928i
31:10 41c 635d 986k	**33:18** 438ae 589b	**36:1** 741t	**4:7** 557e
31:11 102d 194t	761p	**36:2** 110s 131i	**4:10** 184s 188h 222g
31:14 783f	**33:19** 209ae 589b	**36:3** 752b 963j	350p
31:15 169c 783f	761p 967g	**36:4** 188f 561y 741t	**4:11** 222g 350p
31:21 459w 599b	982m	**36:5** 110z 131i 914w	**4:12** 164s 235j 738c
32:1 712g	**33:20** 361af 364l 741t	**36:6** 747o	**4:13** 804f
32:3 342i	**33:21** 110u 131g 741t	**36:7** 786i	**4:15** 459ae 589d
32:5 235i 656ad 662i	**33:22** 914w 982m	**36:8** 589b 741t	738c
723i	**33:23** 872k	**36:9** 110s 131g 914w	**4:16** 222g 350p
32:6 855d	**33:24** 362w 623g	**36:10** 188f 741t	**4:17** 222g 350p 460i
32:7 160c 162l 854ai	**33:25** 362ah 741t	**36:11** 110z 131g	588b
855a	**34:1** 110ab 131g	**36:12** 579z 871f 914w	**4:18** 579m
32:8 89d 371q 703b	741t	**36:13** 602b 738b	**4:19** 459ae 738c
716a	**34:2** 913r	**36:16** 851b	**4:20** 222g 350p 804f
32:9 712d	**34:3** 130h 165k	**36:17** 362ak	**4:21** 145a 757e
32:10 485a	209ah 459w	**36:18** 786i	**4:23** 579m
32:11 495c 636f	967i 982q	**36:19** 165g 235m	**4:24** 990w
32:12 209ah 990g	**34:4** 332f 364i 967e	381g	**5:1** 579z^2
32:13 668w	967i	**36:20** 188d	**5:2** 164aa 990w
32:17 588a 668w	**34:5** 363h	**36:21** 110ae 683l	**5:3** 222g 737d
921a	**34:8** 549a 656ad	725d	**5:5** 660a 757e

5:6	222g 588b
5:8	218l 344r 990w
5:9	737d
5:11	164aa 742a
5:12	728e 891l
5:13	164aa 737d
5:14	194k
5:15	164aa
5:16	214d
5:17	459ae 737d
6:1	459ae 589d
6:2	589d
6:3	164aa 195a 737d 990w
6:4	344r 631d 809i
6:5	194k
6:7	620t
6:8	804b 809i
6:9	781r
6:10	761r
6:11	218l 641i
6:12	561g
6:14	$579z^2$ 725g 990w
6:15	108p
6:16	876g 988l
6:17	99m 981y
6:18	53x 589g
6:19	108e 988e
6:20	648x
6:21	46aq 148p
6:22	110o 824o 855c
7:1	148p 169a
7:6	586v 703d 953h
7:9	108e 108i 703d
7:10	534l 536a 953h
7:11	22b 586v 737d 986d
7:12	586v 741u 986d
7:14	691h
7:15	797i
7:19	194k
7:21	586v 986d
7:24	804f
7:25	534l 957d
7:26	954c 963i
7:27	923l
7:28	703d
8:1	169c 741aa
8:15	350s 986ab
8:16	986ab
8:18	703d
8:21	350s 761r 872i 946g
8:22	703d 872o
8:23	761r 946g
8:24	986e

8:25	194k 322e 797l
8:31	350s 703d
8:33	322e
8:35	981p
9:1	46aq 371v 894w
9:2	43c
9:3	259d 259m 836g
9:4	854e
9:6	761r 872o
9:7	728e
9:8	41q
9:9	742p
9:10	607h
9:11	649o
9:12	894w
9:13	41o
9:14	891g 894w
9:15	41o 913b
10:1	836w
10:2	894w
10:3	765j 896e
10:4	855a
10:5	532k
10:6	836w 946m
10:8	300u
10:9	108m 350ac
10:10	894w
10:11	46aq 526p 896e
10:13	350ac
10:15	704f
10:18	894w
10:19	896e 981ad
10:44	894w

Nehemiah

1:1	108m
1:3	41o 235m 264c
1:4	761p 836ag 946g
1:5	768c
1:6	455b 526p
1:7	954c
1:8	75c
1:9	74b 561g 605j
1:10	792n
1:11	455b 686d 727b
2:1	108e 834c 949d
2:3	165d 364h
2:4	761p
2:5	164s 364h 751l
2:7	222g 588b
2:8	366q 588b 631d 703d
2:9	222g 588b
2:10	825h
2:12	129f 267l 525k

2:13	129f $264d^2$ 339e 438r
2:14	264d 346a
2:15	129f 264d
2:16	491ac 525k
2:17	164s 165d 264c 381f 872ab
2:18	164s 703d
2:19	851b
2:20	727b 775a
3:1	164s $209al^2$ 235j 264d 656ad 986k
3:3	264d
3:5	706e
3:6	264d
3:7	222g
3:8	686e 686g
3:11	209al
3:13	$264d^2$
3:14	264d
3:15	264d 346a 370c
3:16	346a 364h
3:20	986k
3:26	264d
3:28	264d
3:29	264d
3:31	264d
3:32	264d 686g
4:1	851b 891v
4:3	163k 365t
4:4	280c 922l
4:5	909j
4:6	235j
4:7	891v
4:8	623g 716f
4:9	457f 761p
4:10	163g 641i 684a
4:11	145a 362o 491ab
4:12	524e
4:13	723m
4:14	505f 716d 854af
4:15	702j
4:16	92d 723m
4:17	723m
4:18	414f
4:19	183b
4:20	716a
4:21	92d 723m
4:23	229r
5:1	924n
5:3	636a 803d
5:4	785b
5:5	18f 745g
5:6	891v

5:7	803h
5:8	578e 792l 793g
5:9	854a
5:10	784d 803h
5:11	102k
5:12	532k
5:13	488c 621q
5:14	301av
5:15	804g 854f
5:16	792a
5:18	301l 301av
5:19	505a
6:1	264c 524d
6:2	295d 348a
6:3	145a 638b
6:4	97a
6:5	522d 588b
6:6	529n 738c 741k
6:7	579aj 691l
6:8	541g
6:9	854z
6:10	129g 295d 362o 990w
6:11	620n
6:12	792g
6:13	$854z^2$
6:14	505a 854z
6:15	108j 235j 725g
6:16	703c
6:17	588b
6:18	532j 894w
6:19	588b 854z 923t
7:1	235j
7:2	854f
7:3	263ah
7:4	105c 183b
7:5	148p $169c^2$ 589e
7:61	169c
7:65	301aw 605s
7:68	365ax
7:70	797l
8:1	264d 579k 589g 953h
8:3	264d 455n
8:4	218h
8:5	215b
8:6	311f 488c 923f
8:7	520e
8:9	836w
8:10	301z 801i 824g
8:12	516f 801i
8:14	108k 192y 988i
8:15	366c
8:16	$264d^2$
8:17	21l
8:18	110o 579k

9:1	836*j* 836*l* 946*g*	**10:34**	385*c* 605*r*	**13:30**	46*aq*	**3:12**	108*e* 557*e* 558*a*
9:2	46*aq* 526*p*	**10:35**	171*l*	**13:31**	385*c* 505*a*		586*v* 588*b* 743*k*
9:3	98*b* 579*k*	**10:36**	119*a*			**3:13**	108*p* 362*al*
9:4	577*g*	**10:37**	102*d* 986*aa*	**Esther**			790*g*
9:5	115*d* 923*l*	**10:39**	458*a*	**1:1**	741*u*	**3:14**	528*m*
9:6	21*c* 164*a* 360*i*	**11:1**	102*g* 605*r*	**1:2**	743*c*	**3:15**	184*bd* 474*a*
9:7	304*a* 561*w* 605*b*	**11:2**	597*b*	**1:3**	882*f*		882*b*
9:8	184*b* 371*v* 725*b*	**11:3**	169*c*	**1:4**	110*s* 800*f*	**4:1**	836*g* 836*j* 836*l*
	765*b*	**11:17**	907*e*	**1:5**	184*bd* 882*f*	**4:2**	263*i*
9:9	825*f*	**11:19**	264*i*	**1:6**	218*q* 218*ab*	**4:3**	836*aa* 946*g*
9:10	864*b* 866*f*	**11:22**	169*c* 413*a*		436*a* 436*b* 624*l*	**4:4**	228*x*
9:11	46*l* 342*a* 362*bi*	**11:25**	184*ad*	**1:7**	194*l* 949*d*	**4:5**	172*j* 459*h* 529*p*
9:12	355*c* 381*q* 417*i*	**11:31**	184*ad*	**1:8**	740*c*	**4:7**	809*n*
	689*d*	**12:1**	986*g*	**1:9**	882*f*	**4:8**	737*d* 761*al* 905*i*
9:13	209*k* 953*c*	**12:8**	907*e*	**1:10**	172*j* 949*i*	**4:9**	529*p*
9:14	683*a* 953*a*	**12:10**	169*b* 986*k*	**1:11**	841*h*	**4:11**	743*l* 919*a* 963*n*
9:15	184*e* 301*ae*	**12:23**	589*e*	**1:12**	760*b* 891*w*	**4:13**	661*b*
	339*k*	**12:25**	264*i*	**1:13**	500*e*	**4:14**	137*d* 582*k*
9:16	602*b* 871*f* 954*c*	**12:27**	235*j* 414*b* 876*g*	**1:15**	738*d*	**4:16**	110*l* 761*o* 946*g*
9:17	506*f* 602*b* 621*g*	**12:28**	413*a*	**1:17**	894*k* 922*g*	**5:1**	228*o* 743*c*
	823*f* 909*a*	**12:30**	648*x*	**1:19**	272*b* 737*d* 752*b*	**5:2**	743*l* 826*p* 919*a*
9:18	304*b* 982*j*	**12:31**	413*a*		752*d*	**5:3**	92*e* 761*ao*
9:19	355*c* 381*q* 621*g*	**12:36**	586*u*	**1:20**	866*ab* 894*k*	**5:4**	882*f*
	689*d*	**12:37**	264*d*² 308*m*	**1:21**	826*l*	**5:6**	92*e* 761*ao*
9:20	301*ae* 339*k*	**12:38**	209*al* 235*e*	**1:22**	557*e* 558*a* 588*b*	**5:8**	882*f*
	534*f* 965*ab*	**12:39**	209*al*² 264*d*⁵		733*ac*	**5:9**	263*l* 891*w*
9:21	110*ac* 633*b*	**12:43**	824*o*	**2:2**	841*i* 895*b*	**5:11**	285*a* 800*f*
	655*c*	**12:44**	102*d* 171*l* 632*a*	**2:3**	172*j* 843*a*	**5:12**	882*f*
9:22	184*p*	**12:46**	413*a*	**2:6**	188*f*	**5:13**	263*l* 829*f*
9:23	104*e*	**12:47**	301*ad*	**2:7**	779*a* 841*h*	**5:14**	195*b* 217*b* 964*c*
9:24	727*i*	**13:1**	59*i* 371*y* 579*k*	**2:9**	301*l* 826*m* 843*a*	**6:1**	579*m* 589*b* 678*a*
9:25	339*f* 366*j* 635*d*		589*g*	**2:10**	371*ae* 525*k*	**6:2**	172*j* 264*j* 362*o*
	771*e* 786*j*	**13:2**	792*g* 899*j*²	**2:11**	8*a*	**6:3**	923*s*
9:26	362*ao* 738*g*	**13:3**	43*c* 46*aq* 59*i*	**2:12**	110*t* 396*l* 843*a*	**6:4**	217*b*
	954*c*	**13:4**	986*k*	**2:14**	172*j* 952*c*	**6:6**	923*s*²
9:27	455*g* 668*g* 728*e*	**13:5**	194*t*	**2:15**	826*p*	**6:8**	228*o* 365*bg*
	761*q*	**13:6**	761*al*	**2:16**	108*n*		743*h*
9:28	455*g* 621*b*	**13:7**	194*t*	**2:17**	743*f* 826*p* 890*a*	**6:9**	528*m*
9:29	360*n* 602*b* 676*e*	**13:8**	300*o*	**2:18**	882*f*	**6:10**	263*l* 365*bg*
	871*f*	**13:9**	648*s*	**2:19**	263*l*	**6:11**	228*o* 528*m*
9:30	456*f* 600*i* 728*e*	**13:10**	102*d*	**2:20**	371*ae* 525*k*	**6:12**	226*f* 263*l* 836*aa*
	965*aa*	**13:11**	924*k*	**2:21**	263*l* 362*o*	**6:13**	371*ae*
9:31	621*g* 905*d*	**13:14**	505*a*	**2:22**	524*e*	**6:14**	680*a* 882*f*
9:32	160*a* 768*c*	**13:15**	370*l* 683*i* 924*k*	**2:23**	217*b* 362*af*	**7:2**	92*e* 761*ao*
9:33	913*a* 929*a*	**13:16**	683*i* 793*c*		589*b* 964*c*	**7:3**	360*e* 371*ae*
9:34	954*c*	**13:17**	683*h* 924*k*	**3:1**	285*a*		761*al*
9:35	184*c*	**13:19**	264*g* 418*b*	**3:2**	263*l* 311*a* 311*c*	**7:4**	362*al* 582*f* 745*g*
9:36	742*p*	**13:20**	794*a*		923*t*	**7:5**	13*k*
9:38	765*j*	**13:22**	264*i* 648*x*	**3:3**	738*d*	**7:6**	705*g* 854*ae*
10:28	46*aq*	**13:23**	894*w*	**3:4**	371*ae* 524*e*	**7:7**	360*e* 370*c* 891*w*
10:29	532*k* 765*j* 899*e*	**13:24**	557*d*	**3:5**	311*c* 891*w*	**7:8**	226*f* 309*c* 951*aa*
10:30	894*w*	**13:25**	279*d* 532*k*	**3:6**	362*al* 371*ae*	**7:9**	172*j* 195*b* 217*b*
10:31	683*f* 683*k* 792*a*		899*m* 924*k*	**3:7**	108*e* 108*p* 605*r*		964*c*
	803*e*	**13:26**	21*h* 887*f* 914*y*	**3:8**	75*c* 953*b* 954*f*	**8:1**	526*t*
10:32	804*g*	**13:27**	894*w*	**3:9**	362*al* 737*d*	**8:2**	743*k*
10:33	189*d* 941*f*	**13:28**	300*z* 986*k*		809*n*	**8:3**	761*al*
	981*m* 981*n*	**13:29**	505*a*	**3:10**	743*k*	**8:4**	743*l*

8:5	362al 752c	1:18	876a	5:26	162f	10:5	965a
8:7	217b	1:19	88n 352g 361ae	6:2	322g	10:7	935c
8:8	588b 743k 752d	1:20	648j 836g 981f	6:4	287l 854j	10:8	164j
8:9	108g 557e 558a	1:21	229f 781f 786e	6:6	387a 388c	10:9	332d 344d
	586v		923h	6:8	361s	10:10	164j
8:10	267k 743k	1:22	913q 928c	6:12	163b	10:11	319g
8:11	362ba 790l	2:1	968f 969c	6:14	880a	10:12	360i
8:12	108p	2:2	268c	6:15	350j 446b	10:14	455i 914e
8:13	910g	2:3	21h 854f 916g	6:22	612j	10:18	361s
8:14	184bd		929c	6:24	534v 914ae	10:19	2b
8:15	228o 435c 436c	2:4	226x 360e	6:30	914ae	10:20	620t
	743g	2:5	655g 899i	7:1	114r 682a	10:21	361i 418k
8:16	824q	2:6	362q 733ai	7:4	128j 129a	11:2	581a
8:17	371ae 854x	2:7	651d	7:5	651d	11:4	935d
9:1	108p	2:8	333a	7:6	114d	11:6	498k
9:2	854x	2:9	899i	7:7	114c	11:7	183c 211a
9:3	854ae	2:10	501e 645c 913q	7:9	361h	11:12	501c
9:4	866s	2:11	831f 880d	7:11	582k	11:13	761d
9:5	362ba	2:12	491s 836g 836l	7:12	343f	11:17	417r
9:10	790l	2:13	110o 311v 582f	7:13	218aa	11:18	485a
9:12	362ba 761ao	3:1	2b 899s	7:14	438v	12:2	498b
9:13	217b	3:3	110a	7:16	114c 620t	12:4	851d
9:15	108p 790l	3:11	167m 361s	7:17	371e 461a	12:6	730c
9:16	362ba 790l	3:13	683q	7:19	302o 620t	12:7	365a
9:17	108p^2 876f	3:16	2b 172l	7:20	441h 914e	12:10	360i
9:18	108p^2	3:17	683q	7:21	114d 909i	12:11	386b 461j
9:19	108p	3:20	360d 361s	8:3	914c	12:12	133b 498b
9:20	588b	3:25	854r	8:5	459s	12:13	498f
9:21	108p^2 988l	4:2	579g	8:8	125d	12:14	165a 747a
9:24	362al 605r	4:3	162j 534l	8:9	114c	12:15	342c 350b
9:25	217b 280e	4:7	913y 935c	8:11	366d	12:16	498f
9:26	605r	4:8	370h 914s	8:13	506e	12:17	872g
9:27	876f	4:10	365ad	8:14	485aj	12:18	746a
9:29	588b	4:12	438s	8:20	607f 935c	12:19	872g
9:31	946a	4:17	913t	8:21	835b	12:21	922e
9:32	589d	4:18	486c	8:22	872t 888l	12:22	526g
10:1	804f	4:19	163b	9:2	960c	12:23	165a
10:2	589b	4:20	114c	9:3	959b	12:24	268b
10:3	644d	5:1	460a	9:4	162a 498f 711b	13:3	959b
		5:3	501c	9:5	209i	13:4	541e 658b
Job		5:7	381a 827a	9:6	176g	13:5	582a
1:1	854f 929c	5:8	459v	9:7	321q	13:7	542c
1:3	638e 800f	5:9	864a	9:8	321e 343f	13:8	481a
1:4	876a	5:10	350z	9:9	321e	13:9	542c
1:5	128b 899i 979i	5:11	310f 836aj	9:11	444b	13:10	481a
1:6	968f 969c	5:12	623d	9:12	459g	13:11	854j
1:7	268c	5:13	498q 691o	9:17	655g 916g	13:13	582h
1:8	21h 854f 929c	5:14	418m	9:21	922i	13:15	362bc
1:9	854i	5:15	801g	9:22	16a 362bc	13:20	523f
1:10	235s	5:17	827i 924c	9:25	114d	13:21	854j
1:11	655g 899i	5:18	655g 656r	9:28	961i	13:23	914ae
1:12	733ai	5:20	636g 718a	9:29	936a	13:24	523a 705b
1:13	876a	5:21	176e 579j	9:30	648c	13:27	747a
1:14	786f	5:22	365f	9:32	965a	14:1	114c 827a
1:15	88n	5:23	344e 365f	9:33	720a	14:2	114c
1:16	88n 381t	5:24	192v	10:2	961i	14:3	480d
1:17	88n 786f	5:25	104j	10:4	965a	14:4	649q

14:5	131*b* 608*b*	**19:26**	438*f*	**26:5**	361*i*	**31:19**	228*w*
14:6	620*t*	**20:5**	114*m*	**26:6**	361*a*	**31:21**	779*h*
14:7	656*b*	**20:7**	302*i*	**26:7**	164*b*	**31:22**	899*q*
14:10	361*b*	**20:8**	438*y*	**26:8**	350*z*	**31:24**	485*ae* 797*a*
14:12	361*h*	**20:12**	392*i*	**26:10**	250*e*	**31:25**	800*l*
14:13	361*s*	**20:14**	659*c*	**26:11**	218*r*	**31:26**	321*j*
14:14	656*b*	**20:15**	302*q*	**26:12**	343*f*	**31:29**	906*d*
14:15	737*k*	**20:16**	659*c*	**27:2**	391*d* 914*c*	**31:32**	813*d*
14:16	86*g*	**20:17**	635*a*	**27:10**	826*j*	**31:35**	586*l*
14:18	51*c*	**20:19**	786*f* 801*m*	**27:13**	777*p* 938*h*	**31:39**	805*a*
14:19	655*c*	**20:23**	301*j*	**27:14**	859*i*	**31:40**	69*j* 899*q*
14:20	361*d*	**20:29**	938*h*	**27:16**	228*z* 797*o*	**32:1**	913*u*
14:21	491*b*	**21:7**	938*j*	**28:1**	255*i* 359*a*	**32:4**	130*k*
14:22	88*q*	**21:13**	730*c*	**28:3**	255*i*	**32:6**	130*k*
15:2	581*b*	**21:14**	620*t*	**28:11**	350*e*	**32:7**	133*b* 498*b*
15:4	854*q*	**21:15**	13*b* 771*h*	**28:12**	498*d*	**32:8**	516*e*
15:6	961*f*	**21:17**	420*m* 938*j*	**28:15**	792*v* 809*l*	**32:9**	133*b*
15:7	68*f*	**21:18**	323*d*	**28:23**	498*d*	**32:19**	949*s*
15:10	133*h*	**21:19**	169*x*	**28:25**	339*b* 352*f* 465*i*	**32:21**	925*b*
15:11	831*d*	**21:22**	534*a*	**28:28**	498*k* 854*c*	**33:4**	164*j* 965*y*
15:14	371*e* 913*t*	**21:23**	361*f*	**29:2**	125*g*	**33:6**	344*d*
15:15	486*c*	**21:30**	938*j*	**29:3**	417*j*	**33:9**	913*u* 935*d*
15:20	938*h*	**21:34**	831*e*	**29:4**	129*p* 880*b*	**33:10**	705*a*
15:25	704*d*	**22:2**	640*a*	**29:5**	89*h*	**33:14**	579*o*
15:27	357*ah*	**22:5**	914*ab*	**29:6**	357*b*	**33:15**	438*s*
15:31	485*aj*	**22:6**	229*m* 767*d*	**29:7**	263*l*	**33:19**	377*a*
16:2	831*k*	**22:7**	301*ay*	**29:8**	308*j*	**33:20**	301*av* 888*h*
16:3	581*a*	**22:9**	779*g* 896*l*	**29:9**	582*g*	**33:23**	720*b* 968*a*
16:8	198*a*	**22:10**	542*r*	**29:12**	779*d* 801*j*	**33:24**	792*p*
16:9	891*m*	**22:12**	209*a*	**29:13**	896*k*	**34:3**	386*b* 461*j*
16:11	272*d*	**22:13**	490*h*	**29:14**	228*ad*	**34:5**	913*u* 935*d*
16:12	165*a*	**22:14**	355*f*	**29:15**	439*n* 655*q*	**34:10**	914*d*
16:15	836*j*	**22:15**	624*d*	**29:18**	113*b*	**34:11**	676*f*
16:18	335*c*	**22:17**	300*ac*	**29:21**	582*g*	**34:12**	914*d*
16:19	466*k*	**22:21**	717*c*	**29:23**	350*ae*	**34:14**	332*d* 352*b*
16:22	361*h*	**22:22**	534*c*	**29:25**	831*e*	**34:19**	481*a*
17:1	114*d*	**22:23**	148*b*	**30:1**	132*f* 851*d*	**34:21**	441*h*
17:2	851*d*	**22:24**	797*n*	**30:3**	636*d*	**34:28**	924*n*
17:6	496*e*	**22:27**	761*z*	**30:6**	255*h*	**34:35**	499*f*
17:11	114*d*	**23:3**	459*z*	**30:9**	496*e*	**35:3**	771*h*
17:13	361*q*	**23:4**	475*a*	**30:10**	302*l*	**35:6**	914*e*
18:5	938*h*	**23:8**	190*b*	**30:19**	347*b*	**35:7**	913*e*
18:8	542*r*	**23:10**	461*a* 797*r*	**30:20**	460*j*	**35:10**	190*a* 824*aa*
18:19	172*e*	**23:12**	301*ba* 739*h*	**30:21**	735*b* 735*h*	**35:11**	534*b*
19:6	914*c*	**23:13**	88*a*	**30:23**	361*b* 361*f*	**35:12**	761*af*
19:7	914*c*	**24:2**	547*t*	**30:26**	645*c*	**35:16**	581*b*
19:9	867*e*	**24:3**	767*d* 779*g* 896*l*	**30:30**	428*a*	**36:3**	913*d*
19:11	705*a*	**24:4**	801*m*	**31:1**	438*l* 765*r* 859*o*	**36:5**	160*a*
19:12	712*a*	**24:7**	229*f*	**31:4**	86*g*	**36:7**	441*h*
19:13	880*f*	**24:9**	767*d*	**31:6**	322*g* 935*d*	**36:11**	455*k* 730*a*
19:17	888*o*	**24:10**	229*f*	**31:8**	899*q*	**36:14**	114*f*
19:18	132*f*	**24:13**	418*m*	**31:9**	951*k*	**36:22**	160*c*
19:20	256*p* 667*d*	**24:14**	362*b*	**31:10**	899*q*	**36:26**	115*b*
19:22	735*h*	**24:15**	527*a* 951*f*	**31:13**	742*m* 914*ae*	**36:27**	350*z*
19:23	589*i*	**24:19**	914*s*	**31:15**	164*m*	**37:2**	176*k*
19:24	586*p*	**25:4**	913*t*	**31:16**	801*l* 896*l*	**37:6**	350*aj*
19:25	792*r*	**25:6**	365*l* 371*e*	**31:17**	779*d*		

37:9	176*j* 281*e* 281*j* 380*a*	**41:4**	765*r*	**4:5**	485*d* 981*aq*	**9:16**	280*a* 913*a*
37:10	380*b*	**41:5**	837*b*	**4:6**	417*j*	**9:17**	361*v*
37:14	864*a*	**41:11**	773*b*	**4:7**	635*a* 824*h*	**9:18**	505*d*
37:17	281*j* 379*a*	**41:13**	226*w*	**4:8**	660*a* 679*a*	**9:19**	308*a* 480*c*
37:18	321*e*	**41:14**	263*r*	**5:t**	412*k*	**9:20**	371*u*
37:23	160*c* 913*f*	**41:18**	302*s*	**5:1**	455*b*	**10:1**	199*l* 523*a*
37:24	854*g*	**41:19**	381*d*	**5:3**	128*i* 761*g*	**10:2**	619*g* 871*a*
38:1	352*m*	**41:26**	723*r*	**5:4**	914*e*	**10:4**	2*a* 459*ab*
38:2	491*c*	**41:33**	21*i*	**5:5**	877*f*	**10:5**	730*c*
38:3	669*h*	**42:2**	469*a* 623*a*	**5:6**	541*a*	**10:6**	153*u*
38:4	164*b* 214*a*	**42:3**	491*c*	**5:8**	249*b* 913*x*	**10:7**	542*g*
38:5	465*i*	**42:5**	438*d*	**5:9**	364*r* 541*e* 579*j* 925*a*	**10:8**	523*i*
38:6	214*a*	**42:6**	939*d*			**10:11**	506*b*
38:7	968*d*	**42:7**	891*m*	**5:11**	662*a*	**10:12**	308*a*
38:8	343*a*	**42:8**	99*c* 761*k* 981*p*	**5:12**	662*j*	**10:14**	703*b* 779*e*
38:10	236*f*	**42:10**	656*af*	**6:t**	412*k*	**10:16**	741*a*
38:12	128*a*	**42:11**	797*g* 831*f* 844*a*	**6:2**	905*a*	**11:t**	412*k*
38:16	211*a* 343*b*	**42:12**	369*a*	**6:3**	136*a*	**11:1**	620*n* 662*a*
38:17	361*a*	**42:15**	771*a* 841*h*	**6:4**	668*o*	**11:3**	163*g* 214*b*
38:19	417*a*	**42:16**	131*j*	**6:5**	361*i* 923*c*	**11:4**	461*a* 971*a*
38:22	350*af* 350*aj* 632*e*	**42:17**	133*g* 361*ad*	**6:6**	836*w*	**11:5**	888*b*
				6:8	300*q* 455*e*	**11:6**	381*u* 963*a*
38:26	341*b*	**Psalms**		**6:10**	872*p*	**11:7**	438*f* 913*a* 913*e*
38:28	341*e* 350*aa*	**1:1**	311*x* 691*o* 824*k* 851*e* 938*g*	**7:t**	412*k*	**12:t**	412*k*
38:29	380*b*	**1:2**	449*h* 826*k* 953*g*	**7:1**	662*a* 668*d*	**12:2**	545*a* 925*a*
38:31	321*e*	**1:3**	171*q* 342*l* 350*i* 366*x* 730*a*	**7:5**	899*q*	**12:3**	579*j*
38:34	355*a*			**7:6**	308*a*	**12:5**	308*a* 660*a*
38:35	176*k*	**1:4**	323*d* 938*h*	**7:8**	480*e* 927*a*	**12:6**	529*a* 654*c* 950*a*
38:36	498*d*	**1:5**	959*a*	**7:9**	461*a*	**12:7**	660*a*
38:37	194*q* 350*aa*	**1:6**	624*d* 624*g*	**7:11**	957*a*	**13:t**	412*k*
38:39	301*v* 365*ab*	**2:1**	371*u*	**7:12**	256*c* 287*i*	**13:1**	136*a* 506*b* 523*b*
38:41	301*v* 365*al*	**2:2**	357*h*	**7:14**	167*w*	**13:5**	485*e*
39:1	167*l* 365*x*	**2:3**	746*s*	**7:15**	255*a* 280*b*	**13:6**	412*c*
39:5	365*aa*	**2:4**	851*h*	**7:16**	280*a*	**14:t**	412*k*
39:9	365*aa*	**2:5**	854*j*	**7:17**	907*d*	**14:1**	2*a* 501*a*
39:13	365*an*	**2:6**	209*n* 741*c*	**8:t**	412*k*	**14:2**	441*g* 459*x*
39:14	621*v*	**2:7**	167*u* 169*t* 170*m*	**8:1**	866*f*	**14:3**	914*j*
39:15	332*h*			**8:2**	132*h* 923*a*	**14:6**	662*b*
39:17	499*a*	**2:8**	371*z* 777*m*	**8:3**	164*d* 321*e*	**14:7**	656*ag*
39:18	277*b*	**2:9**	46*o* 218*f*	**8:4**	371*e*	**15:t**	412*k*
39:19	365*bg*	**2:10**	664*c*	**8:5**	371*a* 866*v*	**15:1**	192*k* 209*n*
39:24	414*e*	**2:11**	854*a*	**8:6**	365*c* 733*ab* 745*i*	**15:2**	935*a*
39:26	365*al*	**2:12**	662*a* 824*h* 889*f* 891*o*			**15:3**	926*i*
39:27	209*c* 365*aq*			**8:9**	866*f*	**15:5**	153*r* 612*j* 803*h*
39:30	335*j* 363*m*	**3:t**	412*k*	**9:t**	412*k*	**16:t**	412*k*
40:2	924*f*	**3:1**	705*f*	**9:1**	864*a* 907*d*	**16:1**	662*a*
40:7	669*h*	**3:2**	668*f*	**9:2**	923*g*	**16:2**	644*c*
40:8	913*d*	**3:3**	310*f* 310*j* 662*j*	**9:4**	480*h* 927*a*	**16:4**	966*i*
40:9	160*b*	**3:4**	209*l* 460*c* 761*q*	**9:6**	506*g*	**16:5**	777*e*
40:15	164*g* 301*al* 365*au*	**3:5**	679*a*	**9:7**	115*b* 733*b*	**16:7**	923*g*
		3:6	855*h*	**9:8**	480*h*	**16:8**	153*t*
40:16	162*m*	**3:8**	668*a*	**9:9**	662*d*	**16:10**	656*c*
40:21	347*a*	**4:t**	412*k*	**9:10**	485*e*	**16:11**	189*b* 824*h*
40:23	350*l*	**4:1**	460*a*	**9:11**	192*j*	**17:t**	761*r*
41:1	365*au*	**4:3**	455*c* 605*a*	**9:12**	577*k* 910*c*	**17:3**	461*a* 935*d*
41:3	177*g*	**4:4**	891*s*	**9:13**	735*i*	**17:6**	455*b*
				9:15	255*a* 280*a* 280*b*	**17:7**	668*m*

68:17 274*f*	**71:18** 133*c* 607*d*	**75:1** 907*d*	**78:43** 864*b*
68:18 308*b* 745*i* 781*n*	**71:19** 21*b*	**75:3** 218*r*	**78:44** 335*k*
68:19 273*k*	**71:23** 923*g*	**75:4** 877*d*	**78:45** 365*i* 365*m*
68:20 668*a*	**71:24** 872*t* 913*d*	**75:6** 310*e*	**78:46** 365*j*
68:21 362*bc*	**72:t** 412*n*	**75:7** 310*e* 311*r* 480*d*	**78:47** 350*ag* 380*b*
68:24 267*d*	**72:1** 480*n*	**75:8** 949*o*	**78:48** 350*ag*
68:25 413*a*	**72:2** 480*i*	**75:10** 162*b*	**78:51** 119*e*
68:28 162*a*	**72:4** 801*j*	**76:t** 412*m*	**78:52** 369*k*
68:29 781*o*	**72:6** 350*ae*	**76:1** 490*q*	**78:53** 343*j*
68:31 371*z*	**72:8** 183*f* 350*p* 733*w*	**76:2** 192*j*	**78:54** 184*d*
68:32 412*c*	**72:10** 804*e*	**76:6** 267*n*	**78:55** 300*h* 783*a*
68:33 577*c*	**72:12** 668*l* 801*j*	**76:10** 228*ab* 891*s*	**78:56** 461*f*
68:34 162*a*	**72:15** 761*r* 797*h*	**76:11** 532*s*	**78:57** 246*a* 287*h* 641*k*
69:t 412*k*	**72:16** 171*i*	**76:12** 854*b*	**78:58** 911*d* 982*p*
69:1 350*d*	**72:17** 897*j*	**77:t** 412*m*	**78:59** 607*a*
69:2 347*b*	**72:18** 864*a* 923*l*	**77:1** 761*q*	**78:60** 192*i* 621*b*
69:4 104*o* 259*f* 787*c*	**72:19** 54*g*	**77:2** 831*j*	**78:62** 728*e*
788*h* 888*m*	**72:20** 69*j*	**77:5** 125*d*	**78:64** 362*am* 836*ai*
916*f*	**73:t** 412*m*	**77:7** 607*c*	**78:65** 678*e*
69:5 490*i* 499*f*	**73:1** 644*c*	**77:11** 505*g* 864*a*	**78:67** 607*a*
69:6 507*c* 872*y*	**73:2** 309*a*	**77:13** 21*a*	**78:68** 209*m* 605*b*
69:7 922*l*	**73:3** 730*c* 871*e* 912*d*	**77:14** 864*a*	**78:70** 369*f* 605*b*
69:8 59*v*	938*j*	**77:16** 339*b*	**78:71** 777*f*
69:9 818*b* 921*a*	**73:11** 490*h*	**77:17** 176*k*	**79:t** 412*m*
69:10 946*l*	**73:12** 800*k*	**77:19** 624*a*	**79:1** 165*d* 649*a* 712*f*
69:11 496*e*	**73:13** 641*b* 950*d*	**77:20** 283*a*	990*v*
69:12 949*j*	**73:16** 517*a*	**78:t** 412*m*	**79:2** 363*n*
69:13 761*q*	**73:17** 69*i*	**78:2** 519*c* 526*b*	**79:3** 364*o*
69:14 347*c* 668*d*	**73:18** 258*b*	**78:5** 170*b* 466*k* 534*o*	**79:4** 851*b*
69:15 350*d*	**73:19** 165*r*	953*a*	**79:5** 136*a* 891*g*
69:16 460*a*	**73:20** 438*y*	**78:7** 485*d* 739*g*	**79:10** 190*a* 910*c*
69:17 523*a*	**73:21** 391*d*	**78:8** 602*c* 738*g*	**79:12** 280*c* 804*j*
69:20 831*i*	**73:22** 491*c*	**78:10** 769*b*	**80:t** 412*m*
69:21 301*h* 391*a*	**73:23** 89*d* 378*h*	**78:11** 506*f*	**80:1** 369*k* 968*u*
393*a*	**73:24** 69*e* 689*d* 691*d*	**78:12** 864*b*	**80:3** 417*l* 656*ag*
69:23 439*i*	971*i*	**78:13** 46*l* 209*aa*	**80:4** 891*g*
69:24 891*c*	**73:25** 859*a* 971*a*	**78:14** 355*c* 381*q*	**80:5** 301*bc* 836*ac*
69:28 589*l*	**73:26** 162*b* 777*e*	**78:15** 46*m* 339*k*	**80:6** 851*b*
69:30 907*c* 923*g*	**73:28** 200*b* 662*a*	**78:17** 738*g*	**80:7** 417*l* 656*ag*
69:33 455*c*	**74:t** 412*m*	**78:18** 461*f*	**80:8** 300*h* 366*k* 370*p*
69:35 164*r* 668*q*	**74:1** 607*a* 891*g*	**78:19** 301*w*	**80:10** 418*d*
70:t 412*k*	**74:2** 209*l* 505*a* 792*n*	**78:20** 339*k*	**80:11** 350*p*
70:1 703*a*	**74:4** 547*ad*	**78:21** 891*k*	**80:12** 235*m*
70:2 362*k* 872*t*	**74:6** 554*d*	**78:22** 486*d*	**80:13** 365*bj*
70:4 824*g*	**74:7** 381*g*	**78:24** 301*ae*	**80:19** 417*l* 656*ag*
70:5 703*a*	**74:8** 192*q* 381*g*	**78:25** 968*c*	**81:t** 412*m*
71:1 662*a* 872*v*	**74:9** 579*y*	**78:27** 301*x*	**81:1** 824*g*
71:3 344*w*^{2} 662*b*	**74:10** 136*a*	**78:31** 362*bf* 891*j*	**81:3** 108*c* 414*l*
71:4 668*d*	**74:12** 741*a*	**78:32** 486*d*	**81:6** 322*m*
71:6 130*c*	**74:13** 46*l*	**78:34** 362*bf* 459*v*	**81:7** 461*d*
71:7 662*a*	**74:15** 339*l* 342*h*	**78:35** 344*w*	**81:8** 455*q*
71:9 133*c* 607*d*	**74:16** 128*a* 420*a*	**78:36** 542*c*	**81:9** 966*c*
71:11 607*d* 621*e*	**74:17** 128*n* 236*a*	**78:38** 909*f*	**81:10** 263*q* 304*a*
71:12 703*a*	**74:18** 501*a*	**78:39** 319*a* 352*d*	**81:12** 602*h*
71:13 872*t*	**74:20** 768*c*	**78:40** 738*f*	**81:13** 455*q*
71:15 913*d*	**74:22** 308*a* 501*a*	**78:41** 461*f*	**81:14** 745*k*
71:17 130*f* 534*b*	**75:t** 412*m*	**78:42** 506*f*	**81:16** 301*x* 392*b*

82:t	412m	88:t	412l 412n	91:1	192k 418f	95:4	773b
82:1	480f 966n	88:2	455b	91:2	485e 662b 662c 662d^2	95:5	164d 343a 773b
82:2	481e	88:3	361m			95:6	311e 981a
82:3	913i	88:5	506b	91:3	542w	95:7	365bo 369k 371ac 965e
82:6	966a 966n	88:8	880f	91:4	271d 662j		
82:7	361f	88:10	923c	91:5	855h 855i	95:8	602e
82:8	308a 480c 773c	88:14	523a 607d	91:8	804k	95:9	461f
83:t	412m	88:15	130g	91:9	192k	95:10	110ac 491h 624b
83:1	582d	88:18	880f	91:10	645i		
83:3	623f	89:t	412n	91:11	273l 660b 968a 968n	95:11	532q 683o
83:4	165f 506g	89:1	897l			96:1	126e 412g
83:5	765p	89:3	765i	91:12	279n 344l	96:2	923d
83:10	302i	89:4	741q	91:13	279r 365ad	96:4	854b
83:12	771g	89:5	923a	91:14	490n 668o 887l	96:5	321a 966b
83:13	323d	89:6	21a 21b	91:15	460e	96:8	981a
83:17	872t	89:7	854a	91:16	113a	96:9	981a
83:18	21c 490n	89:8	21b	92:t	412j 683d	96:10	153c 480e 733a
84:t	412l	89:9	343g	92:1	907c 923a	96:11	824i
84:1	192a	89:10	343f	92:3	414b	96:12	366q
84:2	859a	89:11	321g	92:7	165r	96:13	295e 480h
84:3	192ai	89:12	209u^2 281t	92:8	866g	97:1	733a
84:4	897d	89:14	897l 913a	92:9	705e	97:2	355e 418h 913a
84:5	897d	89:15	417j	92:10	162b 357k	97:3	381u
84:6	339o	89:17	162b	92:12	153o 366t 366x	97:4	176k
84:8	455b	89:20	357g 742b	92:13	192k	97:5	209i 337b
84:10	192k	89:23	727c	92:14	133c	97:6	321f 913d
84:11	321i 644c 662j	89:24	162b	92:15	344w 929a	97:7	982s^2
84:12	485j	89:26	169s 344w	93:1	153c 228ab 733a	97:9	866g
85:t	412l	89:27	119h			97:10	668g 888g
85:1	656ak	89:28	765i	93:2	115b	97:11	417r
85:2	909f	89:29	741q	93:3	350b	97:12	824g 907a
85:4	656ag	89:30	954c	93:4	160a	98:t	412j
85:5	891g	89:32	963a	93:5	975a 979d	98:1	126e 412g
85:6	656ag	89:35	532o 541b	94:1	910a	98:2	526e 668p
85:8	719a	89:36	741q	94:2	308a 957a	98:4	824g
85:9	854i	89:38	607a	94:3	136a	98:5	414b
85:10	710c 889c 897l	89:40	165d 235m	94:4	871a	98:7	824i
85:12	171g	89:45	114f 872s	94:5	371ae	98:8	412c
86:1	460a 801o	89:46	136a 523b	94:6	59af 362b 779g 896l	98:9	295e 480h
86:5	909a	89:47	114a			99:1	733a^2
86:6	455b	89:48	361f	94:7	439f 456a	99:2	866g
86:7	460b	89:52	488c 923h	94:8	455q	99:3	979a
86:8	21b	90:1	192k	94:9	164k 415b 438c 455i	99:4	913e
86:9	981b	90:2	115b 125a			99:5	218ac 979a
86:10	21c	90:3	332d 361d	94:10	534b 924a	99:6	460c 986e
86:11	534d 624b	90:4	110ah	94:11	352d 449c 490i	99:7	355c 739h
86:12	907d	90:5	114c 362bc 366f	94:12	534b 827i	99:8	460c 909a 910a
86:13	668k			94:14	621g	99:9	979a
86:15	891n	90:8	417j 914e	94:17	703b	100:t	412j
86:17	547c 872t	90:9	352e	94:19	825t 831d	100:1	824g
87:t	412l	90:10	110ae 110af 114a 131a	94:20	706b	100:2	412d
87:1	209o			94:21	961e	100:3	164j 365bo 371ac
87:2	209m 887f	90:12	498b	94:22	662a 662b		
87:3	184aj 866a	90:13	136a	94:23	280d 804k	100:4	297h 907a
87:4	167r 490p	90:14	824h	95:1	344w 824g	100:5	644a
87:6	548e	90:16	676b	95:2	412g 907b	101:t	412k
87:7	339n	90:17	676d 897n	95:3	965d	101:1	923g

101:3	888g	104:14	301v
101:5	926j	104:15	301u 357r
101:7	542n		949c
102:t	825c	104:16	366m
102:1	455b	104:17	192ai
102:2	523a	104:18	209g
102:4	301av 506l	104:19	110c 164d
102:6	365am	104:20	365e 418a
102:7	678a	104:21	301v
102:8	899l	104:23	682a
102:9	301ar 891m	104:24	498g
102:11	114c 418e	104:25	343b
102:12	115b	104:26	275a 365au
102:13	137a	104:27	301v
102:14	344s	104:29	332d 352b
102:16	164s		523b
102:17	455g	104:30	352a
102:18	124d	104:32	176g
102:19	441g	104:34	449i
102:20	746a	104:35	923d
102:23	114d	105:1	526k 907a
102:25	164b 648p	105:3	459aa
102:26	153e 228ac	105:4	459s
	655d	105:8	768c
102:27	115e 144a	105:10	115k
103:t	412k	105:11	184a
103:1	923d	105:12	105a
103:2	923d 923m	105:13	268a
103:3	656r 909a	105:14	757b 924a
103:4	897m	105:15	357k 579x
103:5	130j	105:16	636a 636d
103:6	913f	105:17	745g 793g
103:7	526c 624b	105:18	747o
103:8	823f 891n	105:19	461b
	905d	105:20	746e
103:11	209a 897l	105:21	733ae
103:12	199i 909g	105:22	534l
103:13	169r 905d	105:23	184m
103:14	319a 332c	105:24	104e
103:15	114c	105:25	888j
103:17	115k 897k	105:26	751a
103:19	733a	105:27	864f
103:20	162o 739f	105:28	418i
	923d 968d	105:29	335k 365av
103:21	923d	105:30	365m
103:22	923d	105:31	365i
104:1	228ab 923d	105:32	350ag
104:2	228ab 417e	105:33	366p
104:3	352m 355e	105:34	365j
104:4	352m 381s	105:36	119e
104:5	164b	105:37	304a
104:6	228ac 339b	105:38	854x
104:7	339b	105:39	355e 381q
104:8	209f	105:40	301x 301ae
104:9	236f		633b
104:10	339l	105:41	339k
104:13	341b	105:43	824i

105:44	184a 771e	107:17	501c 914s
105:45	739i	107:18	301av 888h
106:1	897k 923d	107:20	656s
106:3	824k 913l	107:21	907a
106:4	505a	107:22	907b
106:6	914ac	107:23	270a
106:7	506f 738f	107:25	343d 352g
106:8	668o	107:27	152a 949j
106:9	342a 924b	107:28	761q
106:12	485ad	107:29	266b
106:13	506f 691f	107:31	907a
106:14	461f 859r	107:33	342h
106:15	651f 781f	107:34	172q
106:16	912c	107:35	339l
106:17	263s	107:36	184z
106:18	381u	107:37	370m
106:19	982j	107:38	104e
106:20	150e 982a	107:41	801g
106:21	506e 864b	107:43	455q 897l
106:23	362bg 720a	108:t	412k
106:24	486d 922k	108:3	907d
106:25	456e 829a	108:4	897l
106:26	532q	108:5	866g
106:27	75c	108:7	783a
106:28	967c 984a	108:8	773c
106:29	659a 891l	108:9	648v
106:31	480t 913s	108:11	190b 607a
106:32	891l	108:12	371q
106:33	738g 857b	108:13	727a
106:34	362bb	109:t	412k
106:35	43c	109:1	582d
106:36	542y 982n	109:2	541e 926e
106:37	981ah	109:3	916f
106:39	649b 951x	109:4	880f
106:40	888b 891k	109:5	804n
106:41	728d 733ak	109:7	761ag 961b
106:42	735e	109:8	114g 272b
106:45	505c 768c	109:9	779b 896m
106:47	74b	109:10	761ai
106:48	488c 923d	109:13	561aa
	923h	109:14	909j
107:1	897k 907a	109:15	506g
107:2	74b 792o	109:17	280f 899l
107:3	281v	109:18	228ag
107:4	172u 184z	109:22	801o
107:5	859k	109:23	418e
107:6	761q	109:24	196c 946f
107:7	184z 249a	109:27	676b
107:8	907a	109:28	872p 897h
107:9	635f	109:29	228ag 872t
107:10	418k 747o	109:30	923g
107:11	691f 738g	109:31	89f 241a 801g
107:12	682d	110:t	412k
107:13	761q	110:1	218ad 241b
107:14	418n 746a		311z 727k
107:15	907a		745k
107:16	746a	110:2	733w

110:3	597*c*	**116:1**	455*e* 887*m*	**119:16**	505*h* 826*k*	**119:90**	153*c*
110:4	532*o* 599*a*	**116:3**	361*m* 825*g*	**119:18**	516*f*	**119:91**	742*a*
	986*u*	**116:4**	761*t*	**119:19**	59*w*	**119:92**	826*k*
110:5	241*a* 362*bd*	**116:5**	905*c*	**119:20**	859*b*	**119:93**	505*h*
110:7	301*f*	**116:6**	668*l*	**119:21**	282*f* 871*i*	**119:96**	647*c*
111:1	907*d* 923*d*	**116:7**	683*m*	**119:22**	739*h*	**119:97**	449*h* 887*r*
111:2	676*a*	**116:8**	361*au* 668*k*	**119:23**	449*h*	**119:98**	498*l*
111:4	905*d*	**116:11**	545*a*	**119:24**	691*d* 826*k*	**119:99**	449*h* 537*a*
111:5	301*x* 768*c*	**116:12**	781*n*	**119:26**	534*h*	**119:100**	133*b*
111:6	526*e*	**116:13**	301*bc* 668*m*	**119:27**	449*h* 516*f*	**119:102**	282*f* 534*b*
111:7	494*f*		761*t*	**119:28**	162*c*	**119:103**	392*g*
111:10	498*k* 854*c*	**116:14**	532*s*	**119:30**	605*n*	**119:104**	888*g*
112:1	824*k* 826*k*	**116:15**	361*am* 811*b*	**119:31**	872*v*	**119:105**	417*k* 420*j*
	854*e* 923*d*	**116:16**	742*a* 746*a*	**119:32**	277*f*	**119:106**	532*n*
112:2	170*a*	**116:17**	761*t* 907*d*	**119:33**	534*h*	**119:108**	534*h*
112:3	800*a* 913*a*	**116:18**	532*s*	**119:34**	516*f*	**119:109**	505*h*
112:4	417*r*	**116:19**	923*d*	**119:35**	826*k*	**119:110**	542*v*
112:5	784*a*	**117:1**	59*n* 923*d*	**119:37**	438*n*	**119:111**	824*n*
112:6	153*s* 505*m*	**117:2**	923*d*	**119:38**	854*i*	**119:113**	518*a* 887*r*
112:7	485*f* 855*b*	**118:1**	897*k* 907*a*	**119:40**	859*b*	**119:114**	662*b* 662*j*
112:9	801*j* 813*a*	**118:5**	460*c* 761*q*	**119:42**	460*h* 485*ad*	**119:115**	300*q*
	913*a*		825*g*	**119:45**	459*v* 746*b*	**119:116**	872*v*
112:10	891*u*	**118:6**	371*q* 706*a*	**119:46**	872*v*	**119:118**	282*f*
113:1	923*d*	**118:7**	706*a*	**119:47**	826*k* 887*r*	**119:119**	887*r*
113:2	923*h*	**118:8**	371*q* 485*ag*	**119:48**	310*i* 449*h*	**119:120**	854*j*
113:3	923*a*		662*a*		887*r*	**119:124**	534*h*
113:4	866*g*	**118:10**	230*a*	**119:49**	505*a*	**119:125**	516*f* 742*a*
113:5	21*a*	**118:13**	703*b*	**119:50**	831*d*	**119:126**	137*a*
113:6	441*g*	**118:14**	668*b*	**119:51**	282*f* 922*l*	**119:127**	797*r*
113:7	310*f* 801*g*	**118:15**	241*a*	**119:53**	621*k*	**119:128**	888*g*
113:9	171*c* 923*d*	**118:16**	241*a*	**119:54**	412*g*	**119:130**	417*k* 516*e*
114:1	298*b* 557*b*	**118:17**	361*au*	**119:55**	129*j*	**119:131**	263*q* 859*b*
114:3	343*j* 350*l*	**118:18**	827*i*	**119:57**	777*e*	**119:133**	153*j* 733*aj*
114:4	209*i*	**118:19**	263*j* 297*h*	**119:60**	680*b*	**119:134**	735*c*
114:5	343*j* 350*l*	**118:21**	460*c* 668*b*	**119:61**	505*h*	**119:135**	417*l* 534*h*
114:6	209*i*		907*d*	**119:62**	129*j*	**119:136**	836*w*
114:7	854*a*	**118:22**	214*e* 344*x*	**119:64**	534*h*	**119:137**	913*a*
114:8	339*k* 344*q*	**118:23**	676*b*	**119:66**	485*ad* 534*d*	**119:139**	818*b*
115:1	923*l*	**118:24**	110*a*	**119:67**	282*e* 827*i*	**119:140**	654*c* 887*r*
115:2	190*a*	**118:26**	295*e*	**119:68**	534*h* 644*c*	**119:141**	505*h* 922*l*
115:3	826*a* 971*a*	**118:27**	417*j* 747*q*	**119:69**	545*a*	**119:142**	494*d* 913*b*
115:4	982*c*		965*b*	**119:70**	826*k*	**119:143**	824*n*
115:5	439*e* 578*c*	**118:28**	965*e*	**119:71**	827*i*	**119:144**	516*e* 913*g*
115:6	395*a* 416*b*	**118:29**	897*k* 907*a*	**119:72**	800*q*	**119:145**	460*a*
115:7	267*h* 375*c*	**119:1**	529*a* 558*b*	**119:73**	164*j*	**119:147**	128*i*
	578*c*		824*n* 935*a*	**119:75**	827*i*	**119:148**	129*j* 449*h*
115:8	18*m* 485*ak*	**119:2**	459*aa* 739*j*	**119:76**	831*d*	**119:150**	199*m*
115:9	485*d* 662*j*	**119:4**	739*i*	**119:77**	826*k*	**119:151**	200*a*
	703*b*	**119:6**	872*v*	**119:78**	449*h* 872*t*	**119:152**	115*m* 153*f*
115:10	662*j* 703*b*	**119:7**	907*d*	**119:80**	872*v*	**119:153**	505*h*
115:11	662*j* 703*b*	**119:8**	621*f*	**119:82**	136*a*	**119:155**	459*ab*
115:13	854*i* 897*d*	**119:9**	950*b*	**119:83**	194*r* 388*f*	**119:157**	282*f* 735*i*
115:14	171*a*	**119:10**	282*f* 459*v*		505*h*	**119:159**	887*r*
115:15	164*a* 897*c*	**119:11**	914*p*	**119:84**	136*a*	**119:160**	494*d*
115:16	321*g* 971*a*	**119:12**	534*h*	**119:85**	255*a*	**119:161**	735*i* 854*e*
115:17	361*i*	**119:14**	800*q* 826*k*	**119:86**	545*a* 735*i*	**119:162**	790*b* 824*n*
115:18	923*d*	**119:15**	449*h*	**119:89**	115*m* 153*f*	**119:163**	887*r* 888*g*

144:4	114*c* 352*d*
144:5	209*i* 309*e*
144:6	176*k* 287*j*
144:7	59*a* 350*d*
	545*a*
144:9	126*e* 412*g*
	414*b*
144:11	59*a* 545*a*
144:12	170*a* 218*s*
144:13	171*b* 632*b*
144:15	371*ac* 824*h*
145:t	412*k*
145:1	558*b* 923*g*
145:3	923*a*
145:5	449*h*
145:6	526*k*
145:8	823*f* 891*n*
	905*d*
145:9	644*c*
145:10	907*e*
145:11	526*k*
145:13	115*c* 733*w*
145:15	301*v* 441*l*
145:16	635*g*
145:17	913*a*
145:18	200*a*
145:19	455*c* 635*g*
146:1	923*d*
146:2	923*g*
146:3	371*q* 485*ag*
146:4	361*c*
146:5	824*o*
146:6	164*a* 929*a*
146:7	301*u* 746*a*
	913*f*
146:8	439*p* 887*f*
146:9	59*aa* 779*e*
	896*i*
146:10	733*b*
147:1	923*d*
147:2	164*s*
147:3	656*r* 825*i*
147:4	86*g* 321*g*
	561*n*
147:8	350*z* 366*d*
147:9	301*v*
147:10	162*n* 826*c*
147:12	923*d*
147:14	301*u* 717*i*
147:15	277*f*
147:16	350*aj* 380*b*
147:17	380*b*
147:18	337*a*
147:20	21*e* 923*d*
148:1	923*d*[2]
148:3	321*f*
148:5	164*e*

148:8	352*f*
148:13	866*g*
148:14	162*b* 200*a*
	923*d*
149:1	126*e* 412*g*
	923*d*
149:2	824*h*
149:3	835*e*
149:4	826*e*
149:6	90*s* 723*e*
149:7	910*a*
149:8	747*p*
149:9	923*d*
150:1	923*d*[2]
150:3	414*b*

Proverbs

1:1	496*b*
1:2	498*d*
1:3	534*k*
1:4	498*l*
1:5	500*a*
1:7	498*k* 501*c* 854*c*
1:8	455*r*
1:10	612*f*
1:11	527*e* 916*f*
1:13	790*m*
1:14	9*c* 799*b*
1:15	624*d*
1:16	277*g*
1:17	522*e*
1:18	280*a*
1:19	771*j*
1:20	498*e* 577*j*
1:22	136*g*
1:23	965*s*
1:24	456*g*
1:25	691*f* 924*d*
1:26	851*c*
1:28	459*r* 460*k*
1:29	491*a* 854*q*
1:30	691*f* 924*d*
1:31	171*r*
1:32	483*a*
2:2	455*o*
2:4	459*r* 800*q*
2:5	490*r*
2:6	498*k*
2:7	662*j*
2:8	666*a*
2:16	951*j*
2:17	769*c*
2:18	361*v*
2:21	184*g* 929*g*
3:1	505*g*
3:2	113*e*
3:5	485*d* 490*d*

3:6	249*a* 526*j* 624*e*
3:7	498*s* 854*a*
3:8	656*t*
3:9	171*l* 800*p*
3:10	632*b*
3:11	827*i*
3:12	169*r* 887*h* 924*c*
3:14	771*l* 797*r*
3:15	844*m*
3:16	113*e* 800*c* 866*z*
3:17	717*b*
3:18	366*v*
3:19	164*e* 498*g*
3:23	153*i*
3:24	679*a* 855*i*
3:25	854*ai*
3:27	644*d*
3:28	136*h*
3:30	928*a*
3:31	912*b*
3:33	899*b*
3:35	851*h*
4:1	455*r* 498*l*
4:5	498*d*
4:7	498*d*
4:8	866*z*
4:9	844*a*
4:10	113*e*
4:12	153*i*
4:14	624*d*
4:16	678*b*
4:18	417*q* 624*g*
4:19	418*m* 624*d*
4:20	455*o*
4:22	360*q* 650*b*
4:23	457*e*
4:24	542*n*
4:25	249*c*
4:27	249*c*
5:1	455*o*
5:3	392*c* 579*j* 951*j*
5:4	90*s* 256*j* 391*e*
5:5	361*v*
5:6	152*c*
5:7	455*o*
5:8	199*h*
5:15	301*bc* 894*n*
5:19	253*a* 365*x*
	887*aa*
5:20	951*j*
5:21	441*h* 624*d*
6:1	767*c*
6:2	579*e*
6:3	872*i*
6:4	678*b*
6:6	365*i* 679*i*
6:7	734*b*

6:8	370*s*
6:9	679*i*
6:10	679*g*
6:11	801*f*
6:12	938*d*
6:13	547*y*
6:14	709*d*
6:15	116*a*
6:16	888*b*
6:17	362*a* 541*a* 871*i*
6:18	277*g* 623*d*
6:19	466*t* 709*d*
6:20	455*r*
6:23	420*j*
6:24	951*j*[2]
6:25	841*j*
6:27	381*b*
6:29	951*k* 963*s*
6:30	789*c*
6:31	99*i* 787*a*
6:32	951*f*
6:34	911*a*
6:35	792*k*
7:2	534*k*
7:5	951*j*
7:6	951*s*
7:10	228*s*
7:13	889*d*
7:16	226*i*
7:17	396*l*
7:18	887*aa*
7:19	190*h* 267*b*
7:20	108*c*
7:21	612*f*
7:22	362*bn*
7:24	455*o*
7:27	361*v*
8:1	498*e* 577*j*
8:3	263*p*
8:8	246*c*
8:9	249*b*
8:10	797*r*
8:11	21*g* 844*m*
8:13	854*d* 871*i* 888*g*
8:15	733*ad*
8:18	800*c* 866*z*
8:19	797*r*
8:21	800*c*
8:22	68*b*
8:27	164*e*
8:29	214*a* 236*f* 250*e*
8:30	826*a*
8:31	826*e*
8:34	263*p* 455*o*
8:35	360*i* 897*n*
8:36	361*v* 888*f*

9:1	99f 164v 218r
	498e
9:4	499b
9:5	301af
9:6	501g
9:7	924j
9:8	924h
9:10	498k 854c
9:11	113e
9:12	80a
9:13	501e
9:14	263e
9:16	499b
9:17	530g 788e 951i
9:18	361v
10:1	496b 500a 501e
10:2	771j 913aa
10:3	635g 859j
10:4	678h 800e 801f
10:5	679g
10:7	505q
10:8	739j
10:10	547y
10:11	579h
10:12	887a 888a
10:15	800l 801a
10:16	$804d^2$
10:18	525o 926a
10:19	579g 582a
10:22	800e 897b
10:23	$837b^2$
10:24	854r 859c
10:25	153g
10:26	827k
10:27	113c 114f 854d
10:29	662d
10:30	153s 184i
11:1	465e 826b
11:2	871b 872a
11:3	280a 689a
11:4	800n 913aa
11:5	280a
11:7	361i
11:9	926a
11:10	824m 913aa
11:12	582a
11:13	525m
11:14	691b
11:15	767c
11:16	800k 866z 897t
11:17	280a 280h
11:18	75j
11:19	361u
11:20	826b
11:21	963a
11:22	841g
11:23	859c
11:24	75l 816a
11:25	280h 813c
11:26	793a
11:27	459r
11:28	366c 485ae
11:30	366v
11:31	804k
12:1	827h
12:3	153s 153u
12:4	894m
12:5	449d
12:6	527e
12:7	153h
12:9	872c
12:10	369c 735c
12:11	370e 635b
12:14	280g
12:15	691a
12:16	456i
12:18	579h 579j
12:19	114e
12:22	541a 826b
12:23	525m
12:24	678h 679j
12:25	825t
12:28	360n
13:1	827h
13:3	579d 581b
13:4	679h
13:6	914s
13:7	541j
13:8	792k
13:9	417q
13:10	691a
13:11	771j
13:12	366v 852a
13:13	922c
13:14	534k
13:18	827j
13:20	89n
13:21	730a
13:22	777l
13:24	827h 964a
13:25	635g
14:1	164v
14:2	854d
14:3	280f
14:9	851a
14:10	825d
14:12	624d
14:13	824ab
14:15	485c 487a
14:17	892a
14:19	311b
14:20	800m 801c
14:23	682a
14:24	800c
14:25	466a
14:26	854d
14:27	854d
14:28	104q
14:29	823b 892a
14:30	818a
14:31	801k
14:34	913aa 914a
15:1	177g
15:3	441f
15:4	366v 579h
15:6	800e
15:8	826b 981ao
15:9	624d
15:11	447a 522a
15:13	833a
15:15	833a
15:16	33a
15:17	887a
15:18	892a
15:19	624g 679i
15:20	500a 501e
15:21	499a
15:22	691b
15:23	460g
15:24	308h
15:25	871i 896i
15:27	612j
15:28	449d
15:29	199l 455c
15:30	529i
15:32	922i
15:33	854c 872a
16:1	460g 623c
16:2	935i 950d
16:4	938b
16:5	871c
16:6	854i 941k
16:7	719a
16:8	33a 913aa
16:9	623c 689d
16:10	480n
16:11	465a
16:12	741j
16:14	741i 891u
16:15	741i
16:16	498c 797r
16:18	871j
16:19	790a 872c
16:20	485j
16:21	579ao 612d
16:22	339p
16:23	612d
16:24	392g 579ao
16:25	361t 624d
16:26	859h
16:27	579j
16:28	926a
16:29	612f
16:30	547y
16:31	429a
16:32	823b
16:33	605q
17:1	33a
17:2	733ac 771b
17:3	383a 461a
17:4	455t
17:5	801k 851a
17:6	170a
17:7	541i
17:8	612g
17:9	909o
17:10	924j
17:12	772f
17:13	804n
17:14	709b
17:15	960b 961e
17:17	880a
17:18	767c
17:21	501e
17:22	658g 833a
17:23	612h
17:25	501e
17:27	582a 823b
17:28	582a
18:4	339p
18:5	481e
18:6	579e
18:8	390a
18:9	679j
18:10	209an 561f
18:11	800l
18:12	871j 872a
18:13	455p 460g
18:16	612g
18:18	605q
18:21	579a
18:22	894n 897n
18:23	761ai
18:24	880a
19:1	801q
19:2	680d
19:3	891r
19:4	800p 801c 880f
	880g
19:5	466t
19:6	813c 880g
19:7	$801c^2$ 880f
19:8	887v
19:9	466t
19:10	637b
19:11	823b
19:12	891u
19:13	501e

19:14 777*l* 894*m*
19:15 679*g* 859*h*
19:17 784*b* 801*h*
19:18 827*h*
19:20 691*a*
19:21 623*c*
19:22 801*b*
19:23 854*d*
19:24 679*h*
19:26 169*n*
19:28 466*t*
20:1 949*a*
20:2 891*u*
20:3 709*a*
20:4 679*h*
20:6 929*j*
20:8 741*j*
20:9 950*b*
20:10 465*e*
20:12 164*k* 415*b* 438*a*
20:13 679*g* 801*f*
20:14 792*b*
20:15 579*h*
20:16 767*c*
20:17 542*e*
20:18 691*a*
20:19 926*j*
20:20 169*n* 899*a*
20:22 910*i*
20:23 465*e*
20:24 624*e*
20:25 532*t*
20:26 741*j*
20:27 917*a*
20:29 162*e* 429*a*
20:30 655*g*
21:1 689*e*
21:2 480*d* 624*d*
21:3 981*ar*
21:4 871*b* 914*a*
21:5 857*a*
21:9 709*e*
21:11 963*h*
21:13 458*a* 460*j*
21:14 612*g*
21:17 801*f* 837*a*
21:18 792*k*
21:19 709*e*
21:22 727*c*
21:23 582*a*
21:24 871*b*
21:25 679*i*
21:26 813*b*
21:27 981*ao*
21:28 466*t*
21:30 498*j*
21:31 727*a*

22:1 797*r* 866*ae*
22:2 164*m*
22:3 523*j*
22:4 800*e* 962*b*
22:5 256*l*
22:6 534*o*
22:7 785*a* 800*m*
22:8 370*v*
22:9 813*c*
22:11 880*e*
22:13 679*h*
22:14 255*c* 579*j* 951*j*
22:15 499*a* 827*h*
22:16 801*k*
22:17 455*o*
22:19 485*d*
22:21 460*g*
22:22 801*k*
22:23 713*a*
22:24 620*s* 892*a*
22:26 767*c*
22:28 547*t*
22:29 696*a*
23:1 882*a*
23:3 859*h*
23:4 800*k*
23:5 114*m* 800*o*
23:6 816*b*
23:8 302*q*
23:9 415*c*
23:10 547*t*
23:11 713*a*
23:13 827*h* 964*a*
23:17 854*a* 912*b*
23:18 124*i*
23:20 947*b* 948*d*
23:21 801*f*
23:22 455*r*
23:23 494*a* 792*u*
23:24 500*a*
23:27 255*c* 951*s*
23:29 949*a*
23:34 152*a*
24:1 912*b*
24:3 164*o*
24:5 162*e* 500*a*
24:6 691*a* 718*a*
24:11 668*s*
24:12 491*a* 676*f*
24:13 392*g*
24:14 498*c*
24:15 527*e*
24:16 309*a*
24:17 824*m*
24:19 912*b*
24:20 420*m*
24:21 854*a*

24:23 481*e*
24:24 960*b*
24:26 460*g* 889*c*
24:27 669*g*
24:28 466*t* 542*n*
24:29 804*m*
24:30 679*i*
24:31 235*n*
24:33 679*g*
24:34 801*f*
25:1 496*b*
25:2 525*a*
25:4 641*g*
25:6 866*ac*
25:7 310*a*
25:11 579*h*
25:12 844*m*
25:13 382*a* 529*o*
25:14 877*b*
25:15 177*g* 612*d*
25:16 302*q* 392*e*
25:18 466*t*
25:19 485*ag*
25:20 393*b* 834*a*
25:21 301*n* 705*k* 859*i*
     859*l*
25:24 709*e*
25:25 529*i*
25:27 392*e* 866*y*
25:28 943*a*
26:1 501*c* 866*w* 916*e*
26:2 899*a* 916*h*
26:3 964*a*
26:4 460*g*
26:7 496*a*
26:8 866*w*
26:9 496*a*
26:11 302*q*
26:12 498*s*
26:13 679*h*
26:14 315*f* 679*h*
26:15 679*h*
26:17 231*a*
26:18 839*a*
26:20 385*e* 418*q*
26:21 385*e*
26:24 888*a*
26:27 280*b*
26:28 925*a*
27:1 124*b* 491*y* 877*e*
27:2 923*u*
27:3 322*l*
27:4 911*a*
27:5 525*i*
27:6 655*g* 889*d*
27:7 391*a* 392*e* 635*j*
27:8 282*a*

27:10 200*h* 621*r*
27:12 523*j*
27:13 767*c*
27:14 128*h* 897*u*
27:15 709*e*
27:17 256*b*
27:18 370*q* 457*k*
27:20 859*v*
27:21 383*a* 461*e* 461*h*
27:22 279*g*
27:23 455*s*
27:24 114*m* 800*o*
28:1 620*b* 855*b*
28:2 104*u*
28:3 801*k*
28:5 516*e*
28:6 801*q*
28:7 947*b*
28:8 800*k* 803*h*
28:9 761*af*
28:10 280*b*
28:11 498*s*
28:13 525*o* 526*q*
28:15 365*z* 365*ai*
28:17 335*b* 620*m*
28:19 370*e*
28:20 800*k*
28:21 481*e*
28:22 816*a*
28:23 924*j* 925*b*
28:24 788*d*
28:25 485*j* 709*d*
28:26 485*af*
28:27 635*f* 781*u*
28:28 523*j*
29:1 602*g*
29:2 733*ai* 824*m*
29:3 500*a* 634*a* 951*u*
29:4 153*p*
29:5 925*a*
29:6 542*r*
29:7 801*j*
29:8 891*u*
29:11 892*a*
29:13 417*i*
29:14 153*p*
29:15 964*a*
29:17 827*h*
29:18 438*ac*
29:20 579*g* 857*a*
29:21 736*a*
29:22 892*a*
29:23 871*j* 872*a*
29:24 532*r*
29:25 371*q* 485*j*
    854*ac*
30:4 308*g* 561*h*

30:5	473b 662j	**2:1**	641a 837a	**4:13**	498c 691n	**9:1**	733a
30:6	38a	**2:2**	835a 837a	**4:15**	210b	**9:2**	16a
30:8	301w 542m	**2:3**	210c 949c	**4:16**	352i 641a	**9:4**	360d
	801b	**2:4**	164t 370n	**5:1**	415e 981ao	**9:5**	361i 491b
30:9	13b 788d	**2:5**	370c	**5:2**	582b 857a 971a	**9:6**	210b
30:10	742m	**2:6**	341c	**5:3**	581b	**9:8**	357r 427b
30:12	950d	**2:7**	742o	**5:4**	532s	**9:9**	210b 887aa
30:15	365l 781a 859v	**2:8**	797o 952c	**5:5**	532s	**9:10**	361i 571a
30:17	169n 851a	**2:10**	837a 859z	**5:7**	854a	**9:11**	159a 277i
30:18	517a	**2:11**	210b 352i 641a	**5:10**	641a 797m	**9:12**	110f
30:20	935f 951j	**2:12**	498a 503a		887ah	**9:13**	210b
30:21	827k	**2:13**	498a	**5:12**	678a 679a	**9:14**	712a
30:24	196b	**2:14**	418m 501c	**5:15**	229f 361f	**9:15**	506h 668v
30:25	365i	**2:15**	16a 641a	**5:16**	352i	**9:16**	498c
30:26	192aj	**2:16**	361f 506a	**5:18**	301i	**9:18**	498c 723f
30:27	722g 734b	**2:17**	210b 352i 641a	**5:19**	800b	**10:1**	397a 499a
30:29	267f		888h	**6:1**	210b	**10:4**	891u
30:32	582a 866ac	**2:18**	780a 888h	**6:2**	641a 800b	**10:5**	210b
30:33	279g	**2:19**	641a	**6:3**	361i 364o	**10:7**	742o
31:4	949b	**2:20**	853a	**6:6**	361f	**10:8**	280b
31:6	949c	**2:21**	641a 780a	**6:7**	859h	**10:10**	256a 257a
31:7	506k	**2:23**	641a 678a	**6:8**	34h	**10:11**	136h
31:9	713a	**2:24**	301i	**6:9**	352i 641a	**10:14**	511c 581b
31:10	809a 894m	**2:26**	352i 641a	**6:11**	581b 641a	**10:16**	733ak 949g
31:11	485ah	**3:1**	210c	**6:12**	210b	**10:18**	679j
31:12	644d	**3:2**	167c 361f	**7:1**	357a 361q	**10:19**	797a 949c
31:15	128c 301l	**3:3**	362c 656r		866ae	**10:20**	525m 526a
31:16	792a	**3:4**	835a 835c 836a	**7:2**	361f 836a		899a
31:18	420l	**3:5**	344e 889g	**7:3**	825a	**11:1**	287o 339z
31:21	382a 431d	**3:6**	110f 459r 607m	**7:4**	836a	**11:3**	350aa
31:22	436c		778a	**7:5**	924j	**11:4**	75k 370s
31:23	263n	**3:7**	46s 47d 579a	**7:6**	256k 400a 641a	**11:5**	164c 491y
31:24	793a		582a		835a	**11:6**	75k
31:25	228af	**3:8**	717a 718a 887a	**7:7**	612h	**11:7**	417a
31:26	500a		888a	**7:8**	69a 823b	**11:8**	113b 641a
31:27	678h	**3:9**	771h	**7:9**	891u	**11:9**	130i 959a
31:28	897u 923s	**3:11**	115a 484c 841a	**7:10**	125g	**12:1**	130h 164j 505f
31:30	841g 854h	**3:13**	301i	**7:12**	660e 797a	**12:2**	321o 355a
		3:14	38b 39a 115h	**7:13**	246d	**12:3**	332g 457i
Ecclesiastes		**3:15**	126i	**7:16**	913p	**12:4**	332g
1:1	528a	**3:17**	959a	**7:17**	914q	**12:5**	427c 836o 854r
1:2	641a	**3:18**	365b	**7:19**	498c	**12:6**	208a
1:3	210b 771h	**3:19**	361c 641a	**7:20**	914j	**12:7**	332d 361c
1:4	144b	**3:20**	332d	**7:21**	899l	**12:8**	641a
1:5	321c	**3:21**	365b	**7:23**	461j	**12:9**	496b
1:6	352l	**3:22**	824k	**7:26**	391e 542t	**12:11**	256h 369m
1:7	350e	**4:1**	210b 735c 831i	**7:29**	623d 929f	**12:12**	589m
1:8	829f	**4:2**	2b	**8:1**	417q	**12:13**	854a
1:9	126i² 210b	**4:4**	352i 641a 912a	**8:4**	733ae	**12:14**	480d
1:11	506a	**4:5**	679j	**8:8**	320b 361h		
1:12	528a	**4:6**	352i	**8:10**	364c 641a	**Song of Solomon**	
1:13	210c 459r	**4:7**	210b 641a	**8:11**	136a	**1:1**	412f
1:14	352i 641a	**4:8**	641a 682a	**8:12**	113b 854i	**1:2**	887aa 889a
1:15	190i 246a	**4:9**	90a	**8:13**	114f		949e
1:17	352i 498a 503a	**4:10**	310a	**8:14**	641a 916f	**1:3**	396a
	641a	**4:11**	381an	**8:15**	301i	**1:4**	887aa 949e
1:18	498a	**4:12**	94d	**8:17**	484c	**1:5**	428a

1:6 428a 458b	**5:10** 431a 841k	**1:16** 648ad 913j	**5:2** 172r
1:8 841i	**5:11** 213d 259c 428b	**1:17** 779c 896j	**5:4** 172r
1:9 365bi	**5:12** 438i	**1:18** 427f 431g 914n	**5:5** 235r
1:10 844c	**5:13** 239a 263t	**1:20** 738j	**5:6** 256l 342c
1:11 844a	**5:14** 53h 319g	**1:21** 951x	**5:7** 371ad 913e
1:12 396j	**5:15** 53m	**1:22** 641g	924n
1:13 396l	**5:16** 841k	**1:23** 612g 779g 896l	**5:8** 771e
1:14 396l	**6:1** 187b	**1:24** 910a	**5:10** 172p
1:15 841h	**6:2** 370d	**1:25** 654a	**5:11** 128d 136i 949b
1:17 218l	**6:3** 773g	**1:26** 913y	**5:12** 456e
2:1 366e	**6:4** 722g 841h	**1:27** 913y	**5:13** 188e 491c 636d
2:3 366x	**6:5** 259c	**1:28** 607i	859l
2:4 547ab 882f	**6:6** 90c 256o	**1:29** 366s 872p	**5:14** 361b
2:5 887aa	**6:7** 239a	**1:30** 342f 366y	**5:15** 872g
2:6 889g	**6:8** 952c	**1:31** 385e	**5:16** 866g
2:7 821a 887ac	**6:9** 21g 890a	**2:2** 124h 209l	**5:18** 288c
2:9 365x	**6:10** 722g	990aa	**5:19** 680b
2:10 308i	**6:11** 171e 370r	**2:3** 308c 534c 624b	**5:20** 464a 913p 914b
2:11 128m 129q	**6:13** 438o	953a	**5:21** 498s
2:13 171e 308i	**7:1** 53m	**2:4** 480e 719a 719f	**5:22** 949b
2:14 577a	**7:2** 224e 225a	723s	**5:23** 612h 914v
2:15 165aa 171e	**7:3** 90c 253b	**2:5** 417j	**5:24** 953x
365t	**7:4** 206b 237e 438i	**2:6** 621b 983e	**5:25** 363e 891j^2
2:16 773g	**7:5** 213d 259c 436a	**2:7** 274c 800i	**5:26** 371aa 547z
2:17 365x 380d	**7:6** 841h	**2:8** 982n	547ac
3:1 459af	**7:7** 253b 366n	**2:9** 909j	**5:27** 60e 678b
3:3 457i	**7:8** 253b	**2:10** 523e	**5:30** 418k
3:4 786n	**7:9** 949e	**2:11** 866g 872f	**6:1** 361af 438d
3:5 821a 887ac	**7:10** 773g 859n	**2:12** 871i	733a
3:6 396l	**7:12** 171e 887aa	**2:13** 366s	**6:2** 99b 226g 271c
3:7 218w 722c	**7:13** 366i	**2:16** 275h	968w
3:9 218w	**8:1** 889a	**2:17** 866g 872f	**6:3** 979a
3:10 436a	**8:2** 949e	**2:18** 982d	**6:4** 388g
3:11 438o	**8:4** 821a 887ac	**2:19** 255h 854j	**6:5** 438d 649i
4:1 259c 438i 841h	**8:6** 887a 911a	**2:20** 982r	**6:6** 381k
4:2 90c 256o	**8:7** 887a	**2:21** 255h 854j	**6:7** 941k
4:3 239a 431b	**8:8** 253c	**2:22** 371e	**6:8** 751i
4:4 206b 209al 662i	**8:9** 235f 264b	**3:1** 636d	**6:9** 517c
4:5 90c 253b	**8:10** 235f 253b	**3:4** 733ak	**6:11** 136a
4:6 380d 396l	**8:11** 370n 784g	**3:6** 733ak	**6:13** 41k 102g
4:7 646e 841h	809m	**3:10** 937a	**7:1** 716f
4:8 89o 365ab	**8:14** 365x	**3:11** 938h	**7:3** 351a
365aj		**3:12** 495c 733ak	**7:4** 854ah
4:9 821a	**Isaiah**	**3:13** 480f	**7:9** 486e
4:10 887aa 949e	**1:1** 438aa	**3:15** 801k	**7:11** 547f
4:11 263t 392c 396k	**1:2** 534n 738g	**3:16** 871h	**7:12** 461f
4:12 370d	**1:3** 490x 491c	**3:18** 844f	**7:14** 89d 167k 895c
4:13 370r 396l	**1:4** 621i	**3:22** 228m	**7:15** 301ah
4:15 339p	**1:5** 651a	**3:24** 51d 228l	**7:18** 547z
4:16 352k 370d 396j	**1:6** 658e	**4:1** 561q 872ab	**7:20** 371aa 648j
5:1 301i 370d	**1:7** 165e 381e	**4:2** 53v 841m	**7:22** 301ah
5:2 263af 341f 679a	**1:8** 192z	**4:3** 41p 548e 979f	**7:23** 172q 256l
5:3 229p 648e	**1:9** 18l 41o 184aw	**4:4** 648aa	**8:1** 277i 558a 790g
5:5 263z 396l	**1:11** 637a 981an	**4:5** 355e 381q	**8:2** 466d
5:6 190h 459af	**1:12** 279s	**4:6** 662e	**8:3** 167g 277i 790g
5:7 279d 457i	**1:13** 641e 888b	**5:1** 366k 370p 412f	**8:7** 350c
5:8 887aa	**1:15** 761ae	519e	**8:10** 89d

8:12	623f 854ah	**11:15**	342h	**16:6**	871f	**22:1**	213k 438ad
8:13	854a 979a	**11:16**	41p 624i	**16:8**	366k	**22:3**	620f
8:14	344x 542r 662h	**12:1**	831a 907d	**16:10**	145b	**22:4**	831j
8:17	523b	**12:2**	485f 668b 855h	**16:12**	761ag	**22:7**	712g
8:18	170x 864f	**12:3**	339p	**16:14**	110v 114r 867e	**22:9**	263ac 346b
8:19	459f 984b	**12:4**	490o 526k 907a	**17:1**	165o 184bd	**22:10**	86f
8:20	953c	**12:5**	490o		371x 438ad	**22:11**	346b 486d 623a
8:21	859i 899i	**13:1**	184az 371x	**17:2**	184aa	**22:12**	836k
8:22	418o	**13:2**	547ac	**17:4**	196c 867e	**22:13**	301i
9:1	59p 184t	**13:4**	722a	**17:6**	41o	**22:14**	909h
9:2	417m 418n	**13:5**	199a	**17:7**	164j	**22:15**	686d
9:3	104e 790b 824v	**13:6**	108ae 854j	**17:8**	967j	**22:16**	364h
9:4	322m 746a	**13:8**	167o	**17:10**	506e 966h	**22:17**	287n
9:5	385g	**13:9**	108ae	**17:12**	350k 403c	**22:19**	752a
9:6	169q 170n 561k	**13:10**	321o	**17:13**	323d	**22:21**	228z
	691d 717a	**13:11**	872f	**18:1**	371x	**22:22**	263v^2 264l
	733w 965c	**13:12**	636j	**18:2**	195f 275j	**22:23**	153k
9:7	717i 733w 818b	**13:13**	321s	**18:3**	547ad	**22:24**	217g
9:10	164t 631c	**13:16**	362ab 951aa	**18:4**	441g	**23:1**	184bc 275h
9:11	705g	**13:18**	906c	**18:7**	195f 209m 781o		371x 438ad
9:12	891j	**13:19**	184ax 184az	**19:1**	267o 371x		836ah
9:13	459ab	**13:20**	190k		438ad 982d	**23:2**	222h
9:15	579aj	**13:21**	192aj 365e	**19:2**	718g	**23:5**	836ah
9:16	495c	**14:1**	59o 605h	**19:3**	984a	**23:9**	623a
9:17	891j	**14:2**	745g	**19:5**	342d	**23:11**	343f
9:18	381b	**14:4**	145c 741u	**19:6**	397a	**23:14**	275h 836ah
9:20	636d	**14:7**	717i	**19:8**	836ah	**23:15**	110ae 412f
9:21	891j	**14:9**	361j 970a	**19:9**	222k	**23:17**	110ae 951y
10:1	953z	**14:11**	51e	**19:11**	501f 691n	**24:1**	165r
10:4	891j	**14:12**	309f	**19:12**	500e	**24:2**	18e
10:5	371aa 723b	**14:13**	308g	**19:13**	495c	**24:5**	649c 954c
	891k 964b	**14:14**	18c	**19:14**	152a 302q	**24:6**	105c 899b
10:7	617c	**14:15**	311r	**19:16**	373k	**24:8**	824ab
10:10	982k	**14:16**	13m	**19:17**	854x	**24:9**	949a
10:12	871i 963b	**14:18**	364h	**19:18**	557d	**24:10**	264e
10:13	498s	**14:19**	364p	**19:19**	990f	**24:12**	264c
10:15	630d	**14:21**	169x	**19:20**	761q	**24:13**	41f
10:16	651f	**14:22**	184az	**19:21**	490p 526d	**24:18**	214a 620c
10:17	381o	**14:24**	371x	**19:22**	279h 656r	**24:19**	176i
10:19	105f	**14:25**	322m	**19:23**	624i	**24:20**	152a
10:20	41p 485g	**14:27**	623a	**19:24**	897j	**24:21**	963a
10:21	41o	**14:28**	361af	**19:25**	777f	**24:23**	184am 209m
10:25	891n	**14:29**	371x	**20:2**	228l 229k		321q 733a
10:27	322m	**14:30**	636d	**20:3**	110v	**25:1**	623a 965e
10:33	46ab 311r 366y	**14:31**	60e	**20:4**	229c	**25:2**	165b
11:1	41k 53v 366y	**14:32**	153g 460i	**21:1**	352k 438ad^2	**25:4**	418f 662b
11:2	498h 965l	**15:1**	165o 371x	**21:3**	167o	**25:6**	876e
11:3	480i 854i		438ad	**21:5**	357n	**25:7**	226k 421f
11:4	362bc	**15:2**	209ad 229u	**21:6**	457g	**25:8**	165n 361aw
11:5	228ab		836j	**21:8**	457h		831b
11:6	365f	**15:3**	228l	**21:9**	165p 982r	**25:9**	507c 965e
11:7	301al	**15:5**	620d	**21:10**	370aa	**25:10**	279q 302i
11:9	54d 490p 645i	**15:9**	41r	**21:11**	371x 457h	**25:11**	269d 872f
11:10	547ac	**16:1**	781x	**21:13**	438ad	**26:1**	184z 412f
11:11	41o 74b 656aj	**16:2**	222f 365ak	**21:14**	301s	**26:2**	263j
11:12	547ac	**16:3**	525e	**21:15**	620e	**26:3**	485j 717e
11:13	911l	**16:5**	733w	**21:16**	114r	**26:4**	344w 485d

26:5	872f	29:9	949p	32:15	171i 965s	36:15	485i
26:6	279q	29:10	579y 679b	32:16	913y	36:16	370o 719g
26:7	348b	29:11	264p 589a	32:17	717e 913aa	36:17	188a
26:8	507b 859a	29:12	579m	32:20	75k	36:18	966i
26:9	859a	29:13	515a 579f	33:1	168b	36:21	582g
26:10	897o	29:14	498q	33:2	507b	36:22	836g
26:12	676d	29:15	525n	33:5	866g 913y	37:1	836g 836j
26:13	733ai	29:16	164l	33:6	153g 854d	37:2	579z
26:15	104e 197a	29:17	171i	33:8	267c	37:3	167v 827b
26:16	459w	29:18	416c 589a	33:10	308a 866g	37:4	41o 455i
26:17	167o	29:19	824g	33:11	167w	37:6	854ah
26:18	167v 352i	29:21	914v	33:13	199m 200c	37:7	529n
26:19	656c	29:22	872v	33:14	381q	37:10	542b
26:20	523e	29:23	979c	33:15	456h 612j	37:12	966i
26:21	963a	30:1	623d 738i	33:17	741a 841m	37:14	588a
27:1	365au 365bu	30:2	662f	33:18	86f	37:15	761p
	963b	30:3	872p	33:19	557c	37:16	21c 164a
27:2	370p	30:5	771j	33:20	184aj 988a	37:17	455a
27:3	341b	30:6	438ad 771j	33:21	275i 350h	37:19	966j
27:5	719a	30:7	641c	33:22	741a 957a	37:20	21c
27:6	153o 171n	30:8	586c	33:23	275f	37:22	922h
27:8	188e	30:9	738g	33:24	650a 909b	37:23	921a 979a
27:9	332f 941k 990g	30:10	438ac 579v	34:1	200e	37:24	46aa
27:10	190l	30:11	282b	34:2	891b	37:25	342i
27:11	906b	30:13	235e	34:3	397a	37:26	125b 623a
27:12	74c 350p 370aa	30:15	485f 683n	34:4	321s	37:27	366f
27:13	209l 414n	30:16	277i 619i	34:6	357af	37:29	748b
28:1	743g 949g	30:17	547ac 619f	34:8	910b	37:30	370f 370j 547c
28:2	350ah	30:18	507c 905d 913a	34:9	381v 385h 631m	37:31	153o 171n
28:3	279q 743g 949g	30:19	836aj	34:10	388e 963e	37:32	41o 818b
28:5	743i 841m	30:20	301bc	34:11	192aj 365e	37:35	713a
28:7	152a 949g	30:21	282h 415e 624f	34:13	192aj 365e	37:36	362bi
28:8	302q	30:22	982r	34:16	589l	37:38	362x 741u
28:9	534b 611b	30:23	171g 350ab	34:17	783a	38:1	361n 651h
28:10	278a	30:24	301aj 370z 388c	35:1	171i 172aa	38:2	761s
28:11	557b	30:25	350g	35:2	866i	38:5	38d
28:12	456f 683m	30:26	99i 420b 656r	35:4	162l 854ai	38:6	713a
28:13	278a 747h	30:28	648ae		910a	38:7	547c
28:15	541d 765r	30:29	344w 412f	35:5	416c 439p	38:8	418d
28:16	214e 344x 485j	30:30	381u	35:6	312b 339m	38:9	586c
28:17	215a 350ag	30:31	854j 964b		578b 655q	38:10	114d
	465f 913i	30:33	364c 385h	35:8	624i 979x	38:12	114d 222m
28:18	752h 765r	31:1	485ag	35:9	365ab	38:13	46h
28:20	196h	31:3	319a 371q	35:10	115k 148o	38:16	656v
28:21	209u 255j	31:4	365ab		184am 792o	38:17	909g
28:24	370g	31:5	365ak 660a		824v	38:18	361i
28:25	75k	31:6	148a	36:1	712e	38:21	658d
28:26	534b	31:7	982r	36:2	351a	38:22	547c
28:27	370z	31:8	362bi	36:3	549a 586u	39:1	588a
28:28	370z	31:9	383c	36:4	485a	39:2	526v
28:29	498f	32:1	733w	36:6	218e	39:3	199a
29:1	712g	32:2	350i 418f 662e	36:7	485e 990g	39:6	786i
29:2	836ac	32:3	516h	36:8	267l	39:7	786b
29:3	184af	32:9	373j	36:11	557e	39:8	717i
29:4	970a	32:10	172p	36:12	301ar 302h	40:1	831a
29:5	323d	32:11	229c		302k	40:2	91d 717i
29:8	438y^2 859h	32:14	190l 192aj 365e	36:14	495c	40:3	172y 624i 669a

52:8	457h	**56:12**	949g	**60:17**	631j	**65:2**	738g
52:9	831a	**57:1**	937c	**60:18**	176e 668q	**65:4**	301ap 364i
52:10	229t 371z	**57:5**	859o	**60:19**	417b 420c	**65:5**	200k 979h
52:11	194j 296b	**57:10**	684b	**60:20**	115b	**65:6**	804l
52:12	283a 680d	**57:11**	506e	**61:1**	357u 528e 746a	**65:7**	169x
52:13	742k	**57:13**	184f 323e 662a		825i 965l	**65:10**	459x
52:14	647b 864k		771c	**61:2**	108ac 831c	**65:11**	596b 607g
52:15	516b 578e	**57:14**	624i 702c		836aj	**65:12**	460d
53:1	485ad 486d	**57:15**	192e 872d 979c	**61:3**	366s	**65:13**	636f
53:2	342b	**57:16**	891p	**61:4**	164s 656ad	**65:15**	561v 561aa
53:3	523k 607k 825j	**57:19**	199m 200e	**61:5**	59o	**65:16**	532b
53:4	273i 651b 825j		719b	**61:6**	800j 986x	**65:17**	126e 321t
53:5	655h 656t 914m	**57:20**	343e	**61:7**	91a 115k	**65:18**	184am 824r
53:6	282e 365bp	**57:21**	717j	**61:8**	765i 788d 913e	**65:19**	824d 836aj
	914m	**58:1**	914af	**61:10**	228ad 844c	**65:20**	114b 131a
53:7	362bl 365br	**58:2**	200f 459v 826j		913m	**65:23**	641c
	582e	**58:3**	946b 946j	**61:11**	913g	**65:24**	460c
53:9	364k 542d	**58:4**	946b	**62:1**	582d	**65:25**	365f 645i
53:10	170t 826a 981af	**58:5**	946a	**62:2**	561v	**66:1**	218ac 971a
53:11	273i 914m 927b	**58:6**	746e	**62:3**	743j		990aa
53:12	273i 361ai 761i	**58:7**	228w 301n 801i	**62:4**	607f 826e	**66:2**	854n 872d
	790b 914m	**58:8**	417r		894ac	**66:3**	981an
	954b	**58:9**	460c	**62:5**	824d	**66:4**	460d 963a
54:1	104k 171c 824t	**58:10**	417r	**62:6**	457g 505b 683t	**66:5**	300u 854n
54:2	197a	**58:11**	341d 370d 689d	**62:7**	184al	**66:7**	167r
54:3	184ac	**58:12**	656ad	**62:8**	532o	**66:10**	824r
54:4	854ai	**58:13**	683d	**62:10**	547ac 624i	**66:11**	301q 635d
54:5	894ac	**58:14**	826j	**62:11**	962a	**66:12**	719b
54:7	114p 607c	**59:1**	161b 196a 456a	**62:12**	607f 792o 979f	**66:13**	831b
54:8	523b	**59:2**	46ad 523b 914s	**63:1**	891d	**66:15**	274f 381p
54:9	350a 891p	**59:3**	541e	**63:2**	370l 431d	**66:16**	362bc
54:10	209i 768c	**59:4**	167w	**63:3**	88k	**66:17**	301ap 365n
54:11	827f 831i 844a	**59:5**	167w 222m	**63:4**	910b		979h
54:13	534b	**59:7**	362b 914k	**63:5**	88k	**66:18**	449c 490i
54:17	723r 927a	**59:8**	491j 717j	**63:8**	371ac	**66:19**	528e
55:1	339n 792u 812a	**59:9**	418j	**63:9**	825b 968i	**66:22**	126e 153d
	859d	**59:10**	439d	**63:10**	705a 716b		153m 321t
55:3	115k 455q 765i	**59:15**	455i 494b 914e		738g 827m	**66:23**	311e
55:4	466b	**59:16**	190j	**63:11**	505c 965s	**66:24**	51e 381ad 963e
55:5	491r 866aa	**59:17**	228ab^2 662k	**63:12**	46l		
55:6	200c 459s		723f 910a	**63:14**	683n	**Jeremiah**	
55:7	148a 449e 621o		913m	**63:15**	441i	**1:1**	986d
	624d 909a	**59:18**	804j	**63:16**	169s	**1:2**	529f
55:8	371e 449a 624a	**59:19**	350h 854g	**63:17**	282b 602h	**1:3**	188d
55:9	209a 624a	**59:21**	579q 765m	**63:18**	114o	**1:5**	130b 490m 579s
55:10	171f 301u 341a		965aa	**63:19**	734c		979i
	350ae	**60:1**	417p	**64:1**	209i 309e	**1:6**	132g 695a
55:11	529b	**60:2**	418k	**64:2**	381q	**1:8**	89h 854af
55:12	209h 366m 824i	**60:3**	417p 741w	**64:4**	21c 415b	**1:9**	378h 579q
55:13	366m	**60:4**	170x	**64:6**	228ad 649i 913t	**1:10**	751a
56:1	913j	**60:5**	635g 800j	**64:7**	190j 523b	**1:11**	366n 438ab
56:2	683d	**60:6**	396n 797h	**64:8**	164l 169s	**1:12**	455j 457b
56:3	59m 172h	**60:9**	275c	**64:9**	371ac	**1:13**	194o 281f
56:6	59m	**60:10**	59o	**64:10**	184af		438ab
56:7	761a	**60:11**	263j 800j	**64:11**	381g 990v	**1:15**	712g
56:8	74c	**60:14**	184am 311b	**64:12**	582c	**1:16**	607g 966h
56:9	301ak	**60:16**	301q	**65:1**	459ab	**1:17**	669h 834d

1:18	184y 218s 235f	**4:16**	712g	**7:9**	362b 466u 788d	**10:2**	854ah
1:19	89h 716h	**4:19**	414i 718f		951i	**10:3**	982c 982d
2:2	130h 894ad	**4:21**	414i 547ad	**7:11**	789d 990y	**10:5**	161j 273d 578c
2:3	171m 979f	**4:22**	499d 696d	**7:12**	561g	**10:6**	21b
2:5	199m 641k	**4:23**	244a	**7:13**	128b	**10:7**	21b 854b
	914d	**4:25**	190l	**7:14**	990u	**10:8**	499d 982c
2:6	187c 304a	**4:27**	165e	**7:15**	300n	**10:9**	436c 696a
2:7	171f	**4:28**	599a	**7:16**	761x	**10:10**	965b
2:8	187c 579an	**4:29**	190l 344p 620f	**7:18**	967h	**10:11**	966b
2:9	716b	**4:30**	431d 843a²	**7:21**	981an	**10:12**	164e
2:11	150e		844c	**7:22**	304a	**10:13**	176k
2:13	339f 339o 621i	**4:31**	167o	**7:23**	371ac 739a	**10:14**	499d
2:14	742p	**5:1**	909d 929j	**7:25**	128b 579r	**10:16**	164c 777f
2:15	165e	**5:2**	532e	**7:26**	456e	**10:18**	300l
2:17	607g	**5:4**	491h 801c	**7:29**	259i 607a	**10:19**	655f
2:19	391e 607i	**5:6**	365v 365ab	**7:31**	209ae 381ak	**10:21**	459ab
2:20	746d 951x		365aj		981ah	**10:22**	281g
2:21	366k	**5:7**	607g 951i 951u	**7:32**	255k 364q	**10:23**	624e
2:22	648c	**5:8**	859o	**7:33**	301ak 363m	**10:24**	924c
2:24	859o	**5:10**	774e	**7:34**	145c	**11:3**	769c 899e
2:25	229j	**5:12**	545a	**8:1**	363h	**11:4**	304a 383c
2:26	872s	**5:14**	381z 385e 579q	**8:2**	302i 321j 364o	**11:5**	488c 635d
2:27	169v	**5:15**	557b 712f	**8:3**	361s	**11:7**	128b 304a 664a
2:28	104u 190a 966a	**5:19**	607g 966h	**8:5**	603f	**11:8**	602c
2:32	506e 844e	**5:21**	416b 439d	**8:7**	110f 491h	**11:10**	769a
2:35	935f	**5:22**	236f 854a	**8:8**	498q 541c	**11:12**	966i
3:1	896c 951y	**5:23**	602c	**8:9**	498l 500b 607h	**11:13**	104u 966a
3:3	342c 872z	**5:24**	350z	**8:10**	771j		967b 990f
3:4	169s 880b	**5:26**	542v	**8:11**	656ac 717k	**11:14**	761x
3:5	891p	**5:28**	801m	**8:12**	872z	**11:16**	366x
3:6	951x	**5:31**	579aj 986s	**8:13**	172p	**11:17**	967b
3:8	548d 896f 951x	**6:1**	281f² 414i 620o	**8:14**	659c	**11:19**	362m 365bq
3:9	951l	**6:4**	712g	**8:17**	365o		561aa 623i
3:12	148a 281a	**6:6**	46ab	**8:19**	190a	**11:20**	480h 910d
3:13	526p	**6:9**	41r	**8:20**	128n	**11:21**	362m 579v
3:14	148a 894ad	**6:10**	456d	**8:22**	656ac 658b	**11:23**	41r
3:15	301y 369g 490a	**6:11**	684a		658f	**12:1**	730d 913b 938j
3:16	194f	**6:13**	771j	**9:1**	836s	**12:2**	199m 515a
3:17	184am 743a	**6:14**	656ac 717k	**9:2**	951l	**12:3**	365bq 490i
3:18	184k 281i	**6:15**	872z	**9:3**	287h 491e 541e	**12:5**	277e 684a
3:19	169s	**6:16**	127a 624f 683n	**9:4**	486o	**12:7**	621b
3:20	930a 951l	**6:17**	414h 457g	**9:5**	541e	**12:8**	365ai
3:21	506e	**6:20**	981ao	**9:7**	461a 654a	**12:10**	369i
3:22	148a	**6:21**	702j	**9:8**	542g	**12:13**	370x
3:23	209ag	**6:22**	281g	**9:11**	165b 190k	**12:15**	656aj
3:25	130g	**6:23**	906c	**9:12**	500a	**12:16**	532b 532e
4:1	148a	**6:24**	167o	**9:13**	607h 954c	**13:1**	228e
4:3	75k	**6:26**	836ae	**9:15**	301ar 391b	**13:4**	525h
4:4	988q	**6:27**	461i		659c	**13:7**	641f
4:5	414h	**6:29**	654a	**9:16**	75c	**13:9**	165b 871i
4:6	547ac	**6:30**	607a 641g	**9:17**	836ag	**13:11**	866b
4:7	168a 190k	**7:2**	263o	**9:22**	302i 363e	**13:12**	949d
	365ab	**7:3**	939a	**9:23**	160j 498s 800l	**13:13**	949p
4:8	836k	**7:4**	485aj 990y		877d 877g	**13:14**	906b
4:10	542b	**7:5**	939a	**9:24**	490q	**13:16**	418j
4:11	352k	**7:7**	184a	**9:25**	988q	**13:17**	747i
4:14	648ad	**7:8**	485aj	**9:26**	259j 974a 974c	**13:19**	188d

44:17 967*h*	**49:14** 716*g*	**51:13** 69*h*	**1:10** 59*f* 990*v*
44:25 967*h*	**49:15** 196*e*	**51:14** 532*o*	**1:12** 21*k* 825*d*
44:26 561*i*	**49:16** 209*c* 311*r* 542*i*	**51:15** 164*b*	**1:13** 542*r*
44:29 547*d*	**49:18** 184*ax* 190*k*	**51:16** 176*k* 352*f*	**1:15** 370*l*
44:30 728*h*	**49:19** 21*a*	**51:17** 499*d* 982*d*	**1:16** 831*i*
45:1 586*c* 589*i*	**49:20** 623*b*	**51:19** 164*c*	**1:17** 649*b* 831*i*
45:3 825*d*	**49:22** 365*at*	**51:20** 165*a* 723*b*	**1:18** 913*a*
45:4 165*a*	**49:23** 371*x*	**51:25** 209*h*	**1:21** 831*i*
45:5 638*d* 790*c*	**49:24** 167*o*	**51:27** 547*ac*	**2:1** 218*ac* 558*b*
46:2 371*x* 727*f*	**49:27** 381*e*	**51:29** 190*k*	891*d*
46:5 854*r*	**49:28** 371*x*	**51:44** 967*n*	**2:3** 381*o*
46:6 350*p*	**49:29** 854*r*	**51:45** 298*f*	**2:4** 287*l* 705*a*
46:7 350*r*	**49:30** 620*n*	**51:48** 824*m*	**2:5** 705*a*
46:8 350*c*	**49:31** 264*h* 683*s*	**51:50** 505*f*	**2:7** 607*b*
46:10 281*h* 350*p*	**49:32** 790*h*	**51:51** 59*f*	**2:9** 438*ac* 953*x*
46:11 658*c* 658*f*	**49:33** 190*k*	**51:56** 910*a*	**2:10** 311*y*
46:19 188*g* 669*g*	**49:34** 371*x*	**51:57** 949*p*	**2:13** 21*k*
46:20 281*f* 365*i*	**49:36** 75*a* 352*l*	**51:60** 589*i*	**2:15** 824*s* 841*c*
365*ba*	**49:38** 743*a*	**51:61** 579*k*	**2:19** 310*i* 636*b*
46:23 46*aa* 104*r*	**49:39** 656*ah*	**51:63** 344*t* 350*p*	**2:20** 301*at* 362*am*
46:24 281*g*	**50:1** 371*x*	**51:64** 69*j* 322*j*	**2:21** 362*bg*
46:26 728*h*	**50:2** 547*ac* 967*n*	**52:1** 110*z* 131*i*	**2:22** 854*r*
46:27 854*ai*	**50:3** 281*h*	**52:2** 914*w*	**3:1** 558*b*
46:28 89*d* 854*ai*	**50:4** 459*x* 836*w*	**52:3** 300*n*	**3:2** 418*j*
47:1 371*x*	**50:5** 115*k* 624*i* 765*l*	**52:4** 108*n* 712*g*	**3:4** 46*h*
47:2 281*f* 350*c*	**50:6** 369*i* 495*c*	**52:6** 108*h* 636*a*	**3:6** 361*i* 418*j*
47:4 362*bi*	**50:8** 298*f* 620*n*	**52:8** 619*g*	**3:8** 761*ae*
47:5 46*g* 229*u*	**50:9** 281*h*	**52:9** 786*a*	**3:9** 246*d*
47:6 226*j* 723*a*	**50:12** 872*p*	**52:10** 362*aa*	**3:10** 365*z* 365*ah*
47:7 737*b*	**50:13** 190*k*	**52:11** 188*f* 439*k* 747*o*	**3:12** 287*l*
48:1 165*o* 371*x*	**50:15** 280*c*	**52:12** 108*i*	**3:14** 851*d*
48:6 620*n*	**50:18** 365*ai*	**52:13** 381*g* 990*v*	**3:19** 391*b* 391*d*
48:7 485*ae*	**50:19** 148*o*	**52:14** 235*m*	**3:22** 146*d* 905*d*
48:9 271*a*	**50:20** 909*b*	**52:15** 188*d*	**3:23** 126*d* 128*h* 929*a*
48:10 458*c* 899*m*	**50:23** 630*e*	**52:16** 41*n* 801*o*	**3:24** 777*e*
48:11 41*e* 130*g* 386*a*	**50:24** 542*r*	**52:17** 218*g* 218*p*	**3:25** 459*aa* 507*c*
683*s*	**50:25** 723*b*	343*p* 786*i*	**3:27** 130*l*
48:12 46*o* 220*a*	**50:26** 165*a*	**52:18** 194*k*	**3:30** 279*f*
48:13 872*p* 967*k*	**50:28** 620*e*	**52:20** 99*n* 218*g* 218*p*	**3:31** 607*f*
48:21 184*bd*	**50:29** 280*c*	322*h* 343*p*	**3:32** 905*d*
48:26 302*q* 949*p*	**50:33** 747*h*	554*c*	**3:33** 598*a* 827*i*
48:29 871*f*	**50:34** 162*a*	**52:21** 195*a*	**3:37** 725*c*
48:32 366*k*	**50:36** 501*b*	**52:22** 195*a* 554*c*	**3:40** 148*b* 461*l*
48:33 145*b*	**50:38** 342*d*	**52:24** 986*k*	**3:41** 310*i*
48:37 46*g* 229*u* 836*k*	**50:39** 365*an*	**52:27** 362*am* 747*i*	**3:42** 909*i*
48:47 656*ah*	**50:40** 184*aw* 190*k*	**52:28** 188*f*	**3:43** 619*j*
49:1 371*x* 438*ad*	**50:41** 281*h*	**52:31** 108*p* 310*j* 746*f*	**3:44** 355*e* 761*ae*
771*f*	**50:43** 167*o*	**52:33** 228*i* 301*l*	**3:45** 641*j*
49:2 381*e*	**50:44** 21*a*		**3:50** 441*i*
49:3 188*g* 967*m*	**50:45** 623*b*	**Lamentations**	**3:52** 619*b*
49:4 485*ae*	**51:2** 165*o*	**1:1** 88*l* 190*m* 558*b*	**3:55** 255*c*
49:6 656*ah*	**51:5** 621*g*	**1:2** 831*i* 880*f*	**3:57** 854*ah*
49:7 371*x* 498*m*	**51:6** 620*n*	**1:3** 188*d*	**3:65** 899*b*
49:9 41*f*	**51:7** 503*b* 949*r*	**1:4** 988*a*	**3:66** 619*j*
49:11 896*i*	**51:10** 927*a*	**1:7** 125*g* 505*q*	**4:1** 558*b*
49:12 949*o*	**51:11** 910*a*	**1:8** 229*b* 649*b*	**4:2** 809*a*
49:13 165*o*	**51:12** 527*c* 547*ac*	**1:9** 831*i*	**4:3** 365*t* 365*an*

4:4 859*l*	**2:4** 602*c*	**7:4** 906*b*	**11:10** 490*n*
4:5 436*c*	**2:6** 256*l* 365*s*	**7:6** 69*h*	**11:12** 490*n*
4:6 184*aw*	854*af*	**7:12** 792*b*	**11:13** 361*ad*
4:7 427*e*	**2:8** 301*ba*	**7:14** 414*i*	**11:15** 184*g* 199*m*
4:8 428*a*	**2:9** 589*k*	**7:17** 163*b*	**11:16** 75*c*
4:9 636*b*	**2:10** 238*b* 836*b*	**7:18** 229*u* 836*k*	**11:17** 74*b* 184*k*
4:10 301*at* 381*m*	**3:1** 301*ba*	**7:19** 797*q*	**11:19** 126*g* 447*e*
4:15 649*k*	**3:3** 392*g*	**7:25** 717*j*	**11:20** 371*ac* 965*e*
4:19 619*g*	**3:5** 557*c*	**7:26** 438*ac*	**11:23** 209*q*
4:21 949*p*	**3:7** 456*e*	**7:27** 490*n*	**11:24** 310*d* 965*y*
5:1 505*a*	**3:8** 602*i*	**8:1** 108*j*	**12:2** 416*b* 439*d* 738*g*
5:2 59*f*	**3:9** 854*af*	**8:2** 381*o*	**12:3** 188*b* 777*q*
5:3 779*a*	**3:12** 310*d* 965*y*	**8:3** 259*d* 310*d* 911*d*	**12:5** 263*ac*
5:4 339*g* 385*c*	**3:13** 271*c* 315*b* 398*a*	965*y*	**12:6** 226*g* 547*e*
5:7 169*x*	**3:14** 310*d* 965*y*	**8:5** 281*c* 982*p*	**12:11** 188*b* 547*e*
5:8 733*ak*	**3:15** 110*o* 188*f* 350*v*	**8:7** 263*ac*	**12:12** 226*g*
5:9 661*a*	**3:17** 180*a* 457*g* 664*b*	**8:8** 263*ac*	**12:13** 439*k* 542*r*
5:10 383*d* 636*b*	**3:18** 180*a* 361*u*	**8:10** 554*e*	**12:15** 75*c* 490*n*
5:11 951*aa*	**3:20** 180*a* 361*u*	**8:11** 99*s* 396*f*	**12:16** 41*o* 490*n*
5:12 217*e*	**3:23** 311*g* 350*v*	**8:12** 439*f* 530*g* 554*e*	**12:18** 825*t*
5:15 835*c*	**3:24** 965*y*	607*a* 982*n*	**12:19** 854*r*
5:18 365*t*	**3:25** 747*o*	**8:14** 836*r*	**12:20** 490*n*
5:19 733*b*	**3:26** 578*a*	**8:16** 311*l* 321*j*	**12:22** 136*b* 496*c* 726*c*
5:20 506*b* 621*b*	**4:1** 551*a* 631*n*	**8:18** 906*b*	**12:23** 725*c*
5:21 656*al*	**4:2** 712*g*	**9:2** 586*v* 723*c* 963*k*	**12:25** 135*c* 725*c*
	4:4 242*b* 273*i*	**9:3** 968*u*	**12:27** 124*h*
Ezekiel	311*ab* 914*z*	**9:4** 237*b* 547*q* 836*x*	**12:28** 135*c*
1:1 108*h* 263*ag*	**4:5** 110*b* 110*s*	**9:6** 362*bg*	**13:2** 579*aj*
350*v* 438*aa*	110*ag*	**9:9** 439*f*	**13:4** 365*u*
1:3 350*v* 986*d*	**4:6** 110*b* 110*r*	**9:10** 906*b*	**13:8** 541*e* 704*c*
1:4 281*e* 352*k*	110*ac* 241*c*	**10:1** 743*a*	**13:9** 490*n* 589*e*
1:5 96*b* 365*bt* 968*u*	273*i* 311*ab*	**10:2** 315*b* 381*y* 968*u*	**13:10** 427*g* 717*k*
1:6 96*d* 237*a* 271*c*	914*z*	**10:3** 355*d* 968*v*	**13:11** 235*n*
1:7 53*m*	**4:8** 747*o*	**10:4** 355*d*	**13:14** 490*n*
1:8 53*h*	**4:9** 110*s* 301*ah*	**10:5** 271*c* 398*a* 577*c*	**13:16** 717*k*
1:9 249*d* 271*c* 285*c*	**4:10** 322*d*	**10:6** 365*bt*	**13:18** 226*f* 983*c*
1:10 237*a* 365*ae*	**4:11** 465*d*	**10:8** 53*h*	**13:21** 226*f* 490*n*
365*ar* 365*az*	**4:12** 302*h* 381*m* 385*f*	**10:9** 315*b* 968*u*	**13:22** 855*g*
371*d*	**4:14** 301*ap* 363*o*	**10:10** 315*b*	**13:23** 490*n*
1:11 226*a* 271*c*	**4:15** 302*h* 385*f*	**10:11** 249*d*	**14:3** 459*b* 982*n*
1:12 249*d* 285*c*	**4:16** 636*d*	**10:12** 438*j*	**14:4** 982*n*
1:13 176*k* 381*q*	**5:1** 95*c* 256*e* 322*f*	**10:13** 315*b*	**14:6** 982*f*
1:15 315*b*	381*f* 648*j*	**10:14** 96*d* 237*a*	**14:7** 982*n*
1:16 315*b*	**5:2** 75*c*	365*ae* 365*ar*	**14:8** 490*n* 496*d* 704*c*
1:17 249*d*	**5:3** 41*i*	371*d* 968*v*	**14:11** 371*ac* 965*e*
1:18 438*j*	**5:8** 704*c*	**10:15** 350*v*	**14:13** 636*d*
1:21 320*c*	**5:10** 75*c* 301*at*	**10:17** 320*c*	**14:14** 668*x* 937*b*
1:22 422*a*	**5:12** 75*c*	**10:20** 350*v* 968*v*	**14:15** 365*e*
1:23 226*a* 271*c*	**5:16** 636*d*	**10:21** 53*h* 96*d* 237*a*	**14:19** 659*a*
1:24 271*c* 339*c* 398*a*	**5:17** 365*e*	271*c*	**14:20** 668*x*
577*c*	**6:3** 165*c* 209*ag*	**10:22** 237*a* 249*d* 350*v*	**14:21** 636*d*
1:26 743*a* 965*a*	**6:5** 363*e* 363*h*	**11:1** 310*d* 965*y*	**14:22** 41*o*
1:27 381*o*	**6:8** 41*o*	**11:3** 164*w* 194*o*	**15:2** 366*j* 366*k* 631*c*
1:28 250*c* 445*g*	**6:9** 505*i* 888*t*	**11:5** 449*c* 490*i* 965*n*	**15:4** 385*b*
2:1 215*b*	**6:10** 490*n*	**11:6** 362*f*	**15:7** 490*n* 704*c*
2:2 215*b* 965*y*	**6:14** 490*n*	**11:7** 304*c*	**16:3** 167*x* 169*v* 169*ai*
2:3 738*g*	**7:2** 69*h* 184*j*	**11:9** 59*c*	**16:7** 36*b* 229*j*

16:8 226a 765c
16:9 357r 648f
16:10 228v 631o
16:11 844a
16:13 631o 841c
16:15 485af 951y
16:17 951x
16:20 981ah
16:22 506f
16:25 951y
16:28 951y
16:32 951l
16:33 951y
16:35 951x
16:37 229b
16:39 229b
16:43 506f
16:44 496c
16:45 169v 169ai
16:46 11g 184aw
16:49 801m 871h
16:53 656ai
16:59 769a
16:60 115k 505c 765i
16:62 490n
16:63 505r 909b
17:2 519e 530j
17:3 365at 366k 366t
      437b
17:9 342k
17:13 765n
17:15 738b 769d
17:20 542r
17:22 366t 519e
17:23 192ai 365ak
      366t
18:2 169x 393c 496c
18:4 361u 773c
18:6 45j 209ad 951g
18:7 228w 301n
      767a 788h
18:8 803h
18:9 360n
18:11 209ad 951g
18:12 767a 788d 801l
18:13 361u 803i
18:15 209ad 951g
18:16 228w 301n
      767a 788h
18:17 360n 803h
18:18 361u
18:19 169y
18:20 169y 361u
18:21 360n
18:23 361i 826c
18:24 361u
18:25 624a 624c 914c

18:26 361u
18:28 360n
18:29 624a 624c
18:31 126g 361v 447e
18:32 826c 939a
19:1 836ag
19:2 365af
19:4 748b
19:9 748b
19:10 366k
19:12 342k
20:1 108i 459b
20:3 459e
20:5 490o 532p 605h
      965e
20:6 635d
20:7 982f
20:8 738f
20:9 561i
20:11 360n 676e 953a
20:12 547b 683a 979e
20:13 360n 676e 683h
20:14 561i
20:15 635d
20:16 683h
20:17 919a
20:19 965e
20:20 490n 547b 683d
20:21 360n 676e 683h
20:22 561i
20:23 75c
20:24 683h
20:25 360o 953m
20:26 119g 490n
      981ah
20:28 209ad
20:29 209ad
20:31 459e
20:32 18k
20:33 741a
20:34 74b
20:38 490n
20:40 209n
20:41 74b
20:42 184k 490n
20:43 505r
20:44 490n
20:47 381v
20:49 519a
21:3 704c
21:4 362bc
21:6 836b
21:9 256c 723c
21:14 279u
21:17 279u
21:19 547u
21:21 605t 983e

21:22 712g
21:24 747h
21:27 165b 295e
21:28 371x 438ad
      723c
21:32 385e 506g
22:4 936a
22:5 851b
22:7 59af 169n
22:8 683h 922d
22:10 45j 951q
22:11 951r
22:12 506e 612h 803i
22:15 75c
22:16 490n
22:18 641j
22:20 337c 383a
22:22 383a
22:26 15a 953x
22:27 365w
22:28 427g
22:29 59af
22:30 720a
23:2 519e
23:3 253a 951x
23:5 859o
23:6 436c
23:7 859o
23:8 253a
23:9 859o
23:10 229b
23:12 859o
23:14 553a
23:16 859o
23:20 302c 859o
23:21 253a
23:23 716f
23:28 728e
23:29 229b
23:31 301bc
23:35 506e
23:37 951l
23:38 683h
23:39 981ah 990v
23:40 843a
23:49 490n
24:2 712g
24:3 194o^2 519e
24:5 385a
24:6 51b
24:11 51b
24:16 836ai
24:18 361ae
24:19 514a
24:21 990u
24:23 836ai
24:24 490n 547e

24:27 490n 578b
25:2 371x 438ad
25:3 188d 990v
25:4 281m
25:7 165o 490n
25:8 18k 371x
25:9 184bd
25:10 281m
25:11 490n
25:12 910g
25:14 910a
25:15 371x 910g
25:17 490n 910a
26:2 184bc 371x
26:3 704b
26:4 165p 209ak
      229i 333a 344v
26:6 490n
26:7 281g
26:8 712b
26:9 209ak 279m
26:13 145c
26:14 229i 344v
26:17 165o 836ah
26:21 2e
27:2 836ah
27:3 646e 841e
27:4 275f 646e
27:5 631e^2
27:6 631e^2
27:7 435e 631o
27:8 269b
27:11 646e 841e
27:12 631h 791b 795a
27:14 365bg
27:15 631k
27:16 436a
27:25 275e
27:26 165y
27:30 836ah
27:32 21f
27:36 2e
28:2 966l
28:3 498m
28:4 800c
28:5 871h
28:7 59c
28:9 966l
28:12 646e^2 836ah
      841e
28:13 370b 844c
28:14 209p 381q
28:15 914i
28:16 209p 300p 381q
28:17 841e 871h
28:21 184bc 371x
28:22 490n 704b

28:23	490*n*	**33:22**	578*b*
28:24	490*n*	**33:25**	184*i* 335*g*
28:25	74*b* 184*k*	**33:29**	490*n*
28:26	490*n*	**33:31**	677*b*
29:1	108*n*	**33:32**	412*h*
29:2	371*x*	**34:2**	301*y* 369*i*
29:3	350*r* 704*b*	**34:4**	735*e*
29:4	365*av* 748*b*	**34:5**	75*g* 369*j*
29:5	301*ak*	**34:8**	301*y*
29:6	218*e* 490*n*	**34:10**	704*b*
29:9	350*r* 490*n*	**34:11**	459*ad*
29:10	704*b*	**34:12**	369*k*
29:11	110*ac*	**34:13**	74*b* 301*y*
29:12	75*a*	**34:16**	459*ad*
29:13	74*c*	**34:17**	480*f*
29:14	639*d* 656*ah*	**34:18**	279*t*
29:16	490*n*	**34:19**	301*ar*
29:17	108*e*	**34:20**	480*f*
29:18	229*u*	**34:22**	480*f*
29:19	790*h* 804*b*	**34:23**	301*y* 369*f*
29:21	160*h* 490*n*	**34:25**	365*g* 765*l*
30:2	836*ah*	**34:26**	350*ab* 897*b*
30:3	108*ae*	**34:27**	171*g* 490*n*
30:8	490*n*		660*a* 746*a*
30:12	165*o* 342*h*	**34:29**	636*i*
30:13	165*c* 982*r*	**34:30**	89*d* 371*ac*
30:19	490*n*	**34:31**	369*k* 965*e*
30:20	108*e*	**35:2**	209*u* 371*x*
30:21	658*e*	**35:3**	704*b*
30:23	75*a*	**35:4**	490*n*
30:25	490*n*	**35:6**	362*j*
30:26	75*a* 490*n*	**35:9**	190*k*
31:1	108*g*	**35:10**	189*a* 773*h*
31:2	21*f*	**35:15**	490*n*
31:3	366*x*	**36:1**	209*h*
31:6	365*ak*	**36:9**	706*a*
31:10	871*i*	**36:10**	104*i* 164*s*
31:12	46*ab*	**36:11**	490*n*
32:1	108*p*	**36:19**	75*c*
32:2	365*af* 836*ah*	**36:20**	561*i*
32:3	542*r*	**36:22**	561*i*
32:7	321*o*	**36:23**	490*n*
32:19	841*e*	**36:24**	74*b*
32:22	361*j*	**36:25**	648*aa*
33:2	180*a* 457*g* 664*b*	**36:26**	126*g* 447*e*
33:3	414*h*	**36:27**	953*w* 965*p*
33:4	180*a*	**36:28**	184*k* 965*e*
33:6	180*a* 414*h*	**36:29**	636*i*
33:7	457*g* 664*b*	**36:30**	636*i*
33:8	180*a* 361*u*	**36:31**	505*r*
33:11	826*c* 939*a*	**36:35**	370*b*
33:13	485*af* 506*d*	**36:37**	104*c*
33:15	767*a* 787*c*	**36:38**	490*n*
33:16	506*d*	**37:1**	255*k* 363*i*
33:17	624*c* 914*c*		965*ae*
33:20	624*c*	**37:2**	342*j*
33:21	108*n* 165*d*	**37:3**	656*b*

37:4	579*u*	**40:16**	554*c*
37:5	352*a*	**40:22**	554*c*
37:6	490*n*	**40:31**	554*c*
37:7	45*b*	**40:34**	554*c*
37:9	352*a*	**40:37**	554*c*
37:10	215*b* 352*a*	**40:38**	648*s*
37:12	148*o* 184*k* 364*j*	**40:39**	218*ae*
	656*m*	**41:4**	28*l* 979*z*
37:13	490*n*	**41:18**	237*a* 554*c* 968*u*
37:14	184*k* 965*p*	**41:19**	365*ae* 371*d*
37:16	45*m* 218*d*	**41:21**	28*n*
	371*ah* 586*n*	**41:22**	218*ae*
37:21	74*b*	**41:25**	554*c* 968*u*
37:22	371*ah*	**41:26**	554*c*
37:23	371*ac*	**42:13**	301*ab* 979*x*
37:24	369*f* 741*c*		979*aa*
37:25	184*k*	**42:14**	989*a*
37:26	115*k* 765*i* 990*z*	**42:16**	28*m*
37:27	192*e* 371*ac*	**43:2**	577*c* 866*e*
37:28	990*z*	**43:3**	311*g* 350*v*
38:2	371*x*	**43:5**	310*d* 866*e* 965*y*
38:3	704*b*	**43:7**	192*e* 743*a*
38:4	748*b*	**43:9**	192*e*
38:8	124*h* 712*f*	**43:10**	872*s*
38:10	623*d*	**43:12**	979*aa*
38:15	281*g*	**43:13**	195*a* 990*a*
38:16	712*f*	**43:19**	981*y*
38:17	13*m*	**43:26**	941*f*
38:19	176*i*	**44:1**	264*f*
38:21	362*ai*	**44:3**	301*z*
38:22	350*ag* 385*h*	**44:4**	311*g* 866*e*
38:23	490*n*	**44:7**	59*g*
39:1	704*b*	**44:9**	59*g*
39:2	281*g*	**44:10**	936*d*
39:3	161*i*	**44:13**	986*y*
39:4	301*ak*	**44:14**	986*y*
39:6	381*t* 490*n*	**44:15**	986*a*
39:7	490*n*	**44:17**	259*n* 989*b*
39:9	110*y* 385*g*	**44:18**	302*p* 989*i*
39:11	364*h* 364*q*	**44:19**	989*a*
39:12	110*s*	**44:20**	259*h* 648*k*
39:14	110*s*	**44:21**	948*a*
39:17	301*ak* 363*m*	**44:22**	894*f*
	981*ai*	**44:23**	534*l*
39:22	490*n*	**44:24**	480*l*
39:23	523*b*	**44:25**	363*b* 986*a*
39:24	523*b*	**44:27**	981*y*
39:25	656*ah* 905*d*	**44:28**	777*k*
	911*c*	**44:29**	301*ab*
39:27	74*b*	**44:30**	171*l*
39:28	188*e* 490*n*	**44:31**	301*ap*
39:29	523*d* 965*s*	**45:1**	605*r* 783*a* 979*x*
40:2	209*x*	**45:2**	28*m*
40:3	465*f*	**45:3**	990*ac*
40:5	195*a* 235*e* 990*z*	**45:10**	465*a*
40:6	264*c*	**45:11**	465*c*
40:11	263*j*	**45:12**	465*b*^{2}

45:14	465c	**1:17**	438w 490w 500c	**4:4**	683s	**6:4**	928h
45:17	781r	**1:20**	500c	**4:5**	438v	**6:6**	360c
45:18	108e	**2:1**	438v	**4:6**	520a	**6:7**	365ac 761x
45:20	108e 491w	**2:2**	500e 983f	**4:9**	520b	**6:8**	153a 752d
45:21	108e 988c	**2:3**	438v	**4:10**	366y 438u	**6:9**	586l
45:25	108e	**2:4**	520b	**4:12**	365ak	**6:10**	139a 586l 761g
46:1	263ah	**2:5**	526v	**4:14**	46ac	**6:12**	153a 761x
46:4	981n 981p	**2:9**	526v	**4:15**	41k 341f 365ba	**6:13**	139a 761g
46:9	249d 988a	**2:11**	700a	**4:16**	110y 447d	**6:15**	153a
46:11	988a	**2:12**	362n	**4:17**	733a 733ad	**6:16**	287m 365ac
46:13	981m	**2:16**	520a	**4:18**	520a	**6:17**	344i 743k
46:17	988j	**2:17**	761o	**4:20**	366y	**6:18**	678a 946k
46:20	381m	**2:18**	905a	**4:21**	365ak	**6:19**	128f 680c
47:1	339n	**2:19**	438w 526g	**4:23**	41k 46ac 110y 341f 365ba	**6:20**	668f
47:3	211c	**2:20**	498f 923l	**4:25**	341f 365ba 733a 733ad	**6:21**	360c
47:4	211c	**2:21**	498k 733ad			**6:22**	264o 935c 968l
47:5	211c	**2:22**	417c 418h 526g	**4:26**	41k 733a	**6:23**	310b 485g
47:7	366v	**2:24**	520a	**4:27**	914p	**6:24**	287m
47:8	392h	**2:28**	526g	**4:30**	877b	**6:25**	588b
47:9	365av	**2:29**	526g	**4:31**	752a	**6:26**	115b 360g
47:10	686c	**2:31**	438u 554f	**4:32**	110y 301ar 365ba 733a 733ad	**6:27**	864a
47:12	171i 366v 656t	**2:32**	631l			**7:1**	438u
47:13	236b 783a	**2:33**	43b	**4:33**	53g 259g 301ar 341f 365ba	**7:2**	343d 352l
47:15	236b	**2:34**	332f 344x			**7:3**	96b 343c 365bu
47:18	350m	**2:35**	323e 344x	**4:34**	502a 733b	**7:4**	215c 271a 365ae
47:20	343m	**2:37**	733ad 733al	**4:35**	595c 639d		
47:22	59o 605r	**2:41**	43b	**4:36**	502a 656af	**7:5**	301ak 365y
48:1	184q	**2:42**	330a	**4:37**	871i	**7:6**	96d 213g 271a 365aj
48:2	184q	**2:44**	332f 733w	**5:1**	882f		
48:3	184q	**2:45**	124k 344x	**5:2**	194k	**7:7**	99k 254f 256n
48:4	184q	**2:46**	311a 981aj	**5:4**	966j	**7:8**	254b 438j 877b
48:5	184q	**2:47**	965d	**5:5**	53g 586t	**7:9**	133i 228t 259c 259n 381q 427a 743a
48:6	184q	**2:49**	761al	**5:7**	436c 500e 520b 844a		
48:7	184q	**3:1**	348a 982o			**7:10**	104v 381o 589n
48:10	979x	**3:2**	876g	**5:8**	520b	**7:11**	362bo
48:20	28m	**3:5**	311l 414d 982o	**5:11**	500e	**7:13**	133i 355i 371j
48:23	184q	**3:6**	383b	**5:16**	436c 844a	**7:14**	115k 733w
48:24	184q	**3:7**	414d	**5:17**	520a	**7:16**	520b
48:25	184q	**3:10**	311l 414d	**5:18**	733ad	**7:17**	96c 733al
48:26	184q	**3:11**	383b	**5:20**	752b 871j	**7:18**	733ag
48:27	184q	**3:12**	982o	**5:21**	301ar 341f 365ba 733a 733ad	**7:19**	256n
48:29	605r 783a	**3:14**	982o			**7:20**	99k 254f 438j 877b
48:30	99n 264c	**3:15**	383b 414d 668f	**5:22**	872k		
48:35	189a	**3:16**	460k	**5:23**	194k 352b 866k 966j	**7:21**	718j
		3:17	668f			**7:22**	133i 979j
Daniel		**3:18**	982o	**5:25**	590a	**7:23**	733al
1:1	712g	**3:19**	99i 379c 383b	**5:26**	114g	**7:24**	$99k^2$
1:2	194k 727j	**3:20**	747o	**5:27**	322g	**7:25**	110w 979j
1:4	557d 646e 841l	**3:21**	287m	**5:28**	46ak	**7:26**	752a
1:5	110v 301ap	**3:24**	747o	**5:29**	228m 436c 844a	**7:27**	115c
1:7	561y	**3:25**	746a			**8:1**	438aa
1:8	301ap	**3:28**	485g	**5:30**	362x	**8:2**	184bd 351b
1:9	826p	**3:29**	668f	**5:31**	131g 741u	**8:3**	254c 365bs
1:12	301ap 461h	**3:30**	285a	**6:3**	285a	**8:4**	281t
1:14	461h	**4:2**	864b			**8:5**	254b 281r 365bs
1:15	195e	**4:3**	115c 733b				

8:8	46d 96d 254d
8:9	254b
8:10	321p
8:11	981m
8:14	110x
8:16	968x
8:17	69e 311g
8:18	215b 378h 679c
8:19	69e
8:20	365bs 741x
8:21	254b 365bs
8:22	254d
8:26	525c
8:27	651g
9:2	110ae 165d 579z 589i
9:3	761r 836j 946g
9:5	914ac
9:7	872o 913b
9:8	872o
9:9	905c
9:12	21k
9:13	953d
9:15	304a 561a
9:16	184aj 209l
9:18	441i 561g² 905c
9:21	108q 968x
9:24	110ag 115k 941k
9:25	110ac 110ag 164s 357u
9:26	361ai
9:27	165x 765p
10:2	836ag
10:3	357s 946g
10:4	108e 350v
10:5	228p
10:7	523e
10:9	679c
10:10	378h
10:12	854ah
10:13	110q 968x 969t
10:16	378h
10:18	162k 378h
10:19	162l 854ah
10:20	969t²
10:21	968x
11:2	741x
11:5	281j
11:6	281a
11:15	712b
11:16	184c
11:30	275g
11:31	165x 981m
11:32	490p
11:33	498m
11:36	866y 980b

11:41	184c
11:45	192u
12:1	589l 827b 968x
12:2	656k²
12:3	417q 498m
12:4	264p 525c
12:7	110w
12:9	264p 525c
12:10	914r
12:11	110x 165x 981m
12:12	110x

Hosea

1:2	951i 951l
1:3	167i
1:4	963c
1:6	167i 561o 906b
1:8	167i
1:9	371al 561o
1:10	104c 170t 371ak
2:1	371ac 561o² 905d
2:2	951k
2:3	229b
2:6	700b
2:10	229b
2:11	145c
2:13	506e
2:15	255k 304a 852b
2:16	894ac
2:18	365f 719a 765l
2:19	894ad 913y
2:20	490n
2:23	371ak
3:1	887f
3:2	792e 809d
3:4	734a
3:5	459x
4:1	491e 929j
4:6	491c 506b 607b
4:9	18e
4:10	636d
4:12	459f 951x 982n
4:13	209ad
4:14	951u
4:16	365ba 602c
4:19	872p
5:1	542v
5:3	490m 951x
5:4	951x
5:5	871g
5:6	459v 484c 523b
5:7	954g
5:8	414h
5:10	547t 891h
5:12	51d
5:13	656ac

5:14	365ah
5:15	459ab
6:1	148b
6:3	350ae 490r
6:4	114o 341h
6:5	579r
6:6	490q 905h 981ar
6:7	18e 769a
6:11	656ah
7:2	505e
7:4	383d 951i
7:5	949g
7:6	383d
7:7	761x
7:8	43c 59y
7:9	429a 491z
7:10	148d 459ab 871g
7:11	365ap 499d
7:12	542r
7:13	282e 541e 738f 792n
7:16	723b
8:1	365at 414h 769b
8:2	490p
8:4	741l 982c
8:5	982k
8:7	352i
8:9	792g
8:11	990f
8:13	505e
9:1	951l
9:2	636d
9:3	148m
9:7	501i 503e
9:8	457g
9:9	505e
9:10	18m 171n 366k
9:11	271e
9:12	772g
9:14	172k
9:15	887aj
9:17	268a
10:1	366k 990f
10:2	165c
10:3	734a
10:5	982k
10:8	209j 226c
10:11	365ba 370g
10:12	75j 370j 459s 913i
10:13	485ag
11:1	132e 304a 737k 887f
11:3	267f 491i 534b

11:4	689d
11:5	148m
11:8	184aw 621b 905d
11:9	965a
11:10	365ah 403a
11:11	365ak
12:1	352i
12:2	963c
12:3	300ad 716c
12:6	148a
12:7	465e
12:8	800f
12:9	192u 988i
12:10	519a
12:12	804b 894z
12:13	579s
13:2	982n
13:3	114o 323d 341h
13:4	21d
13:6	506e
13:7	365ah 365aj
13:8	365z 772f
13:9	704d
13:10	741l
13:11	733ad
13:13	167q
13:14	256j 361aw 792n
13:16	263x
14:1	148a
14:3	779e
14:4	603j 656t
14:5	341g 366x
14:8	171q
14:9	500a 624a

Joel

1:4	165aa 365j
1:5	949b
1:8	836ab
1:9	981u
1:11	172p
1:13	836k 981u
1:14	946h
1:15	108ae
1:20	342d
2:1	108ae 414n
2:2	418h
2:4	365bh
2:5	722g
2:7	60e
2:8	722g
2:11	722a
2:12	148a

2:13	823*f* 836*i* 891*n* 905*d*	**2:8**	767*d*	**5:27**	188*b*	**Jonah**	
2:14	981*u*	**2:9**	195*g*	**6:1**	683*s*	**1:2**	184*bb*
2:15	414*l* 946*h*	**2:10**	110*ac* 304*a*	**6:4**	218*x*	**1:3**	275*c* 620*p* 809*n*
2:17	190*a*	**2:11**	46*ah* 579*r*	**6:5**	412*h*	**1:4**	176*j* 352*g*
2:18	911*c*	**2:12**	46*ah* 579*v* 949*k*	**6:6**	836*ai*	**1:5**	270*a* 323*b* 679*c*
2:19	635*g*	**2:14**	620*b*	**6:7**	188*b*		761*ah*
2:20	281*i*	**2:16**	229*d*	**6:8**	871*i* 888*b*	**1:6**	678*g*
2:21	676*a*	**3:1**	304*a*	**6:10**	364*b*	**1:7**	605*r*
2:23	350*z* 824*g*	**3:2**	371*ad* 605*h*	**6:12**	391*e*	**1:9**	164*a* 371*ae*
2:24	635*g*		963*c*	**7:1**	165*aa*	**1:10**	620*p*
2:25	110*b* 365*j* 787*c*	**3:3**	89*n* 295*b*	**7:3**	603*b*	**1:12**	266*b* 287*m*
2:26	635*g* 872*v*	**3:4**	403*a*	**7:4**	381*u*	**1:13**	269*a*
2:27	89*a*	**3:5**	542*r*	**7:6**	603*b*	**1:14**	180*f* 761*p* 826*a*
2:28	438*s* 438*z* 579*ag*	**3:6**	414*h* 645*c*	**7:7**	215*a*	**1:15**	266*b* 287*m*
	965*s*	**3:7**	526*g*	**7:10**	623*f* 986*r*	**1:16**	854*l*
2:30	864*b*	**3:8**	403*a* 579*u*	**7:11**	188*b* 362*w*	**1:17**	110*l* 365*av*
2:31	108*ae* 321*o*	**3:10**	491*h*	**7:12**	300*z* 438*af*	**2:1**	761*p*
2:32	667*a* 761*t*	**3:11**	705*g*	**7:13**	579*v*	**2:2**	460*c*
3:1	656*ah*	**3:12**	53*k*	**7:14**	369*a* 579*s*	**2:3**	350*d*
3:2	75*d* 480*e*	**3:14**	254*i*	**7:17**	188*b* 951*t*	**2:4**	300*n*
3:3	605*r* 793*g* 809*d*	**3:15**	192*ad*	**8:1**	171*k*	**2:6**	310*f*
3:8	793*h*	**4:1**	365*ba* 801*m*	**8:2**	69*h*	**2:7**	505*i*
3:9	718*e*	**4:2**	748*b*	**8:3**	363*e*	**2:9**	532*s* 668*a* 907*d*
3:10	723*i*	**4:4**	102*a* 914*r*	**8:4**	801*k*	**2:10**	302*q*
3:12	480*e*	**4:5**	323*f*	**8:5**	465*e* 683*h*	**3:2**	184*bb*
3:13	370*l*	**4:6**	148*d* 636*b*	**8:6**	641*f* 809*d*	**3:3**	184*bb*
3:14	108*ae* 605*n*	**4:7**	342*c* 350*ad*	**8:8**	350*r*	**3:4**	110*r*
3:15	321*o*	**4:8**	148*d*	**8:9**	418*c*	**3:5**	228*l* 485*g* 946*h*
3:16	403*a* 662*b* 662*d*	**4:9**	148*d*	**8:10**	836*ab*	**3:9**	603*b*
3:17	59*h* 192*j* 209*m*	**4:10**	148*d* 397*a* 659*a*	**8:11**	636*k*	**3:10**	603*b*
	490*n*	**4:11**	148*d* 184*aw*	**8:12**	459*v*	**4:1**	891*v*
3:18	339*n*		381*ae* 668*l*	**9:1**	438*d*	**4:2**	761*p* 823*f*
3:21	192*j* 910*c*	**4:12**	295*b* 669*b*	**9:2**	183*h*	**4:3**	361*s*
		4:13	164*d* 449*a*	**9:4**	645*b*	**4:4**	891*v*
Amos		**5:1**	836*ag*	**9:5**	350*r*	**4:5**	418*d*
1:1	176*h* 369*a*	**5:2**	309*b*	**9:6**	343*a*	**4:6**	366*g*
1:2	403*a*	**5:3**	41*i*	**9:7**	304*a*	**4:7**	365*l*
1:3	914*aa*	**5:4**	459*s*	**9:9**	176*c* 648*ae*	**4:8**	361*s* 379*a*
1:4	381*u*	**5:5**	188*b*	**9:11**	164*r*	**4:11**	905*d*
1:5	188*g*	**5:6**	381*o* 459*s*	**9:12**	371*z*		
1:6	914*aa*	**5:7**	391*e*	**9:13**	171*i* 370*e* 370*u*	**Micah**	
1:7	381*u*	**5:8**	164*d* 321*b* 343*a*	**9:14**	164*r* 656*ai*	**1:2**	466*k*
1:9	184*bc* 914*aa*	**5:10**	888*j*			**1:4**	209*i* 255*l*
1:10	381*u*	**5:11**	801*k*	**Obadiah**		**1:5**	914*z*
1:12	381*u*	**5:12**	612*g*	**1**	371*x*	**1:6**	165*b*
1:13	263*x* 914*aa*	**5:13**	110*f* 582*a*	**3**	311*r* 542*i* 871*a*	**1:7**	165*c* 804*b*
1:14	381*u*	**5:14**	89*d* 913*j*	**4**	209*c*	**1:8**	836*ag*
1:15	188*g*	**5:16**	836*ab*	**5**	41*f*	**1:10**	525*l*
2:1	363*h* 914*aa*	**5:18**	108*ae* 418*h*	**8**	500*b*	**1:16**	188*b* 229*u*
2:2	381*u*	**5:19**	365*o* 365*y*	**10**	176*a*	**2:1**	218*aa*
2:4	541*d* 914*aa*	**5:20**	108*ae* 418*h*	**11**	605*r* 883*d*	**2:2**	859*w*
	954*c*	**5:21**	988*b*	**15**	108*ae* 280*a*	**2:6**	579*v*
2:5	381*u*	**5:22**	981*ao*	**16**	2*e*	**2:7**	644*c* 857*b*
2:6	793*g* 809*d*	**5:23**	412*i*	**17**	668*q* 773*f*	**2:11**	949*j*
	914*aa*	**5:24**	350*i* 913*i*	**18**	381*t*	**2:12**	74*c*
2:7	951*q*	**5:25**	110*ac*	**21**	733*a*	**3:1**	913*i*
		5:26	967*q*			**3:2**	887*ag* 888*i*

3:3	229v 301at	**1:3**	352f 823f 961b	**3:10**	176g	**2:6**	318b 321s
3:4	460j 523b	**1:4**	342a	**3:11**	321q	**2:7**	318b
3:5	495c 579al	**1:5**	176g	**3:13**	668q	**2:8**	797a
	717k	**1:7**	644a 662b	**3:15**	343f	**2:9**	717i 866a
3:6	418k	**1:9**	623c	**3:17**	172s 824aa	**2:10**	108l
3:7	460j 872p	**1:11**	623d	**3:19**	162b	**2:12**	979u
3:8	160m	**1:13**	746a			**2:13**	649h
3:9	246d	**1:14**	165c	**Zephaniah**		**2:16**	636b
3:11	89a 612h	**1:15**	53m 529k	**1:2**	165o	**2:18**	108l
3:12	165d 370h	**2:2**	656ag	**1:3**	371f	**2:20**	108l
4:1	124h 209l	**2:6**	263k	**1:4**	704c	**2:21**	318b
4:2	308c 371z 534c	**2:8**	184bb 620d	**1:5**	311l	**2:23**	743k
	624b 953a	**2:9**	790d	**1:6**	459ab 603f		
4:3	480e 719a 719f	**2:11**	365ag	**1:7**	108ae 582b	**Zechariah**	
	723s	**2:13**	145c 704b	**1:12**	677d	**1:1**	108l 579z
4:4	366j 366r	**3:3**	363e	**1:13**	164x 370k	**1:2**	891j
4:5	561f	**3:5**	229b 704b	**1:14**	108ae	**1:3**	148c
4:7	41n 733a	**3:7**	184bb	**1:15**	108ae	**1:4**	456e
4:9	734a	**3:8**	350q	**1:16**	414i	**1:7**	108o
4:10	167o	**3:10**	188h	**1:18**	69h 668w 797q	**1:8**	365bg 427e
4:12	370aa 623b	**3:11**	949p	**2:2**	891d		430a 431e
4:13	370aa	**3:13**	263k 373k	**2:3**	459s 525e	**1:10**	457j 751i
5:1	712f	**3:15**	104j 365j	**2:7**	656ah	**1:12**	110ae 136a
5:2	125a 184ao	**3:19**	655f	**2:8**	922h		906b 968g
	369l 741c			**2:9**	184ax	**1:14**	911c
5:5	717c	**Habakkuk**		**2:15**	1e 21f	**1:16**	164aa 465f
5:7	41p 341g	**1:1**	579z	**3:1**	738c	**1:17**	605k 831a
5:8	365ag	**1:2**	136a 456a 703a	**3:2**	200f 486d	**1:18**	96d 254d
5:12	983i	**1:4**	954c	**3:3**	365w 365ai	**1:19**	75c
5:14	967j	**1:5**	486d	**3:4**	579ak 986s	**1:20**	96c 686g
6:2	928d	**1:8**	365as	**3:5**	913a	**2:1**	465f
6:3	684f	**1:10**	851b	**3:11**	871i	**2:4**	104i
6:4	304a	**1:11**	162n 966l	**3:12**	872d	**2:5**	230a 235f 381o
6:6	981an	**1:12**	115b 344w	**3:13**	541i	**2:6**	620n
6:7	119g 781s		480m	**3:14**	824p	**2:8**	438k
	981ag	**1:13**	582c 938j 950a	**3:15**	89a	**2:10**	192e
6:8	89g 627a 872c	**1:14**	365av 734b	**3:16**	854ah	**2:12**	605k
	913i	**1:15**	542u	**3:17**	89a 582c 824d	**3:1**	928e 969i 986k
6:11	465e	**1:16**	981ak		887c	**3:2**	381ae 668l
6:14	636d	**2:2**	277e 586c	**3:20**	74c 656ah	**3:3**	228i 228ad
6:15	370x	**2:3**	135c			**3:8**	53v 742k
7:2	542v 937c	**2:4**	485s 913v	**Haggai**		**3:9**	914n
7:3	612h	**2:5**	361b 859q 949a	**1:1**	108j 579z	**4:2**	99f 420h
7:5	485ag	**2:6**	114m	**1:2**	138a	**4:3**	90f 366x
7:6	11i 705h	**2:8**	280a	**1:4**	138a 192ad	**4:6**	160m 965x
7:7	507b	**2:9**	788d	**1:6**	172p 772c	**4:7**	209i
7:8	417b	**2:12**	164o	**1:8**	164aa	**4:9**	725g
7:10	190a	**2:14**	54d 490p	**1:9**	33a 192ad	**4:10**	215a 441f 922k
7:11	164s	**2:15**	229j 949k	**1:10**	172p	**4:11**	90f
7:14	369k	**2:16**	949o	**1:11**	342c	**4:14**	357k
7:15	864a	**2:18**	485ak 982c	**1:13**	89d	**5:1**	271e 589k
7:17	301am	**2:20**	990aa	**1:15**	108j	**5:2**	195a
7:18	21a 909a	**3:1**	579z 761p	**2:1**	108k	**5:3**	899f
		3:2	656al	**2:2**	986k	**5:6**	465c
Nahum		**3:3**	209u	**2:3**	639e	**5:7**	322i
1:1	184bb 371x	**3:8**	350e	**2:4**	89d 162l	**5:8**	914h
1:2	910a 911b	**3:9**	350e	**2:5**	89a	**5:9**	271a

6:1	96e	**11:7**	45m 218d 369j	**3:2**	648o	**2:12**	148l 438t 664d
6:2	428c 431e	**11:10**	46r 218d	**3:3**	648x 654a	**2:13**	362p 438t 445a
6:3	427e 437a	**11:12**	804b 809c		986ab		459ag 620n
6:6	281a 281j 427e	**11:14**	45m 46r 218d	**3:5**	983j		968g
	428c 437a		371ah	**3:6**	144a	**2:14**	129f
6:7	457j	**11:16**	369i	**3:7**	148c	**2:15**	170m 361af
6:8	281a	**11:17**	621r	**3:8**	102a 788n		725e 737k
6:11	743e	**12:1**	164b	**3:9**	899e	**2:16**	108aa 131e
6:12	53v 164ab 561k	**12:2**	949o	**3:10**	461g		362al 372f
6:13	986u	**12:3**	344l	**3:14**	742a		542k 698b 741v
7:1	108m	**12:4**	503b	**3:15**	461g	**2:17**	579z 725e
7:3	108i 946e	**12:8**	18d	**3:16**	589l 854h	**2:18**	2f 831j 836s
7:5	108i 108k	**12:10**	441c 655l 836u	**3:17**	777f	**2:19**	361af 438t 445a
	110ae 946b	**13:1**	350ak 648ab	**3:18**	15a		968g
	946e	**13:2**	982r	**4:1**	323d 381aa	**2:20**	184d 362p
7:9	913i	**13:3**	579y		383b	**2:22**	184u 438t 664d
7:12	602b	**13:4**	228e	**4:2**	271b 420i 656t		741v 854ad
7:14	75c	**13:6**	655f	**4:3**	279r	**2:23**	53v 184aq 561k
8:2	911c	**13:7**	75g 365bq 369j	**4:4**	953g		725e
8:3	184am 192j	**13:9**	95b 371ac 460c	**4:5**	108ae 579s	**3:1**	172x 172y 528b
	209l		461a	**4:6**	169j		988s
8:4	133c	**14:2**	188b 786j			**3:2**	200d 733f 939b
8:5	132d 837b		951aa	**Matthew**		**3:3**	66b 172y 249a
8:6	701a	**14:3**	716a	**1:1**	169b 357v 589j		579z 624i 669a
8:7	668p	**14:4**	46n 209q	**1:6**	741o		725e
8:8	371ac 965e	**14:5**	176h 295e	**1:11**	188d	**3:4**	228j 259b 301ai
8:9	162l	**14:7**	417j	**1:12**	188d		365j 392a
8:12	171g	**14:8**	339n	**1:16**	357v	**3:6**	350o 526r 988s
8:13	162l	**14:9**	88a 741a	**1:17**	99o 188d	**3:7**	124e 365q 620q
8:14	645b	**14:10**	209al 264d^2	**1:18**	167g 167k		708b 988t
8:15	644c	**14:12**	659a		894ab 965af	**3:8**	171o 939e
8:16	540b	**14:14**	800j	**1:19**	530i 872u 896e	**3:9**	169b 344e
8:17	888b	**14:15**	659a		937b		371ai
8:19	108h 108i 108k	**14:16**	988i	**1:20**	438t 445a	**3:10**	46ac 172t
	108n 946e	**14:20**	979w		965af 968g		381aa
8:21	459s			**1:21**	561k 668j	**3:11**	160e 229n 284i
8:22	371z	**Malachi**		**1:22**	725e		339t 381z 916a
8:23	89a 786n	**1:1**	529r	**1:23**	89d 167k 895c		939d 965w
9:1	704c	**1:2**	887f 888b	**1:24**	894z		988s 988y
9:4	343c	**1:6**	169r 866u	**1:25**	45h 561k	**3:12**	74c 323d 370w
9:9	267j 668e 824p	**1:7**	301aa 649n	**2:1**	167k 184ao		381aa
9:10	183f 350p 733w	**1:8**	439b		281m 500e	**3:13**	350o 988u
9:11	335o 746a 765e	**1:10**	264f 981ao		741v 983f	**3:14**	757g 988u
9:13	287k	**1:11**	183g	**2:2**	321k 741c 981g	**3:15**	756a 913k 915h
9:16	369k 844h	**1:12**	301aa	**2:3**	854l	**3:16**	263ag 365ap
10:1	350ab	**1:14**	647a 899e	**2:4**	167k 187d 357x		965l 971c
10:2	369j	**2:2**	899b		459i 586w	**3:17**	170m 577c
10:5	89a	**2:3**	302i		986n		826d 887d
10:6	460c	**2:4**	765c	**2:5**	184ao 586e	**4:1**	172z 612p 689f
10:8	104i	**2:7**	529r 986s	**2:6**	369l 639e 741c		926d 965ae
10:9	75c 505f	**2:10**	164m 169q	**2:7**	108aa 321k 530h		969d
10:10	74b	**2:11**	894x		983f	**4:2**	110r 859k 946f
10:11	350r	**2:13**	836w 981ao	**2:8**	459ag 981g	**4:3**	13c 170o 301c
10:12	561f	**2:14**	894i	**2:9**	283b 321k		344q
11:1	366q	**2:16**	896a	**2:10**	824u	**4:4**	301k 529c 586e
11:4	369j	**2:17**	684e	**2:11**	311k 396n 781o	**4:5**	209am 990y
11:6	906b	**3:1**	529r 669a 990y		797h 981g		

8:28	90*k* 176*a* 184*x* 364*i* 656*z* 969*u*	**9:38**	370*w* 686*a* 751*k* 761*u*

8:28 90*k* 176*a* 184*x* 364*i* 656*z* 969*u*
8:29 10*a* 827*n*
8:30 365*bj*
8:31 761*v*
8:32 297*n* 300*b* 309*h* 361*ah*
8:33 524*c* 620*k*
8:34 296*c* 607*k* 761*v*
9:1 184*ar* 222*h* 275*j*
9:2 218*z* 485*v* 651*l* 656*z* 855*f* 909*f*
9:3 586*y* 980*c*
9:4 490*l*
9:5 701*c*
9:6 218*z* 371*j* 733*aa*
9:8 74*s* 733*aa*
9:9 284*b* 804*h*
9:10 882*c* 938*k*
9:12 650*c* 658*a*
9:13 737*l* 905*h* 938*k* 981*ar*
9:14 538*c* 708*f* 946*c*
9:15 89*m* 786*d* 836*ak* 946*c*
9:16 47*e* 126*h* 127*f* 656*ad*
9:17 46*w* 126*h* 127*f* 194*r* 949*n*
9:18 170*i* 361*ae* 378*y* 656*z*
9:19 284*h*
9:20 110*z* 234*a* 302*e* 378*p*
9:21 228*f*
9:22 485*z* 656*z* 855*f*
9:23 61*a* 413*e* 656*o*
9:24 300*r* 679*e* 851*f*
9:25 378*k* 656*z*
9:26 526*k*
9:27 439*q* 905*b*
9:28 485*z*
9:29 378*j* 485*z* 656*z*
9:30 525*d*
9:31 526*k*
9:32 578*a* 969*u*
9:33 21*j* 578*b* 579*b* 656*z* 864*r*
9:34 300*c* 708*j* 969*v*
9:35 192*m* 528*f* 534*i*^{2} 656*x* 733*h*
9:36 74*t* 365*bq* 369*j* 905*e*
9:37 105*e* 171*s* 370*w*

9:38 370*w* 686*a* 751*k* 761*u*
10:1 99*m* 300*d* 538*a* 656*aa* 733*ag* 751*c* 969*aa*
10:2 11*o*^{2}
10:3 804*h*
10:4 272*e* 708*m*
10:5 59*y* 751*k*
10:6 365*bp* 371*al* 772*j*
10:7 200*d* 528*c* 733*f*
10:8 300*d* 648*j* 656*n* 656*aa* 781*v* 812*d* 969*aa*
10:9 670*d* 797*p*
10:10 218*c* 228*j* 301*c* 915*e*
10:11 266*e* 915*c*
10:12 297*b* 719*e* 884*b*
10:14 299*h* 332*b* 456*f* 621*q*
10:15 108*ai* 184*ay* 827*c*
10:16 365*q* 365*w* 365*ap* 365*bq* 498*n* 751*k* 935*a*
10:17 192*r* 279*j* 371*q* 692*b*
10:18 466*s* 741*w*
10:19 579*q* 670*c* 781*k* 825*w*
10:20 579*q* 965*k* 965*aa*
10:21 11*i* 169*m* 170*e* 272*h* 704*g*
10:22 69*f* 600*c* 668*n* 888*k*
10:23 184*ac* 295*g* 371*j* 620*o* 735*k*
10:24 35*a* 537*b* 742*l*
10:25 83*b* 969*v*
10:26 526*a* 854*af*
10:27 526*a*
10:28 161*i* 320*a* 362*bc* 854*a* 854*af* 972*a*
10:29 309*d* 365*am* 809*h* 812*b*
10:30 86*g* 259*k*
10:31 638*c* 809*a*
10:32 371*t* 526*n*
10:33 371*t* 533*b*
10:34 717*k*
10:35 169*l* 704*g*
10:36 11*i* 705*h*

10:37 887*p* 916*a*
10:38 284*e* 361*ar* 825*m* 916*a* 964*d*
10:39 361*ar* 772*i*
10:40 28*c* 299*c*
10:41 579*ah* 937*a* 962*c*
10:42 339*q* 962*c*
11:1 99*m* 534*i*
11:2 357*y*
11:3 13*c*
11:5 267*g* 416*c* 439*q* 528*e* 648*y* 655*q* 656*n* 656*x* 801*j*
11:6 702*g*
11:7 74*t* 152*b* 172*y*
11:8 192*aa* 228*n*
11:9 579*ab*
11:10 529*r* 669*a*
11:11 34*c* 34*f* 35*b* 733*n*
11:12 176*b* 733*c*
11:13 579*u*
11:14 13*i*
11:15 455*q*
11:16 18*n* 132*k*
11:17 829*d* 835*c* 836*ai*
11:18 946*d* 969*v*
11:19 371*k* 498*c* 880*d* 938*k* 947*a* 949*l*
11:20 184*ac* 924*e* 940*b*
11:21 184*bc* 184*bf* 228*l* 830*e* 864*c* 939*f*
11:22 108*ai* 736*b* 827*c*
11:23 184*as* 184*ay* 864*c*
11:24 108*ai* 736*b* 827*c*
11:25 132*h* 500*b* 525*a* 526*g* 923*g* 965*b*
11:26 826*a*
11:27 170*q* 490*t* 526*i* 781*c*
11:28 289*c* 322*n* 682*d* 683*m*
11:29 177*b* 536*a* 683*n* 747*u* 872*l*
11:30 323*c* 701*d* 747*u*
12:1 301*ai* 370*t* 683*g*

12:2 683*j* 708*j* 916*c*
12:3 579*l* 859*k*
12:4 189*d* 301*ac* 916*c* 990*q*
12:5 579*l* 683*j* 954*d*
12:6 34*b* 990*ab*
12:7 905*h* 961*e* 981*ar*
12:8 371*j* 683*b* 733*aa*
12:9 192*m* 683*g*
12:10 53*f* 342*k* 656*y* 683*j* 915*j* 928*f*
12:11 310*k* 683*j*
12:12 371*e* 638*c* 683*b* 809*a*
12:13 53*f* 656*z*
12:14 362*bk* 490*j* 623*i* 708*h*
12:15 284*c* 656*x* 883*e*
12:16 525*d* 664*f*
12:17 579*z* 725*e*
12:18 59*p* 605*d* 742*k* 826*d* 887*d* 965*l*
12:19 577*h* 582*e* 709*l*
12:20 46*r* 177*b* 218*e* 379*c* 418*p*
12:21 59*p* 852*d*
12:22 439*q* 578*b* 579*b* 656*z* 969*u*
12:23 13*c* 74*s* 864*r*
12:24 300*c* 708*j* 969*a* 969*v*
12:25 46*ak* 490*l*
12:26 300*c* 969*c*
12:27 300*c* 300*g* 969*a* 969*v*
12:28 300*c* 733*f* 965*l*
12:29 162*a* 747*p* 790*n*
12:30 74*d* 75*i* 703*j* 704*e*
12:31 909*h* 980*d*
12:32 124*f* 371*m* 909*c* 965*ah* 980*d*
12:33 171*t* 463*b* 644*f* 645*d*
12:34 365*q* 447*b* 579*a* 938*e*
12:35 799*f*
12:36 108*ai* 579*e*
12:37 579*e* 960*a* 961*i*
12:38 547*f* 586*w* 708*j*
12:39 547*o* 547*p* 579*z* 951*l*
12:40 110*l*^{2} 365*av*

17:1 89*l* 110*n* 209*s*
17:2 147*a* 228*u* 417*d* 427*a*
17:3 445*e* 579*ac* 584*a*
17:4 93*c* 192*y* 644*i*
17:5 170*m* 355*i* 455*k* 826*d* 887*d*
17:6 311*g* 854*p*
17:7 308*i* 854*ah*
17:8 88*o*
17:9 371*j* 525*d* 656*e* 737*g*
17:10 283*f* 586*w*
17:11 656*ag*
17:12 13*i* 371*j* 491*s* 825*j*
17:13 988*s*
17:14 74*t* 311*j*
17:15 309*c* 651*l* 905*b*
17:16 161*f*
17:17 136*d* 200*g* 486*g*
17:18 656*z* 924*e* 969*u*
17:19 161*f* 300*f* 459*l*
17:20 196*f* 209*i* 469*c* 486*g*
17:21 761*e* 946*i*
17:22 184*v* 371*j*
17:23 110*l* 362*bk* 656*e* 834*g*
17:24 184*ar* 797*b* 804*g*
17:25 59*b* 804*g*
17:26 919*f*
17:27 542*z* 702*c* 797*b*
18:1 34*d* 733*o*
18:2 132*g*
18:3 147*d* 297*j* 733*p*
18:4 34*e* 733*o* 872*i*
18:5 28*c* 132*i* 299*c*
18:6 132*i* 217*f* 322*j* 343*c* 485*q* 702*d* 963*m*
18:7 473*b* 702*d* 830*e*[2]
18:8 46*b* 53*c*[2] 297*i* 381*ab* 655*n* 702*h* 963*e* 963*f* 972*a*
18:9 304*g* 438*l* 702*h* 972*a*
18:10 132*i* 922*n* 968*f*
18:12 99*t* 282*b* 365*bp* 459*ad* 519*d* 621*c*
18:13 824*e*
18:14 132*i* 595*a* 598*a*

18:15 88*p* 771*m* 914*u* 924*h*
18:16 90*d* 90*g* 456*f* 466*a*
18:17 59*z* 985*b*
18:18 746*p* 747*p* 971*f*
18:19 90*g* 710*b* 761*e*
18:20 74*j* 89*j* 90*g*
18:21 99*g* 99*h* 106*b* 909*r*
18:22 99*t*
18:23 18*o* 519*d* 733*i* 804*i*
18:24 803*c*
18:25 793*h*
18:26 311*a* 804*i* 823*f*
18:27 905*d* 909*q*
18:28 786*n* 803*c*
18:29 804*i* 823*f*
18:30 747*f*
18:31 524*a*
18:33 905*h*
18:34 827*i*
18:35 909*r*
19:1 184*v* 184*x*
19:2 74*p* 656*x*
19:3 461*k* 708*j* 896*b* 915*j*
19:4 164*h* 372*a* 579*l*
19:5 45*a* 169*k* 621*p*
19:6 45*a* 46*am*
19:7 548*d* 896*b*
19:8 68*f* 602*d* 896*b*
19:9 896*c* 951*h*
19:10 894*d*
19:11 781*l*
19:12 172*h* 733*d*
19:13 132*h* 200*g* 378*o* 924*l*
19:14 132*h* 620*s* 702*c* 733*k*
19:15 378*o*
19:16 360*k* 676*g*
19:17 644*a* 739*g*
19:18 362*a* 466*t* 788*d* 951*k*
19:19 169*i* 866*u* 887*t*
19:20 627*c*
19:21 284*b* 646*d* 781*v* 793*d* 800*r* 971*g*
19:22 800*f* 834*g*
19:23 297*i* 700*c* 733*q* 800*n*
19:24 256*g* 263*ad* 365*bc* 701*c* 733*q*

19:25 668*l* 864*l*
19:26 371*b* 469*a* 470*a*
19:27 284*d* 621*m*
19:28 99*m* 371*j* 480*p* 733*x* 733*ag* 743*b* 743*c*
19:29 360*p* 621*n* 782*b*
19:30 68*j* 69*c*
20:1 18*o* 519*d* 686*a* 733*i* 792*g*
20:2 710*b* 797*b* 804*b* 809*n*
20:3 108*s* 679*k*
20:5 108*u* 108*v*
20:6 108*w* 679*k*
20:8 129*b* 804*a*
20:9 108*w* 797*b*
20:10 797*b*
20:11 829*c*
20:12 28*h* 110*h* 379*a*
20:13 710*b* 797*b*
20:14 28*h*
20:15 816*b* 915*j*
20:16 68*j* 69*c*
20:17 184*ah* 538*a*
20:18 362*bk* 371*j* 586*y* 961*a* 986*n*
20:19 59*c* 110*l* 279*i* 656*e* 851*f*
20:20 169*ad* 311*k* 761*w*
20:21 241*g* 859*ac*
20:22 491*k* 949*m*
20:23 241*g* 669*e*
20:24 891*x*
20:25 59*b* 733*am*
20:26 19*a* 34*e* 742*j*
20:27 68*j*
20:28 361*aj* 371*k* 742*k* 792*q*
20:29 74*p* 184*au*
20:30 90*k* 439*q* 905*b*
20:31 578*h*
20:32 859*f* 859*ac*
20:33 438*a*
20:34 284*c* 378*j* 656*z* 905*e*
21:1 90*h* 184*ah* 209*q*
21:2 365*bd* 746*q*
21:3 627*b*
21:4 725*e*
21:5 177*b* 267*j* 741*c*
21:7 226*i* 267*j*
21:8 53*u* 366*c* 624*h*
21:9 74*q* 295*e* 561*e* 668*c*

21:10 13*c* 821*b*
21:11 13*d* 184*aq* 579*ae*
21:12 218*ag* 221*a* 300*r* 365*ao* 794*a* 990*r*
21:13 255*f* 586*e* 761*a* 789*d* 990*y*
21:14 439*q* 655*q* 656*x*
21:15 132*h* 586*y* 668*x* 891*y* 986*p*
21:16 132*h* 923*a*
21:17 192*ah* 883*e*
21:18 128*f* 859*k*
21:19 172*t* 342*k* 366*r*
21:20 864*s*
21:21 209*i* 485*aa*
21:22 485*ac* 761*ad*
21:23 534*i* 733*z* 986*p* 986*af* 990*r*
21:24 459*k* 460*g*
21:25 371*p* 475*b* 486*n* 988*s*
21:26 579*ab* 854*ad*
21:27 491*k* 525*d* 733*z*
21:28 90*k* 519*d*
21:29 598*e* 603*d*
21:31 283*g* 595*h* 733*q* 938*k* 951*s*
21:32 485*ad* 486*n* 603*d* 913*q*
21:33 370*ab* 519*d* 784*g*
21:34 171*o* 370*t*
21:35 279*d* 362*ao*
21:37 170*q* 920*a*
21:38 362*p* 776*b*
21:39 300*y* 362*bl*
21:41 171*o* 784*g*
21:42 214*e* 344*x* 579*l* 607*k* 864*i*
21:43 171*o* 371*al* 733*t* 786*l*
21:44 332*h* 344*x*
21:45 516*f* 708*c*
21:46 579*ae* 747*n* 854*ad*
22:1 519*b*
22:2 18*o* 519*d* 733*i* 876*b* 894*ae*
22:3 598*e* 737*l*
22:4 669*k*
22:5 456*e*
22:6 362*ao*
22:7 362*bc* 381*v*
22:8 669*k* 916*a*
22:9 624*j* 737*l*

22:10 54k 624j
22:11 228p
22:12 228p 578e
22:13 223h 418o
747o 827c
22:14 104n 105e
605a 737l
22:15 542x 579d
691m 708h
22:16 481d 494d 534k
22:17 804g 915j
22:18 461k 545f
22:19 797e
22:20 22d 590a
22:21 741h 781n
781x 915e
22:22 864l
22:23 656b 708e
22:24 172c 894l
22:25 99d 172c
22:28 894r
22:29 160d 491h
495d 975h
22:30 894r 968c
22:31 579l
22:32 361k 965a 965f
22:33 74s 452b 864l
22:34 578e 708e
22:35 459m 461k
958a
22:36 638b 737e
22:37 887l
22:39 200l 887t
22:40 975d
22:41 459k
22:42 170p 357x 965j
22:43 741d
22:44 241b 727k
22:46 459n 578e
23:1 74t
23:2 534l 586w 708f
23:3 20g 579f 739m
23:4 322k
23:5 194s 234a 371n
875a
23:6 192p 866x 882f
23:7 537a 796a 884a
23:8 11o 537b
23:9 169q
23:10 357y 537b
23:11 34e 742j
23:12 872h
23:13 264l 545f 708g
733r 830g
23:14 545f 708g 830g
896l 961b

23:15 91e 147f 267b
545f 708g
830g 972b
23:16 439c 532d
689a 830g
990y
23:17 501b 638b
23:19 439d 638b
23:22 743a
23:23 102e 366g
458c 545f
708g 830g
953x
23:24 365i 365bc
439c 464b
689a
23:25 223b 224a 545f
648s 708g
788c 830g
943a
23:26 224a 439d 708g
23:27 223a 224a
364r 427g
545f 708g
830g 841f
23:28 224a 543b 954a
23:29 364h 545f 548a
708g 830g
23:30 362ao
23:31 170y 362ao
466g
23:32 725i
23:33 365q 667a
963g 972a
23:34 192r 279j
362aq 500f
579r 586w 735f
23:35 180d 362ac
362ao^2 579z
23:37 74c 184ag
362ao 365al
598e
23:38 990v
23:39 295e 439h 561e
24:1 522f 990y
24:2 165g
24:3 69e 108ag 209q
295g 547j
24:4 495b
24:5 13g 357ad
561m
24:6 718b 854ah
24:7 176i 636f
24:8 167p
24:9 362aq 888k
24:10 603g 888o

24:11 495e 542j
579al
24:12 887q 954a
24:13 69f 600c 668n
24:14 69e 466s 528c
733h
24:15 165x 516a 579z
24:16 620o
24:17 213k
24:18 228c
24:19 167h 301p 830e
24:20 129q 620o
683e 761r
24:21 21k 827b
24:22 114i 605g
24:23 357ad 486p
24:24 357ad 495e
545g 579al
605g 864h
24:25 511b
24:26 486p
24:27 183j 295h
24:28 363m 365aq
24:29 309f 321o 418c
24:30 160f 295g 355i
371j 547j 836u
866q
24:31 74b 414n 605g
968s
24:32 128n 366r 519d
24:33 200m
24:35 2c 115m 153e
321s 529a
24:36 108ag 490f
491q 968b
24:37 295h 508a
24:38 275d 301i 894s
24:40 90k 786d
24:41 90k 786d
24:42 108ag 295h
457c 491q^2
24:43 108ah 789f
24:44 108ag 295h
371k 508a 669c
24:45 301y 751h
24:46 676m
24:48 136b
24:49 279d 949g
24:50 108ag 508a
24:51 46a 545f 827c
25:1 18o 99k 420l
519d 733i 895e
25:2 99a 500a 501f
25:3 357a 670d
25:5 136b 679d
25:6 129o 295b
25:7 60d

25:8 418q
25:9 636j 792d
25:10 264l
25:11 263ae
25:12 491u
25:13 108ag 457c
25:14 267b 519d 751h
25:15 99a 160j 797e
25:16 771k 791b
25:17 771k
25:18 525h
25:19 113h 804i
25:20 771k
25:21 733ag 824f 929i
25:22 771k
25:23 733ag 824f 929i
25:24 370y 735a
25:25 525h
25:26 370y 679k
25:27 803j
25:29 38c 39b 772a
773a 781l 786k
25:30 223h 287m
418o 827c
25:31 295g 371j 519d
733x 743b 968t
25:32 46as 74c 365bp
25:33 241c
25:34 68c 669e 733k
777n
25:35 59ad 299c
301n 859g
859m
25:36 228w 229g
651b 747e
25:37 859g 859m
25:38 59ad 229g
25:39 651b 747e
25:40 11l 28c
25:41 300q 963e
963f^2
25:42 859g 859m
25:43 59af 228w
229g 651b
747e
25:44 59ad 229g
651b 747e
859g 859m
25:45 28e
25:46 360p 963f 963g
26:1 69j
26:2 110k 362bk 371j
988f
26:3 362bk 986k
986p
26:4 362bk 542x 623i
747n

26:5   61*a* 988*f*
26:6   184*at* 651*l*
26:7   213*e* 311*ad*
     350*x* 396*j* 811*a*
26:8   634*a*
26:9   781*w* 811*a*
26:10   490*l* 644*d* 702*c*
26:11   89*m* 801*a*
26:12   364*b* 669*l*
26:13   183*i* 505*m* 528*i*
26:14   986*o*
26:15   809*e*
26:16   137*e* 272*e*
26:17   669*j* 988*f*
26:18   108*ab* 537*e*
26:20   129*d* 311*ad*
26:21   272*f*
26:22   13*n* 834*g*
26:23   272*f* 882*e*
26:24   2*b* 371*j* 586*f*
     830*e*
26:25   13*n* 488*a*
26:26   46*p* 319*e* 907*i*
26:27   301*h*
26:28   335*o* 765*m* 909*l*
26:29   126*h* 733*v* 948*c*
26:30   209*q* 412*d*
26:31   75*g* 365*bq* 369*j*
     603*g*
26:32   184*w* 283*c* 656*e*
26:33   603*g*
26:34   94*b* 409*c* 533*b*
26:35   361*r* 533*b*
26:36   761*h*
26:37   89*l* 825*j*
26:38   457*d* 834*e*
26:39   311*g* 469*b*
     595*e* 761*h*
     949*m*
26:40   110*h* 457*d* 679*c*
26:41   163*e* 319*a*
     320*a* 457*d*
     597*c* 612*m*
26:42   595*f* 761*h*
26:43   679*c*
26:44   106*a* 761*h*
26:45   108*ab* 272*g*
     371*j* 679*c*
26:46   272*g*
26:47   74*n* 723*n* 986*o*
26:48   547*f* 889*e*
26:49   537*e* 884*d*
26:50   747*n* 880*f*
26:51   46*b* 415*h* 655*i*
26:53   99*m* 722*j* 968*n*
26:54   725*e*

26:55   74*t* 534*i* 723*n*
     789*g*
26:56   589*i* 620*k* 725*e*
26:57   986*k*
26:58   199*f* 235*d* 284*f*
26:59   466*v* 692*c*
26:60   90*e*
26:61   110*l* 164*ab*
     165*h* 990*x*
26:62   460*l*
26:63   13c^2 13*f* 357*w*
     532*r* 582*e*
26:64   241*b* 311*ah*
     355*i* 371*j*[2]
     488*a*
26:65   46*t* 836*g* 891*t*
     980*c*
26:66   915*f*
26:67   279*i* 302*m*
26:68   579*af*
26:69   89*j* 235*d*
26:70   491*n* 533*b*
26:71   89*j* 184*aq*
26:72   491*n*
26:73   580*a*
26:74   409*c* 491*n*
     532*g* 899*p*
26:75   94*b* 409*c* 505*r*
     836*ae*
27:1   128*e* 362*bk*
     623*i* 691*m*
     986*p*
27:2   272*a* 747*t*
27:3   272*e* 809*e* 830*c*
     961*e*
27:4   335*e* 860*a*
     914*ad*
27:5   217*d* 287*o*
     362*ae*
27:6   335*e* 799*d* 809*n*
     916*c*
27:7   235*q* 364*g* 792*c*
27:8   235*q* 335*e*
27:9   579*z* 725*e* 809*e*
27:10   235*q*
27:11   459*o* 488*a* 741*c*
27:12   582*e* 928*f* 986*p*
27:13   466*f*
27:14   582*e* 864*k*
27:15   127*c* 746*f*
27:16   750*a*
27:17   746*f* 988*f*
27:18   912*c*
27:19   10*f* 438*v* 620*t*
     956*a*
27:20   74*n* 612*b* 986*p*
27:22   357*w* 362*bk*

27:23   914*af*
27:24   61*a* 648*b* 935*d*
27:25   180*c*
27:26   279*i* 746*f*
27:27   722*n*
27:28   228*m* 229*l* 431*d*
27:29   218*c* 241*c*
     256*m* 311*i*
     741*c* 743*d* 851*f*
27:30   279*i* 302*m*
27:31   229*l* 851*f*
27:32   273*f* 740*a* 964*d*
27:33   363*g* 561*u*
27:34   375*a* 598*b* 948*c*
27:35   228*aa* 362*bl*
     605*r* 783*c*
27:36   457*f*
27:37   741*c* 928*f*
27:38   90*l* 241*g* 362*bl*
     789*e*
27:39   921*a*
27:40   13*c* 110*l* 164*ab*
     165*h* 170*o*
     309*g* 668*x* 990*x*
27:41   851*f* 986*p*
27:42   309*g* 485*r* 668*x*
27:43   170*o* 485*g* 668*f*
     826*d*
27:44   921*a*
27:45   108*u* 108*v* 418*b*
27:46   108*v* 577*d* 621*e*
27:47   579*ac*
27:48   218*c* 301*h* 393*a*
27:49   579*ac*
27:50   361*ai* 577*d*
27:51   46*m* 46*u* 176*i*
     421*e*
27:52   364*j* 656*m* 979*j*
27:53   445*e*
27:54   13*e* 170*n* 854*u*
27:55   199*f* 373*e*
27:56   169*ad*
27:57   129*e* 538*a* 800*f*
27:58   363*l* 761*al*
27:59   226*d* 364*k*
27:60   126*e* 315*c* 344*i*
     364*l*
27:61   240*a*
27:62   669*j* 708*c* 986*p*
27:63   110*l* 542*d* 656*e*
27:64   364*k* 655*a*
     660*h* 788*l*
27:66   264*m*
28:1   108*b* 364*k* 683*f*
28:2   176*f* 315*d* 344*j*
     968*o*
28:3   228*t* 417*g* 427*a*

28:4   854*m*
28:5   459*ag* 854*ah*
28:6   190*e* 656*f*
28:7   184*w* 277*h* 283*c*
     524*c*
28:8   824*u* 854*m*
28:9   295*b* 378*c* 884*d*
     981*g*
28:10   11*l* 184*w* 854*ah*
28:11   524*a*
28:12   612*i* 691*m* 986*p*
28:13   129*f* 679*c* 788*l*
28:14   415*d*
28:15   528*n*
28:16   99*l* 184*w* 209*s*
28:17   486*l* 981*g*
28:18   733*aa*
28:19   93*a* 538*d* 988*w*
28:20   69*e* 89*j* 115*e*
     534*q* 739*k*

Mark

1:1   68*l* 170*n* 357*v*
     529*l* 965*i*
1:2   66*b* 579*z* 669*a*
1:3   172*y* 249*a* 624*i*
     669*a*
1:4   172*y* 528*b* 909*m*
     939*d* 988*s*
1:5   350*o* 526*r*
1:6   228*j* 259*b* 301*ai*
     365*j* 392*a*
1:7   160*e* 284*i* 746*t*
     916*a*
1:8   339*t* 965*w* 988*s*
     988*y*
1:9   184*aq* 988*u*
1:10   263*ag* 365*ap*
     965*l*
1:11   170*m* 826*d*
1:12   172*z* 300*y*
     965*ae*
1:13   110*r* 365*f* 612*p*
     968*n* 969*d*
1:14   184*v* 528*f* 747*b*
1:15   108*z* 200*d* 485*n*
     733*f* 939*b*
1:16   11*c* 343*l* 686*c*
1:17   284*b* 686*c*
1:18   284*b* 621*m*
1:19   11*c* 275*j* 656*ad*
1:20   284*b* 621*m*
1:21   184*as* 192*m*
     534*i* 683*g*
1:22   733*aa* 864*l*
1:23   577*e* 969*u*

7:35 498c 927d	**8:31** 761v 972c	**9:23** 284e 361ar	**10:8** 301d
7:36 708i 882d	**8:32** 297n 365bj	533f 825m	**10:9** 200d 656aa
7:37 396j 938k	756a	964d	733f
7:38 357u 648e	**8:33** 309h 361ah	**9:24** 361ar 772i	**10:10** 299h
836ae 889f	**8:35** 228a 311af	**9:25** 771h 772i	**10:11** 200d 332b
7:39 490l 579af 938k	502a 854o	**9:26** 295g 371j 866q	621q 733f
7:41 90k 519d 803c	**8:37** 275j 607k 854o	872q 968t	**10:12** 184ay 827c
7:42 887p 909q	**8:38** 89l	**9:27** 733f	**10:13** 184bc 184bf
7:44 648e	**8:39** 676d^2	**9:28** 89l 110p 209s^2	830e 864c 939f
7:45 889f	**8:40** 74r	761h	**10:14** 827c
7:46 357s	**8:41** 192o 311j 656z	**9:29** 147a 228u 427a	**10:15** 184as 311r
7:47 887p 909f	**8:42** 74p 88h 131g	**9:30** 445e 579ac	**10:16** 28c 28e 455v
7:48 909f	**8:43** 110z 302e 651k	866t	**10:17** 99s 969aa
7:49 13c 909n	658b	**9:31** 184ah 296e	**10:18** 309f 969x
7:50 485t	**8:44** 234a 378p 656z	**9:32** 679c	**10:19** 365p 645h
8:1 528f 733h	**8:45** 74p 378c	**9:33** 93c 192y	733ag 969aa
8:2 99e 373e 656z	**8:46** 160f	**9:34** 355i	**10:20** 548e 824t
969y	**8:47** 311j	**9:35** 170m 605d	**10:21** 132h 500b
8:3 686d	**8:48** 485z	**9:36** 88o 525d	525a 526g
8:4 74p 370ab 519d	**8:49** 361ae 656o	**9:37** 74r	826a
8:5 75m 279t 365ak	**8:50** 485z 854ai	**9:38** 88h	**10:22** 490t 526i 781c
624j	**8:51** 89l 757d	**9:39** 318a 969u	**10:23** 490u
8:6 344m	**8:52** 679e 836q	**9:40** 161f 300f	**10:24** 859a
8:7 256k 362v	**8:53** 851f	**9:41** 136d 486g	**10:25** 360k 360p
8:8 36f 99t 171j	**8:54** 308i 310c 378k	**9:42** 318a 656z 924e	461k 676g
455q	656z	**9:43** 864r	777n 958a
8:10 517c 519c 526g	**8:55** 301s	**9:44** 272g 371j	**10:26** 586d
733g 781i	**8:56** 525d 864r	**9:45** 459n 517d 854p	**10:27** 200l 887l 887t
8:11 75m 370ab	**9:1** 656aa 733ag	**9:46** 34d 709h	**10:28** 676e
529h	969aa	**9:47** 132i 490l	**10:29** 200l 927h
8:12 485t 485x 624j	**9:2** 528c 656aa	**9:48** 28c 34e 35b	**10:30** 184au 229l
786k 969g	733h	299c	519d 789e
8:13 114o 344m	**9:3** 218c 228j 670d	**9:49** 89t 300g 757g	**10:31** 986s
824n	797p	**9:50** 706d	**10:32** 986ad
8:14 172r 256k 362v	**9:4** 266e	**9:51** 184ah 310h	**10:33** 59t 371ab 905i
800l 825w	**9:5** 299h 332b 621q	599c	**10:34** 357t 658e
8:15 171o 600c	**9:6** 528c 656aa	**9:52** 371ab 529r	**10:35** 457k 797e
8:16 420k 519d 526a	**9:7** 13d 474a 656m	**9:53** 184ah 299f	**10:36** 200l
8:17 526a	741v	**9:54** 381t	**10:37** 20d
8:18 38c 39b 772a	**9:9** 13c 362ar	**9:55** 924e	**10:39** 311af 455k
773a 781l 786k	**9:10** 184bf 883e	**9:56** 668e	**10:40** 703i
8:19 11k 74q 169af	**9:11** 74p 656x 733h	**9:57** 284d	**10:41** 825u
8:21 11l 169ag 739a	**9:12** 301t	**9:58** 192al	**10:42** 596a
8:22 222h 275j	**9:13** 99a 301ai	**9:59** 169i 284b 364n	**11:1** 534i 761d 761h
8:23 54a 176j 679c	**9:14** 99r 99u 311ac	**9:60** 364n 528c 733h	**11:2** 169q 733j 761e
8:24 266b 343g 352o	**9:16** 907i	**9:61** 284d 882i	979c
678g 924e	**9:17** 41c 99n 635f	**9:62** 370e 603i 733m	**11:3** 141a 301x
8:25 13c 343g 352o	**9:18** 13c 459k 761h	916a	**11:4** 612m 909r
486g 739e	**9:19** 13d	**10:1** 90h 99s 751c	**11:5** 129k 519d 784a
8:26 184x	**9:20** 13e 357v 459k	**10:2** 105e 370w^2	**11:7** 620t
8:27 192ak 229j 364i	965i	686a 761u	**11:8** 600h
969u	**9:21** 525d	**10:3** 365w 365bq	**11:9** 263ae 279p
8:28 10a 170n 311j	**9:22** 110l 362bk 371j	751k	459r 484b
827n	607k 656e	**10:4** 670d 797p 884i	761ac
8:29 300b 656z 747o	825j 986n	**10:5** 719e	**11:11** 301c 301as
8:30 104s 297n		**10:6** 719e	761am
561ab		**10:7** 266e 301d 804a	

11:13	781*a* 781*j* 914*j* 938*e* 965*u*	**12:4**	161*i* 319*j* 362*g* 854*af*	**12:49**	381*w*	**14:5**	310*k* 683*j*
11:14	300*a* 578*b* 579*b* 656*z* 864*r*	**12:5**	362*bc* 854*a* 972*a*	**12:50**	988*v*	**14:6**	578*e*
				12:51	46*ao* 717*k*	**14:7**	519*d* 866*x*
11:15	300*c* 969*v*	**12:6**	365*am* 505*d* 809*h* 812*b*	**12:52**	46*ao* 704*g*	**14:9**	309*i* 872*n*
11:16	461*k* 547*f*			**12:53**	169*l*	**14:10**	308*k* 872*c*
11:17	46*ak*	**12:7**	86*g* 259*k* 638*c*	**12:54**	340*b*	**14:11**	872*h*
11:18	300*c* 969*c*	**12:8**	371*j* 371*t* 526*n*	**12:56**	121*a* 520*d* 545*f*	**14:12**	804*i* 876*d*
11:19	300*g*	**12:9**	371*t* 533*b* 968*s*	**12:57**	480*a* 959*c*	**14:13**	439*n* 655*n* 801*i*
11:20	53*p* 378*s* 733*f* 965*l*	**12:10**	909*h* 965*ah* 980*d*	**12:58**	719*h*	**14:14**	656*k* 804*k*
				12:59	804*i*	**14:15**	733*v* 876*e*
11:22	162*e* 747*p*	**12:11**	192*r* 670*c* 781*k* 825*w*	**13:1**	335*n* 981*ah*	**14:16**	519*d* 882*f*
11:23	74*d* 75*i* 704*e*			**13:2**	938*i*	**14:17**	669*k*
11:24	969*o*	**12:12**	579*q* 965*aa*	**13:3**	939*b*	**14:18**	614*a*
11:25	60*c*	**12:13**	783*d*	**13:4**	209*al* 938*i*	**14:21**	439*n* 655*n* 801*i*
11:26	99*e* 655*a*	**12:14**	480*j* 957*b*	**13:5**	939*b*	**14:22**	183*a*
11:27	167*b* 169*af* 301*p*	**12:15**	457*a* 777*b* 859*w*	**13:6**	172*t* 366*r* 519*d*	**14:23**	54*k* 740*a*
				13:7	46*ac*	**14:25**	74*p*
11:28	739*j*	**12:16**	171*j* 519*d*	**13:8**	171*f* 620*t*	**14:26**	169*l* 538*c* 888*p*
11:29	547*p* 579*z* 938*a*	**12:18**	632*d* 777*b*	**13:9**	46*ac*	**14:27**	284*e* 361*ar* 825*m* 964*d*
11:30	184*bb* 547*e*[2]	**12:19**	301*i*	**13:10**	192*m* 534*i* 683*g*		
11:31	34*b* 199*a* 498*m* 961*b*	**12:20**	501*b*	**13:11**	110*z* 246*b* 969*u*	**14:28**	209*aj* 809*o*
		12:21	800*n* 800*r*	**13:12**	746*n*	**14:29**	726*a*
11:32	34*b* 184*bb*	**12:22**	228*v* 301*x* 825*w*	**13:13**	378*x* 656*z*	**14:31**	691*a* 718*e*
11:33	420*k* 526*a*	**12:23**	319*i* 360*a*	**13:14**	656*y* 683*j* 891*y*	**14:32**	719*i*
11:34	44*a* 417*o* 418*l* 438*i*	**12:24**	301*v* 365*ak* 370*y* 638*c*	**13:15**	545*f* 683*j*	**14:33**	538*c* 621*m*
				13:16	110*z* 170*v* 746*n* 969*h*	**14:34**	387*a* 641*e*
11:35	417*s*	**12:25**	113*f* 825*w*			**14:35**	455*q*
11:37	708*i* 882*d*	**12:27**	222*l* 228*n*	**13:18**	18*o* 75*n* 370*ab* 519*d* 733*i*	**15:1**	938*k*
11:38	648*d* 864*k*	**12:28**	114*l* 228*v* 486*g*			**15:2**	299*b* 708*j* 829*c* 882*c*
11:39	224*a* 648*s* 788*c*	**12:29**	825*w*	**13:19**	36*f* 192*ai* 196*f* 365*ak*		
11:40	224*b*	**12:30**	59*a* 490*g* 980*d*			**15:3**	519*d*
11:41	224*b* 648*r*	**12:31**	38*c* 459*t* 733*j*	**13:20**	18*o*	**15:4**	99*t* 365*bp* 459*ad* 621*c* 772*j*
11:42	102*e* 458*c* 830*g*	**12:32**	365*bp* 733*k* 826*e* 854*ah*	**13:21**	93*c* 323*g*		
11:43	192*p* 830*g* 866*x* 884*a*			**13:22**	184*ah* 534*i*		
		12:33	51*f* 781*v* 788*i* 793*d* 800*r* 971*g*	**13:23**	105*e*	**15:5**	824*e*
11:44	364*r* 830*g*			**13:24**	104*n* 105*e* 161*g* 206*a* 297*f* 716*k*	**15:6**	772*j*
11:45	921*c* 958*a*	**12:34**	800*r*			**15:7**	824*e* 939*b* 971*b*
11:46	322*k* 830*g* 958*a*	**12:35**	420*l* 669*c*			**15:8**	420*d* 519*d* 772*j*
11:47	362*ao* 364*h* 830*g*	**12:36**	148*r* 263*af* 279*p* 507*e* 519*d*	**13:25**	263*ae* 264*e* 279*p* 491*u*	**15:9**	772*j* 824*e*
				13:27	300*q* 491*u*	**15:10**	824*e* 939*b* 968*d*
11:48	923*w*			**13:28**	300*q* 733*v* 827*c*	**15:11**	90*k* 519*d*
11:49	362*aq* 498*h* 579*r*	**12:37**	742*k*	**13:29**	183*i* 876*e*	**15:12**	783*d*
		12:38	108*ag*	**13:30**	68*j* 69*c*	**15:13**	199*b* 634*a*
11:50	180*d* 335*c* 362*ao* 480*u* 579*x*	**12:39**	108*ah* 491*q* 789*f*	**13:31**	362*bk* 708*h* 741*v*	**15:14**	636*a*
						15:15	301*aj*
		12:40	108*ag* 371*j* 508*a* 669*c*	**13:32**	110*l* 300*b* 365*u* 656*x*	**15:16**	301*ar*
11:51	579*z*					**15:17**	502*a*
11:52	263*v* 297*k* 490*a* 830*g* 958*a*	**12:42**	301*y*	**13:33**	184*ag* 362*ao*	**15:18**	914*ad*
		12:43	676*m*	**13:34**	74*c* 184*ag* 365*al* 598*e*	**15:19**	742*a* 916*a*
		12:44	751*h*			**15:20**	199*m* 889*a* 905*d*
11:53	459*m* 704*e*	**12:45**	136*b* 279*d* 949*g*	**13:35**	295*e* 561*e*		
11:54	579*d*	**12:46**	46*a* 108*ag* 486*j* 508*a*	**14:1**	708*i* 882*d*	**15:21**	914*ad* 916*a*
12:1	74*q* 323*h* 457*a* 543*b*			**14:2**	651*k*	**15:22**	228*m* 743*k*
		12:47	490*v* 963*d*	**14:3**	656*y* 683*j* 915*j* 958*a*	**15:23**	876*c*
		12:48	491*x* 736*b* 781*l* 915*g* 963*d*			**15:24**	360*m* 361*x* 772*j* 824*e*
12:2	526*a*			**14:4**	378*k* 582*g* 656*z*	**15:25**	412*a* 835*c*

1:9	417d	**2:7**	54a	**3:36**	360u 485u 738l	**5:3**	651j
1:10	164f 491g	**2:9**	386b		891f	**5:5**	110ab
1:11	299f	**2:11**	68l 184bf 485p	**4:1**	988w	**5:6**	859f
1:12	170t 299e 485u		547g 866l	**4:2**	988w	**5:7**	283g
1:13	167s 595a 595e	**2:12**	184ar	**4:3**	184u	**5:8**	267g 273b 308i
1:14	88i 192f 319d	**2:13**	184ah 988f	**4:4**	184s		656z
	371g 494c	**2:14**	365ao 794a 990r	**4:5**	184s	**5:9**	267g 683j
	866l 897q	**2:15**	221a 300r 794a	**4:6**	108x 339d 684b	**5:10**	683j 916c
1:15	34b	**2:16**	365ao 796b	**4:7**	339q 373e	**5:11**	267g
1:16	54j 782d 897q	**2:17**	818b 990y	**4:9**	371ab 883a	**5:13**	491n
1:17	494c 897q 953a	**2:18**	547f 547o	**4:10**	339o 339q 781g	**5:14**	939b
1:18	88i 438e 520g	**2:19**	110l 164ab	**4:11**	211a	**5:16**	683j
	526i 965h		165h 990x	**4:12**	34b	**5:17**	146d 676a
1:19	13i 466o	**2:20**	110ac	**4:13**	859l	**5:18**	28a 169t 362bk
1:20	13i 357ae	**2:21**	319d 990ab	**4:14**	339o 360s 635h		965h
1:21	$13i^2$ 579ae	**2:22**	485ad 505g		859d	**5:19**	20a 745j
1:22	13i˙	**2:23**	184ah 485p	**4:15**	859d	**5:20**	864s 887d
1:23	66b 249a 579z		547h 864c	**4:16**	894z	**5:21**	360s 656k
	624i 669a	**2:24**	490l	**4:18**	99a 951d	**5:22**	480i
1:24	708j	**3:1**	708i	**4:19**	579ae	**5:23**	866p
1:25	988s	**3:2**	89i 129f 547g	**4:20**	184ak 209v	**5:24**	360u 480k 485u
1:26	339t 491g 988s		864c		981b	**5:25**	360w 361x 656k
1:27	916a	**3:3**	167s 733p	**4:22**	371af 491e	**5:26**	360h
1:28	184be	**3:4**	167c	**4:23**	320a 459ad	**5:27**	371i 480i 733aa
1:29	365br 941m	**3:5**	167s 297j 733p		494h 981b	**5:28**	656k
1:30	34b	**3:6**	167s	**4:24**	320a 320c 494h	**5:29**	656l
1:31	339t 491m	**3:7**	167s		965a	**5:30**	161c 480i 595e
	526m 988s	**3:8**	167s 352n	**4:25**	357v		745j
1:32	365ap 466m	**3:10**	517e 537a	**4:26**	13f 965i	**5:31**	466m
	965l	**3:11**	466n 490w	**4:27**	864k	**5:32**	466o
1:33	339t 491m 965l	**3:12**	486i 971d	**4:28**	621u	**5:33**	466m
	965w 988y	**3:13**	371l 971d	**4:29**	13e 965i	**5:35**	420k
1:34	170n 466o	**3:14**	310g 365p 371j	**4:31**	301d	**5:36**	466m
1:36	365br	**3:15**	360u 485u	**4:34**	301ba 595e	**5:37**	438e 466m
1:37	284b	**3:16**	88i 360u 485u		739b	**5:38**	486h
1:38	192ah		781g 887i	**4:35**	110s 370w 427e	**5:39**	360q 360s 466m
1:39	108t 192ah	**3:17**	480j 668e 961b		669i		975c
1:40	11c	**3:18**	88i $480k^2$ 485w	**4:36**	74d 75j 370u	**5:41**	371r
1:41	357v 965i		486j 961b		804c	**5:42**	887q
1:42	344y	**3:19**	417d 418l 480k	**4:37**	75j 370w	**5:43**	299f
1:43	284b		887ag	**4:38**	370y	**5:44**	88a 486i
1:44	184bf	**3:20**	417h 526t 888e	**4:39**	466o 485p	**5:45**	928d
1:45	184aq 586g 975c	**3:21**	417o 676k	**4:40**	192ah	**5:46**	485ad 586g
1:46	184ap	**3:22**	988w	**4:41**	485p		975c
1:47	371ag 542k	**3:23**	184be 339t 988s	**4:42**	668e	**6:1**	222h 343l
1:48	366r	**3:25**	648u	**4:43**	184u	**6:2**	74p 547h
1:49	170n 741c	**3:26**	466m 988w	**4:44**	579w 867b	**6:3**	209s
1:50	366r	**3:27**	781l	**4:46**	184as 184bf	**6:4**	988f
1:51	263ag 308f	**3:28**	13i 357ae	**4:47**	656z	**6:5**	301t
	968n 971c	**3:29**	824f	**4:48**	486h 547o	**6:6**	461d
2:1	169af 184bf	**3:30**	872m	**4:49**	361p	**6:7**	809m
	894z	**3:31**	638a 971d	**4:50**	485p	**6:9**	99a 301ai
2:3	636c 949d	**3:32**	466p	**4:52**	108y 654b	**6:10**	99u 311ac
2:4	10a 108ab	**3:33**	494c	**4:53**	485p	**6:11**	907i
2:5	739a	**3:34**	579p 965l	**4:54**	547g	**6:12**	635f
2:6	99b 339x 465d	**3:35**	781c 887d	**5:1**	184ah 988a	**6:13**	41c 99n
	648u			**5:2**	264d 346a	**6:14**	547g 579ae

6:15	209s 740a 741l 883e
6:17	222h 275j
6:19	269a 269e 854p
6:20	1c 854ai
6:21	295j
6:22	275j
6:24	184ar 459ag
6:26	459ag 547h
6:27	301ba 360s 360v 371i 751g
6:28	676g
6:29	485m
6:30	547f 547o
6:31	301ae
6:32	301af
6:33	301af² 971d
6:35	13h 301af 485j 635h 859e
6:36	486h
6:37	300s 781d
6:38	595e 745j
6:39	595a 772j 781d
6:40	360u 485u 656k
6:41	13h 301af 971d
6:42	13d 309e 971d
6:44	289c 656k
6:45	534f
6:46	438e
6:47	360u
6:48	13h 301af
6:50	301af 971d
6:51	13h 301af 319e 360v 971d
6:52	319e
6:53	301af 335h 371m
6:54	319e 360v 656k
6:56	319e
6:57	360h
6:58	301af 360v
6:59	184as 192m
6:60	700d
6:61	702g
6:62	308f 371l
6:63	319l 320d²
6:64	272f 486h 490l
6:65	289c
6:66	282d
6:68	360q
6:69	13e
6:70	605e 969j
6:71	272e
7:1	184v 362bk
7:2	988i
7:3	11k
7:4	526l

7:5	486g
7:6	108ab
7:7	466p 888e
7:8	108ab
7:9	184u
7:10	530f
7:12	542d 937b
7:13	573a 854ab
7:14	534i
7:15	493a 864l
7:16	452b
7:17	452b 595g
7:18	932a
7:19	362bk 738h 953a
7:20	969v
7:21	864r
7:22	683j 988m²
7:23	891y
7:24	445f 480a
7:25	362bk
7:26	357w
7:27	187d 357x 491l 965j
7:28	491g
7:29	490t
7:30	108ab 747n
7:31	357v 485p 547i
7:32	747n
7:33	89m 114h
7:34	459ag
7:35	75c
7:36	459ag
7:37	69a 859d
7:38	339o 350i 485j
7:39	866n 965t²
7:40	579ae
7:41	13e 184t 357v 357x
7:42	184ao 357x
7:43	46ao
7:44	747n
7:46	579p
7:47	495c
7:48	486g
7:49	493b
7:51	455p 480a 961g
7:52	184t 579af
8:1	209q
8:2	534i 990r
8:3	951i
8:5	963r
8:6	53p 461k 586n 928f
8:7	935i
8:8	586n
8:10	961g

8:11	939b
8:12	13h 417d 417n
8:13	466m
8:14	490k 491l
8:15	480a 480j
8:16	480i
8:17	90d 466a
8:18	466m²
8:19	491g
8:20	108ab 534i 799c
8:21	361u 459ag
8:22	362ae
8:23	209b
8:24	1b 361u 485w
8:25	13c
8:26	494c
8:27	169q
8:28	1b 88r 310g 371j
8:29	89i 826d
8:30	485p
8:31	538c
8:32	494a 746m
8:33	371ai
8:34	745m 914s
8:35	115e
8:36	746m 746o
8:37	362bk
8:39	169p
8:40	362bk
8:41	169q
8:42	88r 169aa 887q
8:43	517e
8:44	169aa 362b 494i 543a 545c 969f² 969n
8:45	486h
8:46	935g
8:47	455k
8:48	371ab 969v
8:49	866u
8:50	866m
8:51	360q
8:52	969v
8:53	13c 34b
8:54	866m 866n
8:55	490t 491e
8:56	824u
8:57	131g
8:58	1b
8:59	344n 362bk 523h
9:1	130d 439q 656z
9:2	914ae
9:3	526k 651c
9:4	128l 129n

9:5	417d
9:6	302n 344c 658e
9:7	346a 648h
9:8	13m 761ai
9:11	344c 648h 658e
9:13	708j
9:14	683j
9:15	344c 648h 658e
9:16	46ao 547g
9:17	579ae
9:18	169o
9:19	13m 130d
9:20	130d
9:21	134b
9:22	192s 300w 357ab 854ab
9:23	134b
9:24	938m
9:25	490v 491o
9:27	456e
9:28	538c
9:29	187d 491l
9:31	456b
9:32	130d
9:34	167m 300w 938e
9:35	371h 485p
9:36	13c
9:38	485o 981g
9:39	439j 480i
9:40	439d
10:1	369l 519d 789a
10:2	297h
10:3	263af 561ac 577b
10:4	283e 284a
10:5	59y 577b
10:6	517d
10:7	13h 264b
10:8	789a
10:9	13h 264b 297f
10:10	360j 362b 789a
10:11	13h 361aj 369l
10:12	365v 620b 792b
10:14	13h 369l 490m
10:15	490t
10:16	88e 369l
10:17	361ai 887d
10:19	46ao
10:20	503d 969v
10:22	988l
10:23	129q 263i 990r
10:24	13c 136a 357w 573a
10:25	466m 486j
10:26	486j

16:11	480e 961b 969a 969z	**18:12**	747n	**19:30**	361ai 725a	**21:8**	199j 288b
16:13	124l 494g 965k	**18:13**	986k	**19:31**	363c 669j 683f	**21:9**	381m
16:14	526m 866o	**18:14**	361aj 640c	**19:32**	46i	**21:11**	99t
16:15	773e	**18:15**	284f	**19:33**	363l	**21:12**	13j
16:16	114h 438g	**18:17**	533b	**19:34**	239c 335p 655l	**21:14**	445c
16:20	824x 836t	**18:18**	380c 381am	**19:35**	466n 494g	**21:15**	301y 887p
16:21	167c 167n	**18:19**	459o	**19:36**	46i 725e	**21:16**	369g
16:22	824x	**18:20**	192m 522d 534i 579p 990q	**19:37**	441c 655l	**21:17**	94b 301y 490j
16:23	459n 761ad			**19:38**	363l 538a 854ab	**21:18**	133f 228a 598c
16:24	824x	**18:21**	459o			**21:19**	284b 361al 362ar 866j
16:25	519b 573a	**18:22**	279i 460i	**19:39**	129f 322d 396n		
16:26	761i	**18:24**	986k	**19:40**	226d 364d 364k	**21:20**	887j
16:27	887i	**18:25**	381am 533b	**19:41**	126a 370c	**21:22**	284b 361as
16:28	148q	**18:26**	46b 89j	**19:42**	364l 669j	**21:23**	361au
16:29	573a	**18:27**	409c	**20:1**	108b 263ab 344j	**21:24**	466s
16:30	490j	**18:28**	192af 649l 988f			**21:25**	586i 589m
16:32	75g 89i	**18:29**	928f	**20:2**	786d 887j		
16:33	717d 727k 974e	**18:31**	963l	**20:4**	277d	**Acts**	
17:1	108ab 761i 866n	**18:32**	361ai 725b	**20:5**	364d	**1:1**	534i
		18:33	192af 741c	**20:6**	226d	**1:2**	308b 737f 965l
17:2	360s 733aa 781d	**18:36**	716j 733x	**20:8**	485o	**1:3**	110r 466p 733f
		18:37	455o 466p 488a 494d 741c	**20:9**	517d 656e	**1:4**	764g
17:3	88b 360r 490u			**20:11**	836t	**1:5**	339t 965w 988y
17:4	725a 866j			**20:12**	90m 427a 968o	**1:6**	656ag 733e
17:5	68c 866n	**18:38**	494a 935g	**20:13**	786d	**1:7**	108z 491q 733a
17:6	526i 781d	**18:39**	746f 988f	**20:14**	491m	**1:8**	68n 160m 183i 184s 184ai 466n 782c 965x
17:8	579p	**18:40**	789e	**20:15**	459ag 686f		
17:9	781d	**19:1**	279i	**20:16**	537e		
17:10	773e	**19:2**	228m 256m 743d	**20:17**	148q 308b² 378c 786n		
17:11	88e 561e					**1:9**	308b 355i
17:12	165w 660b 725e	**19:3**	279i	**20:19**	108b 129e 264e 717b 854ab	**1:10**	90m 427a 968o
		19:4	935g			**1:11**	148r
17:13	824f	**19:5**	13d 371g 436c			**1:12**	199k 209q
17:14	10c 888k	**19:6**	362bk 935g	**20:20**	53i 239c 526m 655l	**1:13**	194t 708m
17:15	660b	**19:7**	13f 170o 965i			**1:14**	11k 169af 761u
17:16	10c 974e	**19:8**	854o	**20:21**	717b 751k	**1:15**	99t
17:17	494d 979n	**19:9**	187b 582e	**20:22**	352a 782c 965u	**1:16**	725e
17:18	751k	**19:10**	733ad	**20:23**	909c	**1:18**	46d 224g 235q 309c 361ad
17:19	979n	**19:11**	733ad 914z	**20:24**	190f		
17:20	485q	**19:12**	741c 746f	**20:25**	239c 378c 486l 547f	**1:19**	335e
17:21	88e 224d 485m	**19:13**	624k 956a			**1:20**	190o
17:22	866r	**19:14**	108r 669j 741c	**20:26**	717b	**1:22**	466n 988s
17:23	224d 751k	**19:15**	362bk	**20:27**	53i 239c 378c 486l	**1:24**	490i 605e 761u
17:24	68c 89j 781d 887d	**19:17**	273f 363g 964d			**1:26**	99l 605r 754c
		19:18	90l 362bl²	**20:28**	965h	**2:1**	74h 988h
17:25	490t 751k 974e	**19:19**	184aq 590a 741c	**20:29**	485m	**2:2**	352n
17:26	224d 526i 887d			**20:30**	547i 864c	**2:3**	381p
18:1	255j 370c	**19:20**	557e	**20:31**	170n 357ab 360u 485u 586h	**2:4**	54i 557f 965q
18:3	420d 723n	**19:21**	741c			**2:6**	557a
18:4	459ag 490j	**19:22**	586n			**2:7**	864u
18:5	1c 184aq	**19:23**	98c 228aa 783c	**21:1**	343l 445c	**2:8**	557a
18:6	311j	**19:24**	605r 725e	**21:3**	172ab 542z	**2:12**	864u
18:7	184aq 459ag	**19:26**	170j 887j	**21:4**	491m	**2:13**	851e 949l
18:9	772h 781d	**19:27**	169af	**21:5**	172ab	**2:14**	99l
18:10	46b 655i	**19:28**	490k 725a 725e² 859m	**21:6**	171u 241c	**2:15**	108s 949l
18:11	226j 949m			**21:7**	13f 229r 741d 887j	**2:16**	579z
		19:29	218c 393a			**2:17**	69d 438s 438z 579ag 965s

2:19	335e 547j 864b	**3:21**	108aj 125f
2:20	108af 418c		656ag
2:21	668m 761t	**3:22**	455k 579ae
2:22	184aq 547g	**3:23**	456f
	864c	**3:24**	579z
2:23	362bl 608a	**3:25**	371iai 765b
2:24	656g		897j
2:25	89i 153t 241a	**3:26**	68n 656g
2:27	51f	**4:1**	708e
2:28	189b	**4:2**	656a
2:29	361af 364l	**4:3**	747b
2:30	532o 579z	**4:4**	99u 104l 485p
2:31	656e	**4:6**	986k 986o
2:32	466n 656g	**4:7**	160e 561m
2:33	241b 764g 965u	**4:8**	54i 965q
2:34	241b 311z 727k	**4:10**	184aq 362bm
2:35	218ad		561k 656g
2:36	357ac 362bm	**4:11**	214e 344x 607k
	965h	**4:12**	561k 668e
2:37	676g 818e	**4:13**	89j 493a
2:38	781j 909m 939d	**4:14**	578e
	965u 988w	**4:15**	692b
2:39	199m 737m	**4:16**	547l 864g
	764g	**4:17**	578h 664f
2:40	668x	**4:19**	739c
2:41	99u 104l 988w	**4:22**	131g
2:42	9b 301ag 534p	**4:24**	164a 761p
	761u	**4:26**	357aa 741w
2:43	547k 864g	**4:27**	357u 741v
2:44	775b	**4:28**	608a
2:45	783g	**4:29**	529h 900a
2:46	990s	**4:30**	547l 656aa 864g
2:47	38e 104l 866ad	**4:31**	54i 74h 176f
3:1	108v 656ab		529h 855b
	761g 990s		965q
3:2	130b 263i 264d	**4:32**	88f 775b
	655n 655q	**4:33**	466n 656h
	761ai	**4:34**	635i 793d
3:4	455r	**4:35**	783g
3:6	267g 781w 797p	**4:36**	561y 855f
3:7	310c 378n	**4:37**	793b
3:8	267g 312b 923i	**5:1**	793b
3:10	263i 264d 761ai	**5:2**	778a
	864r	**5:3**	541a 541d 969f
3:11	48b 263i	**5:4**	541a
3:12	160k 267g	**5:5**	361ad 854l
3:13	866n	**5:6**	364l
3:14	533c	**5:8**	809j
3:15	360h 362bl	**5:9**	461f 710d
	466n 656g	**5:10**	361ad 364l
3:16	485z 650b	**5:11**	854l 985b
3:17	491w	**5:12**	74h 263i 547k
3:18	357z 511a 725e		864g
	825j	**5:13**	856b 866ad
3:19	685b 909m 939b	**5:14**	104l 485p
3:20	357v	**5:15**	418f 651j
		5:16	656aa

5:17	708e 911g 986l	**7:18**	491r
5:18	747b	**7:20**	167i
5:19	746b 968p	**7:21**	170k 534n
5:21	534p 692a 990s	**7:22**	534v
5:23	190o 264e	**7:23**	131g
5:26	854ad	**7:24**	910g
5:27	459o	**7:25**	517d 668t
5:28	180e 578h	**7:26**	719g
5:29	371p 739c	**7:27**	957g
5:30	217c 362bm	**7:28**	362k
	656g	**7:29**	620i
5:31	241b 866o	**7:30**	110ac 209k
	909m 939c		366o 381p
5:32	466m 466n 466r	**7:32**	13a 965f
	739l 781j	**7:33**	229p 979x
	965aa	**7:34**	746c
5:33	362ar 891y	**7:35**	668t 957g
5:34	537d 692b 708i	**7:36**	110ac 343i 547k
5:36	75b		864f
5:37	75b 86b	**7:37**	579ae
5:38	371p 620t	**7:38**	209k 968k
5:39	704d	**7:39**	148m
5:40	279k 578h	**7:40**	491v 982j
5:41	824aa 872r	**7:42**	110ac 321j
	915d		586e 589i 982n
5:42	357ac 528g	**7:43**	188b 967m
6:1	104l 301l 557e		967q
	829c	**7:44**	23a 990l
6:3	54h 500f 965r	**7:46**	192d 826f
6:4	761u	**7:47**	192d
6:5	54i 147f 485h	**7:48**	192b
	965q	**7:49**	218ac 971a
6:6	378v 761m	**7:50**	164c
6:7	104l² 986e	**7:51**	602b 715b 974c
6:8	547l 864g	**7:52**	362bl 511a
6:9	192o 709i		735f
6:10	500f	**7:53**	720b 954c 968k
6:11	980c	**7:54**	891x
6:12	692b	**7:55**	54i 241b 965q
6:13	466v	**7:56**	263ag 371j
6:14	127f 165h	**7:57**	456d
	184aq	**7:58**	228b 362ar
6:15	968c	**7:59**	344n
7:3	11j 184d	**7:60**	909e
7:4	361ad	**8:1**	75h 184s 488b
7:5	774a		735g 923w
7:6	59u 742p		985b
7:8	99m 131f 765b	**8:2**	364l 836r
	988m 988n	**8:3**	165i 747f 985b
7:9	89h 793g 911i	**8:4**	75h 528g
7:10	826p	**8:5**	59t 184s 357ac
7:11	636a	**8:6**	547l
7:13	526t	**8:7**	300e 656aa
7:14	99s	**8:8**	824w
7:15	361ad	**8:9**	638d 983e
7:16	364e 792c	**8:10**	455t
7:17	104e 108z	**8:12**	733h 988w

8:13	547*l* 864*g* 864*u*	9:42	104*l*	11:13	968*p*	13:11	439*i*

14:22	162k 733q 827f 855d		
14:23	751e 761e 946i 985c 986ag		
14:26	269c		
14:27	59q 74h 263h 526k 985e		
14:28	113i		
15:1	988o		
15:2	709h		
15:3	147e 824w 985e		
15:4	985e		
15:5	708i 739i 988o		
15:6	74h 986ag		
15:7	59q 59r 605f		
15:8	466k 490i 965u		
15:9	16c 648r		
15:10	461f 747u		
15:11	897q		
15:12	547k 582g 864g		
15:14	59q 68o		
15:15	586e		
15:16	164y 371z		
15:17	59p		
15:18	125f		
15:20	335g 362u 951e 982h		
15:21	192o 579k 683g 975i		
15:22	985e		
15:23	588f		
15:26	661a		
15:28	322n		
15:29	335g 362u 951e 982h		
15:30	74h		
15:31	579n		
15:32	162k 855d		
15:35	534p		
15:36	148e		
15:38	621s		
15:39	46am 709j		
15:41	162k 985c		
16:3	988n		
16:5	104l 162k 985c		
16:6	757c		
16:7	757c		
16:9	438aa 703i 761ap		
16:10	528d		
16:11	269c		
16:13	761f		
16:14	263af 436a 455u		
16:15	192ah 988w		
16:16	969y 983e		
16:18	300e		

16:19	288a
16:21	954e
16:22	229l 279k
16:23	747b
16:24	747t
16:25	129l 412d 761p
16:26	47g 176f 263g 746b
16:27	362ae 678g
16:29	311a 420d
16:30	668r 676g
16:31	485t 668m
16:33	648f 658e 988w
16:34	301r 485p 824w
16:35	746f
16:37	191a 279k
16:38	854ad
16:39	296c
17:1	192n
17:2	127i 475b
17:3	13e 357z 357ac 656e 825j
17:5	61a 911g
17:6	221b 288a 827d
17:7	741c
17:9	767b
17:10	129g 192n
17:11	782d 929c 975i
17:12	104l
17:16	982o
17:17	192n 475b
17:18	449g 656a 966h
17:19	126e 209v
17:21	126e
17:22	209v 973b
17:23	491e
17:24	164a 192b
17:25	352b 360i 627a 742a 781e
17:26	110d 164m 236a 371u^2
17:27	200a 459y
17:28	1d 170r 360i
17:29	982c
17:30	456c 491a 939b
17:31	108ai 466o 480i 656h
17:32	656b 851g
17:34	485p
18:2	300z
18:3	686h
18:4	192n 475b 612c 683g
18:5	13e 357ac
18:6	59r 180b 621q
18:8	485p 988w
18:9	854ai

18:10	89h 104l
18:11	110t 534p
18:12	956a^2
18:13	954e
18:16	300z
18:17	279k 860a
18:18	259i 269c 532w
18:19	192n 475b
18:21	269c 595b
18:22	985e 985g
18:23	162k
18:24	579ap 975h
18:25	818d 988t
18:26	192n 520e
18:27	588f
18:28	13e 357ac 479a
19:2	782c 965u
19:3	988t
19:4	939d
19:5	988w
19:6	378w 557f 579ai 965u
19:7	99m
19:8	110s 192n 475b
19:9	475b 539a 624m 883f 926b
19:10	110u
19:11	864g
19:12	228g 300e 656aa
19:13	300g
19:14	99d 986d
19:15	13j 490z
19:16	229d 655j
19:17	854h
19:18	526r
19:19	589o 809k 983e
19:20	36h
19:23	624m
19:24	686g 967q 990ae
19:26	966j 982c
19:27	752b 967q
19:28	967q
19:29	61a 724a
19:32	61a 491ab
19:33	547x
19:34	110i 967q
19:35	578h 967q
19:38	928h
19:40	61a
20:1	61a
20:3	110s 623q
20:6	110o 269c 988f

20:7	46q 74h 108b 113i 129l 301ag
20:8	74h 420d
20:9	132d 309c 361ad 679e
20:10	378n 656o
20:11	46q 113i
20:12	656o 831g
20:13	269c
20:15	269c
20:16	680c 988h
20:17	986ag
20:18	68o
20:19	872m
20:20	534p
20:21	485n 939b
20:22	491ab
20:24	361ar 600c 725h
20:25	439h
20:26	935h
20:27	528h
20:28	369g 457f 792q 985a
20:29	365w
20:30	495e
20:31	110v
20:32	529g 777n
20:33	859y
20:35	682c 781a
20:36	311e 761n
20:37	836ad 889a
20:38	439h
21:1	269c
21:4	110o 184ai 664g
21:5	311e 761n
21:7	269c
21:8	528b
21:9	96c 579aa 895c
21:10	579z
21:11	664g 747t
21:12	184ai
21:13	184ai 361an 669d 836ad
21:14	595f
21:17	184ai
21:19	59r
21:20	104l
21:21	127f 988o
21:23	532w
21:24	648i 648x 739i
21:25	335g 362u 951e 982h
21:27	990s
21:28	59g 649a
21:30	264g 288a

21:31	362*l* 722*f*
21:32	279*k*
21:33	13*j* 47*f* 747*t*
21:35	273*g*
21:37	557*e*
21:38	708*m*
21:39	191*a*
21:40	547*x* 557*e*
22:2	557*e* 582*g*
22:3	311*af* 818*d*
22:4	362*ar* 624*m*
	735*g* 747*f*
22:5	588*c*
22:6	417*f*
22:7	735*g*
22:8	13*c* 184*aq* 735*g*
22:10	676*g*
22:11	439*i* 689*b*
22:13	656*ab*
22:14	438*g* 455*m*
	490*v*
22:15	466*n*
22:16	648*ad* 988*w*
22:17	438*aa*
22:19	192*r* 279*k* 747*f*
22:20	228*b* 488*b*
	923*w*
22:21	59*r* 199*b*
22:23	332*b* 621*q*
22:24	279*k* 459*o* 722*f*
22:25	191*a* 747*t*
22:26	722*f*
22:28	792*d*
22:29	854*u*
22:30	692*a*
23:1	917*a*
23:2	279*k*
23:3	427*g*
23:4	921*c* 986*l*
23:5	586*e* 926*i*
23:6	656*c* 708*b* 708*i*
23:7	709*j*
23:8	656*b* 708*e* 708*f*
	968*e*
23:9	935*h* 968*e*
23:10	46*a* 722*f*
23:11	466*s*
23:12	362*ar* 532*h*
	623*i* 946*n*
23:13	99*r*
23:14	946*n*
23:15	692*b* 722*f*
23:20	623*i* 692*b*
23:21	527*d* 899*r* 946*n*
23:22	525*l* 722*f*
23:23	722*m*
23:24	267*l*

23:25	588*c*
23:27	191*a*
23:28	692*b*
23:29	928*h*
23:30	623*i*
23:31	129*g*
24:1	928*h* 986*k*
24:2	654*d* 717*g*
24:3	907*l*
24:5	184*ap* 659*e*
	708*k*
24:6	980*c* 990*p*
24:7	722*f*
24:10	547*x*
24:11	981*f*
24:14	485*ad* 624*m*
	708*k* 975*a* 981*f*
24:15	656*c*
24:16	917*a*
24:17	781*w*
24:21	656*c*
24:22	624*m* 722*f*
24:23	880*d*
24:24	485*n*
24:25	124*e* 137*d*
	480*d* 823*g*
	854*l* 913*h*
24:26	612*i*
25:2	928*h*
25:3	527*d*
25:7	928*h*
25:8	935*h*
25:11	761*ao*
25:13	741*v*
25:16	127*g*
25:19	361*ai* 973*b*
25:21	761*ao*
25:23	875*b*
25:25	761*ao* 935*h*
25:27	928*h*
26:1	547*x* 741*v*
26:3	492*a*
26:4	130*f*
26:5	708*i*
26:6	764*c*
26:7	99*m*
26:8	486*m* 656*b*
26:9	184*aq* 704*e*
26:10	747*f* 923*w* 979*l*
26:11	192*r* 980*e*
26:12	751*f*
26:13	417*f*
26:14	256*f* 279*q* 557*e*
	735*g*
26:15	13*c* 735*g*
26:16	308*i* 466*s*
26:17	59*r*

26:18	417*n* 438*a*
	439*p* 777*m*
	909*c* 969*aa*
	979*o*
26:19	438*z* 739*b*
26:20	939*b* 939*e*
26:21	362*ar*
26:22	975*a*
26:23	68*k* 357*z* 417*n*
	656*e* 825*j*
26:24	503*d*
26:26	741*v*
26:27	485*ad*
26:28	116*c* 561*l*
26:29	47*f*
26:31	935*h*
26:32	746*f* 761*ao*
27:1	722*e*
27:2	269*c*
27:3	880*d*
27:4	702*h*
27:7	278*b* 700*b*
27:9	661*b* 941*b*
27:10	772*d*
27:12	129*r*
27:13	281*j*
27:14	165*y* 176*j* 281*e*
	352*k*
27:16	349*b*
27:17	218*ah*
27:18	323*b* 607*m*
27:19	275*b* 607*m*
27:21	946*k*
27:23	968*p*
27:24	854*ai*
27:25	485*e* 855*f*
27:26	349*b*
27:27	110*q* 129*l*
27:28	211*c*^{2}
27:29	47*i*
27:30	47*i* 275*j* 541*j*
	667*a*
27:32	275*j*
27:33	110*q* 301*d* 946*k*
27:34	259*k*
27:35	46*q* 907*i*
27:37	99*t*
27:38	323*b* 607*m*
27:40	47*i* 275*b*
27:41	46*y*
27:42	269*d* 362*k*
27:44	207*a*
28:1	349*b*
28:2	350*ac* 380*c*
	381*am*
28:3	365*p* 385*a*
28:4	362*b*

28:5	318*c*
28:6	36*d* 966*l*
28:8	378*z* 651*k*
	656*ab* 761*s*
28:9	656*aa*
28:11	90*b* 269*c*
28:13	281*j* 352*k*
28:15	855*f* 907*m*
28:17	127*e*
28:18	935*h*
28:19	761*ao*
28:20	47*f* 852*b*
28:22	708*k* 924*g*
28:23	733*h* 975*e*
28:24	486*j*
28:25	579*z* 709*j*
	965*aa*
28:26	517*c*
28:27	439*d* 456*d*
28:28	59*q*
28:30	110*u*
28:31	528*g*

Romans

1:1	529*l* 742*h* 754*c*
1:2	764*a* 975*f*
1:3	170*p* 357*x*
1:4	170*n* 656*h* 979*a*
1:5	59*q* 739*e* 751*c*
1:6	737*p*
1:7	887*i* 979*k*
1:8	485*q* 907*m*
1:9	466*k* 761*n*
1:11	781*m* 859*ab*
1:13	171*s* 702*h*
1:14	59*r* 500*b* 803*b*
1:16	68*n* 160*n* 371*aj*
	529*l* 872*y*
1:17	485*s* 913*v* 913*x*
1:18	494*i* 525*n* 526*e*
	891*f*
1:19	522*b*
1:20	115*c* 164*c* 180*h*
	444*b* 936*a*
	965*a*
1:21	449*e* 475*a* 490*s*
	866*k* 908*a*
1:22	499*d*
1:23	115*b* 150*e* 365*c*
	982*a*
1:24	272*d* 319*j* 867*f*
	951*d*
1:25	115*d* 150*e* 164*m*
	543*b* 742*d*
	981*aj*
1:26	150*e* 272*d* 951*o*
1:27	859*p* 963*a*

1:28	272d 447c 449e	**3:21**	913v 975f	**5:18**	927b 961b	**8:4**	319n 725f 953w
1:29	362b 542e 709d	**3:22**	16a 485s	**5:19**	738k 739d		965ad
	859q 898a	**3:23**	307a 914j	**5:20**	897r 953i	**8:5**	319l 965ad
	912a 914k 926c	**3:24**	792s 927b	**5:21**	360s 733aj 897r	**8:6**	319l 361x 717e
1:30	169m 738a	**3:25**	919e 941m		914k	**8:7**	161g 319l 704d
	871a 877a	**3:26**	485s 913a 927b	**6:1**	914r	**8:8**	826g
	888e	**3:27**	81b 877f	**6:2**	361ao	**8:9**	319n 965ah
1:31	499d 887aj 906c	**3:28**	480t 485s 676h	**6:3**	988x	**8:10**	360r 361x
	930a		927c	**6:4**	126f 364s 656g	**8:11**	656j
1:32	490v 923w 963s	**3:29**	16c 965f	**6:5**	45k 361ao 656j	**8:12**	803b
2:1	180h 961f	**3:30**	88a 485s 927c	**6:6**	127k 361ao	**8:13**	319l 361u 361ap
2:4	823f 897q 939c		988p		745m	**8:14**	170t 689f 965ae
2:5	108ai 602g	**3:31**	752e 953w	**6:7**	361ao 746m	**8:15**	169u 170l 745n
	891d 940a	**4:1**	169p	**6:8**	361ao		855h
2:6	676f 804k 962b	**4:2**	877f 927f	**6:9**	361aw	**8:16**	170t 466r 965ab
2:7	360n	**4:3**	480t 485s 913v	**6:10**	360h 361aj	**8:17**	776c 825k 866r
2:8	738l 891f	**4:4**	676h 804a	**6:11**	360aa 361ap	**8:18**	121a 462a 825r
2:9	68n 371aj 827c	**4:5**	485s 913v 927b		480u		866r
2:10	68n	**4:6**	913v	**6:12**	733aj	**8:19**	507e 526o
2:11	481a	**4:7**	909c	**6:13**	53a 360aa 630d	**8:20**	321h 641a
2:12	914s 953o 953q	**4:9**	480t 485s 913v	**6:14**	733aj 897r 953r	**8:21**	321h 746p
2:13	676e 739l		988p	**6:15**	914r	**8:22**	167p 321h 825r
2:14	953q	**4:10**	974d	**6:16**	745m	**8:23**	170l 171m 507d
2:15	449e 586r 917g	**4:11**	169p 485s 913v	**6:17**	739e 745m		825r
	928j		988p	**6:18**	742h 746m	**8:24**	852a
2:16	108ai 480i	**4:12**	169p 371ai	**6:19**	53a 742h 979q	**8:25**	439g
2:17	371af 877g	**4:13**	764c 913v 953m	**6:21**	361u 872n	**8:26**	163j 703b 761d
	953n	**4:14**	485x 752f	**6:22**	360p 742b 979q		761i
2:18	595d	**4:15**	891a 953k 953q	**6:23**	360s 361u 781h	**8:27**	459ac 979m
2:19	417s 439c	**4:16**	104b 169p 170v		804d 914s	**8:28**	644c 737m
2:20	534m		485s	**7:1**	953n	**8:29**	11l 18d 83a
2:21	534m 788d	**4:17**	1d 169p 656c	**7:2**	361e 746k 894h		119h 510a
2:22	788m 951i 982b	**4:19**	131h 172a 319h	**7:3**	746k 951h		608c
2:23	867a 877b	**4:20**	485g	**7:4**	171o 361ao 953r	**8:30**	608c 737m 866r
2:24	586e 926c	**4:21**	725b 764a	**7:5**	171t 859z 953l		927b
2:25	739i 988o	**4:22**	480t 913v	**7:6**	126f 746k 953r	**8:31**	704k 706a
2:26	480t 974d	**4:23**	586e	**7:7**	859w 953j 953l	**8:32**	781e 919c
2:28	223c 371ai 988q	**4:24**	480t 656g 913v	**7:8**	859w 953l	**8:33**	927a 961h
2:29	224b 923q	**4:25**	361aj 656i 927b	**7:9**	361y	**8:34**	241b 361ai 656g
3:1	34h 371af	**5:1**	485s 717d 927c	**7:10**	361y		761i
3:2	975h	**5:2**	824x	**7:11**	361y 542i	**8:35**	46af 229f 362as
3:3	486e	**5:3**	600f 825o	**7:12**	953j		636g 661c
3:4	371b 494c 545a	**5:4**	852a 933a	**7:13**	914h		827f 887i
3:5	914c	**5:5**	350y 887i 965z	**7:14**	319l 320d 793i	**8:36**	362aq 365bq
3:6	480h	**5:6**	108ab 137b 161g		953j	**8:37**	727l 887i
3:8	914r		361aj	**7:15**	517b 676n	**8:38**	46af 121b 124j
3:9	371aj 914j	**5:7**	361an	**7:16**	953j²		361am 969q
3:10	914j	**5:8**	361aj 887i	**7:18**	319l 644k		969s
3:11	459ab 517c	**5:9**	335p 891p 927b	**7:21**	81a	**8:39**	209e 211b
3:13	542g 579j 659d	**5:10**	360h 705b 719c	**7:22**	953j	**9:1**	466r
3:14	391e 899l	**5:11**	824x	**7:24**	668k	**9:2**	834h 836ag
3:15	277g 362b	**5:12**	361u 914g	**7:25**	319l 907g	**9:3**	46ae 371al 899c
3:17	717j	**5:13**	914h 953q	**8:1**	961h	**9:4**	170l 764c 765b
3:18	854q	**5:14**	23b 361t 371c	**8:2**	81a 81b 746m		953a
3:19	180g 578d	**5:15**	781h	**8:3**	18i 161g 961b	**9:5**	115e 169d 357x
3:20	490v 676h 927f	**5:16**	927b 961b		981ac		965h
	953m	**5:17**	360r 361t 733ag			**9:6**	371ai

9:7	170h
9:8	319n 764d
9:10	167i
9:11	605f 676j 737m
9:12	130i 742q
9:13	887f 888b
9:14	914d
9:15	905c
9:18	602h 905c
9:19	160c 595c 928d
9:20	164l 371e 460f
9:21	686h 866r 867c
9:22	608d 823f 891f
9:23	608d 669b 866r
	905c
9:24	371ak
9:25	887g
9:26	170t
9:27	41o 104e
9:29	18l 41o 184aw
9:30	485s 913u 913v
9:32	485x 676e 702g
9:33	344x 485j 509a
10:1	761u 859ac
10:2	491h 818d
10:3	913u
10:4	69b 485s 913v
	953r
10:5	676e
10:6	308g 311s 485s
10:7	309j 310h 656g
	972d
10:8	200d
10:9	485t 526n 656i
	668r 741f
10:10	447f 485s 579a
10:11	485j 509a
10:12	16b 371ak 741e
10:13	668m 761t
10:14	455m 486h
	528k 761e
10:15	53m 529k 751k
	841n
10:16	486d
10:17	455m 485a
10:18	183g 455m
10:19	911f
10:20	459ab 484b
10:21	602c 738g
11:1	371ag 607f
11:2	371al 510a
11:3	41h 88j 362ao
	990h
11:4	41m 99u
11:5	41q 605f 676j
	897r
11:7	602h

11:8	375b 439j 456d
11:10	439j
11:11	309b 911f
11:12	54l 371al 800s
11:13	59r
11:14	911f
11:15	607c 656p
11:16	53w
11:17	45n 46ad
11:18	871d
11:20	153n 486e
	854a 871d
11:21	919d
11:22	46ad 735a 897r
11:23	45n
11:24	45n^2
11:25	54l 371al 602h
11:26	54l 668p
11:27	765m 909c
11:28	169z 705d 887f
11:29	473b 737n 781h
11:30	738l
11:32	738l 905c
11:33	490e 498f 517a
	800t
11:34	691c
11:35	781n
11:36	115d 866f
12:1	319i 981at
12:2	83d 126f 147b
	595d
12:3	482a 871d
12:4	17a 53b 319g
12:5	88d 319f
12:6	17a 579ai 781m
12:7	534q
12:8	612c 781v 905h
12:9	542n 887b 888g
12:10	866v 887x
12:11	818b
12:12	600a 761c
	824a 827f 852d
12:13	781v 813d
12:14	735k 897t
12:15	824a 836d
12:16	498s 872c
12:17	804m 910i
12:18	717f
12:19	910a 910i
12:20	301n 859i 859l
12:21	727l
13:1	733ad 745b
13:2	704d
13:3	854v
13:4	963h
13:5	745b 917b
13:6	804g

13:7	854ac 866v
	915e
13:8	725f 803a 887t
	953w
13:9	362a 788d 859w
	887t 951k
13:10	645h 725f 887a
	953w
13:11	108ac 135d
	668r 678f
13:12	128k 129o 418l
	723f
13:13	128l 709d 911k
	949a 951e
13:14	228af 319n
14:1	163i 299d
	301aq
14:3	922j 922n
14:4	153l 480r
14:5	110e 473a
14:6	907i
14:7	360aa 361an
	931a
14:8	773e
14:9	361k 741d
14:10	480f 922n 956b
14:11	311e
14:12	180g
14:13	480b 702c
14:14	648r
14:15	301aq 361aj
	834h 887ak
14:17	301k 717e 733c
	824t 913l 965z
14:18	923s
14:19	164ad 719f
14:20	301aq 648r
14:21	702c
14:22	485b 961f
14:23	486a
15:1	162k 163i 932c
15:2	826n
15:3	826d 924f 931a
15:4	125f 586e 975g
15:5	600e 710b 855c
15:6	710b 866j
15:7	299c
15:8	371aj 742k
	764c
15:9	59n
15:10	59n
15:11	59n
15:12	59p
15:13	160m 717e
	824y 852d 965x
15:14	490w 664e
15:15	505n

15:16	742j 981at 986x
15:17	877g
15:18	739e 864g
15:19	160m 528h
	547k 965x
15:20	491n 528d
15:22	702h
15:23	859ab
15:25	184ai
15:26	781w
15:27	803b
15:30	761o
15:31	979m
15:33	717a
16:1	742g 923s 985e
16:2	299d 703i
16:3	884g
16:4	661a 985e
16:5	68o 147e 985g
16:7	750c 754c
16:15	979k
16:16	884c 884e 889a
16:17	620s 702a 709b
16:18	301k 542e
	859h 925a
16:19	498n 935a
16:20	135d 717a 727l
	969aa
16:21	884f
16:22	586j
16:23	798a
16:25	153l 526g
16:26	115b 739e 975f
	985e
16:27	88b 115d 498f
	866f

1 Corinthians

1:1	595b 754c
1:2	761t 979k 979o
	985e
1:4	907m
1:5	800s
1:7	507d 526m
	635h 781m
1:8	108af 146d
	153l 935b
1:9	9a 929a
1:10	46ap 710b
1:11	709k
1:13	46ap 362bl
	988x
1:17	498q 528d 641b
1:18	160n 499c 964f
1:19	498q
1:20	499d
1:21	485t 491e 498j
	499c

1:22 498q 547o
1:23 362bl 499c 702f
1:24 160e 357y 498i 737p
1:25 162a 163a 499c
1:26 105e 499c
1:27 163j 499g 605f 872t
1:28 2g 639b 922m
1:29 877f
1:30 498i 792r 913x 979q
1:31 877g
2:1 499c 579ap
2:2 362bl 491d
2:3 163e 854u
2:4 160o 579ap 965x
2:5 485d
2:6 2e 134a 498k
2:7 125b 498i 530c 608c
2:8 362bl 517d
2:9 491p 669e 887o
2:10 211b 526g 965ab
2:11 320b
2:12 490o 965ab
2:14 499c 517c 965ah
2:15 480p
2:16 447g
3:1 132k 319l
3:2 301ba
3:3 319l 911j
3:5 5a 742i
3:6 36i 341d 370i
3:8 962b
3:9 164ac 235r 707a
3:10 164ac 214f
3:11 15c 214e
3:12 631b
3:13 381z
3:14 962b
3:15 772a
3:16 192c 990ab
3:17 165i 979f
3:18 499g 542h
3:19 498q
3:20 499g 641a
3:21 877d
3:22 121b 124j 773f
3:23 773e
4:1 742i
4:2 929g

4:3 480r
4:4 480g
4:5 480b 526a
4:6 871d
4:7 782d 877f
4:8 54j
4:9 361o 445h 754b 968q
4:10 163e 501i 867c
4:11 192al 228j 801p 859j
4:12 600d 682c 735k 897t 924g
4:13 641j 926f
4:14 664e 872u
4:15 169w
4:16 20c
4:17 170w 505n 985d
4:18 871f
4:20 160o 579ap 733c
4:21 964a
5:1 894e 951q
5:2 300x 836ae 871f
5:3 480p
5:4 74i 160e
5:5 108af 319j 969ab
5:6 877a
5:7 126h 127k 323i 357z 988g
5:8 323h 494g
5:9 883c 951e
5:11 789b 859x 883c 921e 949h 982g
5:12 480p
5:13 300x 480e
6:1 959c 979l
6:2 480p 979l
6:3 968b
6:7 728c 788j
6:8 788n
6:9 733s 774d 951b 951f 951o 982t
6:10 789b 859x 921e 949h
6:11 648ac 927b 979o
6:12 641e 733aj 915i^2
6:13 224e 301c 319i 951e
6:14 656j
6:15 53b 951v

6:16 45a
6:17 45k
6:18 319l 620r 951e
6:19 319i 990ab
6:20 792q 866j
7:1 378r 894d
7:3 894i
7:4 319h
7:5 612m 760c 761e
7:6 758a
7:7 18f 781m
7:8 895h
7:9 823g 859o
7:10 46am 896a
7:11 896a 896c^2
7:12 896a
7:14 170a 979n
7:15 717f
7:16 668s
7:17 7a 985d
7:18 988p
7:19 739i 988p
7:20 7a
7:21 746i
7:22 742h 742n
7:23 745f 792q
7:25 451a 895h
7:26 7a
7:27 895h 896a
7:28 827a 894d
7:29 114i 894d
7:30 792a 824c 836e
7:31 2e
7:32 825w 826h 895h
7:33 826m 894d
7:34 826m 895h
7:36 895h
7:38 894d
7:39 361e 746k 894g 894h
7:40 7a
8:1 164ae 490a 871b 887a 982h
8:2 490b
8:3 490m 887l
8:4 21c 88a 641h
8:5 966a
8:6 88a 164f 965g
8:7 163i 491k 917e
8:8 301k 923r
8:9 702c
8:10 917e
8:11 165i 361aj 490b
8:12 28e 914ab 917e
8:13 301ax 702c

9:1 438g 746o 754c
9:2 751g 754c
9:4 301c
9:5 11k 894a
9:7 369h 370m 722o 804a
9:9 365ay 365ba 747x
9:10 370u
9:11 75j 370u
9:12 600d 702i
9:13 301ab
9:14 804c
9:15 877c
9:16 528d 740b
9:18 812d 962g
9:19 83c 745b 771m
9:20 371ag 953p
9:21 953s 953y
9:22 163e
9:24 716l 962d
9:25 115l 823g
9:26 641d
9:27 279f 300ae 319j
10:1 343i 355h
10:2 988r
10:3 301ae
10:4 344q 344x
10:5 826g
10:6 23b 664c 859z
10:7 837b 982f 982i
10:8 951e
10:9 365o 461f
10:10 829e
10:11 23b 69d 534g 664c
10:12 309a 457e
10:13 612m 667e 929a
10:14 620r 982f 982h
10:16 46q 319e 335q 775c
10:17 88d 319f
10:20 969l
10:21 969m
10:22 911d
10:23 641e 915i
10:24 932c
10:25 301aq
10:26 321g
10:27 301d
10:28 917b
10:30 907i
10:31 866j
10:32 702c 985b
10:33 826n
11:1 20a 20c

11:2 127*j*

11:3 213*i* 373*i* 741*d*

11:4 226*f* 867*d*

11:5 229*s* 867*d*

11:7 18*a* 866*d*

11:9 164*i* 373*a*

11:10 733*ah* 968*q*

11:11 12*b*

11:13 229*s*

11:14 259*h* 872*n*

11:15 226*e* 259*g* 866*d*

11:16 709*h* 985*d*

11:17 74*i* 301*ag*

11:18 46*ap* 985*c*

11:21 859*j* 949*i*

11:22 985*b*

11:23 272*f*

11:24 46*p* 319*e* 505*f* 907*i*

11:25 126*e* 335*o* 505*f* 765*m*

11:26 295*i* 528*l*

11:27 916*d* 936*g*

11:28 461*l*

11:29 961*b*

11:30 361*u* 651*a* 679*e*

11:31 480*s*

11:32 827*i*

11:34 859*j*

12:1 491*k* 781*m*

12:2 578*c* 982*d*

12:3 741*f* 899*h* 965*aa*^{2}

12:4 17*a* 93*a* 781*m* 965*ad*

12:8 490*w* 498*k*

12:9 485*a* 656*aa*

12:10 463*a* 520*c* 557*f* 579*ag* 864*e*

12:11 783*h* 965*ad*

12:12 53*b* 88*d* 319*f*

12:13 965*w* 988*x* 988*y*

12:15 53*j*

12:16 415*g*

12:17 394*b* 438*h*

12:20 88*d*

12:21 213*c* 438*h* 627*c*

12:23 867*c*

12:25 46*ap*

12:26 825*l*

12:27 319*f*

12:28 537*f* 557*f* 579*ag* 656*aa* 689*c* 703*i* 751*c* 754*a* 864*e* 985*a*

12:29 579*ag*

12:30 520*c* 557*i* 656*aa*

12:31 859*e*

13:1 400*a* 557*i* 887*a*

13:2 209*i* 485*aa* 490*c* 579*ai* 639*a*

13:3 639*a* 781*u*

13:4 823*a* 871*b* 887*a* 911*k*

13:5 892*c* 932*d*

13:6 824*b*

13:7 485*a* 600*c* 852*a*

13:8 145*e* 153*b* 490*b* 557*i* 579*ai* 887*a*

13:9 490*d* 579*ai*

13:10 646*d*

13:11 132*k* 134*a*

13:12 200*a* 440*c* 442*b* 490*c* 490*d*

13:13 485*a* 852*a* 887*a*

14:1 579*ah* 859*e* 887*b*

14:2 557*g*

14:3 579*ai*

14:4 164*ae* 557*g* 985*c*

14:5 520*c* 557*g* 557*h* 985*c*

14:6 557*h*

14:7 414*e*

14:8 414*e* 718*f*

14:9 516*g*

14:10 557*a*

14:11 59*v*

14:12 164*af* 985*c*

14:13 520*c* 557*j*

14:14 557*h* 761*d*

14:15 412*g* 761*d*

14:16 488*c*

14:17 164*ae*

14:18 557*g*

14:19 985*c*

14:20 132*g* 132*k* 134*a*

14:21 557*b*

14:22 486*j* 547*m* 579*ah*

14:23 74*i* 503*e* 557*h*

14:24 579*ah* 928*j*

14:25 89*a* 526*s* 981*f*

14:26 74*i* 164*af* 412*d* 520*c* 557*j*

14:27 65*b* 520*c* 557*j*

14:28 582*i*

14:29 480*q* 579*ah*

14:30 582*i*

14:31 65*b* 579*ai*

14:32 579*ai*

14:33 61*c* 717*a* 979*k* 985*d*

14:34 373*i* 582*j* 721*c* 985*c*

14:35 459*j* 985*c*

14:37 737*f*

14:39 557*j* 579*ah* 579*ai*

14:40 60*a*

15:1 153*n* 529*l*

15:2 668*r*

15:3 361*aj* 941*m* 975*e*

15:4 110*l* 364*l* 656*g*

15:5 445*c*^{2}

15:6 445*c*

15:7 445*c*^{2}

15:8 138*b* 445*c*

15:9 35*c* 735*g* 754*c* 985*b*

15:10 682*c* 897*q*

15:12 656*g*

15:13 656*b*

15:14 641*b*

15:15 466*w*

15:16 656*b*

15:17 641*b* 914*t*

15:18 361*am*

15:19 852*e*

15:20 68*k* 171*m* 656*f* 679*e*

15:21 361*i* 656*a*

15:22 360*w* 361*f*

15:23 65*a* 68*k* 171*m*

15:24 69*e* 733*u*

15:25 727*k* 733*x*

15:26 361*aw* 705*e*

15:27 745*i*

15:28 745*j*

15:29 988*z*

15:30 661*c*

15:31 361*aq*

15:32 124*c* 301*i* 365*e* 716*k*

15:33 89*n*

15:34 491*e* 914*p*

15:35 319*c* 656*l*

15:36 75*p* 361*am*

15:39 17*b* 319*c*

15:40 17*b*

15:41 321*b*

15:42 75*p* 114*n* 115*l*

15:43 163*f* 867*c*

15:44 319*c* 320*d*

15:45 360*i* 371*c* 371*g*

15:46 65*a*

15:47 371*c*

15:49 18*d* 18*e*

15:50 114*n* 319*m* 733*s* 774*d*

15:51 147*b* 361*g* 679*e*

15:52 115*l* 116*c* 414*n* 656*l*

15:53 114*n* 228*af*

15:54 361*aw* 727*l*

15:55 256*j* 361*aw*

15:56 953*l*

15:57 727*l* 907*g*

15:58 146*e* 599*d* 641*d* 676*k*

16:1 781*w* 979*m* 985*d*

16:2 108*b*

16:3 588*f*

16:6 129*r*

16:8 988*h*

16:9 263*h* 705*d*

16:11 922*n*

16:13 162*l* 457*e* 600*a*

16:14 887*b*

16:15 171*m* 742*r* 979*m*

16:16 721*b*

16:18 685*d*

16:19 884*e*^{2} 985*g*

16:20 884*c* 889*a*

16:21 586*j*

16:22 295*i* 887*q* 899*n*

16:23 897*p*

16:24 887*ae*

2 Corinthians

1:1 595*b* 979*k* 985*e*

1:2 897*p*

1:3 831*a* 905*c*

1:5 825*k*

1:7 825*o* 831*c*

1:8 825*n* 853*a*

1:9 361*aq* 485*e* 485*af* 656*c*

1:10 668*f*

1:11 761*o*

1:12 979*p*

1:13 516*g*

1:14 108*af*

1:15 882*g*

1:17 152*c* 601*b*

1:19 601*b* 603*a*

1:20 488*d*^{2} 764*a*

1:21 153*l* 357*k*

1:22	547*q* 767*f* 781*j* 965*u* 965*v*
1:23	919*a*
1:24	600*a* 733*am*
2:2	834*h*
2:3	588*e*
2:4	834*h*
2:7	909*r*
2:8	887*z*
2:9	461*i*
2:10	909*s*
2:11	490*w* 623*j* 969*k*
2:12	263*h*
2:13	683*t*
2:14	396*h* 727*l* 907*g*
2:17	540*b* 794*b*
3:1	588*f* 923*t*
3:2	588*f*
3:3	586*r* 965*ac*
3:5	915*d*
3:6	126*e* 320*d* 765*m* 953*k* 965*ac*
3:7	361*y* 586*a* 866*r*
3:9	913*w* 961*d*
3:12	573*b*
3:13	226*f* 421*f*
3:14	765*g*
3:17	746*o*
3:18	18*d* 147*b* 438*g* 442*b*
4:1	855*b*
4:2	540*b* 917*b* 923*v*
4:3	525*b*
4:4	18*b* 439*l* 967*r* 969*a* 969*g*
4:5	528*l* 741*f* 742*j*
4:6	417*m* 490*p*
4:7	160*k* 344*d* 869*b*
4:8	825*o* 853*a*
4:9	621*g* 735*k*
4:10	360*z* 361*aq*
4:13	485*l*
4:14	656*g* 656*j*
4:15	907*k*
4:16	51*d* 126*f* 855*b*
4:17	21*m* 114*j* 115*k* 825*o* 866*r*
4:18	114*l* 115*a* 444*a*
5:1	115*l* 192*l*
5:2	228*af*
5:3	229*h*
5:5	767*f* 781*j* 965*u*
5:6	190*d*
5:7	438*b* 485*b*
5:8	89*k*
5:9	826*h*

5:10	480*f* 676*f* 804*k* 956*b*
5:11	612*c* 854*h*
5:12	445*f* 871*h* 923*u*
5:13	502*b* 503*e*
5:14	361*aj* 887*k*
5:15	656*i* 932*c*
5:16	319*d* 319*n*
5:17	126*f* 127*k*
5:18	719*c* 719*e*
5:19	529*l* 909*f*
5:20	754*e* 761*an*
5:21	913*x* 914*m*
6:1	641*d*
6:2	108*ac* 121*c* 668*j*
6:3	702*c*
6:4	600*d* 825*o* 923*v*
6:5	279*j* 678*c* 747*d* 859*j*
6:6	490*w* 823*e* 887*z* 950*c* 965*ac*
6:7	160*k* 241*f* 494*d* 723*e*
6:8	542*o* 866*ad* 926*f*
6:9	361*aq* 491*t*
6:10	146*c* 773*f* 774*c* 801*p* 834*f*
6:14	10*b*² 29*a* 43*a* 43*c* 417*a* 913*ac*
6:15	10*b* 969*c*
6:16	89*g* 371*ac* 965*e* 982*f* 990*ab*
6:17	46*aq* 298*f* 649*e*
6:18	160*a* 169*q* 170*t*
7:1	648*ad* 764*e* 979*g*
7:3	961*h*
7:5	683*t* 825*n* 854*u*
7:6	831*a*
7:8	588*e*
7:9	834*f* 939*f*
7:10	361*f*
7:11	818*b* 935*e*
7:15	739*m*
8:1	985*e*
8:2	801*p* 813*c*
8:3	781*w*
8:4	761*an* 979*m*
8:5	781*t*
8:7	485*ab* 635*i*
8:9	800*s* 801*b* 801*p* 897*q*
8:10	451*a*
8:13	28*h*
8:14	635*i*

8:15	32*a* 33*a* 635*c* 637*b*
8:16	907*g*
8:20	924*m*
8:21	371*s*
8:23	754*c*
9:1	637*c* 979*m*
9:2	669*d* 818*b*
9:4	872*s*
9:6	75*l* 370*v* 813*c*
9:7	740*c* 781*a* 833*b*
9:8	635*h*
9:9	115*c* 781*e* 801*j* 913*a*
9:10	75*l* 301*u* 370*v* 913*l*
9:11	800*s* 813*c* 907*k*
9:12	979*m*
9:13	739*e*
9:15	781*g* 907*h*
10:1	177*b*
10:3	319*o* 718*d*
10:4	165*l* 723*e*
10:5	477*a* 490*q* 739*e*
10:6	738*l*
10:7	223*a*
10:8	164*ad* 733*ag* 877*c*
10:9	588*e*
10:10	163*e* 588*d*
10:12	462*b* 923*u*
10:13	877*c*
10:14	68*o*
10:15	877*c*
10:17	877*g*
10:18	923*r* 923*u*
11:1	499*h*
11:2	894*ad* 895*d* 911*h*
11:3	44*b* 282*g* 365*r* 542*p* 969*d*
11:4	15*c*²
11:5	34*g* 754*d*
11:6	490*w*
11:7	812*d*
11:8	788*n*
11:9	322*l*
11:10	877*c*
11:13	527*b* 545*g* 754*d*
11:14	527*b* 969*d* 969*q*
11:15	69*i*
11:16	499*h*
11:17	877*c*
11:22	371*ag*
11:23	279*k* 503*e* 682*c* 747*d* 827*g*
11:24	99*a* 99*r* 279*b*

11:25	94*c* 110*j* 165*y* 279*k* 344*n*
11:26	267*b* 545*g* 661*b* 789*b*
11:27	380*c* 678*c* 859*k*
11:28	825*u* 985*c*
11:29	163*e*
11:30	163*h* 877*c*
11:32	741*u*
11:33	194*s* 311*n*
12:1	438*z* 877*c*
12:2	971*h*
12:4	578*f* 971*h*
12:5	163*h* 877*c*
12:7	256*m* 827*g* 969*h*
12:8	94*b* 761*r*
12:9	160*k* 163*h*² 877*c* 897*q*
12:10	163*h* 828*b*
12:11	34*g* 754*d*
12:12	547*k* 754*a* 864*g*
12:13	322*l*
12:14	94*b* 169*j*
12:15	806*a*
12:20	61*c* 709*k* 911*j* 926*i*
12:21	940*c* 951*e*
13:1	90*d* 94*b* 466*a*
13:3	160*l*
13:4	160*f* 163*a* 163*e* 362*bl*
13:5	461*l*
13:8	494*i*
13:9	163*e*
13:10	164*ad* 733*ag*
13:11	89*b* 710*b* 717*a* 717*f* 887*c*
13:12	884*c* 889*a*
13:13	884*e* 979*k*
13:14	9*a* 93*a* 887*c* 897*p*

Galatians

1:1	656*g* 754*c*
1:2	985*e*
1:4	121*a* 595*e* 668*j*
1:5	115*d*
1:6	15*c* 621*j* 864*o*
1:8	899*n* 968*q*
1:10	371*r* 826*m*
1:11	371*p* 529*l*
1:12	526*m*
1:13	735*g* 973*c* 985*b*
1:14	127*e* 818*d* 973*c*
1:15	130*b* 526*m* 737*o*

1:16 371*p* 528*d*
1:17 754*b* 883*g*
1:18 110*q* 110*v*
1:19 11*k*
1:22 491*t* 985*e*
1:23 528*h*
2:1 110*z*
2:2 526*g* 529*l* 641*c*
2:3 988*o*
2:4 545*g* 745*n*
2:6 481*a* 866*s*
2:7 59*r* 974*b*
2:9 9*b* 241*d* 866*s*
2:10 505*o* 801*i*
2:11 704*i*
2:12 708*l* 854*aa*
　　　882*c* 883*f*
2:13 545*f*
2:14 740*c*
2:15 371*ag*
2:16 485*s* 676*h* 927*c*
　　　953*m*
2:17 914*r*
2:19 361*ao*
2:20 360*z* 361*ao* 887*j*
2:21 641*b* 752*f* 953*m*
3:1 362*bl* 499*d*
　　　522*b* 983*h*
3:2 455*m* 676*j* 782*c*
　　　953*m* 965*u*
3:3 319*l*
3:4 641*d*
3:5 455*m* 864*a*
　　　953*m*
3:6 480*t* 485*s* 913*v*
3:7 170*v* 485*s*
3:8 371*z* 528*j*
3:10 586*e* 899*e* 953*o*
3:11 485*s* 913*v*
3:12 676*e*
3:13 217*a* 586*e* 792*s*
　　　899*e* 899*g*
3:14 764*g* 965*u*
3:15 765*s*
3:16 170*v* 764*c*
3:17 110*ag* 752*e*
　　　765*b*
3:18 764*c*
3:19 720*b* 953*i* 968*k*
3:20 88*a*
3:21 360*o* 953*m*
3:22 914*j*
3:23 485*w* 747*u*
3:24 690*b* 927*c* 953*i*
3:26 170*t*
3:27 228*af* 988*x*

3:28 16*b²* 88*d* 371*ak*
　　　372*b* 742*n*
3:29 170*v* 776*c*
4:1 16*a* 130*k* 776*c*
4:3 156*a* 745*l*
4:4 108*z* 167*k* 953*n*
　　　953*v*
4:5 170*l* 792*s*
4:6 169*u* 170*t* 965*k*
4:7 742*n* 776*c*
4:8 966*a*
4:9 156*a* 490*m*
　　　490*q* 745*n*
4:10 110*e*
4:11 641*c*
4:13 651*i*
4:14 28*c* 299*c* 968*c*
4:15 304*g* 438*k*
4:16 540*c* 705*i*
4:19 167*o* 825*u*
4:21 953*n*
4:22 745*n* 746*o*
4:23 764*c*
4:24 209*k* 765*c*
4:25 184*ag* 745*n*
4:26 169*ah* 184*an*
　　　746*o*
4:27 171*c*
4:28 764*d*
4:29 735*f*
4:30 300*v*
5:1 745*n* 746*o*
5:2 988*o*
5:3 953*n*
5:4 46*ad* 655*b* 927*f*
5:5 852*d* 913*v*
5:6 485*b* 988*p*
5:7 702*h*
5:8 612*o*
5:9 323*h*
5:11 702*f* 735*j* 964*f*
　　　988*o*
5:12 172*i*
5:13 742*r* 746*l*
5:14 887*t* 953*u*
5:16 965*ad*
5:17 319*l*
5:18 953*r* 965*ae*
5:19 319*l* 676*n* 914*k*
　　　951*a*
5:20 708*a* 709*a* 709*d*
　　　881*a* 891*z*
　　　911*j* 982*a* 983*a*
5:21 733*s* 912*a* 949*f*

5:22 171*p* 644*f* 717*e*
　　　823*a* 824*t*
　　　887*y* 897*t* 929*f*
　　　965*ad*
5:23 177*c* 823*g* 953*r*
5:24 361*ao* 859*t*
5:25 965*ad*
5:26 877*d* 912*b*
6:1 177*e* 612*m*
　　　656*am*
6:2 273*j* 322*l* 953*y*
6:3 482*a* 542*h* 871*d*
6:5 273*j*
6:6 537*f* 783*g*
6:7 75*j* 370*v* 542*m*
　　　851*h*
6:8 51*b* 319*l* 360*p*
　　　965*ad*
6:9 370*v* 855*a*
6:10 11*n* 644*d*
6:11 558*a* 586*j*
6:12 735*j* 964*f* 988*o*
6:13 877*a* 988*o*
6:14 46*aq* 877*h* 964*e*
6:15 126*f* 371*ai* 988*p*
6:16 717*f*
6:17 655*m* 827*g*
6:18 897*p*

Ephesians

1:1 595*b* 754*c* 979*k*
1:2 717*c*
1:3 169*r* 897*s* 923*l*
　　　971*f*
1:4 68*c* 605*f* 935*b*
　　　979*f*
1:5 170*l* 608*c*
1:6 887*d* 897*q*
1:7 335*p* 792*q* 909*l*
　　　941*m*
1:8 498*f*
1:9 526*g* 595*d*
1:10 74*c* 108*z*
1:11 595*c* 608*c* 777*m*
1:12 923*n*
1:13 547*q* 764*g* 965*v*
1:14 767*f*
1:15 485*q* 887*z* 979*m*
1:16 761*n* 907*m*
1:17 498*h* 526*g*
1:18 516*h* 737*o* 777*g*
　　　800*t* 852*a* 979*k*
1:19 160*k*
1:20 241*b* 311*z* 656*i*
1:21 124*f* 733*aa*
1:22 213*i* 741*d* 745*i*
　　　985*a*

1:23 54*f* 319*f*
2:1 361*x*
2:2 738*k* 969*a* 969*t*
2:3 859*u* 891*f*
2:4 887*i* 905*c*
2:5 360*t* 361*x* 668*r*
　　　897*r*
2:6 308*e* 656*j* 971*f*
2:7 897*q*
2:8 485*t* 668*r* 676*h*
　　　781*h* 897*r*
2:9 877*f*
2:10 608*a* 676*d* 676*k*
2:11 371*ak* 974*c*
2:12 46*ad* 59*a* 853*b*
　　　965*ah*
2:13 199*m* 200*e*
　　　335*q*
2:14 88*e* 235*o* 371*ak*
　　　717*c* 719*d*
2:15 126*f* 881*a* 953*v*
2:16 88*d* 719*d* 964*e*
2:17 199*m* 200*e* 717*c*
2:18 297*g*
2:19 11*n* 59*o* 191*b*
　　　371*ak* 979*k*
2:20 164*ac* 214*e*
　　　214*f* 579*ag*
　　　754*a*
2:21 36*i* 45*l* 990*ab*
2:22 192*c*
3:1 750*c*
3:3 526*g* 530*c*
3:4 530*b*
3:5 125*f* 579*ag*
　　　754*a* 965*ab*
3:6 371*ak* 764*d* 775*c*
3:7 742*j* 781*h*
3:8 35*c* 528*d* 800*s*
　　　979*l*
3:9 164*c* 525*a*
3:10 498*i* 969*s* 985*a*
3:11 115*c* 617*a*
3:12 297*g*
3:13 855*a*
3:14 169*q* 311*e* 761*n*
　　　965*g*
3:15 11*m*
3:16 162*d* 224*c*
3:17 192*c* 887*i*
3:18 490*u* 887*j*
3:19 54*j* 517*a*
3:20 160*k*
3:21 115*d* 923*k* 985*a*
4:1 750*c* 915*d*
4:2 823*c* 872*c*

4:3	47k 88f 319f 717f	**5:21**	721b	**1:17**	747d	**3:14**	962d
4:4	88d 93a	**5:22**	721c 894k	**1:18**	528l	**3:17**	83f
4:5	485b 988x	**5:23**	213i² 668e 741d 985a	**1:19**	633a 668h 761o	**3:18**	705b 964f
4:8	308b 750d 781m	**5:24**	721a	**1:20**	866p 872u	**3:19**	69i 319l 859r
4:9	309j	**5:25**	887j 887aa 894j 985a	**1:21**	360z 361am 771l	**3:20**	191h 507d 971f
4:10	54f 308b	**5:26**	648ac 979n	**1:22**	171s	**3:21**	83a 147b 160f 745i
4:11	369g 528k 537f 579ag 754a	**5:27**	646d 935b	**1:23**	89k 361am	**4:1**	600a 743j
4:12	164ad 319f 669c 979m	**5:28**	319b 887aa	**1:24**	596a	**4:2**	710b
4:13	54f 88f 134a	**5:29**	985a	**1:27**	600a 688a 716k 915d	**4:3**	589l 703i
4:14	132k 152b 535a	**5:30**	53b 319f	**1:28**	547m 854af	**4:4**	146c 824g
4:15	213i 540b 741d	**5:31**	45a 169k 621p	**1:29**	825m	**4:5**	177d 200a 200d
4:16	36i 45l 164ad 213i 319f	**5:32**	985a	**2:1**	9a 817a 855f	**4:6**	761c 825w 907a
4:17	59a 641k	**5:33**	887aa 920b	**2:2**	710b	**4:7**	517a 660c 717c
4:18	491f 602g	**6:1**	169i 739m	**2:3**	871d 872c 932c	**4:8**	449f 494a 841a 866af 950e
4:19	859q 951d	**6:2**	113d 169i 764b 866u 920b	**2:4**	932c	**4:9**	20c 717a
4:20	536a	**6:4**	534o 891aa	**2:5**	447g	**4:10**	137c
4:21	494c	**6:5**	44a 739m	**2:6**	28b 965h	**4:11**	8d 828b
4:22	127k 688a	**6:6**	28d² 371r 595f	**2:7**	18i 371g 742k 872l	**4:12**	635i 636h
4:23	126f	**6:8**	804k	**2:8**	361ak 739d	**4:13**	162d 469c
4:24	126f 228af 913l	**6:9**	481a 741y 900b	**2:9**	561k 866o	**4:15**	781w
4:25	53b 540b	**6:10**	162a 162l	**2:10**	311k	**4:18**	54e 396h 826i
4:26	891s	**6:11**	600a 723f 969aa	**2:11**	526n 741f 866j	**4:19**	635h 800s
4:27	137f 969aa	**6:12**	319o 716m 969s²	**2:12**	676m 854a	**4:20**	115d 923k
4:28	781v 788d	**6:14**	494g 913m	**2:13**	595a 676d	**4:21**	884e 884g
4:29	579d	**6:15**	53m 528k 669i	**2:14**	829e	**4:22**	884e 979k
4:30	108aj 547q 827m 965v	**6:16**	287h 485b 662j	**2:15**	170u 420k 935b 950c	**4:23**	897p
4:31	391f 891z 898a 926i	**6:17**	529b 662k 668r 723d 723g	**2:16**	108af 641d		
4:32	905h 909r	**6:18**	146a 761c 979m	**2:17**	981t	**Colossians**	
5:1	20a 170u	**6:19**	526g 530b	**2:21**	932a	**1:1**	595b 754c
5:2	396h 887j 981ac	**6:20**	747d 754e	**2:22**	170w	**1:2**	717c 897p 979k
5:3	859q 951e 979k	**6:22**	831f	**2:24**	289b	**1:3**	169t 761n 907m
5:4	839b 907f	**6:23**	717c	**2:25**	722o	**1:4**	485q 887z 979m
5:5	733s 774d 859x 951b 982b	**6:24**	887o 897p	**2:26**	651i	**1:5**	529l 852d
5:6	542m 738k 891f			**2:29**	299d 920b	**1:6**	171s
5:7	10e	**Philippians**		**2:30**	661a	**1:8**	887z
5:8	417p² 418k	**1:1**	742g 742i 979k 986ag	**3:1**	106a 824g	**1:9**	595d 761n²
5:9	171p	**1:2**	717b 897p	**3:2**	46c 365bm 457a 708l	**1:10**	171o 490q 826h 915d
5:10	826h	**1:3**	761n 907m	**3:3**	319n 485ag 877h 981b 988q	**1:11**	162d
5:11	10e 418l 676n	**1:6**	68m 108af 146d 725a	**3:5**	131f 371ag 708i 988n	**1:12**	777n 907f 979k
5:12	530g	**1:7**	747d	**3:6**	735g 818d 935d 985b	**1:13**	418n 733k
5:13	443a	**1:8**	466k 817a	**3:7**	772i	**1:14**	792r 909l
5:14	656j 678f	**1:9**	463a 887b	**3:8**	302i 490u 641i	**1:15**	18b 119h 444b
5:15	457e 500a	**1:10**	108af 923w 935b	**3:9**	485s 913u 913v	**1:16**	164f 969s
5:16	108a	**1:11**	171p 913l 923p	**3:10**	83a 490u 656i 825k	**1:17**	1d 48c 119h
5:17	595d	**1:13**	747d	**3:11**	656k	**1:18**	68k 119h 213i 638a 741d 985a
5:18	54h 949f 965r	**1:14**	855e	**3:12**	646d	**1:19**	54f
5:19	412d	**1:15**	912c	**3:13**	506k	**1:20**	335p 719c
5:20	907f					**1:21**	704d
						1:22	719c 935b 979n
						1:23	183i 528j 600a 742j
						1:24	825k 985a

1:25	742*j*	**3:20**	169*i* 739*m* 826*i*	**3:2**	153*n* 162*k*
1:26	530*c* 979*k*	**3:21**	891*aa*	**3:3**	825*m*
1:27	192*c* 526*g* 852*c*	**3:22**	44*a* 739*m*	**3:4**	735*j*
1:28	134*a* 528*l*	**3:23**	28*d*	**3:5**	612*o* 641*c*
1:29	160*k* 682*c*	**3:24**	742*i* 962*b*	**3:6**	859*ab*
2:2	45*l* 490*u* 530*b*	**3:25**	481*a*	**3:7**	831*g*
2:3	490*a* 498*i* 800*s*	**4:1**	741*y* 913*i*	**3:8**	153*n*
2:4	542*m*	**4:2**	761*c* 907*f*	**3:9**	824*w* 907*m*
2:5	60*a* 153*n* 190*f*	**4:3**	263*h* 528*l* 530*b*	**3:10**	146*b* 761*n*
2:6	688*a* 782*d*		747*d*	**3:12**	887*b*
2:7	153*n* 907*f*	**4:5**	59*ag* 137*c* 223*i*	**3:13**	153*l* 295*f* 935*b*
2:8	127*e* 156*a* 449*g*	**4:6**	388*d* 460*h*		979*l*
	542*f*	**4:10**	299*d* 750*c* 884*e*	**4:1**	826*h*
2:9	54*f* 319*d* 965*h*	**4:11**	708*l*	**4:2**	737*f*
2:10	54*j* 213*i* 741*d*	**4:12**	134*a* 761*n*	**4:3**	595*a* 951*e* 979*p*
2:11	988*q*	**4:14**	658*b*	**4:5**	59*a* 491*e* 859*o*
2:12	364*s* 656*i* 988*x*	**4:15**	884*g* 985*g*	**4:6**	788*e* 963*a*
2:13	360*t* 361*x* 909*f*	**4:16**	579*n* 588*d* 985*e*	**4:7**	951*e*
	974*c*	**4:17**	725*h*	**4:8**	371*p* 781*j* 965*u*
2:14	752*f* 803*f* 964*e*	**4:18**	586*j* 747*d*	**4:9**	534*e* 887*z*
2:15	161*i* 727*k* 969*s*			**4:11**	719*f*
2:16	301*aq* 480*r*	## 1 Thessalonians		**4:12**	59*ag* 920*c*
	988*a*	**1:1**	717*b* 897*p* 985*e*	**4:13**	361*am* 836*ak*
2:17	22*c*	**1:2**	761*n* 907*m*		853*b*
2:18	447*c* 872*b* 968*a*	**1:3**	676*k* 852*d*	**4:14**	89*c* 656*j* 679*e*
	969*q* 981*al*	**1:4**	605*f*	**4:15**	283*h* 295*f*
2:19	36*i* 45*l* 47*k* 213*i*	**1:5**	160*o* 579*f*	**4:16**	309*e* 414*n* 656*k*
	741*d*	**1:6**	20*a* 825*n*		968*t*
2:20	156*a* 361*ao*	**1:7**	83*f*	**4:17**	89*k* 115*l* 340*a*
2:21	378*q* 386*d*	**1:8**	528*j*		355*i*
2:22	371*o*	**1:9**	982*f*	**4:18**	831*e*
2:23	872*b* 944*a* 945*a*	**1:10**	124*e* 507*d* 656*g*	**5:1**	108*z*
3:1	241*b* 311*z* 459*t*		668*e*	**5:2**	108*ah* 129*o*
	656*j* 971*f*	**2:1**	641*d*		789*f*
3:2	449*f*	**2:2**	704*f* 825*n*	**5:3**	165*s* 167*p* 717*k*
3:3	361*ao* 525*g*	**2:3**	495*f* 542*o* 951*b*	**5:4**	108*ah* 418*n*
3:4	445*d* 526*m*	**2:4**	371*r* 461*a* 826*i*		789*f*
	526*o*		923*r*	**5:5**	128*l* 129*m* 417*p*
3:5	53*a* 361*ap*	**2:5**	466*k* 859*t* 925*b*		418*n*
	859*q*^{2} 951*e*	**2:6**	371*r* 754*b* 866*x*	**5:6**	679*f*
	982*b*	**2:7**	177*f* 301*y*	**5:7**	129*m* 679*f* 949*f*
3:6	891*f*	**2:8**	887*z*	**5:8**	128*l* 485*b* 662*k*
3:8	891*z* 926*i*	**2:9**	682*c*		668*r* 723*f*
3:9	127*k* 541*i*	**2:10**	466*k*		723*g* 887*y*
3:10	18*d* 126*f* 228*af*	**2:11**	169*w*	**5:9**	608*d* 668*r* 891*p*
3:11	16*b* 371*ak*	**2:12**	733*l* 737*m*	**5:10**	360*z* 361*aj*
	742*n* 988*p*		915*d*		679*d*
3:12	177*d* 228*af*	**2:13**	371*p* 529*g*	**5:11**	164*af* 855*e*
	605*f* 823*c*	**2:14**	20*d* 825*n* 985*e*	**5:12**	920*b*
	872*c* 905*h*	**2:15**	300*w* 362*ao*	**5:13**	717*f*
3:13	909*r*		362*bl* 704*j*	**5:14**	163*i* 664*e* 823*c*
3:14	47*k* 887*b*	**2:16**	579*q* 702*h* 891*f*	**5:15**	804*m*
3:15	88*d* 717*d* 907*a*	**2:17**	859*ab*	**5:16**	146*c* 824*a*
3:16	412*d* 529*g*	**2:18**	702*h* 969*h*	**5:17**	146*a* 761*c*
3:17	561*l* 907*f*	**2:19**	743*j*	**5:18**	8*d* 595*a* 907*a*
3:18	721*c* 894*k*	**2:20**	866*b*	**5:19**	418*p* 965*ag*
3:19	887*aa* 894*j*	**3:1**	88*n* 621*s*	**5:20**	579*t* 922*k*

5:21	461*j*		
5:22	620*r*		
5:23	295*f* 979*p*		
5:24	929*a*		
5:25	761*o*		
5:26	884*c* 889*a*		
5:27	532*r* 579*n* 588*d*		
5:28	897*p*		

2 Thessalonians

1:1	985*e*
1:2	717*c* 897*p*
1:3	485*ab* 887*z*
	907*m*
1:4	600*b* 735*k*
1:5	733*m* 913*f* 915*d*
1:6	804*k* 825*s* 913*a*
1:7	381*u* 381*w* 831*c*
	968*f*
1:8	491*f* 738*l* 910*a*
1:9	46*ad* 115*k* 963*e*
	963*f*
1:10	295*f* 864*q* 923*o*
	979*l*
1:11	761*n* 915*d*
1:12	923*o*
2:1	74*c* 295*f*
2:2	108*ah* 588*d*
2:3	165*x* 542*m*
	603*h* 914*ag*
	954*a*
2:4	866*y* 967*r* 990*t*
2:6	526*t* 747*v*
2:7	530*g* 954*a*
2:8	165*m* 295*g*
	954*a*
2:9	864*h*
2:10	361*v*
2:11	485*aj* 542*b*
2:12	826*s* 961*b*
2:13	68*d* 605*f* 907*m*
	979*q*
2:14	737*o* 866*r*
2:15	127*j* 588*e* 600*a*
2:16	115*k* 831*c*
2:17	162*d* 831*d*
3:1	529*h* 761*o*
3:2	486*b* 668*d*
3:3	660*a* 929*a*
3:5	600*e* 887*c*
3:6	127*j* 620*s*
3:7	20*b*
3:8	322*l* 682*c* 805*a*
3:9	20*b* 83*f*
3:10	676*l*
3:11	679*k*
3:13	684*g*

3:14 620*s* 872*t* 883*c*
3:15 664*e* 705*i*
3:16 89*b* 717*a* 717*c*
3:17 586*j*
3:18 897*p*

1 Timothy
1:1 754*c* 852*c*
1:2 170*w* 717*c* 897*p*
1:3 535*b*
1:4 169*f* 543*c*
1:5 485*b* 887*b* 917*a*
1:7 517*e* 537*a*
1:8 953*j*
1:9 362*b* 953*i*
1:10 545*d* 788*a* 951*o*
1:11 529*l*
1:12 929*d*
1:13 486*k* 491*w* 735*g*
905*f* 980*e*
1:14 897*q*
1:15 35*c* 473*c* 668*j*
938*k*
1:16 83*e* 360*u* 823*f*
1:17 21*c* 88*a* 115*d*
741*a* 866*f*
1:18 579*ah* 716*k*
1:19 165*z* 917*a* 917*f*
1:20 969*ab* 980*f*
2:1 761*c*
2:2 717*f* 741*h*
2:3 668*p*
2:4 597*a*
2:5 88*a* 371*g* 720*a*
2:6 792*q*
2:7 754*c*
2:8 310*i* 372*e* 761*c*
2:9 228*h* 373*i* 676*k*
844*m*
2:11 373*i* 536*a* 582*j*
721*c*
2:12 373*i* 534*r* 582*j*
733*ak*
2:13 164*i*
2:14 542*p*
2:15 167*u*
3:1 986*ah*
3:2 537*f* 813*d* 894*g*
929*g*
3:3 177*d* 797*n*
887*ai* 948*d*
3:4 733*ah*
3:5 985*c*
3:6 130*l* 147*e* 871*d*
969*e*
3:7 59*ag* 866*ad*
969*e*

3:8 742*g* 926*i* 948*d*
3:9 530*b* 917*a*
3:10 461*i*
3:11 373*i* 926*i*
3:12 733*ah* 894*g*
3:14 289*b*
3:15 218*s* 688*a* 985*c*
3:16 308*b* 485*q* 528*l*
530*b* 927*a*
968*n*
4:1 452*c* 542*q* 603*h*
969*p*
4:2 545*b* 917*f*
4:3 301*aq* 757*g*
894*c* 895*i* 907*i*
4:6 452*a*
4:7 495*b* 543*c*
979*ac*
4:8 124*f* 534*w*
4:9 473*c*
4:10 668*e* 682*c*
4:11 534*q*
4:12 83*g* 130*i* 922*n*
4:13 534*s* 579*k*
4:14 378*v* 579*ah*
781*m*
4:15 654*b*
4:16 452*a* 457*e*
5:1 11*o* 133*d* 924*h*
5:3 896*g*
5:4 11*h* 633*c*
5:6 361*v*
5:8 11*h* 533*e* 633*c*
5:9 131*c* 894*g*
5:10 53*l* 648*e* 813*d*
979*m*
5:11 859*o*
5:13 679*k* 926*i*
5:14 894*b* 926*g*
5:15 282*d* 969*l*
5:16 11*h* 985*c*
5:17 91*c* 534*s* 804*a*
986*ah*
5:18 365*ay* 586*e*
747*x* 915*e*
5:19 90*d* 466*a* 928*a*
986*ah*
5:20 924*h*
5:21 481*c*
5:22 378*v* 857*a*
5:23 651*i* 658*f* 949*c*
5:24 522*c* 914*l*
6:1 742*l*
6:2 920*b*
6:3 15*c*
6:4 709*a* 709*b* 871*a*
6:5 771*i* 979*ac*

6:6 828*b* 979*ac*
6:8 228*a* 301*c* 828*b*
6:9 542*y* 800*l*
6:10 282*e* 655*k*
797*m* 887*ah*
6:11 177*d* 485*b* 600*g*
620*r* 887*b* 913*i*
6:12 360*l* 360*x* 466*s*
485*b* 716*k*
6:13 466*p*
6:14 445*d*
6:15 88*b* 741*e*^{2}
6:16 115*c* 417*e* 438*e*
6:17 474*c* 485*ae*
633*a* 800*l*
824*o* 871*h*
6:18 676*k* 800*r* 813*b*
6:19 360*l* 800*s*
6:20 490*d* 515*b*
6:21 282*e*

2 Timothy
1:1 754*c*
1:2 717*c* 897*p*
1:3 146*b* 761*n*
907*m* 917*a*
1:4 859*ab*
1:5 169*ac* 485*q*
1:6 378*v* 781*m*
1:7 160*m* 177*c*
855*h* 887*y*
1:8 825*l* 872*y*
1:9 125*b* 668*j* 676*h*
737*o* 897*q*
1:10 360*s* 361*aw*
445*b*
1:11 751*c* 754*c* 825*n*
1:12 485*o* 660*d* 872*y*
1:13 452*a*
1:14 192*f* 660*d* 965*s*
1:15 621*s*
1:16 47*f* 685*d* 872*aa*
1:17 459*af*
2:1 162*l*
2:2 534*q*
2:3 722*o* 825*l*
2:4 826*h*
2:5 716*l*
2:6 370*u*
2:7 516*e*
2:8 170*p* 505*f* 656*f*
2:9 746*o* 747*t*
2:10 115*k* 600*d* 605*g*
668*r* 866*r*
2:11 361*ao* 473*c*
600*c*
2:12 533*c* 733*ag*

2:13 470*b* 533*a* 929*a*
930*a*
2:14 505*n* 709*b*
2:15 529*g* 686*a* 872*y*
923*r*
2:16 515*b*
2:17 651*f*
2:18 282*e* 656*d*
2:19 214*e* 490*m* 561*l*
620*r*
2:20 194*p* 631*l* 866*r*
867*c*
2:21 640*a* 648*ad*
866*r*
2:22 130*l* 485*b* 619*k*
620*r* 717*f* 859*z*
887*b* 913*i*
2:23 474*b* 709*a*
2:24 537*f* 709*b*
2:25 177*e* 939*c*
2:26 542*y* 667*d* 969*e*
3:1 700*b*
3:2 169*m* 738*a*
797*m* 871*a*
877*a* 887*v*
887*ah* 908*a*
932*a* 980*a*
3:3 829*d* 887*aj* 888*i*
898*a* 926*c*
943*a*
3:4 272*h* 826*r* 857*a*
871*a* 887*q*
3:5 161*d* 620*s* 973*a*
3:6 373*k*
3:7 490*s* 536*b*
3:8 704*f*
3:9 499*d*
3:10 20*c* 534*p*
3:11 668*h* 825*n*
3:12 735*j* 979*ac*
3:13 542*e*^{2} 655*a*
3:15 130*f* 498*l* 668*r*
975*h*
3:16 352*c* 534*g* 640*c*
913*o* 924*h*
975*a*
3:17 669*c* 696*c*
4:1 480*f* 480*i*
4:2 137*c* 528*k* 669*c*
924*h*
4:3 456*d* 537*c*
4:4 456*d* 495*e* 543*c*
4:5 528*k* 600*g* 825*l*
4:6 361*al* 981*t*
4:7 485*b* 716*k* 725*h*
4:8 743*i* 913*w*

4:10	121*a* 621*s*
	887*ag* 974*f*
4:11	89*r* 640*b*
4:13	228*c* 589*p*
4:14	645*f* 686*g* 804*k*
4:15	704*f*
4:16	621*s*
4:17	89*f* 162*d* 365*ad*
	528*d*
4:18	115*d* 668*h* 733*k*
	971*f*
4:19	884*g*
4:20	651*i*
4:21	129*q* 884*e*
4:22	89*b* 897*p*

Titus

1:1	494*g* 754*c*
1:2	125*b* 360*j* 470*b*
	540*a* 764*e*
1:3	526*c*
1:4	170*w* 717*c* 897*p*
1:5	751*e* 986*ag*
1:6	738*a* 894*g* 929*g*
	986*ah*
1:7	602*f* 771*i* 891*z*
	929*g* 948*d*
1:8	813*d*
1:9	452*a*
1:10	708*l* 988*o*
1:11	535*a* 578*d* 771*i*
1:12	545*a* 579*am*
	679*k* 947*a*
1:13	924*h*
1:14	495*b* 543*c*
1:15	447*c* 917*f* 950*c*
1:16	490*s* 533*b* 641*k*
	676*k*
2:1	452*a* 534*t*
2:2	133*a*
2:3	133*a* 926*i* 948*d*
2:4	534*q* 887*aa*
	894*k*
2:5	721*c*
2:7	83*g* 534*t*
2:8	872*t*
2:9	742*l*
2:10	534*t* 788*d* 844*n*
2:11	668*r*
2:12	913*l*
2:13	445*d* 507*d*
	852*d* 965*h*
2:14	371*ac* 792*s*
	818*c*
2:15	855*e* 922*n*
3:1	739*a* 745*b*
3:2	177*d* 926*i*

3:3	499*g* 542*m* 738*k*
	745*m* 826*r*
	888*f* 912*d*
3:4	887*i*
3:5	126*f* 648*ac* 668*j*
	676*h* 965*ac*
3:6	965*s*
3:7	360*x* 776*c* 927*b*
3:8	473*c* 676*k*
3:9	169*f* 641*e* 709*b*
3:10	46*ap* 664*e*
3:12	129*r*
3:13	703*i* 958*a*
3:14	171*p* 676*k*
3:15	884*e* 884*g* 897*p*

Philemon

1	750*c*
2	722*o* 985*g*
3	897*p*
4	761*n* 907*m*
5	485*q* 887*z*
	979*m*
7	685*d* 831*f* 887*z*
	979*m*
9	750*c*
10	170*w* 640*b*
11	640*b* 641*j*
16	11*o*
17	28*f* 299*c*
18	803*g*
19	586*j*
20	685*d*
22	192*ah* 194*t*
	761*o*
23	750*c* 884*e*
25	897*p*

Hebrews

1:1	125*f* 579*r*
1:2	164*f* 170*q* 579*o*
	776*b*
1:3	18*b* 241*b* 311*z*
	866*l* 941*m*
1:4	968*b*
1:5	169*t* 170*m*
1:6	968*b* 981*g*
1:7	352*m* 381*s* 968*a*
1:8	115*g* 743*b* 743*l*
	965*h*
1:9	357*u* 824*f*
1:10	2*c* 68*b* 164*b*
	648*p*
1:11	2*c* 153*e* 228*ac*
1:12	115*e*
1:13	218*ad* 241*b*
	311*z* 727*k*

1:14	968*a*
2:1	455*q*
2:2	968*k*
2:3	458*c* 667*d*
2:4	466*l* 547*k* 781*m*
	783*h* 864*g*
2:5	124*f* 968*b*
2:6	371*e*
2:7	114*h* 733*ab*
	866*s* 872*l* 968*b*
2:8	745*a*
2:9	114*h* 361*ak*
	866*o* 872*l* 968*b*
2:10	68*k* 170*t* 646*b*
	825*j* 915*h*
2:11	11*l* 872*x*
2:13	170*x*
2:14	165*m* 319*d*
	361*ak* 969*b*
2:15	361*l* 745*l* 854*s*
2:16	968*b*
2:17	11*l* 18*i* 941*m*
	986*w*
2:18	612*p* 703*b*
3:1	737*o* 754*a* 986*v*
3:2	929*b*
3:3	866*l*
3:4	164*c*
3:5	742*b*
3:6	170*q* 192*c* 600*a*
3:7	975*b*
3:8	602*e*
3:9	110*ac* 461*f*
3:10	282*e* 624*b* 891*j*
3:11	683*o*
3:12	486*b* 603*h*
3:13	542*i* 855*e*
3:14	600*a* 775*c*
3:15	602*e*
3:16	738*f*
3:17	110*ac*
3:18	683*o* 738*j*
3:19	486*b*
4:1	854*a*
4:2	486*b*
4:3	485*u* 683*n* 683*o*
	725*a*
4:4	683*a*
4:5	683*o*
4:6	738*j*
4:7	602*e*
4:8	683*o*
4:9	683*n*
4:10	676*i*
4:11	738*l*
4:12	90*s* 256*i* 529*b*
	617*c* 723*d*

4:13	522*a*
4:14	600*a* 971*e* 986*v*
4:15	163*j* 612*p* 935*g*
	986*v*
4:16	200*e* 743*a* 905*f*
5:1	986*h*
5:2	163*d* 177*f*
5:3	981*ac*
5:4	751*b*
5:5	170*m* 986*v*
5:6	115*e* 986*u*
5:7	761*h* 836*y*
5:8	739*d* 825*j*
5:9	115*k* 646*b* 668*e*
	739*e*
5:10	986*u*
5:11	456*d* 517*e*
5:12	301*ba* 534*u*
	537*f*
5:13	132*k*
5:14	134*a*
6:1	134*a* 485*d* 534*u*
	676*i* 939*b*
6:2	378*u* 648*w* 656*a*
	963*e*
6:3	756*a*
6:4	386*c* 603*i* 775*d*
6:5	124*f* 386*c*
6:6	362*bm* 940*c*
6:7	171*f*
6:8	69*i* 172*t* 256*k*
	381*aa*
6:9	668*r*
6:10	505*d* 913*a*
	979*m*
6:11	600*a*
6:12	20*d* 764*f* 823*e*
6:13	532*o*
6:14	104*b*
6:15	764*c* 823*e*
6:16	532*o*
6:17	153*g*
6:18	470*b* 541*b* 662*a*
6:19	47*j* 153*n* 297*l*
	421*e* 852*d*
	990*ad*
6:20	66*a* 115*e* 986*u*
7:1	741*u* 986*q*
7:2	102*f* 717*g* 741*u*
	913*x*
7:3	115*e*^{2} 169*e*
	986*u*
7:4	102*f* 638*e*
7:5	102*a* 986*c*
7:7	897*a*
7:10	224*g*
7:11	986*u* 986*v*

7:14	169*d*	**9:24**	297*l* 971*e*	**11:9**	59*u* 192*t*	**12:17**	607*e* 940*c*
7:16	115*e* 360*h*	**9:25**	106*c*^{2} 941*b*	**11:10**	184*z*	**12:18**	209*k*
7:17	115*e* 986*u*	**9:26**	69*d* 88*g* 445*b*	**11:11**	167*i* 929*a*	**12:19**	414*g*
7:18	752*f*	**9:27**	361*f* 480*d*	**11:12**	104*e*	**12:20**	344*o* 378*d*
7:19	200*e* 647*c* 852*d*	**9:28**	88*g* 668*e* 981*ac*	**11:13**	59*w* 199*e*	**12:21**	854*l*
	953*m*	**10:1**	22*c* 106*c* 647*c*	**11:14**	184*l*	**12:22**	184*an* 209*l*
7:20	532*o*		953*i*	**11:16**	184*l* 184*z* 872*x*		968*f*
7:21	115*e* 599*a* 986*u*	**10:3**	106*c* 505*l*		965*e* 971*f*	**12:23**	119*h* 548*e* 589*l*
7:22	765*m*	**10:4**	941*i*	**11:17**	461*b* 981*ag*		646*d* 957*a*
7:23	104*v*	**10:5**	319*d* 981*an*	**11:18**	170*h*		971*f* 985*a*
7:24	115*e*^{2} 986*u*	**10:6**	826*i* 981*an*	**11:19**	656*c*	**12:24**	126*e* 335*p* 579*i*
7:25	200*e* 761*i*	**10:7**	739*b*	**11:20**	124*f* 897*v*		720*a* 765*l*
7:26	915*h* 935*g* 986*w*	**10:8**	826*i* 981*an*	**11:21**	897*v*	**12:25**	667*d* 760*d*
7:27	88*g* 106*c* 981*ac*	**10:10**	88*g* 981*ac*	**11:22**	296*e* 363*f*	**12:26**	2*c* 321*s*
7:28	115*e* 163*d* 646*b*	**10:11**	106*c*^{2}	**11:23**	110*s* 525*e* 841*l*	**12:27**	165*t*
	986*v*	**10:12**	88*g* 241*b* 311*z*	**11:24**	170*k*	**12:28**	153*s* 733*c* 907*j*
8:1	241*b* 311*z* 725*a*		725*a* 981*ac*	**11:25**	826*q*	**12:29**	381*o*
	986*w*	**10:13**	218*ad* 727*k*	**11:26**	800*r* 924*f* 962*d*	**13:1**	887*x*
8:2	990*m*	**10:14**	88*g* 646*d*	**11:27**	444*b*	**13:2**	59*ab* 813*d* 968*c*
8:3	986*h*	**10:16**	447*e* 953*g*	**11:28**	988*e*	**13:3**	747*e*
8:5	22*c* 23*a*	**10:17**	506*c* 909*b*	**11:29**	342*a*	**13:4**	894*i* 951*b*
8:6	720*a* 765*m*	**10:18**	909*l* 981*ap*	**11:30**	184*au* 235*k*	**13:5**	621*g* 797*n* 828*a*
8:7	765*l*	**10:19**	297*g*		309*d*		887*ai*
8:8	126*e* 765*m*	**10:20**	126*e* 319*d*	**11:31**	951*t*	**13:6**	371*q* 703*b* 855*h*
8:9	769*b*		421*e* 990*ad*	**11:33**	263*r* 365*ad*	**13:7**	20*b*
8:10	371*ac* 447*e*	**10:21**	986*v*		727*c*	**13:8**	115*e* 144*a*
	586*r* 953*g* 965*e*	**10:22**	200*e* 648*ac*	**11:34**	163*h* 381*c*	**13:9**	301*k* 452*a*
8:11	490*q*		917*c*		418*p* 667*e*	**13:10**	990*i*
8:12	506*c* 909*b*	**10:23**	600*a* 929*a*	**11:35**	656*m* 827*f*	**13:11**	223*e*
8:13	126*e* 127*b* 765*l*	**10:24**	612*c*	**11:36**	279*j* 747*e* 851*e*	**13:12**	223*f*
9:2	218*ae* 301*aa*	**10:25**	74*j*	**11:37**	92*a* 228*j* 344*n*	**13:13**	924*f*
	420*f* 979*x* 990*l*	**10:26**	914*r* 981*ap*	**11:38**	268*a* 916*a*	**13:14**	124*f* 184*z*
9:3	421*d* 979*z*	**10:27**	381*w* 480*f*	**11:39**	764*f* 923*r*	**13:15**	907*f* 923*d*
	990*ac*	**10:28**	90*d* 466*a* 953*k*	**11:40**	646*d*		981*as*
9:4	194*a*^{3} 218*b*	**10:29**	335*o* 649*a*	**12:1**	355*b* 466*s* 702*h*	**13:16**	783*g* 981*ar*
	990*c*		765*m* 921*a*		716*l*	**13:17**	721*b*
9:5	226*m* 941*e*		963*d*	**12:2**	68*k* 241*b* 311*z*	**13:18**	761*o* 917*a*
	968*u*	**10:30**	480*f* 910*a*		455*q* 485*a*	**13:20**	115*k* 335*o* 369*l*
9:7	941*b* 986*h*	**10:31**	854*b*		824*f* 872*x*		656*g* 717*a*
9:9	121*a* 647*b* 917*d*	**10:32**	505*p* 825*n*		922*e* 964*d*		765*m*
9:10	301*k* 319*k*	**10:33**	445*h*	**12:3**	684*g* 704*e*	**13:21**	115*d* 633*a*
9:11	124*g* 986*w*	**10:34**	747*e* 777*b* 788*j*	**12:4**	715*a*		676*k* 826*h*
	990*aa*		824*aa*	**12:5**	169*r* 827*i*	**13:22**	569*a*
9:12	88*g* 115*k* 335*p*	**10:35**	962*c*	**12:6**	887*h*	**13:23**	746*f*
	792*r* 990*ad*	**10:36**	600*g*	**12:7**	170*u*	**13:24**	884*e* 884*g* 979*k*
9:13	319*k*	**10:37**	114*i* 135*c*	**12:8**	954*g*	**13:25**	897*p*
9:14	115*f* 335*p* 646*c*	**10:38**	485*s* 855*j* 913*v*	**12:9**	169*q* 721*a*		
	648*ab* 917*c*	**10:39**	485*t*	**12:10**	979*g*	**James**	
9:15	115*k* 126*e*	**11:1**	485*a*	**12:11**	171*p* 827*i* 913*z*	**1:1**	75*h* 99*m*
	361*aj* 720*a*	**11:2**	923*r*	**12:12**	53*f* 53*k* 162*j*	**1:2**	461*e* 824*aa*
	765*l*	**11:3**	164*e* 444*a* 529*d*		163*i*	**1:3**	600*f*
9:16	335*o*	**11:4**	466*k* 485*a* 579*i*	**12:13**	46*e* 249*a* 624*e*	**1:4**	646*d*
9:18	765*e*		981*h*		655*n*	**1:5**	498*k* 761*ac*^{2}
9:19	335*m*	**11:5**	361*au* 826*e*	**12:14**	438*f* 619*k* 717*f*		781*e*
9:20	765*e*	**11:6**	1*a* 826*i*		719*f* 979*p*	**1:6**	343*e* 485*ac*
9:22	335*m* 648*q* 909*l*	**11:7**	275*d* 913*v* 961*c*	**12:15**	391*e* 897*r*		486*a*
9:23	22*c*	**11:8**	491*y* 739*d*	**12:16**	119*d* 793*e* 951*e*	**1:8**	152*b* 601*a*

1:9 869a	**3:5** 381b 381j 579d	**5:15** 656aa 909c	**2:12** 676k
1:10 114e 366f 800l	**3:6** 579d 972b	**5:16** 526r 656aa	**2:13** 741h 745b
1:12 600f 743i 887o	**3:7** 365f 745o	761ad	**2:14** 963h
1:13 612n	**3:8** 579d 659d 745o	**5:17** 18f 110w 342c	**2:15** 578d
1:14 612n 859z	**3:9** 18a 899l 923j	**5:18** 350ab	**2:16** 746l
1:15 167w^2 361u	**3:10** 899l	**5:19** 656am	**2:17** 854a 866v 887x
1:16 542h	**3:11** 339j 391c 392h	**5:20** 668s	**2:18** 721b 735e
1:17 144a 169q 418g	**3:12** 171t 388a		**2:19** 825p
420i 781e	**3:13** 498d	**1 Peter**	**2:21** 20a 83e 825j
1:18 167s 171m 529g	**3:14** 541i 871d 912a	**1:1** 59w 75h 605f	825k
595a	932b	754c	**2:22** 542d 935g
1:19 277f 278b 455p	**3:15** 498r	**1:2** 93a 335p 510a	**2:23** 900b 921e
579g 823c 891z	**3:16** 61c 912a 932b	717b 739e	**2:24** 273i 361ap
1:20 891z	**3:17** 177a 498c 717f	897p 979p	655g 656x 964e
1:21 529g 649b 872c	950a	**1:3** 167s 169t 656i	**2:25** 282e 365bp
1:22 415f 455n 542h	**3:18** 75j 171p 719f	923l	369l
739j	913z	**1:4** 115l 777m 971f	**3:1** 721c 894k
1:23 442c	**4:1** 709d 826r	**1:5** 69e 526k 668r	**3:3** 373i 844m
1:24 506j	**4:2** 362b 761c 859z	**1:6** 114j 824x 825p	**3:4** 177d
1:25 746l	912a	**1:7** 381k 461e 485q	**3:5** 721c
1:26 542h 579g 641b	**4:3** 761af	526m	**3:6** 169ac
973a	**4:4** 705b 880g 951l	**1:8** 444b 824x	**3:7** 163b 373k 702i
1:27 648ad 779c	974f	887m	761e 894j 920b
801i 896k 973a	**4:5** 911c	**1:9** 668r	**3:8** 710b
2:1 481c	**4:6** 871i 872d	**1:10** 459d 579u	**3:9** 804m 910i
2:2 228n 800m	**4:7** 620u 715a 721a	**1:11** 108z 357z 511a	**3:10** 113c 542n
2:3 218ad	969aa	825j 866o	**3:11** 619k 717f
2:5 605f 733k 800r	**4:8** 200e 601a 648c	**1:12** 968b 968n	**3:12** 441h 704a
801p 887o	**4:9** 836f	**1:13** 526m 669h	761aa
2:6 800m 801m	**4:10** 872h	**1:14** 83d 739a	**3:13** 818c
959c	**4:11** 480r 926i	**1:15** 979d	**3:14** 825p 854ah
2:7 926j	**4:12** 480r 957a	**1:17** 480d 854a	**3:15** 177e 460h 741d
2:8 887t	**4:13** 124b 771k	**1:18** 114m 361aj	**3:16** 872t 917a 926g
2:9 481c	**4:14** 114c 124a 124b	792q 797q	**3:17** 825p
2:10 936a 954c	355j	**1:19** 335p 365br	**3:18** 361aj
2:11 362a 951k	**4:15** 595f 597a	646c	**3:19** 528f 748a
2:12 480g 746l 953y	**4:16** 877e	**1:20** 68c 69d 510b	**3:20** 99j 275d
2:13 480b 905h 906a	**4:17** 914a	526m	**3:21** 917c 988x
2:14 485y 676l	**5:1** 800l 836f	**1:21** 485d 656g	**3:22** 241b 745i 969s
2:15 229g 636h	**5:2** 51b	**1:22** 887x	969x 971e
2:16 381am	**5:3** 69d 466g	**1:23** 115l 167s 529g	**4:1** 825j 825k
2:17 485y 676l	**5:4** 804a 924n	**1:24** 114c 366f	**4:3** 125h 949h 982t
2:18 485y 676l	**5:5** 195e 826r	**1:25** 115m 529a	**4:4** 926f
2:19 88a 485g 969c	**5:6** 715c	**2:1** 542n 912b 926i	**4:5** 480e
2:20 485y 676l	**5:7** 295f 350aa	**2:2** 36g 132g 301ba	**4:6** 528f
2:21 676l 927e	823d	**2:3** 386c	**4:7** 69d 200m 761e
2:22 485y 676l	**5:8** 200m 295g	**2:4** 344x 607k	**4:8** 887a 887x
2:23 480t 485s 880c	**5:9** 829e 957a	**2:5** 164ac 344y	**4:9** 813d
913v	**5:10** 83f 579x 823e	981at 986x	**4:10** 742r 781m 897p
2:24 485y 927e	**5:11** 600d 600f 823e	**2:6** 214e 344x 485j	**4:11** 115d 579q 866j
2:25 676l 927e 951t	905d	**2:7** 214e 344x 607k	**4:12** 461e 827f
2:26 485y 676l	**5:12** 532f^2	**2:8** 344x 702g	**4:13** 824aa 825k
3:1 537f	**5:13** 412e 761c 825g	**2:9** 417m 418n 605i	**4:14** 921b
3:2 495a 646e	833a	777f 923n 979f	**4:15** 362b 789b 825p
3:3 365bf 689a	**5:14** 357t 651b 658e	986x	**4:16** 561l 708k
748c	761e 985c	**2:10** 371ak 905f	**4:17** 69i 480f
3:4 270a 275b 689a	986ah	**2:11** 59w 859s	**4:18** 700c

4:19 595f 825p
5:1 466n 775d
986ah
5:2 369g 740c 771i
5:3 83g 733am
5:4 369l 743i 866r
5:5 228af 721b 871i
872c 872d
5:6 872c 872h
5:7 825w
5:8 365ai 403b
705g 969i
5:9 600a 715a
5:10 114j 115k 153l
825p
5:12 569a 586j 897r
5:13 884e
5:14 717d 884c 889a

2 Peter

1:1 485q 754c
1:2 717b 897p
1:3 633a
1:4 764e 775d 859s
1:5 38c 490c
1:6 600g 823g
1:7 887z
1:8 171p 640a
1:9 439c 440d 506j
1:10 605f 737n
1:11 297i 733k
1:12 153n 505g
1:14 361al
1:16 160e 441k 495f
543c
1:17 170m 826d
1:18 209s
1:19 128k 420j
1:20 520h 975a
1:21 975b
2:1 533b 535b
545g² 579al
792t
2:2 926c
2:3 125c 961b
2:4 919d 969r 972a
972c
2:5 350a 528b 919d
2:6 184ay 664h
2:7 929e
2:9 108ai 668m
963a
2:10 871a 926c
2:11 928g 968a
2:12 365b 448a 476a
926c
2:13 280b 804k

2:14 951i
2:15 282e 797m
887ah
2:16 365bd 579c
2:17 342f 355j 418o
2:18 859z
2:19 745m 746s
2:20 655a
2:21 282d
2:22 302q 365bk
496c 649q
3:1 505n 588f
3:3 851e
3:4 153c 295h 764f
3:5 339a 529d
3:6 165r 165t 350a
3:7 108ai 381x
3:8 110ah
3:9 135c 823f 939c
3:10 2c 108ah 165t
789f
3:11 979p
3:12 108af 165t 381x
680a
3:13 126e 321t
3:14 717f 935a
3:15 588d 823d
3:16 165s 517c 588d
3:17 495b
3:18 36g 115d 490u

1 John

1:1 68b 378c 438g
529d
1:2 360h 360r 466n
1:3 9a 9b 438g
1:4 586h 824a
1:5 417b 418h 965a
1:6 9a 10d 418l
542h
1:7 9b 335p 417o
648ab
1:8 542h 935i
1:9 526r 909a 929a
1:10 541c 935i
2:1 703b 703f 913c
914p
2:2 941m
2:3 490u 739k
2:4 545b
2:5 887n
2:6 688a
2:7 126e 737f
2:8 417d
2:9 418l 888n
2:10 702i 887y
2:11 418l 439l 888n

2:12 132j 909f
2:13 68b 132j 169q
169w 727l
969aa
2:14 169w 727l
969aa
2:15 887ag 974f²
2:16 859u 974e
2:17 2e 115l 595g
859u
2:18 69d 705c
2:19 298g
2:20 357k 490q
2:21 490q 543a
2:22 13f 357v 533c
545b 705c
2:23 533c
2:24 68m
2:25 360j² 764e
2:27 357k 534f
2:28 445d
2:29 913c
3:1 170v 491g 887i
3:2 18d 170t 438f
445d
3:3 648ad
3:4 954a
3:5 914m 941m
3:6 438e 490s 914r
3:7 542m 913c
929h
3:8 68g 165m 914b
969b
3:9 167t 914r
3:10 463b 887ak
914r
3:11 887x
3:12 362ac
3:13 888k
3:14 360aa 887z
3:15 360y 362b 888n
3:16 361an 887j
3:17 906c
3:18 579f 887b
3:20 490e 961f
3:22 761ad 826h
3:23 485m 737f
887w
3:24 965ab
4:1 320e 461j 545g
579al
4:2 319d
4:3 705c
4:4 160l 638a
4:5 455v
4:6 455v 494g
4:7 887c 887x 887y

4:8 887c 887ak
965a
4:9 887i
4:10 887c 941m
4:11 887w
4:12 438e 887y
4:13 965ab
4:14 668e
4:15 170q
4:16 887c 965a
4:17 28c 108ai
4:18 855h 887a
4:19 887w
4:20 545b
4:21 887w
5:1 167s
5:2 887n
5:3 322n 739k 887n
5:4 167t 485t 727l
5:6 335p 339v
5:7 466m 466r
5:8 93e 335p 339v
5:9 466m
5:10 541c
5:11 360r
5:13 360u 490v
5:14 761ad
5:16 361u 761j 914a
5:17 914a
5:18 167t 914r
5:19 969l
5:20 360g 360r 490u
5:21 982f

2 John

2 115m 494g
3 717c 897p
5 126e 737f 887w
6 739k 887n
7 319d 542e 705c
8 962d
9 452d
10 299g 452d 884h
11 775e
12 586k
13 170x 884f

3 John

2 650c
4 494g
7 59z 561l
8 703i
9 588f 871f
10 299h 300x
11 20f 438e 644d
12 466h
13 586k

14	717b 884f 884g

Jude

1	737p
2	717b 905g
3	716k 979k
4	125c 533c 951d
5	362bf
6	108ai 418o
	963e 963f 969r
7	115k 184av
	664h 951d
	951p 963e
8	649d 926c
9	928g 968x
10	365b 448a 476a
	926c
12	129p 172r 342f
	355b 369i
13	343e 418o 963e
	963f
14	579z
15	480e
16	829d 925a
17	505p
18	851e
19	46ap 965ah
20	164ad 761c
21	360s 507d 887h
23	381ae
24	935b
25	88a 115d 923k

Revelation

1:1	135d 526m
1:2	466s
1:3	579k
1:4	1a 99d 99e 717c
	965k 985e
1:5	119h 335q 466p
	656f 741e
	746m
1:6	115d 169t 986x
1:7	355i 438g 655l
	836u
1:8	1a 68a 160a
1:9	349b 466o 775c
1:10	108b 414e 577c
	965n
1:11	99d 586i 985e
1:12	99f 420h
1:13	228m 228p
	253b
1:14	259c 259n 427c
	438i
1:15	53m 339c 577c
	631l

1:16	90s 99f 237a
	321m 420i
	723d
1:17	68a 309c 378h
	854ah
1:18	115e 263v 656h
1:19	586i
1:20	99d 99e 99f^2
	321m 420h
	968q 985e
2:1	99f 321m 420h
	588g 985f
2:2	461i 676k 754d
2:3	600b 684g
2:4	607h 887aj
2:5	420h 786l 939b
2:6	888b
2:7	301af 366v
	455q 727m
	971i
2:8	68a 588g 656f
	985f
2:9	192q 371ai
	801p 969l
2:10	110q 743i 747f
	854ah 929g
2:11	361at 455q
	727m
2:12	90s 588g 723d
	985f
2:13	466o 533d 743c
	969l
2:14	535a 951d 982i^2
2:15	535a
2:16	135d 716b 939b
2:17	301af 344x
	455q 561v
	727m
2:18	53m 438i 588g
	631l 985f
2:19	600d 654e 676k
	742r
2:20	495c 579al
	951d 982i
2:21	940b
2:23	362bi 459ac
	804k
2:24	211b 322n
2:26	600c 727m
	733ag
2:27	169t 733aa
2:28	128k 321m
2:29	455q
3:1	99e 99f 321m
	361x 588g
	676k 965k 985f
3:2	678f 726a

3:3	491q 505p 789f
	939b
3:4	228t 427b 648n
	915d
3:5	427b 466q 589l
	727m
3:6	455q
3:7	263v^2 264l 494c
	588g 985f
3:8	163g 263h 533d
	676k
3:9	192q 311b
	371ai 969l
3:10	827b
3:11	135d 295g 743i
3:12	126e 184an
	218s 561d
	586s 727m
	971i 990ab
3:13	455q
3:14	68a 164f 466p
	488d 588g 985f
3:15	30a 380e 676k
	860c
3:16	302r
3:17	229j 439c 800l
	801p
3:18	228t 427b 658f
	792u 797r
3:19	924c 939b
3:20	263af 279p
	455k 882d
3:21	727m 733ag
3:22	455q
4:1	263ag 414e
	577c 971c
4:2	743a
4:3	250c 844i^2
4:4	99p 228t 427b
	743c 743i
	986ag
4:5	99e 99f 176l
	420i 965k
4:6	96b 343q 365bt
	422a
4:7	365ae 365ar
	365az 371d
4:8	1a 160a 438j
	979a
4:9	115b 923k
4:10	99p 115b 743i
	986ag
4:11	1d 164e 595c
	915a
5:1	99f 223j 264p
	589k
5:2	263ai 915b

5:3	916b
5:5	99f 263ai
	365ah
5:6	99e 99f 254e
	362bl 365br
	965k
5:8	99p 311j 396d
	414b 761a
	979k 986ag
5:9	126e 371z 412g
	792q 915b
5:10	733ag 986x
5:11	104m 968n
5:12	160e 162a 915b
5:13	115d 923k
6:1	99f 263aj
6:2	365bg 427e
	727n 743i
6:3	263aj
6:4	365bg 431e
	718g
6:5	263aj 365bg
	428c 465a
6:6	809m
6:7	263aj
6:8	98a 361a 365e
	365bg 434a
	636f
6:9	263aj 362aq
	466o 990i
6:10	136a 910c
6:11	54l 228t 427b
6:12	176f 263aj 321o
	335k 428c
6:13	309f 321l
6:14	209i 349a
6:15	209j 255h 523e
6:16	344p 525e 891d
6:17	108ai
7:1	96a 352h 968r
7:2	547q 968r
7:3	547q
7:4	99m 99v 104m
7:5	99v
7:9	53u 104m 228t
	427b
7:10	668a
7:11	311g 981e
7:12	115d 923k
7:13	13j 228t 427b
7:14	228ae 335q
	427f 648ab
	827b
7:15	742a
7:16	379b 635h
7:17	339n 369l 831b

8:1	110g 263aj 399a 971b	**10:11**	579u	**13:4**	21i 981am	**16:2**	547s 651d
8:2	99e 99f 414o 968r	**11:1**	465f 990z	**13:5**	110w 733al	**16:3**	335k 339h 343h
8:3	396d 761a 979k 990c	**11:2**	59f 110w 235c 279s	**13:6**	980b	**16:4**	335k 339h
8:4	979k	**11:3**	90f 110w 466s 579u	**13:7**	371w 718j 733al 979l	**16:5**	1a 913f
8:5	176f 176l 381y	**11:4**	366l 420h	**13:8**	68c 362bl 589l 981am	**16:6**	280e 335i 339h 979k
8:6	99e 99f 968r	**11:5**	381z	**13:9**	455q	**16:7**	160a 913f
8:7	95a 350af 381x 414p	**11:6**	335k 342c	**13:10**	600d 747g 979k	**16:8**	321o 381x
8:8	95a 209x 335k 339h 343h 414p	**11:7**	365bu 972c	**13:11**	254c 365bs 365bu	**16:9**	940b
8:9	275a	**11:8**	184ax 184ba 364o	**13:12**	655h 656w 981am	**16:10**	418o 743c
8:10	95a 309f 321p 414p	**11:9**	110l	**13:13**	381b 547n	**16:11**	940b
8:11	339h 391c	**11:10**	579u 827d	**13:14**	982o	**16:12**	342a 350p
8:12	95a 321o 414p	**11:11**	360i 854u	**13:15**	656q	**16:13**	365m 365bu 969o
8:13	365aq 830h	**11:12**	308e	**13:16**	237c 241c 547s	**16:14**	108af 160a 547n 718j
9:1	263w 309f 321p 414p 972c	**11:13**	102h 165t 176f	**13:17**	792a	**16:15**	229e 295h 789f
9:2	263w 388e	**11:14**	830h	**13:18**	99t	**16:16**	74e 718j
9:3	365j 365s	**11:15**	115c 414p 733b 733u	**14:1**	99v 209l 237b 365br 586s	**16:17**	340a 725a
9:4	547q	**11:16**	99p 311g 986ag	**14:2**	176m 339c 413c	**16:18**	176f 176l
9:5	110s 365s	**11:17**	1a 160a 733u	**14:3**	99v 126e 412g	**16:19**	95d 165t 184az 891e 949q
9:6	361s	**11:18**	165m 168b 891b 962a 979k	**14:4**	171m 792r 895f	**16:20**	209i 349a
9:7	365bh 371d 743h	**11:19**	176f 176l 194e 263ah 350af 990aa	**14:5**	540c 541i	**16:21**	322d 350af 899i
9:8	256o 259g 365ae 373f	**12:1**	99n 321l 373f 547a 743i	**14:6**	529m 968r	**17:1**	99e 99f 350k 951y
9:9	274f	**12:2**	167p	**14:7**	108ai 164a 480e 854a	**17:2**	949r 951m
9:10	110s 238c 365s	**12:3**	99f² 99k 254f 365bu 431e 547a 743h	**14:8**	165t 184az 949r 968r	**17:3**	99f 99k 254f 431e 980b
9:11	168b 969r 972c	**12:4**	95a 167k 238c 321p	**14:9**	237c 547s 968r 981am	**17:4**	228n 431d 436c 844c 951m
9:12	830h	**12:5**	733w	**14:10**	381ac 949q 963e	**17:5**	169ah 184ba 237c 530g 951y
9:13	254h 414p 990c	**12:6**	110w 620k	**14:11**	388e 963e 963f	**17:6**	335i 949r 979k
9:14	96a 350p 746r 969r	**12:7**	718j 968x	**14:12**	600d 979k	**17:7**	99f 99k 254f
9:15	95a 96a	**12:9**	300p 365r 365bu 542q 969a 969r	**14:13**	361am	**17:8**	2e 68c 589l 608c 972c
9:16	99v	**12:10**	733x 928e 969i	**14:14**	355i 630a 743f	**17:9**	99f 209y 741x
9:17	365ae 365bh 431f 433a 435g	**12:11**	335q 466o 661a 727l	**14:15**	108ai 370w	**17:10**	99f
9:18	95a	**12:12**	114i 969i	**14:17**	370l 630a	**17:11**	2e
9:19	365q 655i	**12:13**	735f	**14:19**	370l 891d	**17:12**	99k² 254f
9:20	940b 969p 982t	**12:14**	110w 271a 365ar	**14:20**	199k 335f	**17:13**	733al
9:21	362b 788f 951d 983g	**12:15**	350w	**15:1**	69g 99e 99f 659b	**17:14**	365br 605f 727k 737n 741d
10:1	250c 355b 968r	**12:17**	466o	**15:2**	343q 381s 414b 422a 727l	**17:15**	350k
10:2	589k	**13:1**	99f 99k² 254f 365bu 743h 980b	**15:3**	115b 160a 412f 624a	**17:16**	99k 229l 254f 888s
10:3	99f 176m 403a	**13:2**	365y 365ae 365aj 733al	**15:4**	854a 979b	**17:17**	710d
10:4	99f 525c	**13:3**	655h 656w 864v	**15:5**	263ah 990aa	**17:18**	184ba
10:6	115b 135d 164a 532n			**15:6**	99e 99f 228m 228u 968r	**18:1**	417q 968r
10:7	530c 725b			**15:7**	99e 99f 115b 194q	**18:2**	165t 184az
10:8	589k			**15:8**	99e 99f 381y	**18:3**	800d 949r 951m
10:9	301ba 391a 392g			**16:1**	99e 99f	**18:4**	298f
						18:6	804j
						18:7	896m
						18:8	659b

18:9 184*ba* 836*ah*
18:11 836*ah*
18:12 795*a*
18:15 836*ah*
18:16 431*d* 436*c*
631*o* 844*c*
18:17 165*t*
18:18 21*m*
18:19 275*e* 800*d*
836*ah*
18:20 480*e*
18:21 165*t* 184*az*
343*c* 344*t*
18:22 412*b*
18:23 145*c* 983*g*
18:24 335*c* 979*k*
19:1 668*a*
19:2 910*c*
19:3 388*e* 963*e* 963*f*
19:4 99*p* 311*g*
19:6 160*a* 176*m*
339*c* 733*a*
19:7 669*c* 894*ae*
19:8 228*ad* 631*o*
913*n* 979*k*
19:9 876*e* 894*ae*
19:10 466*o* 579*ai*
968*a*^{2} 981*a*
981*al*
19:11 263*ag* 365*bg*
427*e* 718*k*
929*b* 971*c*
19:12 438*i* 561*k* 743*d*
19:13 228*ae* 335*d*
529*d* 561*k*
19:14 228*t* 365*bg*
427*b* 427*e*
631*o* 722*j*
19:15 160*a* 723*d*
891*d*
19:16 741*e*
19:17 301*ak* 363*m*
19:19 718*j*
19:20 381*ac* 547*n*
19:21 301*ak*
20:1 47*f* 263*w* 972*c*
20:2 110*ah* 365*r*
365*bu* 969*a*
20:3 114*k* 264*m*
20:4 46*f* 110*ah* 480*p*
547*s* 733*ag*
981*am*
20:5 656*c*
20:6 361*at* 733*ag*
986*x*
20:7 110*ah* 746*r*
20:8 104*s* 542*q*

20:9 381*t* 979*l*
20:10 381*ac* 963*e*
963*f*
20:11 427*e* 480*d*
620*q* 743*a*
20:12 589*l* 589*n*
20:13 343*g* 361*aw*
656*c* 676*f*
20:14 361*at* 361*aw*
381*ac*
20:15 381*ac* 589*l*
21:1 2*d* 126*e* 321*s*
321*t* 343*g*
21:2 126*e* 184*an*
894*ae* 971*i*
21:3 89*a* 192*e* 371*ac*
21:4 2*d* 361*aw* 831*b*
21:5 126*d*
21:6 68*a*^{2} 339*o* 812*d*
859*d*
21:7 170*t* 727*m* 965*e*
21:8 362*b* 381*ac*
486*j* 545*d*
856*a* 951*b*
963*f* 982*t* 983*b*
21:9 99*e* 99*f*^{2} 894*ae*
21:10 184*an* 209*x*
971*i*
21:11 844*j*
21:12 99*m*^{2} 99*n* 235*h*
264*c* 297*m*
21:14 99*n* 214*c* 235*h*
754*b*
21:15 465*f*
21:16 28*l* 99*v*
21:17 99*t* 235*h*
21:19 214*c* 844*j*
21:21 99*n* 264*c* 297*m*
422*a* 624*l* 844*k*
21:22 160*a* 990*aa*
21:23 321*i* 420*c* 420*i*
21:24 866*c*
21:25 129*a* 263*ah*
21:26 866*c*
21:27 589*l* 951*b*
22:1 339*n* 350*h* 422*a*
743*b*
22:2 99*n* 171*i* 360*j*
366*v* 656*t*
22:3 742*a* 743*b* 899*g*
22:4 237*b* 438*f* 561*l*
22:5 2*d* 129*a* 417*j*
420*i* 733*ag*
22:6 135*d*
22:7 135*d* 295*g*
22:8 968*a* 981*al*
22:9 968*a* 981*a*

22:10 264*q* 526*a*
22:11 914*r*
22:12 135*d* 676*f* 962*b*
22:13 68*a*^{3}
22:14 297*f* 366*v*
648*ad*
22:15 223*g* 362*b*
365*bm* 545*d*
951*b* 982*t* 983*b*
22:16 128*k* 170*p*
22:17 812*d* 859*d*
965*aa*
22:18 38*a*
22:19 39*a* 366*v*
22:20 135*d* 295*g*
22:21 897*p*

Subject index

Aaron
Aaronic priesthood
986b
Abaddon 168b
Abana and Pharpar
350s
abandon 621
abandoning for God
621l
abandoning God
621h
abandoning in haste
621u
abandoning people
621p
animals abandoning
621v
God abandoning
individuals 621d
God abandoning
people 621a
not abandoned by
God 621f
reject 607
relinquish 621
remnant abandoned
41r
abase 311r
abased 872h
abate 37c
Abba! Father! 169u
ABC 558a
abdomen 224e
abduct
kidnap 788a
abhor 888b
Abib 108e

abide
be 1
dwell 192
ability
Power 160
ablaze 381
able
be able 160
not able 161
unable 161
Abode 192
abolish 752d
abolition 752d
abominations 165w
abomination of
desolation 165x
detestable thing 888c
abort
miscarry 172k
abortion
miscarriage 172k
abound 635h
about-turn
Change of mind
603
above
not superior 35
superior 34
up above 209a
Abraham
Abraham's bosom
971i
children of
Abraham 170v
Father Abraham
169p

Abraham (cont.)
genealogy of
Abraham 169a
patriarch 169p
promise to Abraham
764c
abrogate 752
Abrogation 752
abscess 651d
abscond
flee 620
Absence 190
Absence of intellect
448
Absence of thought
450
absent 190
God absent 190a
absolution
forgiveness 909
absolve
exempt 919
forgive 909
abstain
avoid 620r
abstemious 948
abstention
not drinking 948
absurd
foolish 499
abundance
excess 637
more than enough
637a
Much 32
Sufficiency 635
abuse
ill-treat 735d
pledges abused 767d
rape 951z
abyss
hell 972c
accent 580a
accept
welcome 299a
acceptable 782a
acceptable anger
891s
access 297
access to God 297g
accessible 297g

accession
becoming king 741k
accident 618
accidental
unintentional 618
acclaim
praise 923
Accompaniment 89
accomplice 707
accomplish 676
accord 710
according to
in proportion 12a
position in rank 73
account 808a
accounting 808
give account 180g
settle accounts 804i
accountability 180g
accountable 180g
accountant
Treasurer 798
Accounts 808
accumulate
accumulating money
797o
accursed 899
Accusation 928
rules about
accusations 928a
accuse 928
accused of being
demonised 969v
accused of
drunkenness 949l
accusing angels
928g
accusing God 928c
accusing Jesus 928f
accusing men 928h
God and scripture
accuse 928d
Satan accuses 928e
accustomed
tradition 127c
achieve
do 676
health achieved 650b
succeed 727b

Note
Category names are shown in bold, such as **Power**. Side-headings are shown in italics, such as *assenting*. Numerals indicate category numbers. Italic letters represent paragraphs within those categories as a suggestion for where to begin a search for the item required.

ailing 651
ailment 651
 people with
  specified ailments
  651*k*
aim
 aim at love 887*b*
Air 340
alacrity
 promptness 135
 speed 277*h*
alarm
 Warning 664
alas! 830*e*
alcohol 949
 avoiding alcohol
  949*a*
alcoholic 949*b*
ale 949
alert
 attentive 455
alias 561*v*
alien 59
alienation
 Enmity 881
alight
 burning 381
alike 18
 all treated alike 16*a*
alive 360*b*
all
 all have sinned 914*j*
 all Israel 54*l*
 complete 54
 creator of all 164*m*
 God knows all
  things 490*e*
 God wants to save
  all 668*p*
all sorts 17
all things
 circumstances 8*d*
 I can do all things
  469*c*
all times
 unceasing 146
all treated alike 16*a*
allegation
 Accusation 928
allegiance 706
 change of
  allegiance 603*e*
allegory
 allegorical food and
  drink 301*ba*
 Metaphor 519

alleluia!
 praise the Lord!
  923*d*
alley
 path 624
alliance
 Cooperation 706
 Marriage 894
allied 706*c*
all kinds 17
allocate
 portion out 783*a*
allocation 783*a*
 ration 26*a*
allot
 portion out 783*a*
allow 756
 marriage allowed
  894*a*
 not allow 757
 uncleanness not
  allowed 649*j*
allowance
 wage 804*a*
ally 707
Almighty 160*a*
 God Almighty 965*c*
 Power 160
almonds 171*k*
 almond tree 366*n*
alms 781*u*
alone
 leaving others alone
  620*s*
 living alone 88*l*
 not acting alone 88*r*
 on one's own 88*n*
alongside
 alongside to help
  703*e*
 near 200
along with 89
aloof 883*d*
Alpha and Omega
 Beginning 68
alphabet 558
 letters of the
  alphabet 558*a*
altar 990*a*
 altar of burnt
  offering 990*b*
 altar of incense 990*d*
 altars in general
  990*a*
 destroying altars
  990*g*

altar (cont.)
 heavenly altar 990*i*
 horns on altars 254*g*
 various altars 990*f*
 who built altars 990*e*
alter
 change 147
alternating 141*b*
alternative
 alternatives to
  money 797*r*
always
 always rejoicing
  146*c*
 God always works
  146*d*
 unceasing 146
am
 exist 1
 Identity 13
 who am I? 639*a*
Amalek 371*x*
amalgam 43
amanuensis 586*j*
amazed 864*i*
 amazed by God 864*i*
 amazed by Jesus
  864*k*
 amazed by miracles
  864*r*
 amazed by people
  864*n*
 amazed by teaching
  864*w*
 crowds amazed 74*s*
 Jesus amazed 864*m*
amazement 864*i*
amazing 864*i*
ambassadors 754*e*
ambidextrous 242*a*
Ambiguity 518
ambush 527*c*
amen! 488*c*
amend
 repair 656*ad*
amicable
 friendly 880
amiss
 incense offered
  amiss 396*e*
Ammon 371*x*
amnesia
 loss of memory 506
among
 accompanying 89
Amorites 371*v*

amorphous 244
amount
 amounts of food 26*a*
 amounts of
  resources 26*c*
 amounts of spices
  26*b*
 Quantity 26
amuse 837*c*
Amusement 837
amusing 837*c*
anaesthetic 375*a*
Anakim 195*g*
analogous 18
Anammelech 967*o*
Anarchy 734
anathema 899
ancestor 169*a*
anchors 47*i*
ancient
 ancient times 125*e*
 Oldness 127
anew 126
Angel 968
 accusing angels
  928*g*
 afraid of angels
  854*m*
 angel of the Lord
  968*g*
 angels and the
  church 968*p*
 angels and Jesus
  968*n*
 angels and the law
  968*k*
 angels at the end
  968*r*
 angels before Jesus'
  birth 968*l*
 angels in heaven
  968*f*
 angels' strength
  162*o*
 evil angels 969*q*
 four angels 96*a*
 named angels 968*x*
 nature of angels
  968*a*
 two angels 90*m*
 worshipping angels
  981*al*
Anger 891
 acceptable anger
  891*s*
 anger of people 891*u*

anger (cont.)
avoid anger 891*z*
God's anger 891*a*
*God turning from
anger* 891*p*
Jesus' anger 891*q*
*speed of God's
anger* 891*n*
*tearing clothes in
anger* 891*t*
angry 891
angry people 891*v*
angry with God 891*r*
angry with Jesus
891*y*
*God angry with his
people* 891*j*
*God angry with
individuals* 891*m*
God will be angry
891*h*
*people angry with
others* 891*w*
will God be angry?
891*g*
anguish 825
anguish of heart
834*a*
Animals 365
animal horns 254*a*
Animal husbandry
369
animal mothers
169*aj*
Animal sounds 409
animals abandoning
621*v*
animals eating 301*aj*
animals in general
365*a*
animals killing
362*bp*
animals released
746*q*
clean animals 648*z*
dead animals 363*o*
death of animals
361*ah*
*domesticated
animals* 365*aw*
female animals 373*l*
killing animals
362*bn*
lifting animals 310*k*
male animals 372*g*
red animals 431*e*

animals (cont.)
seven animals 99*c*
sex with an animal
951*n*
strength of animals
162*m*
tending animals
369*a*
two animals 90*o*
unclean animals
649*m*
wild animals 365*e*
young animal 132*l*
animosity
Enmity 881
annals 589*b*
annihilating 362*aw*
anniversary 141*f*
announce
disclose 526
proclaim 528
annoy 827*k*
annoyance 827*k*
annoying 827*k*
annoying people
827*k*
annual 141
annuity
wage 804*a*
annul 752*d*
marriage annulled
896
annulment 896
anoint 357*c*
anointing kings 357*e*
anointing oil 357*c*
anointing priests
357*d*
anointing prophets
357*i*
anointing things 357*l*
anoint with
medicine 658*e*
cosmetic anointing
357*r*
medicinal anointing
357*u*
*perfumed anointing
oil* 396*a*
anointed 357*d*
anointed Christ 357*u*
anointed people 357*j*
another
different 15
Answer 460
answering God 460*d*

answer (cont.)
answering men 460*g*
could not answer
578*e*
God answering 460*a*
God answers prayer
761*z*
no answer 460*j*
not answer 582*g*
prayer not answered
761*ae*
ant 365*i*
antagonism
Enmity 881
antichrist 705*c*
anticipate 507
shortage anticipated
636*d*
antidote 658*d*
antimony 844*a*
antipathy
Hatred 888
antiquated
Oldness 127
antitype 23*b*
anxiety 825*t*
anxious 825*t*
do not be anxious
825*v*
apathy 860
ape
Imitation 20
aperture 263*x*
Apollyon 168*b*
apostasy 603*f*
apostate 603*f*
apostles 754*a*
false apostles 754*d*
particular apostles
754*c*
apparel 228*b*
apparent
Appearing 445
evident 522*b*
apparition 445*a*
appeal
Request 761
appear
manifest oneself
445*a*
Appearance 445
appearances 445*f*
appearing 445*a*
for appearance sake
875*a*

appearance (cont.)
outward appearance
223*a*
appearing 445*d*
appease 719
appetising 390
appetite 859*h*
apple tree 366*x*
appliance
tool 630
appoint 751*a*
appointment 295*b*
apportion 783
*apportioning
carcasses* 783*i*
Apportionment 783
apprehend
arrest 747*l*
understand 516
apprehension
anxiety 825*t*
understanding 516
apprentice 538
Approach 289
come to 289
draw near 200*e*
approbation 923
appropriate
fitting 915
Approval 923
approval to kill 362*s*
approve 923
things approved
923*w*
apron 228
apt
fitting 915*f*
aqueous 339
Aramaic
language 557*e*
arbiter
judge 957
arbitrate 720
arbitration 720
arbitrator 720*a*
archaic
Oldness 127
archangel 968*x*
archetype 23*b*
archives 589*d*
arch priest 986*h*
archer 287*e*
ardent
zealous 818*a*
ardour
zeal 818*a*

be (cont.)
  Nature 5
  not to be 2
be content! 828*a*
be like 20
be strong! 162*l*
beams 218*k*
  bar 218*k*
bear
  armour bearers 723*q*
  bearing people's
    burdens 273*j*
  bearing sin 273*i*
  bears (animals) 365*y*
  carry 273*a*
  endure 600
  give birth 167*c*
  unbearable 827*k*
Bear (constellation)
  321*e*
bear witness 466
  bearing witness 466*b*
  bearing witness to
    Jesus 466*m*
  Jesus bearing
    witness 466*p*
beards 259*l*
bearer 273
bearing
  direction 281
beast
  animal 365
beat
  hit 279
  win 727
beaten
  defeated 728
beating 279*c*
  beating believers
    279*j*
  beating Jesus 279*i*
  beating with a rod
    964*a*
beatitudes 897*h*
Beautification 843
beautiful 841
Beauty 841
  beauty of God's
    people 841*n*
  God's beauty 841*m*
becoming like God 18*c*
bed 218*v*
  seats and beds 218*v*
bedeck 844
bee 365*k*
beer 949

befitting 915*d*
before
  coming
  coming before 283*f*
  Forerunner 66
  former times 125
  Jesus going before
    283*c*
befriend 880
beg 761*ai*
  begging 761*ai*
  begging Jesus 761*v*
beget 167*c*
begin 68
Beginning 68
  beginning of the
    gospel 68*k*
  God the beginning
    68*a*
begotten 167*c*
  only begotten Son
    88*i*
behaviour
  Conduct 688
beheading 46*f*
Behemoth 365*au*
behind 238*d*
behold 438
being 1
being changed 147*b*
being pursued 619*f*
Bel 967*n*
Belial
  son of Belial 938*d*
Belief 485
  Unbelief 486
believe 485
  believe in Jesus
    485*m*
  believing for
    miracles 485*z*
  believing in Christ
    357*ab*
  believing the
    prophets 485*ad*
  not believe 486
  not believing in
    Jesus 486*g*
  not believing people
    486*n*
  not believing the
    gospel 486*j*
  unbelieving 486
believer
  beating believers
    279*j*
  believers bound 747*t*

believer (cont.)
  believers
    imprisoned 747*d*
  believers in God
    485*g*
  believers in Jesus
    485*o*
  death of believers
    361*al*
  imitating believers
    20*b*
  unbeliever 486
belittle
  underestimate 483
bell 414*a*
belly 224*e*
  on the belly 311*u*
belong
  are possessed 773
belongings
  Property 777
beloved 887
belt 228*x*
  priest's belt 989*h*
benediction 897
beneficial 644
  useful 640
benefit 640
  benefits of youth
    130*g*
  praise God for his
    benefits 923*m*
  thanks for benefits
    907*j*
  use 640
Benevolence 897
benevolent 897
Ben-hinnom 255*j*
Benjamin
  wives for Benjamin
    894*y*
bent
  crooked 246*a*
bequeathing 780*a*
Beracah 255*j*
berate
  reproach 924
bereaved 772*e*
bereavement 772*e*
bereft
  bereft of the
    kingdom 733*s*
beseech 761
beside
  beside oneself 503*e*
besiege 712*a*

Besor 350*t*
best 644
bestiality 951*n*
Bethany
  Bethany beyond
    Jordan 184*be*
  Bethany near
    Jerusalem 184*at*
Bethel 192*g*
Bethlehem 184*ao*
Bethsaida 184*bf*
betraying 272*e*
betrothal 894*ab*
better 644
  a better land 184*l*
  get better 654*b*
  two are better 90*a*
between ourselves 525*l*
bewail 836
beware 457*a*
  beware of
    hindrances 702*a*
  beware of men 371*q*
  beware of your
    speech 579*d*
beyond
  beyond comparison
    462*a*
  beyond weighing
    322*h*
  certain beyond
    doubt 473*b*
  surpassing 306*a*
bias 481
  unbiased 481
Bible 975
bicker 709
bid
  summon 737*i*
bier 364*b*
big
  tall 195*f*
big amount 32
bigamy 894*t*
big toe 53*o*
big-headed 871*a*
bill
  bills of divorce 548*d*
billow
  wave 350*d*
bind 747*o*
  believers bound 747*t*
  binding 747*o*
  binding clothing 47*d*
  tie up 747*o*
birds 365*ak*

birth
  births 167*j*
  born of God 167*r*
  childbirth 167*c*
  *conceptions and
    births* 167*i*
  from birth 130*c*
  physical birth 167*c*
  premature birth
    138*b*
  spiritual birth 167*v*
birth pangs 167*n*
birthdays 141*f*
birthrights 119*c*
  *birthrights
    transferred* 119*d*
  *rights of the
    firstborn* 119*c*
bisect 92
bishop
  elders 986*ae*
bit
  bridle 748*c*
bit by bit 278
bitter 391
  bitter food 391*a*
  bitter water 391*c*
bitterness 391
  bitterness of heart
    391*d*
black 428
  black and white
    437*a*
  black people 428*a*
  black things 428*b*
black magic
  Sorcery 983
Blackness 428
blacksmith 686*g*
blame
  Guilt 936
blameless
  innocent 935
  upright 929*e*
bland
  tasteless 387*a*
blaspheme 980*b*
blasphemy 980*b*
bleach 648*o*
bleat
  lowing and bleating
    409*b*
bleeding 302*e*
blemish 647
  blemished creatures
    647*a*

blemish (cont.)
  blemished people
    647*b*
  unblemished 646*c*
  without blemish
    646*c*
blend 43
bless 897
  bless the Lord 923
blessed
  being blessed 897
  *God's people
    blessed* 897*h*
  happy 824
  *those blessed by
    God* 897*e*
blessing 897*a*
  adding blessing 38*c*
  blessing and curse
    897*i*
  *blessing not through
    the law* 953*m*
  *blessing through
    God's people* 897*j*
  *blessings of
    obedience* 739*l*
  God's blessing 897*b*
  marriage blessings
    894*m*
  people blessing 897*u*
  subtracting blessing
    39*b*
blind 439
  blinded 439*i*
  blind healed 439*p*
  blind ones 439*a*
  *dealings with the
    blind* 439*n*
  to blind 439*i*
  blindfold 439*m*
Blindness 439
  blinkered 439*l*
bliss
  Joy 824
  blissful 824
blood 335*b*
  blood of Christ 335*p*
  blood of sacrifices
    335*m*
  *blood of the
    covenant* 335*o*
  blood on one's head
    180
  blood on the door
    335*l*
  eating blood 335*g*

blood (cont.)
  flesh and blood 319*a*
  flow of blood 302*e*
  killing 362
  Life 360
  lifeblood 335*b*
  sea turned to blood
    343*h*
  turned to blood 335*k*
bloodguilt 936*h*
bloodshed 362
  *prospect of
    bloodshed* 362*h*
bloodthirsty 362*e*
blooming
  wilderness blooming
    172*aa*
blossoming 171*e*
blot
  blemish 647
blot out
  blot out name 561*z*
  blot out sins 909*a*
  blotted out 165*v*
  blotting out 506*g*
  name blotted out
    561*z*
blow
  blow trumpet 412*a*
  hit 279
blue 435
  blue and purple 435*e*
  blue cloth 435*a*
  blue cords 435*d*
  blue things 435*g*
  dirty jokes 839*b*
blue, purple and
  scarlet 435*f*
Blueness 435
blueprint 23*a*
blunder 495
blunt 257*a*
Bluntness 257
blurred
  dim vision 440
boards 207*a*
boast 877
  boast, those who
    877*a*
  boastful existence 1*e*
  boasting excluded
    877*f*
  boasting in God
    877*g*
  do not boast 877*d*
Boasting 877

boats 275*j*
  ships 275*a*
body
  *church as Christ's
    body* 319*f*
  Corpse 363
  covering the body
    226*a*
  dividing up a body
    46*a*
  eating Christ's body
    319*e*
  flesh and blood 319*a*
  frame 319
  gashing bodies 46*g*
  growth in body 36*a*
  halving bodies 92*a*
  Jesus' body 319*d*
  our bodies 319*g*
  right parts of body
    241*e*
  *severing parts of the
    body* 46*b*
  side of body 239*b*
  stealing the body
    788*l*
body life
  Fellowship 9
bodyguard 660*g*
bog
  Marsh 347
boil
  abscess 651*d*
  heat 381*m*
bold 855*b*
boldly 855*b*
boldness 855*a*
  plain speaking 573*a*
bolt
  flee 620
  lock 264*e*
Bond 47
  spiritual bonds 47*k*
bones 363*f*
  bones and flesh 319*a*
  breaking bones 46*h*
Book 589
  book of the covenant
    589*f*
  book of the law 589*g*
  books in general
    589*a*
  books in prophecy
    589*k*
  books of scripture
    589*i*

Choice 605
  choosing 605
choir 413*a*
choke 362*u*
choose 605
  choosing in
    judgement 605*m*
  God choosing 605*a*
  God choosing a
    place 605*j*
  people choosing
    605*n*
chop 46
Chorazin 184*bf*
chosen 605
  chosen disciples
    605*e*
  chosen people 605*h*
  chosen son 605*d*
Christ
  anointed Christ 357*v*
  baptised into Christ
    988*x*
  believing in Christ
    357*ab*
  blood of Christ 335*p*
  Christ forbidding
    757*d*
  Christ foreknown
    510*b*
  Christ humbled
    himself 872*l*
  Christ is Lord 741*c*
  Christ is righteous
    913*c*
  Christ is risen 656*f*
  Christ knowing God
    490*t*
  Christ like God 18*b*
  Christ like people
    18*i*
  Christ made perfect
    646*b*
  Christ our
    righteousness
    913*x*
  Christ pleasing God
    826*d*
  Christ preached
    357*ac*
  Christ rejoicing 824*f*
  Christ silent 582*e*
  Christ suffering 357*z*
  Christ the firstborn
    119*h*
  Christ the rock 344*x*

Christ (cont.)
  Christ the servant
    742*k*
  Christ the sin
    offering 981*ac*
  Christ's earthly
    family 11*k*
  Christ's hands 53*i*
  Christ's life 360*h*
  Christ's life was
    short 114*h*
  Christ's limbs 53*b*
  Christ's love 887*j*
  Christ's nature 357*y*
  Christ's origin 357*x*
  Christ's throne 743*b*
  Christ's true family
    11*l*
  church as Christ's
    body 319*f*
  Crowns for Christ
    743*d*
  death of Christ 361*ai*
  denying Christ 533*b*
  eating Christ's body
    319*e*
  equality with Christ
    28*c*
  eternal Christ 115*e*
  eternal life through
    Christ 360*r*
  false Christs 357*ad*
  father of the Christ
    169*t*
  freedom through
    Christ 746*m*
  genealogy of Christ
    169*a*
  gentleness of Christ
    177*b*
  glory through Christ
    866*r*
  God the Son 965*h*
  God's love in Christ
    887*i*
  grace through
    Christ 897*p*
  greatness of Christ
    34*b*
  hope in Christ 852*c*
  human nature of
    Christ 371*g*
  ignorant of Christ
    491*l*
  ignorant of Christ's
    return 491*q*

Christ (cont.)
  Jesus called Christ
    357*v*
  Jesus is the Christ
    13*e*
  killing Christ 362*bk*
  knowing Christ 490*u*
  law of Christ 953*y*
  name of Christ 561*k*
  nature of Christ 5*b*
  peace through
    Christ 719*c*
  power of Christ 160*e*
  preaching Christ
    528*l*
  predicting Christ
    511*a*
  prisoners for Christ
    750*c*
  redemption in
    Christ 792*q*
  resurrection of
    Christ 656*e*
  sanctification in
    Christ 979*n*
  seeing Christ 438*g*
  servants of Christ
    742*h*
  sharing in Christ
    775*c*
  signs of Christ's
    return 547*j*
  signs of the Christ
    547*f*
  Spirit on Christ 965*l*
  subject to Christ
    745*i*
  suffering of Christ
    825*j*
  suffering of Christ's
    disciples 825*l*
  suffering with Christ
    825*k*
  yes in Christ 488*d*
Christian 708*k*
  christian baptism
    988*w*
  christian traditions
    127*j*
  christians 708*k*
  weapons of the
    Christian 723*e*
chronicle 589*b*
chum
  friend 880

church 985
  angels and the
    church 968*p*
  building the church
    164*ac*
  Church, the 985
  church as Christ's
    body 319*f*
  church foundation
    214*e*
  church scattered 75*h*
  church universal
    985*a*
  destruction of the
    church 165*i*
  disorder in the
    church 61*c*
  growth of the
    church 36*i*
  leaving the church
    298*g*
  letters to churches
    588*f*
  local church 985*c*
  local churches 985*e*
  one church 88*d*
  prophecy in the
    church 579*ag*
  teachers in the
    church 537*f*
  teaching in the
    church 534*p*
  The church 985
  wise men in the
    church 500*f*
churlish 898*a*
circle
  go around 314*a*
  ring 250
Circling 314
circuit
  go round 314
  circular 250*d*
Circularity 250
circumcise 988*m*
  uncircumcised 974*a*
circumcision 988*m*
  circumcision party
    708*l*
  circumcision
    performed 988*n*
  is circumcision
    necessary? 988*o*
  true circumcision
    988*q*

Circumstance 8
circumstances 8*d*
cisterns 339*f*
citizen 191
citizens of heaven
191*b*
Roman citizens 191*a*
citizenship 191
city 184*y*
building cities 164*p*
burning cities 381*e*
capturing cities 786*j*
cities for the tribes
184*ad*
cities in general
184*y*
cities in Israel 184*aa*
cities of refuge
184*ae*
cities of the plain
184*av*
city foundation 214*c*
city of God 184*aj*
fortified cities 713*c*
looking for a city
184*z*
other cities 184*bd*
civil war 718*g*
killing one another
362*ai*
clairvoyant
medium 984*a*
clan 11
clapping 279*u*
clasp
clasps, fastenings
47*a*
grab 786*n*
Class 77
kind 77
Clauda 349*b*
clay 344*c*
clean 648
be clean from sin
648*ad*
clean animals 648*z*
clean clothes 648*l*
not clean 649
unclean 649
cleanliness 648
ritual cleanliness
648*q*
Cleanness 648
Uncleanliness 649

cleanse 648
cleansing lepers
648*y*
cleansing of sin
648*aa*
cleansing people
648*w*
cleansing the
conscience 917*c*
cleansing things
648*s*
cleave
cling 48
divide 46
clever
intelligent 498
climb 308*j*
cling 48
clinging to God 48*a*
clinging to people
48*b*
clinging to things
48*c*
clique 708
cloak
garment 228
close
close to people 200*h*
closed eyes and ears
456*d*
near 200
shut 264*e*
Closure 264
closet
lavatory 302*f*
cloth 631*o*
blue cloth 435*a*
purple cloth 436*a*
swaddling cloths
226*b*
clothe 228 (*see also*
clothing)
clothed 228*a*
clothing the needy
228*w*
God clothing people
228*v*
unclothed 229*a*
clothes 228*b* (*see also*
clothing)
bright clothes 228*t*
clean clothes 648*l*
figurative clothes
228*ab*
giving clothes 228*x*
fine clothes 228*m*

clothes (cont.)
fringe of clothes
234*a*
modest clothes 228*h*
purple clothes 436*c*
red clothes 431*d*
special clothes 228*o*
tearing clothes in
anger 891*t*
tearing clothes in
grief 836*g*
transferred clothes
228*z*
using clothes 228*d*
white clothes 427*a*
clothing 228
binding clothing 47*d*
clothing the needy
228*w*
God clothing people
228*v*
wolf in sheep's
clothing 527*b*
Cloud 355
clouds 355*a*
Jesus in a cloud 355*i*
God in a cloud 355*c*
club
weapon 723*n*
clutch
grasp 786*n*
coal 381*k*
burning 381
coat 228
coax
tempt 612*l*
cobra 365*o*
venonous creature
659*c*
cock
cock crow 409*c*
cogitate
think 449
cohere 48
Cohesion 48
coin 797*b*
coitus 45*a*
Cold 380
cold and heat 380*a*
cold of snow 382*a*
cold things 380*e*
cold weather 380*a*
colleague 707
Colour 425
coloured 425
multi-coloured 437*b*

column
pillars 218*n*
Combatant 722
combination
mixture 43
combined directions
281*t*
combustion 381
come (*see also*
coming)
Arrival 295
come to 289
coming to Jesus
289*c*
coming to people
289*a*
kingdom coming
733*u*
things to come 124*e*
come after 284*i*
come before
coming before 283*f*
come down
come down! 309*g*
coming down from
heaven 309*e*
come from 187*a*
come out 298
coming out of
people 298*e*
come to pass 725*c*
comely
beautiful 841
Comfort 831
Comforter 965*t*
God comforting
831*a*
human comfort 831*e*
no comfort 831*i*
comic
Wit 839
coming
coming to Jesus
289*c*
coming to people
289*a*
Future time 124
Jesus coming again
148*r*
Lord's coming 295*e*
waiting for the
second coming
507*d*
coming after 284*i*

dappled 437*a*
dare 855
  not dare 856*b*
dark 418
darken 418
  sky darkened 321*n*
Darkness 418
  darkness of evil 418*l*
  *darkness over the
    earth* 418*a*
  *from darkness to
    light* 417*m*
  God and darkness
    418*h*
  outer darkness 418*o*
  out of darkness 418*n*
  people in darkness
    418*j*
Darling 890
dart
  missile 287*h*
  rush 680
date palms 366*n*
daughter 170
David
  *bowing before
    David* 311*d*
dawdle 136
dawn 128*a*
  dawn from heaven
    128*k*
day
  bygone days 125*d*
  cool of the day 380*d*
  day and night 128*a*
  day of atonement
    941*a*
  day of judgement
    108*ai*
  days of a hireling
    114*r*
  days old 131
  daytime 128*a*
  Period 110
  periods of days 110*j*
  provision of day
    128*a*
  Time 108
  using the day 128*l*
day of atonement 941*a*
day of judgement 108*ai*
day of rest 683*a*
day of the Lord 108*ae*
  *timing of the day of
    the Lord* 108*ag*
daybreak 128*b*

daysman 720*a*
daytime 128*a*
deacons 742*g*
dead 361
  are the dead raised?
    656*b*
  *baptised for the
    dead* 988*z*
  *condition of the
    dead* 361*i*
  dead animals 363*o*
  dead body 363
  Dead Sea 343*n*
  raise the dead 656*n*
  spiritually dead 361*x*
  dead are raised 656*c*
Deafness 416
  deaf 416*a*
  deaf healed 656*x*
  deaf hearing 416*c*
  unhearing 416*b*
dealing
  *dealing with the
    nations* 371*y*
  *dealings with the
    blind* 439*n*
  eternal dealings
    115*h*
  have no dealings 10*e*
  no dealings 883*a*
dear
  expensive 811*a*
Dearness 811
Death 361 (*see also*
  death penalty)
  age at death 131*j*
  death as punishment
    361*z*
  death avoided 361*au*
  *death due to God's
    presence* 361*aa*
  death due to sin 361*t*
  death is near 361*m*
  death may happen
    361*p*
  death of animals
    361*ah*
  death of believers
    361*al*
  death of Christ 361*ai*
  death of groups
    361*ag*
  death of individuals
    361*ad*
  death of kings 361*af*

death (cont.)
  *death of office
    holders* 361*ac*
  *death of the
    firstborn* 119*e*
  death overcome
    361*aw*
  death postponed
    361*as*
  desire for death 361*s*
  dying 361
  effect of death 361*c*
  fear of death 361*l*
  *God delivers from
    sin and death* 668*j*
  finality of death
    361*h*
  inevitability of death
    361*f*
  killing 362
  losing one's life 772*i*
  *mourning after a
    death* 836*o*
  nature of death 361*a*
  resigned to death
    361*q*
  *responsible for
    others' death* 180*c*
  *responsible for own
    death* 180*b*
  rest in death 683*q*
  second death 361*at*
  sleep of death 679*e*
  striking to death
    279*l*
death penalty 963*k*
  *death penalty for
    heresy* 963*p*
  *death penalty for
    killing* 963*k*
  *death penalty for
    profanity* 963*o*
  *death penalty for
    sexual sin* 963*r*
  *death penalty for
    violence* 963*m*
death sentence 963*k*
debate
  discussions 475*b*
Debt 803
  being in debt 803*a*
  cancelling debts
    803*e*
  people in debt 803*c*
decay 51
  no decay 51*f*

decay (cont.)
  people decaying 51*d*
  things decaying 51*a*
decease 361
deceit 542
  avoid deceit 542*m*
  God and deceit 542*b*
  *Jesus and deceit
    542d*
  *laws about deceit
    542a*
  *prophesying deceit
    542j*
  *Satan and deceit
    542p*
deceitful 542
  *deceitful tongues
    542g*
deceive 542
  *deceiving oneself
    542h*
  men deceive 542*e*
  *those who deceived
    542k*
Deceiver 545
Deception 542
decide 605
  *deciding by lots
    605q*
  indecision 601
  undecided 601
decision 605
  indecision 601
declare
  *declaring that God
    is just* 913*d*
deck
  bedeck 844
  deck of ship 194*u*
  decks 194*u*
decompose 51
Decomposition 51
decorate 844
Decrease 37
decree 737*d*
dedication 876*g*
  celebrate 876*g*
  Feast of Dedication
    988*l*
deduction
  Subtraction 39
deed
  Action 676
  bad deeds 676*n*
  *making God's deeds
    known* 526*k*

deed (cont.)
repaid for deeds
676f
title deed 767g
deep 211a
deep places 211a
not deep 212
sea 343
deer 365x
defeat
be conquered 728a
conquer 727c
defeat of Israel 728d
defeat of Judah 728e
defeat of others 728g
defeated by their
fellows 728f
prospect of defeat
728a
defeated 728a
undefeated 727
defecate
defecation and dung
302f
defect 647
Speech defect 580
without defect 646c
Defective vision 440
Defence 713
defend 713
defending 713a
defer
dawdle 136
Defiance 711
deficiency
deficiencies of
priests 986s
money's
deficiencies 797q
deficit
Debt 803
defile 649a
defraud 788e
defy 711
defying 711a
Deities in general 966
Deity 965
God 965
national deities 967o
other gods 966
various deities 967q
dejected 834a
delapidated 655c
delay 136h
God will not delay
135c

delay (cont.)
God's delay 136a
hinder 702b
Lateness 136
no delay 135c
people who delayed
136e
delayed 136
people who delayed
136e
delegate
authority delegated
to people 733ab
delegate authority
751h
deliberate
intentional 617
delicacy 390
delicious 390
delight
delight to the eyes
841b
Joy 824
pleasure 826a
delight in 826
deliver
deliver us! 668c
God delivers from
enemies 668g
God delivers from
sin and death 668j
save 668
Deliverance 668
deliverance is of
God 668a
deliverer 668e
delude 542
deluge
flood 350a
delusion 542
demise 361
demolish 165
demon 969
demons entering
297n
Jesus casting out
demons 300a
people casting out
demons 300d
demonised 969u
accused of being
demonised 969v
demon-possessed 969u
demonstrate
prove 478
Demonstration 478

demote 752a
den
cave 255f
denarius 797b
denomination
faction 708
deny 533
denying Christ 533b
denying oneself 533f
God denying 533a
depart 296
depart from me!
300q
Departure 296
dependent
independent 88r
interdependent 12b
depend on
trust 485
deplore
disapprove 924
deport 188c
deportation 188c
depose 752a
deposed priests 986t
deposit
lay 187e
Security 767
depositing 187e
deprecate
disapprove 924
depression 834b
depth 211
no depth 212a
sounding depths
211c
depths
dejection 834a
deride
show contempt 922
derision
Contempt 922
Ridicule 851
descend 309
Descendant 170
spiritual
descendants 170w
Descent 309
line of descent 169a
Description 590
inscription 590a
desecrate 649a
desecrating the
temple 990p
desert
abandon 621

desert (cont.)
dry place 342h
what one deserves
915f
wilderness 172u
deserted
uninhabited 190k
deserve 915f
not deserve 916a
design
pattern 23a
designate
choose 605
designation
name 561
Desire 859
desire for death 361s
desire for God 859a
desire for God's
word 859b
desires satisfied in
God 859c
evil desires 859z
right desires 859ab
sexual desire 859n
desist
cease 145
desolate 165
desolation 165
abomination of
desolation 165x
despair
despairing 853a
Hopelessness 853
despise 922
despising God 922a
despising God's
things 922c
despising people
922g
despising things
922k
do not despise 922n
God despising 922e
those who are
despised 922l
destination 295j
destined
predetermined 608
destiny 596b
destroy (*see also*
destruction)
demolish 165
destroying angel
168b

don
wear 228
donate 781
donkeys 365*bd*
wild donkey 365*aa*
wild man 84
doors 264*a*
blood on the door
335*l*
door of opportunity
263*h*
doorposts 263*f*
doorways 263*d*
shutting doors 264*e*
shutting temple
doors 264*f*
do right! 913*i*
dot 196*g*
do the same
Imitation 20
double-cross
deceive 542
double-minded 601*a*
Doubling 91
double portion 91*a*
doubly 91*e*
doubt 486
certain beyond
doubt 473*b*
doubting God 486*d*
doubting the
resurrection 486*l*
God doubting 486*c*
doubtful 486
doubtless
believing 485
certainly 473
dove
doves and pigeons
365*ao*
down
come down! 309*g*
coming down from
heaven 309*e*
going down 309*h*
downcast 834*a*
downhearted 834*a*
downpour 350*z*
do wrong
done nothing wrong
935*f*
dowry 809*g*
doze 679*a*
dozen 99*m*
drachma 797*b*
drag 288

dragon
creature 365*bu*
devil 969*a*
draw
draw water 304*d*
drawing 551*a*
sketch 551*a*
drawback
drawbacks to riches
800*n*
draw near 200*e*
drawing near to
God 200*e*
drawing near to
Jesus 200*g*
drawing water 304*d*
dreams 438*s*
dreams interpreted
438*w*
interpreting dreams
520*a*
like a dream 438*y*
misleading dreams
438*x*
dreamer 438*u*
dregs
lees 41*e*
useless 641
drench 341*a*
dressed 228*a*
undressed 229*a*
Dressing 228
drift 282
drink
allegorical foor and
drink 301*ba*
eat, drink and be
merry 301*i*
eating, drinking and
rejoicing 824*z*
drink offering 981*s*
drinking 301*f*
drinking no wine
948*a*
drinking water 339*g*
strong drink 949
drive
drive away 300*v*
driven from God's
people 300*u*
driven from God's
presence 300*m*
driving vehicle 267*i*
drive out 300*h*
driving Israel out
300*l*

drive out (cont.)
driving out the
people of the land
300*h*
Jesus driven out
300*y*
other driving out
300*z*
droll
funny 839
drop
descend 309
fall 309*a*
dropsy 651*k*
dross 641*g*
drought 342*c*
drowse 679*a*
drugged 375*a*
drunk 949
do not get drunk
949*f*
evil making drunk
949*r*
God making drunk
949*o*
making others drunk
949*k*
not drunk 948*e*
drunkard 949*g*
drunken 949*i*
drunken people 949*i*
Drunkenness 949
accused of
drunkenness 949*l*
dry 342
dry land 342*a*
dry things 342*j*
dry up 342*a*
Dryness 342
dual
Doubling 91
dub
name 561*n*
duck
baptise 988*r*
due
due return 915*f*
due rights 915*e*
fitting 915
honour due 866*u*
not due 916
undue 916
Dueness 915
Undueness 916
dumb 578*a*

dunce
fool 501
dung 641*i*
defecation and dung
302*f*
dung for fuel 385*f*
dungeon 748*a*
dunk
baptise 988*r*
duplicate
transcript 22*a*
Doubling 91
duration
length of time 110
Long duration 113
dust 332*a*
ashes/dust on head
836*l*
creatures from dust
332*c*
as many as the dust
104*d*
Duty 917
marriage duties 894*i*
tax 804*g*
dwarf 196*a*
dwell 192
dwelling 192
God's dwelling 192*a*
dwelling-place 192
dye 425*a*
dyeing 425*a*
dying 361
dynasty 741*q*
dysentery 651*k*

eager 818*b*
eager to speak 581*c*
eagerness 818*a*
eagles 365*aq*
ear
close ears 456*d*
ears 415*g*
stop their ears 416*b*
Earliness 135
early
in the morning 128*e*
promptly 135
rising early 128*b*
earnings
wage 804*a*
ear-ring 844*f*
ears 415*g*
earth 344*a*
darkness over the
earth 418*a*

flesh and blood 319*a*

flesh
human 371
matter 319*a*
meat 301*ah*
one flesh 45*a*

fleshly
carnal 319*l*

flexible
inflexible, obstinate
602

flight
put to flight 619*c*
running away 620
tired in flight 684*d*

flimsy 163*k*

fling
throw 287

flint 256*e*
like a flint 599*c*

float 323*a*

flock
animals 365*bn*
feeding the flock
301*y*
people 371*ac*

flog
beat 279

flood 350*a*

flow
flow of blood 302*e*
flowing with milk
and honey 635*a*

fluid 335

flute 414*b*

flute-player 413*e*

fly
Escape 667
insect 365*i*
soar 271*a*

flying things 271*e*

foam 355*k*

fold
sheepfold 369*d*

foliage 366*c*

Following 284
accompanying 89
following evil 914*x*
following Jesus 284*a*
following others
284*h*
following the devil
969*l*
go after 284
Imitation 20

follow after
pursue 619

follower
followers of Baal
967*d*

folly 499
folly in general 499*a*
wordy folly 581*b*

Food 301
*allegorical food and
drink* 301*ba*
amounts of food 26*a*
bitter food 391*a*
dividing food 783*e*
food defined 301*a*
food left over 41*b*
food offered to idols
982*h*
food to be avoided
301*ao*
God gives food 301*u*
going without food
946*k*
Jesus our food 301*af*
limitations of food
301*k*
need for food 301*c*
no food 301*ay*
not much food 33*a*
particular food
301*ah*
plenty of food 635*a*
preparing food 669*j*
price of food 809*m*
providing food 301*l*
repulsive food 301*ar*
savoury food 390*a*
*shortage other than
food* 636*j*
stores of food 632*a*
thanks for food 907*i*

Fool 501
counted as fools
501*h*
fools against God
501*a*
God against fools
501*b*
nature of fools 501*c*
*those who were
fools* 501*f*
work of fools 501*d*

foolish 499
foolish person 501

foolishness 499
foolishness of God
499*c*
foolishness of men
499*d*

foot (*see also* feet)
feet and legs 53*j*
limb 53
severed foot 363*k*

footing
firm footing 153*i*

footstool 218*ac*
stool 218*ac*
Subjection 745
triumph 727*l*

for
for God 706*b*
for people 706*c*
God fights for you
716*a*
God for us 706*a*
*his resurrection for
us* 656*i*
on the side of 706*a*

For ever 115
priest for ever 986*u*

forbearance 823*c*

forbid 757
Christ forbidding
757*d*
God forbidding 757*a*
people forbidding
757*e*

force 176*a*
by force 176*a*
compel 740
forced labour 682*e*

ford 222*f*

forecast 511

foreheads 237*b*

foreign
foreign temples
990*ae*
*rejecting foreign
gods* 607*l*

Foreigner 59
exiled foreigners
188*g*
foreigners avoided
59*y*
foreigners' hope 59*l*
*foreigners in the
holy places* 59*f*
foreigners restricted
59*i*

foreigner (cont.)
obstinate foreigners
602*a*
*reckoned as
foreigners* 59*u*
specific foreigners
59*s*
*suffering from
foreigners* 59*c*
*wisdom towards
foreigners* 59*ag*

foreknowledge 510

foreknown 510
Christ foreknown
510*b*
elect foreknown
510*a*

foremost 638
foremost of sinners
35*c*

foreordain
predestine 608

Forerunner 66

foreshadowing
shadows of the true
22*c*

Foresight 510

foreskin 167*a*

forests 366*q*

foretell 511

foretold 511

forfeit 772*i*

forget 506
forgetting God 506*e*
forgetting people
506*h*
forgetting things
506*i*
God forgetting 506*b*

Forgetfulness 506

forgive 909
a forgiving God
909*a*
forgive one another
909*r*
God, forgive! 909*e*
God has forgiven
909*f*
God not forgiving
909*h*
God will forgive
909*b*
man forgiving 909*o*
not forgive 909*h*
unforgiving 909*h*

God (cont.)

God clothing people
228v

God comforting
831a

God commissioning
751a

God cursing 899b

God delivers from
enemies 668g

God delivers from
sin and death 668j

God denying 533a

God despising 922e

God destroying 165a

God disciplining
924c

God does good 644b

God does what is
right 913f

God doubting 486c

God enduring 600i

God establishes us
153l

God far away 199l

God feeds his
people 301x

God fighting you
716b

God fights for you
716a

God forbidding 757a

God forgetting 506b

God, forgive! 909e

God forgiving 909a

God for us 706a

God gathering 74b

God going up 308a

God gives food 301u

God gives light 417i

God gives peace
719a

God gives
repentance 939c

God gives
understanding
516e

God gives wealth
800a

God gives wisdom
498k

God giving freely
781e

God giving life 360i

God giving rest
683m

God (cont.)

God giving to the
Son 781c

God giving words
781k

God guiding 689d

God hardening 602h

God has forgiven
909f

God has
understanding
516d

God hating 888b

God healing sorrow
825i

God heals 656r

God heard 455e

God hears prayer
455c

God heeding 455h

God, help! 703a

God helping 703b

God helps orphans
779e

God helps the poor
801g

God helps the weak
163j

God hiding 523a

God hiding people
525f

God humbling
people 872e

God in a cloud 355c

God in heaven 971a

God in secret 530a

God is a fortress
662d

God is a light 420i

God is exalted 866g

God is faithful 929a

God is good 644a

God is great 638a

God is holy 979a

God is jealous 911b

God is King 741a

God is light 417b

God is perfect 646a

God is pure 950a

God is righteous
913a

God is the same
144a

God is to be feared
854b

God is true 494c

God (cont.)

God is unique 21a

God is witness 466k

God is worthy 915a

God, judge! 480c

God judges 480d

God judges his
people 480f

God judges
righteously 480h

God keeping 666a

God keeping silent
582c

God keeps covenant
768c

God killing 362bc

God killing his
people 362bf

God killing
individuals 362be

God killing others
362bi

God knowing his
people 490m

God knows all
things 490e

God knows the heart
490i

God leading the way
283a

God lifting up 310d

God lives in
Jerusalem 192j

God lives with men
192e

God living in the
tabernacle 192h

God loves right 913e

God make you
numerous 104a

God making drunk
949o

God making himself
known 526c

God making
mysteries known
526f

God manifest 522b

God multiplied his
people 104f

God naming 561n

God near 200a

God not forgiving
909h

God not heeding
456a

God (cont.)

God not rejecting
607f

God of his people
965e

God of peace 717a

God opposing 704a

God our Father 169q

God performs
miracles 864a

God pleased with
people 826e

God possessing 773b

God provides rivers
350g

God providing 633a

God providing
water 339k

God punishing 963a

God pursuing 619j

God receiving 782a

God redeeming his
people 792n

God rejecting
individuals 607d

God rejecting Israel
607a

God rejoicing 824d

God releasing
captives 746a

God remembering
505c

God renaming 561v

God reproaching
924a

God resolute 599a

God saves because
of love 668o

God saves his
people 668q

God saves the needy
668l

God saves those
who turn to him
668m

God searching
459ac

God seeing 438c

God seeking 459ad

God sending
prophets 579r

God shows mercy
905c

God speaking 579o

God suing 959a

God suffering 825b

gullibility 487*a*
gully 201
gush
  pouring 350*w*

habit
  traditions 127*c*
habitation 192
hack 46
Hades
  place of the dead
    361*a*
haemorrhage 302*e*
hail
  greet 884
  hailing 577*j*
  hailstones 350*af*
hair 259
  grey hair 429*a*
  hair cut 259*i*
  hair of the head 259*c*
  hairs protected 259*k*
  long hair 259*g*
  white hair 427*c*
haircut 259*i*
hairless
  bald 229*u*
hairy 259*a*
Half 92
  half an hour 110*g*
  half of groups 92*c*
half-hearted 518*a*
hallow 979
halt 145
halving 92
  halving bodies 92*a*
  halving possessions
    92*e*
  halving things 92*b*
hammer 630*e*
hamper
  hinder 702
hand 53*c*
  at hand 200*a*
  Christ's hands 53*i*
  crossing hands 222*j*
  given into their
    hands 727*i*
  hands and fingers
    53*c*
  hands laid on for
    the Holy Spirit
    378*w*
  hands laid on to
    commission 378*v*

hand (cont.)
  hands laid on to
    condemn 378*aa*
  hands laid on to
    heal 378*x*
  handwriting 586*j*
  laying on of hands
    378*t*
  left handed 242*a*
  lifting hands 310*i*
  limb 53
  mighty hand 160*b*
  right hand 241*a*
  severed hand 363*k*
  washing hands 648*b*
  wave hand 317*d*
hand over
  handing over 272*a*
  handing over to the
    devil 969*ab*
handbreadth 205*a*
handing over 272*a*
handle
  Touch 378
hand-made
  hand-made gods
    966*j*
  idols are hand-made
    982*c*
handsome 841
  handsome men 841*k*
handwriting 586*j*
hang 217
  hang on his words
    455*u*
Hanging 217
  people hanging 217*a*
  things hanging 217*f*
happy
  joyful 824
harass 827
harassed 825
hard
  difficult 700
  hard tasks 700*a*
  hard to be saved
    700*c*
  obstinate 602
  severe 735*a*
  working hard 682*a*
hard of hearing 416*a*
hard up
  poor 801*a*
hard work 682*a*
harden
  God hardening 602*h*

harden (cont.)
  harden one's heart
    602
hardened
  Israel hardened
    371*al*
  obstinate 602
hard-hearted
  merciless 906
hardship 827
  transient hardship
    114*p*
hard-working 678*h*
harlot 951*s*
harm 645
  doing harm 645*f*
  stones for harming
    344*k*
  unable to harm 161*h*
harp
  harpist 413*c*
  making harps 414*a*
harpist 413*c*
harrow 370*g*
harsh 735*e*
hart
  deer 365*x*
harvest
  harvesting 370*s*
  feast of harvest 988*h*
  fruitfulness 171
Haste 680
  abandoning in haste
    621*u*
hasten 680
hasty
  rash 857
hate 888
  God hating 888*b*
  hating 888*a*
  hating evil 888*g*
  hating God 888*e*
  hating good 888*i*
  hating life 888*h*
  hating one another
    888*n*
  hating the righteous
    888*j*
  hating without a
    cause 888*m*
  not hating 888*u*
  those who hated
    888*q*
hateful 888
Hatred 888

haul
  Booty 790
  drag 288
have
  possess 773
have no dealings 10*e*
hawker 794
hazard 661
Hazor 371*x*
heads 213*c*
  ashes/dust on head
    836*l*
  Hair of the head
    259*c*
  lifting heads 310*j*
  Master 741
  severed head 363*j*
heal 656*r*
  blind healed 439*p*
  God healing sorrow
    825*i*
  God heals 656*r*
  hands laid on to
    heal 378*x*
  healing in the name
    of Jesus 656*aa*
  Jesus healing 656*x*
  no healing 656*ac*
  people healed 656*u*
  praying for healing
    761*s*
  those Jesus healed
    656*z*
healer 658*a*
Health 650
  health achieved 650*b*
  health promised
    650*a*
healthy 650
  unhealthy 651
heap 209*z*
hear
  deaf hearing 416*c*
  God heard 455*e*
  God hears prayer
    455*c*
  hear our prayer!
    455*a*
  hear prayer! 761*y*
  hearing the word
    455*m*
  listening 415*a*
  pay attention 455
  refusing to hear the
    word 456*d*
hearer 415

hit
 strike 279
Hittites 371*v*
Hivites 371*v*
hoard
 Store 632
hold fast 599
hold
 handle 378*c*
 take hold 786*n*
hold together 48*c*
hole
 cave 255*d*
 dwelling 192*al*
 hiding holes 662*l*
 hollow 255*o*
 openings 263*x*
Holiness 979
 lack of holiness 980*a*
hollow 255*o*
holy 979
 be holy for I am
  holy 979*d*
 carrying holy things
  273*a*
 covering holy things
  226*n*
 foreigners in the
  holy places 59*f*
 God is holy 979*a*
 holy garments 989*a*
 holy of holies 990*ac*
 holy people 979*f*
 holy things 979*t*
 looking at holy
  things 441*a*
 most holy place
  990*ac*
 most holy things
  979*z*
 unholy 980
Holy Spirit 965*k*
 hands laid on for
  the Holy Spirit
  378*w*
 promise of the Holy
  Spirit 764*g*
home 192
 go home! 148*h*
 going home 148*k*
 homeless 192*al*
 let them go home
  148*f*
homer
 bushel 465*c*
homeland 184*a*

homeless 192*al*
homicide 362
homosexuality 951*o*
hone
 sharpen 256*a*
honest 929*c*
honey 392*a*
 flowing with milk
  and honey 635*a*
 Sweetness 392
honour 866*u*
 honour due 866*u*
 honouring 866*ab*
 losing honour 867*e*
 praise 923
 Respect 920
 seeking honour 866*x*
 source of honour
  866*z*
 without honour 867
hooks 748*b*
Hope 852
 concerning hope
  852*a*
 foreigners' hope 59*l*
 future hope 124*i*
 hope in Christ 852*c*
 hope in old age 133*c*
 hope of Israel 852*b*
 without hope 853*b*
hopeful 852
hopeless 853
 hopeless morning
  128*j*
 without hope 853*b*
Hopelessness 853
Horeb
 Mount Sinai 209*k*
horn
 animal horns 254*a*
 blow horn 414*g*
 horns of the altar
  990*c*
 horns on altars 254*g*
 power 160*h*
Prominence 254
Strength 162*b*
hornet 365*k*
horror
 bywords of horror
  496*d*
horsefly 365*i*
horses 365*bf*
hosanna 668*c*
hospitable 813*d*
 inhospitable 813*f*

hospitable (cont.)
 not hospitable 813*f*
hospitality 813*d*
host
 army 722*a*
 host of heaven 321*j*
hostage 750*b*
hostile 704*d*
hostility 704*d*
hot 379
 hot things 379*c*
 hot weather 379*a*
hot-tempered 892*a*
hound
 oppress 735*c*
hour
 one hour 110*h*
 periods of hours
  110*g*
 Time 108
house
 building houses 164*t*
 house of God 192*g*
 houses 192*aa*
 Lord's house 990*n*
 moving house 272*i*
 outside the house
  223*d*
house of God 990*n*
household
 family 11
housetop 213*j*
how
 how God created
  164*e*
 how to greet 884*c*
 how to live long
  113*c*
 how to pray 761*d*
 how to fast 946*a*
 how to worship 981*b*
 how you judge 480*a*
how is? 8*a*
how long? 136*a*
howl
 barking and
  howling 409*a*
hug 889*g*
human
 human comfort 831*e*
 human doctors 658*b*
 human friendship
  880*d*
 human guides 690*a*
 human judges 957*d*
 human law 953*z*

human (cont.)
 human nature of
  Christ 371*g*
 human sacrifices
  981*ag*
 human weakness
  163*b*
 Mankind 371
humble 872*a*
 be humble! 872*c*
 Christ humbled
  himself 872*l*
 God and the humble
  872*d*
 God humbling
  people 872*e*
 humble people 872*m*
 humbling and
  exalting 872*h*
 humbling oneself
  872*i*
humiliated 872*o*
humiliation 872*o*
Humility 872
humour
 sense of humour 839
hundred 99*t*
 100s 99*t*
 100s of years 110*ag*
 100 years lifespan
  131*a*
 144 000 99*v*
hundredfold 99*t*
hung 217
 hung on his words
  455*u*
 people hanging 217*a*
 things hanging 217*f*
hunger 859*g*
 not hunger 635*a*
 physical hunger
  859*g*
 shortage 636
hungry 859*g*
 Fasting 946
 hungry people 859*k*
hunt 619*a*
 hunting 619*a*
 pursue 619
hunter 619*a*
hurl 287
hurry 680
 acting hurriedly
  680*b*
 hurrying others on
  680*a*

hurt
  feel pain 377
  cause pain 827
  harm 645
husband 894
hush 578*h*
hut 192*y*
hyacinth 435*g*
hybrid 43
hygiene 648
hymn 412*d*
hypocrisy 543*b*
hypocrites 545*e*
hyssop 366*g*

I
  I am! 1*a*
  I am God 13*a*
  I am nothing 639*a*
  I am the ... 13*h*
  it is I 1*c*
ice 380*b*
Idea 451
  opinion 451*a*
  Thought 449
identical
  the same 16
Identity 13
  true identity 13*o*
idiot 501
idiotic
  foolish 499
idleness 679*h*
idol 982*c*
  burning idols 381*h*
  destroying idols
    982*q*
  food offered to idols
    982*h*
  idols are handmade
    982*c*
  idols are useless
    982*d*
  impotence of idols
    161*j*
  trusting in idols
    485*ak*
idolater 982*a*
  fate of idolaters 982*s*
Idolatry 982
  Gentiles and
    idolatry 982*o*
  God and idolatry
    982*p*
  idolatry at Sinai 982*j*

idolatry (cont.)
  idolatry in Samaria
    982*k*
  Jews and idolatry
    982*l*
  nature of idolatry
    982*a*
  shun idolatry 982*e*
ignite 381
Ignoramus 493
Ignorance 491
  ignorance in
    general 491*a*
  sinning through
    ignorance 491*w*
ignorant 491
  ignorant of Christ
    491*l*
  ignorant of Christ's
    return 491*q*
  not educated 493
  not knowing 491
ignore
  neglect 458
  not heed 456
ill
  Ill health 651
  people who were ill
    651*g*
Ill health 651
illegal 954
Illegality 954
illegitimate 954*g*
illicit 954
illiterate 579*m*
illness 651*a*
ill-treat
  do harm 645*f*
  oppress 735*d*
illuminate
  light up 417*n*
illustration
  parable 519
ill will 898
image
  idol 982
  likeness 18
imagine
  think 449
imitating 20
  imitating believers
    20*b*
  imitating evil 20*g*
  imitating God 20*a*
  imitating good 20*f*
  imitating others 20*e*

Imitation 20
Immanuel 89*d*
immature 130
immediately 116
immerse
  dip 303*c*
  baptise 988*r*
immigrant
  Foreigner 59
imminent
  short time 114
immorality 951
  about immorality
    951*a*
  avoid immorality
    951*e*
  they committed
    immorality 951*d*
immortal 115
Impact 279
impaling 303*a*
impartial 481
impatient 857*b*
impecunious 801
impede
  hinder 702
impediment 580*b*
  speech impediment
    580*b*
Impenitence 940
impenitent 940
imperfect 647
Imperfection 647
imperishable 115
Impiety 980
import 791*b*
  Trade 791
Importance 638
  Unimportance 639
important 638
  not important 639
  unimportant 639
importunate
  persisting 600*h*
Impossibility 470
impossible 470
  impossible for God
    470*b*
  impossible for men
    470*a*
  nothing impossible
    469*a*
impostor 545*g*
Impotence 161
  impotence of idols
    161*j*

impotence (cont.)
  impotence of Satan
    161*i*
impotent
  powerless 161
imprecation 899
imprison 747*a*
  believers
    imprisoned 747*d*
  imprisoned 747*a*
improve 654
  people improved
    654*a*
  things improved
    654*c*
Improvement 654
Impurity 951
impute 480*t*
in
  in one another 224*d*
  in the heart 224*a*
  in the midst 89*a*
  Inside 224
  in a short time 116*c*
  in order 65*a*
  in sequence 65
  orderliness 60*a*
  put in sequence 73
  in the evening 129*b*
  in the morning 128*e*
  in turn 65*a*
  in vain 641*b*
Inaction 677
Inactivity 679
inadequate
  inadequate burial
    364*o*
Inattention 456
inattentive 456
incapable 161
incense 396*b*
  altar of incense 990*d*
  incense and prayer
    396*d*
  incense offered
    amiss 396*e*
incest 951*q*
incite 612*l*
included in 224*h*
income
  wages 804*a*
incomparable 21
incomplete 726
  incomplete works
    726*a*
incomprehensible 517

inconsistent 709*m*
  disagree 709*m*
Increase 36
  Addition 38
  increase in number
    104
incredible 486*m*
incurable 651*k*
incurring guilt 936*c*
in danger 661*b*
indebted 803*b*
indecision 601
indecisive 601
indemnify
  make restitution 787
independent
  not acting alone 88*r*
Indication 547
indict
  accuse 928
Indifference 860
indifferent 860
indiscriminate 464
Indiscrimination 464
indulge
  pamper 736*a*
indulgence 944
  self-indulgence 943*a*
industriousness 678*h*
inebriated 949*f*
ineffective
  sorcery ineffective
    983*i*
inept 695
Inequality 29
inevitable 473*b*
inevitability of death
    361*f*
Inexcitability 823
inexhaustible
  Sufficiency 635
inexpensive 812*a*
inexperienced 695*a*
inexpert 695
infant 132
infection 651
Inferiority 35
infidel 486
inflexible
  obstinate 602
influence 612
inform 524
  not inform 525*i*
Information 524
  giving vital
    information 524*d*

Infrequency 140
infuriated
  angry 891
Ingathering 988*i*
Ingratitude 908
Inhabitant 191
inherit 771*a*
  inheriting 771*a*
  inheriting from God
    777*m*
  inheriting property
    777*l*
  inheriting the land
    771*c*
  the land inherited
    184*e*
inheritance
  dividing inheritance
    783*d*
  land an inheritance,
    the 777*h*
  no earthly
    inheritance 774*a*
  no heavenly
    inheritance 774*d*
  possession 777
  priestly inheritance
    777*j*
  the land an
    inheritance 777*h*
inheritor 776
inhospitable 813*f*
iniquity 914
initial
  First 119
initially
  Beginning 68
initiate
  begin action 68*h*
injure 655*f*
injury 655*f*
injustice 914
ink
  pen and ink 586*k*
inner 224
  inner compulsion
    740*b*
Innocence 935
  innocence of Jesus
    935*g*
  innocence of Paul
    935*h*
  need for innocence
    935*a*
  plea of innocence
    935*c*

innocent 935
  acquitted 960
  condemning the
    innocent 961*e*
  guiltless 935
  innocent? 935*i*
in proportion 12*a*
inquire 459
insane 503
  reckoned insane
    503*c*
  striking insane 503*b*
Insanity 503
  studying insanity
    503*a*
insatiable 859*v*
inscription 590*a*
inscrutable 517*a*
insects etc. 365*h*
  insects jumping 312*c*
insensibility
  Physical
    insensibility 375
Insertion 303
Inside 224
insight
  Knowledge 490
insignia 743
insincerity
  deceit 542
Insipidness 387
insist
  compel 740
insomnia 678*a*
inspecting 438*q*
instability 152
instant
  Instantly 116
  Time 108
instantaneous 116
Instantly 116
instead of 150
instinct 476*a*
institute
  sabbath instituted
    683*a*
instruct 534
instructing 534
instruction
  instruction about
    mourning 836*c*
  instructions
    regarding women
    373*g*
instructor
  Teacher 537

instrument
  making musical
    instruments 414*a*
  Musical
    instruments 414
  musical instruments
    in worship 414*b*
  Tool 630
instrumentalists 413*b*
Insufficiency 636
insufficient 636
insult 921
  insulted for God
    921*b*
  insulting God 921*a*
  insulting people
    921*c*
insurrection 738*c*
integrity 929*c*
Intellect 447
  Absence of intellect
    448
Intelligence 498
  Unintelligence 499
intelligent 498
  unintelligent 499
Intelligibility 516
  Unintelligibility 517
intelligible 516
  unintelligible 517
Intemperance 943
  Drunkenness 949
  self-indulgence 943*a*
intend 617
Intention 617
  unintentional 618*a*
inter
  bury 364
intercede 761*j*
  none to plead 190*j*
intercession 761*j*
intercourse
  homosexual
    intercourse 951*o*
  sex with a near
    relative 951*q*
  sex with an animal
    951*n*
  sexual intercourse
    45*a*
interdependent 12*b*
interest
  charging interest
    803*h*
  usury 803*h*
interfering 231*a*

lust
greed 859*q*
sexual desire 859*n*
luxury 637*b*
Lycaonian
language 557*e*
lye 648*o*
lying 541
deceiving 542
lyre
making lyres 414*a*

mad
insane 503
made 164
hand-made gods
966*j*
made like God 18*a*
made white 427*f*
madman 503
madness 503
maggot
corruption 51*e*
creature 365*l*
magi
wise men 500
magic
Sorcery 983
magicians 500*e*
Wise man 500
Magistrate 957
magnify
exalt 923
magos
Wise man 500
maid
maidservant 742*a*
virgin 895*a*
maim 655*f*
main
important 638
majesty 866
make 164
making disciples
538*d*
making God a liar
541*c*
making kings 741*k*
making musical
instruments 414*a*
making unclean
649*a*
people making
peace 719*g*

make drunk
evil making drunk
949*r*
God making drunk
949*o*
making others drunk
949*k*
make fun 837*c*
making fun 837*c*
make known 526
God making himself
known 526*c*
God making
mysteries known
526*f*
making God known
526*i*
making God's deeds
known 526*k*
making Jesus known
526*l*
make money 800*g*
make perfect
being made perfect
646*d*
Christ made perfect
646*b*
make ready 669
make sport 837*c*
make sure
investigate 459*p*
make the best of
be content! 828*a*
make-up
cosmetics 843*a*
make vows
making vows 532*s*
people who made
vows 532*w*
maker 164
Making 164
malady 651
Male 372
killing all males 372*f*
male and female
372*a*
male animals 372*g*
males 372*c*
male prostitutes 951*w*
malediction 899
Malevolence 898
malice 898*a*
malign
defame 926
Malta 349*b*

mammon
Wealth 800
man (*see also* men)
breaking man's law
954*e*
creation of man
164*h*
greatness of man
638*c*
love of man and
woman 887*aa*
male 372
man a mere breath
352*d*
man avenging 910*e*
man commissioning
751*a*
man forgiving 909*o*
man from dust 332*c*
man naming 561*p*
man naming places
561*s*
man of sin 914*ag*
man possessing 773*g*
man providing a
meal 301*r*
man providing
water 339*q*
man renaming 561*y*
man suing man 959*c*
man tested 461*e*
man trapping 542*t*
man vindicates 927*g*
Mankind 371
man's counsel 691*k*
man's knowledge
490*v*
man's needs 627*c*
man's plans 623*c*
man's purposes 617*b*
man's spirit 320*a*
man's teaching 371*o*
man's thoughts 449*c*
man's value 371*e*
man's ways 624*d*
mature person 134
nature of man 371*a*
receiving from man
782*e*
seen by man 371*n*
'*Son of man*' 371*h*
Management 689
mandrakes 366*i*
maneh 465*b*
manger 301*an*
maniac 503

manifest 522
evident 522*b*
God manifest 522*b*
manifest to God
522*a*
things manifest 522*c*
Manifestation 522
Mankind 371
manna 301*ae*
manner
manner of life 688*a*
mansion 192*ad*
manslaughter 362*d*
manslayer
manslayers fleeing
620*m*
mantle 228*e*
many 104
many enemies 104*o*
many gods 966*a*
many ministering
104*v*
many ruling 104*u*
many sins 104*y*
many thoughts 104*x*
many words 581
not many 105
too many words
581*a*
many-coloured 437*b*
Maranatha 295*i*
maraud 788*c*
marching 267*d*
order of march 65*c*
Marduk 967*n*
mare 365*bf*
marine
ships 275*a*
Mariner 270
marital 894
mark
boundary marks 547*t*
marks on people
547*q*
sign 547*q*
wound 655*f*
Market 796
market place 796*a*
temple a market
796*b*
maroon
abandon 621
marred
imperfect 647

merciful 905
  be merciful! 905a
merciless 906
  God without mercy
    906a
  people without
    mercy 906c
Mercury
  Hermes 967s
mercy 905
  God shows mercy
    905c
  God without mercy
    906a
  need for mercy 905h
  people showing
    mercy 905i
  people without
    mercy 906c
  receiving mercy 905f
  without mercy 906
mercy seat 226l
merit
  deserve 915f
merry
  eat, drink and be
    merry 301i
Meshech and Tubal
  371x
message 529
  conveying the
    message 516g
  sealing the message
    264p
  understanding the
    message 517c
messenger 529o
  messengers 529o
  messengers of the
    Lord 529r
Messiah
  Christ 357v
metal
  Materials 631
  metals and ivory
    631g
  Mineral 359
Metaphor 519
  metaphorical
    carrying 273l
  metaphorical tools
    630d
  metaphorical trees
    366u
  parable 519
mice 365n

middle
  middle watch 108q
middling
  average 30
midget 196a
Midianites 371y
midnight 129k
midst
  in the midst 89
midwife 658b
might
  Strength 162
  Vigour 571
mighty
  mighty men 722c
  powerful 160
  strong 162
mikhtam 412k
Milcom 967m
  Molech / Milcom
    967m
milk 335a
  food 301
  flowing with milk
    and honey 635a
millenium 110ah
million 99v
millstone
  burdens 322k
  stones 344e
mimic 20
mind
  Change of mind
    603
  God changing his
    mind 603a
  Intellect 447
  out of one's mind
    503d
  people changing
    their minds 603c
  right mind 502a
  set your mind 449f
mine
  belonging to me
    773b
  excavation 255i
  mine for ore 255i
Mineral 359
  minerals 359a
minister
  many ministering
    104v
  Servant 742
mint 366g

minus
  subtract 39
minute
  small 196e
  minutiae 196g
miracle 864a
  amazed by miracles
    864r
  believing for ·
    miracles 485z
  false miracles 864h
  God performs
    miracles 864a
  Jesus' miracles 864c
  performing miracles
    864e
mire 347a
mirrors 442a
miscarriage 172k
miserly 816
mislead 495
  do not mislead 495a
  misleading dreams
    438x
  no misleading 495f
misled 495
  do not be misled
    495b
  people misled 495c
miss
  missing eternal life
    360y
  notice absence 190f
Misjudgement 481
missile 287
missing
  absent 190
  people missing 190f
mist 355j
mistake 495
Misteaching 535
mistress
  concubine 952
misuse
  misusing God's
    name 980g
mite
  coin 797j
mix 43
  mixing people 43c
  mixing unlike things
    43a
  unequal 29
  Unmixed 44
Mixture 43
Moab 371x

moan
  grumbling 829a
  mourn 836
mob 74
mock 851
  mocked by youths
    132f
  mocking and God
    851h
  mocking Jesus 851f
  mocking people 851a
Model 23
  example 83e
moderate 177
moderation 177
modest 872
  modest clothes 228h
moist
  moist things 341i
Moisture 341
Molech 967m
  Molech / Milcom
    967m
molest 645f
mollify 719
Moloch 967m
molten
  moulded 554b
moment
  Instantly 116
  short time 114
  Time 108
Money 797
  about money 797a
  accumulating
    money 797o
  alternatives to
    money 797r
  friendship and
    money 880g
  love of money 797m
  loving money 887ah
  money for the
    temple 797i
  money's
    deficiencies 797q
  transfer of money
    797c
moneybag 799b
money box 799a
money-changer 794a
moneyless 801a
month
  a month and more
    110r
  42 months 110w

not proud
  do not be proud
    871*d*
not rash
  do not be rash 857*a*
not reject
  God not rejecting
    607*f*
not remember 506
not repent 940
not resemble 19
not resisting 715*c*
not respect 921*d*
not ruled 734*b*
not satisfied 829*f*
not seeing 439*f*
not seeking God 459*ab*
not selfish
  do not be selfish
    932*c*
  unselfish 931*a*
not similar 19
not slander
  do not slander 926*i*
not sleep
  do not sleep 679*f*
  sleeplessness 678*a*
not smell
  unable to smell 395*a*
no stealing 788*h*
not stingy
  do not be stingy
    816*b*
not sparing 919*c*
Not speaking 582
  not speaking of evil
    582*m*
not speech alone 579*f*
not swearing 532*f*
not telling 525*i*
not the time 138*a*
not threatening 900*b*
not too much wine
  948*d*
not touching 378*q*
not turning aside 249*c*
not weary
  do not grow weary
    684*g*
not welcome
  not welcoming
    people 299*f*
not works
  grace not works
    676*h*

not worship
  do not worship
    other gods 966*d*
notable 866*s*
noteworthy 866*s*
nothing
  I am nothing 639*a*
  unimportant 639
  useless 641
  nothing good 644*k*
nothing like
  Uniqueness 21
nothing new 126*i*
nothing to do with
  avoid 620*s*
  no relationship 10
now 121*c*
nullify 752*e*
Number 85
  total 85*a*
  Counting 86
  numbers of
    concubines 952*c*
numeration
  Counting 86
Numerous 104
  God make you
    numerous 104*a*
  numerous after exile
    104*i*
  numerous armies
    104*q*
nurse
  breast-feeding 301*o*
nurture 534*n*
nut
  food 301

oaks 366*s*
oath
  God swearing oaths
    532*o*
  swearing oaths 532*a*
Obedience 739
  blessings of
    obedience 739*l*
  right by obedience
    913*s*
obedient 739
obeisance 311*a*
obese 195*d*
obey 739
  obey! 739*a*
  obeying people 739*m*
  those who obeyed
    739*d*

obey (cont.)
  we obey 739*b*
obliged
  grateful 907
oblivion
  Forgetfulness 506
obscure
  puzzling 517
Observance 768
observe
  adhere to 768
  keep commands
    739*b*
  not keep covenant
    769*a*
  not keep the law
    954*c*
  sabbath observed
    683*d*
  watch 441
observer 441
obsolete 127*a*
Obstinacy 602
  avoid obstinacy 602*e*
  consequences of
    obstinacy 602*g*
obstinate 602
  obstinate foreigners
    602*a*
  obstinate Israel 602*b*
obtain
  gain 771*h*
  obtaining eternal
    life 360*k*
obtuse
  unintelligent 499
occasion
  right time 137
  right time for God
    137*a*
  right time for people
    137*c*
occult 984
Occultism 984
occupations 686*b*
Ocean 343
o'clock 108*q*
odious
  hateful 888
Odour 394
  Fragrance 396
  Stench 397
Odourlessness 395
of age 134*b*
offence
  give offence 702

offend 827*l*
  hinder 702
Offer 759
  food offered to idols
    982*h*
  give 781
offering
  altar of burnt
    offering 990*b*
  burnt offering 981*l*
  cereal offerings and
    libations 981*r*
  Christ the sin
    offering 981*ac*
  eating offerings
    301*aa*
  gift 781
  guilt offering 981*ad*
  offerings left over
    41*a*
  peace offerings 981*v*
  regular burnt
    offerings 141*e*
  sacrifice 981*h*
  sacrificial offerings
    981*h*
  sin offering 981*x*
  thank offering 981*v*
  wave offering 317*a*
office
  death of office
    holders 361*ac*
officer
  officers 722*d*
offscouring 641*j*
offspring 170
oil 357*a*
  anointing oil 357*c*
  medicines 658*c*
  oil on sacrifices
    357*o*
  perfumed amoining
    oil 396*a*
Oiliness 357
ointment
  medicines 658*c*
old 127
  Age 131
  character of old
    people 133*a*
  old is good 127*a*
  old nature 127*k*
  Old person 133
  old sayings 496*c*
  returning to the old
    148*m*

reconcile 719*c*
reconciliation 719*c*
Record 548
  historical records
    589*b*
  written records 548*f*
recorded 548*f*
Recorder 549
recover
  improve 654*b*
  retrieve 656*ae*
recuperate 656*v*
red 431
  red animals 431*e*
  red clothes 431*d*
  red cord 431*b*
  red material 431*c*
  red people 431*a*
  Red Sea 343*i*
  red things 431*f*
redeem
  about redeeming
    792*h*
  actual redeeming
    792*l*
  buy back 792*h*
  God redeeming his
    people 792*n*
redemption
  buying back 792*h*
  redemption in
    Christ 792*q*
  redemption once for
    all 88*g*
  timing of
    redemption 108*z*
Redness 431
reduce 198*a*
  reduce in quantity 37
  reduce in size 198
  subtract 39
reducing 37*a*
reduction
  reduction in
    quantity 37
  Subtraction 39
reed
  reed sea 343*i*
reeling
  staggering 152*a*
referee
  mediator 720
refine 654*a*
reform 654*d*
refresh 685
  refreshed 685*a*

refreshing 685*b*
Refreshment 685
Refrigeration 382
Refuge 662
  cities of refuge
    184*ae*
  other refuge 662*e*
  refuge in God 662*a*
  refuge under God's
    wings 662*c*
  sanctuary of refuge
    662*g*
refugee 188*f*
Refusal 760
refuse
  refusing God 760*d*
  refusing people 760*a*
  refusing to hear the
    word 456*d*
  refusing to heed the
    word 456*e*
  rubbish 641*i*
  say no 760
refuting 479*a*
regain
  regaining sanity
    502*a*
regard
  attentive 455
  no regard 456*b*
Region 184
  Jesus in various
    regions 184*x*
  regions 184*p*
register
  books registering
    people 589*e*
Regression 286
Regret 830
  mourning in regret
    836*z*
  regretting 830*a*
Regularity 141
  fasting regularly
    946*d*
  periodic 141
  regular burnt
    offerings 141*e*
  regular feasts and
    fasts 141*c*
  regular periods 141*a*
regulations
  regulating sacrifices
    981*j*

regulations (cont.)
  regulations on
    striking people
    279*a*
reign 733
  eternal reign 115*g*
reinstate
  reinstating people
    656*af*
reject 607
  God not rejecting
    607*f*
  God rejecting
    individuals 607*d*
  God rejecting Israel
    607*a*
  rejecting foreign
    gods 607*l*
  rejecting God 607*g*
  rejecting Jesus 607*k*
  rejecting the law
    953*x*
Rejection 607 (*see*
  also reject)
rejoice 824
  always rejoicing
    146*c*
  Christ rejoicing 824*f*
  eating, drinking and
    rejoicing 824*z*
  God rejoicing 824*d*
  lack of rejoicing
    824*ab*
  rejoicing 824*a*
  rejoicing in God's
    word 824*n*
  rejoicing in God's
    works 824*o*
  rejoicing in
    Jerusalem 824*r*
  rejoicing in right
    living 824*k*
  rejoicing in
    salvation 824*t*
  rejoicing in the Lord
    824*g*
  rejoicing in trial
    824*aa*
  rejoicing over
    justice 824*m*
relate
  have fellowship 9
  not relate 10
  unrelated 10
relatedness
  Fellowship 9

relatedness (cont.)
  Unrelatedness 10
  related nations 11*g*
  related people 11*a*
  relations 11
  Relations of
    kindred 11
  relationship 9
  no relationship 10
  relatives
    kin 11
    marrying relatives
      11*d*
  relays 141*b*
  release
    animals released
      746*q*
    God releasing
      captives 746*a*
  Liberation 746
    men releasing
      captives 746*e*
    things released 746*t*
  reliable 473*b*
  relief
  Comfort 831
  relieve
    give relief 831
    relieve oneself 302*f*
  Religion 973
    Irreligion 974
  religious 973*a*
    irreligious 974
  Relinquishment 621
  rely on 485
  remain
    left over 41
    staying put 266*d*
  Remainder 41
  remarry 894*f*
  Remedy 658
  remember 505
    God remembering
      505*c*
    not remember 506
    people remembering
      505*q*
    remember! 505*o*
    remember, O God!
      505*a*
    remembering God
      505*f*
  remembrance 505
    no remembrance
      506*a*
  remind 505*n*

Superiority 34
  not superior 35
superlative 34*g*
supper
  Lord's supper 301*ag*
supplanting 300*ad*
supplication 761*c*
supplies
  provides 633
supply
  Provision 633
Support 218
  lift up 218*ah*
  giving support 218*ah*
  help 703
  supports 218*g*
suppress
  conceal 525
sure 473
  sure knowledge 473*a*
surefooted 153
surety
  pledge 767*a*
surpass 306*a*
surplus 637*b*
surprise 864*i*
surround 230*a*
Surroundings 230
survivors 41*h*
Susa 184*bd*
suspect
  unsuspecting 670*a*
suspend
  hang 217
swaddling cloths 226*b*
swag
  Booty 790
swallow
  destroy 165*u*
  not discriminate
    464*b*
swallowing up 165*u*
swamp
  flood 350*a*
  Marsh 347
  swamped 350*d*
swap 150
swarm
  crowd 74
  teem 104
swarthy 428*a*
sway
  influence 612
swayed
  changeable 152*b*

swear
  God swearing oaths
    532*o*
  not swearing 532*f*
  people who swore
    532*g*
  swearing oaths 532*a*
sweat 302*p*
sweet 392*f*
Sweetness 392
swell
  grow 36
  swell up 36*d*
swift
  fast 277*a*
  life is swiftly gone
    114*d*
Swiftness 277
swimming 269*d*
swindler
  Thief 789
swine 365*bj*
sword 723*a*
  sharp sword 256*e*
sworn 532*a*
synagogue 192*m*
  persecution from
    synagogues 192*r*

tabernacle 990*k*
  Feast of Booths
    (Tabernacles) 988*i*
  God living in the
    tabernacle 192*h*
  the tabernacle 990*k*
table 218*ae*
tablet
  stone tablet 548*c*
  tablets 548*c*
taciturn 582
tackle
  rigging 275*b*
  ships' tackle 275*b*
tails 238*c*
take
  capture 786*a*
  subtract 39
  take away 786*a*
  take away sins 941*m*
  take by the hand
    378*k*
  take hold of 378
  taken captive 747*g*
  Taking 786
  taking away sin
    786*m*

take (cont.)
  taking away the
    things of God 786*k*
  taking people 786*a*
  taking possession
    771*e*
  taking property 786*e*
  taking temple
    treasures 786*i*
take care
  taking care 457*k*
take off
  doff 229*o*
take rest
  taking rest 683*r*
take to heart
  taking the law to
    heart 953*g*
tale
  myths 543*c*
talk
  converse 584
  speak 579
Talkativeness 581
tall
  high 209
  not short 195*f*
  tall people 195*f*
tamarisk tree 366*n*
tambourine 414*b*
tame 745*p*
  taming 745*o*
tanner 686*h*
tar
  bricks and tar 631*m*
tare
  parable of the tares
    370*ab*
Tartak 967*o*
task
  hard tasks 700*a*
tassels 234*a*
Taste 386
  tasteless 387*a*
  tasting 386*b*
  unable to taste 387*b*
tasteless 387*a*
tasty 390
taught (*see* teach)
tax
  money levied 804*e*
  paying tax 804*g*
tax collector
  taxman 804*h*
  wicked person 938*k*
taxman 804*h*

teach 534
  God teaching 534*b*
  Jesus teaching 534*i*
  misteach 535
  people teaching 534*v*
  people who taught
    534*l*
  scripture teaching
    534*g*
  sitting to teach
    311*ae*
  Spirit teaching 534*f*
  taught by the Spirit
    965*ab*
  teaching God 534*a*
  teaching in the
    church 534*p*
  teach the way of
    God 534*j*
  untaught 493
Teacher 537
  about teachers 537*a*
  Jesus the teacher
    537*e*
  specific teachers
    537*d*
  teachers in the
    church 537*f*
Teaching 534
  amazed by teaching
    864*w*
  instructing 534
  man's teaching 371*o*
  what is taught 452
  wrong teaching 535
tear
  tearing 46*s*
  tearing clothes in
    anger 891*t*
  tearing clothes in
    grief 836*g*
tears
  weeping 836*m*
Tebeth 108*n*
teem 104
teeth 256*n*
tell
  Command 737
  inform 524
  not telling 525*i*
tell off
  rebuke 924
temper
  hot temper 892
  lose temper 892
  Quick temper 892

two (cont.)
two people 90*j*
two things 90*q*
two times 91
two witnesses 90*d*
two years 110*u*
two years old 131*e*
type 23*b*
copy 22*c*
kind 77
Nature 5
prototype 23
tyranny 735*e*
Tyre
people of Tyre 371*x*
Tyre and Sidon
184*bc*

Ulai canal 351*b*
unable 161
unable to expel 161*e*
unable to harm 161*h*
unable to serve God
161*g*
unable to smell 395*a*
unable to taste 387*b*
unadulterated 44
unalloyed 44
unaware
unaware of
nakedness 229*j*
unbearable 827*k*
Unbelief 486
unbelief in general
486*a*
unbelieving 486
unbiased 481
unblemished 646*c*
unborn 2*b*
unburied 364*o*
Unceasing 146
uncertain 474
uncertain things
474*b*
Uncertainty 474
unchanging 144
fixed 153
unchanging things
153*a*
uncircumcised 974*a*
uncle 11
unclean 649
making unclean
649*a*
restrictions on the
unclean 649*k*

unclean (cont.)
touching the
unclean 649*e*
unclean animals
649*m*
unclean people 649*h*
unclean things 649*o*
unclean through sex
45*j*
Uncleanness 649
uncleanness not
allowed 649*j*
unclean spirit 969*o*
unclothed 229*a*
unconcerned 860*a*
uncontrolled 943
uncovered 229*a*
manifest 522
Uncovering 229
unction
anointing 357*c*
uncut 670*b*
undecided 601
undefeated 727
under
refuge under God's
wings 662*c*
under God's wings
271*d*
under one's breath
578*i*
under the law 953*n*
under the sun 210*b*
underneath 210*a*
underclothes 989*i*
underestimating 483*a*
Underestimation 483
undergarments 989*i*
underneath 210*a*
understand 516
understanding 516
God gives
understanding
516*e*
God has
understanding
516*d*
need for
understanding
516*a*
passes
understanding
517*a*
understanding
God's word 516*f*

understanding (cont.)
understanding
mysteries 517*a*
understanding the
message 517*c*
undeviating 249*c*
undressed 229*a*
undue 916
unduly quiet 582*k*
Undueness 916
uneducated 493*a*
unequal 29
unequal mates 29*a*
unequal weights 29*b*
unequally yoked 29*a*
unequipped 670*d*
unexpected 508*a*
unfailing 153*b*
unfaithful 930*a*
adulterous 951*f*
Unfaithfulness 930
unfathomable 517*a*
unfeeling
not feel 375*c*
unfitting 916*c*
unfitting action 916*c*
unforgiving 909*h*
unfruitful 172
burning the
unfruitful 381*aa*
unfulfilled 726
unfulfilled word
726*c*
ungodly
cursing the ungodly
899*m*
end of the ungodly
69*h*
multitudes of the
ungodly 104*n*
suffering of the
ungodly 825*h*
ungodly cursing 899*l*
ungodly world 974*e*
ungrateful 908*a*
unguarded 661*d*
unhealthy 651
unhearing 416*b*
unholy 980
uniform grace 16*b*
Uniformity 16
unify
gather into one 88*e*
Unimportance 639

unimportant 639
unimportant people
639*c*
unimportant things
639*e*
uninhabited 190*k*
Unintelligence 499
unintelligent 499
Unintelligibility 517
unintelligible 517
unintentional 618*a*
union 45
physical union 45*a*
sexual union 45*c*
spiritual union 45*k*
unique 21
God is unique 21*a*
unique creatures 21*i*
unique events 21*j*
unique feasts 21*l*
unique nations 21*e*
unique people 21*f*
unique things 21*m*
unique trouble 21*k*
Uniqueness 21
unite 45
gathering together
74*h*
gather into one 88*e*
united 45
unity
Joining 45
one 88
oneness 88
universal
the church universal
985*a*
Universe 321
creation of the
universe 321*a*
curbing the universe
321*q*
God and the
universe 321*e*
measuring out the
universe 465*i*
new universe 321*t*
universe passing
away 321*s*
worshipping the
universe 321*j*
unjust 914
is God unjust? 914*c*
unkindness
unkindness to
strangers 59*ae*

unknowable 517*a*
unknown 491*t*
unlawful 954
unleavened 323*i*
Unleavened Bread
988*c*
unlettered 493
unlike 19
mixing unlike 43*a*
unlock 263*v*
unloose 746
unmarried 895*h*
unmatching 19
Unmixed 44
unmoved
unshaken 153*r*
unpeopled 190*k*
unpremeditated 618*b*
unprepared 670*a*
Unpreparedness 670
Unproductiveness 172
unquenchable
unquenchable fire
381*ad*
unready 670
unreasoning 448*a*
Unrelatedness 10
unrepentant 940*a*
unrighteous 914
unrighteousness 914
unsatisfactory
unsatisfactory rulers
733*ak*
Unsavouriness 391
unsearchable 517*a*
unseeing 439*f*
unseen 444*c*
invisible 444
unselfish 931*a*
Unselfishness 931
unshakable 153*s*
unshaken 153*s*
unshifting 144
Unskilfulness 695
unskilled 695
Unsociability 883
unsociable 883
unsound
unsound doctrine
452*c*
unspotted 646*c*
unstable
fickleness 152*b*
staggering 152*a*
unsteady
fickleness 152*b*

unsteady (cont.)
staggering 152*a*
unsuspecting 670*a*
untaught 493
Untimeliness 138
untried 126*a*
untrustworthy 930
Untruth 543
Untruthfulness 541
untutored 493
unused 126*a*
unwilling 598
God unwilling 598*a*
people unwilling
598*c*
Unwillingness 598
unworthy 916*a*
people unworthy
916*a*
up
getting up 308*i*
God going up 308*a*
going up to God
308*c*
going up to heaven
308*e*
upright
faithful 929
uproar
Disorder 61
uproot
exile 188*b*
upward 308
urge 612*a*
Urim and Thummim
605*s*
urinating 302*j*
us
God with us 89*d*
use
Jesus using
parables 519*b*
right use of wealth
800*p*
unused 126*a*
use of the scriptures
975*g*
use of wine 949*c*
using clothes 228*d*
using parables 519*a*
using weakness 163*h*
utility 640
useful 640
useful people 640*a*
useful things 640*c*
Usefulness 640

useless 641
idols are useless
982*d*
useless endeavour
641*a*
useless people 641*j*
useless things 641*e*
weapons are useless
723*r*
Uselessness 641
using the day 128*l*
using the night 129*f*
usury 803*h*
utensil 194*g*
temple utensils 194*g*
Tool 630
utility 640
inutility 641

vacated 190*k*
vacillate 601
vagrant 268*a*
vain
in vain 641*b*
proud 871
valiant
bold 855*a*
valley 255*j*
valuation 809*b*
value 809*a*
Jerusalem's value
184*aj*
man's value 371*e*
valued
precious 644*i*
vanish
disappear 446
pass away 2*c*
vanishing 446*a*
vanity
Pride 871
useless 641*a*
variable
not variable 144
variegated 437
Variegation 437
variety 17
variety of function
17*a*
variety of form 17*b*
various 17
vegetable 366
vegetation 366
Vehicle 274
driving vehicle 267*i*

veil
cover 226*e*
curtains 421*a*
the veil 421*d*
various veils 421*f*
veiled
concealed 525*b*
velocity 277*h*
venerate
Respect 920
vengeance 910
venom 659*c*
venture
at a venture 159*a*
veracity
Truthfulness 540
verbose 581
verify
bear witness 466
verity 494
vernacular
accent 580*a*
Vertical 215
plumb line 215*a*
vessel
Receptacle 194
ships 275
various vessels 194*l*
vicarious substitution
150*a*
vicinity
Nearness 200
victor 727
victorious 727
God victorious 727*a*
victory 727
various victories
727*n*
victory over enemies
727*c*
viewing 438*n*
vigorous 571
vigorously 571*a*
Vigour 571
vindicate 927
God vindicates 927*a*
man vindicates 927*g*
Vindication 927
vine
vines and olives 366*j*
vinegar 393*a*
irritant 827*k*
vineyards 370*k*
violate
sabbath violated
683*h*